SUMMA THEOLOGIÆ

The
SUMMA THEOLOGIÆ
of
SAINT THOMAS AQUINAS

LATIN-ENGLISH
EDITION

VOLUME III
Prima Secundae, Q. 1-70

Treatise on the Last End
Treatise on Human Acts: Acts Peculiar to Man
Treatise on the Passions
Treatise on Habits
Treatise on Habits in Particular
― *Good Habits, i.e., Virtues* ―

NOVANTIQUA

Copyright © 2010 NovAntiqua
www.novantiqua.com

All Rights Reserved

ISBN-13: 978-1450563260

Printed in the United States of America

Without limiting the rights under the copyright reserved above, no part of this publication may be reproduced, stored in or introduced into a retrieval system, or transmitted in any form or by any means (electronic, mechanical, by photocopying, or otherwise) without the prior written permission of the copyright owner and the publisher of the book. The scanning, uploading, and distribution of this book via the Internet or by any other means without permission is illegal and punishable by law.

Preface

The *Summa Theologiæ* of Saint Thomas Aquinas is a work that has held a place of prominence in the disciplines of theology and philosophy since the time of Saint Thomas himself. It was written when Latin was the language of scholarship, a common tongue that crossed Europe's volatile political boundaries and facilitated the growth of universities, many of which are still standing today.

The universities remain standing, but the language in which they took root no longer thrives as it once did, and thousands of works lie now nearly inaccessible—never translated, gathering dust, forgotten because the language in which they were written is "dead."

Translations of the *Summa Theologiæ* are readily available. It is the hope, however, of those responsible for this edition, that having the original Latin text and a respected English translation side by side will not only give those who are not ready to tackle the Latin of Saint Thomas unaided access to his own words, but will inspire them and assist them in their pursuit of this language. They will likely discover, as many have before them, that Saint Thomas is more easily understood in the tongue in which he wrote than he is in any other.

The English translation used for this edition of the *Summa Theologiæ* is that of the Fathers of the English Dominican Province, originally published in the United States by Benziger Brothers. Multiple editions of the work have been consulted in the creation of this Latin-English edition.

TABLE OF CONTENTS

Preface — iii

Treatise on the Last End

- Q. 1 - *Of Man's Last End* — 1
- Q. 2 - *Of Those Things in Which Man's Happiness Consists* — 16
- Q. 3 - *What Is Happiness* — 31
- Q. 4 - *Of Those Things That Are Required for Happiness* — 48
- Q. 5 - *Of the Attainment of Happiness* — 64

Treatise on Human Acts: Acts Peculiar to Man

- Q. 6 - *Of the Voluntary and the Involuntary* — 80
- Q. 7 - *Of the Circumstances of Human Acts* — 97
- Q. 8 - *Of the Will, in Regard to What It Wills* — 105
- Q. 9 - *Of That Which Moves the Will* — 111
- Q. 10 - *Of the Manner in Which the Will Is Moved* — 123
- Q. 11 - *Of Enjoyment, Which Is an Act of the Will* — 131
- Q. 12 - *Of Intention* — 138
- Q. 13 - *Of Choice, Which Is an Act of the Will with Regard to the Means* — 146
- Q. 14 - *Of Counsel, Which Precedes Choice* — 156
- Q. 15 - *Of Consent, Which Is an Act of the Will with Regard to the Means* — 166
- Q. 16 - *Of Use, Which Is an Act of the Will in Regard to the Means* — 173
- Q. 17 - *Of the Acts Commanded by the Will* — 179
- Q. 18 - *Of the Good and Evil of Human Acts, in General* — 195
- Q. 19 - *Of the Goodness and Malice of the Interior Act of the Will* — 217
- Q. 20 - *Of Goodness and Malice in External Human Affairs* — 238
- Q. 21 - *Of the Consequences of Human Actions by Reason of Their Goodness and Malice* — 250

Treatise on the Passions

- Q. 22 - *Of the Subject of the Soul's Passions* — 258
- Q. 23 - *How the Passions Differ from One Another* — 264
- Q. 24 - *Of Good and Evil in the Passions of the Soul* — 273
- Q. 25 - *Of the Order of the Passions to One Another* — 280
- Q. 26 - *Of the Passions of the Soul in Particular: and First, of Love* — 289
- Q. 27 - *Of the Cause of Love* — 296
- Q. 28 - *Of the Effects of Love* — 303
- Q. 29 - *Of Hatred* — 314
- Q. 30 - *Of Concupiscence* — 324

Q. 31 - *Of Delight, Considered in Itself*	332
Q. 32 - *Of the Cause of Pleasure*	347
Q. 33 - *Of the Effects of Pleasure*	361
Q. 34 - *Of the Goodness and Malice of Pleasures*	369
Q. 35 - *Of Pain or Sorrow, in Itself*	377
Q. 36 - *Of the Causes of Sorrow or Pain*	396
Q. 37 - *Of the Effects of Pain or Sorrow*	403
Q. 38 - *Of the Remedies of Sorrow or Pain*	410
Q. 39 - *Of the Goodness and Malice of Sorrow or Pain*	418
Q. 40 - *Of the Irascible Passions, and First, of Hope and Despair*	424
Q. 41 - *Of Fear, in Itself*	437
Q. 42 - *Of the Object of Fear*	444
Q. 43 - *Of the Cause of Fear*	454
Q. 44 - *Of the Effects of Fear*	457
Q. 45 - *Of Daring*	464
Q. 46 - *Of Anger, in Itself*	471
Q. 47 - *Of the Cause That Provokes Anger, and of the Remedies of Anger*	486
Q. 48 - *Of the Effects of Anger*	493

TREATISE ON HABITS

Q. 49 - *Of Habits in General, as to Their Substance*	501
Q. 50 - *Of the Subjects of Habits*	512
Q. 51 - *Of the Cause of Habits, as to Their Formation*	526
Q. 52 - *Of the Increase of Habits*	534
Q. 53 - *How the Habits Are Corrupted or Diminished*	543
Q. 54 - *Of the Distinction of Habits*	550

TREATISE ON HABITS IN PARTICULAR
❧ GOOD HABITS, I.E., VIRTUES

Q. 55 - *Of the Virtues, as to Their Essence*	558
Q. 56 - *Of the Subject of Virtue*	567
Q. 57 - *Of the Intellectual Virtues*	579
Q. 58 - *Of the Difference Between Moral and Intellectual Virtues*	593
Q. 59 - *Of Moral Virtue in Relation to the Passions*	603
Q. 60 - *How the Moral Virtues Differ from One Another*	612
Q. 61 - *Of the Cardinal Virtues*	624
Q. 62 - *Of the Theological Virtues*	636
Q. 63 - *Of the Cause of Virtues*	643
Q. 64 - *Of the Mean of Virtue*	652

Q. 65 - *Of the Connection of Virtues*   660
Q. 66 - *Of Equality Among the Virtues*   672
Q. 67 - *Of the Duration of Virtues After This Life*   686
Q. 68 - *Of the Gifts*   700
Q. 69 - *Of the Beatitudes*   721
Q. 70 - *Of the Fruits of the Holy Spirit*   733

Prima Secundae

Q. I-LXX

First Part of the Second Part

Q. 1-70

PRIMA SECUNDAE

Prologus

Quia, sicut Damascenus dicit, homo factus ad imaginem Dei dicitur, secundum quod per imaginem significatur *intellectuale et arbitrio liberum et per se potestativum;* postquam praedictum est de exemplari, scilicet de Deo, et de his quae processerunt ex divina potestate secundum eius voluntatem; restat ut consideremus de eius imagine, idest de homine, secundum quod et ipse est suorum operum principium, quasi liberum arbitrium habens et suorum operum potestatem.

Prologue

Since, as Damascene states (De Fide Orth. ii, 12), man is said to be made in God's image, in so far as the image implies "an intelligent being endowed with free-will and self-movement": now that we have treated of the exemplar, i.e., God, and of those things which came forth from the power of God in accordance with His will; it remains for us to treat of His image, i.e., man, inasmuch as he too is the principle of his actions, as having free-will and control of his actions.

TREATISE ON THE LAST END

Quaestio I

Ubi primo considerandum occurrit de ultimo fine humanae vitae; et deinde de his per quae homo ad hunc finem pervenire potest, vel ab eo deviare, ex fine enim oportet accipere rationes eorum quae ordinantur ad finem. Et quia ultimus finis humanae vitae ponitur esse beatitudo, oportet *primo* considerare de ultimo fine in communi; *deinde* de beatitudine. Circa primum quaeruntur octo. *Primo,* utrum hominis sit agere propter finem. *Secundo,* utrum hoc sit proprium rationalis naturae. *Tertio,* utrum actus hominis recipiant speciem a fine. *Quarto,* utrum sit aliquis ultimus finis humanae vitae. *Quinto,* utrum unius hominis possint esse plures ultimi fines. *Sexto,* utrum homo ordinet omnia in ultimum finem. *Septimo,* utrum idem sit finis ultimus omnium hominum. *Octavo,* utrum in illo ultimo fine omnes aliae creaturae conveniant.

Question 1
Of Man's Last End

In this matter we shall consider first the last end of human life; and secondly, those things by means of which man may advance towards this end, or stray from the path: for the end is the rule of whatever is ordained to the end. And since the last end of human life is stated to be happiness, we must consider 1. the last end in general; 2. happiness. Under the first head there are eight points of inquiry: 1. Whether it belongs to man to act for an end? 2. Whether this is proper to the rational nature? 3. Whether a man's actions are specified by their end? 4. Whether there is any last end of human life? 5. Whether one man can have several last ends? 6. Whether man ordains all to the last end? 7. Whether all men have the same last end? 8. Whether all other creatures concur with man in that last end?

Articulus 1

Ad primum sic proceditur. Videtur quod homini non conveniat agere propter finem. Causa enim naturaliter prior est. Sed finis habet rationem ultimi, ut ipsum nomen sonat. Ergo finis non habet rationem causae.

Article 1
Whether it belongs to man to act for an end?

Objection 1: It would seem that it does not belong to man to act for an end. For a cause is naturally first. But an end, in its very name, implies something that is last. Therefore an end is not a cause.

Sed propter illud agit homo, quod est causa actionis, cum haec praepositio *propter* designet habitudinem causae. Ergo homini non convenit agere propter finem.

Praeterea, illud quod est ultimus finis, non est propter finem. Sed in quibusdam actiones sunt ultimus finis; ut patet per philosophum in I Ethic. Ergo non omnia homo agit propter finem.

Praeterea, tunc videtur homo agere propter finem, quando deliberat. Sed multa homo agit absque deliberatione, de quibus etiam quandoque nihil cogitat; sicut cum aliquis movet pedem vel manum aliis intentus, vel fricat barbam. Non ergo homo omnia agit propter finem.

Sed contra, omnia quae sunt in aliquo genere, derivantur a principio illius generis. Sed finis est principium in operabilibus ab homine; ut patet per philosophum in II Physic. Ergo homini convenit omnia agere propter finem.

Respondeo dicendum quod actionum quae ab homine aguntur, illae solae proprie dicuntur *humanae,* quae sunt propriae hominis inquantum est homo. Differt autem homo ab aliis irrationalibus creaturis in hoc, quod est suorum actuum dominus. Unde illae solae actiones vocantur proprie humanae, quarum homo est dominus. Est autem homo dominus suorum actuum per rationem et voluntatem, unde et liberum arbitrium esse dicitur *facultas voluntatis et rationis*. Illae ergo actiones proprie humanae dicuntur, quae ex voluntate deliberata procedunt. Si quae autem aliae actiones homini conveniant, possunt dici quidem *hominis* actiones; sed non proprie *humanae,* cum non sint hominis inquantum est homo. Manifestum est autem quod omnes actiones quae procedunt ab aliqua potentia, causantur ab ea secundum rationem sui obiecti. Obiectum autem voluntatis est finis et bonum. Unde oportet quod omnes actiones humanae propter finem sint.

Ad primum ergo dicendum quod finis, etsi sit postremus in executione, est tamen primus in intentione agentis. Et hoc modo habet rationem causae.

But that for which a man acts, is the cause of his action; since this preposition "for" indicates a relation of causality. Therefore it does not belong to man to act for an end.

Objection 2: Further, that which is itself the last end is not for an end. But in some cases the last end is an action, as the Philosopher states (Ethic. i, 1). Therefore man does not do everything for an end.

Objection 3: Further, then does a man seem to act for an end, when he acts deliberately. But man does many things without deliberation, sometimes not even thinking of what he is doing; for instance when one moves one's foot or hand, or scratches one's beard, while intent on something else. Therefore man does not do everything for an end.

On the contrary, All things contained in a genus are derived from the principle of that genus. Now the end is the principle in human operations, as the Philosopher states (Phys. ii, 9). Therefore it belongs to man to do everything for an end.

I answer that, Of actions done by man those alone are properly called "human," which are proper to man as man. Now man differs from irrational animals in this, that he is master of his actions. Wherefore those actions alone are properly called human, of which man is master. Now man is master of his actions through his reason and will; whence, too, the free-will is defined as "the faculty and will of reason." Therefore those actions are properly called human which proceed from a deliberate will. And if any other actions are found in man, they can be called actions "of a man," but not properly "human" actions, since they are not proper to man as man. Now it is clear that whatever actions proceed from a power, are caused by that power in accordance with the nature of its object. But the object of the will is the end and the good. Therefore all human actions must be for an end.

Reply to Objection 1: Although the end be last in the order of execution, yet it is first in the order of the agent's intention. And it is this way that it is a cause.

Ad secundum dicendum quod, si qua actio humana sit ultimus finis, oportet eam esse voluntariam, alias non esset humana, ut dictum est. Actio autem aliqua dupliciter dicitur voluntaria, uno modo, quia imperatur a voluntate, sicut ambulare vel loqui; alio modo, quia elicitur a voluntate, sicut ipsum velle. Impossibile autem est quod ipse actus a voluntate elicitus sit ultimus finis. Nam obiectum voluntatis est finis, sicut obiectum visus est color, unde sicut impossibile est quod primum visibile sit ipsum videre, quia omne videre est alicuius obiecti visibilis; ita impossibile est quod primum appetibile, quod est finis, sit ipsum velle. Unde relinquitur quod, si qua actio humana sit ultimus finis, quod ipsa sit imperata a voluntate. Et ita ibi aliqua actio hominis, ad minus ipsum velle, est propter finem. Quidquid ergo homo faciat, verum est dicere quod homo agit propter finem, etiam agendo actionem quae est ultimus finis.

Ad tertium dicendum quod huiusmodi actiones non sunt proprie humanae, quia non procedunt ex deliberatione rationis, quae est proprium principium humanorum actuum. Et ideo habent quidem finem imaginatum, non autem per rationem praestitutum.

Reply to Objection 2: If any human action be the last end, it must be voluntary, else it would not be human, as stated above. Now an action is voluntary in one of two ways: first, because it is commanded by the will, e.g., to walk, or to speak; secondly, because it is elicited by the will, for instance the very act of willing. Now it is impossible for the very act elicited by the will to be the last end. For the object of the will is the end, just as the object of sight is color: wherefore just as the first visible cannot be the act of seeing, because every act of seeing is directed to a visible object; so the first appetible, i.e., the end, cannot be the very act of willing. Consequently it follows that if a human action be the last end, it must be an action commanded by the will: so that there, some action of man, at least the act of willing, is for the end. Therefore whatever a man does, it is true to say that man acts for an end, even when he does that action in which the last end consists.

Reply to Objection 3: Such like actions are not properly human actions; since they do not proceed from deliberation of the reason, which is the proper principle of human actions. Therefore they have indeed an imaginary end, but not one that is fixed by reason.

Articulus 2

Ad secundum sic proceditur. Videtur quod agere propter finem sit proprium rationalis naturae. Homo enim, cuius est agere propter finem, nunquam agit propter finem ignotum. Sed multa sunt quae non cognoscunt finem, vel quia omnino carent cognitione, sicut creaturae insensibiles; vel quia non apprehendunt rationem finis, sicut bruta animalia. Videtur ergo proprium esse rationalis naturae agere propter finem.

Praeterea, agere propter finem est ordinare suam actionem ad finem. Sed hoc est rationis opus. Ergo non convenit his quae ratione carent.

Article 2
Whether it is proper to the rational nature to act for an end?

Objection 1: It would seem that it is proper to the rational nature to act for an end. For man, to whom it belongs to act for an end, never acts for an unknown end. On the other hand, there are many things that have no knowledge of an end; either because they are altogether without knowledge, as insensible creatures: or because they do not apprehend the idea of an end as such, as irrational animals. Therefore it seems proper to the rational nature to act for an end.

Objection 2: Further, to act for an end is to order one's action to an end. But this is the work of reason. Therefore it does not belong to things that lack reason.

PRAETEREA, bonum et finis est obiectum voluntatis. Sed *voluntas in ratione est,* ut dicitur in III de anima. Ergo agere propter finem non est nisi rationalis naturae.

SED CONTRA est quod philosophus probat in II Physic., quod *non solum intellectus, sed etiam natura agit propter finem.*

RESPONDEO dicendum quod omnia agentia necesse est agere propter finem. Causarum enim ad invicem ordinatarum, si **prima subtrahatur, necesse est alias subtrahi.** Prima autem inter omnes causas est causa finalis. Cuius ratio est, quia materia non consequitur formam nisi secundum quod movetur ab agente, nihil enim reducit se de potentia in actum. Agens autem non movet nisi ex intentione finis. Si enim agens non esset determinatum ad aliquem effectum, non magis ageret hoc quam illud, ad hoc ergo quod determinatum effectum producat, necesse est quod determinetur ad aliquid certum, quod habet rationem finis. Haec autem determinatio, sicut in rationali natura fit per *rationalem appetitum,* qui dicitur voluntas; ita in aliis fit per inclinationem naturalem, quae dicitur *appetitus naturalis.* Tamen considerandum est quod aliquid sua actione vel motu tendit ad finem dupliciter, uno modo, sicut seipsum ad finem movens, ut homo; alio modo, sicut ab alio motum ad finem, sicut sagitta tendit ad determinatum finem ex hoc quod movetur a sagittante, qui suam actionem dirigit in finem. Illa ergo quae ra tionem habent, seipsa movent ad finem, quia habent dominium suorum actuum per liberum arbitrium, quod est *facultas voluntatis et rationis.* Illa vero quae ratione carent, tendunt in finem per naturalem inclinationem, quasi ab alio mota, non autem a seipsis, cum non cognoscant rationem finis, et ideo nihil in finem ordinare possunt, sed solum in finem ab alio ordinantur. Nam tota irrationalis natura comparatur ad Deum sicut instrumentum ad agens principale, ut supra habitum est. Et ideo proprium est naturae rationalis ut tendat in finem quasi se agens vel ducens ad

Objection 3: Further, the good and the end is the object of the will. But "the will is in the reason" (De Anima iii, 9). Therefore to act for an end belongs to none but a rational nature.

On the contrary, The Philosopher proves (Phys. ii, 5) that "not only mind but also nature acts for an end."

I answer that, Every agent, of necessity, acts for an end. For if, in a number of causes ordained to one another, the first be removed, the others must, of necessity, be removed also. Now the first of all causes is the final cause. The reason of which is that matter does not receive form, save in so far as it is moved by an agent; for nothing reduces itself from potentiality to act. But an agent does not move except out of intention for an end. For if the agent were not determinate to some particular effect, it would not do one thing rather than another: consequently in order that it produce a determinate effect, it must, of necessity, be determined to some certain one, which has the nature of an end. And just as this determination is effected, in the rational nature, by the "rational appetite," which is called the will; so, in other things, it is caused by their natural inclination, which is called the "natural appetite." Nevertheless it must be observed that a thing tends to an end, by its action or movement, in two ways: first, as a thing, moving itself to the end, as man; secondly, as a thing moved by another to the end, as an arrow tends to a determinate end through being moved by the archer who directs his action to the end. Therefore those things that are possessed of reason, move themselves to an end; because they have dominion over their actions through their free-will, which is the "faculty of will and reason." But those things that lack reason tend to an end, by natural inclination, as being moved by another and not by themselves; since they do not know the nature of an end as such, and consequently cannot ordain anything to an end, but can be ordained to an end only by another. For the entire irrational nature is in comparison to God as an instrument to the principal agent, as stated above (I, q. 22, a. 2, ad 4; q. 103, a. 1, ad 3). Consequently it is proper to the rational nature to tend to an end, as directing [*agens*] and leading itself to

finem, naturae vero irrationalis, quasi ab alio acta vel ducta, sive in finem apprehensum, sicut ruta animalia, sive in finem non apprehensum, sicut ea quae omnino cognitione carent.

AD PRIMUM ergo dicendum quod homo, quando per seipsum agit propter finem, cognoscit finem, sed quando ab alio agitur vel ducitur, puta cum agit ad imperium alterius, vel cum movetur altero impellente, non est necessarium quod cognoscat finem. Et ita est in creaturis irrationalibus.

AD SECUNDUM dicendum quod ordinare in finem est eius quod seipsum agit in finem. Eius vero quod ab alio in finem agitur, est ordinari in finem. Quod potest esse irrationalis naturae, sed ab aliquo rationem habente.

AD TERTIUM dicendum quod obiectum voluntatis est finis et bonum in universali. Unde non potest esse voluntas in his quae carent ratione et intellectu, cum non possint apprehendere universale, sed est in eis appetitus naturalis vel sensitivus, determinatus ad aliquod bonum particulare. Manifestum autem est quod particulares causae moventur a causa universali, sicut rector civitatis, qui intendit bonum commune, movet suo imperio omnia particularia officia civitatis. Et ideo necesse est quod omnia quae carent ratione, moveantur in fines particulares ab aliqua voluntate rationali, quae se extendit in bonum universale, scilicet a voluntate divina.

the end: whereas it is proper to the irrational nature to tend to an end, as directed or led by another, whether it apprehend the end, as do irrational animals, or do not apprehend it, as is the case of those things which are altogether void of knowledge.

Reply to Objection 1: When a man of himself acts for an end, he knows the end: but when he is directed or led by another, for instance, when he acts at another's command, or when he is moved under another's compulsion, it is not necessary that he should know the end. And it is thus with irrational creatures.

Reply to Objection 2: To ordain towards an end belongs to that which directs itself to an end: whereas to be ordained to an end belongs to that which is directed by another to an end. And this can belong to an irrational nature, but owing to some one possessed of reason.

Reply to Objection 3: The object of the will is the end and the good in universal. Consequently there can be no will in those things that lack reason and intellect, since they cannot apprehend the universal; but they have a natural appetite or a sensitive appetite, determinate to some particular good. Now it is clear that particular causes are moved by a universal cause: thus the governor of a city, who intends the common good, moves, by his command, all the particular departments of the city. Consequently all things that lack reason are, of necessity, moved to their particular ends by some rational will which extends to the universal good, namely by the Divine will.

ARTICULUS 3

AD TERTIUM sic proceditur. Videtur quod actus humani non recipiant speciem a fine. Finis enim est causa extrinseca. Sed unumquodque habet speciem ab aliquo principio intrinseco. Ergo actus humani non recipiunt speciem a fine.

PRAETEREA, illud quod dat speciem, oportet esse prius. Sed finis est posterior in esse.

ARTICLE 3
Whether human acts are specified by their end?

Objection 1: It would seem that human acts are not specified by their end. For the end is an extrinsic cause. But everything is specified by an intrinsic principle. Therefore human acts are not specified by their end.

Objection 2: Further, that which gives a thing its species should exist before it. But the end comes into existence afterwards.

Ergo actus humanus non habet speciem a fine.

PRAETEREA, idem non potest esse nisi in una specie. Sed eundem numero actum contingit ordinari ad diversos fines. Ergo finis non dat speciem actibus humanis.

SED CONTRA est quod dicit Augustinus, in libro de moribus Ecclesiae et Manichaeorum, *secundum quod finis est culpabilis vel laudabilis, secundum hoc sunt opera nostra culpabilia vel laudabilia.*

RESPONDEO dicendum quod unumquodque sortitur speciem secundum actum, et non secundum potentiam, unde ea quae sunt composita ex materia et forma, constituuntur in suis speciebus per proprias formas. Et hoc etiam considerandum est in motibus propriis. Cum enim motus quodammodo distinguatur per actionem et passionem, utrumque horum ab actu speciem sortitur, actio quidem ab actu qui est principium agendi; passio vero ab actu qui est terminus motus. Unde calefactio actio nihil aliud est quam motio quaedam a calore procedens, calefactio vero passio nihil aliud est quam motus ad calorem, definitio autem manifestat rationem speciei. Et utroque modo actus humani, sive considerentur per modum actionum, sive per modum passionum, a fine speciem sortiuntur. Utroque enim modo possunt considerari actus humani, eo quod homo movet seipsum, et movetur a seipso. Dictum est autem supra quod actus dicuntur humani, inquantum procedunt a voluntate deliberata. Obiectum autem voluntatis est bonum et finis. Et ideo manifestum est quod principium humanorum actuum, inquantum sunt humani, est finis. Et similiter est terminus eorundem, nam id ad quod terminatur actus humanus, est id quod voluntas intendit tanquam finem; sicut in agentibus naturalibus forma generati est conformis formae generantis. Et quia, ut Ambrosius dicit, super Lucam, *mores proprie dicuntur humani,* actus morales proprie speciem sortiuntur ex fine, nam idem sunt actus morales et actus humani.

Therefore a human act does not derive its species from the end.

Objection 3: Further, one thing cannot be in more than one species. But one and the same act may happen to be ordained to various ends. Therefore the end does not give the species to human acts.

On the contrary, Augustine says (De Mor. Eccl. et Manich. ii, 13): "According as their end is worthy of blame or praise so are our deeds worthy of blame or praise."

I answer that, Each thing receives its species in respect of an act and not in respect of potentiality; wherefore things composed of matter and form are established in their respective species by their own forms. And this is also to be observed in proper movements. For since movements are, in a way, divided into action and passion, each of these receives its species from an act; action indeed from the act which is the principle of acting, and passion from the act which is the terminus of the movement. Wherefore heating, as an action, is nothing else than a certain movement proceeding from heat, while heating as a passion is nothing else than a movement towards heat: and it is the definition that shows the specific nature. And either way, human acts, whether they be considered as actions, or as passions, receive their species from the end. For human acts can be considered in both ways, since man moves himself, and is moved by himself. Now it has been stated above (I-II, q. 1, a. 1) that acts are called human, inasmuch as they proceed from a deliberate will. Now the object of the will is the good and the end. And hence it is clear that the principle of human acts, in so far as they are human, is the end. In like manner it is their terminus: for the human act terminates at that which the will intends as the end; thus in natural agents the form of the thing generated is conformed to the form of the generator. And since, as Ambrose says (Prolog. super Luc.) "morality is said properly of man," moral acts properly speaking receive their species from the end, for moral acts are the same as human acts.

Ad primum ergo dicendum quod finis non est omnino aliquid extrinsecum ab actu, quia comparatur ad actum ut principium vel terminus; et hoc ipsum est de ratione actus, ut scilicet sit ab aliquo, quantum ad actionem, et ut sit ad aliquid, quantum ad passionem.

Ad secundum dicendum quod finis secundum quod est prior in intentione, ut dictum est, secundum hoc pertinet ad voluntatem. Et hoc modo dat speciem actui humano sive morali.

Ad tertium dicendum quod idem actus numero, secundum quod semel egreditur ab agente, non ordinatur nisi ad unum finem proximum, a quo habet speciem, sed potest ordinari ad plures fines remotos, quorum unus est finis alterius. Possibile tamen est quod unus actus secundum speciem naturae, ordinetur ad diversos fines voluntatis, sicut hoc ipsum quod est *occidere hominem,* quod est idem secundum speciem naturae, potest ordinari sicut in finem ad conservationem iustitiae, et ad satisfaciendum irae. Et ex hoc erunt diversi actus secundum speciem moris, quia uno modo erit actus virtutis, alio modo erit actus vitii. Non enim motus recipit speciem ab eo quod est terminus per accidens, sed solum ab eo quod est terminus per se. Fines autem morales accidunt rei naturali; et e converso ratio naturalis finis accidit morali. Et ideo nihil prohibet actus qui sunt iidem secundum speciem naturae, esse diversos secundum speciem moris, et e converso.

Reply to Objection 1: The end is not altogether extrinsic to the act, because it is related to the act as principle or terminus; and thus it just this that is essential to an act, *viz.* to proceed from something, considered as action, and to proceed towards something, considered as passion.

Reply to Objection 2: The end, in so far as it pre-exists in the intention, pertains to the will, as stated above (I-II, q. 1, a. 1, ad 1). And it is thus that it gives the species to the human or moral act.

Reply to Objection 3: One and the same act, in so far as it proceeds once from the agent, is ordained to but one proximate end, from which it has its species: but it can be ordained to several remote ends, of which one is the end of the other. It is possible, however, that an act which is one in respect of its natural species, be ordained to several ends of the will: thus this act "to kill a man," which is but one act in respect of its natural species, can be ordained, as to an end, to the safeguarding of justice, and to the satisfying of anger: the result being that there would be several acts in different species of morality: since in one way there will be an act of virtue, in another, an act of vice. For a movement does not receive its species from that which is its terminus accidentally, but only from that which is its *per se* terminus. Now moral ends are accidental to a natural thing, and conversely the relation to a natural end is accidental to morality. Consequently there is no reason why acts which are the same considered in their natural species, should not be diverse, considered in their moral species, and conversely.

Articulus 4

Ad quartum sic proceditur. Videtur quod non sit aliquis ultimus finis humanae vitae, sed procedatur in finibus in infinitum. Bonum enim, secundum suam rationem, est diffusivum sui; ut patet per Dionysium, IV cap. de Div. Nom. Si ergo quod procedit ex bono, ipsum etiam est bonum, oportet quod illud bonum diffundat aliud bonum, et sic processus boni est in infinitum. Sed bonum

Article 4
Whether there is one last end of human life?

Objection 1: It would seem that there is no last end of human life, but that we pro-ceed to infinity. For good is essentially diffusive, as Dionysius states (Div. Nom. iv). Consequently if that which proceeds from good is itself good, the latter must needs diffuse some other good: so that the diffusion of good goes on indefinitely. But good

habet rationem finis. Ergo in finibus est processus in infinitum.

Praeterea, ea quae sunt rationis, in infinitum multiplicari possunt, unde et mathematicae quantitates in infinitum augentur. Species etiam numerorum propter hoc sunt infinitae, quia, dato quolibet numero, ratio alium maiorem excogitare potest. Sed desiderium finis sequitur apprehensionem rationis. Ergo videtur quod etiam in finibus procedatur in infinitum.

Praeterea, bonum et finis est obiectum voluntatis. Sed voluntas infinities potest reflecti supra seipsam, possum enim velle aliquid, et velle me velle illud, et sic in infinitum. Ergo in finibus humanae voluntatis proceditur in infinitum, et non est aliquis ultimus finis humanae voluntatis.

Sed contra est quod philosophus dicit, II Metaphys., quod *qui infinitum faciunt, auferunt naturam boni.* Sed bonum est quod habet rationem finis. Ergo contra rationem finis est quod procedatur in infinitum. Necesse est ergo ponere unum ultimum finem.

Respondeo dicendum quod, per se loquendo, impossibile est in finibus procedere in infinitum, ex quacumque parte. In omnibus enim quae per se habent ordinem ad invicem, oportet quod, remoto primo, removeantur ea quae sunt ad primum. Unde philosophus probat, in VIII Physic., quod non est possibile in causis moventibus procedere in infinitum, quia iam non esset primum movens, quo subtracto alia movere non possunt, cum non moveant nisi per hoc quod moventur a primo movente. In finibus autem invenitur duplex ordo, scilicet ordo intentionis, et ordo executionis, et in utroque ordine oportet esse aliquid primum. Id enim quod est primum in ordine intentionis est quasi principium movens appetitum, unde, subtracto principio, appetitus a nullo moveretur. Id autem quod est principium in executione, est unde incipit operatio, unde, isto principio subtracto, nullus inciperet aliquid operari. Principium autem intentionis est ultimus finis, principium autem executionis est primum

has the nature of an end. Therefore there is an indefinite series of ends.

Objection 2: Further, things pertaining to the reason can be multiplied to infinity: thus mathematical quantities have no limit. For the same reason the species of numbers are infinite, since, given any number, the reason can think of one yet greater. But desire of the end is consequent on the apprehension of the reason. Therefore it seems that there is also an infinite series of ends.

Objection 3: Further, the good and the end is the object of the will. But the will can react on itself an infinite number of times: for I can will something, and will to will it, and so on indefinitely. Therefore there is an infinite series of ends of the human will, and there is no last end of the human will.

On the contrary, The Philosopher says (Metaph. ii, 2) that "to suppose a thing to be indefinite is to deny that it is good." But the good is that which has the nature of an end. Therefore it is contrary to the nature of an end to proceed indefinitely. Therefore it is necessary to fix one last end.

I answer that, Absolutely speaking, it is not possible to proceed indefinitely in the matter of ends, from any point of view. For in whatsoever things there is an essential order of one to another, if the first be removed, those that are ordained to the first, must of necessity be removed also. Wherefore the Philosopher proves (Phys. viii, 5) that we cannot proceed to infinitude in causes of movement, because then there would be no first mover, without which neither can the others move, since they move only through being moved by the first mover. Now there is to be observed a twofold order in ends—the order of intention and the order of execution: and in either of these orders there must be something first. For that which is first in the order of intention, is the principle, as it were, moving the appetite; consequently, if you remove this principle, there will be nothing to move the appetite. On the other hand, the principle in execution is that wherein operation has its beginning; and if this principle be taken away, no one will begin to work. Now the principle in the intention is the last end; while the principle in execution is the first

eorum quae sunt ad finem. Sic ergo ex neutra parte possibile est in infinitum procedere, quia si non esset ultimus finis, nihil appeteretur, nec aliqua actio terminaretur, nec etiamquiesceret intentio agentis; si autem non esset primum in his quae sunt ad finem, nullus inciperet aliquid operari, nec terminaretur consilium, sed in infinitum procederet. Ea vero quae non habent ordinem per se, sed per accidens sibi invicem coniunguntur, nihil prohibet infinitatem habere, causae enim per accidens indeterminatae sunt. Et hoc etiam modo contingit esse infinitatem per accidens in finibus, et in his quae sunt ad finem.

AD PRIMUM ergo dicendum quod de ratione boni est quod aliquid ab ipso effluat, non tamen quod ipsum ab alio procedat. Et ideo, cum bonum habeat rationem finis, et primum bonum sit ultimus finis, ratio ista non probat quod non sit ultimus finis; sed quod a fine primo supposito procedatur in infinitum inferius versus ea quae sunt ad finem. Et hoc quidem competeret, si consideraretur sola virtus primi boni, quae est infinita. Sed quia primum bonum habet diffusionem secundum intellectum, cuius est secundum aliquam certam formam profluere in causata; aliquis certus modus adhibetur bonorum effluxui a primo bono, a quo omnia alia bona participant virtutem diffusivam. Et ideo diffusio bonorum non procedit in infinitum, sed, sicut dicitur Sap. XI, Deus omnia disposuit *in numero, pondere et mensura*.

AD SECUNDUM dicendum quod in his quae sunt per se, ratio incipit a principiis naturaliter notis, et ad aliquem terminum progreditur. Unde philosophus probat, in I Poster., quod in demonstrationibus non est processus in infinitum, quia in demonstrationibus attenditur ordo aliquorum per se ad invicem connexorum, et non per accidens. In his autem quae per accidens connectuntur, nihil prohibet rationem in infinitum procedere. Accidit autem quantitati aut numero praeexistenti, inquantum huiusmodi, quod ei addatur quantitas aut unitas.

of the things which are ordained to the end. Consequently, on neither side is it possible to go to infinity since if there were no last end, nothing would be desired, nor would any action have its term, nor would the intention of the agent be at rest; while if there is no first thing among those that are ordained to the end, none would begin to work at anything, and counsel would have no term, but would continue indefinitely. On the other hand, nothing hinders infinity from being in things that are ordained to one another not essentially but accidentally; for accidental causes are indeterminate. And in this way it happens that there is an accidental infinity of ends, and of things ordained to the end.

Reply to Objection 1: The very nature of good is that something flows from it, but not that it flows from something else. Since, therefore, good has the nature of end, and the first good is the last end, this argument does not prove that there is no last end; but that from the end, already supposed, we may proceed downwards indefinitely towards those things that are ordained to the end. And this would be true if we considered but the power of the First Good, which is infinite. But, since the First Good diffuses itself according to the intellect, to which it is proper to flow forth into its effects according to a certain fixed form; it follows that there is a certain measure to the flow of good things from the First Good from Which all other goods share the power of diffusion. Consequently the diffusion of goods does not proceed indefinitely but, as it is written (Wis. 11:21), God disposes all things "in number, weight and measure."

Reply to Objection 2: In things which are of themselves, reason begins from principles that are known naturally, and advances to some term. Wherefore the Philosopher proves (Poster. i, 3) that there is no infinite process in demonstrations, because there we find a process of things having an essential, not an accidental, connection with one another. But in those things which are accidentally connected, nothing hinders the reason from proceeding indefinitely. Now it is accidental to a stated quantity or number, as such, that quantity or unity be added to it.

Unde in huiusmodi nihil prohibet rationem procedere in infinitum.

Ad tertium dicendum quod illa multiplicatio actuum voluntatis reflexae supra seipsam, per accidens se habet ad ordinem finium. Quod patet ex hoc, quod circa unum et eundem finem indifferenter semel vel pluries supra seipsam voluntas reflectitur.

Articulus 5

Ad quintum sic proceditur. Videtur quod possibile sit voluntatem unius hominis in plura ferri simul, sicut in ultimos fines. Dicit enim Augustinus, XIX de Civ. Dei, quod quidam ultimum hominis finem posuerunt in quatuor, scilicet *in voluptate, in quiete, in primis naturae, et in virtute.* Haec autem manifeste sunt plura. Ergo unus homo potest constituere ultimum finem suae voluntatis in multis.

Praeterea, ea quae non opponuntur ad invicem, se invicem non excludunt. Sed multa inveniuntur in rebus quae sibi invicem non opponuntur. Ergo si unum ponatur ultimus finis voluntatis, non propter hoc alia excluduntur.

Praeterea, voluntas per hoc quod constituit ultimum finem in aliquo, suam liberam potentiam non amittit. Sed antequam constitueret ultimum finem suum in illo, puta in voluptate, poterat constituere finem suum ultimum in alio, puta in divitiis. Ergo etiam postquam constituit aliquis ultimum finem suae voluntatis in voluptate, potest simul constituere ultimum finem in divitiis. Ergo possibile est voluntatem unius hominis simul ferri in diversa, sicut in ultimos fines.

Sed contra, illud in quo quiescit aliquis sicut in ultimo fine, hominis affectui dominatur, quia ex eo totius vitae suae regulas accipit. Unde de gulosis dicitur Philipp. III, *quorum Deus venter est,* quia scilicet constituunt ultimum finem in deliciis ventris. Sed sicut dicitur Matth. VI, *nemo potest duobus dominis servire,* ad invicem scilicet non ordinatis. Ergo impossibile est esse plures ultimos fines unius hominis ad invicem non ordinatos.

Respondeo dicendum quod impossibile est quod voluntas unius hominis simul se

Wherefore in such like things nothing hinders the reason from an indefinite process.

Reply to Objection 3: This multiplication of acts of the will reacting on itself, is accidental to the order of ends. This is clear from the fact that in regard to one and the same end, the will reacts on itself indifferently once or several times.

Article 5
Whether one man can have several last ends?

Objection 1: It would seem possible for one man's will to be directed at the same time to several things, as last ends. For Augustine says (De Civ. Dei xix, 1) that some held man's last end to consist in four things, *viz.* "in pleasure, repose, the gifts of nature, and virtue." But these are clearly more than one thing. Therefore one man can place the last end of his will in many things.

Objection 2: Further, things not in opposition to one another do not exclude one another. Now there are many things which are not in opposition to one another. Therefore the supposition that one thing is the last end of the will does not exclude others.

Objection 3: Further, by the fact that it places its last end in one thing, the will does not lose its freedom. But before it placed its last end in that thing, e.g., pleasure, it could place it in something else, e.g., riches. Therefore even after having placed his last end in pleasure, a man can at the same time place his last end in riches. Therefore it is possible for one man's will to be directed at the same time to several things, as last ends.

On the contrary, That in which a man rests as in his last end, is master of his affections, since he takes therefrom his entire rule of life. Hence of gluttons it is written (Phil. 3:19): "Whose god is their belly": *viz.* because they place their last end in the pleasures of the belly. Now according to Mat. 6:24, "No man can serve two masters," such, namely, as are not ordained to one another. Therefore it is impossible for one man to have several last ends not ordained to one another.

I answer that, It is impossible for one man's will to be directed at the same time

habeat ad diversa, sicut ad ultimos fines. Cuius ratio potest triplex assignari. Prima est quia, cum unumquodque appetat suam perfectionem, illud appetit aliquis ut ultimum finem, quod appetit, ut bonum perfectum et completivum sui ipsius. Unde Augustinus dicit, XIX de Civ. Dei, *finem boni nunc dicimus, non quod consumatur ut non sit, sed quod perficiatur ut plenum sit.* Oportet igitur quod ultimus finis ita impleat totum hominis appetitum, quod nihil extra ipsum appetendum relinquatur. Quod esse non potest, si aliquid extraneum ad ipsius perfectionem requiratur. Unde non potest esse quod in duo sic tendat appetitus, ac si utrumque sit bonum perfectum ipsius. Secunda ratio est quia, sicut in processu rationis principium est id quod naturaliter cognoscitur, ita in processu rationalis appetitus, qui est voluntas, oportet esse principium id quod naturaliter desideratur. Hoc autem oportet esse unum, quia natura non tendit nisi ad unum. Principium autem in processu rationalis appetitus est ultimus finis. Unde oportet id in quod tendit voluntas sub ratione ultimi finis, esse unum. Tertia ratio est quia, cum actiones voluntarie ex fine speciem sortiantur, sicut supra habitum est, oportet quod a fine ultimo, qui est communis, sortiantur rationem generis, sicut et naturalia ponuntur in genere secundum formalem rationem communem. Cum igitur omnia appetibilia voluntatis, inquantum huiusmodi, sint unius generis, oportet ultimum finem esse unum. Et praecipue quia in quolibet genere est unum primum principium, ultimus autem finis habet rationem primi principii, ut dictum est. Sicut autem se habet ultimus finis hominis simpliciter ad totum humanum genus, ita se habet ultimus finis huius hominis ad hunc hominem. Unde oportet quod, sicut omnium hominum est naturaliter unus finis ultimus, ita huius hominis voluntas in uno ultimo fine statuatur.

AD PRIMUM ergo dicendum quod omnia illa plura accipiebantur in ratione unius boni perfecti ex his constituti, ab his qui in eis ultimum finem ponebant.

to diverse things, as last ends. Three reasons may be assigned for this. First, because, since everything desires its own perfection, a man desires for his ultimate end, that which he desires as his perfect and crowning good. Hence Augustine (De Civ. Dei xix, 1): "In speaking of the end of good we mean now, not that it passes away so as to be no more, but that it is perfected so as to be complete." It is therefore necessary for the last end so to fill man's appetite, that nothing is left besides it for man to desire. Which is not possible, if something else be required for his perfection. Consequently it is not possible for the appetite so to tend to two things, as though each were its perfect good. The second reason is because, just as in the process of reasoning, the principle is that which is naturally known, so in the process of the rational appetite, i.e., the will, the principle needs to be that which is naturally desired. Now this must needs be one: since nature tends to one thing only. But the principle in the process of the rational appetite is the last end. Therefore that to which the will tends, as to its last end, is one. The third reason is because, since voluntary actions receive their species from the end, as stated above (I-II, q. 1, a. 3), they must needs receive their genus from the last end, which is common to them all: just as natural things are placed in a genus according to a common form. Since, then, all things that can be desired by the will, belong, as such, to one genus, the last end must needs be one. And all the more because in every genus there is one first principle; and the last end has the nature of a first principle, as stated above. Now as the last end of man, simply as man, is to the whole human race, so is the last end of any individual man to that individual. Therefore, just as of all men there is naturally one last end, so the will of an individual man must be fixed on one last end.

Reply to Objection 1: All these several objects were considered as one perfect good resulting therefrom, by those who placed in them the last end.

Articulus 6

Ad sextum sic proceditur. Videtur quod non omnia quaecumque homo vult, propter ultimum finem velit. Ea enim quae ad finem ultimum ordinantur, seriosa dicuntur, quasi utilia. Sed iocosa a seriis distinguuntur. Ergo ea quae homo iocose agit, non ordinat in ultimum finem.

Praeterea, philosophus dicit, in principio Metaphys., quod scientiae speculativae propter seipsas quaeruntur. Nec tamen potest dici quod quaelibet earum sit ultimus finis. Ergo non omnia quae homo appetit, appetit propter ultimum finem.

Praeterea, quicumque ordinat aliquid in finem aliquem, cogitat de illo fine. Sed non semper homo cogitat de ultimo fine in omni eo quod appetit aut facit. Non ergo omnia homo appetit aut facit propter ultimum finem.

Sed contra est quod dicit Augustinus, XIX de Civ. Dei, *illud est finis boni nostri, propter quod amantur cetera, illud autem propter seipsum.*

Respondeo dicendum quod necesse est quod omnia quae homo appetit, appetat propter ultimum finem. Et hoc apparet duplici ratione. Primo quidem, quia quidquid homo appetit, appetit sub ratione boni. Quod quidem si non appetitur ut bonum perfectum, quod est ultimus finis, necesse est ut appetatur ut tendens in bonum perfectum, quia semper inchoatio alicuius ordinatur ad consummationem ipsius; sicut patet tam in his quae fiunt a natura, quam in his quae fiunt ab arte. Et ideo omnis inchoatio

Reply to Objection 2: Although it is possible to find several things which are not in opposition to one another, yet it is contrary to a thing's perfect good, that anything besides be required for that thing's perfection.

Reply to Objection 3: The power of the will does not extend to making opposites exist at the same time. Which would be the case were it to tend to several diverse objects as last ends, as has been shown above (ad 2).

Article 6
Whether man wills all, whatsoever he wills, for the last end?

Objection 1: It would seem that man does not will all, whatsoever he wills, for the last end. For things ordained to the last end are said to be serious matter, as being useful. But jests are foreign to serious matter. Therefore what man does in jest, he ordains not to the last end.

Objection 2: Further, the Philosopher says at the beginning of his Metaphysics 1, 2 that speculative science is sought for its own sake. Now it cannot be said that each speculative science is the last end. Therefore man does not desire all, whatsoever he desires, for the last end.

Objection 3: Further, whosoever ordains something to an end, thinks of that end. But man does not always think of the last end in all that he desires or does. Therefore man neither desires nor does all for the last end.

On the contrary, Augustine says (De Civ. Dei xix, 1): "That is the end of our good, for the sake of which we love other things, whereas we love it for its own sake."

I answer that, Man must, of necessity, desire all, whatsoever he desires, for the last end. This is evident for two reasons. First, because whatever man desires, he desires it under the aspect of good. And if he desire it, not as his perfect good, which is the last end, he must, of necessity, desire it as tending to the perfect good, because the beginning of anything is always ordained to its completion; as is clearly the case in effects both of nature and of art. Wherefore every beginning

perfectionis ordinatur in perfectionem consummatam, quae est per ultimum finem. Secundo, quia ultimus finis hoc modo se habet in movendo appetitum, sicut se habet in aliis motionibus primum movens. Manifestum est autem quod causae secundae moventes non movent nisi secundum quod moventur a primo movente. Unde secunda appetibilia non movent appetitum nisi in ordine ad primum appetibile, quod est ultimus finis.

Ad primum ergo dicendum quod actiones ludicrae non ordinantur ad aliquem finem extrinsecum; sed tamen ordinantur ad bonum ipsius ludentis, prout sunt delectantes vel requiem praestantes. Bonum autem consummatum hominis est ultimus finis eius.

Et similiter dicendum ad secundum, de scientia speculativa; quae appetitur ut bonum quoddam speculantis, quod comprehenditur sub bono completo et perfecto, quod est ultimus finis.

Ad tertium dicendum quod non oportet ut semper aliquis cogitet de ultimo fine, quandocumque aliquid appetit vel operatur, sed virtus primae intentionis, quae est respectu ultimi finis, manet in quolibet appetitu cuiuscumque rei, etiam si de ultimo fine actu non cogitetur. Sicut non oportet quod qui vadit per viam, in quolibet passu cogitet de fine.

of perfection is ordained to complete perfection which is achieved through the last end. Secondly, because the last end stands in the same relation in moving the appetite, as the first mover in other movements. Now it is clear that secondary moving causes do not move save inasmuch as they are moved by the first mover. Therefore secondary objects of the appetite do not move the appetite, except as ordained to the first object of the appetite, which is the last end.

Reply to Objection 1: Actions done jestingly are not directed to any external end; but merely to the good of the jester, in so far as they afford him pleasure or relaxation. But man's consummate good is his last end.

Reply to Objection 2: The same applies to speculative science; which is desired as the scientist's good, included in complete and perfect good, which is the ultimate end.

Reply to Objection 3: One need not always be thinking of the last end, whenever one desires or does something: but the virtue of the first intention, which was in respect of the last end, remains in every desire directed to any object whatever, even though one's thoughts be not actually directed to the last end. Thus while walking along the road one needs not to be thinking of the end at every step.

Articulus 7

Ad septimum sic proceditur. Videtur quod non omnium hominum sit unus finis ultimus. Maxime enim videtur hominis ultimus finis esse incommutabile bonum. Sed quidam avertuntur ab incommutabili bono, peccando. Non ergo omnium hominum est unus ultimus finis.

Praeterea, secundum ultimum finem tota vita hominis regulatur. Si igitur esset unus ultimus finis omnium hominum, sequeretur quod in hominibus non essent diversa studia vivendi. Quod patet esse falsum.

Praeterea, finis est actionis terminus. Actiones autem sunt singularium. Homines autem, etsi conveniant in natura speciei,

Article 7
Whether all men have the same last end?

Objection 1: It would seem that all men have not the same last end. For before all else the unchangeable good seems to be the last end of man. But some turn away from the unchangeable good, by sinning. Therefore all men have not the same last end.

Objection 2: Further, man's entire life is ruled according to his last end. If, therefore, all men had the same last end, they would not have various pursuits in life. Which is evidently false.

Objection 3: Further, the end is the term of action. But actions are of individuals. Now although men agree in their specific nature,

tamen differunt secundum ea quae ad individua pertinent. Non ergo omnium hominum est unus ultimus finis.

SED CONTRA est quod Augustinus dicit, XIII de Trin., quod omnes homines conveniunt in appetendo ultimum finem, qui est beatitudo.

RESPONDEO dicendum quod de ultimo fine possumus loqui dupliciter, uno modo, secundum rationem ultimi finis; alio modo, secundum id in quo finis ultimi ratio invenitur. Quantum igitur ad rationem ultimi finis, omnes conveniunt in appetitu finis ultimi, quia omnes appetunt suam perfectionem adimpleri, quae est ratio ultimi finis, ut dictum est. Sed quantum ad id in quo ista ratio invenitur, non omnes homines conveniunt in ultimo fine, nam quidam appetunt divitias tanquam consummatum bonum, quidam autem voluptatem, quidam vero quodcumque aliud. Sicut et omni gustui delectabile est dulce, sed quibusdam maxime delectabilis est dulcedo vini, quibusdam dulcedo mellis, aut alicuius talium. Illud tamen dulce oportet esse simpliciter melius delectabile, in quo maxime delectatur qui habet optimum gustum. Et similiter illud bonum oportet esse completissimum, quod tanquam ultimum finem appetit habens affectum bene dispositum.

AD PRIMUM ergo dicendum quod illi qui peccant, avertuntur ab eo in quo vere invenitur ratio ultimi finis, non autem ab ipsa ultimi finis intentione, quam quaerunt falso in aliis rebus.

AD SECUNDUM dicendum quod diversa studia vivendi contingunt in hominibus propter diversas res in quibus quaeritur ratio summi boni.

AD TERTIUM dicendum quod, etsi actiones sint singularium, tamen primum principium agendi in eis est natura, quae tendit ad unum, ut dictum est.

ARTICULUS 8

AD OCTAVUM sic proceditur. Videtur quod in ultimo fine hominis etiam omnia alia conveniant. Finis enim respondet principio.

yet they differ in things pertaining to individuals. Therefore all men have not the same last end.

On the contrary, Augustine says (De Trin. xiii, 3) that all men agree in desiring the last end, which is happiness.

I answer that, We can speak of the last end in two ways: first, considering only the aspect of last end; secondly, considering the thing in which the aspect of last end is realized. So, then, as to the aspect of last end, all agree in desiring the last end: since all desire the fulfilment of their perfection, and it is precisely this fulfilment in which the last end consists, as stated above (I-II, q. 1, a. 5). But as to the thing in which this aspect is realized, all men are not agreed as to their last end: since some desire riches as their consummate good; some, pleasure; others, something else. Thus to every taste the sweet is pleasant but to some, the sweetness of wine is most pleasant, to others, the sweetness of honey, or of something similar. Yet that sweet is absolutely the best of all pleasant things, in which he who has the best taste takes most pleasure. In like manner that good is most complete which the man with well disposed affections desires for his last end.

Reply to Objection 1: Those who sin turn from that in which their last end really consists: but they do not turn away from the intention of the last end, which intention they mistakenly seek in other things.

Reply to Objection 2: Various pursuits in life are found among men by reason of the various things in which men seek to find their last end.

Reply to Objection 3: Although actions are of individuals, yet their first principle of action is nature, which tends to one thing, as stated above (I-II, q. 1, a. 5).

ARTICLE 8
Whether other creatures concur in that last end?

Objection 1: It would seem that all other creatures concur in man's last end. For the end corresponds to the beginning.

Sed illud quod est principium hominum, scilicet Deus, est etiam principium omnium aliorum. Ergo in ultimo fine hominis omnia alia communicant.

PRAETEREA, Dionysius dicit, in libro de Div. Nom., quod *Deus convertit omnia ad seipsum, tanquam ad ultimum finem.* Sed ipse est etiam ultimus finis hominis, quia solo ipso fruendum est, ut Augustinus dicit. Ergo in fine ultimo hominis etiam alia conveniunt.

PRAETEREA, finis ultimus hominis est obiectum voluntatis. Sed obiectum voluntatis est bonum universale, quod est finis omnium. Ergo necesse est quod in ultimo fine hominis omnia conveniant.

SED CONTRA est quod ultimus finis hominum est beatitudo; quam omnes appetunt, ut Augustinus dicit. Sed *non cadit in animalia rationis expertia ut beata sint,* sicut Augustinus dicit in libro octoginta trium quaest. Non ergo in ultimo fine hominis alia conveniunt.

RESPONDEO dicendum quod, sicut philosophus dicit in II Physic. et in V Metaphys., finis dupliciter dicitur, scilicet *cuius,* et *quo,* idest ipsa res in qua ratio boni invenitur, et usus sive adeptio illius rei. Sicut si dicamus quod motus corporis gravis finis est vel locus inferior ut *res,* vel hoc quod est esse in loco inferiori, ut *usus,* et finis avari est vel pecunia ut *res,* vel possessio pecuniae ut *usus.* Si ergo loquamur de ultimo fine hominis quantum ad ipsam rem quae est finis, sic in ultimo fine hominis omnia alia conveniunt, quia Deus est ultimus finis hominis et omnium aliarum rerum. Si autem loquamur de ultimo fine hominis quantum ad consecutionem finis, sic in hoc fine hominis non communicant creaturae irrationales. Nam homo et aliae rationales creaturae consequuntur ultimum finem cognoscendo et amando Deum, quod non competit aliis creaturis, quae adipiscuntur ultimum finem inquantum participant aliquam similitudinem Dei, secundum quod sunt, vel vivunt, vel etiam cognoscunt.

Et per hoc patet responsio ad obiecta.

But man's beginning—i.e., God—is also the beginning of all else. Therefore all other things concur in man's last end.

Objection 2: Further, Dionysius says (Div. Nom. iv) that "God turns all things to Himself as to their last end." But He is also man's last end; because He alone is to be enjoyed by man, as Augustine says (De Doctr. Christ. i, 5, 22). Therefore other things, too, concur in man's last end.

Objection 3: Further, man's last end is the object of the will. But the object of the will is the universal good, which is the end of all. Therefore other things, too, concur in man's last end.

On the contrary, man's last end is happiness; which all men desire, as Augustine says (De Trin. xiii, 3, 4). But "happiness is not possible for animals bereft of reason," as Augustine says (QQ. 83, qu. 5). Therefore other things do not concur in man's last end.

I answer that, As the Philosopher says (Phys. ii, 2), the end is twofold—the end "for which" and the end "by which"; *viz.* the thing itself in which is found the aspect of good, and the use or acquisition of that thing. Thus we say that the end of the movement of a weighty body is either a lower place as "thing," or to be in a lower place, as "use"; and the end of the miser is money as "thing," or possession of money as "use." If, therefore, we speak of man's last end as of the thing which is the end, thus all other things concur in man's last end, since God is the last end of man and of all other things. If, however, we speak of man's last end, as of the acquisition of the end, then irrational creatures do not concur with man in this end. For man and other rational creatures attain to their last end by knowing and loving God: this is not possible to other creatures, which acquire their last end, in so far as they share in the Divine likeness, inasmuch as they are, or live, or even know.

Hence it is evident how the objections are solved: since happiness means the acquisition of the last end.

Quaestio II

Deinde considerandum est de beatitudine, nam beatitudo nominat adeptionem ultimi finis. *Primo* quidem, in quibus sit; *secundo,* quid sit; *tertio,* qualiter eam consequi possimus. Circa primum quaeruntur octo. *Primo,* utrum beatitudo consistat in divitiis. *Secundo,* utrum in honoribus. *Tertio,* utrum in fama, sive in gloria. *Quarto,* utrum in potestate. *Quinto,* utrum in aliquo corporis bono. *Sexto,* utrum in voluptate. *Septimo,* utrum in aliquo bono animae. *Octavo,* utrum in aliquo bono creato.

Question 2
Of Those Things in Which Man's Happiness Consists

We have now to consider happiness: and 1. in what it consists; 2. what it is; 3. how we can obtain it. Concerning the first there are eight points of inquiry: 1. Whether happiness consists in wealth? 2. Whether in honor? 3. Whether in fame or glory? 4. Whether in power? 5. Whether in any good of the body? 6. Whether in pleasure? 7. Whether in any good of the soul? 8. Whether in any created good?

Articulus 1

Ad primum sic proceditur. Videtur quod beatitudo hominis in divitiis consistat. Cum enim beatitudo sit ultimus finis hominis, in eo consistit quod maxime in hominis affectu dominatur. Huiusmodi autem sunt divitiae, dicitur enim Eccle. X, *pecuniae obediunt omnia.* Ergo in divitiis beatitudo hominis consistit.

Praeterea, secundum Boetium, in III de Consol., beatitudo est *status omnium bonorum aggregatione perfectus.* Sed in pecuniis omnia possideri videntur, quia, ut philosophus dicit in V Ethic., ad hoc nummus est inventus, ut sit quasi fideiussor habendi pro eo quodcumque homo voluerit. Ergo in divitiis beatitudo consistit.

Praeterea, desiderium summi boni, cum nunquam deficiat, videtur esse infinitum. Sed hoc maxime in divitiis invenitur, quia *avarus non implebitur pecunia,* ut dicitur Eccle. V. Ergo in divitiis beatitudo consistit.

Sed contra, bonum hominis in retinendo beatitudinem magis consistit quam in emittendo ipsam. Sed sicut Boetius in II de Consol. dicit, *divitiae effundendo, magis quam coacervando, melius nitent, siquidem avaritia semper odiosos, claros largitas facit.* Ergo in divitiis beatitudo non consistit.

Article 1
Whether man's happiness consists in wealth?

Objection 1: It would seem that man's happiness consists in wealth. For since happiness is man's last end, it must consist in that which has the greatest hold on man's affections. Now this is wealth: for it is written (Eccles. 10:19): "All things obey money." Therefore man's happiness consists in wealth.

Objection 2: Further, according to Boethius (De Consol. iii), happiness is "a state of life made perfect by the aggregate of all good things." Now money seems to be the means of possessing all things: for, as the Philosopher says (Ethic. v, 5), money was invented, that it might be a sort of guarantee for the acquisition of whatever man desires. Therefore happiness consists in wealth.

Objection 3: Further, since the desire for the sovereign good never fails, it seems to be infinite. But this is the case with riches more than anything else; since "a covetous man shall not be satisfied with riches" (Eccles. 5:9). Therefore happiness consists in wealth.

On the contrary, Man's good consists in retaining happiness rather than in spreading it. But as Boethius says (De Consol. ii), "wealth shines in giving rather than in hoarding: for the miser is hateful, whereas the generous man is applauded." Therefore man's happiness does not consist in wealth.

RESPONDEO dicendum quod impossibile est beatitudinem hominis in divitiis consistere. Sunt enim duplices divitiae, ut philosophus dicit in I Polit., scilicet naturales, et artificiales. Naturales quidem divitiae sunt, quibus homini subvenitur ad defectus naturales tollendos, sicut cibus, potus, vestimenta, vehicula et habitacula, et alia huiusmodi. Divitiae autem artificiales sunt, quibus secundum se natura non iuvatur, ut denarii; sed ars humana eos adinvenit propter facilitatem commutationis, ut sint quasi mensura quaedam rerum venalium. Manifestum est autem quod in divitiis naturalibus beatitudo hominis esse non potest. Quaeruntur enim huiusmodi divitiae propter aliud, scilicet ad sustentandam naturam hominis, et ideo non possunt esse ultimus finis hominis, sed magis ordinantur ad hominem sicut ad finem. Unde in ordine naturae omnia huiusmodi sunt infra hominem, et propter hominem facta; secundum illud Psalmi VIII, *omnia subiecisti sub pedibus eius*. Divitiae autem artificiales non quaeruntur nisi propter naturales, non enim quaererentur, nisi quia per eas emuntur res ad usum vitae necessariae. Unde multo minus habent rationem ultimi finis. Impossibile est igitur beatitudinem, quae est ultimus finis hominis, in divitiis esse.

AD PRIMUM ergo dicendum quod omnia corporalia obediunt pecuniae, quantum ad multitudinem stultorum, qui sola corporalia bona cognoscunt, quae pecunia acquiri possunt. Iudicium autem de bonis humanis non debet sumi a stultis, sed a sapientibus, sicut et iudicium de saporibus ab his qui habent gustum bene dispositum.

AD SECUNDUM dicendum quod pecunia possunt haberi omnia venalia, non autem spiritualia, quae vendi non possunt. Unde dicitur Proverb. XVII, *quid prodest stulto divitias habere, cum sapientiam emere non possit?*

AD TERTIUM dicendum quod appetitus naturalium divitiarum non est infinitus, quia secundum certam mensuram naturae sufficiunt. Sed appetitus divitiarum artificialium est infinitus, quia deservit concupiscentiae inordinatae, quae non modificatur, ut patet per philosophum in I

I answer that, It is impossible for man's happiness to consist in wealth. For wealth is twofold, as the Philosopher says (Polit. i, 3), *viz.* natural and artificial. Natural wealth is that which serves man as a remedy for his natural wants: such as food, drink, clothing, cars, dwellings, and such like, while artificial wealth is that which is not a direct help to nature, as money, but is invented by the art of man, for the convenience of exchange, and as a measure of things salable. Now it is evident that man's happiness cannot consist in natural wealth. For wealth of this kind is sought for the sake of something else, *viz.* as a support of human nature: consequently it cannot be man's last end, rather is it ordained to man as to its end. Wherefore in the order of nature, all such things are below man, and made for him, according to Ps. 8:8: "Thou hast subjected all things under his feet." And as to artificial wealth, it is not sought save for the sake of natural wealth; since man would not seek it except because, by its means, he procures for himself the necessaries of life. Consequently much less can it be considered in the light of the last end. Therefore it is impossible for happiness, which is the last end of man, to consist in wealth.

Reply to Objection 1: All material things obey money, so far as the multitude of fools is concerned, who know no other than material goods, which can be obtained for money. But we should take our estimation of human goods not from the foolish but from the wise: just as it is for a person whose sense of taste is in good order, to judge whether a thing is palatable.

Reply to Objection 2: All things salable can be had for money: not so spiritual things, which cannot be sold. Hence it is written (Prov. 17:16): "What doth it avail a fool to have riches, seeing he cannot buy wisdom."

Reply to Objection 3: The desire for natural riches is not infinite: because they suffice for nature in a certain measure. But the desire for artificial wealth is infinite, for it is the servant of disordered concupiscence, which is not curbed, as the Philosopher makes clear

Polit. Aliter tamen est infinitum desiderium divitiarum, et desiderium summi boni. Nam summum bonum quanto perfectius possidetur, tanto ipsummet magis amatur, et alia contemnuntur, quia quanto magis habetur, magis cognoscitur. Et ideo dicitur Eccli. XXIV, *qui edunt me, adhuc esurient*. Sed in appetitu divitiarum, et quorumcumque temporalium bonorum, est e converso, nam quando iam habentur, ipsa contemnuntur, et **alia appetuntur; secundum quod significatur** Ioan. IV, cum dominus dicit, *qui bibit ex hac aqua,* per quam temporalia significantur, *sitiet iterum.* Et hoc ideo, quia eorum insufficientia magis cognoscitur cum habentur. Et ideo hoc ipsum ostendit eorum imperfectionem, et quod in eis summum bonum non consistit.

(Polit. i, 3). Yet this desire for wealth is infinite otherwise than the desire for the sovereign good. For the more perfectly the sovereign good is possessed, the more it is loved, and other things despised: because the more we possess it, the more we know it. Hence it is written (Ecclus. 24:29): "They that eat me shall yet hunger." Whereas in the desire for wealth and for whatsoever temporal goods, the contrary is the case: for when we **already possess them, we despise them, and** seek others: which is the sense of Our Lord's words (Jn. 4:13): "Whosoever drinketh of this water," by which temporal goods are signified, "shall thirst again." The reason of this is that we realize more their insufficiency when we possess them: and this very fact shows that they are imperfect, and the sovereign good does not consist therein.

Articulus 2

Ad secundum sic proceditur. Videtur quod beatitudo hominis in honoribus consistat. Beatitudo enim, sive felicitas, est *praemium virtutis,* ut philosophus dicit in I Ethic. Sed honor maxime videtur esse id quod est virtutis praemium, ut philosophus dicit in IV Ethic. Ergo in honore maxime consistit beatitudo.

Praeterea, illud quod convenit Deo et excellentissimis, maxime videtur esse beatitudo, quae est bonum perfectum. Sed huiusmodi est honor, ut philosophus dicit in IV Ethic. Et etiam I Tim. I, dicit apostolus, *soli Deo honor et gloria*. Ergo in honore consistit beatitudo.

Praeterea, illud quod est maxime desideratum ab hominibus, est beatitudo. Sed nihil videtur esse magis desiderabile ab hominibus quam honor, quia homines patiuntur iacturam in omnibus aliis rebus ne patiantur aliquod detrimentum sui honoris. Ergo in honore beatitudo consistit.

Sed contra, beatitudo est in beato. Honor autem non est in eo qui honoratur, sed magis in honorante, qui reverentiam exhibet honorato, ut philosophus dicit in I Ethic. Ergo in honore beatitudo non consistit.

Article 2
Whether man's happiness consists in honors?

Objection 1: It would seem that man's happiness consists in honors. For happiness or bliss is "the reward of virtue," as the Philosopher says (Ethic. i, 9). But honor more than anything else seems to be that by which virtue is rewarded, as the Philosopher says (Ethic. iv, 3). Therefore happiness consists especially in honor.

Objection 2: Further, that which belongs to God and to persons of great excellence seems especially to be happiness, which is the perfect good. But that is honor, as the Philosopher says (Ethic. iv, 3). Moreover, the Apostle says (1 Tim. 1:17): "To . . . the only God be honor and glory." Therefore happiness consists in honor.

Objection 3: Further, that which man desires above all is happiness. But nothing seems more desirable to man than honor: since man suffers loss in all other things, lest he should suffer loss of honor. Therefore happiness consists in honor.

On the contrary, Happiness is in the happy. But honor is not in the honored, but rather in him who honors, and who offers deference to the person honored, as the Philosopher says (Ethic. i, 5). Therefore happiness does not consist in honor.

Respondeo dicendum quod impossibile est beatitudinem consistere in honore. Honor enim exhibetur alicui propter aliquam eius excellentiam; et ita est signum et testimonium quoddam illius excellentiae quae est in honorato. Excellentia autem hominis maxime attenditur secundum beatitudinem, quae est hominis bonum perfectum; et secundum partes eius, idest secundum illa bona quibus aliquid beatitudinis participatur. Et ideo honor potest quidem consequi beatitudinem, sed principaliter in eo beatitudo consistere non potest.

Ad primum ergo dicendum quod, sicut philosophus ibidem dicit, honor non est praemium virtutis propter quod virtuosi operantur, sed accipiunt honorem ab hominibus loco praemii, *quasi a non habentibus aliquid maius ad dandum*. Verum autem praemium virtutis est ipsa beatitudo, propter quam virtuosi operantur. Si autem propter honorem operarentur, iam non esset virtus, sed magis ambitio.

Ad secundum dicendum quod honor debetur Deo et excellentissimis, in signum vel testimonium excellentiae praeexistentis, non quod ipse honor faciat eos excellentes.

Ad tertium dicendum quod ex naturali desiderio beatitudinis, quam consequitur honor, ut dictum est, contingit quod homines maxime honorem desiderant. Unde quaerunt homines maxime honorari a sapientibus, quorum iudicio credunt se esse excellentes vel felices.

I answer that, It is impossible for happiness to consist in honor. For honor is given to a man on account of some excellence in him; and consequently it is a sign and attestation of the excellence that is in the person honored. Now a man's excellence is in proportion, especially to his happiness, which is man's perfect good; and to its parts, i.e., those goods by which he has a certain share of happiness. And therefore honor can result from happiness, but happiness cannot principally consist therein.

Reply to Objection 1: As the Philosopher says (Ethic. i, 5), honor is not that reward of virtue, for which the virtuous work: but they receive honor from men by way of reward, "as from those who have nothing greater to offer." But virtue's true reward is happiness itself, for which the virtuous work: whereas if they worked for honor, it would no longer be a virtue, but ambition.

Reply to Objection 2: Honor is due to God and to persons of great excellence as a sign of attestation of excellence already existing: not that honor makes them excellent.

Reply to Objection 3: That man desires honor above all else, arises from his natural desire for happiness, from which honor results, as stated above. Wherefore man seeks to be honored especially by the wise, on whose judgment he believes himself to be excellent or happy.

Articulus 3

Article 3
Whether man's happiness consists in fame or glory?

Ad tertium sic proceditur. Videtur quod beatitudo hominis consistat in gloria. In eo enim videtur beatitudo consistere, quod redditur sanctis pro tribulationibus quas in mundo patiuntur. Huiusmodi autem est gloria, dicit enim apostolus, Rom. VIII, *non sunt condignae passiones huius temporis ad futuram gloriam, quae revelabitur in nobis.* Ergo beatitudo consistit in gloria.

Praeterea, bonum est diffusivum sui, ut patet per Dionysium, IV cap. de Div. Nom. Sed per gloriam bonum hominis maxime diffunditur in notitiam aliorum,

Objection 1: It would seem that man's happiness consists in glory. For happiness seems to consist in that which is paid to the saints for the trials they have undergone in the world. But this is glory: for the Apostle says (Rom. 8:18): "The sufferings of this time are not worthy to be compared with the glory to come, that shall be revealed in us." Therefore happiness consists in glory.

Objection 2: Further, good is diffusive of itself, as stated by Dionysius (Div. Nom. iv). But man's good is spread abroad in the knowledge of others by glory more than by

quia gloria, ut Ambrosius dicit, nihil aliud est quam *clara cum laude notitia.* Ergo beatitudo hominis consistit in gloria.

Praeterea, beatitudo est stabilissimum bonorum. Hoc autem videtur esse fama vel gloria, quia per hanc quodammodo homines aeternitatem sortiuntur. Unde Boetius dicit, in libro de Consol., *vos immortalitatem vobis propagare videmini, cum futuri famam temporis cogitatis.* Ergo beatitudo hominis consistit in fama seu gloria.

Sed contra, beatitudo est verum hominis bonum. Sed famam seu gloriam contingit esse falsam, ut enim dicit Boetius, in libro III de Consol., *plures magnum saepe nomen falsis vulgi opinionibus abstulerunt. Quo quid turpius excogitari potest? Nam qui falso praedicantur, suis ipsi necesse est laudibus erubescant.* Non ergo beatitudo hominis consistit in fama seu gloria.

Respondeo dicendum quod impossibile est beatitudinem hominis in fama seu gloria humana consistere. Nam gloria nihil aliud est quam *clara notitia cum laude,* ut Ambrosius dicit. Res autem cognita aliter comparatur ad cognitionem humanam, et aliter ad cognitionem divinam, humana enim cognitio a rebus cognitis causatur, sed divina cognitio est causa rerum cognitarum. Unde perfectio humani boni, quae beatitudo dicitur, non potest causari a notitia humana, sed magis notitia humana de beatitudine alicuius procedit et quodammodo causatur ab ipsa humana beatitudine, vel inchoata vel perfecta. Et ideo in fama vel in gloria non potest consistere hominis beatitudo. Sed bonum hominis dependet, sicut ex causa, ex cognitione Dei. Et ideo ex gloria quae est apud Deum, dependet beatitudo hominis sicut ex causa sua, secundum illud Psalmi XC, *eripiam eum, et glorificabo eum, longitudine dierum replebo eum, et ostendam illi salutare meum.* Est etiam aliud considerandum, quod humana notitia saepe fallitur, et praecipue in singularibus contingentibus, cuiusmodi sunt actus humani. Et ideo frequenter humana gloria fallax est. Sed quia Deus falli non potest,

anything else: since, according to Ambrose,[*] glory consists "in being well known and praised." Therefore man's happiness consists in glory.

Objection 3: Further, happiness is the most enduring good. Now this seems to be fame or glory; because by this men attain to eternity after a fashion. Hence Boethius says (De Consol. ii): "You seem to beget unto yourselves eternity, when you think of your fame in future time." Therefore man's happiness consists in fame or glory.

On the contrary, Happiness is man's true good. But it happens that fame or glory is false: for as Boethius says (De Consol. iii), "many owe their renown to the lying reports spread among the people. Can anything be more shameful? For those who receive false fame, must needs blush at their own praise." Therefore man's happiness does not consist in fame or glory.

I answer that, Man's happiness cannot consist in human fame or glory. For glory consists "in being well known and praised," as Ambrose[†] says. Now the thing known is related to human knowledge otherwise than to God's knowledge: for human knowledge is caused by the things known, whereas God's knowledge is the cause of the things known. Wherefore the perfection of human good, which is called happiness, cannot be caused by human knowledge: but rather human knowledge of another's happiness proceeds from, and, in a fashion, is caused by, human happiness itself, inchoate or perfect. Consequently man's happiness cannot consist in fame or glory. On the other hand, man's good depends on God's knowledge as its cause. And therefore man's beatitude depends, as on its cause, on the glory which man has with God; according to Ps. 90:15, 16: "I will deliver him, and I will glorify him; I will fill him with length of days, and I will show him my salvation." Furthermore, we must observe that human knowledge often fails, especially in contingent singulars, such as are human acts. For this reason human glory is frequently deceptive. But since God cannot be deceived,

---

[*] Augustine, Contra Maxim. Arian. ii. 13
[†] Ibid.

eius gloria semper vera est. Propter quod dicitur, II ad Cor. X, *ille probatus est, quem Deus commendat.*

AD PRIMUM ergo dicendum quod apostolus non loquitur ibi de gloria quae est ab hominibus, sed de gloria quae est a Deo coram angelis eius. Unde dicitur Marc. VIII, *filius hominis confitebitur eum in gloria patris sui, coram angelis eius.*

AD SECUNDUM dicendum quod bonum alicuius hominis quod per famam vel gloriam est in cognitione multorum, si cognitio quidem vera sit, oportet quod derivetur a bono existente in ipso homine, et sic praesupponit beatitudinem perfectam vel inchoatam. Si autem cognitio falsa sit, non concordat rei, et sic bonum non invenitur in eo cuius fama celebris habetur. Unde patet quod fama nullo modo potest facere hominem beatum.

AD TERTIUM dicendum quod fama non habet stabilitatem, immo falso rumore de facili perditur. Et si stabilis aliquando perseveret, hoc est per accidens. Sed beatitudo habet per se stabilitatem, et semper.

His glory is always true; hence it is written (2 Cor. 10:18): "He . . . is approved . . . whom God commendeth."

Reply to Objection 1: The Apostle speaks, then, not of the glory which is with men, but of the glory which is from God, with His Angels. Hence it is written (Mk. 8:38): "The Son of Man shall confess him in the glory of His Father, before His angels."*

Reply to Objection 2: A man's good which, through fame or glory, is in the knowledge of many, if this knowledge be true, must needs be derived from good existing in the man himself: and hence it presupposes perfect or inchoate happiness. But if the knowledge be false, it does not harmonize with the thing: and thus good does not exist in him who is looked upon as famous. Hence it follows that fame can nowise make man happy.

Reply to Objection 3: Fame has no stability; in fact, it is easily ruined by false report. And if sometimes it endures, this is by accident. But happiness endures of itself, and for ever.

ARTICULUS 4

AD QUARTUM sic proceditur. Videtur quod beatitudo consistat in potestate. Omnia enim appetunt assimilari Deo, tanquam ultimo fini et primo principio. Sed homines qui in potestatibus sunt, propter similitudinem potestatis, maxime videntur esse Deo conformes, unde et in Scriptura *dii* vocantur, ut patet Exod. XXII, *diis non detrahes.* Ergo in potestate beatitudo consistit.

PRAETEREA, beatitudo est bonum perfectum. Sed perfectissimum est quod homo etiam alios regere possit, quod convenit his qui in potestatibus sunt constituti. Ergo beatitudo consistit in potestate.

PRAETEREA, beatitudo, cum sit maxime appetibilis, opponitur ei quod maxime est fugiendum. Sed homines maxime fugiunt servitutem, cui contraponitur potestas. Ergo in potestate beatitudo consistit.

ARTICLE 4
Whether man's happiness consists in power?

Objection 1: It would seem that happiness consists in power. For all things desire to become like to God, as to their last end and first beginning. But men who are in power, seem, on account of the similarity of power, to be most like to God: hence also in Scripture they are called "gods" (Ex. 22:28), "Thou shalt not speak ill of the gods." Therefore happiness consists in power.

Objection 2: Further, happiness is the perfect good. But the highest perfection for man is to be able to rule others; which belongs to those who are in power. Therefore happiness consists in power.

Objection 3: Further, since happiness is supremely desirable, it is contrary to that which is before all to be shunned. But, more than aught else, men shun servitude, which is contrary to power. Therefore happiness consists in power.

---

* St. Thomas joins Mk. 8:38 with Lk. 12:8 owing to a possible variant in his text, or to the fact that he was quoting from memory.

Sed contra, beatitudo est perfectum bonum. Sed potestas est maxime imperfecta. Ut enim dicit Boetius, III de Consol., *potestas humana sollicitudinum morsus expellere, formidinum aculeos vitare nequit. Et postea, potentem censes cui satellites latus ambiunt qui quos terret, ipse plus metuit? Non igitur beatitudo consistit in potestate.*

Respondeo dicendum quod impossibile est beatitudinem in potestate consistere, propter duo. Primo quidem, quia potestas habet rationem principii, ut patet in V Metaphys. Beatitudo autem habet rationem ultimi finis. Secundo, quia potestas se habet ad bonum et ad malum. Beatitudo autem est proprium et perfectum hominis bonum. Unde magis posset consistere beatitudo aliqua in bono usu potestatis, qui est per virtutem, quam in ipsa potestate. Possunt autem quatuor generales rationes induci ad ostendendum quod in nullo praemissorum exteriorum bonorum beatitudo consistat. Quarum prima est quia, cum beatitudo sit summum hominis bonum, non compatitur secum aliquod malum. Omnia autem praedicta possunt inveniri et in bonis et in malis. Secunda ratio est quia, cum de ratione beatitudinis sit quod sit *per se sufficiens,* ut patet in I Ethic., necesse est quod, beatitudine adepta, nullum bonum homini necessarium desit. Adeptis autem singulis praemissorum, possunt adhuc multa bona homini necessaria deesse, puta sapientia, sanitas corporis, et huiusmodi. Tertia, quia, cum beatitudo sit bonum perfectum, ex beatitudine non potest aliquod malum alicui provenire. Quod non convenit praemissis, dicitur enim Eccle. V, quod *divitiae* interdum *conservantur in malum domini sui;* et simile patet in aliis tribus. Quarta ratio est quia ad beatitudinem homo ordinatur per principia interiora, cum ad ipsam naturaliter ordinetur. Praemissa autem quatuor bona magis sunt a causis exterioribus, et ut plurimum a fortuna, unde et bona fortunae dicuntur. Unde patet quod in praemissis nullo modo beatitudo consistit.

Ad primum ergo dicendum quod divina potestas est sua bonitas, unde uti sua potestate non potest nisi bene. Sed hoc in hominibus non invenitur. Unde non sufficit ad

On the contrary, Happiness is the perfect good. But power is most imperfect. For as Boethius says (De Consol. iii), "the power of man cannot relieve the gnawings of care, nor can it avoid the thorny path of anxiety": and further on: "Think you a man is powerful who is surrounded by attendants, whom he inspires with fear indeed, but whom he fears still more?"

I answer that, It is impossible for happiness to consist in power; and this for two reasons. First because power has the nature of principle, as is stated in Metaph. v, 12, whereas happiness has the nature of last end. Secondly, because power has relation to good and evil: whereas happiness is man's proper and perfect good. Wherefore some happiness might consist in the good use of power, which is by virtue, rather than in power itself. Now four general reasons may be given to prove that happiness consists in none of the foregoing external goods. First, because, since happiness is man's supreme good, it is incompatible with any evil. Now all the foregoing can be found both in good and in evil men. Secondly, because, since it is the nature of happiness to "satisfy of itself," as stated in Ethic. i, 7, having gained happiness, man cannot lack any needful good. But after acquiring any one of the foregoing, man may still lack many goods that are necessary to him; for instance, wisdom, bodily health, and such like. Thirdly, because, since happiness is the perfect good, no evil can accrue to anyone therefrom. This cannot be said of the foregoing: for it is written (Eccles. 5:12) that "riches" are sometimes "kept to the hurt of the owner"; and the same may be said of the other three. Fourthly, because man is ordained to happiness through principles that are in him; since he is ordained thereto naturally. Now the four goods mentioned above are due rather to external causes, and in most cases to fortune; for which reason they are called goods of fortune. Therefore it is evident that happiness nowise consists in the foregoing.

Reply to Objection 1: God's power is His goodness: hence He cannot use His power otherwise than well. But it is not so with men. Consequently it is not enough for

beatitudinem hominis quod assimiletur Deo quantum ad potestatem, nisi etiam assimiletur ei quantum ad bonitatem.

Ad secundum dicendum quod, sicut optimum est quod aliquis utatur bene potestate in regimine multorum, ita pessimum est si male utatur. Et ita potestas se habet et ad bonum et ad malum.

Ad tertium dicendum quod servitus est impedimentum boni usus potestatis, et ideo naturaliter homines eam fugiunt, et non quasi in potestate hominis sit summum bonum.

man's happiness, that he become like God in power, unless he become like Him in goodness also.

Reply to Objection 2: Just as it is a very good thing for a man to make good use of power in ruling many, so is it a very bad thing if he makes a bad use of it. And so it is that power is towards good and evil.

Reply to Objection 3: Servitude is a hindrance to the good use of power: therefore is it that men naturally shun it; not because man's supreme good consists in power.

Articulus 5

Ad quintum sic proceditur. Videtur quod beatitudo hominis consistat in bonis corporis. Dicitur enim Eccli. XXX, *non est census supra censum salutis corporis.* Sed in eo quod est optimum, consistit beatitudo. Ergo consistit in corporis salute.

Praeterea, Dionysius dicit, V cap. de Div. Nom., quod *esse* est melius quam *vivere,* et *vivere* melius quam alia quae consequuntur. Sed ad esse et vivere hominis requiritur salus corporis. Cum ergo beatitudo sit summum bonum hominis, videtur quod salus corporis maxime pertineat ad beatitudinem.

Praeterea, quanto aliquid est communius, tanto ab altiori principio dependet quia quanto causa est superior, tanto eius virtus ad plura se extendit. Sed sicut causalitas causae efficientis consideratur secundum influentiam, ita causalitas finis attenditur secundum appetitum. Ergo sicut prima causa efficiens est quae in omnia influit, ita ultimus finis est quod ab omnibus desideratur. Sed ipsum esse est quod maxime desideratur ab omnibus. Ergo in his quae pertinent ad esse hominis, sicut est salus corporis, maxime consistit eius beatitudo.

Sed contra, secundum beatitudinem homo excellit omnia alia animalia. Sed secundum bona corporis, a multis animalibus superatur, sicut ab elephante in diuturnitate vitae, a leone in fortitudine, a cervo in cursu.

Article 5
Whether man's happiness consists in any bodily good?

Objection 1: It would seem that man's happiness consists in bodily goods. For it is written (Ecclus. 30:16): "There is no riches above the riches of the health of the body." But happiness consists in that which is best. Therefore it consists in the health of the body.

Objection 2: Further, Dionysius says (Div. Nom. v), that "to be" is better than "to live," and "to live" is better than all that follows. But for man's being and living, the health of the body is necessary. Since, therefore, happiness is man's supreme good, it seems that health of the body belongs more than anything else to happiness.

Objection 3: Further, the more universal a thing is, the higher the principle from which it depends; because the higher a cause is, the greater the scope of its power. Now just as the causality of the efficient cause consists in its flowing into something, so the causality of the end consists in its drawing the appetite. Therefore, just as the First Cause is that which flows into all things, so the last end is that which attracts the desire of all. But being itself is that which is most desired by all. Therefore man's happiness consists most of all in things pertaining to his being, such as the health of the body.

On the contrary, Man surpasses all other animals in regard to happiness. But in bodily goods he is surpassed by many animals; for instance, by the elephant in longevity, by the lion in strength, by the stag in fleetness.

Ergo beatitudo hominis non consistit in bonis corporis.

Respondeo dicendum quod impossibile est beatitudinem hominis in bonis corporis consistere, propter duo. Primo quidem, quia impossibile est quod illius rei quae ordinatur ad aliud sicut ad finem, ultimus finis sit eiusdem conservatio in esse. Unde gubernator non intendit, sicut ultimum finem, conservationem navis sibi commissae; eo quod navis ad aliud ordinatur sicut ad finem, scilicet ad navigandum. Sicut autem navis committitur gubernatori ad dirigendum, ita homo est suae voluntati et rationi commissus; secundum illud quod dicitur Eccli. XV, *Deus ab initio constituit hominem, et reliquit eum in manu consilii sui.* Manifestum est autem quod homo ordinatur ad aliquid sicut ad finem, non enim homo est summum bonum. Unde impossibile est quod ultimus finis rationis et voluntatis humanae sit conservatio humani esse. Secundo quia, dato quod finis rationis et voluntatis humanae esset conservatio humani esse, non tamen posset dici quod finis hominis esset aliquod corporis bonum. Esse enim hominis consistit in anima et corpore, et quamvis esse corporis dependeat ab anima, esse tamen humanae animae non dependet a corpore, ut supra ostensum est; ipsumque corpus est propter animam, sicut materia propter formam, et instrumenta propter motorem, ut per ea suas actiones exerceat. Unde omnia bona corporis ordinantur ad bona animae, sicut ad finem. Unde impossibile est quod in bonis corporis beatitudo consistat, quae est ultimus hominis finis.

Ad primum ergo dicendum quod, sicut corpus ordinatur ad animam sicut ad finem, ita bona exteriora ad ipsum corpus. Et ideo rationabiliter bonum corporis praefertur bonis exterioribus, quae per *censum* significantur, sicut et bonum animae praefertur omnibus bonis corporis.

Ad secundum dicendum quod esse simpliciter acceptum, secundum quod includit in se omnem perfectionem essendi, praeeminet vitae et omnibus subsequentibus, sic enim ipsum esse praehabet in se omnia subsequentia. Et hoc modo Dionysius loquitur. Sed si consideretur ipsum esse prout participatur in hac re vel in illa, quae non capiunt totam

Therefore man's happiness does not consist in goods of the body.

I answer that, It is impossible for man's happiness to consist in the goods of the body; and this for two reasons. First, because, if a thing be ordained to another as to its end, its last end cannot consist in the preservation of its being. Hence a captain does not intend as a last end, the preservation of the ship entrusted to him, since a ship is ordained to something else as its end, *viz.* to navigation. Now just as the ship is entrusted to the captain that he may steer its course, so man is given over to his will and reason; according to Ecclus. 15:14: "God made man from the beginning and left him in the hand of his own counsel." Now it is evident that man is ordained to something as his end: since man is not the supreme good. Therefore the last end of man's reason and will cannot be the preservation of man's being. Secondly, because, granted that the end of man's will and reason be the preservation of man's being, it could not be said that the end of man is some good of the body. For man's being consists in soul and body; and though the being of the body depends on the soul, yet the being of the human soul depends not on the body, as shown above (I, q. 75, a. 2); and the very body is for the soul, as matter for its form, and the instruments for the man that puts them into motion, that by their means he may do his work. Wherefore all goods of the body are ordained to the goods of the soul, as to their end. Consequently happiness, which is man's last end, cannot consist in goods of the body.

Reply to Objection 1: Just as the body is ordained to the soul, as its end, so are external goods ordained to the body itself. And therefore it is with reason that the good of the body is preferred to external goods, which are signified by "riches," just as the good of the soul is preferred to all bodily goods.

Reply to Objection 2: Being taken simply, as including all perfection of being, surpasses life and all that follows it; for thus being itself includes all these. And in this sense Dionysius speaks. But if we consider being itself as participated in this or that thing, which does not possess the whole

perfectionem essendi, sed habent esse imperfectum, sicut est esse cuiuslibet creaturae; sic manifestum est quod ipsum esse cum perfectione superaddita est eminentius. Unde et Dionysius ibidem dicit quod viventia sunt meliora existentibus, et intelligentia viventibus.

AD TERTIUM dicendum quod, quia finis respondet principio, ex illa ratione probatur quod ultimus finis est primum principium essendi, in quo est omnis essendi perfectio, cuius similitudinem appetunt, secundum suam proportionem, quaedam quidem secundum esse tantum, quaedam secundum esse vivens, quaedam secundum esse vivens et intelligens et beatum. Et hoc paucorum est.

perfection of being, but has imperfect being, such as the being of any creature; then it is evident that being itself together with an additional perfection is more excellent. Hence in the same passage Dionysius says that things that live are better than things that exist, and intelligent better than living things.

Reply to Objection 3: Since the end corresponds to the beginning; this argument proves that the last end is the first beginning of being, in Whom every perfection of being is: Whose likeness, according to their proportion, some desire as to being only, some as to living being, some as to being which is living, intelligent and happy. And this belongs to few.

ARTICULUS 6

AD SEXTUM sic proceditur. Videtur quod beatitudo hominis in voluptate consistat. Beatitudo enim, cum sit ultimus finis, non appetitur propter aliud, sed alia propter ipsam. Sed hoc maxime convenit delectationi, *ridiculum est enim ab aliquo quaerere propter quid velit delectari,* ut dicitur in X Ethic. Ergo beatitudo maxime in voluptate et delectatione consistit.

PRAETEREA, *causa prima vehementius imprimit quam secunda,* ut dicitur in libro de causis. Influentia autem finis attenditur secundum eius appetitum. Illud ergo videtur habere rationem finis ultimi, quod maxime movet appetitum. Hoc autem est voluptas, cuius signum est quod delectatio intantum absorbet hominis voluntatem et rationem, quod alia bona contemnere facit. Ergo videtur quod ultimus finis hominis, qui est beatitudo, maxime in voluptate consistat.

PRAETEREA, cum appetitus sit boni, illud quod omnia appetunt, videtur esse optimum. Sed delectationem omnia appetunt, et sapientes et insipientes, et etiam ratione carentia. Ergo delectatio est optimum. Consistit ergo in voluptate beatitudo, quae est summum bonum.

ARTICLE 6
Whether man's happiness consists in pleasure?

Objection 1: It would seem that man's happiness consists in pleasure. For since happiness is the last end, it is not desired for something else, but other things for it. But this answers to pleasure more than to anything else: "for it is absurd to ask anyone what is his motive in wishing to be pleased" (Ethic. x, 2). Therefore happiness consists principally in pleasure and delight.

Objection 2: Further, "the first cause goes more deeply into the effect than the second cause" (De Causis i). Now the causality of the end consists in its attracting the appetite. Therefore, seemingly that which moves most the appetite, answers to the notion of the last end. Now this is pleasure: and a sign of this is that delight so far absorbs man's will and reason, that it causes him to despise other goods. Therefore it seems that man's last end, which is happiness, consists principally in pleasure.

Objection 3: Further, since desire is for good, it seems that what all desire is best. But all desire delight; both wise and foolish, and even irrational creatures. Therefore delight is the best of all. Therefore happiness, which is the supreme good, consists in pleasure.

Sed contra est quod Boetius dicit, in III de Consol., *tristes exitus esse voluptatum, quisquis reminisci libidinum suarum volet, intelliget. Quae si beatos efficere possent, nihil causae est quin pecudes quoque beatae esse dicantur.*

Respondeo dicendum quod, quia delectationes corporales pluribus notae sunt, *assumpserunt sibi nomen voluptatum,* ut dicitur VII Ethic., cum tamen sint aliae delectationes potiores. **In quibus tamen beatitudo principaliter non consistit.** Quia in unaquaque re aliud est quod pertinet ad essentiam eius, aliud est proprium accidens ipsius, sicut in homine aliud est quod est animal rationale mortale, aliud quod est risibile. Est igitur considerandum quod omnis delectatio est quoddam proprium accidens quod consequitur beatitudinem, vel aliquam beatitudinis partem, ex hoc enim aliquis delectatur quod habet bonum aliquod sibi conveniens, vel in re, vel in spe, vel saltem in memoria. Bonum autem conveniens, si quidem sit perfectum, est ipsa hominis beatitudo si autem sit imperfectum est quaedam beatitudinis participatio, vel propinqua, vel remota, vel saltem apparens. Unde manifestum est quod nec ipsa delectatio quae consequitur bonum perfectum, est ipsa essentia beatitudinis; sed quoddam consequens ad ipsam sicut per se accidens. Voluptas autem corporalis non potest etiam modo praedicto sequi bonum perfectum. Nam sequitur bonum quod apprehendit sensus, qui est virtus animae corpore utens. Bonum autem quod pertinet ad corpus, quod apprehenditur secundum sensum, non potest esse perfectum hominis bonum. Cum enim anima rationalis excedat proportionem materiae corporalis, pars animae quae est ab organo corporeo absoluta, quandam habet infinitatem respectu ipsius corporis et partium animae corpori concretarum, sicut immaterialia sunt quodammodo infinita respectu materialium, eo quod forma per materiam quodammodo contrahitur et finitur, unde forma a materia absoluta est quodammodo infinita. Et ideo sensus, qui est vis corporalis, cognoscit singulare, quod est determinatum per materiam, intellectus vero, qui est vis a materia absoluta, cognoscit universale, quod est abstractum

On the contrary, Boethius says (De Consol. iii): "Any one that chooses to look back on his past excesses, will perceive that pleasures had a sad ending: and if they can render a man happy, there is no reason why we should not say that the very beasts are happy too."

I answer that, Because bodily delights are more generally known, "the name of pleasure has been appropriated to them" (Ethic. vii, 13), although other delights excel them: **and yet happiness does not consist in them.** Because in every thing, that which pertains to its essence is distinct from its proper accident: thus in man it is one thing that he is a mortal rational animal, and another that he is a risible animal. We must therefore consider that every delight is a proper accident resulting from happiness, or from some part of happiness; since the reason that a man is delighted is that he has some fitting good, either in reality, or in hope, or at least in memory. Now a fitting good, if indeed it be the perfect good, is precisely man's happiness: and if it is imperfect, it is a share of happiness, either proximate, or remote, or at least apparent. Therefore it is evident that neither is delight, which results from the perfect good, the very essence of happiness, but something resulting therefrom as its proper accident. But bodily pleasure cannot result from the perfect good even in that way. For it results from a good apprehended by sense, which is a power of the soul, which power makes use of the body. Now good pertaining to the body, and apprehended by sense, cannot be man's perfect good. For since the rational soul excels the capacity of corporeal matter, that part of the soul which is independent of a corporeal organ, has a certain infinity in regard to the body and those parts of the soul which are tied down to the body: just as immaterial things are in a way infinite as compared to material things, since a form is, after a fashion, contracted and bounded by matter, so that a form which is independent of matter is, in a way, infinite. Therefore sense, which is a power of the body, knows the singular, which is determinate through matter: whereas the intellect, which is a power independent of matter, knows the universal, which is abstracted

a materia, et continet sub se infinita singularia. Unde patet quod bonum conveniens corpori, quod per apprehensionem sensus delectationem corporalem causat, non est perfectum bonum hominis, sed est minimum quiddam in comparatione ad bonum animae. Unde Sap. VII, dicitur quod *omne aurum, in comparatione sapientiae, arena est exigua.* Sic igitur neque voluptas corporalis est ipsa beatitudo, nec est per se accidens beatitudinis.

AD PRIMUM ergo dicendum quod eiusdem rationis est quod appetatur bonum, et quod appetatur delectatio, quae nihil est aliud quam quietatio appetitus in bono, sicut ex eadem virtute naturae est quod grave feratur deorsum, et quod ibi quiescat. Unde sicut bonum propter seipsum appetitur, ita et delectatio propter se, et non propter aliud appetitur, si ly *propter* dicat causam finalem. Si vero dicat causam formalem, vel potius motivam, sic delectatio est appetibilis propter aliud, idest propter bonum, quod est delectationis obiectum, et per consequens est principium eius, et dat ei formam, ex hoc enim delectatio habet quod appetatur, quia est quies in bono desiderato.

AD SECUNDUM dicendum quod vehemens appetitus delectationis sensibilis contingit ex hoc quod operationes sensuum, quia sunt principia nostrae cognitionis, sunt magis perceptibiles. Unde etiam a pluribus delectationes sensibiles appetuntur.

AD TERTIUM dicendum quod eo modo omnes appetunt delectationem, sicut et appetunt bonum, et tamen delectationem appetunt ratione boni, et non e converso, ut dictum est. Unde non sequitur quod delectatio sit maximum et per se bonum, sed quod unaquaeque delectatio consequatur aliquod bonum, et quod aliqua delectatio consequatur id quod est per se et maximum bonum.

from matter, and contains an infinite number of singulars. Consequently it is evident that good which is fitting to the body, and which causes bodily delight through being apprehended by sense, is not man's perfect good, but is quite a trifle as compared with the good of the soul. Hence it is written (Wis. 7:9) that "all gold in comparison of her, is as a little sand." And therefore bodily pleasure is neither happiness itself, nor a proper accident of happiness.

Reply to Objection 1: It comes to the same whether we desire good, or desire delight, which is nothing else than the appetite's rest in good: thus it is owing to the same natural force that a weighty body is borne downwards and that it rests there. Consequently just as good is desired for itself, so delight is desired for itself and not for anything else, if the preposition "for" denote the final cause. But if it denote the formal or rather the motive cause, thus delight is desirable for something else, i.e., for the good, which is the object of that delight, and consequently is its principle, and gives it its form: for the reason that delight is desired is that it is rest in the thing desired.

Reply to Objection 2: The vehemence of desire for sensible delight arises from the fact that operations of the senses, through being the principles of our knowledge, are more perceptible. And so it is that sensible pleasures are desired by the majority.

Reply to Objection 3: All desire delight in the same way as they desire good: and yet they desire delight by reason of the good and not conversely, as stated above (ad 1). Consequently it does not follow that delight is the supreme and essential good, but that every delight results from some good, and that some delight results from that which is the essential and supreme good.

ARTICULUS 7

AD SEPTIMUM sic proceditur. Videtur quod beatitudo consistat in aliquo bono animae. Beatitudo enim est quoddam hominis bonum. Hoc autem per tria dividitur, quae sunt bona exteriora, bona corporis, et

ARTICLE 7
Whether some good of the soul constitutes man's happiness?

Objection 1: It would seem that some good of the soul constitutes man's happiness. For happiness is man's good. Now this is threefold: external goods, goods of the body, and

bona animae. Sed beatitudo non consistit in bonis exterioribus, neque in bonis corporis, sicut supra ostensum est. Ergo consistit in bonis animae.

PRAETEREA, illud cui appetimus aliquod bonum, magis amamus quam bonum quod ei appetimus, sicut magis amamus amicum cui appetimus pecuniam, quam pecuniam. Sed unusquisque quodcumque bonum sibi appetit. Ergo seipsum amat magis quam omnia alia bona. Sed beatitudo est quod maxime amatur, quod patet ex hoc quod propter ipsam omnia alia amantur et desiderantur. Ergo beatitudo consistit in aliquo bono ipsius hominis. Sed non in bonis corporis. Ergo in bonis animae.

PRAETEREA, perfectio est aliquid eius quod perficitur. Sed beatitudo est quaedam perfectio hominis. Ergo beatitudo est aliquid hominis. Sed non est aliquid corporis, ut ostensum est. Ergo beatitudo est aliquid animae. Et ita consistit in bonis animae.

SED CONTRA, sicut Augustinus dicit in libro de Doctr. Christ., *id in quo constituitur beata vita, propter se diligendum est.* Sed homo non est propter seipsum diligendus, sed quidquid est in homine, est diligendum propter Deum. Ergo in nullo bono animae beatitudo consistit.

RESPONDEO dicendum quod, sicut supra dictum est, finis dupliciter dicitur, scilicet ipsa res quam adipisci desideramus; et usus, seu adeptio aut possessio illius rei. Si ergo loquamur de ultimo fine hominis quantum ad ipsam rem quam appetimus sicut ultimum finem, impossibile est quod ultimus finis hominis sit ipsa anima, vel aliquid eius. Ipsa enim anima, in se considerata, est ut in potentia existens, fit enim de potentia sciente actu sciens, et de potentia virtuosa actu virtuosa. Cum autem potentia sit propter actum, sicut propter complementum, impossibile est quod id quod est secundum se in potentia existens, habeat rationem ultimi finis. Unde impossibile est quod ipsa anima sit ultimus finis sui ipsius. Similiter etiam neque aliquid eius, sive sit potentia, sive habitus, sive actus. Bonum enim quod est ultimus finis,

goods of the soul. But happiness does not consist in external goods, nor in goods of the body, as shown above (I-II, q. 2, a. 4; a. 5). Therefore it consists in goods of the soul.

Objection 2: Further, we love that for which we desire good, more than the good that we desire for it: thus we love a friend for whom we desire money, more than we love money. But whatever good a man desires, he desires it for himself. Therefore he loves himself more than all other goods. Now happiness is what is loved above all: which is evident from the fact that for its sake all else is loved and desired. Therefore happiness consists in some good of man himself: not, however, in goods of the body; therefore, in goods of the soul.

Objection 3: Further, perfection is something belonging to that which is perfected. But happiness is a perfection of man. Therefore happiness is something belonging to man. But it is not something belonging to the body, as shown above (II-I, q. 2, a. 5). Therefore it is something belonging to the soul; and thus it consists in goods of the soul.

On the contrary, As Augustine says (De Doctr. Christ. i, 22), "that which constitutes the life of happiness is to be loved for its own sake." But man is not to be loved for his own sake, but whatever is in man is to be loved for God's sake. Therefore happiness consists in no good of the soul.

I answer that, As stated above (I-II, q. 1, a. 8), the end is twofold: namely, the thing itself, which we desire to attain, and the use, namely, the attainment or possession of that thing. If, then, we speak of man's last end, it is impossible for man's last end to be the soul itself or something belonging to it. Because the soul, considered in itself, is as something existing in potentiality: for it becomes knowing actually, from being potentially knowing; and actually virtuous, from being potentially virtuous. Now since potentiality is for the sake of act as for its fulfilment, that which in itself is in potentiality cannot be the last end. Therefore the soul itself cannot be its own last end. In like manner neither can anything belonging to it, whether power, habit, or act. For that good which is the last end,

est bonum perfectum complens appetitum. Appetitus autem humanus, qui est voluntas, est boni universalis. Quodlibet bonum autem inhaerens ipsi animae, est bonum participatum, et per consequens particulatum. Unde impossibile est quod aliquod eorum sit ultimus finis hominis. Sed si loquamur de ultimo fine hominis quantum ad ipsam adeptionem vel possessionem, seu quemcumque usum ipsius rei quae appetitur ut finis, sic ad ultimum finem pertinet aliquid hominis ex parte animae, quia homo per animam beatitudinem consequitur. Res ergo ipsa quae appetitur ut finis, est id in quo beatitudo consistit, et quod beatum facit, sed huius rei adeptio vocatur beatitudo. Unde dicendum est quod beatitudo est aliquid animae; sed id in quo consistit beatitudo, est aliquid extra animam.

AD PRIMUM ergo dicendum quod, secundum quod sub illa divisione comprehenduntur omnia bona quae homini sunt appetibilia, sic bonum animae dicitur non solum potentia aut habitus aut actus, sed etiam obiectum, quod est extrinsecum. Et hoc modo nihil prohibet dicere id in quo beatitudo consistit, esse quoddam bonum animae.

AD SECUNDUM dicendum, quantum ad propositum pertinet, quod beatitudo maxime amatur tanquam bonum concupitum, amicus autem amatur tanquam id cui concupiscitur bonum; et sic etiam homo amat seipsum. Unde non est eadem ratio amoris utrobique. Utrum autem amore amicitiae aliquid homo supra se amet, erit locus considerandi cum de caritate agetur.

AD TERTIUM dicendum quod beatitudo ipsa, cum sit perfectio animae, est quoddam animae bonum inhaerens, sed id in quo beatitudo consistit, quod scilicet beatum facit, est aliquid extra animam, ut dictum est.

ARTICULUS 8

AD OCTAVUM sic proceditur. Videtur quod beatitudo hominis consistat in aliquo bono creato. Dicit enim Dionysius, VII cap. de Div. Nom., quod divina sapientia *coniungit fines primorum principiis secundorum,* ex quo

is the perfect good fulfilling the desire. Now man's appetite, otherwise the will, is for the universal good. And any good inherent to the soul is a participated good, and consequently a portioned good. Therefore none of them can be man's last end. But if we speak of man's last end, as to the attainment or possession thereof, or as to any use whatever of the thing itself desired as an end, thus does something of man, in respect of his soul, belong to his last end: since man attains happiness through his soul. Therefore the thing itself which is desired as end, is that which constitutes happiness, and makes man happy; but the attainment of this thing is called happiness. Consequently we must say that happiness is something belonging to the soul; but that which constitutes happiness is something outside the soul.

Reply to Objection 1: Inasmuch as this division includes all goods that man can desire, thus the good of the soul is not only power, habit, or act, but also the object of these, which is something outside. And in this way nothing hinders us from saying that what constitutes happiness is a good of the soul.

Reply to Objection 2: As far as the proposed objection is concerned, happiness is loved above all, as the good desired; whereas a friend is loved as that for which good is desired; and thus, too, man loves himself. Consequently it is not the same kind of love in both cases. As to whether man loves anything more than himself with the love of friendship there will be occasion to inquire when we treat of Charity.

Reply to Objection 3: Happiness, itself, since it is a perfection of the soul, is an inherent good of the soul; but that which constitutes happiness, *viz.* which makes man happy, is something outside his soul, as stated above.

ARTICLE 8
Whether any created good constitutes man's happiness?

Objection 1: It would seem that some created good constitutes man's happiness. For Dionysius says (Div. Nom. vii) that Divine wisdom "unites the ends of first things to the beginnings of second things," from which

potest accipi quod summum inferioris naturae sit attingere infimum naturae superioris. Sed summum hominis bonum est beatitudo. Cum ergo angelus naturae ordine sit supra hominem, ut in primo habitum est; videtur quod beatitudo hominis consistat in hoc quod aliquo modo attingit ad angelum.

PRAETEREA, ultimus finis cuiuslibet rei est in suo perfecto, unde pars est propter totum, sicut propter finem. Sed tota universitas creaturarum, quae dicitur maior mundus, comparatur ad hominem, qui in VIII Physic. dicitur minor mundus, sicut perfectum ad imperfectum. Ergo beatitudo hominis consistit in tota universitate creaturarum.

PRAETEREA, per hoc homo efficitur beatus, quod eius naturale desiderium quietat. Sed naturale desiderium hominis non extenditur ad maius bonum quam quod ipse capere potest. Cum ergo homo non sit capax boni quod excedit limites totius creaturae, videtur quod per aliquod bonum creatum homo beatus fieri possit. Et ita beatitudo hominis in aliquo bono creato consistit.

SED CONTRA est quod Augustinus dicit, XIX de Civ. Dei, *ut vita carnis anima est, ita beata vita hominis Deus est; de quo dicitur, beatus populus cuius dominus Deus eius.*

RESPONDEO dicendum quod impossibile est beatitudinem hominis esse in aliquo bono creato. Beatitudo enim est bonum perfectum, quod totaliter quietat appetitum, alioquin non esset ultimus finis, si adhuc restaret aliquid appetendum. Obiectum autem voluntatis, quae est appetitus humanus, est universale bonum; sicut obiectum intellectus est universale verum. Ex quo patet quod nihil potest quietare voluntatem hominis, nisi bonum universale. Quod non invenitur in aliquo creato, sed solum in Deo, quia omnis creatura habet bonitatem participatam. Unde solus Deus voluntatem hominis implere potest; secundum quod dicitur in Psalmo CII, *qui replet in bonis desiderium tuum.* In solo igitur Deo beatitudo hominis consistit.

AD PRIMUM ergo dicendum quod superius hominis attingit quidem infimum angelicae naturae per quandam similitudinem; non tamen ibi sistit sicut in ultimo fine, sed procedit usque ad ipsum universalem fontem

we may gather that the summit of a lower nature touches the base of the higher nature. But man's highest good is happiness. Since then the angel is above man in the order of nature, as stated in (I-II, q. 111, a. 1), it seems that man's happiness consists in man somehow reaching the angel.

Objection 2: Further, the last end of each thing is that which, in relation to it, is perfect: hence the part is for the whole, as for its end. But the universe of creatures which is called the macrocosm, is compared to man who is called the microcosm (Phys. viii, 2), as perfect to imperfect. Therefore man's happiness consists in the whole universe of creatures.

Objection 3: Further, man is made happy by that which lulls his natural desire. But man's natural desire does not reach out to a good surpassing his capacity. Since then man's capacity does not include that good which surpasses the limits of all creation, it seems that man can be made happy by some created good. Consequently some created good constitutes man's happiness.

On the contrary, Augustine says (De Civ. Dei xix, 26): "As the soul is the life of the body, so God is man's life of happiness: of Whom it is written: 'Happy is that people whose God is the Lord' (Ps. 143:15)."

I answer that, It is impossible for any created good to constitute man's happiness. For happiness is the perfect good, which lulls the appetite altogether; else it would not be the last end, if something yet remained to be desired. Now the object of the will, i.e., of man's appetite, is the universal good; just as the object of the intellect is the universal true. Hence it is evident that naught can lull man's will, save the universal good. This is to be found, not in any creature, but in God alone; because every creature has goodness by participation. Wherefore God alone can satisfy the will of man, according to the words of Ps. 102:5: "Who satisfieth thy desire with good things." Therefore God alone constitutes man's happiness.

Reply to Objection 1: The summit of man does indeed touch the base of the angelic nature, by a kind of likeness; but man does not rest there as in his last end, but reaches out to the universal fount itself

boni, qui est universale obiectum beatitudinis omnium beatorum, tanquam infinitum et perfectum bonum existens.

AD SECUNDUM dicendum quod, si totum aliquod non sit ultimus finis, sed ordinetur ad finem ulteriorem, ultimus finis partis non est ipsum totum, sed aliquid aliud. Universitas autem creaturarum, ad quam comparatur homo ut pars ad totum, non est ultimus finis, sed ordinatur in Deum sicut in ultimum finem. Unde bonum universi non est ultimus finis hominis, sed ipse Deus.

AD TERTIUM dicendum quod bonum creatum non est minus quam bonum cuius homo est capax ut rei intrinsecae et inhaerentis, est tamen minus quam bonum cuius est capax ut obiecti, quod est infinitum. Bonum autem quod participatur ab angelo, et a toto universo, est bonum finitum et contractum.

of good, which is the common object of happiness of all the blessed, as being the infinite and perfect good.

Reply to Objection 2: If a whole be not the last end, but ordained to a further end, then the last end of a part thereof is not the whole itself, but something else. Now the universe of creatures, to which man is compared as part to whole, is not the last end, but is ordained to God, as to its last end. Therefore the last end of man is not the good of the universe, but God himself.

Reply to Objection 3: Created good is not less than that good of which man is capable, as of something intrinsic and inherent to him: but it is less than the good of which he is capable, as of an object, and which is infinite. And the participated good which is in an angel, and in the whole universe, is a finite and restricted good.

QUAESTIO III

Deinde considerandum est quid sit beatitudo; et quae requirantur ad ipsam. Circa primum quaeruntur octo. *Primo,* utrum beatitudo sit aliquid increatum. *Secundo,* si est aliquid creatum, utrum sit operatio. *Tertio,* utrum sit operatio sensitivae partis, an intellectivae tantum. *Quarto,* si est operatio intellectivae partis, utrum sit operatio intellectus, an voluntatis. *Quinto,* si est operatio intellectus, utrum sit operatio intellectus speculativi, aut practici. *Sexto,* si est operatio intellectus speculativi, utrum consistat in speculatione scientiarum speculativarum. *Septimo,* utrum consistat in speculatione substantiarum separatarum, scilicet angelorum. *Octavo,* utrum in sola speculatione Dei qua per essentiam videtur.

QUESTION 3
What Is Happiness

We have now to consider 1. what happiness is, and 2. what things are required for it. Concerning the first there are eight points of inquiry: 1. Whether happiness is something uncreated? 2. If it be something created, whether it is an operation? 3. Whether it is an operation of the sensitive, or only of the intellectual part? 4. If it be an operation of the intellectual part, whether it is an operation of the intellect, or of the will? 5. If it be an operation of the intellect, whether it is an operation of the speculative or of the practical intellect? 6. If it be an operation of the speculative intellect, whether it consists in the consideration of speculative sciences? 7. Whether it consists in the consideration of separate substances *viz.* angels? 8. Whether it consists in the sole contemplation of God seen in His Essence?

ARTICULUS 1

AD PRIMUM sic proceditur. Videtur quod beatitudo sit aliquid increatum. Dicit enim Boetius, in III de Consol., *Deum esse ipsam beatitudinem necesse est confiteri.*

ARTICLE 1
Whether happiness is something uncreated?

Objection 1: It would seem that happiness is something uncreated. For Boethius says (De Consol. iii): "We must needs confess that God is happiness itself."

PRAETEREA, beatitudo est summum bonum. Sed esse summum bonum convenit Deo. Cum ergo non sint plura summa bona, videtur quod beatitudo sit idem quod Deus.

PRAETEREA, beatitudo est ultimus finis, in quem naturaliter humana voluntas tendit. Sed in nullum aliud voluntas tanquam in finem tendere debet nisi in Deum; quo solo fruendum est, ut Augustinus dicit. Ergo beatitudo est idem quod Deus.

SED CONTRA, nullum factum est increatum. Sed beatitudo hominis est aliquid factum, quia secundum Augustinum, I de Doctr. Christ., *illis rebus fruendum est, quae nos beatos faciunt*. Ergo beatitudo non est aliquid increatum.

RESPONDEO dicendum quod, sicut supra dictum est, finis dicitur dupliciter. Uno modo, ipsa res quam cupimus adipisci, sicut avaro est finis pecunia. Alio modo, ipsa adeptio vel possessio, seu usus aut fruitio eius rei quae desideratur, sicut si dicatur quod possessio pecuniae est finis avari, et frui re voluptuosa est finis intemperati. Primo ergo modo, ultimus hominis finis est bonum increatum, scilicet Deus, qui solus sua infinita bonitate potest voluntatem hominis perfecte implere. Secundo autem modo, ultimus finis hominis est aliquid creatum in ipso existens, quod nihil est aliud quam adeptio vel fruitio finis ultimi. Ultimus autem finis vocatur beatitudo. Si ergo beatitudo hominis consideretur quantum ad causam vel obiectum, sic est aliquid increatum, si autem consideretur quantum ad ipsam essentiam beatitudinis, sic est aliquid creatum.

AD PRIMUM ergo dicendum quod Deus est beatitudo per essentiam suam, non enim per adeptionem aut participationem alicuius alterius beatus est, sed per essentiam suam. Homines autem sunt beati, sicut ibidem dicit Boetius, per participationem; sicut et *dii* per participationem dicuntur. Ipsa autem participatio beatitudinis secundum quam homo dicitur beatus, aliquid creatum est.

AD SECUNDUM dicendum quod beatitudo dicitur esse summum hominis bonum, quia est adeptio vel fruitio summi boni.

Objection 2: Further, happiness is the supreme good. But it belongs to God to be the supreme good. Since, then, there are not several supreme goods, it seems that happiness is the same as God.

Objection 3: Further, happiness is the last end, to which man's will tends naturally. But man's will should tend to nothing else as an end, but to God, Who alone is to be enjoyed, as Augustine says (De Doctr. Christ. i, 5,22). Therefore happiness is the same as God.

On the contrary, Nothing made is uncreated. But man's happiness is something made; because according to Augustine (De Doctr. Christ. i, 3): "Those things are to be enjoyed which make us happy." Therefore happiness is not something uncreated.

I answer that, As stated above (I-II, q. 1, a. 8; q. 2, a. 7), our end is twofold. First, there is the thing itself which we desire to attain: thus for the miser, the end is money. Secondly there is the attainment or possession, the use or enjoyment of the thing desired; thus we may say that the end of the miser is the possession of money; and the end of the intemperate man is to enjoy something pleasurable. In the first sense, then, man's last end is the uncreated good, namely, God, Who alone by His infinite goodness can perfectly satisfy man's will. But in the second way, man's last end is something created, existing in him, and this is nothing else than the attainment or enjoyment of the last end. Now the last end is called happiness. If, therefore, we consider man's happiness in its cause or object, then it is something uncreated; but if we consider it as to the very essence of happiness, then it is something created.

Reply to Objection 1: God is happiness by His Essence: for He is happy not by acquisition or participation of something else, but by His Essence. On the other hand, men are happy, as Boethius says (De Consol. iii), by participation; just as they are called "gods," by participation. And this participation of happiness, in respect of which man is said to be happy, is something created.

Reply to Objection 2: Happiness is called man's supreme good, because it is the attainment or enjoyment of the supreme good.

AD TERTIUM dicendum quod beatitudo dicitur ultimus finis, per modum quo adeptio finis dicitur finis.

ARTICULUS 2

AD SECUNDUM sic proceditur. Videtur quod beatitudo non sit operatio. Dicit enim apostolus, Rom. VI, *habetis fructum vestrum in sanctificationem, finem vero vitam aeternam.* Sed vita non est operatio, sed ipsum esse viventium. Ergo ultimus finis, qui est beatitudo, non est operatio.

PRAETEREA, Boetius dicit, in III de Consol., quod beatitudo est *status omnium bonorum aggregatione perfectus.* Sed status non nominat operationem. Ergo beatitudo non est operatio.

PRAETEREA, beatitudo significat aliquid in beato existens, cum sit ultima perfectio hominis. Sed operatio non significat ut aliquid existens in operante, sed magis ut ab ipso procedens. Ergo beatitudo non est operatio.

PRAETEREA, beatitudo permanet in beato. Operatio autem non permanet, sed transit. Ergo beatitudo non est operatio.

PRAETEREA, unius hominis est una beatitudo. Operationes autem sunt multae. Ergo beatitudo non est operatio.

PRAETEREA, beatitudo inest beato absque interruptione. Sed operatio humana frequenter interrumpitur puta somno, vel aliqua alia occupatione, vel quiete. Ergo beatitudo non est operatio.

SED CONTRA est quod philosophus dicit, in I Ethic., quod *felicitas est operatio secundum virtutem perfectam.*

RESPONDEO dicendum quod, secundum quod beatitudo hominis est aliquid creatum in ipso existens necesse est dicere quod beatitudo hominis sit operatio. Est enim beatitudo ultima hominis perfectio. Unumquodque autem intantum perfectum est, inquantum est actu, nam potentia sine actu imperfecta est. Oportet ergo beatitudinem in ultimo actu hominis consistere. Manifestum est autem quod operatio est ultimus actus operantis;

Reply to Objection 3: Happiness is said to be the last end, in the same way as the attainment of the end is called the end.

ARTICLE 2
Whether happiness is an operation?

Objection 1: It would seem that happiness is not an operation. For the Apostle says (Rom. 6:22): "You have your fruit unto sanctification, and the end, life everlasting." But life is not an operation, but the very being of living things. Therefore the last end, which is happiness, is not an operation.

Objection 2: Further, Boethius says (De Consol. iii) that happiness is "a state made perfect by the aggregate of all good things." But state does not indicate operation. Therefore happiness is not an operation.

Objection 3: Further, happiness signifies something existing in the happy one: since it is man's final perfection. But the meaning of operation does not imply anything existing in the operator, but rather something proceeding therefrom. Therefore happiness is not an operation.

Objection 4: Further, happiness remains in the happy one. Now operation does not remain, but passes. Therefore happiness is not an operation.

Objection 5: Further, to one man there is one happiness. But operations are many. Therefore happiness is not an operation.

Objection 6: Further, happiness is in the happy one uninterruptedly. But human operation is often interrupted; for instance, by sleep, or some other occupation, or by cessation. Therefore happiness is not an operation.

On the contrary, The Philosopher says (Ethic. i, 13) that "happiness is an operation according to perfect virtue."

I answer that, In so far as man's happiness is something created, existing in him, we must needs say that it is an operation. For happiness is man's supreme perfection. Now each thing is perfect in so far as it is actual; since potentiality without act is imperfect. Consequently happiness must consist in man's last act. But it is evident that operation is the last act of the operator,

unde et *actus secundus* a philosopho nominatur, in II de anima, nam habens formam potest esse in potentia operans, sicut sciens est in potentia considerans. Et inde est quod in aliis quoque rebus res unaquaeque dicitur esse *propter suam operationem,* ut dicitur in II de caelo. Necesse est ergo beatitudinem hominis operationem esse.

AD PRIMUM ergo dicendum quod vita dicitur dupliciter. Uno modo, ipsum esse viventis. Et sic beatitudo non est vita, ostensum est enim quod esse unius hominis, qualecumque sit, non est hominis beatitudo; solius enim Dei beatitudo est suum esse. Alio modo dicitur vita ipsa operatio viventis, secundum quam principium vitae in actum reducitur, et sic nominamus vitam activam, vel contemplativam, vel voluptuosam. Et hoc modo vita aeterna dicitur ultimus finis. Quod patet per hoc quod dicitur Ioan. XVII, *haec est vita aeterna, ut cognoscant te, Deum verum unum.*

AD SECUNDUM dicendum quod Boetius, definiendo beatitudinem, consideravit ipsam communem beatitudinis rationem. Est enim communis ratio beatitudinis quod sit bonum commune perfectum; et hoc significavit cum dixit quod est *status omnium bonorum aggregatione perfectus,* per quod nihil aliud significatur nisi quod beatus est in statu boni perfecti. Sed Aristoteles expressit ipsam essentiam beatitudinis, ostendens per quid homo sit in huiusmodi statu, quia per operationem quandam. Et ideo in I Ethic. ipse etiam ostendit quod beatitudo est *bonum perfectum.*

AD TERTIUM dicendum quod, sicut dicitur in IX Metaphys., duplex est actio. Una quae procedit ab operante in exteriorem materiam, sicut *urere* et *secare.* Et talis operatio non potest esse beatitudo, nam talis operatio non est actio et perfectio agentis, sed magis patientis, ut ibidem dicitur. Alia est actio manens in ipso agente, ut sentire, intelligere et velle, et huiusmodi actio est perfectio et actus agentis. Et talis operatio potest esse beatitudo.

wherefore the Philosopher calls it "second act" (De Anima ii, 1): because that which has a form can be potentially operating, just as he who knows is potentially considering. And hence it is that in other things, too, each one is said to be "for its operation" (De Coel ii, 3). Therefore man's happiness must of necessity consist in an operation.

Reply to Objection 1: Life is taken in two senses. First for the very being of the living. And thus happiness is not life: since it has been shown (I-II, q. 2, a. 5) that the being of a man, no matter in what it may consist, is not that man's happiness; for of God alone is it true that His Being is His Happiness. Secondly, life means the operation of the living, by which operation the principle of life is made actual: thus we speak of active and contemplative life, or of a life of pleasure. And in this sense eternal life is said to be the last end, as is clear from Jn. 17:3: "This is eternal life, that they may know Thee, the only true God."

Reply to Objection 2: Boethius, in defining happiness, considered happiness in general: for considered thus it is the perfect common good; and he signified this by saying that happiness is "a state made perfect by the aggregate of all good things," thus implying that the state of a happy man consists in possessing the perfect good. But Aristotle expressed the very essence of happiness, showing by what man is established in this state, and that it is by some kind of operation. And so it is that he proves happiness to be "the perfect good" (Ethic. i, 7).

Reply to Objection 3: As stated in Metaph. ix, 7 action is twofold. One proceeds from the agent into outward matter, such as "to burn" and "to cut." And such an operation cannot be happiness: for such an operation is an action and a perfection, not of the agent, but rather of the patient, as is stated in the same passage. The other is an action that remains in the agent, such as to feel, to understand, and to will: and such an action is a perfection and an act of the agent. And such an operation can be happiness.

AD QUARTUM dicendum quod, cum beatitudo dicat quandam ultimam perfectionem, secundum quod diversae res beatitudinis capaces ad diversos gradus perfectionis pertingere possunt, secundum hoc necesse est quod diversimode beatitudo dicatur. Nam in Deo est beatitudo per essentiam, quia ipsum esse eius est operatio eius, qua non fruitur alio, sed seipso. In angelis autem beatis est ultima perfectio secundum aliquam operationem, qua coniunguntur bono increato, et haec operatio in eis est unica et sempiterna. In hominibus autem, secundum statum praesentis vitae, est ultima perfectio secundum operationem qua homo coniungitur Deo, sed haec operatio nec continua potest esse, et per consequens nec unica est, quia operatio intercisione multiplicatur. Et propter hoc in statu praesentis vitae, perfecta beatitudo ab homine haberi non potest. Unde philosophus, in I Ethic., ponens beatitudinem hominis in hac vita, dicit eam imperfectam, post multa concludens, *beatos autem dicimus ut homines.* Sed promittitur nobis a Deo beatitudo perfecta, quando erimus *sicut angeli in caelo,* sicut dicitur Matth. XXII. Quantum ergo ad illam beatitudinem perfectam, cessat obiectio, quia una et continua et sempiterna operatione in illo beatitudinis statu mens hominis Deo coniungetur. Sed in praesenti vita, quantum deficimus ab unitate et continuitate talis operationis, tantum deficimus a beatitudinis perfectione. Est tamen aliqua participatio beatitudinis, et tanto maior, quanto operatio potest esse magis continua et una. Et ideo in activa vita, quae circa multa occupatur, est minus de ratione beatitudinis quam in vita contemplativa, quae versatur circa unum, idest circa veritatis contemplationem. Et si aliquando homo actu non operetur huiusmodi operationem, tamen quia in promptu habet eam semper operari; et quia etiam ipsam cessationem, puta somni vel occupationis alicuius naturalis, ad operationem praedictam ordinat; quasi videtur operatio continua esse.

Et per hoc patet solutio ad quintum, et ad sextum.

Reply to Objection 4: Since happiness signifies some final perfection; according as various things capable of happiness can attain to various degrees of perfection, so must there be various meanings applied to happiness. For in God there is happiness essentially; since His very Being is His operation, whereby He enjoys no other than Himself. In the happy angels, the final perfection is in respect of some operation, by which they are united to the Uncreated Good: and this operation of theirs is one only and everlasting. But in men, according to their present state of life, the final perfection is in respect of an operation whereby man is united to God: but this operation neither can be continual, nor, consequently, is it one only, because operation is multiplied by being discontinued. And for this reason in the present state of life, perfect happiness cannot be attained by man. Wherefore the Philosopher, in placing man's happiness in this life (Ethic. i, 10), says that it is imperfect, and after a long discussion, concludes: "We call men happy, but only as men." But God has promised us perfect happiness, when we shall be "as the angels . . . in heaven" (Mat. 22:30). Consequently in regard to this perfect happiness, the objection fails: because in that state of happiness, man's mind will be united to God by one, continual, everlasting operation. But in the present life, in as far as we fall short of the unity and continuity of that operation so do we fall short of perfect happiness. Nevertheless it is a participation of happiness: and so much the greater, as the operation can be more continuous and more one. Consequently the active life, which is busy with many things, has less of happiness than the contemplative life, which is busied with one thing, i.e., the contemplation of truth. And if at any time man is not actually engaged in this operation, yet since he can always easily turn to it, and since he ordains the very cessation, by sleeping or occupying himself otherwise, to the aforesaid occupation, the latter seems, as it were, continuous.

From these remarks the replies to Objections 5 and 6 are evident.

Articulus 3

AD TERTIUM sic proceditur. Videtur quod beatitudo consistat etiam in operatione sensus. Nulla enim operatio invenitur in homine nobilior operatione sensitiva, nisi intellectiva. Sed operatio intellectiva dependet in nobis ab operatione sensitiva, quia *non possumus intelligere sine phantasmate,* ut dicitur in III de anima. Ergo beatitudo consistit etiam in operatione sensitiva.

PRAETEREA, Boetius dicit, in III de Consol., quod beatitudo est *status omnium bonorum aggregatione perfectus.* Sed quaedam bona sunt sensibilia, quae attingimus per sensus operationem. Ergo videtur quod operatio sensus requiratur ad beatitudinem.

PRAETEREA, beatitudo est bonum perfectum, ut probatur in I Ethic., quod non esset, nisi homo perficeretur per ipsam secundum omnes partes suas. Sed per operationes sensitivas quaedam partes animae perficiuntur. Ergo operatio sensitiva requiritur ad beatitudinem.

SED CONTRA, in operatione sensitiva communicant nobiscum bruta animalia. Non autem in beatitudine. Ergo beatitudo non consistit in operatione sensitiva.

RESPONDEO dicendum quod ad beatitudinem potest aliquid pertinere tripliciter, *uno modo,* essentialiter; *alio modo,* antecedenter; *tertio modo,* consequenter. Essentialiter quidem non potest pertinere operatio sensus ad beatitudinem. Nam beatitudo hominis consistit essentialiter in coniunctione ipsius ad bonum increatum, quod est ultimus finis, ut supra ostensum est, cui homo coniungi non potest per sensus operationem. Similiter etiam quia, sicut ostensum est, in corporalibus bonis beatitudo hominis non consistit, quae tamen sola per operationem sensus attingimus. Possunt autem operationes sensus pertinere ad beatitudinem antecedenter et consequenter. Antecedenter quidem, secundum beatitudinem imperfectam, qualis in praesenti vita haberi potest, nam operatio intellectus praeexigit operationem sensus. Consequenter autem, in illa perfecta

ARTICLE 3
Whether happiness is an operation of the sensitive part, or of the intellective part only?

Objection 1: It would seem that happiness consists in an operation of the senses also. For there is no more excellent operation in man than that of the senses, except the intellective operation. But in us the intellective operation depends on the sensitive: since "we cannot understand without a phantasm" (De Anima iii, 7). Therefore happiness consists in an operation of the senses also.

Objection 2: Further, Boethius says (De Consol. iii) that happiness is "a state made perfect by the aggregate of all good things." But some goods are sensible, which we attain by the operation of the senses. Therefore it seems that the operation of the senses is needed for happiness.

Objection 3: Further, happiness is the perfect good, as we find proved in Ethic. i, 7: which would not be true, were not man perfected thereby in all his parts. But some parts of the soul are perfected by sensitive operations. Therefore sensitive operation is required for happiness.

On the contrary, Irrational animals have the sensitive operation in common with us: but they have not happiness in common with us. Therefore happiness does not consist in a sensitive operation.

I answer that, A thing may belong to happiness in three ways: 1. essentially, 2. antecedently, 3. consequently. Now the operation of sense cannot belong to happiness essentially. For man's happiness consists essentially in his being united to the Uncreated Good, Which is his last end, as shown above (I-II, q. 3, a. 1): to Which man cannot be united by an operation of his senses. Again, in like manner, because, as shown above (I-II, q. 2, a. 5), man's happiness does not consist in goods of the body, which goods alone, however, we attain through the operation of the senses.Nevertheless the operations of the senses can belong to happiness, both antecedently and consequently: antecedently, in respect of imperfect happiness, such as can be had in this life, since the operation of the intellect demands a previous operation of the sense; consequently, in that perfect

beatitudine quae expectatur in caelo, quia post resurrectionem, *ex ipsa beatitudine animae,* ut Augustinus dicit in epistola ad Dioscorum, *fiet quaedam refluentia in corpus et in sensus corporeos, ut in suis operationibus perficiantur;* ut infra magis patebit, cum de resurrectione agetur. Non autem tunc operatio qua mens humana Deo coniungetur, a sensu dependebit.

AD PRIMUM ergo dicendum quod obiectio illa probat quod operatio sensus requiritur antecedenter ad beatitudinem imperfectam, qualis in hac vita haberi potest.

AD SECUNDUM dicendum quod beatitudo perfecta, qualem angeli habent, habet congregationem omnium bonorum per coniunctionem ad universalem fontem totius boni; non quod indigeat singulis particularibus bonis. Sed in hac beatitudine imperfecta, requiritur congregatio bonorum sufficientium ad perfectissimam operationem huius vitae.

AD TERTIUM dicendum quod in perfecta beatitudine perficitur totus homo, sed in inferiori parte per redundantiam a superiori. In beatitudine autem imperfecta praesentis vitae, e converso a perfectione inferioris partis proceditur ad perfectionem superioris.

happiness which we await in heaven; because at the resurrection, "from the very happiness of the soul," as Augustine says (Ep. ad Dioscor.) "the body and the bodily senses will receive a certain overflow, so as to be perfected in their operations"; a point which will be explained further on when we treat of the resurrection (II-II, qq. 82-85). But then the operation whereby man's mind is united to God will not depend on the senses.

Reply to Objection 1: This objection proves that the operation of the senses is required antecedently for imperfect happiness, such as can be had in this life.

Reply to Objection 2: Perfect happiness, such as the angels have, includes the aggregate of all good things, by being united to the universal source of all good; not that it requires each individual good. But in this imperfect happiness, we need the aggregate of those goods that suffice for the most perfect operation of this life.

Reply to Objection 3: In perfect happiness the entire man is perfected, in the lower part of his nature, by an overflow from the higher. But in the imperfect happiness of this life, it is otherwise; we advance from the perfection of the lower part to the perfection of the higher part.

ARTICULUS 4

AD QUARTUM sic proceditur. Videtur quod beatitudo consistat in actu voluntatis. Dicit enim Augustinus, XIX de Civ. Dei, quod beatitudo hominis in pace consistit, unde in Psalmo CXLVII, *qui posuit fines tuos pacem.* Sed pax ad voluntatem pertinet. Ergo beatitudo hominis in voluntate consistit.

PRAETEREA, beatitudo est summum bonum. Sed bonum est obiectum voluntatis. Ergo beatitudo in operatione voluntatis consistit.

PRAETEREA, primo moventi respondet ultimus finis, sicut ultimus finis totius exercitus est victoria, quae est finis

ARTICLE 4
Whether, if happiness is in the intellective part, it is an operation of the intellect or of the will?

Objection 1: It would seem that happiness consists in an act of the will. For Augustine says (De Civ. Dei xix, 10, 11), that man's happiness consists in peace; wherefore it is written (Ps. 147:3): "Who hath placed peace in thy end.*" But peace pertains to the will. Therefore man's happiness is in the will.

Objection 2: Further, happiness is the supreme good. But good is the object of the will. Therefore happiness consists in an operation of the will.

Objection 3: Further, the last end corresponds to the first mover: thus the last end of the whole army is victory, which is the end

---

* Douay: 'borders'

I-II, q. 3, a. 4, arg. 3

ducis, qui omnes movet. Sed primum movens ad operandum est voluntas, quia movet alias vires, ut infra dicetur. Ergo beatitudo ad voluntatem pertinet.

Praeterea, si beatitudo est aliqua operatio, oportet quod sit nobilissima operatio hominis. Sed nobilior operatio est dilectio Dei, quae est actus voluntatis, quam cognitio, quae est operatio intellectus, ut patet per **apostolum,** I ad Cor. XIII. **Ergo** videtur quod beatitudo consistat in actu voluntatis.

Praeterea, Augustinus dicit, in XIII de Trin., quod *beatus est qui habet omnia quae vult, et nihil vult male.* Et post pauca subdit, *propinquat beato qui bene vult quodcumque vult, bona enim beatum faciunt, quorum bonorum iam habet aliquid, ipsam scilicet bonam voluntatem.* Ergo beatitudo in actu voluntatis consistit.

Sed contra est quod dominus dicit, Ioan. XVII, *haec est vita aeterna, ut cognoscant te, Deum verum unum.* Vita autem aeterna est ultimus finis, ut dictum est. Ergo beatitudo hominis in cognitione Dei consistit, quae est actus intellectus.

Respondeo dicendum quod ad beatitudinem, sicut supra dictum est, duo requiruntur, unum quod est essentia beatitudinis; aliud quod est quasi per se accidens eius, scilicet delectatio ei adiuncta. Dico ergo quod, quantum ad id quod est essentialiter ipsa beatitudo, impossibile est quod consistat in actu voluntatis. Manifestum est enim ex praemissis quod beatitudo est consecutio finis ultimi. Consecutio autem finis non consistit in ipso actu voluntatis. Voluntas enim fertur in finem et absentem, cum ipsum desiderat; et praesentem, cum in ipso requiescens delectatur. Manifestum est autem quod ipsum desiderium finis non est consecutio finis, sed est motus ad finem. Delectatio autem advenit voluntati ex hoc quod finis est praesens, non autem e converso ex hoc aliquid fit praesens, quia voluntas delectatur in ipso.

WHAT IS HAPPINESS

of the general, who moves all the men. But the first mover in regard to operations is the will: because it moves the other powers, as we shall state further on (I-II, q. 9, a. 1; a. 3). Therefore happiness regards the will.

Objection 4: Further, if happiness be an operation, it must needs be man's most excellent operation. But the love of God, which is an act of the will, is a more excellent operation than knowledge, which is an operation of the intellect, as the Apostle declares (1 Cor. 13). Therefore it seems that happiness consists in an act of the will.

Objection 5: Further, Augustine says (De Trin. xiii, 5) that "happy is he who has whatever he desires, and desires nothing amiss." And a little further on (6) he adds: "He is most happy who desires well, whatever he desires: for good things make a man happy, and such a man already possesses some good—i.e., a good will." Therefore happiness consists in an act of the will.

On the contrary, Our Lord said (Jn. 17:3): "This is eternal life: that they may know Thee, the only true God." Now eternal life is the last end, as stated above (I-II, q. 3, a. 2, ad 1). Therefore man's happiness consists in the knowledge of God, which is an act of the intellect.

I answer that, As stated above (I-II, q. 2, a. 6) two things are needed for happiness: one, which is the essence of happiness: the other, that is, as it were, its proper accident, i.e., the delight connected with it. I say, then, that as to the very essence of happiness, it is impossible for it to consist in an act of the will. For it is evident from what has been said (I-II, q. 3, a. 1; a. 2; q. 2, a. 7) that happiness is the attainment of the last end. But the attainment of the end does not consist in the very act of the will. For the will is directed to the end, both absent, when it desires it; and present, when it is delighted by resting therein. Now it is evident that the desire itself of the end is not the attainment of the end, but is a movement towards the end: while delight comes to the will from the end being present; and not conversely, is a thing made present, by the fact that the will delights in it.

Oportet igitur aliquid aliud esse quam actum voluntatis, per quod fit ipse finis praesens volenti. Et hoc manifeste apparet circa fines sensibiles. Si enim consequi pecuniam esset per actum voluntatis, statim a principio cupidus consecutus esset pecuniam, quando vult eam habere. Sed a principio quidem est absens ei; consequitur autem ipsam per hoc quod manu ipsam apprehendit, vel aliquo huiusmodi; et tunc iam delectatur in pecunia habita. Sic igitur et circa intelligibilem finem contingit. Nam a principio volumus consequi finem intelligibilem; consequimur autem ipsum per hoc quod fit praesens nobis per actum intellectus; et tunc voluntas delectata conquiescit in fine iam adepto. Sic igitur essentia beatitudinis in actu intellectus consistit, sed ad voluntatem pertinet delectatio beatitudinem consequens; secundum quod Augustinus dicit, X Confess., quod beatitudo est *gaudium de veritate*; quia scilicet ipsum gaudium est consummatio beatitudinis.

AD PRIMUM ergo dicendum quod pax pertinet ad ultimum hominis finem, non quasi essentialiter sit ipsa beatitudo; sed quia antecedenter et consequenter se habet ad ipsam. Antecedenter quidem, inquantum iam sunt remota omnia perturbantia, et impedientia ab ultimo fine. Consequenter vero, inquantum iam homo, adepto ultimo fine, remanet pacatus, suo desiderio quietato.

AD SECUNDUM dicendum quod primum obiectum voluntatis non est actus eius sicut nec primum obiectum visus est visio, sed visibile. Unde ex hoc ipso quod beatitudo pertinet ad voluntatem tanquam primum obiectum eius, sequitur quod non pertineat ad ipsam tanquam actus ipsius.

AD TERTIUM dicendum quod finem primo apprehendit intellectus quam voluntas, tamen motus ad finem incipit in voluntate. Et ideo voluntati debetur id quod ultimo consequitur consecutionem finis, scilicet delectatio vel fruitio.

AD QUARTUM dicendum quod dilectio praeeminet cognitioni in movendo, sed cognitio praevia est dilectioni in attingendo, *non enim diligitur nisi cognitum,* ut dicit Augustinus in X de Trin. Et ideo intelligibilem finem primo attingimus per actionem intellectus;

Therefore, that the end be present to him who desires it, must be due to something else than an act of the will. This is evidently the case in regard to sensible ends. For if the acquisition of money were through an act of the will, the covetous man would have it from the very moment that he wished for it. But at the moment it is far from him; and he attains it, by grasping it in his hand, or in some like manner; and then he delights in the money got. And so it is with an intelligible end. For at first we desire to attain an intelligible end; we attain it, through its being made present to us by an act of the intellect; and then the delighted will rests in the end when attained. So, therefore, the essence of happiness consists in an act of the intellect: but the delight that results from happiness pertains to the will. In this sense Augustine says (Confess. x, 23) that happiness is "joy in truth," because, to wit, joy itself is the consummation of happiness.

Reply to Objection 1: Peace pertains to man's last end, not as though it were the very essence of happiness; but because it is antecedent and consequent thereto: antecedent, in so far as all those things are removed which disturb and hinder man in attaining the last end: consequent inasmuch as when man has attained his last end, he remains at peace, his desire being at rest.

Reply to Objection 2: The will's first object is not its act: just as neither is the first object of the sight, vision, but a visible thing. Wherefore, from the very fact that happiness belongs to the will, as the will's first object, it follows that it does not belong to it as its act.

Reply to Objection 3: The intellect apprehends the end before the will does: yet motion towards the end begins in the will. And therefore to the will belongs that which last of all follows the attainment of the end, *viz.* delight or enjoyment.

Reply to Objection 4: Love ranks above knowledge in moving, but knowledge precedes love in attaining: for "naught is loved save what is known," as Augustine says (De Trin. x, 1). Consequently we first attain an intelligible end by an act of the intellect;

sicut et finem sensibilem primo attingimus per actionem sensus.

Ad quintum dicendum quod ille qui habet omnia quae vult, ex hoc est beatus, quod habet ea quae vult, quod quidem est per aliud quam per actum voluntatis. Sed nihil male velle requiritur ad beatitudinem sicut quaedam debita dispositio ad ipsam. Voluntas autem bona ponitur in numero bonorum quae beatum faciunt, prout est inclinatio quaedam in ipsa, sicut motus reducitur ad genus sui termini, ut *alteratio* ad *qualitatem.*

just as we first attain a sensible end by an act of sense.

Reply to Objection 5: He who has whatever he desires, is happy, because he has what he desires: and this indeed is by something other than the act of his will. But to desire nothing amiss is needed for happiness, as a necessary disposition thereto. And a good will is reckoned among the good things which make a man happy, forasmuch as it is an inclination of the will: just as a movement is reduced to the genus of its terminus, for instance, "alteration" to the genus "quality."

Articulus 5

Ad quintum sic proceditur. Videtur quod beatitudo consistat in operatione intellectus practici. Finis enim ultimus cuiuslibet creaturae consistit in assimilatione ad Deum. Sed homo magis assimilatur Deo per intellectum practicum, qui est causa rerum intellectarum, quam per intellectum speculativum, cuius scientia accipitur a rebus. Ergo beatitudo hominis magis consistit in operatione intellectus practici quam speculativi.

Praeterea, beatitudo est perfectum hominis bonum. Sed intellectus practicus magis ordinatur ad bonum quam speculativus, qui ordinatur ad verum. Unde et secundum perfectionem practici intellectus, dicimur boni, non autem secundum perfectionem speculativi intellectus, sed secundum eam dicimur scientes vel intelligentes. Ergo beatitudo hominis magis consistit in actu intellectus practici quam speculativi.

Praeterea, beatitudo est quoddam bonum ipsius hominis. Sed speculativus intellectus occupatur magis circa ea quae sunt extra hominem, practicus autem intellectus occupatur circa ea quae sunt ipsius hominis, scilicet circa operationes et passiones eius. Ergo beatitudo hominis magis consistit in operatione intellectus practici quam intellectus speculativi.

Sed contra est quod Augustinus dicit, in I de Trin., quod *contemplatio promittitur*

Article 5
Whether happiness is an operation of the speculative, or of the practical intellect?

Objection 1: It would seem that happiness is an operation of the practical intellect. For the end of every creature consists in becoming like God. But man is like God, by his practical intellect, which is the cause of things understood, rather than by his speculative intellect, which derives its knowledge from things. Therefore man's happiness consists in an operation of the practical intellect rather than of the speculative.

Objection 2: Further, happiness is man's perfect good. But the practical intellect is ordained to the good rather than the speculative intellect, which is ordained to the true. Hence we are said to be good, in reference to the perfection of the practical intellect, but not in reference to the perfection of the speculative intellect, according to which we are said to be knowing or understanding. Therefore man's happiness consists in an act of the practical intellect rather than of the speculative.

Objection 3: Further, happiness is a good of man himself. But the speculative intellect is more concerned with things outside man; whereas the practical intellect is concerned with things belonging to man himself, *viz.* his operations and passions. Therefore man's happiness consists in an operation of the practical intellect rather than of the speculative.

On the contrary, Augustine says (De Trin. i, 8) that "contemplation is promised

nobis, actionum omnium finis, atque aeterna perfectio gaudiorum.

Respondeo dicendum quod beatitudo magis consistit in operatione speculativi intellectus quam practici. Quod patet ex tribus. Primo quidem, ex hoc quod, si beatitudo hominis est operatio, oportet quod sit optima operatio hominis. Optima autem operatio hominis est quae est optimae potentiae respectu optimi obiecti. Optima autem potentia est intellectus, cuius optimum obiectum est bonum divinum, quod quidem non est obiectum practici intellectus, sed speculativi. Unde in tali operatione, scilicet in contemplatione divinorum, maxime consistit beatitudo. Et quia unusquisque *videtur esse id quod est optimum in eo,* ut dicitur in IX et X Ethic., ideo talis operatio est maxime propria homini, et maxime delectabilis. Secundo apparet idem ex hoc quod contemplatio maxime quaeritur propter seipsam. Actus autem intellectus practici non quaeritur propter seipsum, sed propter actionem. Ipsae etiam actiones ordinantur ad aliquem finem. Unde manifestum est quod ultimus finis non potest consistere in vita activa, quae pertinet ad intellectum practicum. Tertio idem apparet ex hoc quod in vita contemplativa homo communicat cum superioribus, scilicet cum Deo et angelis, quibus per beatitudinem assimilatur. Sed in his quae pertinent ad vitam activam, etiam alia animalia cum homine aliqualiter communicant, licet imperfectae. Et ideo ultima et perfecta beatitudo, quae expectatur in futura vita, tota consistit in contemplatione. Beatitudo autem imperfecta, qualis hic haberi potest, primo quidem et principaliter consistit in contemplatione, secundario vero in operatione practici intellectus ordinantis actiones et passiones humanas, ut dicitur in X Ethic.

Ad primum ergo dicendum quod similitudo praedicta intellectus practici ad Deum, est secundum proportionalitatem; quia scilicet se habet ad suum cognitum, sicut Deus ad suum. Sed assimilatio intellectus speculativi ad Deum, est secundum unionem vel informationem; quae est multo maior assimilatio. Et tamen dici potest quod, respectu principalis cogniti,

us, as being the goal of all our actions, and the everlasting perfection of our joys."

I answer that, Happiness consists in an operation of the speculative rather than of the practical intellect. This is evident for three reasons. First because if man's happiness is an operation, it must needs be man's highest operation. Now man's highest operation is that of his highest power in respect of its highest object: and his highest power is the intellect, whose highest object is the Divine Good, which is the object, not of the practical but of the speculative intellect. Consequently happiness consists principally in such an operation, *viz.* in the contemplation of Divine things. And since that "seems to be each man's self, which is best in him," according to Ethic. ix, 8, and x, 7, therefore such an operation is most proper to man and most delightful to him. Secondly, it is evident from the fact that contemplation is sought principally for its own sake. But the act of the practical intellect is not sought for its own sake but for the sake of action: and these very actions are ordained to some end. Consequently it is evident that the last end cannot consist in the active life, which pertains to the practical intellect. Thirdly, it is again evident, from the fact that in the contemplative life man has something in common with things above him, *viz.* with God and the angels, to whom he is made like by happiness. But in things pertaining to the active life, other animals also have something in common with man, although imperfectly. Therefore the last and perfect happiness, which we await in the life to come, consists entirely in contemplation. But imperfect happiness, such as can be had here, consists first and principally, in an operation of the practical intellect directing human actions and passions, as stated in Ethic. x, 7, 8.

Reply to Objection 1: The asserted likeness of the practical intellect to God is one of proportion; that is to say, by reason of its standing in relation to what it knows, as God does to what He knows. But the likeness of the speculative intellect to God is one of union and "information"; which is a much greater likeness. And yet it may be answered that, in regard to the principal thing known,

quod est sua essentia, non habet Deus practicam cognitionem, sed speculativam tantum.

AD SECUNDUM dicendum quod intellectus practicus ordinatur ad bonum quod est extra ipsum, sed intellectus speculativus habet bonum in seipso, scilicet contemplationem veritatis. Et si illud bonum sit perfectum, ex eo totus homo perficitur et fit bonus, quod quidem intellectus practicus non habet sed ad illud ordinat.

AD TERTIUM dicendum quod ratio illa procederet, si ipsemet homo esset ultimus finis suus, tunc enim consideratio et ordinatio actuum et passionum eius esset eius beatitudo. Sed quia ultimus hominis finis est aliquod bonum extrinsecum, scilicet Deus, ad quem per operationem intellectus speculativi attingimus; ideo magis beatitudo hominis in operatione intellectus speculativi consistit, quam in operatione intellectus practici.

which is His Essence, God has not practical but merely speculative knowledge.

Reply to Objection 2: The practical intellect is ordained to good which is outside of it: but the speculative intellect has good within it, *viz.* the contemplation of truth. And if this good be perfect, the whole man is perfected and made good thereby: such a good the practical intellect has not; but it directs man thereto.

Reply to Objection 3: This argument would hold, if man himself were his own last end; for then the consideration and direction of his actions and passions would be his happiness. But since man's last end is something outside of him, to wit, God, to Whom we reach out by an operation of the speculative intellect; therefore, man's happiness consists in an operation of the speculative intellect rather than of the practical intellect.

ARTICULUS 6

AD SEXTUM sic proceditur. Videtur quod beatitudo hominis consistat in consideratione speculativarum scientiarum. Philosophus enim dicit, in libro Ethic., quod *felicitas est operatio secundum perfectam virtutem*. Et distinguens virtutes, non ponit speculativas nisi tres, *scientiam, sapientiam* et *intellectum;* quae omnes pertinent ad considerationem scientiarum speculativarum. Ergo ultima hominis beatitudo in consideratione scientiarum speculativarum consistit.

PRAETEREA, illud videtur esse ultima hominis beatitudo, quod naturaliter desideratur ab omnibus propter seipsum. Sed huiusmodi est consideratio speculativarum scientiarum, quia, ut dicitur in I Metaphys., *omnes homines natura scire desiderant;* et post pauca subditur quod speculativae scientiae propter seipsas quaeruntur. Ergo in consideratione scientiarum speculativarum consistit beatitudo.

PRAETEREA, beatitudo est ultima hominis perfectio. Unumquodque autem perficitur secundum quod reducitur de potentia in actum. Intellectus autem humanus reducitur in actum per considerationem scientiarum speculativarum. Ergo videtur quod in

ARTICLE 6
Whether happiness consists in the consideration of speculative sciences?

Objection 1: It would seem that man's happiness consists in the consideration of speculative sciences. For the Philosopher says (Ethic. i, 13) that "happiness is an operation according to perfect virtue." And in distinguishing the virtues, he gives no more than three speculative virtues—"knowledge," "wisdom" and "understanding," which all belong to the consideration of speculative sciences. Therefore man's final happiness consists in the consideration of speculative sciences.

Objection 2: Further, that which all desire for its own sake, seems to be man's final happiness. Now such is the consideration of speculative sciences; because, as stated in Metaph. i, 1, "all men naturally desire to know"; and, a little farther on (2), it is stated that speculative sciences are sought for their own sakes. Therefore happiness consists in the consideration of speculative sciences.

Objection 3: Further, happiness is man's final perfection. Now everything is perfected, according as it is reduced from potentiality to act. But the human intellect is reduced to act by the consideration of speculative sciences. Therefore it seems that in the

huiusmodi consideratione ultima hominis beatitudo consistat.

SED CONTRA est quod dicitur Ierem. IX, *non glorietur sapiens in sapientia sua;* et loquitur de sapientia speculativarum scientiarum. Non ergo consistit in harum consideratione ultima hominis beatitudo.

RESPONDEO dicendum quod, sicut supra dictum est, duplex est hominis beatitudo, una perfecta, et alia imperfecta. Oportet autem intelligere perfectam beatitudinem, quae attingit ad veram beatitudinis rationem, beatitudinem autem imperfectam, quae non attingit, sed participat quandam particularem beatitudinis similitudinem. Sicut perfecta prudentia invenitur in homine, apud quem est ratio rerum agibilium, imperfecta autem prudentia est in quibusdam animalibus brutis, in quibus sunt quidam particulares instinctus ad quaedam opera similia operibus prudentiae. Perfecta igitur beatitudo in consideratione scientiarum speculativarum essentialiter consistere non potest. Ad cuius evidentiam, considerandum est quod consideratio speculativae scientiae non se extendit ultra virtutem principiorum illius scientiae, quia in principiis scientiae virtualiter tota scientia continetur. Prima autem principia scientiarum speculativarum sunt per sensum accepta; ut patet per philosophum in principio Metaphys., et in fine Poster. Unde tota consideratio scientiarum speculativarum non potest ultra extendi quam sensibilium cognitio ducere potest. In cognitione autem sensibilium non potest consistere ultima hominis beatitudo, quae est ultima eius perfectio. Non enim aliquid perficitur ab aliquo inferiori, nisi secundum quod in inferiori est aliqua participatio superioris. Manifestum est autem quod forma lapidis, vel cuiuslibet rei sensibilis, est inferior homine. Unde per formam lapidis non perficitur intellectus inquantum est talis forma, sed inquantum in ea participatur aliqua similitudo alicuius quod est supra intellectum humanum, scilicet lumen intelligibile, vel aliquid huiusmodi. Omne autem quod est per aliud, reducitur ad id quod est per se. Unde oportet quod ultima perfectio hominis sit per cognitionem alicuius rei quae sit supra intellectum humanum. Ostensum est autem quod per sensibilia non

consideration of these sciences, man's final happiness consists.

On the contrary, It is written (Jer. 9:23): "Let not the wise man glory in his wisdom": and this is said in reference to speculative sciences. Therefore man's final happiness does not consist in the consideration of these.

I answer that, As stated above (I-II, q. 3, a. 2, ad 4), man's happiness is twofold, one perfect, the other imperfect. And by perfect happiness we are to understand that which attains to the true notion of happiness; and by imperfect happiness that which does not attain thereto, but partakes of some particular likeness of happiness. Thus perfect prudence is in man, with whom is the idea of things to be done; while imperfect prudence is in certain irrational animals, who are possessed of certain particular instincts in respect of works similar to works of prudence. Accordingly perfect happiness cannot consist essentially in the consideration of speculative sciences. To prove this, we must observe that the consideration of a speculative science does not extend beyond the scope of the principles of that science: since the entire science is virtually contained in its principles. Now the first principles of speculative sciences are received through the senses, as the Philosopher clearly states at the beginning of the Metaphysics (i, 1), and at the end of the Posterior Analytics (ii, 15). Wherefore the entire consideration of speculative sciences cannot extend farther than knowledge of sensibles can lead. Now man's final happiness, which is his final perfection cannot consist in the knowledge of sensibles. For a thing is not perfected by something lower, except in so far as the lower partakes of something higher. Now it is evident that the form of a stone or of any sensible, is lower than man. Consequently the intellect is not perfected by the form of a stone, as such, but inasmuch as it partakes of a certain likeness to that which is above the human intellect, *viz.* the intelligible light, or something of the kind. Now whatever is by something else is reduced to that which is of itself. Therefore man's final perfection must needs be through knowledge of something above the human intellect. But it has been shown (I, q. 88, a. 2), that man can-

potest deveniri in cognitionem substantiarum separatarum, quae sunt supra intellectum humanum. Unde relinquitur quod ultima hominis beatitudo non possit esse in consideratione speculativarum scientiarum. Sed sicut in formis sensibilibus participatur aliqua similitudo superiorum substantiarum, ita consideratio scientiarum speculativarum est quaedam participatio verae et perfectae beatitudinis.

AD PRIMUM ergo dicendum quod philosophus loquitur in libro Ethicorum de felicitate imperfecta, qualiter in hac vita haberi potest, ut supra dictum est.

AD SECUNDUM dicendum quod naturaliter desideratur non solum perfecta beatitudo, sed etiam qualiscumque similitudo vel participatio ipsius.

AD TERTIUM dicendum quod per considerationem scientiarum speculativarum reducitur intellectus noster aliquo modo in actum, non autem in ultimum et completum.

not acquire through sensibles, the knowledge of separate substances, which are above the human intellect. Consequently it follows that man's happiness cannot consist in the consideration of speculative sciences. However, just as in sensible forms there is a participation of the higher substances, so the consideration of speculative sciences is a certain participation of true and perfect happiness.

Reply to Objection 1: In his book on Ethics the Philosopher treats of imperfect happiness, such as can be had in this life, as stated above (I-II, q. 3, a. 2, ad 4).

Reply to Objection 2: Not only is perfect happiness naturally desired, but also any likeness or participation thereof.

Reply to Objection 3: Our intellect is reduced to act, in a fashion, by the consideration of speculative sciences, but not to its final and perfect act.

ARTICULUS 7

AD SEPTIMUM sic proceditur. Videtur quod beatitudo hominis consistat in cognitione substantiarum separatarum, idest angelorum. Dicit enim Gregorius, in quadam homilia, *nihil prodest interesse festis hominum, si non contingat interesse festis angelorum;* per quod finalem beatitudinem designat. Sed festis angelorum interesse possumus per eorum contemplationem. Ergo videtur quod in contemplatione angelorum ultima hominis beatitudo consistat.

PRAETEREA, ultima perfectio uniuscuiusque rei est ut coniungatur suo principio, unde et circulus dicitur esse figura perfecta, quia habet idem principium et finem. Sed principium cognitionis humanae est ab ipsis angelis, per quos homines illuminantur, ut dicit Dionysius, IV cap. Cael. Hier. Ergo perfectio humani intellectus est in contemplatione angelorum.

PRAETEREA, unaquaeque natura perfecta est, quando coniungitur superiori naturae, sicut ultima perfectio corporis est ut coniungatur naturae spirituali. Sed supra intellectum humanum, ordine naturae, sunt

ARTICLE 7
Whether happiness consists in the knowledge of separate substances, namely, angels?

Objection 1: It would seem that man's happiness consists in the knowledge of separate substances, namely, angels. For Gregory says in a homily (xxvi in Evang.): "It avails nothing to take part in the feasts of men, if we fail to take part in the feasts of angels"; by which he means final happiness. But we can take part in the feasts of the angels by contemplating them. Therefore it seems that man's final happiness consists in contemplating the angels.

Objection 2: Further, the final perfection of each thing is for it to be united to its principle: wherefore a circle is said to be a perfect figure, because its beginning and end coincide. But the beginning of human knowledge is from the angels, by whom men are enlightened, as Dionysius says (Coel. Hier. iv). Therefore the perfection of the human intellect consists in contemplating the angels.

Objection 3: Further, each nature is perfect, when united to a higher nature; just as the final perfection of a body is to be united to the spiritual nature. But above the human intellect, in the natural order, are the

angeli. Ergo ultima perfectio intellectus humani est ut coniungatur per contemplationem ipsis angelis.

SED CONTRA est quod dicitur Ierem. IX, *in hoc glorietur qui gloriatur, scire et nosse me.* Ergo ultima hominis gloria, vel beatitudo, non consistit nisi in cognitione Dei.

RESPONDEO dicendum quod, sicut dictum est, perfecta hominis beatitudo non consistit in eo quod est perfectio intellectus secundum alicuius participationem, sed in eo quod est per essentiam tale. Manifestum est autem quod unumquodque intantum est perfectio alicuius potentiae, inquantum ad ipsum pertinet ratio proprii obiecti illius potentiae. Proprium autem obiectum intellectus est verum. Quidquid ergo habet veritatem participatam, contemplatum non facit intellectum perfectum ultima perfectione. Cum autem eadem sit dispositio rerum in esse sicut in veritate, ut dicitur in II Metaphys.; quaecumque sunt entia per participationem, sunt vera per participationem. Angeli autem habent esse participatum, quia solius Dei suum esse est sua essentia, ut in primo ostensum est. Unde relinquitur quod solus Deus sit veritas per essentiam, et quod eius contemplatio faciat perfecte beatum. Aliqualem autem beatitudinem imperfectam nihil prohibet attendi in contemplatione angelorum; et etiam altiorem quam in consideratione scientiarum speculativarum.

AD PRIMUM ergo dicendum quod festis angelorum intererimus non solum contemplantes angelos, sed simul cum ipsis, Deum.

AD SECUNDUM dicendum quod, secundum illos qui ponunt animas humanas esse ab angelis creatas, satis conveniens videtur quod beatitudo hominis sit in contemplatione angelorum, quasi in coniunctione ad suum principium. Sed hoc est erroneum, ut in primo dictum est. Unde ultima perfectio intellectus humani est per coniunctionem ad Deum, qui est primum principium et creationis animae et illuminationis eius. Angelus autem illuminat tanquam minister, ut in primo habitum est. Unde suo ministerio adiuvat

angels. Therefore the final perfection of the human intellect is to be united to the angels by contemplation.

On the contrary, It is written (Jer. 9:24): "Let him that glorieth, glory in this, that he understandeth and knoweth Me." Therefore man's final glory or happiness consists only in the knowledge of God.

I answer that, As stated above (I-II, q. 3, a. 6), man's perfect happiness consists not in that which perfects the intellect by some participation, but in that which is so by its essence. Now it is evident that whatever is the perfection of a power is so in so far as the proper formal object of that power belongs to it. Now the proper object of the intellect is the true. Therefore the contemplation of whatever has participated truth, does not perfect the intellect with its final perfection. Since, therefore, the order of things is the same in being and in truth (Metaph ii, 1); whatever are beings by participation, are true by participation. Now angels have being by participation: because in God alone is His Being His Essence, as shown in the I, q. 44, a. 1. It follows that contemplation of Him makes man perfectly happy. However, there is no reason why we should not admit a certain imperfect happiness in the contemplation of the angels; and higher indeed than in the consideration of speculative science.

Reply to Objection 1: We shall take part in the feasts of the angels, by contemplating not only the angels, but, together with them, also God Himself.

Reply to Objection 2: According to those that hold human souls to be created by the angels, it seems fitting enough, that man's happiness should consist in the contemplation of the angels, in the union, as it were, of man with his beginning. But this is erroneous, as stated in I, q. 90, a. 3. Wherefore the final perfection of the human intellect is by union with God, Who is the first principle both of the creation of the soul and of its enlightenment. Whereas the angel enlightens as a minister, as stated in the I, q. 111, a. 2, ad 2. Consequently, by his ministration he helps

hominem ut ad beatitudinem perveniat, non autem est humanae beatitudinis obiectum.

Ad tertium dicendum quod attingi superiorem naturam ab inferiori contingit dupliciter. Uno modo, secundum gradum potentiae participantis, et sic ultima perfectio hominis erit in hoc quod homo attinget ad contemplandum sicut angeli contemplantur. Alio modo, sicut obiectum attingitur a potentia, et hoc modo ultima perfectio cuiuslibet potentiae est ut attingat ad id in quo plene invenitur ratio sui obiecti.

man to attain to happiness; but he is not the object of man's happiness.

Reply to Objection 3: The lower nature may reach the higher in two ways. First, according to a degree of the participating power: and thus man's final perfection will consist in his attaining to a contemplation such as that of the angels. Secondly, as the object is attained by the power: and thus the final perfection of each power is to attain that in which is found the fulness of its formal object.

Articulus 8

Ad octavum sic proceditur. Videtur quod beatitudo hominis non sit in visione ipsius divinae essentiae. Dicit enim Dionysius, in I cap. Myst. Theol., quod per id quod est supremum intellectus, homo Deo coniungitur sicut omnino ignoto. Sed id quod videtur per essentiam, non est omnino ignotum. Ergo ultima intellectus perfectio, seu beatitudo, non consistit in hoc quod Deus per essentiam videtur.

Praeterea, altioris naturae altior est perfectio. Sed haec est perfectio divini intellectus propria, ut suam essentiam videat. Ergo ultima perfectio intellectus humani ad hoc non pertingit, sed infra subsistit.

Sed contra est quod dicitur I Ioan. III, *cum apparuerit, similes ei erimus, et videbimus eum sicuti ipse est.*

Respondeo dicendum quod ultima et perfecta beatitudo non potest esse nisi in visione divinae essentiae. Ad cuius evidentiam, duo consideranda sunt. Primo quidem, quod homo non est perfecte beatus, quandiu restat sibi aliquid desiderandum et quaerendum. Secundum est, quod uniuscuiusque potentiae perfectio attenditur secundum rationem sui obiecti. Obiectum autem intellectus est *quod quid est,* idest essentia rei, ut dicitur in III de anima. Unde intantum procedit perfectio intellectus, inquantum cognoscit essentiam alicuius rei. Si ergo intellectus aliquis cognoscat essentiam alicuius effectus, per quam

Article 8
Whether man's happiness consists in the vision of the divine essence?

Objection 1: It would seem that man's happiness does not consist in the vision of the Divine Essence. For Dionysius says (Myst. Theol. i) that by that which is highest in his intellect, man is united to God as to something altogether unknown. But that which is seen in its essence is not altogether unknown. Therefore the final perfection of the intellect, namely, happiness, does not consist in God being seen in His Essence.

Objection 2: Further, the higher the perfection belongs to the higher nature. But to see His own Essence is the perfection proper to the Divine intellect. Therefore the final perfection of the human intellect does not reach to this, but consists in something less.

On the contrary, It is written (1 Jn. 3:2): "When He shall appear, we shall be like to Him; and* we shall see Him as He is."

I answer that, Final and perfect happiness can consist in nothing else than the vision of the Divine Essence. To make this clear, two points must be observed. First, that man is not perfectly happy, so long as something remains for him to desire and seek: secondly, that the perfection of any power is determined by the nature of its object. Now the object of the intellect is "what a thing is," i.e., the essence of a thing, according to De Anima iii, 6. Wherefore the intellect attains perfection, in so far as it knows the essence of a thing. If therefore an intellect knows the essence of some effect, whereby

---

* Vulg.: 'because'

non possit cognosci essentia causae, ut scilicet sciatur de causa quid est; non dicitur intellectus attingere ad causam simpliciter, quamvis per effectum cognoscere possit de causa an sit. Et ideo remanet naturaliter homini desiderium, cum cognoscit effectum, et scit eum habere causam, ut etiam sciat de causa *quid est*. Et illud desiderium est admirationis, et causat inquisitionem, ut dicitur in principio Metaphys. Puta si aliquis cognoscens eclipsim solis, considerat quod ex aliqua causa procedit, de qua, quia nescit quid sit, admiratur, et admirando inquirit. Nec ista inquisitio quiescit quousque perveniat ad cognoscendum essentiam causae. Si igitur intellectus humanus, cognoscens essentiam alicuius effectus creati, non cognoscat de Deo nisi *an est*; nondum perfectio eius attingit simpliciter ad causam primam, sed remanet ei adhuc naturale desiderium inquirendi causam. Unde nondum est perfecte beatus. Ad perfectam igitur beatitudinem requiritur quod intellectus pertingat ad ipsam essentiam primae causae. Et sic perfectionem suam habebit per unionem ad Deum sicut ad obiectum, in quo solo beatitudo hominis consistit, ut supra dictum est.

AD PRIMUM ergo dicendum quod Dionysius loquitur de cognitione eorum qui sunt in via, tendentes ad beatitudinem.

AD SECUNDUM dicendum quod, sicut supra dictum est, finis potest accipi dupliciter. Uno modo, quantum ad rem ipsam quae desideratur, et hoc modo idem est finis superioris et inferioris naturae, immo omnium rerum, ut supra dictum est. Alio modo, quantum ad consecutionem huius rei, et sic diversus est finis superioris et inferioris naturae, secundum diversam habitudinem ad rem talem. Sic igitur altior est beatitudo Dei suam essentiam intellectu comprehendentis, quam hominis vel angeli videntis, et non comprehendentis.

it is not possible to know the essence of the cause, i.e., to know of the cause "what it is"; that intellect cannot be said to reach that cause simply, although it may be able to gather from the effect the knowledge of that the cause is. Consequently, when man knows an effect, and knows that it has a cause, there naturally remains in the man the desire to know about the cause, "what it is." And this desire is one of wonder, and causes inquiry, as is stated in the beginning of the Metaphysics (i, 2). For instance, if a man, knowing the eclipse of the sun, consider that it must be due to some cause, and know not what that cause is, he wonders about it, and from wondering proceeds to inquire. Nor does this inquiry cease until he arrive at a knowledge of the essence of the cause. If therefore the human intellect, knowing the essence of some created effect, knows no more of God than "that He is"; the perfection of that intellect does not yet reach simply the First Cause, but there remains in it the natural desire to seek the cause. Wherefore it is not yet perfectly happy. Consequently, for perfect happiness the intellect needs to reach the very Essence of the First Cause. And thus it will have its perfection through union with God as with that object, in which alone man's happiness consists, as stated above (I-II, q. 3, a. 1; a. 7; q. 2, a. 8).

Reply to Objection 1: Dionysius speaks of the knowledge of wayfarers journeying towards happiness.

Reply to Objection 2: As stated above (I-II, q. 1, a. 8), the end has a twofold acceptation. First, as to the thing itself which is desired: and in this way, the same thing is the end of the higher and of the lower nature, and indeed of all things, as stated above (I-II, q. 1, a. 8). Secondly, as to the attainment of this thing; and thus the end of the higher nature is different from that of the lower, according to their respective habitudes to that thing. So then in the happiness of God, Who, in understanding his Essence, comprehends It, is higher than that of a man or angel who sees It indeed, but comprehends It not.

Quaestio IV

Deinde, considerandum est de his quae exiguntur ad beatitudinem. Et circa hoc quaeruntur octo. *Primo,* utrum delectatio requiratur ad beatitudinem. *Secundo,* quid sit principalius in beatitudine, utrum delectatio vel visio. *Tertio,* utrum requiratur comprehensio. *Quarto,* utrum requiratur rectitudo voluntatis. *Quinto,* utrum ad beatitudinem hominis requiratur corpus. *Sexto,* utrum perfectio corporis. *Septimo,* utrum aliqua exteriora bona. *Octavo,* utrum requiratur societas amicorum.

Articulus 1

Ad primum sic proceditur. Videtur quod delectatio non requiratur ad beatitudinem. Dicit enim Augustinus, in I de Trin., quod *visio est tota merces fidei.* Sed id quod est praemium vel merces virtutis, est beatitudo, ut patet per philosophum in I Ethic. Ergo nihil aliud requiritur ad beatitudinem nisi sola visio.

Praeterea, beatitudo est *per se sufficientissimum bonum,* ut philosophus dicit I Ethic. Quod autem eget aliquo alio, non est per se sufficiens. Cum igitur essentia beatitudinis in visione Dei consistat, ut ostensum est; videtur quod ad beatitudinem non requiratur delectatio.

Praeterea, *operationem felicitatis seu beatitudinis oportet esse non impeditam,* ut dicitur in VII Ethic. Sed delectatio impedit actionem intellectus corrumpit enim aestimationem prudentiae, ut dicitur in VI Ethic. Ergo delectatio non requiritur ad beatitudinem.

Sed contra est quod Augustinus dicit, X Confess., quod beatitudo est *gaudium de veritate.*

Respondeo dicendum quod quadrupliciter aliquid requiritur ad aliud. Uno modo, sicut praeambulum vel praeparatorium ad ipsum, sicut disciplina requiritur ad scientiam. Alio modo, sicut perficiens aliquid, sicut anima requiritur ad vitam corporis. Tertio modo, sicut coadiuvans extrinsecum,

Question 4
Of Those Things That Are Required for Happiness

We have now to consider those things that are required for happiness: and concerning this there are eight points of inquiry: 1. Whether delight is required for happiness? 2. Which is of greater account in happiness, delight or vision? 3. Whether comprehension is required? 4. Whether rectitude of the will is required? 5. Whether the body is necessary for man's happiness? 6. Whether any perfection of the body is necessary? 7. Whether any external goods are necessary? 8. Whether the fellowship of friends is necessary?

Article 1
Whether delight is required for happiness?

Objection 1: It would seem that delight is not required for happiness. For Augustine says (De Trin. i, 8) that "vision is the entire reward of faith." But the prize or reward of virtue is happiness, as the Philosopher clearly states (Ethic. i, 9). Therefore nothing besides vision is required for happiness.

Objection 2: Further, happiness is "the most self-sufficient of all goods," as the Philosopher declares (Ethic. i, 7). But that which needs something else is not self-sufficient. Since then the essence of happiness consists in seeing God, as stated above (I-II, q. 3, a. 8); it seems that delight is not necessary for happiness.

Objection 3: Further, the "operation of bliss or happiness should be unhindered" (Ethic. vii, 13). But delight hinders the operation of the intellect: since it destroys the estimate of prudence (Ethic. vi, 5). Therefore delight is not necessary for happiness.

On the contrary, Augustine says (Confess. x, 23) that happiness is "joy in truth."

I answer that, One thing may be necessary for another in four ways. First, as a preamble and preparation to it: thus instruction is necessary for science. Secondly, as perfecting it: thus the soul is necessary for the life of the body. Thirdly, as helping it from without:

sicut amici requiruntur ad aliquid agendum. Quarto modo, sicut aliquid concomitans, ut si dicamus quod calor requiritur ad ignem. Et hoc modo delectatio requiritur ad beatitudinem. Delectatio enim causatur ex hoc quod appetitus requiescit in bono adepto. Unde, cum beatitudo nihil aliud sit quam adeptio summi boni, non potest esse beatitudo sine delectatione concomitante.

Ad primum ergo dicendum quod ex hoc ipso quod merces alicui redditur, voluntas merentis requiescit, quod est delectari. Unde in ipsa ratione mercedis redditae delectatio includitur.

Ad secundum dicendum quod ex ipsa visione Dei causatur delectatio. Unde ille qui Deum videt, delectatione indigere non potest.

Ad tertium dicendum quod delectatio concomitans operationem intellectus, non impedit ipsam, sed magis eam confortat, ut dicitur, in X Ethic., ea enim quae delectabiliter facimus, attentius et perseverantius operamur. Delectatio autem extranea impedit operationem, quandoque quidem ex intentionis distractione; quia, sicut dictum est, ad ea in quibus delectamur, magis intenti sumus; et dum uni vehementer intendimus, necesse est quod ab alio intentio retrahatur. Quandoque autem etiam ex contrarietate, sicut delectatio sensus contraria rationi, impedit aestimationem prudentiae magis quam aestimationem speculativi intellectus.

thus friends are necessary for some undertaking. Fourthly, as something attendant on it: thus we might say that heat is necessary for fire. And in this way delight is necessary for happiness. For it is caused by the appetite being at rest in the good attained. Wherefore, since happiness is nothing else but the attainment of the Sovereign Good, it cannot be without concomitant delight.

Reply to Objection 1: From the very fact that a reward is given to anyone, the will of him who deserves it is at rest, and in this consists delight. Consequently, delight is included in the very notion of reward.

Reply to Objection 2: The very sight of God causes delight. Consequently, he who sees God cannot need delight.

Reply to Objection 3: Delight that is attendant upon the operation of the intellect does not hinder it, rather does it perfect it, as stated in Ethic. x, 4: since what we do with delight, we do with greater care and perseverance. On the other hand, delight which is extraneous to the operation is a hindrance thereto: sometimes by distracting the attention because, as already observed, we are more attentive to those things that delight us; and when we are very attentive to one thing, we must needs be less attentive to another: sometimes on account of opposition; thus a sensual delight that is contrary to reason, hinders the estimate of prudence more than it hinders the estimate of the speculative intellect.

Articulus 2

Ad secundum sic proceditur. Videtur quod delectatio sit principalius in beatitudine quam visio. *Delectatio* enim, ut dicitur in X Ethic., *est perfectio operationis.* Sed perfectio est potior perfectibili. Ergo delectatio est potior operatione intellectus, quae est visio.

Praeterea, illud propter quod aliquid est appetibile, est potius. Sed operationes appetuntur propter delectationem ipsarum, unde et natura operationibus necessariis ad conservationem individui et speciei, delectationem apposuit,

Article 2
Whether in happiness vision ranks before delight?

Objection 1: It would seem that in happiness, delight ranks before vision. For "delight is the perfection of operation" (Ethic. x, 4). But perfection ranks before the thing perfected. Therefore delight ranks before the operation of the intellect, i.e., vision.

Objection 2: Further, that by reason of which a thing is desirable, is yet more desirable. But operations are desired on account of the delight they afford: hence, too, nature has adjusted delight to those operations which are necessary for the preservation of the individual and of the species,

ut huiusmodi operationes ab animalibus non negligantur. Ergo delectatio est potior in beatitudine quam operatio intellectus, quae est visio.

PRAETEREA, visio respondet fidei, delectatio autem, sive fruitio, caritati. Sed caritas est maior fide, ut dicit apostolus I ad Cor. XIII. Ergo delectatio, sive fruitio, est potior visione.

SED CONTRA, causa est potior effectu. Sed visio est causa delectationis. Ergo visio est potior quam delectatio.

RESPONDEO dicendum quod istam quaestionem movet philosophus in X Ethic., et eam insolutam dimittit. Sed si quis diligenter consideret, ex necessitate oportet quod operatio intellectus, quae est visio, sit potior delectatione. Delectatio enim consistit in quadam quietatione voluntatis. Quod autem voluntas in aliquo quietetur, non est nisi propter bonitatem eius in quo quietatur. Si ergo voluntas quietatur in aliqua operatione, ex bonitate operationis procedit quietatio voluntatis. Nec voluntas quaerit bonum propter quietationem, sic enim ipse actus voluntatis esset finis, quod est contra praemissa. Sed ideo quaerit quod quietetur in operatione, quia operatio est bonum eius. Unde manifestum est quod principalius bonum est ipsa operatio in qua quietatur voluntas, quam quietatio voluntatis in ipso.

AD PRIMUM ergo dicendum quod, sicut philosophus ibidem dicit, *delectatio perficit operationem sicut decor iuventutem,* qui est ad iuventutem consequens. Unde delectatio est quaedam perfectio concomitans visionem; non sicut perfectio faciens visionem esse in sua specie perfectam.

AD SECUNDUM dicendum quod apprehensio sensitiva non attingit ad communem rationem boni, sed ad aliquod bonum particulare quod est delectabile. Et ideo secundum appetitum sensitivum, qui est in animalibus, operationes quaeruntur propter delectationem. Sed intellectus apprehendit universalem rationem boni, ad cuius consecutionem sequitur delectatio. Unde principalius intendit bonum quam delectationem. Et inde est quod divinus intellectus, qui est institutor naturae, delectationes apposuit propter operationes.

lest animals should disregard such operations. Therefore, in happiness, delight ranks before the operation of the intellect, which is vision.

Objection 3: Further, vision corresponds to faith; while delight or enjoyment corresponds to charity. But charity ranks before faith, as the Apostle says (1 Cor. 13:13). Therefore delight or enjoyment ranks before vision.

On the contrary, The cause is greater than its effect. But vision is the cause of delight. Therefore vision ranks before delight.

I answer that, The Philosopher discusses this question (Ethic. x, 4), and leaves it unsolved. But if one consider the matter carefully, the operation of the intellect which is vision, must needs rank before delight. For delight consists in a certain repose of the will. Now that the will finds rest in anything, can only be on account of the goodness of that thing in which it reposes. If therefore the will reposes in an operation, the will's repose is caused by the goodness of the operation. Nor does the will seek good for the sake of repose; for thus the very act of the will would be the end, which has been disproved above (I-II, q. 1, a. 1, ad 2; q. 3, a. 4): but it seeks to be at rest in the operation, because that operation is its good. Consequently it is evident that the operation in which the will reposes ranks before the resting of the will therein.

Reply to Objection 1: As the Philosopher says (Ethic. x, 4) "delight perfects operation as vigor perfects youth," because it is a result of youth. Consequently delight is a perfection attendant upon vision; but not a perfection whereby vision is made perfect in its own species.

Reply to Objection 2: The apprehension of the senses does not attain to the universal good, but to some particular good which is delightful. And consequently, according to the sensitive appetite which is in animals, operations are sought for the sake of delight. But the intellect apprehends the universal good, the attainment of which results in delight: wherefore its purpose is directed to good rather than to delight. Hence it is that the Divine intellect, which is the Author of nature, adjusted delights to operations on account of the operations.

Non est autem aliquid aestimandum simpliciter secundum ordinem sensitivi appetitus, sed magis secundum ordinem appetitus intellectivi.

AD TERTIUM dicendum quod caritas non quaerit bonum dilectum propter delectationem, sed hoc est ei consequens, ut delectetur in bono adepto quod amat. Et sic delectatio non respondet ei ut finis, sed magis visio, per quam primo finis fit ei praesens.

And we should form our estimate of things not simply according to the order of the sensitive appetite, but rather according to the order of the intellectual appetite.

Reply to Objection 3: Charity does not seem the beloved good for the sake of delight: it is for charity a consequence that it delights in the good gained which it loves. Thus delight does not answer to charity as its end, but vision does, whereby the end is first made present to charity.

ARTICULUS 3

AD TERTIUM sic proceditur. Videtur quod ad beatitudinem non requiratur comprehensio. Dicit enim Augustinus, ad Paulinam de videndo Deum, *attingere mente Deum magna est beatitudo, comprehendere autem est impossibile.* Ergo sine comprehensione est beatitudo.

PRAETEREA, beatitudo est perfectio hominis secundum intellectivam partem, in qua non sunt aliae potentiae quam intellectus et voluntas, ut in primo dictum est. Sed intellectus sufficienter perficitur per visionem Dei, voluntas autem per delectationem in ipso. Ergo non requiritur comprehensio tanquam aliquod tertium.

PRAETEREA, beatitudo in operatione consistit. Operationes autem determinantur secundum obiecta. Obiecta autem generalia sunt duo, verum et bonum, verum correspondet visioni, et bonum correspondet delectationi. Ergo non requiritur comprehensio quasi aliquod tertium.

SED CONTRA est quod apostolus dicit, I ad Cor. IX, *sic currite ut comprehendatis.* Sed spiritualis cursus terminatur ad beatitudinem, unde ipse dicit, II ad Tim. ult., *bonum certamen certavi, cursum consummavi, fidem servavi; in reliquo reposita est mihi corona iustitiae.* Ergo comprehensio requiritur ad beatitudinem.

RESPONDEO dicendum quod, cum beatitudo consistat in consecutione ultimi finis, ea quae requiruntur ad beatitudinem sunt consideranda

ARTICLE 3
Whether comprehension is necessary for happiness?

Objection 1: It would seem that comprehension is not necessary for happiness. For Augustine says (Ad Paulinam de Videndo Deum;*): "To reach God with the mind is happiness, to comprehend Him is impossible." Therefore happiness is without comprehension.

Objection 2: Further, happiness is the perfection of man as to his intellective part, wherein there are no other powers than the intellect and will, as stated in the I, q. 79 and following. But the intellect is sufficiently perfected by seeing God, and the will by enjoying Him. Therefore there is no need for comprehension as a third.

Objection 3: Further, happiness consists in an operation. But operations are determined by their objects: and there are two universal objects, the true and the good: of which the true corresponds to vision, and good to delight. Therefore there is no need for comprehension as a third.

On the contrary, The Apostle says (1 Cor. 9:24): "So run that you may comprehend.†" But happiness is the goal of the spiritual race: hence he says (2 Tim. 4:7, 8): "I have fought a good fight, I have finished my course, I have kept the faith; as to the rest there is laid up for me a crown of justice." Therefore comprehension is necessary for Happiness.

I answer that, Since Happiness consists in gaining the last end, those things that are required for Happiness must be gathered

---

* Cf. Serm. xxxciii De Verb. Dom.
† Douay: 'obtain'

ex ipso ordine hominis ad finem. Ad finem autem intelligibilem ordinatur homo partim quidem per intellectum, partim autem per voluntatem. Per intellectum quidem, inquantum in intellectu praeexistit aliqua cognitio finis imperfecta. Per voluntatem autem, primo quidem per amorem, qui est primus motus voluntatis in aliquid, secundo autem, per realem habitudinem amantis ad amatum, quae quidem potest esse triplex. Quandoque enim amatum est praesens amanti, et tunc iam non quaeritur. Quandoque autem non est praesens, sed impossibile est ipsum adipisci, et tunc etiam non quaeritur. Quandoque autem possibile est ipsum adipisci, sed est elevatum supra facultatem adipiscentis, ita ut statim haberi non possit, et haec est habitudo sperantis ad speratum, quae sola habitudo facit finis inquisitionem. Et istis tribus respondent aliqua in ipsa beatitudine. Nam perfecta cognitio finis respondet imperfectae; praesentia vero ipsius finis respondet habitudini spei; sed delectatio in fine iam praesenti consequitur dilectionem, ut supra dictum est. Et ideo necesse est ad beatitudinem ista tria concurrere, scilicet visionem, quae est cognitio perfecta intelligibilis finis; comprehensionem, quae importat praesentiam finis; delectationem, vel fruitionem, quae importat quietationem rei amantis in amato.

AD PRIMUM ergo dicendum quod comprehensio dicitur dupliciter. Uno modo, inclusio comprehensi in comprehendente, et sic omne quod comprehenditur a finito, est finitum. Unde hoc modo Deus non potest comprehendi ab aliquo intellectu creato. Alio modo comprehensio nihil aliud nominat quam tentionem alicuius rei iam praesentialiter habitae, sicut aliquis consequens aliquem, dicitur eum comprehendere quando tenet eum. Et hoc modo comprehensio requiritur ad beatitudinem.

AD SECUNDUM dicendum quod, sicut ad voluntatem pertinet spes et amor, quia eiusdem est amare aliquid et tendere in illud non habitum; ita etiam

from the way in which man is ordered to an end. Now man is ordered to an intelligible end partly through his intellect, and partly through his will: through his intellect, in so far as a certain imperfect knowledge of the end pre-exists in the intellect: through the will, first by love which is the will's first movement towards anything; secondly, by a real relation of the lover to the thing beloved, which relation may be threefold. For sometimes the thing beloved is present to the lover: and then it is no longer sought for. Sometimes it is not present, and it is impossible to attain it: and then, too, it is not sought for. But sometimes it is possible to attain it, yet it is raised above the capability of the attainer, so that he cannot have it forthwith; and this is the relation of one that hopes, to that which he hopes for, and this relation alone causes a search for the end. To these three, there are a corresponding three in Happiness itself. For perfect knowledge of the end corresponds to imperfect knowledge; presence of the end corresponds to the relation of hope; but delight in the end now present results from love, as already stated (I-II, q. 4, a. 2, ad 3). And therefore these three must concur with Happiness; to wit, vision, which is perfect knowledge of the intelligible end; comprehension, which implies presence of the end; and delight or enjoyment, which implies repose of the lover in the object beloved.

Reply to Objection 1: Comprehension is twofold. First, inclusion of the comprehended in the comprehensor; and thus whatever is comprehended by the finite, is itself finite. Wherefore God cannot be thus comprehended by a created intellect. Secondly, comprehension means nothing but the holding of something already present and possessed: thus one who runs after another is said to comprehend* him when he lays hold on him. And in this sense comprehension is necessary for Happiness.

Reply to Objection 2: Just as hope and love pertain to the will, because it is the same one that loves a thing, and that tends towards it while not possessed, so, too,

---

* In English we should say 'catch.'

ad voluntatem pertinet et comprehensio et delectatio, quia eiusdem est habere aliquid et quiescere in illo.

AD TERTIUM dicendum quod comprehensio non est aliqua operatio praeter visionem, sed est quaedam habitudo ad finem iam habitum. Unde etiam ipsa visio, vel res visa secundum quod praesentialiter adest, est obiectum comprehensionis.

comprehension and delight belong to the will, since it is the same that possesses a thing and reposes therein.

Reply to Objection 3: Comprehension is not a distinct operation from vision; but a certain relation to the end already gained. Wherefore even vision itself, or the thing seen, inasmuch as it is present, is the object of comprehension.

ARTICULUS 4

AD QUARTUM sic proceditur. Videtur quod rectitudo voluntatis non requiratur ad beatitudinem. Beatitudo enim essentialiter consistit in operatione intellectus, ut dictum est. Sed ad perfectam intellectus operationem non requiritur rectitudo voluntatis, per quam homines mundi dicuntur, dicit enim Augustinus, in libro Retract., non approbo quod in oratione dixi, Deus qui non nisi mundos verum scire voluisti. Responderi enim potest multos etiam non mundos multa scire vera. Ergo rectitudo voluntatis non requiritur ad beatitudinem.

PRAETEREA, prius non dependet a posteriori. Sed operatio intellectus est prior quam operatio voluntatis. Ergo beatitudo, quae est perfecta operatio intellectus, non dependet a rectitudine voluntatis.

PRAETEREA, quod ordinatur ad aliquid tanquam ad finem, non est necessarium adepto iam fine, sicut navis postquam pervenitur ad portum. Sed rectitudo voluntatis, quae est per virtutem, ordinatur ad beatitudinem tanquam ad finem. Ergo, adepta beatitudine, non est necessaria rectitudo voluntatis.

SED CONTRA est quod dicitur Matth. V, *beati mundo corde, quoniam ipsi Deum videbunt.* Et Heb. XII, *pacem sequimini cum omnibus, et sanctimoniam, sine qua nemo videbit Deum.*

RESPONDEO dicendum quod rectitudo voluntatis requiritur ad beatitudinem et antecedenter et concomitanter. Antecedenter quidem, quia rectitudo voluntatis est per debitum ordinem ad finem ultimum. Finis autem

ARTICLE 4
Whether rectitude of the will is necessary for happiness?

Objection 1: It would seem that rectitude of the will is not necessary for Happiness. For Happiness consists essentially in an operation of the intellect, as stated above (I-II, q. 3, a. 4). But rectitude of the will, by reason of which men are said to be clean of heart, is not necessary for the perfect operation of the intellect: for Augustine says (Retract. i, 4) "I do not approve of what I said in a prayer: O God, Who didst will none but the clean of heart to know the truth. For it can be answered that many who are not clean of heart, know many truths." Therefore rectitude of the will is not necessary for Happiness.

Objection 2: Further, what precedes does not depend on what follows. But the operation of the intellect precedes the operation of the will. Therefore Happiness, which is the perfect operation of the intellect, does not depend on rectitude of the will.

Objection 3: Further, that which is ordained to another as its end, is not necessary, when the end is already gained; as a ship, for instance, after arrival in port. But rectitude of will, which is by reason of virtue, is ordained to Happiness as to its end. Therefore, Happiness once obtained, rectitude of the will is no longer necessary.

On the contrary, It is written (Mat. 5:8): "Blessed are the clean of heart; for they shall see God": and (Heb. 12:14): "Follow peace with all men, and holiness; without which no man shall see God."

I answer that, Rectitude of will is necessary for Happiness both antecedently and concomitantly. Antecedently, because rectitude of the will consists in being duly ordered to the last end. Now the end

comparatur ad id quod ordinatur ad finem, sicut forma ad materiam. Unde sicut materia non potest consequi formam, nisi sit debito modo disposita ad ipsam, ita nihil consequitur finem, nisi sit debito modo ordinatum ad ipsum. Et ideo nullus potest ad beatitudinem pervenire, nisi habeat rectitudinem voluntatis. Concomitanter autem, quia, sicut dictum est, beatitudo ultima consistit in visione divinae essentiae, quae est ipsa essentia bonitatis. Et ita **voluntas videntis Dei essentiam, ex necessitate amat quidquid amat, sub ordine ad Deum**; sicut voluntas non videntis Dei essentiam, ex necessitate amat quidquid amat, sub communi ratione boni quam novit. Et hoc ipsum est quod facit voluntatem rectam. Unde manifestum est quod beatitudo non potest esse sine recta voluntate.

AD PRIMUM ergo dicendum quod Augustinus loquitur de cognitione veri quod non est ipsa essentia bonitatis.

AD SECUNDUM dicendum quod omnis actus voluntatis praeceditur ab aliquo actu intellectus, aliquis tamen actus voluntatis est prior quam aliquis actus intellectus. Voluntas enim tendit in finalem actum intellectus, qui est beatitudo. Et ideo recta inclinatio voluntatis praeexigitur ad beatitudinem, sicut rectus motus sagittae ad percussionem signi.

AD TERTIUM dicendum quod non omne quod ordinatur ad finem, cessat adveniente fine, sed id tantum quod se habet in ratione imperfectionis, ut motus. Unde instrumenta motus non sunt necessaria postquam pervenitur ad finem, sed debitus ordo ad finem est necessarius.

in comparison to what is ordained to the end is as form compared to matter. Wherefore, just as matter cannot receive a form, unless it be duly disposed thereto, so nothing gains an end, except it be duly ordained thereto. And therefore none can obtain Happiness, without rectitude of the will. Concomitantly, because as stated above (I-II, q. 3, a. 8), final Happiness consists in the vision of the Divine Essence, Which is the very essence of goodness. **So that the will of him who sees the Essence of God, of necessity, loves, whatever he loves, in subordination to God**; just as the will of him who sees not God's Essence, of necessity, loves whatever he loves, under the common notion of good which he knows. And this is precisely what makes the will right. Wherefore it is evident that Happiness cannot be without a right will.

Reply to Objection 1: Augustine is speaking of knowledge of truth that is not the essence of goodness itself.

Reply to Objection 2: Every act of the will is preceded by an act of the intellect: but a certain act of the will precedes a certain act of the intellect. For the will tends to the final act of the intellect which is happiness. And consequently right inclination of the will is required antecedently for happiness, just as the arrow must take a right course in order to strike the target.

Reply to Objection 3: Not everything that is ordained to the end, ceases with the getting of the end: but only that which involves imperfection, such as movement. Hence the instruments of movement are no longer necessary when the end has been gained: but the due order to the end is necessary.

ARTICULUS 5

ARTICLE 5
Whether the body is necessary for man's happiness?

AD QUINTUM sic proceditur. Videtur quod ad beatitudinem requiratur corpus. Perfectio enim virtutis et gratiae praesupponit perfectionem naturae. Sed beatitudo est perfectio virtutis et gratiae. Anima autem sine corpore non habet perfectionem naturae, cum sit pars naturaliter humanae naturae, omnis autem pars est imperfecta a

Objection 1: It would seem that the body is necessary for Happiness. For the perfection of virtue and grace presupposes the perfection of nature. But Happiness is the perfection of virtue and grace. Now the soul, without the body, has not the perfection of nature; since it is naturally a part of human nature, and every part is imperfect while

suo toto separata. Ergo anima sine corpore non potest esse beata.

Praeterea, beatitudo est operatio quaedam perfecta, ut supra dictum est. Sed operatio perfecta sequitur esse perfectum, quia nihil operatur nisi secundum quod est ens in actu. Cum ergo anima non habeat esse perfectum quando est a corpore separata, sicut nec aliqua pars quando separata est a toto; videtur quod anima sine corpore non possit esse beata.

Praeterea, beatitudo est perfectio hominis. Sed anima sine corpore non est homo. Ergo beatitudo non potest esse in anima sine corpore.

Praeterea, secundum philosophum, in VII Ethic., *felicitatis operatio,* in qua consistit beatitudo, est *non impedita.* Sed operatio animae separatae est impedita, quia, ut dicit Augustinus XII super Gen. ad Litt., *inest ei naturalis quidam appetitus corpus administrandi, quo appetitu retardatur quodammodo ne tota intentione pergat in illud summum caelum,* idest in visionem essentiae divinae. Ergo anima sine corpore non potest esse beata.

Praeterea, beatitudo est sufficiens bonum, et quietat desiderium. Sed hoc non convenit animae separatae, quia adhuc appetit corporis unionem, ut Augustinus dicit. Ergo anima separata a corpore non est beata.

Praeterea, homo in beatitudine est angelis aequalis. Sed anima sine corpore non aequatur angelis, ut Augustinus dicit. Ergo non est beata.

Sed contra est quod dicitur Apoc. XIV, *beati mortui qui in domino moriuntur.*

Respondeo dicendum quod duplex est beatitudo, una imperfecta, quae habetur in hac vita; et alia perfecta, quae in Dei visione consistit. Manifestum est autem quod ad beatitudinem huius vitae, de necessitate requiritur corpus. Est enim beatitudo huius vitae operatio intellectus, vel speculativi vel practici. Operatio autem intellectus in hac vita non potest esse sine phantasmate, quod

separated from its whole. Therefore the soul cannot be happy without the body.

Objection 2: Further, Happiness is a perfect operation, as stated above (I-II, q. 3, a. 2; a. 5). But perfect operation follows perfect being: since nothing operates except in so far as it is an actual being. Since, therefore, the soul has not perfect being, while it is separated from the body, just as neither has a part, while separate from its whole; it seems that the soul cannot be happy without the body.

Objection 3: Further, Happiness is the perfection of man. But the soul, without the body, is not man. Therefore Happiness cannot be in the soul separated from the body.

Objection 4: Further, according to the Philosopher (Ethic. vii, 13) "the operation of bliss," in which operation happiness consists, is "not hindered." But the operation of the separate soul is hindered; because, as Augustine says (Gen. ad lit. xii, 35), the soul "has a natural desire to rule the body, the result of which is that it is held back, so to speak, from tending with all its might to the heavenward journey," i.e., to the vision of the Divine Essence. Therefore the soul cannot be happy without the body.

Objection 5: Further, Happiness is the sufficient good and lulls desire. But this cannot be said of the separated soul; for it yet desires to be united to the body, as Augustine says (Gen. ad lit. xii, 35). Therefore the soul is not happy while separated from the body.

Objection 6: Further, in Happiness man is equal to the angels. But the soul without the body is not equal to the angels, as Augustine says (Gen. ad lit. xii, 35). Therefore it is not happy.

On the contrary, It is written (Apoc. 14:13): "Happy* are the dead who die in the Lord."

I answer that, Happiness is twofold; the one is imperfect and is had in this life; the other is perfect, consisting in the vision of God. Now it is evident that the body is necessary for the happiness of this life. For the happiness of this life consists in an operation of the intellect, either speculative or practical. And the operation of the intellect in this life cannot be without a phantasm, which

---

* Douay: 'blessed'

non est nisi in organo corporeo, ut in primo habitum est. Et sic beatitudo quae in hac vita haberi potest, dependet quodammodo ex corpore. Sed circa beatitudinem perfectam, quae in Dei visione consistit, aliqui posuerunt quod non potest animae advenire sine corpore existenti; dicentes quod animae sanctorum a corporibus separatae, ad illam beatitudinem non perveniunt usque ad diem iudicii, quando corpora resument. Quod **quidem apparet esse falsum et auctoritate, et ratione**. Auctoritate quidem, quia apostolus dicit, II ad Cor. V, *quandiu sumus in corpore, peregrinamur a domino;* et quae sit ratio peregrinationis ostendit, subdens, *per fidem enim ambulamus, et non per speciem.* Ex quo apparet quod quandiu aliquis ambulat per fidem et non per speciem, carens visione divinae essentiae, nondum est Deo praesens. Animae autem sanctorum a corporibus separatae, sunt Deo praesentes, unde subditur, *audemus autem, et bonam voluntatem habemus peregrinari a corpore, et praesentes esse ad dominum.* Unde manifestum est quod animae sanctorum separatae a corporibus, *ambulant per speciem,* Dei essentiam videntes, in quo est vera beatitudo. Hoc etiam per rationem apparet. Nam intellectus ad suam operationem non indiget corpore nisi propter phantasmata, in quibus veritatem intelligibilem contuetur, ut in primo dictum est. Manifestum est autem quod divina essentia per phantasmata videri non potest, ut in primo ostensum est. Unde, cum in visione divinae essentiae perfecta hominis beatitudo consistat, non dependet beatitudo perfecta hominis a corpore. Unde sine corpore potest anima esse beata. Sed sciendum quod ad perfectionem alicuius rei dupliciter aliquid pertinet. Uno modo, ad constituendam essentiam rei, sicut anima requiritur ad perfectionem hominis. Alio modo requiritur ad perfectionem rei quod pertinet ad bene esse eius, sicut pulchritudo corporis, et velocitas ingenii pertinet ad perfectionem hominis. Quamvis ergo corpus primo modo ad perfectionem beatitudinis humanae non pertineat, pertinet tamen secundo modo. Cum enim operatio dependeat ex natura rei, quando anima perfectior erit in sua natura, tanto perfectius habebit suam propriam

is only in a bodily organ, as was shown in the I, q. 84, a. 6; a. 7. Consequently that happiness which can be had in this life, depends, in a way, on the body. But as to perfect Happiness, which consists in the vision of God, some have maintained that it is not possible to the soul separated from the body; and have said that the souls of saints, when separated from their bodies, do not attain to that Happiness until the Day of Judgment, when they will **receive their bodies back again. And this is shown to be false, both by authority and by reason.** By authority, since the Apostle says (2 Cor. 5:6): "While we are in the body, we are absent from the Lord"; and he points out the reason of this absence, saying: "For we walk by faith and not by sight." Now from this it is clear that so long as we walk by faith and not by sight, bereft of the vision of the Divine Essence, we are not present to the Lord. But the souls of the saints, separated from their bodies, are in God's presence; wherefore the text continues: "But we are confident and have a good will to be absent . . . from the body, and to be present with the Lord." Whence it is evident that the souls of the saints, separated from their bodies, "walk by sight," seeing the Essence of God, wherein is true Happiness. Again this is made clear by reason. For the intellect needs not the body, for its operation, save on account of the phantasms, wherein it looks on the intelligible truth, as stated in the I, q. 84, a. 7. Now it is evident that the Divine Essence cannot be seen by means of phantasms, as stated in the I, q. 12, a. 3. Wherefore, since man's perfect Happiness consists in the vision of the Divine Essence, it does not depend on the body. Consequently, without the body the soul can be happy. We must, however, notice that something may belong to a thing's perfection in two ways. First, as constituting the essence thereof; thus the soul is necessary for man's perfection. Secondly, as necessary for its well-being: thus, beauty of body and keenness of perfection belong to man's perfection. Wherefore though the body does not belong in the first way to the perfection of human Happiness, yet it does in the second way. For since operation depends on a thing's nature, the more perfect is the soul in its nature, the more perfectly it has its proper

operationem, in qua felicitas consistit. Unde Augustinus, in XII super Gen. ad Litt., cum quaesivisset, *utrum spiritibus defunctorum sine corporibus possit summa illa beatitudo praeberi,* respondet *quod non sic possunt videre incommutabilem substantiam, ut sancti angeli vident; sive alia latentiore causa, sive ideo quia est in eis naturalis quidam appetitus corpus administrandi.*

AD PRIMUM ergo dicendum quod beatitudo est perfectio animae ex parte intellectus, secundum quem anima transcendit corporis organa, non autem secundum quod est forma naturalis corporis. Et ideo illa naturae perfectio manet secundum quam ei beatitudo debetur, licet non maneat illa naturae perfectio secundum quam est corporis forma.

AD SECUNDUM dicendum quod anima aliter se habet ad esse quam aliae partes. Nam esse totius non est alicuius suarum partium, unde vel pars omnino desinit esse, destructo toto, sicut partes animalis destructo animali; vel, si remanent, habent aliud esse in actu, sicut pars lineae habet aliud esse quam tota linea. Sed animae humanae remanet esse compositi post corporis destructionem, et hoc ideo, quia idem est esse formae et materia, et hoc est esse compositi. Anima autem subsistit in suo esse, ut in primo ostensum est. Unde relinquitur quod post separationem a corpore perfectum esse habeat, unde et perfectam operationem habere potest; licet non habeat perfectam naturam speciei.

AD TERTIUM dicendum quod beatitudo est hominis secundum intellectum, et ideo, remanente intellectu, potest inesse ei beatitudo. Sicut dentes Aethiopis possunt esse albi, etiam post evulsionem, secundum quos Aethiops dicitur albus.

AD QUARTUM dicendum quod dupliciter aliquid impeditur ab alio. Uno modo, per modum contrarietatis, sicut frigus impedit actionem caloris, et tale impedimentum operationis repugnat felicitati. Alio modo, per modum cuiusdam defectus, quia scilicet

operation, wherein its happiness consists. Hence, Augustine, after inquiring (Gen. ad lit. xii, 35) "whether that perfect Happiness can be ascribed to the souls of the dead separated from their bodies," answers "that they cannot see the Unchangeable Substance, as the blessed angels see It; either for some other more hidden reason, or because they have a natural desire to rule the body."

Reply to Objection 1: Happiness is the perfection of the soul on the part of the intellect, in respect of which the soul transcends the organs of the body; but not according as the soul is the natural form of the body. Wherefore the soul retains that natural perfection in respect of which happiness is due to it, though it does not retain that natural perfection in respect of which it is the form of the body.

Reply to Objection 2: The relation of the soul to being is not the same as that of other parts: for the being of the whole is not that of any individual part: wherefore, either the part ceases altogether to be, when the whole is destroyed, just as the parts of an animal, when the animal is destroyed; or, if they remain, they have another actual being, just as a part of a line has another being from that of the whole line. But the human soul retains the being of the composite after the destruction of the body: and this because the being of the form is the same as that of its matter, and this is the being of the composite. Now the soul subsists in its own being, as stated in the I, q. 75, a. 2. It follows, therefore, that after being separated from the body it has perfect being and that consequently it can have a perfect operation; although it has not the perfect specific nature.

Reply to Objection 3: Happiness belongs to man in respect of his intellect: and, therefore, since the intellect remains, it can have Happiness. Thus the teeth of an Ethiopian, in respect of which he is said to be white, can retain their whiteness, even after extraction.

Reply to Objection 4: One thing is hindered by another in two ways. First, by way of opposition; thus cold hinders the action of heat: and such a hindrance to operation is repugnant to Happiness. Secondly, by way of some kind of defect, because, to wit,

res impedita non habet quidquid ad omnimodam sui perfectionem requiritur, et tale impedimentum operationis non repugnat felicitati, sed omnimodae perfectioni ipsius. Et sic separatio a corpore dicitur animam retardare, ne tota intentione tendat in visionem divinae essentiae. Appetit enim anima sic frui Deo, quod etiam ipsa fruitio derivetur ad corpus per redundantiam, sicut est possibile. Et ideo quandiu ipsa fruitur Deo sine corpore, **appetitus eius sic quiescit in eo quod habet**, quod tamen adhuc ad participationem eius vellet suum corpus pertingere.

AD QUINTUM dicendum quod desiderium animae separatae totaliter quiescit ex parte appetibilis, quia scilicet habet id quod suo appetitui sufficit. Sed non totaliter requiescit ex parte appetentis, quia illud bonum non possidet secundum omnem modum quo possidere vellet. Et ideo, corpore resumpto, beatitudo crescit non intensive, sed extensive.

AD SEXTUM dicendum quod id quod ibidem dicitur, quod *spiritus defunctorum non sic vident Deum sicut angeli,* non est intelligendum secundum inaequalitatem quantitatis, quia etiam modo aliquae animae beatorum sunt assumptae ad superiores ordines angelorum, clarius videntes Deum quam inferiores angeli. Sed intelligitur secundum inaequalitatem proportionis, quia angeli, etiam infimi, habent omnem perfectionem beatitudinis quam sunt habituri, non autem animae separatae sanctorum.

that which is hindered has not all that is necessary to make it perfect in every way: and such a hindrance to operation is not incompatible with Happiness, but prevents it from being perfect in every way. And thus it is that separation from the body is said to hold the soul back from tending with all its might to the vision of the Divine Essence. For the soul desires to enjoy God in such a way that the enjoyment also may overflow into the body, as far as possible. And therefore, as long as it enjoys God, without the fellowship of the body, its appetite is at rest in that which it has, in such a way, that it would still wish the body to attain to its share.

Reply to Objection 5: The desire of the separated soul is entirely at rest, as regards the thing desired; since, to wit, it has that which suffices its appetite. But it is not wholly at rest, as regards the desirer, since it does not possess that good in every way that it would wish to possess it. Consequently, after the body has been resumed, Happiness increases not in intensity, but in extent.

Reply to Objection 6: The statement made (Gen. ad lit. xii, 35) to the effect that "the souls of the departed see not God as the angels do," is not to be understood as referring to inequality of quantity; because even now some souls of the Blessed are raised to the higher orders of the angels, thus seeing God more clearly than the lower angels. But it refers to inequality of proportion: because the angels, even the lowest, have every perfection of Happiness that they ever will have, whereas the separated souls of the saints have not.

ARTICULUS 6

AD SEXTUM sic proceditur. Videtur quod perfectio corporis non requiratur ad beatitudinem hominis perfectam. Perfectio enim corporis est quoddam corporale bonum. Sed supra ostensum est quod beatitudo non consistit in corporalibus bonis. Ergo ad beatitudinem hominis non requiritur aliqua perfecta dispositio corporis.

ARTICLE 6
Whether perfection of the body is necessary for happiness?

Objection 1: It would seem that perfection of the body is not necessary for man's perfect Happiness. For perfection of the body is a bodily good. But it has been shown above (I-II, q. 2) that Happiness does not consist in bodily goods. Therefore no perfect disposition of the body is necessary for man's Happiness.

PRAETEREA, beatitudo hominis consistit in visione divinae essentiae, ut ostensum est. Sed ad hanc operationem nihil exhibet corpus, ut dictum est. Ergo nulla dispositio corporis requiritur ad beatitudinem.

PRAETEREA, quanto intellectus est magis abstractus a corpore, tanto perfectius intelligit. Sed beatitudo consistit in perfectissima operatione intellectus. Ergo oportet omnibus modis animam esse abstractam a corpore. Nullo ergo modo requiritur aliqua dispositio corporis ad beatitudinem.

SED CONTRA, praemium virtutis est beatitudo, unde dicitur Ioan. XIII, *beati eritis, si feceritis ea*. Sed sanctis repromittitur pro praemio non solum visio Dei et delectatio, sed etiam corporis bona dispositio, dicitur enim Isaiae ult., *videbitis, et gaudebit cor vestrum, et ossa vestra quasi herba germinabunt*. Ergo bona dispositio corporis requiritur ad beatitudinem.

RESPONDEO dicendum quod, si loquamur de beatitudine hominis qualis in hac vita potest haberi, manifestum est quod ad eam ex necessitate requiritur bona dispositio corporis. Consistit enim haec beatitudo, secundum philosophum, in *operatione virtutis perfectae*. Manifestum est autem quod per invaletudinem corporis, in omni operatione virtutis homo impediri potest. Sed si loquamur de beatitudine perfecta, sic quidam posuerunt quod non requiritur ad beatitudinem aliqua corporis dispositio, immo requiritur ad eam ut omnino anima sit a corpore separata. Unde Augustinus, XXII de Civ. Dei, introducit verba Porphyrii dicentis quod *ad hoc quod beata sit anima, omne corpus fugiendum est*. Sed hoc est inconveniens. Cum enim naturale sit animae corpori uniri, non potest esse quod perfectio animae naturalem eius perfectionem excludat. Et ideo dicendum est quod ad beatitudinem omnibus modis perfectam, requiritur perfecta dispositio corporis et antecedenter et consequenter. Antecedenter quidem, quia, ut Augustinus dicit XII super Gen. ad Litt., *si tale sit corpus, cuius sit difficilis et gravis administratio, sicut*

Objection 2: Further, man's Happiness consists in the vision of the Divine Essence, as shown above (I-II, q. 3, a. 8). But the body has not part in this operation, as shown above (I-II, q. 4, a. 5). Therefore no disposition of the body is necessary for Happiness.

Objection 3: Further, the more the intellect is abstracted from the body, the more perfectly it understands. But Happiness consists in the most perfect operation of the intellect. Therefore the soul should be abstracted from the body in every way. Therefore, in no way is a disposition of the body necessary for Happiness.

On the contrary, Happiness is the reward of virtue; wherefore it is written (Jn. 13:17): "You shall be blessed, if you do them." But the reward promised to the saints is not only that they shall see and enjoy God, but also that their bodies shall be well-disposed; for it is written (Is. 66:14): "You shall see and your heart shall rejoice, and your bones shall flourish like a herb." Therefore good disposition of the body is necessary for Happiness.

I answer that, If we speak of that happiness which man can acquire in this life, it is evident that a well-disposed body is of necessity required for it. For this happiness consists, according to the Philosopher (Ethic. i, 13) in "an operation according to perfect virtue"; and it is clear that man can be hindered, by indisposition of the body, from every operation of virtue. But speaking of perfect Happiness, some have maintained that no disposition of body is necessary for Happiness; indeed, that it is necessary for the soul to be entirely separated from the body. Hence Augustine (De Civ. Dei xxii, 26) quotes the words of Porphyry who said that "for the soul to be happy, it must be severed from everything corporeal." But this is unreasonable. For since it is natural to the soul to be united to the body; it is not possible for the perfection of the soul to exclude its natural perfection. Consequently, we must say that perfect disposition of the body is necessary, both antecedently and consequently, for that Happiness which is in all ways perfect. Antecedently, because, as Augustine says (Gen. ad lit. xii, 35), "if body be such, that the governance thereof is difficult and burdensome, like

unto flesh which is corruptible and weighs upon the soul, the mind is turned away from that vision of the highest heaven." Whence he concludes that, "when this body will no longer be 'natural,' but 'spiritual,' then will it be equalled to the angels, and that will be its glory, which erstwhile was its burden." Consequently, because from the Happiness of the soul there will be an overflow on to the body, so that this too will obtain its perfection. Hence Augustine says (Ep. ad Dioscor.) that "God gave the soul such a powerful nature that from its exceeding fulness of happiness the vigor of incorruption overflows into the lower nature."

Reply to Objection 1: Happiness does not consist in bodily good as its object: but bodily good can add a certain charm and perfection to Happiness.

Reply to Objection 2: Although the body has not part in that operation of the intellect whereby the Essence of God is seen, yet it might prove a hindrance thereto. Consequently, perfection of the body is necessary, lest it hinder the mind from being lifted up.

Reply to Objection 3: The perfect operation of the intellect requires indeed that the intellect be abstracted from this corruptible body which weighs upon the soul; but not from the spiritual body, which will be wholly subject to the spirit. On this point we shall treat in the Third Part of this work (II-II, q. 82, seqq.).

ARTICLE 7
Whether any external goods are necessary for happiness?

Objection 1: It would seem that external goods also are necessary for Happiness. For that which is promised the saints for reward, belongs to Happiness. But external goods are promised the saints; for instance, food and drink, wealth and a kingdom: for it is said (Lk. 22:30): "That you may eat and drink at My table in My kingdom": and (Mat. 6:20): "Lay up to yourselves treasures in heaven": and (Mat. 25:34): "Come, ye blessed of My Father, possess you the kingdom." Therefore external goods are necessary for Happiness.

Praeterea, secundum Boetium, in III de Consol., beatitudo est *status omnium bonorum aggregatione perfectus*. Sed exteriora sunt aliqua hominis bona, licet minima, ut Augustinus dicit. Ergo ipsa etiam requiruntur ad beatitudinem.

Praeterea, dominus, Matth. V, dicit, *merces vestra multa est in caelis*. Sed esse in caelis significat esse in loco. Ergo saltem locus exterior requiritur ad beatitudinem.

Sed contra est quod dicitur in Psalmo LXXII, *quid enim mihi est in caelo? Et a te quid volui super terram?* Quasi dicat, *nihil aliud volo nisi hoc quod sequitur, mihi adhaerere Deo bonum est*. Ergo nihil aliud exterius ad beatitudinem requiritur.

Respondeo dicendum quod ad beatitudinem imperfectam, qualis in hac vita potest haberi, requiruntur exteriora bona, non quasi de essentia beatitudinis existentia, sed quasi instrumentaliter deservientia beatitudini, quae consistit in operatione virtutis, ut dicitur in I Ethic. Indiget enim homo in hac vita necessariis corporis tam ad operationem virtutis contemplativae quam etiam ad operationem virtutis activae, ad quam etiam plura alia requiruntur, quibus exerceat opera activae virtutis. Sed ad beatitudinem perfectam, quae in visione Dei consistit, nullo modo huiusmodi bona requiruntur. Cuius ratio est quia omnia huiusmodi bona exteriora vel requiruntur ad sustentationem animalis corporis; vel requiruntur ad aliquas operationes quas per animale corpus exercemus, quae humanae vitae conveniunt. Illa autem perfecta beatitudo quae in visione Dei consistit, vel erit in anima sine corpore; vel erit in anima corpori unita non iam animali, sed spirituali. Et ideo nullo modo huiusmodi exteriora bona requiruntur ad illam beatitudinem, cum ordinentur ad vitam animalem. Et quia in hac vita magis accedit ad similitudinem illius perfectae beatitudinis felicitas contemplativa quam activa, utpote etiam Deo similior, ut ex dictis patet; ideo minus indiget huiusmodi bonis corporis, ut dicitur in X Ethic.

Objection 2: Further, according to Boethius (De Consol. iii): happiness is "a state made perfect by the aggregate of all good things." But some of man's goods are external, although they be of least account, as Augustine says (De Lib. Arb. ii, 19). Therefore they too are necessary for Happiness.

Objection 3: Further, Our Lord said (Mat. 5:12): "Your reward is very great in heaven." But to be in heaven implies being in a place. Therefore at least external place is necessary for Happiness.

On the contrary, It is written (Ps. 72:25): "For what have I in heaven? and besides Thee what do I desire upon earth?" As though to say: "I desire nothing but this,"—"It is good for me to adhere to my God." Therefore nothing further external is necessary for Happiness.

I answer that, For imperfect happiness, such as can be had in this life, external goods are necessary, not as belonging to the essence of happiness, but by serving as instruments to happiness, which consists in an operation of virtue, as stated in Ethic. i, 13. For man needs in this life, the necessaries of the body, both for the operation of contemplative virtue, and for the operation of active virtue, for which latter he needs also many other things by means of which to perform its operations. On the other hand, such goods as these are nowise necessary for perfect Happiness, which consists in seeing God. The reason of this is that all suchlike external goods are requisite either for the support of the animal body; or for certain operations which belong to human life, which we perform by means of the animal body: whereas that perfect Happiness which consists in seeing God, will be either in the soul separated from the body, or in the soul united to the body then no longer animal but spiritual. Consequently these external goods are nowise necessary for that Happiness, since they are ordained to the animal life. And since, in this life, the felicity of contemplation, as being more Godlike, approaches nearer than that of action to the likeness of that perfect Happiness, therefore it stands in less need of these goods of the body as stated in Ethic. x, 8.

Ad primum ergo dicendum quod omnes illae corporales promissiones quae in sacra Scriptura continentur, sunt metaphorice intelligendae, secundum quod in Scripturis solent spiritualia per corporalia designari, *ut ex his quae novimus, ad desiderandum incognita consurgamus,* sicut Gregorius dicit in quadam homilia. Sicut per cibum et potum intelligitur delectatio beatitudinis; per divitias, sufficientia qua homini sufficiet Deus; per regnum, exaltatio hominis usque ad coniunctionem cum Deo.

Ad secundum dicendum quod bona ista deservientia animali vitae, non competunt vitae spirituali in qua beatitudo perfecta consistit. Et tamen erit in illa beatitudine omnium bonorum congregatio, quia quidquid boni invenitur in istis, totum habebitur in summo fonte bonorum.

Ad tertium dicendum quod, secundum Augustinum in libro de Serm. Dom. in monte, merces sanctorum non dicitur esse in corporeis caelis, sed per caelos intelligitur altitudo spiritualium bonorum. Nihilominus tamen locus corporeus, scilicet caelum Empyreum, aderit beatis, non propter necessitatem beatitudinis, sed secundum quandam congruentiam et decorem.

Reply to Objection 1: All those material promises contained in Holy Scripture, are to be understood metaphorically, inasmuch as Scripture is wont to express spiritual things under the form of things corporeal, in order "that from things we know, we may rise to the desire of things unknown," as Gregory says (Hom. xi in Evang.). Thus food and drink signify the delight of Happiness; wealth, the sufficiency of God for man; the kingdom, the lifting up of man to union of God.

Reply to Objection 2: These goods that serve for the animal life, are incompatible with that spiritual life wherein perfect Happiness consists. Nevertheless in that Happiness there will be the aggregate of all good things, because whatever good there be in these things, we shall possess it all in the Supreme Fount of goodness.

Reply to Objection 3: According to Augustine (De Serm. Dom. in Monte i, 5), it is not material heaven that is described as the reward of the saints, but a heaven raised on the height of spiritual goods. Nevertheless a bodily place, *viz.* the empyrean heaven, will be appointed to the Blessed, not as a need of Happiness, but by reason of a certain fitness and adornment.

Articulus 8

Ad octavum sic proceditur. Videtur quod amici sint necessarii ad beatitudinem. Futura enim beatitudo in Scripturis frequenter nomine *gloriae* designatur. Sed gloria consistit in hoc quod bonum hominis ad notitiam multorum deducitur. Ergo ad beatitudinem requiritur societas amicorum.

Praeterea, Boetius dicit quod *nullius boni sine consortio iucunda est possessio.* Sed ad beatitudinem requiritur delectatio. Ergo etiam requiritur societas amicorum.

Praeterea, caritas in beatitudine perficitur. Sed caritas se extendit ad dilectionem Dei et proximi. Ergo videtur

Article 8
Whether the fellowship of friend is necessary for happiness?

Objection 1: It would seem that friends are necessary for Happiness. For future Happiness is frequently designated by Scripture under the name of "glory." But glory consists in man's good being brought to the notice of many. Therefore the fellowship of friends is necessary for Happiness.

Objection 2: Further, Boethius* says that "there is no delight in possessing any good whatever, without someone to share it with us." But delight is necessary for Happiness. Therefore fellowship of friends is also necessary.

Objection 3: Further, charity is perfected in Happiness. But charity includes the love of God and of our neighbor. Therefore it seems

---

* Seneca, Ep. 6

quod ad beatitudinem requiratur societas amicorum.

Sed contra est quod dicitur Sap. VII, *venerunt mihi omnia bona pariter cum illa,* scilicet cum divina sapientia, quae consistit in contemplatione Dei. Et sic ad beatitudinem nihil aliud requiritur.

Respondeo dicendum quod, si loquamur de felicitate praesentis vitae, sicut philosophus dicit in IX Ethic., felix indiget amicis, non quidem propter utilitatem, cum sit sibi sufficiens; nec propter delectationem, quia habet in seipso delectationem perfectam in operatione virtutis; sed propter bonam operationem, ut scilicet eis benefaciat, et ut eos inspiciens benefacere delectetur, et ut etiam ab eis in benefaciendo adiuvetur. Indiget enim homo ad bene operandum auxilio amicorum, tam in operibus vitae activae, quam in operibus vitae contemplativae. Sed si loquamur de perfecta beatitudine quae erit in patria, non requiritur societas amicorum de necessitate ad beatitudinem, quia homo habet totam plenitudinem suae perfectionis in Deo. Sed ad bene esse beatitudinis facit societas amicorum. Unde Augustinus dicit, VIII super Gen. ad Litt., quod *creatura spiritualis, ad hoc quod beata sit, non nisi intrinsecus adiuvatur aeternitate, veritate, caritate creatoris. Extrinsecus vero, si adiuvari dicenda est, fortasse hoc solo adiuvatur, quod invicem vident, et de sua societate gaudent in Deo.*

Ad primum ergo dicendum quod gloria quae est essentialis beatitudini, est quam habet homo non apud hominem, sed apud Deum.

Ad secundum dicendum quod verbum illud intelligitur, quando in eo bono quod habetur, non est plena sufficientia. Quod in proposito dici non potest, quia omnis boni sufficientiam habet homo in Deo.

Ad tertium dicendum quod perfectio caritatis est essentialis beatitudini quantum ad dilectionem Dei, non autem quantum ad dilectionem proximi. Unde si esset una sola anima fruens Deo, beata esset, non habens proximum quem diligeret. Sed supposito proximo, sequitur dilectio eius ex

that fellowship of friends is necessary for Happiness.

On the contrary, It is written (Wis. 7:11): "All good things came to me together with her," i.e., with divine wisdom, which consists in contemplating God. Consequently nothing else is necessary for Happiness.

I answer that, If we speak of the happiness of this life, the happy man needs friends, as the Philosopher says (Ethic. ix, 9), not, indeed, to make use of them, since he suffices himself; nor to delight in them, since he possesses perfect delight in the operation of virtue; but for the purpose of a good operation, *viz.* that he may do good to them; that he may delight in seeing them do good; and again that he may be helped by them in his good work. For in order that man may do well, whether in the works of the active life, or in those of the contemplative life, he needs the fellowship of friends. But if we speak of perfect Happiness which will be in our heavenly Fatherland, the fellowship of friends is not essential to Happiness; since man has the entire fulness of his perfection in God. But the fellowship of friends conduces to the well-being of Happiness. Hence Augustine says (Gen. ad lit. viii, 25) that "the spiritual creatures receive no other interior aid to happiness than the eternity, truth, and charity of the Creator. But if they can be said to be helped from without, perhaps it is only by this that they see one another and rejoice in God, at their fellowship."

Reply to Objection 1: That glory which is essential to Happiness, is that which man has, not with man but with God.

Reply to Objection 2: This saying is to be understood of the possession of good that does not fully satisfy. This does not apply to the question under consideration; because man possesses in God a sufficiency of every good.

Reply to Objection 3: Perfection of charity is essential to Happiness, as to the love of God, but not as to the love of our neighbor. Wherefore if there were but one soul enjoying God, it would be happy, though having no neighbor to love. But supposing one neighbor to be there, love of him results from

perfecta dilectione Dei. Unde quasi concomitanter se habet amicitia ad beatitudinem perfectam.

perfect love of God. Consequently, friendship is, as it were, concomitant with perfect Happiness.

Quaestio V

Deinde considerandum est de ipsa adeptione beatitudinis. Et circa hoc quaeruntur octo. *Primo,* utrum homo possit consequi beatitudinem. *Secundo,* utrum unus homo possit esse alio beatior. *Tertio,* utrum aliquis possit esse in hac vita beatus. *Quarto,* utrum beatitudo habita possit amitti. *Quinto,* utrum, homo per sua naturalia possit acquirere beatitudinem. *Sexto,* utrum homo consequatur beatitudinem per actionem alicuius superioris creaturae. *Septimo,* utrum requirantur opera hominis aliqua ad hoc quod homo beatitudinem consequatur a Deo. *Octavo,* utrum omnis homo appetat beatitudinem.

Question 5
Of the Attainment of Happiness

We must now consider the attainment of Happiness. Under this heading there are eight points of inquiry: 1. Whether man can attain Happiness? 2. Whether one man can be happier than another? 3. Whether any man can be happy in this life? 4. Whether Happiness once had can be lost? 5. Whether man can attain Happiness by means of his natural powers? 6. Whether man attains Happiness through the action of some higher creature? 7. Whether any actions of man are necessary in order that man may obtain Happiness of God? 8. Whether every man desires Happiness?

Articulus 1

Ad primum sic proceditur. Videtur quod homo beatitudinem adipisci non possit. Sicut enim natura rationalis est supra sensibilem ita natura intellectualis est supra rationalem ut patet per Dionysium in libro de Div. Nom., in multis locis. Sed bruta animalia, quae habent naturam sensibilem tantum, non possunt pervenire ad finem rationalis naturae. Ergo nec homo, qui est rationalis naturae, potest pervenire ad finem intellectualis naturae, qui est beatitudo.

Praeterea, beatitudo vera consistit in visione Dei, qui est veritas pura. Sed homini est connaturale ut veritatem intueatur in rebus materialibus, unde *species intelligibiles in phantasmatibus intelligit,* ut dicitur in III de anima. Ergo non potest ad beatitudinem pervenire.

Praeterea, beatitudo consistit in adeptione summi boni. Sed aliquis non potest pervenire ad summum, nisi transcendat

Article 1
Whether man can attain happiness?

Objection 1: It would seem that man cannot attain happiness. For just as the rational is above the sensible nature, so the intellectual is above the rational, as Dionysius declares (Div. Nom. iv, vi, vii) in several passages. But irrational animals that have the sensitive nature only, cannot attain the end of the rational nature. Therefore neither can man, who is of rational nature, attain the end of the intellectual nature, which is Happiness.

Objection 2: Further, True Happiness consists in seeing God, Who is pure Truth. But from his very nature, man considers truth in material things: wherefore "he understands the intelligible species in the phantasm" (De Anima iii, 7). Therefore he cannot attain Happiness.

Objection 3: Further, Happiness consists in attaining the Sovereign Good. But we cannot arrive at the top without surmounting the

media. Cum igitur inter Deum et naturam humanam media sit natura angelica, quam homo transcendere non potest; videtur quod non possit beatitudinem adipisci.

SED CONTRA est quod dicitur in Psalmo XCIII, *beatus homo quem tu erudieris, domine.*

RESPONDEO dicendum quod beatitudo nominat adeptionem perfecti boni. Quicumque ergo est capax perfecti boni, potest ad beatitudinem pervenire. Quod autem homo perfecti boni sit capax, ex hoc apparet, quia et eius intellectus apprehendere potest universale et perfectum bonum, et eius voluntas appetere illud. Et ideo homo potest beatitudinem adipisci. Apparet etiam idem ex hoc quod homo est capax visionis divinae essentiae, sicut in primo habitum est; in qua quidem visione perfectam hominis beatitudinem consistere diximus.

AD PRIMUM ergo dicendum quod aliter excedit natura rationalis sensitivam, et aliter intellectualis rationalem. Natura enim rationalis excedit sensitivam quantum ad cognitionis obiectum, quia sensus nullo modo potest cognoscere universale, cuius ratio est cognoscitiva. Sed intellectualis natura excedit rationalem quantum ad modum cognoscendi eandem intelligibilem veritatem, nam intellectualis natura statim apprehendit veritatem, ad quam rationalis natura per inquisitionem rationis pertingit, ut patet ex his quae in primo dicta sunt. Et ideo ad id quod intellectus apprehendit, ratio per quendam motum pertingit. Unde rationalis natura consequi potest beatitudinem, quae est perfectio intellectualis naturae, tamen alio modo quam angeli. Nam angeli consecuti sunt eam statim post principium suae conditionis, homines autem per tempus ad ipsam perveniunt. Sed natura sensitiva ad hunc finem nullo modo pertingere potest.

AD SECUNDUM dicendum quod homini, secundum statum praesentis vitae, est connaturalis modus cognoscendi veritatem intelligibilem per phantasmata. Sed post huius vitae statum, habet alium modum connaturalem, ut in primo dictum est.

AD TERTIUM dicendum quod homo non potest transcendere angelos gradu naturae,

middle. Since, therefore, the angelic nature through which man cannot mount is midway between God and human nature; it seems that he cannot attain Happiness.

On the contrary, It is written (Ps. 93:12): "Blessed is the man whom Thou shalt instruct, O Lord."

I answer that, Happiness is the attainment of the Perfect Good. Whoever, therefore, is capable of the Perfect Good can attain Happiness. Now, that man is capable of the Perfect Good, is proved both because his intellect can apprehend the universal and perfect good, and because his will can desire it. And therefore man can attain Happiness. This can be proved again from the fact that man is capable of seeing God, as stated in I, q. 12, a. 1: in which vision, as we stated above (I-II, q. 3, a. 8) man's perfect Happiness consists.

Reply to Objection 1: The rational exceeds the sensitive nature, otherwise than the intellectual surpasses the rational. For the rational exceeds the sensitive nature in respect of the object of its knowledge: since the senses have no knowledge whatever of the universal, whereas the reason has knowledge thereof. But the intellectual surpasses the rational nature, as to the mode of knowing the same intelligible truth: for the intellectual nature grasps forthwith the truth which the rational nature reaches by the inquiry of reason, as was made clear in the I, q. 58, a. 3; I, q. 79, a. 8. Therefore reason arrives by a kind of movement at that which the intellect grasps. Consequently the rational nature can attain Happiness, which is the perfection of the intellectual nature: but otherwise than the angels. Because the angels attained it forthwith after the beginning of their creation: whereas man attains if after a time. But the sensitive nature can nowise attain this end.

Reply to Objection 2: To man in the present state of life the natural way of knowing intelligible truth is by means of phantasms. But after this state of life, he has another natural way, as was stated in the I, q. 84, a. 7; I, q. 89, a. 1.

Reply to Objection 3: Man cannot surmount the angels in the degree of nature

ut scilicet naturaliter sit eis superior. Potest tamen eos transcendere per operationem intellectus, dum intelligit aliquid super angelos esse, quod homines beatificat; quod cum perfecte consequetur, perfecte beatus erit.

so as to be above them naturally. But he can surmount them by an operation of the intellect, by understanding that there is above the angels something that makes men happy; and when he has attained it, he will be perfectly happy.

Articulus 2

Ad secundum sic proceditur. Videtur quod unus homo alio non possit esse beatior. Beatitudo enim est *praemium virtutis,* ut philosophus dicit in I Ethic. Sed pro operibus virtutum omnibus aequalis merces redditur, dicitur enim Matth. XX, quod omnes qui operati sunt in vinea, *acceperunt singulos denarios;* quia, ut dicit Gregorius, *aequalem aeternae vitae retributionem sortiti sunt.* Ergo unus non erit alio beatior.

Praeterea, beatitudo est summum bonum. Sed summo non potest esse aliquid maius. Ergo beatitudine unius hominis non potest esse alia maior beatitudo.

Praeterea, beatitudo, cum sit *perfectum et sufficiens bonum,* desiderium hominis quietat. Sed non quietatur desiderium, si aliquod bonum deest quod suppleri possit. Si autem nihil deest quod suppleri possit, non poterit esse aliquid aliud maius bonum. Ergo vel homo non est beatus, vel, si est beatus, non potest alia maior beatitudo esse.

Sed contra est quod dicitur Ioan. XIV, *in domo patris mei mansiones multae sunt;* per quas, ut Augustinus dicit, *diversae meritorum dignitates intelliguntur in vita aeterna.* Dignitas autem vitae aeternae, quae pro merito datur, est ipsa beatitudo. Ergo sunt diversi gradus beatitudinis, et non omnium est aequalis beatitudo.

Respondeo dicendum quod, sicut supra dictum est, in ratione beatitudinis duo includuntur, scilicet ipse finis ultimus, qui est summum bonum; et adeptio vel fruitio ipsius boni. Quantum igitur ad ipsum bonum quod est beatitudinis obiectum et causa, non potest esse una beatitudo alia maior, quia non est nisi unum summum bonum, scilicet Deus, cuius fruitione

Article 2
Whether one man can be happier than another?

Objection 1: It would seem that one man cannot be happier than another. For Happiness is "the reward of virtue," as the Philosopher says (Ethic. i, 9). But equal reward is given for all the works of virtue; because it is written (Mat. 20:10) that all who labor in the vineyard "received every man a penny"; for, as Gregory says (Hom. xix in Evang.), "each was equally rewarded with eternal life." Therefore one man cannot be happier than another.

Objection 2: Further, Happiness is the supreme good. But nothing can surpass the supreme. Therefore one man's Happiness cannot be surpassed by another's.

Objection 3: Further, since Happiness is "the perfect and sufficient good" (Ethic. i, 7) it brings rest to man's desire. But his desire is not at rest, if he yet lacks some good that can be got. And if he lack nothing that he can get, there can be no still greater good. Therefore either man is not happy; or, if he be happy, no other Happiness can be greater.

On the contrary, It is written (Jn. 14:2): "In My Father's house there are many mansions"; which, according to Augustine (Tract. lxvii in Joan.) signify "the diverse dignities of merits in the one eternal life." But the dignity of eternal life which is given according to merit, is Happiness itself. Therefore there are diverse degrees of Happiness, and Happiness is not equally in all.

I answer that, As stated above (I-II, q. 1, a. 8; q. 2, a. 7), Happiness implies two things, to wit, the last end itself, i.e., the Sovereign Good; and the attainment or enjoyment of that same Good. As to that Good itself, Which is the object and cause of Happiness, one Happiness cannot be greater than another, since there is but one Sovereign Good, namely, God, by enjoying Whom,

homines sunt beati. Sed quantum ad adeptionem huiusmodi boni vel fruitionem, potest aliquis alio esse beatior, quia quanto magis hoc bono fruitur, tanto beatior est. Contingit autem aliquem perfectius frui Deo quam alium, ex eo quod est melius dispositus vel ordinatus ad eius fruitionem. Et secundum hoc potest aliquis alio beatior esse.

AD PRIMUM ergo dicendum quod unitas denarii significat unitatem beatitudinis ex parte obiecti. Sed diversitas mansionum significat diversitatem beatitudinis secundum diversum gradum fruitionis.

AD SECUNDUM dicendum quod beatitudo dicitur esse summum bonum, inquantum est summi boni perfecta possessio sive fruitio.

AD TERTIUM dicendum quod nulli beato deest aliquod bonum desiderandum, cum habeat ipsum bonum infinitum, quod est *bonum omnis boni,* ut Augustinus dicit. Sed dicitur aliquis alio beatior, ex diversa eiusdem boni participatione. Additio autem aliorum bonorum non auget beatitudinem, unde Augustinus dicit, in V Confess., *qui te et alia novit, non propter illa beatior, sed propter te solum beatus.*

men are made happy. But as to the attainment or enjoyment of this Good, one man can be happier than another; because the more a man enjoys this Good the happier he is. Now, that one man enjoys God more than another, happens through his being better disposed or ordered to the enjoyment of Him. And in this sense one man can be happier than another.

Reply to Objection 1: The one penny signifies that Happiness is one in its object. But the many mansions signify the manifold Happiness in the divers degrees of enjoyment.

Reply to Objection 2: Happiness is said to be the supreme good, inasmuch as it is the perfect possession or enjoyment of the Supreme Good.

Reply to Objection 3: None of the Blessed lacks any desirable good; since they have the Infinite Good Itself, Which is "the good of all good," as Augustine says (Enarr. in Ps. 134). But one is said to be happier than another, by reason of diverse participation of the same good. And the addition of other goods does not increase Happiness, since Augustine says (Confess. v, 4): "He who knows Thee, and others besides, is not the happier for knowing them, but is happy for knowing Thee alone."

ARTICULUS 3

AD TERTIUM sic proceditur. Videtur quod beatitudo possit in hac vita haberi. Dicitur enim in Psalmo CXVIII, *beati immaculati in via, qui ambulant in lege domini.* Hoc autem in hac vita contingit. Ergo aliquis in hac vita potest esse beatus.

PRAETEREA, imperfecta participatio summi boni non adimit rationem beatitudinis, alioquin unus non esset alio beatior. Sed in hac vita homines possunt participare summum bonum, cognoscendo et amando Deum, licet imperfecte. Ergo homo in hac vita potest esse beatus.

PRAETEREA, quod a pluribus dicitur, non potest totaliter falsum esse, videtur enim esse naturale quod in pluribus est; natura autem non totaliter deficit. Sed plures ponunt

ARTICLE 3
Whether one can be happy in this life?

Objection 1: It would seem that Happiness can be had in this life. For it is written (Ps. 118:1): "Blessed are the undefiled in the way, who walk in the law of the Lord." But this happens in this life. Therefore one can be happy in this life.

Objection 2: Further, imperfect participation in the Sovereign Good does not destroy the nature of Happiness, otherwise one would not be happier than another. But men can participate in the Sovereign Good in this life, by knowing and loving God, albeit imperfectly. Therefore man can be happy in this life.

Objection 3: Further, what is said by many cannot be altogether false: since what is in many, comes, apparently, from nature; and nature does not fail altogether. Now many say

beatitudinem in hac vita, ut patet per illud Psalmi CXLIII, *beatum dixerunt populum cui haec sunt,* scilicet praesentis vitae bona. Ergo aliquis in hac vita potest esse beatus.

SED CONTRA est quod dicitur Iob XIV, *homo natus de muliere, brevi vivens tempore, repletur multis miseriis.* Sed beatitudo excludit miseriam. Ergo homo in hac vita non potest esse beatus.

RESPONDEO dicendum quod aliqualis beatitudinis participatio in hac vita haberi potest, perfecta autem et vera beatitudo non potest haberi in hac vita. Et hoc quidem considerari potest dupliciter. Primo quidem, ex ipsa communi beatitudinis ratione. Nam beatitudo, cum sit *perfectum et sufficiens bonum,* omne malum excludit, et omne desiderium implet. In hac autem vita non potest omne malum excludi. Multis enim malis praesens vita subiacet, quae vitari non possunt, et ignorantiae ex parte intellectus, et inordinatae affectioni ex parte appetitus, et multiplicibus poenalitatibus ex parte corporis; ut Augustinus diligenter prosequitur XIX de Civ. Dei. Similiter etiam desiderium boni in hac vita satiari non potest. Naturaliter enim homo desiderat permanentiam eius boni quod habet. Bona autem praesentis vitae transitoria sunt, cum et ipsa vita transeat, quam naturaliter desideramus, et eam perpetuo permanere vellemus, quia naturaliter homo refugit mortem. Unde impossibile est quod in hac vita vera beatitudo habeatur. Secundo, si consideretur id in quo specialiter beatitudo consistit, scilicet visio divinae essentiae, quae non potest homini provenire in hac vita, ut in primo ostensum est. Ex quibus manifeste apparet quod non potest aliquis in hac vita veram et perfectam beatitudinem adipisci.

AD PRIMUM ergo dicendum quod beati dicuntur aliqui in hac vita, vel propter spem beatitudinis adipiscendae in futura vita, secundum illud Rom. VIII, *spe salvi facti sumus,* vel propter aliquam participationem beatitudinis, secundum aliqualem summi boni fruitionem.

AD SECUNDUM dicendum quod participatio beatitudinis potest esse imperfecta dupliciter. Uno modo, ex parte ipsius obiecti

that Happiness can be had in this life, as appears from Ps. 143:15: "They have called the people happy that hath these things," to wit, the good things in this life. Therefore one can be happy in this life.

On the contrary, It is written (Job 14:1): "Man born of a woman, living for a short time, is filled with many miseries." But Happiness excludes misery. Therefore man cannot be happy in this life.

I answer that, A certain participation of Happiness can be had in this life: but perfect and true Happiness cannot be had in this life. This may be seen from a twofold consideration. First, from the general notion of happiness. For since happiness is a "perfect and sufficient good," it excludes every evil, and fulfils every desire. But in this life every evil cannot be excluded. For this present life is subject to many unavoidable evils; to ignorance on the part of the intellect; to inordinate affection on the part of the appetite, and to many penalties on the part of the body; as Augustine sets forth in De Civ. Dei xix, 4. Likewise neither can the desire for good be satiated in this life. For man naturally desires the good, which he has, to be abiding. Now the goods of the present life pass away; since life itself passes away, which we naturally desire to have, and would wish to hold abidingly, for man naturally shrinks from death. Wherefore it is impossible to have true Happiness in this life. Secondly, from a consideration of the specific nature of Happiness, *viz.* the vision of the Divine Essence, which man cannot obtain in this life, as was shown in the I, q. 12, a. 11. Hence it is evident that none can attain true and perfect Happiness in this life.

Reply to Objection 1: Some are said to be happy in this life, either on account of the hope of obtaining Happiness in the life to come, according to Rom. 8:24: "We are saved by hope"; or on account of a certain participation of Happiness, by reason of a kind of enjoyment of the Sovereign Good.

Reply to Objection 2: The imperfection of participated Happiness is due to one of two causes. First, on the part of the object

beatitudinis, quod quidem secundum sui essentiam non videtur. Et talis imperfectio tollit rationem verae beatitudinis. Alio modo potest esse imperfecta ex parte ipsius participantis, qui quidem ad ipsum obiectum beatitudinis secundum seipsum attingit, scilicet Deum, sed imperfecte, per respectum ad modum quo Deus seipso fruitur. Et talis imperfectio non tollit veram rationem beatitudinis, quia, cum beatitudo sit operatio quaedam, ut supra dictum est, vera ratio beatitudinis, consideratur ex obiecto, quod dat speciem actui, non autem ex subiecto.

AD TERTIUM dicendum quod homines reputant in hac vita esse aliquam beatitudinem, propter aliquam similitudinem verae beatitudinis. Et sic non ex toto in sua aestimatione deficiunt.

of Happiness, which is not seen in Its Essence: and this imperfection destroys the nature of true Happiness. Secondly, the imperfection may be on the part of the participator, who indeed attains the object of Happiness, in itself, namely, God: imperfectly, however, in comparison with the way in which God enjoys Himself. This imperfection does not destroy the true nature of Happiness; because, since Happiness is an operation, as stated above (I-II, q. 3, a. 2), the true nature of Happiness is taken from the object, which specifies the act, and not from the subject.

Reply to Objection 3: Men esteem that there is some kind of happiness to be had in this life, on account of a certain likeness to true Happiness. And thus they do not fail altogether in their estimate.

ARTICULUS 4

AD QUARTUM sic proceditur. Videtur quod beatitudo possit amitti. Beatitudo enim est perfectio quaedam. Sed omnis perfectio inest perfectibili secundum modum ipsius. Cum igitur homo secundum suam naturam sit mutabilis, videtur quod beatitudo mutabiliter ab homine participetur. Et ita videtur quod homo beatitudinem possit amittere.

PRAETEREA, beatitudo consistit in actione intellectus, qui subiacet voluntati. Sed voluntas se habet ad opposita. Ergo videtur quod possit desistere ab operatione qua homo beatificatur, et ita homo desinet esse beatus.

PRAETEREA, principio respondet finis. Sed beatitudo hominis habet principium, quia homo non semper fuit beatus. Ergo videtur quod habeat finem.

SED CONTRA est quod dicitur Matth. XXV, de iustis, quod *ibunt in vitam aeternam;* quae, ut dictum est, est beatitudo sanctorum. Quod autem est aeternum, non deficit. Ergo beatitudo non potest amitti.

RESPONDEO dicendum quod, si loquamur de beatitudine imperfecta, qualis in hac vita potest haberi, sic potest amitti. Et hoc patet in felicitate contemplativa, quae amittitur vel per oblivionem, puta cum corrumpitur scientia ex aliqua aegritudine; vel etiam per

ARTICLE 4
Whether happiness once had can be lost?

Objection 1: It would seem that Happiness can be lost. For Happiness is a perfection. But every perfection is in the thing perfected according to the mode of the latter. Since then man is, by his nature, changeable, it seems that Happiness is participated by man in a changeable manner. And consequently it seems that man can lose Happiness.

Objection 2: Further, Happiness consists in an act of the intellect; and the intellect is subject to the will. But the will can be directed to opposites. Therefore it seems that it can desist from the operation whereby man is made happy: and thus man will cease to be happy.

Objection 3: Further, the end corresponds to the beginning. But man's Happiness has a beginning, since man was not always happy. Therefore it seems that it has an end.

On the contrary, It is written (Mat. 25:46) of the righteous that "they shall go . . . into life everlasting," which, as above stated (I-II, q. 5, a. 2), is the Happiness of the saints. Now what is eternal ceases not. Therefore Happiness cannot be lost.

I answer that, If we speak of imperfect happiness, such as can be had in this life, in this sense it can be lost. This is clear of contemplative happiness, which is lost either by forgetfulness, for instance, when knowledge is lost through sickness; or again

aliquas occupationes, quibus totaliter abstrahitur aliquis a contemplatione. Patet etiam idem in felicitate activa, voluntas enim hominis transmutari potest, ut in vitium degeneret a virtute, in cuius actu principaliter consistit felicitas. Si autem virtus remaneat integra, exteriores transmutationes possunt quidem beatitudinem talem perturbare, inquantum impediunt multas operationes virtutum, non tamen possunt eam totaliter auferre, quia adhuc remanet operatio virtutis, dum ipsas adversitates homo laudabiliter sustinet. Et quia beatitudo huius vitae amitti potest, quod videtur esse contra rationem beatitudinis; ideo philosophus dicit, in I Ethic., aliquos esse in hac vita beatos, non simpliciter, sed *sicut homines* quorum natura mutationi subiecta est. Si vero loquamur de beatitudine perfecta quae expectatur post hanc vitam, sciendum est quod Origenes posuit, quorundam Platonicorum errorem sequens, quod post ultimam beatitudinem homo potest fieri miser. Sed hoc manifeste apparet esse falsum dupliciter. Primo quidem, ex ipsa communi ratione beatitudinis. Cum enim ipsa beatitudo sit *perfectum bonum et sufficiens,* oportet quod desiderium hominis quietet, et omne malum excludat. Naturaliter autem homo desiderat retinere bonum quod habet, et quod eius retinendi securitatem obtineat, alioquin necesse est quod timore amittendi, vel dolore de certitudine amissionis, affligatur. Requiritur igitur ad veram beatitudinem quod homo certam habeat opinionem bonum quod habet, nunquam se amissurum. Quae quidem opinio si vera sit, consequens est quod beatitudinem nunquam amittet. Si autem falsa sit, hoc ipsum est quoddam malum, falsam opinionem habere, nam falsum est malum intellectus, sicut verum est bonum ipsius, ut dicitur in VI Ethic. Non igitur iam vere erit beatus, si aliquod malum ei inest. Secundo idem apparet, si consideretur ratio beatitudinis in speciali. Ostensum est enim supra quod perfecta beatitudo hominis in visione divinae essentiae consistit. Est autem impossibile quod aliquis videns divinam essentiam, velit eam non videre. Quia omne bonum habitum quo quis carere vult,

by certain occupations, whereby a man is altogether withdrawn from contemplation. This is also clear of active happiness: since man's will can be changed so as to fall to vice from the virtue, in whose act that happiness principally consists. If, however, the virtue remain unimpaired, outward changes can indeed disturb such like happiness, in so far as they hinder many acts of virtue; but they cannot take it away altogether because there still remains an act of virtue, whereby man bears these trials in a praiseworthy manner. And since the happiness of this life can be lost, a circumstance that appears to be contrary to the nature of happiness, therefore did the Philosopher state (Ethic. i, 10) that some are happy in this life, not simply, but "as men," whose nature is subject to change. But if we speak of that perfect Happiness which we await after this life, it must be observed that Origen (Peri Archon. ii, 3), following the error of certain Platonists, held that man can become unhappy after the final Happiness. This, however, is evidently false, for two reasons. First, from the general notion of happiness. For since happiness is the "perfect and sufficient good," it must needs set man's desire at rest and exclude every evil. Now man naturally desires to hold to the good that he has, and to have the surety of his holding: else he must of necessity be troubled with the fear of losing it, or with the sorrow of knowing that he will lose it. Therefore it is necessary for true Happiness that man have the assured opinion of never losing the good that he possesses. If this opinion be true, it follows that he never will lose happiness: but if it be false, it is in itself an evil that he should have a false opinion: because the false is the evil of the intellect, just as the true is its good, as stated in Ethic. vi, 2. Consequently he will no longer be truly happy, if evil be in him. Secondly, it is again evident if we consider the specific nature of Happiness. For it has been shown above (I-II, q. 3, a. 8) that man's perfect Happiness consists in the vision of the Divine Essence. Now it is impossible for anyone seeing the Divine Essence, to wish not to see It. Because every good that one possesses and yet wishes to be without,

aut est insufficiens, et quaeritur aliquid sufficientius loco eius, aut habet aliquod incommodum annexum, propter quod in fastidium venit. Visio autem divinae essentiae replet animam omnibus bonis, cum coniungat fonti totius bonitatis, unde dicitur in Psalmo XVI, *satiabor cum apparuerit gloria tua;* et Sap. VII, dicitur, *venerunt mihi omnia bona pariter cum illa,* scilicet cum contemplatione sapientiae. Similiter etiam non habet aliquod incommodum adiunctum, quia de contemplatione sapientiae dicitur, Sap. VIII, *non habet amaritudinem conversatio illius, nec taedium convictus eius.* Sic ergo patet quod propria voluntate beatus non potest beatitudinem deserere. Similiter etiam non potest eam perdere, Deo subtrahente. Quia, cum subtractio beatitudinis sit quaedam poena, non potest talis subtractio a Deo, iusto iudice, provenire, nisi pro aliqua culpa, in quam cadere non potest qui Dei essentiam videt, cum ad hanc visionem ex necessitate sequatur rectitudo voluntatis, ut supra ostensum est. Similiter etiam nec aliquod aliud agens potest eam subtrahere. Quia mens Deo coniuncta super omnia alia elevatur; et sic ab huiusmodi coniunctione nullum aliud agens potest ipsam excludere. Unde inconveniens videtur quod per quasdam alternationes temporum transeat homo de beatitudine ad miseriam, et e converso, quia huiusmodi temporales alternationes esse non possunt, nisi circa ea quae subiacent tempori et motui.

AD PRIMUM ergo dicendum quod beatitudo est perfectio consummata, quae omnem defectum excludit a beato. Et ideo absque mutabilitate advenit eam habenti, faciente hoc virtute divina, quae hominem sublevat in participationem aeternitatis transcendentis omnem mutationem.

AD SECUNDUM dicendum quod voluntas ad opposita se habet in his quae ad finem ordinantur, sed ad ultimum finem naturali necessitate ordinatur. Quod patet ex hoc, quod homo non potest non velle esse beatus.

is either insufficient, something more sufficing being desired in its stead; or else has some inconvenience attached to it, by reason of which it becomes wearisome. But the vision of the Divine Essence fills the soul with all good things, since it unites it to the source of all goodness; hence it is written (Ps. 16:15): "I shall be satisfied when Thy glory shall appear"; and (Wis. 7:11): "All good things came to me together with her," i.e., with the contemplation of wisdom. In like manner neither has it any inconvenience attached to it; because it is written of the contemplation of wisdom (Wis. 8:16): "Her conversation hath no bitterness, nor her company any tediousness." It is thus evident that the happy man cannot forsake Happiness of his own accord. Moreover, neither can he lose Happiness, through God taking it away from him. Because, since the withdrawal of Happiness is a punishment, it cannot be enforced by God, the just Judge, except for some fault; and he that sees God cannot fall into a fault, since rectitude of the will, of necessity, results from that vision as was shown above (I-II, q. 4, a. 4). Nor again can it be withdrawn by any other agent. Because the mind that is united to God is raised above all other things: and consequently no other agent can sever the mind from that union. Therefore it seems unreasonable that as time goes on, man should pass from happiness to misery, and vice versa; because such like vicissitudes of time can only be for such things as are subject to time and movement.

Reply to Objection 1: Happiness is consummate perfection, which excludes every defect from the happy. And therefore whoever has happiness has it altogether unchangeably: this is done by the Divine power, which raises man to the participation of eternity which transcends all change.

Reply to Objection 2: The will can be directed to opposites, in things which are ordained to the end; but it is ordained, of natural necessity, to the last end. This is evident from the fact that man is unable not to wish to be happy.

I-II, q. 5, a. 4, ad 3

AD TERTIUM dicendum quod beatitudo habet principium ex conditione participantis, sed caret fine, propter conditionem boni cuius participatio facit beatum. Unde ab alio est initium beatitudinis; et ab alio est quod caret fine.

Reply to Objection 3: Happiness has a beginning owing to the condition of the participator: but it has no end by reason of the condition of the good, the participation of which makes man happy. Hence the beginning of happiness is from one cause, its endlessness is from another.

ARTICULUS 5

ARTICLE 5
Whether man can attain happiness by his natural powers?

AD QUINTUM sic proceditur. Videtur quod homo per sua naturalia possit beatitudinem consequi. Natura enim non deficit in necessariis. Sed nihil est homini tam necessarium quam id per quod finem ultimum consequitur. Ergo hoc naturae humanae non deest. Potest igitur homo per sua naturalia beatitudinem consequi.

PRAETEREA, homo, cum sit nobilior irrationalibus creaturis, videtur esse sufficientior. Sed irrationales creaturae per sua naturalia possunt consequi suos fines. Ergo multo magis homo per sua naturalia potest beatitudinem consequi.

PRAETEREA, beatitudo est *operatio perfecta,* secundum philosophum. Eiusdem autem est incipere rem, et perficere ipsam. Cum igitur operatio imperfecta, quae est quasi principium in operationibus humanis, subdatur naturali hominis potestati, qua suorum actuum est dominus; videtur quod per naturalem potentiam possit pertingere ad operationem perfectam, quae est beatitudo.

SED CONTRA, homo est principium naturaliter actuum suorum per intellectum et voluntatem. Sed ultima beatitudo sanctis praeparata, excedit intellectum hominis et voluntatem, dicit enim apostolus, I ad Cor. II, *oculus non vidit, et auris non audivit, et in cor hominis non ascendit, quae praeparavit Deus diligentibus se.* Ergo homo per sua naturalia non potest beatitudinem consequi.

RESPONDEO dicendum quod beatitudo imperfecta quae in hac vita haberi potest, potest ab homine acquiri per sua naturalia, eo modo quo et virtus, in cuius operatione

Objection 1: It would seem that man can attain Happiness by his natural powers. For nature does not fail in necessary things. But nothing is so necessary to man as that by which he attains the last end. Therefore this is not lacking to human nature. Therefore man can attain Happiness by his natural powers.

Objection 2: Further, since man is more noble than irrational creatures, it seems that he must be better equipped than they. But irrational creatures can attain their end by their natural powers. Much more therefore can man attain Happiness by his natural powers.

Objection 3: Further, Happiness is a "perfect operation," according to the Philosopher (Ethic. vii, 13). Now the beginning of a thing belongs to the same principle as the perfecting thereof. Since, therefore, the imperfect operation, which is as the beginning in human operations, is subject to man's natural power, whereby he is master of his own actions; it seems that he can attain to perfect operation, i.e., Happiness, by his natural powers.

On the contrary, Man is naturally the principle of his action, by his intellect and will. But final Happiness prepared for the saints, surpasses the intellect and will of man; for the Apostle says (1 Cor. 2:9) "Eye hath not seen, nor ear heard, neither hath it entered into the heart of man, what things God hath prepared for them that love Him." Therefore man cannot attain Happiness by his natural powers.

I answer that, Imperfect happiness that can be had in this life, can be acquired by man by his natural powers, in the same way as virtue, in whose operation

consistit, de quo infra dicetur. Sed beatitudo hominis perfecta, sicut supra dictum est, consistit in visione divinae essentiae. Videre autem Deum per essentiam est supra naturam non solum hominis, sed etiam omnis creaturae, ut in primo ostensum est. Naturalis enim cognitio cuiuslibet creaturae est secundum modum substantiae eius, sicut de intelligentia dicitur in libro de causis, quod cognoscit ea quae sunt supra se, et ea quae sunt infra se, secundum modum substantiae suae. Omnis autem cognitio quae est secundum modum substantiae creatae, deficit a visione divinae essentiae, quae in infinitum excedit omnem substantiam creatam. Unde nec homo, nec aliqua creatura, potest consequi beatitudinem ultimam per sua naturalia.

AD PRIMUM ergo dicendum quod, sicut natura non deficit homini in necessariis, quamvis non dederit sibi arma et tegumenta sicut aliis animalibus quia dedit ei rationem et manus, quibus possit haec sibi conquirere; ita nec deficit homini in necessariis, quamvis non daret sibi aliquod principium quo posset beatitudinem consequi; hoc enim erat impossibile. Sed dedit ei liberum arbitrium, quo possit converti ad Deum, qui eum faceret beatum. Quae enim per amicos possumus, per nos aliqualiter possumus, ut dicitur in III Ethic.

AD SECUNDUM dicendum quod nobilioris conditionis est natura quae potest consequi perfectum bonum, licet indigeat exteriori auxilio ad hoc consequendum, quam natura quae non potest consequi perfectum bonum, sed consequitur quoddam bonum imperfectum, licet ad consecutionem eius non indigeat exteriori auxilio, ut philosophus dicit in II de caelo. Sicut melius est dispositus ad sanitatem qui potest consequi perfectam sanitatem, licet hoc sit per auxilium medicinae; quam qui solum potest consequi quandam imperfectam sanitatem, sine medicinae auxilio. Et ideo creatura rationalis, quae potest consequi perfectum beatitudinis bonum, indigens ad hoc divino auxilio, est perfectior quam creatura irrationalis, quae huiusmodi boni non est capax, sed

it consists: on this point we shall speak further on (I-II, q. 63). But man's perfect Happiness, as stated above (I-II, q. 3, a. 8), consists in the vision of the Divine Essence. Now the vision of God's Essence surpasses the nature not only of man, but also of every creature, as was shown in the I, q. 12, a. 4. For the natural knowledge of every creature is in keeping with the mode of his substance: thus it is said of the intelligence (De Causis; Prop. viii) that "it knows things that are above it, and things that are below it, according to the mode of its substance." But every knowledge that is according to the mode of created substance, falls short of the vision of the Divine Essence, which infinitely surpasses all created substance. Consequently neither man, nor any creature, can attain final Happiness by his natural powers.

Reply to Objection 1: Just as nature does not fail man in necessaries, although it has not provided him with weapons and clothing, as it provided other animals, because it gave him reason and hands, with which he is able to get these things for himself; so neither did it fail man in things necessary, although it gave him not the wherewithal to attain Happiness: since this it could not do. But it did give him free-will, with which he can turn to God, that He may make him happy. "For what we do by means of our friends, is done, in a sense, by ourselves" (Ethic. iii, 3).

Reply to Objection 2: The nature that can attain perfect good, although it needs help from without in order to attain it, is of more noble condition than a nature which cannot attain perfect good, but attains some imperfect good, although it need no help from without in order to attain it, as the Philosopher says (De Coel. ii, 12). Thus he is better disposed to health who can attain perfect health, albeit by means of medicine, than he who can attain but imperfect health, without the help of medicine. And therefore the rational creature, which can attain the perfect good of happiness, but needs the Divine assistance for the purpose, is more perfect than the irrational creature, which is not capable of attaining this good, but

quoddam imperfectum bonum consequitur virtute suae naturae.

AD TERTIUM dicendum quod, quando imperfectum et perfectum sunt eiusdem speciei, ab eadem virtute causari possunt. Non autem hoc est necesse, si sunt alterius speciei, non enim quidquid potest causare dispositionem materiae, potest ultimam perfectionem conferre. Imperfecta autem operatio, quae subiacet naturali hominis potestati, non est eiusdem speciei cum operatione illa perfecta quae est hominis beatitudo, cum operationis species dependeat ex obiecto. Unde ratio non sequitur.

attains some imperfect good by its natural powers.

Reply to Objection 3: When imperfect and perfect are of the same species, they can be caused by the same power. But this does not follow of necessity, if they be of different species: for not everything, that can cause the disposition of matter, can produce the final perfection. Now the imperfect operation, which is subject to man's natural power, is not of the same species as that perfect operation which is man's happiness: since operation takes its species from its object. Consequently the argument does not prove.

ARTICULUS 6

AD SEXTUM sic proceditur. Videtur quod homo possit fieri beatus per actionem alicuius superioris creaturae, scilicet angeli. Cum enim duplex ordo inveniatur in rebus, unus partium universi ad invicem, alius totius universi ad bonum quod est extra universum; primus ordo ordinatur ad secundum sicut ad finem, ut dicitur XII Metaphys.; sicut ordo partium exercitus ad invicem est propter ordinem totius exercitus ad ducem. Sed ordo partium universi ad invicem attenditur secundum quod superiores creaturae agunt in inferiores, ut in primo dictum est, beatitudo autem consistit in ordine hominis ad bonum quod est extra universum, quod est Deus. Ergo per actionem superioris creaturae, scilicet angeli, in hominem, homo beatus efficitur.

PRAETEREA, quod est in potentia tale, potest reduci in actum per id quod est actu tale, sicut quod est potentia calidum, fit actu calidum per id quod est actu calidum. Sed homo est in potentia beatus. Ergo potest fieri actu beatus per angelum, qui est actu beatus.

PRAETEREA, beatitudo consistit in operatione intellectus, ut supra dictum est. Sed angelus potest illuminare intellectum hominis, ut in primo habitum est. Ergo angelus potest facere hominem beatum.

SED CONTRA est quod dicitur in Psalmo LXXXIII, *gratiam et gloriam dabit dominus.*

ARTICLE 6
Whether man attains happiness through the action of some higher creature?

Objection 1: It would seem that man can be made happy through the action of some higher creature, *viz.* an angel. For since we observe a twofold order in things—one, of the parts of the universe to one another, the other, of the whole universe to a good which is outside the universe; the former order is ordained to the second as to its end (Metaph. xii, 10). Thus the mutual order of the parts of an army is dependent on the order of the parts of an army is dependent on the order of the whole army to the general. But the mutual order of the parts of the universe consists in the higher creatures acting on the lower, as stated in the I, q. 109, a. 2: while happiness consists in the order of man to a good which is outside the universe, i.e., God. Therefore man is made happy, through a higher creature, *viz.* an angel, acting on him.

Objection 2: Further, that which is such in potentiality, can be reduced to act, by that which is such actually: thus what is potentially hot, is made actually hot, by something that is actually hot. But man is potentially happy. Therefore he can be made actually happy by an angel who is actually happy.

Objection 3: Further, Happiness consists in an operation of the intellect as stated above (I-II, q. 3, a. 4). But an angel can enlighten man's intellect as shown in the I, q. 111, a. 1. Therefore an angel can make a man happy.

On the contrary, It is written (Ps. 83:12): "The Lord will give grace and glory."

RESPONDEO dicendum quod, cum omnis creatura naturae legibus sit subiecta, utpote habens limitatam virtutem et actionem; illud quod excedit naturam creatam, non potest fieri virtute alicuius creaturae. Et ideo si quid fieri oporteat quod sit supra naturam, hoc fit immediate a Deo; sicut suscitatio mortui, illuminatio caeci, et cetera huiusmodi. Ostensum est autem quod beatitudo est quoddam bonum excedens naturam creatam. Unde impossibile est quod per actionem alicuius creaturae conferatur, sed homo beatus fit solo Deo agente, si loquamur de beatitudine perfecta. Si vero loquamur de beatitudine imperfecta, sic eadem ratio est de ipsa et de virtute, in cuius actu consistit.

AD PRIMUM ergo dicendum quod plerumque contingit in potentiis activis ordinatis, quod perducere ad ultimum finem pertinet ad supremam potentiam, inferiores vero potentiae coadiuvant ad consecutionem illius ultimi finis disponendo, sicut ad artem gubernativam, quae praeest navifactivae, pertinet usus navis, propter quem navis ipsa fit. Sic igitur et in ordine universi, homo quidem adiuvatur ab angelis ad consequendum ultimum finem, secundum aliqua praecedentia, quibus disponitur ad eius consecutionem, sed ipsum ultimum finem consequitur per ipsum primum agentem, qui est Deus.

AD SECUNDUM dicendum quod, quando aliqua forma actu existit in aliquo secundum esse perfectum et naturale, potest esse principium actionis in alterum; sicut calidum per calorem calefacit. Sed si forma existit in aliquo imperfecte, et non secundum esse naturale, non potest esse principium communicationis sui ad alterum, sicut intentio coloris quae est in pupilla, non potest facere album; neque etiam omnia quae sunt illuminata aut calefacta, possunt alia calefacere et illuminare; sic enim illuminatio at calefactio essent usque ad infinitum. Lumen autem gloriae, per quod Deus videtur, in Deo quidem est perfecte secundum esse naturale, in qualibet autem creatura est imperfecte, et secundum esse similitudinarium vel participatum. Unde nulla creatura beata potest communicare suam beatitudinem alteri.

I answer that, Since every creature is subject to the laws of nature, from the very fact that its power and action are limited: that which surpasses created nature, cannot be done by the power of any creature. Consequently if anything need to be done that is above nature, it is done by God immediately; such as raising the dead to life, restoring sight to the blind, and such like. Now it has been shown above (I-II, q. 5, a. 5) that Happiness is a good surpassing created nature. Therefore it is impossible that it be bestowed through the action of any creature: but by God alone is man made happy, if we speak of perfect Happiness. If, however, we speak of imperfect happiness, the same is to be said of it as of the virtue, in whose act it consists.

Reply to Objection 1: It often happens in the case of active powers ordained to one another, that it belongs to the highest power to reach the last end, while the lower powers contribute to the attainment of that last end, by causing a disposition thereto: thus to the art of sailing, which commands the art of shipbuilding, it belongs to use a ship for the end for which it was made. Thus, too, in the order of the universe, man is indeed helped by the angels in the attainment of his last end, in respect of certain preliminary dispositions thereto: whereas he attains the last end itself through the First Agent, which is God.

Reply to Objection 2: When a form exists perfectly and naturally in something, it can be the principle of action on something else: for instance a hot thing heats through heat. But if a form exist in something imperfectly, and not naturally, it cannot be the principle whereby it is communicated to something else: thus the "intention" of color which is in the pupil, cannot make a thing white; nor indeed can everything enlightened or heated give heat or light to something else; for if they could, enlightening and heating would go on to infinity. But the light of glory, whereby God is seen, is in God perfectly and naturally; whereas in any creature, it is imperfectly and by likeness or participation. Consequently no creature can communicate its Happiness to another.

I-II, q. 5, a. 6, ad 3

AD TERTIUM dicendum quod angelus beatus illuminat intellectum hominis, vel etiam inferioris angeli, quantum ad aliquas rationes divinorum operum non autem quantum ad visionem divinae essentiae, ut in primo dictum est. Ad eam enim videndam, omnes immediate illuminantur a Deo.

ARTICULUS 7

AD SEPTIMUM sic proceditur. Videtur quod non requirantur aliqua opera hominis ad hoc ut beatitudinem consequatur a Deo. Deus enim, cum sit agens infinitae virtutis, non praeexigit in agendo materiam, aut dispositionem materiae, sed statim potest totum producere. Sed opera hominis, cum non requirantur ad beatitudinem eius sicut causa efficiens, ut dictum est, non possunt requiri ad eam nisi sicut dispositiones. Ergo Deus, qui dispositiones non praeexigit in agendo, beatitudinem sine praecedentibus operibus confert.

PRAETEREA, sicut Deus est auctor beatitudinis immediate, ita et naturam immediate instituit. Sed in prima institutione naturae, produxit creaturas nulla dispositione praecedente vel actione creaturae; sed statim fecit unumquodque perfectum in sua specie. Ergo videtur quod beatitudinem conferat homini sine aliquibus operationibus praecedentibus.

PRAETEREA, apostolus dicit, Rom. IV, beatitudinem hominis esse *cui Deus confert iustitiam sine operibus.* Non ergo requiruntur aliqua opera hominis ad beatitudinem consequendam.

SED CONTRA est quod dicitur Ioan. XIII, *si haec scitis, beati eritis si feceritis ea.* Ergo per actionem ad beatitudinem pervenitur.

RESPONDEO dicendum quod rectitudo voluntatis, ut supra dictum est, requiritur ad beatitudinem, cum nihil aliud sit quam debitus ordo voluntatis ad ultimum finem; quae ita exigitur ad consecutionem ultimi finis, sicut debita dispositio materiae ad consecutionem formae. Sed ex hoc non ostenditur quod aliqua operatio hominis debeat praecedere eius beatitudinem, posset

THE ATTAINMENT OF HAPPINESS

Reply to Objection 3: A happy angel enlightens the intellect of a man or of a lower angel, as to certain notions of the Divine works: but not as to the vision of the Divine Essence, as was stated in the I, q. 106, a. 1: since in order to see this, all are immediately enlightened by God.

ARTICLE 7
Whether any good works are necessary that man may receive happiness from God?

Objection 1: It would seem that no works of man are necessary that he may obtain Happiness from God. For since God is an agent of infinite power, He requires before acting, neither matter, nor disposition of matter, but can forthwith produce the whole effect. But man's works, since they are not required for Happiness, as the efficient cause thereof, as stated above (I-II, q. 5, a. 6), can be required only as dispositions thereto. Therefore God who does not require dispositions before acting, bestows Happiness without any previous works.

Objection 2: Further, just as God is the immediate cause of Happiness, so is He the immediate cause of nature. But when God first established nature, He produced creatures without any previous disposition or action on the part of the creature, but made each one perfect forthwith in its species. Therefore it seems that He bestows Happiness on man without any previous works.

Objection 3: Further, the Apostle says (Rom. 4:6) that Happiness is of the man "to whom God reputeth justice without works." Therefore no works of man are necessary for attaining Happiness.

On the contrary, It is written (Jn. 13:17): "If you know these things, you shall be blessed if you do them." Therefore Happiness is obtained through works.

I answer that, Rectitude of the will, as stated above (I-II, q. 4, a. 4), is necessary for Happiness; since it is nothing else than the right order of the will to the last end; and it is therefore necessary for obtaining the end, just as the right disposition of matter, in order to receive the form. But this does not prove that any work of man need precede his Happiness:

enim Deus simul facere voluntatem recte tendentem in finem, et finem consequentem; sicut quandoque simul materiam disponit, et inducit formam. Sed ordo divinae sapientiae exigit ne hoc fiat, ut enim dicitur in II de caelo, *eorum quae nata sunt habere bonum perfectum, aliquid habet ipsum sine motu, aliquid uno motu, aliquid pluribus.* Habere autem perfectum bonum sine motu, convenit ei quod naturaliter habet illud. Habere autem beatitudinem naturaliter est solius Dei. Unde solius Dei proprium est quod ad beatitudinem non moveatur per aliquam operationem praecedentem. Cum autem beatitudo excedat omnem naturam creatam, nulla pura creatura convenienter beatitudinem consequitur absque motu operationis, per quam tendit in ipsam. Sed angelus, qui est superior ordine naturae quam homo, consecutus est eam, ex ordine divinae sapientiae, uno motu operationis meritoriae, ut in primo expositum est. Homines autem consequuntur ipsam multis motibus operationum, qui merita dicuntur. Unde etiam, secundum philosophum, beatitudo est praemium virtuosarum operationum.

AD PRIMUM ergo dicendum quod operatio hominis non praeexigitur ad consecutionem beatitudinis propter insufficientiam divinae virtutis beatificantis, sed ut servetur ordo in rebus.

AD SECUNDUM dicendum quod primas creaturas statim Deus perfectas produxit, absque aliqua dispositione vel operatione creaturae praecedente, quia sic instituit prima individua specierum, ut per ea natura propagaretur ad posteros. Et similiter, quia per Christum, qui est Deus et homo, beatitudo erat ad alios derivanda, secundum illud apostoli ad Heb. II, *qui multos filios in gloriam adduxerat;* statim a principio suae conceptionis, absque aliqua operatione meritoria praecedente, anima eius fuit beata. Sed hoc est singulare in ipso, nam pueris baptizatis subvenit meritum Christi ad beatitudinem consequendam, licet desint eis merita propria, eo quod per Baptismum sunt Christi membra effecti.

for God could make a will having a right tendency to the end, and at the same time attaining the end; just as sometimes He disposes matter and at the same time introduces the form. But the order of Divine wisdom demands that it should not be thus; for as is stated in De Coel. ii, 12, "of those things that have a natural capacity for the perfect good, one has it without movement, some by one movement, some by several." Now to possess the perfect good without movement, belongs to that which has it naturally: and to have Happiness naturally belongs to God alone. Therefore it belongs to God alone not to be moved towards Happiness by any previous operation. Now since Happiness surpasses every created nature, no pure creature can becomingly gain Happiness, without the movement of operation, whereby it tends thereto. But the angel, who is above man in the natural order, obtained it, according to the order of Divine wisdom, by one movement of a meritorious work, as was explained in the I, q. 62, a. 5; whereas man obtains it by many movements of works which are called merits. Wherefore also according to the Philosopher (Ethic. i, 9), happiness is the reward of works of virtue.

Reply to Objection 1: Works are necessary to man in order to gain Happiness; not on account of the insufficiency of the Divine power which bestows Happiness, but that the order in things be observed.

Reply to Objection 2: God produced the first creatures so that they are perfect forthwith, without any previous disposition or operation of the creature; because He instituted the first individuals of the various species, that through them nature might be propagated to their progeny. In like manner, because Happiness was to be bestowed on others through Christ, who is God and Man, "Who," according to Heb. 2:10, "had brought many children into glory"; therefore, from the very beginning of His conception, His soul was happy, without any previous meritorious operation. But this is peculiar to Him: for Christ's merit avails baptized children for the gaining of Happiness, though they have no merits of their own; because by Baptism they are made members of Christ.

AD TERTIUM dicendum quod apostolus loquitur de beatitudine spei, quae habetur per gratiam iustificantem, quae quidem non datur propter opera praecedentia. Non enim habet rationem termini motus, ut beatitudo, sed magis est principium motus quo ad beatitudinem tenditur.

Articulus 8

AD OCTAVUM sic proceditur. Videtur quod non omnes appetant beatitudinem. Nullus enim potest appetere quod ignorat, cum bonum apprehensum sit obiectum appetitus, ut dicitur in III de anima. Sed multi nesciunt quid sit beatitudo, quod, sicut Augustinus dicit in XIII de Trin., patet ex hoc, quod *quidam posuerunt beatitudinem in voluptate corporis, quidam in virtute animi, quidam in aliis rebus.* Non ergo omnes beatitudinem appetunt.

PRAETEREA, essentia beatitudinis est visio essentiae divinae, ut dictum est. Sed aliqui opinantur hoc esse impossibile, quod Deus per essentiam ab homine videatur, unde hoc non appetunt. Ergo non omnes homines appetunt beatitudinem.

PRAETEREA, Augustinus dicit, in XIII de Trin. quod *beatus est qui habet omnia quae vult, et nihil male vult.* Sed non omnes hoc volunt, quidam enim male aliqua volunt, et tamen volunt illa se velle. Non ergo omnes volunt beatitudinem.

SED CONTRA est quod Augustinus dicit, XIII de Trin., *si minus dixisset, omnes beati esse vultis, miseri esse non vultis, dixisset aliquid quod nullus in sua non cognosceret voluntate.* Quilibet ergo vult esse beatus.

RESPONDEO dicendum quod beatitudo dupliciter potest considerari. Uno modo, secundum communem rationem beatitudinis. Et sic necesse est quod omnis homo beatitudinem velit. Ratio autem beatitudinis communis est ut sit bonum perfectum, sicut dictum est. Cum autem bonum sit obiectum voluntatis, perfectum bonum est alicuius, quod totaliter eius voluntati satisfacit. Unde appetere beatitudinem nihil aliud est quam appetere ut voluntas satietur. Quod quilibet vult. Alio modo possumus loqui de

Reply to Objection 3: The Apostle is speaking of the Happiness of Hope, which is bestowed on us by sanctifying grace, which is not given on account of previous works. For grace is not a term of movement, as Happiness is; rather is it the principle of the movement that tends towards Happiness.

Article 8
Whether every man desires happiness?

Objection 1: It would seem that not all desire Happiness. For no man can desire what he knows not; since the apprehended good is the object of the appetite (De Anima iii, 10). But many know not what Happiness is. This is evident from the fact that, as Augustine says (De Trin. xiii, 4), "some thought that Happiness consists in pleasures of the body; some, in a virtue of the soul; some in other things." Therefore not all desire Happiness.

Objection 2: Further, the essence of Happiness is the vision of the Divine Essence, as stated above (I-II, q. 3, a. 8). But some consider it impossible for man to see the Divine Essence; wherefore they desire it not. Therefore all men do not desire Happiness.

Objection 3: Further, Augustine says (De Trin. xiii, 5) that "happy is he who has all he desires, and desires nothing amiss." But all do not desire this; for some desire certain things amiss, and yet they wish to desire such things. Therefore all do not desire Happiness.

On the contrary, Augustine says (De Trin. xiii, 3): "If that actor had said: 'You all wish to be happy; you do not wish to be unhappy,' he would have said that which none would have failed to acknowledge in his will." Therefore everyone desires to be happy.

I answer that, Happiness can be considered in two ways. First according to the general notion of happiness: and thus, of necessity, every man desires happiness. For the general notion of happiness consists in the perfect good, as stated above (I-II, q. 5, a. 3; a. 4). But since good is the object of the will, the perfect good of a man is that which entirely satisfies his will. Consequently to desire happiness is nothing else than to desire that one's will be satisfied. And this everyone desires. Secondly we may speak of

beatitudine secundum specialem rationem, quantum ad id in quo beatitudo consistit. Et sic non omnes cognoscunt beatitudinem, quia nesciunt cui rei communis ratio beatitudinis conveniat. Et per consequens, quantum ad hoc, non omnes eam volunt.

Unde patet responsio ad primum.

AD SECUNDUM dicendum quod, cum voluntas sequatur apprehensionem intellectus seu rationis, sicut contingit quod aliquid est idem secundum rem, quod tamen est diversum secundum rationis considerationem; ita contingit quod aliquid est idem secundum rem, et tamen uno modo appetitur, alio modo non appetitur. Beatitudo ergo potest considerari sub ratione finalis boni et perfecti, quae est communis ratio beatitudinis, et sic naturaliter et ex necessitate voluntas in illud tendit, ut dictum est. Potest etiam considerari secundum alias speciales considerationes, vel ex parte ipsius operationis, vel ex parte potentiae operativae, vel ex parte obiecti, et sic non ex necessitate voluntas tendit in ipsam.

AD TERTIUM dicendum quod ista definitio beatitudinis quam quidam posuerunt, *beatus est qui habet omnia quae vult,* vel, *cui omnia optata succedunt,* quodam modo intellecta, est bona et sufficiens; alio vero modo, est imperfecta. Si enim intelligatur simpliciter de omnibus quae vult homo naturali appetitu, sic verum est quod qui habet omnia quae vult, est beatus, nihil enim satiat naturalem hominis appetitum, nisi bonum perfectum, quod est beatitudo. Si vero intelligatur de his quae homo vult secundum apprehensionem rationis, sic habere quaedam quae homo vult, non pertinet ad beatitudinem, sed magis ad miseriam inquantum huiusmodi habita impediunt hominem ne habeat quaecumque naturaliter vult, sicut etiam ratio accipit ut vera interdum quae impediunt a cognitione veritatis. Et secundum hanc considerationem, Augustinus addidit ad perfectionem beatitudinis, quod *nihil mali velit.* Quamvis primum posset sufficere, si recte intelligeretur, scilicet quod *beatus est qui habet omnia quae vult.*

Happiness according to its specific notion, as to that in which it consists. And thus all do not know Happiness; because they know not in what thing the general notion of happiness is found. And consequently, in this respect, not all desire it.

Wherefore the reply to the first Objection is clear.

Reply to Objection 2: Since the will follows the apprehension of the intellect or reason; just as it happens that where there is no real distinction, there may be a distinction according to the consideration of reason; so does it happen that one and the same thing is desired in one way, and not desired in another. So that happiness may be considered as the final and perfect good, which is the general notion of happiness: and thus the will naturally and of necessity tends thereto, as stated above. Again it can be considered under other special aspects, either on the part of the operation itself, or on the part of the operating power, or on the part of the object; and thus the will does not tend thereto of necessity.

Reply to Objection 3: This definition of Happiness given by some—"Happy is the man that has all he desires," or, "whose every wish is fulfilled" is a good and adequate definition; but an inadequate definition if understood in another. For if we understand it simply of all that man desires by his natural appetite, thus it is true that he who has all that he desires, is happy: since nothing satisfies man's natural desire, except the perfect good which is Happiness. But if we understand it of those things that man desires according to the apprehension of the reason, thus it does not belong to Happiness, to have certain things that man desires; rather does it belong to unhappiness, in so far as the possession of such things hinders man from having all that he desires naturally; thus it is that reason sometimes accepts as true things that are a hindrance to the knowledge of truth. And it was through taking this into consideration that Augustine added so as to include perfect Happiness—that he "desires nothing amiss": although the first part suffices if rightly understood, to wit, that "happy is he who has all he desires."

TREATISE ON HUMAN ACTS: ACTS PECULIAR TO MAN

Quaestio VI

Quia igitur ad beatitudinem per actus aliquos necesse est pervenire, oportet consequenter de humanis actibus considerare, ut sciamus quibus actibus perveniatur ad beatitudinem, vel impediatur beatitudinis via. Sed quia **operationes et actus circa singularia sunt**, ideo omnis operativa scientia in particulari consideratione perficitur. Moralis igitur consideratio quia est humanorum actuum, primo quidem tradenda est in universali secundo vero, in particulari. Circa universalem autem considerationem humanorum actuum, *primo* quidem considerandum occurrit de ipsis actibus humanis; *secundo,* de principiis eorum. Humanorum autem actuum quidam sunt hominis proprii; quidam autem sunt homini et aliis animalibus communes. Et quia beatitudo est proprium hominis bonum, propinquius se habent ad beatitudinem actus qui sunt proprie humani, quam actus qui sunt homini aliisque animalibus communes. Primo ergo considerandum est de actibus qui sunt proprii hominis; secundo, de actibus qui sunt homini aliisque animalibus communes, qui dicuntur animae passiones. Circa primum duo consideranda occurrunt, *primo,* de conditione humanorum actuum; *secundo,* de distinctione eorum. Cum autem actus humani proprie dicantur qui sunt voluntarii, eo quod voluntas est rationalis appetitus, qui est proprius hominis; oportet considerare de actibus inquantum sunt voluntarii. Primo ergo considerandum est de voluntario et involuntario in communi; secundo, de actibus qui sunt voluntarii quasi ab ipsa voluntate eliciti, ut immediate ipsius voluntatis existentes; tertio, de actibus qui sunt voluntarii quasi a voluntate imperati, qui sunt ipsius voluntatis mediantibus aliis potentiis. Et quia actus voluntarii habent quasdam circumstantias, secundum quas diiudicantur, primo considerandum est de voluntario et involuntario; et consequenter de circumstantiis ipsorum actuum in quibus voluntarium et involuntarium invenitur. Circa primum

Question 6
Of the Voluntary and the Involuntary

Since therefore Happiness is to be gained by means of certain acts, we must in due sequence consider human acts, in order to know by what acts we may obtain Happiness, and by what acts we are prevented from obtaining it. But because operations and acts are concerned with things singular, consequently all practical knowledge is incomplete unless it take account of things in detail. The study of Morals, therefore, since it treats of human acts, should consider first the general principles; and secondly matters of detail. In treating of the general principles, the points that offer themselves for our consideration are 1. human acts themselves; 2. their principles. Now of human acts some are proper to man; others are common to man and animals. And since Happiness is man's proper good, those acts which are proper to man have a closer connection with Happiness than have those which are common to man and the other animals. First, then, we must consider those acts which are proper to man; secondly, those acts which are common to man and the other animals, and are called Passions. The first of these points offers a twofold consideration: 1. What makes a human act? 2. What distinguishes human acts? And since those acts are properly called human which are voluntary, because the will is the rational appetite, which is proper to man; we must consider acts in so far as they are voluntary. First, then, we must consider the voluntary and involuntary in general; secondly, those acts which are voluntary, as being elicited by the will, and as issuing from the will immediately; thirdly, those acts which are voluntary, as being commanded by the will, which issue from the will through the medium of the other powers. And because voluntary acts have certain circumstances, according to which we form our judgment concerning them, we must first consider the voluntary and the involuntary, and afterwards, the circumstances of those acts which are found to be voluntary or involuntary. Under the first head

quaeruntur octo. *Primo,* utrum in humanis actibus inveniatur voluntarium. *Secundo,* utrum inveniatur in animalibus brutis. *Tertio,* utrum voluntarium esse possit absque omni actu. *Quarto,* utrum violentia voluntati possit inferri. *Quinto,* utrum violentia causet involuntarium. *Sexto,* utrum metus causet involuntarium. *Septimo,* utrum concupiscentia involuntarium causet. *Octavo,* utrum ignorantia.

there are eight points of inquiry: 1. Whether there is anything voluntary in human acts? 2. Whether in irrational animals? 3. Whether there can be voluntariness without any action? 4. Whether violence can be done to the will? 5. Whether violence causes involuntariness? 6. Whether fear causes involuntariness? 7. Whether concupiscence causes involuntariness? 8. Whether ignorance causes involuntariness?

Articulus 1

Ad primum sic proceditur. Videtur quod in humanis actibus non inveniatur voluntarium. Voluntarium enim est *cuius principium est in ipso;* ut patet per Gregorium Nyssenum, et Damascenum, et Aristotelem. Sed principium humanorum actuum non est in ipso homine, sed est extra, nam appetitus hominis movetur ad agendum ab appetibili quod est extra quod est sicut *movens non motum,* ut dicitur in III de anima. Ergo in humanis actibus non invenitur voluntarium.

Praeterea, philosophus in VIII Physic. probat quod non invenitur in animalibus aliquis motus novus, qui non praeveniatur ab alio motu exteriori. Sed omnes actus hominis sunt novi, nullus enim actus hominis aeternus est. Ergo principium omnium humanorum actuum est ab extra. Non igitur in eis invenitur voluntarium.

Praeterea, qui voluntarie agit, per se agere potest. Sed hoc homini non convenit, dicitur enim Ioan. XV, *sine me nihil potestis facere.* Ergo voluntarium in humanis actibus non invenitur.

Sed contra est quod dicit Damascenus, in II libro, quod *voluntarium est actus qui est operatio rationalis.* Tales autem sunt actus humani. Ergo in actibus humanis invenitur voluntarium.

Respondeo dicendum quod oportet in actibus humanis voluntarium esse. Ad cuius evidentiam, considerandum est quod quorundam actuum seu motuum principium est in agente, seu in eo quod movetur;

Article 1
Whether there is anything voluntary in human acts?

Objection 1: It would seem that there is nothing voluntary in human acts. For that is voluntary "which has its principle within itself." as Gregory of Nyssa,* Damascene (De Fide Orth. ii, 24), and Aristotle (Ethic. iii, 1) declare. But the principle of human acts is not in man himself, but outside him: since man's appetite is moved to act, by the appetible object which is outside him, and is as a "mover unmoved" (De Anima iii, 10). Therefore there is nothing voluntary in human acts.

Objection 2: Further, the Philosopher (Phys. viii, 2) proves that in animals no new movement arises that is not preceded by a motion from without. But all human acts are new, since none is eternal. Consequently, the principle of all human acts is from without: and therefore there is nothing voluntary in them.

Objection 3: Further, he that acts voluntarily, can act of himself. But this is not true of man; for it is written (Jn. 15:5): "Without Me you can do nothing." Therefore there is nothing voluntary in human acts.

On the contrary, Damascene says (De Fide Orth. ii) that "the voluntary is an act consisting in a rational operation." Now such are human acts. Therefore there is something voluntary in human acts.

I answer that, There must needs be something voluntary in human acts. In order to make this clear, we must take note that the principle of some acts or movements is within the agent, or that which is moved;

---

* Nemesius, De Natura Hom. xxxii.

quorundam autem motuum vel actuum principium est extra. Cum enim lapis movetur sursum, principium huius motionis est extra lapidem, sed cum movetur deorsum, principium huius motionis est in ipso lapide. Eorum autem quae a principio intrinseco moventur, quaedam movent seipsa, quaedam autem non. Cum enim omne agens seu motum agat seu moveatur propter finem, ut supra habitum est; illa perfecte moventur a principio intrinseco, in quibus est aliquod intrinsecum principium non solum ut moveantur, sed ut moveantur in finem. Ad hoc autem quod fiat aliquid propter finem, requiritur cognitio finis aliqualis. Quodcumque igitur sic agit vel movetur a principio intrinseco, quod habet aliquam notitiam finis, habet in seipso principium sui actus non solum ut agat, sed etiam ut agat propter finem. Quod autem nullam notitiam finis habet, etsi in eo sit principium actionis vel motus; non tamen eius quod est agere vel moveri propter finem est principium in ipso, sed in alio, a quo ei imprimitur principium suae motionis in finem. Unde huiusmodi non dicuntur movere seipsa, sed ab aliis moveri. Quae vero habent notitiam finis dicuntur seipsa movere, quia in eis est principium non solum ut agant, sed etiam ut agant propter finem. Et ideo, cum utrumque sit ab intrinseco principio, scilicet quod agunt, et quod propter finem agunt, horum motus et actus dicuntur voluntarii, hoc enim importat nomen *voluntarii*, quod motus et actus sit a propria inclinatione. Et inde est quod voluntarium dicitur esse, secundum definitionem Aristotelis et Gregorii Nysseni et Damasceni, non solum cuius *principium est intra*, sed cum additione *scientiae*. Unde, cum homo maxime cognoscat finem sui operis et moveat seipsum, in eius actibus maxime voluntarium invenitur.

whereas the principle of some movements or acts is outside. For when a stone is moved upwards, the principle of this movement is outside the stone: whereas when it is moved downwards, the principle of this movement is in the stone. Now of those things that are moved by an intrinsic principle, some move themselves, some not. For since every agent or thing moved, acts or is moved for an end, as stated above (I-II, q. 1, a. 2); those are perfectly moved by an intrinsic principle, whose intrinsic principle is one not only of movement but of movement for an end. Now in order for a thing to be done for an end, some knowledge of the end is necessary. Therefore, whatever so acts or is moved by an intrinsic principle, that it has some knowledge of the end, has within itself the principle of its act, so that it not only acts, but acts for an end. On the other hand, if a thing has no knowledge of the end, even though it have an intrinsic principle of action or movement, nevertheless the principle of acting or being moved for an end is not in that thing, but in something else, by which the principle of its action towards an end is not in that thing, but in something else, by which the principle of its action towards an end is imprinted on it. Wherefore such like things are not said to move themselves, but to be moved by others. But those things which have a knowledge of the end are said to move themselves because there is in them a principle by which they not only act but also act for an end. And consequently, since both are from an intrinsic principle, to wit, that they act and that they act for an end, the movements of such things are said to be voluntary: for the word "voluntary" implies that their movements and acts are from their own inclination. Hence it is that, according to the definitions of Aristotle, Gregory of Nyssa, and Damascene,* the voluntary is defined not only as having "a principle within" the agent, but also as implying "knowledge." Therefore, since man especially knows the end of his work, and moves himself, in his acts especially is the voluntary to be found.

---

* See Objection 1

AD PRIMUM ergo dicendum quod non omne principium est principium primum. Licet ergo de ratione voluntarii sit quod principium eius sit intra, non tamen est contra rationem voluntarii quod principium intrinsecum causetur vel moveatur ab exteriori principio, quia non est de ratione voluntarii quod principium intrinsecum sit principium primum. Sed tamen sciendum quod contingit aliquod principium motus esse primum in genere, quod tamen non est primum simpliciter sicut in genere alterabilium primum alterans est corpus caeleste, quod tamen non est primum movens simpliciter, sed movetur motu locali a superiori movente. Sic igitur principium intrinsecum voluntarii actus, quod est vis cognoscitiva et appetitiva, est primum principium in genere appetitivi motus, quamvis moveatur ab aliquo exteriori secundum alias species motus.

AD SECUNDUM dicendum quod motus animalis novus praevenitur quidem ab aliquo exteriori motu quantum ad duo. Uno modo, inquantum per motum exteriorem praesentatur sensui animalis aliquod sensibile, quod apprehensum movet appetitum, sicut leo videns cervum per eius motum appropinquantem, incipit moveri ad ipsum. Alio modo, inquantum per exteriorem motum incipit aliqualiter immutari naturali immutatione corpus animalis, puta per frigus vel calorem; corpore autem immutato per motum exterioris corporis, immutatur etiam per accidens appetitus sensitivus, qui est virtus organi corporei; sicut cum ex aliqua alteratione corporis commovetur appetitus ad concupiscentiam alicuius rei. Sed hoc non est contra rationem voluntarii, ut dictum est huiusmodi enim motiones ab exteriori principio sunt alterius generis.

AD TERTIUM dicendum quod Deus movet hominem ad agendum non solum sicut proponens sensui appetibile, vel sicut immutans corpus, sed etiam sicut movens ipsam voluntatem, quia omnis motus tam voluntatis quam naturae, ab eo procedit sicut a primo movente. Et sicut non est contra

Reply to Objection 1: Not every principle is a first principle. Therefore, although it is essential to the voluntary act that its principle be within the agent, nevertheless it is not contrary to the nature of the voluntary act that this intrinsic principle be caused or moved by an extrinsic principle: because it is not essential to the voluntary act that its intrinsic principle be a first principle. Yet again it must be observed that a principle of movement may happen to be first in a genus, but not first simply: thus in the genus of things subject to alteration, the first principle of alteration is a heavenly body, which is nevertheless, is not the first mover simply, but is moved locally by a higher mover. And so the intrinsic principle of the voluntary act, i.e., the cognitive and appetitive power, is the first principle in the genus of appetitive movement, although it is moved by an extrinsic principle according to other species of movement.

Reply to Objection 2: New movements in animals are indeed preceded by a motion from without; and this in two respects. First, in so far as by means of an extrinsic motion an animal's senses are confronted with something sensible, which, on being apprehended, moves the appetite. Thus a lion, on seeing a stag in movement and coming towards him, begins to be moved towards the stag. Secondly, in so far as some extrinsic motion produces a physical change in an animal's body, as in the case of cold or heat; and through the body being affected by the motion of an outward body, the sensitive appetite which is the power of a bodily organ, is also moved indirectly; thus it happens that through some alteration in the body the appetite is roused to the desire of something. But this is not contrary to the nature of voluntariness, as stated above (ad 1), for such movements caused by an extrinsic principle are of another genus of movement.

Reply to Objection 3: God moves man to act, not only by proposing the appetible to the senses, or by effecting a change in his body, but also by moving the will itself; because every movement either of the will or of nature, proceeds from God as the First Mover. And just as it is not incompatible with

rationem naturae quod motus naturae sit a Deo sicut a primo movente, inquantum natura est quoddam instrumentum Dei moventis; ita non est contra rationem actus voluntarii quod sit a Deo, inquantum voluntas a Deo movetur. Est tamen communiter de ratione naturalis et voluntarii motus, quod sint a principio intrinseco.

nature that the natural movement be from God as the First Mover, inasmuch as nature is an instrument of God moving it: so it is not contrary to the essence of a voluntary act, that it proceed from God, inasmuch as the will is moved by God. Nevertheless both natural and voluntary movements have this in common, that it is essential that they should proceed from a principle within the agent.

Articulus 2

Article 2
Whether there is anything voluntary in irrational animals?

Ad secundum sic proceditur. Videtur quod voluntarium non sit in brutis animalibus. *Voluntarium* enim a *voluntate* dicitur. Voluntas autem, cum sit in ratione, ut dicitur in III de anima, non potest esse in brutis animalibus. Ergo neque voluntarium in eis invenitur.

Praeterea, secundum hoc quod actus humani sunt voluntarii, homo dicitur esse dominus suorum actuum. Sed bruta animalia non habent dominium sui actus, non enim agunt, sed magis aguntur, ut Damascenus dicit. Ergo in brutis animalibus non est voluntarium.

Praeterea, Damascenus dicit quod *actus voluntarios sequitur laus et vituperium*. Sed actibus brutorum animalium non debetur neque laus neque vituperium. Ergo in eis non est voluntarium.

Sed contra est quod dicit philosophus, in III Ethic., quod *pueri et bruta animalia communicant voluntario*. Et idem dicunt Damascenus et Gregorius Nyssenus.

Respondeo dicendum quod, sicut dictum est, ad rationem voluntarii requiritur quod principium actus sit intra, cum aliqua cognitione finis. Est autem duplex cognitio finis, perfecta scilicet, et imperfecta. Perfecta quidem finis cognitio est quando non solum apprehenditur res quae est finis sed etiam cognoscitur ratio finis, et proportio eius quod ordinatur in finem ad ipsum. Et talis cognitio finis competit

Objection 1: It would seem that there is nothing voluntary in irrational animals. For a thing is called "voluntary" from *voluntas* [will]. Now since the will is in the reason (De Anima iii, 9), it cannot be in irrational animals. Therefore neither is there anything voluntary in them.

Objection 2: Further, according as human acts are voluntary, man is said to be master of his actions. But irrational animals are not masters of their actions; for "they act not; rather are they acted upon," as Damascene says (De Fide Orth. ii, 27). Therefore there is no such thing as a voluntary act in irrational animals.

Objection 3: Further, Damascene says (De Fide Orth. 24) that "voluntary acts lead to praise and blame." But neither praise nor blame is due to the acts of irrational minds. Therefore such acts are not voluntary.

On the contrary, The Philosopher says (Ethic. iii, 2) that "both children and irrational animals participate in the voluntary." The same is said by Damascene (De Fide Orth. 24) and Gregory of Nyssa.*

I answer that, As stated above (I-II, q. 6, a. 1), it is essential to the voluntary act that its principle be within the agent, together with some knowledge of the end. Now knowledge of the end is twofold; perfect and imperfect. Perfect knowledge of the end consists in not only apprehending the thing which is the end, but also in knowing it under the aspect of end, and the relationship of the means to that end. And such knowledge belongs to

---

* Nemesius, De Nat. Hom. xxxii.

soli rationali naturae. Imperfecta autem cognitio finis est quae in sola finis apprehensione consistit, sine hoc quod cognoscatur ratio finis, et proportio actus ad finem. Et talis cognitio finis invenitur in brutis animalibus, per sensum et aestimationem naturalem. Perfectam igitur cognitionem finis sequitur voluntarium secundum rationem perfectam, prout scilicet, apprehenso fine, aliquis potest, deliberans de fine et de his quae sunt ad finem, moveri in finem vel non moveri. Imperfectam autem cognitionem finis sequitur voluntarium secundum rationem imperfectam, prout scilicet apprehendens finem non deliberat, sed subito movetur in ipsum. Unde soli rationali naturae competit voluntarium secundum rationem perfectam, sed secundum rationem imperfectam, competit etiam brutis animalibus.

AD PRIMUM ergo dicendum quod voluntas nominat rationalem appetitum, et ideo non potest esse in his quae ratione carent. *Voluntarium* autem denominative dicitur a *voluntate,* et potest trahi ad ea in quibus est aliqua participatio voluntatis, secundum aliquam convenientiam ad voluntatem. Et hoc modo voluntarium attribuitur animalibus brutis, inquantum scilicet per cognitionem aliquam moventur in finem.

AD SECUNDUM dicendum quod ex hoc contingit quod homo est dominus sui actus, quod habet deliberationem de suis actibus, ex hoc enim quod ratio deliberans se habet ad opposita, voluntas in utrumque potest. Sed secundum hoc voluntarium non est in brutis animalibus, ut dictum est.

AD TERTIUM dicendum quod laus et vituperium consequuntur actum voluntarium secundum perfectam voluntarii rationem; qualis non invenitur in brutis.

ARTICULUS 3

AD TERTIUM sic proceditur. Videtur quod voluntarium non possit esse sine actu. Voluntarium enim dicitur quod est a voluntate. Sed nihil potest esse a voluntate nisi per aliquem actum, ad minus ipsius voluntatis.

none but the rational nature. But imperfect knowledge of the end consists in mere apprehension of the end, without knowing it under the aspect of end, or the relationship of an act to the end. Such knowledge of the end is exercised by irrational animals, through their senses and their natural estimative power. Consequently perfect knowledge of the end leads to the perfect voluntary; inasmuch as, having apprehended the end, a man can, from deliberating about the end and the means thereto, be moved, or not, to gain that end. But imperfect knowledge of the end leads to the imperfect voluntary; inasmuch as the agent apprehends the end, but does not deliberate, and is moved to the end at once. Wherefore the voluntary in its perfection belongs to none but the rational nature: whereas the imperfect voluntary is within the competency of even irrational animals.

Reply to Objection 1: The will is the name of the rational appetite; and consequently it cannot be in things devoid of reason. But the word "voluntary" is derived from *voluntas* [will], and can be extended to those things in which there is some participation of will, by way of likeness thereto. It is thus that voluntary action is attributed to irrational animals, in so far as they are moved to an end, through some kind of knowledge.

Reply to Objection 2: The fact that man is master of his actions, is due to his being able to deliberate about them: for since the deliberating reason is indifferently disposed to opposite things, the will can be inclined to either. But it is not thus that voluntariness is in irrational animals, as stated above.

Reply to Objection 3: Praise and blame are the result of the voluntary act, wherein is the perfect voluntary; such as is not to be found in irrational animals.

ARTICLE 3
Whether there can be voluntariness without any act?

Objection 1: It would seem that voluntariness cannot be without any act. For that is voluntary which proceeds from the will. But nothing can proceed from the will, except through some act, at least an act of the will.

I-II, q. 6, a. 3, arg. 1

Ergo voluntarium non potest esse sine actu.

Praeterea, sicut per actum voluntatis dicitur aliquis velle, ita cessante actu voluntatis dicitur non velle. Sed non velle involuntarium causat, quod opponitur voluntario. Ergo voluntarium non potest esse, actu voluntatis cessante.

Praeterea, de ratione voluntarii est **cognitio, ut dictum est**. Sed cognitio est per aliquem actum. Ergo voluntarium non potest esse absque aliquo actu.

Sed contra, illud cuius domini sumus, dicitur esse *voluntarium*. Sed nos domini sumus eius quod est agere et non agere, velle et non velle. Ergo sicut agere et velle est voluntarium, ita et non agere et non velle.

Respondeo dicendum quod voluntarium dicitur quod est a voluntate. Ab aliquo autem dicitur esse aliquid dupliciter. Uno modo, directe, quod scilicet procedit ab aliquo inquantum est agens, sicut calefactio a calore. Alio modo, indirecte, ex hoc ipso quod non agit, sicut submersio navis dicitur esse a gubernatore, inquantum desistit a gubernando. Sed sciendum quod non semper id quod sequitur ad defectum actionis, reducitur sicut in causam in agens, ex eo quod non agit, sed solum tunc cum potest et debet agere. Si enim gubernator non posset navem dirigere, vel non esset ei commissa gubernatio navis, non imputaretur ei navis submersio, quae per absentiam gubernatoris contingeret. Quia igitur voluntas, volendo et agendo, potest impedire hoc quod est non velle et non agere, et aliquando debet; hoc quod est non velle et non agere, imputatur ei, quasi ab ipsa existens. Et sic voluntarium potest esse absque actu, quandoque quidem absque actu exteriori, cum actu interiori, sicut cum vult non agere; aliquando autem et absque actu interiori, sicut cum non vult.

THE VOLUNTARY AND THE INVOLUNTARY

Therefore there cannot be voluntariness without act.

Objection 2: Further, just as one is said to wish by an act of the will, so when the act of the will ceases, one is said not to wish. But not to wish implies involuntariness, which is contrary to voluntariness. Therefore there can be nothing voluntary when the act of the will ceases.

Objection 3: Further, knowledge is **essential to the voluntary, as stated above** (I-II, q. 6, a. 1; a. 2). But knowledge involves an act. Therefore voluntariness cannot be without some act.

On the contrary, The word "voluntary" is applied to that of which we are masters. Now we are masters in respect of to act and not to act, to will and not to will. Therefore just as to act and to will are voluntary, so also are not to act and not to will.

I answer that, Voluntary is what proceeds from the will. Now one thing proceeds from another in two ways. First, directly; in which sense something proceeds from another inasmuch as this other acts; for instance, heating from heat. Secondly, indirectly; in which sense something proceeds from another through this other not acting; thus the sinking of a ship is set down to the helmsman, from his having ceased to steer. But we must take note that the cause of what follows from want of action is not always the agent as not acting; but only then when the agent can and ought to act. For if the helmsman were unable to steer the ship or if the ship's helm be not entrusted to him, the sinking of the ship would not be set down to him, although it might be due to his absence from the helm. Since, then, the will by willing and acting, is able, and sometimes ought, to hinder not-willing and not-acting; this not-willing and not-acting is imputed to, as though proceeding from, the will. And thus it is that we can have the voluntary without an act; sometimes without outward act, but with an interior act; for instance, when one wills not to act; and sometimes without even an interior act, as when one does not will to act.

Ad primum ergo dicendum quod *voluntarium* dicitur non solum quod procedit a voluntate directe, sicut ab agente; sed etiam quod est ab ea indirecte, sicut a non agente.

Ad secundum dicendum quod *non velle* dicitur dupliciter. Uno modo, prout sumitur in vi unius dictionis, secundum quod est infinitivum huius verbi *nolo*. Unde sicut cum dico *nolo legere*, sensus est, *volo non legere*; ita hoc quod est *non velle legere*, significat *velle non legere*. Et sic *non velle* causat involuntarium. Alio modo sumitur in vi orationis. Et tunc non affirmatur actus voluntatis. Et huiusmodi *non velle* non causat involuntarium.

Ad tertium dicendum quod eo modo requiritur ad voluntarium actus cognitionis, sicut et actus voluntatis; ut scilicet sit in potestate alicuius considerare et velle et agere. Et tunc sicut non velle et non agere, cum tempus fuerit, est voluntarium, ita etiam non considerare.

Reply to Objection 1: We apply the word "voluntary" not only to that which proceeds from the will directly, as from its action; but also to that which proceeds from it indirectly as from its inaction.

Reply to Objection 2: "Not to wish" is said in two senses. First, as though it were one word, and the infinitive of "I-do-not-wish." Consequently just as when I say "I do not wish to read," the sense is, "I wish not to read"; so "not to wish to read" is the same as "to wish not to read," and in this sense "not to wish" implies involuntariness. Secondly it is taken as a sentence: and then no act of the will is affirmed. And in this sense "not to wish" does not imply involuntariness.

Reply to Objection 3: Voluntariness requires an act of knowledge in the same way as it requires an act of will; namely, in order that it be in one's power to consider, to wish and to act. And then, just as not to wish, and not to act, when it is time to wish and to act, is voluntary, so is it voluntary not to consider.

Articulus 4

Ad quartum sic proceditur. Videtur quod voluntati possit violentia inferri. Unumquodque enim potest cogi a potentiori. Sed aliquid est humana voluntate potentius, scilicet Deus. Ergo saltem ab eo cogi potest.

Praeterea, omne passivum cogitur a suo activo, quando immutatur ab eo. Sed voluntas est vis passiva, est enim *movens motum*, ut dicitur in III de anima. Cum ergo aliquando moveatur a suo activo, videtur quod aliquando cogatur.

Praeterea, motus violentus est qui est contra naturam. Sed motus voluntatis aliquando est contra naturam; ut patet de motu voluntatis ad peccandum, qui est contra naturam, ut Damascenus dicit. Ergo motus voluntatis potest esse coactus.

Sed contra est quod Augustinus dicit, in V de Civ. Dei, quod si aliquid fit voluntate, non fit ex necessitate. Omne autem coactum fit ex necessitate. Ergo quod fit ex voluntate,

Article 4
Whether violence can be done to the will?

Objection 1: It would seem that violence can be done to the will. For everything can be compelled by that which is more powerful. But there is something, namely, God, that is more powerful than the human will. Therefore it can be compelled, at least by Him.

Objection 2: Further, every passive subject is compelled by its active principle, when it is changed by it. But the will is a passive force: for it is a "mover moved" (De Anima iii, 10). Therefore, since it is sometimes moved by its active principle, it seems that sometimes it is compelled.

Objection 3: Further, violent movement is that which is contrary to nature. But the movement of the will is sometimes contrary to nature; as is clear of the will's movement to sin, which is contrary to nature, as Damascene says (De Fide Orth. iv, 20). Therefore the movement of the will can be compelled.

On the contrary, Augustine says (De Civ. Dei v, 10) that what is done by the will is not done of necessity. Now, whatever is done under compulsion is done of necessity: consequently what is done by the will,

non potest esse coactum. Ergo voluntas non potest cogi ad agendum.

RESPONDEO dicendum quod duplex est actus voluntatis, unus quidem qui est eius immediate, velut ab ipsa elicitus, scilicet *velle*; alius autem est actus voluntatis a voluntate imperatus, et mediante alia potentia exercitus, ut *ambulare* et *loqui*, qui a voluntate imperantur mediante potentia motiva. Quantum igitur ad actus a voluntate imperatos, **voluntas violentiam pati potest,** inquantum per violentiam exteriora membra impediri possunt ne imperium voluntatis exequantur. Sed quantum ad ipsum proprium actum voluntatis, non potest ei violentia inferri. Et huius ratio est quia actus voluntatis nihil est aliud quam inclinatio quaedam procedens ab interiori principio cognoscente, sicut appetitus naturalis est quaedam inclinatio ab interiori principio et sine cognitione. Quod autem est coactum vel violentum, est ab exteriori principio. Unde contra rationem ipsius actus voluntatis est quod sit coactus vel violentus, sicut etiam est contra rationem naturalis inclinationis vel motus. Potest enim lapis per violentiam sursum ferri, sed quod iste motus violentus sit ex eius naturali inclinatione, esse non potest. Similiter etiam potest homo per violentiam trahi, sed quod hoc sit ex eius voluntate, repugnat rationi violentiae.

AD PRIMUM ergo dicendum quod Deus, qui est potentior quam voluntas humana, potest voluntatem humanam movere; secundum illud Prov. XXI, *cor regis in manu Dei est, et quocumque voluerit, vertet illud.* Sed si hoc esset per violentiam, iam non esset cum actu voluntatis nec ipsa voluntas moveretur, sed aliquid contra voluntatem.

AD SECUNDUM dicendum quod non semper est motus violentus, quando passivum immutatur a suo activo, sed quando hoc fit contra interiorem inclinationem passivi. Alioquin omnes alterationes et generationes simplicium corporum essent innaturales et violentae. Sunt autem naturales, propter naturalem aptitudinem interiorem materiae

cannot be compelled. Therefore the will cannot be compelled to act.

I answer that, The act of the will is twofold: one is its immediate act, as it were, elicited by it, namely, "to wish"; the other is an act of the will commanded by it, and put into execution by means of some other power, such as "to walk" and "to speak," which are commanded by the will to be executed by means of the motive power. **As regards the commanded acts of the will,** then, the will can suffer violence, in so far as violence can prevent the exterior members from executing the will's command. But as to the will's own proper act, violence cannot be done to the will. The reason of this is that the act of the will is nothing else than an inclination proceeding from the interior principle of knowledge: just as the natural appetite is an inclination proceeding from an interior principle without knowledge. Now what is compelled or violent is from an exterior principle. Consequently it is contrary to the nature of the will's own act, that it should be subject to compulsion and violence: just as it is also contrary to the nature of a natural inclination or movement. For a stone may have an upward movement from violence, but that this violent movement be from its natural inclination is impossible. In like manner a man may be dragged by force: but it is contrary to the very notion of violence, that he be dragged of his own will.

Reply to Objection 1: God Who is more powerful than the human will, can move the will of man, according to Prov. 21:1: "The heart of the king is in the hand of the Lord; whithersoever He will He shall turn it." But if this were by compulsion, it would no longer be by an act of the will, nor would the will itself be moved, but something else against the will.

Reply to Objection 2: It is not always a violent movement, when a passive subject is moved by its active principle; but only when this is done against the interior inclination of the passive subject. Otherwise every alteration and generation of simply bodies would be unnatural and violent: whereas they are natural by reason of the natural interior aptitude of the matter

vel subiecti ad talem dispositionem. Et similiter quando voluntas movetur ab appetibili secundum propriam inclinationem, non est motus violentus, sed voluntarius.

AD TERTIUM dicendum quod id in quod voluntas tendit peccando, etsi sit malum et contra rationalem naturam secundum rei veritatem, apprehenditur tamen ut bonum et conveniens naturae, inquantum est conveniens homini secundum aliquam passionem sensus, vel secundum aliquem habitum corruptum.

or subject to such a disposition. In like manner when the will is moved, according to its own inclination, by the appetible object, this movement is not violent but voluntary.

Reply to Objection 3: That to which the will tends by sinning, although in reality it is evil and contrary to the rational nature, nevertheless is apprehended as something good and suitable to nature, in so far as it is suitable to man by reason of some pleasurable sensation or some vicious habit.

ARTICULUS 5

AD QUINTUM sic proceditur. Videtur quod violentia non causet involuntarium. Voluntarium enim et involuntarium secundum voluntatem dicuntur. Sed voluntati violentia inferri non potest, ut ostensum est. Ergo violentia involuntarium causare non potest.

PRAETEREA, id quod est involuntarium, est cum tristitia, ut Damascenus et philosophus dicunt. Sed aliquando patitur aliquis violentiam, nec tamen inde tristatur. Ergo violentia non causat involuntarium.

PRAETEREA, id quod est a voluntate, non potest esse involuntarium. Sed aliqua violenta sunt a voluntate, sicut cum aliquis cum corpore gravi sursum ascendit; et sicut cum aliquis inflectit membra contra naturalem eorum flexibilitatem. Ergo violentia non causat involuntarium.

SED CONTRA est quod philosophus et Damascenus dicunt, quod *aliquid est involuntarium per violentiam.*

RESPONDEO dicendum quod violentia directe opponitur voluntario, sicut etiam et naturali. Commune est enim voluntario et naturali quod utrumque sit a principio intrinseco, violentum autem est a principio extrinseco. Et propter hoc, sicut in rebus quae cognitione carent, violentia aliquid facit contra naturam; ita in rebus cognoscentibus facit aliquid esse contra voluntatem. Quod autem est contra naturam, dicitur esse *innaturale,* et

ARTICLE 5
Whether violence causes involuntariness?

Objection 1: It would seem that violence does not cause involuntariness. For we speak of voluntariness and involuntariness in respect of the will. But violence cannot be done to the will, as shown above (I-II, q. 6, a. 4). Therefore violence cannot cause involuntariness.

Objection 2: Further, that which is done involuntarily is done with grief, as Damascene (De Fide Orth. ii, 24) and the Philosopher (Ethic. iii, 5) say. But sometimes a man suffers compulsion without being grieved thereby. Therefore violence does not cause involuntariness.

Objection 3: Further, what is from the will cannot be involuntary. But some violent actions proceed from the will: for instance, when a man with a heavy body goes upwards; or when a man contorts his limbs in a way contrary to their natural flexibility. Therefore violence does not cause involuntariness.

On the contrary, The Philosopher (Ethic. iii, 1) and Damascene (De Fide Orth. ii, 24) say that "things done under compulsion are involuntary."

I answer that, Violence is directly opposed to the voluntary, as likewise to the natural. For the voluntary and the natural have this in common, that both are from an intrinsic principle; whereas violence is from an extrinsic principle. And for this reason, just as in things devoid of knowledge, violence effects something against nature: so in things endowed with knowledge, it effects something against the will. Now that which is against nature is said to be "unnatural"; and

similiter quod est contra voluntatem, dicitur esse *involuntarium*. Unde violentia involuntarium causat.

Ad primum ergo dicendum quod involuntarium voluntario opponitur. Dictum est autem supra quod voluntarium dicitur non solum actus qui est immediate ipsius voluntatis, sed etiam actus a voluntate imperatus. Quantum igitur ad actum qui est immediate ipsius voluntatis, ut supra dictum est, **violentia voluntati inferri non potest, unde talem actum violentia involuntarium facere non potest**. Sed quantum ad actum imperatum, voluntas potest pati violentiam. Et quantum ad hunc actum, violentia involuntarium facit.

Ad secundum dicendum quod, sicut naturale dicitur quod est secundum inclinationem naturae, ita voluntarium dicitur quod est secundum inclinationem voluntatis. Dicitur autem aliquid naturale dupliciter. Uno modo, quia est a natura sicut a principio activo, sicut calefacere est naturale igni. Alio modo, secundum principium passivum, quia scilicet est in natura inclinatio ad recipiendum actionem a principio extrinseco, sicut motus caeli dicitur esse naturalis, propter aptitudinem naturalem caelestis corporis ad talem motum, licet movens sit voluntarium. Et similiter voluntarium potest aliquid dici dupliciter, uno modo, secundum actionem, puta cum aliquis vult aliquid agere; alio modo, secundum passionem, scilicet cum aliquis vult pati ab alio. Unde cum actio infertur ab aliquo exteriori, manente in eo qui patitur voluntate patiendi, non est simpliciter violentum, quia licet ille qui patitur non conferat agendo, confert tamen volendo pati. Unde non potest dici involuntarium.

Ad tertium dicendum quod, sicut philosophus dicit in VIII Physic., motus animalis quo interdum movetur animal contra naturalem inclinationem corporis, etsi non sit naturalis corpori, est tamen quodammodo naturalis animali, cui naturale est quod secundum appetitum moveatur. Et ideo hoc non est violentum simpliciter, sed secundum quid. Et similiter

in like manner that which is against the will is said to be "involuntary." Therefore violence causes involuntariness.

Reply to Objection 1: The involuntary is opposed to the voluntary. Now it has been said (I-II, q. 6, a. 4) that not only the act, which proceeds immediately from the will, is called voluntary, but also the act commanded by the will. Consequently, as to the act which proceeds immediately from the will, violence **cannot be done to the will, as stated above** (I-II, q. 6, a. 4): wherefore violence cannot make that act involuntary. But as to the commanded act, the will can suffer violence: and consequently in this respect violence causes involuntariness.

Reply to Objection 2: As that is said to be natural, which is according to the inclination of nature; so that is said to be voluntary, which is according to the inclination of the will. Now a thing is said to be natural in two ways. First, because it is from nature as from an active principle: thus it is natural for fire to produce heat. Secondly, according to a passive principle; because, to wit, there is in nature an inclination to receive an action from an extrinsic principle: thus the movement of the heavens is said to be natural, by reason of the natural aptitude in a heavenly body to receive such movement; although the cause of that movement is a voluntary agent. In like manner an act is said to be voluntary in two ways. First, in regard to action, for instance, when one wishes to be passive to another. Hence when action is brought to bear on something, by an extrinsic agent, as long as the will to suffer that action remains in the passive subject, there is not violence simply: for although the patient does nothing by way of action, he does something by being willing to suffer. Consequently this cannot be called involuntary.

Reply to Objection 3: As the Philosopher says (Phys. viii, 4) the movement of an animal, whereby at times an animal is moved against the natural inclination of the body, although it is not natural to the body, is nevertheless somewhat natural to the animal, to which it is natural to be moved according to its appetite. Accordingly this is violent, not simply but in a certain respect. The same

est dicendum cum aliquis inflectit membra contra naturalem dispositionem. Hoc enim est violentum secundum quid, scilicet quantum ad membrum particulare non tamen simpliciter, quantum ad ipsum hominem.

remark applies in the case of one who contorts his limbs in a way that is contrary to their natural disposition. For this is violent in a certain respect, i.e., as to that particular limb; but not simply, i.e., as to the man himself.

Articulus 6

Ad sextum sic proceditur. Videtur quod metus causet involuntarium simpliciter. Sicut enim violentia est respectu eius quod contrariatur praesentialiter voluntati, ita metus est respectu mali futuri quod repugnat voluntati. Sed violentia causat involuntarium simpliciter. Ergo et metus involuntarium simpliciter causat.

Praeterea, quod est secundum se tale, quolibet addito remanet tale, sicut quod secundum se est calidum, cuicumque coniungatur, nihilominus est calidum, ipso manente. Sed illud quod per metum agitur, secundum se est involuntarium. Ergo etiam adveniente metu est involuntarium.

Praeterea, quod sub conditione est tale, secundum quid est tale; quod autem absque conditione est tale, simpliciter est tale, sicut quod est necessarium ex conditione, est necessarium secundum quid; quod autem est necessarium absolute, est necessarium simpliciter. Sed id quod per metum agitur, est involuntarium absolute, non est autem voluntarium nisi sub conditione, scilicet ut vitetur malum quod timetur. Ergo id quod per metum agitur, est simpliciter involuntarium.

Sed contra est quod Gregorius Nyssenus dicit, et etiam philosophus quod huiusmodi quae per metum aguntur, sunt *magis voluntaria quam involuntaria*.

Respondeo dicendum quod, sicut philosophus dicit in III Ethic., et idem dicit Gregorius Nyssenus in libro suo de homine, huiusmodi quae per metum aguntur, *mixta sunt* ex voluntario et involuntario. Id enim quod per metum agitur, in se consideratum, non est voluntarium, sed fit voluntarium in casu, scilicet ad vitandum

Article 6
Whether fear causes involuntariness simply?

Objection 1: It would seem that fear causes involuntariness simply. For just as violence regards that which is contrary to the will at the time, so fear regards a future evil which is repugnant to the will. But violence causes involuntariness simply. Therefore fear too causes involuntariness simply.

Objection 2: Further, that which is such of itself, remains such, whatever be added to it: thus what is hot of itself, as long as it remains, is still hot, whatever be added to it. But that which is done through fear, is involuntary in itself. Therefore, even with the addition of fear, it is involuntary.

Objection 3: Further, that which is such, subject to a condition, is such in a certain respect; whereas what is such, without any condition, is such simply: thus what is necessary, subject to a condition, is necessary in some respect: but what is necessary absolutely, is necessary simply. But that which is done through fear, is absolutely involuntary; and is not voluntary, save under a condition, namely, in order that the evil feared may be avoided. Therefore that which is done through fear, is involuntary simply.

On the contrary, Gregory of Nyssa* and the Philosopher (Ethic. iii, 1) say that such things as are done through fear are "voluntary rather than involuntary."

I answer that, As the Philosopher says (Ethic. iii) and likewise Gregory of Nyssa in his book on Man (Nemesius, De Nat. Hom. xxx), such things are done through fear "are of a mixed character," being partly voluntary and partly involuntary. For that which is done through fear, considered in itself, is not voluntary; but it becomes voluntary in this particular case, in order, namely, to avoid the

---

* Nemesius, De Nat. Hom. xxx.

malum quod timetur. Sed si quis recte consideret, magis sunt huiusmodi voluntaria quam involuntaria, sunt enim voluntaria simpliciter, involuntaria autem secundum quid. Unumquodque enim simpliciter esse dicitur secundum quod est in actu, secundum autem quod est in sola apprehensione, non est simpliciter, sed secundum quid. Hoc autem quod per metum agitur, secundum hoc est in actu, secundum quod fit, cum enim actus in singularibus sint, singulare autem, inquantum huiusmodi, est hic et nunc; secundum hoc id quod fit est in actu, secundum quod est hic et nunc et sub aliis conditionibus individualibus. Sic autem hoc quod fit per metum, est voluntarium, inquantum scilicet est hic et nunc, prout scilicet in hoc casu est impedimentum maioris mali quod timebatur, sicut proiectio mercium in mare fit voluntarium tempore tempestatis, propter timorem periculi. Unde manifestum est quod simpliciter voluntarium est. Unde et competit ei ratio voluntarii, quia principium eius est intra. Sed quod accipiatur id quod per metum fit, ut extra hunc casum existens, prout repugnat voluntati, hoc non est nisi secundum considerationem tantum. Et ideo est involuntarium secundum quid, idest prout consideratur extra hunc casum existens.

AD PRIMUM ergo dicendum quod ea quae aguntur per metum et per vim, non solum differunt secundum praesens et futurum, sed etiam secundum hoc, quod in eo quod agitur per vim, voluntas non consentit, sed omnino est contra motum voluntatis, sed id quod per metum agitur, fit voluntarium, ideo quia motus voluntatis fertur in id, licet non propter seipsum, sed propter aliud, scilicet ad repellendum malum quod timetur. Sufficit enim ad rationem voluntarii quod sit propter aliud voluntarium, voluntarium enim est non solum quod propter seipsum volumus ut finem, sed etiam quod propter aliud volumus ut propter finem. Patet ergo quod in eo quod per vim agitur, voluntas interior nihil agit, sed in eo quod per metum agitur, voluntas aliquid agit.

evil feared. But if the matter be considered aright, such things are voluntary rather than involuntary; for they are voluntary simply, but involuntary in a certain respect. For a thing is said to be simply, according as it is in act; but according as it is only in apprehension, it is not simply, but in a certain respect. Now that which is done through fear, is in act in so far as it is done. For, since acts are concerned with singulars; and the singular, as such, is here and now; that which is done is in act, in so far as it is here and now and under other individuating circumstances. And that which is done through fear is voluntary, inasmuch as it is here and now, that is to say, in so far as, under the circumstances, it hinders a greater evil which was feared; thus the throwing of the cargo into the sea becomes voluntary during the storm, through fear of the danger: wherefore it is clear that it is voluntary simply. And hence it is that what is done out of fear is essentially voluntary, because its principle is within. But if we consider what is done through fear, as outside this particular case, and inasmuch as it is repugnant to the will, this is merely a consideration of the mind. And consequently what is done through fear is involuntary, considered in that respect, that is to say, outside the actual circumstances of the case.

Reply to Objection 1: Things done through fear and compulsion differ not only according to present and future time, but also in this, that the will does not consent, but is moved entirely counter to that which is done through compulsion: whereas what is done through fear, becomes voluntary, because the will is moved towards it, albeit not for its own sake, but on account of something else, that is, in order to avoid an evil which is feared. For the conditions of a voluntary act are satisfied, if it be done on account of something else voluntary: since the voluntary is not only what we wish, for its own sake, as an end, but also what we wish for the sake of something else, as an end. It is clear therefore that in what is done from compulsion, the will does nothing inwardly; whereas in what is done through fear, the will does something.

Et ideo, ut Gregorius Nyssenus dicit, ad excludendum ea quae per metum aguntur, in definitione violenti non solum dicitur quod violentum est *cuius principium est extra,* sed additur, *nihil conferente vim passo,* quia ad id quod agitur per metum, voluntas timentis aliquid confert.

AD SECUNDUM dicendum quod ea quae absolute dicuntur, quolibet addito remanent talia, sicut calidum et album, sed ea quae relative dicuntur, variantur secundum comparationem ad diversa; quod enim est magnum comparatum huic, est parvum comparatum alteri. Voluntarium autem dicitur aliquid non solum propter seipsum, quasi absolute, sed etiam propter aliud, quasi relative. Et ideo nihil prohibet aliquid quod non esset voluntarium alteri comparatum fieri voluntarium per comparationem ad aliud.

AD TERTIUM dicendum quod illud quod per metum agitur, absque conditione est voluntarium, idest secundum quod actu agitur, sed involuntarium est sub conditione, idest si talis metus non immineret. Unde secundum illam rationem magis potest concludi oppositum.

ARTICULUS 7

AD SEPTIMUM sic proceditur. Videtur quod concupiscentia causet involuntarium. Sicut enim metus est quaedam passio, ita et concupiscentia. Sed metus causat quodammodo involuntarium. Ergo etiam concupiscentia.

PRAETEREA, sicut per timorem timidus agit contra id quod proponebat, ita incontinens propter concupiscentiam. Sed timor aliquo modo causat involuntarium. Ergo et concupiscentia.

PRAETEREA, ad voluntarium requiritur cognitio. Sed concupiscentia corrumpit cognitionem, dicit enim philosophus, in VI Ethic., quod *delectatio,* sive concupiscentia

Accordingly, as Gregory of Nyssa* says, in order to exclude things done through fear, a violent action is defined as not only one, "the principal whereof is from without," but with the addition, "in which he that suffers violence concurs not at all"; because the will of him that is in fear, does concur somewhat in that which he does through fear.

Reply to Objection 2: Things that are such absolutely, remain such, whatever be added to them; for instance, a cold thing, or a white thing: but things that are such relatively, vary according as they are compared with different things. For what is big in comparison with one thing, is small in comparison with another. Now a thing is said to be voluntary, not only for its own sake, as it were absolutely; but also for the sake of something else, as it were relatively. Accordingly, nothing prevents a thing which was not voluntary in comparison with one thing, from becoming voluntary when compared with another.

Reply to Objection 3: That which is done through fear, is voluntary without any condition, that is to say, according as it is actually done: but it is involuntary, under a certain condition, that is to say, if such a fear were not threatening. Consequently, this argument proves rather the opposite.

ARTICLE 7
Whether concupiscence causes involuntariness?

Objection 1: It would seem that concupiscence causes involuntariness. For just as fear is a passion, so is concupiscence. But fear causes involuntariness to a certain extent. Therefore concupiscence does so too.

Objection 2: Further, just as the timid man through fear acts counter to that which he proposed, so does the incontinent, through concupiscence. But fear causes involuntariness to a certain extent. Therefore concupiscence does so also.

Objection 3: Further, knowledge is necessary for voluntariness. But concupiscence impairs knowledge; for the Philosopher says (Ethic. vi, 5) that "delight," or the lust

---

* Nemesius, De Nat. Hom. xxx.

delectationis, *corrumpit aestimationem prudentiae.* Ergo concupiscentia causat involuntarium.

Sed contra est quod Damascenus dicit, *involuntarium est misericordia vel indulgentia dignum, et cum tristitia agitur.* Sed neutrum horum competit ei quod per concupiscentiam agitur. Ergo concupiscentia non causat involuntarium.

Respondeo dicendum quod concupiscentia non causat involuntarium, sed magis facit aliquid voluntarium. Dicitur enim aliquid voluntarium ex eo quod voluntas in id fertur. Per concupiscentiam autem voluntas inclinatur ad volendum id quod concupiscitur. Et ideo concupiscentia magis facit ad hoc quod aliquid sit voluntarium, quam quod sit involuntarium.

Ad primum ergo dicendum quod timor est de malo, concupiscentia autem respicit bonum. Malum autem secundum se contrariatur voluntati, sed bonum est voluntati consonum. Unde magis se habet timor ad causandum involuntarium quam concupiscentia.

Ad secundum dicendum quod in eo qui per metum aliquid agit, manet repugnantia voluntatis ad id quod agitur, secundum quod in se consideratur. Sed in eo qui agit aliquid per concupiscentiam, sicut est incontinens, non manet prior voluntas, qua repudiabat illud quod concupiscitur, sed mutatur ad volendum id quod prius repudiabat. Et ideo quod per metum agitur, quodammodo est involuntarium, sed quod per concupiscentiam agitur, nullo modo. Nam incontinens concupiscentiae agit contra id quod prius proponebat, non autem contra id quod nunc vult, sed timidus agit contra id quod etiam nunc secundum se vult.

Ad tertium dicendum quod, si concupiscentia totaliter cognitionem auferret, sicut contingit in illis qui propter concupiscentiam fiunt amentes, sequeretur quod concupiscentia voluntarium tolleret. Nec tamen proprie esset ibi involuntarium, quia in his quae usum rationis non habent, neque voluntarium est neque involuntarium. Sed quandoque in his

of pleasure, "destroys the judgment of prudence." Therefore concupiscence causes involuntariness.

On the contrary, Damascene says (De Fide Orth. ii, 24): "The involuntary act deserves mercy or indulgence, and is done with regret." But neither of these can be said of that which is done out of concupiscence. Therefore concupiscence does not cause involuntariness.

I answer that, Concupiscence does not cause involuntariness, but on the contrary makes something to be voluntary. For a thing is said to be voluntary, from the fact that the will is moved to it. Now concupiscence inclines the will to desire the object of concupiscence. Therefore the effect of concupiscence is to make something to be voluntary rather than involuntary.

Reply to Objection 1: Fear regards evil, but concupiscence regards good. Now evil of itself is counter to the will, whereas good harmonizes with the will. Therefore fear has a greater tendency than concupiscence to cause involuntariness.

Reply to Objection 2: He who acts from fear retains the repugnance of the will to that which he does, considered in itself. But he that acts from concupiscence, e.g., an incontinent man, does not retain his former will whereby he repudiated the object of his concupiscence; for his will is changed so that he desires that which previously he repudiated. Accordingly, that which is done out of fear is involuntary, to a certain extent, but that which is done from concupiscence is nowise involuntary. For the man who yields to concupiscence acts counter to that which he purposed at first, but not counter to that which he desires now; whereas the timid man acts counter to that which in itself he desires now.

Reply to Objection 3: If concupiscence were to destroy knowledge altogether, as happens with those whom concupiscence has rendered mad, it would follow that concupiscence would take away voluntariness. And yet properly speaking it would not result in the act being involuntary, because in things bereft of reason, there is neither voluntary nor involuntary. But sometimes in

quae per concupiscentiam aguntur, non totaliter tollitur cognitio, quia non tollitur potestas cognoscendi; sed solum consideratio actualis in particulari agibili. Et tamen hoc ipsum est voluntarium, secundum quod voluntarium dicitur quod est in potestate voluntatis, ut *non agere* et *non velle,* similiter autem et *non considerare,* potest enim voluntas passioni resistere, ut infra dicetur.

those actions which are done from concupiscence, knowledge is not completely destroyed, because the power of knowing is not taken away entirely, but only the actual consideration in some particular possible act. Nevertheless, this itself is voluntary, according as by voluntary we mean that which is in the power of the will, for example "not to act" or "not to will," and in like manner "not to consider"; for the will can resist the passion, as we shall state later on (I-II, q. 10, a. 3; q. 77, a. 7).

Articulus 8

Ad octavum sic proceditur. Videtur quod ignorantia non causet involuntarium. *Involuntarium enim veniam meretur,* ut Damascenus dicit. Sed interdum quod per ignorantiam agitur, veniam non meretur; secundum illud I ad Cor. XIV, *si quis ignorat, ignorabitur.* Ergo ignorantia non causat involuntarium.

Praeterea, omne peccatum est cum ignorantia; secundum illud Prov. XIV, *errant qui operantur malum.* Si igitur ignorantia involuntarium causet, sequeretur quod omne peccatum esset involuntarium. Quod est contra Augustinum dicentem quod *omne peccatum est voluntarium.*

Praeterea, *involuntarium cum tristitia est,* ut Damascenus dicit. Sed quaedam ignoranter aguntur, et sine tristitia, puta si aliquis occidit hostem quem quaerit occidere, putans occidere cervum. Ergo ignorantia non causat involuntarium.

Sed contra est quod Damascenus et philosophus dicunt, quod *involuntarium quoddam est per ignorantiam.*

Respondeo dicendum quod ignorantia habet causare involuntarium ea ratione qua privat cognitionem, quae praeexigitur ad voluntarium, ut supra dictum est. Non tamen quaelibet ignorantia huiusmodi cognitionem privat. Et ideo sciendum quod ignorantia tripliciter se habet ad actum voluntatis,

Article 8
Whether ignorance causes involuntariness?

Objection 1: It would seem that ignorance does not cause involuntariness. For "the involuntary act deserves pardon," as Damascene says (De Fide Orth. ii, 24). But sometimes that which is done through ignorance does not deserve pardon, according to 1 Cor. 14:38: "If any man know not, he shall not be known." Therefore ignorance does not cause involuntariness.

Objection 2: Further, every sin implies ignorance; according to Prov. 14: 22: "They err, that work evil." If, therefore, ignorance causes involuntariness, it would follow that every sin is involuntary: which is opposed to the saying of Augustine, that "every sin is voluntary" (De Vera Relig. xiv).

Objection 3: Further, "involuntariness is not without sadness," as Damascene says (De Fide Orth. ii, 24). But some things are done out of ignorance, but without sadness: for instance, a man may kill a foe, whom he wishes to kill, thinking at the time that he is killing a stag. Therefore ignorance does not cause involuntariness.

On the contrary, Damascene (De Fide Orth. ii, 24) and the Philosopher (Ethic. iii, 1) say that "what is done through ignorance is involuntary."

I answer that, If ignorance causes involuntariness, it is in so far as it deprives one of knowledge, which is a necessary condition of voluntariness, as was declared above (I-II, q. 6, a. 1). But it is not every ignorance that deprives one of this knowledge. Accordingly, we must take note that ignorance has a threefold relationship to the act of the will:

uno modo, *concomitanter;* alio modo, *consequenter;* tertio modo, *antecedenter. Concomitanter* quidem, quando ignorantia est de eo quod agitur, tamen, etiam si sciretur, nihilominus ageretur. Tunc enim ignorantia non inducit ad volendum ut hoc fiat, sed accidit simul esse aliquid factum et ignoratum, sicut, in exemplo posito, cum aliquis vellet quidem occidere hostem, sed ignorans occidit eum, putans occidere cervum. Et talis ignorantia non facit involuntarium, ut philosophus dicit, quia non causat aliquid quod sit repugnans voluntati, sed facit *non voluntarium,* quia non potest esse actu volitum quod ignoratum est. *Consequenter* autem se habet ignorantia ad voluntatem, inquantum ipsa ignorantia est voluntaria. Et hoc contingit dupliciter, secundum duos modos voluntarii supra positos. Uno modo, quia actus voluntatis fertur in ignorantiam, sicut cum aliquis ignorare vult ut excusationem peccati habeat, vel ut non retrahatur a peccando, secundum illud Iob XXI, *scientiam viarum tuarum nolumus.* Et haec dicitur *ignorantia affectata.* Alio modo dicitur ignorantia voluntaria eius quod quis potest scire et debet, sic enim *non agere* et *non velle* voluntarium dicitur, ut supra dictum est. Hoc igitur modo dicitur ignorantia, sive cum aliquis actu non considerat quod considerare potest et debet, quae est *ignorantia malae electionis,* vel ex passione vel ex habitu proveniens, sive cum aliquis notitiam quam debet habere, non curat acquirere; et secundum hunc modum, ignorantia universalium iuris, quae quis scire tenetur, voluntaria dicitur, quasi per negligentiam proveniens. Cum autem ipsa ignorantia sit voluntaria aliquo istorum modorum, non potest causare simpliciter involuntarium. Causat tamen secundum quid involuntarium, inquantum praecedit motum voluntatis ad aliquid agendum, qui non esset scientia praesente. *Antecedenter* autem se habet ad voluntatem ignorantia, quando non est voluntaria, et tamen est causa volendi quod

in one way, "concomitantly"; in another, "consequently"; in a third way, "antecedently." "Concomitantly," when there is ignorance of what is done; but, so that even if it were known, it would be done. For then, ignorance does not induce one to wish this to be done, but it just happens that a thing is at the same time done, and not known: thus in the example given (arg. 3) a man did indeed wish to kill his foe, but killed him in ignorance, **thinking to kill a stag. And ignorance of this kind**, as the Philosopher states (Ethic. iii, 1), does not cause involuntariness, since it is not the cause of anything that is repugnant to the will: but it causes "non-voluntariness," since that which is unknown cannot be actually willed. Ignorance is "consequent" to the act of the will, in so far as ignorance itself is voluntary: and this happens in two ways, in accordance with the two aforesaid modes of voluntary (I-II, q. 6, a. 3). First, because the act of the will is brought to bear on the ignorance: as when a man wishes not to know, that he may have an excuse for sin, or that he may not be withheld from sin; according to Job 21:14: "We desire not the knowledge of Thy ways." And this is called "affected ignorance." Secondly, ignorance is said to be voluntary, when it regards that which one can and ought to know: for in this sense "not to act" and "not to will" are said to be voluntary, as stated above (I-II, q. 6, a. 3). And ignorance of this kind happens, either when one does not actually consider what one can and ought to consider; this is called "ignorance of evil choice," and arises from some passion or habit: or when one does not take the trouble to acquire the knowledge which one ought to have; in which sense, ignorance of the general principles of law, which one to know, is voluntary, as being due to negligence. Accordingly, if in either of these ways, ignorance is voluntary, it cannot cause involuntariness simply. Nevertheless it causes involuntariness in a certain respect, inasmuch as it precedes the movement of the will towards the act, which movement would not be, if there were knowledge. Ignorance is "antecedent" to the act of the will, when it is not voluntary, and yet is the cause of man's willing

alias homo non vellet. Sicut cum homo ignorat aliquam circumstantiam actus quam non tenebatur scire, et ex hoc aliquid agit, quod non faceret si sciret, puta cum aliquis, diligentia adhibita, nesciens aliquem transire per viam, proiicit sagittam, qua interficit transeuntem. Et talis ignorantia causat involuntarium simpliciter.

Et per hoc patet responsio ad obiecta. Nam prima ratio procedebat de ignorantia eorum quae quis tenetur scire. Secunda autem, de ignorantia electionis, quae quodammodo est voluntaria, ut dictum est. Tertia vero, de ignorantia quae concomitanter se habet ad voluntatem.

what he would not will otherwise. Thus a man may be ignorant of some circumstance of his act, which he was not bound to know, the result being that he does that which he would not do, if he knew of that circumstance; for instance, a man, after taking proper precaution, may not know that someone is coming along the road, so that he shoots an arrow and slays a passer-by. Such ignorance causes involuntariness simply.

From this may be gathered the solution of the objections. For the first objection deals with ignorance of what a man is bound to know. The second, with ignorance of choice, which is voluntary to a certain extent, as stated above. The third, with that ignorance which is concomitant with the act of the will.

Quaestio VII

Deinde considerandum est de circumstantiis humanorum actuum. Et circa hoc quaeruntur quatuor. *Primo,* quid sit circumstantia. *Secundo,* utrum circumstantiae sint circa humanos actus attendendae a theologo. *Tertio,* quot sunt circumstantiae. *Quarto,* quae sunt in eis principaliores.

Articulus 1

Ad primum sic proceditur. Videtur quod circumstantia non sit accidens actus humani. Dicit enim Tullius, in rhetoricis, quod circumstantia est per *quam argumentationi auctoritatem et firmamentum adiungit oratio.* Sed oratio dat firmamentum argumentationi praecipue ab his quae sunt de substantia rei, ut definitio, genus, species, et alia huiusmodi; a quibus etiam Tullius oratorem argumentari docet. Ergo circumstantia non est accidens humani actus.

Praeterea, accidentis proprium est *inesse.* Quod autem circumstat, non inest, sed magis est extra. Ergo circumstantiae non sunt accidentia humanorum actuum.

Question 7
Of the Circumstances of Human Acts

We must now consider the circumstances of human acts: under which head there are four points of inquiry: 1. What is a circumstance? 2. Whether a theologian should take note of the circumstances of human acts? 3. How many circumstances are there? 4. Which are the most important of them?

Article 1
Whether a circumstance is an accident of a human act?

Objection 1: It would seem that a circumstance is not an accident of a human act. For Tully says (De Invent. Rhetor. i) that a circumstance is that from "which an orator adds authority and strength to his argument." But oratorical arguments are derived principally from things pertaining to the essence of a thing, such as the definition, the genus, the species, and the like, from which also Tully declares that an orator should draw his arguments. Therefore a circumstance is not an accident of a human act.

Objection 2: Further, "to be in" is proper to an accident. But that which surrounds [*circumstat*] is rather out than in. Therefore the circumstances are not accidents of human acts.

PRAETEREA, accidentis non est accidens. Sed ipsi humani actus sunt quaedam accidentia. Non ergo circumstantiae sunt accidentia actuum.

SED CONTRA, particulares conditiones cuiuslibet rei singularis dicuntur accidentia individuantia ipsam. Sed philosophus, in III Ethic., circumstantias nominat particularia, idest particulares singulorum actuum conditiones. Ergo circumstantiae sunt accidentia individualia humanorum actuum.

RESPONDEO dicendum quod, quia *nomina,* secundum philosophum, *sunt signa intellectuum,* necesse est quod secundum processum intellectivae cognitionis, sit etiam nominationis processus. Procedit autem nostra cognitio intellectualis a notioribus ad minus nota. Et ideo apud nos a notioribus nomina transferuntur ad significandum res minus notas. Et inde est quod, sicut dicitur in X Metaphys., *ab his quae sunt secundum locum, processit nomen distantiae ad omnia contraria,* et similiter nominibus pertinentibus ad motum localem, utimur ad significandum alios motus, eo quod corpora, quae loco circumscribuntur, sunt maxime nobis nota. Et inde est quod nomen *circumstantiae* ab his quae in loco sunt, derivatur ad actus humanos. Dicitur autem in localibus aliquid circumstare, quod est quidem extrinsecum a re, tamen attingit ipsam, vel appropinquat ei secundum locum. Et ideo quaecumque conditiones sunt extra substantiam actus, et tamen attingunt aliquo modo actum humanum, circumstantiae dicuntur. Quod autem est extra substantiam rei ad rem ipsam pertinens, accidens eius dicitur. Unde circumstantiae actuum humanorum accidentia eorum dicenda sunt.

AD PRIMUM ergo dicendum quod oratio quidem dat firmamentum argumentationi, primo ex substantia actus, secundario vero, ex his quae circumstant actum. Sicut primo accusabilis redditur aliquis ex hoc quod homicidium fecit, secundario vero, ex hoc quod dolo fecit, vel propter lucrum, vel in tempore aut loco sacro, aut aliquid aliud huiusmodi.

Objection 3: Further, an accident has no accident. But human acts themselves are accidents. Therefore the circumstances are not accidents of acts.

On the contrary, The particular conditions of any singular thing are called its individuating accidents. But the Philosopher (Ethic. iii, 1) calls the circumstances particular things,* i.e., the particular conditions of each act. Therefore the circumstances are individual accidents of human acts.

I answer that, Since, according to the Philosopher (Peri Herm. i), "words are the signs of what we understand," it must needs be that in naming things we follow the process of intellectual knowledge. Now our intellectual knowledge proceeds from the better known to the less known. Accordingly with us, names of more obvious things are transferred so as to signify things less obvious: and hence it is that, as stated in Metaph. x, 4, "the notion of distance has been transferred from things that are apart locally, to all kinds of opposition": and in like manner words that signify local movement are employed to designate all other movements, because bodies which are circumscribed by place, are best known to us. And hence it is that the word "circumstance" has passed from located things to human acts. Now in things located, that is said to surround something, which is outside it, but touches it, or is placed near it. Accordingly, whatever conditions are outside the substance of an act, and yet in some way touch the human act, are called circumstances. Now what is outside a thing's substance, while it belongs to that thing, is called its accident. Wherefore the circumstances of human acts should be called their accidents.

Reply to Objection 1: The orator gives strength to his argument, in the first place, from the substance of the act; and secondly, from the circumstances of the act. Thus a man becomes indictable, first, through being guilty of murder; secondly, through having done it fraudulently, or from motives of greed or at a holy time or place, and so forth.

---

* τα καθ' ἕκαστα.

Et ideo signanter dicit quod per circumstantiam oratio *argumentationi firmamentum adiungit,* quasi secundario.

AD SECUNDUM dicendum quod aliquid dicitur accidens alicuius dupliciter. Uno modo, quia inest ei, sicut album dicitur accidens Socratis. Alio modo quia est simul cum eo in eodem subiecto, sicut dicitur quod album accidit musico, inquantum conveniunt, et quodammodo se contingunt, in uno subiecto. Et per hunc modum dicuntur circumstantiae accidentia actuum.

AD TERTIUM dicendum quod, sicut dictum est, accidens dicitur accidenti accidere propter convenientiam in subiecto. Sed hoc contingit dupliciter. Uno modo, secundum quod duo accidentia comparantur ad unum subiectum absque aliquo ordine, sicut album et musicum ad Socratem. Alio modo, cum aliquo ordine, puta quia subiectum recipit unum accidens alio mediante, sicut corpus recipit colorem mediante superficie. Et sic unum accidens dicitur etiam alteri inesse, dicimus enim colorem esse in superficie. Utroque autem modo circumstantiae se habent ad actus. Nam aliquae circumstantiae ordinatae ad actum, pertinent ad agentem non mediante actu, puta locus et conditio personae, aliquae vero mediante ipso actu, sicut modus agendi.

And so in the passage quoted, it is said pointedly that the orator "adds strength to his argument," as though this were something secondary.

Reply to Objection 2: A thing is said to be an accident of something in two ways. First, from being in that thing: thus, whiteness is said to be an accident of Socrates. Secondly, because it is together with that thing in the same subject: thus, whiteness is an accident of the art of music, inasmuch as they meet in the same subject, so as to touch one another, as it were. And in this sense circumstances are said to be the accidents of human acts.

Reply to Objection 3: As stated above (ad 2), an accident is said to be the accident of an accident, from the fact that they meet in the same subject. But this happens in two ways. First, in so far as two accidents are both related to the same subject, without any relation to one another; as whiteness and the art of music in Socrates. Secondly, when such accidents are related to one another; as when the subject receives one accident by means of the other; for instance, a body receives color by means of its surface. And thus also is one accident said to be in another; for we speak of color as being in the surface. Accordingly, circumstances are related to acts in both these ways. For some circumstances that have a relation to acts, belong to the agent otherwise than through the act; as place and condition of person; whereas others belong to the agent by reason of the act, as the manner in which the act is done.

ARTICULUS 2

AD SECUNDUM sic proceditur. Videtur quod circumstantiae humanorum actuum non sint considerandae a theologo. Non enim considerantur a theologo actus humani, nisi secundum quod sunt aliquales, idest boni vel mali. Sed circumstantiae non videntur posse facere actus aliquales, quia nihil qualificatur, formaliter loquendo, ab eo quod est extra ipsum, sed ab eo quod in ipso est. Ergo circumstantiae actuum non sunt a theologo considerandae.

ARTICLE 2
Whether theologians should take note of the circumstances of human acts?

Objection 1: It would seem that theologians should not take note of the circumstances of human acts. Because theologians do not consider human acts otherwise than according to their quality of good or evil. But it seems that circumstances cannot give quality to human acts; for a thing is never qualified, formally speaking, by that which is outside it; but by that which is in it. Therefore theologians should not take note of the circumstances of acts.

Praeterea, circumstantiae sunt accidentia actuum. Sed uni infinita accidunt, et ideo, ut dicitur in VI Metaphys., *nulla ars vel scientia est circa ens per accidens, nisi sola sophistica.* Ergo theologos non habet considerare circumstantias humanorum actuum.

Praeterea, circumstantiarum consideratio pertinet ad rhetorem. Rhetorica autem non est pars theologiae. Ergo consideratio circumstantiarum non pertinet ad theologum.

Sed contra, ignorantia circumstantiarum causat involuntarium, ut Damascenus et Gregorius Nyssenus dicunt. Sed involuntarium excusat a culpa, cuius consideratio pertinet ad theologum. Ergo et consideratio circumstantiarum ad theologum pertinet.

Respondeo dicendum quod circumstantiae pertinent ad considerationem theologi triplici ratione. Primo quidem, quia theologus considerat actus humanos secundum quod per eos homo ad beatitudinem ordinatur. Omne autem quod ordinatur ad finem, oportet esse proportionatum fini. Actus autem proportionantur fini secundum commensurationem quandam, quae fit per debitas circumstantias. Unde consideratio circumstantiarum ad theologum pertinet. Secundo, quia theologus considerat actus humanos secundum quod in eis invenitur bonum et malum, et melius et peius, et hoc diversificatur secundum circumstantias, ut infra patebit. Tertio, quia theologus considerat actus humanos secundum quod sunt meritorii vel demeritorii, quod convenit actibus humanis; ad quod requiritur quod sint voluntarii. Actus autem humanus iudicatur voluntarius vel involuntarius, secundum cognitionem vel ignorantiam circumstantiarum, ut dictum est. Et ideo consideratio circumstantiarum pertinet ad theologum.

Ad primum ergo dicendum quod bonum ordinatum ad finem dicitur utile, quod importat relationem quandam, unde philosophus dicit, in I Ethic., quod *in*

Objection 2: Further, circumstances are the accidents of acts. But one thing may be subject to an infinity of accidents; hence the Philosopher says (Metaph. vi, 2) that "no art or science considers accidental being, except only the art of sophistry." Therefore the theologian has not to consider circumstances.

Objection 3: Further, the consideration of circumstances belongs to the orator. But oratory is not a part of theology. Therefore it is not a theologian's business to consider circumstances.

On the contrary, Ignorance of circumstances causes an act to be involuntary, according to Damascene (De Fide Orth. ii, 24) and Gregory of Nyssa.* But involuntariness excuses from sin, the consideration of which belongs to the theologian. Therefore circumstances also should be considered by the theologian.

I answer that, Circumstances come under the consideration of the theologian, for a threefold reason. First, because the theologian considers human acts, inasmuch as man is thereby directed to Happiness. Now, everything that is directed to an end should be proportionate to that end. But acts are made proportionate to an end by means of a certain commensurateness, which results from the due circumstances. Hence the theologian has to consider the circumstances. Secondly, because the theologian considers human acts according as they are found to be good or evil, better or worse: and this diversity depends on circumstances, as we shall see further on (I-II, q. 18, a. 10; a. 11; q. 73, a. 7). Thirdly, because the theologian considers human acts under the aspect of merit and demerit, which is proper to human acts; and for this it is requisite that they be voluntary. Now a human act is deemed to be voluntary or involuntary, according to knowledge or ignorance of circumstances, as stated above (I-II, q. 6, a. 8). Therefore the theologian has to consider circumstances.

Reply to Objection 1: Good directed to the end is said to be useful; and this implies some kind of relation: wherefore the Philosopher says (Ethic. i, 6) that "the

---

* Nemesius, De Nat. Hom. xxxi.

ad aliquid bonum est utile. In his autem quae *ad aliquid* dicuntur, denominatur aliquid non solum ab eo quod inest, sed etiam ab eo quod extrinsecus adiacet, ut patet in *dextro* et *sinistro, aequali* et *inaequali,* et similibus. Et ideo, cum bonitas actuum sit inquantum sunt utiles ad finem, nihil prohibet eos bonos vel malos dici secundum proportionem ad aliqua quae exterius adiacent.

AD SECUNDUM dicendum quod accidentia quae omnino per accidens se habent, relinquuntur ab omni arte, propter eorum incertitudinem et infinitatem. Sed talia accidentia non habent rationem circumstantiae, quia, ut dictum est, sic circumstantiae sunt extra actum, quod tamen actum aliquo modo contingunt, ordinatae ad ipsum. Accidentia autem per se cadunt sub arte.

AD TERTIUM dicendum quod consideratio circumstantiarum pertinet ad moralem, et politicum, et ad rhetorem. Ad moralem quidem, prout secundum eas invenitur vel praetermittitur medium virtutis in humanis actibus et passionibus. Ad politicum autem et rhetorem, secundum quod ex circumstantiis actus redduntur laudabiles vel vituperabiles, excusabiles vel accusabiles. Diversimode tamen, nam quod rhetor persuadet, politicus diiudicat. Ad theologum autem, cui omnes aliae artes deserviunt, pertinent omnibus modis praedictis, nam ipse habet considerationem de actibus virtuosis et vitiosis, cum morali; et considerat actus secundum quod merentur poenam vel praemium, cum rhetore et politico.

good in the genus 'relation' is the useful." Now, in the genus "relation" a thing is denominated not only according to that which is inherent in the thing, but also according to that which is extrinsic to it: as may be seen in the expressions "right" and "left," "equal" and "unequal," and such like. Accordingly, since the goodness of acts consists in their utility to the end, nothing hinders their being called good or bad according to their proportion to extrinsic things that are adjacent to them.

Reply to Objection 2: Accidents which are altogether accidental are neglected by every art, by reason of their uncertainty and infinity. But such like accidents are not what we call circumstances; because circumstances although, as stated above (I-II, q. 7, a. 1), they are extrinsic to the act, nevertheless are in a kind of contact with it, by being related to it. Proper accidents, however, come under the consideration of art.

Reply to Objection 3: The consideration of circumstances belongs to the moralist, the politician, and the orator. To the moralist, in so far as with respect to circumstances we find or lose the mean of virtue in human acts and passions. To the politician and to the orator, in so far as circumstances make acts to be worthy of praise or blame, of excuse or indictment. In different ways, however: because where the orator persuades, the politician judges. To the theologian this consideration belongs, in all the aforesaid ways: since to him all the other arts are subservient: for he has to consider virtuous and vicious acts, just as the moralist does; and with the orator and politician he considers acts according as they are deserving of reward or punishment.

ARTICULUS 3

AD TERTIUM sic proceditur. Videtur quod inconvenienter circumstantiae numerentur in III Ethic. Circumstantia enim actus dicitur quod exterius se habet ad actum. Huiusmodi autem sunt tempus et locus. Ergo solae duae sunt circumstantiae, scilicet *quando* et *ubi.*

ARTICLE 3
Whether the circumstances are properly set forth in the third book of Ethics?

Objection 1: It would seem that the circumstances are not properly set forth in Ethic. iii, 1. For a circumstance of an act is described as something outside the act. Now time and place answer to this description. Therefore there are only two circumstances, to wit, "when" and "where."

I-II, q. 7, a. 3, arg. 2

Praeterea, ex circumstantiis accipitur quid bene vel male fiat. Sed hoc pertinet ad modum actus. Ergo omnes circumstantiae concluduntur sub una, quae est *modus agendi.*

Praeterea, circumstantiae non sunt de substantia actus. Sed ad substantiam actus pertinere videntur causae ipsius actus. Ergo nulla circumstantia debet sumi ex causa ipsius actus. Sic ergo neque *quis,* neque *propter quid,* neque *circa quid,* sunt circumstantiae, nam *quis* pertinet ad causam efficientem, *propter quid* ad finalem, *circa quid* ad materialem.

Sed contra est auctoritas philosophi in III Ethicorum.

Respondeo dicendum quod Tullius, in sua rhetorica, assignat septem circumstantias, quae hoc versu continentur, *quis, quid, ubi, quibus auxiliis, cur, quomodo, quando.* Considerandum est enim in actibus *quis* fecit, *quibus auxiliis* vel *instrumentis* fecerit, *quid* fecerit, *ubi* fecerit, *cur* fecerit, *quomodo* fecerit, et *quando* fecerit. Sed Aristoteles, in III Ethic., addit aliam, scilicet *circa quid,* quae a Tullio comprehenditur sub *quid.* Et ratio huius annumerationis sic accipi potest. Nam circumstantia dicitur quod, extra substantiam actus existens, aliquo modo attingit ipsum. Contingit autem hoc fieri tripliciter, uno modo, inquantum attingit ipsum actum; alio modo, inquantum attingit causam actus; tertio modo, inquantum attingit effectum. Ipsum autem actum attingit, vel per modum mensurae, sicut *tempus* et *locus;* vel per modum qualitatis actus, sicut *modus agendi.* Ex parte autem effectus, ut cum consideratur *quid* aliquis fecerit. Ex parte vero causae actus, quantum ad causam finalem, accipitur *propter quid;* ex parte autem causae materialis, sive obiecti, accipitur *circa quid;* ex parte vero causae agentis principalis, accipitur *quis* egerit; ex parte vero causae agentis instrumentalis, accipitur *quibus auxiliis.*

Ad primum ergo dicendum quod tempus et locus circumstant actum per modum mensurae, sed alia circumstant actum inquantum attingunt ipsum quocumque alio modo, extra substantiam eius existentia.

Objection 2: Further, we judge from the circumstances whether a thing is well or ill done. But this belongs to the mode of an act. Therefore all the circumstances are included under one, which is the "mode of acting."

Objection 3: Further, circumstances are not part of the substance of an act. But the causes of an act seem to belong to its substance. Therefore no circumstance should be taken from the cause of the act itself. Accordingly, neither "who," nor "why," nor "about what," are circumstances: since "who" refers to the efficient cause, "why" to the final cause, and "about what" to the material cause.

On the contrary is the authority of the Philosopher in Ethic. iii, 1.

I answer that, Tully, in his Rhetoric (De Invent. Rhetor. i), gives seven circumstances, which are contained in this verse: *Quis, quid, ubi, quibus auxiliis, cur, quomodo, quando*— "Who, what, where, by what aids, why, how, and when." For in acts we must take note of "who" did it, "by what aids" or "instruments" he did it, "what" he did, "where" he did it, "why" he did it, "how" and "when" he did it. But Aristotle in Ethic. iii, 1 adds yet another, to wit, "about what," which Tully includes in the circumstance "what." The reason of this enumeration may be set down as follows. For a circumstance is described as something outside the substance of the act, and yet in a way touching it. Now this happens in three ways: first, inasmuch as it touches the act itself; secondly, inasmuch as it touches the cause of the act; thirdly, inasmuch as it touches the effect. It touches the act itself, either by way of measure, as "time" and "place"; or by qualifying the act as the "mode of acting." It touches the effect when we consider "what" is done. It touches the cause of the act, as to the final cause, by the circumstance "why"; as to the material cause, or object, in the circumstance "about what"; as to the principal efficient cause, in the circumstance "who"; and as to the instrumental efficient cause, in the circumstance "by what aids."

Reply to Objection 1: Time and place surround [*circumstant*] the act by way of measure; but the others surround the act by touching it in any other way, while they are extrinsic to the substance of the act.

AD SECUNDUM dicendum quod iste modus qui est *bene* vel *male,* non ponitur circumstantia, sed consequens ad omnes circumstantias. Sed specialis circumstantia ponitur modus qui pertinet ad qualitatem actus, puta quod aliquis ambulet velociter vel tarde, et quod aliquis percutit fortiter vel remisse, et sic de aliis.

AD TERTIUM dicendum quod illa conditio causae ex qua substantia actus dependet, non dicitur circumstantia; sed aliqua conditio adiuncta. Sicut in obiecto non dicitur circumstantia furti quod sit alienum, hoc enim pertinet ad substantiam furti; sed quod sit magnum vel parvum. Et similiter est de aliis circumstantiis quae accipiuntur ex parte aliarum causarum. Non enim finis qui dat speciem actus, est circumstantia; sed aliquis finis adiunctus. Sicut quod fortis fortiter agat propter bonum fortitudinis, non est circumstantia; sed si fortiter agat propter liberationem civitatis, vel populi Christiani, vel aliquid huiusmodi. Similiter etiam ex parte eius quod est *quid,* nam quod aliquis perfundens aliquem aqua, abluat ipsum, non est circumstantia ablutionis; sed quod abluendo infrigidet vel calefaciat, et sanet vel noceat, hoc est circumstantia.

Reply to Objection 2: This mode "well" or "ill" is not a circumstance, but results from all the circumstances. But the mode which refers to a quality of the act is a special circumstance; for instance, that a man walk fast or slowly; that he strike hard or gently, and so forth.

Reply to Objection 3: A condition of the cause, on which the substance of the act depends, is not a circumstance; it must be an additional condition. Thus, in regard to the object, it is not a circumstance of theft that the object is another's property, for this belongs to the substance of the act; but that it be great or small. And the same applies to the other circumstances which are considered in reference to the other causes. For the end that specifies the act is not a circumstance, but some additional end. Thus, that a valiant man act "valiantly for the sake of" the good of the virtue or fortitude, is not a circumstance; but if he act valiantly for the sake of the delivery of the state, or of Christendom, or some such purpose. The same is to be said with regard to the circumstance "what"; for that a man by pouring water on someone should happen to wash him, is not a circumstance of the washing; but that in doing so he give him a chill, or scald him; heal him or harm him, these are circumstances.

ARTICULUS 4

AD QUARTUM sic proceditur. Videtur quod non sint principales circumstantiae *propter quid,* et ea *in quibus est operatio,* ut dicitur in III Ethic. Ea enim in quibus est operatio, videntur esse locus et tempus, quae non videntur esse principalia inter circumstantias, cum sint maxime extrinseca ab actu. Ea ergo in quibus est operatio non sunt principalissimae circumstantiarum.

PRAETEREA, finis est extrinsecus rei. Non ergo videtur esse principalissima circumstantiarum.

ARTICLE 4
Whether the most important circumstances are "why" and "in what the act consists"?

Objection 1: It would seem that these are not the most important circumstances, namely, "why" and those "in which the act is,"* as stated in Ethic. iii, 1. For those in which the act is seem to be place and time: and these do not seem to be the most important of the circumstances, since, of them all, they are the most extrinsic to the act. Therefore those things in which the act is are not the most important circumstances.

Objection 2: Further, the end of a thing is extrinsic to it. Therefore it is not the most important circumstance.

---

* ἐν οἷς ἡ πρᾶξις (*en hois he praxis*).

PRAETEREA, principalissimum in unoquoque est causa eius et forma ipsius. Sed causa ipsius actus est persona agens; forma autem actus est modus ipsius. Ergo istae duae circumstantiae videntur esse principalissimae.

SED CONTRA est quod Gregorius Nyssenus dicit, quod *principalissimae circumstantiae* sunt *cuius gratia agitur,* et *quid est quod agitur.*

RESPONDEO dicendum quod actus proprie dicuntur humani, sicut supra dictum est, prout sunt voluntarii. Voluntatis autem motivum et obiectum est finis. Et ideo principalissima est omnium circumstantiarum illa quae attingit actum ex parte finis, scilicet *cuius gratia,* secundaria vero, quae attingit ipsam substantiam actus, idest *quid fecit.* Aliae vero circumstantiae sunt magis vel minus principales, secundum quod magis vel minus ad has appropinquant.

AD PRIMUM ergo dicendum quod per ea *in quibus est operatio,* philosophus non intelligit tempus et locum, sed ea quae adiunguntur ipsi actui. Unde Gregorius Nyssenus, quasi exponens dictum philosophi, loco eius quod philosophus dixit, *in quibus est operatio,* dicit *quid agitur.*

AD SECUNDUM dicendum quod finis, etsi non sit de substantia actus, est tamen causa actus principalissima, inquantum movet ad agendum. Unde et maxime actus moralis speciem habet ex fine.

AD TERTIUM dicendum quod persona agens causa est actus secundum quod movetur a fine; et secundum hoc principaliter ordinatur ad actum. Aliae vero conditiones personae non ita principaliter ordinantur ad actum. Modus etiam non est substantialis forma actus, hoc enim attenditur in actu secundum obiectum et terminum vel finem, sed est quasi quaedam qualitas accidentalis.

Objection 3: Further, that which holds the foremost place in regard to each thing, is its cause and its form. But the cause of an act is the person that does it; while the form of an act is the manner in which it is done. Therefore these two circumstances seem to be of the greatest importance.

On the contrary, Gregory of Nyssa* says that "the most important circumstances" are "why it is done" and "what is done."

I answer that, As stated above (I-II, q. 1, a. 1), acts are properly called human, inasmuch as they are voluntary. Now, the motive and object of the will is the end. Therefore that circumstance is the most important of all which touches the act on the part of the end, *viz.* the circumstance "why": and the second in importance, is that which touches the very substance of the act, *viz.* the circumstance "what he did." As to the other circumstances, they are more or less important, according as they more or less approach to these.

Reply to Objection 1: By those things "in which the act is" the Philosopher does not mean time and place, but those circumstances that are affixed to the act itself. Wherefore Gregory of Nyssa,† as though he were explaining the dictum of the Philosopher, instead of the latter's term—"in which the act is"—said, "what is done."

Reply to Objection 2: Although the end is not part of the substance of the act, yet it is the most important cause of the act, inasmuch as it moves the agent to act. Wherefore the moral act is specified chiefly by the end.

Reply to Objection 3: The person that does the act is the cause of that act, inasmuch as he is moved thereto by the end; and it is chiefly in this respect that he is directed to the act; while other conditions of the person have not such an important relation to the act. As to the mode, it is not the substantial form of the act, for in an act the substantial form depends on the object and term or end; but it is, as it were, a certain accidental quality of the act.

---

* Nemesius, De Nat. Hom. xxxi.
† Ibid.

Quaestio VIII

Deinde considerandum est de ipsis actibus voluntariis in speciali. Et primo, de actibus qui sunt immediate ipsius voluntatis velut ab ipsa voluntate eliciti; secundo de actibus imperatis a voluntate. Voluntas autem movetur et in finem, et in ea quae sunt ad finem. *Primo* igitur considerandum est de actibus voluntatis quibus movetur in finem; et *deinde* de actibus eius quibus movetur in ea quae sunt ad finem. Actus autem voluntatis in finem videntur esse tres, scilicet *velle, frui* et *intendere*. *Primo* ergo considerabimus de voluntate; *secundo,* de fruitione; *tertio,* de intentione. Circa primum consideranda sunt tria, *primo* quidem, quorum voluntas sit; *secundo,* a quo moveatur; *tertio,* quomodo moveatur. Circa primum quaeruntur tria. *Primo,* utrum voluntas sit tantum boni. *Secundum,* utrum sit tantum finis, an etiam eorum quae sunt ad finem. *Tertio,* si est aliquo modo eorum quae sunt ad finem, utrum uno motu moveatur in finem et in ea quae sunt ad finem.

Articulus 1

Ad primum sic proceditur. Videtur quod voluntas non tantum sit boni. Eadem enim est potentia oppositorum, sicut visus albi et nigri. Sed bonum et malum sunt opposita. Ergo voluntas non solum est boni, sed etiam mali.

Praeterea, potentiae rationales se habent ad opposita prosequenda, secundum philosophum. Sed voluntas est potentia rationalis, est enim *in ratione,* ut dicitur in III de anima. Ergo voluntas se habet ad opposita. Non ergo tantum ad volendum bonum, sed etiam ad volendum malum.

Praeterea, bonum et ens convertuntur. Sed voluntas non solum est entium, sed etiam non entium, volumus enim quandoque *non ambulare* et *non loqui.* Volumus etiam interdum quaedam futura, quae non sunt entia in actu. Ergo voluntas non tantum est boni.

Question 8
Of the Will, in Regard to What It Wills

We must now consider the different acts of the will; and in the first place, those acts which belong to the will itself immediately, as being elicited by the will; secondly, those acts which are commanded by the will. Now the will is moved to the end, and to the means to the end; we must therefore consider: 1. those acts of the will whereby it is moved to the end; and 2. those whereby it is moved to the means. And since it seems that there are three acts of the will in reference to the end; viz. "volition," "enjoyment," and "intention"; we must consider: 1. volition; 2. enjoyment; 3. intention. Concerning the first, three things must be considered: 1. Of what things is the will? 2. By what is the will moved? 3. How is it moved? Under the first head there are three points of inquiry: 1. Whether the will is of good only? 2. Whether it is of the end only, or also of the means? 3. If in any way it be of the means, whether it be moved to the end and to the means, by the same movement?

Article 1
Whether the will is of good only?

Objection 1: It would seem that the will is not of good only. For the same power regards opposites; for instance, sight regards white and black. But good and evil are opposites. Therefore the will is not only of good, but also of evil.

Objection 2: Further, rational powers can be directed to opposite purposes, according to the Philosopher (Metaph. ix, 2). But the will is a rational power, since it is "in the reason," as is stated in De Anima iii, 9. Therefore the will can be directed to opposites; and consequently its volition is not confined to good, but extends to evil.

Objection 3: Further, good and being are convertible. But volition is directed not only to beings, but also to non-beings. For sometimes we wish "not to walk," or "not to speak"; and again at times we wish for future things, which are not actual beings. Therefore the will is not of good only.

Sed contra est quod Dionysius dicit, IV cap. de Div. Nom., quod *malum est praeter voluntatem,* et quod *omnia bonum appetunt.*

Respondeo dicendum quod voluntas est appetitus quidam rationalis. Omnis autem appetitus non est nisi boni. Cuius ratio est quia appetitus nihil aliud est quam inclinatio appetentis in aliquid. Nihil autem inclinatur nisi in aliquid simile et conveniens. Cum igitur omnis res, inquantum est ens et substantia, sit quoddam bonum, necesse est ut omnis inclinatio sit in bonum. Et inde est quod philosophus dicit, in I Ethic., quod *bonum est quod omnia appetunt.* Sed considerandum est quod, cum omnis inclinatio consequatur aliquam formam, appetitus naturalis consequitur formam in natura existentem, appetitus autem sensitivus, vel etiam intellectivus seu rationalis, qui dicitur voluntas, sequitur formam apprehensam. Sicut igitur id in quod tendit appetitus naturalis, est bonum existens in re; ita id in quod tendit appetitus animalis vel voluntarius, est bonum apprehensum. Ad hoc igitur quod voluntas in aliquid tendat, non requiritur quod sit bonum in rei veritate, sed quod apprehendatur in ratione boni. Et propter hoc philosophus dicit, in II Physic., quod *finis est bonum, vel apparens bonum.*

Ad primum ergo dicendum quod eadem potentia est oppositorum, sed non eodem modo se habet ad utrumque. Voluntas igitur se habet et ad bonum et ad malum, sed ad bonum, appetendo ipsum; ad malum vero, fugiendo illud. Ipse ergo actualis appetitus boni vocatur *voluntas,* secundum quod nominat actum voluntatis, sic enim nunc loquimur de voluntate. Fuga autem mali magis dicitur *noluntas.* Unde sicut voluntas est boni, ita noluntas est mali.

Ad secundum dicendum quod potentia rationalis non se habet ad quaelibet opposita prosequenda, sed ad ea quae sub suo obiecto convenienti continentur, nam nulla potentia prosequitur nisi suum conveniens obiectum. Obiectum autem voluntatis

On the contrary, Dionysius says (Div. Nom. iv) that "evil is outside the scope of the will," and that "all things desire good."

I answer that, The will is a rational appetite. Now every appetite is only of something good. The reason of this is that the appetite is nothing else than an inclination of a person desirous of a thing towards that thing. Now every inclination is to something like and suitable to the thing inclined. Since, therefore, everything, inasmuch as it is being and substance, is a good, it must needs be that every inclination is to something good. And hence it is that the Philosopher says (Ethic. i, 1) that "the good is that which all desire." But it must be noted that, since every inclination results from a form, the natural appetite results from a form existing in the nature of things: while the sensitive appetite, as also the intellective or rational appetite, which we call the will, follows from an apprehended form. Therefore, just as the natural appetite tends to good existing in a thing; so the animal or voluntary appetite tends to a good which is apprehended. Consequently, in order that the will tend to anything, it is requisite, not that this be good in very truth, but that it be apprehended as good. Wherefore the Philosopher says (Phys. ii, 3) that "the end is a good, or an apparent good."

Reply to Objection 1: The same power regards opposites, but it is not referred to them in the same way. Accordingly, the will is referred both to good and evil: but to good by desiring it: to evil, by shunning it. Wherefore the actual desire of good is called "volition,"* meaning thereby the act of the will; for it is in this sense that we are now speaking of the will. On the other hand, the shunning of evil is better described as "nolition": wherefore, just as volition is of good, so nolition is of evil.

Reply to Objection 2: A rational power is not to be directed to all opposite purposes, but to those which are contained under its proper object; for no power seeks other than its proper object. Now, the object of the will

---

* In Latin, *voluntas*. To avoid confusion with *voluntas* (the will), St. Thomas adds a word of explanation, which in the translation may appear superfluous.

est bonum. Unde ad illa opposita prosequenda se habet voluntas, quae sub bono comprehenduntur, sicut moveri et quiescere, loqui et tacere, et alia huiusmodi, in utrumque enim horum fertur voluntas sub ratione boni.

AD TERTIUM dicendum quod illud quod non est ens in rerum natura, accipitur ut ens in ratione, unde negationes et privationes dicuntur *entia rationis*. Per quem etiam modum futura, prout apprehenduntur, sunt entia. Inquantum igitur sunt huiusmodi entia, apprehenduntur sub ratione boni, et sic voluntas in ea tendit. Unde philosophus dicit, in V Ethic., quod *carere malo habet rationem boni*.

is good. Wherefore the will can be directed to such opposite purposes as are contained under good, such as to be moved or to be at rest, to speak or to be silent, and such like: for the will can be directed to either under the aspect of good.

Reply to Objection 3: That which is not a being in nature, is considered as a being in the reason, wherefore negations and privations are said to be "beings of reason." In this way, too, future things, in so far as they are apprehended, are beings. Accordingly, in so far as such like are beings, they are apprehended under the aspect of good; and it is thus that the will is directed to them. Wherefore the Philosopher says (Ethic. v, 1) that "to lack evil is considered as a good."

ARTICULUS 2

AD SECUNDUM sic proceditur. Videtur quod voluntas non sit eorum quae sunt ad finem, sed tantum finis. Dicit enim philosophus, in III Ethic., quod *voluntas est finis, electio autem eorum quae sunt ad finem.*

PRAETEREA, *ad ea quae sunt diversa genere, diversae potentiae animae ordinantur,* ut dicitur in VI Ethic. Sed finis et ea quae sunt ad finem sunt in diverso genere boni, nam finis, qui est bonum honestum vel delectabile, est in genere *qualitatis,* vel *actionis* aut *passionis;* bonum autem quod dicitur utile, quod est ad finem, est in *ad aliquid,* ut dicitur in I Ethic. Ergo, si voluntas est finis, non erit eorum quae sunt ad finem.

PRAETEREA, habitus proportionantur potentis, cum sint earum perfectiones. Sed in habitibus qui dicuntur artes operativae, ad aliud pertinet finis, et ad aliud quod est ad finem, sicut ad gubernatorem pertinet usus navis, qui est finis eius; ad navifactivam vero constructio navis, quae est propter finem. Ergo, cum voluntas sit finis, non erit eorum quae sunt ad finem.

SED CONTRA est, quia in rebus naturalibus per eandem potentiam aliquid pertransit media, et pertingit ad terminum.

ARTICLE 2
Whether volition is of the end only, or also of the means?

Objection 1: It would seem that volition is not of the means, but of the end only. For the Philosopher says (Ethic. iii, 2) that "volition is of the end, while choice is of the means."

Objection 2: Further, "For objects differing in genus there are corresponding different powers of the soul" (Ethic. vi, 1). Now, the end and the means are in different genera of good: because the end, which is a good either of rectitude or of pleasure, is in the genus "quality," or "action," or "passion"; whereas the good which is useful, and is directed to and end, is in the genus "relation" (Ethic. i, 6). Therefore, if volition is of the end, it is not of the means.

Objection 3: Further, habits are proportionate to powers, since they are perfections thereof. But in those habits which are called practical arts, the end belongs to one, and the means to another art; thus the use of a ship, which is its end, belongs to the [art of the] helmsman; whereas the building of the ship, which is directed to the end, belongs to the art of the shipwright. Therefore, since volition is of the end, it is not of the means.

On the contrary, In natural things, it is by the same power that a thing passes through the middle space, and arrives at the terminus.

Sed ea quae sunt ad finem, sunt quaedam media per quae pervenitur ad finem sicut ad terminum. Ergo, si voluntas est finis, ipsa etiam est eorum quae sunt ad finem.

RESPONDEO dicendum quod *voluntas* quandoque dicitur ipsa potentia qua volumus; quandoque autem ipse voluntatis actus. Si ergo loquamur de voluntate secundum quod nominat potentiam, sic se extendit et ad finem, et ad ea quae sunt ad finem. Ad ea enim se extendit unaquaeque potentia, in quibus inveniri potest quocumque modo ratio sui obiecti, sicut visus se extendit ad omnia quaecumque participant quocumque modo colorem. Ratio autem boni, quod est obiectum potentiae voluntatis, invenitur non solum in fine, sed etiam in his quae sunt ad finem. Si autem loquamur de voluntate secundum quod nominat proprie actum, sic, proprie loquendo, est finis tantum. Omnis enim actus denominatus a potentia, nominat simplicem actum illius potentiae, sicut *intelligere* nominat simplicem actum intellectus. Simplex autem actus potentiae est in id quod est secundum se obiectum potentiae. Id autem quod est propter se bonum et volitum, est finis. Unde voluntas proprie est ipsius finis. Ea vero quae sunt ad finem, non sunt bona vel volita propter seipsa, sed ex ordine ad finem. Unde voluntas in ea non fertur, nisi quatenus fertur in finem, unde hoc ipsum quod in eis vult, est finis. Sicut et intelligere proprie est eorum quae secundum se cognoscuntur, scilicet principiorum, eorum autem quae cognoscuntur per principia, non dicitur esse intelligentia, nisi inquantum in eis ipsa principia considerantur, sic enim se habet finis in appetibilibus, sicut se habet principium in intelligibilibus, ut dicitur in VII Ethic.

AD PRIMUM ergo dicendum quod philosophus loquitur de voluntate, secundum quod proprie nominat simplicem actum voluntatis, non autem secundum quod nominat potentiam.

AD SECUNDUM dicendum quod ad ea quae sunt diversa genere ex aequo se habentia, ordinantur diversae potentiae, sicut sonus et color sunt diversa genera sensibilium, ad quae ordinantur auditus et visus. Sed utile et

But the means are a kind of middle space, through which one arrives at the end or terminus. Therefore, if volition is of the end, it is also of the means.

I answer that, The word *voluntas* sometimes designates the power of the will, sometimes its act.* Accordingly, if we speak of the will as a power, thus it extends both to the end and to the means. For every power extends to those things in which may be considered the aspect of the object of that power in any way whatever: thus the sight extends to all things whatsoever that are in any way colored. Now the aspect of good, which is the object of the power of the will, may be found not only in the end, but also in the means. If, however, we speak of the will in regard to its act, then, properly speaking, volition is of the end only. Because every act denominated from a power, designates the simple act of that power: thus "to understand" designates the simple act of the understanding. Now the simple act of a power is referred to that which is in itself the object of that power. But that which is good and willed in itself is the end. Wherefore volition, properly speaking, is of the end itself. On the other hand, the means are good and willed, not in themselves, but as referred to the end. Wherefore the will is directed to them, only in so far as it is directed to the end: so that what it wills in them, is the end. Thus, to understand, is properly directed to things that are known in themselves, i.e., first principles: but we do not speak of understanding with regard to things known through first principles, except in so far as we see the principles in those things. For in morals the end is what principles are in speculative science (Ethic. viii, 8).

Reply to Objection 1: The Philosopher is speaking of the will in reference to the simple act of the will; not in reference to the power of the will.

Reply to Objection 2: There are different powers for objects that differ in genus and are on an equality; for instance, sound and color are different genera of sensibles, to which are referred hearing and sight. But the useful and

---

* See note: above a. 1, ad 1

honestum non ex aequo se habent, sed sicut quod est secundum se et secundum alterum. Huiusmodi autem semper referuntur ad eandem potentiam, sicut per potentiam visivam sentitur et color, et lux, per quam color videtur.

AD TERTIUM dicendum quod non quidquid diversificat habitum, diversificat potentiam, habitus enim sunt quaedam determinationes potentiarum ad aliquos speciales actus. Et tamen quaelibet ars operativa considerat et finem et id quod est ad finem. Nam ars gubernativa considerat quidem finem, ut quem operatur, id autem quod est ad finem, ut quod imperat. E contra vero navifactiva considerat id quod est ad finem, ut quod operatur, id vero quod est finis, ut ad quod ordinat id quod operatur. Et iterum in unaquaque arte operativa est aliquis finis proprius, et aliquid quod est ad finem, quod proprie ad illam artem pertinet.

Articulus 3

AD TERTIUM sic proceditur. Videtur quod eodem actu voluntas feratur in finem, et in id quod est ad finem. Quia secundum philosophum, *ubi est unum propter alterum, ibi est unum tantum.* Sed voluntas non vult id quod est ad finem, nisi propter finem. Ergo eodem actu movetur in utrumque.

PRAETEREA, finis est ratio volendi ea quae sunt ad finem, sicut lumen est ratio visionis colorum. Sed eodem actu videtur lumen et color. Ergo idem est motus voluntatis quo vult finem, et ea quae sunt ad finem.

PRAETEREA, idem numero motus naturalis est qui per media tendit ad ultimum. Sed ea quae sunt ad finem, comparantur ad finem sicut media ad ultimum. Ergo idem motus voluntatis est quo voluntas fertur in finem, et in ea quae sunt ad finem.

SED CONTRA, actus diversificantur secundum obiecta. Sed diversae species boni sunt finis, et id quod est ad finem, quod dicitur utile. Ergo non eodem actu voluntas fertur in utrumque.

the righteous are not on an equality, but are as that which is of itself, and that which is in relation to another. Now such like objects are always referred to the same power; for instance, the power of sight perceives both color and light by which color is seen.

Reply to Objection 3: Not everything that diversifies habits, diversifies the powers: since habits are certain determinations of powers to certain special acts. Moreover, every practical art considers both the end and the means. For the art of the helmsman does indeed consider the end, as that which it effects; and the means, as that which it commands. On the other hand, the ship-building art considers the means as that which it effects; but it considers that which is the end, as that to which it refers what it effects. And again, in every practical art there is an end proper to it and means that belong properly to that art.

Article 3
Whether the will is moved by the same act to the end and to the means?

Objection 1: It would seem that the will is moved by the same act, to the end and to the means. Because according to the Philosopher (Topic. iii, 2) "where one thing is on account of another there is only one." But the will does not will the means save on account of the end. Therefore it is moved to both by the same act.

Objection 2: Further, the end is the reason for willing the means, just as light is the reason of seeing colors. But light and colors are seen by the same act. Therefore it is the same movement of the will, whereby it wills the end and the means.

Objection 3: Further, it is one and the same natural movement which tends through the middle space to the terminus. But the means are in comparison to the end, as the middle space is to the terminus. Therefore it is the same movement of the will whereby it is directed to the end and to the means.

On the contrary, Acts are diversified according to their objects. But the end is a different species of good from the means, which are a useful good. Therefore the will is not moved to both by the same act.

Respondeo dicendum quod, cum finis sit secundum se volitus, id autem quod est ad finem, inquantum huiusmodi, non sit volitum nisi propter finem; manifestum est quod voluntas potest ferri in finem sine hoc quod feratur in ea quae sunt ad finem; sed in ea quae sunt ad finem, inquantum huiusmodi, non potest ferri, nisi feratur in ipsum finem. Sic ergo voluntas in ipsum finem dupliciter fertur, uno modo, absolute secundum se; alio modo, sicut in rationem volendi ea quae sunt ad finem. Manifestum est ergo quod unus et idem motus voluntatis est quo fertur in finem, secundum quod est ratio volendi ea quae sunt ad finem, et in ipsa quae sunt ad finem. Sed alius actus est quod fertur in ipsum finem absolute. Et quandoque praecedit tempore, sicut cum aliquis primo vult sanitatem, et postea, deliberans quomodo possit sanari, vult conducere medicum ut sanetur. Sicut etiam et circa intellectum accidit, nam primo aliquis intelligit ipsa principia secundum se; postmodum autem intelligit ea in ipsis conclusionibus, secundum quod assentit conclusionibus propter principia.

Ad primum ergo dicendum quod ratio illa procedit secundum quod voluntas fertur in finem, ut est ratio volendi ea quae sunt ad finem.

Ad secundum dicendum quod quandocumque videtur color, eodem actu videtur lumen, potest tamen videri lumen sine hoc quod videatur color. Et similiter quandocumque quis vult ea quae sunt ad finem, vult eodem actu finem, non tamen e converso.

Ad tertium dicendum quod in executione operis, ea quae sunt ad finem se habent ut media, et finis ut terminus. Unde sicut motus naturalis interdum sistit in medio, et non pertingit ad terminum; ita quandoque operatur aliquis id quod est ad finem, et tamen non consequitur finem. Sed in volendo est e converso, nam voluntas per finem devenit ad volendum ea quae sunt ad finem; sicut et intellectus devenit in conclusiones per principia, quae *media* dicuntur. Unde intellectus aliquando intelligit medium, et ex eo non procedit ad conclusionem. Et similiter voluntas aliquando

I answer that, Since the end is willed in itself, whereas the means, as such, are only willed for the end, it is evident that the will can be moved to the end, without being moved to the means; whereas it cannot be moved to the means, as such, unless it is moved to the end. Accordingly the will is moved to the end in two ways: first, to the end absolutely and in itself; secondly, as the reason for willing the means. Hence it is **evident that the will is moved by one and the same movement, to the end, as the reason for willing the means; and to the means themselves. But it is another act whereby the will is moved to the end absolutely. And sometimes this act precedes the other in time;** for example when a man first wills to have health, and afterwards deliberating by what means to be healed, wills to send for the doctor to heal him. The same happens in regard to the intellect: for at first a man understands the principles in themselves; but afterwards he understands them in the conclusions, inasmuch as he assents to the conclusions on account of the principles.

Reply to Objection 1: This argument holds in respect of the will being moved to the end as the reason for willing the means.

Reply to Objection 2: Whenever color is seen, by the same act the light is seen; but the light can be seen without the color being seen. In like manner whenever a man wills the means, by the same act he wills the end; but not the conversely.

Reply to Objection 3: In the execution of a work, the means are as the middle space, and the end, as the terminus. Wherefore just as natural movement sometimes stops in the middle and does not reach the terminus; so sometimes one is busy with the means, without gaining the end. But in willing it is the reverse: the will through [willing] the end comes to will the means; just as the intellect arrives at the conclusions through the principles which are called "means." Hence it is that sometimes the intellect understands a mean, and does not proceed thence to the conclusion. And in like manner the will

vult finem, et tamen non procedit ad volendum id quod est ad finem.

Ad illud vero quod in contrarium obiicitur, patet solutio per ea quae supra dicta sunt. Nam utile et honestum non sunt species boni ex aequo divisae, sed se habent sicut propter se et propter alterum. Unde actus voluntatis in unum potest ferri sine hoc quod feratur in alterum, sed non e converso.

sometimes wills the end, and yet does not proceed to will the means.

The solution to the argument in the contrary sense is clear from what has been said above (I-II, q. 8, a. 2, ad 2). For the useful and the righteous are not species of good in an equal degree, but are as that which is for its own sake and that which is for the sake of something else: wherefore the act of the will can be directed to one and not to the other; but not conversely.

Quaestio IX

Deinde considerandum est de motivo voluntatis. Et circa hoc quaeruntur sex. *Primo,* utrum voluntas moveatur ab intellectu. *Secundo,* utrum moveatur ab appetitu sensitivo. *Tertio,* utrum voluntas moveat seipsam. *Quarto,* utrum moveatur ab aliquo exteriori principio. *Quinto,* utrum moveatur a corpore caelesti. *Sexto,* utrum voluntas moveatur a solo Deo, sicut ab exteriori principio.

Question 9
Of That Which Moves the Will

We must now consider what moves the will: and under this head there are six points of inquiry: 1. Whether the will is moved by the intellect? 2. Whether it is moved by the sensitive appetite? 3. Whether the will moves itself? 4. Whether it is moved by an extrinsic principle? 5. Whether it is moved by a heavenly body? 6. Whether the will is moved by God alone as by an extrinsic principle?

Articulus 1

Ad primum sic proceditur. Videtur quod voluntas non moveatur ab intellectu. Dicit enim Augustinus, super illud Psalmi, *concupivit anima mea desiderare iustificationes tuas, praevolat intellectus, sequitur tardus aut nullus affectus, scimus bonum, nec delectat agere.* Hoc autem non esset, si voluntas ab intellectu moveretur, quia motus mobilis sequitur motionem moventis. Ergo intellectus non movet voluntatem.

Praeterea, intellectus se habet ad voluntatem ut demonstrans appetibile, sicut imaginatio demonstrat appetibile appetitui sensitivo. Sed imaginatio demonstrans appetibile non movet appetitum sensitivum, immo quandoque ita nos habemus ad ea quae imaginamur, sicut ad ea quae in pictura nobis ostenduntur, ex quibus non movemur, ut dicitur in libro de anima.

Article 1
Whether the will is moved by the intellect?

Objection 1: It would seem that the will is not moved by the intellect. For Augustine says on Ps. 118:20: "My soul hath coveted to long for Thy justifications: The intellect flies ahead, the desire follows sluggishly or not at all: we know what is good, but deeds delight us not." But it would not be so, if the will were moved by the intellect: because movement of the movable results from motion of the mover. Therefore the intellect does not move the will.

Objection 2: Further, the intellect in presenting the appetible object to the will, stands in relation to the will, as the imagination in representing the appetible will to the sensitive appetite. But the imagination, does not remove the sensitive appetite: indeed sometimes our imagination affects us no more than what is set before us in a picture, and moves us not at all (De Anima ii, 3).

Ergo neque etiam intellectus movet voluntatem.

PRAETEREA, idem respectu eiusdem non est movens et motum. Sed voluntas movet intellectum, intelligimus enim quando volumus. Ergo intellectus non movet voluntatem.

SED CONTRA est quod philosophus dicit, in III de anima, quod *appetibile intellectum est movens non motum, voluntas autem est movens motum.*

RESPONDEO dicendum quod intantum aliquid indiget moveri ab aliquo, inquantum est in potentia ad plura, oportet enim ut id quod est in potentia, reducatur in actum per aliquid quod est actu; et hoc est movere. Dupliciter autem aliqua vis animae invenitur esse in potentia ad diversa, uno modo, quantum ad agere et non agere; alio modo, quantum ad agere hoc vel illud. Sicut visus quandoque videt actu, et quandoque non videt; et quandoque videt album, et quandoque videt nigrum. Indiget igitur movente quantum ad duo, scilicet quantum ad exercitium vel usum actus; et quantum ad determinationem actus. Quorum primum est ex parte subiecti, quod quandoque invenitur agens, quandoque non agens, aliud autem est ex parte obiecti, secundum quod specificatur actus. Motio autem ipsius subiecti est ex agente aliquo. Et cum omne agens agat propter finem, ut supra ostensum est, principium huius motionis est ex fine. Et inde est quod ars ad quam pertinet finis, movet suo imperio artem ad quam pertinet id quod est ad finem, sicut *gubernatoria ars imperat navifactivae,* ut in II Physic. dicitur. Bonum autem in communi, quod habet rationem finis, est obiectum voluntatis. Et ideo ex hac parte voluntas movet alias potentias animae ad suos actus, utimur enim aliis potentiis cum volumus. Nam fines et perfectiones omnium aliarum potentiarum comprehenduntur sub obiecto voluntatis, sicut quaedam particularia bona, semper autem ars vel potentia ad quam pertinet finis universalis, movet ad agendum artem vel potentiam ad quam pertinet finis particularis sub illo universali comprehensus; sicut dux exercitus, qui intendit bonum commune, scilicet ordinem totius exercitus,

Therefore neither does the intellect move the will.

Objection 3: Further, the same is not mover and moved in respect of the same thing. But the will moves the intellect; for we exercise the intellect when we will. Therefore the intellect does not move the will.

On the contrary, The Philosopher says (De Anima iii, 10) that "the appetible object is a mover not moved, whereas the will is a mover moved."

I answer that, A thing requires to be moved by something in so far as it is in potentiality to several things; for that which is in potentiality needs to be reduced to act by something actual; and to do this is to move. Now a power of the soul is seen to be in potentiality to different things in two ways: first, with regard to acting and not acting; secondly, with regard to this or that action. Thus the sight sometimes sees actually, and sometimes sees not: and sometimes it sees white, and sometimes black. It needs therefore a mover in two respects, *viz.* as to the exercise or use of the act, and as to the determination of the act. The first of these is on the part of the subject, which is sometimes acting, sometimes not acting: while the other is on the part of the object, by reason of which the act is specified. The motion of the subject itself is due to some agent. And since every agent acts for an end, as was shown above (I-II, q. 1, a. 2), the principle of this motion lies in the end. And hence it is that the art which is concerned with the end, by its command moves the art which is concerned with the means; just as the "art of sailing commands the art of shipbuilding" (Phys. ii, 2). Now good in general, which has the nature of an end, is the object of the will. Consequently, in this respect, the will moves the other powers of the soul to their acts, for we make use of the other powers when we will. For the end and perfection of every other power, is included under the object of the will as some particular good: and always the art or power to which the universal end belongs, moves to their acts the arts or powers to which belong the particular ends included in the universal end. Thus the leader of an army, who intends the common good—i.e., the order

movet suo imperio aliquem ex tribunis, qui intendit ordinem unius aciei. Sed obiectum movet, determinando actum, ad modum principii formalis, a quo in rebus naturalibus actio specificatur, sicut calefactio a calore. Primum autem principium formale est *ens* et *verum* universale, quod est obiectum intellectus. Et ideo isto modo motionis intellectus movet voluntatem, sicut praesentans ei obiectum suum.

Ad primum ergo dicendum quod ex illa auctoritate non habetur quod intellectus non moveat, sed quod non moveat ex necessitate.

Ad secundum dicendum quod, sicut imaginatio formae sine aestimatione convenientis vel nocivi, non movet appetitum sensitivum; ita nec apprehensio veri sine ratione boni et appetibilis. Unde intellectus speculativus non movet, sed intellectus practicus, ut dicitur in III de anima.

Ad tertium dicendum quod voluntas movet intellectum quantum ad exercitium actus, quia et ipsum verum, quod est perfectio intellectus, continetur sub universali bono ut quoddam bonum particulare. Sed quantum ad determinationem actus, quae est ex parte obiecti, intellectus movet voluntatem, quia et ipsum bonum apprehenditur secundum quandam specialem rationem comprehensam sub universali ratione veri. Et sic patet quod non est idem movens et motum secundum idem.

Articulus 2

Ad secundum sic proceditur. Videtur quod voluntas ab appetitu sensitivo moveri non possit. *Movens enim et agens est praestantius patiente,* ut Augustinus dicit, XII super Gen. ad Litt. Sed appetitus sensitivus est inferior voluntate, quae est appetitus intellectivus; sicut sensus est inferior intellectu. Ergo appetitus sensitivus non movet voluntatem.

Praeterea, nulla virtus particularis potest facere effectum universalem. Sed appetitus sensitivus est virtus particularis,

of the whole army—by his command moves one of the captains, who intends the order of one company. On the other hand, the object moves, by determining the act, after the manner of a formal principle, whereby in natural things actions are specified, as heating by heat. Now the first formal principle is universal "being" and "truth," which is the object of the intellect. And therefore by this kind of motion the intellect moves the will, as presenting its object to it.

Reply to Objection 1: The passage quoted proves, not that the intellect does not move, but that it does not move of necessity.

Reply to Objection 2: Just as the imagination of a form without estimation of fitness or harmfulness, does not move the sensitive appetite; so neither does the apprehension of the true without the aspect of goodness and desirability. Hence it is not the speculative intellect that moves, but the practical intellect (De Anima iii, 9).

Reply to Objection 3: The will moves the intellect as to the exercise of its act; since even the true itself which is the perfection of the intellect, is included in the universal good, as a particular good. But as to the determination of the act, which the act derives from the object, the intellect moves the will; since the good itself is apprehended under a special aspect as contained in the universal true. It is therefore evident that the same is not mover and moved in the same respect.

Article 2
Whether the will is moved by the sensitive appetite?

Objection 1: It would seem that the will cannot be moved by the sensitive appetite. For "to move and to act is more excellent than to be passive," as Augustine says (Gen. ad lit. xii, 16). But the sensitive appetite is less excellent than the will which is the intellectual appetite; just as sense is less excellent than intellect. Therefore the sensitive appetite does not move the will.

Objection 2: Further, no particular power can produce a universal effect. But the sensitive appetite is a particular power,

consequitur enim particularem sensus apprehensionem. Ergo non potest causare motum voluntatis, qui est universalis, velut consequens apprehensionem universalem intellectus.

Praeterea, ut probatur in VIII Physic., movens non movetur ab eo quod movet, ut sit motio reciproca. Sed voluntas movet appetitum sensitivum, inquantum appetitus sensitivus obedit rationi. Ergo appetitus sensitivus non movet voluntatem.

Sed contra est quod dicitur Iac. I, *unusquisque tentatur a concupiscentia sua abstractus et illectus.* Non autem abstraheretur quis a concupiscentia, nisi voluntas eius moveretur ab appetitu sensitivo, in quo est concupiscentia. Ergo appetitus sensitivus movet voluntatem.

Respondeo dicendum quod, sicut supra dictum est, id quod apprehenditur sub ratione boni et convenientis, movet voluntatem per modum obiecti. Quod autem aliquid videatur bonum et conveniens, ex duobus contingit, scilicet ex conditione eius quod proponitur, et eius cui proponitur. Conveniens enim secundum relationem dicitur, unde ex utroque extremorum dependet. Et inde est quod gustus diversimode dispositus, non eodem modo accipit aliquid ut conveniens et ut non conveniens. Unde, ut philosophus dicit in III Ethic., *qualis unusquisque est, talis finis videtur ei.* Manifestum est autem quod secundum passionem appetitus sensitivi, immutatur homo ad aliquam dispositionem. Unde secundum quod homo est in passione aliqua, videtur sibi aliquid conveniens, quod non videtur extra passionem existenti, sicut irato videtur bonum, quod non videtur quieto. Et per hunc modum, ex parte obiecti, appetitus sensitivus movet voluntatem.

Ad primum ergo dicendum quod nihil prohibet id quod est simpliciter et secundum se praestantius, quoad aliquid esse debilius. Voluntas igitur simpliciter praestantior est quam appetitus sensitivus, sed quoad istum in quo passio dominatur,

because it follows the particular apprehension of sense. Therefore it cannot cause the movement of the will, which movement is universal, as following the universal apprehension of the intellect.

Objection 3: Further, as is proved in Phys. viii, 5, the mover is not moved by that which it moves, in such a way that there be reciprocal motion. But the will moves the sensitive appetite, inasmuch as the sensitive appetite obeys the reason. Therefore the sensitive appetite does not move the will.

On the contrary, It is written (James 1:14): "Every man is tempted by his own concupiscence, being drawn away and allured." But man would not be drawn away by his concupiscence, unless his will were moved by the sensitive appetite, wherein concupiscence resides. Therefore the sensitive appetite moves the will.

I answer that, As stated above (I-II, q. 9, a. 1), that which is apprehended as good and fitting, moves the will by way of object. Now, that a thing appear to be good and fitting, happens from two causes: namely, from the condition, either of the thing proposed, or of the one to whom it is proposed. For fitness is spoken of by way of relation; hence it depends on both extremes. And hence it is that taste, according as it is variously disposed, takes to a thing in various ways, as being fitting or unfitting. Wherefore as the Philosopher says (Ethic. iii, 5): "According as a man is, such does the end seem to him." Now it is evident that according to a passion of the sensitive appetite man is changed to a certain disposition. Wherefore according as man is affected by a passion, something seems to him fitting, which does not seem so when he is not so affected: thus that seems good to a man when angered, which does not seem good when he is calm. And in this way, the sensitive appetite moves the will, on the part of the object.

Reply to Objection 1: Nothing hinders that which is better simply and in itself, from being less excellent in a certain respect. Accordingly the will is simply more excellent than the sensitive appetite: but in respect of the man in whom a passion is predominant,

inquantum subiacet passioni, praeeminet appetitus sensitivus.

AD SECUNDUM dicendum quod actus et electiones hominum sunt circa singularia. Unde ex hoc ipso quod appetitus sensitivus est virtus particularis, habet magnam virtutem ad hoc quod per ipsum sic disponatur homo, ut ei aliquid videatur sic vel aliter, circa singularia.

AD TERTIUM dicendum quod, sicut philosophus dicit in I Polit., ratio, in qua est voluntas, movet suo imperio irascibilem et concupiscibilem, non quidem *despotico principatu,* sicut movetur servus a domino; sed *principatu regali seu politico,* sicut liberi homines reguntur a gubernante, qui tamen possunt contra movere. Unde et irascibilis et concupiscibilis possunt in contrarium movere ad voluntatem. Et sic nihil prohibet voluntatem aliquando ab eis moveri.

in so far as he is subject to that passion, the sensitive appetite is more excellent.

Reply to Objection 2: Men's acts and choices are in reference to singulars. Wherefore from the very fact that the sensitive appetite is a particular power, it has great influence in disposing man so that something seems to him such or otherwise, in particular cases.

Reply to Objection 3: As the Philosopher says (Polit. i, 2), the reason, in which resides the will, moves, by its command, the irascible and concupiscible powers, not, indeed, "by a despotic sovereignty," as a slave is moved by his master, but by a "royal and politic sovereignty," as free men are ruled by their governor, and can nevertheless act counter to his commands. Hence both irascible and concupiscible can move counter to the will: and accordingly nothing hinders the will from being moved by them at times.

Articulus 3

AD TERTIUM sic proceditur. Videtur quod voluntas non moveat seipsam. Omne enim movens, inquantum huiusmodi, est in actu, quod autem movetur, est in potentia, nam *motus est actus existentis in potentia, inquantum huiusmodi.* Sed non est idem in potentia et in actu respectu eiusdem. Ergo nihil movet seipsum. Neque ergo voluntas seipsam movere potest.

PRAETEREA, mobile movetur ad praesentiam moventis. Sed voluntas semper sibi est praesens. Si ergo ipsa seipsam moveret, semper moveretur. Quod patet esse falsum.

PRAETEREA, voluntas movetur ab intellectu, ut dictum est. Si igitur voluntas movet seipsam, sequitur quod idem simul moveatur a duobus motoribus immediate, quod videtur inconveniens. Non ergo voluntas movet seipsam.

SED CONTRA est quia voluntas domina est sui actus, et in ipsa est velle et non velle. Quod non esset, si non haberet in

ARTICLE 3
Whether the will moves itself?

Objection 1: It would seem that the will does not move itself. For every mover, as such, is in act: whereas what is moved, is in potentiality; since "movement is the act of that which is in potentiality, as such."* Now the same is not in potentiality and in act, in respect of the same. Therefore nothing moves itself. Neither, therefore, can the will move itself.

Objection 2: Further, the movable is moved on the mover being present. But the will is always present to itself. If, therefore, it moved itself, it would always be moving itself, which is clearly false.

Objection 3: Further, the will is moved by the intellect, as stated above (I-II, q. 9, a. 1). If, therefore, the will move itself, it would follow that the same thing is at once moved immediately by two movers; which seems unreasonable. Therefore the will does not move itself.

On the contrary, The will is mistress of its own act, and to it belongs to will and not to will. But this would not be so, had it not

---

* Aristotle, Phys. iii, 1

potestate movere seipsum ad volendum. Ergo ipsa movet seipsam.

Respondeo dicendum quod, sicut supra dictum est, ad voluntatem pertinet movere alias potentias ex ratione finis, qui est voluntatis obiectum. Sed sicut dictum est, hoc modo se habet finis in appetibilibus, sicut principium in intelligibilibus. Manifestum est autem quod intellectus per hoc quod cognoscit principium, reducit seipsum de potentia in actum, quantum ad cognitionem conclusionum, et hoc modo movet seipsum. Et similiter voluntas per hoc quod vult finem, movet seipsam ad volendum ea quae sunt ad finem.

Ad primum ergo dicendum quod voluntas non secundum idem movet et movetur. Unde nec secundum idem est in actu et in potentia. Sed inquantum actu vult finem, reducit se de potentia in actum respectu eorum quae sunt ad finem, ut scilicet actu ea velit.

Ad secundum dicendum quod potentia voluntatis semper actu est sibi praesens, sed actus voluntatis, quo vult finem aliquem, non semper est in ipsa voluntate. Per hunc autem movet seipsam. Unde non sequitur quod semper seipsam moveat.

Ad tertium dicendum quod non eodem modo voluntas movetur ab intellectu, et a seipsa. Sed ab intellectu quidem movetur secundum rationem obiecti, a seipsa vero, quantum ad exercitium actus, secundum rationem finis.

the power to move itself to will. Therefore it moves itself.

I answer that, As stated above (I-II, q. 9, a. 1), it belongs to the will to move the other powers, by reason of the end which is the will's object. Now, as stated above (I-II, q. 8, a. 2), the end is in things appetible, what the principle is in things intelligible. But it is evident that the intellect, through its knowledge of the principle, reduces itself from potentiality to act, as to its knowledge of the conclusions; and thus it moves itself. And, in like manner, the will, through its volition of the end, moves itself to will the means.

Reply to Objection 1: It is not in respect of the same that the will moves itself and is moved: wherefore neither is it in act and in potentiality in respect of the same. But forasmuch as it actually wills the end, it reduces itself from potentiality to act, in respect of the means, so as, in a word, to will them actually.

Reply to Objection 2: The power of the will is always actually present to itself; but the act of the will, whereby it wills an end, is not always in the will. But it is by this act that it moves itself. Accordingly it does not follow that it is always moving itself.

Reply to Objection 3: The will is moved by the intellect, otherwise than by itself. By the intellect it is moved on the part of the object: whereas it is moved by itself, as to the exercise of its act, in respect of the end.

Articulus 4

Ad quartum sic proceditur. Videtur quod voluntas non moveatur ab aliquo exteriori. Motus enim voluntatis est voluntarius. Sed de ratione voluntarii est quod sit a principio intrinseco, sicut et de ratione naturalis. Non ergo motus voluntatis est ab aliquo extrinseco.

Praeterea, voluntas violentiam pati non potest, ut supra ostensum est. Sed violentum est *cuius principium est extra.*

Article 4
Whether the will is moved by an exterior principle?

Objection 1: It would seem that the will is not moved by anything exterior. For the movement of the will is voluntary. But it is essential to the voluntary act that it be from an intrinsic principle, just as it is essential to the natural act. Therefore the movement of the will is not from anything exterior.

Objection 2: Further, the will cannot suffer violence, as was shown above (I-II, q. 6, a. 4). But the violent act is one "the principle of which is outside the agent."*

---

* Aristotle, Ethic. iii, 1

Ergo voluntas non potest ab aliquo exteriori moveri.

PRAETEREA, quod sufficienter movetur ab uno motore, non indiget moveri ab alio. Sed voluntas sufficienter movet seipsam. Non ergo movetur ab aliquo exteriori.

SED CONTRA, voluntas movetur ab obiecto, ut dictum est. Sed obiectum voluntatis potest esse aliqua exterior res sensui proposita. Ergo voluntas potest ab aliquo exteriori moveri.

RESPONDEO dicendum quod, secundum quod voluntas movetur ab obiecto, manifestum est quod moveri potest ab aliquo exteriori. Sed eo modo quo movetur quantum ad exercitium actus, adhuc necesse est ponere voluntatem ab aliquo principio exteriori moveri. Omne enim quod quandoque est agens in actu et quandoque in potentia, indiget moveri ab aliquo movente. Manifestum est autem quod voluntas incipit velle aliquid, cum hoc prius non vellet. Necesse est ergo quod ab aliquo moveatur ad volendum. Et quidem, sicut dictum est, ipsa movet seipsam, inquantum per hoc quod vult finem, reducit seipsam ad volendum ea quae sunt ad finem. Hoc autem non potest facere nisi consilio mediante, cum enim aliquis vult sanari, incipit cogitare quomodo hoc consequi possit, et per talem cogitationem pervenit ad hoc quod potest sanari per medicum, et hoc vult. Sed quia non semper sanitatem actu voluit, necesse est quod inciperet velle sanari, aliquo movente. Et si quidem ipsa moveret seipsam ad volendum, oportuisset quod mediante consilio hoc ageret, ex aliqua voluntate praesupposita. Hoc autem non est procedere in infinitum. Unde necesse est ponere quod in primum motum voluntatis voluntas prodeat ex instinctu alicuius exterioris moventis, ut Aristoteles concludit in quodam capitulo Ethicae Eudemicae.

AD PRIMUM ergo dicendum quod de ratione voluntarii est quod principium eius sit intra, sed non oportet quod hoc principium intrinsecum sit primum principium non motum ab alio. Unde motus voluntarius etsi habeat principium proximum intrinsecum, tamen principium primum est ab extra. Sicut

Therefore the will cannot be moved by anything exterior.

Objection 3: Further, that which is sufficiently moved by one mover, needs not to be moved by another. But the will moves itself sufficiently. Therefore it is not moved by anything exterior.

On the contrary, The will is moved by the object, as stated above (I-II, q. 9, a. 1). But the object of the will can be something exterior, offered to the sense. Therefore the will can be moved by something exterior.

I answer that, As far as the will is moved by the object, it is evident that it can be moved by something exterior. But in so far as it is moved in the exercise of its act, we must again hold it to be moved by some exterior principle. For everything that is at one time an agent actually, and at another time an agent in potentiality, needs to be moved by a mover. Now it is evident that the will begins to will something, whereas previously it did not will it. Therefore it must, of necessity, be moved by something to will it. And, indeed, it moves itself, as stated above (I-II, q. 9, a. 3), in so far as through willing the end it reduces itself to the act of willing the means. Now it cannot do this without the aid of counsel: for when a man wills to be healed, he begins to reflect how this can be attained, and through this reflection he comes to the conclusion that he can be healed by a physician: and this he wills. But since he did not always actually will to have health, he must, of necessity, have begun, through something moving him, to will to be healed. And if the will moved itself to will this, it must, of necessity, have done this with the aid of counsel following some previous volition. But this process could not go on to infinity. Wherefore we must, of necessity, suppose that the will advanced to its first movement in virtue of the instigation of some exterior mover, as Aristotle concludes in a chapter of the Eudemian Ethics (vii, 14).

Reply to Objection 1: It is essential to the voluntary act that its principle be within the agent: but it is not necessary that this inward principle be the first principle unmoved by another. Wherefore though the voluntary act has an inward proximate principle, nevertheless its first principle is from without. Thus,

et primum principium motus naturalis est ab extra, quod scilicet movet naturam.

Ad secundum dicendum quod hoc non sufficit ad rationem violenti, quod principium sit extra, sed oportet addere quod *nil conferat vim patiens*. Quod non contingit, dum voluntas ab exteriori movetur, nam ipsa est quae vult, ab alio tamen mota. Esset autem motus iste violentus, si esset contrarius motui voluntatis. Quod in proposito esse non potest, quia sic idem vellet et non vellet.

Ad tertium dicendum quod voluntas quantum ad aliquid sufficienter se movet, et in suo ordine, scilicet sicut agens proximum, sed non potest seipsam movere quantum ad omnia, ut ostensum est. Unde indiget moveri ab alio sicut a primo movente.

Articulus 5

Ad quintum sic proceditur. Videtur quod voluntas humana a corpore caelesti moveatur. Omnes enim motus varii et multiformes reducuntur, sicut in causam, in motum uniformem, qui est motus caeli ut probatur VIII Physic. Sed motus humani sunt varii et multiformes, incipientes postquam prius non fuerant. Ergo reducuntur in motum caeli sicut in causam, qui est uniformis secundum naturam.

Praeterea, secundum Augustinum, in III de Trin., *corpora inferiora moventur per corpora superiora*. Sed motus humani corporis, qui causantur a voluntate, non possent reduci in motum caeli sicut in causam, nisi etiam voluntas a caelo moveretur. Ergo caelum movet voluntatem humanam.

Praeterea, per observationem caelestium corporum astrologi quaedam vera praenuntiant de humanis actibus futuris, qui sunt a voluntate. Quod non esset, si corpora caelestia voluntatem hominis movere non possent. Movetur ergo voluntas humana a caelesti corpore.

too, the first principle of the natural movement is from without, that, to wit, which moves nature.

Reply to Objection 2: For an act to be violent it is not enough that its principle be extrinsic, but we must add "without the concurrence of him that suffers violence." This does not happen when the will is moved by an exterior principle: for it is the will that wills, though moved by another. But this movement would be violent, if it were counter to the movement of the will: which in the present case is impossible; since then the will would will and not will the same thing.

Reply to Objection 3: The will moves itself sufficiently in one respect, and in its own order, that is to say as proximate agent; but it cannot move itself in every respect, as we have shown. Wherefore it needs to be moved by another as first mover.

Article 5
Whether the will is moved by a heavenly body?

Objection 1: It would seem that the human will is moved by a heavenly body. For all various and multiform movements are reduced, as to their cause, to a uniform movement which is that of the heavens, as is proved in Phys. viii, 9. But human movements are various and multiform, since they begin to be, whereas previously they were not. Therefore they are reduced, as to their cause, to the movement of the heavens, which is uniform according to its nature.

Objection 2: Further, according to Augustine (De Trin. iii, 4) "the lower bodies are moved by the higher." But the movements of the human body, which are caused by the will, could not be reduced to the movement of the heavens, as to their cause, unless the will too were moved by the heavens. Therefore the heavens move the human will.

Objection 3: Further, by observing the heavenly bodies astrologers foretell the truth about future human acts, which are caused by the will. But this would not be so, if the heavenly bodies could not move man's will. Therefore the human will is moved by a heavenly body.

SED CONTRA est quod Damascenus dicit, in II libro, quod *corpora caelestia non sunt causae nostrorum actuum*. Essent autem, si voluntas, quae est humanorum actuum principium, a corporibus caelestibus moveretur. Non ergo movetur voluntas a corporibus caelestibus.

RESPONDEO dicendum quod eo modo quo voluntas movetur ab exteriori obiecto, manifestum est quod voluntas potest moveri a corporibus caelestibus, inquantum scilicet corpora exteriora, quae sensui proposita movent voluntatem, et etiam ipsa organa potentiarum sensitivarum, subiacent motibus caelestium corporum. Sed eo modo quo voluntas movetur, quantum ad exercitium actus, ab aliquo exteriori agente, adhuc quidam posuerunt corpora caelestia directe imprimere in voluntatem humanam. Sed hoc est impossibile. *Voluntas* enim, ut dicitur in III de anima, *est in ratione*. Ratio autem est potentia animae non alligata organo corporali. Unde relinquitur quod voluntas sit potentia omnino immaterialis et incorporea. Manifestum est autem quod nullum corpus agere potest in rem incorpoream, sed potius e converso, eo quod res incorporeae et immateriales sunt formalioris et universalioris virtutis quam quaecumque res corporales. Unde impossibile est quod corpus caeleste imprimat directe in intellectum aut voluntatem. Et propter hoc Aristoteles, in libro de anima, opinionem dicentium quod *talis est voluntas in hominibus, qualem in diem ducit pater deorum virorumque* (scilicet Iupiter, per quem totum caelum intelligunt), attribuit eis qui ponebant intellectum non differre a sensu. Omnes enim vires sensitivae, cum sint actus organorum corporalium, per accidens moveri possunt a caelestibus corporibus, motis scilicet corporibus quorum sunt actus. Sed quia dictum est quod appetitus intellectivus quodammodo movetur ab appetitu sensitivo, indirecte redundat motus caelestium corporum in voluntatem, inquantum scilicet per passiones appetitus sensitivi voluntatem moveri contingit.

On the contrary, Damascene says (De Fide Orth. ii, 7) that "the heavenly bodies are not the causes of our acts." But they would be, if the will, which is the principle of human acts, were moved by the heavenly bodies. Therefore the will is not moved by the heavenly bodies.

I answer that, It is evident that the will can be moved by the heavenly bodies in the same way as it is moved by its object; that is to say, in so far as exterior bodies, which move the will, through being offered to the senses, and also the organs themselves of the sensitive powers, are subject to the movements of the heavenly bodies. But some have maintained that heavenly bodies have an influence on the human will, in the same way as some exterior agent moves the will, as to the exercise of its act. But this is impossible. For the "will," as stated in De Anima iii, 9, "is in the reason." Now the reason is a power of the soul, not bound to a bodily organ: wherefore it follows that the will is a power absolutely incorporeal and immaterial. But it is evident that no body can act on what is incorporeal, but rather the reverse: because things incorporeal and immaterial have a power more formal and more universal than any corporeal things whatever. Therefore it is impossible for a heavenly body to act directly on the intellect or will. For this reason Aristotle (De Anima iii, 3) ascribed to those who held that intellect differs not from sense, the theory that "such is the will of men, as is the day which the father of men and of gods bring on"* (referring to Jupiter, by whom they understand the entire heavens). For all the sensitive powers, since they are acts of bodily organs, can be moved accidentally, by the heavenly bodies, i.e., through those bodies being moved, whose acts they are. But since it has been stated (I-II, q. 9, a. 2) that the intellectual appetite is moved, in a fashion, by the sensitive appetite, the movements of the heavenly bodies have an indirect bearing on the will; in so far as the will happens to be moved by the passions of the sensitive appetite.

---

* Odyssey xviii. 135

AD PRIMUM ergo dicendum quod multiformes motus voluntatis humanae reducuntur in aliquam causam uniformem, quae tamen est intellectu et voluntate superior. Quod non potest dici de aliquo corpore, sed de aliqua superiori substantia immateriali. Unde non oportet quod motus voluntatis in motum caeli reducatur sicut in causam.

AD SECUNDUM dicendum quod motus corporales humani reducuntur in motum **caelestis corporis sicut in causam,** inquantum ipsa dispositio organorum congrua ad motum, est aliqualiter ex impressione caelestium corporum; et inquantum etiam appetitus sensitivus commovetur ex impressione caelestium corporum; et ulterius inquantum corpora exteriora moventur secundum motum caelestium corporum, ex quorum occursu voluntas incipit aliquid velle vel non velle, sicut adveniente frigore incipit aliquis velle facere ignem. Sed ista motio voluntatis est ex parte obiecti exterius praesentati, non ex parte interioris instinctus.

AD TERTIUM dicendum quod, sicut dictum est, appetitus sensitivus est actus organi corporalis. Unde nihil prohibet ex impressione corporum caelestium aliquos esse habiles ad irascendum vel concupiscendum, vel aliquam huiusmodi passionem, sicut et ex complexione naturali. Plures autem hominum sequuntur passiones, quibus soli sapientes resistunt. Et ideo ut in pluribus verificantur ea quae praenuntiantur de actibus hominum secundum considerationem caelestium corporum. Sed tamen, ut Ptolomaeus dicit in Centiloquio, *sapiens dominatur astris,* scilicet quia, resistens passionibus, impedit per voluntatem liberam, et nequaquam motui caelesti subiectam, huiusmodi corporum caelestium effectus. Vel, ut Augustinus dicit II super Gen. ad Litt., *fatendum est, quando ab astrologis vera dicuntur, instinctu quodam occultissimo dici, quem nescientes humanae mentes patiuntur. Quod cum ad decipiendum homines fit, spirituum seductorum operatio est.*

Reply to Objection 1: The multiform movements of the human will are reduced to some uniform cause, which, however, is above the intellect and will. This can be said, not of any body, but of some superior immaterial substance. Therefore there is no need for the movement of the will to be referred to the movement of the heavens, as to its cause.

Reply to Objection 2: The movements of the human body are reduced, as to their cause, **to the movement of a heavenly body,** in so far as the disposition suitable to a particular movement, is somewhat due to the influence of heavenly bodies; also, in so far as the sensitive appetite is stirred by the influence of heavenly bodies; and again, in so far as exterior bodies are moved in accordance with the movement of heavenly bodies, at whose presence, the will begins to will or not to will something; for instance, when the body is chilled, we begin to wish to make the fire. But this movement of the will is on the part of the object offered from without: not on the part of an inward instigation.

Reply to Objection 3: As stated above (Cf. I, q. 84, a. 6; a. 7) the sensitive appetite is the act of a bodily organ. Wherefore there is no reason why man should not be prone to anger or concupiscence, or some like passion, by reason of the influence of heavenly bodies, just as by reason of his natural complexion. But the majority of men are led by the passions, which the wise alone resist. Consequently, in the majority of cases predictions about human acts, gathered from the observation of heavenly bodies, are fulfilled. Nevertheless, as Ptolemy says (Centiloquium v), "the wise man governs the stars"; which is a though to say that by resisting his passions, he opposes his will, which is free and nowise subject to the movement of the heavens, to such like effects of the heavenly bodies. Or, as Augustine says (Gen. ad lit. ii, 15): "We must confess that when the truth is foretold by astrologers, this is due to some most hidden inspiration, to which the human mind is subject without knowing it. And since this is done in order to deceive man, it must be the work of the lying spirits."

Articulus 6

Ad sextum sic proceditur. Videtur quod voluntas non a solo Deo moveatur sicut ab exteriori principio. Inferius enim natum est moveri a suo superiori, sicut corpora inferiora a corporibus caelestibus. Sed voluntas hominis habet aliquid superius post Deum; scilicet angelum. Ergo voluntas hominis potest moveri, sicut ab exteriori principio, etiam ab angelo.

Praeterea, actus voluntatis sequitur actum intellectus. Sed intellectus hominis reducitur in suum actum non solum a Deo, sed etiam ab angelo per illuminationes, ut Dionysius dicit. Ergo eadem ratione et voluntas.

Praeterea, Deus non est causa nisi bonorum; secundum illud Gen. I, *vidit Deus cuncta quae fecerat, et erant valde bona*. Si ergo a solo Deo voluntas hominis moveretur, nunquam moveretur ad malum, cum tamen voluntas sit qua *peccatur et recte vivitur,* ut Augustinus dicit.

Sed contra est quod apostolus dicit, ad Philipp. II, *Deus est qui operatur in nobis velle et perficere.*

Respondeo dicendum quod motus voluntatis est ab intrinseco, sicut et motus naturalis. Quamvis autem rem naturalem possit aliquid movere quod non est causa naturae rei motae, tamen motum naturalem causare non potest nisi quod est aliqualiter causa naturae. Movetur enim lapis sursum ab homine, qui naturam lapidis non causat, sed hic motus non est lapidi naturalis, naturalis autem motus eius non causatur nisi ab eo quod causat naturam. Unde dicitur in VIII Physic. quod generans movet secundum locum gravia et levia. Sic ergo hominem, voluntatem habentem, contingit moveri ab aliquo qui non est causa eius, sed quod motus voluntarius eius sit ab aliquo principio extrinseco quod non est causa voluntatis, est impossibile.

Article 6
Whether the will is moved by God alone, as exterior principle?

Objection 1: It would seem that the will is not moved by God alone as exterior principle. For it is natural that the inferior be moved by its superior: thus the lower bodies are moved by the heavenly bodies. But there is something which is higher than the will of man and below God, namely, the angel. Therefore man's will can be moved by an angel also, as exterior principle.

Objection 2: Further, the act of the will follows the act of the intellect. But man's intellect is reduced to act, not by God alone, but also by the angel who enlightens it, as Dionysius says (Coel. Hier. iv). For the same reason, therefore, the will also is moved by an angel.

Objection 3: Further, God is not the cause of other than good things, according to Gn. 1:31: "God saw all the things that He had made, and they were very good." If, therefore man's will were moved by God alone, it would never be moved to evil: and yet it is the will whereby "we sin and whereby we do right," as Augustine says (Retract. i, 9).

On the contrary, It is written (Phil. 2:13): "It is God Who worketh in us[*] both to will and to accomplish."

I answer that, The movement of the will is from within, as also is the movement of nature. Now although it is possible for something to move a natural thing, without being the cause of the thing moved, yet that alone, which is in some way the cause of a thing's nature, can cause a natural movement in that thing. For a stone is moved upwards by a man, who is not the cause of the stone's nature, but this movement is not natural to the stone; but the natural movement of the stone is caused by no other than the cause of its nature. Wherefore it is said in Phys. vii, 4, that the generator moves locally heavy and light things. Accordingly man endowed with a will is sometimes moved by something that is not his cause; but that his voluntary movement be from an exterior principle that is not the cause of his will, is impossible.

---

[*] Vulg. "you"

I-II, q. 9, a. 6, co.

Voluntatis autem causa nihil aliud esse potest quam Deus. Et hoc patet dupliciter. Primo quidem, ex hoc quod voluntas est potentia animae rationalis, quae a solo Deo causatur per creationem, ut in primo dictum est. Secundo vero ex hoc patet, quod voluntas habet ordinem ad universale bonum. Unde nihil aliud potest esse voluntatis causa, nisi ipse Deus, qui est universale bonum. Omne autem aliud bonum per participationem dicitur, et est quoddam particulare bonum, particularis autem causa non dat inclinationem universalem. Unde nec materia prima, quae est in potentia ad omnes formas, potest causari ab aliquo particulari agente.

AD PRIMUM ergo dicendum quod angelus non sic est supra hominem, quod sit causa voluntatis eius; sicut corpora caelestia sunt causa formarum naturalium, ad quas consequuntur naturales motus corporum naturalium.

AD SECUNDUM dicendum quod intellectus hominis movetur ab angelo ex parte obiecti, quod sibi proponitur virtute angelici luminis ad cognoscendum. Et sic etiam voluntas ab exteriori creatura potest moveri, ut dictum est.

AD TERTIUM dicendum quod Deus movet voluntatem hominis, sicut universalis motor, ad universale obiectum voluntatis, quod est bonum. Et sine hac universali motione homo non potest aliquid velle. Sed homo per rationem determinat se ad volendum hoc vel illud, quod est vere bonum vel apparens bonum. Sed tamen interdum specialiter Deus movet aliquos ad aliquid determinate volendum, quod est bonum, sicut in his quos movet per gratiam, ut infra dicetur.

THAT WHICH MOVES THE WILL

Now the cause of the will can be none other than God. And this is evident for two reasons. First, because the will is a power of the rational soul, which is caused by God alone, by creation, as was stated in the I, q. 90, a. 2. Secondly, it is evident from the fact that the will is ordained to the universal good. Wherefore nothing else can be the cause of the will, except God Himself, Who is the universal good: while every other good is good by participation, and is some particular good, and a particular cause does not give a universal inclination. Hence neither can primary matter, which is potentiality to all forms, be created by some particular agent.

Reply to Objection 1: An angel is not above man in such a way as to be the cause of his will, as the heavenly bodies are the causes of natural forms, from which result the natural movements of natural bodies.

Reply to Objection 2: Man's intellect is moved by an angel, on the part of the object, which by the power of the angelic light is proposed to man's knowledge. And in this way the will also can be moved by a creature from without, as stated above (I-II, q. 9, a. 4).

Reply to Objection 3: God moves man's will, as the Universal Mover, to the universal object of the will, which is good. And without this universal motion, man cannot will anything. But man determines himself by his reason to will this or that, which is true or apparent good. Nevertheless, sometimes God moves some specially to the willing of something determinate, which is good; as in the case of those whom He moves by grace, as we shall state later on (I-II, q. 109, a. 2).

Quaestio X

Deinde considerandum est de modo quo voluntas movetur. Et circa hoc quaeruntur quatuor. *Primo,* utrum voluntas ad aliquid naturaliter moveatur. *Secundo,* utrum de necessitate moveatur a suo obiecto. *Tertio,* utrum de necessitate moveatur ab appetitu inferiori. *Quarto,* utrum de necessitate moveatur ab exteriori motivo quod est Deus.

Articulus 1

Ad primum sic proceditur. Videtur quod voluntas non moveatur ad aliquid naturaliter. Agens enim naturale dividitur contra agens voluntarium, ut patet in principio II Physic. Non ergo voluntas ad aliquid naturaliter movetur.

Praeterea, id quod est naturale, inest alicui semper; sicut igni *esse calidum.* Sed nullus motus inest voluntati semper. Ergo nullus motus est naturalis voluntati.

Praeterea, natura est determinata ad unum. Sed voluntas se habet ad opposita. Ergo voluntas nihil naturaliter vult.

Sed contra est quod motus voluntatis sequitur actum intellectus. Sed intellectus aliqua intelligit naturaliter. Ergo et voluntas aliqua vult naturaliter.

Respondeo dicendum quod, sicut Boetius dicit in libro de duabus naturis, et philosophus in V Metaphys., *natura* dicitur multipliciter. Quandoque enim dicitur principium intrinsecum in rebus mobilibus. Et talis natura est vel materia, vel forma materialis, ut patet ex II Physic. Alio modo dicitur natura quaelibet substantia, vel etiam quodlibet ens. Et secundum hoc, illud dicitur esse naturale rei, quod convenit ei secundum suam substantiam. Et hoc est quod per se inest rei. In omnibus autem, ea quae non per se insunt, reducuntur in aliquid quod per se inest, sicut in principium. Et ideo necesse est quod, hoc modo accipiendo naturam, semper principium in his quae conveniunt rei, sit

Question 10
Of the Manner in Which the Will Is Moved

We must now consider the manner in which the will is moved. Under this head there are four points of inquiry: 1. Whether the will is moved to anything naturally? 2. Whether it is moved of necessity by its object? 3. Whether it is moved of necessity by the lower appetite? 4. Whether it is moved of necessity by the exterior mover which is God?

Article 1
Whether the will is moved to anything naturally?

Objection 1: It would seem that the will is not moved to anything naturally. For the natural agent is condivided with the voluntary agent, as stated at the beginning of Phys. ii, 1. Therefore the will is not moved to anything naturally.

Objection 2: Further, that which is natural is in a thing always: as "being hot" is in fire. But no movement is always in the will. Therefore no movement is natural to the will.

Objection 3: Further, nature is determinate to one thing: whereas the will is referred to opposites. Therefore the will wills nothing naturally.

On the contrary, The movement of the will follows the movement of the intellect. But the intellect understands some things naturally. Therefore the will, too, wills some things naturally.

I answer that, As Boethius says (De Duabus Nat.) and the Philosopher also (Metaph. v, 4) the word "nature" is used in a manifold sense. For sometimes it stands for the intrinsic principle in movable things. In this sense nature is either matter or the material form, as stated in Phys. ii, 1. In another sense nature stands for any substance, or even for any being. And in this sense, that is said to be natural to a thing which befits it in respect of its substance. And this is that which of itself is in a thing. Now all things that do not of themselves belong to the thing in which they are, are reduced to something which belongs of itself to that thing, as to their principle. Wherefore, taking nature in this sense, it is necessary that the principle of whatever belongs to a thing, be

naturale. Et hoc manifeste apparet in intellectu, nam principia intellectualis cognitionis sunt naturaliter nota. Similiter etiam principium motuum voluntariorum oportet esse aliquid naturaliter volitum. Hoc autem est bonum in communi, in quod voluntas naturaliter tendit, sicut etiam quaelibet potentia in suum obiectum, et etiam ipse finis ultimus, qui hoc modo se habet in appetibilibus, sicut prima principia demonstrationum in intelligibilibus, et universaliter omnia illa quae conveniunt volenti secundum suam naturam. Non enim per voluntatem appetimus solum ea quae pertinent ad potentiam voluntatis; sed etiam ea quae pertinent ad singulas potentias, et ad totum hominem. Unde naturaliter homo vult non solum obiectum voluntatis, sed etiam alia quae conveniunt aliis potentiis, ut cognitionem veri, quae convenit intellectui; et esse et vivere et alia huiusmodi, quae respiciunt consistentiam naturalem; quae omnia comprehenduntur sub obiecto voluntatis, sicut quadam particularia bona.

AD PRIMUM ergo dicendum quod voluntas dividitur contra naturam, sicut una causa contra aliam, quaedam enim fiunt naturaliter, et quaedam fiunt voluntarie. Est autem alius modus causandi proprius voluntati, quae est domina sui actus, praeter modum qui convenit naturae, quae est determinata ad unum. Sed quia voluntas in aliqua natura fundatur, necesse est quod motus proprius naturae, quantum ad aliquid, participetur in voluntate, sicut quod est prioris causae, participatur a posteriori. Est enim prius in unaquaque re ipsum esse, quod est per naturam, quam velle, quod est per voluntatem. Et inde est quod voluntas naturaliter aliquid vult.

AD SECUNDUM dicendum quod in rebus naturalibus id quod est naturale quasi consequens formam tantum, semper actu inest, sicut calidum igni. Quod autem est naturale sicut consequens materiam, non semper actu inest, sed quandoque secundum potentiam tantum. Nam forma est actus, materia vero potentia. Motus autem est *actus existentis in potentia*. Et ideo illa quae pertinent ad motum, vel quae consequuntur motum, in rebus naturalibus,

a natural principle. This is evident in regard to the intellect: for the principles of intellectual knowledge are naturally known. In like manner the principle of voluntary movements must be something naturally willed. Now this is good in general, to which the will tends naturally, as does each power to its object; and again it is the last end, which stands in the same relation to things appetible, as the first principles of demonstrations to things intelligible: and, speaking generally, it is all those things which belong to the willer according to his nature. For it is not only things pertaining to the will that the will desires, but also that which pertains to each power, and to the entire man. Wherefore man wills naturally not only the object of the will, but also other things that are appropriate to the other powers; such as the knowledge of truth, which befits the intellect; and to be and to live and other like things which regard the natural well-being; all of which are included in the object of the will, as so many particular goods.

Reply to Objection 1: The will is distinguished from nature as one kind of cause from another; for some things happen naturally and some are done voluntarily. There is, however, another manner of causing that is proper to the will, which is mistress of its act, besides the manner proper to nature, which is determinate to one thing. But since the will is founded on some nature, it is necessary that the movement proper to nature be shared by the will, to some extent: just as what belongs to a previous cause is shared by a subsequent cause. Because in every thing, being itself, which is from nature, precedes volition, which is from the will. And hence it is that the will wills something naturally.

Reply to Objection 2: In the case of natural things, that which is natural, as a result of the form only, is always in them actually, as heat is in fire. But that which is natural as a result of matter, is not always in them actually, but sometimes only in potentiality: because form is act, whereas matter is potentiality. Now movement is "the act of that which is in potentiality" (Aristotle, Phys. iii, 1). Wherefore that which belongs to, or results from, movement, in regard to natural things,

non semper insunt, sicut ignis non semper movetur sursum, sed quando est extra locum suum. Et similiter non oportet quod voluntas, quae de potentia in actum reducitur dum aliquid vult, semper actu velit, sed solum quando est in aliqua dispositione determinata. Voluntas autem Dei, quae est actus purus, semper est in actu volendi.

Ad tertium dicendum quod naturae semper respondet unum, proportionatum tamen naturae. Naturae enim in genere, respondet aliquid unum in genere; et naturae in specie acceptae, respondet unum in specie; naturae autem individuatae respondet aliquid unum individuale. Cum igitur voluntas sit quaedam vis immaterialis sicut et intellectus, respondet sibi naturaliter aliquod unum commune, scilicet bonum, sicut etiam intellectui aliquod unum commune, scilicet verum, vel ens, vel *quod quid est*. Sub bono autem communi multa particularia bona continentur, ad quorum nullum voluntas determinatur.

is not always in them. Thus fire does not always move upwards, but only when it is outside its own place.* And in like manner it is not necessary that the will (which is reduced from potentiality to act, when it wills something), should always be in the act of volition; but only when it is in a certain determinate disposition. But God's will, which is pure act, is always in the act of volition.

Reply to Objection 3: To every nature there is one thing corresponding, proportionate, however, to that nature. For to nature considered as a genus, there corresponds something one generically; and to nature as species there corresponds something one specifically; and to the individualized nature there corresponds some one individual. Since, therefore, the will is an immaterial power like the intellect, some one general thing corresponds to it, naturally which is the good; just as to the intellect there corresponds some one general thing, which is the true, or being, or "what a thing is." And under good in general are included many particular goods, to none of which is the will determined.

Articulus 2

Ad secundum sic proceditur. Videtur quod voluntas de necessitate moveatur a suo obiecto. Obiectum enim voluntatis comparatur ad ipsam sicut motivum ad mobile, ut patet in III de anima. Sed motivum, si sit sufficiens, ex necessitate movet mobile. Ergo voluntas ex necessitate potest moveri a suo obiecto.

Praeterea, sicut voluntas est vis immaterialis, ita et intellectus, et utraque potentia ad obiectum universale ordinatur, ut dictum est. Sed intellectus ex necessitate movetur a suo obiecto. Ergo et voluntas a suo.

Praeterea, omne quod quis vult, aut est finis, aut aliquid ordinatum ad finem. Sed finem aliquis ex necessitate vult, ut videtur, quia est sicut principium in speculativis, cui

Article 2
Whether the will is moved, of necessity, by its object?

Objection 1: It seems that the will is moved, of necessity, by its object. For the object of the will is compared to the will as mover to movable, as stated in De Anima iii, 10. But a mover, if it be sufficient, moves the movable of necessity. Therefore the will can be moved of necessity by its object.

Objection 2: Further, just as the will is an immaterial power, so is the intellect: and both powers are ordained to a universal object, as stated above (I-II, q. 10, a. 1, ad 3). But the intellect is moved, of necessity, by its object: therefore the will also, by its object.

Objection 3: Further, whatever one wills, is either the end, or something ordained to an end. But, seemingly, one wills an end necessarily: because it is like the principle in speculative matters, to which principle

---

* The Aristotelian theory was that fire's proper place is the fiery heaven, i.e., the Empyrean.

ex necessitate assentimus. Finis autem est ratio volendi ea quae sunt ad finem, et sic videtur quod etiam ea quae sunt ad finem, ex necessitate velimus. Voluntas ergo ex necessitate movetur a suo obiecto.

SED CONTRA est quod potentiae rationales, secundum philosophum, sunt ad opposita. Sed voluntas est potentia rationalis, est enim in ratione, ut dicitur in III de anima. Ergo voluntas se habet ad opposita. Non ergo ex necessitate movetur ad alterum oppositorum.

RESPONDEO dicendum quod voluntas movetur dupliciter, uno modo, quantum ad exercitium actus; alio modo, quantum ad specificationem actus, quae est ex obiecto. Primo ergo modo, voluntas a nullo obiecto ex necessitate movetur, potest enim aliquis de quocumque obiecto non cogitare, et per consequens neque actu velle illud. Sed quantum AD SECUNDUM motionis modum, voluntas ab aliquo obiecto ex necessitate movetur, ab aliquo autem non. In motu enim cuiuslibet potentiae a suo obiecto, consideranda est ratio per quam obiectum movet potentiam. Visibile enim movet visum sub ratione coloris actu visibilis. Unde si color proponatur visui, ex necessitate movet visum, nisi aliquis visum avertat, quod pertinet ad exercitium actus. Si autem proponeretur aliquid visui quod non omnibus modis esset color in actu, sed secundum aliquid esset tale, secundum autem aliquid non tale, non ex necessitate visus tale obiectum videret, posset enim intendere in ipsum ex ea parte qua non est coloratum in actu, et sic ipsum non videret. Sicut autem coloratum in actu est obiectum visus, ita bonum est obiectum voluntatis. Unde si proponatur aliquod obiectum voluntati quod sit universaliter bonum et secundum omnem considerationem, ex necessitate voluntas in illud tendet, si aliquid velit, non enim poterit velle oppositum. Si autem proponatur sibi aliquod obiectum quod non secundum quamlibet considerationem sit bonum, non ex necessitate voluntas feretur in illud. Et quia defectus cuiuscumque boni habet rationem non boni, ideo illud solum bonum quod est perfectum et cui nihil deficit, est tale bonum quod voluntas non potest non velle, quod est beatitudo.

one assents of necessity. Now the end is the reason for willing the means; and so it seems that we will the means also necessarily. Therefore the will is moved of necessity by its object.

On the contrary, The rational powers, according to the Philosopher (Metaph. ix, 2) are directed to opposites. But the will is a rational power, since it is in the reason, as stated in De Anima iii, 9. Therefore the will is directed to opposites. Therefore it is not moved, of necessity, to either of the opposites.

I answer that, The will is moved in two ways: first, as to the exercise of its act; secondly, as to the specification of its act, derived from the object. As to the first way, no object moves the will necessarily, for no matter what the object be, it is in man's power not to think of it, and consequently not to will it actually. But as to the second manner of motion, the will is moved by one object necessarily, by another not. For in the movement of a power by its object, we must consider under what aspect the object moves the power. For the visible moves the sight, under the aspect of color actually visible. Wherefore if color be offered to the sight, it moves the sight necessarily: unless one turns one's eyes away; which belongs to the exercise of the act. But if the sight were confronted with something not in all respects colored actually, but only so in some respects, and in other respects not, the sight would not of necessity see such an object: for it might look at that part of the object which is not actually colored, and thus it would not see it. Now just as the actually colored is the object of sight, so is good the object of the will. Wherefore if the will be offered an object which is good universally and from every point of view, the will tends to it of necessity, if it wills anything at all; since it cannot will the opposite. If, on the other hand, the will is offered an object that is not good from every point of view, it will not tend to it of necessity. And since lack of any good whatever, is a non-good, consequently, that good alone which is perfect and lacking in nothing, is such a good that the will cannot not-will it: and this is Happiness.

Alia autem quaelibet particularia bona, inquantum deficiunt ab aliquo bono, possunt accipi ut non bona, et secundum hanc considerationem, possunt repudiari vel approbari a voluntate, quae potest in idem ferri secundum diversas considerationes.

AD PRIMUM ergo dicendum quod sufficiens motivum alicuius potentiae non est nisi obiectum quod totaliter habet rationem motivi. Si autem in aliquo deficiat, non ex necessitate movebit, ut dictum est.

AD SECUNDUM dicendum quod intellectus ex necessitate movetur a tali obiecto quod est semper et ex necessitate verum, non autem ab eo quod potest esse verum et falsum, scilicet a contingenti, sicut et de bono dictum est.

AD TERTIUM dicendum quod finis ultimus ex necessitate movet voluntatem, quia est bonum perfectum. Et similiter illa quae ordinantur ad hunc finem, sine quibus finis haberi non potest, sicut *esse* et *vivere* et huiusmodi. Alia vero, sine quibus finis haberi potest, non ex necessitate vult qui vult finem, sicut conclusiones sine quibus principia possunt esse vera, non ex necessitate credit qui credit principia.

Whereas any other particular goods, in so far as they are lacking in some good, can be regarded as non-goods: and from this point of view, they can be set aside or approved by the will, which can tend to one and the same thing from various points of view.

Reply to Objection 1: The sufficient mover of a power is none but that object that in every respect presents the aspect of the mover of that power. If, on the other hand, it is lacking in any respect, it will not move of necessity, as stated above.

Reply to Objection 2: The intellect is moved, of necessity, by an object which is such as to be always and necessarily true: but not by that which may be either true or false—*viz.* by that which is contingent: as we have said of the good.

Reply to Objection 3: The last end moves the will necessarily, because it is the perfect good. In like manner whatever is ordained to that end, and without which the end cannot be attained, such as "to be" and "to live," and the like. But other things without which the end can be gained, are not necessarily willed by one who wills the end: just as he who assents to the principle, does not necessarily assent to the conclusions, without which the principles can still be true.

ARTICULUS 3

AD TERTIUM sic proceditur. Videtur quod voluntas ex necessitate moveatur a passione appetitus inferioris. Dicit enim apostolus, Rom. VII, *non enim quod volo bonum, hoc ago; sed quod odi malum, illud facio,* quod dicitur propter concupiscentiam, quae est passio quaedam. Ergo voluntas ex necessitate movetur a passione.

PRAETEREA, sicut dicitur in III Ethic., *qualis unusquisque est, talis finis videtur ei.* Sed non est in potestate voluntatis quod statim passionem abiiciat. Ergo non est in potestate voluntatis quod non velit illud ad quod passio se inclinat.

PRAETEREA, causa universalis non applicatur ad effectum particularem nisi mediante causa particulari, unde et ratio universalis non movet nisi

ARTICLE 3
Whether the will is moved, of necessity, by the lower appetite?

Objection 1: It would seem that the will is moved of necessity by a passion of the lower appetite. For the Apostle says (Rom. 7:19): "The good which I will I do not; but the evil which I will not, that I do": and this is said by reason of concupiscence, which is a passion. Therefore the will is moved of necessity by a passion.

Objection 2: Further, as stated in Ethic. iii, 5, "according as a man is, such does the end seem to him." But it is not in man's power to cast aside a passion once. Therefore it is not in man's power not to will that to which the passion inclines him.

Objection 3: Further, a universal cause is not applied to a particular effect, except by means of a particular cause: wherefore the universal reason does not move save by

mediante aestimatione particulari, ut dicitur in III de anima. Sed sicut se habet ratio universalis ad aestimationem particularem, ita se habet voluntas ad appetitum sensitivum. Ergo ad aliquod particulare volendum non movetur voluntas nisi mediante appetitu sensitivo. Ergo si appetitus sensitivus sit per aliquam passionem ad aliquid dispositus, voluntas non poterit in contrarium moveri.

Sed contra est quod dicitur Gen. IV, *subter te erit appetitus tuus, et tu dominaberis illius.* Non ergo voluntas hominis ex necessitate movetur ab appetitu inferiori.

Respondeo dicendum quod, sicut supra dictum est, passio appetitus sensitivi movet voluntatem ex ea parte qua voluntas movetur ab obiecto, inquantum scilicet homo aliqualiter dispositus per passionem, iudicat aliquid esse conveniens et bonum quod extra passionem existens non iudicaret. Huiusmodi autem immutatio hominis per passionem duobus modis contingit. Uno modo, sic quod totaliter ratio ligatur, ita quod homo usum rationis non habet, sicut contingit in his qui propter vehementem iram vel concupiscentiam furiosi vel amentes fiunt, sicut et propter aliquam aliam perturbationem corporalem; huiusmodi enim passiones non sine corporali transmutatione accidunt. Et de talibus eadem est ratio sicut et de animalibus brutis, quae ex necessitate sequuntur impetum passionis, in his enim non est aliquis rationis motus, et per consequens nec voluntatis. Aliquando autem ratio non totaliter absorbetur a passione, sed remanet quantum ad aliquid iudicium rationis liberum. Et secundum hoc remanet aliquid de motu voluntatis. Inquantum ergo ratio manet libera et passioni non subiecta, intantum voluntatis motus qui manet, non ex necessitate tendit ad hoc ad quod passio inclinat. Et sic aut motus voluntatis non est in homine, sed sola passio dominatur, aut, si motus voluntatis sit, non ex necessitate sequitur passionem.

means of a particular estimation, as stated in De Anima iii, 11. But as the universal reason is to the particular estimation, so is the will to the sensitive appetite. Therefore the will is not moved to will something particular, except through the sensitive appetite. Therefore, if the sensitive appetite happen to be disposed to something, by reason of a passion, the will cannot be moved in a contrary sense.

On the contrary, It is written (Gn. 4:7): "Thy lust* shall be under thee, and thou shalt have dominion over it." Therefore man's will is not moved of necessity by the lower appetite.

I answer that, As stated above (I-II, q. 9, a. 2), the passion of the sensitive appetite moves the will, in so far as the will is moved by its object: inasmuch as, to wit, man through being disposed in such and such a way by a passion, judges something to be fitting and good, which he would not judge thus were it not for the passion. Now this influence of a passion on man occurs in two ways. First, so that his reason is wholly bound, so that he has not the use of reason: as happens in those who through a violent access of anger or concupiscence become furious or insane, just as they may from some other bodily disorder; since such like passions do not take place without some change in the body. And of such the same is to be said as of irrational animals, which follow, of necessity, the impulse of their passions: for in them there is neither movement of reason, nor, consequently, of will. Sometimes, however, the reason is not entirely engrossed by the passion, so that the judgment of reason retains, to a certain extent, its freedom: and thus the movement of the will remains in a certain degree. Accordingly in so far as the reason remains free, and not subject to the passion, the will's movement, which also remains, does not tend of necessity to that whereto the passion inclines it. Consequently, either there is no movement of the will in that man, and the passion alone holds its sway: or if there be a movement of the will, it does not necessarily follow the passion.

---

* Vulg. 'The lust thereof'

AD PRIMUM ergo dicendum quod, etsi voluntas non possit facere quin motus concupiscentiae insurgat, de quo apostolus dicit Rom. VII, *quod odi malum, illud facio,* idest concupisco; tamen potest voluntas non velle concupiscere, aut concupiscentiae non consentire. Et sic non ex necessitate sequitur concupiscentiae motum.

AD SECUNDUM dicendum quod, cum in homine duae sint naturae, intellectualis scilicet et sensitiva, quandoque quidem est homo aliqualis uniformiter secundum totam animam, quia scilicet vel pars sensitiva totaliter subiicitur rationi, sicut contingit in virtuosis; vel e converso ratio totaliter absorbetur a passione sicut accidit in amentibus. Sed aliquando, etsi ratio obnubiletur a passione, remanet tamen aliquid rationis liberum. Et secundum hoc potest aliquis vel totaliter passionem repellere; vel saltem se tenere ne passionem sequatur. In tali enim dispositione, quia homo secundum diversas partes animae diversimode disponitur, aliud ei videtur secundum rationem, et aliud secundum passionem.

AD TERTIUM dicendum quod voluntas non solum movetur a bono universali apprehenso per rationem, sed etiam a bono apprehenso per sensum. Et ideo potest moveri ad aliquod particulare bonum absque passione appetitus sensitivi. Multa enim volumus et operamur absque passione, per solam electionem, ut maxime patet in his in quibus ratio renititur passioni.

ARTICULUS 4

AD QUARTUM sic proceditur. Videtur quod voluntas ex necessitate moveatur a Deo. Omne enim agens cui resisti non potest, ex necessitate movet. Sed Deo, cum sit infinitae virtutis, resisti non potest, unde dicitur Rom. IX, *voluntati eius quis resistit?* Ergo Deus ex necessitate movet voluntatem.

PRAETEREA, voluntas ex necessitate movetur in illa quae naturaliter vult, ut dictum est. Sed *hoc est unicuique rei naturale, quod Deus in ea operatur,* ut Augustinus dicit, XXVI

Reply to Objection 1: Although the will cannot prevent the movement of concupiscence from arising, of which the Apostle says: "The evil which I will not, that I do"—i.e., I desire; yet it is in the power of the will not to will to desire or not to consent to concupiscence. And thus it does not necessarily follow the movement of concupiscence.

Reply to Objection 2: Since there is in man a twofold nature, intellectual and sensitive; sometimes man is such and such uniformly in respect of his whole soul: either because the sensitive part is wholly subject to this reason, as in the virtuous; or because reason is entirely engrossed by passion, as in a madman. But sometimes, although reason is clouded by passion, yet something of this reason remains free. And in respect of this, man can either repel the passion entirely, or at least hold himself in check so as not to be led away by the passion. For when thus disposed, since man is variously disposed according to the various parts of the soul, a thing appears to him otherwise according to his reason, than it does according to a passion.

Reply to Objection 3: The will is moved not only by the universal good apprehended by the reason, but also by good apprehended by sense. Wherefore he can be moved to some particular good independently of a passion of the sensitive appetite. For we will and do many things without passion, and through choice alone; as is most evident in those cases wherein reason resists passion.

ARTICLE 4
Whether the will is moved of necessity by the exterior mover which is God?

Objection 1: It would seem that the will is moved of necessity by God. For every agent that cannot be resisted moves of necessity. But God cannot be resisted, because His power is infinite; wherefore it is written (Rom. 9:19): "Who resisteth His will?" Therefore God moves the will of necessity.

Objection 2: Further, the will is moved of necessity to whatever it wills naturally, as stated above (I-II, q. 10, a. 2, ad 3). But "whatever God does in a thing is natural to it," as Augustine says (Contra Faust. xxvi, 3).

contra Faustum. Ergo voluntas ex necessitate vult omne illud ad quod a Deo movetur.

Praeterea, possibile est quo posito non sequitur impossibile. Sequitur autem impossibile, si ponatur quod voluntas non velit hoc ad quod Deus eam movet, quia secundum hoc, operatio Dei esset inefficax. Non ergo est possibile voluntatem non velle hoc ad quod Deus eam movet. Ergo necesse est eam hoc velle.

Sed contra est quod dicitur Eccli. XV, *Deus ab initio constituit hominem, et reliquit eum in manu consilii sui.* Non ergo ex necessitate movet voluntatem eius.

Respondeo dicendum quod, sicut Dionysius dicit, IV cap. de Div. Nom., *ad providentiam divinam non pertinet naturam rerum corrumpere, sed servare.* Unde omnia movet secundum eorum conditionem, ita quod ex causis necessariis per motionem divinam consequuntur effectus ex necessitate; ex causis autem contingentibus sequuntur effectus contingenter. Quia igitur voluntas est activum principium non determinatum ad unum, sed indifferenter se habens ad multa, sic Deus ipsam movet, quod non ex necessitate ad unum determinat, sed remanet motus eius contingens et non necessarius, nisi in his ad quae naturaliter movetur.

Ad primum ergo dicendum quod voluntas divina non solum se extendit ut aliquid fiat per rem quam movet, sed ut etiam eo modo fiat quo congruit naturae ipsius. Et ideo magis repugnaret divinae motioni, si voluntas ex necessitate moveretur, quod suae naturae non competit; quam si moveretur libere, prout competit suae naturae.

Ad secundum dicendum quod naturale est unicuique quod Deus operatur in ipso ut sit ei naturale, sic enim unicuique convenit aliquid, secundum quod Deus vult quod ei conveniat. Non autem vult quod quidquid operatur in rebus, sit eis naturale, puta quod mortui resurgant. Sed hoc vult unicuique esse naturale, quod potestati divinae subdatur.

Therefore the will wills of necessity everything to which God moves it.

Objection 3: Further, a thing is possible, if nothing impossible follows from its being supposed. But something impossible follows from the supposition that the will does not will that to which God moves it: because in that case God's operation would be ineffectual. Therefore it is not possible for the will not to will that to which God moves it. Therefore it wills it of necessity.

On the contrary, It is written (Ecclus. 15:14): "God made man from the beginning, and left him in the hand of his own counsel." Therefore He does not of necessity move man's will.

I answer that, As Dionysius says (Div. Nom. iv) "it belongs to Divine providence, not to destroy but to preserve the nature of things." Wherefore it moves all things in accordance with their conditions; so that from necessary causes through the Divine motion, effects follow of necessity; but from contingent causes, effects follow contingently. Since, therefore, the will is an active principle, not determinate to one thing, but having an indifferent relation to many things, God so moves it, that He does not determine it of necessity to one thing, but its movement remains contingent and not necessary, except in those things to which it is moved naturally.

Reply to Objection 1: The Divine will extends not only to the doing of something by the thing which He moves, but also to its being done in a way which is fitting to the nature of that thing. And therefore it would be more repugnant to the Divine motion, for the will to be moved of necessity, which is not fitting to its nature; than for it to be moved freely, which is becoming to its nature.

Reply to Objection 2: That is natural to a thing, which God so works in it that it may be natural to it: for thus is something becoming to a thing, according as God wishes it to be becoming. Now He does not wish that whatever He works in things should be natural to them, for instance, that the dead should rise again. But this He does wish to be natural to each thing—that it be subject to the Divine power.

AD TERTIUM dicendum quod, si Deus movet voluntatem ad aliquid, incompossibile est huic positioni quod voluntas ad illud non moveatur. Non tamen est impossibile simpliciter. Unde non sequitur quod voluntas a Deo ex necessitate moveatur.

Reply to Objection 3: If God moves the will to anything, it is incompatible with this supposition, that the will be not moved thereto. But it is not impossible simply. Consequently it does not follow that the will is moved by God necessarily.

Quaestio XI

Deinde considerandum est de fruitione. Et circa hoc quaeruntur quatuor. *Primo*, utrum frui sit actus appetitivae potentiae. *Secundo*, utrum soli rationali creaturae conveniat, an etiam animalibus brutis. *Tertio*, utrum fruitio sit tantum ultimi finis. *Quarto*, utrum sit solum finis habiti.

Question 11
Of Enjoyment,* Which Is an Act of the Will

We must now consider enjoyment: concerning which there are four points of inquiry:
1. Whether to enjoy is an act of the appetitive power? 2. Whether it belongs to the rational creature alone, or also to irrational animals? 3. Whether enjoyment is only of the last end? 4. Whether it is only of the end possessed?

Articulus 1

AD PRIMUM sic proceditur. Videtur quod frui non sit solum appetitivae potentiae. Frui enim nihil aliud esse videtur quam fructum capere. Sed fructum humanae vitae, qui est beatitudo, capit intellectus, in cuius actu beatitudo consistit, ut supra ostensum est. Ergo frui non est appetitivae potentiae, sed intellectus.

PRAETEREA, quaelibet potentia habet proprium finem, qui est eius perfectio, sicut visus finis est cognoscere visibile, auditus percipere sonos, et sic de aliis. Sed finis rei est fructus eius. Ergo frui est potentiae cuiuslibet, et non solum appetitivae.

PRAETEREA, fruitio delectationem quandam importat. Sed delectatio sensibilis pertinet ad sensum, qui delectatur in suo obiecto, et eadem ratione, delectatio intellectualis ad intellectum. Ergo fruitio pertinet ad apprehensivam potentiam, et non ad appetitivam.

SED CONTRA est quod Augustinus dicit, I de Doctr. Christ., et in X de Trin.,

Article 1
Whether to enjoy is an act of the appetitive power?

Objection 1: It would seem that to enjoy belongs not only to the appetitive power. For to enjoy seems nothing else than to receive the fruit. But it is the intellect, in whose act Happiness consists, as shown above (I-II, q. 3, a. 4), that receives the fruit of human life, which is Happiness. Therefore to enjoy is not an act of the appetitive power, but of the intellect.

Objection 2: Further, each power has its proper end, which is its perfection: thus the end of sight is to know the visible; of the hearing, to perceive sounds; and so forth. But the end of a thing is its fruit. Therefore to enjoy belongs to each power, and not only to the appetite.

Objection 3: Further, enjoyment implies a certain delight. But sensible delight belongs to sense, which delights in its object: and for the same reason, intellectual delight belongs to the intellect. Therefore enjoyment belongs to the apprehensive, and not to the appetitive power.

On the contrary, Augustine says (De Doctr. Christ. i, 4; and De Trin. x, 10,11):

---
* Or, Fruition

frui est amore inhaerere alicui rei propter seipsam. Sed amor pertinet ad appetitivam potentiam. Ergo et frui est actus appetitivae potentiae.

Respondeo dicendum quod *fruitio* et *fructus* ad idem pertinere videntur, et unum ex altero derivari. Quid autem a quo, nihil ad propositum refert; nisi quod hoc probabile videtur, quod id quod magis est manifestum, prius etiam fuerit nominatum. Sunt autem nobis primo manifesta quae sunt sensibilia magis. Unde a sensibilibus fructibus nomen *fruitionis* derivatum videtur. Fructus autem sensibilis est id quod ultimum ex arbore expectatur, et cum quadam suavitate percipitur. Unde fruitio pertinere videtur ad amorem vel delectationem quam aliquis habet de ultimo expectato, quod est finis. Finis autem et bonum est obiectum appetitivae potentiae. Unde manifestum est quod fruitio est actus appetitivae potentiae.

Ad primum ergo dicendum quod nihil prohibet unum et idem, secundum diversas rationes, ad diversas potentias pertinere. Ipsa igitur visio Dei, inquantum est visio, est actus intellectus, inquantum autem est bonum et finis, est voluntatis obiectum. Et hoc modo est eius fruitio. Et sic hunc finem intellectus consequitur tanquam potentia agens, voluntas autem tanquam potentia movens ad finem, et fruens fine iam adepto.

Ad secundum dicendum quod perfectio et finis cuiuslibet alterius potentiae, continetur sub obiecto appetitivae, sicut proprium sub communi, ut dictum est supra. Unde perfectio et finis cuiuslibet potentiae, inquantum est quoddam bonum, pertinet ad appetitivam. Propter quod appetitiva potentia movet alias ad suos fines; et ipsa consequitur finem, quando quaelibet aliarum pertingit ad finem.

Ad tertium dicendum quod in delectatione duo sunt, scilicet perceptio convenientis, quae pertinet ad apprehensivam potentiam; et complacentia eius quod offertur ut conveniens. Et hoc pertinet ad appetitivam potentiam, in qua ratio delectationis completur.

"To enjoy is to adhere lovingly to something for its own sake." But love belongs to the appetitive power. Therefore also to enjoy is an act of the appetitive power.

I answer that, Fruitio [enjoyment] and *fructus* [fruit] seem to refer to the same, one being derived from the other; which from which, matters not for our purpose; though it seems probable that the one which is more clearly known, was first named. Now those things are most manifest to us which appeal most to the senses: wherefore it seems that the word "fruition" is derived from sensible fruits. But sensible fruit is that which we expect the tree to produce in the last place, and in which a certain sweetness is to be perceived. Hence fruition seems to have relation to love, or to the delight which one has in realizing the longed-for term, which is the end. Now the end and the good is the object of the appetitive power. Wherefore it is evident that fruition is the act of the appetitive power.

Reply to Objection 1: Nothing hinders one and the same thing from belonging, under different aspects, to different powers. Accordingly the vision of God, as vision, is an act of the intellect, but as a good and an end, is the object of the will. And as such is the fruition thereof: so that the intellect attains this end, as the executive power, but the will as the motive power, moving [the powers] towards the end and enjoying the end attained.

Reply to Objection 2: The perfection and end of every other power is contained in the object of the appetitive power, as the proper is contained in the common, as stated above (I-II, q. 9, a. 1). Hence the perfection and end of each power, in so far as it is a good, belongs to the appetitive power. Wherefore the appetitive power moves the other powers to their ends; and itself realizes the end, when each of them reaches the end.

Reply to Objection 3: In delight there are two things: perception of what is becoming; and this belongs to the apprehensive power; and complacency in that which is offered as becoming: and this belongs to the appetitive power, in which power delight is formally completed.

Articulus 2

Ad secundum sic proceditur. Videtur quod frui solummodo sit hominum. Dicit enim Augustinus, in I de Doct. Christ., quod *nos homines sumus qui fruimur et utimur.* Non ergo alia animalia frui possunt.

Praeterea, frui est ultimi finis. Sed ad ultimum finem non possunt pertingere bruta animalia. Ergo eorum non est frui.

Praeterea, sicut appetitus sensitivus est sub intellectivo, ita appetitus naturalis est sub sensitivo. Si igitur frui pertinet ad appetitum sensitivum, videtur quod pari ratione possit ad naturalem pertinere. Quod patet esse falsum, quia eius non est delectari. Ergo appetitus sensitivi non est frui. Et ita non convenit brutis animalibus.

Sed contra est quod Augustinus dicit, in libro octoginta trium quaest., *frui quidem cibo et qualibet corporali voluptate, non absurde existimantur et bestiae.*

Respondeo dicendum quod, sicut ex praedictis habetur, frui non est actus potentiae pervenientis ad finem sicut exequentis, sed potentiae imperantis executionem, dictum est enim quod est appetitivae potentiae. In rebus autem cognitione carentibus invenitur quidem potentia pertingens ad finem per modum exequentis, sicut qua grave tendit deorsum et leve sursum. Sed potentia ad quam pertineat finis per modum imperantis, non invenitur in eis; sed in aliqua superiori natura, quae sic movet totam naturam per imperium, sicut in habentibus cognitionem appetitus movet alias potentias ad suos actus. Unde manifestum est quod in his quae cognitione carent, quamvis pertingant ad finem, non invenitur fruitio finis; sed solum in his quae cognitionem habent. Sed cognitio finis est duplex, perfecta, et imperfecta. Perfecta quidem, qua non solum cognoscitur id quod est finis et bonum, sed universalis ratio finis et boni, et talis cognitio

Article 2
Whether to enjoy belongs to the rational creature alone, or also to irrational animals?

Objection 1: It would seem that to enjoy belongs to men alone. For Augustine says (De Doctr. Christ. i, 22) that "it is given to us men to enjoy and to use." Therefore other animals cannot enjoy.

Objection 2: Further, to enjoy relates to the last end. But irrational animals cannot obtain the last end. Therefore it is not for them to enjoy.

Objection 3: Further, just as the sensitive appetite is beneath the intellectual appetite, so is the natural appetite beneath the sensitive. If, therefore, to enjoy belongs to the sensitive appetite, it seems that for the same reason it can belong to the natural appetite. But this is evidently false, since the latter cannot delight in anything. Therefore the sensitive appetite cannot enjoy: and accordingly enjoyment is not possible for irrational animals.

On the contrary, Augustine says (QQ. 83, qu. 30): "It is not so absurd to suppose that even beasts enjoy their food and any bodily pleasure."

I answer that, As was stated above (I-II, q. 11, a. 1) to enjoy is not the act of the power that achieves the end as executor, but of the power that commands the achievement; for it has been said to belong to the appetitive power. Now things void of reason have indeed a power of achieving an end by way of execution, as that by which a heavy body has a downward tendency, whereas a light body has an upward tendency. Yet the power of command in respect of the end is not in them, but in some higher nature, which moves all nature by its command, just as in things endowed with knowledge, the appetite moves the other powers to their acts. Wherefore it is clear that things void of knowledge, although they attain an end, have no enjoyment of the end: this is only for those that are endowed with knowledge. Now knowledge of the end is twofold: perfect and imperfect. Perfect knowledge of the end, is that whereby not only is that known which is the end and the good, but also the universal formality of the end and the good; and such knowledge

est solius rationalis naturae. Imperfecta autem cognitio est qua cognoscitur particulariter finis et bonum, et talis cognitio est in brutis animalibus. Quorum etiam virtutes appetitivae non sunt imperantes libere; sed secundum naturalem instinctum ad ea quae apprehenduntur, moventur. Unde rationali naturae convenit fruitio secundum rationem perfectam, brutis autem animalibus secundum rationem imperfectam, aliis autem creaturis nullo modo.

AD PRIMUM ergo dicendum quod Augustinus loquitur de fruitione perfecta.

AD SECUNDUM dicendum quod non oportet quod fruitio sit ultimi finis simpliciter, sed eius quod habetur ab unoquoque pro ultimo fine.

AD TERTIUM dicendum quod appetitus sensitivus consequitur aliquam cognitionem, non autem appetitus naturalis, praecipue prout est in his quae cognitione carent.

AD QUARTUM dicendum, quod Augustinus ibi loquitur de fruitione imperfecta. Quod ex ipso modo loquendi apparet, dicit enim quod *frui non adeo absurde existimantur et bestiae,* scilicet sicut *uti* absurdissime dicerentur.

belongs to the rational nature alone. On the other hand, imperfect knowledge is that by which the end and the good are known in the particular. Such knowledge is in irrational animals: whose appetitive powers do not command with freedom, but are moved according to a natural instinct to whatever they apprehend. Consequently, enjoyment belongs to the rational nature, in a perfect degree; to irrational animals, imperfectly; to other creatures, not at all.

Reply to Objection 1: Augustine is speaking there of perfect enjoyment.

Reply to Objection 2: Enjoyment need not be of the last end simply; but of that which each one chooses for his last end.

Reply to Objection 3: The sensitive appetite follows some knowledge; not so the natural appetite, especially in things void of knowledge.

Reply to Objection 4: Augustine is speaking there of imperfect enjoyment. This is clear from his way of speaking: for he says that "it is not so absurd to suppose that even beasts enjoy," that is, as it would be, if one were to say that they "use."

ARTICULUS 3

AD TERTIUM sic proceditur. Videtur quod fruitio non sit tantum ultimi finis. Dicit enim apostolus, ad Philem., *ita, frater, ego te fruar in domino.* Sed manifestum est quod Paulus non posuerat ultimum suum finem in homine. Ergo frui non tantum est ultimi finis.

PRAETEREA, fructus est quo aliquis fruitur. Sed apostolus dicit, ad Galat. V, *fructus spiritus est caritas, gaudium, pax,* et cetera huiusmodi; quae non habent rationem ultimi finis. Non ergo fruitio est tantum ultimi finis.

PRAETEREA, actus voluntatis supra seipsos reflectuntur, volo enim me velle, et amo me amare. Sed frui est actus voluntatis, *voluntas enim est per quam fruimur,* ut Augustinus dicit X de Trin. Ergo aliquis fruitur sua fruitione. Sed fruitio non est ultimus finis hominis, sed solum bonum increatum, quod est Deus. Non ergo fruitio est solum ultimi finis.

ARTICLE 3
Whether enjoyment is only of the last end?

Objection 1: It would seem that enjoyment is not only of the last end. For the Apostle says (Philem. 20): "Yea, brother, may I enjoy thee in the Lord." But it is evident that Paul had not placed his last end in a man. Therefore to enjoy is not only of the last end.

Objection 2: Further, what we enjoy is the fruit. But the Apostle says (Gal. 5:22): "The fruit of the Spirit is charity, joy, peace," and other like things, which are not in the nature of the last end. Therefore enjoyment is not only of the last end.

Objection 3: Further, the acts of the will reflect on one another; for I will to will, and I love to love. But to enjoy is an act of the will: since "it is the will with which we enjoy," as Augustine says (De Trin. x, 10). Therefore a man enjoys his enjoyment. But the last end of man is not enjoyment, but the uncreated good alone, which is God. Therefore enjoyment is not only of the last end.

SED CONTRA est quod Augustinus dicit, X de Trin., *non fruitur si quis id quod in facultatem voluntatis assumit, propter aliud appetit.* Sed solum ultimus finis est qui non propter aliud appetitur. Ergo solius ultimi finis est fruitio.

RESPONDEO dicendum quod, sicut dictum est, ad rationem fructus duo pertinent, scilicet quod sit ultimum; et quod appetitum quietet quadam dulcedine vel delectatione. Ultimum autem est simpliciter, et secundum quid, simpliciter quidem, quod ad aliud non refertur; sed secundum quid, quod est aliquorum ultimum. Quod ergo est simpliciter ultimum, in quo aliquid delectatur sicut in ultimo fine, hoc proprie dicitur fructus, et eo proprie dicitur aliquis frui. Quod autem in seipso non est delectabile, sed tantum appetitur in ordine ad aliud, sicut potio amara ad sanitatem; nullo modo fructus dici potest. Quod autem in se habet quandam delectationem, ad quam quaedam praecedentia referuntur, potest quidem aliquo modo dici fructus, sed non proprie, et secundum completam rationem fructus, eo dicimur frui. Unde Augustinus, in X de Trin., dicit quod *fruimur cognitis in quibus voluntas delectata conquiescit.* Non autem quiescit simpliciter nisi in ultimo, quia quandiu aliquid expectatur, motus voluntatis remanet in suspenso, licet iam ad aliquid pervenerit. Sicut in motu locali, licet illud quod est medium in magnitudine, sit principium et finis; non tamen accipitur ut finis in actu, nisi quando in eo quiescitur.

AD PRIMUM ergo dicendum quod, sicut Augustinus dicit in I de Doctr. Christ., *si dixisset te fruar, et non addidisset in domino, videretur finem dilectionis in eo posuisse. Sed quia illud addidit, in domino se posuisse finem, atque eo se frui significavit.* Ut sic fratre se frui dixerit non tanquam termino, sed tanquam medio.

AD SECUNDUM dicendum quod fructus aliter comparatur ad arborem producentem, et aliter ad hominem fruentem. Ad arborem quidem producentem comparatur ut

On the contrary, Augustine says (De Trin. x, 11): "A man does not enjoy that which he desires for the sake of something else." But the last end alone is that which man does not desire for the sake of something else. Therefore enjoyment is of the last end alone.

I answer that, As stated above (I-II, q. 11, a. 1) the notion of fruit implies two things: first that it should come last; second, that it should calm the appetite with a certain sweetness and delight. Now a thing is last either simply or relatively; simply, if it be referred to nothing else; relatively, if it is the last in a particular series. Therefore that which is last simply, and in which one delights as in the last end, is properly called fruit; and this it is that one is properly said to enjoy. But that which is delightful not in itself, but is desired, only as referred to something else, e.g., a bitter potion for the sake of health, can nowise be called fruit. And that which has something delightful about it, to which a number of preceding things are referred, may indeed by called fruit in a certain manner; but we cannot be said to enjoy it properly or as though it answered perfectly to the notion of fruit. Hence Augustine says (De Trin. x, 10) that "we enjoy what we know, when the delighted will is at rest therein." But its rest is not absolute save in the possession of the last end: for as long as something is looked for, the movement of the will remains in suspense, although it has reached something. Thus in local movement, although any point between the two terms is a beginning and an end, yet it is not considered as an actual end, except when the movement stops there.

Reply to Objection 1: As Augustine says (De Doctr. Christ. i, 33), "if he had said, 'May I enjoy thee,' without adding 'in the Lord,' he would seem to have set the end of his love in him. But since he added that he set his end in the Lord, he implied his desire to enjoy Him": as if we were to say that he expressed his enjoyment of his brother not as a term but as a means.

Reply to Objection 2: Fruit bears one relation to the tree that bore it, and another to man that enjoys it. To the tree indeed that bore it, it is compared as

effectus ad causam, ad fruentem autem, sicut ultimum expectatum et delectans. Dicuntur igitur ea quae enumerat ibi apostolus, fructus, quia sunt effectus quidam spiritus sancti in nobis, unde et *fructus spiritus* dicuntur, non autem ita quod eis fruamur tanquam ultimo fine. Vel aliter dicendum quod dicuntur fructus, secundum Ambrosium, quia *propter se petenda sunt,* non quidem ita quod ad beatitudinem non referantur; sed quia in **seipsis habent unde nobis placere debeant.**

AD TERTIUM dicendum quod, sicut supra dictum est finis dicitur dupliciter, uno modo, ipsa res; alio modo, adeptio rei. Quae quidem non sunt duo fines, sed unus finis, in se consideratus, et alteri applicatus. Deus igitur est ultimus finis sicut res quae ultimo quaeritur, fruitio autem sicut adeptio huius ultimi finis. Sicut igitur non est alius finis Deus, et fruitio Dei; ita eadem ratio fruitionis est qua fruimur Deo, et qua fruimur divina fruitione. Et eadem ratio est de beatitudine creata, quae in fruitione consistit.

ARTICULUS 4

AD QUARTUM sic proceditur. Videtur quod fruitio non sit nisi finis habiti. Dicit enim Augustinus, X de Trin., quod *frui est cum gaudio uti, non adhuc spei, sed iam rei.* Sed quandiu non habetur, non est gaudium rei, sed spei. Ergo fruitio non est nisi finis habiti.

PRAETEREA, sicut dictum est, fruitio non est proprie nisi ultimi finis, quia solus ultimus finis quietat appetitum. Sed appetitus non quietatur nisi in fine iam habito. Ergo fruitio, proprie loquendo, non est nisi finis habiti.

effect to cause; to the one enjoying it, as the final object of his longing and the consummation of his delight. Accordingly these fruits mentioned by the Apostle are so called because they are certain effects of the Holy Ghost in us, wherefore they are called "fruits of the spirit": but not as though we are to enjoy them as our last end. Or we may say with Ambrose that they are called fruits because "we should desire them for their own sake": **not indeed as though they were not ordained to the last end; but because they are such that we ought to find pleasure in them.**

Reply to Objection 3: As stated above (I-II, q. 1, a. 8; q. 2, a. 7), we speak of an end in a twofold sense: first, as being the thing itself; secondly, as the attainment thereof. These are not, of course, two ends, but one end, considered in itself, and in its relation to something else. Accordingly God is the last end, as that which is ultimately sought for: while the enjoyment is as the attainment of this last end. And so, just as God is not one end, and the enjoyment of God, another: so it is the same enjoyment whereby we enjoy God, and whereby we enjoy our enjoyment of God. And the same applies to created happiness which consists in enjoyment.

ARTICLE 4
Whether enjoyment is only of the end possessed?

Objection 1: It would seem that enjoyment is only of the end possessed. For Augustine says (De Trin. x, 1) that "to enjoy is to use joyfully, with the joy, not of hope, but of possession." But so long as a thing is not had, there is joy, not of possession, but of hope. Therefore enjoyment is only of the end possessed.

Objection 2: Further, as stated above (I-II, q. 11, a. 3), enjoyment is not properly otherwise than of the last end: because this alone gives rest to the appetite. But the appetite has no rest save in the possession of the end. Therefore enjoyment, properly speaking, is only of the end possessed.

PRAETEREA, frui est capere fructum. Sed non capitur fructus, nisi quando iam finis habetur. Ergo fruitio non est nisi finis habiti.

SED CONTRA, *frui est amore inhaerere alicui rei propter seipsam,* ut Augustinus dicit. Sed hoc potest fieri etiam de re non habita. Ergo frui potest esse etiam finis non habiti.

RESPONDEO dicendum quod frui importat comparationem quandam voluntatis ad ultimum finem, secundum quod voluntas habet aliquid pro ultimo fine. Habetur autem finis dupliciter, uno modo, perfecte; et alio modo, imperfecte. Perfecte quidem, quando habetur non solum in intentione, sed etiam in re, imperfecte autem, quando habetur in intentione tantum. Est ergo perfecta fruitio finis iam habiti realiter. Sed imperfecta est etiam finis non habiti realiter, sed in intentione tantum.

AD PRIMUM ergo dicendum quod Augustinus loquitur de fruitione perfecta.

AD SECUNDUM dicendum quod quies voluntatis dupliciter impeditur, uno modo, ex parte obiecti, quia scilicet non est ultimus finis, sed ad aliud ordinatur; alio modo, ex parte appetentis finem qui nondum adipiscitur finem. Obiectum autem est quod dat speciem actui, sed ab agente dependet modus agendi, ut sit perfectus vel imperfectus, secundum conditionem agentis. Et ideo eius quod non est ultimus finis, fruitio est impropria, quasi deficiens a specie fruitionis. Finis autem ultimi non habiti, est fruitio propria quidem, sed imperfecta, propter imperfectum modum habendi ultimum finem.

AD TERTIUM dicendum quod finem accipere vel habere dicitur aliquis, non solum secundum rem, sed etiam secundum intentionem, ut dictum est.

Objection 3: Further, to enjoy is to lay hold of the fruit. But one does not lay hold of the fruit until one is in possession of the end. Therefore enjoyment is only of the end possessed.

On the contrary, "to enjoy is to adhere lovingly to something for its own sake," as Augustine says (De Doctr. Christ. i, 4). But this is possible, even in regard to a thing which is not in our possession. Therefore it is possible to enjoy the end even though it be not possessed.

I answer that, To enjoy implies a certain relation of the will to the last end, according as the will has something by way of last end. Now an end is possessed in two ways; perfectly and imperfectly. Perfectly, when it is possessed not only in intention but also in reality; imperfectly, when it is possessed in intention only. Perfect enjoyment, therefore, is of the end already possessed: but imperfect enjoyment is also of the end possessed not really, but only in intention.

Reply to Objection 1: Augustine speaks there of perfect enjoyment.

Reply to Objection 2: The will is hindered in two ways from being at rest. First on the part of the object; by reason of its not being the last end, but ordained to something else: secondly on the part of the one who desires the end, by reason of his not being yet in possession of it. Now it is the object that specifies an act: but on the agent depends the manner of acting, so that the act be perfect or imperfect, as compared with the actual circumstances of the agent. Therefore enjoyment of anything but the last end is not enjoyment properly speaking, as falling short of the nature of enjoyment. But enjoyment of the last end, not yet possessed, is enjoyment properly speaking, but imperfect, on account of the imperfect way in which it is possessed.

Reply to Objection 3: One is said to lay hold of or to have an end, not only in reality, but also in intention, as stated above.

Quaestio XII

Deinde considerandum est de intentione. Et circa hoc quaeruntur quinque. *Primo,* utrum intentio sit actus intellectus, vel voluntatis. *Secundo,* utrum sit tantum finis ultimi. *Tertio,* utrum aliquis possit simul duo intendere. *Quarto,* utrum intentio finis sit idem actus cum voluntate eius quod est ad finem. *Quinto,* utrum intentio conveniat brutis animalibus.

Articulus 1

Ad primum sic proceditur. Videtur quod intentio sit actus intellectus, et non voluntatis. Dicitur enim Matth. VI, *si oculus tuus fuerit simplex, totum corpus tuum lucidum erit,* ubi per oculum significatur intentio, ut dicit Augustinus in libro de Serm. Dom. in Mont. Sed oculus, cum sit instrumentum visus, significat apprehensivam potentiam. Ergo intentio non est actus appetitivae potentiae, sed apprehensivae.

Praeterea, ibidem Augustinus dicit quod intentio lumen vocatur a domino, ubi dicit, *si lumen quod in te est, tenebrae sunt,* et cetera. Sed lumen ad cognitionem pertinet. Ergo et intentio.

Praeterea, intentio designat ordinationem quandam in finem. Sed ordinare est rationis. Ergo intentio non pertinet ad voluntatem, sed ad rationem.

Praeterea, actus voluntatis non est nisi vel finis, vel eorum quae sunt ad finem. Sed actus voluntatis respectu finis, vocatur voluntas seu fruitio, respectu autem eorum quae sunt ad finem, est electio, a quibus differt intentio. Ergo intentio non est actus voluntatis.

Sed contra est quod Augustinus dicit, in XI de Trin., quod *voluntatis intentio copulat corpus visum visui, et similiter speciem in memoria existentem ad aciem animi interius cogitantis.* Est igitur intentio actus voluntatis.

Question 12
Of Intention

We must now consider Intention: concerning which there are five points of inquiry: 1. Whether intention is an act of intellect or of the will? 2. Whether it is only of the last end? 3. Whether one can intend two things at the same time? 4. Whether intention of the end is the same act as volition of the means? 5. Whether intention is within the competency of irrational animals?

Article 1
Whether intention is an act of the intellect or of the will?

Objection 1: It would seem that intention is an act of the intellect, and not of the will. For it is written (Mat. 6:22): "If thy eye be single, thy whole body shall be lightsome": where, according to Augustine (De Serm. Dom. in Monte ii, 13) the eye signifies intention. But since the eye is the organ of sight, it signifies the apprehensive power. Therefore intention is not an act of the appetitive but of the apprehensive power.

Objection 2: Further, Augustine says (De Serm. Dom. in Monte ii, 13) that Our Lord spoke of intention as a light, when He said (Mat. 6:23): "If the light that is in thee be darkness," etc. But light pertains to knowledge. Therefore intention does too.

Objection 3: Further, intention implies a kind of ordaining to an end. But to ordain is an act of reason. Therefore intention belongs not to the will but to the reason.

Objection 4: Further, an act of the will is either of the end or of the means. But the act of the will in respect of the end is called volition, or enjoyment; with regard to the means, it is choice, from which intention is distinct. Therefore it is not an act of the will.

On the contrary, Augustine says (De Trin. xi, 4,8,9) that "the intention of the will unites the sight to the object seen; and the images retained in the memory, to the penetrating gaze of the soul's inner thought." Therefore intention is an act of the will.

RESPONDEO dicendum quod intentio, sicut ipsum nomen sonat, significat *in aliquid tendere.* In aliquid autem tendit et actio moventis, et motus mobilis. Sed hoc quod motus mobilis in aliquid tendit, ab actione moventis procedit. Unde intentio primo et principaliter pertinet ad id quod movet ad finem, unde dicimus architectorem, et omnem praecipientem, movere suo imperio alios ad id quod ipse intendit. Voluntas autem movet omnes alias vires animae ad finem, ut supra habitum est. Unde manifestum est quod intentio proprie est actus voluntatis.

AD PRIMUM ergo dicendum quod intentio nominatur oculus metaphorice, non quia ad cognitionem pertineat; sed quia cognitionem praesupponit, per quam proponitur voluntati finis ad quem movet; sicut oculo praevidemus quo tendere corporaliter debeamus.

AD SECUNDUM dicendum quod intentio dicitur lumen, quia manifesta est intendenti. Unde et opera dicuntur tenebrae, quia homo scit quid intendit, sed nescit quid ex opere sequatur, sicut Augustinus ibidem exponit.

AD TERTIUM dicendum quod voluntas quidem non ordinat, sed tamen in aliquid tendit secundum ordinem rationis. Unde hoc nomen *intentio* nominat actum voluntatis, praesupposita ordinatione rationis ordinantis aliquid in finem.

AD QUARTUM dicendum quod intentio est actus voluntatis respectu finis. Sed voluntas respicit finem tripliciter. Uno modo, absolute, et sic dicitur *voluntas,* prout absolute volumus vel sanitatem, vel si quid aliud est huiusmodi. Alio modo consideratur finis secundum quod in eo quiescitur, et hoc modo *fruitio* respicit finem. Tertio modo consideratur finis secundum quod est terminus alicuius quod in ipsum ordinatur, et sic *intentio* respicit finem. Non enim solum ex hoc intendere dicimur sanitatem, quia volumus eam, sed quia volumus ad eam per aliquid aliud pervenire.

I answer that, Intention, as the very word denotes, signifies, "to tend to something." Now both the action of the mover and the movement of thing moved, tend to something. But that the movement of the thing moved tends to anything, is due to the action of the mover. Consequently intention belongs first and principally to that which moves to the end: hence we say that an architect or anyone who is in authority, by his command moves others to that which he intends. Now the will moves all the other powers of the soul to the end, as shown above (I-II, q. 9, a. 1). Wherefore it is evident that intention, properly speaking, is an act of the will.

Reply to Objection 1: The eye designates intention figuratively, not because intention has reference to knowledge, but because it presupposes knowledge, which proposes to the will the end to which the latter moves; thus we foresee with the eye whither we should tend with our bodies.

Reply to Objection 2: Intention is called a light because it is manifest to him who intends. Wherefore works are called darkness because a man knows what he intends, but knows not what the result may be, as Augustine expounds (De Serm. Dom. in Monte ii, 13).

Reply to Objection 3: The will does not ordain, but tends to something according to the order of reason. Consequently this word "intention" indicates an act of the will, presupposing the act whereby the reason orders something to the end.

Reply to Objection 4: Intention is an act of the will in regard to the end. Now the will stands in a threefold relation to the end. First, absolutely; and thus we have "volition," whereby we will absolutely to have health, and so forth. Secondly, it considers the end, as its place of rest; and thus "enjoyment" regards the end. Thirdly, it considers the end as the term towards which something is ordained; and thus "intention" regards the end. For when we speak of intending to have health, we mean not only that we have it, but that we will have it by means of something else.

Articulus 2

Ad secundum sic proceditur. Videtur quod intentio sit tantum ultimi finis. Dicitur enim in libro sententiarum prosperi, *clamor ad Deum est intentio cordis*. Sed Deus est ultimus finis humani cordis. Ergo intentio semper respicit ultimum finem.

Praeterea, intentio respicit finem secundum quod est terminus, ut dictum est. Sed terminus habet rationem ultimi. Ergo intentio semper respicit ultimum finem.

Praeterea, sicut intentio respicit finem, ita et fruitio. Sed fruitio semper est ultimi finis. Ergo et intentio.

Sed contra, ultimus finis humanarum voluntatum est unus, scilicet beatitudo, ut supra dictum est. Si igitur intentio esset tantum ultimi finis, non essent diversae hominum intentiones. Quod patet esse falsum.

Respondeo dicendum quod, sicut dictum est, intentio respicit finem secundum quod est terminus motus voluntatis. In motu autem potest accipi terminus dupliciter, uno modo, ipse terminus ultimus, in quo quiescitur, qui est terminus totius motus; alio modo, aliquod medium, quod est principium unius partis motus, et finis vel terminus alterius. Sicut in motu quo itur de *a* in *c* per *b*, *c* est terminus ultimus, *b* autem est terminus, sed non ultimus. Et utriusque potest esse intentio. Unde etsi semper sit finis, non tamen oportet quod semper sit ultimi finis.

Ad primum ergo dicendum quod intentio cordis dicitur clamor ad Deum, non quod Deus sit obiectum intentionis semper, sed quia est intentionis cognitor. Vel quia, cum oramus, intentionem nostram ad Deum dirigimus, quae quidem intentio vim clamoris habet.

Ad secundum dicendum quod terminus habet rationem ultimi; sed non semper ultimi respectu totius, sed quandoque respectu alicuius partis.

Ad tertium dicendum quod fruitio importat quietem in fine, quod pertinet

Article 2
Whether intention is only of the last end?

Objection 1: It would seem that intention is only of the last end. For it is said in the book of Prosper's Sentences (Sent. 100): "The intention of the heart is a cry to God." But God is the last end of the human heart. Therefore intention is always regards the last end.

Objection 2: Further, intention regards the end as the terminus, as stated above (I-II, q. 12, a. 1, ad 4). But a terminus is something last. Therefore intention always regards the last end.

Objection 3: Further, just as intention regards the end, so does enjoyment. But enjoyment is always of the last end. Therefore intention is too.

On the contrary, There is but one last end of human wills, *viz.* Happiness, as stated above (I-II, q. 1, a. 7). If, therefore, intentions were only of the last end, men would not have different intentions: which is evidently false.

I answer that, As stated above (I-II, q. 12, a. 1, ad 4), intention regards the end as a terminus of the movement of the will. Now a terminus of movement may be taken in two ways. First, the very last terminus, when the movement comes to a stop; this is the terminus of the whole movement. Secondly, some point midway, which is the beginning of one part of the movement, and the end or terminus of the other. Thus in the movement from A to C through B, C is the last terminus, while B is a terminus, but not the last. And intention can be both. Consequently though intention is always of the end, it need not be always of the last end.

Reply to Objection 1: The intention of the heart is called a cry to God, not that God is always the object of intention, but because He sees our intention. Or because, when we pray, we direct our intention to God, which intention has the force of a cry.

Reply to Objection 2: A terminus is something last, not always in respect of the whole, but sometimes in respect of a part.

Reply to Objection 3: Enjoyment implies rest in the end; and this belongs to the

Articulus 3

AD TERTIUM sic proceditur. Videtur quod non possit aliquis simul plura intendere. Dicit enim Augustinus, in libro de Serm. Dom. in monte, quod non potest homo simul intendere Deum et commodum corporale. Ergo pari ratione, neque aliqua alia duo.

PRAETEREA, intentio nominat motum voluntatis ad terminum. Sed unius motus non possunt esse plures termini ex una parte. Ergo voluntas non potest simul multa intendere.

PRAETEREA, intentio praesupponit actum rationis sive intellectus. Sed *non contingit simul plura intelligere,* secundum philosophum. Ergo etiam neque contingit simul plura intendere.

SED CONTRA, ars imitatur naturam. Sed natura ex uno instrumento intendit duas utilitates, sicut *lingua ordinatur et ad gustum et ad locutionem,* ut dicitur in II de anima. Ergo, pari ratione ars vel ratio potest simul aliquid unum ad duos fines ordinare. Et ita potest aliquis simul plura intendere.

RESPONDEO dicendum quod *aliqua duo* possunt accipi dupliciter, vel ordinata ad invicem, vel ad invicem non ordinata. Et si quidem ad invicem fuerint ordinata, manifestum est ex praemissis quod homo potest simul multa intendere. Est enim intentio non solum finis ultimi, ut dictum est, sed etiam finis medii. Simul autem intendit aliquis et finem proximum, et ultimum; sicut confectionem medicinae, et sanitatem. Si autem accipiantur duo ad invicem non ordinata, sic etiam simul homo potest plura intendere. Quod patet ex hoc, quod homo unum alteri praeeligit, quia melius est altero, inter alias

solum ad ultimum finem. Sed intentio importat motum in finem, non autem quietem. Unde non est similis ratio.

ARTICLE 3
Whether one can intend two things at the same time?

Objection 1: It would seem that one cannot intend several things at the same time. For Augustine says (De Serm. Dom. in Monte ii, 14,16,17) that man's intention cannot be directed at the same time to God and to bodily benefits. Therefore, for the same reason, neither to any other two things.

Objection 2: Further, intention designates a movement of the will towards a terminus. Now there cannot be several termini in the same direction of one movement. Therefore the will cannot intend several things at the same time.

Objection 3: Further, intention presupposes an act of reason or of the intellect. But "it is not possible to understand several things at the same time," according to the Philosopher (Topic. ii, 10). Therefore neither is it possible to intend several things at the same time.

On the contrary, Art imitates nature. Now nature intends two purposes by means of one instrument: thus "the tongue is for the purpose of taste and speech" (De Anima ii, 8). Therefore, for the same reason, art or reason can at the same time direct one thing to two ends: so that one can intend several ends at the same time.

I answer that, The expression "two things" may be taken in two ways: they may be ordained to one another or not so ordained. And if they be ordained to one another, it is evident, from what has been said, that a man can intend several things at the same time. For intention is not only of the last end, as stated above (I-II, q. 12, a. 2), but also of an intermediary end. Now a man intends at the same time, both the proximate and the last end; as the mixing of a medicine and the giving of health. But if we take two things that are not ordained to one another, thus also a man can intend several things at the same time. This is evident from the fact that a man prefers one thing to another because it is the better of the two. Now one of the

last end alone. But intention implies movement towards an end, not rest. Wherefore the comparison proves nothing.

autem conditiones quibus aliquid est melius altero, una est quod ad plura valet, unde potest aliquid praeeligi alteri, ex hoc quod ad plura valet. Et sic manifeste homo simul plura intendit.

AD PRIMUM ergo dicendum quod Augustinus intelligit hominem non posse simul Deum et commodum temporale intendere, sicut ultimos fines, quia, ut supra ostensum est, non possunt esse plures fines ultimi unius hominis.

AD SECUNDUM dicendum quod unius motus possunt ex una parte esse plures termini, si unus ad alium ordinetur, sed duo termini ad invicem non ordinati, ex una parte, unius motus esse non possunt. Sed tamen considerandum est quod id quod non est unum secundum rem, potest accipi ut unum secundum rationem. Intentio autem est motus voluntatis in aliquid praeordinatum in ratione, sicut dictum est. Et ideo ea quae sunt plura secundum rem, possunt accipi ut unus terminus intentionis, prout sunt unum secundum rationem, vel quia aliqua duo concurrunt ad integrandum aliquid unum, sicut ad sanitatem concurrunt calor et frigus commensurata; vel quia aliqua duo sub uno communi continentur, quod potest esse intentum. Puta acquisitio vini et vestis continetur sub lucro, sicut sub quodam communi, unde nihil prohibet quin ille qui intendit lucrum, simul haec duo intendat.

AD TERTIUM dicendum quod, sicut in primo dictum est, contingit simul plura intelligere, inquantum sunt aliquo modo unum.

Articulus 4

AD QUARTUM sic proceditur. Videtur quod non sit unus et idem motus intentio finis, et voluntas eius quod est ad finem. Dicit enim Augustinus, in XI de Trin., quod *voluntas videndi fenestram, finem habet fenestrae visionem; et altera est voluntas per fenestram videndi transeuntes.* Sed hoc pertinet ad intentionem, quod velim videre transeuntes per fenestram,

reasons for which one thing is better than another is that it is available for more purposes: wherefore one thing can be chosen in preference to another, because of the greater number of purposes for which it is available: so that evidently a man can intend several things at the same time.

Reply to Objection 1: Augustine means to say that man cannot at the same time direct his attention to God and to bodily benefits, as to two last ends: since, as stated above (I-II, q. 1, a. 5), one man cannot have several last ends.

Reply to Objection 2: There can be several termini ordained to one another, of the same movement and in the same direction; but not unless they be ordained to one another. At the same time it must be observed that what is not one in reality may be taken as one by the reason. Now intention is a movement of the will to something already ordained by the reason, as stated above (I-II, q. 12, a. 1, ad 3). Wherefore where we have many things in reality, we may take them as one term of intention, in so far as the reason takes them as one: either because two things concur in the integrity of one whole, as a proper measure of heat and cold conduce to health; or because two things are included in one which may be intended. For instance, the acquiring of wine and clothing is included in wealth, as in something common to both; wherefore nothing hinders the man who intends to acquire wealth, from intending both the others.

Reply to Objection 3: As stated in the I, q. 12, a. 10; q. 58, a. 2; q. 85, a. 4, it is possible to understand several things at the same time, in so far as, in some way, they are one.

Article 4
Whether intention of the end is the same act as the volition of the means?

Objection 1: It would seem that the intention of the end and the volition of the means are not one and the same movement. For Augustine says (De Trin. xi, 6) that "the will to see the window, has for its end the seeing of the window; and is another act from the will to see, through the window, the passersby." But that I should will to see the passersby, through the window, belongs to intention;

hoc autem ad voluntatem eius quod est ad finem, quod velim videre fenestram. Ergo alius est motus voluntatis intentio finis, et alius voluntas eius quod est ad finem.

PRAETEREA, actus distinguuntur secundum obiecta. Sed finis, et id quod est ad finem, sunt diversa obiecta. Ergo alius motus voluntatis est intentio finis, et voluntas eius quod est ad finem.

PRAETEREA, voluntas eius quod est ad finem, dicitur electio. Sed non est idem electio et intentio. Ergo non est idem motus intentio finis, cum voluntate eius quod est ad finem.

SED CONTRA, id quod est ad finem, se habet ad finem ut medium ad terminum. Sed idem motus est qui per medium transit ad terminum, in rebus naturalibus. Ergo et in rebus voluntariis idem motus est intentio finis, et voluntas eius quod est ad finem.

RESPONDEO dicendum quod motus voluntatis in finem et in id quod est ad finem, potest considerari dupliciter. Uno modo, secundum quod voluntas in utrumque fertur absolute et secundum se. Et sic sunt simpliciter duo motus voluntatis in utrumque. Alio modo potest considerari secundum quod voluntas fertur in id quod est ad finem, propter finem. Et sic unus et idem subiecto motus voluntatis est tendens ad finem, et in id quod est ad finem. Cum enim dico, *volo medicinam propter sanitatem,* non designo nisi unum motum voluntatis. Cuius ratio est quia finis ratio est volendi ea quae sunt ad finem. Idem autem actus cadit super obiectum, et super rationem obiecti, sicut eadem visio est coloris et luminis, ut supra dictum est. Et est simile de intellectu, quia si absolute principium et conclusionem consideret, diversa est consideratio utriusque; in hoc autem quod conclusioni propter principia assentit, est unus actus intellectus tantum.

AD PRIMUM ergo dicendum quod Augustinus loquitur de visione fenestrae, et visione transeuntium per fenestram, secundum quod voluntas in utrumque absolute fertur.

whereas that I will to see the window, belongs to the volition of the means. Therefore intention of the end and the willing of the means are distinct movements of the will.

Objection 2: Further, acts are distinct according to their objects. But the end and the means are distinct objects. Therefore the intention of the end and the willing of the means are distinct movements of the will.

Objection 3: Further, the willing of the means is called choice. But choice and intention are not the same. Therefore intention of the end and the willing of the means are not the same movement of the will.

On the contrary, The means in relation to the end, are as the mid-space to the terminus. Now it is all the same movement that passes through the mid-space to the terminus, in natural things. Therefore in things pertaining to the will, the intention of the end is the same movement as the willing of the means.

I answer that, The movement of the will to the end and to the means can be considered in two ways. First, according as the will is moved to each of the aforesaid absolutely and in itself. And thus there are really two movements of the will to them. Secondly, it may be considered accordingly as the will is moved to the means for the sake of the end: and thus the movement of the will to the end and its movement to the means are one and the same thing. For when I say: "I wish to take medicine for the sake of health," I signify no more than one movement of my will. And this is because the end is the reason for willing the means. Now the object, and that by reason of which it is an object, come under the same act; thus it is the same act of sight that perceives color and light, as stated above (I-II, q. 8, a. 3, ad 2). And the same applies to the intellect; for if it consider principle and conclusion absolutely, it considers each by a distinct act; but when it assents to the conclusion on account of the principles, there is but one act of the intellect.

Reply to Objection 1: Augustine is speaking of seeing the window and of seeing, through the window, the passersby, according as the will is moved to either absolutely.

AD SECUNDUM dicendum quod finis, inquantum est res quaedam, est aliud voluntatis obiectum quam id quod est ad finem. Sed inquantum est ratio volendi id quod est ad finem, est unum et idem obiectum.

AD TERTIUM dicendum quod motus qui est unus subiecto, potest ratione differre secundum principium et finem, ut ascensio et descensio, sicut dicitur in III Physic. Sic igitur inquantum motus voluntatis fertur in id **quod est ad finem, prout ordinatur ad finem,** est *electio*. Motus autem voluntatis qui fertur in finem, secundum quod acquiritur per ea quae sunt ad finem, vocatur *intentio*. Cuius signum est quod intentio finis esse potest, etiam nondum determinatis his quae sunt ad finem, quorum est electio.

ARTICULUS 5

AD QUINTUM sic proceditur. Videtur quod bruta animalia intendant finem. Natura enim in his quae cognitione carent, magis distat a rationali natura, quam natura sensitiva, quae est in animalibus brutis. Sed natura intendit finem etiam in his quae cognitione carent, ut probatur in II Physic. Ergo multo magis bruta animalia intendunt finem.

PRAETEREA, sicut intentio est finis, ita et fruitio. Sed fruitio convenit brutis animalibus, ut dictum est. Ergo et intentio.

PRAETEREA, eius est intendere finem, cuius est agere propter finem, cum intendere nihil sit nisi in aliud tendere. Sed bruta animalia agunt propter finem, movetur enim animal vel ad cibum quaerendum, vel ad aliquid huiusmodi. Ergo bruta animalia intendunt finem.

SED CONTRA, intentio finis importat ordinationem alicuius in finem quod est rationis. Cum igitur bruta animalia non habeant rationem, videtur quod non intendant finem.

RESPONDEO dicendum quod, sicut supra dictum est, intendere est in aliud tendere; quod quidem est et moventis, et moti. Secundum quidem igitur quod dicitur intendere finem id quod movetur ad finem ab alio, sic natura dicitur intendere finem, quasi

Reply to Objection 2: The end, considered as a thing, and the means to that end, are distinct objects of the will. But in so far as the end is the formal object in willing the means, they are one and the same object.

Reply to Objection 3: A movement which is one as to the subject, may differ, according to our way of looking at it, as to its beginning and end, as in the case of ascent and descent (Phys. iii, 3). Accordingly, in so far as the **movement of the will is to the means,** as ordained to the end, it is called "choice": but the movement of the will to the end as acquired by the means, it is called "intention." A sign of this is that we can have intention of the end without having determined the means which are the object of choice.

ARTICLE 5
Whether intention is within the competency of irrational animals?

Objection 1: It would seem that irrational animals intend the end. For in things void of reason nature stands further apart from the rational nature, than does the sensitive nature in irrational animals. But nature intends the end even in things void of reason, as is proved in Phys. ii, 8. Much more, therefore, do irrational animals intend the end.

Objection 2: Further, just as intention is of the end, so is enjoyment. But enjoyment is in irrational animals, as stated above (I-II, q. 11, a. 2). Therefore intention is too.

Objection 3: Further, to intend an end belongs to one who acts for an end; since to intend is nothing else than to tend to something. But irrational animals act for an end; for an animal is moved either to seek food, or to do something of the kind. Therefore irrational animals intend an end.

On the contrary, Intention of an end implies ordaining something to an end: which belongs to reason. Since therefore irrational animals are void of reason, it seems that they do not intend an end.

I answer that, As stated above (I-II, q. 12, a. 1), to intend is to tend to something; and this belongs to the mover and to the moved. According, therefore, as that which is moved to an end by another is said to intend the end, thus nature is said to intend an end, as

mota ad suum finem a Deo, sicut sagitta a sagittante. Et hoc modo etiam bruta animalia intendunt finem, inquantum moventur instinctu naturali ad aliquid. Alio modo intendere finem est moventis, prout scilicet ordinat motum alicuius, vel sui vel alterius, in finem. Quod est rationis tantum. Unde per hunc modum bruta non intendunt finem, quod est proprie et principaliter intendere, ut dictum est.

AD PRIMUM ergo dicendum quod ratio illa procedit secundum quod intendere est eius quod movetur ad finem.

AD SECUNDUM dicendum quod fruitio non importat ordinationem alicuius in aliquid, sicut intentio; sed absolutam quietem in fine.

AD TERTIUM dicendum quod bruta animalia moventur ad finem, non quasi considerantia quod per motum suum possunt consequi finem, quod est proprie intendentis, sed concupiscentia finem naturali instinctu, moventur ad finem quasi ab alio mota, sicut et cetera quae moventur naturaliter.

being moved to its end by God, as the arrow is moved by the archer. And in this way, irrational animals intend an end, inasmuch as they are moved to something by natural instinct. The other way of intending an end belongs to the mover; according as he ordains the movement of something, either his own or another's, to an end. This belongs to reason alone. Wherefore irrational animals do not intend an end in this way, which is to intend properly and principally, as stated above (I-II, q. 12, a. 1).

Reply to Objection 1: This argument takes intention in the sense of being moved to an end.

Reply to Objection 2: Enjoyment does not imply the ordaining of one thing to another, as intention does, but absolute repose in the end.

Reply to Objection 3: Irrational animals are moved to an end, not as though they thought that they can gain the end by this movement; this belongs to one that intends; but through desiring the end by natural instinct, they are moved to an end, moved, as it were, by another, like other things that are moved naturally.

Question 13
Of Choice, Which Is an Act of the Will with Regard to the Means

We must now consider the acts of the will with regard to the means. There are three of them: to choose, to consent, and to use. And choice is preceded by counsel. First of all, then, we must consider choice: secondly, counsel; thirdly, consent; fourthly, use. Concerning choice there are six points of inquiry: 1. Of what power is it the act; of the will or of the reason? 2. Whether choice is to be found in irrational animals? 3. Whether choice is only the means, or sometimes also of the end? 4. Whether choice is only of things that we do ourselves? 5. Whether choice is only of possible things? 6. Whether man chooses of necessity or freely?

Article 1
Whether choice is an act of will or of reason?

Objection 1: It would seem that choice is an act, not of will but of reason. For choice implies comparison, whereby one is given preference to another. But to compare is an act of reason. Therefore choice is an act of reason.

Objection 2: Further, it is for the same faculty to form a syllogism, and to draw the conclusion. But, in practical matters, it is the reason that forms syllogisms. Since therefore choice is a kind of conclusion in practical matters, as stated in Ethic. vii, 3, it seems that it is an act of reason.

Objection 3: Further, ignorance does not belong to the will but to the cognitive power. Now there is an "ignorance of choice," as is stated in Ethic. iii, 1. Therefore it seems that choice does not belong to the will but to the reason.

On the contrary, The Philosopher says (Ethic. iii, 3) that choice is "the desire of things in our power." But desire is an act of will. Therefore choice is too.

I answer that, The word choice implies something belonging to the reason or intellect, and something belonging to the will: for the Philosopher says (Ethic. vi, 2) that choice is either "intellect influenced by appetite or appetite influenced by intellect." Now

Quandocumque autem duo concurrunt ad aliquid unum constituendum, unum eorum est ut formale respectu alterius. Unde Gregorius Nyssenus dicit quod electio *neque est appetitus secundum seipsam, neque consilium solum, sed ex his aliquid compositum. Sicut enim dicimus animal ex anima et corpore compositum esse, neque vero corpus esse secundum seipsum, neque animam solam, sed utrumque; ita et electionem.* Est autem considerandum in actibus animae, quod actus qui est essentialiter unius potentiae vel habitus, recipit formam et speciem a superiori potentia vel habitu, secundum quod ordinatur inferius a superiori, si enim aliquis actum fortitudinis exerceat propter Dei amorem, actus quidem ille materialiter est fortitudinis, formaliter vero caritatis. Manifestum est autem quod ratio quodammodo voluntatem praecedit, et ordinat actum eius, inquantum scilicet voluntas in suum obiectum tendit secundum ordinem rationis, eo quod vis apprehensiva appetitivae suum obiectum repraesentat. Sic igitur ille actus quo voluntas tendit in aliquid quod proponitur ut bonum, ex eo quod per rationem est ordinatum ad finem, materialiter quidem est voluntatis, formaliter autem rationis. In huiusmodi autem substantia actus materialiter se habet ad ordinem qui imponitur a superiori potentia. Et ideo electio substantialiter non est actus rationis, sed voluntatis, perficitur enim electio in motu quodam animae ad bonum quod eligitur. Unde manifeste actus est appetitivae potentiae.

AD PRIMUM ergo dicendum quod electio importat collationem quandam praecedentem, non quod essentialiter sit ipsa collatio.

AD SECUNDUM dicendum quod conclusio etiam syllogismi qui fit in operabilibus, ad rationem pertinet; et dicitur *sententia* vel *iudicium,* quam sequitur *electio.* Et ob hoc ipsa conclusio pertinere videtur ad electionem, tanquam ad consequens.

AD TERTIUM dicendum quod ignorantia dicitur esse electionis, non quod ipsa electio sit scientia, sed quia ignoratur quid sit eligendum.

whenever two things concur to make one, one of them is formal in regard to the other. Hence Gregory of Nyssa* says that choice "is neither desire only, nor counsel only, but a combination of the two. For just as we say that an animal is composed of soul and body, and that it is neither a mere body, nor a mere soul, but both; so is it with choice." Now we must observe, as regards the acts of the soul, that an act belonging essentially to some power or habit, receives a form or species from a higher power or habit, according as an inferior is ordained by a superior: for if a man were to perform an act of fortitude for the love of God, that act is materially an act of fortitude, but formally, an act of charity. Now it is evident that, in a sense, reason precedes the will and ordains its act: in so far as the will tends to its object, according to the order of reason, since the apprehensive power presents the object to the appetite. Accordingly, that act whereby the will tends to something proposed to it as being good, through being ordained to the end by the reason, is materially an act of the will, but formally an act of the reason. Now in such like matters the substance of the act is as the matter in comparison to the order imposed by the higher power. Wherefore choice is substantially not an act of the reason but of the will: for choice is accomplished in a certain movement of the soul towards the good which is chosen. Consequently it is evidently an act of the appetitive power.

Reply to Objection 1: Choice implies a previous comparison; not that it consists in the comparison itself.

Reply to Objection 2: It is quite true that it is for the reason to draw the conclusion of a practical syllogism; and it is called "a decision" or "judgment," to be followed by "choice." And for this reason the conclusion seems to belong to the act of choice, as to that which results from it.

Reply to Objection 3: In speaking "of ignorance of choice," we do not mean that choice is a sort of knowledge, but that there is ignorance of what ought to be chosen.

---

* Nemesius, De Nat. Hom. xxxiii.

Articulus 2

Ad secundum sic proceditur. Videtur quod electio brutis animalibus conveniat. Electio enim *est appetitus aliquorum propter finem,* ut dicitur in III Ethic. Sed bruta animalia appetunt aliquid propter finem, agunt enim propter finem, et ex appetitu. Ergo in brutis animalibus est electio.

Praeterea, ipsum nomen *electionis* significare videtur quod aliquid prae aliis accipiatur. Sed bruta animalia accipiunt aliquid prae aliis, sicut manifeste apparet quod ovis unam herbam comedit, et aliam refutat. Ergo in brutis animalibus est electio.

Praeterea, ut dicitur in VI Ethic., *ad prudentiam pertinet quod aliquis bene eligat ea quae sunt ad finem.* Sed prudentia convenit brutis animalibus, unde dicitur in principio Metaphys., quod *prudentia sunt sine disciplina quaecumque sonos audire non potentia sunt, ut apes.* Et hoc etiam sensui manifestum videtur, apparent enim mirabiles sagacitates in operibus animalium, ut apum et aranearum et canum. Canis enim insequens cervum, si ad trivium venerit, odoratu quidem explorat an cervus per primam vel secundam viam transiverit, quod si invenerit non transisse, iam securus per tertiam viam incedit non explorando, quasi utens syllogismo divisivo, quo concludi posset cervum per illam viam incedere, ex quo non incedit per alias duas, cum non sint plures. Ergo videtur quod electio brutis animalibus conveniat.

Sed contra est quod Gregorius Nyssenus dicit, quod *pueri et irrationalia voluntarie quidem faciunt, non tamen eligentia.* Ergo in brutis animalibus non est electio.

Respondeo dicendum quod, cum electio sit praeacceptio unius respectu alterius, necesse est quod electio sit respectu plurium quae eligi possunt. Et ideo in his quae sunt penitus determinata ad unum, electio locum non habet. Est autem differentia inter appetitum sensitivum et voluntatem,

Article 2
Whether choice is to be found in irrational animals?

Objection 1: It would seem that irrational animals are able to choose. For choice "is the desire of certain things on account of an end," as stated in Ethic. iii, 2,3. But irrational animals desire something on account of an end: since they act for an end, and from desire. Therefore choice is in irrational animals.

Objection 2: Further, the very word *electio* [choice] seems to signify the taking of something in preference to others. But irrational animals take something in preference to others: thus we can easily see for ourselves that a sheep will eat one grass and refuse another. Therefore choice is in irrational animals.

Objection 3: Further, according to Ethic. vi, 12, "it is from prudence that a man makes a good choice of means." But prudence is found in irrational animals: hence it is said in the beginning of Metaph. i, 1 that "those animals which, like bees, cannot hear sounds, are prudent by instinct." We see this plainly, in wonderful cases of sagacity manifested in the works of various animals, such as bees, spiders, and dogs. For a hound in following a stag, on coming to a crossroad, tries by scent whether the stag has passed by the first or the second road: and if he find that the stag has not passed there, being thus assured, takes to the third road without trying the scent; as though he were reasoning by way of exclusion, arguing that the stag must have passed by this way, since he did not pass by the others, and there is no other road. Therefore it seems that irrational animals are able to choose.

On the contrary, Gregory of Nyssa* says that "children and irrational animals act willingly but not from choice." Therefore choice is not in irrational animals.

I answer that, Since choice is the taking of one thing in preference to another it must of necessity be in respect of several things that can be chosen. Consequently in those things which are altogether determinate to one there is no place for choice. Now the difference between the sensitive appetite and the will

---

* Nemesius, De Nat. Hom. xxxiii.

quia, ut ex praedictis patet, appetitus sensitivus est determinatus ad unum aliquid particulare secundum ordinem naturae; voluntas autem est quidem, secundum naturae ordinem, determinata ad unum commune, quod est bonum, sed indeterminate se habet respectu particularium bonorum. Et ideo proprie voluntatis est eligere, non autem appetitus sensitivi, qui solus est in brutis animalibus. Et propter hoc brutis animalibus electio non convenit.

AD PRIMUM ergo dicendum quod non omnis appetitus alicuius propter finem, vocatur electio, sed cum quadam discretione unius ab altero. Quae locum habere non potest, nisi ubi appetitus potest ferri ad plura.

AD SECUNDUM dicendum quod brutum animal accipit unum prae alio, quia appetitus eius est naturaliter determinatus ad ipsum. Unde statim quando per sensum vel per imaginationem repraesentatur sibi aliquid ad quod naturaliter inclinatur eius appetitus, absque electione in illud solum movetur. Sicut etiam absque electione ignis movetur sursum, et non deorsum.

AD TERTIUM dicendum quod, sicut dicitur in III Physic., *motus est actus mobilis a movente*. Et ideo virtus moventis apparet in motu mobilis. Et propter hoc in omnibus quae moventur a ratione, apparet ordo rationis moventis, licet ipsa rationem non habeant, sic enim sagitta directe tendit ad signum ex motione sagittantis, ac si ipsa rationem haberet dirigentem. Et idem apparet in motibus horologiorum, et omnium ingeniorum humanorum, quae arte fiunt. Sicut autem comparantur artificialia ad artem humanam, ita comparantur omnia naturalia ad artem divinam. Et ideo ordo apparet in his quae moventur secundum naturam, sicut et in his quae moventur per rationem, ut dicitur in II Physic. Et ex hoc contingit quod in operibus brutorum animalium apparent quaedam sagacitates, inquantum habent inclinationem naturalem ad quosdam ordinatissimos processus, utpote

is that, as stated above (I-II, q. 1, a. 2, ad 3), the sensitive appetite is determinate to one particular thing, according to the order of nature; whereas the will, although determinate to one thing in general, *viz.* the good, according to the order of nature, is nevertheless indeterminate in respect of particular goods. Consequently choice belongs properly to the will, and not to the sensitive appetite which is all that irrational animals have. Wherefore irrational animals are not competent to choose.

Reply to Objection 1: Not every desire of one thing on account of an end is called choice: there must be a certain discrimination of one thing from another. And this cannot be except when the appetite can be moved to several things.

Reply to Objection 2: An irrational animal takes one thing in preference to another, because its appetite is naturally determinate to that thing. Wherefore as soon as an animal, whether by its sense or by its imagination, is offered something to which its appetite is naturally inclined, it is moved to that alone, without making any choice. Just as fire is moved upwards and not downwards, without its making any choice.

Reply to Objection 3: As stated in Phys. iii, 3 "movement is the act of the movable, caused by a mover." Wherefore the power of the mover appears in the movement of that which it moves. Accordingly, in all things moved by reason, the order of reason which moves them is evident, although the things themselves are without reason: for an arrow through the motion of the archer goes straight towards the target, as though it were endowed with reason to direct its course. The same may be seen in the movements of clocks and all engines put together by the art of man. Now as artificial things are in comparison to human art, so are all natural things in comparison to the Divine art. And accordingly order is to be seen in things moved by nature, just as in things moved by reason, as is stated in Phys. ii. And thus it is that in the works of irrational animals we notice certain marks of sagacity, in so far as they have a natural inclination to set about their actions in a most orderly manner through

a summa arte ordinatos. Et propter hoc etiam quaedam animalia dicuntur prudentia vel sagacia, non quod in eis sit aliqua ratio vel electio. Quod ex hoc apparet, quod omnia quae sunt unius naturae, similiter operantur.

being ordained by the Supreme art. For which reason, too, certain animals are called prudent or sagacious; and not because they reason or exercise any choice about things. This is clear from the fact that all that share in one nature, invariably act in the same way.

Articulus 3

Ad tertium sic proceditur. Videtur quod electio non sit tantum eorum quae sunt ad finem. Dicit enim philosophus, in VI Ethic., quod *electionem rectam facit virtus, quaecumque autem illius gratia nata sunt fieri, non sunt virtutis, sed alterius potentiae.* Illud autem cuius gratia fit aliquid, est finis. Ergo electio est finis.

Praeterea, electio importat praeacceptionem unius respectu alterius. Sed sicut eorum quae sunt ad finem unum potest praeaccipi alteri, ita etiam et diversorum finium. Ergo electio potest esse finis, sicut et eorum quae sunt ad finem.

Sed contra est quod philosophus dicit, in III Ethic., quod *voluntas est finis, electio autem eorum quae sunt ad finem.*

Respondeo dicendum quod, sicut iam dictum est, electio consequitur sententiam vel iudicium, quod est sicut conclusio syllogismi operativi. Unde illud cadit sub electione, quod se habet ut conclusio in syllogismo operabilium. Finis autem in operabilibus se habet ut principium, et non ut conclusio, ut philosophus dicit in II Physic. Unde finis, inquantum est huiusmodi, non cadit sub electione. Sed sicut in speculativis nihil prohibet id quod est unius demonstrationis vel scientiae principium, esse conclusionem alterius demonstrationis vel scientiae; primum tamen principium indemonstrabile non potest esse conclusio alicuius demonstrationis vel scientiae; ita etiam contingit id quod est in una operatione ut finis, ordinari ad aliquid ut ad finem. Et hoc modo sub electione cadit. Sicut in operatione medici, sanitas se habet ut finis, unde hoc non cadit sub electione medici, sed hoc supponit tanquam principium. Sed sanitas corporis ordinatur ad

Article 3
Whether choice is only of the means, or sometimes also of the end?

Objection 1: It would seem that choice is not only of the means. For the Philosopher says (Ethic. vi, 12) that "virtue makes us choose aright; but it is not the part of virtue, but of some other power to direct aright those things which are to be done for its sake." But that for the sake of which something is done is the end. Therefore choice is of the end.

Objection 2: Further, choice implies preference of one thing to another. But just as there can be preference of means, so can there be preference of ends. Therefore choice can be of ends, just as it can be of means.

On the contrary, The Philosopher says (Ethic. iii, 2) that "volition is of the end, but choice of the means."

I answer that, As already stated (I-II, q. 13, a. 1, ad 2), choice results from the decision or judgment which is, as it were, the conclusion of a practical syllogism. Hence that which is the conclusion of a practical syllogism, is the matter of choice. Now in practical things the end stands in the position of a principle, not of a conclusion, as the Philosopher says (Phys. ii, 9). Wherefore the end, as such, is not a matter of choice. But just as in speculative knowledge nothing hinders the principle of one demonstration or of one science, from being the conclusion of another demonstration or science; while the first indemonstrable principle cannot be the conclusion of any demonstration or science; so too that which is the end in one operation, may be ordained to something as an end. And in this way it is a matter of choice. Thus in the work of a physician health is the end: wherefore it is not a matter of choice for a physician, but a matter of principle. Now the health of the body is ordained to

bonum animae, unde apud eum qui habet curam de animae salute, potest sub electione cadere esse sanum vel esse infirmum; nam apostolus dicit, II ad Cor. XII, *cum enim infirmor, tunc potens sum. Sed ultimus finis nullo modo sub electione cadit.*

AD PRIMUM ergo dicendum quod fines proprii virtutum ordinantur ad beatitudinem sicut ad ultimum finem. Et hoc modo potest esse eorum electio.

AD SECUNDUM dicendum quod, sicut supra habitum est, ultimus finis est unus tantum. Unde ubicumque occurrunt plures fines, inter eos potest esse electio, secundum quod ordinantur ad ulteriorem finem.

the good of the soul, consequently with one who has charge of the soul's health, health or sickness may be a matter of choice; for the Apostle says (2 Cor. 12:10): "For when I am weak, then am I powerful." But the last end is nowise a matter of choice.

Reply to Objection 1: The proper ends of virtues are ordained to Happiness as to their last end. And thus it is that they can be a matter of choice.

Reply to Objection 2: As stated above (I-II, q. 1, a. 5), there is but one last end. Accordingly wherever there are several ends, they can be the subject of choice, in so far as they are ordained to a further end.

ARTICULUS 4

AD QUARTUM sic proceditur. Videtur quod electio non sit solum respectu humanorum actuum. Electio enim est eorum quae sunt ad finem. Sed ea quae sunt ad finem non solum sunt actus, sed etiam organa, ut dicitur in II Physic. Ergo electiones non sunt tantum humanorum actuum.

PRAETEREA, actio a contemplatione distinguitur. Sed electio etiam in contemplatione locum habet; prout scilicet una opinio alteri praeeligitur. Ergo electio non est solum humanorum actuum.

PRAETEREA, eliguntur homines ad aliqua officia, vel saecularia vel ecclesiastica, ab his qui nihil erga eos agunt. Ergo electio non solum est humanorum actuum.

SED CONTRA est quod philosophus dicit, in III Ethic., quod *nullus eligit nisi ea quae existimat fieri per ipsum.*

RESPONDEO dicendum quod, sicut intentio est finis, ita electio est eorum quae sunt ad finem. Finis autem vel est actio, vel res aliqua. Et cum res aliqua fuerit finis, necesse est quod aliqua humana actio interveniat, vel inquantum homo facit rem illam quae est finis, sicut medicus facit sanitatem, quae est finis eius (unde et facere sanitatem dicitur finis medici); vel inquantum homo aliquo modo utitur vel fruitur re quae est finis, sicut avaro est finis pecunia, vel possessio pecuniae. Et

ARTICLE 4
Whether choice is of those things only that are done by us?

Objection 1: It would seem that choice is not only in respect of human acts. For choice regards the means. Now, not only acts, but also the organs, are means (Phys. ii, 3). Therefore choice is not only concerned with human acts.

Objection 2: Further, action is distinct from contemplation. But choice has a place even in contemplation; in so far as one opinion is preferred to another. Therefore choice is not concerned with human acts alone.

Objection 3: Further, men are chosen for certain posts, whether secular or ecclesiastical, by those who exercise no action in their regard. Therefore choice is not concerned with human acts alone.

On the contrary, The Philosopher says (Ethic. iii, 2) that "no man chooses save what he can do himself."

I answer that, Just as intention regards the end, so does choice regard the means. Now the end is either an action or a thing. And when the end is a thing, some human action must intervene; either in so far as man produces the thing which is the end, as the physician produces health (wherefore the production of health is said to be the end of the physician); or in so far as man, in some fashion, uses or enjoys the thing which is the end; thus for the miser, money or the possession of money is the end. The

eodem modo dicendum est de eo quod est ad finem. Quia necesse est ut id quod est ad finem, vel sit actio; vel res aliqua, interveniente aliqua actione, per quam facit id quod est ad finem, vel utitur eo. Et per hunc modum electio semper est humanorum actuum.

AD PRIMUM ergo dicendum quod organa ordinantur ad finem, inquantum homo utitur eis propter finem.

AD SECUNDUM dicendum quod in ipsa contemplatione est aliquis actus intellectus assentientis huic opinioni vel illi. Actio vero exterior est quae contra contemplationem dividitur.

AD TERTIUM dicendum quod homo qui eligit episcopum vel principem civitatis, eligit nominare ipsum in talem dignitatem. Alioquin, si nulla esset eius actio ad constitutionem episcopi vel principis, non competeret ei electio. Et similiter dicendum est quod quandocumque dicitur aliqua res praeeligi alteri, adiungitur ibi aliqua operatio eligentis.

same is to be said of the means. For the means must needs be either an action; or a thing, with some action intervening whereby man either makes the thing which is the means, or puts it to some use. And thus it is that choice is always in regard to human acts.

Reply to Objection 1: The organs are ordained to the end, inasmuch as man makes use of them for the sake of the end.

Reply to Objection 2: In contemplation itself there is the act of the intellect assenting to this or that opinion. It is exterior action that is put in contradistinction to contemplation.

Reply to Objection 3: When a man chooses someone for a bishopric or some high position in the state, he chooses to name that man to that post. Else, if he had no right to act in the appointment of the bishop or official, he would have no right to choose. Likewise, whenever we speak of one thing being chosen in preference to another, it is in conjunction with some action of the chooser.

ARTICULUS 5

AD QUINTUM sic proceditur. Videtur quod electio non sit solum possibilium. Electio enim est actus voluntatis, ut dictum est. Sed *voluntas est impossibilium,* ut dicitur in III Ethic. Ergo et electio.

PRAETEREA, electio est eorum quae per nos aguntur, sicut dictum est. Nihil ergo refert, quantum ad electionem, utrum eligatur id quod est impossibile simpliciter, vel id quod est impossibile eligenti. Sed frequenter ea quae eligimus, perficere non possumus, et sic sunt impossibilia nobis. Ergo electio est impossibilium.

PRAETEREA, nihil homo tentat agere nisi eligendo. Sed beatus Benedictus dicit quod, si praelatus aliquid impossibile praeceperit, tentandum est. Ergo electio potest esse impossibilium.

SED CONTRA est quod philosophus dicit, in III Ethic., quod *electio non est impossibilium.*

ARTICLE 5
Whether choice is only of possible things?

Objection 1: It would seem that choice in not only of possible things. For choice is an act of the will, as stated above (I-II, q. 13, a. 1). Now there is "a willing of impossibilities" (Ethic. iii, 2). Therefore there is also a choice of impossibilities.

Objection 2: Further, choice is of things done by us, as stated above (I-II, q. 13, a. 4). Therefore it matters not, as far as the act of choosing is concerned, whether one choose that which is impossible in itself, or that which is impossible to the chooser. Now it often happens that we are unable to accomplish what we choose: so that this proves to be impossible to us. Therefore choice is of the impossible.

Objection 3: Further, to try to do a thing is to choose to do it. But the Blessed Benedict says (Regula lxviii) that if the superior command what is impossible, it should be attempted. Therefore choice can be of the impossible.

On the contrary, The Philosopher says (Ethic. iii, 2) that "there is no choice of impossibilities."

RESPONDEO dicendum quod, sicut dictum est, electiones nostrae referuntur semper ad nostras actiones. Ea autem quae per nos aguntur, sunt nobis possibilia. Unde necesse est dicere quod electio non sit nisi possibilium. Similiter etiam ratio eligendi aliquid est ex hoc quod ducit ad finem. Per id autem quod est impossibile, non potest aliquis consequi finem. Cuius signum est quia, cum in consiliando perveniunt homines ad id quod est eis impossibile, discedunt, quasi non valentes ulterius procedere. Apparet etiam hoc manifeste ex processu rationis praecedente. Sic enim se habet id quod est ad finem, de quo electio est, ad finem, sicut conclusio ad principium. Manifestum est autem quod conclusio impossibilis non sequitur ex principio possibili. Unde non potest esse quod finis sit possibilis, nisi id quod est ad finem fuerit possibile. Ad id autem quod est impossibile, nullus movetur. Unde nullus tenderet in finem, nisi per hoc quod apparet id quod est ad finem esse possibile. Unde id quod est impossibile sub electione non cadit.

AD PRIMUM ergo dicendum quod voluntas media est inter intellectum et exteriorem operationem, nam intellectus proponit voluntati suum obiectum, et ipsa voluntas causat exteriorem actionem. Sic igitur principium motus voluntatis consideratur ex parte intellectus, qui apprehendit aliquid ut bonum in universali, sed terminatio, seu perfectio actus voluntatis attenditur secundum ordinem ad operationem, per quam aliquis tendit ad consecutionem rei; nam motus voluntatis est ab anima ad rem. Et ideo perfectio actus voluntatis attenditur secundum hoc quod est aliquid bonum alicui ad agendum. Hoc autem est possibile. Et ideo voluntas completa non est nisi de possibili, quod est bonum volenti. Sed voluntas incompleta est de impossibili, quae secundum quosdam *velleitas* dicitur, quia scilicet aliquis vellet illud, si esset possibile. Electio autem nominat actum voluntatis iam determinatum ad id quod est huic agendum. Et ideo nullo modo est nisi possibilium.

I answer that, As stated above (I-II, q. 13, a. 4), our choice is always concerned with our actions. Now whatever is done by us, is possible to us. Therefore we must needs say that choice is only of possible things. Moreover, the reason for choosing a thing is that it conduces to an end. But what is impossible cannot conduce to an end. A sign of this is that when men in taking counsel together come to something that is impossible to them, they depart, as being unable to proceed with the business. Again, this is evident if we examine the previous process of the reason. For the means, which are the object of choice, are to the end, as the conclusion is to the principle. Now it is clear that an impossible conclusion does not follow from a possible principle. Wherefore an end cannot be possible, unless the means be possible. Now no one is moved to the impossible. Consequently no one would tend to the end, save for the fact that the means appear to be possible. Therefore the impossible is not the object of choice.

Reply to Objection 1: The will stands between the intellect and the external action: for the intellect proposes to the will its object, and the will causes the external action. Hence the principle of the movement in the will is to be found in the intellect, which apprehends something under the universal notion of good: but the term or perfection of the will's act is to be observed in its relation to the action whereby a man tends to the attainment of a thing; for the movement of the will is from the soul to the thing. Consequently the perfect act of the will is in respect of something that is good for one to do. Now this cannot be something impossible. Wherefore the complete act of the will is only in respect of what is possible and good for him that wills. But the incomplete act of the will is in respect of the impossible; and by some is called "velleity," because, to wit, one would will [*vellet*] such a thing, were it possible. But choice is an act of the will, fixed on something to be done by the chooser. And therefore it is by no means of anything but what is possible.

AD SECUNDUM dicendum quod, cum obiectum voluntatis sit bonum apprehensum, hoc modo iudicandum est de obiecto voluntatis, secundum quod cadit sub apprehensione. Et ideo sicut quandoque voluntas est alicuius quod apprehenditur ut bonum, et tamen non est vere bonum; ita quandoque est electio eius quod apprehenditur ut possibile eligenti, quod tamen non est ei possibile.

AD TERTIUM dicendum quod hoc ideo dicitur, quia an aliquid sit possibile, subditus non debet suo iudicio definire; sed in unoquoque, iudicio superioris stare.

Reply to Objection 2: Since the object of the will is the apprehended good, we must judge of the object of the will according as it is apprehended. And so, just as sometimes the will tends to something which is apprehended as good, and yet is not really good; so is choice sometimes made of something apprehended as possible to the chooser, and yet impossible to him.

Reply to Objection 3: The reason for this is that the subject should not rely on his own judgment to decide whether a certain thing is possible; but in each case should stand by his superior's judgment.

ARTICULUS 6

AD SEXTUM sic proceditur. Videtur quod homo ex necessitate eligat. Sic enim se habet finis ad eligibilia, ut principia ad ea quae ex principiis consequuntur, ut patet in VII Ethic. Sed ex principiis ex necessitate deducuntur conclusiones. Ergo ex fine de necessitate movetur aliquis ad eligendum.

PRAETEREA, sicut dictum est, electio consequitur iudicium rationis de agendis. Sed ratio ex necessitate iudicat de aliquibus, propter necessitatem praemissarum. Ergo videtur quod etiam electio ex necessitate sequatur.

PRAETEREA, si aliqua duo sunt penitus aequalia, non magis movetur homo ad unum quam ad aliud, sicut famelicus, si habet cibum aequaliter appetibilem in diversis partibus, et secundum aequalem distantiam, non magis movetur ad unum quam ad alterum, ut Plato dixit, assignans rationem quietis terrae in medio, sicut dicitur in II de caelo. Sed multo minus potest eligi quod accipitur ut minus, quam quod accipitur ut aequale. Ergo si proponantur duo vel plura, inter quae unum maius appareat, impossibile est aliquod aliorum eligere. Ergo ex necessitate eligitur illud quod eminentius apparet. Sed omnis electio est de

ARTICLE 6
Whether man chooses of necessity or freely?

Objection 1: It would seem that man chooses of necessity. For the end stands in relation to the object of choice, as the principle of that which follows from the principles, as declared in Ethic. vii, 8. But conclusions follow of necessity from their principles. Therefore man is moved of necessity from [willing] the end of the choice [of the means].

Objection 2: Further, as stated above (I-II, q. 13, a. 1, ad 2), choice follows the reason's judgment of what is to be done. But reason judges of necessity about some things: on account of the necessity of the premises. Therefore it seems that choice also follows of necessity.

Objection 3: Further, if two things are absolutely equal, man is not moved to one more than to the other; thus if a hungry man, as Plato says (Cf. De Coelo ii, 13), be confronted on either side with two portions of food equally appetizing and at an equal distance, he is not moved towards one more than to the other; and he finds the reason of this in the immobility of the earth in the middle of the world. Now, if that which is equally [eligible] with something else cannot be chosen, much less can that be chosen which appears as less [eligible]. Therefore if two or more things are available, of which one appears to be more [eligible], it is impossible to choose any of the others. Therefore that which appears to hold the first place is chosen of necessity. But every act of choosing is in regard

omni eo quod videtur aliquo modo melius. Ergo omnis electio est ex necessitate.

Sed contra est quod electio est actus potentiae rationalis; quae se habet ad opposita, secundum philosophum.

Respondeo dicendum quod homo non ex necessitate eligit. Et hoc ideo, quia quod possibile est non esse, non necesse est esse. Quod autem possibile sit non eligere vel eligere, huius ratio ex duplici hominis potestate accipi potest. Potest enim homo velle et non velle, agere et non agere, potest etiam velle hoc aut illud, et agere hoc aut illud. Cuius ratio ex ipsa virtute rationis accipitur. Quidquid enim ratio potest apprehendere ut bonum, in hoc voluntas tendere potest. Potest autem ratio apprehendere ut bonum non solum hoc quod est *velle* aut *agere*; sed hoc etiam quod est *non velle* et *non agere*. Et rursum in omnibus particularibus bonis potest considerare rationem boni alicuius, et defectum alicuius boni, quod habet rationem mali, et secundum hoc, potest unumquodque huiusmodi bonorum apprehendere ut eligibile, vel fugibile. Solum autem perfectum bonum, quod est beatitudo, non potest ratio apprehendere sub ratione mali, aut alicuius defectus. Et ideo ex necessitate beatitudinem homo vult, nec potest velle non esse beatus, aut miser. Electio autem, cum non sit de fine, sed de his quae sunt ad finem, ut iam dictum est; non est perfecti boni, quod est beatitudo, sed aliorum particularium bonorum. Et ideo homo non ex necessitate, sed libere eligit.

Ad primum ergo dicendum quod non semper ex principiis ex necessitate procedit conclusio, sed tunc solum quando principia non possunt esse vera si conclusio non sit vera. Et similiter non oportet quod semper ex fine insit homini necessitas ad eligendum ea quae sunt ad finem, quia non omne quod est ad finem, tale est ut sine eo finis haberi non possit; aut, si tale sit, non semper sub tali ratione consideratur.

Ad secundum dicendum quod sententia sive iudicium rationis de rebus agendis est circa contingentia, quae a nobis fieri possunt, in quibus conclusiones non

to something that seems in some way better. Therefore every choice is made necessarily.

On the contrary, Choice is an act of a rational power; which according to the Philosopher (Metaph. ix, 2) stands in relation to opposites.

I answer that, Man does not choose of necessity. And this is because that which is possible not to be, is not of necessity. Now the reason why it is possible not to choose, or to choose, may be gathered from a twofold power in man. For man can will and not will, act and not act; again, he can will this or that, and do this or that. The reason of this is seated in the very power of the reason. For the will can tend to whatever the reason can apprehend as good. Now the reason can apprehend as good, not only this, *viz.* "to will" or "to act," but also this, *viz.* "not to will" or "not to act." Again, in all particular goods, the reason can consider an aspect of some good, and the lack of some good, which has the aspect of evil: and in this respect, it can apprehend any single one of such goods as to be chosen or to be avoided. The perfect good alone, which is Happiness, cannot be apprehended by the reason as an evil, or as lacking in any way. Consequently man wills Happiness of necessity, nor can he will not to be happy, or to be unhappy. Now since choice is not of the end, but of the means, as stated above (I-II, q. 13, a. 3); it is not of the perfect good, which is Happiness, but of other particular goods. Therefore man chooses not of necessity, but freely.

Reply to Objection 1: The conclusion does not always of necessity follow from the principles, but only when the principles cannot be true if the conclusion is not true. In like manner, the end does not always necessitate in man the choosing of the means, because the means are not always such that the end cannot be gained without them; or, if they be such, they are not always considered in that light.

Reply to Objection 2: The reason's decision or judgment of what is to be done is about things that are contingent and possible to us. In such matters the conclusions do not

ex necessitate sequuntur ex principiis necessariis absoluta necessitate, sed necessariis solum ex conditione, ut, *si currit, movetur.*

AD TERTIUM dicendum quod nihil prohibet, si aliqua duo aequalia proponantur secundum unam considerationem, quin circa alterum consideretur aliqua conditio per quam emineat, et magis flectatur voluntas in ipsum quam in aliud.

follow of necessity from principles that are absolutely necessary, but from such as are so conditionally; as, for instance, "If he runs, he is in motion."

Reply to Objection 3: If two things be proposed as equal under one aspect, nothing hinders us from considering in one of them some particular point of superiority, so that the will has a bent towards that one rather than towards the other.

QUAESTIO XIV

Deinde considerandum est de consilio. Et circa hoc quaeruntur sex. *Primo,* utrum consilium sit inquisitio. *Secundo,* utrum consilium sit de fine, vel solum de his quae sunt ad finem. *Tertio,* utrum consilium sit solum de his quae a nobis aguntur. *Quarto,* utrum consilium sit de omnibus quae a nobis aguntur. *Quinto,* utrum consilium procedat ordine resolutorio. *Sexto,* utrum consilium procedat in infinitum.

QUESTION 14
Of Counsel, Which Precedes Choice

We must now consider counsel; concerning which there are six points of inquiry: 1. Whether counsel is an inquiry? 2. Whether counsel is of the end or of the means? 3. Whether counsel is only of things that we do? 4. Whether counsel is of all things that we do? 5. Whether the process of counsel is one of analysis? 6. Whether the process of counsel is indefinite?

ARTICULUS 1

AD PRIMUM sic proceditur. Videtur quod consilium non sit inquisitio. Dicit enim Damascenus quod *consilium est appetitus.* Sed ad appetitum non pertinet inquirere. Ergo consilium non est inquisitio.

PRAETEREA, inquirere intellectus discurrentis est; et sic Deo non convenit, cuius cognitio non est discursiva, ut in primo habitum est. Sed consilium Deo attribuitur, dicitur enim ad Ephes. I, quod *operatur omnia secundum consilium voluntatis suae.* Ergo consilium non est inquisitio.

PRAETEREA, inquisitio est de rebus dubiis. Sed consilium datur de his quae sunt certa bona; secundum illud apostoli, I ad Cor. VII, *de virginibus autem praeceptum domini non habeo, consilium autem do.* Ergo consilium non est inquisitio.

ARTICLE 1
Whether counsel is an inquiry?

Objection 1: It would seem that counsel is not an inquiry. For Damascene says (De Fide Orth. ii, 22) that counsel is "an act of the appetite." But inquiry is not an act of the appetite. Therefore counsel is not an inquiry.

Objection 2: Further, inquiry is a discursive act of the intellect: for which reason it is not found in God, Whose knowledge is not discursive, as we have shown in the I, q. 14, a. 7. But counsel is ascribed to God: for it is written (Eph. 1:11) that "He worketh all things according to the counsel of His will." Therefore counsel is not inquiry.

Objection 3: Further, inquiry is of doubtful matters. But counsel is given in matters that are certainly good; thus the Apostle says (1 Cor. 7:25): "Now concerning virgins I have no commandment of the Lord: but I give counsel." Therefore counsel is not an inquiry.

On the contrary, Gregory of Nyssa* says: "Every counsel is an inquiry; but not every inquiry is a counsel."

I answer that, Choice, as stated above (I-II, q. 13, a. 1, ad. 2; a. 3), follows the judgment of the reason about what is to be done. Now there is much uncertainty in things that have to be done; because actions are concerned with contingent singulars, which by reason of their vicissitude, are uncertain. Now in things doubtful and uncertain the reason does not pronounce judgment, without previous inquiry: wherefore the reason must of necessity institute an inquiry before deciding on the objects of choice; and this inquiry is called counsel. Hence the Philosopher says (Ethic. iii, 2) that choice is the "desire of what has been already counselled."

Reply to Objection 1: When the acts of two powers are ordained to one another, in each of them there is something belonging to the other power: consequently each act can be denominated from either power. Now it is evident that the act of the reason giving direction as to the means, and the act of the will tending to these means according to the reason's direction, are ordained to one another. Consequently there is to be found something of the reason, *viz.* order, in that act of the will, which is choice: and in counsel, which is an act of reason, something of the will—both as matter (since counsel is of what man wills to do)—and as motive (because it is from willing the end, that man is moved to take counsel in regard to the means). And therefore, just as the Philosopher says (Ethic. vi, 2) that choice "is intellect influenced by appetite," thus pointing out that both concur in the act of choosing; so Damascene says (De Fide Orth. ii, 22) that counsel is "appetite based on inquiry," so as to show that counsel belongs, in a way, both to the will, on whose behalf and by whose impulsion the inquiry is made, and to the reason that executes the inquiry.

Reply to Objection 2: The things that we say of God must be understood without any of the defects which are to be found in us: thus in us science is of conclusions derived by

---

* Nemesius, De Nat. Hom. xxxiv.

discursum a causis in effectus; sed scientia dicta de Deo, significat certitudinem de omnibus effectibus in prima causa, absque omni discursu. Et similiter consilium attribuitur Deo quantum ad certitudinem sententiae vel iudicii, quae in nobis provenit ex inquisitione consilii. Sed huiusmodi inquisitio in Deo locum non habet, et ideo consilium secundum hoc Deo non attribuitur. Et secundum hoc Damascenus dicit quod *Deus non consiliatur, ignorantis enim est consiliari.*

AD TERTIUM dicendum quod nihil prohibet aliqua esse certissima bona secundum sententiam sapientum et spiritualium virorum, quae tamen non sunt certa bona secundum sententiam plurium, vel carnalium hominum. Et ideo de talibus consilia dantur.

ARTICULUS 2

AD SECUNDUM sic proceditur. Videtur quod consilium non solum sit de his quae sunt ad finem, sed etiam de fine. Quaecumque enim dubitationem habent, de his potest inquiri. Sed circa operabilia humana contingit esse dubitationem de fine, et non solum de his quae sunt ad finem. Cum igitur inquisitio circa operabilia sit consilium, videtur quod consilium possit esse de fine.

PRAETEREA, materia consilii sunt operationes humanae. Sed quaedam operationes humanae sunt fines, ut dicitur in I Ethic. ergo consilium potest esse de fine.

SED CONTRA est quod Gregorius Nyssenus dicit, quod *non de fine, sed de his quae sunt ad finem, est consilium.*

RESPONDEO dicendum quod finis in operabilibus habet rationem principii, eo quod rationes eorum quae sunt ad finem, ex fine sumuntur. Principium autem non cadit sub quaestione, sed principia oportet supponere in omni inquisitione. Unde cum consilium sit quaestio, de fine non est consilium, sed solum de his quae sunt ad finem. Tamen contingit id quod est finis respectu quorundam, ordinari ad alium finem, sicut etiam id quod est principium unius demonstrationis, est conclusio alterius. Et ideo id quod accipitur

reasoning from causes to effects: but science when said of God means sure knowledge of all effects in the First Cause, without any reasoning process. In like manner we ascribe counsel to God, as to the certainty of His knowledge or judgment, which certainty in us arises from the inquiry of counsel. But such inquiry has no place in God; wherefore in this respect it is not ascribed to God: in which sense Damascene says (De Fide Orth. ii, 22): "**God takes not counsel: those only take counsel who lack knowledge.**"

Reply to Objection 3: It may happen that things which are most certainly good in the opinion of wise and spiritual men are not certainly good in the opinion of many, or at least of carnal-minded men. Consequently in such things counsel may be given.

ARTICLE 2
Whether counsel is of the end, or only of the means?

Objection 1: It would seem that counsel is not only of the means but also of the end. For whatever is doubtful, can be the subject of inquiry. Now in things to be done by man there happens sometimes a doubt as to the end and not only as to the means. Since therefore inquiry as to what is to be done is counsel, it seems that counsel can be of the end.

Objection 2: Further, the matter of counsel is human actions. But some human actions are ends, as stated in Ethic. i, 1. Therefore counsel can be of the end.

On the contrary, Gregory of Nyssa* says that "counsel is not of the end, but of the means."

I answer that, The end is the principle in practical matters: because the reason of the means is to be found in the end. Now the principle cannot be called in question, but must be presupposed in every inquiry. Since therefore counsel is an inquiry, it is not of the end, but only of the means. Nevertheless it may happen that what is the end in regard to some things, is ordained to something else; just as also what is the principle of one demonstration, is the conclusion of another: and consequently that which is looked upon

---

* Nemesius, De Nat. Hom. xxxiv.

ut finis in una inquisitione, potest accipi ut ad finem in alia inquisitione. Et sic de eo erit consilium.

AD PRIMUM ergo dicendum quod id quod accipitur ut finis, est iam determinatum. Unde quandiu habetur ut dubium, non habetur ut finis. Et ideo si de eo consilium habetur, non erit consilium de fine, sed de eo quod est ad finem.

AD SECUNDUM dicendum quod de operationibus est consilium, inquantum ordinantur ad aliquem finem. Unde si aliqua operatio humana sit finis, de ea, inquantum huiusmodi, non est consilium.

as the end in one inquiry, may be looked upon as the means in another; and thus it will become an object of counsel.

Reply to Objection 1: That which is looked upon as an end, is already fixed: consequently as long as there is any doubt about it, it is not looked upon as an end. Wherefore if counsel is taken about it, it will be counsel not about the end, but about the means.

Reply to Objection 2: Counsel is about operations, in so far as they are ordained to some end. Consequently if any human act be an end, it will not, as such, be the matter of counsel.

ARTICULUS 3

AD TERTIUM sic proceditur. Videtur quod consilium non sit solum de his quae aguntur a nobis. Consilium enim collationem quandam importat. Sed collatio inter multos potest fieri etiam de rebus immobilibus, quae non fiunt a nobis, puta de naturis rerum. Ergo consilium non solum est de his quae aguntur a nobis.

PRAETEREA, homines interdum consilium quaerunt de his quae sunt lege statuta, unde et iurisconsulti dicuntur. Et tamen eorum qui quaerunt huiusmodi consilium, non est leges facere. Ergo consilium non solum est de his quae a nobis aguntur.

PRAETEREA, dicuntur etiam quidam consultationes facere de futuris eventibus; qui tamen non sunt in potestate nostra. Ergo consilium non solum est de his quae a nobis fiunt.

PRAETEREA, si consilium esset solum de his quae a nobis fiunt, nullus consiliaretur de his quae sunt per alium agenda. Sed hoc patet esse falsum. Ergo consilium non solum est de his quae a nobis fiunt.

SED CONTRA est quod Gregorius Nyssenus dicit, *consiliamur de his quae sunt in nobis, et per nos fieri possunt.*

RESPONDEO dicendum quod consilium proprie importat collationem inter plures habitam. Quod et ipsum nomen designat, dicitur enim *consilium* quasi *considium*, eo quod multi consident ad

ARTICLE 3
Whether counsel is only of things that we do?

Objection 1: It would seem that counsel is not only of things that we do. For counsel implies some kind of conference. But it is possible for many to confer about things that are not subject to movement, and are not the result of our actions, such as the nature of various things. Therefore counsel is not only of things that we do.

Objection 2: Further, men sometimes seek counsel about things that are laid down by law; hence we speak of counsel at law. And yet those who seek counsel thus, have nothing to do in making the laws. Therefore counsel is not only of things that we do.

Objection 3: Further, some are said to take consultation about future events; which, however, are not in our power. Therefore counsel is not only of things that we do.

Objection 4: Further, if counsel were only of things that we do, no would take counsel about what another does. But this is clearly untrue. Therefore counsel is not only of things that we do.

On the contrary, Gregory of Nyssa* says: "We take counsel of things that are within our competency and that we are able to do."

I answer that, Counsel properly implies a conference held between several; the very word [*consilium*] denotes this, for it means a sitting together [*considium*], from the fact that many sit together in order to

---

* Nemesius, De Nat. Hom. xxxiv.

simul conferendum. Est autem considerandum quod in particularibus contingentibus, ad hoc quod aliquid certum cognoscatur, plures conditiones seu circumstantias considerare oportet, quas ab uno non facile est considerari, sed a pluribus certius percipiuntur, dum quod unus considerat, alii non occurrit, in necessariis autem et universalibus est absolutior et simplicior consideratio, ita quod magis ad huiusmodi considerationem unus per se sufficere potest. Et ideo inquisitio consilii proprie pertinet ad contingentia singularia. Cognitio autem veritatis in talibus non habet aliquid magnum, ut per se sit appetibilis, sicut cognitio universalium et necessariorum, sed appetitur secundum quod est utilis ad operationem, quia actiones sunt circa contingentia singularia. Et ideo dicendum est quod proprie consilium est circa ea quae aguntur a nobis.

AD PRIMUM ergo dicendum quod consilium importat collationem non quamcumque, sed collationem de rebus agendis, ratione iam dicta.

AD SECUNDUM dicendum quod id quod est lege positum, quamvis non sit ex operatione quaerentis consilium, tamen est directivum eius ad operandum, quia ista est una ratio aliquid operandi, mandatum legis.

AD TERTIUM dicendum quod consilium non solum est de his quae aguntur, sed de his quae ordinantur ad operationes. Et propter hoc consultatio dicitur fieri de futuris eventibus, inquantum homo per futuros eventus cognitos dirigitur ad aliquid faciendum vel vitandum.

AD QUARTUM dicendum quod de aliorum factis consilium quaerimus, inquantum sunt quodammodo unum nobiscum, vel per unionem affectus, sicut amicus sollicitus est de his quae ad amicum spectant, sicut de suis; vel per modum instrumenti, nam agens principale et instrumentale sunt quasi una causa, cum unum agat per alterum; et sic dominus consiliatur de his quae sunt agenda per servum.

confer with one another. Now we must take note that in contingent particular cases, in order that anything be known for certain, it is necessary to take several conditions or circumstances into consideration, which it is not easy for one to consider, but are considered by several with greater certainty, since what one takes note of, escapes the notice of another; whereas in necessary and universal things, our view is brought to bear on matters **much more absolute and simple, so that one man by himself may be sufficient to consider** these things. Wherefore the inquiry of counsel is concerned, properly speaking, with contingent singulars. Now the knowledge of the truth in such matters does not rank so high as to be desirable of itself, as is the knowledge of things universal and necessary; but it is desired as being useful towards action, because actions bear on things singular and contingent. Consequently, properly speaking, counsel is about things done by us.

Reply to Objection 1: Counsel implies conference, not of any kind, but about what is to be done, for the reason given above.

Reply to Objection 2: Although that which is laid down by the law is not due to the action of him who seeks counsel, nevertheless it directs him in his action: since the mandate of the law is one reason for doing something.

Reply to Objection 3: Counsel is not only about what is done, but also about whatever has relation to what is done. And for this reason we speak of consulting about future events, in so far as man is induced to do or omit something, through the knowledge of future events.

Reply to Objection 4: We seek counsel about the actions of others, in so far as they are, in some way, one with us; either by union of affection—thus a man is solicitous about what concerns his friend, as though it concerned himself; or after the manner of an instrument, for the principal agent and the instrument are, in a way, one cause, since one acts through the other; thus the master takes counsel about what he would do through his servant.

Articulus 4

Ad quartum sic proceditur. Videtur quod consilium sit de omnibus quae sunt per nos agenda. Electio enim est *appetitus praeconsiliati,* ut dictum est. Sed electio est de omnibus quae per nos aguntur. Ergo et consilium.

Praeterea, consilium importat inquisitionem rationis. Sed in omnibus quae non per impetum passionis agimus, procedimus ex inquisitione rationis. Ergo de omnibus quae aguntur a nobis, est consilium.

Praeterea, philosophus dicit, in III Ethic., quod *si per plura aliquid fieri potest, consilio inquiritur per quod facillime et optime fiat; si autem per unum, qualiter per illud fiat.* Sed omne quod fit, fit per unum vel per multa. Ergo de omnibus quae fiunt a nobis, est consilium.

Sed contra est quod Gregorius Nyssenus dicit, quod *de his quae secundum disciplinam vel artem sunt operibus, non est consilium.*

Respondeo dicendum quod consilium est inquisitio quaedam, ut dictum est. De illis autem inquirere solemus, quae in dubium veniunt, unde et ratio inquisitiva, quae dicitur argumentum, *est rei dubiae faciens fidem.* Quod autem aliquid in operabilibus humanis non sit dubitabile, ex duobus contingit. Uno modo, quia per determinatas vias proceditur ad determinatos fines, sicut contingit in artibus quae habent certas vias operandi; sicut scriptor non consiliatur quomodo debeat trahere litteras, hoc enim determinatum est per artem. Alio modo, quia non multum refert utrum sic vel sic fiat, et ista sunt minima, quae parum adiuvant vel impediunt respectu finis consequendi; quod autem parum est, quasi nihil accipit ratio. Et ideo de duobus non consiliamur, quamvis ordinentur ad finem, ut philosophus dicit,

Article 4
Whether counsel is about all things that we do?

Objection 1: It would seem that counsel is about all things that we have to do. For choice is the "desire of what is counselled" as stated above (I-II, q. 14, a. 1). But choice is about all things that we do. Therefore counsel is too.

Objection 2: Further, counsel implies the reason's inquiry. But, whenever we do not act through the impulse of passion, we act in virtue of the reason's inquiry. Therefore there is counsel about everything that we do.

Objection 3: Further, the Philosopher says (Ethic. iii, 3) that "if it appears that something can be done by more means than one, we take counsel by inquiring whereby it may be done most easily and best; but if it can be accomplished by one means, how it can be done by this." But whatever is done, is done by one means or by several. Therefore counsel takes place in all things that we do.

On the contrary, Gregory of Nyssa* says that "counsel has no place in things that are done according to science or art."

I answer that, Counsel is a kind of inquiry, as stated above (I-II, q. 14, a. 1). But we are wont to inquire about things that admit of doubt; hence the process of inquiry, which is called an argument, "is a reason that attests something that admitted of doubt."† Now, that something in relation to human acts admits of no doubt, arises from a twofold source. First, because certain determinate ends are gained by certain determinate means: as happens in the arts which are governed by certain fixed rules of action; thus a writer does not take counsel how to form his letters, for this is determined by art. Secondly, from the fact that it little matters whether it is done this or that way; this occurs in minute matters, which help or hinder but little with regard to the end aimed at; and reason looks upon small things as mere nothings. Consequently there are two things of which we do not take counsel, although they conduce to the end, as the Philosopher says (Ethic. iii, 3):

---
* Nemesius, De Nat. Hom. xxxiv.
† Cicero, Topic. ad Trebat.

scilicet de rebus parvis; et de his quae sunt determinata qualiter fieri debent, sicut est in operibus artium, praeter quasdam coniecturales, ut Gregorius Nyssenus dicit, ut puta medicinalis, negotiativa, et huiusmodi.

AD PRIMUM ergo dicendum quod electio praesupponit consilium ratione iudicii vel sententiae. Unde quando iudicium vel sententia manifesta est absque inquisitione, non requiritur consilii inquisitio.

AD SECUNDUM dicendum quod ratio in rebus manifestis non inquirit, sed statim iudicat. Et ideo non oportet in omnibus quae ratione aguntur, esse inquisitionem consilii.

AD TERTIUM dicendum quod quando aliquid per unum potest fieri, sed diversis modis, potest dubitationem habere, sicut et quando fit per plura, et ideo opus est consilio. Sed quando determinatur non solum res, sed modus, tunc non est opus consilio.

namely, minute things, and those which have a fixed way of being done, as in works produced by art, with the exception of those arts that admit of conjecture such as medicine, commerce, and the like, as Gregory of Nyssa says.*

Reply to Objection 1: Choice presupposes counsel by reason of its judgment or decision. Consequently when the judgment or decision is evident without inquiry, there is no need for the inquiry of counsel.

Reply to Objection 2: In matters that are evident, the reason makes no inquiry, but judges at once. Consequently there is no need of counsel in all that is done by reason.

Reply to Objection 3: When a thing can be accomplished by one means, but in different ways, doubt may arise, just as when it can be accomplished by several means: hence the need of counsel. But when not only the means, but also the way of using the means, is fixed, then there is no need of counsel.

ARTICULUS 5

AD QUINTUM sic proceditur. Videtur quod consilium non procedat modo resolutorio. Consilium enim est de his quae a nobis aguntur. Sed operationes nostrae non procedunt modo resolutorio, sed magis modo compositivo, scilicet de simplicibus ad composita. Ergo consilium non semper procedit modo resolutorio.

PRAETEREA, consilium est inquisitio rationis. Sed ratio a prioribus incipit, et ad posteriora devenit, secundum convenientiorem ordinem cum igitur praeterita sint priora praesentibus, et praesentia priora futuris, in consiliando videtur esse procedendum a praesentibus et praeteritis in futura. Quod non pertinet ad ordinem resolutorium. Ergo in consiliis non servatur ordo resolutorius.

PRAETEREA, consilium non est nisi de his quae sunt nobis possibilia, ut dicitur in III Ethic. Sed an sit nobis aliquid possibile, perpenditur ex eo quod possumus facere, vel non possumus facere,

ARTICLE 5
Whether the process of counsel is one of analysis?

Objection 1: It would seem that the process of counsel is not one of analysis. For counsel is about things that we do. But the process of our actions is not one of analysis, but rather one of synthesis, *viz.* from the simple to the composite. Therefore counsel does not always proceed by way of analysis.

Objection 2: Further, counsel is an inquiry of the reason. But reason proceeds from things that precede to things that follow, according to the more appropriate order. Since then, the past precedes the present, and the present precedes the future, it seems that in taking counsel one should proceed from the past and present to the future: which is not an analytical process. Therefore the process of counsel is not one of analysis.

Objection 3: Further, counsel is only of such things as are possible to us, according to Ethic. iii, 3. But the question as to whether a certain thing is possible to us, depends on what we are able or unable to do,

---

*   Nemesius, De Nat. Hom. xxiv.

ut perveniamus in illud. Ergo in inquisitione consilii a praesentibus incipere oportet.

SED CONTRA est quod philosophus dicit, in III Ethic., quod *ille qui consiliatur, videtur quaerere et resolvere.*

RESPONDEO dicendum quod in omni inquisitione oportet incipere ab aliquo principio. Quod quidem si, sicut est prius in cognitione, ita etiam sit prius in esse, non est processus resolutorius, sed magis compositivus, procedere enim a causis in effectus, est processus compositivus, nam causae sunt simpliciores effectibus. Si autem id quod est prius in cognitione, sit posterius in esse, est processus resolutorius, utpote cum de effectibus manifestis iudicamus, resolvendo in causas simplices. Principium autem in inquisitione consilii est finis, qui quidem est prior in intentione, posterior tamen in esse. Et secundum hoc, oportet quod inquisitio consilii sit resolutiva, incipiendo scilicet ab eo quod in futuro intenditur, quousque perveniatur ad id quod statim agendum est.

AD PRIMUM ergo dicendum quod consilium est quidem de operationibus. Sed ratio operationum accipitur ex fine, et ideo ordo ratiocinandi de operationibus, est contrarius ordini operandi.

AD SECUNDUM dicendum quod ratio incipit ab eo quod est prius secundum rationem, non autem semper ab eo quod est prius tempore.

AD TERTIUM dicendum quod de eo quod est agendum propter finem, non quaereremus scire an sit possibile, si non esset congruum fini. Et ideo prius oportet inquirere an conveniat ad ducendum in finem, quam consideretur an sit possibile.

ARTICULUS 6

AD SEXTUM sic proceditur. Videtur quod inquisitio consilii procedat in infinitum. Consilium enim est inquisitio de particularibus, in quibus est operatio. Sed singularia sunt infinita. Ergo inquisitio consilii est infinita.

in order to gain such and such an end. Therefore the inquiry of counsel should begin from things present.

On the contrary, The Philosopher says (Ethic. iii, 3) that "he who takes counsel seems to inquire and analyze."

I answer that, In every inquiry one must begin from some principle. And if this principle precedes both in knowledge and in being, the process is not analytic, but synthetic: because to proceed from cause to effect is to proceed synthetically, since causes are more simple than effects. But if that which precedes in knowledge is later in the order of being, the process is one of analysis, as when our judgment deals with effects, which by analysis we trace to their simple causes. Now the principle in the inquiry of counsel is the end, which precedes indeed in intention, but comes afterwards into execution. Hence the inquiry of counsel must needs be one of analysis, beginning that is to say, from that which is intended in the future, and continuing until it arrives at that which is to be done at once.

Reply to Objection 1: Counsel is indeed about action. But actions take their reason from the end; and consequently the order of reasoning about actions is contrary to the order of actions.

Reply to Objection 2: Reason begins with that which is first according to reason; but not always with that which is first in point of time.

Reply to Objection 3: We should not want to know whether something to be done for an end be possible, if it were not suitable for gaining that end. Hence we must first inquire whether it be conducive to the end, before considering whether it be possible.

ARTICLE 6
Whether the process of counsel is indefinite?

Objection 1: It would seem that the process of counsel is indefinite. For counsel is an inquiry about the particular things with which action is concerned. But singulars are infinite. Therefore the process of counsel is indefinite.

I-II, q. 14, a. 6, arg. 2

PRAETEREA, sub inquisitione consilii cadit considerare non solum quid agendum sit, sed etiam quomodo impedimenta tollantur. Sed quaelibet humana actio potest impediri, et impedimentum tolli potest per aliquam rationem humanam. Ergo in infinitum remanet quaerere de impedimentis tollendis.

PRAETEREA, inquisitio scientiae demonstrativae non procedit in infinitum, quia est devenire in aliqua principia per se nota, quae **omnimodam certitudinem habent**. Sed talis certitudo non potest inveniri in singularibus contingentibus, quae sunt variabilia et incerta. Ergo inquisitio consilii procedit in infinitum.

SED CONTRA, *nullus movetur ad id ad quod impossibile est quod perveniat,* ut dicitur in I de caelo. Sed infinitum impossibile est transire. Si igitur inquisitio consilii sit infinita, nullus consiliari inciperet. Quod patet esse falsum.

RESPONDEO dicendum quod inquisitio consilii est finita in actu ex duplici parte, scilicet ex parte principii, et ex parte termini. Accipitur enim in inquisitione consilii duplex principium. Unum proprium, ex ipso genere operabilium, et hoc est finis, de quo non est consilium, sed supponitur in consilio ut principium, ut dictum est. Aliud quasi ex alio genere assumptum sicut et in scientiis demonstrativis una scientia supponit aliqua ab alia, de quibus non inquirit. Huiusmodi autem principia quae in inquisitione consilii supponuntur, sunt quaecumque sunt per sensum accepta, utpote quod hoc sit panis vel ferrum; et quaecumque sunt per aliquam scientiam speculativam vel practicam in universali cognita, sicut quod moechari est a Deo prohibitum, et quod homo non potest vivere nisi nutriatur nutrimento convenienti. Et de istis non inquirit consiliator. Terminus autem inquisitionis est id quod statim est in potestate nostra ut faciamus. Sicut enim finis habet rationem principii, ita id quod agitur propter finem, habet rationem conclusionis. Unde id quod primo agendum occurrit, habet rationem ultimae conclusionis, ad quam inquisitio terminatur. Nihil autem prohibet consilium

COUNSEL, WHICH PRECEDES CHOICE

Objection 2: Further, the inquiry of counsel has to consider not only what is to be done, but how to avoid obstacles. But every human action can be hindered, and an obstacle can be removed by some human reason. Therefore the inquiry about removing obstacles can go on indefinitely.

Objection 3: Further, the inquiry of demonstrative science does not go on indefinitely, because one can come to principles **that are self-evident, which are absolutely certain**. But such like certainty is not to be had in contingent singulars, which are variable and uncertain. Therefore the inquiry of counsel goes on indefinitely.

On the contrary, "No one is moved to that which he cannot possibly reach" (De Coelo i, 7). But it is impossible to pass through the infinite. If therefore the inquiry of counsel is infinite, no one would begin to take counsel. Which is clearly untrue.

I answer that, The inquiry of counsel is actually finite on both sides, on that of its principle and on that of its term. For a twofold principle is available in the inquiry of counsel. One is proper to it, and belongs to the very genus of things pertaining to operation: this is the end which is not the matter of counsel, but is taken for granted as its principle, as stated above (I-II, q. 14, a. 2). The other principle is taken from another genus, so to speak; thus in demonstrative sciences one science postulates certain things from another, without inquiring into them. Now these principles which are taken for granted in the inquiry of counsel are any facts received through the senses—for instance, that this is bread or iron: and also any general statements known either through speculative or through practical science; for instance, that adultery is forbidden by God, or that man cannot live without suitable nourishment. Of such things counsel makes no inquiry. But the term of inquiry is that which we are able to do at once. For just as the end is considered in the light of a principle, so the means are considered in the light of a conclusion. Wherefore that which presents itself as to be done first, holds the position of an ultimate conclusion whereat the inquiry comes to an end. Nothing however prevents counsel

potentia infinitum esse, secundum quod in infinitum possunt aliqua occurrere consilio inquirenda.

AD PRIMUM ergo dicendum quod singularia non sunt infinita actu, sed in potentia tantum.

AD SECUNDUM dicendum quod, licet humana actio possit impediri, non tamen semper habet impedimentum paratum. Et ideo non semper oportet consiliari de impedimento tollendo.

AD TERTIUM dicendum quod in singularibus contingentibus potest aliquid accipi certum, etsi non simpliciter, tamen ut nunc, prout assumitur in operatione. Socratem enim sedere non est necessarium, sed eum sedere, dum sedet, est necessarium. Et hoc per certitudinem accipi potest.

from being infinite potentially, for as much as an infinite number of things may present themselves to be inquired into by means of counsel.

Reply to Objection 1: Singulars are infinite; not actually, but only potentially.

Reply to Objection 2: Although human action can be hindered, the hindrance is not always at hand. Consequently it is not always necessary to take counsel about removing the obstacle.

Reply to Objection 3: In contingent singulars, something may be taken for certain, not simply, indeed, but for the time being, and as far as it concerns the work to be done. Thus that Socrates is sitting is not a necessary statement; but that he is sitting, as long as he continues to sit, is necessary; and this can be taken for a certain fact.

Question 15
Of Consent, Which Is an Act of the Will in Regard to the Means

We must now consider consent; concerning which there are four points of inquiry: 1. Whether consent is an act of the appetitive or of the apprehensive power? 2. Whether it is to be found in irrational animals? 3. Whether it is directed to the end or to the means? 4. Whether consent to an act belongs to the higher part of the soul only?

Article 1
Whether consent is an act of the appetitive or of the apprehensive power?

Objection 1: It would seem that consent belongs only to the apprehensive part of the soul. For Augustine (De Trin. xii, 12) ascribes consent to the higher reason. But the reason is an apprehensive power. Therefore consent belongs to an apprehensive power.

Objection 2: Further, consent is "co-sense." But sense is an apprehensive power. Therefore consent is the act of an apprehensive power.

Objection 3: Further, just as assent is an application of the intellect to something, so is consent. But assent belongs to the intellect, which is an apprehensive power. Therefore consent also belongs to an apprehensive power.

On the contrary, Damascene says (De Fide Orth. ii, 22) that "if a man judge without affection for that of which he judges, there is no sentence," i.e., consent. But affection belongs to the appetitive power. Therefore consent does also.

I answer that, Consent implies application of sense to something. Now it is proper to sense to take cognizance of things present; for the imagination apprehends the similitude of corporeal things, even in the absence of the things of which they bear the likeness; while the intellect apprehends universal ideas, which it can apprehend indifferently, whether the singulars be present or absent. And since the act of an appetitive power is a kind of inclination to the thing itself, the application of the appetitive power to the

rem, secundum quod ei inhaeret, accipit nomen sensus, quasi experientiam quandam sumens de re cui inhaeret, inquantum complacet sibi in ea. Unde et Sap. I, dicitur, *sentite de domino in bonitate.* Et secundum hoc, consentire est actus appetitivae virtutis.

AD PRIMUM ergo dicendum quod, sicut dicitur in III de anima, *voluntas in ratione est.* Unde cum Augustinus attribuit consensum rationi, accipit rationem secundum quod in ea includitur voluntas.

AD SECUNDUM dicendum, quod sentire proprie dictum ad apprehensivam potentiam pertinet, sed secundum similitudinem cuiusdam experientiae, pertinet ad appetitivam, ut dictum est.

AD TERTIUM dicendum quod *assentire* est quasi *ad aliud sentire,* et sic importat quandam distantiam ad id cui assentitur. Sed *consentire* est *simul sentire,* et sic importat quandam coniunctionem ad id cui consentitur. Et ideo voluntas, cuius est tendere ad ipsam rem, magis proprie dicitur consentire, intellectus autem, cuius operatio non est secundum motum ad rem, sed potius e converso, ut in primo dictum est, magis proprie dicitur assentire, quamvis unum pro alio poni soleat. Potest etiam dici quod intellectus assentit, inquantum a voluntate movetur.

thing, in so far as it cleaves to it, gets by a kind of similitude, the name of sense, since, as it were, it acquires direct knowledge of the thing to which it cleaves, in so far as it takes complacency in it. Hence it is written (Wis. 1:1): "Think of [*Sentite*] the Lord in goodness." And on these grounds consent is an act of the appetitive power.

Reply to Objection 1: As stated in De Anima iii, 9, "the will is in the reason." Hence, when Augustine ascribes consent to the reason, he takes reason as including the will.

Reply to Objection 2: Sense, properly speaking, belongs to the apprehensive faculty; but by way of similitude, in so far as it implies seeking acquaintance, it belongs to the appetitive power, as stated above.

Reply to Objection 3: Assentire [to assent] is, to speak, *ad aliud sentire* [to feel towards something]; and thus it implies a certain distance from that to which assent is given. But *consentire* [to consent] is "to feel with," and this implies a certain union to the object of consent. Hence the will, to which it belongs to tend to the thing itself, is more properly said to consent: whereas the intellect, whose act does not consist in a movement towards the thing, but rather the reverse, as we have stated in the I, q. 16, a. 1; q. 27, a. 4; q. 59, a. 2, is more properly said to assent: although one word is wont to be used for the other.* We may also say that the intellect assents, in so far as it is moved by the will.

ARTICULUS 2

AD SECUNDUM sic proceditur. Videtur quod consensus conveniat brutis animalibus. Consensus enim importat determinationem appetitus ad unum. Sed appetitus brutorum animalium sunt determinati ad unum. Ergo consensus in brutis animalibus invenitur.

ARTICLE 2
Whether consent is to be found in irrational animals?

Objection 1: It would seem that consent is to be found in irrational animals. For consent implies a determination of the appetite to one thing. But the appetite of irrational animals is determinate to one thing. Therefore consent is to be found in irrational animals.

---

* In Latin rather than in English.

PRAETEREA, remoto priori, removetur posterius. Sed consensus praecedit operis executionem. Si ergo in brutis non esset consensus, non esset in eis operis executio. Quod patet esse falsum.

PRAETEREA, homines interdum consentire dicuntur in aliquid agendum ex aliqua passione, puta concupiscentia vel ira. Sed bruta animalia ex passione agunt. Ergo in eis est consensus.

SED CONTRA est quod Damascenus dicit quod *post iudicium, homo disponit et amat quod ex consilio iudicatum est, quod vocatur sententia,* idest consensus. Sed consilium non est in brutis animalibus. Ergo nec consensus.

RESPONDEO dicendum quod consensus, proprie loquendo, non est in brutis animalibus. Cuius ratio est quia consensus importat applicationem appetitivi motus ad aliquid agendum. Eius autem est applicare appetitivum motum ad aliquid agendum, in cuius potestate est appetitivus motus, sicut tangere lapidem convenit quidem baculo, sed applicare baculum ad tactum lapidis, est eius qui habet in potestate movere baculum. Bruta autem animalia non habent in sui potestate appetitivum motum, sed talis motus in eis est ex instinctu naturae. Unde brutum animal appetit quidem, sed non applicat appetitivum motum ad aliquid. Et propter hoc non proprie dicitur consentire, sed solum rationalis natura, quae habet in potestate sua appetitivum motum, et potest ipsum applicare vel non applicare ad hoc vel ad illud.

AD PRIMUM ergo dicendum quod in brutis animalibus invenitur determinatio appetitus ad aliquid passive tantum. Consensus vero importat determinationem appetitus non solum passivam, sed magis activam.

AD SECUNDUM dicendum quod, remoto priori, removetur posterius quod proprie ex eo tantum sequitur. Si autem aliquid ex pluribus sequi possit, non propter hoc posterius removetur, uno priorum remoto, sicut si induratio possit fieri et a calido et frigido

Objection 2: Further, if you remove what is first, you remove what follows. But consent precedes the accomplished act. If therefore there were no consent in irrational animals, there would be no act accomplished; which is clearly false.

Objection 3: Further, men are sometimes said to consent to do something, through some passion; desire, for instance, or anger. But irrational animals act through passion. Therefore they consent.

On the contrary, Damascene says (De Fide Orth. ii, 22) that "after judging, man approves and embraces the judgment of his counselling, and this is called the sentence," i.e., consent. But counsel is not in irrational animals. Therefore neither is consent.

I answer that, Consent, properly speaking, is not in irrational animals. The reason of this is that consent implies an application of the appetitive movement to something as to be done. Now to apply the appetitive movement to the doing of something, belongs to the subject in whose power it is to move the appetite: thus to touch a stone is an action suitable to a stick, but to apply the stick so that it touch the stone, belongs to one who has the power of moving the stick. But irrational animals have not the command of the appetitive movement; for this is in them through natural instinct. Hence in the irrational animal, there is indeed the movement of the appetite, but it does not apply that movement to some particular thing. And hence it is that the irrational animal is not properly said to consent: this is proper to the rational nature, which has the command of the appetitive movement, and is able to apply or not to apply it to this or that thing.

Reply to Objection 1: In irrational animals the determination of the appetite to a particular thing is merely passive: whereas consent implies a determination of the appetite, which is active rather than merely passive.

Reply to Objection 2: If the first be removed, then what follows is removed, provided that, properly speaking, it follow from that only. But if something can follow from several things, it is not removed by the fact that one of them is removed; thus if hardening is the effect of heat and of cold

(nam lateres indurantur ab igne, et aqua congelata induratur ex frigore), non oportet quod, remoto calore, removeatur induratio. Executio autem operis non solum sequitur ex consensu, sed etiam ex impetuoso appetitu, qualis est in brutis animalibus.

AD TERTIUM dicendum quod homines qui ex passione agunt, possunt passionem non sequi. Non autem bruta animalia. Unde non est similis ratio.

ARTICULUS 3

AD TERTIUM sic proceditur. Videtur quod consensus sit de fine. Quia propter quod unumquodque, illud magis. Sed his quae sunt ad finem consentimus propter finem. Ergo fini consentimus magis.

PRAETEREA, actio intemperati est finis eius, sicut et actio virtuosi est finis eius. Sed intemperatus consentit in proprium actum. Ergo consensus potest esse de fine.

PRAETEREA, appetitus eorum quae sunt ad finem, est electio, ut supra dictum est. Si igitur consensus esset solum de his quae sunt ad finem, in nullo ab electione differre videretur. Quod patet esse falsum per Damascenum, qui dicit quod *post dispositionem,* quam vocaverat *sententiam, fit electio.* Non ergo consensus est solum de his quae sunt ad finem.

SED CONTRA est quod Damascenus ibidem dicit, quod *sententia,* sive consensus, est *quando homo disponit et amat quod ex consilio iudicatum est.* Sed consilium non est nisi de his quae sunt ad finem. Ergo nec consensus.

RESPONDEO dicendum quod consensus nominat applicationem appetitivi motus ad aliquid praeexistens in potestate applicantis in ordine autem agibilium, primo quidem oportet sumere apprehensionem finis; deinde appetitum finis; deinde consilium de his quae sunt ad finem; deinde appetitum eorum quae sunt ad finem. Appetitus autem in ultimum finem tendit naturaliter, unde et applicatio motus appetitivi in finem apprehensum,

(since bricks are hardened by the fire, and frozen water is hardened by the cold), then by removing heat it does not follow that there is no hardening. Now the accomplishment of an act follows not only from consent, but also from the impulse of the appetite, such as is found in irrational animals.

Reply to Objection 3: The man who acts through passion is able not to follow the passion: whereas irrational animals have not that power. Hence the comparison fails.

ARTICLE 3
Whether consent is directed to the end or to the means?

Objection 1: It would seem that consent is directed to the end. Because that on account of which a thing is such is still more such. But it is on account of the end that we consent to the means. Therefore, still more do we consent to the end.

Objection 2: Further, the act of the intemperate man is his end, just as the act of the virtuous man is his end. But the intemperate man consents to his own act. Therefore consent can be directed to the end.

Objection 3: Further, desire of the means is choice, as stated above (I-II, q. 13, a. 1). If therefore consent were only directed to the means it would nowise differ from choice. And this is proved to be false by the authority of Damascene who says (De Fide Orth. ii, 22) that "after the approval" which he calls "the sentence," "comes the choice." Therefore consent is not only directed to the means.

On the contrary, Damascene says (De Fide Orth. ii, 22) that the "sentence," i.e., the consent, takes place "when a man approves and embraces the judgment of his counsel." But counsel is only about the means. Therefore the same applies to consent.

I answer that, Consent is the application of the appetitive movement to something that is already in the power of him who causes the application. Now the order of action is this: First there is the apprehension of the end; then the desire of the end; then the counsel about the means; then the desire of the means. Now the appetite tends to the last end naturally: wherefore the application of the appetitive movement to the apprehended end

non habet rationem consensus, sed simplicis voluntatis. De his autem quae sunt post ultimum finem, inquantum sunt ad finem, sub consilio cadunt, et sic potest esse de eis consensus, inquantum motus appetitivus applicatur ad id quod ex consilio iudicatum est. Motus vero appetitivus in finem, non applicatur consilio, sed magis consilium ipsi, quia consilium praesupponit appetitum finis. Sed appetitus eorum quae sunt ad finem, **praesupponit determinationem consilii.** Et ideo applicatio appetitivi motus ad determinationem consilii, proprie est consensus. Unde, cum consilium non sit nisi de his quae sunt ad finem, consensus, proprie loquendo, non est nisi de his quae sunt ad finem.

AD PRIMUM ergo dicendum quod, sicut conclusiones scimus per principia, horum tamen non est scientia, sed quod maius est, scilicet intellectus; ita consentimus his quae sunt ad finem propter finem, cuius tamen non est consensus, sed quod maius est, scilicet voluntas.

AD SECUNDUM dicendum quod intemperatus habet pro fine delectationem operis, propter quam consentit in opus, magis quam ipsam operationem.

AD TERTIUM dicendum quod electio addit supra consensum quandam relationem respectu eius cui aliquid praeeligitur, et ideo post consensum, adhuc remanet electio. Potest enim contingere quod per consilium inveniantur plura ducentia ad finem, quorum dum quodlibet placet, in quodlibet eorum consentitur, sed ex multis quae placent, praeaccipimus unum eligendo. Sed si inveniatur unum solum quod placeat, non differunt re consensus et electio, sed ratione tantum, ut consensus dicatur secundum quod placet ad agendum; electio autem, secundum quod praefertur his quae non placent.

has not the nature of consent, but of simple volition. But as to those things which come under consideration after the last end, in so far as they are directed to the end, they come under counsel: and so counsel can be applied to them, in so far as the appetitive movement is applied to the judgment resulting from counsel. But the appetitive movement to the end is not applied to counsel: rather is counsel applied to it, because counsel presupposes the desire of the end. On the other hand, the desire of the means presupposes the decision of counsel. And therefore the application of the appetitive movement to counsel's decision is consent, properly speaking. Consequently, since counsel is only about the means, consent, properly speaking, is of nothing else but the means.

Reply to Objection 1: Just as the knowledge of conclusions through the principles is science, whereas the knowledge of the principles is not science, but something higher, namely, understanding; so do we consent to the means on account of the end, in respect of which our act is not consent but something greater, namely, volition.

Reply to Objection 2: Delight in his act, rather than the act itself, is the end of the intemperate man, and for sake of this delight he consents to that act.

Reply to Objection 3: Choice includes something that consent has not, namely, a certain relation to something to which something else is preferred: and therefore after consent there still remains a choice. For it may happen that by aid of counsel several means have been found conducive to the end, and through each of these meeting with approval, consent has been given to each: but after approving of many, we have given our preference to one by choosing it. But if only one meets with approval, then consent and choice do not differ in reality, but only in our way of looking at them; so that we call it consent, according as we approve of doing that thing; but choice according as we prefer it to those that do not meet with our approval.

Articulus 4
Whether consent to the act belongs only to the higher part of the soul?

AD QUARTUM sic proceditur. Videtur quod consensus ad agendum non semper pertineat ad superiorem rationem. *Delectatio enim consequitur operationem, et perficit eam, sicut decor iuventutem,* sicut dicitur in X Ethic. Sed consensus in delectationem pertinet ad inferiorem rationem, ut dicit Augustinus in XII de Trin. Ergo consensus in actum non pertinet ad solam superiorem rationem.

PRAETEREA, actio in quam consentimus, dicitur esse voluntaria. Sed multarum potentiarum est producere actiones voluntarias. Ergo non sola superior ratio consentit in actum.

PRAETEREA, *superior ratio intendit aeternis inspiciendis ac consulendis,* ut Augustinus dicit in XII de Trin. Sed multoties homo consentit in actum non propter rationes aeternas, sed propter aliquas rationes temporales, vel etiam propter aliquas animae passiones. Non ergo consentire in actum pertinet ad solam superiorem rationem.

SED CONTRA est quod Augustinus dicit, XII de Trin., *non potest peccatum efficaciter perpetrandum mente decerni, nisi illa mentis intentio penes quam summa potestas est membra in opus movendi vel ab opere cohibendi, malae actioni cedat et serviat.*

RESPONDEO dicendum quod finalis sententia semper pertinet ad eum qui superior est, ad quem pertinet de aliis iudicare, quandiu enim iudicandum restat quod proponitur, nondum datur finalis sententia. Manifestum est autem quod superior ratio est quae habet de omnibus iudicare, quia de sensibilibus per rationem iudicamus; de his vero quae ad rationes humanas pertinent, iudicamus secundum rationes divinas, quae pertinent ad rationem superiorem. Et ideo quandiu incertum est an secundum rationes divinas resistatur vel non, nullum iudicium rationis habet rationem finalis sententiae. Finalis autem sententia de agendis

Article 4
Whether consent to the act belongs only to the higher part of the soul?

Objection 1: It would seem that consent to the act does not always belong to the higher reason. For "delight follows action, and perfects it, just as beauty perfects youth"* (Ethic. x, 4). But consent to delight belongs to the lower reason, as Augustine says (De Trin. xii, 12). Therefore consent to the act does not belong only to the higher reason.

Objection 2: Further, an act to which we consent is said to be voluntary. But it belongs to many powers to produce voluntary acts. Therefore the higher reason is not alone in consenting to the act.

Objection 3: Further, "the higher reason is that which is intent on the contemplation and consultation of things eternal," as Augustine says (De Trin. xii, 7). But man often consents to an act not for eternal, but for temporal reasons, or even on account of some passion of the soul. Therefore consent to an act does not belong to the higher reason alone.

On the contrary, Augustine says (De Trin. xii, 12): "It is impossible for man to make up his mind to commit a sin, unless that mental faculty which has the sovereign power of urging his members to, or restraining them from, act, yield to the evil deed and become its slave."

I answer that, The final decision belongs to him who holds the highest place, and to whom it belongs to judge of the others; for as long as judgment about some matter remains to be pronounced, the final decision has not been given. Now it is evident that it belongs to the higher reason to judge of all: since it is by the reason that we judge of sensible things; and of things pertaining to human principles we judge according to Divine principles, which is the function of the higher reason. Wherefore as long as a man is uncertain whether he resists or not, according to Divine principles, no judgment of the reason can be considered in the light of a final decision. Now the final decision of what is to be done

---

* οἷον τοῖς ἀκμαίοις ἡ ὥρα—as youthful vigor perfects a man in his prime.

est consensus in actum. Et ideo consensus in actum pertinet ad rationem superiorem, secundum tamen quod in ratione voluntas includitur, sicut supra dictum est.

AD PRIMUM ergo dicendum quod consensus in delectationem operis pertinet ad superiorem rationem, sicut et consensus in opus, sed consensus in delectationem cogitationis, pertinet ad rationem inferiorem, sicut ad ipsam pertinet cogitare. Et tamen de hoc ipso quod est cogitare vel non cogitare, inquantum consideratur ut actio quaedam, habet iudicium superior ratio, et similiter de delectatione consequente. Sed inquantum accipitur ut ad actionem aliam ordinatum, sic pertinet ad inferiorem rationem. Quod enim ad aliud ordinatur, ad inferiorem artem vel potentiam pertinet quam finis ad quem ordinatur, unde ars quae est de fine, architectonica, seu principalis, vocatur.

AD SECUNDUM dicendum quod, quia actiones dicuntur voluntariae ex hoc quod eis consentimus, non oportet quod consensus sit cuiuslibet potentiae, sed voluntatis, a qua dicitur voluntarium; quae est in ratione, sicut dictum est.

AD TERTIUM dicendum quod ratio superior dicitur consentire, non solum quia secundum rationes aeternas semper moveat ad agendum; sed etiam quia secundum rationes aeternas non dissentit.

is consent to the act. Therefore consent to the act belongs to the higher reason; but in that sense in which the reason includes the will, as stated above (I-II, q. 15, a. 1, ad 1).

Reply to Objection 1: Consent to delight in the work done belongs to the higher reason, as also does consent to the work; but consent to delight in thought belongs to the lower reason, just as to the lower reason it belongs to think. Nevertheless the higher reason **exercises judgment on the fact of thinking or not thinking, considered as an action;** and in like manner on the delight that results. But in so far as the act of thinking is considered as ordained to a further act, it belongs to the lower reason. For that which is ordained to something else, belongs to a lower art or power than does the end to which it is ordained: hence the art which is concerned with the end is called the master or principal art.

Reply to Objection 2: Since actions are called voluntary from the fact that we consent to them, it does not follow that consent is an act of each power, but of the will which is in the reason, as stated above (I-II, q. 15, a. 1, ad 1), and from which the voluntary act is named.

Reply to Objection 3: The higher reason is said to consent not only because it always moves to act, according to the eternal reasons; but also because it fails to dissent according to those same reasons.

Quaestio XVI

Deinde considerandum est de usu. Et circa hoc quaeruntur quatuor. *Primo,* utrum uti sit actus voluntatis. *Secundo,* utrum conveniat brutis animalibus. *Tertio,* utrum sit tantum eorum quae sunt ad finem, vel etiam finis. *Quarto,* de ordine usus ad electionem.

Articulus 1

Ad primum sic proceditur. Videtur quod uti non sit actus voluntatis. Dicit enim Augustinus, in I de Doctr. Christ., quod *uti est id quod in usum venerit, ad aliud obtinendum referre.* Sed *referre* aliquid ad aliud est rationis, cuius est conferre et ordinare. Ergo uti est actus rationis. Non ergo voluntatis.

Praeterea, Damascenus dicit quod homo *impetum facit ad operationem, et dicitur impetus, deinde utitur, et dicitur usus.* Sed operatio pertinet ad potentiam executivam. Actus autem voluntatis non sequitur actum executivae potentiae, sed executio est ultimum. Ergo usus non est actus voluntatis.

Praeterea, Augustinus dicit, in libro octoginta trium quaest., *omnia quae facta sunt, in usum hominis facta sunt, quia omnibus utitur iudicando ratio quae hominibus data est.* Sed iudicare de rebus a Deo creatis pertinet ad rationem speculativam; quae omnino separata videtur a voluntate, quae est principium humanorum actuum. Ergo uti non est actus voluntatis.

Sed contra est quod Augustinus dicit, in X de Trin., *uti est assumere aliquid in facultatem voluntatis.*

Respondeo dicendum quod usus rei alicuius importat applicationem rei illius ad aliquam operationem, unde et operatio ad quam applicamus rem aliquam, dicitur usus eius; sicut equitare est usus equi, et percutere est usus baculi. Ad operationem autem applicamus et principia interiora agendi, scilicet ipsas potentias animae vel membra corporis, ut intellectum ad intelligendum, et oculum

Question 16
Of Use, Which Is an Act of the Will in Regard to the Means

We must now consider use; concerning which there are four points of inquiry: 1. Whether use is an act of the will? 2. Whether it is to be found in irrational animals? 3. Whether it regards the means only, or the end also? 4. Of the relation of use to choice.

Article 1
Whether use is an act of the will?

Objection 1: It would seem that use is not an act of the will. For Augustine says (De Doctr. Christ. i, 4) that "to use is to refer that which is the object of use to the obtaining of something else." But "to refer" something to another is an act of the reason to which it belongs to compare and to direct. Therefore use is an act of the reason and not of the will.

Objection 2: Further, Damascene says (De Fide Orth. ii, 22) that man "goes forward to the operation, and this is called impulse; then he makes use [of the powers] and this is called use." But operation belongs to the executive power; and the act of the will does not follow the act of the executive power, on the contrary execution comes last. Therefore use is not an act of the will.

Objection 3: Further, Augustine says (QQ. 83, qu. 30): "All things that were made were made for man's use, because reason with which man is endowed uses all things by its judgment of them." But judgment of things created by God belongs to the speculative reason; which seems to be altogether distinct from the will, which is the principle of human acts. Therefore use is not an act of the will.

On the contrary, Augustine says (De Trin. x, 11): "To use is to apply to something to purpose of the will."

I answer that, The use of a thing implies the application of that thing to an operation: hence the operation to which we apply a thing is called its use; thus the use of a horse is to ride, and the use of a stick is to strike. Now we apply to an operation not only the interior principles of action, *viz.* the powers of the soul or the members of the body; as the intellect, to understand; and the eye,

ad videndum; et etiam res exteriores, sicut baculum ad percutiendum. Sed manifestum est quod res exteriores non applicamus ad aliquam operationem nisi per principia intrinseca, quae sunt potentiae animae, aut habitus potentiarum, aut organa, quae sunt corporis membra. Ostensum est autem supra quod voluntas est quae movet potentias animae ad suos actus; et hoc est applicare eas ad operationem. Unde manifestum est quod uti primo et principaliter est voluntatis, tanquam primi moventis; rationis autem tanquam dirigentis; sed aliarum potentiarum tanquam exequentium, quae comparantur ad voluntatem, a qua applicantur ad agendum, sicut instrumenta ad principale agens. Actio autem proprie non attribuitur instrumento, sed principali agenti, sicut aedificatio aedificatori, non autem instrumentis. Unde manifestum est quod uti proprie est actus voluntatis.

AD PRIMUM ergo dicendum quod ratio quidem in aliud refert, sed voluntas tendit in id quod est in aliud relatum per rationem. Et secundum hoc dicitur quod uti est referre aliquid in alterum.

AD SECUNDUM dicendum quod Damascenus loquitur de usu, secundum quod pertinet ad executivas potentias.

AD TERTIUM dicendum quod etiam ipsa ratio speculativa applicatur ad opus intelligendi vel iudicandi, a voluntate. Et ideo intellectus speculativus uti dicitur tanquam a voluntate motus, sicut aliae executivae potentiae.

to see; but also external things, as a stick, to strike. But it is evident that we do not apply external things to an operation save through the interior principles which are either the powers of the soul, or the habits of those powers, or the organs which are parts of the body. Now it has been shown above (I-II, q. 9, a. 1) that it is the will which moves the soul's powers to their acts, and this is to apply them to operation. Hence it is evident that **first and principally use belongs to the will as** first mover; to the reason, as directing; and to the other powers as executing the operation, which powers are compared to the will which applies them to act, as the instruments are compared to the principal agent. Now action is properly ascribed, not to the instrument, but to the principal agent, as building is ascribed to the builder, not to his tools. Hence it is evident that use is, properly speaking, an act of the will.

Reply to Objection 1: Reason does indeed refer one thing to another; but the will tends to that which is referred by the reason to something else. And in this sense to use is to refer one thing to another.

Reply to Objection 2: Damascene is speaking of use in so far as it belongs to the executive powers.

Reply to Objection 3: Even the speculative reason is applied by the will to the act of understanding or judging. Consequently the speculative reason is said to use, in so far as it is moved by the will, in the same way as the other powers.

ARTICULUS 2

AD SECUNDUM sic proceditur. Videtur quod uti conveniat brutis animalibus. Frui enim est nobilius quam uti, quia, ut Augustinus dicit in X de Trin., *utimur eis quae ad aliud referimus, quo fruendum est.* Sed frui convenit brutis animalibus, ut supra dictum est. Ergo multo magis convenit eis uti.

PRAETEREA, applicare membra ad agendum est uti membris. Sed bruta animalia applicant membra ad aliquid agendum;

ARTICLE 2
Whether use is to be found in irrational animals?

Objection 1: It would seem that use is to be found in irrational animals. For it is better to enjoy than to use, because, as Augustine says (De Trin. x, 10): "We use things by referring them to something else which we are to enjoy." But enjoyment is to be found in irrational animals, as stated above (I-II, q. 11, a. 2). Much more, therefore, is it possible for them to use.

Objection 2: Further, to apply the members to action is to use them. But irrational animals apply their members to action;

sicut pedes ad ambulandum, cornua ad percutiendum. Ergo brutis animalibus convenit uti.

SED CONTRA est quod Augustinus dicit, in libro octoginta trium quaest., *uti aliqua re non potest nisi animal quod rationis est particeps.*

RESPONDEO dicendum quod, sicut dictum est, uti est applicare aliquod principium actionis ad actionem, sicut consentire est applicare motum appetitivum ad aliquid appetendum, ut dictum est. Applicare autem aliquid ad alterum non est nisi eius quod habet arbitrium super illud, quod non est nisi eius qui scit referre aliquid in alterum, quod ad rationem pertinet. Et ideo solum animal rationale et consentit, et utitur.

AD PRIMUM ergo dicendum quod frui importat absolutum motum appetitus in appetibile, sed uti importat motum appetitus ad aliquid in ordine ad alterum. Si ergo comparentur uti et frui quantum ad obiecta, sic frui est nobilius quam uti, quia id quod est absolute appetibile, est melius quam id quod est appetibile solum in ordine ad aliud. Sed si comparentur quantum ad vim apprehensivam praecedentem, maior nobilitas requiritur ex parte usus, quia ordinare aliquid in alterum est rationis; absolute autem aliquid apprehendere potest etiam sensus.

AD SECUNDUM dicendum quod animalia per sua membra aliquid agunt instinctu naturae, non per hoc quod cognoscant ordinem membrorum ad illas operationes. Unde non dicuntur proprie applicare membra ad agendum, nec uti membris.

for instance, their feet, to walk; their horns, to strike. Therefore it is possible for irrational animals to use.

On the contrary, Augustine says (QQ. 83, qu. 30): "None but a rational animal can make use of a thing."

I answer that, as stated above (I-II, q. 16, a. 1), to use is to apply an active principle to action: thus to consent is to apply the appetitive movement to the desire of something, as stated above (I-II, q. 15, a. 1; a. 2; a. 3). Now he alone who has the disposal of a thing, can apply it to something else; and this belongs to him alone who knows how to refer it to something else, which is an act of the reason. And therefore none but a rational animal consents and uses.

Reply to Objection 1: To enjoy implies the absolute movement of the appetite to the appetible: whereas to use implies a movement of the appetite to something as directed to something else. If therefore we compare use and enjoyment in respect of their objects, enjoyment is better than use; because that which is appetible absolutely is better than that which is appetible only as directed to something else. But if we compare them in respect of the apprehensive power that precedes them, greater excellence is required on the part of use: because to direct one thing to another is an act of reason; whereas to apprehend something absolutely is within the competency even of sense.

Reply to Objection 2: Animals by means of their members do something from natural instinct; not through knowing the relation of their members to these operations. Wherefore, properly speaking, they do not apply their members to action, nor do they use them.

ARTICULUS 3

AD TERTIUM sic proceditur. Videtur quod usus possit esse etiam ultimi finis. Dicit enim Augustinus, in X de Trin., *omnis qui fruitur, utitur.* Sed ultimo fine fruitur aliquis. Ergo ultimo fine aliquis utitur.

ARTICLE 3
Whether use regards also the last end?

Objection 1: It would seem that use can regard also the last end. For Augustine says (De Trin. x, 11): "Whoever enjoys, uses." But man enjoys the last end. Therefore he uses the last end.

PRAETEREA, *uti est assumere aliquid in facultatem voluntatis,* ut ibidem dicitur. Sed nihil magis assumitur a voluntate quam ultimus finis. Ergo usus potest esse ultimi finis.

PRAETEREA, Hilarius dicit, in II de Trin., quod *aeternitas est in patre, species in imagine,* idest in filio, *usus in munere,* idest in spiritu sancto. Sed spiritus sanctus, cum sit Deus, est ultimus finis. Ergo ultimo fine contingit uti.

SED CONTRA est quod dicit Augustinus, in libro octoginta trium quaest., *Deo nullus recte utitur, sed fruitur.* Sed solus Deus est ultimus finis. Ergo ultimo fine non est utendum.

RESPONDEO dicendum quod uti, sicut dictum est, importat applicationem alicuius ad aliquid. Quod autem applicatur ad aliud, se habet in ratione eius quod est ad finem. Et ideo uti semper est eius quod est ad finem. Propter quod et ea quae sunt ad finem accommoda, *utilia* dicuntur; et ipsa utilitas interdum usus nominatur. Sed considerandum est quod ultimus finis dicitur dupliciter, uno modo, simpliciter; et alio modo, quoad aliquem. Cum enim finis, ut supra dictum est, dicatur quandoque quidem res, quandoque autem adeptio rei vel possessio eius, sicut avaro finis est vel pecunia vel possessio pecuniae; manifestum est quod, simpliciter loquendo, ultimus finis est ipsa res, non enim possessio pecuniae est bona, nisi propter bonum pecuniae. Sed quoad hunc, adeptio pecuniae est finis ultimus, non enim quaereret pecuniam avarus, nisi ut haberet eam. Ergo, simpliciter loquendo et proprie, pecunia homo aliquis fruitur, quia in ea ultimum finem constituit, sed inquantum refert eam ad possessionem, dicitur uti ea.

AD PRIMUM ergo dicendum quod Augustinus loquitur de usu communiter, secundum quod importat ordinem finis ad ipsam finis fruitionem, quam aliquis quaerit de fine.

AD SECUNDUM dicendum quod finis assumitur in facultatem voluntatis, ut voluntas in illo quiescat. Unde ipsa requies in fine, quae fruitio est, dicitur hoc modo usus finis. Sed id quod est ad finem, assumitur in facultatem voluntatis non solum

Objection 2: Further, "to use is to apply something to the purpose of the will" (De Trin. x, 11). But the last end, more than anything else, is the object of the will's application. Therefore it can be the object of use.

Objection 3: Further, Hilary says (De Trin. ii) that "Eternity is in the Father, Likeness in the Image," i.e., in the Son, "Use in the Gift," i.e., in the Holy Ghost. But the Holy Ghost, since He is God, is the last end. Therefore the last end can be the object of use.

On the contrary, Augustine says (QQ. 83, qu. 30): "No one rightly uses God, but one enjoys Him." But God alone is the last end. Therefore we cannot use the last end.

I answer that, Use, as stated above (I-II, q. 16, a. 1), implies the application of one thing to another. Now that which is applied to another is regarded in the light of means to an end; and consequently use always regards the means. For this reason things that are adapted to a certain end are said to be "useful"; in fact their very usefulness is sometimes called use. It must, however, be observed that the last end may be taken in two ways: first, simply; secondly, in respect of an individual. For since the end, as stated above (I-II, q. 1, a. 8; q. 2, a. 7), signifies sometimes the thing itself, and sometimes the attainment or possession of that thing (thus the miser's end is either money or the possession of it); it is evident that, simply speaking, the last end is the thing itself; for the possession of money is good only inasmuch as there is some good in money. But in regard to the individual, the obtaining of money is the last end; for the miser would not seek for money, save that he might have it. Therefore, simply and properly speaking, a man enjoys money, because he places his last end therein; but in so far as he seeks to possess it, he is said to use it.

Reply to Objection 1: Augustine is speaking of use in general, in so far as it implies the relation of an end to the enjoyment which a man seeks in that end.

Reply to Objection 2: The end is applied to the purpose of the will, that the will may find rest in it. Consequently this rest in the end, which is the enjoyment thereof, is in this sense called use of the end. But the means are applied to the will's purpose, not only

in ordine ad usum eius quod est ad finem, sed in ordine ad aliam rem, in qua voluntas quiescit.

AD TERTIUM dicendum quod usus accipitur in verbis Hilarii pro quiete in ultimo fine, eo modo quo aliquis, communiter loquendo, dicitur uti fine ad obtinendum ipsum, sicut dictum est. Unde Augustinus, in VI de Trin., dicit quod *illa dilectio, delectatio, felicitas vel beatitudo usus ab eo appellatur.*

in being used as means, but as ordained to something else in which the will finds rest.

Reply to Objection 3: The words of Hilary refer to use as applicable to rest in the last end; just as, speaking in a general sense, one may be said to use the end for the purpose of attaining it, as stated above. Hence Augustine says (De Trin. vi, 10) that "this love, delight, felicity, or happiness, is called use by him."

ARTICULUS 4

AD QUARTUM sic proceditur. Videtur quod usus praecedat electionem. Post electionem enim nihil sequitur nisi executio. Sed usus, cum pertineat ad voluntatem, praecedit executionem. Ergo praecedit etiam electionem.

PRAETEREA, absolutum est ante relatum. Ergo minus relatum est ante magis relatum. Sed electio importat duas relationes, unam eius quod eligitur ad finem, aliam vero ad id cui praeeligitur, usus autem importat solam relationem ad finem. Ergo usus est prior electione.

PRAETEREA, voluntas utitur aliis potentiis inquantum movet eas. Sed voluntas movet etiam seipsam ut dictum est. Ergo etiam utitur seipsa, applicando se ad agendum. Sed hoc facit cum consentit. Ergo in ipso consensu est usus. Sed consensus praecedit electionem ut dictum est. Ergo et usus.

SED CONTRA est quod Damascenus dicit, quod *voluntas post electionem impetum facit ad operationem, et postea utitur.* Ergo usus sequitur electionem.

RESPONDEO dicendum quod voluntas duplicem habitudinem habet ad volitum. Unam quidem, secundum quod volitum est quodammodo in volente, per quandam proportionem vel ordinem ad volitum. Unde et res quae naturaliter sunt proportionatae ad aliquem finem, dicuntur appetere illum naturaliter. Sed sic habere finem, est imperfecte habere ipsum. Omne autem imperfectum tendit in perfectionem. Et ideo tam appetitus naturalis, quam voluntarius, tendit ut habeat ipsum finem realiter,

ARTICLE 4
Whether use precedes choice?

Objection 1: It would seem that use precedes choice. For nothing follows after choice, except execution. But use, since it belongs to the will, precedes execution. Therefore it precedes choice also.

Objection 2: Further, the absolute precedes the relative. Therefore the less relative precedes the more relative. But choice implies two relations: one, of the thing chosen, in relation to the end; the other, of the thing chosen, in respect of that to which it is preferred; whereas use implies relation to the end only. Therefore use precedes choice.

Objection 3: Further, the will uses the other powers in so far as it removes them. But the will moves itself, too, as stated above (I-II, q. 9, a. 3). Therefore it uses itself, by applying itself to act. But it does this when it consents. Therefore there is use in consent. But consent precedes choice as stated above (I-II, q. 15, a. 3, ad 3). Therefore use does also.

On the contrary, Damascene says (De Fide Orth. ii, 22) that "the will after choosing has an impulse to the operation, and afterwards it uses [the powers]." Therefore use follows choice.

I answer that, The will has a twofold relation to the thing willed. One, according as the thing willed is, in a way, in the willing subject, by a kind of proportion or order to the thing willed. Wherefore those things that are naturally proportionate to a certain end, are said to desire that end naturally. Yet to have an end thus is to have it imperfectly. Now every imperfect thing tends to perfection. And therefore both the natural and the voluntary appetite tend to have the end in reality; and

quod est perfecte habere ipsum. Et haec est secunda habitudo voluntatis ad volitum. Volitum autem non solum est finis, sed id quod est ad finem. Ultimum autem quod pertinet ad primam habitudinem voluntatis, respectu eius quod est ad finem, est electio, ibi enim completur proportio voluntatis, ut complete velit id quod est ad finem. Sed usus iam pertinet ad secundam habitudinem voluntatis, qua tendit ad consequendum rem volitam. Unde manifestum est quod usus sequitur electionem, si tamen accipiatur usus, secundum quod voluntas utitur executiva potentia movendo ipsam. Sed quia voluntas etiam quodammodo rationem movet, et utitur ea, potest intelligi usus eius quod est ad finem, secundum quod est in consideratione rationis referentis ipsum in finem. Et hoc modo usus praecedit electionem.

AD PRIMUM ergo dicendum quod ipsam executionem operis praecedit motio qua voluntas movet ad exequendum, sequitur autem electionem. Et sic, cum usus pertineat ad praedictam motionem voluntatis, medium est inter electionem et executionem.

AD SECUNDUM dicendum quod id quod est per essentiam suam relatum, posterius est absoluto, sed id cui attribuuntur relationes, non oportet quod sit posterius. Immo quanto causa est prior, tanto habet relationem ad plures effectus.

AD TERTIUM dicendum quod electio praecedit usum, si referantur ad idem. Nihil autem prohibet quod usus unius praecedat electionem alterius. Et quia actus voluntatis reflectuntur supra seipsos, in quolibet actu voluntatis potest accipi et consensus, et electio, et usus, ut si dicatur quod voluntas consentit se eligere, et consentit se consentire, et utitur se ad consentiendum et eligendum. Et semper isti actus ordinati ad id quod est prius, sunt priores.

this is to have it perfectly. This is the second relation of the will to the thing willed. Now the thing willed is not only the end, but also the means. And the last act that belongs to the first relation of the will to the means, is choice; for there the will becomes fully proportionate, by willing the means fully. Use, on the other hand, belongs to the second relation of the will, in respect of which it tends to the realization of the thing willed. Wherefore it is evident that use follows choice; provided that by use we mean the will's use of the executive power in moving it. But since the will, in a way, moves the reason also, and uses it, we may take the use of the means, as consisting in the consideration of the reason, whereby it refers the means to the end. In this sense use precedes choice.

Reply to Objection 1: The motion of the will to the execution of the work, precedes execution, but follows choice. And so, since use belongs to that very motion of the will, it stands between choice and execution.

Reply to Objection 2: What is essentially relative is after the absolute; but the thing to which relation is referred need not come after. Indeed, the more a cause precedes, the more numerous the effects to which it has relation.

Reply to Objection 3: Choice precedes use, if they be referred to the same object. But nothing hinders the use of one thing preceding the choice of another. And since the acts of the will react on one another, in each act of the will we can find both consent and choice and use; so that we may say that the will consents to choose, and consents to consent, and uses itself in consenting and choosing. And such acts as are ordained to that which precedes, precede also.

Quaestio XVII

Deinde considerandum est de actibus imperatis a voluntate. Et circa hoc quaeruntur novem. *Primo,* utrum imperare sit actus voluntatis, vel rationis. *Secundo,* utrum imperare pertineat ad bruta animalia. *Tertio,* de ordine imperii ad usum. *Quarto,* utrum imperium et actus imperatus sint unus actus, vel diversi. *Quinto,* utrum actus voluntatis imperetur. *Sexto,* utrum actus rationis. *Septimo,* utrum actus appetitus sensitivi. *Octavo,* utrum actus animae vegetabilis. *Nono,* utrum actus exteriorum membrorum.

Articulus 1

Ad primum sic proceditur. Videtur quod imperare non sit actus rationis, sed voluntatis. Imperare enim est movere quoddam, dicit enim Avicenna quod quadruplex est movens, scilicet *perficiens, disponens, imperans et consilians.* Sed ad voluntatem pertinet movere omnes alias vires animae, ut dictum est supra. Ergo imperare est actus voluntatis.

Praeterea, sicut imperari pertinet ad id quod est subiectum, ita imperare pertinere videtur ad id quod est maxime liberum. Sed radix libertatis est maxime in voluntate. Ergo voluntatis est imperare.

Praeterea, ad imperium statim sequitur actus. Sed ad actum rationis non statim sequitur actus, non enim qui iudicat aliquid esse faciendum, statim illud operatur. Ergo imperare non est actus rationis, sed voluntatis.

Sed contra est quod Gregorius Nyssenus dicit, et etiam philosophus quod *appetitivum obedit rationi.* Ergo rationis est imperare.

Respondeo dicendum quod imperare est actus rationis, praesupposito tamen actu voluntatis. Ad cuius evidentiam, considerandum est quod, quia actus voluntatis et rationis

Question 17
Of the Acts Commanded by the Will

We must now consider the acts commanded by the will; under which head there are nine points of inquiry: 1. Whether command is an act of the will or of the reason? 2. Whether command belongs to irrational animals? 3. Of the order between command and use. 4. Whether command and the commanded act are one act or distinct? 5. Whether the act of the will is commanded? 6. Whether the act of the reason is commanded? 7. Whether the act of the sensitive appetite is commanded? 8. Whether the act of the vegetal soul is commanded? 9. Whether the acts of the external members are commanded?

Article 1
Whether command is an act of the reason or of the will?

Objection 1: It would seem that command is not an act of the reason but of the will. For command is a kind of motion; because Avicenna says that there are four ways of moving, "by perfecting, by disposing, by commanding, and by counselling." But it belongs to the will to move all the other powers of the soul, as stated above (I-II, q. 9, a. 1). Therefore command is an act of the will.

Objection 2: Further, just as to be commanded belongs to that which is subject, so, seemingly, to command belongs to that which is most free. But the root of liberty is especially in the will. Therefore to command belongs to the will.

Objection 3: Further, command is followed at once by act. But the act of the reason is not followed at once by act: for he who judges that a thing should be done, does not do it at once. Therefore command is not an act of the reason, but of the will.

On the contrary, Gregory of Nyssa* and the Philosopher (Ethic. i, 13) say that "the appetite obeys reason." Therefore command is an act of the reason.

I answer that, Command is an act of the reason presupposing, however, an act of the will. In proof of this, we must take note that, since the acts of the reason and of the will

---

* Nemesius, De Nat. Hom. xvi.

supra se invicem possunt ferri, prout scilicet ratio ratiocinatur de volendo, et voluntas vult ratiocinari; contingit actum voluntatis praeveniri ab actu rationis, et e converso. Et quia virtus prioris actus remanet in actu sequenti, contingit quandoque quod est aliquis actus voluntatis, secundum quod manet virtute in ipso aliquid de actu rationis, ut dictum est de usu et de electione; et e converso aliquis est actus rationis, secundum quod virtute manet in ipso aliquid de actu voluntatis. Imperare autem est quidem essentialiter actus rationis, imperans enim ordinat eum cui imperat, ad aliquid agendum, intimando vel denuntiando; sic autem ordinare per modum cuiusdam intimationis, est rationis. Sed ratio potest aliquid intimare vel denuntiare dupliciter. Uno modo, absolute, quae quidem intimatio exprimitur per verbum indicativi modi; sicut si aliquis alicui dicat, *hoc est tibi faciendum*. Aliquando autem ratio intimat aliquid alicui, movendo ipsum ad hoc, et talis intimatio exprimitur per verbum imperativi modi; puta cum alicui dicitur, *fac hoc*. Primum autem movens in viribus animae ad exercitium actus, est voluntas, ut supra dictum est. Cum ergo secundum movens non moveat nisi in virtute primi moventis, sequitur quod hoc ipsum quod ratio movet imperando, sit ei ex virtute voluntatis. Unde relinquitur quod imperare sit actus rationis, praesupposito actu voluntatis, in cuius virtute ratio movet per imperium ad exercitium actus.

AD PRIMUM ergo dicendum quod imperare non est movere quocumque modo, sed cum quadam intimatione denuntiativa ad alterum. Quod est rationis.

AD SECUNDUM dicendum quod radix libertatis est voluntas sicut subiectum, sed sicut causa, est ratio. Ex hoc enim voluntas libere potest ad diversa ferri, quia ratio potest habere diversas conceptiones boni. Et ideo philosophi definiunt liberum arbitrium quod est *liberum de ratione iudicium,* quasi ratio sit causa libertatis.

can be brought to bear on one another, in so far as the reason reasons about willing, and the will wills to reason, the result is that the act of the reason precedes the act of the will, and conversely. And since the power of the preceding act continues in the act that follows, it happens sometimes that there is an act of the will in so far as it retains in itself something of an act of the reason, as we have stated in reference to use and choice; and conversely, that there is an act of the reason in so far as it retains in itself something of an act of the will. Now, command is essentially indeed an act of the reason: for the commander orders the one commanded to do something, by way of intimation or declaration; and to order thus by intimating or declaring is an act of the reason. Now the reason can intimate or declare something in two ways. First, absolutely: and this intimation is expressed by a verb in the indicative mood, as when one person says to another: "This is what you should do." Sometimes, however, the reason intimates something to a man by moving him thereto; and this intimation is expressed by a verb in the imperative mood; as when it is said to someone: "Do this." Now the first mover, among the powers of the soul, to the doing of an act is the will, as stated above (I-II, q. 9, a. 1). Since therefore the second mover does not move, save in virtue of the first mover, it follows that the very fact that the reason moves by commanding, is due to the power of the will. Consequently it follows that command is an act of the reason, presupposing an act of the will, in virtue of which the reason, by its command, moves [the power] to the execution of the act.

Reply to Objection 1: To command is to move, not anyhow, but by intimating and declaring to another; and this is an act of the reason.

Reply to Objection 2: The root of liberty is the will as the subject thereof; but it is the reason as its cause. For the will can tend freely towards various objects, precisely because the reason can have various perceptions of good. Hence philosophers define the free-will as being "a free judgment arising from reason," implying that reason is the root of liberty.

AD TERTIUM dicendum quod ratio illa concludit quod imperium non sit actus rationis absolute, sed cum quadam motione, ut dictum est.

ARTICULUS 2

AD SECUNDUM sic proceditur. Videtur quod imperare conveniat brutis animalibus. Quia secundum Avicennam, *virtus imperans motum est appetitiva, et virtus exequens motum est in musculis et in nervis.* Sed utraque virtus est in brutis animalibus. Ergo imperium invenitur in brutis animalibus.

PRAETEREA, de ratione servi est quod ei imperetur. Sed corpus comparatur ad animam sicut servus ad dominum, sicut dicit philosophus in I Polit. Ergo corpori imperatur ab anima, etiam in brutis, quae sunt composita ex anima et corpore.

PRAETEREA, per imperium homo facit impetum ad opus. Sed impetus in opus invenitur in brutis animalibus, ut Damascenus dicit. Ergo in brutis animalibus invenitur imperium.

SED CONTRA, imperium est actus rationis, ut dictum est. Sed in brutis non est ratio. Ergo neque imperium.

RESPONDEO dicendum quod imperare nihil aliud est quam ordinare aliquem ad aliquid agendum, cum quadam intimativa motione. Ordinare autem est proprius actus rationis. Unde impossibile est quod in brutis animalibus, in quibus non est ratio, sit aliquo modo imperium.

AD PRIMUM ergo dicendum quod vis appetitiva dicitur imperare motum, inquantum movet rationem imperantem. Sed hoc est solum in hominibus. In brutis autem animalibus virtus appetitiva non est proprie imperativa, nisi imperativum sumatur large pro motivo.

AD SECUNDUM dicendum quod in brutis animalibus corpus quidem habet unde obediat, sed anima non habet unde imperet, quia non habet unde ordinet. Et ideo

Reply to Objection 3: This argument proves that command is an act of reason not absolutely, but with a kind of motion as stated above.

ARTICLE 2
Whether command belongs to irrational animals?

Objection 1: It would seem that command belongs to irrational animals. Because, according to Avicenna, "the power that commands movement is the appetite; and the power that executes movement is in the muscles and nerves." But both powers are in irrational animals. Therefore command is to be found in irrational animals.

Objection 2: Further, the condition of a slave is that of one who receives commands. But the body is compared to the soul as a slave to his master, as the Philosopher says (Polit. i, 2). Therefore the body is commanded by the soul, even in irrational animals, since they are composed of soul and body.

Objection 3: Further, by commanding, man has an impulse towards an action. But impulse to action is to be found in irrational animals, as Damascene says (De Fide Orth. ii, 22). Therefore command is to be found in irrational animals.

On the contrary, Command is an act of reason, as stated above (I-II, q. 17, a. 1). But in irrational animals there is no reason. Neither, therefore, is there command.

I answer that, To command is nothing else than to direct someone to do something, by a certain motion of intimation. Now to direct is the proper act of reason. Wherefore it is impossible that irrational animals should command in any way, since they are devoid of reason.

Reply to Objection 1: The appetitive power is said to command movement, in so far as it moves the commanding reason. But this is only in man. In irrational animals the appetitive power is not, properly speaking, a commanding faculty, unless command be taken loosely for motion.

Reply to Objection 2: The body of the irrational animal is competent to obey; but its soul is not competent to command, because it is not competent to direct. Consequently

non est ibi ratio imperantis et imperati; sed solum moventis et moti.

AD TERTIUM dicendum quod aliter invenitur impetus ad opus in brutis animalibus, et aliter in hominibus. Homines enim faciunt impetum ad opus per ordinationem rationis, unde habet in eis impetus rationem imperii. In brutis autem fit impetus ad opus per instinctum naturae, quia scilicet appetitus eorum statim apprehenso convenienti vel inconvenienti, **naturaliter movetur ad prosecutionem vel fugam.** Unde ordinantur ab alio ad agendum, non autem ipsa seipsa ordinant ad actionem. Et ideo in eis est impetus, sed non imperium.

ARTICULUS 3

AD TERTIUM sic proceditur. Videtur quod usus praecedat imperium. Imperium enim est actus rationis praesupponens actum voluntatis, ut supra dictum est. Sed usus est actus voluntatis, ut supra dictum est. Ergo usus praecedit imperium.

PRAETEREA, imperium est aliquid eorum quae ad finem ordinantur. Eorum autem quae sunt ad finem, est usus. Ergo videtur quod usus sit prius quam imperium.

PRAETEREA, omnis actus potentiae motae a voluntate, usus dicitur, quia voluntas utitur aliis potentiis, ut supra dictum est. Sed imperium est actus rationis prout mota est a voluntate, sicut dictum est. Ergo imperium est quidam usus. Commune autem est prius proprio. Ergo usus est prius quam imperium.

SED CONTRA est quod Damascenus dicit, quod impetus ad operationem praecedit usum. Sed impetus ad operationem fit per imperium. Ergo imperium praecedit usum.

RESPONDEO dicendum quod usus eius quod est ad finem, secundum quod est in ratione referente ipsum in finem, praecedit electionem, ut supra dictum est. Unde multo magis praecedit imperium. Sed usus eius quod est ad finem, secundum quod subditur potentiae executivae, sequitur imperium, eo quod usus utentis coniunctus est cum actu eius quo quis utitur; non enim utitur aliquis baculo, antequam

there is no ratio there of commander and commanded; but only of mover and moved.

Reply to Objection 3: Impulse to action is in irrational animals otherwise than in man. For the impulse of man to action arises from the directing reason; wherefore his impulse is one of command. On the other hand, the impulse of the irrational animal arises from natural instinct; because as soon as they apprehend the fitting or the unfitting, their appetite is moved naturally to pursue or to avoid. Wherefore they are directed by another to act; and they themselves do not direct themselves to act. Consequently in them is impulse but not command.

ARTICLE 3
Whether use precedes command?

Objection 1: It would seem that use precedes command. For command is an act of the reason presupposing an act of the will, as stated above (I-II, q. 17, a. 1). But, as we have already shown (I-II, q. 16, a. 1), use is an act of the will. Therefore use precedes command.

Objection 2: Further, command is one of those things that are ordained to the end. But use is of those things that are ordained to the end. Therefore it seems that use precedes command.

Objection 3: Further, every act of a power moved by the will is called use; because the will uses the other powers, as stated above (I-II, q. 16, a. 1). But command is an act of the reason as moved by the will, as stated above (I-II, q. 17, a. 1). Therefore command is a kind of use. Now the common precedes the proper. Therefore use precedes command.

On the contrary, Damascene says (De Fide Orth. ii, 22) that impulse to action precedes use. But impulse to operation is given by command. Therefore command precedes use.

I answer that, use of that which is directed to the end, in so far as it is in the reason referring this to the end, precedes choice, as stated above (I-II, q. 16, a. 4). Wherefore still more does it precede command. On the other hand, use of that which is directed to the end, in so far as it is subject to the executive power, follows command; because use in the user is united to the act of the thing used; for one does not use a stick before doing

aliquo modo per baculum operetur. Imperium autem non est simul cum actu eius cui imperatur, sed naturaliter prius est imperium quam imperio obediatur, et aliquando etiam est prius tempore. Unde manifestum est quod imperium est prius quam usus.

AD PRIMUM ergo dicendum quod non omnis actus voluntatis praecedit hunc actum rationis qui est imperium, sed aliquis praecedit, scilicet electio; et aliquis sequitur, scilicet usus. Quia post determinationem consilii, quae est iudicium rationis, voluntas eligit; et post electionem, ratio imperat ei per quod agendum est quod eligitur; et tunc demum voluntas alicuius incipit uti, exequendo imperium rationis; quandoque quidem voluntas alterius, cum aliquis imperat alteri; quandoque autem voluntas ipsius imperantis, cum aliquis imperat sibi ipsi.

AD SECUNDUM dicendum quod, sicut actus sunt praevii potentiis, ita obiecta actibus. Obiectum autem usus est id quod est ad finem. Ex hoc ergo quod ipsum imperium est ad finem, magis potest concludi quod imperium sit prius usu, quam quod sit posterius.

AD TERTIUM dicendum quod, sicut actus voluntatis utentis ratione ad imperandum, praecedit ipsum imperium; ita etiam potest dici quod et istum usum voluntatis praecedit aliquod imperium rationis, eo quod actus harum potentiarum supra seipsos invicem reflectuntur.

something with the stick. But command is not simultaneous with the act of the thing to which the command is given: for it naturally precedes its fulfilment, sometimes, indeed, by priority of time. Consequently it is evident that command precedes use.

Reply to Objection 1: Not every act of the will precedes this act of the reason which is command; but an act of the will precedes, *viz.* choice; and an act of the will follows, *viz.* use. Because after counsel's decision, which is reason's judgment, the will chooses; and after choice, the reason commands that power which has to do what was chosen; and then, last of all, someone's will begins to use, by executing the command of reason; sometimes it is another's will, when one commands another; sometimes the will of the one that commands, when he commands himself to do something.

Reply to Objection 2: Just as act ranks before power, so does the object rank before the act. Now the object of use is that which is directed to the end. Consequently, from the fact that command precedes, rather than that it follows use.

Reply to Objection 3: Just as the act of the will in using the reason for the purpose of command, precedes the command; so also we may say that this act whereby the will uses the reason, is preceded by a command of reason; since the acts of these powers react on one another.

ARTICULUS 4

AD QUARTUM sic proceditur. Videtur quod actus imperatus non sit unus actus cum ipso imperio. Diversarum enim potentiarum diversi sunt actus. Sed alterius potentiae est actus imperatus, et alterius ipsum imperium, quia alia est potentia quae imperat, et alia cui imperatur. Ergo non est idem actus imperatus cum imperio.

PRAETEREA, quaecumque possunt ab invicem separari, sunt diversa, nihil enim separatur a seipso. Sed aliquando

ARTICLE 4
Whether command and the commanded act are one act, or distinct?

Objection 1: It would seem that the commanded act is not one with the command itself. For the acts of different powers are themselves distinct. But the commanded act belongs to one power, and the command to another; since one is the power that commands, and the other is the power that receives the command. Therefore the commanded act is not one with the command.

Objection 2: Further, whatever things can be separate from one another, are distinct: for nothing is severed from itself. But sometimes

I-II, q. 17, a. 4, arg. 2

actus imperatus separatur ab imperio, praecedit enim quandoque imperium, et non sequitur actus imperatus. Ergo alius actus est imperium ab actu imperato.

Praeterea, quaecumque se habent secundum prius et posterius, sunt diversa. Sed imperium naturaliter praecedit actum imperatum. Ergo sunt diversa.

Sed contra est quod philosophus dicit, *quod ubi est unum propter alterum, ibi est unum tantum.* Sed actus imperatus non est nisi propter imperium. Ergo sunt unum.

Respondeo dicendum quod nihil prohibet aliqua esse secundum quid multa, et secundum quid unum. Quinimmo omnia multa sunt secundum aliquid unum, ut Dionysius dicit, ult. cap. de Div. Nom. Est tamen differentia attendenda in hoc, quod quaedam sunt simpliciter multa, et secundum quid unum, quaedam vero e converso. *Unum* autem hoc modo dicitur sicut et *ens*. Ens autem simpliciter est substantia, sed ens secundum quid est accidens, vel etiam ens *rationis*. Et ideo quaecumque sunt unum secundum substantiam, sunt unum simpliciter, et multa secundum quid. Sicut totum in genere substantiae, compositum ex suis partibus vel integralibus vel essentialibus, est unum simpliciter, nam totum est ens et substantia simpliciter, partes vero sunt entia et substantiae in toto. Quae vero sunt diversa secundum substantiam, et unum secundum accidens, sunt diversa simpliciter, et unum secundum quid, sicut multi homines sunt unus populus, et multi lapides sunt unus acervus; quae est unitas compositionis, aut ordinis. Similiter etiam multa individua, quae sunt unum genere vel specie, sunt simpliciter multa, et secundum quid unum, nam esse unum genere vel specie, est esse unum secundum rationem. Sicut autem in genere rerum naturalium, aliquod totum componitur ex materia et forma, ut homo ex anima et corpore, qui est unum ens naturale, licet habeat multitudinem partium; ita etiam in actibus humanis, actus inferioris potentiae materialiter se habet ad actum superioris, inquantum inferior potentia agit in virtute superioris

THE ACTS COMMANDED BY THE WILL

the commanded act is separate from the command: for sometimes the command is given, and the commanded act follows not. Therefore command is a distinct act from the act commanded.

Objection 3: Further, whatever things are related to one another as precedent and consequent, are distinct. But command naturally precedes the commanded act. Therefore they are distinct.

On the contrary, The Philosopher says (Topic. iii, 2) that "where one thing is by reason of another, there is but one." But there is no commanded act unless by reason of the command. Therefore they are one.

I answer that, Nothing prevents certain things being distinct in one respect, and one in another respect. Indeed, every multitude is one in some respect, as Dionysius says (Div. Nom. xiii). But a difference is to be observed in this, that some are simply many, and one in a particular aspect: while with others it is the reverse. Now "one" is predicated in the same way as "being." And substance is being simply, whereas accident or being "of reason" is a being only in a certain respect. Wherefore those things that are one in substance are one simply, though many in a certain respect. Thus, in the genus substance, the whole composed of its integral or essential parts, is one simply: because the whole is being and substance simply, and the parts are being and substances in the whole. But those things which are distinct in substance, and one according to an accident, are distinct simply, and one in a certain respect: thus many men are one people, and many stones are one heap; which is unity of composition or order. In like manner also many individuals that are one in genus or species are many simply, and one in a certain respect: since to be one in genus or species is to be one according to the consideration of the reason. Now just as in the genus of natural things, a whole is composed of matter and form (e.g., man, who is one natural being, though he has many parts, is composed of soul and body); so, in human acts, the act of a lower power is in the position of matter in regard to the act of a higher power, in so far as the lower power acts in virtue of the higher power

moventis ipsam, sic enim et actus moventis primi formaliter se habet ad actum instrumenti. Unde patet quod imperium et actus imperatus sunt unus actus humanus, sicut quoddam totum est unum, sed est secundum partes multa.

AD PRIMUM ergo dicendum quod, si essent potentiae diversae ad invicem non ordinatae, actus earum essent simpliciter diversi. Sed quando una potentia est movens alteram, tunc actus earum sunt quodammodo unus, nam *idem est actus moventis et moti,* ut dicitur in III Physic.

AD SECUNDUM dicendum quod ex hoc quod imperium et actus imperatus possunt ab invicem separari, habetur quod sunt multa partibus. Nam partes hominis possunt ab invicem separari, quae tamen sunt unum toto.

AD TERTIUM dicendum quod nihil prohibet in his quae sunt multa partibus et unum toto, unum esse prius alio. Sicut anima quodammodo est prius corpore, et cor est prius aliis membris.

moving it: for thus also the act of the first mover is as the form in regard to the act of its instrument. Hence it is evident that command and the commanded act are one human act, just as a whole is one, yet in its parts, many.

Reply to Objection 1: If the distinct powers are not ordained to one another, their acts are diverse simply. But when one power is the mover of the other, then their acts are, in a way, one: since "the act of the mover and the act of the thing moved are one act" (Phys. iii, 3).

Reply to Objection 2: The fact that command and the commanded act can be separated from one another shows that they are different parts. Because the parts of a man can be separated from one another, and yet they form one whole.

Reply to Objection 3: In those things that are many in parts, but one as a whole, nothing hinders one part from preceding another. Thus the soul, in a way, precedes the body; and the heart, the other members.

ARTICULUS 5

AD QUINTUM sic proceditur. Videtur quod actus voluntatis non sit imperatus. Dicit enim Augustinus, in VIII Confess., *imperat animus ut velit animus, nec tamen facit.* Velle autem est actus voluntatis. Ergo actus voluntatis non imperatur.

PRAETEREA, ei convenit imperari, cui convenit imperium intelligere. Sed voluntatis non est intelligere imperium, differt enim voluntas ab intellectu, cuius est intelligere. Ergo actus voluntatis non imperatur.

PRAETEREA, si aliquis actus voluntatis imperatur, pari ratione omnes imperantur. Sed si omnes actus voluntatis imperantur, necesse est in infinitum procedere, quia actus voluntatis praecedit actum imperantis rationis, ut dictum est; qui voluntatis actus si iterum imperatur, illud iterum imperium praecedet alius rationis actus, et sic

ARTICLE 5
Whether the act of the will is commanded?

Objection 1: It would seem that the act of the will is not commanded. For Augustine says (Confess. viii, 9): "The mind commands the mind to will, and yet it does not." But to will is the act of the will. Therefore the act of the will is not commanded.

Objection 2: Further, to receive a command belongs to one who can understand the command. But the will cannot understand the command; for the will differs from the intellect, to which it belongs to understand. Therefore the act of the will is not commanded.

Objection 3: Further, if one act of the will is commanded, for the same reason all are commanded. But if all the acts of the will are commanded, we must needs proceed to infinity; because the act of the will precedes the act of reason commanding, as stated above (I-II, q. 17, a. 1); for if that act of the will be also commanded, this command will be precedes by another act of the reason, and so

in infinitum. Hoc autem est inconveniens, quod procedatur in infinitum. Non ergo actus voluntatis imperatur.

SED CONTRA, omne quod est in potestate nostra, subiacet imperio nostro. Sed actus voluntatis sunt maxime in potestate nostra, nam omnes actus nostri intantum dicuntur in potestate nostra esse, inquantum voluntarii sunt. Ergo actus voluntatis imperantur a nobis.

RESPONDEO dicendum quod, sicut dictum est, imperium nihil aliud est quam actus rationis ordinantis, cum quadam motione, aliquid ad agendum. Manifestum est autem quod ratio potest ordinare de actu voluntatis, sicut enim potest iudicare quod bonum sit aliquid velle, ita potest ordinare imperando quod homo velit. Ex quo patet quod actus voluntatis potest esse imperatus.

AD PRIMUM ergo dicendum quod, sicut Augustinus ibidem dicit, animus, quando perfecte imperat sibi ut velit, tunc iam vult, sed quod aliquando imperet et non velit, hoc contingit ex hoc quod non perfecte imperat. Imperfectum autem imperium contingit ex hoc, quod ratio ex diversis partibus movetur ad imperandum vel non imperandum, unde fluctuat inter duo, et non perfecte imperat.

AD SECUNDUM dicendum quod, sicut in membris corporalibus quodlibet membrum operatur non sibi soli, sed toti corpori, ut oculus videt toti corpori; ita etiam est in potentiis animae. Nam intellectus intelligit non solum sibi, sed omnibus potentiis; et voluntas vult non solum sibi, sed omnibus potentiis. Et ideo homo imperat sibi ipsi actum voluntatis, inquantum est intelligens et volens.

AD TERTIUM dicendum quod, cum imperium sit actus rationis, ille actus imperatur, qui rationi subditur. Primus autem voluntatis actus non est ex rationis ordinatione, sed ex instinctu naturae, aut superioris causae, ut supra dictum est. Et ideo non oportet quod in infinitum procedatur.

on to infinity. But to proceed to infinity is not possible. Therefore the act of the will is not commanded.

On the contrary, Whatever is in our power, is subject to our command. But the acts of the will, most of all, are in our power; since all our acts are said to be in our power, in so far as they are voluntary. Therefore the acts of the will are commanded by us.

I answer that, As stated above (I-II, q. 17, a. 1), command is nothing else than the act of the reason directing, with a certain motion, something to act. Now it is evident that the reason can direct the act of the will: for just as it can judge it to be good to will something, so it can direct by commanding man to will. From this it is evident that an act of the will can be commanded.

Reply to Objection 1: As Augustine says (Confess. viii, 9) when the mind commands itself perfectly to will, then already it wills: but that sometimes it commands and wills not, is due to the fact that it commands imperfectly. Now imperfect command arises from the fact that the reason is moved by opposite motives to command or not to command: wherefore it fluctuates between the two, and fails to command perfectly.

Reply to Objection 2: Just as each of the members of the body works not for itself alone but for the whole body; thus it is for the whole body that the eye sees; so is it with the powers of the soul. For the intellect understands, not for itself alone, but for all the powers; and the will wills not only for itself, but for all the powers too. Wherefore man, in so far as he is endowed with intellect and will, commands the act of the will for himself.

Reply to Objection 3: Since command is an act of reason, that act is commanded which is subject to reason. Now the first act of the will is not due to the direction of the reason but to the instigation of nature, or of a higher cause, as stated above (I-II, q. 9, a. 4). Therefore there is no need to proceed to infinity.

Articulus 6

Ad sextum sic proceditur. Videtur quod actus rationis non possit esse imperatus. Inconveniens enim videtur quod aliquid imperet sibi ipsi. Sed ratio est quae imperat, ut supra dictum est. Ergo rationis actus non imperatur.

Praeterea, id quod est per essentiam, diversum est ab eo quod est per participationem. Sed potentia cuius actus imperatur a ratione, est ratio per participationem, ut dicitur in I Ethic. Ergo illius potentiae actus non imperatur, quae est ratio per essentiam.

Praeterea, ille actus imperatur, qui est in potestate nostra. Sed cognoscere et iudicare verum, quod est actus rationis, non est semper in potestate nostra. Non ergo actus rationis potest esse imperatus.

Sed contra, id quod libero arbitrio agimus, nostro imperio agi potest. Sed actus rationis exercentur per liberum arbitrium, dicit enim Damascenus quod *libero arbitrio homo exquirit, et scrutatur, et iudicat, et disponit.* Ergo actus rationis possunt esse imperati.

Respondeo dicendum quod, quia ratio supra seipsam reflectitur, sicut ordinat de actibus aliarum potentiarum, ita etiam potest ordinare de actu suo. Unde etiam actus suus potest esse imperatus. Sed attendendum est quod actus rationis potest considerari dupliciter. Uno modo, quantum ad exercitium actus. Et sic actus rationis semper imperari potest, sicut cum indicitur alicui quod attendat, et ratione utatur. Alio modo, quantum ad obiectum, respectu cuius, duo actus rationis attenduntur. Primo quidem, ut veritatem circa aliquid apprehendat. Et hoc non est in potestate nostra, hoc enim contingit per virtutem alicuius luminis, vel naturalis vel supernaturalis. Et ideo quantum ad hoc, actus rationis non est in potestate nostra, nec imperari potest. Alius autem actus rationis est, dum his quae apprehendit assentit. Si igitur fuerint talia apprehensa, quibus naturaliter intellectus assentiat, sicut prima principia, assensus talium vel dissensus non est in potestate nostra, sed in ordine naturae,

Article 6
Whether the act of the reason is commanded?

Objection 1: It would seem that the act of the reason cannot be commanded. For it seems impossible for a thing to command itself. But it is the reason that commands, as stated above (I-II, q. 17, a. 1). Therefore the act of the reason is not commanded.

Objection 2: Further, that which is essential is different from that which is by participation. But the power whose act is commanded by reason, is rational by participation, as stated in Ethic. i, 13. Therefore the act of that power, which is essentially rational, is not commanded.

Objection 3: Further, that act is commanded, which is in our power. But to know and judge the truth, which is the act of reason, is not always in our power. Therefore the act of the reason cannot be commanded.

On the contrary, That which we do of our free-will, can be done by our command. But the acts of the reason are accomplished through the free-will: for Damascene says (De Fide Orth. ii, 22) that "by his free-will man inquires, considers, judges, approves." Therefore the acts of the reason can be commanded.

I answer that, Since the reason reacts on itself, just as it directs the acts of other powers, so can it direct its own act. Consequently its act can be commanded. But we must take note that the act of the reason may be considered in two ways. First, as to the exercise of the act. And considered thus, the act of the reason can always be commanded: as when one is told to be attentive, and to use one's reason. Secondly, as to the object; in respect of which two acts of the reason have to be noticed. One is the act whereby it apprehends the truth about something. This act is not in our power: because it happens in virtue of a natural or supernatural light. Consequently in this respect, the act of the reason is not in our power, and cannot be commanded. The other act of the reason is that whereby it assents to what it apprehends. If, therefore, that which the reason apprehends is such that it naturally assents thereto, e.g., the first principles, it is not in our power to assent or dissent to the like: assent follows naturally,

et ideo, proprie loquendo, nec imperio subiacet. Sunt autem quaedam apprehensa, quae non adeo convincunt intellectum, quin possit assentire vel dissentire, vel saltem assensum vel dissensum suspendere, propter aliquam causam, et in talibus assensus ipse vel dissensus in potestate nostra est, et sub imperio cadit.

AD PRIMUM ergo dicendum quod ratio hoc modo imperat sibi ipsi, sicut et voluntas movet seipsam, ut supra dictum est, inquantum scilicet utraque potentia reflectitur supra suum actum, et ex uno in aliud tendit.

AD SECUNDUM dicendum quod, propter diversitatem obiectorum quae actui rationis subduntur, nihil prohibet rationem seipsam participare, sicut in cognitione conclusionum participatur cognitio principiorum.

AD TERTIUM patet responsio ex dictis.

ARTICULUS 7

AD SEPTIMUM sic proceditur. Videtur quod actus sensitivi appetitus non sit imperatus. Dicit enim apostolus, Rom. VII, *non enim quod volo bonum, hoc ago,* et Glossa exponit quod homo vult non concupiscere, et tamen concupiscit. Sed concupiscere est actus appetitus sensitivi. Ergo actus appetitus sensitivi non subditur imperio nostro.

PRAETEREA, materia corporalis soli Deo obedit, quantum ad transmutationem formalem, ut in primo habitum est. Sed actus appetitus sensitivi habet quandam formalem transmutationem corporis, scilicet calorem vel frigus. Ergo actus appetitus sensitivi non subditur imperio humano.

PRAETEREA, proprium motivum appetitus sensitivi est apprehensum secundum sensum vel imaginationem. Sed non est in potestate nostra semper quod aliquid apprehendamus sensu vel imaginatione. Ergo actus appetitus sensitivi non subiacet imperio nostro.

and consequently, properly speaking, is not subject to our command. But some things which are apprehended do not convince the intellect to such an extent as not to leave it free to assent or dissent, or at least suspend its assent or dissent, on account of some cause or other; and in such things assent or dissent is in our power, and is subject to our command.

Reply to Objection 1: Reason commands itself, just as the will moves itself, as stated above (I-II, q. 9, a. 3), that is to say, in so far as each power reacts on its own acts, and from one thing tends to another.

Reply to Objection 2: On account of the diversity of objects subject to the act of the reason, nothing prevents the reason from participating in itself: thus the knowledge of principles is participated in the knowledge of the conclusions.

The reply to the third objection is evident from what has been said.

ARTICLE 7
Whether the act of the sensitive appetite is commanded?

Objection 1: It would seem that the act of the sensitive appetite is not commanded. For the Apostle says (Rom. 7:15): "For I do not that good which I will": and a gloss explains this by saying that man lusts, although he wills not to lust. But to lust is an act of the sensitive appetite. Therefore the act of the sensitive appetite is not subject to our command.

Objection 2: Further, corporeal matter obeys God alone, to the effect of formal transmutation, as was shown in the I, q. 65, a. 4; q. 91, a. 2; q. 110, a. 2. But the act of the sensitive appetite is accompanied by a formal transmutation of the body, consisting in heat or cold. Therefore the act of the sensitive appetite is not subject to man's command.

Objection 3: Further, the proper motive principle of the sensitive appetite is something apprehended by sense or imagination. But it is not always in our power to apprehend something by sense or imagination. Therefore the act of the sensitive appetite is not subject to our command.

THE ACTS COMMANDED BY THE WILL

Sed contra est quod Gregorius Nyssenus dicit, *quod obediens rationi dividitur in duo, in desiderativum et irascitivum,* quae pertinent ad appetitum sensitivum. Ergo actus appetitus sensitivi subiacet imperio rationis.

Respondeo dicendum quod secundum hoc aliquis actus imperio nostro subiacet, prout est in potestate nostra, ut supra dictum est. Et ideo ad intelligendum qualiter actus appetitus sensitivi subdatur imperio rationis, oportet considerare qualiter sit in potestate nostra. Est autem sciendum quod appetitus sensitivus in hoc differt ab appetitu intellectivo, qui dicitur voluntas, quod appetitus sensitivus est virtus organi corporalis, non autem voluntas. Omnis autem actus virtutis utentis organo corporali, dependet non solum ex potentia animae, sed etiam ex corporalis organi dispositione, sicut visio ex potentia visiva, et qualitate oculi, per quam iuvatur vel impeditur. Unde et actus appetitus sensitivi non solum dependet ex vi appetitiva, sed etiam ex dispositione corporis. Illud autem quod est ex parte potentiae animae, sequitur apprehensionem. Apprehensio autem imaginationis, cum sit particularis, regulatur ab apprehensione rationis, quae est universalis, sicut virtus activa particularis a virtute activa universali. Et ideo ex ista parte, actus appetitus sensitivi subiacet imperio rationis. Qualitas autem et dispositio corporis non subiacet imperio rationis. Et ideo ex hac parte, impeditur quin motus sensitivi appetitus totaliter subdatur imperio rationis. Contingit etiam quandoque quod motus appetitus sensitivi subito concitatur ad apprehensionem imaginationis vel sensus. Et tunc ille motus est praeter imperium rationis, quamvis potuisset impediri a ratione, si praevidisset. Unde philosophus

On the contrary, Gregory of Nyssa* says: "That which obeys reason is twofold, the concupiscible and the irascible," which belong to the sensitive appetite. Therefore the act of the sensitive appetite is subject to the command of reason.

I answer that, An act is subject to our command, in so far as it is in our power, as stated above (I-II, q. 17, a. 5). Consequently in order to understand in what manner the act of the sensitive appetite is subject to the command of reason, we must consider in what manner it is in our power. Now it must be observed that the sensitive appetite differs from the intellective appetite, which is called the will, in the fact that the sensitive appetite is a power of a corporeal organ, whereas the will is not. Again, every act of a power that uses a corporeal organ, depends not only on a power of the soul, but also on the disposition of that corporeal organ: thus the act of vision depends on the power of sight, and on the condition of the eye, which condition is a help or a hindrance to that act. Consequently the act of the sensitive appetite depends not only on the appetitive power, but also on the disposition of the body. Now whatever part the power of the soul takes in the act, follows apprehension. And the apprehension of the imagination, being a particular apprehension, is regulated by the apprehension of reason, which is universal; just as a particular active power is regulated by a universal active power. Consequently in this respect the act of the sensitive appetite is subject to the command of reason. On the other hand, condition or disposition of the body is not subject to the command of reason: and consequently in this respect, the movement of the sensitive appetite is hindered from being wholly subject to the command of reason. Moreover it happens sometimes that the movement of the sensitive appetite is aroused suddenly in consequence of an apprehension of the imagination of sense. And then such movement occurs without the command of reason: although reason could have prevented it, had it foreseen. Hence the Philosopher

---

* Nemesius, De Nat. Hom. xvi.

dicit, in I Polit., quod ratio praeest irascibili et concupiscibili *non principatu despotico,* qui est domini ad servum; sed *principatu politico aut regali,* qui est ad liberos, qui non totaliter subduntur imperio.

AD PRIMUM ergo dicendum quod hoc quod homo vult non concupiscere, et tamen concupiscit, contingit ex dispositione corporis, per quam impeditur appetitus sensitivus **ne totaliter sequatur imperium rationis.** Unde et apostolus ibidem subdit, *video aliam legem in membris meis, repugnantem legi mentis meae.* Hoc etiam contingit propter subitum motum concupiscentiae, ut dictum est.

AD SECUNDUM dicendum quod qualitas corporalis dupliciter se habet ad actum appetitus sensitivi. Uno modo, ut praecedens, prout aliquis est aliqualiter dispositus secundum corpus, ad hanc vel illam passionem. Alio modo, ut consequens, sicut cum ex ira aliquis incalescit. Qualitas igitur praecedens non subiacet imperio rationis, quia vel est ex natura, vel ex aliqua praecedenti motione, quae non statim quiescere potest. Sed qualitas consequens sequitur imperium rationis, quia sequitur motum localem cordis, quod diversimode movetur secundum diversos actus sensitivi appetitus.

AD TERTIUM dicendum quod, quia ad apprehensionem sensus requiritur sensibile exterius, non est in potestate nostra apprehendere aliquid sensu, nisi sensibili praesente; cuius praesentia non semper est in potestate nostra. Tunc enim homo potest uti sensu cum voluerit, nisi sit impedimentum ex parte organi. Apprehensio autem imaginationis subiacet ordinationi rationis, secundum modum virtutis vel debilitatis imaginativae potentiae. Quod enim homo non possit imaginari quae ratio considerat, contingit vel ex hoc quod non sunt imaginabilia, sicut incorporalia; vel propter debilitatem virtutis imaginativae, quae est ex aliqua indispositione organi.

says (Polit. i, 2) that the reason governs the irascible and concupiscible not by a "despotic supremacy," which is that of a master over his slave; but by a "politic and royal supremacy," whereby the free are governed, who are not wholly subject to command.

Reply to Objection 1: That man lusts, although he wills not to lust, is due to a disposition of the body, whereby the sensitive appetite is hindered from perfect compliance with the **command of reason.** Hence the Apostle adds (Rom. 7:15): "I see another law in my members, fighting against the law of my mind." This may also happen through a sudden movement of concupiscence, as stated above.

Reply to Objection 2: The condition of the body stands in a twofold relation to the act of the sensitive appetite. First, as preceding it: thus a man may be disposed in one way or another, in respect of his body, to this or that passion. Secondly, as consequent to it: thus a man becomes heated through anger. Now the condition that precedes, is not subject to the command of reason: since it is due either to nature, or to some previous movement, which cannot cease at once. But the condition that is consequent, follows the command of reason: since it results from the local movement of the heart, which has various movements according to the various acts of the sensitive appetite.

Reply to Objection 3: Since the external sensible is necessary for the apprehension of the senses, it is not in our power to apprehend anything by the senses, unless the sensible be present; which presence of the sensible is not always in our power. For it is then that man can use his senses if he will so to do; unless there be some obstacle on the part of the organ. On the other hand, the apprehension of the imagination is subject to the ordering of reason, in proportion to the strength or weakness of the imaginative power. For that man is unable to imagine the things that reason considers, is either because they cannot be imagined, such as incorporeal things; or because of the weakness of the imaginative power, due to some organic indisposition.

Articulus 8

Ad octavum sic proceditur. Videtur quod actus vegetabilis animae imperio rationis subdantur. Vires enim sensitivae nobiliores sunt viribus animae vegetabilis. Sed vires animae sensitivae subduntur imperio rationis. Ergo multo magis vires animae vegetabilis.

Praeterea, homo dicitur *minor mundus*, quia sic est anima in corpore, sicut Deus in mundo. Sed Deus sic est in mundo, quod omnia quae sunt in mundo, obediunt eius imperio. Ergo et omnia quae sunt in homine, obediunt imperio rationis, etiam vires vegetabilis animae.

Praeterea, laus et vituperium non contingit nisi in actibus qui subduntur imperio rationis. Sed in actibus nutritivae et generativae potentiae, contingit esse laudem et vituperium, et virtutem et vitium, sicut patet in gula et luxuria, et virtutibus oppositis. Ergo actus harum potentiarum subduntur imperio rationis.

Sed contra est quod Gregorius Nyssenus dicit, quod *id quod non persuadetur a ratione, est nutritivum et generativum.*

Respondeo dicendum quod actuum quidam procedunt ex appetitu naturali, quidam autem ex appetitu animali vel intellectuali, omne enim agens aliquo modo appetit finem. Appetitus autem naturalis non consequitur aliquam apprehensionem, sicut sequitur appetitus animalis et intellectualis. Ratio autem imperat per modum apprehensivae virtutis. Et ideo actus illi qui procedunt ab appetitu intellectivo vel animali, possunt a ratione imperari, non autem actus illi qui procedunt ex appetitu naturali. Huiusmodi autem sunt actus vegetabilis animae, unde Gregorius Nyssenus dicit *quod vocatur naturale quod generativum et nutritivum.* Et propter hoc, actus vegetabilis animae non subduntur imperio rationis.

Ad primum ergo dicendum quod, quanto aliquis actus est immaterialior, tanto est nobilior, et magis subditus imperio rationis.

Article 8
Whether the act of the vegetal soul is commanded?

Objection 1: It would seem that the acts of the vegetal soul are subject to the command of reason. For the sensitive powers are of higher rank than the vegetal powers. But the powers of the sensitive soul are subject to the command of reason. Much more, therefore, are the powers of the vegetal soul.

Objection 2: Further, man is called a "little world,"* because the soul is in the body, as God is in the world. But God is in the world in such a way, that everything in the world obeys His command. Therefore all that is in man, even the powers of the vegetal soul, obey the command of reason.

Objection 3: Further, praise and blame are awarded only to such acts as are subject to the command of reason. But in the acts of the nutritive and generative power, there is room for praise and blame, virtue and vice: as in the case of gluttony and lust, and their contrary virtues. Therefore the acts of these powers are subject to the command of reason.

On the contrary, Gregory of Nyssa† states that "the nutritive and generative power is one over which the reason has no control."

I answer that, Some acts proceed from the natural appetite, others from the animal, or from the intellectual appetite: for every agent desires an end in some way. Now the natural appetite does not follow from some apprehension, as to the animal and the intellectual appetite. But the reason commands by way of apprehensive power. Wherefore those acts that proceed from the intellective or the animal appetite, can be commanded by reason: but not those acts that proceed from the natural appetite. And such are the acts of the vegetal soul; wherefore Gregory of Nyssa‡ says "that generation and nutrition belong to what are called natural powers." Consequently the acts of the vegetal soul are not subject to the command of reason.

Reply to Objection 1: The more immaterial an act is, the more noble it is, and the more is it subject to the command of reason.

---

* Aristotle, Phys. viii. 2
† Nemesius, De Nat. Hom. xxii.
‡ Ibid.

Unde ex hoc ipso quod vires animae vegetabilis non obediunt rationi, apparet has vires infimas esse.

AD SECUNDUM dicendum quod similitudo attenditur quantum ad aliquid, quia scilicet, sicut Deus movet mundum, ita anima movet corpus. Non autem quantum ad omnia, non enim anima creavit corpus ex nihilo, sicut Deus mundum; propter quod totaliter subditur eius imperio.

AD TERTIUM dicendum quod virtus et vitium, laus et vituperium, non debentur ipsis actibus nutritivae vel generativae potentiae, qui sunt digestio et formatio corporis humani; sed actibus sensitivae partis ordinatis ad actus generativae vel nutritivae; puta in concupiscendo delectationem cibi et venereorum, et utendo, secundum quod oportet, vel non secundum quod oportet.

ARTICULUS 9

AD NONUM sic proceditur. Videtur quod membra corporis non obediant rationi quantum ad actus suos. Constat enim quod membra corporis magis distant a ratione quam vires animae vegetabilis. Sed vires animae vegetabilis non obediunt rationi, ut dictum est. Ergo multo minus membra corporis.

PRAETEREA, cor est principium motus animalis. Sed motus cordis non subditur imperio rationis, dicit enim Gregorius Nyssenus quod *pulsativum non est persuasibile ratione.* Ergo motus membrorum corporalium non subiacet imperio rationis.

PRAETEREA, Augustinus dicit, XIV de Civ. Dei, quod *motus membrorum genitalium aliquando importunus est, nullo poscente, aliquando autem destituit inhiantem, et cum in animo concupiscentia ferveat, friget in corpore.* Ergo motus membrorum non obediunt rationi.

Hence the very fact that the acts of the vegetal soul do not obey reason, shows that they rank lowest.

Reply to Objection 2: The comparison holds in a certain respect: because, to wit, as God moves the world, so the soul moves the body. But it does not hold in every respect: for the soul did not create the body out of nothing, as God created the world; for which reason the world is wholly subject to His command.

Reply to Objection 3: Virtue and vice, praise and blame do not affect the acts themselves of the nutritive and generative power, i.e., digestion, and formation of the human body; but they affect the acts of the sensitive part, that are ordained to the acts of generation and nutrition; for example the desire for pleasure in the act of taking food or in the act of generation, and the right or wrong use thereof.

ARTICLE 9
Whether the acts of the external members are commanded?

Objection 1: It would seem that the members of the body do not obey reason as to their acts. For it is evident that the members of the body are more distant from the reason, than the powers of the vegetal soul. But the powers of the vegetal soul do not obey reason, as stated above (I-II, q. 17, a. 8). Therefore much less do the members of the body obey.

Objection 2: Further, the heart is the principle of animal movement. But the movement of the heart is not subject to the command of reason: for Gregory of Nyssa* says that "the pulse is not controlled by reason." Therefore the movement of the bodily members is not subject to the command of reason.

Objection 3: Further, Augustine says (De Civ. Dei xiv, 16) that "the movement of the genital members is sometimes inopportune and not desired; sometimes when sought it fails, and whereas the heart is warm with desire, the body remains cold." Therefore the movements of the members are not obedient to reason.

---

* Nemesius, De Nat. Hom. xxii.

SED CONTRA est quod Augustinus dicit, VIII Confess., *imperat animus ut moveatur manus, et tanta est facilitas, ut vix a servitio discernatur imperium.*

RESPONDEO dicendum quod membra corporis sunt organa quaedam potentiarum animae. Unde eo modo quo potentiae animae se habent ad hoc quod obediant rationi, hoc modo se habent etiam corporis membra. Quia igitur vires sensitivae subduntur imperio rationis, non autem vires naturales; ideo omnes motus membrorum quae moventur a potentiis sensitivis, subduntur imperio rationis; motus autem membrorum qui consequuntur vires naturales, non subduntur imperio rationis.

AD PRIMUM ergo dicendum quod membra non movent seipsa, sed moventur per potentias animae; quarum quaedam sunt rationi viciniores quam vires animae vegetabilis.

AD SECUNDUM dicendum quod in his quae ad intellectum et voluntatem pertinent, primum invenitur id quod est secundum naturam, ex quo alia derivantur, ut a cognitione principiorum naturaliter notorum, cognitio conclusionum; et a voluntate finis naturaliter desiderati, derivatur electio eorum quae sunt ad finem. Ita etiam in corporalibus motibus principium est secundum naturam. Principium autem corporalis motus est a motu cordis. Unde motus cordis est secundum naturam, et non secundum voluntatem, consequitur enim sicut per se accidens vitam, quae est ex unione animae et corporis. Sicut motus gravium et levium consequitur formam substantialem ipsorum, unde et a generante moveri dicuntur, secundum philosophum in VIII Physic. Et propter hoc motus iste *vitalis* dicitur. Unde Gregorius Nyssenus dicit quod sicut generativum et nutritivum non obedit rationi, ita nec pulsativum, quod est vitale. Pulsativum

On the contrary, Augustine says (Confess. viii, 9): "The mind commands a movement of the hand, and so ready is the hand to obey, that scarcely can one discern obedience from command."

I answer that, The members of the body are organs of the soul's powers. Consequently according as the powers of the soul stand in respect of obedience to reason, so do the members of the body stand in respect thereof. Since then the sensitive powers are subject to the command of reason, whereas the natural powers are not; therefore all movements of members, that are moved by the sensitive powers, are subject to the command of reason; whereas those movements of members, that arise from the natural powers, are not subject to the command of reason.

Reply to Objection 1: The members do not move themselves, but are moved through the powers of the soul; of which powers, some are in closer contact with the reason than are the powers of the vegetal soul.

Reply to Objection 2: In things pertaining to intellect and will, that which is according to nature stands first, whence all other things are derived: thus from the knowledge of principles that are naturally known, is derived knowledge of the conclusions; and from volition of the end naturally desired, is derived the choice of the means. So also in bodily movements the principle is according to nature. Now the principle of bodily movements begins with the movement of the heart. Consequently the movement of the heart is according to nature, and not according to the will: for like a proper accident, it results from life, which follows from the union of soul and body. Thus the movement of heavy and light things results from their substantial form: for which reason they are said to be moved by their generator, as the Philosopher states (Phys. viii, 4). Wherefore this movement is called "vital." For which reason Gregory of Nyssa[*] says that, just as the movement of generation and nutrition does not obey reason, so neither does the pulse which is a vital movement. By the pulse

---

[*] Nemesius, De Nat. Hom. xxii.

autem appellat motum cordis, qui manifestatur per venas pulsatiles.

Ad tertium dicendum quod, sicut Augustinus dicit in XIV de Civ. Dei, hoc quod motus genitalium membrorum rationi non obedit, est ex poena peccati, ut scilicet anima suae inobedientiae ad Deum in illo praecipue membro poenam inobedientiae patiatur, per quod peccatum originale ad posteros traducitur. Sed quia per peccatum primi parentis, ut **infra dicetur**, natura est sibi relicta, subtracto supernaturali dono quod homini divinitus erat collatum; ideo consideranda est ratio naturalis quare motus huiusmodi membrorum specialiter rationi non obedit. Cuius causam assignat Aristoteles in libro de causis motus animalium, dicens *involuntarios esse motus cordis et membri pudendi,* quia scilicet ex aliqua apprehensione huiusmodi membra commoventur, inquantum scilicet intellectus et phantasia repraesentant aliqua ex quibus consequuntur passiones animae, ad quas consequitur motus horum membrorum. Non tamen moventur secundum iussum rationis aut intellectus, quia scilicet ad motum horum membrorum requiritur aliqua alteratio naturalis, scilicet caliditatis et frigiditatis, quae quidem alteratio non subiacet imperio rationis. Specialiter autem hoc accidit in his duobus membris, quia utrumque istorum membrorum est quasi quoddam animal separatum, inquantum est principium vitae, principium autem est virtute totum. Cor enim principium est sensuum, et ex membro genitali virtus exit seminalis, quae est virtute totum animal. Et ideo habent proprios motus naturaliter, quia principia oportet esse naturalia, ut dictum est.

he means the movement of the heart which is indicated by the pulse veins.

Reply to Objection 3: As Augustine says (De Civ. Dei xiv, 17,20) it is in punishment of sin that the movement of these members does not obey reason: in this sense, that the soul is punished for its rebellion against God, by the insubmission of that member whereby original sin is transmitted to posterity. But because, as we shall state later on, **the effect of the sin of our first parent was that his nature was left to itself, through the withdrawal of the supernatural gift which God had bestowed on man,** we must consider the natural cause of this particular member's insubmission to reason. This is stated by Aristotle (De Causis Mot. Animal.) who says that "the movements of the heart and of the organs of generation are involuntary," and that the reason of this is as follows. These members are stirred at the occasion of some apprehension; in so far as the intellect and imagination represent such things as arouse the passions of the soul, of which passions these movements are a consequence. But they are not moved at the command of the reason or intellect, because these movements are conditioned by a certain natural change of heat and cold, which change is not subject to the command of reason. This is the case with these two organs in particular, because each is as it were a separate animal being, in so far as it is a principle of life; and the principle is virtually the whole. For the heart is the principle of the senses; and from the organ of generation proceeds the seminal virtue, which is virtually the entire animal. Consequently they have their proper movements naturally: because principles must needs be natural, as stated above (ad 2).

Question 18
Of the Good and Evil of Human Acts, in General

We must now consider the good and evil of human acts. First, how a human act is good or evil; secondly, what results from the good or evil of a human act, as merit or demerit, sin and guilt. Under the first head there will be a threefold consideration: the first will be of the good and evil of human acts, in general; the second, of the good and evil of internal acts; the third, of the good and evil of external acts. Concerning the first there are eleven points of inquiry: 1. Whether every human action is good, or are there evil actions? 2. Whether the good or evil of a human action is derived from its object? 3. Whether it is derived from a circumstance? 4. Whether it is derived from the end? 5. Whether a human action is good or evil in its species? 6. Whether an action has the species of good or evil from its end? 7. Whether the species derived from the end is contained under the species derived from the object, as under its genus, or conversely? 8. Whether any action is indifferent in its species? 9. Whether an individual action can be indifferent? 10. Whether a circumstance places a moral action in the species of good or evil? 11. Whether every circumstance that makes an action better or worse, places the moral action in the species of good or evil?

Article 1
Whether every human action is good, or are there evil actions?

Objection 1: It would seem that every human action is good, and that none is evil. For Dionysius says (Div. Nom. iv) that evil acts not, save in virtue of the good. But no evil is done in virtue of the good. Therefore no action is evil.

Objection 2: Further, nothing acts except in so far as it is in act. Now a thing is evil, not according as it is in act, but according as its potentiality is void of act; whereas in so far as its potentiality is perfected by act, it is good, as stated in Metaph. ix, 9. Therefore nothing acts in so far as it is evil, but only according

est bonum. Omnis ergo actio est bona, et nulla mala.

Praeterea, malum non potest esse causa nisi per accidens, ut patet per Dionysium, IV cap. de Div. Nom. Sed omnis actionis est aliquis per se effectus. Nulla ergo actio est mala, sed omnis actio est bona.

Sed contra est quod dominus dicit, Ioan. III, *omnis qui male agit, odit lucem*. Est ergo aliqua actio hominis mala.

Respondeo dicendum quod de bono et malo in actionibus oportet loqui sicut de bono et malo in rebus, eo quod unaquaeque res talem actionem producit, qualis est ipsa. In rebus autem unumquodque tantum habet de bono, quantum habet de esse, bonum enim et ens convertuntur, ut in primo dictum est. Solus autem Deus habet totam plenitudinem sui esse secundum aliquid unum et simplex, unaquaeque vero res alia habet plenitudinem essendi sibi convenientem secundum diversa. Unde in aliquibus contingit quod quantum ad aliquid habent esse, et tamen eis aliquid deficit ad plenitudinem essendi eis debitam. Sicut ad plenitudinem esse humani requiritur quod sit quoddam compositum ex anima et corpore, habens omnes potentias et instrumenta cognitionis et motus, unde si aliquid horum deficiat alicui homini deficit ei aliquid de plenitudine sui esse. Quantum igitur habet de esse, tantum habet de bonitate, inquantum vero aliquid ei deficit de plenitudine essendi, intantum deficit a bonitate, et dicitur malum, sicut homo caecus habet de bonitate quod vivit, et malum est ei quod caret visu. Si vero nihil haberet de entitate vel bonitate, neque malum neque bonum dici posset. Sed quia de ratione boni est ipsa plenitudo essendi, si quidem alicui aliquid defuerit de debita essendi plenitudine, non dicetur simpliciter bonum, sed secundum quid, inquantum est ens, poterit tamen dici simpliciter ens et secundum quid non ens, ut in primo dictum est. Sic igitur dicendum est quod omnis actio, inquantum habet aliquid de esse, intantum habet de bonitate, inquantum vero deficit ei aliquid de plenitudine essendi quae debetur actioni humanae, intantum deficit a bonitate,

as it is good. Therefore every action is good, and none is evil.

Objection 3: Further, evil cannot be a cause, save accidentally, as Dionysius declares (Div. Nom. iv). But every action has some effect which is proper to it. Therefore no action is evil, but every action is good.

On the contrary, Our Lord said (Jn. 3:20): "Every one that doth evil, hateth the light." Therefore some actions of man are evil.

I answer that, We must speak of good and evil in actions as of good and evil in things: because such as everything is, such is the act that it produces. Now in things, each one has so much good as it has being: since good and being are convertible, as was stated in the I, q. 5, a. 1; a. 3. But God alone has the whole plenitude of His Being in a certain unity: whereas every other thing has its proper fulness of being in a certain multiplicity. Wherefore it happens with some things, that they have being in some respect, and yet they are lacking in the fulness of being due to them. Thus the fulness of human being requires a compound of soul and body, having all the powers and instruments of knowledge and movement: wherefore if any man be lacking in any of these, he is lacking in something due to the fulness of his being. So that as much as he has of being, so much has he of goodness: while so far as he is lacking in goodness, and is said to be evil: thus a blind man is possessed of goodness inasmuch as he lives; and of evil, inasmuch as he lacks sight. That, however, which has nothing of being or goodness, could not be said to be either evil or good. But since this same fulness of being is of the very essence of good, if a thing be lacking in its due fulness of being, it is not said to be good simply, but in a certain respect, inasmuch as it is a being; although it can be called a being simply, and a non-being in a certain respect, as was stated in the I, q. 5, a. 1, ad 1. We must therefore say that every action has goodness, in so far as it has being; whereas it is lacking in goodness, in so far as it is lacking in something that is due to its fulness of being;

et sic dicitur mala, puta si deficiat ei vel determinata quantitas secundum rationem, vel debitus locus, vel aliquid huiusmodi.

AD PRIMUM ergo dicendum quod malum agit in virtute boni deficientis. Si enim nihil esset ibi de bono, neque esset ens, neque agere posset. Si autem non esset deficiens, non esset malum. Unde et actio causata est quoddam bonum deficiens, quod secundum quid est bonum, simpliciter autem malum.

AD SECUNDUM dicendum quod nihil prohibet aliquid esse secundum quid in actu, unde agere possit; et secundum aliud privari actu, unde causet deficientem actionem. Sicut homo caecus actu habet virtutem gressivam, per quam ambulare potest, sed inquantum caret visu, qui dirigit in ambulando, patitur defectum in ambulando, dum ambulat cespitando.

AD TERTIUM dicendum quod actio mala potest habere aliquem effectum per se, secundum id quod habet de bonitate et entitate. Sicut adulterium est causa generationis humanae, inquantum habet commixtionem maris et feminae, non autem inquantum caret ordine rationis.

and thus it is said to be evil: for instance if it lacks the quantity determined by reason, or its due place, or something of the kind.

Reply to Objection 1: Evil acts in virtue of deficient goodness. For it there were nothing of good there, there would be neither being nor possibility of action. On the other hand if good were not deficient, there would be no evil. Consequently the action done is a deficient good, which is good in a certain respect, but simply evil.

Reply to Objection 2: Nothing hinders a thing from being in act in a certain respect, so that it can act; and in a certain respect deficient in act, so as to cause a deficient act. Thus a blind man has in act the power of walking, whereby he is able to walk; but inasmuch as he is deprived of sight he suffers a defect in walking by stumbling when he walks.

Reply to Objection 3: An evil action can have a proper effect, according to the goodness and being that it has. Thus adultery is the cause of human generation, inasmuch as it implies union of male and female, but not inasmuch as it lacks the order of reason.

ARTICULUS 2

ARTICLE 2
Whether the good or evil of a man's action is derived from its object?

AD SECUNDUM sic proceditur. Videtur quod actio non habeat bonitatem vel malitiam ex obiecto. Obiectum enim actionis est res. *In rebus autem non est malum, sed in usu peccantium,* ut Augustinus dicit in libro III de Doct. Christ. Ergo actio humana non habet bonitatem vel malitiam ex obiecto.

PRAETEREA, obiectum comparatur ad actionem ut materia. Bonitas autem rei non est ex materia, sed magis ex forma, quae est actus. Ergo bonum et malum non est in actibus ex obiecto.

PRAETEREA, obiectum potentiae activae comparatur ad actionem sicut effectus ad causam. Sed bonitas causae non dependet ex effectu, sed magis e converso. Ergo actio humana non habet bonitatem vel malitiam ex obiecto.

Objection 1: It would seem that the good or evil of an action is not derived from its object. For the object of any action is a thing. But "evil is not in things, but in the sinner's use of them," as Augustine says (De Doctr. Christ. iii, 12). Therefore the good or evil of a human action is not derived from their object.

Objection 2: Further, the object is compared to the action as its matter. But the goodness of a thing is not from its matter, but rather from the form, which is an act. Therefore good and evil in actions is not derived from their object.

Objection 3: Further, the object of an active power is compared to the action as effect to cause. But the goodness of a cause does not depend on its effect; rather is it the reverse. Therefore good or evil in actions is not derived from their object.

Sed contra est quod dicitur Osee IX, *facti sunt abominabiles, sicut ea quae dilexerunt*. Fit autem homo Deo abominabilis propter malitiam suae operationis. Ergo malitia operationis est secundum obiecta mala quae homo diligit. Et eadem ratio est de bonitate actionis.

Respondeo dicendum quod, sicut dictum est, bonum et malum actionis, sicut et ceterarum rerum, attenditur ex plenitudine essendi vel defectu ipsius. Primum autem quod ad plenitudinem essendi pertinere videtur, est id quod dat rei speciem. Sicut autem res naturalis habet speciem ex sua forma, ita actio habet speciem ex obiecto; sicut et motus ex termino. Et ideo sicut prima bonitas rei naturalis attenditur ex sua forma, quae dat speciem ei, ita et prima bonitas actus moralis attenditur ex obiecto convenienti; unde et a quibusdam vocatur *bonum ex genere*; puta, *uti re sua*. Et sicut in rebus naturalibus primum malum est, si res generata non consequitur formam specificam, puta si non generetur homo, sed aliquid loco hominis; ita primum malum in actionibus moralibus est quod est ex obiecto, sicut *accipere aliena*. Et dicitur *malum ex genere*, genere pro specie accepto, eo modo loquendi quo dicimus *humanum* genus totam humanam speciem.

Ad primum ergo dicendum quod, licet res exteriores sint in seipsis bonae, tamen non semper habent debitam proportionem ad hanc vel illam actionem. Et ideo inquantum considerantur ut obiecta talium actionum, non habent rationem boni.

Ad secundum dicendum quod obiectum non est materia *ex qua*, sed materia *circa quam*, et habet quodammodo rationem formae, inquantum dat speciem.

Ad tertium dicendum quod non semper obiectum actionis humanae est obiectum activae potentiae. Nam appetitiva potentia est quodammodo passiva, inquantum movetur ab appetibili, et tamen est principium humanorum actuum. Neque etiam

On the contrary, It is written (Osee 9:10): "They became abominable as those things which they loved." Now man becomes abominable to God on account of the malice of his action. Therefore the malice of his action is according to the evil objects that man loves. And the same applies to the goodness of his action.

I answer that, as stated above (I-II, q. 18, a. 1) the good or evil of an action, as of other things, depends on its fulness of being or its lack of that fulness. Now the first thing that belongs to the fulness of being seems to be that which gives a thing its species. And just as a natural thing has its species from its form, so an action has its species from its object, as movement from its term. And therefore just as the primary goodness of a natural thing is derived from its form, which gives it its species, so the primary goodness of a moral action is derived from its suitable object: hence some call such an action "good in its genus"; for instance, "to make use of what is one's own." And just as, in natural things, the primary evil is when a generated thing does not realize its specific form (for instance, if instead of a man, something else be generated); so the primary evil in moral actions is that which is from the object, for instance, "to take what belongs to another." And this action is said to be "evil in its genus," genus here standing for species, just as we apply the term "mankind" to the whole human species.

Reply to Objection 1: Although external things are good in themselves, nevertheless they have not always a due proportion to this or that action. And so, inasmuch as they are considered as objects of such actions, they have not the quality of goodness.

Reply to Objection 2: The object is not the matter "of which" [a thing is made], but the matter "about which" [something is done]; and stands in relation to the act as its form, as it were, through giving it its species.

Reply to Objection 3: The object of the human action is not always the object of an active power. For the appetitive power is, in a way, passive; in so far as it is moved by the appetible object; and yet it is a principle of human actions. Nor again

potentiarum activarum obiecta semper habent rationem effectus, sed quando iam sunt transmutata, sicut alimentum transmutatum est effectus nutritivae potentiae, sed alimentum nondum transmutatum comparatur ad potentiam nutritivam sicut materia circa quam operatur. Ex hoc autem quod obiectum est aliquo modo effectus potentiae activae, sequitur quod sit terminus actionis eius, et per consequens quod det ei formam et speciem, motus enim habet speciem a terminis. Et quamvis etiam bonitas actionis non causetur ex bonitate effectus, tamen ex hoc dicitur actio bona, quod bonum effectum inducere potest. Et ita ipsa proportio actionis ad effectum, est ratio bonitatis ipsius.

have the objects of the active powers always have the nature of an effect, but only when they are already transformed: thus food when transformed is the effect of the nutritive power; whereas food before being transformed stands in relation to the nutritive power as the matter about which it exercises its operation. Now since the object is in some way the effect of the active power, it follows that it is the term of its action, and consequently that it gives it its form and species, since movement derives its species from its term. Moreover, although the goodness of an action is not caused by the goodness of its effect, yet an action is said to be good from the fact that it can produce a good effect. Consequently the very proportion of an action to its effect is the measure of its goodness.

Articulus 3

Ad tertium sic proceditur. Videtur quod actio non sit bona vel mala ex circumstantia. Circumstantiae enim circumstant actum sicut extra ipsum existentes, ut dictum est. Sed *bonum et malum sunt in ipsis rebus,* ut dicitur in VI Metaphys. Ergo actio non habet bonitatem vel malitiam ex circumstantia.

Praeterea, bonitas vel malitia actus maxime consideratur in doctrina morum. Sed circumstantiae, cum sint quaedam accidentia actuum, videntur esse praeter considerationem artis, quia *nulla ars considerat id quod est per accidens,* ut dicitur in VI Metaphys. Ergo bonitas vel malitia actionis non est ex circumstantia.

Praeterea, id quod convenit alicui secundum suam substantiam, non attribuitur ei per aliquod accidens. Sed bonum et malum convenit actioni secundum suam substantiam, quia actio ex suo genere potest esse bona vel mala, ut dictum est. Ergo non convenit actioni ex circumstantia quod sit bona vel mala.

Sed contra est quod philosophus dicit, in libro Ethic., quod virtuosus operatur secundum quod oportet, et quando oportet, et secundum alias circumstantias.

Article 3
Whether man's action is good or evil from a circumstance?

Objection 1: It would seem that an action is not good or evil from a circumstance. For circumstances stand around [*circumstant*] an action, as being outside it, as stated above (I-II, q. 7, a. 1). But "good and evil are in things themselves," as is stated in Metaph. vi, 4. Therefore an action does not derive goodness or malice from a circumstance.

Objection 2: Further, the goodness or malice of an action is considered principally in the doctrine of morals. But since circumstances are accidents of actions, it seems that they are outside the scope of art: because "no art takes notice of what is accidental" (Metaph. vi, 2). Therefore the goodness or malice of an action is not taken from a circumstance.

Objection 3: Further, that which belongs to a thing, in respect of its substance, is not ascribed to it in respect of an accident. But good and evil belong to an action in respect of its substance; because an action can be good or evil in its genus as stated above (I-II, q. 18, a. 2). Therefore an action is not good or bad from a circumstance.

On the contrary, the Philosopher says (Ethic. ii, 3) that a virtuous man acts as he should, and when he should, and so on in respect of the other circumstances.

Ergo ex contrario vitiosus, secundum unumquodque vitium, operatur quando non oportet, ubi non oportet, et sic de aliis circumstantiis. Ergo actiones humanae secundum circumstantias sunt bonae vel malae.

Respondeo dicendum quod in rebus naturalibus non invenitur tota plenitudo perfectionis quae debetur rei, ex forma substantiali, quae dat speciem; sed multum **superadditur ex supervenientibus accidentibus**, sicut in homine ex figura, ex colore, et huiusmodi; quorum si aliquod desit ad decentem habitudinem, consequitur malum. Ita etiam est in actione. Nam plenitudo bonitatis eius non tota consistit in sua specie, sed aliquid additur ex his quae adveniunt tanquam accidentia quaedam. Et huiusmodi sunt circumstantiae debitae. Unde si aliquid desit quod requiratur ad debitas circumstantias, erit actio mala.

Ad primum ergo dicendum quod circumstantiae sunt extra actionem, inquantum non sunt de essentia actionis, sunt tamen in ipsa actione velut quaedam accidentia eius. Sicut et accidentia quae sunt in substantiis naturalibus, sunt extra essentias earum.

Ad secundum dicendum quod non omnia accidentia per accidens se habent ad sua subiecta, sed quaedam sunt per se accidentia; quae in unaquaque arte considerantur. Et per hunc modum considerantur circumstantiae actuum in doctrina morali.

Ad tertium dicendum quod, cum bonum convertatur cum ente, sicut ens dicitur secundum substantiam et secundum accidens, ita et bonum attribuitur alicui et secundum esse suum essentiale, et secundum esse accidentale, tam in rebus naturalibus, quam in actionibus moralibus.

Articulus 4

Ad quartum sic proceditur. Videtur quod bonum et malum in actibus humanis non sint ex fine. Dicit enim Dionysius, IV cap. de Div. Nom., quod *nihil respiciens ad malum operatur.* Si igitur ex fine derivaretur operatio bona vel mala, nulla actio esset mala. Quod patet esse falsum.

Therefore, on the other hand, the vicious man, in the matter of each vice, acts when he should not, or where he should not, and so on with the other circumstances. Therefore human actions are good or evil according to circumstances.

I answer that, In natural things, it is to be noted that the whole fulness of perfection due to a thing, is not from the mere substantial form, that gives it its species; since a thing derives much from **supervening accidents**, as man does from shape, color, and the like; and if any one of these accidents be out of due proportion, evil is the result. So it is with action. For the plenitude of its goodness does not consist wholly in its species, but also in certain additions which accrue to it by reason of certain accidents: and such are its due circumstances. Wherefore if something be wanting that is requisite as a due circumstance the action will be evil.

Reply to Objection 1: Circumstances are outside an action, inasmuch as they are not part of its essence; but they are in an action as accidents thereof. Thus, too, accidents in natural substances are outside the essence.

Reply to Objection 2: Every accident is not accidentally in its subject; for some are proper accidents; and of these every art takes notice. And thus it is that the circumstances of actions are considered in the doctrine of morals.

Reply to Objection 3: Since good and being are convertible; according as being is predicated of substance and of accident, so is good predicated of a thing both in respect of its essential being, and in respect of its accidental being; and this, both in natural things and in moral actions.

Article 4
Whether a human action is good or evil from its end?

Objection 1: It would seem that the good and evil in human actions are not from the end. For Dionysius says (Div. Nom. iv) that "nothing acts with a view to evil." If therefore an action were good or evil from its end, no action would be evil. Which is clearly false.

PRAETEREA, bonitas actus est aliquid in ipso existens. Finis autem est causa extrinseca. Non ergo secundum finem dicitur actio bona vel mala.

PRAETEREA, contingit aliquam bonam operationem ad malum finem ordinari, sicut cum aliquis dat eleemosynam propter inanem gloriam, et e converso aliquam malam operationem ordinari ad bonum finem, sicut cum quis furatur ut det pauperi. Non ergo est ex fine actio bona vel mala.

SED CONTRA est quod Boetius dicit, in Topic., quod *cuius finis bonus est, ipsum quoque bonum est, et cuius finis malus est, ipsum quoque malum est.*

RESPONDEO dicendum quod eadem est dispositio rerum in bonitate, et in esse. Sunt enim quaedam quorum esse ex alio non dependet, et in his sufficit considerare ipsum eorum esse absolute. Quaedam vero sunt quorum esse dependet ab alio, unde oportet quod consideretur per considerationem ad causam a qua dependet. Sicut autem esse rei dependet ab agente et forma, ita bonitas rei dependet a fine. Unde in personis divinis, quae non habent bonitatem dependentem ab alio, non consideratur aliqua ratio bonitatis ex fine. Actiones autem humanae, et alia quorum bonitas dependet ab alio, habent rationem bonitatis ex fine a quo dependent, praeter bonitatem absolutam quae in eis existit. Sic igitur in actione humana bonitas quadruplex considerari potest. Una quidem secundum genus, prout scilicet est actio, quia quantum habet de actione et entitate, tantum habet de bonitate, ut dictum est. Alia vero secundum speciem, quae accipitur secundum obiectum conveniens. Tertia secundum circumstantias, quasi secundum accidentia quaedam. Quarta autem secundum finem, quasi secundum habitudinem ad causam bonitatis.

AD PRIMUM ergo dicendum quod bonum ad quod aliquis respiciens operatur, non semper est verum bonum; sed

Objection 2: Further, the goodness of an action is something in the action. But the end is an extrinsic cause. Therefore an action is not said to be good or bad according to its end.

Objection 3: Further, a good action may happen to be ordained to an evil end, as when a man gives an alms from vainglory; and conversely, an evil action may happen to be ordained to a good end, as a theft committed in order to give something to the poor. Therefore an action is not good or evil from its end.

On the contrary, Boethius says (De Differ. Topic. ii) that "if the end is good, the thing is good, and if the end be evil, the thing also is evil."

I answer that, The disposition of things as to goodness is the same as their disposition as to being. Now in some things the being does not depend on another, and in these it suffices to consider their being absolutely. But there are things the being of which depends on something else, and hence in their regard we must consider their being in its relation to the cause on which it depends. Now just as the being of a thing depends on the agent, and the form, so the goodness of a thing depends on its end. Hence in the Divine Persons, Whose goodness does not depend on another, the measure of goodness is not taken from the end. Whereas human actions, and other things, the goodness of which depends on something else, have a measure of goodness from the end on which they depend, besides that goodness which is in them absolutely. Accordingly a fourfold goodness may be considered in a human action. First, that which, as an action, it derives from its genus; because as much as it has of action and being so much has it of goodness, as stated above (I-II, q. 18, a. 1). Secondly, it has goodness according to its species; which is derived from its suitable object. Thirdly, it has goodness from its circumstances, in respect, as it were, of its accidents. Fourthly, it has goodness from its end, to which it is compared as to the cause of its goodness.

Reply to Objection 1: The good in view of which one acts is not always a true good; but

quandoque verum bonum, et quandoque apparens. Et secundum hoc, ex fine sequitur actio mala.

AD SECUNDUM dicendum quod, quamvis finis sit causa extrinseca, tamen debita proportio ad finem et relatio in ipsum, inhaeret actioni.

AD TERTIUM dicendum quod nihil prohibet actioni habenti unam praedictarum bonitatum, deesse aliam. Et secundum hoc, contingit actionem quae est bona secundum speciem suam vel secundum circumstantias, ordinari ad finem malum, et e converso. Non tamen est actio bona simpliciter, nisi omnes bonitates concurrant, quia *quilibet singularis defectus causat malum, bonum autem causatur ex integra causa,* ut Dionysius dicit, IV cap. de Div. Nom.

sometimes it is a true good, sometimes an apparent good. And in the latter event, an evil action results from the end in view.

Reply to Objection 2: Although the end is an extrinsic cause, nevertheless due proportion to the end, and relation to the end, are inherent to the action.

Reply to Objection 3: Nothing hinders an action that is good in one of the way mentioned above, from lacking goodness in another way. And thus it may happen that an action which is good in its species or in its circumstances is ordained to an evil end, or vice versa. However, an action is not good simply, unless it is good in all those ways: since "evil results from any single defect, but good from the complete cause," as Dionysius says (Div. Nom. iv).

ARTICULUS 5

AD QUINTUM sic proceditur. Videtur quod actus morales non differant specie secundum bonum et malum. Bonum enim et malum in actibus invenitur conformiter rebus, ut dictum est. Sed in rebus bonum et malum non diversificant speciem, idem enim specie est homo bonus et malus. Ergo neque etiam bonum et malum in actibus diversificant speciem.

PRAETEREA, malum, cum sit privatio, est quoddam non ens. Sed non ens non potest esse differentia, secundum philosophum, in III Metaphys. Cum ergo differentia constituat speciem, videtur quod aliquis actus, ex hoc quod est malus, non constituatur in aliqua specie. Et ita bonum et malum non diversificant speciem humanorum actuum.

PRAETEREA, diversorum actuum secundum speciem, diversi sunt effectus. Sed idem specie effectus potest consequi ex actu bono et malo, sicut homo generatur ex adulterio, et ex matrimoniali concubitu. Ergo actus bonus et malus non differunt specie.

PRAETEREA, bonum et malum dicitur in actibus quandoque secundum circumstantiam, ut dictum est. Sed circumstantia, cum sit accidens, non dat speciem actui. Ergo

ARTICLE 5
Whether a human action is good or evil in its species?

Objection 1: It would seem that good and evil in moral actions do not make a difference of species. For the existence of good and evil in actions is in conformity with their existence in things, as stated above (I-II, q. 18, a. 1). But good and evil do not make a specific difference in things; for a good man is specifically the same as a bad man. Therefore neither do they make a specific difference in actions.

Objection 2: Further, since evil is a privation, it is a non-being. But non-being cannot be a difference, according to the Philosopher (Metaph. iii, 3). Since therefore the difference constitutes the species, it seems that an action is not constituted in a species through being evil. Consequently good and evil do not diversify the species of human actions.

Objection 3: Further, acts that differ in species produce different effects. But the same specific effect results from a good and from an evil action: thus a man is born of adulterous or of lawful wedlock. Therefore good and evil actions do not differ in species.

Objection 4: Further, actions are sometimes said to be good or bad from a circumstance, as stated above (I-II, q. 18, a. 3). But since a circumstance is an accident, it does not give an action its species. Therefore

actus humani non differunt specie propter bonitatem et malitiam.

SED CONTRA, secundum philosophum, in II Ethic., *similes habitus similes actus reddunt.* Sed habitus bonus et malus differunt specie, ut liberalitas et prodigalitas. Ergo et actus bonus et malus differunt specie.

RESPONDEO dicendum quod omnis actus speciem habet ex suo obiecto, sicut supra dictum est. Unde oportet quod aliqua differentia obiecti faciat diversitatem speciei in actibus. Est autem considerandum quod aliqua differentia obiecti facit differentiam speciei in actibus, secundum quod referuntur ad unum principium activum, quod non facit differentiam in actibus, secundum quod referuntur ad aliud principium activum. Quia nihil quod est per accidens, constituit speciem, sed solum quod est per se, potest autem aliqua differentia obiecti esse per se in comparatione ad unum activum principium, et per accidens in comparatione ad aliud; sicut cognoscere colorem et sonum, per se differunt per comparationem ad sensum, non autem per comparationem ad intellectum. In actibus autem humanis bonum et malum dicitur per comparationem ad rationem, quia, ut Dionysius dicit, IV cap. de Div. Nom., *bonum hominis est secundum rationem esse,* malum autem quod est *praeter rationem.* Unicuique enim rei est bonum quod convenit ei secundum suam formam; et malum quod est ei praeter ordinem suae formae. Patet ergo quod differentia boni et mali circa obiectum considerata, comparatur per se ad rationem, scilicet secundum quod obiectum est ei conveniens vel non conveniens. Dicuntur autem aliqui actus humani, vel morales, secundum quod sunt a ratione. Unde manifestum est quod bonum et malum diversificant speciem in actibus moralibus, differentiae enim per se diversificant speciem.

AD PRIMUM ergo dicendum quod etiam in rebus naturalibus bonum et malum, quod est secundum naturam et contra naturam, diversificant speciem naturae, corpus enim mortuum et corpus vivum non sunt eiusdem speciei. Et similiter bonum, inquantum est secundum rationem, et malum,

human actions do not differ in species on account of their goodness or malice.

On the contrary, According to the Philosopher (Ethic ii. 1) "like habits produce like actions." But a good and a bad habit differ in species, as liberality and prodigality. Therefore also good and bad actions differ in species.

I answer that, Every action derives its species from its object, as stated above (I-II, q. 18, a. 2). Hence it follows that a difference of object causes a difference of species in actions. Now, it must be observed that a difference of objects causes a difference of species in actions, according as the latter are referred to one active principle, which does not cause a difference in actions, according as they are referred to another active principle. Because nothing accidental constitutes a species, but only that which is essential; and a difference of object may be essential in reference to one active principle, and accidental in reference to another. Thus to know color and to know sound, differ essentially in reference to sense, but not in reference to the intellect. Now in human actions, good and evil are predicated in reference to the reason; because as Dionysius says (Div. Nom. iv), "the good of man is to be in accordance with reason," and evil is "to be against reason." For that is good for a thing which suits it in regard to its form; and evil, that which is against the order of its form. It is therefore evident that the difference of good and evil considered in reference to the object is an essential difference in relation to reason; that is to say, according as the object is suitable or unsuitable to reason. Now certain actions are called human or moral, inasmuch as they proceed from the reason. Consequently it is evident that good and evil diversify the species in human actions; since essential differences cause a difference of species.

Reply to Objection 1: Even in natural things, good and evil, inasmuch as something is according to nature, and something against nature, diversify the natural species; for a dead body and a living body are not of the same species. In like manner, good, inasmuch as it is in accord with reason, and evil,

inquantum est praeter rationem, diversificant speciem moris.

Ad secundum dicendum quod malum importat privationem non absolutam, sed consequentem talem potentiam. Dicitur enim malus actus secundum suam speciem, non ex eo quod nullum habeat obiectum; sed quia habet obiectum non conveniens rationi, sicut tollere aliena. Unde inquantum obiectum est aliquid positive, potest constituere speciem mali actus.

Ad tertium dicendum quod actus coniugalis et adulterium, secundum quod comparantur ad rationem, differunt specie, et habent effectus specie differentes, quia unum eorum meretur laudem et praemium, aliud vituperium et poenam. Sed secundum quod comparantur ad potentiam generativam, non differunt specie. Et sic habent unum effectum secundum speciem.

Ad quartum dicendum quod circumstantia quandoque sumitur ut differentia essentialis obiecti, secundum quod ad rationem comparatur, et tunc potest dare speciem actui morali. Et hoc oportet esse, quandocumque circumstantia transmutat actum de bonitate in malitiam, non enim circumstantia faceret actum malum, nisi per hoc quod rationi repugnat.

inasmuch as it is against reason, diversify the moral species.

Reply to Objection 2: Evil implies privation, not absolute, but affecting some potentiality. For an action is said to be evil in its species, not because it has no object at all; but because it has an object in disaccord with reason, for instance, to appropriate another's property. Wherefore in so far as the object is something positive, it can constitute the species of an evil act.

Reply to Objection 3: The conjugal act and adultery, as compared to reason, differ specifically and have effects specifically different; because the other deserves praise and reward, the other, blame and punishment. But as compared to the generative power, they do not differ in species; and thus they have one specific effect.

Reply to Objection 4: A circumstance is sometimes taken as the essential difference of the object, as compared to reason; and then it can specify a moral act. And it must needs be so whenever a circumstance transforms an action from good to evil; for a circumstance would not make an action evil, except through being repugnant to reason.

Articulus 6

Ad sextum sic proceditur. Videtur quod bonum et malum quod est ex fine, non diversificent speciem in actibus. Actus enim habent speciem ex obiecto. Sed finis est praeter rationem obiecti. Ergo bonum et malum quod est ex fine, non diversificant speciem actus.

Praeterea, id quod est per accidens, non constituit speciem, ut dictum est. Sed accidit alicui actui quod ordinetur ad aliquem finem; sicut quod aliquis det eleemosynam propter inanem gloriam. Ergo secundum bonum et malum quod est ex fine, non diversificantur actus secundum speciem.

Praeterea, diversi actus secundum speciem, ad unum finem ordinari possunt,

Article 6
Whether an action has the species of good or evil from its end?

Objection 1: It would seem that the good and evil which are from the end do not diversify the species of actions. For actions derive their species from the object. But the end is altogether apart from the object. Therefore the good and evil which are from the end do not diversify the species of an action.

Objection 2: Further, that which is accidental does not constitute the species, as stated above (I-II, q. 18, a. 5). But it is accidental to an action to be ordained to some particular end; for instance, to give alms from vainglory. Therefore actions are not diversified as to species, according to the good and evil which are from the end.

Objection 3: Further, acts that differ in species, can be ordained to the same end:

sicut ad finem inanis gloriae ordinari possunt actus diversarum virtutum, et diversorum vitiorum. Non ergo bonum et malum quod accipitur secundum finem, diversificat speciem actuum.

SED CONTRA est quod supra ostensum est, quod actus humani habent speciem a fine. Ergo bonum et malum quod accipitur secundum finem, diversificat speciem actuum.

RESPONDEO dicendum quod aliqui actus dicuntur humani, inquantum sunt voluntarii, sicut supra dictum est. In actu autem voluntario invenitur duplex actus, scilicet actus interior voluntatis, et actus exterior, et uterque horum actuum habet suum obiectum. Finis autem proprie est obiectum interioris actus voluntarii, id autem circa quod est actio exterior, est obiectum eius. Sicut igitur actus exterior accipit speciem ab obiecto circa quod est; ita actus interior voluntatis accipit speciem a fine, sicut a proprio obiecto. Ita autem quod est ex parte voluntatis, se habet ut formale ad id quod est ex parte exterioris actus, quia voluntas utitur membris ad agendum, sicut instrumentis; neque actus exteriores habent rationem moralitatis, nisi inquantum sunt voluntarii. Et ideo actus humani species formaliter consideratur secundum finem, materialiter autem secundum obiectum exterioris actus. Unde philosophus dicit, in V Ethic., quod *ille qui furatur ut committat adulterium, est, per se loquendo, magis adulter quam fur.*

AD PRIMUM ergo dicendum quod etiam finis habet rationem obiecti, ut dictum est.

AD SECUNDUM dicendum quod ordinari ad talem finem, etsi accidat exteriori actui, non tamen accidit actui interiori voluntatis, qui comparatur ad exteriorem sicut formale ad materiale.

AD TERTIUM dicendum quod quando multi actus specie differentes ordinantur ad unum finem, est quidem diversitas speciei ex parte exteriorum actuum; sed unitas speciei ex parte actus interioris.

thus to the end of vainglory, actions of various virtues and vices can be ordained. Therefore the good and evil which are taken from the end, do not diversify the species of action.

On the contrary, It has been shown above (I-II, q. 1, a. 3) that human actions derive their species from the end. Therefore good and evil in respect of the end diversify the species of actions.

I answer that, Certain actions are called human, inasmuch as they are voluntary, as stated above (I-II, q. 1, a. 1). Now, in a voluntary action, there is a twofold action, *viz.* the interior action of the will, and the external action: and each of these actions has its object. The end is properly the object of the interior act of the will: while the object of the external action, is that on which the action is brought to bear. Therefore just as the external action takes its species from the object on which it bears; so the interior act of the will takes its species from the end, as from its own proper object. Now that which is on the part of the will is formal in regard to that which is on the part of the external action: because the will uses the limbs to act as instruments; nor have external actions any measure of morality, save in so far as they are voluntary. Consequently the species of a human act is considered formally with regard to the end, but materially with regard to the object of the external action. Hence the Philosopher says (Ethic. v, 2) that "he who steals that he may commit adultery, is strictly speaking, more adulterer than thief."

Reply to Objection 1: The end also has the character of an object, as stated above.

Reply to Objection 2: Although it is accidental to the external action to be ordained to some particular end, it is not accidental to the interior act of the will, which act is compared to the external act, as form to matter.

Reply to Objection 3: When many actions, differing in species, are ordained to the same end, there is indeed a diversity of species on the part of the external actions; but unity of species on the part of the internal action.

Articulus 7

Ad septimum sic proceditur. Videtur quod species bonitatis quae est ex fine, contineatur sub specie bonitatis quae est ex obiecto, sicut species sub genere, puta cum aliquis vult furari ut det eleemosynam. Actus enim habet speciem ex obiecto, ut dictum est. Sed impossibile est quod aliquid contineatur in aliqua alia specie, quae sub propria specie non continetur, quia idem non potest esse in diversis speciebus non subalternis. Ergo species quae est ex fine, continetur sub specie quae est ex obiecto.

Praeterea, semper ultima differentia constituit speciem specialissimam. Sed differentia quae est ex fine, videtur esse posterior quam differentia quae est ex obiecto, quia finis habet rationem ultimi. Ergo species quae est ex fine, continetur sub specie quae est ex obiecto, sicut species specialissima.

Praeterea, quanto aliqua differentia est magis formalis, tanto magis est specialis, quia differentia comparatur ad genus ut forma ad materiam. Sed species quae est ex fine, est formalior ea quae est ex obiecto, ut dictum est. Ergo species quae est ex fine, continetur sub specie quae est ex obiecto, sicut species specialissima sub genere subalterno.

Sed contra, cuiuslibet generis sunt determinatae differentiae. Sed actus eiusdem speciei ex parte obiecti, potest ad infinitos fines ordinari, puta furtum ad infinita bona vel mala. Ergo species quae est ex fine, non continetur sub specie quae est ex obiecto, sicut sub genere.

Respondeo dicendum quod obiectum exterioris actus dupliciter potest se habere ad finem voluntatis, uno modo, sicut per se ordinatum ad ipsum, sicut bene pugnare per se

Article 7
Whether the species derived from the end is contained under the species derived from the object, as under its genus, or conversely?

Objection 1: It would seem that the species of goodness derived from the end is contained under the species of goodness derived from the object, as a species is contained under its genus; for instance, when a man commits a theft in order to give alms. For an action takes its species from its object, as stated above (I-II, q. 18, a. 2; a. 6). But it is impossible for a thing to be contained under another species, if this species be not contained under the proper species of that thing; because the same thing cannot be contained in different species that are not subordinate to one another. Therefore the species which is taken from the end, is contained under the species which is taken from the object.

Objection 2: Further, the last difference always constitutes the most specific species. But the difference derived from the end seems to come after the difference derived from the object: because the end is something last. Therefore the species derived from the end, is contained under the species derived from the object, as its most specific species.

Objection 3: Further, the more formal a difference is compared to genus, as form to matter. But the species derived from the end, is more formal than that which is derived from the object, as stated above (I-II, q. 18, a. 6). Therefore the species derived from the end is contained under the species derived from the object, as the most specific species is contained under the subaltern genus.

On the contrary, Each genus has its determinate differences. But an action of one same species on the part of its object, can be ordained to an infinite number of ends: for instance, theft can be ordained to an infinite number of good and bad ends. Therefore the species derived from the end is not contained under the species derived from the object, as under its genus.

I answer that, The object of the external act can stand in a twofold relation to the end of the will: first, as being of itself ordained thereto; thus to fight well is of itself

ordinatur ad victoriam; alio modo, per accidens, sicut accipere rem alienam per accidens ordinatur ad dandum eleemosynam. Oportet autem, ut philosophus dicit in VII Metaphys., quod differentiae dividentes aliquod genus, et constituentes speciem illius generis, per se dividant illud. Si autem per accidens, non recte procedit divisio, puta si quis dicat, *animalium aliud rationale, aliud irrationale; et animalium irrationalium aliud alatum, aliud non alatum, alatum* enim et *non alatum* non sunt per se determinativa eius quod est irrationale. Oportet autem sic dividere, *animalium aliud habens pedes, aliud non habens pedes; et habentium pedes, aliud habet duos, aliud quatuor, aliud multos,* haec enim per se determinant priorem differentiam. Sic igitur quando obiectum non est per se ordinatum ad finem, differentia specifica quae est ex obiecto, non est per se determinativa eius quae est ex fine, nec e converso. Unde una istarum specierum non est sub alia, sed tunc actus moralis est sub duabus speciebus quasi disparatis. Unde dicimus quod ille qui furatur ut moechetur, committit duas malitias in uno actu. Si vero obiectum per se ordinetur ad finem, una dictarum differentiarum est per se determinativa alterius. Unde una istarum specierum continebitur sub altera. Considerandum autem restat quae sub qua. Ad cuius evidentiam, primo considerandum est quod quanto aliqua differentia sumitur a forma magis particulari, tanto magis est specifica. Secundo, quod quanto agens est magis universale, tanto ex eo est forma magis universalis. Tertio, quod quanto aliquis finis est posterior, tanto respondet agenti universaliori, sicut victoria, quae est ultimus finis exercitus, est finis intentus a summo duce; ordinatio autem huius aciei vel illius, est finis intentus ab aliquo inferiorum ducum. Et ex istis sequitur quod differentia specifica quae est ex fine, est magis generalis; et

ordained to victory; secondly, as being ordained thereto accidentally; thus to take what belongs to another is ordained accidentally to the giving of alms. Now the differences that divide a genus, and constitute the species of that genus, must, as the Philosopher says (Metaph. vii, 12), divide that genus essentially: and if they divide it accidentally, the division is incorrect: as, if one were to say: "Animals are divided into rational and irrational; and the irrational into animals with wings, and animals without wings"; for "winged" and "wingless" are not essential determinations of the irrational being. But the following division would be correct: "Some animals have feet, some have no feet: and of those that have feet, some have two feet, some four, some many": because the latter division is an essential determination of the former. Accordingly when the object is not of itself ordained to the end, the specific difference derived from the object is not an essential determination of the species derived from the end, nor is the reverse the case. Wherefore one of these species is not under the other; but then the moral action is contained under two species that are disparate, as it were. Consequently we say that he that commits theft for the sake of adultery, is guilty of a twofold malice in one action. On the other hand, if the object be of itself ordained to the end, one of these differences is an essential determination of the other. Wherefore one of these species will be contained under the other. It remains to be considered which of the two is contained under the other. In order to make this clear, we must first of all observe that the more particular the form is from which a difference is taken, the more specific is the difference. Secondly, that the more universal an agent is, the more universal a form does it cause. Thirdly, that the more remote an end is, the more universal the agent to which it corresponds; thus victory, which is the last end of the army, is the end intended by the commander in chief; while the right ordering of this or that regiment is the end intended by one of the lower officers. From all this it follows that the specific difference derived from the end, is more general; and

differentia quae est ex obiecto per se ad talem finem ordinato, est specifica respectu eius. Voluntas enim, cuius proprium obiectum est finis, est universale motivum respectu omnium potentiarum animae, quarum propria obiecta sunt obiecta particularium actuum.

AD PRIMUM ergo dicendum quod secundum substantiam suam non potest aliquid esse in duabus speciebus, quarum una sub altera non ordinetur. Sed secundum ea quae rei adveniunt, potest aliquid sub diversis speciebus contineri. Sicut hoc pomum, secundum colorem, continetur sub hac specie, scilicet albi, et secundum odorem, sub specie bene redolentis. Et similiter actus qui secundum substantiam suam est in una specie naturae, secundum conditiones morales supervenientes, ad duas species referri potest, ut supra dictum est.

AD SECUNDUM dicendum quod finis est postremum in executione; sed est primum in intentione rationis, secundum quam accipiuntur moralium actuum species.

AD TERTIUM dicendum quod differentia comparatur ad genus ut forma ad materiam, inquantum facit esse genus in actu. Sed etiam genus consideratur ut formalius specie, secundum quod est absolutius, et minus contractum. Unde et partes definitionis reducuntur ad genus causae formalis, ut dicitur in libro Physic. Et secundum hoc, genus est causa formalis speciei, et tanto erit formalius, quanto communius.

that the difference derived from an object which of itself is ordained to that end, is a specific difference in relation to the former. For the will, the proper object of which is the end, is the universal mover in respect of all the powers of the soul, the proper objects of which are the objects of their particular acts.

Reply to Objection 1: One and the same thing, considered in its substance, cannot be in two species, one of which is not subordinate to the other. But in respect of those things which are superadded to the substance, one thing can be contained under different species. Thus one and the same fruit, as to its color, is contained under one species, i.e., a white thing: and, as to its perfume, under the species of sweet-smelling things. In like manner an action which, as to its substance, is in one natural species, considered in respect to the moral conditions that are added to it, can belong to two species, as stated above (I-II, q. 1, a. 3, ad 3).

Reply to Objection 2: The end is last in execution; but first in the intention of the reason, in regard to which moral actions receive their species.

Reply to Objection 3: Difference is compared to genus as form to matter, inasmuch as it actualizes the genus. On the other hand, the genus is considered as more formal than the species, inasmuch as it is something more absolute and less contracted. Wherefore also the parts of a definition are reduced to the genus of formal cause, as is stated in Phys. ii, 3. And in this sense the genus is the formal cause of the species; and so much the more formal, as it is more universal.

ARTICULUS 8

ARTICLE 8
Whether any action is indifferent in its species?

AD OCTAVUM sic proceditur. Videtur quod non sit aliquis actus indifferens secundum suam speciem. Malum enim est privatio boni, secundum Augustinum. Sed privatio et habitus sunt opposita immediata, secundum philosophum. Ergo non est aliquis actus qui secundum speciem suam sit indifferens, quasi medium existens inter bonum et malum.

Objection 1: It would seem that no action is indifferent in its species. For evil is the privation of good, according to Augustine (Enchiridion xi). But privation and habit are immediate contraries, according to the Philosopher (Categor. viii). Therefore there is not such thing as an action that is indifferent in its species, as though it were between good and evil.

PRAETEREA, actus humani habent speciem a fine vel obiecto, ut dictum est. Sed omne obiectum, et omnis finis habet rationem boni vel mali. Ergo omnis actus humanus secundum suam speciem est bonus vel malus. Nullus ergo est indifferens secundum speciem.

PRAETEREA, sicut dictum est, actus dicitur bonus, qui habet debitam perfectionem bonitatis; malus, cui aliquid de hoc deficit. Sed necesse est quod omnis actus vel habeat totam plenitudinem suae bonitatis, vel aliquid ei deficiat. Ergo necesse est quod omnis actus secundum speciem suam sit bonus vel malus, et nullus indifferens.

SED CONTRA est quod Augustinus dicit, in libro de Serm. Dom. in Mont., *quod sunt quaedam facta media, quae possunt bono vel malo animo fieri, de quibus est temerarium iudicare.* Sunt ergo aliqui actus secundum speciem suam indifferentes.

RESPONDEO dicendum quod, sicut dictum est, actus omnis habet speciem ab obiecto; et actus humanus, qui dicitur moralis, habet speciem ab obiecto relato ad principium actuum humanorum, quod est ratio. Unde si obiectum actus includat aliquid quod conveniat ordini rationis, erit actus bonus secundum suam speciem, sicut dare eleemosynam indigenti. Si autem includat aliquid quod repugnet ordini rationis, erit malus actus secundum speciem, sicut furari, quod est tollere aliena. Contingit autem quod obiectum actus non includit aliquid pertinens ad ordinem rationis, sicut levare festucam de terra, ire ad campum, et huiusmodi, et tales actus secundum speciem suam sunt indifferentes.

AD PRIMUM ergo dicendum quod duplex est privatio. Quaedam quae consistit in *privatum esse,* et haec nihil relinquit, sed totum aufert; ut caecitas totaliter aufert visum, et tenebrae lucem, et mors vitam. Et inter hanc privationem et habitum oppositum, non potest esse aliquod medium circa proprium susceptibile. Est autem alia privatio quae consistit in *privari,*

Objection 2: Further, human actions derive their species from their end or object, as stated above (I-II, q. 18, a. 6; q. 1, a. 3). But every end and every object is either good or bad. Therefore every human action is good or evil according to its species. None, therefore, is indifferent in its species.

Objection 3: Further, as stated above (I-II, q. 18, a. 1), an action is said to be good, when it has its due complement of goodness; and evil, when it lacks that complement. But every action must needs either have the entire plenitude of its goodness, or lack it in some respect. Therefore every action must needs be either good or bad in its species, and none is indifferent.

On the contrary, Augustine says (De Serm. Dom. in Monte ii, 18) that "there are certain deeds of a middle kind, which can be done with a good or evil mind, of which it is rash to form a judgment." Therefore some actions are indifferent according to their species.

I answer that, As stated above (I-II, q. 18, a. 2; a. 5), every action takes its species from its object; while human action, which is called moral, takes its species from the object, in relation to the principle of human actions, which is the reason. Wherefore if the object of an action includes something in accord with the order of reason, it will be a good action according to its species; for instance, to give alms to a person in want. On the other hand, if it includes something repugnant to the order of reason, it will be an evil act according to its species; for instance, to steal, which is to appropriate what belongs to another. But it may happen that the object of an action does not include something pertaining to the order of reason; for instance, to pick up a straw from the ground, to walk in the fields, and the like: and such actions are indifferent according to their species.

Reply to Objection 1: Privation is twofold. One is privation "as a result" [*privatum esse*], and this leaves nothing, but takes all away: thus blindness takes away sight altogether; darkness, light; and death, life. Between this privation and the contrary habit, there can be no medium in respect of the proper subject. The other is privation "in process" [*privari*]:

sicut aegritudo est privatio sanitatis, non quod tota sanitas sit sublata, sed quod est quasi quaedam via ad totalem ablationem sanitatis, quae fit per mortem. Et ideo talis privatio, cum aliquid relinquat, non semper est immediata cum opposito habitu. Et hoc modo malum est privatio boni, ut Simplicius dicit in commento super librum Praedic., quia non totum bonum aufert, sed aliquid relinquit. Unde potest esse aliquod medium **inter bonum et malum.**

AD SECUNDUM dicendum quod omne obiectum vel finis habet aliquam bonitatem vel malitiam, saltem naturalem, non tamen semper importat bonitatem vel malitiam moralem, quae consideratur per comparationem ad rationem, ut dictum est. Et de hac nunc agitur.

AD TERTIUM dicendum quod non quidquid habet actus, pertinet ad speciem eius. Unde etsi in ratione suae speciei non contineatur quidquid pertinet ad plenitudinem bonitatis ipsius, non propter hoc est ex specie sua malus, nec etiam bonus, sicut homo secundum suam speciem neque virtuosus, neque vitiosus est.

Articulus 9

AD NONUM sic proceditur. Videtur quod aliquis actus secundum individuum sit indifferens. Nulla enim species est quae sub se non contineat vel continere possit aliquod individuum. Sed aliquis actus est indifferens secundum suam speciem, ut dictum est. Ergo aliquis actus individualis potest esse indifferens.

PRAETEREA, ex individualibus actibus causantur habitus conformes ipsis, ut dicitur in II Ethic. Sed aliquis habitus est indifferens. Dicit enim philosophus, in IV Ethic., de quibusdam, sicut de placidis et prodigis, quod non sunt mali, et tamen constat quod non sunt boni, cum recedant a virtute, et sic sunt indifferentes secundum habitum. Ergo aliqui actus individuales sunt indifferentes.

PRAETEREA, bonum morale pertinet ad virtutem, malum autem morale pertinet ad vitium. Sed contingit quandoque quod homo

thus sickness is privation of health; not that it takes health away altogether, but that it is a kind of road to the entire loss of health, occasioned by death. And since this sort of privation leaves something, it is not always the immediate contrary of the opposite habit. In this way evil is a privation of good, as Simplicius says in his commentary on the Categories: because it does not take away all good, but leaves some. Consequently there can be something **between good and evil.**

Reply to Objection 2: Every object or end has some goodness or malice, at least natural to it: but this does not imply moral goodness or malice, which is considered in relation to the reason, as stated above. And it is of this that we are here treating.

Reply to Objection 3: Not everything belonging to an action belongs also to its species. Wherefore although an action's specific nature may not contain all that belongs to the full complement of its goodness, it is not therefore an action specifically bad; nor is it specifically good. Thus a man in regard to his species is neither virtuous nor wicked.

Article 9
Whether an individual action can be indifferent?

Objection 1: It would seem that an individual action can be indifferent. For there is no species that does not, cannot, contain an individual. But an action can be indifferent in its species, as stated above (I-II, q. 18, a. 8). Therefore an individual action can be indifferent.

Objection 2: Further, individual actions cause like habits, as stated in Ethic. ii, 1. But a habit can be indifferent: for the Philosopher says (Ethic. iv, 1) that those who are of an even temper and prodigal disposition are not evil; and yet it is evident that they are not good, since they depart from virtue; and thus they are indifferent in respect of a habit. Therefore some individual actions are indifferent.

Objection 3: Further, moral good belongs to virtue, while moral evil belongs to vice. But it happens sometimes that a man

actum qui ex specie sua est indifferens, non ordinat ad aliquem finem vel vitii vel virtutis. Ergo contingit aliquem actum individualem esse indifferentem.

SED CONTRA est quod Gregorius dicit in quadam homilia, *otiosum verbum est quod utilitate rectitudinis, aut ratione iustae necessitatis aut piae utilitatis, caret.* Sed verbum otiosum est malum, quia *de eo reddent homines rationem in die iudicii,* ut dicitur Matth. XII. Si autem non caret ratione iustae necessitatis aut piae utilitatis, est bonum. Ergo omne verbum aut est bonum aut malum. Pari ergo ratione, et quilibet alius actus vel est bonus vel malus. Nullus ergo individualis actus est indifferens.

RESPONDEO dicendum quod contingit quandoque aliquem actum esse indifferentem secundum speciem, qui tamen est bonus vel malus in individuo consideratus. Et hoc ideo, quia actus moralis, sicut dictum est, non solum habet bonitatem ex obiecto, a quo habet speciem; sed etiam ex circumstantiis, quae sunt quasi quaedam accidentia; sicut aliquid convenit individuo hominis secundum accidentia individualia, quod non convenit homini secundum rationem speciei. Et oportet quod quilibet individualis actus habeat aliquam circumstantiam per quam trahatur ad bonum vel malum, ad minus ex parte intentionis finis. Cum enim rationis sit ordinare, actus a ratione deliberativa procedens, si non sit ad debitum finem ordinatus, ex hoc ipso repugnat rationi, et habet rationem mali. Si vero ordinetur ad debitum finem, convenit cum ordine rationis, unde habet rationem boni. Necesse est autem quod vel ordinetur, vel non ordinetur ad debitum finem. Unde necesse est omnem actum hominis a deliberativa ratione procedentem, in individuo consideratum, bonum esse vel malum. Si autem non procedit a ratione deliberativa, sed ex quadam imaginatione, sicut cum aliquis fricat barbam, vel movet manum aut pedem; talis actus non est, proprie loquendo, moralis vel humanus; cum hoc habeat actus a ratione. Et sic erit indifferens, quasi extra genus moralium actuum existens.

fails to ordain a specifically indifferent action to a vicious or virtuous end. Therefore an individual action may happen to be indifferent.

On the contrary, Gregory says in a homily (vi in Evang.): "An idle word is one that lacks either the usefulness of rectitude or the motive of just necessity or pious utility." But an idle word is an evil, because "men ... shall render an account of it in the day of judgment" (Mat. 12:36): while if it does not lack the motive of just necessity or pious utility, it is good. Therefore every word is either good or bad. For the same reason every other action is either good or bad. Therefore no individual action is indifferent.

I answer that, It sometimes happens that an action is indifferent in its species, but considered in the individual it is good or evil. And the reason of this is because a moral action, as stated above (I-II, q. 18, a. 3), derives its goodness not only from its object, whence it takes its species; but also from the circumstances, which are its accidents, as it were; just as something belongs to a man by reason of his individual accidents, which does not belong to him by reason of his species. And every individual action must needs have some circumstance that makes it good or bad, at least in respect of the intention of the end. For since it belongs to the reason to direct; if an action that proceeds from deliberate reason be not directed to the due end, it is, by that fact alone, repugnant to reason, and has the character of evil. But if it be directed to a due end, it is in accord with reason; wherefore it has the character of good. Now it must needs be either directed or not directed to a due end. Consequently every human action that proceeds from deliberate reason, if it be considered in the individual, must be good or bad. If, however, it does not proceed from deliberate reason, but from some act of the imagination, as when a man strokes his beard, or moves his hand or foot; such an action, properly speaking, is not moral or human; since this depends on the reason. Hence it will be indifferent, as standing apart from the genus of moral actions.

AD PRIMUM ergo dicendum quod aliquem actum esse indifferentem secundum suam speciem, potest esse multipliciter. Uno modo, sic quod ex sua specie debeatur ei quod sit indifferens. Et sic procedit ratio. Sed tamen isto modo nullus actus ex sua specie est indifferens, non enim est aliquod obiectum humani actus, quod non possit ordinari vel ad bonum vel ad malum, per finem vel circumstantiam. Alio modo potest dici indifferens ex sua specie, quia non habet ex sua specie quod sit bonus vel malus. Unde per aliquid aliud potest fieri bonus vel malus. Sicut homo non habet ex sua specie quod sit albus vel niger, nec tamen habet ex sua specie quod non sit albus aut niger, potest enim albedo vel nigredo supervenire homini aliunde quam a principiis speciei.

AD SECUNDUM dicendum quod philosophus dicit illum esse malum proprie, qui est aliis hominibus nocivus. Et secundum hoc, dicit prodigum non esse malum, quia nulli alteri nocet nisi sibi ipsi. Et similiter de omnibus aliis qui non sunt proximis nocivi. Nos autem hic dicimus malum communiter omne quod est rationi rectae repugnans. Et secundum hoc, omnis individualis actus est bonus vel malus, ut dictum est.

AD TERTIUM dicendum quod omnis finis a ratione deliberativa intentus, pertinet ad bonum alicuius virtutis, vel ad malum alicuius vitii. Nam hoc ipsum quod aliquis agit ordinate ad sustentationem vel quietem sui corporis, ad bonum virtutis ordinatur in eo qui corpus suum ordinat ad bonum virtutis. Et idem patet in aliis.

Reply to Objection 1: For an action to be indifferent in its species can be understood in several ways. First in such a way that its species demands that it remain indifferent; and the objection proceeds along this line. But no action can be specifically indifferent thus: since no object of human action is such that it cannot be directed to good or evil, either through its end or through a circumstance. Secondly, specific indifference of an action may be due to the fact that as far as its species is concerned, it is neither good nor bad. Wherefore it can be made good or bad by something else. Thus man, as far as his species is concerned, is neither white nor black; nor is it a condition of his species that he should not be black or white; but blackness or whiteness is superadded to man by other principles than those of his species.

Reply to Objection 2: The Philosopher states that a man is evil, properly speaking, if he be hurtful to others. And accordingly, because he hurts none save himself. And the same applies to all others who are not hurtful to other men. But we say here that evil, in general, is all that is repugnant to right reason. And in this sense every individual action is either good or bad, as stated above.

Reply to Objection 3: Whenever an end is intended by deliberate reason, it belongs either to the good of some virtue, or to the evil of some vice. Thus, if a man's action is directed to the support or repose of his body, it is also directed to the good of virtue, provided he direct his body itself to the good of virtue. The same clearly applies to other actions.

ARTICULUS 10

ARTICLE 10
Whether a circumstance places a moral action in the species of good or evil?

AD DECIMUM sic proceditur. Videtur quod circumstantia non possit constituere aliquam speciem boni vel mali actus. Species enim actus est ex obiecto. Sed circumstantiae differunt ab obiecto. Ergo circumstantiae non dant speciem actus.

Objection 1: It would seem that a circumstance cannot place a moral action in the species of good or evil. For the species of an action is taken from its object. But circumstances differ from the object. Therefore circumstances do not give an action its species.

Praeterea, circumstantiae comparantur ad actum moralem sicut accidentia eius, ut dictum est. Sed accidens non constituit speciem. Ergo circumstantia non constituit aliquam speciem boni vel mali.

Praeterea, unius rei non sunt plures species. Unius autem actus sunt plures circumstantiae. Ergo circumstantia non constituit actum moralem in aliqua specie boni vel mali.

Sed contra, locus est circumstantia quaedam. Sed locus constituit actum moralem in quadam specie mali, furari enim aliquid de loco sacro est sacrilegium. Ergo circumstantia constituit actum moralem in aliqua specie boni vel mali.

Respondeo dicendum quod, sicut species rerum naturalium constituuntur ex naturalibus formis, ita species moralium actuum constituuntur ex formis prout sunt a ratione conceptae, sicut ex supradictis patet. Quia vero natura determinata est ad unum, nec potest esse processus naturae in infinitum, necesse est pervenire ad aliquam ultimam formam, ex qua sumatur differentia specifica, post quam alia differentia specifica esse non possit. Et inde est quod in rebus naturalibus, id quod est accidens alicui rei, non potest accipi ut differentia constituens speciem. Sed processus rationis non est determinatus ad aliquid unum, sed quolibet dato, potest ulterius procedere. Et ideo quod in uno actu accipitur ut circumstantia superaddita obiecto quod determinat speciem actus, potest iterum accipi a ratione ordinante ut principalis conditio obiecti determinantis speciem actus. Sicut tollere alienum habet speciem ex ratione *alieni,* ex hoc enim constituitur in specie furti, et si consideretur super hoc ratio loci vel temporis, se habebit in ratione circumstantiae. Sed quia ratio etiam de loco vel de tempore, et aliis huiusmodi, ordinare potest; contingit conditionem loci circa obiectum accipi ut contrariam ordini rationis; puta quod ratio ordinat non esse iniuriam faciendam loco sacro. Unde tollere aliquid alienum de loco sacro addit specialem repugnantiam ad ordinem

Objection 2: Further, circumstances are as accidents in relation to the moral action, as stated above (I-II, q. 17, a. 1). But an accident does not constitute the species. Therefore a circumstance does not constitute a species of good or evil.

Objection 3: Further, one thing is not in several species. But one action has several circumstances. Therefore a circumstance does not place a moral action in a species of good or evil.

On the contrary, Place is a circumstance. But place makes a moral action to be in a certain species of evil; for theft of a thing from a holy place is a sacrilege. Therefore a circumstance makes a moral action to be specifically good or bad.

I answer that, Just as the species of natural things are constituted by their natural forms, so the species of moral actions are constituted by forms as conceived by the reason, as is evident from what was said above (I-II, q. 18, a. 5). But since nature is determinate to one thing, nor can a process of nature go on to infinity, there must needs be some ultimate form, giving a specific difference, after which no further specific difference is possible. Hence it is that in natural things, that which is accidental to a thing, cannot be taken as a difference constituting the species. But the process of reason is not fixed to one particular term, for at any point it can still proceed further. And consequently that which, in one action, is taken as a circumstance added to the object that specifies the action, can again be taken by the directing reason, as the principal condition of the object that determines the action's species. Thus to appropriate another's property is specified by reason of the property being "another's," and in this respect it is placed in the species of theft; and if we consider that action also in its bearing on place or time, then this will be an additional circumstance. But since the reason can direct as to place, time, and the like, it may happen that the condition as to place, in relation to the object, is considered as being in disaccord with reason: for instance, reason forbids damage to be done to a holy place. Consequently to steal from a holy place has an additional repugnance to the order

rationis. Et ideo locus, qui prius considerabatur ut circumstantia, nunc consideratur ut principalis conditio obiecti rationi repugnans. Et per hunc modum, quandocumque aliqua circumstantia respicit specialem ordinem rationis vel pro vel contra, oportet quod circumstantia det speciem actui morali vel bono vel malo.

AD PRIMUM ergo dicendum quod circumstantia secundum quod dat speciem actui, **consideratur ut quaedam conditio obiecti,** sicut dictum est, et quasi quaedam specifica differentia eius.

AD SECUNDUM dicendum quod circumstantia manens in ratione circumstantiae, cum habeat rationem accidentis, non dat speciem, sed inquantum mutatur in principalem conditionem obiecti, secundum hoc dat speciem.

AD TERTIUM dicendum quod non omnis circumstantia constituit actum moralem in aliqua specie boni vel mali, cum non quaelibet circumstantia importet aliquam consonantiam vel dissonantiam ad rationem. Unde non oportet, licet sint multae circumstantiae unius actus, quod unus actus sit in pluribus speciebus. Licet etiam non sit inconveniens quod unus actus moralis sit in pluribus speciebus moris etiam disparatis, ut dictum est.

of reason. And thus place, which was first of all considered as a circumstance, is considered here as the principal condition of the object, and as itself repugnant to reason. And in this way, whenever a circumstance has a special relation to reason, either for or against, it must needs specify the moral action whether good or bad.

Reply to Objection 1: A circumstance, in so far as it specifies an action, is considered **as a condition of the object,** as stated above, and as being, as it were, a specific difference thereof.

Reply to Objection 2: A circumstance, so long as it is but a circumstance, does not specify an action, since thus it is a mere accident: but when it becomes a principal condition of the object, then it does specify the action.

Reply to Objection 3: It is not every circumstance that places the moral action in the species of good or evil; since not every circumstance implies accord or disaccord with reason. Consequently, although one action may have many circumstances, it does not follow that it is in many species. Nevertheless there is no reason why one action should not be in several, even disparate, moral species, as said above (I-II, q. 18, a. 7, ad 1; q. 1, a. 3, ad 3).

ARTICULUS 11

ARTICLE 11
Whether every circumstance that makes an action better or worse, places a moral action in a species of good or evil?

AD UNDECIMUM sic proceditur. Videtur quod omnis circumstantia pertinens ad bonitatem vel malitiam, det speciem actui. Bonum enim et malum sunt differentiae specificae moralium actuum. Quod ergo facit differentiam in bonitate vel malitia moralis actus, facit differre secundum differentiam specificam, quod est differre secundum speciem. Sed id quod addit in bonitate vel malitia actus, facit differre secundum bonitatem et malitiam. Ergo facit differre secundum speciem. Ergo omnis circumstantia addens in bonitate vel malitia actus, constituit speciem.

PRAETEREA, aut circumstantia adveniens habet in se aliquam rationem bonitatis vel malitiae, aut non. Si non,

Objection 1: It would seem that every circumstance relating to good or evil, specifies an action. For good and evil are specific differences of moral actions. Therefore that which causes a difference in the goodness or malice of a moral action, causes a specific difference, which is the same as to make it differ in species. Now that which makes an action better or worse, makes it differ in goodness and malice. Therefore it causes it to differ in species. Therefore every circumstance that makes an action better or worse, constitutes a species.

Objection 2: Further, an additional circumstance either has in itself the character of goodness or malice, or it has not. If not,

non potest addere in bonitate vel malitia actus, quia quod non est bonum, non potest facere maius bonum; et quod non est malum, non potest facere maius malum. Si autem habet in se rationem bonitatis vel malitiae, ex hoc ipso habet quandam speciem boni vel mali. Ergo omnis circumstantia augens bonitatem vel malitiam, constituit novam speciem boni vel mali.

Praeterea, secundum Dionysium, IV cap. de Div. Nom., *malum causatur ex singularibus defectibus.* Quaelibet autem circumstantia aggravans malitiam, habet specialem defectum. Ergo quaelibet circumstantia addit novam speciem peccati. Et eadem ratione, quaelibet augens bonitatem, videtur addere novam speciem boni, sicut quaelibet unitas addita numero, facit novam speciem numeri; bonum enim consistit in *numero, pondere et mensura.*

Sed contra, magis et minus non diversificant speciem. Sed magis et minus est circumstantia addens in bonitate vel malitia. Ergo non omnis circumstantia addens in bonitate vel malitia, constituit actum moralem in specie boni vel mali.

Respondeo dicendum quod, sicut dictum est, circumstantia dat speciem boni vel mali actui morali, inquantum respicit specialem ordinem rationis. Contingit autem quandoque quod circumstantia non respicit ordinem rationis in bono vel malo, nisi praesupposita alia circumstantia, a qua actus moralis habet speciem boni vel mali. Sicut tollere aliquid in magna quantitate vel parva, non respicit ordinem rationis in bono vel malo, nisi praesupposita aliqua alia conditione, per quam actus habeat malitiam vel bonitatem, puta hoc quod est esse alienum, quod repugnat rationi. Unde tollere alienum in magna vel parva quantitate, non diversificat speciem peccati. Tamen potest aggravare vel diminuere peccatum. Et similiter est in aliis malis vel bonis. Unde non omnis circumstantia addens in bonitate vel malitia, variat speciem moralis actus.

it cannot make the action better or worse; because what is not good, cannot make a greater good; and what is not evil, cannot make a greater evil. But if it has in itself the character of good or evil, for this very reason it has a certain species of good or evil. Therefore every circumstance that makes an action better or worse, constitutes a new species of good or evil.

Objection 3: Further, according to Dionysius (Div. Nom. iv), "evil is caused by each single defect." Now every circumstance that increases malice, has a special defect. Therefore every such circumstance adds a new species of sin. And for the same reason, every circumstance that increases goodness, seems to add a new species of goodness: just as every unity added to a number makes a new species of number; since the good consists in "number, weight, and measure" (I, q. 5, a. 5).

On the contrary, More and less do not change a species. But more and less is a circumstance of additional goodness or malice. Therefore not every circumstance that makes a moral action better or worse, places it in a species of good or evil.

I answer that, As stated above (I-II, q. 18, a. 10), a circumstance gives the species of good or evil to a moral action, in so far as it regards a special order of reason. Now it happens sometimes that a circumstance does not regard a special order of reason in respect of good or evil, except on the supposition of another previous circumstance, from which the moral action takes its species of good or evil. Thus to take something in a large or small quantity, does not regard the order of reason in respect of good or evil, except a certain other condition be presupposed, from which the action takes its malice or goodness; for instance, if what is taken belongs to another, which makes the action to be discordant with reason. Wherefore to take what belongs to another in a large or small quantity, does not change the species of the sin. Nevertheless it can aggravate or diminish the sin. The same applies to other evil or good actions. Consequently not every circumstance that makes a moral action better or worse, changes its species.

Ad primum ergo dicendum quod in his quae intenduntur et remittuntur, differentia intensionis et remissionis non diversificat speciem, sicut quod differt in albedine secundum magis et minus, non differt secundum speciem coloris. Et similiter quod facit diversitatem in bono vel malo secundum intensionem et remissionem, non facit differentiam moralis actus secundum speciem.

Ad secundum dicendum quod circumstantia aggravans peccatum, vel augens bonitatem actus, quandoque non habet bonitatem vel malitiam secundum se, sed per ordinem ad aliam conditionem actus, ut dictum est. Et ideo non dat novam speciem, sed auget bonitatem vel malitiam quae est ex alia conditione actus.

Ad tertium dicendum quod non quaelibet circumstantia inducit singularem defectum secundum seipsam, sed solum secundum ordinem ad aliquid aliud. Et similiter non semper addit novam perfectionem, nisi per comparationem ad aliquid aliud. Et pro tanto, licet augeat bonitatem vel malitiam, non semper variat speciem boni vel mali.

Reply to Objection 1: In things which can be more or less intense, the difference of more or less does not change the species: thus by differing in whiteness through being more or less white a thing is not changed in regard to its species of color. In like manner that which makes an action to be more or less good or evil, does not make the action differ in species.

Reply to Objection 2: A circumstance that aggravates a sin, or adds to the goodness of an action, sometimes has no goodness or malice in itself, but in regard to some other condition of the action, as stated above. Consequently it does not add a new species, but adds to the goodness or malice derived from this other condition of the action.

Reply to Objection 3: A circumstance does not always involve a distinct defect of its own; sometimes it causes a defect in reference to something else. In like manner a circumstance does not always add further perfection, except in reference to something else. And, for as much as it does, although it may add to the goodness or malice, it does not always change the species of good or evil.

Quaestio XIX

Deinde considerandum est de bonitate actus interioris voluntatis. Et circa hoc quaeruntur decem. *Primo,* utrum bonitas voluntatis dependeat ex obiecto. *Secundo,* utrum ex solo obiecto dependeat. *Tertio,* utrum dependeat ex ratione. *Quarto,* utrum dependeat ex lege aeterna. *Quinto,* utrum ratio errans obliget. *Sexto,* utrum voluntas contra legem Dei sequens rationem errantem, sit mala. *Septimo,* utrum bonitas voluntatis in his quae sunt ad finem, dependeat ex intentione finis. *Octavo,* utrum quantitas bonitatis vel malitiae in voluntate, sequatur quantitatem boni vel mali in intentione. *Nono,* utrum bonitas voluntatis dependeat ex conformitate ad voluntatem divinam. *Decimo,* utrum necesse sit voluntatem humanam conformari divinae voluntati in volito, ad hoc quod sit bona.

Articulus 1

Ad primum sic proceditur. Videtur quod bonitas voluntatis non dependeat ex obiecto. Voluntas enim non potest esse nisi boni, quia *malum est praeter voluntatem,* ut Dionysius dicit, IV cap. de Div. Nom. Si igitur bonitas voluntatis iudicaretur ex obiecto, sequeretur quod omnis voluntas esset bona, et nulla esset mala.

Praeterea, bonum per prius invenitur in fine, unde bonitas finis, inquantum huiusmodi, non dependet ab aliquo alio. Sed secundum philosophum, in VI Ethic., *bona actio est finis, licet factio nunquam sit finis,* ordinatur enim semper, sicut ad finem, ad aliquid factum. Ergo bonitas actus voluntatis non dependet ex aliquo obiecto.

Praeterea, unumquodque quale est, tale alterum facit. Sed obiectum voluntatis est bonum bonitate naturae. Non ergo potest praestare voluntati bonitatem moralem.

Question 19
Of the Goodness and Malice of the Interior Act of the Will

We must now consider the goodness of the interior act of the will; under which head there are ten points of inquiry: 1. Whether the goodness of the will depends on the subject? 2. Whether it depends on the object alone? 3. Whether it depends on reason? 4. Whether it depends on the eternal law? 5. Whether erring reason binds? 6. Whether the will is evil if it follows the erring reason against the law of God? 7. Whether the goodness of the will in regard to the means, depends on the intention of the end? 8. Whether the degree of goodness or malice in the will depends on the degree of good or evil in the intention? 9. Whether the goodness of the will depends on its conformity to the Divine Will? 10. Whether it is necessary for the human will, in order to be good, to be conformed to the Divine Will, as regards the thing willed?

Article 1
Whether the goodness of the will depends on the object?

Objection 1: It would seem that the goodness of the will does not depend on the object. For the will cannot be directed otherwise than to what is good: since "evil is outside the scope of the will," as Dionysius says (Div. Nom. iv). If therefore the goodness of the will depended on the object, it would follow that every act of the will is good, and none bad.

Objection 2: Further, good is first of all in the end: wherefore the goodness of the end, as such, does not depend on any other. But, according to the Philosopher (Ethic. vi, 5), "goodness of action is the end, but goodness of making is never the end": because the latter is always ordained to the thing made, as to its end. Therefore the goodness of the act of the will does not depend on any object.

Objection 3: Further, such as a thing is, such does it make a thing to be. But the object of the will is good, by reason of the goodness of nature. Therefore it cannot give moral goodness to the will.

Moralis ergo bonitas voluntatis non dependet ex obiecto.

SED CONTRA est quod philosophus dicit, in V Ethic., quod iustitia est *secundum quam aliqui volunt iusta,* et eadem ratione, virtus est secundum quam aliqui volunt bona. Sed bona voluntas est quae est secundum virtutem. Ergo bonitas voluntatis est ex hoc quod aliquis vult bonum.

RESPONDEO dicendum quod bonum et malum sunt per se differentiae actus voluntatis. Nam bonum et malum per se ad voluntatem pertinent; sicut verum et falsum ad rationem, cuius actus per se distinguitur differentia veri et falsi, prout dicimus opinionem esse veram vel falsam. Unde voluntas bona et mala sunt actus differentes secundum speciem. Differentia autem speciei in actibus est secundum obiecta, ut dictum est. Et ideo bonum et malum in actibus voluntatis proprie attenditur secundum obiecta.

AD PRIMUM ergo dicendum quod voluntas non semper est veri boni, sed quandoque est apparentis boni, quod quidem habet aliquam rationem boni, non tamen simpliciter convenientis ad appetendum. Et propter hoc actus voluntatis non est bonus semper, sed aliquando malus.

AD SECUNDUM dicendum quod, quamvis aliquis actus possit esse ultimus finis hominis secundum aliquem modum, non tamen talis actus est actus voluntatis, ut supra dictum est.

AD TERTIUM dicendum quod bonum per rationem repraesentatur voluntati ut obiectum; et inquantum cadit sub ordine rationis, pertinet ad genus moris, et causat bonitatem moralem in actu voluntatis. Ratio enim principium est humanorum et moralium actuum, ut supra dictum est.

ARTICULUS 2

AD SECUNDUM sic proceditur. Videtur quod bonitas voluntatis non dependeat solum ex obiecto. Finis enim affinior est voluntati quam alteri potentiae. Sed actus aliarum potentiarum recipiunt bonitatem non solum ex obiecto, sed etiam ex fine,

Therefore the moral goodness of the will does not depend on the object.

On the contrary, the Philosopher says (Ethic. v, 1) that justice is that habit "from which men wish for just things": and accordingly, virtue is a habit from which men wish for good things. But a good will is one which is in accordance with virtue. Therefore the goodness of the will is from the fact that a man wills that which is good.

I answer that, Good and evil are essential differences of the act of the will. Because good and evil of themselves regard the will; just as truth and falsehood regard reason; the act of which is divided essentially by the difference of truth and falsehood, for as much as an opinion is said to be true or false. Consequently good and evil will are acts differing in species. Now the specific difference in acts is according to objects, as stated above (I-II, q. 18, a. 5). Therefore good and evil in the acts of the will is derived properly from the objects.

Reply to Objection 1: The will is not always directed to what is truly good, but sometimes to the apparent good; which has indeed some measure of good, but not of a good that is simply suitable to be desired. Hence it is that the act of the will is not always good, but sometimes evil.

Reply to Objection 2: Although an action can, in a certain way, be man's last end; nevertheless such action is not an act of the will, as stated above (I-II, q. 1, a. 1, ad 2).

Reply to Objection 3: Good is presented to the will as its object by the reason: and in so far as it is in accord with reason, it enters the moral order, and causes moral goodness in the act of the will: because the reason is the principle of human and moral acts, as stated above (I-II, q. 18, a. 5).

ARTICLE 2
Whether the goodness of the will depends on the object alone?

Objection 1: It would seem that the goodness of the will does not depend on the object alone. For the end has a closer relationship to the will than to any other power. But the acts of the other powers derive goodness not only from the object but also from the end,

ut ex supradictis patet. Ergo etiam actus voluntatis recipit bonitatem non solum ex obiecto, sed etiam ex fine.

PRAETEREA, bonitas actus non solum est ex obiecto, sed etiam ex circumstantiis, ut supra dictum est. Sed secundum diversitatem circumstantiarum contingit esse diversitatem bonitatis et malitiae in actu voluntatis, puta quod aliquis velit quando debet et ubi debet, et quantum debet, et quomodo debet, vel prout non debet. Ergo bonitas voluntatis non solum dependet ex obiecto, sed etiam ex circumstantiis.

PRAETEREA, ignorantia circumstantiarum excusat malitiam voluntatis, ut supra habitum est. Sed hoc non esset, nisi bonitas et malitia voluntatis a circumstantiis dependeret. Ergo bonitas et malitia voluntatis dependet ex circumstantiis, et non a solo obiecto.

SED CONTRA, ex circumstantiis, inquantum huiusmodi, actus non habet speciem, ut supra dictum est. Sed bonum et malum sunt specificae differentiae actus voluntatis, ut dictum est. Ergo bonitas et malitia voluntatis non dependet ex circumstantiis, sed ex solo obiecto.

RESPONDEO dicendum quod in quolibet genere, quanto aliquid est prius, tanto est simplicius et in paucioribus consistens, sicut prima corpora sunt simplicia. Et ideo invenimus quod ea quae sunt prima in quolibet genere, sunt aliquo modo simplicia, et in uno consistunt. Principium autem bonitatis et malitiae humanorum actuum est ex actu voluntatis. Et ideo bonitas et malitia voluntatis secundum aliquid unum attenditur, aliorum vero actuum bonitas et malitia potest secundum diversa attendi. Illud autem unum quod est principium in quolibet genere, non est per accidens, sed per se, quia omne quod est per accidens, reducitur ad id quod est per se, sicut ad principium. Et ideo bonitas voluntatis ex solo uno illo dependet, quod per se facit bonitatem in actu, scilicet

as we have shown above (I-II, q. 18, a. 4). Therefore the act also of the will derives goodness not only from the object but also from the end.

Objection 2: Further, the goodness of an action is derived not only from the object but also from the circumstances, as stated above (I-II, q. 18, a. 3). But according to the diversity of circumstances there may be diversity of goodness and malice in the act of the will: for instance, if a man will, when he ought, where he ought, as much as he ought, and how he ought, or if he will as he ought not. Therefore the goodness of the will depends not only on the object, but also on the circumstances.

Objection 3: Further, ignorance of circumstances excuses malice of the will, as stated above (I-II, q. 6, a. 8). But it would not be so, unless the goodness or malice of the will depended on the circumstances. Therefore the goodness and malice of the will depend on the circumstances, and not only on the object.

On the contrary, An action does not take its species from the circumstances as such, as stated above (I-II, q. 18, a. 10, ad 2). But good and evil are specific differences of the act of the will, as stated above (I-II, q. 19, a. 1). Therefore the goodness and malice of the will depend, not on the circumstances, but on the object alone.

I answer that, In every genus, the more a thing is first, the more simple it is, and the fewer the principles of which it consists: thus primary bodies are simple. Hence it is to be observed that the first things in every genus, are, in some way, simple and consist of one principle. Now the principle of the goodness and malice of human actions is taken from the act of the will. Consequently the goodness and malice of the act of the will depend on some one thing; while the goodness and malice of other acts may depend on several things. Now that one thing which is the principle in each genus, is not something accidental to that genus, but something essential thereto: because whatever is accidental is reduced to something essential, as to its principle. Therefore the goodness of the will's act depends on that one thing alone, which of itself causes goodness in the act; and that

ex obiecto, et non ex circumstantiis, quae sunt quaedam accidentia actus.

AD PRIMUM ergo dicendum quod finis est obiectum voluntatis, non autem aliarum virium. Unde quantum ad actum voluntatis, non differt bonitas quae est ex obiecto, a bonitate quae est ex fine, sicut in actibus aliarum virium, nisi forte per accidens, prout finis dependet ex fine, et voluntas ex voluntate.

AD SECUNDUM dicendum quod, supposito quod voluntas sit boni, nulla circumstantia potest eam facere malam. Quod ergo dicitur quod aliquis vult aliquod bonum quando non debet vel ubi non debet, potest intelligi dupliciter. Uno modo, ita quod ista circumstantia referatur ad volitum. Et sic voluntas non est boni, quia velle facere aliquid quando non debet fieri, non est velle bonum. Alio modo, ita quod referatur ad actum volendi. Et sic impossibile est quod aliquis velit bonum quando non debet, quia semper homo debet velle bonum, nisi forte per accidens, inquantum aliquis, volendo hoc bonum, impeditur ne tunc velit aliquod bonum debitum. Et tunc non incidit malum ex eo quod aliquis vult illud bonum; sed ex eo quod non vult aliud bonum. Et similiter dicendum est de aliis circumstantiis.

AD TERTIUM dicendum quod circumstantiarum ignorantia excusat malitiam voluntatis, secundum quod circumstantiae se tenent ex parte voliti, inquantum scilicet ignorat circumstantias actus quem vult.

ARTICULUS 3

AD TERTIUM sic proceditur. Videtur quod bonitas voluntatis non dependeat a ratione. Prius enim non dependet a posteriori. Sed bonum per prius pertinet ad voluntatem quam ad rationem, ut ex supradictis patet. Ergo bonum voluntatis non dependet a ratione.

one thing is the object, and not the circumstances, which are accidents, as it were, of the act.

Reply to Objection 1: The end is the object of the will, but not of the other powers. Hence, in regard to the act of the will, the goodness derived from the object, does not differ from that which is derived from the end, as they differ in the acts of the other powers; except perhaps accidentally, in so far as one end depends on another, and one act of the will on another.

Reply to Objection 2: Given that the act of the will is fixed on some good, no circumstances can make that act bad. Consequently when it is said that a man wills a good when he ought not, or where he ought not, this can be understood in two ways. First, so that this circumstance is referred to the thing willed. And thus the act of the will is not fixed on something good: since to will to do something when it ought not to be done, is not to will something good. Secondly, so that the circumstance is referred to the act of willing. And thus, it is impossible to will something good when one ought not to, because one ought always to will what is good: except, perhaps, accidentally, in so far as a man by willing some particular good, is prevented from willing at the same time another good which he ought to will at that time. And then evil results, not from his willing that particular good, but from his not willing the other. The same applies to the other circumstances.

Reply to Objection 3: Ignorance of circumstances excuses malice of the will, in so far as the circumstance affects the thing willed: that is to say, in so far as a man ignores the circumstances of the act which he wills.

ARTICLE 3
Whether the goodness of the will depends on reason?

Objection 1: It would seem that the goodness of the will does not depend on reason. For what comes first does not depend on what follows. But the good belongs to the will before it belongs to reason, as is clear from what has been said above (I-II, q. 9, a. 1). Therefore the goodness of the will does not depend on reason.

Praeterea, philosophus dicit, in VI Ethic., quod bonitas intellectus practici est *verum conforme appetitui recto.* Appetitus autem rectus est voluntas bona. Ergo bonitas rationis practicae magis dependet a bonitate voluntatis, quam e converso.

Praeterea, movens non dependet ab eo quod movetur, sed e converso. Voluntas autem movet rationem et alias vires, ut supra dictum est. Ergo bonitas voluntatis non dependet a ratione.

Sed contra est quod Hilarius dicit, in X de Trin., *immoderata est omnis susceptarum voluntatum pertinacia, ubi non rationi voluntas subiicitur.* Sed bonitas voluntatis consistit in hoc quod non sit immoderata. Ergo bonitas voluntatis dependet ex hoc quod sit subiecta rationi.

Respondeo dicendum quod, sicut dictum est, bonitas voluntatis proprie ex obiecto dependet. Obiectum autem voluntatis proponitur ei per rationem. Nam bonum intellectum est obiectum voluntatis proportionatum ei; bonum autem sensibile, vel imaginarium, non est proportionatum voluntati, sed appetitui sensitivo, quia voluntas potest tendere in bonum universale, quod ratio apprehendit; appetitus autem sensitivus non tendit nisi in bonum particulare, quod apprehendit vis sensitiva. Et ideo bonitas voluntatis dependet a ratione, eo modo quo dependet ab obiecto.

Ad primum ergo dicendum quod bonum sub ratione boni, idest appetibilis, per prius pertinet ad voluntatem quam ad rationem. Sed tamen per prius pertinet ad rationem sub ratione veri, quam ad voluntatem sub ratione appetibilis, quia appetitus voluntatis non potest esse de bono, nisi prius a ratione apprehendatur.

Ad secundum dicendum quod philosophus ibi loquitur de intellectu practico, secundum quod est consiliativus et ratiocinativus eorum quae sunt ad finem, sic enim perficitur per prudentiam. In his autem quae sunt ad finem, rectitudo rationis consistit in conformitate ad appetitum finis debiti.

Objection 2: Further, the Philosopher says (Ethic. vi, 2) that the goodness of the practical intellect is "a truth that is in conformity with right desire." But right desire is a good will. Therefore the goodness of the practical reason depends on the goodness of the will, rather than conversely.

Objection 3: Further, the mover does not depend on that which is moved, but vice versa. But the will moves the reason and the other powers, as stated above (I-II, q. 9, a. 1). Therefore the goodness of the will does not depend on reason.

On the contrary, Hilary says (De Trin. x): "It is an unruly will that persists in its desires in opposition to reason." But the goodness of the will consists in not being unruly. Therefore the goodness of the will depends on its being subject to reason.

I answer that, As stated above (I-II, q. 19, a. 1; a. 2), the goodness of the will depends properly on the object. Now the will's object is proposed to it by reason. Because the good understood is the proportionate object of the will; while sensitive or imaginary good is proportionate not to the will but to the sensitive appetite: since the will can tend to the universal good, which reason apprehends; whereas the sensitive appetite tends only to the particular good, apprehended by the sensitive power. Therefore the goodness of the will depends on reason, in the same way as it depends on the object.

Reply to Objection 1: The good considered as such, i.e., as appetible, pertains to the will before pertaining to the reason. But considered as true it pertains to the reason, before, under the aspect of goodness, pertaining to the will: because the will cannot desire a good that is not previously apprehended by reason.

Reply to Objection 2: The Philosopher speaks here of the practical intellect, in so far as it counsels and reasons about the means: for in this respect it is perfected by prudence. Now in regard to the means, the rectitude of the reason depends on its conformity with the desire of a due end:

Sed tamen et ipse appetitus finis debiti praesupponit rectam apprehensionem de fine, quae est per rationem.

Ad tertium dicendum quod voluntas quodam modo movet rationem; et ratio alio modo movet voluntatem, ex parte scilicet obiecti, ut supra dictum est.

nevertheless the very desire of the due end presupposes on the part of reason a right apprehension of the end.

Reply to Objection 3: The will moves the reason in one way: the reason moves the will in another, *viz.* on the part of the object, as stated above (I-II, q. 9, a. 1).

Articulus 4

Article 4
Whether the goodness of the will depends on the eternal law?

Ad quartum sic proceditur. Videtur quod bonitas voluntatis humanae non dependeat a lege aeterna. Unius enim una est regula et mensura. Sed regula humanae voluntatis, ex qua eius bonitas dependet, est ratio recta. Ergo non dependet bonitas voluntatis a lege aeterna.

Praeterea, *mensura est homogenea mensurato*, ut dicitur X Metaphys. Sed lex aeterna non est homogenea voluntati humanae. Ergo lex aeterna non potest esse mensura voluntatis humanae, ut ab ea bonitas eius dependeat.

Praeterea, mensura debet esse certissima. Sed lex aeterna est nobis ignota. Ergo non potest esse nostrae voluntatis mensura, ut ab ea bonitas voluntatis nostrae dependeat.

Sed contra est quod Augustinus dicit, XXII libro contra Faustum, quod *peccatum est factum, dictum vel concupitum aliquid contra aeternam legem*. Sed malitia voluntatis est radix peccati. Ergo, cum malitia bonitati opponatur, bonitas voluntatis dependet a lege aeterna.

Respondeo dicendum quod in omnibus causis ordinatis, effectus plus dependet a causa prima quam a causa secunda, quia causa secunda non agit nisi in virtute primae causae. Quod autem ratio humana sit regula voluntatis humanae, ex qua eius bonitas mensuretur, habet ex lege aeterna, quae est ratio divina. Unde in Psalmo IV, dicitur, *multi dicunt, quis ostendit nobis bona? Signatum est super nos lumen vultus tui, domine,* quasi diceret, *lumen rationis quod in nobis est, intantum potest nobis ostendere bona, et nostram voluntatem regulare, inquantum est lumen vultus tui, idest a vultu tuo derivatum.*

Objection 1: It would seem that the goodness of the human will does not depend on the eternal law. Because to one thing there is one rule and one measure. But the rule of the human will, on which its goodness depends, is right reason. Therefore the goodness of the will does not depend on the eternal law.

Objection 2: Further, "a measure is homogeneous with the thing measured" (Metaph. x, 1). But the eternal law is not homogeneous with the human will. Therefore the eternal law cannot be the measure on which the goodness of the human will depends.

Objection 3: Further, a measure should be most certain. But the eternal law is unknown to us. Therefore it cannot be the measure on which the goodness of our will depends.

On the contrary, Augustine says (Contra Faust. xxii, 27) that "sin is a deed, word or desire against the eternal law." But malice of the will is the root of sin. Therefore, since malice is contrary to goodness, the goodness of the will depends on the eternal law.

I answer that, Wherever a number of causes are subordinate to one another, the effect depends more on the first than on the second cause: since the second cause acts only in virtue of the first. Now it is from the eternal law, which is the Divine Reason, that human reason is the rule of the human will, from which the human derives its goodness. Hence it is written (Ps. 4:6, 7): "Many say: Who showeth us good things? The light of Thy countenance, O Lord, is signed upon us": as though to say: "The light of our reason is able to show us good things, and guide our will, in so far as it is the light (i.e., derived from) Thy countenance."

Unde manifestum est quod multo magis dependet bonitas voluntatis humanae a lege aeterna, quam a ratione humana, et ubi deficit humana ratio, oportet ad rationem aeternam recurrere.

Ad primum ergo dicendum quod unius rei non sunt plures mensurae proximae, possunt tamen esse plures mensurae, quarum una sub alia ordinetur.

Ad secundum dicendum quod mensura proxima est homogenea mensurato, non autem mensura remota.

Ad tertium dicendum quod, licet lex aeterna sit nobis ignota secundum quod est in mente divina; innotescit tamen nobis aliqualiter vel per rationem naturalem, quae ab ea derivatur ut propria eius imago; vel per aliqualem revelationem superadditam.

Articulus 5

Ad quintum sic proceditur. Videtur quod voluntas discordans a ratione errante, non sit mala. Ratio enim est regula voluntatis humanae, inquantum derivatur a lege aeterna, ut dictum est. Sed ratio errans non derivatur a lege aeterna. Ergo ratio errans non est regula voluntatis humanae. Non est ergo voluntas mala, si discordat a ratione errante.

Praeterea, secundum Augustinum, inferioris potestatis praeceptum non obligat, si contrarietur praecepto potestatis superioris, sicut si proconsul iubeat aliquid quod imperator prohibet. Sed ratio errans quandoque proponit aliquid quod est contra praeceptum superioris, scilicet Dei, cuius est summa potestas. Ergo dictamen rationis errantis non obligat. Non est ergo voluntas mala, si discordet a ratione errante.

Praeterea, omnis voluntas mala reducitur ad aliquam speciem malitiae. Sed voluntas discordans a ratione errante, non potest reduci ad aliquam speciem malitiae, puta, si ratio errans errat in hoc, quod dicat

It is therefore evident that the goodness of the human will depends on the eternal law much more than on human reason: and when human reason fails we must have recourse to the Eternal Reason.

Reply to Objection 1: To one thing there are not several proximate measures; but there can be several measures if one is subordinate to the other.

Reply to Objection 2: A proximate measure is homogeneous with the thing measured; a remote measure is not.

Reply to Objection 3: Although the eternal law is unknown to us according as it is in the Divine Mind: nevertheless, it becomes known to us somewhat, either by natural reason which is derived therefrom as its proper image; or by some sort of additional revelation.

Article 5
Whether the will is evil when it is at variance with erring reason?

Objection 1: It would seem that the will is not evil when it is at variance with erring reason. Because the reason is the rule of the human will, in so far as it is derived from the eternal law, as stated above (I-II, q. 19, a. 4). But erring reason is not derived from the eternal law. Therefore erring reason is not the rule of the human will. Therefore the will is not evil, if it be at variance with erring reason.

Objection 2: Further, according to Augustine, the command of a lower authority does not bind if it be contrary to the command of a higher authority: for instance, if a provincial governor command something that is forbidden by the emperor. But erring reason sometimes proposes what is against the command of a higher power, namely, God Whose power is supreme. Therefore the decision of an erring reason does not bind. Consequently the will is not evil if it be at variance with erring reason.

Objection 3: Further, every evil will is reducible to some species of malice. But the will that is at variance with erring reason is not reducible to some species of malice. For instance, if a man's reason err in telling him

esse fornicandum, voluntas eius qui fornicari non vult, ad nullam malitiam reduci potest. Ergo voluntas discordans a ratione errante, non est mala.

Sed contra, sicut in primo dictum est, conscientia nihil aliud est quam applicatio scientiae ad aliquem actum. Scientia autem in ratione est. Voluntas ergo discordans a ratione errante, est contra conscientiam. Sed omnis talis voluntas est mala, dicitur enim Rom. XIV, *omne quod non est ex fide, peccatum est,* idest omne quod est contra conscientiam. Ergo voluntas discordans a ratione errante, est mala.

Respondeo dicendum quod, cum conscientia sit quodammodo dictamen rationis (est enim quaedam applicatio scientiae ad actum, ut in primo dictum est), idem est quaerere utrum voluntas discordans a ratione errante sit mala, quod quaerere *utrum conscientia errans obliget.* Circa quod, aliqui distinxerunt tria genera actuum, quidam enim sunt boni ex genere; quidam sunt indifferentes; quidam sunt mali ex genere. Dicunt ergo quod, si ratio vel conscientia dicat aliquid esse faciendum quod sit bonum ex suo genere, non est ibi error. Similiter, si dicat aliquid non esse faciendum quod est malum ex suo genere, eadem enim ratione praecipiuntur bona, qua prohibentur mala. Sed si ratio vel conscientia dicat alicui quod illa quae sunt secundum se mala, homo teneatur facere ex praecepto; vel quod illa quae sunt secundum se bona, sint prohibita; erit ratio vel conscientia errans. Et similiter si ratio vel conscientia dicat alicui quod id quod est secundum se indifferens, ut levare festucam de terra, sit prohibitum vel praeceptum, erit ratio vel conscientia errans. Dicunt ergo quod ratio vel conscientia errans circa indifferentia, sive praecipiendo sive prohibendo, obligat, ita quod voluntas discordans a tali ratione errante, erit mala et peccatum. Sed ratio vel conscientia errans praecipiendo ea quae sunt per se mala, vel prohibendo ea quae sunt per se bona et necessaria ad salutem, non obligat, unde in talibus voluntas discordans a ratione vel conscientia errante, non est mala. Sed hoc irrationabiliter dicitur. In indifferentibus enim,

to commit fornication, his will in not willing to do so, cannot be reduced to any species of malice. Therefore the will is not evil when it is at variance with erring reason.

On the contrary, As stated in the I, q. 79, a. 13, conscience is nothing else than the application of knowledge to some action. Now knowledge is in the reason. Therefore when the will is at variance with erring reason, it is against conscience. But every such will is evil; for it is written (Rom. 14:23): "All that is not of faith"—i.e., all that is against conscience—"is sin." Therefore the will is evil when it is at variance with erring reason.

I answer that, Since conscience is a kind of dictate of the reason (for it is an application of knowledge to action, as was stated in the I, q. 79, a. 13), to inquire whether the will is evil when it is at variance with erring reason, is the same as to inquire "whether an erring conscience binds." On this matter, some distinguished three kinds of actions: for some are good generically; some are indifferent; some are evil generically. And they say that if reason or conscience tell us to do something which is good generically, there is no error: and in like manner if it tell us not to do something which is evil generically; since it is the same reason that prescribes what is good and forbids what is evil. On the other hand if a man's reason or conscience tells him that he is bound by precept to do what is evil in itself; or that what is good in itself, is forbidden, then his reason or conscience errs. In like manner if a man's reason or conscience tell him, that what is indifferent in itself, for instance to raise a straw from the ground, is forbidden or commanded, his reason or conscience errs. They say, therefore, that reason or conscience when erring in matters of indifference, either by commanding or by forbidding them, binds: so that the will which is at variance with that erring reason is evil and sinful. But they say that when reason or conscience errs in commanding what is evil in itself, or in forbidding what is good in itself and necessary for salvation, it does not bind; wherefore in such cases the will which is at variance with erring reason or conscience is not evil. But this is unreasonable. For in matters of indifference, the

voluntas discordans a ratione vel conscientia errante, est mala aliquo modo propter obiectum, a quo bonitas vel malitia voluntatis dependet, non autem propter obiectum secundum sui naturam; sed secundum quod per accidens a ratione apprehenditur ut malum ad faciendum vel ad vitandum. Et quia obiectum voluntatis est id quod proponitur a ratione, ut dictum est, ex quo aliquid proponitur a ratione ut malum, voluntas, dum in illud fertur, accipit rationem mali. Hoc autem contingit non solum in indifferentibus, sed etiam in per se bonis vel malis. Non solum enim id quod est indifferens, potest accipere rationem boni vel mali per accidens; sed etiam id quod est bonum, potest accipere rationem mali, vel illud quod est malum, rationem boni, propter apprehensionem rationis. Puta, abstinere a fornicatione bonum quoddam est, tamen in hoc bonum non fertur voluntas, nisi secundum quod a ratione proponitur. Si ergo proponatur ut malum a ratione errante, feretur in hoc sub ratione mali. Unde voluntas erit mala, quia vult malum, non quidem id quod est malum per se, sed id quod est malum per accidens, propter apprehensionem rationis. Et similiter credere in Christum est per se bonum, et necessarium ad salutem, sed voluntas non fertur in hoc, nisi secundum quod a ratione proponitur. Unde si a ratione proponatur ut malum, voluntas feretur in hoc ut malum, non quia sit malum secundum se, sed quia est malum per accidens ex apprehensione rationis. Et ideo philosophus dicit, in VII Ethic., quod, *per se loquendo, incontinens est qui non sequitur rationem rectam, per accidens autem, qui non sequitur etiam rationem falsam.* Unde dicendum est simpliciter quod omnis voluntas discordans a ratione, sive recta sive errante, semper est mala.

AD PRIMUM ergo dicendum quod iudicium rationis errantis licet non derivetur a Deo, tamen ratio errans iudicium suum proponit ut verum, et per consequens ut

will that is at variance with erring reason or conscience, is evil in some way on account of the object, on which the goodness or malice of the will depends; not indeed on account of the object according as it is in its own nature; but according as it is accidentally apprehended by reason as something evil to do or to avoid. And since the object of the will is that which is proposed by the reason, as stated above (I-II, q. 19, a. 3), from the very fact that a thing is proposed by the reason as being evil, the will by tending thereto becomes evil. And this is the case not only in indifferent matters, but also in those that are good or evil in themselves. For not only indifferent matters can received the character of goodness or malice accidentally; but also that which is good, can receive the character of evil, or that which is evil, can receive the character of goodness, on account of the reason apprehending it as such. For instance, to refrain from fornication is good: yet the will does not tend to this good except in so far as it is proposed by the reason. If, therefore, the erring reason propose it as an evil, the will tends to it as to something evil. Consequently the will is evil, because it wills evil, not indeed that which is evil in itself, but that which is evil accidentally, through being apprehended as such by the reason. In like manner, to believe in Christ is good in itself, and necessary for salvation: but the will does not tend thereto, except inasmuch as it is proposed by the reason. Consequently if it be proposed by the reason as something evil, the will tends to it as to something evil: not as if it were evil in itself, but because it is evil accidentally, through the apprehension of the reason. Hence the Philosopher says (Ethic. vii, 9) that "properly speaking the incontinent man is one who does not follow right reason; but accidentally, he is also one who does not follow false reason." We must therefore conclude that, absolutely speaking, every will at variance with reason, whether right or erring, is always evil.

Reply to Objection 1: Although the judgment of an erring reason is not derived from God, yet the erring reason puts forward its judgment as being true, and consequently as

a Deo derivatum, a quo est omnis veritas.

AD SECUNDUM dicendum quod verbum Augustini habet locum, quando cognoscitur quod inferior potestas praecipit aliquid contra praeceptum superioris potestatis. Sed si aliquis crederet quod praeceptum proconsulis esset praeceptum imperatoris, contemnendo praeceptum proconsulis, contemneret praeceptum imperatoris. Et similiter si aliquis homo cognosceret quod ratio humana dictaret aliquid contra praeceptum Dei, non teneretur rationem sequi, sed tunc ratio non totaliter esset errans. Sed quando ratio errans proponit aliquid ut praeceptum Dei, tunc idem est contemnere dictamen rationis, et Dei praeceptum.

AD TERTIUM dicendum quod ratio, quando apprehendit aliquid ut malum, semper apprehendit illud sub aliqua ratione mali, puta quia contrariatur divino praecepto, vel quia est scandalum, vel propter aliquid huiusmodi. Et tunc ad talem speciem malitiae reducitur talis mala voluntas.

ARTICULUS 6

AD SEXTUM sic proceditur. Videtur quod voluntas concordans rationi erranti, sit bona. Sicut enim voluntas discordans a ratione tendit in id quod ratio iudicat malum; ita voluntas concordans rationi, tendit in id quod ratio iudicat bonum. Sed voluntas discordans a ratione, etiam errante, est mala. Ergo voluntas concordans rationi, etiam erranti, est bona.

PRAETEREA, voluntas concordans praecepto Dei et legi aeternae, semper est bona. Sed lex aeterna et praeceptum Dei proponitur nobis per apprehensionem rationis, etiam errantis. Ergo voluntas concordans etiam rationi erranti, est bona.

PRAETEREA, voluntas discordans a ratione errante, est mala. Si ergo voluntas concordans rationi erranti sit etiam mala, videtur quod omnis voluntas habentis rationem errantem, sit mala.

being derived from God, from Whom is all truth.

Reply to Objection 2: The saying of Augustine holds good when it is known that the inferior authority prescribes something contrary to the command of the higher authority. But if a man were to believe the command of the proconsul to be the command of the emperor, in scorning the command of the proconsul he would scorn the command of the emperor. In like manner if a man were to know that human reason was dictating something contrary to God's commandment, he would not be bound to abide by reason: but then reason would not be entirely erroneous. But when erring reason proposes something as being commanded by God, then to scorn the dictate of reason is to scorn the commandment of God.

Reply to Objection 3: Whenever reason apprehends something as evil, it apprehends it under some species of evil; for instance, as being something contrary to a divine precept, or as giving scandal, or for some such like reason. And then that evil is reduced to that species of malice.

ARTICLE 6
Whether the will is good when it abides by erring reason?

Objection 1: It would seem that the will is good when it abides by erring reason. For just as the will, when at variance with the reason, tends to that which reason judges to be evil; so, when in accord with reason, it tends to what reason judges to be good. But the will is evil when it is at variance with reason, even when erring. Therefore even when it abides by erring reason, the will is good.

Objection 2: Further, the will is always good, when it abides by the commandment of God and the eternal law. But the eternal law and God's commandment are proposed to us by the apprehension of the reason, even when it errs. Therefore the will is good, even when it abides by erring reason.

Objection 3: Further, the will is evil when it is at variance with erring reason. If, therefore, the will is evil also when it abides by erring reason, it seems that the will is always evil when in conjunction with erring reason:

Et sic talis homo erit perplexus, et ex necessitate peccabit, quod est inconveniens. Ergo voluntas concordans rationi erranti, est bona.

SED CONTRA, voluntas occidentium apostolos erat mala. Sed tamen concordabat rationi erranti ipsorum, secundum illud Ioan. XVI, *venit hora, ut omnis qui interficit vos, arbitretur obsequium se praestare Deo.* Ergo voluntas concordans rationi erranti, potest esse mala.

RESPONDEO dicendum quod, sicut praemissa quaestio eadem est cum quaestione qua quaeritur *utrum conscientia erronea liget;* ita ista quaestio eadem est cum illa qua quaeritur *utrum conscientia erronea excuset.* Haec autem quaestio dependet ab eo quod supra de ignorantia dictum est. Dictum est enim supra quod ignorantia quandoque causat involuntarium, quandoque autem non. Et quia bonum et malum morale consistit in actu inquantum est voluntarius, ut ex praemissis patet; manifestum est quod illa ignorantia quae causat involuntarium, tollit rationem boni et mali moralis; non autem illa quae involuntarium non causat. Dictum est etiam supra quod ignorantia quae est aliquo modo volita, sive directe sive indirecte, non causat involuntarium. Et dico ignorantiam *directe* voluntariam, in quam actus voluntatis fertur, *indirecte* autem, propter negligentiam, ex eo quod aliquis non vult illud scire quod scire tenetur, ut supra dictum est. Si igitur ratio vel conscientia erret errore voluntario, vel directe, vel propter negligentiam, quia est error circa id quod quis scire tenetur; tunc talis error rationis vel conscientiae non excusat quin voluntas concordans rationi vel conscientiae sic erranti, sit mala. Si autem sit error qui causet involuntarium, proveniens ex ignorantia alicuius circumstantiae absque omni negligentia; tunc talis error rationis vel conscientiae excusat, ut voluntas concordans rationi erranti non sit mala. Puta, si ratio errans dicat quod homo teneatur ad uxorem alterius accedere, voluntas concordans huic rationi erranti est mala, eo quod error iste provenit ex ignorantia

so that in such a case a man would be in a dilemma, and, of necessity, would sin: which is unreasonable. Therefore the will is good when it abides by erring reason.

On the contrary, The will of those who slew the apostles was evil. And yet it was in accord with the erring reason, according to Jn. 16:2: "The hour cometh, that whosoever killeth you, will think that he doth a service to God." Therefore the will can be evil, when it abides by erring reason.

I answer that, Whereas the previous question is the same as inquiring "whether an erring conscience binds"; so this question is the same as inquiring "whether an erring conscience excuses." Now this question depends on what has been said above about ignorance. For it was said (I-II, q. 6, a. 8) that ignorance sometimes causes an act to be involuntary, and sometimes not. And since moral good and evil consist in action in so far as it is voluntary, as was stated above (I-II, q. 19, a. 2); it is evident that when ignorance causes an act to be involuntary, it takes away the character of moral good and evil; but not, when it does not cause the act to be involuntary. Again, it has been stated above (I-II, q. 6, a. 8) that when ignorance is in any way willed, either directly or indirectly, it does not cause the act to be involuntary. And I call that ignorance "directly" voluntary, to which the act of the will tends: and that, "indirectly" voluntary, which is due to negligence, by reason of a man not wishing to know what he ought to know, as stated above (I-II, q. 6, a. 8). If then reason or conscience err with an error that is involuntary, either directly, or through negligence, so that one errs about what one ought to know; then such an error of reason or conscience does not excuse the will, that abides by that erring reason or conscience, from being evil. But if the error arise from ignorance of some circumstance, and without any negligence, so that it cause the act to be involuntary, then that error of reason or conscience excuses the will, that abides by that erring reason, from being evil. For instance, if erring reason tell a man that he should go to another man's wife, the will that abides by that erring reason is evil; since this error arises from ignorance of the

legis Dei, quam scire tenetur. Si autem ratio erret in hoc, quod credat aliquam mulierem submissam, esse suam uxorem, et, ea petente debitum, velit eam cognoscere; excusatur voluntas eius, ut non sit mala, quia error iste ex ignorantia circumstantiae provenit, quae excusat, et involuntarium causat.

AD PRIMUM ergo dicendum quod, sicut Dionysius dicit in IV cap. de Div. Nom., *bonum causatur ex integra causa, malum autem ex singularibus defectibus*. Et ideo ad hoc quod dicatur malum id in quod fertur voluntas, sufficit sive quod secundum suam naturam sit malum, sive quod apprehendatur ut malum. Sed ad hoc quod sit bonum, requiritur quod utroque modo sit bonum.

AD SECUNDUM dicendum quod lex aeterna errare non potest, sed ratio humana potest errare. Et ideo voluntas concordans rationi humanae non semper est recta, nec semper est concordans legis aeternae.

AD TERTIUM dicendum quod, sicut in syllogisticis, uno inconvenienti dato, necesse est alia sequi; ita in moralibus, uno inconvenienti posito, ex necessitate alia sequuntur. Sicut, supposito quod aliquis quaerat inanem gloriam, sive propter inanem gloriam faciat quod facere tenetur, sive dimittat, peccabit. Nec tamen est perplexus, quia potest intentionem malam dimittere. Et similiter, supposito errore rationis vel conscientiae qui procedit ex ignorantia non excusante, necesse est quod sequatur malum in voluntate. Nec tamen est homo perplexus, quia potest ab errore recedere, cum ignorantia sit vincibilis et voluntaria.

ARTICULUS 7

AD SEPTIMUM sic proceditur. Videtur quod bonitas voluntatis non dependeat ex intentione finis. Dictum est enim supra quod bonitas voluntatis dependet ex solo obiecto. Sed in his quae sunt ad finem, aliud est obiectum voluntatis, et aliud finis intentus. Ergo in talibus bonitas voluntatis non dependet ab intentione finis.

Divine Law, which he is bound to know. But if a man's reason, errs in mistaking another for his wife, and if he wish to give her her right when she asks for it, his will is excused from being evil: because this error arises from ignorance of a circumstance, which ignorance excuses, and causes the act to be involuntary.

Reply to Objection 1: As Dionysius says (Div. Nom. iv), "good results from the entire cause, evil from each particular defect." Consequently in order that the thing to which the will tends be called evil, it suffices, either that it be evil in itself, or that it be apprehended as evil. But in order for it to be good, it must be good in both ways.

Reply to Objection 2: The eternal law cannot err, but human reason can. Consequently the will that abides by human reason, is not always right, nor is it always in accord with the eternal law.

Reply to Objection 3: Just as in syllogistic arguments, granted one absurdity, others must needs follow; so in moral matters, given one absurdity, others must follow too. Thus suppose a man to seek vainglory, he will sin, whether he does his duty for vainglory or whether he omit to do it. Nor is he in a dilemma about the matter: because he can put aside his evil intention. In like manner, suppose a man's reason or conscience to err through inexcusable ignorance, then evil must needs result in the will. Nor is this man in a dilemma: because he can lay aside his error, since his ignorance is vincible and voluntary.

ARTICLE 7
Whether the goodness of the will, as regards the means, depends on the intention of the end?

Objection 1: It would seem that the goodness of the will does not depend on the intention of the end. For it has been stated above (I-II, q. 19, a. 2) that the goodness of the will depends on the object alone. But as regards the means, the object of the will is one thing, and the end intended is another. Therefore in such matters the goodness of the will does not depend on the intention of the end.

PRAETEREA, velle servare mandatum Dei, pertinet ad voluntatem bonam. Sed hoc potest referri ad malum finem, scilicet ad finem inanis gloriae, vel cupiditatis, dum aliquis vult obedire Deo propter temporalia consequenda. Ergo bonitas voluntatis non dependet ab intentione finis.

PRAETEREA, bonum et malum, sicut diversificant voluntatem, ita diversificant finem. Sed malitia voluntatis non dependet a malitia finis intenti, qui enim vult furari ut det eleemosynam, voluntatem malam habet, licet intendat finem bonum. Ergo etiam bonitas voluntatis non dependet a bonitate finis intenti.

SED CONTRA est quod Augustinus dicit, IX Confess., quod intentio remuneratur a Deo. Sed ex eo aliquid remuneratur a Deo, quia est bonum. Ergo bonitas voluntatis ex intentione finis dependet.

RESPONDEO dicendum quod intentio dupliciter se potest habere ad voluntatem, uno modo, ut praecedens; alio modo, ut concomitans. Praecedit quidem causaliter intentio voluntatem, quando aliquid volumus propter intentionem alicuius finis. Et tunc ordo ad finem consideratur ut ratio quaedam bonitatis ipsius voliti, puta cum aliquis vult ieiunare propter Deum, habet enim ieiunium rationem boni ex hoc ipso quod fit propter Deum. Unde, cum bonitas voluntatis dependeat a bonitate voliti, ut supra dictum est, necesse est quod dependeat ex intentione finis. Consequitur autem intentio voluntatem, quando accedit voluntati praeexistenti, puta si aliquis velit aliquid facere, et postea referat illud in Deum. Et tunc primae voluntatis bonitas non dependet ex intentione sequenti, nisi quatenus reiteratur actus voluntatis cum sequenti intentione.

AD PRIMUM ergo dicendum quod, quando intentio est causa volendi, ordo ad finem accipitur ut quaedam ratio bonitatis in obiecto, ut dictum est.

Objection 2: Further, to wish to keep God's commandment, belongs to a good will. But this can be referred to an evil end, for instance, to vainglory or covetousness, by willing to obey God for the sake of temporal gain. Therefore the goodness of the will does not depend on the intention of the end.

Objection 3: Further, just as good and evil diversify the will, so do they diversify the end. But malice of the will does not depend on the malice of the end intended; since a man who wills to steal in order to give alms, has an evil will, although he intends a good end. Therefore neither does the goodness of the will depend on the goodness of the end intended.

On the contrary, Augustine says (Confess. ix, 3) that God rewards the intention. But God rewards a thing because it is good. Therefore the goodness of the will depends on the intention of the end.

I answer that, The intention may stand in a twofold relation to the act of the will; first, as preceding it, secondly as following* it. The intention precedes the act of the will causally, when we will something because we intend a certain end. And then the order to the end is considered as the reason of the goodness of the thing willed: for instance, when a man wills to fast for God's sake; because the act of fasting is specifically good from the very fact that it is done for God's sake. Wherefore, since the goodness of the will depends on the goodness of the thing willed, as stated above (I-II, q. 19, a. 1; a. 2), it must, of necessity, depend on the intention of the end. On the other hand, intention follows the act of the will, when it is added to a preceding act of the will; for instance, a man may will to do something, and may afterwards refer it to God. And then the goodness of the previous act of the will does not depend on the subsequent intention, except in so far as that act is repeated with the subsequent intention.

Reply to Objection 1: When the intention is the cause of the act of willing, the order to the end is considered as the reason of the goodness of the object, as stated above.

---

* Leonine edn.: "accompanying"

AD SECUNDUM dicendum quod voluntas non potest dici bona, si sit intentio mala causa volendi. Qui enim vult dare eleemosynam propter inanem gloriam consequendam, vult id quod de se est bonum, sub ratione mali, et ideo, prout est volitum ab ipso, est malum. Unde voluntas eius est mala. Sed si intentio sit consequens, tunc voluntas potuit esse bona, et per intentionem sequentem non depravatur ille actus voluntatis qui praecessit, sed actus voluntatis qui iteratur.

AD TERTIUM dicendum quod, sicut iam dictum est, *malum contingit ex singularibus defectibus, bonum vero ex tota et integra causa.* Unde sive voluntas sit eius quod est secundum se malum, etiam sub ratione boni; sive sit boni sub ratione mali; semper voluntas erit mala. Sed ad hoc quod sit voluntas bona, requiritur quod sit boni sub ratione boni; idest quod velit bonum, et propter bonum.

Reply to Objection 2: The act of the will cannot be said to be good, if an evil intention is the cause of willing. For when a man wills to give an alms for the sake of vainglory, he wills that which is good in itself, under a species of evil; and therefore, as willed by him, it is evil. Wherefore his will is evil. If, however, the intention is subsequent to the act of the will, then the latter may be good: and the intention does not spoil that act of the will which preceded, but that which is repeated.

Reply to Objection 3: As we have already stated (I-II, q. 19, a. 6, ad 1), "evil results from each particular defect, but good from the whole and entire cause." Hence, whether the will tend to what is evil in itself, even under the species of good; or to the good under the species of evil, it will be evil in either case. But in order for the will to be good, it must tend to the good under the species of good; in other words, it must will the good for the sake of the good.

ARTICULUS 8

ARTICLE 8
Whether the degree of goodness or malice in the will depends on the degree of good or evil in the intention?

AD OCTAVUM sic proceditur. Videtur quod quantitas bonitatis in voluntate, dependeat ex quantitate bonitatis in intentione. Quia super illud Matth. XII, *bonus homo de thesauro bono cordis sui profert bona,* dicit Glossa, *tantum boni quis facit, quantum intendit.* Sed intentio non solum dat bonitatem actui exteriori, sed etiam voluntati, ut dictum est. Ergo tantum aliquis habet bonam voluntatem, quantum intendit.

PRAETEREA, augmentata causa, augmentatur effectus. Sed intentionis bonitas est causa bonae voluntatis. Ergo quantum quis intendit de bono, tantum voluntas est bona.

PRAETEREA, in malis quantum aliquis intendit, tantum peccat, si enim aliquis proiiciens lapidem, intenderet facere homicidium, reus esset homicidii. Ergo, pari ratione, in bonis tantum est bona voluntas, quantum aliquis bonum intendit.

Objection 1: It would seem that the degree of goodness in the will depends on the degree of good in the intention. Because on Mat. 12:35, "A good man out of the good treasure of his heart bringeth forth that which is good," a gloss says: "A man does as much good as he intends." But the intention gives goodness not only to the external action, but also to the act of the will, as stated above (I-II, q. 19, a. 7). Therefore the goodness of a man's will is according to the goodness of his intention.

Objection 2: Further, if you add to the cause, you add to the effect. But the goodness of the intention is the cause of the good will. Therefore a man's will is good, according as his intention is good.

Objection 3: Further, in evil actions, a man sins in proportion to his intention: for if a man were to throw a stone with a murderous intention, he would be guilty of murder. Therefore, for the same reason, in good actions, the will is good in proportion to the good intended.

SED CONTRA, potest esse intentio bona, et voluntas mala. Ergo, pari ratione, potest esse intentio magis bona, et voluntas minus bona.

RESPONDEO dicendum quod circa actum et intentionem finis, duplex quantitas potest considerari, una ex parte obiecti, quia vult maius bonum, vel agit; alia ex intensione actus, quia intense vult vel agit, quod est maius ex parte agentis. Si igitur loquamur de quantitate utriusque quantum ad obiectum, manifestum est quod quantitas actus non sequitur quantitatem intentionis. Quod quidem ex parte actus exterioris, contingere potest dupliciter. Uno modo, quia obiectum quod ordinatur ad finem intentum, non est proportionatum fini illi, sicut si quis daret decem libras, non posset consequi suam intentionem, si intenderet emere rem valentem centum libras. Alio modo, propter impedimenta quae supervenire possunt circa exteriorem actum, quae non est in potestate nostra removere, puta, aliquis intendit ire usque Romam, et occurrunt ei impedimenta, quod non potest hoc facere. Sed ex parte interioris actus voluntatis, non est nisi uno modo, quia interiores actus voluntatis sunt in potestate nostra, non autem exteriores actus. Sed voluntas potest velle aliquod obiectum non proportionatum fini intento, et sic voluntas quae fertur in illud obiectum absolute consideratum, non est tantum bona, quantum est intentio. Sed quia etiam ipsa intentio quodammodo pertinet ad actum voluntatis, inquantum scilicet est ratio eius; propter hoc redundat quantitas bonae intentionis in voluntatem, inquantum scilicet voluntas vult aliquod bonum magnum ut finem, licet illud per quod vult consequi tantum bonum, non sit dignum illo bono. Si vero consideretur quantitas intentionis et actus secundum intensionem utriusque, sic intensio intentionis redundat in actum interiorem et exteriorem voluntatis, quia ipsa intentio quodammodo se habet formaliter ad utrumque,

On the contrary, The intention can be good, while the will is evil. Therefore, for the same reason, the intention can be better, and the will less good.

I answer that, In regard to both the act, and the intention of the end, we may consider a twofold quantity: one, on the part of the object, by reason of a man willing or doing a good that is greater; the other, taken from the intensity of the act, according as a man wills or acts intensely; and this is more on the part of the agent. If then we speak of these respective quantities from the point of view of the object, it is evident that the quantity in the act does not depend on the quantity in the intention. With regard to the external act this may happen in two ways. First, through the object that is ordained to the intended end not being proportionate to that end; for instance, if a man were to give ten pounds, he could not realize his intention, if he intended to buy a thing worth a hundred pounds. Secondly, on account of the obstacles that may supervene in regard to the exterior action, which obstacles we are unable to remove: for instance, a man intends to go to Rome, and encounters obstacles, which prevent him from going. On the other hand, with regard to the interior act of the will, this happens in only one way: because the interior acts of the will are in our power, whereas the external actions are not. But the will can will an object that is not proportionate to the intended end: and thus the will that tends to that object considered absolutely, is not so good as the intention. Yet because the intention also belongs, in a way, to the act of the will, inasmuch, to wit, as it is the reason thereof; it comes to pass that the quantity of goodness in the intention redounds upon the act of the will; that is to say, in so far as the will wills some great good for an end, although that by which it wills to gain so great a good, is not proportionate to that good. But if we consider the quantity in the intention and in the act, according to their respective intensity, then the intensity of the intention redounds upon the interior act and the exterior act of the will: since the intention stands in relation to them as a kind of form,

ut ex supra dictis patet. Licet materialiter, intentione existente intensa, possit esse actus interior vel exterior non ita intensus, materialiter loquendo, puta cum aliquis non ita intense vult medicinam sumere, sicut vult sanitatem. Tamen hoc ipsum quod est intense intendere sanitatem, redundat formaliter in hoc quod est intense velle medicinam. Sed tamen hoc est considerandum, quod intensio actus interioris vel exterioris potest referri ad **intentionem ut obiectum**, puta cum aliquis intendit intense velle, vel aliquid intense operari. Et tamen non propter hoc intense vult vel operatur, quia quantitatem boni intenti non sequitur bonitas actus interioris vel exterioris, ut dictum est. Et inde est quod non quantum aliquis intendit mereri, meretur, quia quantitas meriti consistit in intensione actus, ut infra dicetur.

AD PRIMUM ergo dicendum quod Glossa illa loquitur quantum ad reputationem Dei, qui praecipue considerat intentionem finis. Unde alia Glossa dicit ibidem quod *thesaurus cordis intentio est, ex qua Deus iudicat opera*. Bonitas enim intentionis, ut dictum est, redundat quodammodo in bonitatem voluntatis, quae facit etiam exteriorem actum meritorium apud Deum.

AD SECUNDUM dicendum quod bonitas intentionis non est tota causa bonae voluntatis. Unde ratio non sequitur.

AD TERTIUM dicendum quod sola malitia intentionis sufficit ad malitiam voluntatis, et ideo etiam quantum mala est intentio, tantum mala est voluntas. Sed non est eadem ratio de bonitate, ut dictum est.

ARTICULUS 9

AD NONUM sic proceditur. Videtur quod bonitas voluntatis humanae non dependeat ex conformitate voluntatis divinae. Impossibile est enim voluntatem hominis conformari voluntati divinae, ut patet per id quod dicitur

as is clear from what has been said above (I-II, q. 12, a. 4; q. 18, a. 6). And yet considered materially, while the intention is intense, the interior or exterior act may be not so intense, materially speaking: for instance, when a man does not will with as much intensity to take medicine as he wills to regain health. Nevertheless the very fact of intending health intensely, redounds, as a formal principle, upon the intense volition of medicine. We must observe, however, that the intensity of the interior or exterior act, may be referred to the intention as its object: as when a man intends to will intensely, or to do something intensely. And yet it does not follow that he wills or acts intensely; because the quantity of goodness in the interior or exterior act does not depend on the quantity of the good intended, as is shown above. And hence it is that a man does not merit as much as he intends to merit: because the quantity of merit is measured by the intensity of the act, as we shall show later on (I-II, q. 20, a. 4; q. 114, a. 4).

Reply to Objection 1: This gloss speaks of good as in the estimation of God, Who considers principally the intention of the end. Wherefore another gloss says on the same passage that "the treasure of the heart is the intention, according to which God judges our works." For the goodness of the intention, as stated above, redounds, so to speak, upon the goodness of the will, which makes even the external act to be meritorious in God's sight.

Reply to Objection 2: The goodness of the intention is not the whole cause of a good will. Hence the argument does not prove.

Reply to Objection 3: The mere malice of the intention suffices to make the will evil: and therefore too, the will is as evil as the intention is evil. But the same reasoning does not apply to goodness, as stated above (ad 2).

ARTICLE 9
Whether the goodness of the will depends on its conformity to the Divine will?

Objection 1: It would seem that the goodness of the human will does not depend on its conformity to the Divine will. Because it is impossible for man's will to be conformed to the Divine will; as appears from the word

Isaiae LV, *sicut exaltantur caeli a terra, ita exaltatae sunt viae meae a viis vestris, et cogitationes meae a cogitationibus vestris.* Si ergo ad bonitatem voluntatis requireretur conformitas ad divinam voluntatem, sequeretur quod impossibile esset hominis voluntatem esse bonam. Quod est inconveniens.

PRAETEREA, sicut voluntas nostra derivatur a voluntate divina, ita scientia nostra derivatur a scientia divina. Sed non requiritur ad scientiam nostram quod sit conformis scientiae divinae, multa enim Deus scit quae nos ignoramus. Ergo non requiritur quod voluntas nostra sit conformis voluntati divinae.

PRAETEREA, voluntas est actionis principium. Sed actio nostra non potest conformari actioni divinae. Ergo nec voluntas voluntati.

SED CONTRA est quod dicitur Matth. XXVI, *non sicut ego volo, sed sicut tu vis,* quod dicit quia *rectum vult esse hominem, et ad Deum dirigi,* ut Augustinus exponit in Enchirid. Rectitudo autem voluntatis est bonitas eius. Ergo bonitas voluntatis dependet ex conformitate ad voluntatem divinam.

RESPONDEO dicendum quod, sicut dictum est, bonitas voluntatis dependet ex intentione finis. Finis autem ultimus voluntatis humanae est summum bonum, quod est Deus, ut supra dictum est. Requiritur ergo ad bonitatem humanae voluntatis, quod ordinetur ad summum bonum, quod est Deus. Hoc autem bonum primo quidem et per se comparatur ad voluntatem divinam ut obiectum proprium eius. Illud autem quod est primum in quolibet genere, est mensura et ratio omnium quae sunt illius generis. Unumquodque autem rectum et bonum est, inquantum attingit ad propriam mensuram. Ergo ad hoc quod voluntas hominis sit bona, requiritur quod conformetur voluntati divinae.

AD PRIMUM ergo dicendum quod voluntas hominis non potest conformari voluntati divinae per aequiparantiam, sed per imitationem. Et similiter conformatur scientia hominis scientiae divinae, inquantum

of Isa. 55:9: "As the heavens are exalted above the earth, so are My ways exalted above your ways, and My thoughts above your thoughts." If therefore goodness of the will depended on its conformity to the Divine will, it would follow that it is impossible for man's will to be good. Which is inadmissible.

Objection 2: Further, just as our wills arise from the Divine will, so does our knowledge flow from the Divine knowledge. But our knowledge does not require to be conformed to God's knowledge; since God knows many things that we know not. Therefore there is no need for our will to be conformed to the Divine will.

Objection 3: Further, the will is a principle of action. But our action cannot be conformed to God's. Therefore neither can our will be conformed to His.

On the contrary, It is written (Mat. 26:39): "Not as I will, but as Thou wilt": which words He said, because "He wishes man to be upright and to tend to God," as Augustine expounds in the Enchiridion.* But the rectitude of the will is its goodness. Therefore the goodness of the will depends on its conformity to the Divine will.

I answer that, As stated above (I-II, q. 19, a. 7), the goodness of the will depends on the intention of the end. Now the last end of the human will is the Sovereign Good, namely, God, as stated above (I-II, q. 1, a. 8; q. 3, a. 1). Therefore the goodness of the human will requires it to be ordained to the Sovereign Good, that is, to God. Now this Good is primarily and essentially compared to the Divine will, as its proper object. Again, that which is first in any genus is the measure and rule of all that belongs to that genus. Moreover, everything attains to rectitude and goodness, in so far as it is in accord with its proper measure. Therefore, in order that man's will be good it needs to be conformed to the Divine will.

Reply to Objection 1: The human will cannot be conformed to the will of God so as to equal it, but only so as to imitate it. In like manner human knowledge is conformed to the Divine knowledge, in so far as it

---

* Enarr. in Ps. 32, serm. i.

cognoscit verum. Et actio hominis actioni divinae, inquantum est agenti conveniens. Et hoc per imitationem, non autem per aequiparantiam.

Unde patet solutio ad secundum, et ad tertium argumentum.

Articulus 10

Ad decimum sic proceditur. Videtur quod voluntas hominis non debeat semper conformari divinae voluntati in volito. Non enim possumus velle quod ignoramus, bonum enim apprehensum est obiectum voluntatis. Sed quid Deus velit, ignoramus in plurimis. Ergo non potest humana voluntas divinae voluntati conformari in volito.

Praeterea, Deus vult damnare aliquem, quem praescit in mortali peccato moriturum. Si ergo homo teneretur conformare voluntatem suam divinae voluntati in volito, sequeretur quod homo teneretur velle suam damnationem. Quod est inconveniens.

Praeterea, nullus tenetur velle aliquid quod est contra pietatem. Sed si homo vellet illud quod Deus vult, hoc esset quandoque contra pietatem, puta, cum Deus vult mori patrem alicuius, si filius hoc idem vellet, contra pietatem esset. Ergo non tenetur homo conformare voluntatem suam voluntati divinae in volito.

Sed contra est quia super illud Psalmi XXXII, *rectos decet collaudatio,* dicit Glossa, rectum cor habet qui vult quod Deus vult. Sed quilibet tenetur habere rectum cor. Ergo quilibet tenetur velle quod Deus vult.

Praeterea, forma voluntatis est ex obiecto sicut et cuiuslibet actus. Si ergo tenetur homo conformare voluntatem suam voluntati divinae, sequitur quod teneatur conformare in volito.

Praeterea, repugnantia voluntatum consistit in hoc, quod homines diversa volunt. Sed quicumque habet voluntatem repugnantem divinae

knows truth: and human action is conformed to the Divine, in so far as it is becoming to the agent: and this by way of imitation, not by way of equality.

From the above may be gathered the replies to the Second and Third Objections.

Article 10
Whether it is necessary for the human will, in order to be good, to be conformed to the Divine will, as regards the thing willed?

Objection 1: It would seem that the human will need not always be conformed to the Divine will, as regards the thing willed. For we cannot will what we know not: since the apprehended good is the object of the will. But in many things we know not what God wills. Therefore the human will cannot be conformed to the Divine will as to the thing willed.

Objection 2: Further, God wills to damn the man whom He foresees about to die in mortal sin. If therefore man were bound to conform his will to the Divine will, in the point of the thing willed, it would follow that a man is bound to will his own damnation. Which is inadmissible.

Objection 3: Further, no one is bound to will what is against filial piety. But if man were to will what God wills, this would sometimes be contrary to filial piety: for instance, when God wills the death of a father: if his son were to will it also, it would be against filial piety. Therefore man is not bound to conform his will to the Divine will, as to the thing willed.

On the contrary, 1. On Ps. 32:1, "Praise becometh the upright," a gloss says: "That man has an upright heart, who wills what God wills." But everyone is bound to have an upright heart. Therefore everyone is bound to will what God wills.

2. Moreover, the will takes its form from the object, as does every act. If therefore man is bound to conform his will to the Divine will, it follows that he is bound to conform it, as to the thing willed.

3. Moreover, opposition of wills arises from men willing different things. But whoever has a will in opposition to the Divine

voluntati, habet malam voluntatem. Ergo quicumque non conformat voluntatem suam voluntati divinae in volito, habet malam voluntatem.

RESPONDEO dicendum quod, sicut ex praedictis patet, voluntas fertur in suum obiectum secundum quod a ratione proponitur. Contingit autem aliquid a ratione considerari diversimode, ita quod sub una ratione est bonum, et secundum aliam rationem non bonum. Et ideo voluntas alicuius, si velit illud esse, secundum quod habet rationem boni, est bona, et voluntas alterius, si velit illud idem non esse, secundum quod habet rationem mali, erit voluntas etiam bona. Sicut iudex habet bonam voluntatem, dum vult occisionem latronis, quia iusta est, voluntas autem alterius, puta uxoris vel filii, qui non vult occidi ipsum, inquantum est secundum naturam mala occisio, est etiam bona. Cum autem voluntas sequatur apprehensionem rationis vel intellectus, secundum quod ratio boni apprehensi fuerit communior, secundum hoc et voluntas fertur in bonum communius. Sicut patet in exemplo proposito, nam iudex habet curam boni communis, quod est iustitia, et ideo vult occisionem latronis, quae habet rationem boni secundum relationem ad statum communem; uxor autem latronis considerare habet bonum privatum familiae, et secundum hoc vult maritum latronem non occidi. Bonum autem totius universi est id quod est apprehensum a Deo, qui est universi factor et gubernator, unde quidquid vult, vult sub ratione boni communis, quod est sua bonitas, quae est bonum totius universi. Apprehensio autem creaturae, secundum suam naturam, est alicuius boni particularis proportionati suae naturae. Contingit autem aliquid esse bonum secundum rationem particularem, quod non est bonum secundum rationem universalem, aut e converso, ut dictum est. Et ideo contingit quod aliqua voluntas est bona volens aliquid secundum rationem particularem consideratum, quod tamen Deus non vult secundum rationem universalem, et e converso. Et inde est etiam quod possunt diversae voluntates diversorum hominum

will, has an evil will. Therefore whoever does not conform his will to the Divine will, as to the thing willed, has an evil will.

I answer that, As is evident from what has been said above (I-II, q. 19, a. 3; a. 5), the will tends to its object, according as it is proposed by the reason. Now a thing may be considered in various ways by the reason, so as to appear good from one point of view, and not good from another point of view. And therefore if a man's will wills a thing to be, according as it appears to be good, his will is good: and the will of another man, who wills that thing not to be, according as it appears evil, is also good. Thus a judge has a good will, in willing a thief to be put to death, because this is just: while the will of another—e.g., the thief's wife or son, who wishes him not to be put to death, inasmuch as killing is a natural evil, is also good. Now since the will follows the apprehension of the reason or intellect; the more universal the aspect of the apprehended good, the more universal the good to which the will tends. This is evident in the example given above: because the judge has care of the common good, which is justice, and therefore he wishes the thief's death, which has the aspect of good in relation to the common estate; whereas the thief's wife has to consider the private, the good of the family, and from this point of view she wishes her husband, the thief, not to be put to death. Now the good of the whole universe is that which is apprehended by God, Who is the Maker and Governor of all things: hence whatever He wills, He wills it under the aspect of the common good; this is His own Goodness, which is the good of the whole universe. On the other hand, the apprehension of a creature, according to its nature, is of some particular good, proportionate to that nature. Now a thing may happen to be good under a particular aspect, and yet not good under a universal aspect, or vice versa, as stated above. And therefore it comes to pass that a certain will is good from willing something considered under a particular aspect, which thing God wills not, under a universal aspect, and vice versa. And hence too it is, that various wills of various men

circa opposita esse bonae, prout sub diversis rationibus particularibus volunt hoc esse vel non esse. Non est autem recta voluntas alicuius hominis volentis aliquod bonum particulare, nisi referat illud in bonum commune sicut in finem, cum etiam naturalis appetitus cuiuslibet partis ordinetur in bonum commune totius. Ex fine autem sumitur quasi formalis ratio volendi illud quod ad finem ordinatur. Unde ad hoc quod aliquis **recta voluntate velit aliquod particulare bonum**, oportet quod illud particulare bonum sit volitum materialiter, bonum autem commune divinum sit volitum formaliter. Voluntas igitur humana tenetur conformari divinae voluntati in volito formaliter, tenetur enim velle bonum divinum et commune, sed non materialiter, ratione iam dicta. Sed tamen quantum ad utrumque, aliquo modo voluntas humana conformatur voluntati divinae. Quia secundum quod conformatur voluntati divinae in communi ratione voliti, conformatur ei in fine ultimo. Secundum autem quod non conformatur ei in volito materialiter, conformatur ei secundum rationem causae efficientis, quia hanc propriam inclinationem consequentem naturam, vel apprehensionem particularem huius rei, habet res a Deo sicut a causa effectiva. Unde consuevit dici quod conformatur, quantum ad hoc, voluntas hominis voluntati divinae, quia vult hoc quod Deus vult eum velle. Est et alius modus conformitatis secundum rationem causae formalis, ut scilicet homo velit aliquid ex caritate, sicut Deus vult. Et ista etiam conformitas reducitur ad conformitatem formalem quae attenditur ex ordine ad ultimum finem, quod est proprium obiectum caritatis.

AD PRIMUM ergo dicendum quod volitum divinum, secundum rationem communem, quale sit, scire possumus. Scimus enim quod Deus quidquid vult, vult sub ratione boni. Et ideo quicumque vult aliquid sub quacumque ratione boni, habet voluntatem conformem voluntati divinae, quantum ad rationem

can be good in respect of opposite things, for as much as, under various aspects, they wish a particular thing to be or not to be. But a man's will is not right in willing a particular good, unless he refer it to the common good as an end: since even the natural appetite of each part is ordained to the common good of the whole. Now it is the end that supplies the formal reason, as it were, of willing whatever is directed to the end. Consequently, in order that a man will some **particular good with a right will**, he must will that particular good materially, and the Divine and universal good, formally. Therefore the human will is bound to be conformed to the Divine will, as to that which is willed formally, for it is bound to will the Divine and universal good; but not as to that which is willed materially, for the reason given above. At the same time in both these respects, the human will is conformed to the Divine, in a certain degree. Because inasmuch as it is conformed to the Divine will in the common aspect of the thing willed, it is conformed thereto in the point of the last end. While, inasmuch as it is not conformed to the Divine will in the thing willed materially, it is conformed to that will considered as efficient cause; since the proper inclination consequent to nature, or to the particular apprehension of some particular thing, comes to a thing from God as its efficient cause. Hence it is customary to say that a man's will, in this respect, is conformed to the Divine will, because it wills what God wishes him to will. There is yet another kind of conformity in respect of the formal cause, consisting in man's willing something from charity, as God wills it. And this conformity is also reduced to the formal conformity, that is in respect of the last end, which is the proper object of charity.

Reply to Objection 1: We can know in a general way what God wills. For we know that whatever God wills, He wills it under the aspect of good. Consequently whoever wills a thing under any aspect of good, has a will conformed to the Divine will, as to the reason

voliti. Sed in particulari nescimus quid Deus velit. Et quantum ad hoc, non tenemur conformare voluntatem nostram divinae voluntati. In statu tamen gloriae, omnes videbunt in singulis quae volent, ordinem eorum ad id quod Deus circa hoc vult. Et ideo non solum formaliter, sed materialiter in omnibus suam voluntatem Deo conformabunt.

AD SECUNDUM dicendum quod Deus non vult damnationem alicuius sub ratione damnationis, nec mortem alicuius inquantum est mors, quia *ipse vult omnes homines salvos fieri,* sed vult ista sub ratione iustitiae. Unde sufficit circa talia quod homo velit iustitiam Dei, et ordinem naturae servari.

Unde patet solutio ad tertium.

AD PRIMUM vero quod in contrarium obiiciebatur, dicendum quod magis vult quod Deus vult, qui conformat voluntatem suam voluntati divinae quantum ad rationem voliti, quam qui conformat quantum ad ipsam rem volitam, quia voluntas principalius fertur in finem, quam in id quod est ad finem.

AD SECUNDUM dicendum quod species et forma actus magis attenditur secundum rationem obiecti, quam secundum id quod est materiale in obiecto.

AD TERTIUM dicendum quod non est repugnantia voluntatum, quando aliqui diversa volunt non secundum eandem rationem. Sed si sub una ratione esset aliquid ab uno volitum, quod alius nollet, hoc induceret repugnantiam voluntatum. Quod tamen non est in proposito.

of the thing willed. But we know not what God wills in particular: and in this respect we are not bound to conform our will to the Divine will. But in the state of glory, every one will see in each thing that he wills, the relation of that thing to what God wills in that particular matter. Consequently he will conform his will to God in all things not only formally, but also materially.

Reply to Objection 2: God does not will the damnation of a man, considered precisely as damnation, nor a man's death, considered precisely as death, because, "He wills all men to be saved" (1 Tim. 2:4); but He wills such things under the aspect of justice. Wherefore in regard to such things it suffices for man to will the upholding of God's justice and of the natural order.

Wherefore the reply to the Third Objection is evident.

To the first argument advanced in a contrary sense, it should be said that a man who conforms his will to God's, in the aspect of reason of the thing willed, wills what God wills, more than the man, who conforms his will to God's, in the point of the very thing willed; because the will tends more to the end, than to that which is on account of the end.

To the second, it must be replied that the species and form of an act are taken from the object considered formally, rather than from the object considered materially.

To the third, it must be said that there is no opposition of wills when several people desire different things, but not under the same aspect: but there is opposition of wills, when under one and the same aspect, one man wills a thing which another wills not. But there is no question of this here.

Quaestio XX

Deinde considerandum est de bonitate et malitia quantum ad exteriores actus. Et circa hoc quaeruntur sex. *Primo,* utrum bonitas et malitia per prius sit in actu voluntatis, vel in actu exteriori. *Secundo,* utrum tota bonitas vel malitia actus exterioris dependeat ex bonitate voluntatis. *Tertio,* utrum sit eadem bonitas et malitia interioris et exterioris actus. *Quarto,* utrum actus exterior aliquid addat de bonitate vel malitia supra actum interiorem. *Quinto,* utrum eventus sequens aliquid addat de bonitate vel malitia ad actum exteriorem. *Sexto,* utrum idem actus exterior possit esse bonus et malus.

Articulus 1

AD PRIMUM sic proceditur. Videtur quod bonum et malum per prius consistat in actu exteriori quam in actu voluntatis. Voluntas enim habet bonitatem ex obiecto, ut supra dictum est. Sed actus exterior est obiectum interioris actus voluntatis, dicimur enim velle furtum, vel velle dare eleemosynam. Ergo malum et bonum per prius est in actu exteriori, quam in actu voluntatis.

PRAETEREA, bonum per prius convenit fini, quia ea quae sunt ad finem, habent rationem boni ex ordine ad finem. Actus autem voluntatis non potest esse finis, ut supra dictum est, actus alicuius alterius potentiae potest esse finis. Ergo per prius consistit bonum in actu potentiae alterius, quam in actu voluntatis.

PRAETEREA, actus voluntatis formaliter se habet ad actum exteriorem, ut supra dictum est. Sed id quod est formale, est posterius, nam forma advenit materiae. Ergo per prius est bonum et malum in actu exteriori quam in actu voluntatis.

SED CONTRA est quod Augustinus dicit, in libro Retract., *quod voluntas est qua peccatur,*

Question 20
Of Goodness and Malice in External Human Affairs

We must next consider goodness and malice as to external actions: under which head there are six points of inquiry: 1. Whether goodness and malice is first in the act of the will, or in the external action? 2. Whether the whole goodness or malice of the external action depends on the goodness of the will? 3. Whether the goodness and malice of the interior act are the same as those of the external action? 4. Whether the external action adds any goodness or malice to that of the interior act? 5. Whether the consequences of an external action increase its goodness or malice? 6. Whether one and the same external action can be both good and evil?

Article 1
Whether goodness or malice is first in the action of the will, or in the external action?

Objection 1: It would seem that good and evil are in the external action prior to being in the act of the will. For the will derives goodness from its object, as stated above (I-II, q. 19, a. 1; a. 2). But the external action is the object of the interior act of the will: for a man is said to will to commit a theft, or to will to give an alms. Therefore good and evil are in the external action, prior to being in the act of the will.

Objection 2: Further, the aspect of good belongs first to the end: since what is directed to the end receives the aspect of good from its relation to the end. Now whereas the act of the will cannot be an end, as stated above (I-II, q. 1, a. 1, ad 2), the act of another power can be an end. Therefore good is in the act of some other power prior to being in the act of the will.

Objection 3: Further, the act of the will stands in a formal relation to the external action, as stated above (I-II, q. 18, a. 6). But that which is formal is subsequent; since form is something added to matter. Therefore good and evil are in the external action, prior to being in the act of the will.

On the contrary, Augustine says (Retract. i, 9) that "it is by the will that we sin,

et recte vivitur. Ergo bonum et malum morale per prius consistit in voluntate.

Respondeo dicendum quod aliqui actus exteriores possunt dici boni vel mali dupliciter. Uno modo, secundum genus suum, et secundum circumstantias in ipsis consideratas, sicut dare eleemosynam, servatis debitis circumstantiis, dicitur esse bonum. Alio modo dicitur aliquid esse bonum vel malum ex ordine ad finem, sicut dare eleemosynam propter inanem gloriam, dicitur esse malum. Cum autem finis sit proprium obiectum voluntatis, manifestum est quod ista ratio boni vel mali quam habet actus exterior ex ordine ad finem, per prius invenitur in actu voluntatis, et ex eo derivatur ad actum exteriorem. Bonitas autem vel malitia quam habet actus exterior secundum se, propter debitam materiam et debitas circumstantias, non derivatur a voluntate, sed magis a ratione. Unde si consideretur bonitas exterioris actus secundum quod est in ordinatione et apprehensione rationis, prior est quam bonitas actus voluntatis, sed si consideretur secundum quod est in executione operis, sequitur bonitatem voluntatis, quae est principium eius.

Ad primum ergo dicendum quod actus exterior est obiectum voluntatis, inquantum proponitur voluntati a ratione ut quoddam bonum apprehensum et ordinatum per rationem, et sic est prius quam bonum actus voluntatis. Inquantum vero consistit in executione operis, est effectus voluntatis, et sequitur voluntatem.

Ad secundum dicendum quod finis est prior in intentione, sed est posterior in executione.

Ad tertium dicendum quod forma, secundum quod est recepta in materia, est posterior in via generationis quam materia, licet sit prior natura, sed secundum quod est in causa agente, est omnibus modis prior. Voluntas autem comparatur ad actum exteriorem sicut causa efficiens. Unde bonitas actus voluntatis est forma exterioris actus, sicut in causa agente existens.

and that we behave aright." Therefore moral good and evil are first in the will.

I answer that, External actions may be said to be good or bad in two ways. First, in regard to their genus, and the circumstances connected with them: thus the giving of alms, if the required conditions be observed, is said to be good. Secondly, a thing is said to be good or evil, from its relation to the end: thus the giving of alms for vainglory is said to be evil. Now, since the end is the will's proper object, it is evident that this aspect of good or evil, which the external action derives from its relation to the end, is to be found first of all in the act of the will, whence it passes to the external action. On the other hand, the goodness or malice which the external action has of itself, on account of its being about due matter and its being attended by due circumstances, is not derived from the will, but rather from the reason. Consequently, if we consider the goodness of the external action, in so far as it comes from reason's ordination and apprehension, it is prior to the goodness of the act of the will: but if we consider it in so far as it is in the execution of the action done, it is subsequent to the goodness of the will, which is its principle.

Reply to Objection 1: The exterior action is the object of the will, inasmuch as it is proposed to the will by the reason, as good apprehended and ordained by the reason: and thus it is prior to the good in the act of the will. But inasmuch as it is found in the execution of the action, it is an effect of the will, and is subsequent to the will.

Reply to Objection 2: The end precedes in the order of intention, but follows in the order of execution.

Reply to Objection 3: A form as received into matter, is subsequent to matter in the order of generation, although it precedes it in the order of nature: but inasmuch as it is in the active cause, it precedes in every way. Now the will is compared to the exterior action, as its efficient cause. Wherefore the goodness of the act of the will, as existing in the active cause, is the form of the exterior action.

ARTICULUS 2

Ad secundum sic proceditur. Videtur quod tota bonitas et malitia actus exterioris dependeat ex voluntate. Dicitur enim Matth. VII, *non potest arbor bona malos fructus facere, nec arbor mala facere fructus bonos.* Per arborem autem intelligitur voluntas, et per fructum opus, secundum Glossam. Ergo non potest esse quod voluntas interior sit bona, et actus exterior sit malus; aut e converso.

Praeterea, Augustinus dicit, in libro Retract., quod non nisi voluntate peccatur. Si ergo non sit peccatum in voluntate, non erit peccatum in exteriori actu. Et ita tota bonitas vel malitia exterioris actus ex voluntate dependet.

Praeterea, bonum et malum de quo nunc loquimur, sunt differentiae moralis actus. Differentiae autem per se dividunt genus, secundum philosophum, in VII Metaphys. Cum igitur actus sit moralis ex eo quod est voluntarius, videtur quod bonum et malum accipitur in actu solum ex parte voluntatis.

Sed contra est quod Augustinus dicit, in libro contra mendacium, quod *quaedam sunt quae nullo quasi bono fine, aut bona voluntate, possunt bene fieri.*

Respondeo dicendum quod, sicut iam dictum est, in actu exteriori potest considerari duplex bonitas vel malitia, una secundum debitam materiam et circumstantias; alia secundum ordinem ad finem. Et illa quidem quae est secundum ordinem ad finem, tota dependet ex voluntate. Illa autem quae est ex debita materia vel circumstantiis, dependet ex ratione, et ex hac dependet bonitas voluntatis, secundum quod in ipsam fertur. Est autem considerandum quod, sicut supra dictum est, ad hoc quod aliquid sit malum, sufficit unus singularis defectus, ad hoc autem quod sit simpliciter bonum, non sufficit unum singulare bonum, sed requiritur integritas bonitatis. Si igitur voluntas sit bona et ex obiecto proprio, et ex fine, consequens est actum exteriorem esse bonum. Sed

ARTICLE 2
Whether the whole goodness and malice of the external action depends on the goodness of the will?

Objection 1: It would seem that the whole goodness and malice of the external action depend on the goodness of the will. For it is written (Mat. 7:18): "A good tree cannot bring forth evil fruit, neither can an evil tree bring forth good fruit." But, according to the gloss, the tree signifies the will, and fruit signifies works. Therefore, it is impossible for the interior act of the will to be good, and the external action evil, or vice versa.

Objection 2: Further, Augustine says (Retract. i, 9) that there is no sin without the will. If therefore there is no sin in the will, there will be none in the external action. And so the whole goodness or malice of the external action depends on the will.

Objection 3: Further, the good and evil of which we are speaking now are differences of the moral act. Now differences make an essential division in a genus, according to the Philosopher (Metaph. vii, 12). Since therefore an act is moral from being voluntary, it seems that goodness and malice in an act are derived from the will alone.

On the contrary, Augustine says (Contra Mendac. vii), that "there are some actions which neither a good end nor a good will can make good."

I answer that, As stated above (I-II, q. 20, a. 1), we may consider a twofold goodness or malice in the external action: one in respect of due matter and circumstances; the other in respect of the order to the end. And that which is in respect of the order to the end, depends entirely on the will: while that which is in respect of due matter or circumstances, depends on the reason: and on this goodness depends the goodness of the will, in so far as the will tends towards it. Now it must be observed, as was noted above (I-II, q. 19, a. 6, ad 1), that for a thing to be evil, one single defect suffices, whereas, for it to be good simply, it is not enough for it to be good in one point only, it must be good in every respect. If therefore the will be good, both from its proper object and from its end, it follows that the external action is good. But

non sufficit ad hoc quod actus exterior sit bonus, bonitas voluntatis quae est ex intentione finis, sed si voluntas sit mala sive ex intentione finis, sive ex actu volito, consequens est actum exteriorem esse malum.

AD PRIMUM ergo dicendum quod voluntas bona, prout significatur per arborem bonam, est accipienda secundum quod habet bonitatem ex actu volito, et ex fine intento.

AD SECUNDUM dicendum quod non solum aliquis voluntate peccat, quando vult malum finem; sed etiam quando vult malum actum.

AD TERTIUM dicendum quod voluntarium dicitur non solum actus interior voluntatis, sed etiam actus exteriores, prout a voluntate procedunt et ratione. Et ideo circa utrosque actus potest esse differentia boni et mali.

if the will be good from its intention of the end, this is not enough to make the external action good: and if the will be evil either by reason of its intention of the end, or by reason of the act willed, it follows that the external action is evil.

Reply to Objection 1: If the good tree be taken to signify the good will, it must be in so far as the will derives goodness from the act willed and from the end intended.

Reply to Objection 2: A man sins by his will, not only when he wills an evil end; but also when he wills an evil act.

Reply to Objection 3: Voluntariness applies not only to the interior act of the will, but also to external actions, inasmuch as they proceed from the will and the reason. Consequently the difference of good and evil is applicable to both the interior and external act.

ARTICULUS 3

ARTICLE 3
Whether the goodness and malice of the external action are the same as those of the interior act?

AD TERTIUM sic proceditur. Videtur quod non eadem sit bonitas vel malitia actus interioris voluntatis, et exterioris actus. Actus enim interioris principium est vis animae interior apprehensiva vel appetitiva, actus autem exterioris principium est potentia exequens motum. Ubi autem sunt diversa principia actionis, ibi sunt diversi actus. Actus autem est subiectum bonitatis vel malitiae. Non potest autem esse idem accidens in diversis subiectis. Ergo non potest esse eadem bonitas interioris et exterioris actus.

PRAETEREA, *virtus est quae bonum facit habentem, et opus eius bonum reddit,* ut dicitur in II Ethic. Sed alia est virtus intellectualis in potentia imperante, et alia virtus moralis in potentia imperata, ut patet ex I Ethic. Ergo alia est bonitas actus interioris, qui est potentiae imperantis, et alia est bonitas actus exterioris, qui est potentiae imperatae.

Objection 1: It would seem that the goodness and malice of the interior act of the will are not the same as those of the external action. For the principle of the interior act is the interior apprehensive or appetitive power of the soul; whereas the principle of the external action is the power that accomplishes the movement. Now where the principles of action are different, the actions themselves are different. Moreover, it is the action which is the subject of goodness or malice: and the same accident cannot be in different subjects. Therefore the goodness of the interior act cannot be the same as that of the external action.

Objection 2: Further, "A virtue makes that, which has it, good, and renders its action good also" (Ethic. ii, 6). But the intellective virtue in the commanding power is distinct from the moral virtue in the power commanded, as is declared in Ethic. i, 13. Therefore the goodness of the interior act, which belongs to the commanding power, is distinct from the goodness of the external action, which belongs to the power commanded.

I-II, q. 20, a. 3, arg. 3

PRAETEREA, causa et effectus idem esse non possunt, nihil enim est causa sui ipsius. Sed bonitas actus interioris est causa bonitatis actus exterioris, aut e converso, ut dictum est. Ergo non potest esse eadem bonitas utriusque.

SED CONTRA est quod supra ostensum est quod actus voluntatis se habet ut formale ad actum exteriorem. Ex formali autem et **materiali fit unum. Ergo est una bonitas actus interioris et exterioris.**

RESPONDEO dicendum quod, sicut supra dictum est, actus interior voluntatis et actus exterior, prout considerantur in genere moris, sunt unus actus. Contingit autem quandoque actum qui est unus subiecto, habere plures rationes bonitatis vel malitiae; et quandoque unam tantum. Sic ergo dicendum quod quandoque est eadem bonitas vel malitia interioris et exterioris actus; quandoque alia et alia. Sicut enim iam dictum est, praedictae duae bonitates vel malitiae, scilicet interioris et exterioris actus, ad invicem ordinantur. Contingit autem in his quae ad aliud ordinantur, quod aliquid est bonum ex hoc solum quod ad aliud ordinatur, sicut potio amara ex hoc solo est bona, quod est sanativa. Unde non est alia bonitas sanitatis et potionis, sed una et eadem. Quandoque vero illud quod ad aliud ordinatur, habet in se aliquam rationem boni, etiam praeter ordinem ad aliud bonum, sicut medicina saporosa habet rationem boni delectabilis, praeter hoc quod est sanativa. Sic ergo dicendum quod, quando actus exterior est bonus vel malus solum ex ordine ad finem, tunc est omnino eadem bonitas vel malitia actus voluntatis, qui per se respicit finem, et actus exterioris, qui respicit finem mediante actu voluntatis. Quando autem actus exterior habet bonitatem vel malitiam secundum se, scilicet secundum materiam vel circumstantias, tunc bonitas

Objection 3: Further, the same thing cannot be cause and effect; since nothing is its own cause. But the goodness of the interior act is the cause of the goodness of the external action, or vice versa, as stated above (I-II, q. 20, a. 1; a. 2). Therefore it is not the same goodness in each.

On the contrary, It was shown above (I-II, q. 18, a. 6) that the act of the will is the form, as it were, of the external action. Now that which results from the material and formal element is one thing. Therefore there is but one goodness of the internal and external act.

I answer that, As stated above (I-II, q. 17, a. 4), the interior act of the will, and the external action, considered morally, are one act. Now it happens sometimes that one and the same individual act has several aspects of goodness or malice, and sometimes that it has but one. Hence we must say that sometimes the goodness or malice of the interior act is the same as that of the external action, and sometimes not. For as we have already said (I-II, q. 20, a. 1; a. 2), these two goodnesses or malices, of the internal and external acts, are ordained to one another. Now it may happen, in things that are subordinate to something else, that a thing is good merely from being subordinate; thus a bitter draught is good merely because it procures health. Wherefore there are not two goodnesses, one the goodness of health, and the other the goodness of the draught; but one and the same. On the other hand it happens sometimes that that which is subordinate to something else, has some aspect of goodness in itself, besides the fact of its being subordinate to some other good: thus a palatable medicine can be considered in the light of a pleasurable good, besides being conducive to health. We must therefore say that when the external action derives goodness or malice from its relation to the end only, then there is but one and the same goodness of the act of the will which of itself regards the end, and of the external action, which regards the end through the medium of the act of the will. But when the external action has goodness or malice of itself, i.e., in regard to its matter and circumstances, then the goodness

exterioris actus est una, et bonitas voluntatis quae est ex fine, est alia, ita tamen quod et bonitas finis ex voluntate redundat in actum exteriorem, et bonitas materiae et circumstantiarum redundat in actum voluntatis, sicut iam dictum est.

AD PRIMUM ergo dicendum quod ratio illa probat quod actus interior et exterior sunt diversi secundum genus naturae. Sed tamen ex eis sic diversis constituitur unum in genere moris, ut supra dictum est.

AD SECUNDUM dicendum quod, sicut dicitur in VI Ethic., virtutes morales ordinantur ad ipsos actus virtutum, qui sunt quasi fines; prudentia autem, quae est in ratione, ad ea quae sunt ad finem. Et propter hoc requiruntur diversae virtutes. Sed ratio recta de ipso fine virtutum non habet aliam bonitatem quam bonitatem virtutis, secundum quod bonitas rationis participatur in qualibet virtute.

AD TERTIUM dicendum quod, quando aliquid ex uno derivatur in alterum sicut ex causa agente univoca, tunc aliud est quod est in utroque, sicut cum calidum calefacit, alius numero est calor calefacientis, et calor calefacti, licet idem specie. Sed quando aliquid derivatur ab uno in alterum secundum analogiam vel proportionem, tunc est tantum unum numero, sicut a sano quod est in corpore animalis, derivatur sanum ad medicinam et urinam; nec alia sanitas est medicinae et urinae, quam sanitas animalis, quam medicina facit, et urina significat. Et hoc modo a bonitate voluntatis derivatur bonitas actus exterioris, et e converso, scilicet secundum ordinem unius ad alterum.

of the external action is distinct from the goodness of the will in regarding the end; yet so that the goodness of the end passes into the external action, and the goodness of the matter and circumstances passes into the act of the will, as stated above (I-II, q. 20, a. 1; a. 2).

Reply to Objection 1: This argument proves that the internal and external actions are different in the physical order: yet distinct as they are in that respect, they combine to form one thing in the moral order, as stated above (I-II, q. 17, a. 4).

Reply to Objection 2: As stated in Ethic. vi, 12, a moral virtue is ordained to the act of that virtue, which act is the end, as it were, of that virtue; whereas prudence, which is in the reason, is ordained to things directed to the end. For this reason various virtues are necessary. But right reason in regard to the very end of a virtue has no other goodness than the goodness of that virtue, in so far as the goodness of the reason is participated in each virtue.

Reply to Objection 3: When a thing is derived by one thing from another, as from a univocal efficient cause, then it is not the same in both: thus when a hot thing heats, the heat of the heater is distinct from the heat of the thing heated, although it be the same specifically. But when a thing is derived from one thing from another, according to analogy or proportion, then it is one and the same in both: thus the healthiness which is in medicine or urine is derived from the healthiness of the animal's body; nor is health as applied to urine and medicine, distinct from health as applied to the body of an animal, of which health medicine is the cause, and urine the sign. It is in this way that the goodness of the external action is derived from the goodness of the will, and vice versa; *viz.* according to the order of one to the other.

ARTICULUS 4

AD QUARTUM sic proceditur. Videtur quod exterior actus non addat in bonitate vel malitia supra actum interiorem. Dicit enim Chrysostomus, super Matth., *voluntas est quae aut remuneratur pro bono, aut condemnatur pro malo.* Opera autem testimonia sunt voluntatis. Non ergo quaerit Deus opera propter se, ut sciat quomodo iudicet; sed propter alios, ut omnes intelligant quia iustus est Deus. Sed malum vel bonum magis est aestimandum secundum iudicium Dei, quam secundum iudicium hominum. Ergo actus exterior nihil addit ad bonitatem vel malitiam super actum interiorem.

PRAETEREA, una et eadem est bonitas interioris et exterioris actus, ut dictum est. Sed augmentum fit per additionem unius ad alterum. Ergo actus exterior non addit in bonitate vel malitia super actum interiorem.

PRAETEREA, tota bonitas creaturae nihil addit supra bonitatem divinam, quia tota derivatur a bonitate divina. Sed bonitas actus exterioris quandoque tota derivatur ex bonitate actus interioris, quandoque autem e converso, ut dictum est. Non ergo unum eorum addit in bonitate vel malitia super alterum.

SED CONTRA, omne agens intendit consequi bonum et vitare malum. Si ergo per actum exteriorem nihil additur de bonitate vel malitia, frustra qui habet bonam voluntatem vel malam, facit opus bonum, aut desistit a malo opere. Quod est inconveniens.

RESPONDEO dicendum quod, si loquamur de bonitate exterioris actus quam habet ex voluntate finis, tunc actus exterior nihil addit ad bonitatem, nisi contingat ipsam voluntatem secundum se fieri meliorem in bonis, vel peiorem in malis. Quod quidem videtur posse contingere tripliciter. Uno modo, secundum numerum. Puta, cum aliquis vult aliquid facere bono fine vel

ARTICLE 4
Whether the external action adds any goodness or malice to that of the interior act?

Objection 1: It would seem that the external action does not add any goodness or malice to that of the interior action. For Chrysostom says (Hom. xix in Mat.): "It is the will that is rewarded for doing good, or punished for doing evil." Now works are the witnesses of the will. Therefore God seeks for works not on His own account, in order to know how to judge; but for the sake of others, that all may understand how just He is. But good or evil is to be estimated according to God's judgment rather than according to the judgment of man. Therefore the external action adds no goodness or malice to that of the interior act.

Objection 2: Further, the goodness and malice of the interior and external acts are one and the same, as stated above (I-II, q. 20, a. 3). But increase is the addition of one thing to another. Therefore the external action does not add to the goodness or malice of the interior act.

Objection 3: Further, the entire goodness of created things does not add to the Divine Goodness, because it is entirely derived therefrom. But sometimes the entire goodness of the external action is derived from the goodness of the interior act, and sometimes conversely, as stated above (I-II, q. 20, a. 1; a. 2). Therefore neither of them adds to the goodness or malice of the other.

On the contrary, Every agent intends to attain good and avoid evil. If therefore by the external action no further goodness or malice be added, it is to no purpose that he who has a good or an evil will, does a good deed or refrains from an evil deed. Which is unreasonable.

I answer that, If we speak of the goodness which the external action derives from the will tending to the end, then the external action adds nothing to this goodness, unless it happens that the will in itself is made better in good things, or worse in evil things. This, seemingly, may happen in three ways. First in point of number; if, for instance, a man wishes to do something with a good or an

malo, et tunc quidem non facit, postmodum autem vult et facit; duplicatur actus voluntatis, et sic fit duplex bonum vel duplex malum. Alio modo, quantum ad extensionem. Puta, cum aliquis vult facere aliquid bono fine vel malo et propter aliquod impedimentum desistit; alius autem continuat motum voluntatis quousque opere perficiat; manifestum est quod huiusmodi voluntas est diuturnior in bono vel malo, et secundum hoc est peior vel melior. Tertio, secundum intensionem. Sunt enim quidam actus exteriores qui, inquantum sunt delectabiles vel poenosi, nati sunt intendere voluntatem vel remittere. Constat autem quod quanto voluntas intensius tendit in bonum vel malum, tanto est melior vel peior. Si autem loquamur de bonitate actus exterioris quam habet secundum materiam et debitas circumstantias, sic comparatur ad voluntatem ut terminus et finis. Et hoc modo addit ad bonitatem vel malitiam voluntatis, quia omnis inclinatio vel motus perficitur in hoc quod consequitur finem, vel attingit terminum. Unde non est perfecta voluntas, nisi sit talis quae, opportunitate data, operetur. Si vero possibilitas desit, voluntate existente perfecta, ut operaretur si posset; defectus perfectionis quae est ex actu exteriori, est simpliciter involuntarium. Involuntarium autem, sicut non meretur poenam vel praemium in operando bonum aut malum, ita non tollit aliquid de praemio vel de poena, si homo involuntarie simpliciter deficiat ad faciendum bonum vel malum.

AD PRIMUM ergo dicendum quod Chrysostomus loquitur, quando voluntas hominis est consummata, et non cessatur ab actu nisi propter impotentiam faciendi.

AD SECUNDUM dicendum quod ratio illa procedit de bonitate actus exterioris quam habet a voluntate finis. Sed bonitas actus exterioris quam habet ex materia et circumstantiis, est alia a bonitate voluntatis quae est ex fine, non autem alia a bonitate voluntatis quam habet ex ipso actu volito, sed comparatur ad ipsam ut ratio et causa eius, sicut supra dictum est.

evil end in view, and does not do it then, but afterwards wills and does it, the act of his will is doubled and a double good, or a double evil is the result. Secondly, in point of extension: when, for instance, a man wishes to do something for a good or an evil end, and is hindered by some obstacle, whereas another man perseveres in the movement of the will until he accomplish it in deed; it is evident that the will of the latter is more lasting in good or evil, and in this respect, is better or worse. Thirdly, in point of intensity: for these are certain external actions, which, in so far as they are pleasurable, or painful, are such as naturally to make the will more intense or more remiss; and it is evident that the more intensely the will tends to good or evil, the better or worse it is. On the other hand, if we speak of the goodness which the external action derives from its matter and due circumstances, thus it stands in relation to the will as its term and end. And in this way it adds to the goodness or malice of the will; because every inclination or movement is perfected by attaining its end or reaching its term. Wherefore the will is not perfect, unless it be such that, given the opportunity, it realizes the operation. But if this prove impossible, as long as the will is perfect, so as to realize the operation if it could; the lack of perfection derived from the external action, is simply involuntary. Now just as the involuntary deserves neither punishment nor reward in the accomplishment of good or evil deeds, so neither does it lessen reward or punishment, if a man through simple involuntariness fail to do good or evil.

Reply to Objection 1: Chrysostom is speaking of the case where a man's will is complete, and does not refrain from the deed save through the impossibility of achievement.

Reply to Objection 2: This argument applies to that goodness which the external action derives from the will as tending to the end. But the goodness which the external action takes from its matter and circumstances, is distinct from that which it derives from the end; but it is not distinct from that which it has from the very act willed, to which it stands in the relation of measure and cause, as stated above (I-II, q. 20, a. 1; a. 2).

Et per hoc etiam patet solutio ad tertium.

From this the reply to the Third Objection is evident.

Articulus 5

Ad quintum sic proceditur. Videtur quod eventus sequens addat ad bonitatem vel malitiam actus. Effectus enim virtute praeexistit in causa. Sed eventus consequuntur actus sicut effectus causas. Ergo virtute praeexistunt in actibus. Sed unumquodque secundum suam virtutem iudicatur bonum vel malum, nam virtus est *quae bonum facit habentem,* ut dicitur in II Ethic. Ergo eventus addunt ad bonitatem vel malitiam actus.

Praeterea, bona quae faciunt auditores, sunt effectus quidam consequentes ex praedicatione doctoris. Sed huiusmodi bona redundant ad meritum praedicatoris, ut patet per id quod dicitur Philipp. IV, *fratres mei carissimi et desideratissimi, gaudium meum et corona mea.* Ergo eventus sequens addit ad bonitatem vel malitiam actus.

Praeterea, poena non additur nisi crescente culpa, unde dicitur Deut. XXV, *pro mensura peccati, erit et plagarum modus.* Sed ex eventu sequente additur ad poenam, dicitur enim Exod. XXI, quod *si bos fuerit cornupeta ab heri et nudius tertius, et contestati sunt dominum eius, nec recluserit eum, occideritque virum aut mulierem; et bos lapidibus obruetur, et dominum eius occident.* Non autem occideretur, si bos non occidisset hominem, etiam non reclusus. Ergo eventus sequens addit ad bonitatem vel malitiam actus.

Praeterea, si aliquis ingerat causam mortis percutiendo vel sententiam dando, et mors non sequatur, non contrahitur irregularitas. Contraheretur autem si mors sequeretur. Ergo eventus sequens addit ad bonitatem vel malitiam actus.

Article 5
Whether the consequences of the external action increase its goodness or malice?

Objection 1: It would seem that the consequences of the external action increase its goodness or malice. For the effect pre-exists virtually in its cause. But the consequences result from the action as an effect from its cause. Therefore they pre-exist virtually in actions. Now a thing is judged to be good or bad according to its virtue, since a virtue "makes that which has it to be good" (Ethic. ii, 6). Therefore the consequences increase the goodness or malice of an action.

Objection 2: Further, the good actions of his hearers are consequences resulting from the words of a preacher. But such goods as these redound to the merit of the preacher, as is evident from Phil. 4:1: "My dearly beloved brethren, my joy and my crown." Therefore the consequences of an action increase its goodness or malice.

Objection 3: Further, punishment is not increased, unless the fault increases: wherefore it is written (Dt. 25:2): "According to the measure of the sin shall the measure also of the stripes be." But the punishment is increased on account of the consequences; for it is written (Ex. 21:29): "But if the ox was wont to push with his horn yesterday and the day before, and they warned his master, and he did not shut him up, and he shall kill a man or a woman, then the ox shall be stoned, and his owner also shall be put to death." But he would not have been put to death, if the ox, although he had not been shut up, had not killed a man. Therefore the consequences increase the goodness or malice of an action.

Objection 4: Further, if a man do something which may cause death, by striking, or by sentencing, and if death does not ensue, he does not contract irregularity: but he would if death were to ensue. Therefore the consequence of an action increase its goodness or malice.

SED CONTRA, eventus sequens non facit actum malum qui erat bonus, nec bonum qui erat malus. Puta si aliquis det eleemosynam pauperi, qua ille abutatur ad peccatum, nihil deperit ei qui eleemosynam fecit, et similiter si aliquis patienter ferat iniuriam sibi factam, non propter hoc excusatur ille qui fecit. Ergo eventus sequens non addit ad bonitatem vel malitiam actus.

RESPONDEO dicendum quod eventus sequens aut est praecogitatus, aut non. Si est praecogitatus, manifestum est quod addit ad bonitatem vel malitiam. Cum enim aliquis cogitans quod ex opere suo multa mala possunt sequi, nec propter hoc dimittit, ex hoc apparet voluntas eius esse magis inordinata. Si autem eventus sequens non sit praecogitatus, tunc distinguendum est. Quia si per se sequitur ex tali actu, et ut in pluribus, secundum hoc eventus sequens addit ad bonitatem vel malitiam actus, manifestum est enim meliorem actum esse ex suo genere, ex quo possunt plura bona sequi; et peiorem, ex quo nata sunt plura mala sequi. Si vero per accidens, et ut in paucioribus, tunc eventus sequens non addit ad bonitatem vel ad malitiam actus, non enim datur iudicium de re aliqua secundum illud quod est per accidens, sed solum secundum illud quod est per se.

AD PRIMUM ergo dicendum quod virtus causae existimatur secundum effectus per se, non autem secundum effectus per accidens.

AD SECUNDUM dicendum quod bona quae auditores faciunt, consequuntur ex praedicatione doctoris sicut effectus per se. Unde redundant ad praemium praedicatoris, et praecipue quando sunt praeintenta.

AD TERTIUM dicendum quod eventus ille pro quo illi poena infligenda mandatur, et per se sequitur ex tali causa, et iterum ponitur ut praecogitatus. Et ideo imputatur ad poenam.

AD QUARTUM dicendum quod ratio illa procederet, si irregularitas sequeretur

On the contrary, The consequences do not make an action that was evil, to be good; nor one that was good, to be evil. For instance, if a man give an alms to a poor man who makes bad use of the alms by committing a sin, this does not undo the good done by the giver; and, in like manner, if a man bear patiently a wrong done to him, the wrongdoer is not thereby excused. Therefore the consequences of an action doe not increase its goodness or malice.

I answer that, The consequences of an action are either foreseen or not. If they are foreseen, it is evident that they increase the goodness or malice. For when a man foresees that many evils may follow from his action, and yet does not therefore desist therefrom, this shows his will to be all the more inordinate. But if the consequences are not foreseen, we must make a distinction. Because if they follow from the nature of the action and in the majority of cases, in this respect, the consequences increase the goodness or malice of that action: for it is evident that an action is specifically better, if better results can follow from it; and specifically worse, if it is of a nature to produce worse results. On the other hand, if the consequences follow by accident and seldom, then they do not increase the goodness or malice of the action: because we do not judge of a thing according to that which belongs to it by accident, but only according to that which belongs to it of itself.

Reply to Objection 1: The virtue of a cause is measured by the effect that flows from the nature of the cause, not by that which results by accident.

Reply to Objection 2: The good actions done by the hearers, result from the preacher's words, as an effect that flows from their very nature. Hence they redound to the merit of the preacher: especially when such is his intention.

Reply to Objection 3: The consequences for which that man is ordered to be punished, both follow from the nature of the cause, and are supposed to be foreseen. For this reason they are reckoned as punishable.

Reply to Objection 4: This argument would prove if irregularity were the result of the

culpam. Non autem sequitur culpam, sed factum, propter aliquem defectum sacramenti.

Articulus 6

Ad sextum sic proceditur. Videtur quod unus actus possit esse bonus et malus. *Motus enim est unus qui est continuus,* ut dicitur in **V Physic. Sed unus motus continuus potest** esse bonus et malus, puta si aliquis, continue ad Ecclesiam vadens, primo quidem intendat inanem gloriam, postea intendat Deo servire. Ergo unus actus potest esse bonus et malus.

Praeterea, secundum philosophum, in III Physic., actio et passio sunt unus actus. Sed potest esse passio bona, sicut Christi; et actio mala, sicut Iudaeorum. Ergo unus actus potest esse bonus et malus.

Praeterea, cum servus sit quasi instrumentum domini, actio servi est actio domini, sicut actio instrumenti est actio artificis. Sed potest contingere quod actio servi procedat ex bona voluntate domini, et sic sit bona, et ex mala voluntate servi, et sic sit mala. Ergo idem actus potest esse bonus et malus.

Sed contra, contraria non possunt esse in eodem. Sed bonum et malum sunt contraria. Ergo unus actus non potest esse bonus et malus.

Respondeo dicendum quod nihil prohibet aliquid esse unum, secundum quod est in uno genere; et esse multiplex, secundum quod refertur ad aliud genus. Sicut superficies continua est una, secundum quod consideratur in genere quantitatis, tamen est multiplex, secundum quod refertur ad genus coloris, si partim sit alba, et partim nigra. Et secundum hoc, nihil prohibet aliquem actum esse unum secundum quod refertur ad genus naturae, qui tamen non est unus secundum quod refertur ad genus moris, sicut et e converso, ut dictum est. Ambulatio enim continua est unus actus secundum genus naturae, potest tamen contingere quod sint plures

fault. But it is not the result of the fault, but of the fact, and of the obstacle to the reception of a sacrament.

Article 6
Whether one and the same external action can be both good and evil?

Objection 1: It would seem that one and the same external action can be both good and evil. For "movement, if continuous, is one and the same" (Phys. v, 4). But one continuous movement can be both good and bad: for instance, a man may go to church continuously, intending at first vainglory, and afterwards the service of God. Therefore one and the same action can be both good and bad.

Objection 2: Further, according to the Philosopher (Phys. iii, 3), action and passion are one act. But the passion may be good, as Christ's was; and the action evil, as that of the Jews. Therefore one and the same act can be both good and evil.

Objection 3: Further, since a servant is an instrument, as it were, of his master, the servant's action is his master's, just as the action of a tool is the workman's action. But it may happen that the servant's action result from his master's good will, and is therefore good: and from the evil will of the servant, and is therefore evil. Therefore the same action can be both good and evil.

On the contrary, The same thing cannot be the subject of contraries. But good and evil are contraries. Therefore the same action cannot be both good and evil.

I answer that, Nothing hinders a thing from being one, in so far as it is in one genus, and manifold, in so far as it is referred to another genus. Thus a continuous surface is one, considered as in the genus of quantity; and yet it is manifold, considered as to the genus of color, if it be partly white, and partly black. And accordingly, nothing hinders an action from being one, considered in the natural order; whereas it is not one, considered in the moral order; and vice versa, as we have stated above (I-II, q. 20, a. 3, ad 1; q. 18, a. 7, ad 1). For continuous walking is one action, considered in the natural order: but it may resolve itself into many actions,

secundum genus moris, si mutetur ambulantis voluntas, quae est principium actuum moralium. Si ergo accipiatur unus actus prout est in genere moris, impossibile est quod sit bonus et malus bonitate et malitia morali. Si tamen sit unus unitate naturae, et non unitate moris, potest esse bonus et malus.

AD PRIMUM ergo dicendum quod ille motus continuus qui procedit ex diversa intentione, licet sit unus unitate naturae, non est tamen unus unitate moris.

AD SECUNDUM dicendum quod actio et passio pertinent ad genus moris, inquantum habent rationem voluntarii. Et ideo secundum quod diversa voluntate dicuntur voluntaria, secundum hoc sunt duo moraliter, et potest ex una parte inesse bonum, et ex alia malum.

AD TERTIUM dicendum quod actus servi, inquantum procedit ex voluntate servi, non est actus domini, sed solum inquantum procedit ex mandato domini. Unde sic non facit ipsum malum mala voluntas servi.

considered in the moral order, if a change take place in the walker's will, for the will is the principle of moral actions. If therefore we consider one action in the moral order, it is impossible for it to be morally both good and evil. Whereas if it be one as to natural and not moral unity, it can be both good and evil.

Reply to Objection 1: This continual movement which proceeds from various intentions, although it is one in the natural order, is not one in the point of moral unity.

Reply to Objection 2: Action and passion belong to the moral order, in so far as they are voluntary. And therefore in so far as they are voluntary in respect of wills that differ, they are two distinct things, and good can be in one of them while evil is in the other.

Reply to Objection 3: The action of the servant, in so far as it proceeds from the will of the servant, is not the master's action: but only in so far as it proceeds from the master's command. Wherefore the evil will of the servant does not make the action evil in this respect.

Question 21
Of the Consequences of Human Actions by Reason of Their Goodness and Malice

We have now to consider the consequences of human actions by reason of their goodness and malice: and under this head there are four points of inquiry: 1. Whether a human action is right or sinful by reason of its being good or evil? 2. Whether it thereby deserves praise or blame? 3. Whether accordingly, it is meritorious or demeritorious? 4. Whether it is accordingly meritorious or demeritorious before God?

Article 1
Whether a human action is right or sinful, in so far as it is good or evil?

Objection 1: It seems that a human action is not right or sinful, in so far as it is good or evil. For "monsters are the sins of nature" (Phys. ii, 8). But monsters are not actions, but things engendered outside the order of nature. Now things that are produced according to art and reason imitate those that are produced according to nature (Phys. ii, 8). Therefore an action is not sinful by reason of its being inordinate and evil.

Objection 2: Further, sin, as stated in Phys. ii, 8 occurs in nature and art, when the end intended by nature or art is not attained. But the goodness or malice of a human action depends, before all, on the intention of the end, and on its achievement. Therefore it seems that the malice of an action does not make it sinful.

Objection 3: Further, if the malice of an action makes it sinful, it follows that wherever there is evil, there is sin. But this is false: since punishment is not a sin, although it is an evil. Therefore an action is not sinful by reason of its being evil.

On the contrary, As shown above (I-II, q. 19, a. 4), the goodness of a human action depends principally on the Eternal Law: and consequently its malice consists in its being in disaccord with the Eternal Law. But this is the very nature of sin; for Augustine says (Contra Faust. xxii, 27) that "sin is a word,

vel factum, vel concupitum aliquid contra legem aeternam. Ergo actus humanus ex hoc quod est malus, habet rationem peccati.

RESPONDEO dicendum quod malum in plus est quam peccatum, sicut et bonum in plus est quam rectum. Quaelibet enim privatio boni in quocumque constituit rationem mali, sed peccatum proprie consistit in actu qui agitur propter finem aliquem, cum non habet debitum ordinem ad finem illum. Debitus autem ordo ad finem secundum aliquam regulam mensuratur. Quae quidem regula in his quae secundum naturam agunt, est ipsa virtus naturae, quae inclinat in talem finem. Quando ergo actus procedit a virtute naturali secundum naturalem inclinationem in finem, tunc servatur rectitudo in actu, quia medium non exit ab extremis, scilicet actus ab ordine activi principii ad finem. Quando autem a rectitudine tali actus aliquis recedit, tunc incidit ratio peccati. In his vero quae aguntur per voluntatem, regula proxima est ratio humana; regula autem suprema est lex aeterna. Quando ergo actus hominis procedit in finem secundum ordinem rationis et legis aeternae, tunc actus est rectus, quando autem ab hac rectitudine obliquatur, tunc dicitur esse peccatum. Manifestum est autem ex praemissis quod omnis actus voluntarius est malus per hoc quod recedit ab ordine rationis et legis aeternae, et omnis actus bonus concordat rationi et legi aeternae. Unde sequitur quod actus humanus ex hoc quod est bonus vel malus, habeat rationem rectitudinis vel peccati.

AD PRIMUM ergo dicendum quod monstra dicuntur esse peccata, inquantum producta sunt ex peccato in actu naturae existente.

AD SECUNDUM dicendum quod duplex est finis, scilicet ultimus, et propinquus. In peccato autem naturae, deficit quidem actus a fine ultimo, qui est perfectio generati; non tamen deficit a quocumque fine proximo; operatur enim natura aliquid formando. Similiter in peccato voluntatis, semper est defectus ab ultimo fine intento, quia nullus actus voluntarius malus est ordinabilis ad beatitudinem, quae est ultimus finis, licet non deficiat ab aliquo fine proximo, quem voluntas intendit et consequitur. Unde

deed, or desire, in opposition to the Eternal Law." Therefore a human action is sinful by reason of its being evil.

I answer that, Evil is more comprehensive than sin, as also is good than right. For every privation of good, in whatever subject, is an evil: whereas sin consists properly in an action done for a certain end, and lacking due order to that end. Now the due order to an end is measured by some rule. In things that act according to nature, this rule is the natural force that inclines them to that end. When therefore an action proceeds from a natural force, in accord with the natural inclination to an end, then the action is said to be right: since the mean does not exceed its limits, *viz.* the action does not swerve from the order of its active principle to the end. But when an action strays from this rectitude, it comes under the notion of sin. Now in those things that are done by the will, the proximate rule is the human reason, while the supreme rule is the Eternal Law. When, therefore, a human action tends to the end, according to the order of reason and of the Eternal Law, then that action is right: but when it turns aside from that rectitude, then it is said to be a sin. Now it is evident from what has been said (I-II, q. 19, a. 3; a. 4) that every voluntary action that turns aside from the order of reason and of the Eternal Law, is evil, and that every good action is in accord with reason and the Eternal Law. Hence it follows that a human action is right or sinful by reason of its being good or evil.

Reply to Objection 1: Monsters are called sins, inasmuch as they result from a sin in nature's action.

Reply to Objection 2: The end is twofold; the last end, and the proximate end. In the sin of nature, the action does indeed fail in respect of the last end, which is the perfection of the thing generated; but it does not fail in respect of any proximate end whatever; since when nature works it forms something. In like manner, the sin of the will always fails as regards the last end intended, because no voluntary evil action can be ordained to happiness, which is the last end: and yet it does not fail in respect of some proximate end: intended and achieved by the will. Wherefore

etiam cum ipsa intentio huius finis ordinetur ad finem ultimum, in ipsa intentione huiusmodi finis potest inveniri ratio rectitudinis et peccati.

AD TERTIUM dicendum quod unumquodque ordinatur ad finem per actum suum, et ideo ratio peccati, quae consistit in deviatione ab ordine ad finem, proprie consistit in actu. Sed poena respicit personam peccantem, ut in primo dictum est.

also, since the very intention of this end is ordained to the last end, this same intention may be right or sinful.

Reply to Objection 3: Each thing is ordained to its end by its action: and therefore sin, which consists in straying from the order to the end, consists properly in an action. On the other hand, punishment regards the person of the sinner, as was stated in the I, q. 48, a. 5, ad 4; a. 6, ad 3.

ARTICULUS 2

AD SECUNDUM sic proceditur. Videtur quod actus humanus, ex hoc quod est bonus vel malus, non habeat rationem laudabilis vel culpabilis. *Peccatum enim contingit etiam in his quae aguntur a natura,* ut dicitur in II Physic. Sed tamen ea quae sunt naturalia, non sunt laudabilia nec culpabilia, ut dicitur in III Ethic. Ergo actus humanus, ex hoc quod est malus vel peccatum, non habet rationem culpae, et per consequens nec ex hoc quod est bonus, habet rationem laudabilis.

PRAETEREA, sicut contingit peccatum in actibus moralibus, ita et in actibus artis, quia, ut dicitur in II Physic., *peccat grammaticus non recte scribens, et medicus non recte dans potionem.* Sed non culpatur artifex ex hoc quod aliquod malum facit, quia ad industriam artificis pertinet quod possit et bonum opus facere et malum, cum voluerit. Ergo videtur quod etiam actus moralis, ex hoc quod est malus, non habeat rationem culpabilis.

PRAETEREA, Dionysius dicit, in IV cap. de Div. Nom., quod malum est *infirmum et impotens.* Sed infirmitas vel impotentia vel tollit vel diminuit rationem culpae. Non ergo actus humanus est culpabilis ex hoc quod est malus.

SED CONTRA est quod philosophus dicit, quod *laudabilia sunt virtutum opera; vituperabilia autem, vel culpabilia, opera contraria.* Sed actus boni sunt actus virtutis, quia virtus est quae bonum facit habentem, et opus eius bonum reddit, ut dicitur in II Ethic., unde actus oppositi sunt actus mali. Ergo

ARTICLE 2

Whether a human action deserves praise or blame, by reason of its being good or evil?

Objection 1: It would seem that a human action does not deserve praise or blame by reason of its being good or evil. For "sin happens even in things done by nature" (Phys. ii, 8). And yet natural things are not deserving of praise or blame (Ethic. iii, 5). Therefore a human action does not deserve blame, by reason of its being evil or sinful; and, consequently, neither does it deserve praise, by reason of its being good.

Objection 2: Further, just as sin occurs in moral actions, so does it happen in the productions of art: because as stated in Phys. ii, 8 "it is a sin in a grammarian to write badly, and in a doctor to give the wrong medicine." But the artist is not blamed for making something bad: because the artist's work is such, that he can produce a good or a bad thing, just as he lists. Therefore it seems that neither is there any reason for blaming a moral action, in the fact that it is evil.

Objection 3: Further, Dionysius says (Div. Nom. iv) that evil is "weak and incapable." But weakness or inability either takes away or diminishes guilt. Therefore a human action does not incur guilt from being evil.

On the contrary, The Philosopher says (De Virt. et Vit. i) that "virtuous deeds deserve praise, while deeds that are opposed to virtue deserve censure and blame." But good actions are virtuous; because "virtue makes that which has it, good, and makes its action good" (Ethic. ii, 6): wherefore actions opposed to virtue are evil. Therefore a

actus humanus ex hoc quod est bonus vel malus, habet rationem laudabilis vel culpabilis.

RESPONDEO dicendum quod, sicut malum est in plus quam peccatum, ita peccatum est in plus quam culpa. Ex hoc enim dicitur aliquis actus culpabilis vel laudabilis, quod imputatur agenti, nihil enim est aliud laudari vel culpari, quam imputari alicui malitiam vel bonitatem sui actus. Tunc autem actus imputatur agenti, quando est in potestate ipsius, ita quod habeat dominium sui actus. Hoc autem est in omnibus actibus voluntariis, quia per voluntatem homo dominium sui actus habet, ut ex supradictis patet. Unde relinquitur quod bonum vel malum in solis actibus voluntariis constituit rationem laudis vel culpae; in quibus idem est malum, peccatum et culpa.

AD PRIMUM ergo dicendum quod actus naturales non sunt in potestate naturalis agentis, cum natura sit determinata ad unum. Et ideo, licet in actibus naturalibus sit peccatum, non tamen est ibi culpa.

AD SECUNDUM dicendum quod ratio aliter se habet in artificialibus et aliter in moralibus. In artificialibus enim ratio ordinatur ad finem particularem, quod est aliquid per rationem excogitatum. In moralibus autem ordinatur ad finem communem totius humanae vitae. Finis autem particularis ordinatur ad finem communem. Cum ergo peccatum sit per deviationem ab ordine ad finem, ut dictum est, in actu artis contingit dupliciter esse peccatum. Uno modo, per deviationem a fine particulari intento ab artifice, et hoc peccatum erit proprium arti; puta si artifex, intendens facere bonum opus, faciat malum, vel intendens facere malum, faciat bonum. Alio modo, per deviationem a fine communi humanae vitae, et hoc modo dicetur peccare, si intendat facere malum opus, et faciat, per quod alius decipiatur. Sed hoc peccatum non est proprium artificis inquantum artifex, sed inquantum homo est. Unde ex primo peccato culpatur artifex inquantum artifex, sed ex secundo culpatur homo inquantum homo. Sed in moralibus, ubi attenditur ordo rationis ad finem communem

human action deserves praise or blame, through being good or evil.

I answer that, Just as evil is more comprehensive than sin, so is sin more comprehensive than blame. For an action is said to deserve praise or blame, from its being imputed to the agent: since to praise or to blame means nothing else than to impute to someone the malice or goodness of his action. Now an action is imputed to an agent, when it is in his power, so that he has dominion over it: because it is through his will that man has dominion over his actions, as was made clear above (I-II, q. 1, a. 1; a. 2). Hence it follows that good or evil, in voluntary actions alone, renders them worthy of praise or blame: and in such like actions, evil, sin and guilt are one and the same thing.

Reply to Objection 1: Natural actions are not in the power of the natural agent: since the action of nature is determinate. And, therefore, although there be sin in natural actions, there is no blame.

Reply to Objection 2: Reason stands in different relations to the productions of art, and to moral actions. In matters of art, reason is directed to a particular end, which is something devised by reason: whereas in moral matters, it is directed to the general end of all human life. Now a particular end is subordinate to the general end. Since therefore sin is a departure from the order to the end, as stated above (I-II, q. 21, a. 1), sin may occur in two ways, in a production of art. First, by a departure from the particular end intended by the artist: and this sin will be proper to the art; for instance, if an artist produce a bad thing, while intending to produce something good; or produce something good, while intending to produce something bad. Secondly, by a departure from the general end of human life: and then he will be said to sin, if he intend to produce a bad work, and does so in effect, so that another is taken in thereby. But this sin is not proper to the artist as such, but as man. Consequently for the former sin the artist is blamed as an artist; while for the latter he is blamed as a man. On the other hand, in moral matters, where we take into consideration the order of reason to the general end

humanae vitae, semper peccatum et malum attenditur per deviationem ab ordine rationis ad finem communem humanae vitae. Et ideo culpatur ex tali peccato homo et inquantum est homo, et inquantum est moralis. Unde philosophus dicit, in VI Ethic., quod *in arte volens peccans est eligibilior; circa prudentiam autem minus, sicut et in virtutibus moralibus,* quarum prudentia est directiva.

AD TERTIUM dicendum quod illa infirmitas quae est in malis voluntariis, subiacet potestati hominis. Et ideo nec tollit nec diminuit rationem culpae.

of human life, sin and evil are always due to a departure from the order of reason to the general end of human life. Wherefore man is blamed for such a sin, both as man and as a moral being. Hence the Philosopher says (Ethic. vi, 5) that "in art, he who sins voluntarily is preferable; but in prudence, as in the moral virtues," which prudence directs, "he is the reverse."

Reply to Objection 3: Weakness that occurs in voluntary evils, is subject to man's power: wherefore it neither takes away nor diminishes guilt.

ARTICULUS 3

AD TERTIUM sic proceditur. Videtur quod actus humanus non habeat rationem meriti et demeriti, propter suam bonitatem vel malitiam. Meritum enim et demeritum dicitur per ordinem ad retributionem, quae locum solum habet in his quae ad alterum sunt. Sed non omnes actus humani boni vel mali sunt ad alterum, sed quidam sunt ad seipsum. Ergo non omnis actus humanus bonus vel malus habet rationem meriti vel demeriti.

PRAETEREA, nullus meretur poenam vel praemium ex hoc quod disponit ut vult de eo cuius est dominus, sicut si homo destruat rem suam, non punitur, sicut si destrueret rem alterius. Sed homo est dominus suorum actuum. Ergo ex hoc quod bene vel male disponit de suo actu, non meretur poenam vel praemium.

PRAETEREA, ex hoc quod aliquis sibi ipsi acquirit bonum, non meretur ut ei bene fiat ab alio, et eadem ratio est de malis. Sed ipse actus bonus est quoddam bonum et perfectio agentis, actus autem inordinatus est quoddam malum ipsius. Non ergo ex hoc quod homo facit malum actum vel bonum, meretur vel demeretur.

SED CONTRA est quod dicitur Isaiae III, *dicite iusto quoniam bene, quoniam fructum adinventionum suarum comedet. Vae impio in malum, retributio enim manuum eius fiet ei.*

ARTICLE 3
Whether a human action is meritorious or demeritorious in so far as it is good or evil?

Objection 1: It would seem that a human action is not meritorious or demeritorious on account of its goodness or malice. For we speak of merit or demerit in relation to retribution, which has no place save in matters relating to another person. But good or evil actions are not all related to another person, for some are related to the person of the agent. Therefore not every good or evil human action is meritorious or demeritorious.

Objection 2: Further, no one deserves punishment or reward for doing as he chooses with that of which he is master: thus if a man destroys what belongs to him, he is not punished, as if he had destroyed what belongs to another. But man is master of his own actions. Therefore a man does not merit punishment or reward, through putting his action to a good or evil purpose.

Objection 3: Further, if a man acquire some good for himself, he does not on that account deserve to be benefited by another man: and the same applies to evil. Now a good action is itself a kind of good and perfection of the agent: while an inordinate action is his evil. Therefore a man does not merit or demerit, from the fact that he does a good or an evil deed.

On the contrary, It is written (Is. 3:10, 11): "Say to the just man that it is well; for he shall eat the fruit of his doings. Woe to the wicked unto evil; for the reward of his hands shall be given him."

Respondeo dicendum quod meritum et demeritum dicuntur in ordine ad retributionem quae fit secundum iustitiam. Retributio autem secundum iustitiam fit alicui ex eo quod agit in profectum vel nocumentum alterius. Est autem considerandum quod unusquisque in aliqua societate vivens, est aliquo modo pars et membrum totius societatis. Quicumque ergo agit aliquid in bonum vel malum alicuius in societate existentis, hoc redundat in totam societatem sicut qui laedit manum, per consequens laedit hominem. Cum ergo aliquis agit in bonum vel malum alterius singularis personae, cadit ibi dupliciter ratio meriti vel demeriti. Uno modo, secundum quod debetur ei retributio a singulari persona quam iuvat vel offendit. Alio modo, secundum quod debetur ei retributio a toto collegio. Quando vero aliquis ordinat actum suum directe in bonum vel malum totius collegii, debetur ei retributio primo quidem et principaliter a toto collegio, secundario vero, ab omnibus collegii partibus. Cum vero aliquis agit quod in bonum proprium vel malum vergit, etiam debetur ei retributio, inquantum etiam hoc vergit in commune secundum quod ipse est pars collegii, licet non debeatur ei retributio inquantum est bonum vel malum singularis personae, quae est eadem agenti, nisi forte a seipso secundum quandam similitudinem, prout est iustitia hominis ad seipsum. Sic igitur patet quod actus bonus vel malus habet rationem laudabilis vel culpabilis, secundum quod est in potestate voluntatis; rationem vero rectitudinis et peccati, secundum ordinem ad finem; rationem vero meriti et demeriti, secundum retributionem iustitiae ad alterum.

Ad primum ergo dicendum quod quandoque actus hominis boni vel mali, etsi non ordinantur ad bonum vel malum alterius singularis personae, tamen ordinantur ad bonum vel ad malum alterius quod est ipsa communitas.

Ad secundum dicendum quod homo, qui habet dominium sui actus, ipse etiam, inquantum est alterius, scilicet communitatis, cuius est pars meretur aliquid vel demeretur, inquantum actus suos bene vel male disponit,

I answer that, We speak of merit and demerit, in relation to retribution, rendered according to justice. Now, retribution according to justice is rendered to a man, by reason of his having done something to another's advantage or hurt. It must, moreover, be observed that every individual member of a society is, in a fashion, a part and member of the whole society. Wherefore, any good or evil, done to the member of a society, redounds on the whole society: thus, who hurts the hand, hurts the man. When, therefore, anyone does good or evil to another individual, there is a twofold measure of merit or demerit in his action: first, in respect of the retribution owed to him by the individual to whom he has done good or harm; secondly, in respect of the retribution owed to him by the whole of society. Now when a man ordains his action directly for the good or evil of the whole society, retribution is owed to him, before and above all, by the whole society; secondarily, by all the parts of society. Whereas when a man does that which conduces to his own benefit or disadvantage, then again is retribution owed to him, in so far as this too affects the community, forasmuch as he is a part of society: although retribution is not due to him, in so far as it conduces to the good or harm of an individual, who is identical with the agent: unless, perchance, he owe retribution to himself, by a sort of resemblance, in so far as man is said to be just to himself. It is therefore evident that a good or evil action deserves praise or blame, in so far as it is in the power of the will: that it is right or sinful, according as it is ordained to the end; and that its merit or demerit depends on the recompense for justice or injustice towards another.

Reply to Objection 1: A man's good or evil actions, although not ordained to the good or evil of another individual, are nevertheless ordained to the good or evil of another, i.e., the community.

Reply to Objection 2: Man is master of his actions; and yet, in so far as he belongs to another, i.e., the community, of which he forms part, he merits or demerits, inasmuch as he disposes his actions well or ill:

sicut etiam si alia sua, de quibus communitati servire debet, bene vel male dispenset.

AD TERTIUM dicendum quod hoc ipsum bonum vel malum quod aliquis sibi facit per suum actum, redundat in communitatem, ut dictum est.

just as if he were to dispense well or ill other belongings of his, in respect of which he is bound to serve the community.

Reply to Objection 3: This very good or evil, which a man does to himself by his action, redounds to the community, as stated above.

ARTICULUS 4

AD QUARTUM sic proceditur. Videtur quod actus hominis bonus vel malus non habeat rationem meriti vel demeriti per comparationem ad Deum. Quia, ut dictum est, meritum et demeritum importat ordinem ad recompensationem profectus vel damni ad alterum illati. Sed actus hominis bonus vel malus non cedit in aliquem profectum vel damnum ipsius Dei, dicitur enim Iob XXXV, *si peccaveris quid ei nocebis? Porro si iuste egeris, quid donabis ei?* Ergo actus hominis bonus vel malus non habet rationem meriti vel demeriti apud Deum.

PRAETEREA, instrumentum nihil meretur vel demeretur apud eum qui utitur instrumento, quia tota actio instrumenti est utentis ipso. Sed homo in agendo est instrumentum divinae virtutis principaliter ipsum moventis, unde dicitur Isaiae X, *numquid gloriabitur securis contra eum qui secat in ea? Aut exaltabitur serra contra eum a quo trahitur?* Ubi manifeste hominem agentem comparat instrumento. Ergo homo, bene agendo vel male, nihil meretur vel demeretur apud Deum.

PRAETEREA, actus humanus habet rationem meriti vel demeriti, inquantum ordinatur ad alterum. Sed non omnes actus humani ordinantur ad Deum. Ergo non omnes actus boni vel mali habent rationem meriti vel demeriti apud Deum.

SED CONTRA est quod dicitur Eccle. ult., *cuncta quae fiunt adducet Deus in iudicium, sive bonum sit sive malum.* Sed iudicium importat retributionem, respectu cuius meritum et demeritum dicitur. Ergo omnis

ARTICLE 4
Whether a human action is meritorious or demeritorious before God, according as it is good or evil?

Objection 1: It would seem that man's actions, good or evil, are not meritorious or demeritorious in the sight of God. Because, as stated above (I-II, q. 21, a. 3), merit and demerit imply relation to retribution for good or harm done to another. But a man's action, good or evil, does no good or harm to God; for it is written (Job 35:6, 7): "If thou sin, what shalt thou hurt Him? . . . And if thou do justly, what shalt thou give Him?" Therefore a human action, good or evil, is not meritorious or demeritorious in the sight of God.

Objection 2: Further, an instrument acquires no merit or demerit in the sight of him that uses it; because the entire action of the instrument belongs to the user. Now when man acts he is the instrument of the Divine power which is the principal cause of his action; hence it is written (Is. 10:15): "Shall the axe boast itself against him that cutteth with it? Or shall the saw exalt itself against him by whom it is drawn?" where man while acting is evidently compared to an instrument. Therefore man merits or demerits nothing in God's sight, by good or evil deeds.

Objection 3: Further, a human action acquires merit or demerit through being ordained to someone else. But not all human actions are ordained to God. Therefore not every good or evil action acquires merit or demerit in God's sight.

On the contrary, It is written (Eccles. 12:14): "All things that are done, God will bring into judgment . . . whether it be good or evil." Now judgment implies retribution, in respect of which we speak of merit and demerit. Therefore every

actus hominis bonus vel malus habet rationem meriti vel demeriti apud Deum.

RESPONDEO dicendum quod, sicut dictum est, actus alicuius hominis habet rationem meriti vel demeriti, secundum quod ordinatur ad alterum, vel ratione eius, vel ratione communitatis. Utroque autem modo actus nostri boni vel mali habent rationem meriti vel demeriti apud Deum. Ratione quidem ipsius, inquantum est ultimus hominis finis, est autem debitum ut ad finem ultimum omnes actus referantur, ut supra habitum est. Unde qui facit actum malum non referibilem in Deum, non servat honorem Dei, qui ultimo fini debetur. Ex parte vero totius communitatis universi, quia in qualibet communitate ille qui regit communitatem, praecipue habet curam boni communis, unde ad eum pertinet retribuere pro his quae bene vel male fiunt in communitate. Est autem Deus gubernator et rector totius universi, sicut in primo habitum est, et specialiter rationalium creaturarum. Unde manifestum est quod actus humani habent rationem meriti vel demeriti per comparationem ad ipsum, alioquin sequeretur quod Deus non haberet curam de actibus humanis.

AD PRIMUM ergo dicendum quod per actum hominis Deo secundum se nihil potest accrescere vel deperire, sed tamen homo, quantum in se est, aliquid subtrahit Deo, vel ei exhibet, cum servat vel non servat ordinem quem Deus instituit.

AD SECUNDUM dicendum quod homo sic movetur a Deo ut instrumentum, quod tamen non excluditur quin moveat seipsum per liberum arbitrium, ut ex supradictis patet. Et ideo per suum actum meretur vel demeretur apud Deum.

AD TERTIUM dicendum quod homo non ordinatur ad communitatem politicam secundum se totum, et secundum omnia sua, et ideo non oportet quod quilibet actus eius sit meritorius vel demeritorius per ordinem ad communitatem politicam. Sed totum quod homo est, et quod potest et habet, ordinandum est ad Deum, et ideo omnis actus hominis bonus vel malus habet rationem meriti vel demeriti apud Deum, quantum est ex ipsa ratione actus.

human action, both good and evil, acquires merit or demerit in God's sight.

I answer that, A human action, as stated above (I-II, q. 21, a. 3), acquires merit or demerit, through being ordained to someone else, either by reason of himself, or by reason of the community: and in each way, our actions, good and evil, acquire merit or demerit, in the sight of God. On the part of God Himself, inasmuch as He is man's last end; and it is our duty to refer all our actions to the last end, as stated above (I-II, q. 19, a. 10). Consequently, whoever does an evil deed, not referable to God, does not give God the honor due to Him as our last end. On the part of the whole community of the universe, because in every community, he who governs the community, cares, first of all, for the common good; wherefore it is his business to award retribution for such things as are done well or ill in the community. Now God is the governor and ruler of the whole universe, as stated in the I, q. 103, a. 5: and especially of rational creatures. Consequently it is evident that human actions acquire merit or demerit in reference to Him: else it would follow that human actions are no business of God's.

Reply to Objection 1: God in Himself neither gains nor losses anything by the action of man: but man, for his part, takes something from God, or offers something to Him, when he observes or does not observe the order instituted by God.

Reply to Objection 2: Man is so moved, as an instrument, by God, that, at the same time, he moves himself by his free-will, as was explained above (I-II, q. 9, a. 6, ad 3). Consequently, by his action, he acquires merit or demerit in God's sight.

Reply to Objection 3: Man is not ordained to the body politic, according to all that he is and has; and so it does not follow that every action of his acquires merit or demerit in relation to the body politic. But all that man is, and can, and has, must be referred to God: and therefore every action of man, whether good or bad, acquires merit or demerit in the sight of God, as far as the action itself is concerned.

TREATISE ON THE PASSIONS

Question 22
Of the Subject of the Soul's Passions

We must now consider the passions of the soul: first, in general; secondly, in particular. Taking them in general, there are four things to be considered: 1. Their subject: 2. The difference between them: 3. Their mutual relationship: 4. Their malice and goodness. Under the first head there are three points of inquiry: 1. Whether there is any passion in the soul? 2. Whether passion is in the appetitive rather than in the apprehensive part? 3. Whether passion is in the sensitive appetite rather than in the intellectual appetite, which is called the will?

Article 1
Whether any passion is in the soul?

Objection 1: It would seem that there is no passion in the soul. Because passivity belongs to matter. But the soul is not composed of matter and form, as stated in the I, q. 75, a. 5. Therefore there is no passion in the soul.

Objection 2: Further, passion is movement, as is stated in Phys. iii, 3. But the soul is not moved, as is proved in De Anima i, 3. Therefore passion is not in the soul.

Objection 3: Further, passion is the road to corruption; since "every passion, when increased, alters the substance," as is stated in Topic. vi, 6. But the soul is incorruptible. Therefore no passion is in the soul.

On the contrary, The Apostle says (Rom. 7:5): "When we were in the flesh, the passions of sins which were by the law, did the work in our members." Now sins are, properly speaking, in the soul. Therefore passions also, which are described as being "of sins," are in the soul.

I answer that, The word "passive" is used in three ways. First, in a general way, according as whatever receives something is passive, although nothing is taken from it: thus we may say that the air is passive when it is lit up. But this is to be perfected rather than to be passive. Secondly, the word "passive" is employed in its proper sense, when something is received, while something else is taken away: and this happens

dupliciter. Quandoque enim abiicitur id quod non est conveniens rei, sicut cum corpus animalis sanatur, dicitur pati, quia recipit sanitatem, aegritudine abiecta. Alio modo, quando e converso contingit, sicut aegrotare dicitur pati, quia recipitur infirmitas, sanitate abiecta. Et hic est propriissimus modus passionis. Nam pati dicitur ex eo quod aliquid trahitur ad agentem, quod autem recedit ab eo quod est sibi conveniens, maxime videtur ad aliud trahi. Et similiter in I de Generat. dicitur quod, quando ex ignobiliori generatur nobilius, est generatio simpliciter, et corruptio secundum quid, e converso autem quando ex nobiliori ignobilius generatur. Et his tribus modis contingit esse in anima passionem. Nam secundum receptionem tantum dicitur quod *sentire et intelligere est quoddam pati*. Passio autem cum abiectione non est nisi secundum transmutationem corporalem, unde passio proprie dicta non potest competere animae nisi per accidens, inquantum scilicet *compositum* patitur. Sed et in hoc est diversitas, nam quando huiusmodi transmutatio fit in deterius, magis proprie habet rationem passionis, quam quando fit in melius. Unde tristitia magis proprie est passio quam laetitia.

AD PRIMUM igitur dicendum quod pati, secundum quod est cum abiectione et transmutatione, proprium est materiae, unde non invenitur nisi in compositis ex materia et forma. Sed pati prout importat receptionem solam, non est necessarium quod sit materiae, sed potest esse cuiuscumque existentis in potentia. Anima autem, etsi non sit composita ex materia et forma, habet tamen aliquid potentialitatis, secundum quam convenit sibi recipere et pati, secundum quod intelligere pati est, ut dicitur in III de anima.

AD SECUNDUM dicendum quod pati et moveri, etsi non conveniat animae per se, convenit tamen ei per accidens, ut in I de anima dicitur.

AD TERTIUM dicendum quod ratio illa procedit de passione quae est cum transmutatione ad deterius. Et huiusmodi passio

in two ways. For sometimes that which is lost is unsuitable to the thing: thus when an animal's body is healed, and loses sickness. At other times the contrary occurs: thus to ail is to be passive; because the ailment is received and health is lost. And here we have passion in its most proper acceptation. For a thing is said to be passive from its being drawn to the agent: and when a thing recedes from what is suitable to it, then especially does it appear to be drawn to something else. Moreover in De Generat. i, 3 it is stated that when a more excellent thing is generated from a less excellent, we have generation simply, and corruption in a particular respect: whereas the reverse is the case, when from a more excellent thing, a less excellent is generated. In these three ways it happens that passions are in the soul. For in the sense of mere reception, we speak of "feeling and understanding as being a kind of passion" (De Anima i, 5). But passion, accompanied by the loss of something, is only in respect of a bodily transmutation; wherefore passion properly so called cannot be in the soul, save accidentally, in so far, to wit, as the "composite" is passive. But here again we find a difference; because when this transmutation is for the worse, it has more of the nature of a passion, than when it is for the better: hence sorrow is more properly a passion than joy.

Reply to Objection 1: It belongs to matter to be passive in such a way as to lose something and to be transmuted: hence this happens only in those things that are composed of matter and form. But passivity, as implying mere reception, need not be in matter, but can be in anything that is in potentiality. Now, though the soul is not composed of matter and form, yet it has something of potentiality, in respect of which it is competent to receive or to be passive, according as the act of understanding is a kind of passion, as stated in De Anima iii, 4.

Reply to Objection 2: Although it does not belong to the soul in itself to be passive and to be moved, yet it belongs accidentally as stated in De Anima i, 3.

Reply to Objection 3: This argument is true of passion accompanied by transmutation to something worse. And passion, in this sense,

Articulus 2

Ad secundum sic proceditur. Videtur quod passio magis sit in parte animae apprehensiva quam in parte appetitiva. Quod enim est primum in quolibet genere videtur esse maximum eorum quae sunt in genere illo, et causa aliorum, ut dicitur in II Metaphys. Sed passio prius invenitur in parte apprehensiva quam in parte appetitiva, non enim patitur pars appetitiva, nisi passione praecedente in parte apprehensiva. Ergo passio est magis in parte apprehensiva quam in parte appetitiva.

Praeterea, quod est magis activum, videtur esse minus passivum, actio enim passioni opponitur. Sed pars appetitiva est magis activa quam pars apprehensiva. Ergo videtur quod in parte apprehensiva magis sit passio.

Praeterea, sicut appetitus sensitivus est virtus in organo corporali, ita et vis apprehensiva sensitiva. Sed passio animae fit, proprie loquendo, secundum transmutationem corporalem. Ergo non magis est passio in parte appetitiva sensitiva quam in apprehensiva sensitiva.

Sed contra est quod Augustinus dicit, in IX de Civ. Dei, quod *motus animi, quos Graeci pathe, nostri autem quidam, sicut Cicero, perturbationes, quidam affectiones vel affectus, quidam vero, sicut in Graeco habetur, expressius passiones vocant*. Ex quo patet quod passiones animae sunt idem quod affectiones. Sed affectiones manifeste pertinent ad partem appetitivam, et non ad apprehensivam. Ergo et passiones magis sunt in appetitiva quam in apprehensiva.

Respondeo dicendum quod, sicut iam dictum est, in nomine *passionis* importatur quod patiens trahatur ad id quod est

Article 2
Whether passion is in the appetitive rather than in the apprehensive part?

Objection 1: It would seem that passion is in the apprehensive part of the soul rather than in the appetitive. Because that which is first in any genus, seems to rank first among all things that are in that genus, and to be their cause, as is stated in Metaph. ii, 1. Now passion is found to be in the apprehensive, before being in the appetitive part: for the appetitive part is not affected unless there be a previous passion in the apprehensive part. Therefore passion is in the apprehensive part more than in the appetitive.

Objection 2: Further, what is more active is less passive; for action is contrary to passion. Now the appetitive part is more active than the apprehensive part. Therefore it seems that passion is more in the apprehensive part.

Objection 3: Further, just as the sensitive appetite is the power of a corporeal organ, so is the power of sensitive apprehension. But passion in the soul occurs, properly speaking, in respect of a bodily transmutation. Therefore passion is not more in the sensitive appetitive than in the sensitive apprehensive part.

On the contrary, Augustine says (De Civ. Dei ix, 4) that "the movement of the soul, which the Greeks called πάθη [pathe], are styled by some of our writers, Cicero* for instance, disturbances; by some, affections or emotions; while others rendering the Greek more accurately, call them passions." From this it is evident that the passions of the soul are the same as affections. But affections manifestly belong to the appetitive, and not to the apprehensive part. Therefore the passions are in the appetitive rather than in the apprehensive part.

I answer that, As we have already stated (I-II, q. 22, a. 1) the word "passion" implies that the patient is drawn to that which belongs to

---

* Those things which the Greeks call πάθη, we prefer to call disturbances rather than diseases (Tusc. iv. 5).

agentis. Magis autem trahitur anima ad rem per vim appetitivam quam per vim apprehensivam. Nam per vim appetitivam anima habet ordinem ad ipsas res, prout in seipsis sunt, unde philosophus dicit, in VI Metaphys., quod *bonum et malum,* quae sunt obiecta appetitivae potentiae, *sunt in ipsis rebus.* Vis autem apprehensiva non trahitur ad rem, secundum quod in seipsa est; sed cognoscit eam secundum *intentionem* rei, quam in se habet vel recipit secundum proprium modum. Unde et ibidem dicitur quod *verum et falsum,* quae ad cognitionem pertinent, *non sunt in rebus, sed in mente.* Unde patet quod ratio passionis magis invenitur in parte appetitiva quam in parte apprehensiva.

AD PRIMUM ergo dicendum quod e contrario se habet in his quae pertinent ad perfectionem, et in his quae pertinent ad defectum. Nam in his quae ad perfectionem pertinent, attenditur intensio per accessum ad unum primum principium, cui quanto est aliquid propinquius, tanto est magis intensum, sicut intensio lucidi attenditur per accessum ad aliquid summe lucidum, cui quanto aliquid magis appropinquat, tanto est magis lucidum. Sed in his quae ad defectum pertinent, attenditur intensio non per accessum ad aliquod summum, sed per recessum a perfecto, quia in hoc ratio privationis et defectus consistit. Et ideo quanto minus recedit a primo, tanto est minus intensum, et propter hoc, in principio semper invenitur parvus defectus, qui postea procedendo magis multiplicatur. Passio autem ad defectum pertinet, quia est alicuius secundum quod est in potentia. Unde in his quae appropinquant primo perfecto, scilicet Deo, invenitur parum de ratione potentiae et passionis, in aliis autem consequenter, plus. Et sic etiam in priori vi animae, scilicet apprehensiva, invenitur minus de ratione passionis.

AD SECUNDUM dicendum quod vis appetitiva dicitur esse magis activa, quia est magis

the agent. Now the soul is drawn to a thing by the appetitive power rather than by the apprehensive power: because the soul has, through its appetitive power, an order to things as they are in themselves: hence the Philosopher says (Metaph. vi, 4) that "good and evil," i.e., the objects of the appetitive power, "are in things themselves." On the other hand the apprehensive power is not drawn to a thing, as it is in itself; but knows it by reason of an "intention" of the thing, which "intention" it has in itself, or receives in its own way. Hence we find it stated (Metaph. vi, 4) that "the true and the false," which pertain to knowledge, "are not in things, but in the mind." Consequently it is evident that the nature of passion is consistent with the appetitive, rather than with the apprehensive part.

Reply to Objection 1: In things relating to perfection the case is the opposite, in comparison to things that pertain to defect. Because in things relating to perfection, intensity is in proportion to the approach to one first principle; to which the nearer a thing approaches, the more intense it is. Thus the intensity of a thing possessed of light depends on its approach to something endowed with light in a supreme degree, to which the nearer a thing approaches the more light it possesses. But in things that relate to defect, intensity depends, not on approach to something supreme, but in receding from that which is perfect; because therein consists the very notion of privation and defect. Wherefore the less a thing recedes from that which stands first, the less intense it is: and the result is that at first we always find some small defect, which afterwards increases as it goes on. Now passion pertains to defect, because it belongs to a thing according as it is in potentiality. Wherefore in those things that approach to the Supreme Perfection, i.e., to God, there is but little potentiality and passion: while in other things, consequently, there is more. Hence also, in the supreme, i.e., the apprehensive, power of the soul, passion is found less than in the other powers.

Reply to Objection 2: The appetitive power is said to be more active, because it is, more than the apprehensive power, the

principium exterioris actus. Et hoc habet ex hoc ipso ex quo habet quod sit magis passiva, scilicet ex hoc quod habet ordinem ad rem ut est in seipsa, per actionem enim exteriorem pervenimus ad consequendas res.

AD TERTIUM dicendum quod, sicut in primo dictum est, dupliciter organum animae potest transmutari. Uno modo, transmutatione spirituali, secundum quod recipit *intentionem* rei. Et hoc per se invenitur in actu **apprehensivae** virtutis sensitivae, sicut oculus immutatur a visibili, non ita quod coloretur, sed ita quod recipiat intentionem coloris. Est autem alia naturalis transmutatio organi, prout organum transmutatur quantum ad suam naturalem dispositionem, puta quod calefit aut infrigidatur, vel alio simili modo transmutatur. Et huiusmodi transmutatio per accidens se habet ad actum apprehensivae virtutis sensitivae, puta cum oculus fatigatur ex forti intuitu, vel dissolvitur ex vehementia visibilis. Sed ad actum appetitus sensitivi per se ordinatur huiusmodi transmutatio, unde in definitione motuum appetitivae partis, materialiter ponitur aliqua naturalis transmutatio organi; sicut dicitur quod *ira est accensio sanguinis circa cor.* Unde patet quod ratio passionis magis invenitur in actu sensitivae virtutis appetitivae, quam in actu sensitivae virtutis apprehensivae, licet utraque sit actus organi corporalis.

principle of the exterior action: and this for the same reason that it is more passive, namely, its being related to things as existing in themselves: since it is through the external action that we come into contact with things.

Reply to Objection 3: As stated in the I, q. 78, a. 3 the organs of the soul can be changed in two ways. First, by a spiritual change, in respect of which the organ receives an "intention" of the object. And this is essential to **the act of the sensitive apprehension: thus is** the eye changed by the object visible, not by being colored, but by receiving an intention of color. But the organs are receptive of another and natural change, which affects their natural disposition; for instance, when they become hot or cold, or undergo some similar change. And whereas this kind of change is accidental to the act of the sensitive apprehension; for instance, if the eye be wearied through gazing intently at something or be overcome by the intensity of the object: on the other hand, it is essential to the act of the sensitive appetite; wherefore the material element in the definitions of the movements of the appetitive part, is the natural change of the organ; for instance, "anger is" said to be "a kindling of the blood about the heart." Hence it is evident that the notion of passion is more consistent with the act of the sensitive appetite, than with that of the sensitive apprehension, although both are actions of a corporeal organ.

ARTICULUS 3

ARTICLE 3
Whether passion is in the sensitive appetite rather than in the intellectual appetite, which is called the will?

AD TERTIUM sic proceditur. Videtur quod passio non magis sit in appetitu sensitivo quam in appetitu intellectivo. Dicit enim Dionysius, II cap. de Div. Nom., quod Hierotheus *ex quadam est doctus diviniore inspiratione, non solum discens, sed etiam patiens divina.* Sed *passio* divinorum non potest pertinere ad appetitum sensitivum, cuius obiectum est bonum sensibile. Ergo passio est in appetitu intellectivo, sicut et in sensitivo.

Objection 1: It would seem that passion is not more in the sensitive than in the intellectual appetite. For Dionysius declares (Div. Nom. ii) Hierotheus "to be taught by a kind of yet more Godlike instruction; not only by learning Divine things, but also by suffering [*patiens*] them." But the sensitive appetite cannot "suffer" Divine things, since its object is the sensible good. Therefore passion is in the intellectual appetite, just as it is also in the sensitive appetite.

PRAETEREA, quanto activum est potentius, tanto passio est fortior. Sed obiectum appetitus intellectivi, quod est bonum universale, est potentius activum quam obiectum appetitus sensitivi, quod est bonum particulare. Ergo ratio passionis magis invenitur in appetitu intellectivo quam in appetitu sensitivo.

PRAETEREA, gaudium et amor passiones quaedam esse dicuntur. Sed haec inveniuntur in appetitu intellectivo, et non solum in sensitivo, alioquin non attribuerentur in Scripturis Deo et angelis. Ergo passiones non magis sunt in appetitu sensitivo quam in intellectivo.

SED CONTRA est quod dicit Damascenus, in II libro, describens animales passiones, *passio est motus appetitivae virtutis sensibilis in imaginatione boni vel mali. Et aliter, passio est motus irrationalis animae per suspicionem boni vel mali.*

RESPONDEO dicendum quod, sicut iam dictum est, passio proprie invenitur ubi est transmutatio corporalis. Quae quidem invenitur in actibus appetitus sensitivi; et non solum spiritualis, sicut est in apprehensione sensitiva, sed etiam naturalis. In actu autem appetitus intellectivi non requiritur aliqua transmutatio corporalis, quia huiusmodi appetitus non est virtus alicuius organi. Unde patet quod ratio passionis magis proprie invenitur in actu appetitus sensitivi quam intellectivi; ut etiam patet per definitiones Damasceni inductas.

AD PRIMUM ergo dicendum quod *passio divinorum* ibi dicitur affectio ad divina, et coniunctio ad ipsa per amorem, quod tamen fit sine transmutatione corporali.

AD SECUNDUM dicendum quod magnitudo passionis non solum dependet ex virtute agentis, sed etiam ex passibilitate patientis, quia quae sunt bene passibilia, multum patiuntur etiam a parvis activis. Licet ergo obiectum appetitus intellectivi sit magis activum quam obiectum appetitus sensitivi, tamen appetitus sensitivus est magis passivus.

Objection 2: Further, the more powerful the active force, the more intense the passion. But the object of the intellectual appetite, which is the universal good, is a more powerful active force than the object of the sensitive appetite, which is a particular good. Therefore passion is more consistent with the intellectual than with the sensitive appetite.

Objection 3: Further, joy and love are said to be passions. But these are to be found in the intellectual and not only in the sensitive appetite: else they would not be ascribed by the Scriptures to God and the angels. Therefore the passions are not more in the sensitive than in the intellectual appetite.

On the contrary, Damascene says (De Fide Orth. ii, 22), while describing the animal passions: "Passion is a movement of the sensitive appetite when we imagine good or evil: in other words, passion is a movement of the irrational soul, when we think of good or evil."

I answer that, As stated above (I-II, q. 22, a. 1) passion is properly to be found where there is corporeal transmutation. This corporeal transmutation is found in the act of the sensitive appetite, and is not only spiritual, as in the sensitive apprehension, but also natural. Now there is no need for corporeal transmutation in the act of the intellectual appetite: because this appetite is not exercised by means of a corporeal organ. It is therefore evident that passion is more properly in the act of the sensitive appetite, than in that of the intellectual appetite; and this is again evident from the definitions of Damascene quoted above.

Reply to Objection 1: By "suffering" Divine things is meant being well affected towards them, and united to them by love: and this takes place without any alteration in the body.

Reply to Objection 2: Intensity of passion depends not only on the power of the agent, but also on the passibility of the patient: because things that are disposed to passion, suffer much even from petty agents. Therefore although the object of the intellectual appetite has greater activity than the object of the sensitive appetite, yet the sensitive appetite is more passive.

AD TERTIUM dicendum quod amor et gaudium et alia huiusmodi, cum attribuuntur Deo vel angelis, aut hominibus secundum appetitum intellectivum, significant simplicem actum voluntatis cum similitudine effectus, absque passione. Unde dicit Augustinus, IX de Civ. Dei, *sancti angeli et sine ira puniunt et sine miseriae compassione subveniunt. Et tamen, istarum nomina passionum, consuetudine locutionis humanae, etiam in eos usurpantur, propter quandam operum similitudinem, non propter affectionum infirmitatem.*

Reply to Objection 3: When love and joy and the like are ascribed to God or the angels, or to man in respect of his intellectual appetite, they signify simple acts of the will having like effects, but without passion. Hence Augustine says (De Civ. Dei ix, 5): "The holy angels feel no anger while they punish . . . no fellow-feeling with misery while they relieve the unhappy: and yet ordinary human speech is wont to ascribe to them also these passions by name, because, although they have none of our weakness, their acts bear a certain resemblance to ours."

Quaestio XXIII

Deinde considerandum est de passionum differentia ad invicem. Et circa hoc quaeruntur quatuor. *Primo,* utrum passiones quae sunt in concupiscibili, sint diversae ab his quae sunt in irascibili. *Secundo,* utrum contrarietas passionum irascibili sit secundum contrarietatem boni et mali. *Tertio,* utrum sit aliqua passio non habens contrarium. *Quarto,* utrum sint aliquae passiones differentes specie, in eadem potentia, non contrariae ad invicem.

Question 23
How the Passions Differ from One Another

We must now consider how the passions differ from one another: and under this head there are four points of inquiry: 1. Whether the passions of the concupiscible part are different from those of the irascible part? 2. Whether the contrariety of passions in the irascible part is based on the contrariety of good and evil? 3. Whether there is any passion that has no contrary? 4. Whether, in the same power, there are any passions, differing in species, but not contrary to one another?

Articulus 1

Article 1
Whether the passions of the concupiscible part are different from those of the irascible part?

AD PRIMUM sic proceditur. Videtur quod passiones eaedem sint in irascibili et in concupiscibili. Dicit enim philosophus, in II Ethic., quod passiones animae sunt *quas sequitur gaudium et tristitia.* Sed gaudium et tristitia sunt in concupiscibili. Ergo omnes passiones sunt in concupiscibili. Non ergo sunt aliae in irascibili, et aliae in concupiscibili.

Objection 1: It would seem that the same passions are in the irascible and concupiscible parts. For the Philosopher says (Ethic. ii, 5) that the passions of the soul are those emotions "which are followed by joy or sorrow." But joy and sorrow are in the concupiscible part. Therefore all the passions are in the concupiscible part, and not some in the irascible, others in the concupiscible part.

PRAETEREA, Matth. XIII, super illud, *simile est regnum caelorum fermento* etc., dicit Glossa Hieronymi, *in ratione possideamus prudentiam, in irascibili odium vitiorum, in concupiscibili desiderium virtutum.* Sed

Objection 2: Further, on the words of Mat. 13:33, "The kingdom of heaven is like to leaven," etc., Jerome's gloss says: "We should have prudence in the reason; hatred of vice in the irascible faculty; desire of virtue, in the concupiscible part." But

odium est in concupiscibili, sicut et amor, cui contrariatur, ut dicitur in II Topic. Ergo eadem passio est in concupiscibili et irascibili.

PRAETEREA, passiones et actus differunt specie secundum obiecta. Sed passionum irascibilis et concupiscibilis eadem obiecta sunt, scilicet bonum et malum. Ergo eaedem sunt passiones irascibilis et concupiscibilis.

SED CONTRA, diversarum potentiarum actus sunt specie diversi, sicut videre et audire. Sed irascibilis et concupiscibilis sunt duae potentiae dividentes appetitum sensitivum, ut in primo dictum est. Ergo, cum passiones sint motus appetitus sensitivi, ut supra dictum est, passiones quae sunt in irascibili, erunt aliae secundum speciem a passionibus quae sunt in concupiscibili.

RESPONDEO dicendum quod passiones quae sunt in irascibili et in concupiscibili, differunt specie. Cum enim diversae potentiae habeant diversa obiecta, ut in primo dictum est, necesse est quod passiones diversarum potentiarum ad diversa obiecta referantur. Unde multo magis passiones diversarum potentiarum specie differunt, maior enim differentia obiecti requiritur ad diversificandam speciem potentiarum, quam ad diversificandam speciem passionum vel actuum. Sicut enim in naturalibus diversitas generis consequitur diversitatem potentiae materiae, diversitas autem speciei diversitatem formae in eadem materia; ita in actibus animae, actus ad diversas potentias pertinentes, sunt non solum specie, sed etiam genere diversi; actus autem vel passiones respicientes diversa obiecta specialia comprehensa sub uno communi obiecto unius potentiae, differunt sicut species illius generis. Ad cognoscendum ergo quae passiones sint in irascibili, et quae in concupiscibili, oportet assumere obiectum utriusque potentiae. Dictum est autem in primo quod obiectum potentiae concupiscibilis est bonum vel malum sensibile simpliciter acceptum, quod est delectabile vel dolorosum. Sed quia necesse est quod interdum anima difficultatem vel pugnam patiatur in adipiscendo aliquod huiusmodi bonum, vel

hatred is in the concupiscible faculty, as also is love, of which it is the contrary, as is stated in Topic. ii, 7. Therefore the same passion is in the concupiscible and irascible faculties.

Objection 3: Further, passions and actions differ specifically according to their objects. But the objects of the irascible and concupiscible passions are the same, *viz.* good and evil. Therefore the same passions are in the irascible and concupiscible faculties.

On the contrary, The acts of the different powers differ in species; for instance, to see, and to hear. But the irascible and the concupiscible are two powers into which the sensitive appetite is divided, as stated in the I, q. 81, a. 2. Therefore, since the passions are movements of the sensitive appetite, as stated above (I-II, q. 22, a. 3), the passions of the irascible faculty are specifically distinct from those of the concupiscible part.

I answer that, The passions of the irascible part differ in species from those of the concupiscible faculty. For since different powers have different objects, as stated in the I, q. 77, a. 3, the passions of different powers must of necessity be referred to different objects. Much more, therefore, do the passions of different faculties differ in species; since a greater difference in the object is required to diversify the species of the powers, than to diversify the species of passions or actions. For just as in the physical order, diversity of genus arises from diversity in the potentiality of matter, while diversity of species arises from diversity of form in the same matter; so in the acts of the soul, those that belong to different powers, differ not only in species but also in genus, while acts and passions regarding different specific objects, included under the one common object of a single power, differ as the species of that genus. In order, therefore, to discern which passions are in the irascible, and which in the concupiscible, we must take the object of each of these powers. For we have stated in the I, q. 81, a. 2, that the object of the concupiscible power is sensible good or evil, simply apprehended as such, which causes pleasure or pain. But, since the soul must, of necessity, experience difficulty or struggle at times, in acquiring some such good, or

fugiendo aliquod huiusmodi malum, inquantum hoc est quodammodo elevatum supra facilem potestatem animalis; ideo ipsum bonum vel malum, secundum quod habet rationem ardui vel difficilis, est obiectum irascibilis. Quaecumque ergo passiones respiciunt absolute bonum vel malum, pertinent ad concupiscibilem; ut gaudium, tristitia, amor, odium, et similia. Quaecumque vero passiones respiciunt bonum vel malum sub ratione ardui, prout est aliquid adipiscibile vel fugibile cum aliqua difficultate, pertinent ad irascibilem; ut audacia, timor, spes, et huiusmodi.

Ad primum ergo dicendum quod, sicut in primo dictum est, ad hoc vis irascibilis data est animalibus, ut tollantur impedimenta quibus concupiscibilis in suum obiectum tendere prohibetur, vel propter difficultatem boni adipiscendi, vel propter difficultatem mali superandi. Et ideo passiones irascibilis omnes terminantur ad passiones concupiscibilis. Et secundum hoc, etiam passiones quae sunt in irascibili, consequitur gaudium et tristitia, quae sunt in concupiscibili.

Ad secundum dicendum quod odium vitiorum attribuit Hieronymus irascibili, non propter rationem odii, quae proprie competit concupiscibili; sed propter impugnationem, quae pertinet ad irascibilem.

Ad tertium dicendum quod bonum inquantum est delectabile, movet concupiscibilem. Sed si bonum habeat quandam difficultatem ad adipiscendum, ex hoc ipso habet aliquid repugnans concupiscibili. Et ideo necessarium fuit esse aliam potentiam quae in id tenderet. Et eadem ratio est de malis. Et haec potentia est irascibilis. Unde ex consequenti passiones concupiscibilis et irascibilis specie differunt.

Articulus 2

Ad secundum sic proceditur. Videtur quod contrarietas passionum irascibilis non sit nisi secundum contrarietatem boni et mali. Passiones enim irascibilis ordinantur ad passiones concupiscibilis, ut dictum est.

in avoiding some such evil, in so far as such good or evil is more than our animal nature can easily acquire or avoid; therefore this very good or evil, inasmuch as it is of an arduous or difficult nature, is the object of the irascible faculty. Therefore whatever passions regard good or evil absolutely, belong to the concupiscible power; for instance, joy, sorrow, love, hatred, and such like: whereas those passions which regard good or bad as arduous, through being difficult to obtain or avoid, belong to the irascible faculty; such are daring, fear, hope and the like.

Reply to Objection 1: As stated in the I, q. 81, a. 2, the irascible faculty is bestowed on animals, in order to remove the obstacles that hinder the concupiscible power from tending towards its object, either by making some good difficult to obtain, or by making some evil hard to avoid. The result is that all the irascible passions terminate in the concupiscible passions: and thus it is that even the passions which are in the irascible faculty are followed by joy and sadness which are in the concupiscible faculty.

Reply to Objection 2: Jerome ascribes hatred of vice to the irascible faculty, not by reason of hatred, which is properly a concupiscible passion; but on account of the struggle, which belongs to the irascible power.

Reply to Objection 3: Good, inasmuch as it is delightful, moves the concupiscible power. But if it prove difficult to obtain, from this very fact it has a certain contrariety to the concupiscible power: and hence the need of another power tending to that good. The same applies to evil. And this power is the irascible faculty. Consequently the concupiscible passions are specifically different from the irascible passions.

Article 2
Whether the contrariety of the irascible passions is based on the contrariety of good and evil?

Objection 1: It would seem that the contrariety of the irascible passions is based on no other contrariety than that of good and evil. For the irascible passions are ordained to the concupiscible passions, as stated above

Sed passiones concupiscibilis non contrariantur nisi secundum contrarietatem boni et mali; sicut amor et odium, gaudium et tristitia. Ergo nec passiones irascibilis.

PRAETEREA, passiones differunt secundum obiecta; sicut et motus secundum terminos. Sed contrarietas non est in motibus nisi secundum contrarietatem terminorum, ut patet in V Physic. Ergo neque in passionibus est contrarietas nisi secundum contrarietatem obiectorum. Obiectum autem appetitus est bonum vel malum. Ergo in nulla potentia appetitiva potest esse contrarietas passionum nisi secundum contrarietatem boni et mali.

PRAETEREA, *omnis passio animae attenditur secundum accessum et recessum,* ut Avicenna dicit, in sexto de naturalibus. Sed accessus causatur ex ratione boni, recessus autem ex ratione mali, quia sicut *bonum est quod omnia appetunt,* ut dicitur in I Ethic., ita malum est quod omnia fugiunt. Ergo contrarietas in passionibus animae non potest esse nisi secundum bonum et malum.

SED CONTRA, timor et audacia sunt contraria, ut patet in III Ethic. sed timor et audacia non differunt secundum bonum et malum, quia utrumque est respectu aliquorum malorum. Ergo non omnis contrarietas passionum irascibilis est secundum contrarietatem boni et mali.

RESPONDEO dicendum quod passio quidam motus est, ut dicitur in III Physic. Unde oportet contrarietatem passionum accipere secundum contrarietatem motuum vel mutationum. Est autem duplex contrarietas in mutationibus vel motibus, ut dicitur in V Physic. Una quidem secundum accessum et recessum ab eodem termino, quae quidem contrarietas est proprie mutationum, idest generationis, quae est mutatio *ad esse,* et corruptionis, quae est mutatio *ab esse.* Alia autem secundum contrarietatem terminorum, quae proprie est contrarietas motuum, sicut dealbatio, quae est motus a nigro in album, opponitur denigrationi, quae est motus ab albo in nigrum. Sic igitur in passionibus animae duplex contrarietas invenitur, una quidem secundum contrarietatem

(I-II, q. 23, a. 1, ad 1). But the contrariety of the concupiscible passions is no other than that of good and evil; take, for instance, love and hatred, joy and sorrow. Therefore the same applies to the irascible passions.

Objection 2: Further, passions differ according to their objects; just as movements differ according to their termini. But there is no other contrariety of movements, except that of the termini, as is stated in Phys. v, 3. Therefore there is no other contrariety of passions, save that of the objects. Now the object of the appetite is good or evil. Therefore in no appetitive power can there be contrariety of passions other than that of good and evil.

Objection 3: Further, "every passion of the soul is by way of approach and withdrawal," as Avicenna declares in his sixth book of Physics. Now approach results from the apprehension of good; withdrawal, from the apprehension of evil: since just as "good is what all desire" (Ethic. i, 1), so evil is what all shun. Therefore, in the passions of the soul, there can be no other contrariety than that of good and evil.

On the contrary, Fear and daring are contrary to one another, as stated in Ethic. iii, 7. But fear and daring do not differ in respect of good and evil: because each regards some kind of evil. Therefore not every contrariety of the irascible passions is that of good and evil.

I answer that, Passion is a kind of movement, as stated in Phys. iii, 3. Therefore contrariety of passions is based on contrariety of movements or changes. Now there is a twofold contrariety in changes and movements, as stated in Phys. v, 5. One is according to approach and withdrawal in respect of the same term: and this contrariety belongs properly to changes, i.e., to generation, which is a change "to being," and to corruption, which is a change "from being." The other contrariety is according to opposition of termini, and belongs properly to movements: thus whitening, which is movement from black to white, is contrary to blackening, which is movement from white to black. Accordingly there is a twofold contrariety in the passions of the soul: one, according to contrariety of

obiectorum, scilicet boni et mali; alia vero secundum accessum et recessum ab eodem termino. In passionibus quidem concupiscibilis invenitur prima contrarietas tantum, quae scilicet est secundum obiecta, in passionibus autem irascibilis invenitur utraque. Cuius ratio est quia obiectum concupiscibilis, ut supra dictum est, est bonum vel malum sensibile absolute. Bonum autem, inquantum bonum, non potest esse terminus ut a quo, **sed solum ut ad quem, quia nihil refugit bonum inquantum bonum, sed omnia appetunt** ipsum. Similiter nihil appetit malum inquantum huiusmodi, sed omnia fugiunt ipsum, et propter hoc, malum non habet rationem termini ad quem, sed solum termini a quo. Sic igitur omnis passio concupiscibilis respectu boni, est ut in ipsum, sicut amor, desiderium et gaudium, omnis vero passio eius respectu mali, est ut ab ipso, sicut odium, fuga seu abominatio, et tristitia. Unde in passionibus concupiscibilis non potest esse contrarietas secundum accessum et recessum ab eodem obiecto. Sed obiectum irascibilis est sensibile bonum vel malum, non quidem absolute, sed sub ratione difficultatis vel arduitatis, ut supra dictum est. Bonum autem arduum sive difficile habet rationem ut in ipsum tendatur, inquantum est bonum, quod pertinet ad passionem *spei;* et ut ab ipso recedatur, inquantum est arduum vel difficile, quod pertinet ad passionem *desperationis*. Similiter malum arduum habet rationem ut vitetur, inquantum est malum, et hoc pertinet ad passionem *timoris,* habet etiam rationem ut in ipsum tendatur, sicut in quoddam arduum, per quod scilicet aliquid evadit subiectionem mali, et sic tendit in ipsum *audacia*. Invenitur ergo in passionibus irascibilis contrarietas secundum contrarietatem boni et mali, sicut inter spem et timorem, et iterum secundum accessum et recessum ab eodem termino, sicut inter audaciam et timorem.

Et per hoc patet responsio ad obiecta.

objects, i.e., of good and evil; the other, according to approach and withdrawal in respect of the same term. In the concupiscible passions the former contrariety alone is to be found; *viz.* that which is based on the objects: whereas in the irascible passions, we find both forms of contrariety. The reason of this is that the object of the concupiscible faculty, as stated above (I-II, q. 23, a. 1), is sensible good or evil considered absolutely. Now **good, as such, cannot be a term wherefrom,** but only a term whereto, since nothing shuns good as such; on the contrary, all things desire it. In like manner, nothing desires evil, as such; but all things shun it: wherefore evil cannot have the aspect of a term whereto, but only of a term wherefrom. Accordingly every concupiscible passion in respect of good, tends to it, as love, desire and joy; while every concupiscible passion in respect of evil, tends from it, as hatred, avoidance or dislike, and sorrow. Wherefore, in the concupiscible passions, there can be no contrariety of approach and withdrawal in respect of the same object. On the other hand, the object of the irascible faculty is sensible good or evil, considered not absolutely, but under the aspect of difficulty or arduousness. Now the good which is difficult or arduous, considered as good, is of such a nature as to produce in us a tendency to it, which tendency pertains to the passion of "hope"; whereas, considered as arduous or difficult, it makes us turn from it; and this pertains to the passion of "despair." In like manner the arduous evil, considered as an evil, has the aspect of something to be shunned; and this belongs to the passion of "fear": but it also contains a reason for tending to it, as attempting something arduous, whereby to escape being subject to evil; and this tendency is called "daring." Consequently, in the irascible passions we find contrariety in respect of good and evil (as between hope and fear): and also contrariety according to approach and withdrawal in respect of the same term (as between daring and fear).

From what has been said the replies to the objections are evident.

Articulus 3

Ad tertium sic proceditur. Videtur quod omnis passio animae habeat aliquid contrarium. Omnis enim passio animae vel est in irascibili vel in concupiscibili, sicut supra dictum est. Sed utraeque passiones habent contrarietatem suo modo. Ergo omnis passio animae habet contrarium.

Praeterea, omnis passio animae habet vel bonum vel malum pro obiecto, quae sunt obiecta universaliter appetitivae partis. Sed passioni cuius obiectum est bonum, opponitur passio cuius obiectum est malum. Ergo omnis passio habet contrarium.

Praeterea, omnis passio animae est secundum accessum vel secundum recessum, ut dictum est. Sed cuilibet accessui contrariatur recessus, et e converso. Ergo omnis passio animae habet contrarium.

Sed contra, ira est quaedam passio animae. Sed nulla passio ponitur contraria irae, ut patet in IV Ethic. Ergo non omnis passio habet contrarium.

Respondeo dicendum quod singulare est in passione irae, quod non potest habere contrarium, neque secundum accessum et recessum, neque secundum contrarietatem boni et mali. Causatur enim ira ex malo difficili iam iniacente. Ad cuius praesentiam, necesse est quod aut appetitus succumbat, et sic non exit terminos *tristitiae,* quae est passio concupiscibilis, aut habet motum ad invadendum malum laesivum, quod pertinet ad *iram.* Motum autem ad fugiendum habere non potest, quia iam malum ponitur praesens vel praeteritum. Et sic motui irae non contrariatur aliqua passio secundum contrarietatem accessus et recessus. Similiter etiam nec secundum contrarietatem boni et mali. Quia malo iam iniacenti opponitur bonum iam adeptum, quod iam non potest habere rationem ardui vel difficilis. Nec post adeptionem boni remanet alius motus, nisi quietatio appetitus in bono

Article 3
Whether any passion of the soul has no contrariety?

Objection 1: It would seem that every passion of the soul has a contrary. For every passion of the soul is either in the irascible or in the concupiscible faculty, as stated above (I-II, q. 23, a. 1). But both kinds of passion have their respective modes of contrariety. Therefore every passion of the soul has its contrary.

Objection 2: Further, every passion of the soul has either good or evil for its object; for these are the common objects of the appetitive part. But a passion having good for its object, is contrary to a passion having evil for its object. Therefore every passion has a contrary.

Objection 3: Further, every passion of the soul is in respect of approach or withdrawal, as stated above (I-II, q. 23, a. 2). But every approach has a corresponding contrary withdrawal, and vice versa. Therefore every passion of the soul has a contrary.

On the contrary, Anger is a passion of the soul. But no passion is set down as being contrary to anger, as stated in Ethic. iv, 5. Therefore not every passion has a contrary.

I answer that, The passion of anger is peculiar in this, that it cannot have a contrary, either according to approach and withdrawal, or according to the contrariety of good and evil. For anger is caused by a difficult evil already present: and when such an evil is present, the appetite must needs either succumb, so that it does not go beyond the limits of "sadness," which is a concupiscible passion; or else it has a movement of attack on the hurtful evil, which movement is that of "anger." But it cannot have a movement of withdrawal: because the evil is supposed to be already present or past. Thus no passion is contrary to anger according to contrariety of approach and withdrawal. In like manner neither can there be according to contrariety of good and evil. Because the opposite of present evil is good obtained, which can be no longer have the aspect of arduousness or difficulty. Nor, when once good is obtained, does there remain any other movement, except the appetite's repose in the good

adepto, quae pertinet ad gaudium, quod est passio concupiscibilis. Unde motus irae non potest habere aliquem motum animae contrarium, sed solummodo opponitur ei cessatio a motu, sicut philosophus dicit, in sua rhetorica, quod *mitescere opponitur ei quod est irasci,* quod non est oppositum contrarie, sed negative vel privative.

Et per hoc patet responsio ad obiecta.

obtained; which repose belongs to joy, which is a passion of the concupiscible faculty. Accordingly no movement of the soul can be contrary to the movement of anger, and nothing else than cessation from its movement is contrary thereto; thus the Philosopher says (Rhet. ii, 3) that "calm is contrary to anger," by opposition not of contrariety but of negation or privation.

From what has been said the replies to the objections are evident.

Articulus 4

Ad quartum sic proceditur. Videtur quod non possint in aliqua potentia esse passiones specie differentes, et non contrariae ad invicem. Passiones enim animae differunt secundum obiecta. Obiecta autem passionum animae sunt bonum et malum, secundum quorum differentiam passiones habent contrarietatem. Ergo nullae passiones eiusdem potentiae, non habentes contrarietatem ad invicem, differunt specie.

Praeterea, differentia speciei est differentia secundum formam. Sed omnis differentia secundum formam, est secundum aliquam contrarietatem, ut dicitur in X Metaphys. Ergo passiones eiusdem potentiae quae non sunt contrariae, non differunt specie.

Praeterea, cum omnis passio animae consistat in accessu vel recessu ad bonum vel ad malum, necesse videtur quod omnis differentia passionum animae sit vel secundum differentiam boni et mali; vel secundum differentiam accessus et recessus; vel secundum maiorem vel minorem accessum aut recessum. Sed primae duae differentiae inducunt contrarietatem in passionibus animae, ut dictum est. Tertia autem differentia non diversificat speciem, quia sic essent infinitae species passionum animae. Ergo non potest esse quod passiones eiusdem potentiae animae differant specie, et non sint contrariae.

Article 4
Whether in the same power, there are any passions, specifically different, but not contrary to one another?

Objection 1: It would seem that there cannot be, in the same power, specifically different passions that are not contrary to one another. For the passions of the soul differ according to their objects. Now the objects of the soul's passions are good and evil; and on this distinction is based the contrariety of the passions. Therefore no passions of the same power, that are not contrary to one another, differ specifically.

Objection 2: Further, difference of species implies a difference of form. But every difference of form is in respect of some contrariety, as stated in Metaph. x, 8. Therefore passions of the same power, that are not contrary to one another, do not differ specifically.

Objection 3: Further, since every passion of the soul consists in approach or withdrawal in respect of good or evil, it seems that every difference in the passions of the soul must needs arise from the difference of good and evil; or from the difference of approach and withdrawal; or from degrees in approach or withdrawal. Now the first two differences cause contrariety in the passions of the soul, as stated above (I-II, q. 23, a. 2) whereas the third difference does not diversify the species; else the species of the soul's passions would be infinite. Therefore it is not possible for passions of the same power to differ in species, without being contrary to one another.

SED CONTRA, amor et gaudium differunt specie, et sunt in concupiscibili. Nec tamen contrariantur ad invicem, quin potius unum est causa alterius. Ergo sunt aliquae passiones eiusdem potentiae quae differunt specie, nec sunt contrariae.

RESPONDEO dicendum quod passiones differunt secundum activa, quae sunt obiecta passionum animae. Differentia autem activorum potest attendi dupliciter, uno modo, secundum speciem vel naturam ipsorum activorum, sicut ignis differt ab aqua; alio modo, secundum diversam virtutem activam. Diversitas autem activi vel motivi quantum ad virtutem movendi, potest accipi in passionibus animae secundum similitudinem agentium naturalium. Omne enim movens trahit quodammodo ad se patiens, vel a se repellit. Trahendo quidem ad se, tria facit in ipso. Nam primo quidem, dat ei inclinationem vel aptitudinem ut in ipsum tendat, sicut cum corpus leve, quod est sursum, dat levitatem corpori generato, per quam habet inclinationem vel aptitudinem ad hoc quod sit sursum. Secundo, si corpus generatum est extra locum proprium, dat ei moveri ad locum. Tertio, dat ei quiescere, in locum cum pervenerit, quia ex eadem causa aliquid quiescit in loco, per quam movebatur ad locum. Et similiter intelligendum est de causa repulsionis. In motibus autem appetitivae partis, bonum habet quasi virtutem attractivam, malum autem virtutem repulsivam. Bonum ergo primo quidem in potentia appetitiva causat quandam inclinationem, seu aptitudinem, seu connaturalitatem ad bonum, quod pertinet ad passionem *amoris.* Cui per contrarium respondet *odium,* ex parte mali. Secundo, si bonum sit nondum habitum, dat ei motum ad assequendum bonum amatum, et hoc pertinet ad passionem *desiderii* vel *concupiscentiae.* Et ex opposito, ex parte mali, est *fuga* vel *abominatio.* Tertio, cum adeptum fuerit bonum, dat appetitus quietationem quandam in ipso bono adepto, et hoc

On the contrary, Love and joy differ in species, and are in the concupiscible power; and yet they are not contrary to one another; rather, in fact, one causes the other. Therefore in the same power there are passions that differ in species without being contrary to one another.

I answer that, Passions differ in accordance with their active causes, which, in the case of the passions of the soul, are their objects. Now, the difference in active causes may be considered in two ways: first, from the point of view of their species or nature, as fire differs from water; secondly, from the point of view of the difference in their active power. In the passions of the soul we can treat the difference of their active or motive causes in respect of their motive power, as if they were natural agents. For every mover, in a fashion, either draws the patient to itself, or repels it from itself. Now in drawing it to itself, it does three things in the patient. Because, in the first place, it gives the patient an inclination or aptitude to tend to the mover: thus a light body, which is above, bestows lightness on the body generated, so that it has an inclination or aptitude to be above. Secondly, if the generated body be outside its proper place, the mover gives it movement towards that place. Thirdly, it makes it to rest, when it shall have come to its proper place: since to the same cause are due, both rest in a place, and the movement to that place. The same applies to the cause of repulsion. Now, in the movements of the appetitive faculty, good has, as it were, a force of attraction, while evil has a force of repulsion. In the first place, therefore, good causes, in the appetitive power, a certain inclination, aptitude or connaturalness in respect of good: and this belongs to the passion of "love": the corresponding contrary of which is "hatred" in respect of evil. Secondly, if the good be not yet possessed, it causes in the appetite a movement towards the attainment of the good beloved: and this belongs to the passion of "desire" or "concupiscence": and contrary to it, in respect of evil, is the passion of "aversion" or "dislike." Thirdly, when the good is obtained, it causes the appetite to rest, as it were, in the good obtained: and this

pertinet ad *delectationem* vel *gaudium*. Cui opponitur ex parte mali *dolor* vel *tristitia*. In passionibus autem irascibilis, praesupponitur quidem aptitudo vel inclinatio ad prosequendum bonum vel fugiendum malum, ex concupiscibili, quae absolute respicit bonum vel malum. Et respectu boni nondum adepti, est *spes* et *desperatio*. Respectu autem mali nondum iniacentis, est *timor* et *audacia*. Respectu autem boni adepti, non est aliqua passio in irascibili, quia iam non habet rationem ardui, ut supra dictum est. Sed ex malo iam iniacenti, sequitur passio *irae*. Sic igitur patet quod in concupiscibili sunt tres coniugationes passionum, scilicet amor et odium, desiderium et fuga gaudium et tristitia. Similiter in irascibili sunt tres, scilicet spes et desperatio, timor et audacia, et ira, cui nulla passio opponitur. Sunt ergo omnes passiones specie differentes undecim, sex quidem in concupiscibili, et quinque in irascibili; sub quibus omnes animae passiones continentur.

Et per hoc patet responsio ad obiecta.

belongs to the passion of "delight" or "joy"; the contrary of which, in respect of evil, is "sorrow" or "sadness." On the other hand, in the irascible passions, the aptitude, or inclination to seek good, or to shun evil, is presupposed as arising from the concupiscible faculty, which regards good or evil absolutely. And in respect of good not yet obtained, we have "hope" and "despair." In respect of evil not yet present we have "fear" and "daring." But in respect of good obtained there is no irascible passion: because it is no longer considered in the light of something arduous, as stated above (I-II, q. 23, a. 3). But evil already present gives rise to the passion of "anger." Accordingly it is clear that in the concupiscible faculty there are three couples of passions; *viz.* love and hatred, desire and aversion, joy and sadness. In like manner there are three groups in the irascible faculty; *viz.* hope and despair, fear and daring, and anger which has not contrary passion. Consequently there are altogether eleven passions differing specifically; six in the concupiscible faculty, and five in the irascible; and under these all the passions of the soul are contained.

From this the replies to the objections are evident.

Quaestio XXIV

Deinde considerandum est de bono et malo circa passiones animae. Et circa hoc quaeruntur quatuor. *Primo,* utrum bonum et malum morale possit in passionibus animae inveniri. *Secundo,* utrum omnis passio animae sit mala moraliter. *Tertio,* utrum omnis passio addat, vel diminuat, ad bonitatem vel malitiam actus. *Quarto,* utrum aliqua passio sit bona vel mala ex sua specie.

Articulus 1

Ad primum sic proceditur. Videtur quod nulla passio animae sit bona vel mala moraliter. Bonum enim et malum morale est proprium hominis, *mores enim proprie dicuntur humani,* ut Ambrosius dicit, super Lucam. Sed passiones non sunt propriae hominum, sed sunt etiam aliis animalibus communes. Ergo nulla passio animae est bona vel mala moraliter.

Praeterea, bonum vel malum hominis est *secundum rationem esse, vel praeter rationem esse,* ut Dionysius dicit, IV cap. de Div. Nom. Sed passiones animae non sunt in ratione, sed in appetitu sensitivo, ut supra dictum est. Ergo non pertinent ad bonum vel malum hominis, quod est bonum morale.

Praeterea, philosophus dicit, in II Ethic., quod *passionibus neque laudamur neque vituperamur.* Sed secundum bona et mala moralia, laudamur et vituperamur. Ergo passiones non sunt bonae vel malae moraliter.

Sed contra est quod Augustinus dicit, in XIV de Civ. Dei, de passionibus animae loquens *mala sunt ista, si malus est amor; bona, si bonus.*

Respondeo dicendum quod passiones animae dupliciter possunt considerari, uno modo, secundum se; alio modo, secundum quod subiacent imperio rationis et voluntatis. Si igitur secundum se considerentur, prout scilicet sunt motus quidam irrationalis appetitus, sic non est in eis bonum vel malum morale, quod dependet a ratione, ut supra dictum est. Si autem considerentur secundum quod subiacent imperio rationis

Question 24

Of Good and Evil in the Passions of the Soul

We must now consider good and evil in the passions of the soul: and under this head there are four points of inquiry: 1. Whether moral good and evil can be found in the passions of the soul? 2. Whether every passion of the soul is morally evil? 3. Whether every passion increases or decreases the goodness of malice of an act? 4. Whether any passion is good or evil specifically?

Article 1

Whether moral good and evil can be found in the passions of the soul?

Objection 1: It would seem that no passion of the soul is morally good or evil. For moral good and evil are proper to man: since "morals are properly predicated of man," as Ambrose says (Super Luc. Prolog.). But passions are not proper to man, for he has them in common with other animals. Therefore no passion of the soul is morally good or evil.

Objection 2: Further, the good or evil of man consists in "being in accord, or in disaccord with reason," as Dionysius says (Div. Nom. iv). Now the passions of the soul are not in the reason, but in the sensitive appetite, as stated above (I-II, q. 22, a. 3). Therefore they have no connection with human, i.e., moral, good or evil.

Objection 3: Further, the Philosopher says (Ethic. ii, 5) that "we are neither praised nor blamed for our passions." But we are praised and blamed for moral good and evil. Therefore the passions are not morally good or evil.

On the contrary, Augustine says (De Civ. Dei xiv, 7) while speaking of the passions of the soul: "They are evil if our love is evil; good if our love is good."

I answer that, We may consider the passions of the soul in two ways: first, in themselves; secondly, as being subject to the command of the reason and will. If then the passions be considered in themselves, to wit, as movements of the irrational appetite, thus there is no moral good or evil in them, since this depends on the reason, as stated above (I-II, q. 18, a. 5). If, however, they be considered as subject to the command of the reason

et voluntatis, sic est in eis bonum et malum morale. Propinquior enim est appetitus sensitivus ipsi rationi et voluntati, quam membra exteriora; quorum tamen motus et actus sunt boni vel mali moraliter, secundum quod sunt voluntarii. Unde multo magis et ipsae passiones, secundum quod sunt voluntariae, possunt dici bonae vel malae moraliter. Dicuntur autem voluntariae vel ex eo quod a voluntate imperantur, vel ex eo quod a voluntate non prohibentur.

AD PRIMUM ergo dicendum quod istae passiones secundum se consideratae, sunt communes hominibus et aliis animalibus, sed secundum quod a ratione imperantur, sunt propriae hominum.

AD SECUNDUM dicendum quod etiam inferiores vires appetitivae dicuntur rationales, secundum quod *participant aliqualiter rationem*, ut dicitur in I Ethic.

AD TERTIUM dicendum quod philosophus dicit quod non laudamur aut vituperamur secundum passiones absolute consideratas, sed non removet quin possint fieri laudabiles vel vituperabiles secundum quod a ratione ordinantur. Unde subdit, *non enim laudatur aut vituperatur qui timet aut irascitur, sed qui aliqualiter, idest secundum rationem vel praeter rationem*.

and will, then moral good and evil are in them. Because the sensitive appetite is nearer than the outward members to the reason and will; and yet the movements and actions of the outward members are morally good or evil, inasmuch as they are voluntary. Much more, therefore, may the passions, in so far as they are voluntary, be called morally good or evil. And they are said to be voluntary, either from being commanded by the will, or from not being checked by the will.

Reply to Objection 1: These passions, considered in themselves, are common to man and other animals: but, as commanded by the reason, they are proper to man.

Reply to Objection 2: Even the lower appetitive powers are called rational, in so far as "they partake of reason in some sort" (Ethic. i, 13).

Reply to Objection 3: The Philosopher says that we are neither praised nor blamed for our passions considered absolutely; but he does not exclude their becoming worthy of praise or blame, in so far as they are subordinate to reason. Hence he continues: "For the man who fears or is angry, is not praised ... or blamed, but the man who is angry in a certain way, i.e., according to, or against reason."

ARTICULUS 2

AD SECUNDUM sic proceditur. Videtur quod omnes passiones animae sint malae moraliter. Dicit enim Augustinus, IX de Civ. Dei, quod *passiones animae quidam vocant morbos vel perturbationes animae*. Sed omnis morbus vel perturbatio animae est aliquid malum moraliter. Ergo omnis passio animae moraliter mala est.

PRAETEREA, Damascenus dicit quod *operatio quidem qui secundum naturam motus est, passio vero qui praeter naturam*. Sed quod est praeter naturam in motibus animae, habet rationem peccati et mali moralis, unde ipse alibi dicit quod *Diabolus versus est ex*

ARTICLE 2
Whether every passion of the soul is evil morally?

Objection 1: It would seem that all the passions of the soul are morally evil. For Augustine says (De Civ. Dei ix, 4) that "some call the soul's passions diseases or disturbances of the soul."* But every disease or disturbance of the soul is morally evil. Therefore every passion of the soul is evil morally.

Objection 2: Further, Damascene says (De Fide Orth. ii, 22) that "movement in accord with nature is an action, but movement contrary to nature is passion." But in movements of the soul, what is against nature is sinful and morally evil: hence he says elsewhere (De Fide Orth. ii, 4) that "the devil turned from

---

* Those things which the Greeks call πάθη (*pathe*), we prefer to call disturbances rather than diseases (Tusc. iv. 5).

eo quod est secundum naturam, in id quod est praeter naturam. Ergo huiusmodi passiones sunt malae moraliter.

PRAETEREA, omne quod inducit ad peccatum, habet rationem mali. Sed huiusmodi passiones inducunt ad peccatum, unde Rom. VII dicuntur *passiones peccatorum*. Ergo videtur quod sint malae moraliter.

SED CONTRA est quod Augustinus dicit, in XIV de Civ. Dei, quod *rectus amor omnes istas affectiones rectas habet. Metuunt enim peccare, cupiunt perseverare, dolent in peccatis, gaudent in operibus bonis.*

RESPONDEO dicendum quod circa hanc quaestionem diversa fuit sententia Stoicorum et Peripateticorum, nam Stoici dixerunt omnes passiones esse malas; Peripatetici vero dixerunt passiones moderatas esse bonas. Quae quidem differentia, licet magna videatur secundum vocem, tamen secundum rem vel nulla est, vel parva, si quis utrorumque intentiones consideret. Stoici enim non discernebant inter sensum et intellectum; et per consequens nec inter intellectivum appetitum et sensitivum. Unde non discernebant passiones animae a motibus voluntatis secundum hoc quod passiones animae sunt in appetitu sensitivo, simplices autem motus voluntatis sunt in intellectivo; sed omnem rationabilem motum appetitivae partis vocabant voluntatem, passionem autem dicebant motum progredientem extra limites rationis. Et ideo, eorum sententiam sequens, Tullius, in III libro de Tusculanis quaestionibus, omnes passiones vocat *animae morbos*. Ex quo argumentatur quod *qui morbosi sunt, sani non sunt; et qui sani non sunt, insipientes sunt*. Unde et insipientes *insanos* dicimus. Peripatetici vero omnes motus appetitus sensitivi *passiones* vocant. Unde eas bonas aestimant, cum sunt a ratione moderatae; malas autem, cum sunt praeter moderationem rationis. Ex quo patet quod Tullius, in eodem libro, Peripateticorum sententiam, qui approbabant mediocritatem passionum, inconvenienter improbat, dicens quod *omne malum, etiam mediocre, vitandum est, nam sicut corpus, etiamsi mediocriter aegrum est, sanum non est; sic ista mediocritas morborum*

that which is in accord with nature to that which is against nature." Therefore these passions are morally evil.

Objection 3: Further, whatever leads to sin, has an aspect of evil. But these passions lead to sin: wherefore they are called "the passions of sins" (Rom. 7:5). Therefore it seems that they are morally evil.

On the contrary, Augustine says (De Civ. Dei xiv, 9) that "all these emotions are right in those whose love is rightly placed . . . For they fear to sin, they desire to persevere; they grieve for sin, they rejoice in good works."

I answer that, On this question the opinion of the Stoics differed from that of the Peripatetics: for the Stoics held that all passions are evil, while the Peripatetics maintained that moderate passions are good. This difference, although it appears great in words, is nevertheless, in reality, none at all, or but little, if we consider the intent of either school. For the Stoics did not discern between sense and intellect; and consequently neither between the intellectual and sensitive appetite. Hence they did not discriminate the passions of the soul from the movements of the will, in so far as the passions of the soul are in the sensitive appetite, while the simple movements of the will are in the intellectual appetite: but every rational movement of the appetitive part they call will, while they called passion, a movement that exceeds the limits of reason. Wherefore Cicero, following their opinion (De Tusc. Quaest. iii, 4) calls all passions "diseases of the soul": whence he argues that "those who are diseased are unsound; and those who are unsound are wanting in sense." Hence we speak of those who are wanting in sense of being "unsound." On the other hand, the Peripatetics give the name of "passions" to all the movements of the sensitive appetite. Wherefore they esteem them good, when they are controlled by reason; and evil when they are not controlled by reason. Hence it is evident that Cicero was wrong in disapproving (De Tusc. Quaest. iii, 4) of the Peripatetic theory of a mean in the passions, when he says that "every evil, though moderate, should be shunned; for, just as a body, though it be moderately ailing, is not sound; so, this mean in the diseases

vel passionum animae, sana non est. Non enim passiones dicuntur *morbi* vel *perturbationes* animae, nisi cum carent moderatione rationis.

Unde patet responsio ad primum.

AD SECUNDUM dicendum quod in omni passione animae additur aliquid, vel diminuitur a naturali motu cordis, inquantum cor intensius vel remissius movetur, secundum systolen aut diastolen, et secundum hoc habet passionis rationem. Non tamen oportet quod passio semper declinet ab ordine naturalis rationis.

AD TERTIUM dicendum quod passiones animae, inquantum sunt praeter ordinem rationis, inclinant ad peccatum, inquantum autem sunt ordinatae a ratione, pertinent ad virtutem.

or passions of the soul, is not sound." For passions are not called "diseases" or "disturbances" of the soul, save when they are not controlled by reason.

Hence the reply to the First Objection is evident.

Reply to Objection 2: In every passion there is an increase or decrease in the natural movement of the heart, according as the heart is moved more or less intensely by contraction and dilatation; and hence it derives the character of passion. But there is no need for passion to deviate always from the order of natural reason.

Reply to Objection 3: The passions of the soul, in so far as they are contrary to the order of reason, incline us to sin: but in so far as they are controlled by reason, they pertain to virtue.

ARTICULUS 3

AD TERTIUM sic proceditur. Videtur quod passio quaecumque semper diminuat de bonitate actus moralis. Omne enim quod impedit iudicium rationis, ex quo dependet bonitas actus moralis, diminuit per consequens bonitatem actus moralis. Sed omnis passio impedit iudicium rationis, dicit enim Sallustius, in Catilinario, *omnes homines qui de rebus dubiis consultant, ab odio, ira, amicitia atque misericordia vacuos esse decet.* Ergo omnis passio diminuit bonitatem moralis actus.

PRAETEREA, actus hominis, quanto est Deo similior, tanto est melior, unde dicit apostolus, Ephes. V, *estote imitatores Dei, sicut filii carissimi.* Sed Deus et sancti angeli sine ira puniunt, sine miseriae compassione subveniunt ut Augustinus dicit, in IX de Civ. Dei. Ergo est melius huiusmodi opera bona agere sine passione animae, quam cum passione.

PRAETEREA, sicut malum morale attenditur per ordinem ad rationem, ita et bonum morale. Sed malum morale diminuitur per passionem, minus enim peccat qui peccat ex passione, quam qui peccat ex industria. Ergo

ARTICLE 3
Whether passion increases or decreases the goodness or malice of an act?

Objection 1: It would seem that every passion decreases the goodness of a moral action. For anything that hinders the judgment of reason, on which depends the goodness of a moral act, consequently decreases the goodness of the moral act. But every passion hinders the judgment of reason: for Sallust says (Catilin.): "All those that take counsel about matters of doubt, should be free from hatred, anger, friendship and pity." Therefore passion decreases the goodness of a moral act.

Objection 2: Further, the more a man's action is like to God, the better it is: hence the Apostle says (Eph. 5:1): "Be ye followers of God, as most dear children." But "God and the holy angels feel no anger when they punish . . . no fellow-feeling with misery when they relieve the unhappy," as Augustine says (De Civ. Dei ix, 5). Therefore it is better to do such like deeds without than with a passion of the soul.

Objection 3: Further, just as moral evil depends on its relation to reason, so also does moral good. But moral evil is lessened by passion: for he sins less, who sins from passion, than he who sins deliberately. Therefore

maius bonum operatur qui operatur bonum sine passione, quam qui operatur cum passione.

SED CONTRA est quod Augustinus dicit, IX de Civ. Dei, quod *passio misericordiae rationi deservit, quando ita praebetur misericordia, ut iustitia conservetur, sive cum indigenti tribuitur, sive cum ignoscitur poenitenti.* Sed nihil quod deservit rationi, diminuit bonum morale. Ergo passio animae non diminuit bonum moris.

RESPONDEO dicendum quod Stoici, sicut ponebant omnem passionem animae esse malam, ita ponebant consequenter omnem passionem animae diminuere actus bonitatem, omne enim bonum ex permixtione mali vel totaliter tollitur, vel fit minus bonum. Et hoc quidem verum est, si dicamus passiones animae solum inordinatos motus sensitivi appetitus, prout sunt perturbationes seu aegritudines. Sed si passiones simpliciter nominemus omnes motus appetitus sensitivi, sic ad perfectionem humani boni pertinet quod etiam ipsae passiones sint moderatae per rationem. Cum enim bonum hominis consistat in ratione sicut in radice, tanto istud bonum erit perfectius, quanto ad plura quae homini conveniunt, derivari potest. Unde nullus dubitat quin ad perfectionem moralis boni pertineat quod actus exteriorum membrorum per rationis regulam dirigantur. Unde, cum appetitus sensitivus possit obedire rationi, ut supra dictum est, ad perfectionem moralis sive humani boni pertinet quod etiam ipsae passiones animae sint regulatae per rationem. Sicut igitur melius est quod homo et velit bonum, et faciat exteriori actu; ita etiam ad perfectionem boni moralis pertinet quod homo ad bonum moveatur non solum secundum voluntatem, sed etiam secundum appetitum sensitivum; secundum illud quod in Psalmo LXXXIII, dicitur, *cor meum et caro mea exultaverunt in Deum vivum,* ut *cor* accipiamus pro appetitu intellectivo, *carnem* autem pro appetitu sensitivo.

AD PRIMUM ergo dicendum quod passiones animae dupliciter se possunt habere ad iudicium rationis. Uno modo, antecedenter. Et sic, cum obnubilent iudicium

he does a better deed, who does well without passion, than he who does with passion.

On the contrary, Augustine says (De Civ. Dei ix, 5) that "the passion of pity is obedient to reason, when pity is bestowed without violating right, as when the poor are relieved, or the penitent forgiven." But nothing that is obedient to reason lessens the moral good. Therefore a passion of the soul does not lessen moral good.

I answer that, As the Stoics held that every passion of the soul is evil, they consequently held that every passion of the soul lessens the goodness of an act; since the admixture of evil either destroys good altogether, or makes it to be less good. And this is true indeed, if by passions we understand none but the inordinate movements of the sensitive appetite, considered as disturbances or ailments. But if we give the name of passions to all the movements of the sensitive appetite, then it belongs to the perfection of man's good that his passions be moderated by reason. For since man's good is founded on reason as its root, that good will be all the more perfect, according as it extends to more things pertaining to man. Wherefore no one questions the fact that it belongs to the perfection of moral good, that the actions of the outward members be controlled by the law of reason. Hence, since the sensitive appetite can obey reason, as stated above (I-II, q. 17, a. 7), it belongs to the perfection of moral or human good, that the passions themselves also should be controlled by reason. Accordingly just as it is better that man should both will good and do it in his external act; so also does it belong to the perfection of moral good, that man should be moved unto good, not only in respect of his will, but also in respect of his sensitive appetite; according to Ps. 83:3: "My heart and my flesh have rejoiced in the living God": where by "heart" we are to understand the intellectual appetite, and by "flesh" the sensitive appetite.

Reply to Objection 1: The passions of the soul may stand in a twofold relation to the judgment of reason. First, antecedently: and thus, since they obscure the judgment of

rationis, ex quo dependet bonitas moralis actus, diminuunt actus bonitatem, laudabilius enim est quod ex iudicio rationis aliquis faciat opus caritatis, quam ex sola passione misericordiae. Alio modo se habent consequenter. Et hoc dupliciter. Uno modo, per modum redundantiae, quia scilicet, cum superior pars animae intense movetur in aliquid, sequitur motum eius etiam pars inferior. Et sic passio existens consequenter **in appetitu sensitivo, est signum intensionis voluntatis.** Et sic indicat bonitatem moralem maiorem. Alio modo, per modum electionis, quando scilicet homo ex iudicio rationis eligit affici aliqua passione, ut promptius operetur, cooperante appetitu sensitivo. Et sic passio animae addit ad bonitatem actionis.

AD SECUNDUM dicendum quod in Deo et in angelis non est appetitus sensitivus, neque etiam membra corporea, et ideo bonum in eis non attenditur secundum ordinationem passionum aut corporeorum actuum, sicut in nobis.

AD TERTIUM dicendum quod passio tendens in malum, praecedens iudicium rationis, diminuit peccatum, sed consequens aliquo praedictorum modorum, auget ipsum, vel significat augmentum eius.

reason, on which the goodness of the moral act depends, they diminish the goodness of the act; for it is more praiseworthy to do a work of charity from the judgment of reason than from the mere passion of pity. In the second place, consequently: and this in two ways. First, by way of redundance: because, to wit, when the higher part of the soul is intensely moved to anything, the lower part also follows that movement: and thus the **passion that results in consequence, in the sensitive appetite, is a sign of the intensity of the will,** and so indicates greater moral goodness. Secondly, by way of choice; when, to wit, a man, by the judgment of his reason, chooses to be affected by a passion in order to work more promptly with the co-operation of the sensitive appetite. And thus a passion of the soul increases the goodness of an action.

Reply to Objection 2: In God and the angels there is no sensitive appetite, nor again bodily members: and so in them good does not depend on the right ordering of passions or of bodily actions, as it does in us.

Reply to Objection 3: A passion that tends to evil, and precedes the judgment of reason, diminishes sin; but if it be consequent in either of the ways mentioned above (ad 1), it aggravates the sin, or else it is a sign of its being more grievous.

ARTICULUS 4

AD QUARTUM sic proceditur. Videtur quod nulla passio animae, secundum speciem suam, sit bona vel mala moraliter. Bonum enim et malum morale attenditur secundum rationem. Sed passiones sunt in appetitu sensitivo, et ita id quod est secundum rationem, accidit eis. Cum ergo nihil quod est per accidens, pertineat ad speciem rei; videtur quod nulla passio secundum suam speciem sit bona vel mala.

PRAETEREA, actus et passiones habent speciem ex obiecto. Si ergo aliqua passio secundum suam speciem esset bona vel mala, oporteret quod passiones quarum obiectum

ARTICLE 4
Whether any passion is good or evil in its species?

Objection 1: It would seem that no passion of the soul is good or evil morally according to its species. Because moral good and evil depend on reason. But the passions are in the sensitive appetite; so that accordance with reason is accidental to them. Since, therefore, nothing accidental belongs to a thing's species, it seems that no passion is good or evil according to its species.

Objection 2: Further, acts and passions take their species from their object. If, therefore, any passion were good or evil, according to its species, it would follow that those passions the object of which

est bonum, bonae essent secundum suam speciem, ut amor, desiderium et gaudium; et passiones quarum obiectum est malum essent malae secundum suam speciem, ut odium, timor et tristitia. Sed hoc patet esse falsum. Non ergo aliqua passio est bona vel mala ex sua specie.

PRAETEREA, nulla species passionum est quae non inveniatur in aliis animalibus. Sed bonum morale non invenitur nisi in homine. Ergo nulla passio animae bona est vel mala ex sua specie.

SED CONTRA est quod Augustinus dicit, IX de Civ. Dei, quod *misericordia pertinet ad virtutem*. Philosophus etiam dicit, in II Ethic., quod verecundia est passio laudabilis. Ergo aliquae passiones sunt bonae vel malae secundum suam speciem.

RESPONDEO dicendum quod sicut de actibus dictum est, ita et de passionibus dicendum videtur, quod scilicet species actus vel passionis dupliciter considerari potest. Uno modo, secundum quod est in genere naturae, et sic bonum vel malum morale non pertinet ad speciem actus vel passionis. Alio modo, secundum quod pertinent ad genus moris, prout scilicet participant aliquid de voluntario et de iudicio rationis. Et hoc modo bonum et malum morale possunt pertinere ad speciem passionis, secundum quod accipitur ut obiectum passionis aliquid de se conveniens rationi, vel dissonum a ratione, sicut patet de *verecundia,* quae est timor turpis; et de *invidia,* quae est tristitia de bono alterius. Sic enim pertinent ad speciem exterioris actus.

AD PRIMUM ergo dicendum quod ratio illa procedit de passionibus secundum quod pertinent ad speciem naturae, prout scilicet appetitus sensitivus in se consideratur. Secundum vero quod appetitus sensitivus obedit rationi, iam bonum et malum rationis non est in passionibus eius per accidens, sed per se.

AD SECUNDUM dicendum quod passiones quae in bonum tendunt, si sit verum bonum, sunt bonae, et similiter quae a vero malo recedunt. E converso vero passiones quae sunt per recessum a

is good, are specifically good, such as love, desire and joy: and that those passions, the object of which is evil, are specifically evil, as hatred, fear and sadness. But this is clearly false. Therefore no passion is good or evil according to its species.

Objection 3: Further, there is no species of passion that is not to be found in other animals. But moral good is in man alone. Therefore no passion of the soul is good or evil according to its species.

On the contrary, Augustine says (De Civ. Dei ix, 5) that "pity is a kind of virtue." Moreover, the Philosopher says (Ethic. ii, 7) that modesty is a praiseworthy passion. Therefore some passions are good or evil according to their species.

I answer that, We ought, seemingly, to apply to passions what has been said in regard to acts (I-II, q. 18, a. 5; a. 6; q. 20, a. 1)—*viz.* that the species of a passion, as the species of an act, can be considered from two points of view. First, according to its natural genus; and thus moral good and evil have no connection with the species of an act or passion. Secondly, according to its moral genus, inasmuch as it is voluntary and controlled by reason. In this way moral good and evil can belong to the species of a passion, in so far as the object to which a passion tends, is, of itself, in harmony or in discord with reason: as is clear in the case of "shame" which is base fear; and of "envy" which is sorrow for another's good: for thus passions belong to the same species as the external act.

Reply to Objection 1: This argument considers the passions in their natural species, in so far as the sensitive appetite is considered in itself. But in so far as the sensitive appetite obeys reason, good and evil of reason are no longer accidentally in the passions of the appetite, but essentially.

Reply to Objection 2: Passions having a tendency to good, are themselves good, if they tend to that which is truly good, and in like manner, if they turn away from that which is truly evil. On the other hand, those passions which consist in aversion from

bono, et per accessum ad malum, sunt malae.

Ad tertium dicendum quod in brutis animalibus appetitus sensitivus non obedit rationi. Et tamen inquantum ducitur quadam aestimativa naturali, quae subiicitur rationi superiori, scilicet divinae, est in eis quaedam similitudo moralis boni, quantum ad animae passiones.

good, and a tendency to evil, are themselves evil.

Reply to Objection 3: In irrational animals the sensitive appetite does not obey reason. Nevertheless, in so far as they are led by a kind of estimative power, which is subject to a higher, i.e., the Divine reason, there is a certain likeness of moral good in them, in regard to the soul's passions.

Quaestio XXV

Deinde considerandum est de ordine passionum ad invicem. Et circa hoc quaeruntur quatuor. *Primo,* de ordine passionum irascibilis ad passiones concupiscibilis. *Secundo,* de ordine passionum concupiscibilis ad invicem. *Tertio,* de ordine passionum irascibilis ad invicem. *Quarto,* de quatuor principalibus passionibus.

Question 25
Of the Order of the Passions to One Another

We must now consider the order of the passions to one another: and under this head there are four points of inquiry: 1. The relation of the irascible passions to the concupiscible passions; 2. The relation of the concupiscible passions to one another; 3. The relation of the irascible passions to one another; 4. The four principal passions.

Articulus 1

Ad primum sic proceditur. Videtur quod passiones irascibilis sint priores passionibus concupiscibilis. Ordo enim passionum est secundum ordinem obiectorum. Sed obiectum irascibilis est bonum arduum, quod videtur esse supremum inter alia bona. Ergo passiones irascibilis videntur praeesse passionibus concupiscibilis.

Praeterea, movens est prius moto. Sed irascibilis comparatur ad concupiscibilem sicut movens ad motum, ad hoc enim datur animalibus, ut tollantur impedimenta quibus concupiscibilis prohibetur frui suo obiecto, ut supra dictum est; *removens autem prohibens habet rationem moventis,* ut dicitur in VIII Physic. Ergo passiones irascibilis sunt priores passionibus concupiscibilis.

Praeterea, gaudium et tristitia sunt passiones concupiscibilis. Sed gaudium et tristitia consequuntur ad passiones irasci-

Article 1
Whether the irascible passions precede the concupiscible passions, or vice versa?

Objection 1: It would seem that the irascible passions precede the concupiscible passions. For the order of the passions is that of their objects. But the object of the irascible faculty is the difficult good, which seems to be the highest good. Therefore the irascible passions seem to precede the concupiscible passions.

Objection 2: Further, the mover precedes that which is moved. But the irascible faculty is compared to the concupiscible, as mover to that which is moved: since it is given to animals, for the purposed of removing the obstacles that hinder the concupiscible faculty from enjoying its object, as stated above (I-II, q. 23, a. 1, ad 1; I, q. 81, a. 2). Now "that which removes an obstacle, is a kind of mover" (Phys. viii, 4). Therefore the irascible passions precede the concupiscible passions.

Objection 3: Further, joy and sadness are concupiscible passions. But joy and sadness succeed to the irascible passions:

bilis, dicit enim philosophus, in IV Ethic., quod *punitio quietat impetum irae, delectationem loco tristitiae faciens.* Ergo passiones concupiscibilis sunt posteriores passionibus irascibilis.

SED CONTRA, passiones concupiscibilis respiciunt bonum absolutum, passiones autem irascibilis respiciunt bonum contractum, scilicet arduum. Cum igitur bonum simpliciter sit prius quam bonum contractum, videtur quod passiones concupiscibilis sint priores passionibus irascibilis.

RESPONDEO dicendum quod passiones concupiscibilis ad plura se habent quam passiones irascibilis. Nam in passionibus concupiscibilis invenitur aliquid pertinens ad motum, sicut desiderium; et aliquid pertinens ad quietem, sicut gaudium et tristitia. Sed in passionibus irascibilis non invenitur aliquid pertinens ad quietem, sed solum pertinens ad motum. Cuius ratio est quia id in quo iam quiescitur, non habet rationem difficilis seu ardui, quod est obiectum irascibilis. Quies autem, cum sit finis motus, est prior in intentione, sed posterior in executione. Si ergo comparentur passiones irascibilis ad passiones concupiscibilis quae significant quietem in bono; manifeste passiones irascibilis praecedunt, ordine executionis, huiusmodi passiones concupiscibilis, sicut spes praecedit gaudium, unde et causat ipsum, secundum illud apostoli, Rom. XII, *spe gaudentes.* Sed passio concupiscibilis importans quietem in malo, scilicet tristitia, media est inter duas passiones irascibilis. Sequitur enim timorem, cum enim occurrerit malum quod timebatur, causatur tristitia. Praecedit autem motum irae, quia cum ex tristitia praecedente aliquis insurgit in vindictam, hoc pertinet ad motum irae. Et quia rependere vicem malis, apprehenditur ut bonum; cum iratus hoc consecutus fuerit, gaudet. Et sic manifestum est quod omnis passio irascibilis terminatur ad passionem concupiscibilis pertinentem ad quietem, scilicet vel ad gaudium vel ad tristitiam. Sed si comparentur passiones irascibilis ad passiones concupiscibilis quae important

for the Philosopher says (Ethic. iv, 5) that "retaliation causes anger to cease, because it produces pleasure instead of the previous pain." Therefore the concupiscible passions follow the irascible passions.

On the contrary, The concupiscible passions regard the absolute good, while the irascible passions regard a restricted, *viz.* the difficult, good. Since, therefore, the absolute good precedes the restricted good, it seems that the concupiscible passions precede the irascible.

I answer that, In the concupiscible passions there is more diversity than in the passions of the irascible faculty. For in the former we find something relating to movement—e.g., desire; and something belonging to repose, e.g., joy and sadness. But in the irascible passions there is nothing pertaining to repose, and only that which belongs to movement. The reason of this is that when we find rest in a thing, we no longer look upon it as something difficult or arduous; whereas such is the object of the irascible faculty. Now since rest is the end of movement, it is first in the order of intention, but last in the order of execution. If, therefore, we compare the passions of the irascible faculty with those concupiscible passions that denote rest in good, it is evident that in the order of execution, the irascible passions take precedence of such like passions of the concupiscible faculty: thus hope precedes joy, and hence causes it, according to the Apostle (Rom. 12:12): "Rejoicing in hope." But the concupiscible passion which denotes rest in evil, *viz.* sadness, comes between two irascible passions: because it follows fear; since we become sad when we are confronted by the evil that we feared: while it precedes the movement of anger; since the movement of self-vindication, that results from sadness, is the movement of anger. And because it is looked upon as a good thing to pay back the evil done to us; when the angry man has achieved this he rejoices. Thus it is evident that every passion of the irascible faculty terminates in a concupiscible passion denoting rest, *viz.* either in joy or in sadness. But if we compare the irascible passions to those concupiscible passions that denote

motum, sic manifeste passiones concupiscibilis sunt priores, eo quod passiones irascibilis addunt supra passiones concupiscibilis; sicut et obiectum irascibilis addit supra obiectum concupiscibilis arduitatem sive difficultatem. Spes enim supra desiderium addit quendam conatum, et quandam elevationem animi ad consequendum bonum arduum. Et similiter timor addit supra fugam seu abominationem, quandam depressionem animi, propter difficultatem mali. Sic ergo passiones irascibilis mediae sunt inter passiones concupiscibilis quae important motum in bonum vel in malum; et inter passiones concupiscibilis quae important quietem in bono vel in malo. Et sic patet quod passiones irascibilis et principium habent a passionibus concupiscibilis, et in passiones concupiscibilis terminantur.

Ad primum ergo dicendum quod illa ratio procederet, si de ratione obiecti concupiscibilis esset aliquid oppositum arduo, sicut de ratione obiecti irascibilis est quod sit arduum. Sed quia obiectum concupiscibilis est bonum absolute, prius naturaliter est quam obiectum irascibilis, sicut commune proprio.

Ad secundum dicendum quod removens prohibens non est movens per se, sed per accidens. Nunc autem loquimur de ordine passionum per se. Et praeterea irascibilis removet prohibens quietem concupiscibilis in suo obiecto. Unde ex hoc non sequitur nisi quod passiones irascibilis praecedunt passiones concupiscibilis ad quietem pertinentes.

De quibus etiam tertia ratio procedit.

Articulus 2

Ad secundum sic proceditur. Videtur quod amor non sit prima passionum concupiscibilis. Vis enim concupiscibilis a concupiscentia denominatur, quae est eadem passio cum desiderio. Sed *denominatio fit a potiori,* ut dicitur in II de anima. Ergo concupiscentia est potior amore.

movement, then it is clear that the latter take precedence: because the passions of the irascible faculty add something to those of the concupiscible faculty; just as the object of the irascible adds the aspect of arduousness or difficulty to the object of the concupiscible faculty. Thus hope adds to desire a certain effort, and a certain raising of the spirits to the realization of the arduous good. In like manner fear adds to aversion or detestation a certain lowness of spirits, on account of difficulty in shunning the evil. Accordingly the passions of the irascible faculty stand between those concupiscible passions that denote movement towards good or evil, and those concupiscible passions that denote rest in good or evil. And it is therefore evident that the irascible passions both arise from and terminate in the passions of the concupiscible faculty.

Reply to Objection 1: This argument would prove, if the formal object of the concupiscible faculty were something contrary to the arduous, just as the formal object of the irascible faculty is that which is arduous. But because the object of the concupiscible faculty is good absolutely, it naturally precedes the object of the irascible, as the common precedes the proper.

Reply to Objection 2: The remover of an obstacle is not a direct but an accidental mover: and here we are speaking of passions as directly related to one another. Moreover, the irascible passion removes the obstacle that hinders the concupiscible from resting in its object. Wherefore it only follows that the irascible passions precede those concupiscible passions that connote rest.

The third object leads to the same conclusion.

Article 2
Whether love is the first of the concupiscible passions?

Objection 1: It would seem that love is not the first of the concupiscible passions. For the concupiscible faculty is so called from concupiscence, which is the same passion as desire. But "things are named from their chief characteristic" (De Anima ii, 4). Therefore desire takes precedence of love.

Praeterea, amor unionem quandam importat, est enim *vis unitiva et concretiva*, ut Dionysius dicit, in IV cap. de Div. Nom. Sed concupiscentia vel desiderium est motus ad unionem rei concupitae vel desideratae. Ergo concupiscentia est prior amore.

Praeterea, causa est prior effectu. Sed delectatio est quandoque causa amoris, quidam enim propter delectationem amant, ut dicitur in VIII Ethic. Ergo delectatio est prior amore. Non ergo prima inter passiones concupiscibilis est amor.

Sed contra est quod Augustinus dicit, in XIV de Civ. Dei, quod omnes passiones ex amore causantur, *amor enim inhians habere quod amatur, cupiditas est; id autem habens, eoque fruens, laetitia est.* Amor ergo est prima passionum concupiscibilis.

Respondeo dicendum quod obiectum concupiscibilis sunt bonum et malum. Naturaliter autem est prius bonum malo, eo quod malum est privatio boni. Unde et omnes passiones quarum obiectum est bonum, naturaliter sunt priores passionibus quarum obiectum est malum, unaquaeque scilicet sua opposita, quia enim bonum quaeritur, ideo refutatur oppositum malum. Bonum autem habet rationem finis, qui quidem est prior in intentione, sed est posterior in consecutione. Potest ergo ordo passionum concupiscibilis attendi vel secundum intentionem, vel secundum consecutionem. Secundum quidem consecutionem, illud est prius quod primo fit in eo quod tendit ad finem. Manifestum est autem quod omne quod tendit ad finem aliquem, primo quidem habet aptitudinem seu proportionem ad finem, nihil enim tendit in finem non proportionatum; secundo, movetur ad finem; tertio, quiescit in fine post eius consecutionem. Ipsa autem aptitudo sive proportio appetitus ad bonum est amor, qui nihil aliud est quam complacentia boni; motus autem ad bonum est desiderium vel concupiscentia; quies autem in bono est gaudium vel delectatio. Et ideo secundum hunc ordinem, amor praecedit desiderium, et desiderium praecedit delectationem. Sed secundum ordinem intentionis, est e converso, nam delectatio intenta causat desiderium et amorem. Delectatio enim est fruitio

Objection 2: Further, love implies a certain union; since it is a "uniting and binding force," as Dionysius says (Div. Nom. iv). But concupiscence or desire is a movement towards union with the thing coveted or desired. Therefore desire precedes love.

Objection 3: Further, the cause precedes its effect. But pleasure is sometimes the cause of love: since some love on account of pleasure (Ethic. viii, 3, 4). Therefore pleasure precedes love; and consequently love is not the first of the concupiscible passions.

On the contrary, Augustine says (De Civ. Dei xiv, 7, 9) that all the passions are caused by love: since "love yearning for the beloved object, is desire; and, having and enjoying it, is joy." Therefore love is the first of the concupiscible passions.

I answer that, Good and evil are the object of the concupiscible faculty. Now good naturally precedes evil; since evil is privation of good. Wherefore all the passions, the object of which is good, are naturally before those, the object of which is evil—that is to say, each precedes its contrary passion: because the quest of a good is the reason for shunning the opposite evil. Now good has the aspect of an end, and the end is indeed first in the order of intention, but last in the order of execution. Consequently the order of the concupiscible passions can be considered either in the order of intention or in the order of execution. In the order of execution, the first place belongs to that which takes place first in the thing that tends to the end. Now it is evident that whatever tends to an end, has, in the first place, an aptitude or proportion to that end, for nothing tends to a disproportionate end; secondly, it is moved to that end; thirdly, it rests in the end, after having attained it. And this very aptitude or proportion of the appetite to good is love, which is complacency in good; while movement towards good is desire or concupiscence; and rest in good is joy or pleasure. Accordingly in this order, love precedes desire, and desire precedes pleasure. But in the order of intention, it is the reverse: because the pleasure intended causes desire and love. For pleasure is the enjoyment of

boni, quae quodammodo est finis sicut et ipsum bonum, ut supra dictum est.

Ad primum ergo dicendum quod hoc modo nominatur aliquid, secundum quod nobis innotescit, *voces enim sunt signa intellectuum,* secundum philosophum. Nos autem, ut plurimum, per effectum cognoscimus causam. Effectus autem amoris, quando quidem habetur ipsum amatum, est delectatio, **quando vero non habetur, est desiderium vel concupiscentia.** Ut autem Augustinus dicit, in X de Trin., *amor magis sentitur, cum eum prodit indigentia.* Unde inter omnes passiones concupiscibilis, magis sensibilis est concupiscentia. Et propter hoc, ab ea denominatur potentia.

Ad secundum dicendum quod duplex est unio amati ad amantem. Una quidem realis, secundum scilicet coniunctionem ad rem ipsam. Et talis unio pertinet ad gaudium vel delectationem, quae sequitur desiderium. Alia autem est unio affectiva, quae est secundum aptitudinem vel proportionem, prout scilicet ex hoc quod aliquid habet aptitudinem ad alterum et inclinationem, iam participat aliquid eius. Et sic amor unionem importat. Quae quidem unio praecedit motum desiderii.

Ad tertium dicendum quod delectatio causat amorem, secundum quod est prior in intentione.

Articulus 3

Ad tertium sic proceditur. Videtur quod spes non sit prima inter passiones irascibilis. Vis enim irascibilis ab ira denominatur. Cum ergo *denominatio fiat a potiori,* videtur quod ira sit potior et prior quam spes.

Praeterea, arduum est obiectum irascibilis. Sed magis videtur esse arduum quod aliquis conetur superare malum contrarium quod imminet ut futurum, quod pertinet ad audaciam; vel quod iniacet iam ut praesens, quod pertinet ad iram; quam quod conetur acquirere simpliciter aliquod bonum. Et similiter magis videtur esse arduum quod conetur vincere malum praesens, quam

the good, which enjoyment is, in a way, the end, just as the good itself is, as stated above (I-II, q. 11, a. 3, ad 3).

Reply to Objection 1: We name a thing as we understand it, for "words are signs of thoughts," as the Philosopher states (Peri Herm. i, 1). Now in most cases we know a cause by its effect. But the effect of love, when the beloved object is possessed, is pleasure: when it is not possessed, it is desire or concupiscence: and, as **Augustine** says (De Trin. x, 12), "we are more sensible to love, when we lack that which we love." Consequently of all the concupiscible passions, concupiscence is felt most; and for this reason the power is named after it.

Reply to Objection 2: The union of lover and beloved is twofold. There is real union, consisting in the conjunction of one with the other. This union belongs to joy or pleasure, which follows desire. There is also an affective union, consisting in an aptitude or proportion, in so far as one thing, from the very fact of its having an aptitude for and an inclination to another, partakes of it: and love betokens such a union. This union precedes the movement of desire.

Reply to Objection 3: Pleasure causes love, in so far as it precedes love in the order of intention.

Article 3
Whether hope is the first of the irascible passions?

Objection 1: It would seem that hope is not the first of the irascible passions. Because the irascible faculty is denominated from anger. Since, therefore, "things are names from their chief characteristic" (cf. a. 2, ad 1), it seems that anger precedes and surpasses hope.

Objection 2: Further, the object of the irascible faculty is something arduous. Now it seems more arduous to strive to overcome a contrary evil that threatens soon to overtake us, which pertains to daring; or an evil actually present, which pertains to anger; than to strive simply to obtain some good. Again, it seems more arduous to strive to overcome a present evil, than a

malum futurum. Ergo ira videtur esse potior passio quam audacia, et audacia quam spes. Et sic spes non videtur esse prior.

PRAETEREA, prius occurrit, in motu ad finem, recessus a termino, quam accessus ad terminum. Sed timor et desperatio important recessum ab aliquo, audacia autem et spes important accessum ad aliquid. Ergo timor et desperatio praecedunt spem et audaciam.

SED CONTRA, quanto aliquid est propinquius primo, tanto est prius. Sed spes est propinquior amori, qui est prima passionum. Ergo spes est prior inter omnes passiones irascibilis.

RESPONDEO dicendum quod, sicut iam dictum est, omnes passiones irascibilis important motum in aliquid. Motus autem ad aliquid in irascibili potest causari ex duobus, uno modo, ex sola aptitudine seu proportione ad finem, quae pertinet ad amorem vel odium; alio modo, ex praesentia ipsius boni vel mali, quae pertinet ad tristitiam vel gaudium. Et quidem ex praesentia boni non causatur aliqua passio in irascibili, ut dictum est, sed ex praesentia mali causatur passio irae. Quia igitur in via generationis seu consecutionis, proportio vel aptitudo ad finem praecedit consecutionem finis; inde est quod ira, inter omnes passiones irascibilis, est ultima, ordine generationis. Inter alias autem passiones irascibilis, quae important motum consequentem amorem vel odium boni vel mali, oportet quod passiones quarum obiectum est bonum, scilicet spes et desperatio, sint naturaliter priores passionibus quarum obiectum est malum, scilicet audacia et timore. Ita tamen quod spes est prior desperatione, quia spes est motus in bonum secundum rationem boni quod de sua ratione est attractivum, et ideo est motus in bonum per se; desperatio autem est recessus a bono, qui non competit bono secundum quod est bonum, sed secundum aliquid aliud, unde est quasi per accidens. Et eadem ratione, timor, cum sit recessus a malo, est prior quam audacia. Quod autem spes et desperatio sint naturaliter priores quam timor et audacia, ex hoc manifestum est, quod, sicut

future evil. Therefore anger seems to be a stronger passion than daring, and daring, than hope. And consequently it seems that hope does not precede them.

Objection 3: Further, when a thing is moved towards an end, the movement of withdrawal precedes the movement of approach. But fear and despair imply withdrawal from something; while daring and hope imply approach towards something. Therefore fear and despair precede hope and daring.

On the contrary, The nearer a thing is to the first, the more it precedes others. But hope is nearer to love, which is the first of the passions. Therefore hope is the first of the passions in the irascible faculty.

I answer that, As stated above (I-II, q. 25, a. 1) all irascible passions imply movement towards something. Now this movement of the irascible faculty towards something may be due to two causes: one is the mere aptitude or proportion to the end; and this pertains to love or hatred, those whose object is good, or evil; and this belongs to sadness or joy. As a matter of fact, the presence of good produces no passion in the irascible, as stated above (I-II, q. 23, a. 3; a. 4); but the presence of evil gives rise to the passion of anger. Since then in order of generation or execution, proportion or aptitude to the end precedes the achievement of the end; it follows that, of all the irascible passions, anger is the last in the order of generation. And among the other passions of the irascible faculty, which imply a movement arising from love of good or hatred of evil, those whose object is good, *viz.* hope and despair, must naturally precede those whose object is evil, *viz.* daring and fear: yet so that hope precedes despair; since hope is a movement towards good as such, which is essentially attractive, so that hope tends to good directly; whereas despair is a movement away from good, a movement which is consistent with good, not as such, but in respect of something else, wherefore its tendency from good is accidental, as it were. In like manner fear, through being a movement from evil, precedes daring. And that hope and despair naturally precede fear and daring is evident from this—that as the

appetitus boni est ratio quare vitetur malum, ita etiam spes et desperatio sunt ratio timoris et audaciae, nam audacia consequitur spem victoriae, et timor consequitur desperationem vincendi. Ira autem consequitur audaciam, nullus enim irascitur vindictam appetens, nisi audeat vindicare, secundum quod Avicenna dicit, in sexto de naturalibus. Sic ergo patet quod spes est prima inter omnes passiones irascibilis. Et si ordinem omnium passionum secundum viam generationis, scire velimus, primo occurrunt amor et odium; secundo, desiderium et fuga; tertio, spes et desperatio; quarto, timor et audacia; quinto, ira; sexto et ultimo, gaudium et tristitia, quae consequuntur ad omnes passiones, ut dicitur in II Ethic. Ita tamen quod amor est prior odio, et desiderium fuga, et spes desperatione, et timor audacia, et gaudium quam tristitia, ut ex praedictis colligi potest.

AD PRIMUM ergo dicendum quod, quia ira causatur ex aliis passionibus sicut effectus a causis praecedentibus, ideo ab ea, tanquam a manifestiori, denominatur potentia.

AD SECUNDUM dicendum quod arduum non est ratio accedendi vel appetendi, sed potius bonum. Et ideo spes, quae directius respicit bonum, est prior, quamvis audacia aliquando sit in magis arduum, vel etiam ira.

AD TERTIUM dicendum quod appetitus primo et per se movetur in bonum, sicut in proprium obiectum; et ex hoc causatur quod recedat a malo. Proportionatur enim motus appetitivae partis, non quidem motui naturali, sed intentioni naturae; quae per prius intendit finem quam remotionem contrarii, quae non quaeritur nisi propter adeptionem finis.

desire of good is the reason for avoiding evil, so hope and despair are the reason for fear and daring: because daring arises from the hope of victory, and fear arises from the despair of overcoming. Lastly, anger arises from daring: for no one is angry while seeking vengeance, unless he dare to avenge himself, as Avicenna observes in the sixth book of his Physics. Accordingly, it is evident that hope is the first of all the irascible passions. And if we wish to know the order of all the passions in the way of generation, love and hatred are first; desire and aversion, second; hope and despair, third; fear and daring, fourth; anger, fifth; sixth and last, joy and sadness, which follow from all the passions, as stated in Ethic. ii, 5: yet so that love precedes hatred; desire precedes aversion; hope precedes despair; fear precedes daring; and joy precedes sadness, as may be gathered from what has been stated above.

Reply to Objection 1: Because anger arises from the other passions, as an effect from the causes that precede it, it is from anger, as being more manifest than the other passions, that the power takes its name.

Reply to Objection 2: It is not the arduousness but the good that is the reason for approach or desire. Consequently hope, which regards good more directly, takes precedence: although at times daring or even anger regards something more arduous.

Reply to Objection 3: The movement of the appetite is essentially and directly towards the good as towards its proper object; its movement from evil results from this. For the movement of the appetitive part is in proportion, not to natural movement, but to the intention of nature, which intends the end before intending the removal of a contrary, which removal is desired only for the sake of obtaining the end.

ARTICULUS 4

AD QUARTUM sic proceditur. Videtur quod non sint istae quatuor principales passiones, gaudium et tristitia, spes et timor. Augustinus enim, in XIV de Civ. Dei, non ponit spem, sed cupiditatem loco eius.

ARTICLE 4
Whether these are the four principal passions: joy, sadness, hope and fear?

Objection 1: It would seem that joy, sadness, hope and fear are not the four principal passions. For Augustine (De Civ. Dei xiv, 3, 7 sqq.) omits hope and puts desire in its place.

Praeterea, in passionibus animae est duplex ordo, scilicet intentionis, et consecutionis seu generationis. Aut ergo principales passiones accipiuntur secundum ordinem intentionis, et sic tantum gaudium et tristitia, quae sunt finales, erunt principales passiones. Aut secundum ordinem consecutionis seu generationis, et sic amor erit principalis passio. Nullo ergo modo debent dici quatuor principales passiones istae quatuor, gaudium et tristitia, spes et timor.

Praeterea, sicut audacia causatur ex spe, ita timor ex desperatione. Aut ergo spes et desperatio debent poni principales passiones, tanquam causae, aut spes et audacia, tanquam sibi ipsis affines.

Sed contra est illud quod Boetius, in libro de Consol., enumerans quatuor principales passiones, dicit, *gaudia pelle, pelle timorem, spemque fugato, nec dolor adsit.*

Respondeo dicendum quod hae quatuor passiones communiter principales esse dicuntur. Quarum duae, scilicet gaudium et tristitia, principales dicuntur, quia sunt completivae et finales simpliciter respectu omnium passionum, unde ad omnes passiones consequuntur, ut dicitur in II Ethic. Timor autem et spes sunt principales, non quidem quasi completivae simpliciter, sed quia sunt completivae in genere motus appetitivi ad aliquid, nam respectu boni, incipit motus in amore, et procedit in desiderium, et terminatur in spe; respectu vero mali, incipit in odio, et procedit ad fugam, et terminatur in timore. Et ideo solet harum quatuor passionum numerus accipi secundum differentiam praesentis et futuri, motus enim respicit futurum, sed quies est in aliquo praesenti. De bono igitur praesenti est gaudium; de malo praesenti est tristitia; de bono vero futuro est spes; de malo futuro est timor. Omnes autem aliae passiones, quae sunt de bono vel de malo praesenti vel futuro, ad has completive reducuntur. Unde etiam a quibusdam dicuntur principales hae praedictae quatuor passiones, quia sunt generales. Quod quidem verum est, si spes et timor designant motum appetitus communiter tendentem in aliquid appetendum vel fugiendum.

Objection 2: Further, there is a twofold order in the passions of the soul: the order of intention, and the order of execution or generation. The principal passions should therefore be taken, either in the order of intention; and thus joy and sadness, which are the final passions, will be the principal passions; or in the order of execution or generation, and thus love will be the principal passion. Therefore joy and sadness, hope and fear should in no way be called the four principal passions.

Objection 3: Further, just as daring is caused by hope, so fear is caused by despair. Either, therefore, hope and despair should be reckoned as principal passions, since they cause others: or hope and daring, from being akin to one another.

On the contrary, Boethius (De Consol. i) in enumerating the four principal passions, says: "Banish joys: banish fears: Away with hope: away with tears."

I answer that, These four are commonly called the principal passions. Two of them, *viz.* joy and sadness, are said to be principal because in them all the other passions have their completion and end; wherefore they arise from all the other passions, as is stated in Ethic. ii, 5. Fear and hope are principal passions, not because they complete the others simply, but because they complete them as regards the movement of the appetite towards something: for in respect of good, movement begins in love, goes forward to desire, and ends in hope; while in respect of evil, it begins in hatred, goes on to aversion, and ends in fear. Hence it is customary to distinguish these four passions in relation to the present and the future: for movement regards the future, while rest is in something present: so that joy relates to present good, sadness relates to present evil; hope regards future good, and fear, future evil. As to the other passions that regard good or evil, present or future, they all culminate in these four. For this reason some have said that these four are the principal passions, because they are general passions; and this is true, provided that by hope and fear we understand the appetite's common tendency to desire or shun something.

Ad primum ergo dicendum quod Augustinus ponit desiderium vel cupiditatem loco spei, inquantum ad idem pertinere videntur, scilicet ad bonum futurum.

Ad secundum dicendum quod passiones istae dicuntur principales, secundum ordinem intentionis et complementi. Et quamvis timor et spes non sint ultimae passiones simpliciter, tamen sunt ultimae in genere passionum tendentium in aliud quasi in futurum. Nec potest esse instantia nisi de ira. Quae tamen non potest poni principalis passio, quia est quidam effectus audaciae, quae non potest esse passio principalis, ut infra dicetur.

Ad tertium dicendum quod desperatio importat recessum a bono, quod est quasi per accidens, et audacia importat accessum ad malum, quod etiam est per accidens. Et ideo hae passiones non possunt esse principales, quia quod est per accidens, non potest dici principale. Et sic etiam nec ira potest dici passio principalis, quae consequitur audaciam.

Reply to Objection 1: Augustine puts desire or covetousness in place of hope, in so far as they seem to regard the same object, *viz.* some future good.

Reply to Objection 2: These are called principal passions, in the order of intention and completion. And though fear and hope are not the last passions simply, yet they are the last of those passions that tend towards something as future. Nor can the argument be pressed any further except in the case of anger: yet neither can anger be reckoned a principal passion, because it is an effect of daring, which cannot be a principal passion, as we shall state further on (ad 3).

Reply to Objection 3: Despair implies movement away from good; and this is, as it were, accidental: and daring implies movement towards evil; and this too is accidental. Consequently these cannot be principal passions; because that which is accidental cannot be said to be principal. And so neither can anger be called a principal passion, because it arises from daring.

Question 26
Of the Passions of the Soul in Particular: and First, of Love

We have now to consider the soul's passions in particular, and 1. the passions of the concupiscible faculty; 2. the passions of the irascible faculty. The first of these considerations will be threefold: since we shall consider 1. Love and hatred; 2. Desire and aversion; 3. Pleasure and sadness. Concerning love, three points must be considered: 1. Love itself; 2. The cause of love; 3. The effects of love. Under the first head there are four points of inquiry: 1. Whether love is in the concupiscible power? 2. Whether love is a passion? 3. Whether love is the same as dilection? 4. Whether love is properly divided into love of friendship, and love of concupiscence?

Article 1
Whether love is in the concupiscible power?

Objection 1: It would seem that love is not in the concupiscible power. For it is written (Wis. 8:2): "Her," namely wisdom, "have I loved, and have sought her out from my youth." But the concupiscible power, being a part of the sensitive appetite, cannot tend to wisdom, which is not apprehended by the senses. Therefore love is not in the concupiscible power.

Objection 2: Further, love seems to be identified with every passion: for Augustine says (De Civ. Dei xiv, 7): "Love, yearning for the object beloved, is desire; having and enjoying it, is joy; fleeing what is contrary to it, is fear; and feeling what is contrary to it, is sadness." But not every passion is in the concupiscible power; indeed, fear, which is mentioned in this passage, is in the irascible power. Therefore we must not say absolutely that love is in the concupiscible power.

Objection 3: Further, Dionysius (Div. Nom. iv) mentions a "natural love." But natural love seems to pertain rather to the natural powers, which belong to the vegetal soul. Therefore love is not simply in the concupiscible power.

On the contrary, The Philosopher says (Topic. ii, 7) that "love is in the concupiscible power."

Respondeo dicendum quod amor est aliquid ad appetitum pertinens, cum utriusque obiectum sit bonum. Unde secundum differentiam appetitus est differentia amoris. Est enim quidam appetitus non consequens apprehensionem ipsius appetentis, sed alterius, et huiusmodi dicitur *appetitus naturalis*. Res enim naturales appetunt quod eis convenit secundum suam naturam, non per apprehensionem propriam, sed per apprehensionem instituentis naturam, ut in I libro dictum est. Alius autem est appetitus consequens apprehensionem ipsius appetentis, sed ex necessitate, non ex iudicio libero. Et talis est *appetitus sensitivus* in brutis, qui tamen in hominibus aliquid libertatis participat, inquantum obedit rationi. Alius autem est appetitus consequens apprehensionem appetentis secundum liberum iudicium. Et talis est appetitus rationalis sive intellectivus, qui dicitur *voluntas*. In unoquoque autem horum appetituum, *amor* dicitur illud quod est principium motus tendentis in finem amatum. In appetitu autem naturali, principium huiusmodi motus est connaturalitas appetentis ad id in quod tendit, quae dici potest amor naturalis, sicut ipsa connaturalitas corporis gravis ad locum medium est per gravitatem, et potest dici *amor naturalis*. Et similiter coaptatio appetitus sensitivi, vel voluntatis, ad aliquod bonum, idest ipsa complacentia boni, dicitur *amor sensitivus*, vel *intellectivus* seu *rationalis*. Amor igitur sensitivus est in appetitu sensitivo, sicut amor intellectivus in appetitu intellectivo. Et pertinet ad concupiscibilem, quia dicitur per respectum ad bonum absolute, non per respectum ad arduum, quod est obiectum irascibilis.

Ad primum ergo dicendum quod auctoritas illa loquitur de amore intellectivo vel rationali.

Ad secundum dicendum quod amor dicitur esse timor, gaudium, cupiditas et tristitia, non quidem essentialiter, sed causaliter.

I answer that, Love is something pertaining to the appetite; since good is the object of both. Wherefore love differs according to the difference of appetites. For there is an appetite which arises from an apprehension existing, not in the subject of the appetite, but in some other: and this is called the "natural appetite." Because natural things seek what is suitable to them according to their nature, by reason of an apprehension which is not in them, but in the Author of their nature, as stated in the I, q. 6, a. 1, ad 2; I, q. 103, a. 1, ad 1; ad 3. And there is another appetite arising from an apprehension in the subject of the appetite, but from necessity and not from free-will. Such is, in irrational animals, the "sensitive appetite," which, however, in man, has a certain share of liberty, in so far as it obeys reason. Again, there is another appetite following freely from an apprehension in the subject of the appetite. And this is the rational or intellectual appetite, which is called the "will." Now in each of these appetites, the name "love" is given to the principle movement towards the end loved. In the natural appetite the principle of this movement is the appetitive subject's connaturalness with the thing to which it tends, and may be called "natural love": thus the connaturalness of a heavy body for the centre, is by reason of its weight and may be called "natural love." In like manner the aptitude of the sensitive appetite or of the will to some good, that is to say, its very complacency in good is called "sensitive love," or "intellectual" or "rational love." So that sensitive love is in the sensitive appetite, just as intellectual love is in the intellectual appetite. And it belongs to the concupiscible power, because it regards good absolutely, and not under the aspect of difficulty, which is the object of the irascible faculty.

Reply to Objection 1: The words quoted refer to intellectual or rational love.

Reply to Objection 2: Love is spoken of as being fear, joy, desire and sadness, not essentially but causally.

AD TERTIUM dicendum quod amor naturalis non solum est in viribus animae vegetativae, sed in omnibus potentiis animae, et etiam in omnibus partibus corporis, et universaliter in omnibus rebus, quia, ut Dionysius dicit, IV cap. de Div. Nom., *omnibus est pulchrum et bonum amabile;* cum unaquaeque res habeat connaturalitatem ad id quod est sibi conveniens secundum suam naturam.

Reply to Objection 3: Natural love is not only in the powers of the vegetal soul, but in all the soul's powers, and also in all the parts of the body, and universally in all things: because, as Dionysius says (Div. Nom. iv), "Beauty and goodness are beloved by all things"; since each single thing has a connaturalness with that which is naturally suitable to it.

Articulus 2

AD SECUNDUM sic proceditur. Videtur quod amor non sit passio. Nulla enim virtus passio est. Sed omnis amor est virtus quaedam, ut dicit Dionysius, IV cap. de Div. Nom. Ergo amor non est passio.

PRAETEREA, amor est unio quaedam vel nexus, secundum Augustinum, in libro de Trin. Sed unio vel nexus non est passio, sed magis relatio. Ergo amor non est passio.

PRAETEREA, Damascenus dicit, in II libro, quod passio est motus quidam. Amor autem non importat motum appetitus, qui est desiderium; sed principium huiusmodi motus. Ergo amor non est passio.

SED CONTRA est quod philosophus dicit, in VIII Ethic., quod *amor est passio.*

RESPONDEO dicendum quod passio est effectus agentis in patiente. Agens autem naturale duplicem effectum inducit in patiens, nam primo quidem dat formam, secundo autem dat motum consequentem formam; sicut generans dat corpori gravitatem, et motum consequentem ipsam. Et ipsa gravitas, quae est principium motus ad locum connaturalem propter gravitatem, potest quodammodo dici *amor naturalis.* Sic etiam ipsum appetibile dat appetitui, primo quidem, quandam coaptationem ad ipsum, quae est complacentia appetibilis; ex qua sequitur motus ad appetibile. Nam *appetitivus motus circulo agitur,* ut dicitur in III de anima, appetibile enim movet appetitum, faciens se quodammodo in eius intentione; et appetitus

Article 2
Whether love is a passion?

Objection 1: It would seem that love is not a passion. For no power is a passion. But every love is a power, as Dionysius says (Div. Nom. iv). Therefore love is not a passion.

Objection 2: Further, love is a kind of union or bond, as Augustine says (De Trin. viii, 10). But a union or bond is not a passion, but rather a relation. Therefore love is not a passion.

Objection 3: Further, Damascene says (De Fide Orth. ii, 22) that passion is a movement. But love does not imply the movement of the appetite; for this is desire, of which movement love is the principle. Therefore love is not a passion.

On the contrary, The Philosopher says (Ethic. viii, 5) that "love is a passion."

I answer that, Passion is the effect of the agent on the patient. Now a natural agent produces a twofold effect on the patient: for in the first place it gives it the form; and secondly it gives it the movement that results from the form. Thus the generator gives the generated body both weight and the movement resulting from weight: so that weight, from being the principle of movement to the place, which is connatural to that body by reason of its weight, can, in a way, be called "natural love." In the same way the appetible object gives the appetite, first, a certain adaptation to itself, which consists in complacency in that object; and from this follows movement towards the appetible object. For "the appetitive movement is circular," as stated in De Anima iii, 10; because the appetible object moves the appetite, introducing itself, as it were, into its intention; while the appetite

tendit in appetibile realiter consequendum, ut sit ibi finis motus, ubi fuit principium. Prima ergo immutatio appetitus ab appetibili vocatur *amor,* qui nihil est aliud quam complacentia appetibilis; et ex hac complacentia sequitur motus in appetibile, qui est *desiderium;* et ultimo quies, quae est *gaudium.* Sic ergo, cum amor consistat in quadam immutatione appetitus ab appetibili, manifestum est quod amor et passio, proprie quidem, secundum quod est in concupiscibili; communiter autem, et extenso nomine, secundum quod est in voluntate.

AD PRIMUM ergo dicendum quod, quia virtus significat principium motus vel actionis, ideo amor, inquantum est principium appetitivi motus, a Dionysio vocatur virtus.

AD SECUNDUM dicendum quod unio pertinet ad amorem, inquantum per complacentiam appetitus amans se habet ad id quod amat, sicut ad seipsum, vel ad aliquid sui. Et sic patet quod amor non est ipsa relatio unionis, sed unio est consequens amorem. Unde et Dionysius dicit quod *amor est virtus unitiva,* et philosophus dicit, in II Polit., quod unio est opus amoris.

AD TERTIUM dicendum quod amor, etsi non nominet motum appetitus tendentem in appetibile, nominat tamen motum appetitus quo immutatur ab appetibili, ut ei appetibile complaceat.

ARTICULUS 3

AD TERTIUM sic proceditur. Videtur quod amor sit idem quod dilectio. Dionysius enim, IV cap. de Div. Nom., dicit quod hoc modo se habent amor et dilectio, *sicut quatuor et bis duo, rectilineum et habens rectas lineas.* Sed ista significant idem. Ergo amor et dilectio significant idem.

PRAETEREA, appetitivi motus secundum obiecta differunt. Sed idem est obiectum dilectionis et amoris. Ergo sunt idem.

PRAETEREA, si dilectio et amor in aliquo differunt, maxime in hoc differre videntur,

moves towards the realization of the appetible object, so that the movement ends where it began. Accordingly, the first change wrought in the appetite by the appetible object is called "love," and is nothing else than complacency in that object; and from this complacency results a movement towards that same object, and this movement is "desire"; and lastly, there is rest which is "joy." Since, therefore, love consists in a change wrought in the appetite by the appetible object, it is evident that love is a passion: properly so called, according as it is in the concupiscible faculty; in a wider and extended sense, according as it is in the will.

Reply to Objection 1: Since power denotes a principle of movement or action, Dionysius calls love a power, in so far as it is a principle of movement in the appetite.

Reply to Objection 2: Union belongs to love in so far as by reason of the complacency of the appetite, the lover stands in relation to that which he loves, as though it were himself or part of himself. Hence it is clear that love is not the very relation of union, but that union is a result of love. Hence, too, Dionysius says that "love is a unitive force" (Div. Nom. iv), and the Philosopher says (Polit. ii, 1) that union is the work of love.

Reply to Objection 3: Although love does not denote the movement of the appetite in tending towards the appetible object, yet it denotes that movement whereby the appetite is changed by the appetible object, so as to have complacency therein.

ARTICLE 3
Whether love is the same as dilection?

Objection 1: It would seem that love is the same as dilection. For Dionysius says (Div. Nom. iv) that love is to dilection, "as four is to twice two, and as a rectilinear figure is to one composed of straight lines." But these have the same meaning. Therefore love and dilection denote the same thing.

Objection 2: Further, the movements of the appetite differ by reason of their objects. But the objects of dilection and love are the same. Therefore these are the same.

Objection 3: Further, if dilection and love differ, it seems that it is chiefly in the fact that

quod *dilectio sit in bono accipienda, amor autem in malo, ut quidam dixerunt,* secundum quod Augustinus narrat, in XIV de Civ. Dei. Sed hoc modo non differunt, quia, ut ibidem Augustinus dicit, in sacris Scripturis utrumque accipitur in bono et in malo. Ergo amor et dilectio non differunt; sicut ipse Augustinus ibidem concludit quod *non est aliud amorem dicere, et aliud dilectionem dicere.*

SED CONTRA est quod Dionysius dicit, IV cap. de Div. Nom., quod *quibusdam sanctorum visum est divinius esse nomen amoris quam nomen dilectionis.*

RESPONDEO dicendum quod quatuor nomina inveniuntur ad idem quodammodo pertinentia, scilicet amor, dilectio, caritas et amicitia. Differunt tamen in hoc, quod *amicitia,* secundum philosophum in VIII Ethic., *est quasi habitus; amor* autem et *dilectio* significantur per modum actus vel passionis; *caritas* autem utroque modo accipi potest. Differenter tamen significatur actus per ista tria. Nam amor communius est inter ea, omnis enim dilectio vel caritas est amor, sed non e converso. Addit enim dilectio supra amorem, electionem praecedentem, ut ipsum nomen sonat. Unde dilectio non est in concupiscibili, sed in voluntate tantum, et est in sola rationali natura. Caritas autem addit supra amorem, perfectionem quandam amoris, inquantum id quod amatur magni pretii aestimatur, ut ipsum nomen designat.

AD PRIMUM ergo dicendum quod Dionysius loquitur de amore et dilectione, secundum quod sunt in appetitu intellectivo, sic enim amor idem est quod dilectio.

AD SECUNDUM dicendum quod obiectum amoris est communius quam obiectum dilectionis, quia ad plura se extendit amor quam dilectio, sicut dictum est.

AD TERTIUM dicendum quod non differunt amor et dilectio secundum differentiam boni et mali, sed sicut dictum est. In parte tamen intellectiva idem est amor et dilectio. Et sic loquitur ibi Augustinus de amore, unde parum post subdit

"dilection refers to good things, love to evil things, as some have maintained," according to Augustine (De Civ. Dei xiv, 7). But they do not differ thus; because as Augustine says (De Civ. Dei xiv, 7) the holy Scripture uses both words in reference to either good or bad things. Therefore love and dilection do not differ: thus indeed Augustine concludes (De Civ. Dei xiv, 7) that "it is not one thing to speak of love, and another to speak of dilection."

On the contrary, Dionysius says (Div. Nom. iv) that "some holy men have held that love means something more Godlike than dilection does."

I answer that, We find four words referring in a way, to the same thing: *viz.* love, dilection, charity and friendship. They differ, however, in this, that "friendship," according to the Philosopher (Ethic. viii, 5), "is like a habit," whereas "love" and "dilection" are expressed by way of act or passion; and "charity" can be taken either way. Moreover these three express act in different ways. For love has a wider signification than the others, since every dilection or charity is love, but not vice versa. Because dilection implies, in addition to love, a choice [*electionem*] made beforehand, as the very word denotes: and therefore dilection is not in the concupiscible power, but only in the will, and only in the rational nature. Charity denotes, in addition to love, a certain perfection of love, in so far as that which is loved is held to be of great price, as the word itself implies.*

Reply to Objection 1: Dionysius is speaking of love and dilection, in so far as they are in the intellectual appetite; for thus love is the same as dilection.

Reply to Objection 2: The object of love is more general than the object of dilection: because love extends to more than dilection does, as stated above.

Reply to Objection 3: Love and dilection differ, not in respect of good and evil, but as stated. Yet in the intellectual faculty love is the same as dilection. And it is in this sense that Augustine speaks of love in the passage quoted: hence a little further on he adds

---

* Referring to the Latin *carus* [dear].

quod *recta voluntas est bonus amor, et perversa voluntas est malus amor.* Quia tamen amor, qui est passio concupiscibilis, plurimos inclinat ad malum, inde habuerunt occasionem qui praedictam differentiam assignaverunt.

AD QUARTUM dicendum quod ideo aliqui posuerunt, etiam in ipsa voluntate, nomen *amoris* esse divinius nomine *dilectionis,* quia amor importat quandam passionem, praecipue secundum quod est in appetitu sensitivo; dilectio autem praesupponit iudicium rationis. Magis autem homo in Deum tendere potest per amorem, passive quodammodo ab ipso Deo attractus, quam ad hoc eum propria ratio ducere possit, quod pertinet ad rationem dilectionis, ut dictum est. Et propter hoc, divinius est amor quam dilectio.

ARTICULUS 4

AD QUARTUM sic proceditur. Videtur quod amor inconvenienter dividatur in amorem amicitiae et concupiscentiae. *Amor enim est passio, amicitia vero est habitus,* ut dicit philosophus, in VIII Ethic. Sed habitus non potest esse pars divisiva passionis. Ergo amor non convenienter dividitur per amorem concupiscentiae et amorem amicitiae.

PRAETEREA, nihil dividitur per id quod ei connumeratur, non enim homo connumeratur *animali.* Sed concupiscentia connumeratur amori, sicut alia passio ab amore. Ergo amor non potest dividi per concupiscentiam.

PRAETEREA, secundum philosophum, in VIII Ethic., triplex est amicitia, *utilis, delectabilis* et *honesta.* Sed amicitia utilis et delectabilis habet concupiscentiam. Ergo concupiscentia non debet dividi contra amicitiam.

SED CONTRA, quaedam dicimur amare quia ea concupiscimus, sicut dicitur *aliquis amare vinum propter dulce quod in eo concupiscit,* ut dicitur in II Topic. Sed ad vinum, et ad huiusmodi, non habemus amicitiam,

that "a right will is well-directed love, and a wrong will is ill-directed love." However, the fact that love, which is concupiscible passion, inclines many to evil, is the reason why some assigned the difference spoken of.

Reply to Objection 4: The reason why some held that, even when applied to the will itself, the word "love" signifies something more Godlike than "dilection," was because love denotes a passion, especially in so far as it is in the sensitive appetite; whereas dilection presupposes the judgment of reason. But it is possible for man to tend to God by love, being as it were passively drawn by Him, more than he can possibly be drawn thereto by his reason, which pertains to the nature of dilection, as stated above. And consequently love is more Godlike than dilection.

ARTICLE 4
Whether love is properly divided into love of friendship and love of concupiscence?

Objection 1: It would seem that love is not properly divided into love of friendship and love of concupiscence. For "love is a passion, while friendship is a habit," according to the Philosopher (Ethic. viii, 5). But habit cannot be the member of a division of passions. Therefore love is not properly divided into love of concupiscence and love of friendship.

Objection 2: Further, a thing cannot be divided by another member of the same division; for man is not a member of the same division as "animal." But concupiscence is a member of the same division as love, as a passion distinct from love. Therefore concupiscence is not a division of love.

Objection 3: Further, according to the Philosopher (Ethic. viii, 3) friendship is threefold, that which is founded on "usefulness," that which is founded on "pleasure," and that which is founded on "goodness." But useful and pleasant friendship are not without concupiscence. Therefore concupiscence should not be contrasted with friendship.

On the contrary, We are said to love certain things, because we desire them: thus "a man is said to love wine, on account of its sweetness which he desires"; as stated in Topic. ii, 3. But we have no friendship for wine and suchlike things, as

ut dicitur in VIII Ethic. Ergo alius est amor concupiscentiae, et alius est amor amicitiae.

Respondeo dicendum quod, sicut philosophus dicit in II Rhetoric., *amare est velle alicui bonum*. Sic ergo motus amoris in duo tendit, scilicet in bonum quod quis vult alicui, vel sibi vel alii; et in illud cui vult bonum. Ad illud ergo bonum quod quis vult alteri, habetur amor concupiscentiae, ad illud autem cui aliquis vult bonum, habetur amor amicitiae. Haec autem divisio est secundum prius et posterius. Nam id quod amatur amore amicitiae, simpliciter et per se amatur, quod autem amatur amore concupiscentiae, non simpliciter et secundum se amatur, sed amatur alteri. Sicut enim ens simpliciter est quod habet esse, ens autem secundum quid quod est in alio; ita bonum, quod convertitur cum ente, simpliciter quidem est quod ipsum habet bonitatem; quod autem est bonum alterius, est bonum secundum quid. Et per consequens amor quo amatur aliquid ut ei sit bonum, est amor simpliciter, amor autem quo amatur aliquid ut sit bonum alterius, est amor secundum quid.

Ad primum ergo dicendum quod amor non dividitur per amicitiam et concupiscentiam, sed per amorem amicitiae et concupiscentiae. Nam ille proprie dicitur amicus, cui aliquod bonum volumus, illud autem dicimur concupiscere, quod volumus nobis.

Et per hoc patet solutio ad secundum.

Ad tertium dicendum quod in amicitia utilis et delectabilis, vult quidem aliquis aliquod bonum amico, et quantum ad hoc salvatur ibi ratio amicitiae. Sed quia illud bonum refert ulterius ad suam delectationem vel utilitatem, inde est quod amicitia utilis et delectabilis, inquantum trahitur ad amorem concupiscentiae, deficit a ratione verae amicitiae.

stated in Ethic. viii, 2. Therefore love of concupiscence is distinct from love of friendship.

I answer that, As the Philosopher says (Rhet. ii, 4), "to love is to wish good to someone." Hence the movement of love has a twofold tendency: towards the good which a man wishes to someone (to himself or to another) and towards that to which he wishes some good. Accordingly, man has love of concupiscence towards the good that he wishes to another, and love of friendship towards him to whom he wishes good. Now the members of this division are related as primary and secondary: since that which is loved with the love of friendship is loved simply and for itself; whereas that which is loved with the love of concupiscence, is loved, not simply and for itself, but for something else. For just as that which has existence, is a being simply, while that which exists in another is a relative being; so, because good is convertible with being, the good, which itself has goodness, is good simply; but that which is another's good, is a relative good. Consequently the love with which a thing is loved, that it may have some good, is love simply; while the love, with which a thing is loved, that it may be another's good, is relative love.

Reply to Objection 1: Love is not divided into friendship and concupiscence, but into love of friendship, and love of concupiscence. For a friend is, properly speaking, one to whom we wish good: while we are said to desire, what we wish for ourselves.

Hence the Reply to the Second Objection.

Reply to Objection 3: When friendship is based on usefulness or pleasure, a man does indeed wish his friend some good: and in this respect the character of friendship is preserved. But since he refers this good further to his own pleasure or use, the result is that friendship of the useful or pleasant, in so far as it is connected with love of concupiscence, loses the character to true friendship.

QUAESTIO XXVII

Deinde considerandum est de causa amoris. Et circa hoc quaeruntur quatuor. *Primo,* utrum bonum sit sola causa amoris. *Secundo,* utrum cognitio sit causa amoris. *Tertio,* utrum similitudo. *Quarto,* utrum aliqua alia animae passionum.

ARTICULUS 1

AD PRIMUM sic proceditur. Videtur quod non solum bonum sit causa amoris. Bonum enim non est causa amoris, nisi quia amatur. Sed contingit etiam malum amari, secundum illud Psalmi X, *qui diligit iniquitatem, odit animam suam,* alioquin omnis amor esset bonus. Ergo non solum bonum est causa amoris.

PRAETEREA, philosophus dicit, in II Rhetoric., quod *eos qui mala sua dicunt, amamus.* Ergo videtur quod malum sit causa amoris.

PRAETEREA, Dionysius dicit, IV cap. de Div. Nom., quod non solum *bonum,* sed etiam *pulchrum est omnibus amabile.*

SED CONTRA est quod Augustinus dicit, VIII de Trin., *non amatur certe nisi bonum.* Solum igitur bonum est causa amoris.

RESPONDEO dicendum quod, sicut supra dictum est, amor ad appetitivam potentiam pertinet, quae est vis passiva. Unde obiectum eius comparatur ad ipsam sicut causa motus vel actus ipsius. Oportet igitur ut illud sit proprie causa amoris quod est amoris obiectum. Amoris autem proprium obiectum est bonum, quia, ut dictum est, amor importat quandam connaturalitatem vel complacentiam amantis ad amatum; unicuique autem est bonum id quod est sibi connaturale et proportionatum. Unde relinquitur quod bonum sit propria causa amoris.

AD PRIMUM ergo dicendum quod malum nunquam amatur nisi sub ratione boni, scilicet inquantum est secundum quid bonum, et apprehenditur ut simpliciter bonum. Et sic aliquis amor est malus, inquantum tendit in id quod non est simpliciter verum bonum. Et per hunc modum homo *diligit iniquitatem,* inquantum

QUESTION 27
Of the Cause of Love

We must now consider the cause of love: and under this head there are four points of inquiry: 1. Whether good is the only cause of love? 2. Whether knowledge is a cause of love? 3. Whether likeness is a cause of love? 4. Whether any other passion of the soul is a cause of love?

ARTICLE 1
Whether good is the only cause of love?

Objection 1: It would seem that good is not the only cause of love. For good does not cause love, except because it is loved. But it happens that evil also is loved, according to Ps. 10:6: "He that loveth iniquity, hateth his own soul": else, every love would be good. Therefore good is not the only cause of love.

Objection 2: Further, the Philosopher says (Rhet. ii, 4) that "we love those who acknowledge their evils." Therefore it seems that evil is the cause of love.

Objection 3: Further, Dionysius says (Div. Nom. iv) that not "the good" only but also "the beautiful is beloved by all."

On the contrary, Augustine says (De Trin. viii, 3): "Assuredly the good alone is beloved." Therefore good alone is the cause of love.

I answer that, As stated above (I-II, q. 26, a. 1), Love belongs to the appetitive power which is a passive faculty. Wherefore its object stands in relation to it as the cause of its movement or act. Therefore the cause of love must needs be love's object. Now the proper object of love is the good; because, as stated above (I-II, q. 26, a. 1; a. 2), love implies a certain connaturalness or complacency of the lover for the thing beloved, and to everything, that thing is a good, which is akin and proportionate to it. It follows, therefore, that good is the proper cause of love.

Reply to Objection 1: Evil is never loved except under the aspect of good, that is to say, in so far as it is good in some respect, and is considered as being good simply. And thus a certain love is evil, in so far as it tends to that which is not simply a true good. It is in this way that man "loves iniquity," inasmuch as,

per iniquitatem adipiscitur aliquod bonum, puta delectationem vel pecuniam vel aliquid huiusmodi.

Ad secundum dicendum quod illi qui mala sua dicunt, non propter mala amantur, sed propter hoc quod dicunt mala, hoc enim quod est dicere mala sua, habet rationem boni, inquantum excludit fictionem seu simulationem.

Ad tertium dicendum quod pulchrum est idem bono, sola ratione differens. Cum enim bonum sit quod omnia appetunt, de ratione boni est quod in eo quietetur appetitus, sed ad rationem pulchri pertinet quod in eius aspectu seu cognitione quietetur appetitus. Unde et illi sensus praecipue respiciunt pulchrum, qui maxime cognoscitivi sunt, scilicet visus et auditus rationi deservientes, dicimus enim pulchra visibilia et pulchros sonos. In sensibilibus autem aliorum sensuum, non utimur nomine *pulchritudinis,* non enim dicimus pulchros sapores aut odores. Et sic patet quod pulchrum addit supra bonum, quendam ordinem ad vim cognoscitivam, ita quod *bonum* dicatur id quod simpliciter complacet appetitui; *pulchrum* autem dicatur id cuius ipsa apprehensio placet.

by means of iniquity, some good is gained; pleasure, for instance, or money, or such like.

Reply to Objection 2: Those who acknowledge their evils, are beloved, not for their evils, but because they acknowledge them, for it is a good thing to acknowledge one's faults, in so far as it excludes insincerity or hypocrisy.

Reply to Objection 3: The beautiful is the same as the good, and they differ in aspect only. For since good is what all seek, the notion of good is that which calms the desire; while the notion of the beautiful is that which calms the desire, by being seen or known. Consequently those senses chiefly regard the beautiful, which are the most cognitive, *viz.* sight and hearing, as ministering to reason; for we speak of beautiful sights and beautiful sounds. But in reference to the other objects of the other senses, we do not use the expression "beautiful," for we do not speak of beautiful tastes, and beautiful odors. Thus it is evident that beauty adds to goodness a relation to the cognitive faculty: so that "good" means that which simply pleases the appetite; while the "beautiful" is something pleasant to apprehend.

Articulus 2

Ad secundum sic proceditur. Videtur quod cognitio non sit causa amoris. Quod enim aliquid quaeratur, hoc contingit ex amore. Sed aliqua quaeruntur quae nesciuntur, sicut scientiae, cum enim *in his idem sit eas habere quod eas nosse,* ut Augustinus dicit in libro octoginta trium quaest., si cognoscerentur, haberentur, et non quaererentur. Ergo cognitio non est causa amoris.

Praeterea, eiusdem rationis videtur esse quod aliquid incognitum ametur, et quod aliquid ametur plus quam cognoscatur. Sed aliqua amantur plus quam cognoscantur, sicut Deus, qui in hac vita potest per seipsum amari, non autem per seipsum cognosci. Ergo cognitio non est causa amoris.

Praeterea, si cognitio esset causa amoris, non posset inveniri amor ubi non est cognitio. Sed in omnibus rebus invenitur amor, ut dicit Dionysius in IV cap. de Div. Nom.,

Article 2
Whether knowledge is a cause of love?

Objection 1: It would seem that knowledge is not a cause of love. For it is due to love that a thing is sought. But some things are sought without being known, for instance, the sciences; for since "to have them is the same as to know them," as Augustine says (QQ 83, qu. 35), if we knew them we should have them, and should not seek them. Therefore knowledge is not the cause of love.

Objection 2: Further, to love what we know not seems like loving something more than we know it. But some things are loved more than they are known: thus in this life God can be loved in Himself, but cannot be known in Himself. Therefore knowledge is not the cause of love.

Objection 3: Further, if knowledge were the cause of love, there would be no love, where there is no knowledge. But in all things there is love, as Dionysius says (Div. Nom.

I-II, q. 27, a. 2, arg. 3

non autem in omnibus invenitur cognitio. Ergo cognitio non est causa amoris.

Sed contra est quod Augustinus probat, in X de Trin., quod *nullus potest amare aliquid incognitum.*

Respondeo dicendum quod, sicut dictum est, bonum est causa amoris per modum obiecti. Bonum autem non est obiectum appetitus, nisi prout est apprehensum. Et ideo amor requirit aliquam apprehensionem boni quod amatur. Et propter hoc philosophus dicit, IX Ethic., quod visio corporalis est principium amoris sensitivi. Et similiter contemplatio spiritualis pulchritudinis vel bonitatis, est principium amoris spiritualis. Sic igitur cognitio est causa amoris, ea ratione qua et bonum, quod non potest amari nisi cognitum.

Ad primum ergo dicendum quod ille qui quaerit scientiam, non omnino ignorat eam, sed secundum aliquid eam praecognoscit, vel in universali, vel in aliquo eius effectu, vel per hoc quod audit eam laudari, ut Augustinus dicit, X de Trin. Sic autem eam cognoscere non est eam habere; sed cognoscere eam perfecte.

Ad secundum dicendum quod aliquid requiritur ad perfectionem cognitionis, quod non requiritur ad perfectionem amoris. Cognitio enim ad rationem pertinet, cuius est distinguere inter ea quae secundum rem sunt coniuncta, et componere quodammodo ea quae sunt diversa, unum alteri comparando. Et ideo ad perfectionem cognitionis requiritur quod homo cognoscat singillatim quidquid est in re, sicut partes et virtutes et proprietates. Sed amor est in vi appetitiva, quae respicit rem secundum quod in se est. Unde ad perfectionem amoris sufficit quod res prout in se apprehenditur, ametur. Ob hoc ergo contingit quod aliquid plus amatur quam cognoscatur, quia potest perfecte amari, etiam si non perfecte cognoscatur. Sicut maxime patet in scientiis, quas aliqui amant propter aliquam summariam cognitionem quam de eis habent, puta quod sciunt rhetoricam esse scientiam per quam homo potest persuadere,

THE CAUSE OF LOVE

iv); whereas there is not knowledge in all things. Therefore knowledge is not the cause of love.

On the contrary, Augustine proves (De Trin. x, 1, 2) that "none can love what he does not know."

I answer that, As stated above (I-II, q. 27, a. 1), good is the cause of love, as being its object. But good is not the object of the appetite, except as apprehended. And therefore **love demands some apprehension of the good** that is loved. For this reason the Philosopher (Ethic. ix, 5, 12) says that bodily sight is the beginning of sensitive love: and in like manner the contemplation of spiritual beauty or goodness is the beginning of spiritual love. Accordingly knowledge is the cause of love for the same reason as good is, which can be loved only if known.

Reply to Objection 1: He who seeks science, is not entirely without knowledge thereof: but knows something about it already in some respect, either in a general way, or in some one of its effects, or from having heard it commended, as Augustine says (De Trin. x, 1,2). But to have it is not to know it thus, but to know it perfectly.

Reply to Objection 2: Something is required for the perfection of knowledge, that is not requisite for the perfection of love. For knowledge belongs to the reason, whose function it is to distinguish things which in reality are united, and to unite together, after a fashion, things that are distinct, by comparing one with another. Consequently the perfection of knowledge requires that man should know distinctly all that is in a thing, such as its parts, powers, and properties. On the other hand, love is in the appetitive power, which regards a thing as it is in itself: wherefore it suffices, for the perfection of love, that a thing be loved according as it is known in itself. Hence it is, therefore, that a thing is loved more than it is known; since it can be loved perfectly, even without being perfectly known. This is most evident in regard to the sciences, which some love through having a certain general knowledge of them: for instance, they know that rhetoric is a science that enables man to persuade

et hoc in rhetorica amant. Et similiter est dicendum circa amorem Dei.

AD TERTIUM dicendum quod etiam amor naturalis, qui est in omnibus rebus, causatur ex aliqua cognitione, non quidem in ipsis rebus naturalibus existente, sed in eo qui naturam instituit, ut supra dictum est.

Articulus 3

AD TERTIUM sic proceditur. Videtur quod similitudo non sit causa amoris. Idem enim non est causa contrariorum. Sed similitudo est causa odii, dicitur enim Prov. XIII, quod *inter superbos semper sunt iurgia;* et philosophus dicit, in VIII Ethic., quod *figuli corrixantur ad invicem.* Ergo similitudo non est causa amoris.

PRAETEREA, Augustinus dicit, in IV Confess., quod *aliquis amat in alio quod esse non vellet, sicut homo amat histrionem, qui non vellet esse histrio.* Hoc autem non contingeret, si similitudo esset propria causa amoris, sic enim homo amaret in altero quod ipse haberet, vel vellet habere. Ergo similitudo non est causa amoris.

PRAETEREA, quilibet homo amat id quo indiget, etiam si illud non habeat, sicut infirmus amat sanitatem, et pauper amat divitias. Sed inquantum indiget et caret eis, habet dissimilitudinem ad ipsa. Ergo non solum similitudo, sed etiam dissimilitudo est causa amoris.

PRAETEREA, philosophus dicit, in II Rhetoric., quod *beneficos in pecunias et salutem amamus, et similiter eos qui circa mortuos servant amicitiam, omnes diligunt.* Non autem omnes sunt tales. Ergo similitudo non est causa amoris.

SED CONTRA est quod dicitur Eccli. XIII, *omne animal diligit simile sibi.*

RESPONDEO dicendum quod similitudo, proprie loquendo, est causa amoris. Sed considerandum est quod similitudo inter aliqua potest attendi dupliciter. Uno modo, ex hoc quod utrumque habet idem in actu, sicut duo habentes albedinem, dicuntur similes. Alio modo, ex hoc quod unum habet in potentia

others; and this is what they love in rhetoric. The same applies to the love of God.

Reply to Objection 3: Even natural love, which is in all things, is caused by a kind of knowledge, not indeed existing in natural things themselves, but in Him Who created their nature, as stated above (I-II, q. 26, a. 1; cf. I, q. 6, a. 1, ad 2).

Article 3
Whether likeness is a cause of love?

Objection 1: It would seem that likeness is not a cause of love. For the same thing is not the cause of contraries. But likeness is the cause of hatred; for it is written (Prov. 13:10) that "among the proud there are always contentions"; and the Philosopher says (Ethic. viii, 1) that "potters quarrel with one another." Therefore likeness is not a cause of love.

Objection 2: Further, Augustine says (Confess. iv, 14) that "a man loves in another that which he would not be himself: thus he loves an actor, but would not himself be an actor." But it would not be so, if likeness were the proper cause of love; for in that case a man would love in another, that which he possesses himself, or would like to possess. Therefore likeness is not a cause of love.

Objection 3: Further, everyone loves that which he needs, even if he have it not: thus a sick man loves health, and a poor man loves riches. But in so far as he needs them and lacks them, he is unlike them. Therefore not only likeness but also unlikeness is a cause of love.

Objection 4: Further, the Philosopher says (Rhet. ii, 4) that "we love those who bestow money and health on us; and also those who retain their friendship for the dead." But all are not such. Therefore likeness is not a cause of love.

On the contrary, It is written (Ecclus. 13:19): "Every beast loveth its like."

I answer that, Likeness, properly speaking, is a cause of love. But it must be observed that likeness between things is twofold. One kind of likeness arises from each thing having the same quality actually: for example, two things possessing the quality of whiteness are said to be alike. Another kind of likeness arises from one thing having potentially

et in quadam inclinatione, illud quod aliud habet in actu, sicut si dicamus quod corpus grave existens extra suum locum, habet similitudinem cum corpore gravi in suo loco existenti. Vel etiam secundum quod potentia habet similitudinem ad actum ipsum, nam in ipsa potentia quodammodo est actus. Primus ergo similitudinis modus causat amorem amicitiae, seu benevolentiae. Ex hoc enim quod aliqui duo sunt similes, quasi habentes unam formam, sunt quodammodo unum in forma illa, sicut duo homines sunt unum in specie humanitatis, et duo albi in albedine. Et ideo affectus unius tendit in alterum, sicut in unum sibi; et vult ei bonum sicut et sibi. Sed secundus modus similitudinis causat amorem concupiscentiae, vel amicitiam utilis seu delectabilis. Quia unicuique existenti in potentia, inquantum huiusmodi, inest appetitus sui actus, et in eius consecutione delectatur, si sit sentiens et cognoscens. Dictum est autem supra quod in amore concupiscentiae amans proprie amat seipsum, cum vult illud bonum quod concupiscit. Magis autem unusquisque seipsum amat quam alium, quia sibi unus est in substantia, alteri vero in similitudine alicuius formae. Et ideo si ex eo quod est sibi similis in participatione formae, impediatur ipsemet a consecutione boni quod amat; efficitur ei odiosus, non inquantum est similis, sed inquantum est proprii boni impeditivus. Et propter hoc *figuli corrixantur ad invicem,* quia se invicem impediunt in proprio lucro, et *inter superbos sunt iurgia,* quia se invicem impediunt in propria excellentia, quam concupiscunt.

Et per hoc patet responsio ad primum.

AD SECUNDUM dicendum quod in hoc etiam quod aliquis in altero amat quod in se non amat, invenitur ratio similitudinis secundum proportionalitatem, nam sicut se habet alius ad hoc quod in eo amatur, ita ipse se habet ad hoc quod in se amat. Puta si bonus cantor bonum amet scriptorem, attenditur ibi similitudo proportionis, secundum quod

and by way of inclination, a quality which the other has actually: thus we may say that a heavy body existing outside its proper place is like another heavy body that exists in its proper place: or again, according as potentiality bears a resemblance to its act; since act is contained, in a manner, in the potentiality itself. Accordingly the first kind of likeness causes love of friendship or well-being. For the very fact that two men are alike, having, as it were, one form, makes them to be, in a manner, one in that form: thus two men are one thing in the species of humanity, and two white men are one thing in whiteness. Hence the affections of one tend to the other, as being one with him; and he wishes good to him as to himself. But the second kind of likeness causes love of concupiscence, or friendship founded on usefulness or pleasure: because whatever is in potentiality, as such, has the desire for its act; and it takes pleasure in its realization, if it be a sentient and cognitive being. Now it has been stated above (I-II, q. 26, a. 4), that in the love of concupiscence, the lover, properly speaking, loves himself, in willing the good that he desires. But a man loves himself more than another: because he is one with himself substantially, whereas with another he is one only in the likeness of some form. Consequently, if this other's likeness to him arising from the participation of a form, hinders him from gaining the good that he loves, he becomes hateful to him, not for being like him, but for hindering him from gaining his own good. This is why "potters quarrel among themselves," because they hinder one another's gain: and why "there are contentions among the proud," because they hinder one another in attaining the position they covet.

Hence the Reply to the First Objection is evident.

Reply to Objection 2: Even when a man loves in another what he loves not in himself, there is a certain likeness of proportion: because as the latter is to that which is loved in him, so is the former to that which he loves in himself: for instance, if a good singer love a good writer, we can see a likeness of proportion, inasmuch as

uterque habet quod convenit ei secundum suam artem.

Ad tertium dicendum quod ille qui amat hoc quo indiget, habet similitudinem ad id quod amat sicut quod est potentia ad actum, ut dictum est.

Ad quartum dicendum quod secundum eandem similitudinem potentiae ad actum, ille qui non est liberalis, amat eum qui est liberalis, inquantum expectat ab eo aliquid quod desiderat. Et eadem ratio est de perseverante in amicitia ad eum qui non perseverat. Utrobique enim videtur esse amicitia propter utilitatem. Vel dicendum quod, licet non omnes homines habeant huiusmodi virtutes secundum habitum completum, habent tamen ea secundum quaedam seminalia rationis, secundum quae, qui non habet virtutem, diligit virtuosum, tanquam suae naturali rationi conformem.

Reply to Objection 3: He that loves what he needs, bears a likeness to what he loves, as potentiality bears a likeness to its act, as stated above.

Reply to Objection 4: According to the same likeness of potentiality to its act, the illiberal man loves the man who is liberal, in so far as he expects from him something which he desires. The same applies to the man who is constant in his friendship as compared to one who is inconstant. For in either case friendship seems to be based on usefulness. We might also say that although not all men have these virtues in the complete habit, yet they have them according to certain seminal principles in the reason, in force of which principles the man who is not virtuous loves the virtuous man, as being in conformity with his own natural reason.

Articulus 4

Ad quartum sic proceditur. Videtur quod aliqua alia passio possit esse causa amoris. Dicit enim philosophus, in VIII Ethic., quod aliqui amantur propter delectationem. Sed delectatio est passio quaedam. Ergo aliqua alia passio est causa amoris.

Praeterea, desiderium quaedam passio est. Sed aliquos amamus propter desiderium alicuius quod ab eis expectamus, sicut apparet in omni amicitia quae est propter utilitatem. Ergo aliqua alia passio est causa amoris.

Praeterea, Augustinus dicit, in X de Trin., *cuius rei adipiscendae spem quisque non gerit, aut tepide amat, aut omnino non amat, quamvis quam pulchra sit videat.* Ergo spes etiam est causa amoris.

Sed contra est quod omnes aliae affectiones animi ex amore causantur, ut Augustinus dicit, XIV de Civ. Dei.

Respondeo dicendum quod nulla alia passio animae est quae non praesupponat aliquem amorem. Cuius ratio est quia omnis alia passio animae vel importat motum ad aliquid, vel quietem in aliquo. Omnis autem motus in aliquid, vel quies in aliquo,

Article 4
Whether any other passion of the soul is a cause of love?

Objection 1: It would seem that some other passion can be the cause of love. For the Philosopher (Ethic. viii, 3) says that some are loved for the sake of the pleasure they give. But pleasure is a passion. Therefore another passion is a cause of love.

Objection 2: Further, desire is a passion. But we love some because we desire to receive something from them: as happens in every friendship based on usefulness. Therefore another passion is a cause of love.

Objection 3: Further, Augustine says (De Trin. x, 1): "When we have no hope of getting a thing, we love it but half-heartedly or not at all, even if we see how beautiful it is." Therefore hope too is a cause of love.

On the contrary, All the other emotions of the soul are caused by love, as Augustine says (De Civ. Dei xiv, 7, 9).

I answer that, There is no other passion of the soul that does not presuppose love of some kind. The reason is that every other passion of the soul implies either movement towards something, or rest in something. Now every movement towards something, or rest in something,

ex aliqua connaturalitate vel coaptatione procedit, quae pertinet ad rationem amoris. Unde impossibile est quod aliqua alia passio animae sit causa universaliter omnis amoris. Contingit tamen aliquam aliam passionem esse causam amoris alicuius, sicut etiam unum bonum est causa alterius.

AD PRIMUM ergo dicendum quod, cum aliquis amat aliquid propter delectationem, amor quidem ille causatur ex delectatione, sed delectatio illa iterum causatur ex alio amore praecedente; nullus enim delectatur nisi in re aliquo modo amata.

AD SECUNDUM dicendum quod desiderium rei alicuius semper praesupponit amorem illius rei. Sed desiderium alicuius rei potest esse causa ut res alia ametur, sicut qui desiderat pecuniam, amat propter hoc eum a quo pecuniam recipit.

AD TERTIUM dicendum quod spes causat vel auget amorem, et ratione delectationis, quia delectationem causat, et etiam ratione desiderii, quia spes desiderium fortificat, non enim ita intense desideramus quae non speramus. Sed tamen et ipsa spes est alicuius boni amati.

arises from some kinship or aptness to that thing; and in this does love consist. Therefore it is not possible for any other passion of the soul to be universally the cause of every love. But it may happen that some other passion is the cause of some particular love: just as one good is the cause of another.

Reply to Objection 1: When a man loves a thing for the pleasure it affords, his love is indeed caused by pleasure; but that very pleasure is caused, in its turn, by another preceding love; for none takes pleasure save in that which is loved in some way.

Reply to Objection 2: Desire for a thing always presupposes love for that thing. But desire of one thing can be the cause of another thing's being loved; thus he that desires money, for this reason loves him from whom he receives it.

Reply to Objection 3: Hope causes or increases love; both by reason of pleasure, because it causes pleasure; and by reason of desire, because hope strengthens desire, since we do not desire so intensely that which we have no hope of receiving. Nevertheless hope itself is of a good that is loved.

Quaestio XXVIII

Deinde considerandum est de effectibus amoris. Et circa hoc quaeruntur sex. *Primo*, utrum unio sit effectus amoris. *Secundo*, utrum mutua inhaesio. *Tertio*, utrum extasis sit effectus amoris. *Quarto*, utrum zelus. *Quinto*, utrum amor sit passio laesiva amantis. *Sexto*, utrum amor sit causa omnium quae amans agit.

Articulus 1

AD PRIMUM sic proceditur. Videtur quod unio non sit effectus amoris. Absentia enim unioni repugnat. Sed amor compatitur secum absentiam, dicit enim apostolus, ad Galat. IV, *bonum aemulamini in bono semper* (loquens de seipso, ut Glossa dicit), *et non tantum cum praesens sum apud vos*. Ergo unio non est effectus amoris.

PRAETEREA, omnis unio aut est per essentiam, sicut forma unitur materiae, et accidens subiecto, et pars toti vel alteri parti ad constitutionem totius, aut est per similitudinem vel generis, vel speciei, vel accidentis. Sed amor non causat unionem essentiae, alioquin nunquam haberetur amor ad ea quae sunt per essentiam divisa. Unionem autem quae est per similitudinem, amor non causat, sed magis ab ea causatur. Ut dictum est. Ergo unio non est effectus amoris.

PRAETEREA, sensus in actu fit sensibile in actu, et intellectus in actu fit intellectum in actu. Non autem amans in actu fit amatum in actu. Ergo unio magis est effectus cognitionis quam amoris.

SED CONTRA est quod dicit Dionysius, IV cap. de Div. Nom., quod amor quilibet est *virtus unitiva*.

RESPONDEO dicendum quod duplex est unio amantis ad amatum. Una quidem secundum rem, puta cum amatum praesentialiter adest amanti. Alia vero secundum affectum. Quae quidem unio consideranda est ex apprehensione praecedente, nam motus appetitivus sequitur apprehensionem. Cum autem sit duplex amor, scilicet

Question 28
Of the Effects of Love

We now have to consider the effects of love: under which head there are six points of inquiry: 1. Whether union is an effect of love? 2. Whether mutual indwelling is an effect of love? 3. Whether ecstasy is an effect of love? 4. Whether zeal is an effect of love? 5. Whether love is a passion that is hurtful to the lover? 6. Whether love is cause of all that the lover does?

Article 1
Whether union is an effect of love?

Objection 1: It would seem that union is not an effect of love. For absence is incompatible with union. But love is compatible with absence; for the Apostle says (Gal. 4:18): "Be zealous for that which is good in a good thing always" (speaking of himself, according to a gloss), "and not only when I am present with you." Therefore union is not an effect of love.

Objection 2: Further, every union is either according to essence, thus form is united to matter, accident to subject, and a part to the whole, or to another part in order to make up the whole: or according to likeness, in genus, species, or accident. But love does not cause union of essence; else love could not be between things essentially distinct. On the other hand, love does not cause union of likeness, but rather is caused by it, as stated above (I-II, q. 27, a. 3). Therefore union is not an effect of love.

Objection 3: Further, the sense in act is the sensible in act, and the intellect in act is the thing actually understood. But the lover in act is not the beloved in act. Therefore union is the effect of knowledge rather than of love.

On the contrary, Dionysius says (Div. Nom. iv) that every love is a "unitive force."

I answer that, The union of lover and beloved is twofold. The first is real union; for instance, when the beloved is present with the lover. The second is union of affection: and this union must be considered in relation to the preceding apprehension; since movement of the appetite follows apprehension. Now love being twofold, *viz.* love of

concupiscentiae et amicitiae, uterque procedit ex quadam apprehensione unitatis amati ad amantem. Cum enim aliquis amat aliquid quasi concupiscens illud, apprehendit illud quasi pertinens ad suum bene esse. Similiter cum aliquis amat aliquem amore amicitiae, vult ei bonum sicut et sibi vult bonum, unde apprehendit eum ut alterum se, inquantum scilicet vult ei bonum sicut et sibi ipsi. Et inde est quod amicus dicitur esse *alter ipse,* et Augustinus dicit, in IV Confess., *bene quidam dixit de amico suo, dimidium animae suae.* Primam ergo unionem amor facit *effective,* quia movet ad desiderandum et quaerendum praesentiam amati, quasi sibi convenientis et ad se pertinentis. Secundam autem unionem facit *formaliter,* quia ipse amor est talis unio vel nexus. Unde Augustinus dicit, in VIII de Trin., quod *amor est quasi vita quaedam duo aliqua copulans, vel copulare appetens, amantem scilicet et quod amatur.* Quod enim dicit *copulans,* refertur ad unionem affectus, sine qua non est amor, quod vero dicit *copulare intendens,* pertinet ad unionem realem.

AD PRIMUM ergo dicendum quod obiectio illa procedit de unione reali. Quam quidem requirit delectatio sicut causam, desiderium vero est in reali absentia amati, amor vero et in absentia et in praesentia.

AD SECUNDUM dicendum quod unio tripliciter se habet ad amorem. Quaedam enim unio est causa amoris. Et haec quidem est unio substantialis, quantum ad amorem quo quis amat seipsum, quantum vero ad amorem quo quis amat alia, est unio similitudinis, ut dictum est. Quaedam vero unio est essentialiter ipse amor. Et haec est unio secundum coaptationem affectus. Quae quidem assimilatur unioni substantiali, inquantum amans se habet ad amatum, in amore quidem amicitiae, ut ad seipsum; in amore autem concupiscentiae, ut ad aliquid sui. Quaedam vero unio est effectus amoris. Et haec est unio realis, quam amans quaerit de re amata. Et haec quidem unio est secundum convenientiam amoris, ut enim philosophus refert, II Politic., *Aristophanes dixit quod*

concupiscence and love of friendship; each of these arises from a kind of apprehension of the oneness of the thing loved with the lover. For when we love a thing, by desiring it, we apprehend it as belonging to our well-being. In like manner when a man loves another with the love of friendship, he wills good to him, just as he wills good to himself: wherefore he apprehends him as his other self, in so far, to wit, as he wills good to him as to himself. Hence a friend is called a man's "other self" (Ethic. ix, 4), and Augustine says (Confess. iv, 6), "Well did one say to his friend: Thou half of my soul." The first of these unions is caused "effectively" by love; because love moves man to desire and seek the presence of the beloved, as of something suitable and belonging to him. The second union is caused "formally" by love; because love itself is this union or bond. In this sense Augustine says (De Trin. viii, 10) that "love is a vital principle uniting, or seeking to unite two together, the lover, to wit, and the beloved." For in describing it as "uniting" he refers to the union of affection, without which there is no love: and in saying that "it seeks to unite," he refers to real union.

Reply to Objection 1: This argument is true of real union. That is necessary to pleasure as being its cause; desire implies the real absence of the beloved: but love remains whether the beloved be absent or present.

Reply to Objection 2: Union has a threefold relation to love. There is union which causes love; and this is substantial union, as regards the love with which one loves oneself; while as regards the love wherewith one loves other things, it is the union of likeness, as stated above (I-II, q. 27, a. 3). There is also a union which is essentially love itself. This union is according to a bond of affection, and is likened to substantial union, inasmuch as the lover stands to the object of his love, as to himself, if it be love of friendship; as to something belonging to himself, if it be love of concupiscence. Again there is a union, which is the effect of love. This is real union, which the lover seeks with the object of his love. Moreover this union is in keeping with the demands of love: for as the Philosopher relates (Polit. ii, 1), "Aristophanes stated that

amantes desiderarent ex ambobus fieri unum, sed quia *ex hoc accideret aut ambos aut alterum corrumpi,* quaerunt unionem quae convenit et decet; ut scilicet simul conversentur, et simul colloquantur, et in aliis huiusmodi coniungantur.

AD TERTIUM dicendum quod cognitio perficitur per hoc quod cognitum unitur cognoscenti secundum suam similitudinem. Sed amor facit quod ipsa res quae amatur, amanti aliquo modo uniatur, ut dictum est. Unde amor est magis unitivus quam cognitio.

lovers would wish to be united both into one," but since "this would result in either one or both being destroyed," they seek a suitable and becoming union—to live together, speak together, and be united together in other like things.

Reply to Objection 3: Knowledge is perfected by the thing known being united, through its likeness, to the knower. But the effect of love is that the thing itself which is loved, is, in a way, united to the lover, as stated above. Consequently the union caused by love is closer than that which is caused by knowledge.

ARTICULUS 2

AD SECUNDUM sic proceditur. Videtur quod amor non causet mutuam inhaesionem, ut scilicet amans sit in amato, et e converso. Quod enim est in altero, continetur in eo. Sed non potest idem esse continens et contentum. Ergo per amorem non potest causari mutua inhaesio, ut amatum sit in amante et e converso.

PRAETEREA, nihil potest penetrare in interiora alicuius integri, nisi per aliquam divisionem. Sed dividere quae sunt secundum rem coniuncta, non pertinet ad appetitum, in quo est amor, sed ad rationem. Ergo mutua inhaesio non est effectus amoris.

PRAETEREA, si per amorem amans est in amato et e converso, sequetur quod hoc modo amatum uniatur amanti, sicut amans amato. Sed ipsa unio est amor, ut dictum est. Ergo sequitur quod semper amans ametur ab amato, quod patet esse falsum. Non ergo mutua inhaesio est effectus amoris.

SED CONTRA est quod dicitur I Ioan. IV, *qui manet in caritate, in Deo manet, et Deus in eo.* Caritas autem est amor Dei. Ergo, eadem ratione, quilibet amor facit amatum esse in amante, et e converso.

ARTICLE 2
Whether mutual indwelling is an effect of love?

Objection 1: It would seem that love does not cause mutual indwelling, so that the lover be in the beloved and vice versa. For that which is in another is contained in it. But the same cannot be container and contents. Therefore love cannot cause mutual indwelling, so that the lover be in the beloved and vice versa.

Objection 2: Further, nothing can penetrate within a whole, except by means of a division of the whole. But it is the function of the reason, not of the appetite where love resides, to divide things that are really united. Therefore mutual indwelling is not an effect of love.

Objection 3: Further, if love involves the lover being in the beloved and vice versa, it follows that the beloved is united to the lover, in the same way as the lover is united to the beloved. But the union itself is love, as stated above (I-II, q. 28, a. 1). Therefore it follows that the lover is always loved by the object of his love; which is evidently false. Therefore mutual indwelling is not an effect of love.

On the contrary, It is written (1 Jn. 4:16): "He that abideth in charity abideth in God, and God in him." Now charity is the love of God. Therefore, for the same reason, every love makes the beloved to be in the lover, and vice versa.

RESPONDEO dicendum quod iste effectus mutuae inhaesionis potest intelligi et quantum ad vim apprehensivam, et quantum ad vim appetitivam. Nam quantum ad vim apprehensivam amatum dicitur esse in amante, inquantum amatum immoratur in apprehensione amantis; secundum illud Philipp. I, *eo quod habeam vos in corde.* Amans vero dicitur esse in amato secundum apprehensionem inquantum amans non est contentus superficiali apprehensione amati, sed nititur singula quae ad amatum pertinent intrinsecus disquirere, et sic ad interiora eius ingreditur. Sicut de spiritu sancto, qui est amor Dei, dicitur, I ad Cor. II, quod *scrutatur etiam profunda Dei.* Sed quantum ad vim appetitivam, amatum dicitur esse in amante, prout est per quandam complacentiam in eius affectu, ut vel delectetur in eo, aut in bonis eius, apud praesentiam; vel in absentia, per desiderium tendat in ipsum amatum per amorem concupiscentiae; vel in bona quae vult amato, per amorem amicitiae; non quidem ex aliqua extrinseca causa, sicut cum aliquis desiderat aliquid propter alterum, vel cum aliquis vult bonum alteri propter aliquid aliud; sed propter complacentiam amati interius radicatam. Unde et amor dicitur *intimus;* et dicuntur *viscera caritatis.* E converso autem amans est in amato aliter quidem per amorem concupiscentiae, aliter per amorem amicitiae. Amor namque concupiscentiae non requiescit in quacumque extrinseca aut superficiali adeptione vel fruitione amati, sed quaerit amatum perfecte habere, quasi ad intima illius perveniens. In amore vero amicitiae, amans est in amato, inquantum reputat bona vel mala amici sicut sua, et voluntatem amici sicut suam, ut quasi ipse in suo amico videatur bona vel mala pati, et affici. Et propter hoc, proprium est amicorum *eadem velle, et in eodem tristari et gaudere* secundum philosophum, in IX Ethic. et in II Rhetoric. Ut sic, inquantum

I answer that, This effect of mutual indwelling may be understood as referring both to the apprehensive and to the appetitive power. Because, as to the apprehensive power, the beloved is said to be in the lover, inasmuch as the beloved abides in the apprehension of the lover, according to Phil. 1:7, "For that I have you in my heart": while the lover is said to be in the beloved, according to apprehension, inasmuch as the lover is not satisfied with a superficial apprehension of the beloved, but strives to gain an intimate knowledge of everything pertaining to the beloved, so as to penetrate into his very soul. Thus it is written concerning the Holy Ghost, Who is God's Love, that He "searcheth all things, yea the deep things of God" (1 Cor. 2:10). As the appetitive power, the object loved is said to be in the lover, inasmuch as it is in his affections, by a kind of complacency: causing him either to take pleasure in it, or in its good, when present; or, in the absence of the object loved, by his longing, to tend towards it with the love of concupiscence, or towards the good that he wills to the beloved, with the love of friendship: not indeed from any extrinsic cause (as when we desire one thing on account of another, or wish good to another on account of something else), but because the complacency in the beloved is rooted in the lover's heart. For this reason we speak of love as being "intimate"; and "of the bowels of charity." On the other hand, the lover is in the beloved, by the love of concupiscence and by the love of friendship, but not in the same way. For the love of concupiscence is not satisfied with any external or superficial possession or enjoyment of the beloved; but seeks to possess the beloved perfectly, by penetrating into his heart, as it were. Whereas, in the love of friendship, the lover is in the beloved, inasmuch as he reckons what is good or evil to his friend, as being so to himself; and his friend's will as his own, so that it seems as though he felt the good or suffered the evil in the person of his friend. Hence it is proper to friends "to desire the same things, and to grieve and rejoice at the same," as the Philosopher says (Ethic. ix, 3 and Rhet. ii, 4). Consequently in so far as

quae sunt amici aestimat sua, amans videatur esse in amato, quasi idem factus amato. Inquantum autem e converso vult et agit propter amicum sicut propter seipsum, quasi reputans amicum idem sibi, sic amatum est in amante. Potest autem et tertio modo mutua inhaesio intelligi in amore amicitiae, secundum viam redamationis, inquantum mutuo se amant amici, et sibi invicem bona volunt et operantur.

A<small>D</small> <small>PRIMUM</small> ergo dicendum quod amatum continetur in amante, inquantum est impressum in affectu eius per quandam complacentiam. E converso vero amans continetur in amato, inquantum amans sequitur aliquo modo illud quod est intimum amati. Nihil enim prohibet diverso modo esse aliquid continens et contentum, sicut genus continetur in specie et e converso.

A<small>D</small> <small>SECUNDUM</small> dicendum quod rationis apprehensio praecedit affectum amoris. Et ideo, sicut ratio disquirit, ita affectus amoris subintrat in amatum, ut ex dictis patet.

A<small>D</small> <small>TERTIUM</small> dicendum quod illa ratio procedit de tertio modo mutuae inhaesionis, qui non invenitur in quolibet amore.

A<small>RTICULUS</small> 3

A<small>D</small> <small>TERTIUM</small> sic proceditur. Videtur quod extasis non sit effectus amoris. Extasis enim quandam alienationem importare videtur. Sed amor non semper facit alienationem, sunt enim amantes interdum sui compotes. Ergo amor non facit extasim.

P<small>RAETEREA</small>, amans desiderat amatum sibi uniri. Magis ergo amatum trahit ad se, quam etiam pergat in amatum, extra se exiens.

P<small>RAETEREA</small>, amor unit amatum amanti, sicut dictum est. Si ergo amans extra se tendit, ut in amatum pergat, sequitur quod semper plus diligat amatum quam seipsum.

he reckons what affects his friend as affecting himself, the lover seems to be in the beloved, as though he were become one with him: but in so far as, on the other hand, he wills and acts for his friend's sake as for his own sake, looking on his friend as identified with himself, thus the beloved is in the lover. In yet a third way, mutual indwelling in the love of friendship can be understood in regard to reciprocal love: inasmuch as friends return love for love, and both desire and do good things for one another.

Reply to Objection 1: The beloved is contained in the lover, by being impressed on his heart and thus becoming the object of his complacency. On the other hand, the lover is contained in the beloved, inasmuch as the lover penetrates, so to speak, into the beloved. For nothing hinders a thing from being both container and contents in different ways: just as a genus is contained in its species, and vice versa.

Reply to Objection 2: The apprehension of the reason precedes the movement of love. Consequently, just as the reason divides, so does the movement of love penetrate into the beloved, as was explained above.

Reply to Objection 3: This argument is true of the third kind of mutual indwelling, which is not to be found in every kind of love.

A<small>RTICLE</small> 3
Whether ecstasy is an effect of love?

Objection 1: It would seem that ecstasy is not an effect of love. For ecstasy seems to imply loss of reason. But love does not always result in loss of reason: for lovers are masters of themselves at times. Therefore love does not cause ecstasy.

Objection 2: Further, the lover desires the beloved to be united to him. Therefore he draws the beloved to himself, rather than betakes himself into the beloved, going forth out from himself as it were.

Objection 3: Further, love unites the beloved to the lover, as stated above (I-II, q. 28, a. 1). If, therefore, the lover goes out from himself, in order to betake himself into the beloved, it follows that the lover always loves the beloved more than himself:

Quod patet esse falsum. Non ergo extasis est effectus amoris.

Sed contra est quod Dionysius dicit, IV cap. de Div. Nom., quod *divinus amor extasim facit,* et quod *ipse Deus propter amorem est extasim passus.* Cum ergo quilibet amor sit quaedam similitudo participata divini amoris, ut ibidem dicitur, videtur quod quilibet amor causet extasim.

Respondeo dicendum quod extasim pati aliquis dicitur, cum extra se ponitur. Quod quidem contingit et secundum vim apprehensivam, et secundum vim appetitivam. Secundum quidem vim apprehensivam aliquis dicitur extra se poni, quando ponitur extra cognitionem sibi propriam, vel quia ad superiorem sublimatur, sicut homo, dum elevatur ad comprehendenda aliqua quae sunt supra sensum et rationem, dicitur extasim pati, inquantum ponitur extra connaturalem apprehensionem rationis et sensus; vel quia ad inferiora deprimitur; puta, cum aliquis in furiam vel amentiam cadit, dicitur extasim passus. Secundum appetitivam vero partem dicitur aliquis extasim pati, quando appetitus alicuius in alterum fertur, exiens quodammodo extra seipsum. Primam quidem extasim facit amor dispositive, inquantum scilicet facit meditari de amato, ut dictum est, intensa autem meditatio unius abstrahit ab aliis. Sed secundam extasim facit amor directe, simpliciter quidem amor amicitiae; amor autem concupiscentiae non simpliciter, sed secundum quid. Nam in amore concupiscentiae, quodammodo fertur amans extra seipsum, inquantum scilicet, non contentus gaudere de bono quod habet, quaerit frui aliquo extra se. Sed quia illud extrinsecum bonum quaerit sibi habere, non exit simpliciter extra se, sed talis affectio in fine infra ipsum concluditur. Sed in amore amicitiae, affectus alicuius simpliciter exit extra se, quia vult amico bonum, et operatur, quasi gerens curam et providentiam ipsius, propter ipsum amicum.

which is evidently false. Therefore ecstasy is not an effect of love.

On the contrary, Dionysius says (Div. Nom. iv) that "the Divine love produces ecstasy," and that "God Himself suffered ecstasy through love." Since therefore according to the same author (Div. Nom. iv), every love is a participated likeness of the Divine Love, it seems that every love causes ecstasy.

I answer that, To suffer ecstasy means to be placed outside oneself. This happens as to the apprehensive power and as to the appetitive power. As to the apprehensive power, a man is said to be placed outside himself, when he is placed outside the knowledge proper to him. This may be due to his being raised to a higher knowledge; thus, a man is said to suffer ecstasy, inasmuch as he is placed outside the connatural apprehension of his sense and reason, when he is raised up so as to comprehend things that surpass sense and reason: or it may be due to his being cast down into a state of debasement; thus a man may be said to suffer ecstasy, when he is overcome by violent passion or madness. As to the appetitive power, a man is said to suffer ecstasy, when that power is borne towards something else, so that it goes forth out from itself, as it were. The first of these ecstasies is caused by love dispositively in so far, namely, as love makes the lover dwell on the beloved, as stated above (I-II, q. 28, a. 2), and to dwell intently on one thing draws the mind from other things. The second ecstasy is caused by love directly; by love of friendship, simply; by love of concupiscence not simply but in a restricted sense. Because in love of concupiscence, the lover is carried out of himself, in a certain sense; in so far, namely, as not being satisfied with enjoying the good that he has, he seeks to enjoy something outside himself. But since he seeks to have this extrinsic good for himself, he does not go out from himself simply, and this movement remains finally within him. On the other hand, in the love of friendship, a man's affection goes out from itself simply; because he wishes and does good to his friend, by caring and providing for him, for his sake.

AD PRIMUM ergo dicendum quod illa ratio procedit de prima extasi.

AD SECUNDUM dicendum quod illa ratio procedit de amore concupiscentiae, qui non facit simpliciter extasim, ut dictum est.

AD TERTIUM dicendum quod ille qui amat, intantum extra se exit, inquantum vult bona amici et operatur. Non tamen vult bona amici magis quam sua. Unde non sequitur quod alterum plus quam se diligat.

Reply to Objection 1: This argument is true of the first kind of ecstasy.

Reply to Objection 2: This argument applies to love of concupiscence, which, as stated above, does not cause ecstasy simply.

Reply to Objection 3: He who loves, goes out from himself, in so far as he wills the good of his friend and works for it. Yet he does not will the good of his friend more than his own good: and so it does not follow that he loves another more than himself.

ARTICULUS 4

AD QUARTUM sic proceditur. Videtur quod zelus non sit effectus amoris. Zelus enim est contentionis principium, unde dicitur I ad Cor. III, *cum sit inter vos zelus et contentio,* et cetera. Sed contentio repugnat amori. Ergo zelus non est effectus amoris.

PRAETEREA, obiectum amoris est bonum, quod est communicativum sui. Sed zelus repugnat communicationi, ad zelum enim pertinere videtur quod aliquis non patiatur consortium in amato; sicut viri dicuntur zelare uxores, quas nolunt habere communes cum ceteris. Ergo zelus non est effectus amoris.

PRAETEREA, zelus non est sine odio, sicut nec sine amore, dicitur enim in Psalmo LXXII, *zelavi super iniquos.* Non ergo debet dici magis effectus amoris quam odii.

SED CONTRA est quod Dionysius dicit, IV cap. de Div. Nom., quod Deus appellatur Zelotes propter multum amorem quem habet ad existentia.

RESPONDEO dicendum quod zelus, quocumque modo sumatur, ex intensione amoris provenit. Manifestum est enim quod quanto aliqua virtus intensius tendit in aliquid, fortius etiam repellit omne contrarium vel repugnans. Cum igitur amor sit *quidam motus in amatum,* ut Augustinus dicit in libro octoginta trium quaest., intensus amor quaerit excludere omne quod sibi repugnat. Aliter tamen hoc contingit

ARTICLE 4
Whether zeal is an effect of love?

Objection 1: It would seem that zeal is not an effect of love. For zeal is a beginning of contention; wherefore it is written (1 Cor. 3:3): "Whereas there is among you zeal* and contention," etc. But contention is incompatible with love. Therefore zeal is not an effect of love.

Objection 2: Further, the object of love is the good, which communicates itself to others. But zeal is opposed to communication; since it seems an effect of zeal, that a man refuses to share the object of his love with another: thus husbands are said to be jealous of [*zelare*] their wives, because they will not share them with others. Therefore zeal is not an effect of love.

Objection 3: Further, there is no zeal without hatred, as neither is there without love: for it is written (Ps. 72:3): "I had a zeal on occasion of the wicked." Therefore it should not be set down as an effect of love any more than of hatred.

On the contrary, Dionysius says (Div. Nom. iv): "God is said to be a zealot, on account of his great love for all things."

I answer that, Zeal, whatever way we take it, arises from the intensity of love. For it is evident that the more intensely a power tends to anything, the more vigorously it withstands opposition or resistance. Since therefore love is "a movement towards the object loved," as Augustine says (QQ. 83, qu. 35), an intense love seeks to remove everything that opposes it. But this happens in different

---

* Douay: 'envying'

in amore concupiscentiae, et aliter in amore amicitiae. Nam in amore concupiscentiae, qui intense aliquid concupiscit, movetur contra omne illud quod repugnat consecutioni vel fruitioni quietae eius quod amatur. Et hoc modo viri dicuntur zelare uxores, ne per consortium aliorum impediatur singularitas quam in uxore quaerunt. Similiter etiam qui quaerunt excellentiam, moventur contra eos qui excellere videntur, quasi impedientes excellentiam eorum. Et iste est zelus invidiae, de quo dicitur in Psalmo XXXVI, *noli aemulari in malignantibus, neque zelaveris facientes iniquitatem*. Amor autem amicitiae quaerit bonum amici, unde quando est intensus, facit hominem moveri contra omne illud quod repugnat bono amici. Et secundum hoc, aliquis dicitur zelare pro amico, quando, si qua dicuntur vel fiunt contra bonum amici, homo repellere studet. Et per hunc etiam modum aliquis dicitur zelare pro Deo, quando ea quae sunt contra honorem vel voluntatem Dei, repellere secundum posse conatur; secundum illud III Reg. XIX, *zelo zelatus sum pro domino exercituum*. Et Ioan. II, super illud, *zelus domus tuae comedit me*, dicit Glossa quod *bono zelo comeditur, qui quaelibet prava quae viderit, corrigere satagit; si nequit, tolerat et gemit*.

AD PRIMUM ergo dicendum quod apostolus ibi loquitur de zelo invidiae; qui quidem est causa contentionis, non contra rem amatam, sed pro re amata contra impedimenta ipsius.

AD SECUNDUM dicendum quod bonum amatur inquantum est communicabile amanti. Unde omne illud quod perfectionem huius communicationis impedit, efficitur odiosum. Et sic ex amore boni zelus causatur. Ex defectu autem bonitatis contingit quod quaedam parva bona non possunt integre simul possideri a multis. Et ex amore talium causatur zelus invidiae. Non autem proprie ex his quae integre possunt a multis possideri, nullus enim invidet alteri de cognitione

ways according to love of concupiscence, and love of friendship. For in love of concupiscence he who desires something intensely, is moved against all that hinders his gaining or quietly enjoying the object of his love. It is thus that husbands are said to be jealous of their wives, lest association with others prove a hindrance to their exclusive individual rights. In like manner those who seek to excel, are moved against those who seem to excel, as though these were a hindrance to their excelling. And this is the zeal of envy, of which it is written (Ps. 36:1): "Be not emulous of evil doers, nor envy [*zelaveris*] them that work iniquity." On the other hand, love of friendship seeks the friend's good: wherefore, when it is intense, it causes a man to be moved against everything that opposes the friend's good. In this respect, a man is said to be zealous on behalf of his friend, when he makes a point of repelling whatever may be said or done against the friend's good. In this way, too, a man is said to be zealous on God's behalf, when he endeavors, to the best of his means, to repel whatever is contrary to the honor or will of God; according to 3 Kings 19:14: "With zeal I have been zealous for the Lord of hosts." Again on the words of Jn. 2:17: "The zeal of Thy house hath eaten me up," a gloss says that "a man is eaten up with a good zeal, who strives to remedy whatever evil he perceives; and if he cannot, bears with it and laments it."

Reply to Objection 1: The Apostle is speaking in this passage of the zeal of envy; which is indeed the cause of contention, not against the object of love, but for it, and against that which is opposed to it.

Reply to Objection 2: Good is loved inasmuch as it can be communicated to the lover. Consequently whatever hinders the perfection of this communication, becomes hateful. Thus zeal arises from love of good. But through defect of goodness, it happens that certain small goods cannot, in their entirety, be possessed by many at the same time: and from the love of such things arises the zeal of envy. But it does not arise, properly speaking, in the case of those things which, in their entirety, can be possessed by many: for no one envies another the knowledge of

veritatis, quae a multis integre cognosci potest; sed forte de excellentia circa cognitionem huius.

AD TERTIUM dicendum quod hoc ipsum quod aliquis odio habet ea quae repugnant amato, ex amore procedit. Unde zelus proprie ponitur effectus amoris magis quam odii.

truth, which can be known entirely by many; except perhaps one may envy another his superiority in the knowledge of it.

Reply to Objection 3: The very fact that a man hates whatever is opposed to the object of his love, is the effect of love. Hence zeal is set down as an effect of love rather than of hatred.

ARTICULUS 5

AD QUINTUM sic proceditur. Videtur quod amor sit passio laesiva. Languor enim significat laesionem quandam languentis. Sed amor causat languorem, dicitur enim Cant. II, *fulcite me floribus, stipate me malis, quia amore langueo.* Ergo amor est passio laesiva.

PRAETEREA, liquefactio est quaedam resolutio. Sed amor est liquefactivus, dicitur enim Cant. V, *anima mea liquefacta est, ut dilectus meus locutus est.* Ergo amor est resolutivus. Est ergo corruptivus et laesivus.

PRAETEREA, fervor designat quendam excessum in caliditate, qui quidem excessus corruptivus est. Sed fervor causatur ex amore, Dionysius enim, VII cap. Cael. Hier., inter ceteras proprietates ad amorem Seraphim pertinentes, ponit *calidum* et *acutum* et *superfervens.* Et Cant. VIII, dicitur de amore quod *lampades eius sunt lampades ignis atque flammarum.* Ergo amor est passio laesiva et corruptiva.

SED CONTRA est quod dicit Dionysius, IV cap. de Div. Nom., quod *singula seipsa amant contentive, idest conservative.* Ergo amor non est passio laesiva, sed magis conservativa et perfectiva.

RESPONDEO dicendum quod, sicut supra dictum est, amor significat coaptationem quandam appetitivae virtutis ad aliquod bonum. Nihil autem quod coaptatur ad aliquid quod est sibi conveniens, ex hoc ipso laeditur, sed magis, si sit possibile, proficit et melioratur. Quod vero coaptatur ad aliquid quod non est sibi conveniens, ex hoc ipso laeditur et deterioratur. Amor ergo boni convenientis est perfectivus et meliorativus amantis, amor autem boni quod non est conveniens

ARTICLE 5
Whether love is a passion that wounds the lover?

Objection 1: It would seem that love wounds the lover. For languor denotes a hurt in the one that languishes. But love causes languor: for it is written (Cant 2:5): "Stay me up with flowers, compass me about with apples; because I languish with love." Therefore love is a wounding passion.

Objection 2: Further, melting is a kind of dissolution. But love melts that in which it is: for it is written (Cant 5:6): "My soul melted when my beloved spoke." Therefore love is a dissolvent: therefore it is a corruptive and a wounding passion.

Objection 3: Further, fervor denotes a certain excess of heat; which excess has a corruptive effect. But love causes fervor: for Dionysius (Coel. Hier. vii) in reckoning the properties belonging to the Seraphim's love, includes "hot" and "piercing" and "most fervent." Moreover it is said of love (Cant 8:6) that "its lamps are fire and flames." Therefore love is a wounding and corruptive passion.

On the contrary, Dionysius says (Div. Nom. iv) that "everything loves itself with a love that holds it together," i.e., that preserves it. Therefore love is not a wounding passion, but rather one that preserves and perfects.

I answer that, As stated above (I-II, q. 26, a. 1; a. 2; q. 27, a. 1), love denotes a certain adapting of the appetitive power to some good. Now nothing is hurt by being adapted to that which is suitable to it; rather, if possible, it is perfected and bettered. But if a thing be adapted to that which is not suitable to it, it is hurt and made worse thereby. Consequently love of a suitable good perfects and betters the lover; but love of a good which is unsuitable to the

amanti, est laesivus et deteriorativus amantis. Unde maxime homo perficitur et melioratur per amorem Dei, laeditur autem et deterioratur per amorem peccati, secundum illud Osee IX, *facti sunt abominabiles, sicut ea quae dilexerunt*. Et hoc quidem dictum sit de amore, quantum ad id quod est formale in ipso, quod est scilicet ex parte appetitus. Quantum vero ad id quod est materiale in passione amoris, quod est immutatio aliqua corporalis, accidit quod amor sit laesivus propter excessum immutationis, sicut accidit in sensu, et in omni actu virtutis animae qui exercetur per aliquam immutationem organi corporalis.

AD EA VERO quae in contrarium obiiciuntur, dicendum quod amori attribui possunt quatuor effectus proximi, scilicet liquefactio, fruitio, languor et fervor. Inter quae primum est *liquefactio,* quae opponitur congelationi. Ea enim quae sunt congelata, in seipsis constricta sunt, ut non possint de facili subintrationem alterius pati. Ad amorem autem pertinet quod appetitus coaptetur ad quandam receptionem boni amati, prout amatum est in amante, sicut iam supra dictum est. Unde cordis congelatio vel duritia est dispositio repugnans amori. Sed liquefactio importat quandam mollificationem cordis, qua exhibet se cor habile ut amatum in ipsum subintret. Si ergo amatum fuerit praesens et habitum, causatur delectatio sive fruitio. Si autem fuerit absens, consequuntur duae passiones, scilicet tristitia de absentia, quae significatur per *languorem* (unde et Tullius, in III de Tusculanis quaest., maxime tristitiam *aegritudinem* nominat); et intensum desiderium de consecutione amati, quod significatur per *fervorem*. Et isti quidem sunt effectus amoris formaliter accepti, secundum habitudinem appetitivae virtutis ad obiectum. Sed in passione amoris, consequuntur aliqui effectus his proportionati, secundum immutationem organi.

lover, wounds and worsens him. Wherefore man is perfected and bettered chiefly by the love of God: but is wounded and worsened by the love of sin, according to Osee 9:10: "They became abominable, as those things which they loved." And let this be understood as applying to love in respect of its formal element, i.e., in regard to the appetite. But in respect of the material element in the passion of love, i.e., a certain bodily change, it happens that **love is hurtful, by reason of this change being excessive: just as it happens in the senses,** and in every act of a power of the soul that is exercised through the change of some bodily organ.

In reply to the objections, it is to be observed that four proximate effects may be ascribed to love: *viz.* melting, enjoyment, languor, and fervor. Of these the first is "melting," which is opposed to freezing. For things that are frozen, are closely bound together, so as to be hard to pierce. But it belongs to love that the appetite is fitted to receive the good which is loved, inasmuch as the object loved is in the lover, as stated above (I-II, q. 28, a. 2). Consequently the freezing or hardening of the heart is a disposition incompatible with love: while melting denotes a softening of the heart, whereby the heart shows itself to be ready for the entrance of the beloved. If, then, the beloved is present and possessed, pleasure or enjoyment ensues. But if the beloved be absent, two passions arise; *viz.* sadness at its absence, which is denoted by "languor" (hence Cicero in De Tusc. Quaest. iii, 11 applies the term "ailment" chiefly to sadness); and an intense desire to possess the beloved, which is signified by "fervor." And these are the effects of love considered formally, according to the relation of the appetitive power to its object. But in the passion of love, other effects ensue, proportionate to the above, in respect of a change in the organ.

Articulus 6

Ad sextum sic proceditur. Videtur quod amans non agat omnia ex amore. Amor enim quaedam passio est, ut supra dictum est. Sed non omnia quae agit homo, agit ex passione, sed quaedam agit ex electione, et quaedam ex ignorantia, ut dicitur in V Ethic. Ergo non omnia quae homo agit, agit ex amore.

Praeterea, appetitus est principium motus et actionis in omnibus animalibus, ut patet in III de anima. Si igitur omnia quae quis agit, agit ex amore, aliae passiones appetitivae partis erunt superfluae.

Praeterea, nihil causatur simul a contrariis causis. Sed quaedam fiunt ex odio. Non ergo omnia sunt ex amore.

Sed contra est quod Dionysius dicit, IV cap. de Div. Nom., quod *propter amorem boni omnia agunt quaecumque agunt.*

Respondeo dicendum quod omne agens agit propter finem aliquem, ut supra dictum est. Finis autem est bonum desideratum et amatum unicuique. Unde manifestum est quod omne agens, quodcumque sit, agit quamcumque actionem ex aliquo amore.

Ad primum ergo dicendum quod obiectio illa procedit de amore qui est passio in appetitu sensitivo existens. Nos autem loquimur nunc de amore communiter accepto, prout comprehendit sub se amorem intellectualem, rationalem, animalem, naturalem, sic enim Dionysius loquitur de amore in IV cap. de Div. Nom.

Ad secundum dicendum quod ex amore, sicut iam dictum est, causantur et desiderium et tristitia et delectatio, et per consequens omnes aliae passiones. Unde omnis actio quae procedit ex quacumque passione, procedit etiam ex amore, sicut ex prima causa. Unde non superfluunt aliae passiones, quae sunt causae proximae.

Ad tertium dicendum quod odium etiam ex amore causatur, sicut infra dicetur.

Article 6
Whether love is cause of all that the lover does?

Objection 1: It would seem that the lover does not do everything from love. For love is a passion, as stated above (I-II, q. 26, a. 2). But man does not do everything from passion: but some things he does from choice, and some things from ignorance, as stated in Ethic. v, 8. Therefore not everything that a man does, is done from love.

Objection 2: Further, the appetite is a principle of movement and action in all animals, as stated in De Anima iii, 10. If, therefore, whatever a man does is done from love, the other passions of the appetitive faculty are superfluous.

Objection 3: Further, nothing is produced at one and the same time by contrary causes. But some things are done from hatred. Therefore all things are not done from love.

On the contrary, Dionysius says (Div. Nom. iv) that "all things, whatever they do, they do for the love of good."

I answer that, Every agent acts for an end, as stated above (I-II, q. 1, a. 2). Now the end is the good desired and loved by each one. Wherefore it is evident that every agent, whatever it be, does every action from love of some kind.

Reply to Objection 1: This objection takes love as a passion existing in the sensitive appetite. But here we are speaking of love in a general sense, inasmuch as it includes intellectual, rational, animal, and natural love: for it is in this sense that Dionysius speaks of love in chapter iv of De Divinis Nominibus.

Reply to Objection 2: As stated above (I-II, q. 28, a. 5; q. 27, a. 4) desire, sadness and pleasure, and consequently all the other passions of the soul, result from love. Wherefore every act proceeds from any passion, proceeds also from love as from a first cause: and so the other passions, which are proximate causes, are not superfluous.

Reply to Objection 3: Hatred also is a result of love, as we shall state further on (I-II, q. 29, a. 2).

Quaestio XXIX

Deinde considerandum est de odio. Et circa hoc quaeruntur sex. *Primo,* utrum causa et obiectum odii sit malum. *Secundo,* utrum odium causetur ex amore. *Tertio,* utrum odium sit fortius quam amor. *Quarto,* utrum aliquis possit habere odio seipsum. *Quinto,* utrum aliquis possit habere odio veritatem. *Sexto,* utrum aliquid possit haberi odio in universali.

Articulus 1

Ad primum sic proceditur. Videtur quod obiectum et causa odii non sit malum. Omne enim quod est, inquantum huiusmodi bonum est. Si igitur obiectum odii sit malum, sequitur quod nulla res odio habeatur, sed solum defectus alicuius rei. Quod patet esse falsum.

Praeterea, odire malum est laudabile, unde in laudem quorundam dicitur II Machab. III, quod *leges optime custodiebantur, propter Oniae pontificis pietatem, et animos odio habentes mala.* Si igitur nihil oditur nisi malum, sequitur quod omne odium sit laudabile. Quod patet esse falsum.

Praeterea, idem non est simul bonum et malum. Sed idem diversis est odibile et amabile. Ergo odium non solum est mali, sed etiam boni.

Sed contra, odium contrariatur amori. Sed obiectum amoris est bonum, ut supra dictum est. Ergo obiectum odii est malum.

Respondeo dicendum quod, cum appetitus naturalis derivetur ab aliqua apprehensione, licet non coniuncta; eadem ratio videtur esse de inclinatione appetitus naturalis, et appetitus animalis, qui sequitur apprehensionem coniunctam, sicut supra dictum est. In appetitu autem naturali hoc manifeste apparet, quod sicut unumquodque habet

Question 29
Of Hatred

We must now consider hatred: concerning which there are six points of inquiry: 1. Whether evil is the cause and the object of hatred? 2. Whether love is the cause of hatred? 3. Whether hatred is stronger than love? 4. Whether a man can hate himself? 5. Whether a man can hate the truth? 6. Whether a thing can be the object of universal hatred?

Article 1
Whether evil is the cause and object of hatred?

Objection 1: It would seem that evil is not the object and cause of hatred. For everything that exists, as such, is good. If therefore evil be the object of hatred, it follows that nothing but the lack of something can be the object of hatred: which is clearly untrue.

Objection 2: Further, hatred of evil is praise-worthy; hence (2 Macc 3:1) some are praised for that "the laws were very well kept, because of the godliness of Onias the high-priest, and the hatred of their souls* had no evil." If, therefore, nothing but evil be the object of hatred, it would follow that all hatred is commendable: and this is clearly false.

Objection 3: Further, the same thing is not at the same time both good and evil. But the same thing is lovable and hateful to different subjects. Therefore hatred is not only of evil, but also of good.

On the contrary, Hatred is the opposite of love. But the object of love is good, as stated above (I-II, q. 26, a. 1; q. 27, a. 1). Therefore the object of hatred is evil.

I answer that, Since the natural appetite is the result of apprehension (though this apprehension is not in the same subject as the natural appetite), it seems that what applies to the inclination of the natural appetite, applies also to the animal appetite, which does result from an apprehension in the same subject, as stated above (I-II, q. 26, a. 1). Now, with regard to the natural appetite, it is evident, that just as each thing is

---

* Douay: 'his soul'

naturalem consonantiam vel aptitudinem ad id quod sibi convenit, quae est amor naturalis; ita ad id quod est ei repugnans et corruptivum, habet dissonantiam naturalem, quae est odium naturale. Sic igitur et in appetitu animali, seu in intellectivo, amor est consonantia quaedam appetitus ad id quod apprehenditur ut conveniens, odium vero est dissonantia quaedam appetitus ad id quod apprehenditur ut repugnans et nocivum. Sicut autem omne conveniens, inquantum huiusmodi, habet rationem boni; ita omne repugnans, inquantum huiusmodi, habet rationem mali. Et ideo, sicut bonum est obiectum amoris, ita malum est obiectum odii.

AD PRIMUM ergo dicendum quod ens, inquantum ens, non habet rationem repugnantis, sed magis convenientis, quia omnia conveniunt in ente. Sed ens inquantum est hoc ens determinatum, habet rationem repugnantis ad aliquod ens determinatum. Et secundum hoc, unum ens est odibile alteri, et est malum, etsi non in se, tamen per comparationem ad alterum.

AD SECUNDUM dicendum quod, sicut aliquid apprehenditur ut bonum, quod non est vere bonum; ita aliquid apprehenditur ut malum, quod non est vere malum. Unde contingit quandoque nec odium mali, nec amorem boni esse bonum.

AD TERTIUM dicendum quod contingit idem esse amabile et odibile diversis, secundum appetitum quidem naturalem, ex hoc quod unum et idem est conveniens uni secundum suam naturam, et repugnans alteri, sicut calor convenit igni, et repugnat aquae. Secundum appetitum vero animalem, ex hoc quod unum et idem apprehenditur ab uno sub ratione boni, et ab alio sub ratione mali.

naturally attuned and adapted to that which is suitable to it, wherein consists natural love; so has it a natural dissonance from that which opposes and destroys it; and this is natural hatred. So, therefore, in the animal appetite, or in the intellectual appetite, love is a certain harmony of the appetite with that which is apprehended as suitable; while hatred is dissonance of the appetite from that which is apprehended as repugnant and hurtful. Now, just as whatever is suitable, as such, bears the aspect of good; so whatever is repugnant, as such, bears the aspect of evil. And therefore, just as good is the object of love, so evil is the object of hatred.

Reply to Objection 1: Being, as such, has not the aspect of repugnance but only of fittingness; because being is common to all things. But being, inasmuch as it is this determinate being, has an aspect of repugnance to some determinate being. And in this way, one being is hateful to another, and is evil; though not in itself, but by comparison with something else.

Reply to Objection 2: Just as a thing may be apprehended as good, when it is not truly good; so a thing may be apprehended as evil, whereas it is not truly evil. Hence it happens sometimes that neither hatred of evil nor love of good is good.

Reply to Objection 3: To different things the same thing may be lovable or hateful: in respect of the natural appetite, owing to one and the same thing being naturally suitable to one thing, and naturally unsuitable to another: thus heat is becoming to fire and unbecoming to water: and in respect of the animal appetite, owing to one and the same thing being apprehended by one as good, by another as bad.

ARTICULUS 2

AD SECUNDUM sic proceditur. Videtur quod amor non sit causa odii. *Ea enim quae ex opposito dividuntur, naturaliter sunt simul,* ut dicitur in praedicamentis. Sed amor et odium, cum sint contraria, ex opposito dividuntur. Ergo naturaliter sunt simul. Non ergo amor est causa odii.

ARTICLE 2
Whether love is a cause of hatred?

Objection 1: It would seem that love is not a cause of hatred. For "the opposite members of a division are naturally simultaneous" (Praedic. x). But love and hatred are opposite members of a division, since they are contrary to one another. Therefore they are naturally simultaneous. Therefore love is not the cause of hatred.

PRAETEREA, unum contrariorum non est causa alterius. Sed amor et odium sunt contraria. Ergo amor non est causa odii.

PRAETEREA, posterius non est causa prioris. Sed odium est prius amore, ut videtur, nam odium importat recessum a malo, amor vero accessum ad bonum. Ergo amor non est causa odii.

SED CONTRA est quod dicit Augustinus, XIV de Civ. Dei, quod omnes affectiones causantur ex amore. Ergo et odium, cum sit quaedam affectio animae, causatur ex amore.

RESPONDEO dicendum quod, sicut dictum est, amor consistit in quadam convenientia amantis ad amatum, odium vero consistit in quadam repugnantia vel dissonantia. Oportet autem in quolibet prius considerare quid ei conveniat, quam quid ei repugnet, per hoc enim aliquid est repugnans alteri, quia est corruptivum vel impeditivum eius quod est conveniens. Unde necesse est quod amor sit prior odio; et quod nihil odio habeatur, nisi per hoc quod contrariatur convenienti quod amatur. Et secundum hoc, omne odium ex amore causatur.

AD PRIMUM ergo dicendum quod in his quae ex opposito dividuntur, quaedam inveniuntur quae sunt naturaliter simul et secundum rem, et secundum rationem, sicut duae species animalis, vel duae species coloris. Quaedam vero sunt simul secundum rationem, sed unum realiter est prius altero et causa eius, sicut patet in speciebus numerorum, figurarum et motuum. Quaedam vero non sunt simul nec secundum rem, nec secundum rationem, sicut substantia et accidens, nam substantia realiter est causa accidentis; et ens secundum rationem prius attribuitur substantiae quam accidenti, quia accidenti non attribuitur nisi inquantum est in substantia. Amor autem et odium naturaliter quidem sunt simul secundum rationem, sed non realiter. Unde nihil prohibet amorem esse causam odii.

AD SECUNDUM dicendum quod amor et odium sunt contraria, quando accipiuntur circa idem. Sed quando sunt de contrariis, non sunt contraria, sed se

Objection 2: Further, of two contraries, one is not the cause of the other. But love and hatred are contraries. Therefore love is not the cause of hatred.

Objection 3: Further, that which follows is not the cause of that which precedes. But hatred precedes love, seemingly: since hatred implies a turning away from evil, whereas love implies a turning towards good. Therefore love is not the cause of hatred.

On the contrary, Augustine says (De Civ. Dei xiv, 7, 9) that all emotions are caused by love. Therefore hatred also, since it is an emotion of the soul, is caused by love.

I answer that, As stated above (I-II, q. 29, a. 1), love consists in a certain agreement of the lover with the object loved, while hatred consists in a certain disagreement or dissonance. Now we should consider in each thing, what agrees with it, before that which disagrees: since a thing disagrees with another, through destroying or hindering that which agrees with it. Consequently love must needs precede hatred; and nothing is hated, save through being contrary to a suitable thing which is loved. And hence it is that every hatred is caused by love.

Reply to Objection 1: The opposite members of a division are sometimes naturally simultaneous, both really and logically; e.g., two species of animal, or two species of color. Sometimes they are simultaneous logically, while, in reality, one precedes, and causes the other; e.g., the species of numbers, figures and movements. Sometimes they are not simultaneous either really or logically; e.g., substance and accident; for substance is in reality the cause of accident; and being is predicated of substance before it is predicated of accident, by a priority of reason, because it is not predicated of accident except inasmuch as the latter is in substance. Now love and hatred are naturally simultaneous, logically but not really. Wherefore nothing hinders love from being the cause of hatred.

Reply to Objection 2: Love and hatred are contraries if considered in respect of the same thing. But if taken in respect of contraries, they are not themselves contrary, but

invicem consequentia, eiusdem enim rationis est quod ametur aliquid, et odiatur eius contrarium. Et sic amor unius rei est causa quod eius contrarium odiatur.

AD TERTIUM dicendum quod in executione prius est recedere ab uno termino, quam accedere ad alterum terminum. Sed in intentione est e converso, propter hoc enim receditur ab uno termino, ut accedatur ad alterum. Motus autem appetitivus magis pertinet ad intentionem quam ad executionem. Et ideo amor est prior odio, cum utrumque sit motus appetitivus.

consequent to one another: for it amounts to the same that one love a certain thing, or that one hate its contrary. Thus love of one thing is the cause of one's hating its contrary.

Reply to Objection 3: In the order of execution, the turning away from one term precedes the turning towards the other. But the reverse is the case in the order of intention: since approach to one term is the reason for turning away from the other. Now the appetitive movement belongs rather to the order of intention than to that of execution. Wherefore love precedes hatred: because each is an appetitive movement.

ARTICULUS 3

AD TERTIUM sic proceditur. Videtur quod odium sit fortius amore. Dicit enim Augustinus, in libro octoginta trium quaest., *nemo est qui non magis dolorem fugiat, quam appetat voluptatem.* Sed fugere dolorem pertinet ad odium, appetitus autem voluptatis pertinet ad amorem. Ergo odium est fortius amore.

PRAETEREA, debilius vincitur a fortiori. Sed amor vincitur ab odio, quando scilicet amor convertitur in odium. Ergo odium est fortius amore.

PRAETEREA, affectio animae per effectum manifestatur. Sed fortius insistit homo ad repellendum odiosum, quam ad prosequendum amatum, sicut etiam bestiae abstinent a delectabilibus propter verbera, ut Augustinus introducit in libro octoginta trium quaest. Ergo odium est fortius amore.

SED CONTRA, bonum est fortius quam malum, quia *malum non agit nisi virtute boni,* ut Dionysius dicit, cap. IV de Div. Nom. Sed odium et amor differunt secundum differentiam boni et mali. Ergo amor est fortior odio.

RESPONDEO dicendum quod impossibile est effectum sua causa esse fortiorem. Omne autem odium procedit ex aliquo amore sicut ex causa, ut supra dictum est. Unde impossibile est quod odium sit fortius amore simpliciter. Sed oportet ulterius quod amor, simpliciter loquendo, sit odio fortior. Fortius enim movetur aliquid in finem, quam in ea quae sunt ad finem.

ARTICLE 3
Whether hatred is stronger than love?

Objection 1: It would seem that hatred is stronger than love. For Augustine says (QQ. 83, qu. 36): "There is no one who does not flee from pain, more than he desires pleasure." But flight from pain pertains to hatred; while desire for pleasure belongs to love. Therefore hatred is stronger than love.

Objection 2: Further, the weaker is overcome by the stronger. But love is overcome by hatred: when, that is to say, love is turned into hatred. Therefore hatred is stronger than love.

Objection 3: Further, the emotions of the soul are shown by their effects. But man insists more on repelling what is hateful, than on seeking what is pleasant: thus also irrational animals refrain from pleasure for fear of the whip, as Augustine instances (QQ. 83, qu. 36). Therefore hatred is stronger than love.

On the contrary, Good is stronger than evil; because "evil does nothing except in virtue of good," as Dionysius says (Div. Nom. iv). But hatred and love differ according to the difference of good and evil. Therefore love is stronger than hatred.

I answer that, It is impossible for an effect to be stronger than its cause. Now every hatred arises from some love as its cause, as above stated (I-II, q. 29, a. 2). Therefore it is impossible for hatred to be stronger than love absolutely. But furthermore, love must needs be, absolutely speaking, stronger than hatred. Because a thing is moved to the end more strongly than to the means.

I-II, q. 29, a. 3, co.

Recessus autem a malo ordinatur ad consecutionem boni, sicut ad finem. Unde, simpliciter loquendo, fortior est motus animae in bonum quam in malum. Sed tamen aliquando videtur odium fortius amore, propter duo. Primo quidem, quia odium est magis sensibile quam amor. Cum enim sensus perceptio sit in quadam immutatione, ex quo aliquid iam immutatum est, non ita sentitur sicut quando est in ipso immutari. Unde calor febris hecticae, quamvis sit maior, non tamen ita sentitur sicut calor tertianae, quia calor hecticae iam versus est quasi in habitum et naturam. Propter hoc etiam, amor magis sentitur in absentia amati, sicut Augustinus dicit, in X de Trin., quod *amor non ita sentitur, cum non prodit eum indigentia.* Et propter hoc etiam, repugnantia eius quod oditur, sensibilius percipitur quam convenientia eius quod amatur. Secundo, quia non comparatur odium ad amorem sibi correspondentem. Secundum enim diversitatem bonorum, est diversitas amorum in magnitudine et parvitate, quibus proportionantur opposita odia. Unde odium quod correspondet maiori amori, magis movet quam minor amor.

Et per hoc patet responsio ad primum. Nam amor voluptatis est minor quam amor conservationis sui ipsius, cui respondet fuga doloris. Et ideo magis fugitur dolor, quam ametur voluptas.

AD SECUNDUM dicendum quod odium nunquam vinceret amorem, nisi propter maiorem amorem cui odium correspondet. Sicut homo magis diligit se quam amicum, et propter hoc quod diligit se, habet odio etiam amicum, si sibi contrarietur.

AD TERTIUM dicendum quod ideo intensius aliquid operatur ad repellendum odiosa, quia odium est magis sensibile.

Now turning away from evil is directed as a means to the gaining of good. Wherefore, absolutely speaking, the soul's movement in respect of good is stronger than its movement in respect of evil. Nevertheless hatred sometimes seems to be stronger than love, for two reasons. First, because hatred is more keenly felt than love. For, since the sensitive perception is accompanied by a certain impression; when once the impression has been received it is not felt so keenly as in the moment of receiving it. Hence the heat of a hectic fever, though greater, is nevertheless not felt so much as the heat of tertian fever; because the heat of the hectic fever is habitual and like a second nature. For this reason, love is felt more keenly in the absence of the object loved; thus Augustine says (De Trin. x, 12) that "love is felt more keenly when we lack what we love." And for the same reason, the unbecomingness of that which is hated is felt more keenly than the becomingness of that which is loved. Secondly, because comparison is made between a hatred and a love which are not mutually corresponding. Because, according to different degrees of good there are different degrees of love to which correspond different degrees of hatred. Wherefore a hatred that corresponds to a greater love, moves us more than a lesser love.

Hence it is clear how to reply to the First Objection. For the love of pleasure is less than the love of self-preservation, to which corresponds flight from pain. Wherefore we flee from pain more than we love pleasure.

Reply to Objection 2: Hatred would never overcome love, were it not for the greater love to which that hatred corresponds. Thus man loves himself, more than he loves his friend: and because he loves himself, his friend is hateful to him, if he oppose him.

Reply to Objection 3: The reason why we act with greater insistence in repelling what is hateful, is because we feel hatred more keenly.

Articulus 4

Ad quartum sic proceditur. Videtur quod aliquis possit seipsum odio habere. Dicitur enim in Psalmo X, *qui diligit iniquitatem, odit animam suam.* Sed multi diligunt iniquitatem. Ergo multi odiunt seipsos.

Praeterea, illum odimus, cui volumus et operamur malum. Sed quandoque aliquis vult et operatur sibi ipsi malum, puta qui interimunt seipsos. Ergo aliqui seipsos habent odio.

Praeterea, Boetius dicit, in II de Consol., quod *avaritia facit homines odiosos,* ex quo potest accipi quod omnis homo odit avarum. Sed aliqui sunt avari. Ergo illi odiunt seipsos.

Sed contra est quod apostolus dicit, ad Ephes. V, quod *nemo unquam carnem suam odio habuit.*

Respondeo dicendum quod impossibile est quod aliquis, per se loquendo, odiat seipsum. Naturaliter enim unumquodque appetit bonum, nec potest aliquis aliquid sibi appetere nisi sub ratione boni, nam *malum est praeter voluntatem,* ut Dionysius dicit, IV cap. de Div. Nom. Amare autem aliquem est velle ei bonum, ut supra dictum est. Unde necesse est quod aliquis amet seipsum; et impossibile est quod aliquis odiat seipsum, per se loquendo. Per accidens tamen contingit quod aliquis seipsum odio habeat. Et hoc dupliciter. Uno modo, ex parte boni quod sibi aliquis vult. Accidit enim quandoque illud quod appetitur ut secundum quid bonum, esse simpliciter malum, et secundum hoc, aliquis per accidens vult sibi malum, quod est odire. Alio modo, ex parte sui ipsius, cui vult bonum. Unumquodque enim maxime est id quod est principalius in ipso, unde civitas dicitur facere quod rex facit, quasi rex sit tota civitas. Manifestum est ergo quod homo maxime est mens hominis. Contingit autem quod aliqui aestimant se esse maxime illud quod sunt secundum naturam corporalem et sensitivam. Unde amant se secundum id quod aestimant se esse, sed odiunt id quod vere sunt, dum volunt contraria rationi. Et utroque modo, *ille qui diligit iniquitatem,*

Article 4
Whether a man can hate himself?

Objection 1: It would seem that a man can hate himself. For it is written (Ps. 10:6): "He that loveth iniquity, hateth his own soul." But many love iniquity. Therefore many hate themselves.

Objection 2: Further, him we hate, to whom we wish and work evil. But sometimes a man wishes and works evil to himself, e.g., a man who kills himself. Therefore some men hate themselves.

Objection 3: Further, Boethius says (De Consol. ii) that "avarice makes a man hateful"; whence we may conclude that everyone hates a miser. But some men are misers. Therefore they hate themselves.

On the contrary, The Apostle says (Eph. 5:29) that "no man ever hated his own flesh."

I answer that, Properly speaking, it is impossible for a man to hate himself. For everything naturally desires good, nor can anyone desire anything for himself, save under the aspect of good: for "evil is outside the scope of the will," as Dionysius says (Div. Nom. iv). Now to love a man is to will good to him, as stated above (I-II, q. 26, a. 4). Consequently, a man must, of necessity, love himself; and it is impossible for a man to hate himself, properly speaking. But accidentally it happens that a man hates himself: and this in two ways. First, on the part of the good which a man wills to himself. For it happens sometimes that what is desired as good in some particular respect, is simply evil; and in this way, a man accidentally wills evil to himself; and thus hates himself. Secondly, in regard to himself, to whom he wills good. For each thing is that which is predominant in it; wherefore the state is said to do what the king does, as if the king were the whole state. Now it is clear that man is principally the mind of man. And it happens that some men account themselves as being principally that which they are in their material and sensitive nature. Wherefore they love themselves according to what they take themselves to be, while they hate that which they really are, by desiring what is contrary to reason. And in both these ways, "he that loveth iniquity

odit non solum *animam suam,* sed etiam seipsum.

Et per hoc patet responsio ad primum.

AD SECUNDUM dicendum quod nullus sibi vult et facit malum, nisi inquantum apprehendit illud sub ratione boni. Nam et illi qui interimunt seipsos, hoc ipsum quod est mori, apprehendunt sub ratione boni, inquantum est terminativum alicuius miseriae vel doloris.

AD TERTIUM dicendum quod avarus odit aliquod accidens suum, non tamen propter hoc odit seipsum, sicut aeger odit suam aegritudinem, ex hoc ipso quod se amat. Vel dicendum quod avaritia odiosos facit aliis, non autem sibi ipsi. Quinimmo causatur ex inordinato sui amore, secundum quem de bonis temporalibus plus sibi aliquis vult quam debeat.

hateth" not only "his own soul," but also himself.

Wherefore the reply to the First Objection is evident.

Reply to Objection 2: No man wills and works evil to himself, except he apprehend it under the aspect of good. For even they who kill themselves, apprehend death itself as a good, considered as putting an end to some unhappiness or pain.

Reply to Objection 3: The miser hates something accidental to himself, but not for that reason does he hate himself: thus a sick man hates his sickness for the very reason that he loves himself. Or we may say that avarice makes man hateful to others, but not to himself. In fact, it is caused by inordinate self-love, in respect of which, man desires temporal goods for himself more than he should.

ARTICULUS 5

AD QUINTUM sic proceditur. Videtur quod aliquis non possit habere odio veritatem. Bonum enim et ens et verum convertuntur. Sed aliquis non potest habere odio bonitatem. Ergo nec veritatem.

PRAETEREA, *omnes homines naturaliter scire desiderant,* ut dicitur in principio Metaphys. Sed scientia non est nisi verorum. Ergo veritas naturaliter desideratur et amatur. Sed quod naturaliter inest, semper inest. Nullus ergo potest habere odio veritatem.

PRAETEREA, philosophus dicit, in II Rhetoric., quod *homines amant non fictos.* Sed non nisi propter veritatem. Ergo homo naturaliter amat veritatem. Non potest ergo eam odio habere.

SED CONTRA est quod apostolus dicit, ad Galat. IV, *factus sum vobis inimicus, verum dicens vobis.*

RESPONDEO dicendum quod bonum et verum et ens sunt idem secundum rem, sed differunt ratione. Bonum enim habet

ARTICLE 5
Whether a man can hate the truth?

Objection 1: It would seem that a man cannot hate the truth. For good, true, and being are convertible. But a man cannot hate good. Neither, therefore, can he hate the truth.

Objection 2: Further, "All men have a natural desire for knowledge," as stated in the beginning of the Metaphysics i, 1. But knowledge is only of truth. Therefore truth is naturally desired and loved. But that which is in a thing naturally, is always in it. Therefore no man can hate the truth.

Objection 3: Further, the Philosopher says (Rhet. ii, 4) that "men love those who are straightforward." But there can be no other motive for this save truth. Therefore man loves the truth naturally. Therefore he cannot hate it.

On the contrary, The Apostle says (Gal. 4:16): "Am I become your enemy because I tell you the truth?"*

I answer that, Good, true and being are the same in reality, but differ as considered by reason. For good is considered in the

---

* St. Thomas quotes the passage, probably from memory, as though it were an assertion: "I am become," etc.

rationem appetibilis, non autem ens vel verum, quia bonum est *quod omnia appetunt*. Et ideo bonum, sub ratione boni, non potest odio haberi, nec in universali nec in particulari. Ens autem et verum in universali quidem odio haberi non possunt, quia dissonantia est causa odii, et convenientia causa amoris; ens autem et verum sunt communia omnibus. Sed in particulari nihil prohibet quoddam ens et quoddam verum odio haberi, inquantum habet rationem contrarii et repugnantis, contrarietas enim et repugnantia non adversatur rationi entis et veri, sicut adversatur rationi boni. Contingit autem verum aliquod particulare tripliciter repugnare vel contrariari bono amato. Uno modo, secundum quod veritas est causaliter et originaliter in ipsis rebus. Et sic homo quandoque odit aliquam veritatem, dum vellet non esse verum quod est verum. Alio modo, secundum quod veritas est in cognitione ipsius hominis, quae impedit ipsum a prosecutione amati. Sicut si aliqui vellent non cognoscere veritatem fidei, ut libere peccarent, ex quorum persona dicitur Iob XXI, *scientiam viarum tuarum nolumus*. Tertio modo habetur odio veritas particularis, tanquam repugnans, prout est in intellectu alterius. Puta, cum aliquis vult latere in peccato, odit quod aliquis veritatem circa peccatum suum cognoscat. Et secundum hoc dicit Augustinus, in X Confess., quod homines *amant veritatem lucentem, oderunt eam redarguentem.*

Et per hoc patet responsio ad primum.

AD SECUNDUM dicendum quod cognoscere veritatem secundum se est amabile, propter quod dicit Augustinus quod amant eam lucentem. Sed per accidens cognitio veritatis potest esse odibilis, inquantum impedit ab aliquo desiderato.

AD TERTIUM dicendum quod ex hoc procedit quod non ficti amantur, quod homo amat secundum se cognoscere veritatem, quam homines non ficti manifestant.

light of something desirable, while being and true are not so considered: because good is "what all things seek." Wherefore good, as such, cannot be the object of hatred, neither in general nor in particular. Being and truth in general cannot be the object of hatred: because disagreement is the cause of hatred, and agreement is the cause of love; while being and truth are common to all things. But nothing hinders some particular being or some particular truth being an object of hatred, in so far as it is considered as hurtful and repugnant; since hurtfulness and repugnance are not incompatible with the notion of being and truth, as they are with the notion of good. Now it may happen in three ways that some particular truth is repugnant or hurtful to the good we love. First, according as truth is in things as in its cause and origin. And thus man sometimes hates a particular truth, when he wishes that what is true were not true. Secondly, according as truth is in man's knowledge, which hinders him from gaining the object loved: such is the case of those who wish not to know the truth of faith, that they may sin freely; in whose person it is said (Job 21:14): "We desire not the knowledge of Thy ways." Thirdly, a particular truth is hated, as being repugnant, inasmuch as it is in the intellect of another man: as, for instance, when a man wishes to remain hidden in his sin, he hates that anyone should know the truth about his sin. In this respect, Augustine says (Confess. x, 23) that men "love truth when it enlightens, they hate it when it reproves."

This suffices for the Reply to the First Objection.

Reply to Objection 2: The knowledge of truth is lovable in itself: hence Augustine says that men love it when it enlightens. But accidentally, the knowledge of truth may become hateful, in so far as it hinders one from accomplishing one's desire.

Reply to Objection 3: The reason why we love those who are straightforward is that they make known the truth, and the knowledge of the truth, considered in itself, is a desirable thing.

Articulus 6

Ad sextum sic proceditur. Videtur quod odium non possit esse alicuius in universali. Odium enim est passio appetitus sensitivi, qui movetur ex sensibili apprehensione. Sed sensus non potest apprehendere universale. Ergo odium non potest esse alicuius in universali.

Praeterea, odium causatur ex aliqua dissonantia; quae communitati repugnat. Sed communitas est de ratione universalis. Ergo odium non potest esse alicuius in universali.

Praeterea, obiectum odii est malum. *Malum autem est in rebus, et non in mente,* ut dicitur in VI Metaphys. Cum ergo universale sit solum in mente, quae abstrahit universale a particulari, videtur quod odium non possit esse alicuius universalis.

Sed contra est quod philosophus dicit, in II Rhetoric., quod *ira semper fit inter singularia odium autem etiam ad genera, furem enim odit et calumniatorem unusquisque.*

Respondeo dicendum quod de universali dupliciter contingit loqui, uno modo, secundum quod subest intentioni universalitatis; alio autem modo, de natura cui talis intentio attribuitur, alia est enim consideratio hominis universalis, et alia hominis in eo quod homo. Si igitur universale accipiatur primo modo, sic nulla potentia sensitivae partis, neque apprehensiva neque appetitiva, ferri potest in universale, quia universale fit per abstractionem a materia individuali, in qua radicatur omnis virtus sensitiva. Potest tamen aliqua potentia sensitiva, et apprehensiva et appetitiva, ferri in aliquid universaliter. Sicut dicimus quod obiectum visus est color secundum genus, non quia visus cognoscat colorem universalem; sed quia quod color sit cognoscibilis a visu, non convenit colori inquantum est hic color, sed inquantum est color simpliciter. Sic ergo odium etiam sensitivae partis, potest respicere aliquid

Article 6
Whether anything can be an object of universal hatred?

Objection 1: It would seem that a thing cannot be an object of universal hatred. Because hatred is a passion of the sensitive appetite, which is moved by an apprehension in the senses. But the senses cannot apprehend the universal. Therefore a thing cannot be an object of universal hatred.

Objection 2: Further, hatred is caused by disagreement; and where there is disagreement, there is nothing in common. But the notion of universality implies something in common. Therefore nothing can be the object of universal hatred.

Objection 3: Further, the object of hatred is evil. But "evil is in things, and not in the mind" (Metaph. vi, 4). Since therefore the universal is in the mind only, which abstracts the universal from the particular, it would seem that hatred cannot have a universal object.

On the contrary, The Philosopher says (Rhet. ii, 4) that "anger is directed to something singular, whereas hatred is also directed to a thing in general; for everybody hates the thief and the backbiter."

I answer that, There are two ways of speaking of the universal: first, as considered under the aspect of universality; secondly, as considered in the nature to which it is ascribed: for it is one thing to consider the universal man, and another to consider a man as man. If, therefore, we take the universal, in the first way, no sensitive power, whether of apprehension or of appetite, can attain the universal: because the universal is obtained by abstraction from individual matter, on which every sensitive power is based. Nevertheless the sensitive powers, both of apprehension and of appetite, can tend to something universally. Thus we say that the object of sight is color considered generically; not that the sight is cognizant of universal color, but because the fact that color is cognizant by the sight, is attributed to color, not as being this particular color, but simply because it is color. Accordingly hatred in the sensitive faculty can regard something

in universali, quia ex natura communi aliquid adversatur animali, et non solum ex eo quod est particularis, sicut lupus ovi. Unde ovis odit lupum generaliter. Sed ira semper causatur ex aliquo particulari, quia ex aliquo actu laedentis; actus autem particularium sunt. Et propter hoc philosophus dicit quod *ira semper est ad aliquid singulare; odium vero potest esse ad aliquid in genere.* Sed odium secundum quod est in parte intellectiva, cum consequatur apprehensionem universalem intellectus, potest utroque modo esse respectu universalis.

AD PRIMUM ergo dicendum quod sensus non apprehendit universale, prout est universale, apprehendit tamen aliquid cui per abstractionem accidit universalitas.

AD SECUNDUM dicendum quod id quod commune est omnibus, non potest esse ratio odii. Sed nihil prohibet aliquid esse commune multis, quod tamen dissonat ab aliis, et sic est eis odiosum.

AD TERTIUM dicendum quod illa obiectio procedit de universali secundum quod substat intentioni universalitatis, sic enim non cadit sub apprehensione vel appetitu sensitivo.

universally: because this thing, by reason of its common nature, and not merely as an individual, is hostile to the animal—for instance, a wolf in regard to a sheep. Hence a sheep hates the wolf universally. On the other hand, anger is always caused by something in particular: because it is caused by some action of the one that hurts us; and actions proceed from individuals. For this reason the Philosopher says (Rhet. ii, 4) that "anger is always directed to something singular, whereas hatred can be directed to a thing in general." But according as hatred is in the intellectual part, since it arises from the universal apprehension of the intellect, it can regard the universal in both ways.

Reply to Objection 1: The senses do not apprehend the universal, as such: but they apprehend something to which the character of universality is given by abstraction.

Reply to Objection 2: That which is common to all cannot be a reason of hatred. But nothing hinders a thing from being common to many, and at variance with others, so as to be hateful to them.

Reply to Objection 3: This argument considers the universal under the aspect of universality: and thus it does not come under the sensitive apprehension or appetite.

Quaestio XXX

Deinde considerandum est de concupiscentia. Et circa hoc quaeruntur quatuor. *Primo,* utrum concupiscentia sit in appetitu sensitivo tantum. *Secundo,* utrum concupiscentia sit passio specialis. *Tertio,* utrum sint aliquae concupiscentiae naturales, et aliquae non naturales. *Quarto,* utrum concupiscentia sit infinita.

Articulus 1

Ad primum sic proceditur. Videtur quod concupiscentia non solum sit in appetitu sensitivo. Est enim quaedam concupiscentia sapientiae, ut dicitur Sap. VI, *concupiscentia sapientiae deducit ad regnum perpetuum.* Sed appetitus sensitivus non potest ferri in sapientiam. Ergo concupiscentia non est in solo appetitu sensitivo.

Praeterea, desiderium mandatorum Dei non est in appetitu sensitivo, immo apostolus dicit, Rom. VII, *non habitat in me, hoc est in carne mea, bonum.* Sed desiderium mandatorum Dei sub concupiscentia cadit, secundum illud Psalmi CXVIII, *concupivit anima mea desiderare iustificationes tuas.* Ergo concupiscentia non est solum in appetitu sensitivo.

Praeterea, cuilibet potentiae est concupiscibile proprium bonum. Ergo concupiscentia est in qualibet potentiae animae, et non solum in appetitu sensitivo.

Sed contra est quod Damascenus dicit, quod *irrationale obediens et persuasibile rationi, dividitur in concupiscentiam et iram. Haec autem est irrationalis pars animae, passiva et appetitiva.* Ergo concupiscentia est in appetitu sensitivo.

Respondeo dicendum quod, sicut philosophus dicit in I Rhetoric., *concupiscentia est appetitus delectabilis.* Est autem duplex delectatio, ut infra dicetur, una quae est in bono intelligibili, quod est

Question 30
Of Concupiscence

We have now to consider concupiscence: under which head there are four points of inquiry: 1. Whether concupiscence is in the sensitive appetite only? 2. Whether concupiscence is a specific passion? 3. Whether some concupiscences are natural, and some not natural? 4. Whether concupiscence is infinite?

Article 1
Whether concupiscence is in the sensitive appetite only?

Objection 1: It would seem that concupiscence is not only in the sensitive appetite. For there is a concupiscence of wisdom, according to Wis. 6:21: "The concupiscence* of wisdom bringeth to the everlasting kingdom." But the sensitive appetite can have no tendency to wisdom. Therefore concupiscence is not only in the sensitive appetite.

Objection 2: Further, the desire for the commandments of God is not in the sensitive appetite: in fact the Apostle says (Rom. 7:18): "There dwelleth not in me, that is to say, in my flesh, that which is good." But desire for God's commandments is an act of concupiscence, according to Ps. 118:20: "My soul hath coveted [*concupivit*] to long for thy justifications." Therefore concupiscence is not only in the sensitive appetite.

Objection 3: Further, to each power, its proper good is a matter of concupiscence. Therefore concupiscence is in each power of the soul, and not only in the sensitive appetite.

On the contrary, Damascene says (De Fide Orth. ii, 12) that "the irrational part which is subject and amenable to reason, is divided into the faculties of concupiscence and anger. This is the irrational part of the soul, passive and appetitive." Therefore concupiscence is in the sensitive appetite.

I answer that, As the Philosopher says (Rhet. i, 11), "concupiscence is a craving for that which is pleasant." Now pleasure is twofold, as we shall state later on (I-II, q. 31, a. 3; a. 4): one is in the intelligible good, which

---

* Douay: 'desire'

bonum rationis; alia quae est in bono secundum sensum. Prima quidem delectatio videtur esse animae tantum. Secunda autem est animae et corporis, quia sensus est virtus in organo corporeo; unde et bonum secundum sensum est bonum totius coniuncti. Talis autem delectationis appetitus videtur esse concupiscentia, quae simul pertineat et ad animam et ad corpus, ut ipsum nomen *concupiscentiae* sonat. Unde concupiscentia, proprie loquendo, est in appetitu sensitivo; et in vi concupiscibili, quae ab ea denominatur.

AD PRIMUM ergo dicendum quod appetitus sapientiae, vel aliorum spiritualium bonorum, interdum concupiscentia nominatur, vel propter similitudinem quandam, vel propter intensionem appetitus superioris partis, ex quo fit redundantia in inferiorem appetitum, ut simul etiam ipse inferior appetitus suo modo tendat in spirituale bonum consequens appetitum superiorem, et etiam ipsum corpus spiritualibus deserviat; sicut in Psalmo LXXXIII, dicitur, *cor meum et caro mea exultaverunt in Deum vivum.*

AD SECUNDUM dicendum quod desiderium magis pertinere potest, proprie loquendo, non solum ad inferiorem appetitum, sed etiam ad superiorem. Non enim importat aliquam consociationem in cupiendo, sicut concupiscentia; sed simplicem motum in rem desideratam.

AD TERTIUM dicendum quod unicuique potentiae animae competit appetere proprium bonum appetitu naturali, qui non sequitur apprehensionem. Sed appetere bonum appetitu animali, qui sequitur apprehensionem, pertinet solum ad vim appetitivam. Appetere autem aliquid sub ratione boni delectabilis secundum sensum, quod proprie est concupiscere, pertinet ad vim concupiscibilem.

ARTICULUS 2

AD SECUNDUM sic proceditur. Videtur quod concupiscentia non sit passio specialis potentiae concupiscibilis. Passiones enim distinguuntur secundum obiecta. Sed obiectum concupiscibilis est delectabile secundum sensum; quod etiam est obiectum

is the good of reason; the other is in good perceptible to the senses. The former pleasure seems to belong to soul alone: whereas the latter belongs to both soul and body: because the sense is a power seated in a bodily organ: wherefore sensible good is the good of the whole composite. Now concupiscence seems to be the craving for this latter pleasure, since it belongs to the united soul and body, as is implied by the Latin word *concupiscentia.* Therefore, properly speaking, concupiscence is in the sensitive appetite, and in the concupiscible faculty, which takes its name from it.

Reply to Objection 1: The craving for wisdom, or other spiritual goods, is sometimes called concupiscence; either by reason of a certain likeness; or on account of the craving in the higher part of the soul being so vehement that it overflows into the lower appetite, so that the latter also, in its own way, tends to the spiritual good, following the lead of the higher appetite, the result being that the body itself renders its service in spiritual matters, according to Ps. 83:3: "My heart and my flesh have rejoiced in the living God."

Reply to Objection 2: Properly speaking, desire may be not only in the lower, but also in the higher appetite. For it does not imply fellowship in craving, as concupiscence does; but simply movement towards the thing desired.

Reply to Objection 3: It belongs to each power of the soul to seek its proper good by the natural appetite, which does not arise from apprehension. But the craving for good, by the animal appetite, which arises from apprehension, belongs to the appetitive power alone. And to crave a thing under the aspect of something delightful to the senses, wherein concupiscence properly consists, belongs to the concupiscible power.

ARTICLE 2
Whether concupiscence is a specific passion?

Objection 1: It would seem that concupiscence is not a specific passion of the concupiscible power. For passions are distinguished by their objects. But the object of the concupiscible power is something delightful to the senses; and this is also the object of

concupiscentiae, secundum philosophum, in I Rhetoric. Ergo concupiscentia non est passio specialis in concupiscibili.

Praeterea, Augustinus dicit, in libro octoginta trium quaest., quod *cupiditas est amor rerum transeuntium,* et sic ab amore non distinguitur. Omnes autem passiones speciales ab invicem distinguuntur. Ergo concupiscentia non est passio specialis in concupiscibili.

Praeterea, cuilibet passioni concupiscibilis opponitur aliqua passio specialis in concupiscibili, ut supra dictum est. Sed concupiscentiae non opponitur aliqua passio specialis in concupiscibili. Dicit enim Damascenus quod *expectatum bonum concupiscentiam constituit, praesens vero laetitiam, similiter expectatum malum timorem, praesens vero tristitiam,* ex quo videtur quod, sicut tristitia contrariatur laetitiae, ita timor contrariatur concupiscentiae. Timor autem non est in concupiscibili, sed in irascibili. Non ergo concupiscentia est specialis passio in concupiscibili.

Sed contra est quod concupiscentia causatur ab amore, et tendit in delectationem, quae sunt passiones concupiscibilis. Et sic distinguitur ab aliis passionibus concupiscibilis, tanquam passio specialis.

Respondeo dicendum quod, sicut dictum est, bonum delectabile secundum sensum est communiter obiectum concupiscibilis. Unde secundum eius differentias, diversae passiones concupiscibilis distinguuntur. Diversitas autem obiecti potest attendi vel secundum naturam ipsius obiecti, vel secundum diversitatem in virtute agendi. Diversitas quidem obiecti activi quae est secundum rei naturam, facit materialem differentiam passionum. Sed diversitas quae est secundum virtutem activam, facit formalem differentiam passionum, secundum quam passiones specie differunt. Est autem alia ratio virtutis motivae ipsius finis vel boni, secundum quod est realiter praesens, et secundum quod est absens, nam secundum quod est praesens, facit in seipso quiescere; secundum autem quod est absens, facit ad seipsum moveri. Unde ipsum

concupiscence, as the Philosopher declares (Rhet. i, 11). Therefore concupiscence is not a specific passion of the concupiscible faculty.

Objection 2: Further, Augustine says (QQ. 83, qu. 33) that "covetousness is the love of transitory things": so that it is not distinct from love. But all specific passions are distinct from one another. Therefore concupiscence is not a specific passion in the concupiscible faculty.

Objection 3: Further, to each passion of the concupiscible faculty there is a specific contrary passion in that faculty, as stated above (I-II, q. 23, a. 4). But no specific passion of the concupiscible faculty is contrary to concupiscence. For Damascene says (De Fide Orth. ii, 12) that "good when desired gives rise to concupiscence; when present, it gives joy: in like manner, the evil we apprehend makes us fear, the evil that is present makes us sad": from which we gather that as sadness is contrary to joy, so is fear contrary to concupiscence. But fear is not in the concupiscible, but in the irascible part. Therefore concupiscence is not a specific passion of the concupiscible faculty.

On the contrary, Concupiscence is caused by love, and tends to pleasure, both of which are passions of the concupiscible faculty. Hence it is distinguished from the other concupiscible passions, as a specific passion.

I answer that, As stated above (I-II, q. 30, a. 1; q. 23, a. 1), the good which gives pleasure to the senses is the common object of the concupiscible faculty. Hence the various concupiscible passions are distinguished according to the differences of that good. Now the diversity of this object can arise from the very nature of the object, or from a diversity in its active power. The diversity, derived from the nature of the active object, causes a material difference of passions: while the difference in regard to its active power causes a formal diversity of passions, in respect of which the passions differ specifically. Now the nature of the motive power of the end or of the good, differs according as it is really present, or absent: because, according as it is present, it causes the faculty to find rest in it; whereas, according as it is absent, it causes the faculty to be moved towards it. Wherefore the object

delectabile secundum sensum, inquantum appetitum sibi adaptat quodammodo et conformat, causat amorem; inquantum vero absens attrahit ad seipsum, causat concupiscentiam; inquantum vero praesens quietat in seipso, causat delectationem. Sic ergo concupiscentia est passio differens *specie* et ab amore et a delectatione. Sed concupiscere hoc delectabile vel illud, facit concupiscentias diversas *numero*.

AD PRIMUM ergo dicendum quod bonum delectabile non est absolute obiectum concupiscentiae, sed sub ratione absentis, sicut et sensibile sub ratione praeteriti, est obiectum memoriae. Huiusmodi enim particulares conditiones diversificant speciem passionum, vel etiam potentiarum sensitivae partis, quae respicit particularia.

AD SECUNDUM dicendum quod illa praedicatio est per causam, non per essentiam, non enim cupiditas est per se amor, sed amoris effectus, vel aliter dicendum, quod Augustinus accipit cupiditatem large pro quolibet motu appetitus qui potest esse respectu boni futuri. Unde comprehendit sub se et amorem et spem.

AD TERTIUM dicendum quod passio quae directe opponitur concupiscentiae, innominata est, quae ita se habet ad malum, sicut concupiscentia ad bonum. Sed quia est mali absentis sicut et timor, quandoque loco eius ponitur timor, sicut et quandoque cupiditas loco spei. Quod enim est parvum bonum vel malum, quasi non reputatur, et ideo pro omni motu appetitus in bonum vel in malum futurum, ponitur spes et timor, quae respiciunt bonum vel malum arduum.

of sensible pleasure causes love, inasmuch as, so to speak, it attunes and conforms the appetite to itself; it causes concupiscence, inasmuch as, when absent, it draws the faculty to itself; and it causes pleasure, inasmuch as, when present, it makes the faculty to find rest in itself. Accordingly, concupiscence is a passion differing "in species" from both love and pleasure. But concupiscences of this or that pleasurable object differ "in number."

Reply to Objection 1: Pleasurable good is the object of concupiscence, not absolutely, but considered as absent: just as the sensible, considered as past, is the object of memory. For these particular conditions diversify the species of passions, and even of the powers of the sensitive part, which regards particular things.

Reply to Objection 2: In the passage quoted we have causal, not essential predication: for covetousness is not essentially love, but an effect of love. We may also say that Augustine is taking covetousness in a wide sense, for any movement of the appetite in respect of good to come: so that it includes both love and hope.

Reply to Objection 3: The passion which is directly contrary to concupiscence has no name, and stands in relation to evil, as concupiscence in regard to good. But since, like fear, it regards the absent evil; sometimes it goes by the name of fear, just as hope is sometimes called covetousness. For a small good or evil is reckoned as though it were nothing: and consequently every movement of the appetite in future good or evil is called hope or fear, which regard good and evil as arduous.

ARTICULUS 3

AD TERTIUM sic proceditur. Videtur quod concupiscentiarum non sint quaedam naturales, et quaedam non naturales. Concupiscentia enim pertinet ad appetitum animalem, ut dictum est. Sed appetitus naturalis dividitur contra animalem. Ergo nulla concupiscentia est naturalis.

ARTICLE 3
Whether some concupiscences are natural, and some not natural?

Objection 1: It would seem that concupiscences are not divided into those which are natural and those which are not. For concupiscence belongs to the animal appetite, as stated above (I-II, q. 30, a. 1, ad 3). But the natural appetite is contrasted with the animal appetite. Therefore no concupiscence is natural.

Praeterea, diversitas materialis non facit diversitatem secundum speciem, sed solum secundum numerum, quae quidem diversitas sub arte non cadit. Sed si quae sint concupiscentiae naturales et non naturales, non differunt nisi secundum diversa concupiscibilia, quod facit materialem differentiam, et secundum numerum tantum. Non ergo dividendae sunt concupiscentiae per naturales et non naturales.

Praeterea, ratio contra naturam dividitur, ut patet in II Physic. Si igitur in homine est aliqua concupiscentia non naturalis, oportet quod sit rationalis. Sed hoc esse non potest, quia concupiscentia cum sit passio quaedam, pertinet ad appetitum sensitivum, non autem ad voluntatem, quae est appetitus rationis. Non ergo sunt concupiscentiae aliquae non naturales.

Sed contra est quod philosophus, in III Ethic. et in I Rhetoric., ponit quasdam concupiscentias naturales, et quasdam non naturales.

Respondeo dicendum quod, sicut dictum est, concupiscentia est appetitus boni delectabilis. Dupliciter autem aliquid est delectabile. Uno modo, quia est conveniens naturae animalis, sicut cibus, potus, et alia huiusmodi. Et huiusmodi concupiscentia delectabilis dicitur naturalis. Alio modo aliquid est delectabile, quia est conveniens animali secundum apprehensionem, sicut cum aliquis apprehendit aliquid ut bonum et conveniens, et per consequens delectatur in ipso. Et huiusmodi delectabilis concupiscentia dicitur non naturalis, et solet magis dici *cupiditas.* Primae ergo concupiscentiae, naturales, communes sunt et hominibus et aliis animalibus, quia utrisque est aliquid conveniens et delectabile secundum naturam. Et in his etiam omnes homines conveniunt, unde et philosophus, in III Ethic., vocat eas *communes* et *necessarias.* Sed secundae concupiscentiae sunt propriae hominum, quorum proprium est excogitare aliquid ut bonum et conveniens, praeter id quod natura requirit. Unde et in I Rhetoric., philosophus dicit primas concupiscentias esse *irrationales,* secundas vero *cum ratione.* Et quia diversi diversimode ratiocinantur, ideo etiam secundae dicuntur,

Objection 2: Further, material differences makes no difference of species, but only numerical difference; a difference which is outside the purview of science. But if some concupiscences are natural, and some not, they differ only in respect of their objects; which amounts to a material difference, which is one of number only. Therefore concupiscences should not be divided into those that are natural and those that are not.

Objection 3: Further, reason is contrasted with nature, as stated in Phys. ii, 5. If therefore in man there is a concupiscence which is not natural, it must needs be rational. But this is impossible: because, since concupiscence is a passion, it belongs to the sensitive appetite, and not to the will, which is the rational appetite. Therefore there are no concupiscences which are not natural.

On the contrary, The Philosopher (Ethic. iii, 11 and Rhetor. i, 11) distinguishes natural concupiscences from those that are not natural.

I answer that, As stated above (I-II, q. 30, a. 1), concupiscence is the craving for pleasurable good. Now a thing is pleasurable in two ways. First, because it is suitable to the nature of the animal; for example, food, drink, and the like: and concupiscence of such pleasurable things is said to be natural. Secondly, a thing is pleasurable because it is apprehended as suitable to the animal: as when one apprehends something as good and suitable, and consequently takes pleasure in it: and concupiscence of such pleasurable things is said to be not natural, and is more wont to be called "cupidity." Accordingly concupiscences of the first kind, or natural concupiscences, are common to men and other animals: because to both is there something suitable and pleasurable according to nature: and in these all men agree; wherefore the Philosopher (Ethic. iii, 11) calls them "common" and "necessary." But concupiscences of the second kind are proper to men, to whom it is proper to devise something as good and suitable, beyond that which nature requires. Hence the Philosopher says (Rhet. i, 11) that the former concupiscences are "irrational," but the latter, "rational." And because different men reason differently, therefore the latter are also called

in III Ethic., *propriae et appositae,* scilicet supra naturales.

Ad primum ergo dicendum quod illud idem quod appetitur appetitu naturali, potest appeti appetitu animali cum fuerit apprehensum. Et secundum hoc cibi et potus et huiusmodi, quae appetuntur naturaliter, potest esse concupiscentia naturalis.

Ad secundum dicendum quod diversitas concupiscentiarum naturalium a non naturalibus, non est materialis tantum; sed etiam quodammodo formalis, inquantum procedit ex diversitate obiecti activi. Obiectum autem appetitus est bonum apprehensum. Unde ad diversitatem activi pertinet diversitas apprehensionis, prout scilicet apprehenditur aliquid ut conveniens absoluta apprehensione, ex qua causantur concupiscentiae naturales, quas philosophus in Rhetoric. vocat *irrationales;* et prout apprehenditur aliquid cum deliberatione, ex quo causantur concupiscentiae non naturales, quae propter hoc in Rhetoric. dicuntur *cum ratione.*

Ad tertium dicendum quod in homine non solum est ratio universalis, quae pertinet ad partem intellectivam; sed etiam ratio particularis, quae pertinet ad partem sensitivam, ut in primo libro dictum est. Et secundum hoc, etiam concupiscentia quae est cum ratione, potest ad appetitum sensitivum pertinere. Et praeterea appetitus sensitivus potest etiam a ratione universali moveri, mediante imaginatione particulari.

(Ethic. iii, 11) "peculiar and acquired," i.e., in addition to those that are natural.

Reply to Objection 1: The same thing that is the object of the natural appetite, may be the object of the animal appetite, once it is apprehended. And in this way there may be an animal concupiscence of food, drink, and the like, which are objects of the natural appetite.

Reply to Objection 2: The difference between those concupiscences that are natural and those that are not, is not merely a material difference; it is also, in a way, formal, in so far as it arises from a difference in the active object. Now the object of the appetite is the apprehended good. Hence diversity of the active object follows from diversity of apprehension: according as a thing is apprehended as suitable, either by absolute apprehension, whence arise natural concupiscences, which the Philosopher calls "irrational" (Rhet. i, 11); or by apprehension together with deliberation, whence arise those concupiscences that are not natural, and which for this very reason the Philosopher calls "rational" (Rhet. i, 11).

Reply to Objection 3: Man has not only universal reason, pertaining to the intellectual faculty; but also particular reason pertaining to the sensitive faculty, as stated in the I, q. 78, a. 4; q. 81, a. 3: so that even rational concupiscence may pertain to the sensitive appetite. Moreover the sensitive appetite can be moved by the universal reason also, through the medium of the particular imagination.

Articulus 4

Ad quartum sic proceditur. Videtur quod concupiscentia non sit infinita. Obiectum enim concupiscentiae est bonum; quod habet rationem finis. Qui autem ponit infinitum, excludit finem, ut dicitur in II Metaphys. Concupiscentia ergo non potest esse infinita.

Praeterea, concupiscentia est boni convenientis, cum procedat ex amore. Sed infinitum, cum sit improportionatum, non potest esse conveniens. Ergo concupiscentia non potest esse infinita.

Article 4

Whether concupiscence is infinite?

Objection 1: It would seem that concupiscence is not infinite. For the object of concupiscence is good, which has the aspect of an end. But where there is infinity there is no end (Metaph. ii, 2). Therefore concupiscence cannot be infinite.

Objection 2: Further, concupiscence is of the fitting good, since it proceeds from love. But the infinite is without proportion, and therefore unfitting. Therefore concupiscence cannot be infinite.

Praeterea, infinita non est transire, et sic in eis non est pervenire ad ultimum. Sed concupiscenti fit delectatio per hoc quod attingit ad ultimum. Ergo si concupiscentia esset infinita, sequeretur quod nunquam fieret delectatio.

Sed contra est quod philosophus dicit, in I Polit., quod, *in infinitum concupiscentia existente homines infinita desiderant.*

Respondeo dicendum quod, sicut dictum est, duplex est concupiscentia, una naturalis, et alia non naturalis. Naturalis quidem igitur concupiscentia non potest esse infinita in actu. Est enim eius quod natura requirit, natura vero semper intendit in aliquid finitum et certum. Unde nunquam homo concupiscit infinitum cibum, vel infinitum potum. Sed sicut in natura contingit esse infinitum in potentia per successionem, ita huiusmodi concupiscentiam contingit infinitam esse per successionem; ut scilicet, post adeptum cibum iterum alia vice desideret cibum, vel quodcumque aliud quod natura requirit, quia huiusmodi corporalia bona, cum adveniunt, non perpetuo manent, sed deficiunt. Unde dixit dominus Samaritanae, Ioan. IV, *qui biberit ex hac aqua, sitiet iterum.* Sed concupiscentia non naturalis omnino est infinita. Sequitur enim rationem, ut dictum est, rationi autem competit in infinitum procedere. Unde qui concupiscit divitias, potest eas concupiscere, non ad aliquem certum terminum, sed simpliciter se divitem esse, quantumcumque potest. Potest et alia ratio assignari, secundum philosophum in I Polit., quare quaedam concupiscentia sit finita, et quaedam infinita. Semper enim concupiscentia finis est infinita, finis enim per se concupiscitur, ut sanitas; unde maior sanitas magis concupiscitur, et sic in infinitum; sicut, si album per se disgregat, magis album magis disgregat. Concupiscentia vero eius quod est ad finem, non est infinita, sed secundum illam mensuram appetitur qua convenit fini. Unde qui finem ponunt in divitiis, habent concupiscentiam divitiarum in infinitum, qui autem divitias appetunt propter necessitatem vitae, concupiscunt divitias finitas, sufficientes

Objection 3: Further, there is no passing through infinite things: and thus there is no reaching an ultimate term in them. But the subject of concupiscence is not delighted until he attain the ultimate term. Therefore, if concupiscence were infinite, no delight would ever ensue.

On the contrary, The Philosopher says (Polit. i, 3) that "since concupiscence is infinite, men desire an infinite number of things."

I answer that, As stated above (I-II, q. 30, a. 3), concupiscence is twofold; one is natural, the other is not natural. Natural concupiscence cannot be actually infinite: because it is of that which nature requires; and nature ever tends to something finite and fixed. Hence man never desires infinite meat, or infinite drink. But just as in nature there is potential successive infinity, so can this kind of concupiscence be infinite successively; so that, for instance, after getting food, a man may desire food yet again; and so of anything else that nature requires: because these bodily goods, when obtained, do not last for ever, but fail. Hence Our Lord said to the woman of Samaria (Jn. 4:13): "Whosoever drinketh of this water, shall thirst again." But non-natural concupiscence is altogether infinite. Because, as stated above (I-II, q. 30, a. 3), it follows from the reason, and it belongs to the reason to proceed to infinity. Hence he that desires riches, may desire to be rich, not up to a certain limit, but to be simply as rich as possible. Another reason may be assigned, according to the Philosopher (Polit. i, 3), why a certain concupiscence is finite, and another infinite. Because concupiscence of the end is always infinite: since the end is desired for its own sake, e.g., health: and thus greater health is more desired, and so on to infinity; just as, if a white thing of itself dilates the sight, that which is more white dilates yet more. On the other hand, concupiscence of the means is not infinite, because the concupiscence of the means is in suitable proportion to the end. Consequently those who place their end in riches have an infinite concupiscence of riches; whereas those who desire riches, on account of the necessities of life, desire a finite measure of riches, sufficient for the

ad necessitatem vitae, ut philosophus dicit ibidem. Et eadem est ratio de concupiscentia, quarumcumque aliarum rerum.

AD PRIMUM ergo dicendum quod omne quod concupiscitur, accipitur ut quoddam finitum, vel quia est finitum secundum rem, prout semel concupiscitur in actu; vel quia est finitum secundum quod cadit sub apprehensione. Non enim potest sub ratione infiniti apprehendi, quia infinitum est, *cuius quantitatem accipientibus, semper est aliquid extra sumere,* ut dicitur in III Physic.

AD SECUNDUM dicendum quod ratio quodammodo est virtutis infinitae inquantum potest in infinitum aliquid considerare, ut apparet in additione numerorum et linearum. Unde infinitum aliquo modo sumptum, est proportionatum rationi. Nam et universale, quod ratio apprehendit, est quodammodo infinitum, inquantum in potentia continet infinita singularia.

AD TERTIUM dicendum quod ad hoc quod aliquis delectetur, non requiritur quod omnia consequatur quae concupiscit, sed in quolibet concupito quod consequitur, delectatur.

necessities of life, as the Philosopher says (Polit. i, 3). The same applies to the concupiscence of any other things.

Reply to Objection 1: Every object of concupiscence is taken as something finite: either because it is finite in reality, as being once actually desired; or because it is finite as apprehended. For it cannot be apprehended as infinite, since the infinite is that "from which, however much we may take, there always remains something to be taken" (Phys. iii, 6).

Reply to Objection 2: The reason is possessed of infinite power, in a certain sense, in so far as it can consider a thing infinitely, as appears in the addition of numbers and lines. Consequently, the infinite, taken in a certain way, is proportionate to reason. In fact the universal which the reason apprehends, is infinite in a sense, inasmuch as it contains potentially an infinite number of singulars.

Reply to Objection 3: In order that a man be delighted, there is no need for him to realize all that he desires: for he delights in the realization of each object of his concupiscence.

Quaestio XXXI

Deinde considerandum est de delectatione et tristitia. Circa delectationem vero consideranda sunt quatuor, *primo,* de ipsa delectatione secundum se; *secundo,* de causis delectationis; *tertio,* de effectibus eius; *quarto,* de bonitate et malitia ipsius. Circa primum **quaeruntur octo.** *Primo,* utrum delectatio sit passio. *Secundo,* utrum sit in tempore. *Tertio,* utrum differat a gaudio. *Quarto,* utrum sit in appetitu intellectivo. *Quinto,* de comparatione delectationum superioris appetitus, ad delectationem inferioris. *Sexto,* de comparatione delectationum sensitivarum ad invicem. *Septimo,* utrum sit aliqua delectatio non naturalis. *Octavo,* utrum delectatio possit esse contraria delectationi.

Articulus 1

Ad primum sic proceditur. Videtur quod delectatio non sit passio. Damascenus enim, in II libro, distinguit operationem a passione, dicens quod *operatio est motus qui est secundum naturam, passio vero est motus contra naturam.* Sed delectatio est operatio, ut philosophus dicit, in VII et X Ethic. Ergo delectatio non est passio.

Praeterea, *pati est moveri,* ut dicitur in III Physic. Sed delectatio non consistit in moveri, sed in motum esse, causatur enim delectatio ex bono iam adepto. Ergo delectatio non est passio.

Praeterea, delectatio consistit in quadam perfectione delectati, *perficit enim operationem,* ut dicitur in X Ethic. Sed perfici non est pati vel alterari, ut dicitur in VII Physic. et in II de anima. Ergo delectatio non est passio.

Sed contra est quod Augustinus, in IX et XIV de Civ. Dei, ponit delectationem, sive gaudium vel laetitiam, inter alias passiones animae.

Question 31
Of Delight, Considered in Itself*

We must now consider delight and sadness. Concerning delight four things must be considered: 1. Delight in itself; 2. The causes of delight; 3. Its effects; 4. Its goodness and malice. Under the first head there are eight points of inquiry: 1. Whether delight is a passion? 2. **Whether delight is subject to time?** 3. Whether it differs from joy? 4. Whether it is in the intellectual appetite? 5. Of the delights of the higher appetite compared with the delight of the lower; 6. Of sensible delights compared with one another; 7. Whether any delight is non-natural? 8. Whether one delight can be contrary to another?

Article 1
Whether delight is a passion?

Objection 1: It would seem that delight is not a passion. For Damascene (De Fide Orth. ii, 22) distinguishes operation from passion, and says that "operation is a movement in accord with nature, while passion is a movement contrary to nature." But delight is an operation, according to the Philosopher (Ethic. vii, 12; x, 5). Therefore delight is not a passion.

Objection 2: Further, "To be passive is to be moved," as stated in Phys. iii, 3. But delight does not consist in being moved, but in having been moved; for it arises from good already gained. Therefore delight is not a passion.

Objection 3: Further, delight is a kind of a perfection of the one who is delighted; since it "perfects operation," as stated in Ethic. x, 4,5. But to be perfected does not consist in being passive or in being altered, as stated in Phys. vii, 3 and De Anima ii, 5. Therefore delight is not a passion.

On the contrary, Augustine (De Civ. Dei ix, 2; xiv, 5 seqq) reckons delight, joy, or gladness among the other passions of the soul.

---

*   Or, Pleasure

RESPONDEO dicendum quod motus appetitus sensitivi proprie passio nominatur, sicut supra dictum est. Affectio autem quaecumque ex apprehensione sensitiva procedens, est motus appetitus sensitivi. Hoc autem necesse est competere delectationi. Nam, sicut philosophus dicit in I Rhetoric., *delectatio est quidam motus animae, et constitutio simul tota et sensibilis in naturam existentem.* Ad cuius intellectum, considerandum est quod, sicut contingit in rebus naturalibus aliqua consequi suas perfectiones naturales, ita hoc contingit in animalibus. Et quamvis moveri ad perfectionem non sit totum simul, tamen consequi naturalem perfectionem est totum simul. Haec autem est differentia inter animalia et alias res naturales, quod aliae res naturales, quando constituuntur in id quod convenit eis secundum naturam, hoc non sentiunt, sed animalia hoc sentiunt. Et ex isto sensu causatur quidam motus animae in appetitu sensitivo, et iste motus est delectatio. Per hoc ergo quod dicitur quod *delectatio est motus animae,* ponitur in genere. Per hoc autem quod dicitur *constitutio in existentem naturam,* idest in id quod existit in natura rei, ponitur causa delectationis, scilicet praesentia connaturalis boni. Per hoc autem quod dicitur *simul tota,* ostendit quod constitutio non debet accipi prout est in constitui, sed prout est in constitutum esse, quasi in termino motus, non enim delectatio est *generatio,* ut Plato posuit, sed magis consistit in *factum esse,* ut dicitur in VII Ethic. Per hoc autem quod dicitur *sensibilis,* excluduntur perfectiones rerum insensibilium, in quibus non est delectatio. Sic ergo patet quod, cum delectatio sit motus in appetitu animali consequens apprehensionem sensus, delectatio est passio animae.

AD PRIMUM ergo dicendum quod operatio connaturalis non impedita, est perfectio secunda, ut habetur in II de anima. Et ideo, quando constituitur res in propria operatione connaturali et non impedita,

I answer that, The movements of the sensitive appetite, are properly called passions, as stated above (I-II, q. 22, a. 3). Now every emotion arising from a sensitive apprehension, is a movement of the sensitive appetite: and this must needs be said of delight, since, according to the Philosopher (Rhet. i, 11) "delight is a certain movement of the soul and a sensible establishing thereof all at once, in keeping with the nature of the thing." In order to understand this, we must observe that just as in natural things some happen to attain to their natural perfections, so does this happen in animals. And though movement towards perfection does not occur all at once, yet the attainment of natural perfection does occur all at once. Now there is this difference between animals and other natural things, that when these latter are established in the state becoming their nature, they do not perceive it, whereas animals do. And from this perception there arises a certain movement of the soul in the sensitive appetite; which movement is called delight. Accordingly by saying that delight is "a movement of the soul," we designate its genus. By saying that it is "an establishing in keeping with the thing's nature," i.e., with that which exists in the thing, we assign the cause of delight, *viz.* the presence of a becoming good. By saying that this establishing is "all at once," we mean that this establishing is to be understood not as in the process of establishment, but as in the fact of complete establishment, in the term of the movement, as it were: for delight is not a "becoming" as Plato* maintained, but a "complete fact," as stated in Ethic. vii, 12. Lastly, by saying that this establishing is "sensible," we exclude the perfections of insensible things wherein there is no delight. It is therefore evident that, since delight is a movement of the animal appetite arising from an apprehension of sense, it is a passion of the soul.

Reply to Objection 1: Connatural operation, which is unhindered, is a second perfection, as stated in De Anima ii, 1: and therefore when a thing is established in its proper connatural and unhindered operation,

---

* Phileb. 32, 33

sequitur delectatio, quae consistit in perfectum esse, ut dictum est. Sic ergo cum dicitur quod delectatio est operatio, non est praedicatio per essentiam, sed per causam.

AD SECUNDUM dicendum quod in animali duplex motus considerari potest, unus secundum intentionem finis, qui pertinet ad appetitum, alius secundum executionem, qui pertinet ad exteriorem operationem licet ergo in eo qui iam consecutus est bonum in quo delectatur, cesset motus executionis, quo tenditur ad finem; non tamen cessat motus appetitivae partis, quae, sicut prius desiderabat non habitum, ita postea delectatur in habito. Licet enim delectatio sit quies quaedam appetitus, considerata praesentia boni delectantis, quod appetitui satisfacit; tamen adhuc remanet immutatio appetitus ab appetibili, ratione cuius delectatio motus quidam est.

AD TERTIUM dicendum quod, quamvis nomen passionis magis proprie conveniat passionibus corruptivis et in malum tendentibus, sicut sunt aegritudines corporales, et tristitia et timor in anima; tamen etiam in bonum ordinantur aliquae passiones, ut supra dictum est. Et secundum hoc delectatio dicitur passio.

delight follows, which consists in a state of completion, as observed above. Accordingly when we say that delight is an operation, we designate, not its essence, but its cause.

Reply to Objection 2: A twofold movement is to be observed in an animal: one, according to the intention of the end, and this belongs to the appetite; the other, according to the execution, and this belongs to the external operation. And so, although in him who has already gained the good in which he delights, the movement of execution ceases, by which the tends to the end; yet the movement of the appetitive faculty does not cease, since, just as before it desired that which it had not, so afterwards does it delight in that which is possesses. For though delight is a certain repose of the appetite, if we consider the presence of the pleasurable good that satisfies the appetite, nevertheless there remains the impression made on the appetite by its object, by reason of which delight is a kind of movement.

Reply to Objection 3: Although the name of passion is more appropriate to those passions which have a corruptive and evil tendency, such as bodily ailments, as also sadness and fear in the soul; yet some passions have a tendency to something good, as stated above (I-II, q. 23, a. 1; a. 4): and in this sense delight is called a passion.

ARTICULUS 2

AD SECUNDUM sic proceditur. Videtur quod delectatio sit in tempore. *Delectatio enim est motus quidam,* ut in I Rhetoric. philosophus dicit. Sed motus omnis est in tempore. Ergo delectatio est in tempore.

PRAETEREA, diuturnum, vel morosum, dicitur aliquid secundum tempus. Sed aliquae delectationes dicuntur morosae. Ergo delectatio est in tempore.

PRAETEREA, passiones animae sunt unius generis. Sed aliquae passiones animae sunt in tempore. Ergo et delectatio.

SED CONTRA est quod philosophus dicit, in X Ethic., quod *secundum nullum tempus accipiet quis delectationem.*

ARTICLE 2
Whether delight is in time?

Objection 1: It would seem that delight is in time. For "delight is a kind of movement," as the Philosopher says (Rhet. i, 11). But all movement is in time. Therefore delight is in time.

Objection 2: Further, a thing is said to last long and to be morose in respect of time. But some pleasures are called morose. Therefore pleasure is in time.

Objection 3: Further, the passions of the soul are of one same genus. But some passions of the soul are in time. Therefore delight is too.

On the contrary, The Philosopher says (Ethic. x, 4) that "no one takes pleasure according to time."

RESPONDEO dicendum quod aliquid contingit esse in tempore dupliciter, uno modo, secundum se; alio modo, per aliud, et quasi per accidens. Quia enim tempus est numerus successivorum, illa secundum se dicuntur esse in tempore, de quorum ratione est successio, vel aliquid ad successionem pertinens, sicut motus, quies, locutio, et alia huiusmodi. Secundum aliud vero, et non per se, dicuntur esse in tempore illa de quorum ratione non est aliqua successio, sed tamen alicui successivo subiacent. Sicut esse hominem de sui ratione non habet successionem, non enim est motus, sed terminus motus vel mutationis, scilicet generationis ipsius, sed quia humanum esse subiacet causis transmutabilibus, secundum hoc esse hominem est in tempore. Sic igitur dicendum est quod delectatio secundum se quidem non est in tempore, est enim delectatio in bono iam adepto, quod est quasi terminus motus. Sed si illud bonum adeptum transmutationi subiaceat, erit delectatio per accidens in tempore. Si autem sit omnino intransmutabile, delectatio non erit in tempore nec per se, nec per accidens.

AD PRIMUM ergo dicendum quod, sicut dicitur in III de anima, motus dupliciter dicitur. Uno modo, qui est *actus imperfecti, scilicet existentis in potentia, inquantum huiusmodi*, et talis motus est successivus, et in tempore. Alius autem motus est *actus perfecti, idest existentis in actu;* sicut intelligere, sentire et velle et huiusmodi, et etiam delectari. Et huiusmodi motus non est successivus, nec per se in tempore.

AD SECUNDUM dicendum quod delectatio dicitur diuturna vel morosa, secundum quod per accidens est in tempore.

AD TERTIUM dicendum quod aliae passiones non habent pro obiecto bonum adeptum, sicut delectatio. Unde plus habent de ratione motus imperfecti, quam delectatio. Et per consequens magis delectationi convenit non esse in tempore.

I answer that, A thing may be in time in two ways: first, by itself; secondly, by reason of something else, and accidentally as it were. For since time is the measure of successive things, those things are of themselves said to be in time, to which succession or something pertaining to succession is essential: such are movement, repose, speech and such like. On the other hand, those things are said to be in time, by reason of something else and not of themselves, to which succession is not essential, but which are subject to something successive. Thus the fact of being a man is not essentially something successive; since it is not a movement, but the term of a movement or change, *viz.* of this being begotten: yet, because human being is subject to changeable causes, in this respect, to be a man is in time. Accordingly, we must say that delight, of itself indeed, is not in time: for it regards good already gained, which is, as it were, the term of the movement. But if this good gained be subject to change, the delight therein will be in time accidentally: whereas if it be altogether unchangeable, the delight therein will not be in time, either by reason of itself or accidentally.

Reply to Objection 1: As stated in De Anima iii, 7, movement is twofold. One is "the act of something imperfect, i.e., of something existing in potentiality, as such": this movement is successive and is in time. Another movement is "the act of something perfect, i.e., of something existing in act," e.g., to understand, to feel, and to will and such like, also to have delight. This movement is not successive, nor is it of itself in time.

Reply to Objection 2: Delight is said to be long lasting or morose, according as it is accidentally in time.

Reply to Objection 3: Other passions have not for their object a good obtained, as delight has. Wherefore there is more of the movement of the imperfect in them than in delight. And consequently it belongs more to delight not to be in time.

Articulus 3

Ad tertium sic proceditur. Videtur quod gaudium sit omnino idem quod delectatio. Passiones enim animae differunt secundum obiecta. Sed idem est obiectum gaudii et delectationis, scilicet bonum adeptum. Ergo gaudium est omnino idem quod delectatio.

Praeterea, unus motus non terminatur ad duos terminos. Sed idem est motus qui terminatur ad gaudium et delectationem, scilicet concupiscentia. Ergo delectatio et gaudium sunt omnino idem.

Praeterea, si gaudium est aliud a delectatione, videtur quod, pari ratione, et laetitia et exultatio et iucunditas significent aliquid aliud a delectatione, et sic erunt omnes diversae passiones. Quod videtur esse falsum. Non ergo gaudium differt a delectatione.

Sed contra est quod in brutis animalibus non dicimus gaudium. Sed in eis dicimus delectationem. Non ergo est idem gaudium et delectatio.

Respondeo dicendum quod gaudium, ut Avicenna dicit in libro suo de anima, est quaedam species delectationis. Est enim considerandum quod, sicut sunt quaedam concupiscentiae naturales, quaedam autem non naturales, sed consequuntur rationem, ut supra dictum est; ita etiam delectationum quaedam sunt naturales, et quaedam non naturales, quae sunt cum ratione. Vel, sicut Damascenus et Gregorius Nyssenus dicunt, *quaedam sunt corporales, quaedam animales,* quod in idem redit. Delectamur enim et in his quae naturaliter concupiscimus, ea adipiscentes; et in his quae concupiscimus secundum rationem. Sed nomen gaudii non habet locum nisi in delectatione quae consequitur rationem, unde gaudium non attribuimus brutis animalibus, sed solum nomen delectationis. Omne autem quod concupiscimus secundum naturam, possumus etiam cum delectatione rationis concupiscere, sed non e converso. Unde de omnibus de quibus est delectatio, potest etiam esse gaudium in habentibus rationem. Quamvis non semper de omnibus sit gaudium, quandoque enim aliquis sentit aliquam delectationem secundum corpus, de qua tamen non

Article 3
Whether delight differs from joy?

Objection 1: It would seem that delight is altogether the same as joy. Because the passions of the soul differ according to their objects. But delight and joy have the same object, namely, a good obtained. Therefore joy is altogether the same as delight.

Objection 2: Further, one movement does not end in two terms. But one and the same movement, that of desire, ends in joy and delight. Therefore delight and joy are altogether the same.

Objection 3: Further, if joy differs from delight, it seems that there is equal reason for distinguishing gladness, exultation, and cheerfulness from delight, so that they would all be various passions of the soul. But this seems to be untrue. Therefore joy does not differ from delight.

On the contrary, We do not speak of joy in irrational animals; whereas we do speak of delight in them. Therefore joy is not the same as delight.

I answer that, Joy, as Avicenna states (De Anima iv), is a kind of delight. For we must observe that, just as some concupiscences are natural, and some not natural, but consequent to reason, as stated above (I-II, q. 30, a. 3), so also some delights are natural, and some are not natural but rational. Or, as Damascene (De Fide Orth. ii, 13) and Gregory of Nyssa* put it, "some delights are of the body, some are of the soul"; which amounts to the same. For we take delight both in those things which we desire naturally, when we get them, and in those things which we desire as a result of reason. But we do not speak of joy except when delight follows reason; and so we do not ascribe joy to irrational animals, but only delight. Now whatever we desire naturally, can also be the object of reasoned desire and delight, but not vice versa. Consequently whatever can be the object of delight, can also be the object of joy in rational beings. And yet everything is not always the object of joy; since sometimes one feels a certain delight in the body, without

---

* Nemesius, De Nat. Hom. xviii.

gaudet secundum rationem. Et secundum hoc, patet quod delectatio est in plus quam gaudium.

AD PRIMUM ergo dicendum quod, cum obiectum appetitus animalis sit bonum apprehensum, diversitas apprehensionis pertinet quodammodo ad diversitatem obiecti. Et sic delectationes animales, quae dicuntur etiam gaudia, distinguuntur a delectationibus corporalibus, quae dicuntur solum delectationes, sicut et de concupiscentiis supra dictum est.

AD SECUNDUM dicendum quod similis differentia invenitur etiam in concupiscentiis, ita quod delectatio respondeat concupiscentiae, et gaudium respondeat desiderio, quod magis videtur pertinere ad concupiscentiam animalem. Et sic secundum differentiam motus, est etiam differentia quietis.

AD TERTIUM dicendum quod alia nomina ad delectationem pertinentia, sunt imposita ab effectibus delectationis, nam *laetitia* imponitur a dilatatione cordis, ac si diceretur *latitia; exultatio* vero dicitur ab exterioribus signis delectationis interioris, quae apparent exterius, inquantum scilicet interius gaudium prosilit ad exteriora; *iucunditas* vero dicitur a quibusdam specialibus laetitiae signis vel effectibus. Et tamen omnia ista nomina videntur pertinere ad gaudium, non enim utimur eis nisi in naturis rationalibus.

rejoicing thereat according to reason. And accordingly delight extends to more things than does joy.

Reply to Objection 1: Since the object of the appetite of the soul is an apprehended good, diversity of apprehension pertains, in a way, to diversity of the object. And so delights of the soul, which are also called joys, are distinct from bodily delights, which are not called otherwise than delights: as we have observed above in regard to concupiscences (I-II, q. 30, a. 3, ad 2).

Reply to Objection 2: A like difference is to be observed in concupiscences also: so that delight corresponds to concupiscence, while joy corresponds to desire, which seems to pertain more to concupiscence of the soul. Hence there is a difference of repose corresponding to the difference of movement.

Reply to Objection 3: These other names pertaining to delight are derived from the effects of delight; for *laetitia* [gladness] is derived from the "dilation" of the heart, as if one were to say *latitia;* "exultation" is derived from the exterior signs of inward delight, which appear outwardly in so far as the inward joy breaks forth from its bounds; and "cheerfulness" is so called from certain special signs and effects of gladness. Yet all these names seem to belong to joy; for we do not employ them save in speaking of rational beings.

ARTICULUS 4

AD QUARTUM sic proceditur. Videtur quod delectatio non sit in appetitu intellectivo. Dicit enim philosophus, in I Rhetoric., quod *delectatio est motus quidam sensibilis.* Sed motus sensibilis non est in parte intellectiva. Ergo delectatio non est in parte intellectiva.

PRAETEREA, delectatio est passio quaedam. Sed omnis passio est in appetitu sensitivo. Ergo delectatio non est nisi in appetitu sensitivo.

PRAETEREA, delectatio est communis nobis et brutis. Ergo non est nisi in parte quae nobis et brutis communis est.

ARTICLE 4
Whether delight is in the intellectual appetite?

Objection 1: It would seem that delight is not in the intellectual appetite. Because the Philosopher says (Rhet. i, 11) that "delight is a sensible movement." But sensible movement is not in an intellectual power. Therefore delight is not in the intellectual appetite.

Objection 2: Further, delight is a passion. But every passion is in the sensitive appetite. Therefore delight is only in the sensitive appetite.

Objection 3: Further, delight is common to us and to the irrational animals. Therefore it is not elsewhere than in that power which we have in common with irrational animals.

SED CONTRA est quod in Psalmo XXXVI, dicitur, *delectare in domino*. Sed ad Deum non potest extendi appetitus sensitivus, sed solum intellectivus. Ergo delectatio potest esse in appetitu intellectivo.

RESPONDEO dicendum quod, sicut dictum est, delectatio quaedam sequitur apprehensionem rationis. Ad apprehensionem autem rationis, non solum commovetur appetitus sensitivus, per applicationem ad aliquid particulare; sed etiam appetitus intellectivus, qui dicitur voluntas. Et secundum hoc, in appetitu intellectivo, sive in voluntate, est delectatio quae dicitur gaudium, non autem delectatio corporalis. Hoc tamen interest inter delectationem utriusque appetitus, quod delectatio appetitus sensibilis est cum aliqua transmutatione corporali, delectatio autem appetitus intellectivi nihil aliud est quam simplex motus voluntatis. Et secundum hoc Augustinus dicit, in XIV de Civ. Dei, quod *cupiditas et laetitia non est aliud quam voluntas in eorum consensione quae volumus*.

AD PRIMUM ergo dicendum quod in illa definitione philosophi, *sensibile* ponitur communiter pro quacumque apprehensione. Dicit enim philosophus in X Ethic., quod *secundum omnem sensum est delectatio; similiter autem et secundum intellectum et speculationem*. Vel potest dici quod ipse definit delectationem appetitus sensitivi.

AD SECUNDUM dicendum quod delectatio habet rationem passionis, proprie loquendo, inquantum est cum aliqua transmutatione corporali. Et sic non est in appetitu intellectivo, sed secundum simplicem motum, sic enim etiam est in Deo et in angelis. Unde dicit philosophus, in VII Ethic., quod *Deus una simplici operatione gaudet*. Et Dionysius dicit, in fine Cael. Hier., quod *angeli non sunt susceptibiles nostrae passibilis delectationis, sed congaudent Deo secundum incorruptionis laetitiam*.

AD TERTIUM dicendum quod in nobis non solum est delectatio in qua communicamus cum brutis, sed etiam in qua communicamus cum angelis. Unde ibidem Dionysius dicit quod *sancti homines multoties fiunt in participatione delectationum angelicarum*. Et ita in nobis est delectatio non solum in appetitu sensitivo, in quo communicamus cum brutis;

On the contrary, It is written (Ps. 36:4): "Delight in the Lord." But the sensitive appetite cannot reach to God; only the intellectual appetite can. Therefore delight can be in the intellectual appetite.

I answer that, As stated above (I-II, q. 31, a. 3), a certain delight arises from the apprehension of the reason. Now on the reason apprehending something, not only the sensitive appetite is moved, as regards its application to some particular thing, but also the intellectual appetite, which is called the will. And accordingly in the intellectual appetite or will there is that delight which is called joy, but not bodily delight. However, there is this difference of delight in either power, that delight of the sensitive appetite is accompanied by a bodily transmutation, whereas delight of the intellectual appetite is nothing but the mere movement of the will. Hence Augustine says (De Civ. Dei xiv, 6) that "desire and joy are nothing else but a volition of consent to the things we wish."

Reply to Objection 1: In this definition of the Philosopher, he uses the word "sensible" in its wide acceptation for any kind of perception. For he says (Ethic. x, 4) that "delight is attendant upon every sense, as it is also upon every act of the intellect and contemplation." Or we may say that he is defining delight of the sensitive appetite.

Reply to Objection 2: Delight has the character of passion, properly speaking, when accompanied by bodily transmutation. It is not thus in the intellectual appetite, but according to simple movement: for thus it is also in God and the angels. Hence the Philosopher says (Ethic. vii, 14) that "God rejoices by one simple act": and Dionysius says at the end of De Coel. Hier., that "the angels are not susceptible to our passible delight, but rejoice together with God with the gladness of incorruption."

Reply to Objection 3: In us there is delight, not only in common with dumb animals, but also in common with angels. Wherefore Dionysius says (De Coel. Hier.) that "holy men often take part in the angelic delights." Accordingly we have delight, not only in the sensitive appetite, which we have in common with dumb animals,

sed etiam in appetitu intellectivo, in quo communicamus cum angelis.

Articulus 5

AD QUINTUM sic proceditur. Videtur quod delectationes corporales et sensibiles sint maiores delectationibus spiritualibus intelligibilibus. Omnes enim aliquam delectationem sequuntur, secundum philosophum, in X Ethic. Sed plures sequuntur delectationes sensibiles, quam delectationes spirituales intelligibiles. Ergo delectationes corporales sunt maiores.

PRAETEREA, magnitudo causae ex effectu cognoscitur. Sed delectationes corporales habent fortiores effectus, *transmutant enim corpus, et quibusdam insanias faciunt,* ut dicitur in VII Ethic. Ergo delectationes corporales sunt fortiores.

PRAETEREA, delectationes corporales oportet temperare et refraenare, propter earum vehementiam. Sed delectationes spirituales non oportet refraenare. Ergo delectationes corporales sunt maiores.

SED CONTRA est quod dicitur in Psalmo CXVIII, *quam dulcia faucibus meis eloquia tua, super mel ori meo.* Et philosophus dicit, in X Ethic., quod *maxima delectatio est quae est secundum operationem sapientiae.*

RESPONDEO dicendum quod, sicut iam dictum est, delectatio provenit ex coniunctione convenientis quae sentitur vel cognoscitur. In operibus autem animae, praecipue sensitivae et intellectivae, est hoc considerandum, quod, cum non transeant in materiam exteriorem, sunt actus vel perfectiones operantis, scilicet intelligere, sentire, velle, et huiusmodi, nam actiones quae transeunt in exteriorem materiam, magis sunt actiones et perfectiones materiae transmutatae; *motus enim est actus mobilis a movente.* Sic igitur praedictae actiones animae sensitivae et intellectivae, et ipsae sunt quoddam bonum operantis, et sunt etiam cognitae per sensum vel intellectum. Unde etiam ex ipsis consurgit delectatio, et non solum ex eorum

but also in the intellectual appetite, which we have in common with the angels.

Article 5
Whether bodily and sensible pleasures are greater than spiritual and intellectual pleasures?

Objection 1: It would seem that bodily and sensible pleasures are greater than spiritual and intelligible pleasures. For all men seek some pleasure, according to the Philosopher (Ethic. x, 2,4). But more seek sensible pleasures, than intelligible spiritual pleasures. Therefore bodily pleasures are greater.

Objection 2: Further, the greatness of a cause is known by its effect. But bodily pleasures have greater effects; since "they alter the state of the body, and in some they cause madness" (Ethic. vii, 3). Therefore bodily pleasures are greater.

Objection 3: Further, bodily pleasures need to be tempered and checked, by reason of their vehemence: whereas there is no need to check spiritual pleasures. Therefore bodily pleasures are greater.

On the contrary, It is written (Ps. 118:103): "How sweet are Thy words to my palate; more than honey to my mouth!" And the Philosopher says (Ethic. x, 7) that "the greatest pleasure is derived from the operation of wisdom."

I answer that, As stated above (I-II, q. 31, a. 1), pleasure arises from union with a suitable object perceived or known. Now, in the operations of the soul, especially of the sensitive and intellectual soul, it must be noted that, since they do not pass into outward matter, they are acts or perfections of the agent, e.g., to understand, to feel, to will and the like: because actions which pass into outward matter, are actions and perfections rather of the matter transformed; for "movement is the act produced by the mover in the thing moved" (Phys. iii, 3). Accordingly the aforesaid actions of the sensitive and intellectual soul, are themselves a certain good of the agent, and are known by sense and intellect. Wherefore from them also does pleasure arise, and not only from their

obiectis. Si igitur comparentur delectationes intelligibiles delectationibus sensibilibus, secundum quod delectamur in ipsis actionibus, puta in cognitione sensus et in cognitione intellectus; non est dubium quod multo sunt maiores delectationes intelligibiles quam sensibiles. Multo enim magis delectatur homo de hoc quod cognoscit aliquid intelligendo, quam de hoc quod cognoscit aliquid sentiendo. Quia intellectualis **cognitio et perfectior est, et etiam magis** cognoscitur, quia intellectus magis reflectitur supra actum suum quam sensus. Est etiam cognitio intellectiva magis dilecta, nullus enim est qui non magis vellet carere visu corporali quam visu intellectuali, eo modo quo bestiae vel stulti carent, sicut Augustinus dicit, in libro de Civ. Dei. Sed si comparentur delectationes intelligibiles spirituales delectationibus sensibilibus corporalibus, sic, secundum se et simpliciter loquendo, delectationes spirituales sunt maiores. Et hoc apparet secundum tria quae requiruntur ad delectationem, scilicet bonum coniunctum, et id cui coniungitur, et ipsa coniunctio. Nam ipsum bonum spirituale et est maius quam corporale bonum; et est magis dilectum. Cuius signum est quod homines etiam a maximis corporalibus voluptatibus abstinent, ut non perdant honorem, qui est bonum intelligibile. Similiter etiam ipsa pars intellectiva est multo nobilior, et magis cognoscitiva, quam pars sensitiva. Coniunctio etiam utriusque est magis intima, et magis perfecta, et magis firma. Intimior quidem est, quia sensus sistit circa exteriora accidentia rei, intellectus vero penetrat usque ad rei essentiam; obiectum enim intellectus est quod quid est. Perfectior autem est, quia coniunctioni sensibilis ad sensum adiungitur motus, qui est actus imperfectus, unde et delectationes sensibiles non sunt totae simul, sed in eis aliquid pertransit, et aliquid expectatur consummandum, ut patet in delectatione ciborum et venereorum. Sed intelligibilia sunt absque motu, unde delectationes tales sunt totae simul. Est etiam firmior, quia delectabilia corporalia sunt corruptibilia, et cito deficiunt; bona vero spiritualia sunt incorruptibilia. Sed

objects. If therefore we compare intellectual pleasures with sensible pleasures, according as we delight in the very actions, for instance in sensitive and in intellectual knowledge; without doubt intellectual pleasures are much greater than sensible pleasures. For man takes much more delight in knowing something, by understanding it, than in knowing something by perceiving it with his sense. Because intellectual knowledge is more **perfect; and because it is better known,** since the intellect reflects on its own act more than sense does. Moreover intellectual knowledge is more beloved: for there is no one who would not forfeit his bodily sight rather than his intellectual vision, as beasts or fools are deprived thereof, as Augustine says in De Civ. Dei (De Trin. xiv, 14). If, however, intellectual spiritual pleasures be compared with sensible bodily pleasures, then, in themselves and absolutely speaking, spiritual pleasures are greater. And this appears from the consideration of the three things needed for pleasure, *viz.* the good which is brought into conjunction, that to which it is conjoined, and the conjunction itself. For spiritual good is both greater and more beloved than bodily good: a sign whereof is that men abstain from even the greatest bodily pleasures, rather than suffer loss of honor which is an intellectual good. Likewise the intellectual faculty is much more noble and more knowing than the sensitive faculty. Also the conjunction is more intimate, more perfect and more firm. More intimate, because the senses stop at the outward accidents of a thing, whereas the intellect penetrates to the essence; for the object of the intellect is "what a thing is." More perfect, because the conjunction of the sensible to the sense implies movement, which is an imperfect act: wherefore sensible pleasures are not perceived all at once, but some part of them is passing away, while some other part is looked forward to as yet to be realized, as is manifest in pleasures of the table and in sexual pleasures: whereas intelligible things are without movement: hence pleasures of this kind are realized all at once. More firm; because the objects of bodily pleasure are corruptible, and soon pass away; whereas spiritual goods are incorruptible. On the

quoad nos, delectationes corporales sunt magis vehementes, propter tria. Primo, quia sensibilia sunt magis nota, quoad nos, quam intelligibilia. Secundo etiam, quia delectationes sensibiles, cum sint passiones sensitivi appetitus, sunt cum aliqua transmutatione corporali. Quod non contingit in delectationibus spiritualibus, nisi per quandam redundantiam a superiori appetitu in inferiorem. Tertio, quia delectationes corporales appetuntur ut medicinae quaedam contra corporales defectus vel molestias, ex quibus tristitiae quaedam consequuntur. Unde delectationes corporales, tristitiis huiusmodi supervenientes, magis sentiuntur, et per consequens magis acceptantur, quam delectationes spirituales quae non habent tristitias contrarias, ut infra dicetur.

Ad primum ergo dicendum quod ideo plures sequuntur delectationes corporales, quia bona sensibilia sunt magis et pluribus nota. Et etiam quia homines indigent delectationibus ut medicinis contra multiplices dolores et tristitias, et cum plures hominum non possint attingere ad delectationes spirituales, quae sunt propriae virtuosorum, consequens et quod declinent ad corporales.

Ad secundum dicendum quod transmutatio corporis magis contingit ex delectationibus corporalibus, inquantum sunt passiones appetitus sensitivi.

Ad tertium dicendum quod delectationes corporales sunt secundum partem sensitivam, quae regulatur ratione, et ideo indigent temperari et refraenari per rationem. Sed delectationes spirituales sunt secundum mentem, quae est ipsa regula, unde sunt secundum seipsas sobriae et moderatae.

Articulus 6

Ad sextum sic proceditur. Videtur quod delectationes quae sunt secundum tactum, non sint maiores delectationibus quae sunt secundum alios sensus. Illa enim delectatio videtur esse maxima, qua exclusa, omne gaudium cessat. Sed talis est delectatio quae est secundum visum, dicitur enim Tobiae V, *quale gaudium erit mihi, qui in tenebris sedeo,*

other hand, in relation to us, bodily pleasures are more vehement, for three reasons. First, because sensible things are more known to us, than intelligible things. Secondly, because sensible pleasures, through being passions of the sensitive appetite, are accompanied by some alteration in the body: whereas this does not occur in spiritual pleasures, save by reason of a certain reaction of the superior appetite on the lower. Thirdly, because bodily pleasures are sought as remedies for bodily defects or troubles, whence various griefs arise. Wherefore bodily pleasures, by reason of their succeeding griefs of this kind, are felt the more, and consequently are welcomed more than spiritual pleasures, which have no contrary griefs, as we shall state farther on (I-II, q. 35, a. 5).

Reply to Objection 1: The reason why more seek bodily pleasures is because sensible goods are known better and more generally: and, again, because men need pleasures as remedies for many kinds of sorrow and sadness: and since the majority cannot attain spiritual pleasures, which are proper to the virtuous, hence it is that they turn aside to seek those of the body.

Reply to Objection 2: Bodily transmutation arises more from bodily pleasures, inasmuch as they are passions of the sensitive appetite.

Reply to Objection 3: Bodily pleasures are realized in the sensitive faculty which is governed by reason: wherefore they need to be tempered and checked by reason. But spiritual pleasures are in the mind, which is itself the rule: wherefore they are in themselves both sober and moderate.

Article 6
Whether the pleasures of touch are greater than the pleasures afforded by the other senses?

Objection 1: It would seem that the pleasures of touch are not greater than the pleasures afforded by the other senses. Because the greatest pleasure seems to be that without which all joy is at an end. But such is the pleasure afforded by the sight, according to the words of Tob. 5:12: "What manner of joy shall be to me, who sit in darkness,

et lumen caeli non video? Ergo delectatio quae est per visum, est maxima inter sensibiles delectationes.

Praeterea, *unicuique fit delectabile illud quod amat,* ut philosophus dicit, in I Rhetoric. Sed *inter alios sensus maxime diligitur visus.* Ergo delectatio quae est secundum visum, est maxima.

Praeterea, principium amicitiae delectabilis maxime est visio. Sed causa talis amicitiae est delectatio. Ergo secundum visum videtur esse maxime delectatio.

Sed contra est quod philosophus dicit, in III Ethic., quod maximae delectationes sunt secundum tactum.

Respondeo dicendum quod, sicut iam dictum est, unumquodque, inquantum amatur, efficitur delectabile. Sensus autem, ut dicitur in principio Metaphys., propter duo diliguntur, scilicet propter cognitionem, et propter utilitatem. Unde et utroque modo contingit esse delectationem secundum sensum. Sed quia apprehendere ipsam cognitionem tanquam bonum quoddam, proprium est hominis; ideo primae delectationes sensuum, quae scilicet sunt secundum cognitionem, sunt propriae hominum, delectationes autem sensuum inquantum diliguntur propter utilitatem, sunt communes omnibus animalibus. Si igitur loquamur de delectatione sensus quae est ratione cognitionis, manifestum est quod secundum visum est maior delectatio quam secundum aliquem alium sensum. Si autem loquamur de delectatione sensus quae est ratione utilitatis, sic maxima delectatio est secundum tactum. Utilitas enim sensibilium attenditur secundum ordinem ad conservationem naturae animalis. Ad hanc autem utilitatem propinquius se habent sensibilia tactus, est enim tactus cognoscitivus eorum ex quibus consistit animal, scilicet calidi et frigidi, et huiusmodi. Unde secundum hoc, delectationes quae sunt secundum tactum, sunt maiores, quasi fini propinquiores. Et propter hoc etiam, alia animalia, quae non habent delectationem secundum sensum nisi ratione utilitatis, non delectantur secundum alios

and see not the light of heaven?" Therefore the pleasure afforded by the sight is the greatest of sensible pleasures.

Objection 2: Further, "every one finds treasure in what he loves," as the Philosopher says (Rhet. i, 11). But "of all the senses the sight is loved most."* Therefore the greatest pleasure seems to be afforded by sight.

Objection 3: Further, the beginning of friendship which is for the sake of the pleasant is principally sight. But pleasure is the cause of such friendship. Therefore the greatest pleasure seems to be afforded by sight.

On the contrary, The Philosopher says (Ethic. iii, 10), that the greatest pleasures are those which are afforded by the touch.

I answer that, As stated above (I-II, q. 25, a. 2, ad 1; q. 27, a. 4, ad 1), everything gives pleasure according as it is loved. Now, as stated in Metaph. i, 1, the senses are loved for two reasons: for the purpose of knowledge, and on account of their usefulness. Wherefore the senses afford pleasure in both these ways. But because it is proper to man to apprehend knowledge itself as something good, it follows that the former pleasures of the senses, i.e., those which arise from knowledge, are proper to man: whereas pleasures of the senses, as loved for their usefulness, are common to all animals. If therefore we speak of that sensible pleasure by which reason of knowledge, it is evident that the sight affords greater pleasure than any other sense. On the other hand, if we speak of that sensible pleasure which is by reason of usefulness, then the greatest pleasure is afforded by the touch. For the usefulness of sensible things is gauged by their relation to the preservation of the animal's nature. Now the sensible objects of touch bear the closest relation to this usefulness: for the touch takes cognizance of those things which are vital to an animal, namely, of things hot and cold and the like. Wherefore in this respect, the pleasures of touch are greater as being more closely related to the end. For this reason, too, other animals which do not experience sensible pleasure save by reason of usefulness, derive no pleasure from the other

---

* Metaph. i, 1

senses except as subordinated to the sensible objects of the touch: "for dogs do not take delight in the smell of hares, but in eating them; ... nor does the lion feel pleasure in the lowing of an ox, but in devouring it" (Ethic. iii, 10). Since then the pleasure afforded by touch is the greatest in respect of usefulness, and the pleasure afforded by sight the greatest in respect of knowledge; if anyone wish to compare these two, he will find that the pleasure of touch is, absolutely speaking, greater than the pleasure of sight, so far as the latter remains within the limits of sensible pleasure. Because it is evident that in everything, that which is natural is most powerful: and it is to these pleasures of the touch that the natural concupiscences, such as those of food, sexual union, and the like, are ordained. If, however, we consider the pleasures of sight, inasmuch sight is the handmaid of the mind, then the pleasures of sight are greater, forasmuch as intellectual pleasures are greater than sensible.

Reply to Objection 1: Joy, as stated above (I-II, q. 31, a. 3), denotes pleasure of the soul; and this belongs principally to the sight. But natural pleasure belongs principally to the touch.

Reply to Objection 2: The sight is loved most, "on account of knowledge, because it helps us to distinguish many things," as is stated in the same passage (Metaph. i, 1).

Reply to Objection 3: Pleasure causes carnal love in one way; the sight, in another. For pleasure, especially that which is afforded by the touch, is the final cause of the friendship which is for the sake of the pleasant: whereas the sight is a cause like that from which a movement has its beginning, inasmuch as the beholder on seeing the lovable object receives an impression of its image, which entices him to love it and to seek its delight.

ARTICLE 7
Whether any pleasure is not natural?

Objection 1: It would seem that no pleasure is not natural. For pleasure is to the emotions of the soul what repose is to bodies. But the appetite of a natural body does not repose save in a connatural place. Neither, therefore, can the repose of the

I-II, q. 31, a. 7, arg. 1

appetitus animalis, quae est delectatio, potest esse nisi in aliquo connaturali. Nulla ergo delectatio est non naturalis.

PRAETEREA, illud quod est contra naturam, est violentum. Sed *omne violentum est contristans,* ut dicitur in V Metaphys. Ergo nihil quod est contra naturam, potest esse delectabile.

PRAETEREA, constitui in propriam naturam, cum sentitur, causat delectationem; ut patet ex definitione philosophi supra posita. Sed constitui in naturam, unicuique est naturale, quia motus naturalis est qui est ad terminum naturalem. Ergo omnis delectatio est naturalis.

SED CONTRA est quod philosophus dicit, in VII Ethic., quod quaedam delectationes sunt *aegritudinales et contra naturam.*

RESPONDEO dicendum quod naturale dicitur quod est secundum naturam, ut dicitur in II Physic. Natura autem in homine dupliciter sumi potest. Uno modo, prout intellectus et ratio est potissime hominis natura, quia secundum eam homo in specie constituitur. Et secundum hoc, naturales delectationes hominum dici possunt quae sunt in eo quod convenit homini secundum rationem, sicut delectari in contemplatione veritatis, et in actibus virtutum, est naturale homini. Alio modo potest sumi natura in homine secundum quod condividitur rationi, id scilicet quod est commune homini et aliis, praecipue quod rationi non obedit. Et secundum hoc, ea quae pertinent ad conservationem corporis, vel secundum individuum, ut cibus, potus, lectus, et huiusmodi, vel secundum speciem, sicut venereorum usus, dicuntur homini delectabilia naturaliter. Secundum utrasque autem delectationes, contingit aliquas esse *innaturales,* simpliciter loquendo, sed *connaturales* secundum quid. Contingit enim in aliquo individuo corrumpi aliquod principiorum naturalium speciei; et sic id quod est contra naturam speciei, fieri per accidens naturale huic individuo; sicut huic aquae calefactae est naturale quod calefaciat. Ita igitur contingit quod id quod est contra naturam hominis,

DELIGHT, CONSIDERED IN ITSELF

animal appetite, which is pleasure, be elsewhere than in something connatural. Therefore no pleasure is non-natural.

Objection 2: Further, what is against nature is violent. But "whatever is violent causes grief" (Metaph. v, 5). Therefore nothing which is unnatural can give pleasure.

Objection 3: Further, the fact of being established in one's own nature, if perceived, gives rise to pleasure, as is evident from the Philosopher's definition quoted above (I-II, q. 31, a. 1). But it is natural to every thing to be established in its nature; because natural movement tends to a natural end. Therefore every pleasure is natural.

On the contrary, The Philosopher says (Ethic. vii, 5,6) that some things are pleasant "not from nature but from disease."

I answer that, We speak of that as being natural, which is in accord with nature, as stated in Phys. ii, 1. Now, in man, nature can be taken in two ways. First, inasmuch as intellect and reason is the principal part of man's nature, since in respect thereof he has his own specific nature. And in this sense, those pleasures may be called natural to man, which are derived from things pertaining to man in respect of his reason: for instance, it is natural to man to take pleasure in contemplating the truth and in doing works of virtue. Secondly, nature in man may be taken as contrasted with reason, and as denoting that which is common to man and other animals, especially that part of man which does not obey reason. And in this sense, that which pertains to the preservation of the body, either as regards the individual, as food, drink, sleep, and the like, or as regards the species, as sexual intercourse, are said to afford man natural pleasure. Under each kind of pleasures, we find some that are "not natural" speaking absolutely, and yet "connatural" in some respect. For it happens in an individual that some one of the natural principles of the species is corrupted, so that something which is contrary to the specific nature, becomes accidentally natural to this individual: thus it is natural to this hot water to give heat. Consequently it happens that something which is not natural to man,

vel quantum ad rationem, vel quantum ad corporis conservationem, fiat huic homini connaturale, propter aliquam corruptionem naturae in eo existentem. Quae quidem corruptio potest esse vel ex parte corporis, sive ex aegritudine, sicut febricitantibus dulcia videntur amara et e converso; sive propter malam complexionem, sicut aliqui delectantur in comestione terrae vel carbonum, vel aliquorum huiusmodi, vel etiam ex parte animae, sicut propter consuetudinem aliqui, delectantur in comedendo homines, vel in coitu bestiarum aut masculorum, aut aliorum huiusmodi, quae non sunt secundum naturam humanam.

Et per hoc patet responsio ad obiecta.

either in regard to reason, or in regard to the preservation of the body, becomes connatural to this individual man, on account of there being some corruption of nature in him. And this corruption may be either on the part of the body—from some ailment; thus to a man suffering from fever, sweet things seem bitter, and vice versa—or from an evil temperament; thus some take pleasure in eating earth and coals and the like; or on the part of the soul; thus from custom some take pleasure in cannibalism or in the unnatural intercourse of man and beast, or other such things, which are not in accord with human nature.

This suffices for the answers to the objections.

Articulus 8

Ad octavum sic proceditur. Videtur quod delectationi non sit delectatio contraria. Passiones enim animae speciem et contrarietatem recipiunt secundum obiecta. Obiectum autem delectationis est bonum. Cum igitur bonum non sit contrarium bono, sed *bonum malo contrarietur, et malum malo,* ut dicitur in praedicamentis; videtur quod delectatio non sit contraria delectationi.

Praeterea, uni unum est contrarium, ut probatur in X Metaphys. Sed delectationi contraria est tristitia. Non ergo delectationi contraria est delectatio.

Praeterea, si delectationi contraria est delectatio hoc non est nisi propter contrarietatem eorum in quibus aliquis delectatur. Sed haec differentia est materialis, contrarietas autem est differentia secundum formam, ut dicitur in X Metaphys. Ergo contrarietas non est delectationis ad delectationem.

Sed contra, ea quae se impediunt, in eodem genere existentia, secundum philosophum, sunt contraria. Sed quaedam delectationes se invicem impediunt ut dicitur in X Ethic. Ergo aliquae delectationes sunt contrariae.

Respondeo dicendum quod delectatio in affectionibus animae, sicut dictum est, proportionatur quieti in corporibus naturalibus. Dicuntur autem duae quietes esse contrariae,

Article 8
Whether one pleasure can be contrary to another?

Objection 1: It would seem that one pleasure cannot be contrary to another. Because the passions of the soul derive their species and contrariety from their objects. Now the object of pleasure is the good. Since therefore good is not contrary to good, but "good is contrary to evil, and evil to good," as stated in Praedic. viii; it seems that one pleasure is not contrary to another.

Objection 2: Further, to one thing there is one contrary, as is proved in Metaph. x, 4. But sadness is contrary to pleasure. Therefore pleasure is not contrary to pleasure.

Objection 3: Further, if one pleasure is contrary to another, this is only on account of the contrariety of the things which give pleasure. But this difference is material: whereas contrariety is a difference of form, as stated in Metaph. x, 4. Therefore there is no contrariety between one pleasure and another.

On the contrary, Things of the same genus that impede one another are contraries, as the Philosopher states (Phys. viii, 8). But some pleasures impede one another, as stated in Ethic. x, 5. Therefore some pleasures are contrary to one another.

I answer that, Pleasure, in the emotions of the soul, is likened to repose in natural bodies, as stated above (I-II, q. 23, a. 4). Now one repose is said to be contrary to another

quae sunt in contrariis terminis; sicut *quies quae est sursum, ei quae est deorsum,* ut dicitur V Physic. Unde et contingit in affectibus animae duas delectationes esse contrarias.

AD PRIMUM ergo dicendum quod verbum illud philosophi est intelligendum secundum quod bonum et malum accipitur in virtutibus et vitiis, nam inveniuntur duo contraria vitia, non autem invenitur virtus contraria virtuti. In aliis autem nil prohibet duo bona esse ad invicem contraria, sicut calidum et frigidum, quorum unum est bonum igni, alterum aquae. Et per hunc modum delectatio potest esse delectationi contraria. Sed hoc in bono virtutis esse non potest, quia bonum virtutis non accipitur nisi per convenientiam ad aliquid unum, scilicet rationem.

AD SECUNDUM dicendum quod delectatio se habet in affectibus animae, sicut quies naturalis in corporibus, est enim in aliquo convenienti et quasi connaturali. Tristitia autem se habet sicut quies violenta, tristabile enim repugnat appetitui animali, sicut locus quietis violentae appetitui naturali. Quieti autem naturali opponitur et quies violenta eiusdem corporis, et quies naturalis alterius, ut dicitur in V Physic. Unde delectationi opponitur et delectatio et tristitia.

AD TERTIUM dicendum quod ea in quibus delectamur, cum sint obiecta delectationis, non solum faciunt differentiam materialem, sed etiam formalem, si sit diversa ratio delectabilitatis. Diversa enim ratio obiecti diversificat speciem actus vel passionis, ut ex supradictis patet.

when they are in contrary termini; thus, "repose in a high place is contrary to repose in a low place" (Phys. v, 6). Wherefore it happens in the emotions of the soul that one pleasure is contrary to another.

Reply to Objection 1: This saying of the Philosopher is to be understood of good and evil as applied to virtues and vices: because one vice may be contrary to another vice, whereas no virtue can be contrary to another virtue. But in other things nothing prevents one good from being contrary to another, such as hot and cold, of which the former is good in relation to fire, the latter, in relation to water. And in this way one pleasure can be contrary to another. That this is impossible with regard to the good of virtue, is due to the fact that virtue's good depends on fittingness in relation to some one thing—i.e., the reason.

Reply to Objection 2: Pleasure, in the emotions of the soul, is likened to natural repose in bodies: because its object is something suitable and connatural, so to speak. But sadness is like a violent repose; because its object is disagreeable to the animal appetite, just as the place of violent repose is disagreeable to the natural appetite. Now natural repose is contrary both to violent repose of the same body, and to the natural repose of another, as stated in Phys. v, 6. Wherefore pleasure is contrary to both to another pleasure and to sadness.

Reply to Objection 3: The things in which we take pleasure, since they are the objects of pleasure, cause not only a material, but also a formal difference, if the formality of pleasurableness be different. Because difference in the formal object causes a specific difference in acts and passions, as stated above (I-II, q. 23, a. 1; a. 4; q. 30, a. 2).

Quaestio XXXII

Deinde considerandum est de causis delectationis. Et circa hoc quaeruntur octo. *Primo,* utrum operatio sit causa propria delectationis. *Secundo,* utrum motus sit causa delectationis. *Tertio,* utrum spes et memoria. *Quarto,* utrum tristitia. *Quinto,* utrum actiones aliorum sint nobis delectationis causa. *Sexto,* utrum benefacere alteri sit causa delectationis. *Septimo,* utrum similitudo sit causa delectationis. *Octavo,* utrum admiratio sit causa delectationis.

Articulus 1

AD PRIMUM sic proceditur. Videtur quod operatio non sit propria et prima causa delectationis. Ut enim philosophus dicit, in I Rhetoric., *delectari consistit in hoc quod sensus aliquid patiatur,* requiritur enim ad delectationem cognitio, sicut dictum est. Sed per prius sunt cognoscibilia obiecta operationum quam ipsae operationes. Ergo operatio non est propria causa delectationis.

PRAETEREA, delectatio potissime consistit in fine adepto, hoc enim est quod praecipue concupiscitur. Sed non semper operatio est finis, sed quandoque ipsum operatum. Non ergo operatio est propria et per se causa delectationis.

PRAETEREA, otium et requies dicuntur per cessationem operationis. Haec autem sunt delectabilia, ut dicitur in I Rhetoric. Non ergo operatio est propria causa delectationis.

SED CONTRA est quod philosophus dicit, VII et X Ethic., quod *delectatio est operatio connaturalis non impedita.*

RESPONDEO dicendum quod, sicut supra dictum est, ad delectationem duo requiruntur, scilicet consecutio boni convenientis, et cognitio huiusmodi adeptionis. Utrumque autem horum in quadam operatione consistit, nam actualis cognitio operatio quaedam est; similiter bonum conveniens adipiscimur aliqua operatione. Ipsa etiam operatio propria est quoddam bonum conveniens. Unde oportet quod omnis delectatio aliquam operationem consequatur.

Question 32
Of the Cause of Pleasure

We must now consider the causes of pleasure: and under this head there are eight points of inquiry: 1. Whether operation is the proper cause of pleasure? 2. Whether movement is a cause of pleasure? 3. Whether hope and memory cause pleasure? 4. Whether sadness causes pleasure? 5. Whether the actions of others are a cause of pleasure to us? 6. Whether doing good to another is a cause of pleasure? 7. Whether likeness is a cause of pleasure? 8. Whether wonder is a cause of pleasure?

Article 1
Whether operation is the proper cause of pleasure?

Objection 1: It would seem that operation is not the proper and first cause of pleasure. For, as the Philosopher says (Rhet. i, 11), "pleasure consists in a perception of the senses," since knowledge is requisite for pleasure, as stated above (I-II, q. 31, a. 1). But the objects of operations are knowable before the operations themselves. Therefore operation is not the proper cause of pleasure.

Objection 2: Further, pleasure consists especially in an end gained: since it is this that is chiefly desired. But the end is not always an operation, but is sometimes the effect of the operation. Therefore operation is not the proper and direct cause of pleasure.

Objection 3: Further, leisure and rest consist in cessation from work: and they are objects of pleasure (Rhet. i, 11). Therefore operation is not the proper cause of pleasure.

On the contrary, The Philosopher says (Ethic. vii, 12,13; x, 4) that "pleasure is a connatural and uninterrupted operation."

I answer that, As stated above (I-II, q. 31, a. 1), two things are requisite for pleasure: namely, the attainment of the suitable good, and knowledge of this attainment. Now each of these consists in a kind of operation: because actual knowledge is an operation; and the attainment of the suitable good is by means of an operation. Moreover, the proper operation itself is a suitable good. Wherefore every pleasure must needs be the result of some operation.

Ad primum ergo dicendum quod ipsa obiecta operationum non sunt delectabilia, nisi inquantum coniunguntur nobis, vel per cognitionem solam, sicut cum delectamur in consideratione vel inspectione aliquorum; vel quocumque alio modo simul cum cognitione, sicut cum aliquis delectatur in hoc quod cognoscit se habere quodcumque bonum, puta divitias vel honorem vel aliquid huiusmodi; quae quidem non essent delectabilia, **nisi inquantum apprehenduntur ut habita.** Ut enim philosophus dicit, in II Polit., *magnam delectationem habet putare aliquid sibi proprium; quae procedit ex naturali amore alicuius ad seipsum.* Habere autem huiusmodi nihil est aliud quam uti eis, vel posse uti. Et hoc est per aliquam operationem. Unde manifestum est quod omnis delectatio in operationem reducitur sicut in causam.

Ad secundum dicendum quod etiam in illis in quibus operationes non sunt fines, sed operata, ipsa operata sunt delectabilia inquantum sunt habita vel facta. Quod refertur ad aliquem usum vel operationem.

Ad tertium dicendum quod operationes sunt delectabiles, inquantum sunt proportionatae et connaturales operanti. Cum autem virtus humana sit finita, secundum aliquam mensuram operatio est sibi proportionata. Unde si excedat illam mensuram, iam non erit sibi proportionata, nec delectabilis, sed magis laboriosa et attaedians. Et secundum hoc, otium et ludus et alia quae ad requiem pertinent, delectabilia sunt, inquantum auferunt tristitiam quae est ex labore.

Reply to Objection 1: The objects of operations are not pleasurable save inasmuch as they are united to us; either by knowledge alone, as when we take pleasure in thinking of or looking at certain things; or in some other way in addition to knowledge; as when a man takes pleasure in knowing that he has something good—riches, honor, or the like; which would not be pleasurable unless they were apprehended as possessed. For as the **Philosopher observes (Polit. ii, 2) "we take great pleasure in looking upon a thing as our own, by reason of the natural love we have for ourselves."** Now to have such like things is nothing else but to use them or to be able to use them: and this is through some operation. Wherefore it is evident that every pleasure is traced to some operation as its cause.

Reply to Objection 2: Even when it is not an operation, but the effect of an operation, that is the end, this effect is pleasant in so far as possessed or effected: and this implies use or operation.

Reply to Objection 3: Operations are pleasant, in so far as they are proportionate and connatural to the agent. Now, since human power is finite, operation is proportionate thereto according to a certain measure. Wherefore if it exceed that measure, it will be no longer proportionate or pleasant, but, on the contrary, painful and irksome. And in this sense, leisure and play and other things pertaining to repose, are pleasant, inasmuch as they banish sadness which results from labor.

Articulus 2

Ad secundum sic proceditur. Videtur quod motus non sit causa delectationis. Quia, sicut supra dictum est, bonum praesentialiter adeptum est causa delectationis, unde philosophus, in VII Ethic., dicit quod delectatio non comparatur generationi, sed operationi rei iam existentis. Id autem quod movetur ad aliquid, nondum habet illud; sed quodammodo est in via generationis respectu illius, secundum quod omni motui adiungitur generatio et corruptio, ut dicitur

Article 2
Whether movement is a cause of pleasure?

Objection 1: It would seem that movement is not a cause of pleasure. Because, as stated above (I-II, q. 31, a. 1), the good which is obtained and is actually possessed, is the cause of pleasure: wherefore the Philosopher says (Ethic. vii, 12) that pleasure is not compared with generation, but with the operation of a thing already in existence. Now that which is being moved towards something has it not as yet; but, so to speak, is being generated in its regard, forasmuch as generation or corruption are united to every movement, as stated

in VIII Physic. Ergo motus non est causa delectationis.

PRAETEREA, motus praecipue laborem et lassitudinem inducit in operibus. Sed operationes, ex hoc quod sunt laboriosae et lassantes, non sunt delectabiles, sed magis afflictivae. Ergo motus non est causa delectationis.

PRAETEREA, motus importat innovationem quandam, quae opponitur consuetudini. Sed ea *quae sunt consueta, sunt nobis delectabilia*, ut philosophus dicit, in I Rhetoric. Ergo motus non est causa delectationis.

SED CONTRA est quod Augustinus dicit, in VIII Confess., *quid est hoc, domine Deus meus, cum tu aeternum tibi tu ipse sis gaudium; et quaedam de te circa te semper gaudeant; quod haec rerum pars alterno defectu et profectu, offensionibus et conciliationibus gaudet?* Ex quo accipitur quod homines gaudent et delectantur in quibusdam alternationibus. Et sic motus videtur esse causa delectationis.

RESPONDEO dicendum quod ad delectationem tria requiruntur, scilicet duo quorum est coniunctio delectabilis; et tertium, quod est cognitio huius coniunctionis. Et secundum haec tria motus efficitur delectabilis, ut philosophus dicit, in VII Ethic. et in I Rhetoric. Nam ex parte nostra qui delectamur, transmutatio efficitur nobis delectabilis propter hoc, quod natura nostra transmutabilis est; et propter hoc, quod est nobis conveniens nunc, non erit nobis conveniens postea; sicut calefieri ad ignem est conveniens homini in hieme, non autem in aestate. Ex parte vero boni delectantis quod nobis coniungitur, fit etiam transmutatio delectabilis. Quia actio continuata alicuius agentis auget effectum, sicut quanto aliquis diutius appropinquat igni, magis calefit et desiccatur. Naturalis autem habitudo in quadam mensura consistit. Et ideo quando continuata praesentia delectabilis superexcedit mensuram naturalis habitudinis, efficitur remotio eius delectabilis. Ex parte vero ipsius cognitionis, quia homo desiderat cognoscere aliquod totum et perfectum. Cum ergo aliqua non poterunt

in Phys. viii, 3. Therefore movement is not a cause of pleasure.

Objection 2: Further, movement is the chief cause of toil and fatigue in our works. But operations through being toilsome and fatiguing are not pleasant but disagreeable. Therefore movement is not a cause of pleasure.

Objection 3: Further, movement implies a certain innovation, which is the opposite of custom. But things "which we are accustomed to, are pleasant," as the Philosopher says (Rhet. i, 11). Therefore movement is not a cause of pleasure.

On the contrary, Augustine says (Confess. viii, 3): "What means this, O Lord my God, whereas Thou art everlasting joy to Thyself, and some things around Thee evermore rejoice in Thee? What means this, that this portion of things ebbs and flows alternately displeased and reconciled?" From these words we gather that man rejoices and takes pleasure in some kind of alterations: and therefore movement seems to cause pleasure.

I answer that, Three things are requisite for pleasure; two, i.e., the one that is pleased and the pleasurable object conjoined to him; and a third, which is knowledge of this conjunction: and in respect of these three, movement is pleasant, as the Philosopher says (Ethic. vii, 14 and Rhetor. i, 11). For as far as we who feel pleasure are concerned, change is pleasant to us because our nature is changeable: for which reason that which is suitable to us at one time is not suitable at another; thus to warm himself at a fire is suitable to man in winter but not in summer. Again, on the part of the pleasing good which is united to us, change is pleasant. Because the continued action of an agent increases its effect: thus the longer a person remains near the fire, the more he is warmed and dried. Now the natural mode of being consists in a certain measure; and therefore when the continued presence of a pleasant object exceeds the measure of one's natural mode of being, the removal of that object becomes pleasant. On the part of the knowledge itself [change becomes pleasant], because man desires to know something whole and perfect: when therefore a thing cannot be

apprehendi tota simul, delectat in his transmutatio, ut unum transeat et alterum succedat, et sic totum sentiatur. Unde Augustinus dicit, in IV Confess., *non vis utique stare syllabam, sed transvolare, ut aliae veniant, et totum audias. Ita semper omnia ex quibus unum aliquid constat, et non sunt omnia simul, plus delectant omnia quam singula, si possint sentiri omnia.* Si ergo sit aliqua res cuius natura sit intransmutabilis; et non possit in ea fieri excessus naturalis habitudinis per continuationem delectabilis; et quae possit totum suum delectabile simul intueri, non erit ei transmutatio delectabilis. Et quanto aliquae delectationes plus ad hoc accedunt, tanto plus continuari possunt.

AD PRIMUM ergo dicendum quod id quod movetur, etsi nondum habeat perfecte id ad quod movetur, incipit tamen iam aliquid habere eius ad quod movetur, et secundum hoc, ipse motus habet aliquid delectationis. Deficit tamen a delectationis perfectione, nam perfectiores delectationes sunt in rebus immobilibus. Motus etiam efficitur delectabilis, inquantum per ipsum fit aliquid conveniens quod prius conveniens non erat, vel desinit esse, ut supra dictum est.

AD SECUNDUM dicendum quod motus laborem et lassitudinem inducit, secundum quod transcendit habitudinem naturalem. Sic autem motus non est delectabilis, sed secundum quod removentur contraria habitudinis naturalis.

AD TERTIUM dicendum quod id quod est consuetum, efficitur delectabile, inquantum efficitur naturale, nam consuetudo est quasi altera natura. Motus autem est delectabilis, non quidem quo receditur a consuetudine, sed magis secundum quod per ipsum impeditur corruptio naturalis habitudinis, quae posset provenire ex assiduitate alicuius operationis. Et sic ex eadem causa connaturalitatis efficitur consuetudo delectabilis, et motus.

apprehended all at once as a whole, change in such a thing is pleasant, so that one part may pass and another succeed, and thus the whole be perceived. Hence Augustine says (Confess. iv, 11): "Thou wouldst not have the syllables stay, but fly away, that others may come, and thou hear the whole. And so whenever any one thing is made up of many, all of which do not exist together, all would please collectively more than they do severally, if all could be perceived collectively." If therefore there be any thing, whose nature is unchangeable; the natural mode of whose being cannot be exceeded by the continuation of any pleasing object; and which can behold the whole object of its delight at once—to such a one change will afford no delight. And the more any pleasures approach to this, the more are they capable of being continual.

Reply to Objection 1: Although the subject of movement has not yet perfectly that to which it is moved, nevertheless it is beginning to have something thereof: and in this respect movement itself has something of pleasure. But it falls short of the perfection of pleasure; because the more perfect pleasures regard things that are unchangeable. Moreover movement becomes the cause of pleasure, in so far as thereby something which previously was unsuitable, becomes suitable or ceases to be, as stated above.

Reply to Objection 2: Movement causes toil and fatigue, when it exceeds our natural aptitude. It is not thus that it causes pleasure, but by removing the obstacles to our natural aptitude.

Reply to Objection 3: What is customary becomes pleasant, in so far as it becomes natural: because custom is like a second nature. But the movement which gives pleasure is not that which departs from custom, but rather that which prevents the corruption of the natural mode of being, that might result from continued operation. And thus from the same cause of connaturalness, both custom and movement become pleasant.

Articulus 3

Ad tertium sic proceditur. Videtur quod memoria et spes non sint causae delectationis. Delectatio enim est de bono praesenti, ut Damascenus dicit. Sed memoria et spes sunt de absenti, est enim memoria praeteritorum, spes vero futurorum. Ergo memoria et spes non sunt causa delectationis.

Praeterea, idem non est causa contrariorum. Sed spes est causa afflictionis, dicitur enim Prov. XIII, *spes quae differtur, affligit animam*. Ergo spes non est causa delectationis.

Praeterea, sicut spes convenit cum delectatione in eo quod est de bono, ita etiam concupiscentia et amor. Non ergo magis debet assignari spes causa delectationis, quam concupiscentia vel amor.

Sed contra est quod dicitur Rom. XII, *spe gaudentes*; et in Psalmo LXXVI, *memor fui Dei, et delectatus sum*.

Respondeo dicendum quod delectatio causatur ex praesentia boni convenientis, secundum quod sentitur, vel qualitercumque percipitur. Est autem aliquid praesens nobis dupliciter, uno modo, secundum cognitionem, prout scilicet cognitum est in cognoscente secundum suam similitudinem; alio modo, secundum rem, prout scilicet unum alteri realiter coniungitur, vel actu vel potentia, secundum quemcumque coniunctionis modum. Et quia maior est coniunctio secundum rem quam secundum similitudinem, quae est coniunctio cognitionis; itemque maior est coniunctio rei in actu quam in potentia, ideo maxima est delectatio quae fit per sensum, qui requirit praesentiam rei sensibilis. Secundum autem gradum tenet delectatio spei, in qua non solum est delectabilis coniunctio secundum apprehensionem, sed etiam secundum facultatem vel potestatem adipiscendi bonum quod delectat. Tertium autem gradum tenet delectatio memoriae, quae habet solam coniunctionem apprehensionis.

Ad primum ergo dicendum quod spes et memoria sunt quidem eorum quae sunt simpliciter absentia, quae tamen secundum quid sunt praesentia, scilicet vel secundum

Article 3
Whether hope and memory causes pleasure?

Objection 1: It would seem that memory and hope do not cause pleasure. Because pleasure is caused by present good, as Damascene says (De Fide Orth. ii, 12). But hope and memory regard what is absent: since memory is of the past, and hope of the future. Therefore memory and hope do not cause pleasure.

Objection 2: Further, the same thing is not the cause of contraries. But hope causes affliction, according to Prov. 13:12: "Hope that is deferred afflicteth the soul." Therefore hope does not cause pleasure.

Objection 3: Further, just as hope agrees with pleasure in regarding good, so also do desire and love. Therefore hope should not be assigned as a cause of pleasure, any more than desire or love.

On the contrary, It is written (Rom. 12:12): "Rejoicing in hope"; and (Ps. 76:4): "I remembered God, and was delighted."

I answer that, Pleasure is caused by the presence of suitable good, in so far as it is felt, or perceived in any way. Now a thing is present to us in two ways. First, in knowledge—i.e., according as the thing known is in the knower by its likeness; secondly, in reality—i.e., according as one thing is in real conjunction of any kind with another, either actually or potentially. And since real conjunction is greater than conjunction by likeness, which is the conjunction of knowledge; and again, since actual is greater than potential conjunction: therefore the greatest pleasure is that which arises from sensation which requires the presence of the sensible object. The second place belongs to the pleasure of hope, wherein there is pleasurable conjunction, not only in respect of apprehension, but also in respect of the faculty or power of obtaining the pleasurable object. The third place belongs to the pleasure of memory, which has only the conjunction of apprehension.

Reply to Objection 1: Hope and memory are indeed of things which, absolutely speaking, are absent: and yet those are, after a fashion, present, i.e., either according to

apprehensionem solam; vel secundum apprehensionem et facultatem, ad minus aestimatam.

Ad secundum dicendum quod nihil prohibet idem, secundum diversa, esse causam contrariorum. Sic igitur spes, inquantum habet praesentem aestimationem boni futuri, delectationem causat, inquantum autem caret praesentia eius, causat afflictionem.

Ad tertium dicendum quod etiam amor et concupiscentia **delectationem causant**. Omne enim amatum fit delectabile amanti, eo quod amor est quaedam unio vel connaturalitas amantis ad amatum. Similiter etiam omne concupitum est delectabile concupiscenti, cum concupiscentia sit praecipue appetitus delectationis. Sed tamen spes, inquantum importat quandam certitudinem realis praesentiae boni delectantis, quam non importat nec amor nec concupiscentia, magis ponitur causa delectationis quam illa. Et similiter magis quam memoria, quae est de eo quod iam transiit.

apprehension only; or according to apprehension and possibility, at least supposed, of attainment.

Reply to Objection 2: Nothing prevents the same thing, in different ways, being the cause of contraries. And so hope, inasmuch as it implies a present appraising of a future good, causes pleasure; whereas, inasmuch as it implies absence of that good, it causes affliction.

Reply to Objection 3: Love and concupiscence also cause pleasure. For everything that is loved becomes pleasing to the lover, since love is a kind of union or connaturalness of lover and beloved. In like manner every object of desire is pleasing to the one that desires, since desire is chiefly a craving for pleasure. However hope, as implying a certainty of the real presence of the pleasing good, that is not implied either by love or by concupiscence, is reckoned in preference to them as causing pleasure; and also in preference to memory, which is of that which has already passed away.

Articulus 4

Ad quartum sic proceditur. Videtur quod tristitia non sit causa delectationis. Contrarium enim non est causa contrarii. Sed tristitia contrariatur delectationi. Ergo non est causa delectationis.

Praeterea, contrariorum contrarii sunt effectus. Sed delectabilia memorata sunt causa delectationis. Ergo tristia memorata sunt causa doloris, et non delectationis.

Praeterea, sicut se habet tristitia ad delectationem, ita odium ad amorem. Sed odium non est causa amoris, sed magis e converso, ut supra dictum est. Ergo tristitia non est causa delectationis.

Sed contra est quod in Psalmo XLI, dicitur, *fuerunt mihi lacrimae meae panes die ac nocte*. Per panem autem refectio delectationis intelligitur. Ergo lacrimae, quae ex tristitia oriuntur, possunt esse delectabiles.

Respondeo dicendum quod tristitia potest dupliciter considerari, uno modo, secundum quod est in actu; alio modo, secundum quod est in memoria. Et utroque modo tristitia potest esse delectationis causa.

Article 4
Whether sadness causes pleasure?

Objection 1: It would seem that sadness does not cause pleasure. For nothing causes its own contrary. But sadness is contrary to pleasure. Therefore it does not cause it.

Objection 2: Further, contraries have contrary effects. But pleasures, when called to mind, cause pleasure. Therefore sad things, when remembered, cause sorrow and not pleasure.

Objection 3: Further, as sadness is to pleasure, so is hatred to love. But hatred does not cause love, but rather the other way about, as stated above (I-II, q. 29, a. 2). Therefore sadness does not cause pleasure.

On the contrary, It is written (Ps. 41:4): "My tears have been my bread day and night": where bread denotes the refreshment of pleasure. Therefore tears, which arise from sadness, can give pleasure.

I answer that, Sadness may be considered in two ways: as existing actually, and as existing in the memory: and in both ways sadness can cause pleasure. Because

Tristitia siquidem in actu existens est causa delectationis, inquantum facit memoriam rei dilectae, de cuius absentia aliquis tristatur, et tamen de sola eius apprehensione delectatur. Memoria autem tristitiae fit causa delectationis, propter subsequentem evasionem. Nam carere malo accipitur in ratione boni, unde secundum quod homo apprehendit se evasisse ab aliquibus tristibus et dolorosis, accrescit ei gaudii materia; secundum quod Augustinus dicit, XXII de Civ. Dei, quod *saepe laeti tristium meminimus, et sani dolorum sine dolore, et inde amplius laeti et grati sumus.* Et in VIII Confess. dicit quod *quanto maius fuit periculum in proelio, tanto maius erit gaudium in triumpho.*

AD PRIMUM ergo dicendum quod contrarium quandoque per accidens est causa contrarii, sicut *frigidum quandoque calefacit,* ut dicitur in VIII Physic. Et similiter tristitia per accidens est delectationis causa, inquantum fit per eam apprehensio alicuius delectabilis.

AD SECUNDUM dicendum quod tristia memorata, inquantum sunt tristia et delectabilibus contraria, non causant delectationem, sed inquantum ab eis homo liberatur. Et similiter memoria delectabilium, ex eo quod sunt amissa, potest causare tristitiam.

AD TERTIUM dicendum quod odium etiam per accidens potest esse causa amoris, prout scilicet aliqui diligunt se, inquantum conveniunt in odio unius et eiusdem.

ARTICULUS 5

AD QUINTUM sic proceditur. Videtur quod actiones aliorum non sint nobis delectationis causa. Causa enim delectationis est proprium bonum coniunctum. Sed aliorum operationes non sunt nobis coniunctae. Ergo non sunt nobis causa delectationis.

PRAETEREA, operatio est proprium bonum operantis. Si igitur operationes

sadness, as actually existing, causes pleasure, inasmuch as it brings to mind that which is loved, the absence of which causes sadness; and yet the mere thought of it gives pleasure. The recollection of sadness becomes a cause of pleasure, on account of the deliverance which ensued: because absence of evil is looked upon as something good; wherefore so far as a man thinks that he has been delivered from that which caused him sorrow and pain, so much reason has he to rejoice. Hence Augustine says in De Civ. Dei xxii, 31* that "oftentimes in joy we call to mind sad things . . . and in the season of health we recall past pains without feeling pain . . . and in proportion are the more filled with joy and gladness": and again (Confess. viii, 3) he says that "the more peril there was in the battle, so much the more joy will there be in the triumph."

Reply to Objection 1: Sometimes accidentally a thing is the cause of its contrary: thus "that which is cold sometimes causes heat," as stated in Phys. viii, 1. In like manner sadness is the accidental cause of pleasure, in so far as it gives rise to the apprehension of something pleasant.

Reply to Objection 2: Sad things, called to mind, cause pleasure, not in so far as they are sad and contrary to pleasant things; but in so far as man is delivered from them. In like manner the recollection of pleasant things, by reason of these being lost, may cause sadness.

Reply to Objection 3: Hatred also can be the accidental cause of love: i.e., so far as some love one another, inasmuch as they agree in hating one and the same thing.

ARTICLE 5
Whether the actions of others are a cause of pleasure to us?

Objection 1: It would seem that the actions of others are not a cause of pleasure to us. Because the cause of pleasure is our own good when conjoined to us. But the actions of others are not conjoined to us. Therefore they are not a cause of pleasure to us.

Objection 2: Further, the action is the agent's own good. If, therefore, the actions of

---

* Gregory, Moral. iv.

aliorum sint nobis causa delectationis, pari ratione omnia alia bona aliorum erunt nobis delectationis causa. Quod patet esse falsum.

PRAETEREA, operatio est delectabilis, inquantum procedit ex habitu nobis innato, unde dicitur in II Ethic., quod *signum generati habitus oportet accipere fientem in opere delectationem.* Sed operationes aliorum non procedunt ex habitibus qui in nobis sunt, sed **interdum ex habitibus qui sunt in operantibus**. Non ergo operationes aliorum sunt nobis delectabiles, sed ipsis operantibus.

SED CONTRA est quod dicitur in secunda canonica Ioannis, *gavisus sum valde, quoniam inveni de filiis tuis ambulantes in veritate.*

RESPONDEO dicendum quod, sicut iam dictum est, ad delectationem duo requiruntur, scilicet consecutio proprii boni, et cognitio proprii boni consecuti. Tripliciter ergo operatio alterius potest esse delectationis causa. Uno modo, inquantum per operationem alicuius consequimur aliquod bonum. Et secundum hoc, operationes illorum qui nobis aliquod bonum faciunt, sunt nobis delectabiles, quia bene pati ab alio est delectabile. Alio modo, secundum quod per operationes aliorum efficitur nobis aliqua cognitio vel aestimatio proprii boni. Et propter hoc homines delectantur in hoc quod laudantur vel honorantur ab aliis, quia scilicet per hoc accipiunt aestimationem in seipsis aliquod bonum esse. Et quia ista aestimatio fortius generatur ex testimonio bonorum et sapientum, ideo in horum laudibus et honoribus homines magis delectantur. Et quia adulator est apparens laudator, propter hoc etiam adulationes quibusdam sunt delectabiles. Et quia amor est alicuius boni, et admiratio est alicuius magni, idcirco amari ab aliis, et in admiratione haberi, est delectabile; inquantum per hoc fit homini aestimatio propriae bonitatis vel magnitudinis, in quibus aliquis delectatur. Tertio modo, inquantum ipsae operationes aliorum, si sint bonae, aestimantur ut bonum proprium, propter vim amoris, qui facit aestimare amicum quasi eundem sibi. Et propter odium, quod facit

others are a cause of pleasure to us, for the same reason all goods belonging to others will be pleasing to us: which is evidently untrue.

Objection 3: Further, action is pleasant through proceeding from an innate habit; hence it is stated in Ethic. ii, 3 that "we must reckon the pleasure which follows after action, as being the sign of a habit existing in us." But the actions of others do not proceed **from habits existing in us, but, sometimes,** from habits existing in the agents. Therefore the actions of others are not pleasing to us, but to the agents themselves.

On the contrary, It is written in the second canonical epistle of John (verse 4): "I was exceeding glad that I found thy children walking in truth."

I answer that, As stated above (I-II, q. 32, a. 1; q. 31, a. 1), two things are requisite for pleasure, namely, the attainment of one's proper good, and the knowledge of having obtained it. Wherefore the action of another may cause pleasure to us in three ways. First, from the fact that we obtain some good through the action of another. And in this way, the actions of those who do some good to us, are pleasing to us: since it is pleasant to be benefited by another. Secondly, from the fact that another's action makes us to know or appreciate our own good: and for this reason men take pleasure in being praised or honored by others, because, to wit, they thus become aware of some good existing in themselves. And since this appreciation receives greater weight from the testimony of good and wise men, hence men take greater pleasure in being praised and honored by them. And because a flatterer appears to praise, therefore flattery is pleasing to some. And as love is for something good, while admiration is for something great, so it is pleasant to be loved and admired by others, inasmuch as a man thus becomes aware of his own goodness or greatness, through their giving pleasure to others. Thirdly, from the fact that another's actions, if they be good, are reckoned as one's own good, by reason of the power of love, which makes a man to regard his friend as one with himself. And on account of hatred, which makes one to

aestimare bonum alterius esse sibi contrarium, efficitur mala operatio inimici delectabilis. Unde dicitur I ad Cor. XIII, quod *caritas non gaudet super iniquitate, congaudet autem veritati.*

AD PRIMUM ergo dicendum quod operatio alterius potest esse mihi coniuncta vel per effectum, sicut in primo modo; vel per apprehensionem, sicut in secundo modo; vel per affectionem, sicut in tertio modo.

AD SECUNDUM dicendum quod ratio illa procedit quantum ad tertium modum, non autem quantum ad duos primos.

AD TERTIUM dicendum quod operationes aliorum etsi non procedant ex habitibus qui in me sunt, causant tamen in me aliquid delectabile; vel faciunt mihi aestimationem sive apprehensionem proprii habitus; vel procedunt ex habitu illius qui est unum mecum per amorem.

reckon another's good as being in opposition to oneself, the evil action of an enemy becomes an object of pleasure: whence it is written (1 Cor. 13:6) that charity "rejoiceth not in iniquity, but rejoiceth with the truth."

Reply to Objection 1: Another's action may be conjoined to me, either by its effect, as in the first way, or by knowledge, as in the second way; or by affection, as in the third way.

Reply to Objection 2: This argument avails for the third mode, but not for the first two.

Reply to Objection 3: Although the actions of another do not proceed from habits that are in me, yet they either produce in me something that gives pleasure; or they make me appreciate or know a habit of mind; or they proceed from the habit of one who is united to me by love.

Articulus 6

AD SEXTUM sic proceditur. Videtur quod benefacere alteri non sit delectationis causa. Delectatio enim causatur ex consecutione proprii boni, sicut supra dictum est. Sed benefacere non pertinet ad consecutionem proprii boni, sed magis ad emissionem. Ergo magis videtur esse causa tristitiae quam delectationis.

PRAETEREA, philosophus dicit, in IV Ethic., quod *illiberalitas connaturalior est hominibus quam prodigalitas.* Sed ad prodigalitatem pertinet benefacere aliis, ad illiberalitatem autem pertinet desistere a benefaciendo. Cum ergo operatio connaturalis sit delectabilis unicuique, ut dicitur in VII et X Ethic., videtur quod benefacere aliis non sit causa delectationis.

PRAETEREA, contrarii effectus ex contrariis causis procedunt. Sed quaedam quae pertinent ad malefacere, sunt naturaliter homini delectabilia, sicut vincere, redarguere vel increpare alios, et etiam punire, quantum ad iratos, ut dicit philosophus in I Rhetoric. Ergo benefacere magis est causa tristitiae quam delectationis.

Article 6
Whether doing good to another is a cause of pleasure?

Objection 1: It would seem that doing good to another is not a cause of pleasure. Because pleasure is caused by one's obtaining one's proper good, as stated above (I-II, q. 32, a. 1; a. 5; q. 31, a. 1). But doing good pertains not to the obtaining but to the spending of one's proper good. Therefore it seems to be the cause of sadness rather than of pleasure.

Objection 2: Further, the Philosopher says (Ethic. iv, 1) that "illiberality is more connatural to man than prodigality." Now it is a mark of prodigality to do good to others; while it is a mark of illiberality to desist from doing good. Since therefore everyone takes pleasure in a connatural operation, as stated in Ethic. vii, 14 and x, 4, it seems that doing good to others is not a cause of pleasure.

Objection 3: Further, contrary effects proceed from contrary causes. But man takes a natural pleasure in certain kinds of ill-doing, such as overcoming, contradicting or scolding others, or, if he be angry, in punishing them, as the Philosopher says (Rhet. i, 11). Therefore doing good to others is a cause of sadness rather than pleasure.

SED CONTRA est quod philosophus dicit, in II Polit., quod *largiri et auxiliari amicis aut extraneis, est delectabilissimum.*

RESPONDEO dicendum quod hoc ipsum quod est benefacere alteri, potest tripliciter esse delectationis causa. Uno modo, per comparationem ad effectum, quod est bonum in altero constitutum. Et secundum hoc, inquantum bonum alterius reputamus quasi nostrum bonum, propter unionem amoris, delectamur in bono quod per nos fit aliis, praecipue amicis, sicut in bono proprio. Alio modo, per comparationem ad finem, sicut cum aliquis, per hoc quod alteri benefacit, sperat consequi aliquod bonum sibi ipsi, vel a Deo vel ab homine. Spes autem delectationis est causa. Tertio modo, per comparationem ad principium. Et sic hoc quod est benefacere alteri, potest esse delectabile per comparationem ad triplex principium. Quorum unum est facultas benefaciendi, et secundum hoc, benefacere alteri fit delectabile, inquantum per hoc fit homini quaedam imaginatio abundantis boni in seipso existentis, ex quo possit aliis communicare. Et ideo homines delectantur in filiis et in propriis operibus, sicut quibus communicant proprium bonum. Aliud principium est habitus inclinans, secundum quem benefacere fit alicui connaturale. Unde liberales delectabiliter dant aliis. Tertium principium est motivum, puta cum aliquis movetur ab aliquo quem diligit, ad benefaciendum alicui, omnia enim quae facimus vel patimur propter amicum, delectabilia sunt, quia amor praecipua causa delectationis est.

AD PRIMUM ergo dicendum quod emissio, inquantum est indicativa proprii boni, est delectabilis. Sed inquantum evacuat proprium bonum potest esse contristans; sicut quando est immoderata.

AD SECUNDUM dicendum quod prodigalitas habet immoderatam emissionem, quae repugnat naturae. Et ideo prodigalitas dicitur esse contra naturam.

AD TERTIUM dicendum quod vincere, redarguere et punire, non est delectabile inquantum est in malum alterius, sed inquantum pertinet ad proprium bonum, quod plus homo amat quam odiat malum alterius.

On the contrary, The Philosopher says (Polit. ii, 2) that "it is most pleasant to give presents or assistance to friends and strangers."

I answer that, Doing good to another may give pleasure in three ways. First, in consideration of the effect, which is the good conferred on another. In this respect, inasmuch as through being united to others by love, we look upon their good as being our own, **we take pleasure in the good we do to others**, especially to our friends, as in our own good. Secondly, in consideration of the end; as when a man, from doing good to another, hopes to get some good for himself, either from God or from man: for hope is a cause of pleasure. Thirdly, in consideration of the principle: and thus, doing good to another, can give pleasure in respect of a threefold principle. One is the faculty of doing good: and in this regard, doing good to another becomes pleasant, in so far as it arouses in man an imagination of abundant good existing in him, whereof he is able to give others a share. Wherefore men take pleasure in their children, and in their own works, as being things on which they bestow a share of their own good. Another principle is man's habitual inclination to do good, by reason of which doing good becomes connatural to him: for which reason the liberal man takes pleasure in giving to others. The third principle is the motive: for instance when a man is moved by one whom he loves, to do good to someone: for whatever we do or suffer for a friend is pleasant, because love is the principal cause of pleasure.

Reply to Objection 1: Spending gives pleasure as showing forth one's good. But in so far as it empties us of our own good it may be a cause of sadness; for instance when it is excessive.

Reply to Objection 2: Prodigality is an excessive spending, which is unnatural: wherefore prodigality is said to be contrary to nature.

Reply to Objection 3: To overcome, to contradict, and to punish, give pleasure, not as tending to another's ill, but as pertaining to one's own good, which man loves more than he hates another's ill.

Vincere enim est delectabile naturaliter, inquantum per hoc homini fit aestimatio propriae excellentiae. Et propter hoc, omnes ludi in quibus est concertatio, et in quibus potest esse victoria, sunt maxime delectabiles, et universaliter omnes concertationes, secundum quod habent spem victoriae. Redarguere autem et increpare potest esse dupliciter delectationis causa. Uno modo, inquantum facit homini imaginationem propriae sapientiae et excellentiae, increpare enim et corripere est sapientum et maiorum alio modo, secundum quod aliquis, increpando et reprehendendo, alteri benefacit, quod est delectabile, ut dictum est. Irato autem est delectabile punire, inquantum videtur removere apparentem minorationem, quae videtur esse ex praecedenti laesione. Cum enim aliquis est ab aliquo laesus, videtur per hoc ab illo minoratus esse, et ideo appetit ab hac minoratione liberari per retributionem laesionis. Et sic patet quod benefacere alteri per se potest esse delectabile, sed malefacere alteri non est delectabile, nisi inquantum videtur pertinere ad proprium bonum.

For it is naturally pleasant to overcome, inasmuch as it makes a man to appreciate his own superiority. Wherefore all those games in which there is a striving for the mastery, and a possibility of winning it, afford the greatest pleasure: and speaking generally all contests, in so far as they admit hope of victory. To contradict and to scold can give pleasure in two ways. First, as making man imagine himself to be wise and excellent; since it belongs to wise men and elders to reprove and to scold. Secondly, in so far as by scolding and reproving, one does good to another: for this gives one pleasure, as stated above. It is pleasant to an angry man to punish, in so far as he thinks himself to be removing an apparent slight, which seems to be due to a previous hurt: for when a man is hurt by another, he seems to be slighted thereby; and therefore he wishes to be quit of this slight by paying back the hurt. And thus it is clear that doing good to another may be of itself pleasant: whereas doing evil to another is not pleasant, except in so far as it seems to affect one's own good.

Articulus 7

Ad septimum sic proceditur. Videtur quod similitudo non sit causa delectationis. Principari enim et praeesse quandam dissimilitudinem importat. Sed *principari et praeesse naturaliter est delectabile,* ut dicitur in I Rhetoric. Ergo dissimilitudo magis est causa delectationis quam similitudo.

Praeterea, nihil magis est dissimile delectationi quam tristitia. Sed illi qui patiuntur tristitias, maxime sequuntur delectationes, ut dicitur in VII Ethic. Ergo dissimilitudo est magis causa delectationis quam similitudo.

Praeterea, illi qui sunt repleti aliquibus delectabilibus, non delectantur in eis, sed magis fastidiunt ea, sicut patet in repletione ciborum. Non ergo similitudo est delectationis causa.

Sed contra est quod similitudo est causa amoris, ut dictum est supra. Amor autem est causa delectationis. Ergo similitudo est causa delectationis.

Article 7
Whether likeness is a cause of pleasure?

Objection 1: It would seem that likeness is not a cause of pleasure. Because ruling and presiding seem to imply a certain unlikeness. But "it is natural to take pleasure in ruling and presiding," as stated in Rhetor. i, 11. Therefore unlikeness, rather than likeness, is a cause of pleasure.

Objection 2: Further, nothing is more unlike pleasure than sorrow. But those who are burdened by sorrow are most inclined to seek pleasures, as the Philosopher says (Ethic. vii, 14). Therefore unlikeness, rather than likeness, is a cause of pleasure.

Objection 3: Further, those who are satiated with certain delights, derive not pleasure but disgust from them; as when one is satiated with food. Therefore likeness is not a cause of pleasure.

On the contrary, Likeness is a cause of love, as above stated (I-II, q. 27, a. 3): and love is the cause of pleasure. Therefore likeness is a cause of pleasure.

Respondeo dicendum quod similitudo est quaedam unitas, unde id quod est simile, inquantum est unum, est delectabile, sicut et amabile, ut supra dictum est. Et si quidem id quod est simile, proprium bonum non corrumpat, sed augeat, est simpliciter delectabile, puta homo homini, et iuvenis iuveni. Si vero sit corruptivum proprii boni, sic per accidens efficitur fastidiosum vel contristans; non quidem inquantum est simile et unum, sed inquantum corrumpit id quod est magis unum. Quod autem aliquid simile corrumpat proprium bonum, contingit dupliciter. Uno modo, quia corrumpit mensuram proprii boni per quendam excessum, bonum enim, praecipue corporale, ut sanitas, in quadam commensuratione consistit. Et propter hoc, superabundantes cibi, vel quaelibet delectationes corporales, fastidiuntur. Alio modo, per directam contrarietatem ad proprium bonum, sicut figuli abominantur alios figulos, non inquantum sunt figuli, sed inquantum per eos amittunt excellentiam propriam, sive proprium lucrum, quae appetunt sicut proprium bonum.

Ad primum ergo dicendum quod, cum sit quaedam communicatio principantis ad subiectum, est ibi quaedam similitudo. Tamen secundum quandam excellentiam, eo quod principari et praeesse pertinent ad excellentiam proprii boni, sapientum enim et meliorum est principari et praeesse. Unde per hoc fit homini propriae bonitatis imaginatio. Vel quia per hoc quod homo principatur et praeest, aliis benefacit, quod est delectabile.

Ad secundum dicendum quod id in quo delectatur tristatus, etsi non sit simile tristitiae, est tamen simile homini contristato. Quia tristitiae contrariantur proprio bono eius qui tristatur. Et ideo appetitur delectatio ab his qui in tristitia sunt, ut conferens ad proprium bonum, inquantum est medicativa contrarii. Et ista est causa quare delectationes corporales, quibus sunt contrariae quaedam tristitiae, magis appetuntur, quam delectationes intellectuales, quae non habent contrarietatem tristitiae, ut infra dicetur. Exinde etiam est quod omnia animalia naturaliter appetunt delectationem, quia semper animal laborat per sensum et motum. Et propter

I answer that, Likeness is a kind of unity; hence that which is like us, as being one with us, causes pleasure; just at it causes love, as stated above (I-II, q. 27, a. 3). And if that which is like us does not hurt our own good, but increase it, it is pleasurable simply; for instance one man in respect of another, one youth in relation to another. But if it be hurtful to our own good, thus accidentally it causes disgust or sadness, not as being like and one with us, but as hurtful to that which is yet more one with us. Now it happens in two ways that something like is hurtful to our own good. First, by destroying the measure of our own good, by a kind of excess; because good, especially bodily good, as health, is conditioned by a certain measure: wherefore superfluous good or any bodily pleasure, causes disgust. Secondly, by being directly contrary to one's own good: thus a potter dislikes other potters, not because they are potters, but because they deprive him of his own excellence or profits, which he seeks as his own good.

Reply to Objection 1: Since ruler and subject are in communion with one another, there is a certain likeness between them: but this likeness is conditioned by a certain superiority, since ruling and presiding pertain to the excellence of a man's own good: because they belong to men who are wise and better than others; the result being that they give man an idea of his own excellence. Another reason is that by ruling and presiding, a man does good to others, which is pleasant.

Reply to Objection 2: That which gives pleasure to the sorrowful man, though it be unlike sorrow, bears some likeness to the man that is sorrowful: because sorrows are contrary to his own good. Wherefore the sorrowful man seeks pleasure as making for his own good, in so far as it is a remedy for its contrary. And this is why bodily pleasures, which are contrary to certain sorrows, are more sought than intellectual pleasures, which have no contrary sorrow, as we shall state later on (I-II, q. 35, a. 5). And this explains why all animals naturally desire pleasure: because animals ever work through sense and movement. For this reason also

hoc etiam iuvenes maxime delectationes appetunt; propter multas transmutationes in eis existentes, dum sunt in statu augmenti. Et etiam melancholici vehementer appetunt delectationes, ad expellendum tristitiam, quia *corpus eorum quasi pravo humore corroditur,* ut dicitur in VII Ethic.

AD TERTIUM dicendum quod bona corporalia in quadam mensura consistunt, et ideo superexcessus similium corrumpit proprium bonum. Et propter hoc efficitur fastidiosum et contristans, inquantum contrariatur bono proprio hominis.

ARTICULUS 8

AD OCTAVUM sic proceditur. Videtur quod admiratio non sit causa delectationis. Admirari enim est ignorantis naturae, ut Damascenus dicit. Sed ignorantia non est delectabilis, sed magis scientia. Ergo admiratio non est causa delectationis.

PRAETEREA, admiratio est principium sapientiae, quasi via ad inquirendum veritatem, ut dicitur in principio Metaphys. Sed *delectabilius est contemplari iam cognita, quam inquirere ignota,* ut philosophus dicit in X Ethic., cum hoc habeat difficultatem et impedimentum, illud autem non habeat; delectatio autem causatur ex operatione non impedita, ut dicitur in VII Ethic. Ergo admiratio non est causa delectationis, sed magis delectationem impedit.

PRAETEREA, unusquisque in consuetis delectatur, unde operationes habituum per consuetudinem acquisitorum, sunt delectabiles. Sed *consueta non sunt admirabilia,* ut dicit Augustinus, super Ioan. Ergo admiratio contrariatur causae delectationis.

SED CONTRA est quod philosophus dicit, in I Rhetoric., quod admiratio est delectationis causa.

RESPONDEO dicendum quod adipisci desiderata est delectabile, ut supra dictum est. Et ideo quanto alicuius rei amatae magis crescit desiderium, tanto magis per adeptionem crescit delectatio. Et etiam in ipso augmento desiderii fit augmentum

young people are most inclined to seek pleasures; on account of the many changes to which they are subject, while yet growing. Moreover this is why the melancholic has a strong desire for pleasures, in order to drive away sorrow: because his "body is corroded by a base humor," as stated in Ethic. vii, 14.

Reply to Objection 3: Bodily goods are conditioned by a certain fixed measure: wherefore surfeit of such things destroys the proper good, and consequently gives rise to disgust and sorrow, through being contrary to the proper good of man.

ARTICLE 8
Whether wonder is a cause of pleasure?

Objection 1: It would seem that wonder is not a cause of pleasure. Because wonder is the act of one who is ignorant of the nature of something, as Damascene says. But knowledge, rather than ignorance, is a cause of pleasure. Therefore wonder is not a cause of pleasure.

Objection 2: Further, wonder is the beginning of wisdom, being as it were, the road to the search of truth, as stated in the beginning of Metaph. i, 2. But "it is more pleasant to think of what we know, than to seek what we know not," as the Philosopher says (Ethic. x, 7): since in the latter case we encounter difficulties and hindrances, in the former not; while pleasure arises from an operation which is unhindered, as stated in Ethic. vii, 12,13. Therefore wonder hinders rather than causes pleasure.

Objection 3: Further, everyone takes pleasure in what he is accustomed to: wherefore the actions of habits acquired by custom, are pleasant. But "we wonder at what is unwonted," as Augustine says (Tract. xxiv in Joan.). Therefore wonder is contrary to the cause of pleasure.

On the contrary, The Philosopher says (Rhet. i, 11) that wonder is the cause of pleasure.

I answer that, It is pleasant to get what one desires, as stated above (I-II, q. 23, a. 4): and therefore the greater the desire for the thing loved, the greater the pleasure when it is attained: indeed the very increase of desire brings with it an increase

delectationis, secundum quod fit etiam spes rei amatae; sicut supra dictum est quod ipsum desiderium ex spe est delectabile. Est autem admiratio desiderium quoddam sciendi, quod in homine contingit ex hoc quod videt effectum et ignorat causam, vel ex hoc quod causa talis effectus excedit cognitionem aut facultatem ipsius. Et ideo admiratio est causa delectationis inquantum habet adiunctam spem consequendi cognitionem eius quod scire desiderat. Et propter hoc omnia mirabilia sunt delectabilia, sicut quae sunt rara, et omnes repraesentationes rerum, etiam quae in se non sunt delectabiles; gaudet enim anima in collatione unius ad alterum, quia conferre unum alteri est proprius et connaturalis actus rationis, ut philosophus dicit in sua poetica. Et propter hoc etiam *liberari a magnis periculis magis est delectabile,* quia est admirabile, ut dicitur in I Rhetoric.

Ad primum ergo dicendum quod admiratio non est delectabilis inquantum habet ignorantiam, sed inquantum habet desiderium addiscendi causam; et inquantum admirans aliquid novum addiscit, scilicet talem esse quem non aestimabat.

Ad secundum dicendum quod delectatio duo habet, scilicet quietem in bono, et huiusmodi quietis perceptionem. Quantum igitur ad primum, cum sit perfectius contemplari veritatem cognitam quam inquirere ignotam, contemplationes rerum scitarum, per se loquendo, sunt magis delectabiles quam inquisitiones rerum ignotarum. Tamen per accidens, quantum ad secundum, contingit quod inquisitiones sunt quandoque delectabiliores, secundum quod ex maiori desiderio procedunt, desiderium autem maius excitatur ex perceptione ignorantiae. Unde maxime homo delectatur in his quae de novo invenit aut addiscit.

Ad tertium dicendum quod ea quae sunt consueta, sunt delectabilia ad operandum, inquantum sunt quasi connaturalia. Sed

of pleasure, according as it gives rise to the hope of obtaining that which is loved, since it was stated above (I-II, q. 32, a. 3, ad 3) that desire resulting from hope is a cause of pleasure. Now wonder is a kind of desire for knowledge; a desire which comes to man when he sees an effect of which the cause either is unknown to him, or surpasses his knowledge or faculty of understanding. Consequently wonder is a cause of pleasure, **in so far as it includes a hope of getting the knowledge which one desires to have.** For this reason whatever is wonderful is pleasing, for instance things that are scarce. Also, representations of things, even of those which are not pleasant in themselves, give rise to pleasure; for the soul rejoices in comparing one thing with another, because comparison of one thing with another is the proper and connatural act of the reason, as the Philosopher says (Poet. iv). This again is why "it is more delightful to be delivered from great danger, because it is something wonderful," as stated in Rhetor. i, 11.

Reply to Objection 1: Wonder gives pleasure, not because it implies ignorance, but in so far as it includes the desire of learning the cause, and in so far as the wonderer learns something new, i.e., that the cause is other than he had thought it to be.*

Reply to Objection 2: Pleasure includes two things; rest in the good, and perception of this rest. As to the former therefore, since it is more perfect to contemplate the known truth, than to seek for the unknown, the contemplation of what we know, is in itself more pleasing than the research of what we do not know. Nevertheless, as to the second, it happens that research is sometimes more pleasing accidentally, in so far as it proceeds from a greater desire: for greater desire is awakened when we are conscious of our ignorance. This is why man takes the greatest pleasure in finding or learning things for the first time.

Reply to Objection 3: It is pleasant to do what we are wont to do, inasmuch as this is connatural to us, as it were. And yet

---

* According to another reading:—that he is other than he thought himself to be.

tamen ea quae sunt rara, possunt esse delectabilia, vel ratione cognitionis, quia desideratur eorum scientia, inquantum sunt mira; vel ratione operationis, quia *ex desiderio magis inclinatur mens ad hoc quod intense in novitate operetur,* ut dicitur in X Ethic.; perfectior enim operatio causat perfectiorem delectationem.

things that are of rare occurrence can be pleasant, either as regards knowledge, from the fact that we desire to know something about them, in so far as they are wonderful; or as regards action, from the fact that "the mind is more inclined by desire to act intensely in things that are new," as stated in Ethic. x, 4, since more perfect operation causes more perfect pleasure.

Quaestio XXXIII

Deinde considerandum est de effectibus delectationis. Et circa hoc quaeruntur quatuor. *Primo,* utrum delectationis sit dilatare. *Secundo,* utrum delectatio causet sui sitim, vel desiderium. *Tertio,* utrum delectatio impediat usum rationis. *Quarto,* utrum delectatio perficiat operationem.

Question 33
Of the Effects of Pleasure

We must now consider the effects of pleasure; and under this head there are four points of inquiry: 1. Whether expansion is an effect of pleasure? 2. Whether pleasure causes thirst or desire for itself? 3. Whether pleasure hinders the use of reason? 4. Whether pleasure perfects operation?

Articulus 1

Ad primum sic proceditur. Videtur quod dilatatio non sit effectus delectationis. Dilatatio enim videtur ad amorem magis pertinere, secundum quod dicit apostolus, II ad Cor. VI, *cor nostrum dilatatum est.* Unde et de praecepto caritatis in Psalmo CXVIII, dicitur, *latum mandatum tuum nimis.* Sed delectatio est alia passio ab amore. Ergo dilatatio non est effectus delectationis.

Praeterea, ex hoc quod aliquid dilatatur, efficitur capacius ad recipiendum. Sed receptio pertinet ad desiderium, quod est rei nondum habitae. Ergo dilatatio magis videtur pertinere ad desiderium quam ad delectationem.

Praeterea, constrictio dilatationi opponitur. Sed constrictio videtur ad delectationem pertinere, nam illud constringimus quod firmiter volumus retinere; et talis est affectio appetitus circa rem delectantem. Ergo dilatatio ad delectationem non pertinet.

Article 1
Whether expansion is an effect of pleasure?

Objection 1: It would seem that expansion is not an effect of pleasure. For expansion seems to pertain more to love, according to the Apostle (2 Cor. 6:11): "Our heart is enlarged." Wherefore it is written (Ps. 118:96) concerning the precept of charity: "Thy commandment is exceeding broad." But pleasure is a distinct passion from love. Therefore expansion is not an effect of pleasure.

Objection 2: Further, when a thing expands it is enabled to receive more. But receiving pertains to desire, which is for something not yet possessed. Therefore expansion seems to belong to desire rather than to pleasure.

Objection 3: Further, contraction is contrary to expansion. But contraction seems to belong to pleasure, for the hand closes on that which we wish to grasp firmly: and such is the affection of appetite in regard to that which pleases it. Therefore expansion does not pertain to pleasure.

Sed contra est quod, ad expressionem gaudii, dicitur Isaiae LX, *videbis, et affluens, et mirabitur et dilatabitur cor tuum.* Ipsa etiam delectatio ex *dilatatione* nomen accepit ut *laetitia* nominetur sicut supra dictum est.

Respondeo dicendum quod latitudo est quaedam dimensio magnitudinis corporalis, unde in affectionibus animae non nisi secundum metaphoram dicitur. Dilatatio autem dicitur quasi motus ad latitudinem. Et competit delectationi secundum duo quae ad delectationem requiruntur. Quorum unum est ex parte apprehensivae virtutis, quae apprehendit coniunctionem alicuius boni convenientis. Ex hac autem apprehensione apprehendit se homo perfectionem quandam adeptum, quae est spiritualis magnitudo, et secundum hoc, animus hominis dicitur per delectationem magnificari, seu dilatari. Aliud autem est ex parte appetitivae virtutis, quae assentit rei delectabili, et in ea quiescit, quodammodo se praebens ei ad eam interius capiendam. Et sic dilatatur affectus hominis per delectationem, quasi se tradens ad continendum interius rem delectantem.

Ad primum ergo dicendum quod nihil prohibet in his quae dicuntur metaphorice, idem diversis attribui secundum diversas similitudines. Et secundum hoc, dilatatio pertinet ad amorem ratione cuiusdam extensionis, inquantum affectus amantis ad alios extenditur, ut curet non solum quae sua sunt, sed quae aliorum. Ad delectationem vero pertinet dilatatio, inquantum aliquid in seipso ampliatur, ut quasi capacius reddatur.

Ad secundum dicendum quod desiderium habet quidem aliquam ampliationem ex imaginatione rei desideratae, sed multo magis ex praesentia rei iam delectantis. Quia magis praebet se animus rei iam delectanti, quam rei non habitae desideratae, cum delectatio sit finis desiderii.

On the contrary, In order to express joy, it is written (Is. 60:5): "Thou shall see and abound, thy heart shall wonder and be enlarged." Moreover pleasure is called by the name of *laetitia* as being derived from *dilatatio* [expansion], as stated above (I-II, q. 31, a. 3, ad 3).

I answer that, Breadth [*latitudo*] is a dimension of bodily magnitude: hence it is not applied to the emotions of the soul, save metaphorically. Now expansion denotes a kind of movement towards breadth; and it belongs to pleasure in respect of the two things requisite for pleasure. One of these is on the part of the apprehensive power, which is cognizant of the conjunction with some suitable good. As a result of this apprehension, man perceives that he has attained a certain perfection, which is a magnitude of the spiritual order: and in this respect man's mind is said to be magnified or expanded by pleasure. The other requisite for pleasure is on the part of the appetitive power, which acquiesces in the pleasurable object, and rests therein, offering, as it were, to enfold it within itself. And thus man's affection is expanded by pleasure, as though it surrendered itself to hold within itself the object of its pleasure.

Reply to Objection 1: In metaphorical expressions nothing hinders one and the same thing from being attributed to different things according to different likenesses. And in this way expansion pertains to love by reason of a certain spreading out, in so far as the affection of the lover spreads out to others, so as to care, not only for his own interests, but also for what concerns others. On the other hand expansion pertains to pleasure, in so far as a thing becomes more ample in itself so as to become more capacious.

Reply to Objection 2: Desire includes a certain expansion arising from the imagination of the thing desired; but this expansion increases at the presence of the pleasurable object: because the mind surrenders itself more to that object when it is already taking pleasure in it, than when it desires it before possessing it; since pleasure is the end of desire.

AD TERTIUM dicendum quod ille qui delectatur, constringit quidem rem delectantem, dum ei fortiter inhaeret, sed cor suum ampliat, ut perfecte delectabili fruatur.

ARTICULUS 2

AD SECUNDUM sic proceditur. Videtur quod delectatio non causet desiderium sui ipsius. Omnis enim motus cessat, cum pervenerit ad quietem. Sed delectatio est quasi quaedam quies motus desiderii, ut supra dictum est. Cessat ergo motus desiderii, cum ad delectationem pervenerit. Non ergo delectatio causat desiderium.

PRAETEREA, oppositum non est causa sui oppositi. Sed delectatio quodammodo desiderio opponitur, ex parte obiecti, nam desiderium est boni non habiti, delectatio vero boni iam habiti. Ergo delectatio non causat desiderium sui ipsius.

PRAETEREA, fastidium desiderio repugnat. Sed delectatio plerumque causat fastidium. Non ergo facit sui desiderium.

SED CONTRA est quod dominus dicit, Ioan. IV, *qui biberit ex hac aqua, sitiet iterum,* per aquam autem significatur, secundum Augustinum, delectatio corporalis.

RESPONDEO dicendum quod delectatio dupliciter potest considerari, uno modo, secundum quod est in actu; alio modo, secundum quod est in memoria. Item sitis, vel desiderium, potest dupliciter accipi, uno modo, proprie, secundum quod importat appetitum rei non habitae; alio modo, communiter, secundum quod importat exclusionem fastidii. Secundum quidem igitur quod est in actu, delectatio non causat sitim vel desiderium sui ipsius, per se loquendo, sed solum per accidens, si tamen sitis vel desiderium dicatur rei non habitae appetitus, nam delectatio est affectio appetitus circa rem praesentem. Sed contingit rem praesentem non perfecte haberi. Et hoc potest esse vel ex parte rei habitae, vel ex parte habentis. Ex parte quidem rei habitae, eo quod res habita non est

Reply to Objection 3: He that takes pleasure in a thing holds it fast, by clinging to it with all his might: but he opens his heart to it that he may enjoy it perfectly.

ARTICLE 2
Whether pleasure causes thirst or desire for itself?

Objection 1: It would seem that pleasure does not cause desire for itself. Because all movement ceases when repose is reached. But pleasure is, as it were, a certain repose of the movement of desire, as stated above (I-II, q. 23, a. 4; q. 25, a. 2). Therefore the movement of desire ceases when pleasure is reached. Therefore pleasure does not cause desire.

Objection 2: Further, a thing does not cause its contrary. But pleasure is, in a way, contrary to desire, on the part of the object: since desire regards a good which is not yet possessed, whereas pleasure regards the good that is possessed. Therefore pleasure does not cause desire for itself.

Objection 3: Further, distaste is incompatible with desire. But pleasure often causes distaste. Therefore it does not cause desire.

On the contrary, Our Lord said (Jn. 4:13): "Whosoever drinketh of this water, shall thirst again": where, according to Augustine (Tract. xv in Joan.), water denotes pleasures of the body.

I answer that, Pleasure can be considered in two ways; first, as existing in reality; secondly, as existing in the memory. Again thirst, or desire, can be taken in two ways; first, properly, as denoting a craving for something not possessed; secondly, in general, as excluding distaste. Considered as existing in reality, pleasure does not of itself cause thirst or desire for itself, but only accidentally; provided we take thirst or desire as denoting a craving for some thing not possessed: because pleasure is an emotion of the appetite in respect of something actually present. But it may happen that what is actually present is not perfectly possessed: and this may be on the part of the thing possessed, or on the part of the possessor. On the part of the thing possessed, this happens through the thing possessed not being a

tota simul, unde successive recipitur, et dum aliquis delectatur in eo quod habet, desiderat potiri eo quod restat; sicut qui audit primam partem versus, et in hoc delectatur, desiderat alteram partem versus audire, ut Augustinus dicit, IV Confess. Et hoc modo omnes fere delectationes corporales faciunt sui ipsarum sitim, quousque consummentur, eo quod tales delectationes consequuntur aliquem motum, sicut patet in delectationibus ciborum. Ex parte autem ipsius habentis, sicut cum aliquis aliquam rem in se perfectam existentem, non statim perfecte habet, sed paulatim acquirit. Sicut in mundo isto, percipientes aliquid imperfecte de divina cognitione, delectamur; et ipsa delectatio excitat sitim vel desiderium perfectae cognitionis; secundum quod potest intelligi quod habetur Eccli. XXIV, *qui bibunt me, adhuc sitient.* Si vero per sitim vel desiderium intelligatur sola intensio affectus tollens fastidium, sic delectationes spirituales maxime faciunt sitim vel desiderium sui ipsarum. Delectationes enim corporales, quia augmentatae, vel etiam continuatae, faciunt superexcrescentiam naturalis habitudinis, efficiuntur fastidiosae; ut patet in delectatione ciborum. Et propter hoc, quando aliquis iam pervenit ad perfectum in delectationibus corporalibus, fastidit eas, et quandoque appetit aliquas alias. Sed delectationes spirituales non superexcrescunt naturalem habitudinem, sed perficiunt naturam. Unde cum pervenitur ad consummationem in ipsis, tunc sunt magis delectabiles, nisi forte per accidens, inquantum operationi contemplativae adiunguntur aliquae operationes virtutum corporalium, quae per assiduitatem operandi lassantur. Et per hunc etiam modum potest intelligi quod dicitur Eccli. XXIV *qui bibit me, adhuc sitiet.* Quia etiam de angelis, qui perfecte Deum cognoscunt, et delectantur in ipso, dicitur I Petri I, quod *desiderant in eum conspicere.* Si vero consideretur delectatio prout est in memoria et non in actu, sic per se nata est causare sui ipsius sitim et desiderium, quando scilicet homo redit ad illam dispositionem in qua

simultaneous whole; wherefore one obtains possession of it successively, and while taking pleasure in what one has, one desires to possess the remainder: thus if a man is pleased with the first part of a verse, he desires to hear the second part, as Augustine says (Confess. iv, 11). In this way nearly all bodily pleasures cause thirst for themselves, until they are fully realized, because pleasures of this kind arise from some movement: as is evident in pleasures of the table. On the part of the possessor, this happens when a man possesses a thing which is perfect in itself, yet does not possess it perfectly, but obtains possession of it little by little. Thus in this life, a faint perception of Divine knowledge affords us delight, and delight sets up a thirst or desire for perfect knowledge; in which sense we may understand the words of Ecclus. 24:29: "They that drink me shall yet thirst." On the other hand, if by thirst or desire we understand the mere intensity of the emotion, that excludes distaste, thus more than all others spiritual pleasures cause thirst or desire for themselves. Because bodily pleasures become distasteful by reason of their causing an excess in the natural mode of being, when they are increased or even when they are protracted; as is evident in the case of pleasures of the table. This is why, when a man arrives at the point of perfection in bodily pleasures, he wearies of them, and sometimes desires another kind. Spiritual pleasures, on the contrary, do not exceed the natural mode of being, but perfect nature. Hence when their point of perfection is reached, then do they afford the greatest delight: except, perchance, accidentally, in so far as the work of contemplation is accompanied by some operation of the bodily powers, which tire from protracted activity. And in this sense also we may understand those words of Ecclus. 24:29: "They that drink me shall yet thirst": for, even of the angels, who know God perfectly, and delight in Him, it is written (1 Pet. 1:12) that they "desire to look at Him." Lastly, if we consider pleasure, not as existing in reality, but as existing in the memory, thus it has of itself a natural tendency to cause thirst and desire for itself: when, to wit, man returns to that disposition, in which

erat sibi delectabile quod praeteriit. Si vero immutatus sit ab illa dispositione, memoria delectationis non causat in eo delectationem, sed fastidium, sicut pleno existenti memoria cibi.

AD PRIMUM ergo dicendum quod, quando delectatio est perfecta, tunc habet omnimodam quietem, et cessat motus desiderii tendentis in non habitum. Sed quando imperfecte habetur, tunc non omnino cessat motus desiderii tendentis in non habitum.

AD SECUNDUM dicendum quod id quod imperfecte habetur, secundum quid habetur, et secundum quid non habetur. Et ideo simul de eo potest esse et desiderium et delectatio.

AD TERTIUM dicendum quod delectationes alio modo causant fastidium, et alio modo desiderium, ut dictum est.

ARTICULUS 3

AD TERTIUM sic proceditur. Videtur quod delectatio non impediat usum rationis. Quies enim maxime confert ad debitum rationis usum, unde dicitur in VII Physic., quod *in sedendo et quiescendo fit anima sciens et prudens;* et Sap. VIII, *intrans in domum meam, conquiescam cum illa,* scilicet sapientia. Sed delectatio est quaedam quies. Ergo non impedit, sed magis iuvat rationis usum.

PRAETEREA, ea quae non sunt in eodem, etiam si sint contraria, non se impediunt. Sed delectatio est in parte appetitiva, usus autem rationis in parte apprehensiva. Ergo delectatio non impedit rationis usum.

PRAETEREA, quod impeditur ab alio, videtur quodammodo transmutari ab ipso. Sed usus apprehensivae virtutis magis movet delectationem quam a delectatione moveatur, est enim causa delectationis. Ergo delectatio non impedit usum rationis.

SED CONTRA est quod philosophus dicit, in VI Ethic., quod *delectatio corrumpit existimationem prudentiae.*

he was when he experienced the pleasure that is past. But if he be changed from that disposition, the memory of that pleasure does not give him pleasure, but distaste: for instance, the memory of food in respect of a man who has eaten to repletion.

Reply to Objection 1: When pleasure is perfect, then it includes complete rest; and the movement of desire, tending to what was not possessed, ceases. But when it is imperfect, then the desire, tending to what was not possessed, does not cease altogether.

Reply to Objection 2: That which is possessed imperfectly, is possessed in one respect, and in another respect is not possessed. Consequently it may be the object of desire and pleasure at the same time.

Reply to Objection 3: Pleasures cause distaste in one way, desire in another, as stated above.

ARTICLE 3
Whether pleasure hinders the use of reason?

Objection 1: It would seem that pleasure does not hinder the use of reason. Because repose facilitates very much the due use of reason: wherefore the Philosopher says (Phys. vii, 3) that "while we sit and rest, the soul is inclined to knowledge and prudence"; and it is written (Wis. 8:16): "When I go into my house, I shall repose myself with her," i.e., wisdom. But pleasure is a kind of repose. Therefore it helps rather than hinders the use of reason.

Objection 2: Further, things which are not in the same subject though they be contraries, do not hinder one another. But pleasure is in the appetitive faculty, while the use of reason is in the apprehensive power. Therefore pleasure does not hinder the use of reason.

Objection 3: Further, that which is hindered by another, seems to be moved, as it were, thereby. But the use of an apprehensive power moves pleasure rather than is moved by it: because it is the cause of pleasure. Therefore pleasure does not hinder the use of reason.

On the contrary, The Philosopher says (Ethic. vi, 5), that "pleasure destroys the estimate of prudence."

RESPONDEO dicendum quod, sicut dicitur in X Ethic., *delectationes propriae adaugent operationes, extraneae vero impediunt.* Est ergo quaedam delectatio quae habetur de ipso actu rationis, sicut cum aliquis delectatur in contemplando vel ratiocinando. Et talis delectatio non impedit usum rationis, sed ipsum adiuvat, quia illud attentius operamur in quo delectamur; attentio autem adiuvat operationem. Sed delectationes corporales impediunt usum rationis triplici ratione. Primo quidem, ratione distractionis. Quia, sicut iam dictum est, ad ea in quibus delectamur, multum attendimus, cum autem attentio fortiter inhaeserit alicui rei, debilitatur circa alias res, vel totaliter ab eis revocatur. Et secundum hoc, si delectatio corporalis fuerit magna, vel totaliter impediet usum rationis, ad se intentionem animi attrahendo; vel multum impediet. Secundo, ratione contrarietatis. Quaedam enim delectationes, maxime superexcedentes, sunt contra ordinem rationis. Et per hunc modum philosophus dicit, in VI Ethic., quod *delectationes corporales corrumpunt existimationem prudentiae, non autem existimationem speculativam,* cui non contrariantur, *puta quod triangulus habet tres angulos aequales duobus rectis.* Secundum autem primum modum, utramque impedit. Tertio modo, secundum quandam ligationem, inquantum scilicet ad delectationem corporalem sequitur quaedam transmutatio corporalis, maior etiam quam in aliis passionibus, quanto vehementius afficitur appetitus ad rem praesentem quam ad rem absentem. Huiusmodi autem corporales perturbationes impediunt usum rationis, sicut patet in vinolentis, qui habent usum rationis ligatum vel impeditum.

AD PRIMUM ergo dicendum quod delectatio corporalis habet quidem quietem appetitus in delectabili, quae quies interdum contrariatur rationi; sed ex parte corporis, semper habet transmutationem. Et quantum ad utrumque, impedit rationis usum.

AD SECUNDUM dicendum quod vis appetitiva et apprehensiva sunt quidem diversae partes, sed unius animae.

I answer that, As is stated in Ethic. x, 5, "appropriate pleasures increase activity ... whereas pleasures arising from other sources are impediments to activity." Accordingly there is a certain pleasure that is taken in the very act of reason, as when one takes pleasure in contemplating or in reasoning: and such pleasure does not hinder the act of reason, but helps it; because we are more attentive in doing that which gives us pleasure, and attention fosters activity. On the other hand bodily pleasures hinder the use of reason in three ways. First, by distracting the reason. Because, as we have just observed, we attend much to that which pleases us. Now when the attention is firmly fixed on one thing, it is either weakened in respect of other things, or it is entirely withdrawn from them; and thus if the bodily pleasure be great, either it entirely hinders the use of reason, by concentrating the mind's attention on itself; or else it hinders it considerably. Secondly, by being contrary to reason. Because some pleasures, especially those that are in excess, are contrary to the order of reason: and in this sense the Philosopher says that "bodily pleasures destroy the estimate of prudence, but not the speculative estimate," to which they are not opposed, "for instance that the three angles of a triangle are together equal to two right angles." In the first sense, however, they hinder both estimates. Thirdly, by fettering the reason: in so far as bodily pleasure is followed by a certain alteration in the body, greater even than in the other passions, in proportion as the appetite is more vehemently affected towards a present than towards an absent thing. Now such bodily disturbances hinder the use of reason; as may be seen in the case of drunkards, in whom the use of reason is fettered or hindered.

Reply to Objection 1: Bodily pleasure implies indeed repose of the appetite in the object of pleasure; which repose is sometimes contrary to reason; but on the part of the body it always implies alteration. And in respect of both points, it hinders the use of reason.

Reply to Objection 2: The powers of the appetite and of apprehension are indeed distinct parts, but belonging to the one soul.

Et ideo cum intentio animae vehementer applicatur ad actum unius, impeditur ab actu contrario alterius.

AD TERTIUM dicendum quod usus rationis requirit debitum usum imaginationis et aliarum virium sensitivarum, quae utuntur organo corporali. Et ideo ex transmutatione corporali usus rationis impeditur, impedito actu virtutis imaginativae et aliarum sensitivarum.

ARTICULUS 4

AD QUARTUM sic proceditur. Videtur quod delectatio non perficiat operationem. Omnis enim humana operatio ab usu rationis dependet. Sed delectatio impedit usum rationis, ut dictum est. Ergo delectatio non perficit, sed debilitat operationem humanam.

PRAETEREA, nihil est perfectivum sui ipsius, vel suae causae. Sed delectatio est operatio, ut dicitur in VII et X Ethic., quod oportet ut intelligatur vel essentialiter, vel causaliter. Ergo delectatio non perficit operationem.

PRAETEREA, si delectatio perficit operationem, aut perficit ipsam sicut finis, aut sicut forma, aut sicut agens. Sed non sicut finis, quia operationes non quaeruntur propter delectationem, sed magis e converso, ut supra dictum est. Nec iterum per modum efficientis, quia magis operatio est causa efficiens delectationis. Nec iterum sicut forma, *non enim perficit delectatio operationem ut habitus quidam,* secundum philosophum, in X Ethic. Delectatio ergo non perficit operationem.

SED CONTRA est quod dicitur ibidem, quod *delectatio operationem perficit.*

RESPONDEO dicendum quod delectatio dupliciter operationem perficit. Uno modo, per modum finis, non quidem secundum quod finis dicitur *id propter quod aliquid est;* sed secundum quod omne bonum completive superveniens, potest dici finis. Et secundum hoc dicit philosophus, in X Ethic., quod *delectatio perficit operationem sicut quidam superveniens finis,* inquantum scilicet super hoc bonum quod est operatio,

Consequently when the soul is very intent on the action of one part, it is hindered from attending to a contrary act of the other part.

Reply to Objection 3: The use of reason requires the due use of the imagination and of the other sensitive powers, which are exercised through a bodily organ. Consequently alteration in the body hinders the use of reason, because it hinders the act of the imagination and of the other sensitive powers.

ARTICLE 4
Whether pleasure perfects operation?

Objection 1: It would seem that pleasure does not perfect operation. For every human operation depends on the use of reason. But pleasure hinders the use of reason, as stated above (I-II, q. 33, a. 3). Therefore pleasure does not perfect, but weakens human operation.

Objection 2: Further, nothing perfects itself or its cause. But pleasure is an operation (Ethic. vii, 12; x, 4), i.e., either in its essence or in its cause. Therefore pleasure does not perfect operation.

Objection 3: Further, if pleasure perfects operation, it does so either as end, or as form, or as agent. But not as end; because operation is not sought for the sake of pleasure, but rather the reverse, as stated above (I-II, q. 4, a. 2): nor as agent, because rather is it the operation that causes pleasure: nor again as form, because, according to the Philosopher (Ethic. x, 4), "pleasure does not perfect operation, as a habit does." Therefore pleasure does not perfect operation.

On the contrary, The Philosopher says (Ethic. x, 4) that "pleasure perfects operation."

I answer that, Pleasure perfects operation in two ways. First, as an end: not indeed according as an end is that on "account of which a thing is"; but according as every good which is added to a thing and completes it, can be called its end. And in this sense the Philosopher says (Ethic. x, 4) that "pleasure perfects operation . . . as some end added to it": that is to say, inasmuch as to this good, which is operation,

supervenit aliud bonum quod est delectatio, quae importat quietationem appetitus in bono praesupposito. Secundo modo, ex parte causae agentis. Non quidem directe, quia philosophus dicit, in X Ethic., quod *perficit delectatio operationem, non sicut medicus sanum, sed sicut sanitas*. Indirecte autem, inquantum scilicet agens, quia delectatur in sua actione, vehementius attendit ad ipsam, et diligentius eam operatur. Et secundum hoc dicitur in X Ethic., quod *delectationes adaugent proprias operationes, et impediunt extraneas.*

AD PRIMUM ergo dicendum quod non omnis delectatio impedit actum rationis, sed delectatio corporalis; quae non consequitur actum rationis, sed actum concupiscibilis, qui per delectationem augetur. Delectatio autem quae consequitur actum rationis, fortificat rationis usum.

AD SECUNDUM dicendum quod, sicut dicitur in II Physic., contingit quod duo sibi invicem sunt causa, ita quod unum sit causa efficiens, et aliud causa finalis alterius. Et per hunc modum, operatio causat delectationem sicut causa efficiens; delectatio autem perficit operationem per modum finis, ut dictum est.

AD TERTIUM patet responsio ex dictis.

there is added another good, which is pleasure, denoting the repose of the appetite in a good that is presupposed. Secondly, as agent; not indeed directly, for the Philosopher says (Ethic. x, 4) that "pleasure perfects operation, not as a physician makes a man healthy, but as health does": but it does so indirectly; inasmuch as the agent, through taking pleasure in his action, is more eagerly intent on it, and carries it out with greater care. And in this sense it is said in Ethic. x, 5 that "pleasures increase their appropriate activities, and hinder those that are not appropriate."

Reply to Objection 1: It is not every pleasure that hinders the act of reason, but only bodily pleasure; for this arises, not from the act of reason, but from the act of the concupiscible faculty, which act is intensified by pleasure. On the contrary, pleasure that arises from the act of reason, strengthens the use of reason.

Reply to Objection 2: As stated in Phys. ii, 3 two things may be causes of one another, if one be the efficient, the other the final cause. And in this way, operation is the efficient cause of pleasure, while pleasure perfects operation by way of final cause, as stated above.

The Reply to the Third Objection is evident for what has been said.

Question 34
Of the Goodness and Malice of Pleasures

We must now consider the goodness and malice of pleasures: under which head there are four points of inquiry: 1. Whether every pleasure is evil? 2. If not, whether every pleasure is good? 3. Whether any pleasure is the greatest good? 4. Whether pleasure is the measure or rule by which to judge of moral good and evil?

Article 1
Whether every pleasure is evil?

Objection 1: It would seem that every pleasure is evil. For that which destroys prudence and hinders the use of reason, seems to be evil in itself: since man's good is to be "in accord with reason," as Dionysius says (Div. Nom. iv). But pleasure destroys prudence and hinders the use of reason; and so much the more, as the pleasure is greater: wherefore "in sexual pleasures," which are the greatest of all, "it is impossible to understand anything," as stated in Ethic. vii, 11. Moreover, Jerome says in his commentary on Matthew* that "at the time of conjugal intercourse, the presence of the Holy Ghost is not vouchsafed, even if it be a prophet that fulfils the conjugal duty." Therefore pleasure is evil in itself; and consequently every pleasure is evil.

Objection 2: Further, that which the virtuous man shuns, and the man lacking in virtue seeks, seems to be evil in itself, and should be avoided; because, as stated in Ethic. x, 5 "the virtuous man is a kind of measure and rule of human actions"; and the Apostle says (1 Cor. 2:15): "The spiritual man judgeth all things." But children and dumb animals, in whom there is no virtue, seek pleasure: whereas the man who is master of himself does not. Therefore pleasures are evil in themselves and should be avoided.

Objection 3: Further, "virtue and art are concerned about the difficult and the good" (Ethic. ii, 3). But no art is ordained to pleasure. Therefore pleasure is not something good.

---

* Origen, Hom. vi in Num.

Sed contra est quod in Psalmo XXXVI, dicitur, *delectare in domino.* Cum igitur ad nihil mali auctoritas divina inducat, videtur quod non omnis delectatio sit mala.

Respondeo dicendum quod, sicut dicitur in X Ethic., aliqui posuerunt omnes delectationes esse malas. Cuius ratio videtur fuisse, quia intentionem suam referebant ad solas delectationes sensibiles et corporales, quae sunt magis manifestae, nam et in ceteris **intelligibilia a sensibilibus antiqui philosophi non distinguebant, nec intellectum a sensu,** ut dicitur in libro de anima. Delectationes autem corporales ut dicitur in libro de anima. Delectationes autem corporales arbitrabantur dicendum omnes esse malas, ut sic homines, qui ad delectationes immoderatas sunt proni, a delectationibus se retrahentes, ad medium virtutis perveniant. Sed haec existimatio non fuit conveniens. Cum enim nullus possit vivere sine aliqua sensibili et corporali delectatione, si illi qui docent omnes delectationes esse malas, deprehendantur aliquas delectationes suscipere; magis homines ad delectationes erunt proclives exemplo operum, verborum doctrina praetermissa. In operationibus enim et passionibus humanis, in quibus experientia plurimum valet, magis movent exempla quam verba. Dicendum est ergo aliquas delectationes esse bonas, et aliquas esse malas. Est enim delectatio quies appetitivae virtutis in aliquo bono amato, et consequens aliquam operationem. Unde huius ratio duplex accipi potest. Una quidem ex parte boni in quo aliquis quiescens delectatur. Bonum enim et malum in moralibus dicitur secundum quod convenit rationi vel discordat ab ea, ut supra dictum est, sicut in rebus naturalibus aliquid dicitur naturale ex eo quod naturae convenit, innaturale vero ex eo quod est a natura discordans. Sicut igitur in naturalibus est quaedam quies naturalis, quae scilicet est in eo quod convenit naturae, ut cum grave quiescit deorsum; et quaedam innaturalis, quae est in eo quod repugnat naturae, sicut cum grave quiescit sursum, ita et in moralibus est quaedam delectatio bona, secundum quod appetitus superior aut inferior requiescit in eo quod convenit rationi; et quaedam mala, ex eo quod

On the contrary, It is written (Ps. 36:4): "Delight in the Lord." Since, therefore, Divine authority leads to no evil, it seems that not every pleasure is evil.

I answer that, As stated in Ethic. x, 2, 3 some have maintained that all pleasure is evil. The reason seems to have been that they took account only of sensible and bodily pleasures which are more manifest; since, also in other respects, the ancient philosophers **did not discriminate between the intelligible and the sensible, nor between intellect and sense** (De Anima iii, 3). And they held that all bodily pleasures should be reckoned as bad, and thus that man, being prone to immoderate pleasures, arrives at the mean of virtue by abstaining from pleasure. But they were wrong in holding this opinion. Because, since none can live without some sensible and bodily pleasure, if they who teach that all pleasures are evil, are found in the act of taking pleasure; men will be more inclined to pleasure by following the example of their works instead of listening to the doctrine of their words: since, in human actions and passions, wherein experience is of great weight, example moves more than words. We must therefore say that some pleasures are good, and that some are evil. For pleasure is a repose of the appetitive power in some loved good, and resulting from some operation; wherefore we assign a twofold reason for this assertion. The first is in respect of the good in which a man reposes with pleasure. For good and evil in the moral order depend on agreement or disagreement with reason, as stated above (I-II, q. 18, a. 5): just as in the order of nature, a thing is said to be natural, if it agrees with nature, and unnatural, if it disagrees. Accordingly, just as in the natural order there is a certain natural repose, whereby a thing rests in that which agrees with its nature, for instance, when a heavy body rests down below; and again an unnatural repose, whereby a thing rests in that which disagrees with its nature, as when a heavy body rests up aloft: so, in the moral order, there is a good pleasure, whereby the higher or lower appetite rests in that which is in accord with reason; and an evil pleasure, whereby the

quiescit in eo quod a ratione discordat, et a lege Dei. Alia ratio accipi potest ex parte operationum, quarum quaedam sunt bonae, et quaedam malae. Operationibus autem magis sunt affines delectationes, quae sunt eis coniunctae, quam concupiscentiae, quae tempore eas praecedunt. Unde, cum concupiscentiae bonarum operationum sint bonae, malarum vero malae; multo magis delectationes bonarum operationum sunt bonae, malarum vero malae.

AD PRIMUM ergo dicendum quod, sicut supra dictum est, delectationes quae sunt de actu rationis, non impediunt rationem, neque corrumpunt prudentiam; sed delectationes extraneae, cuiusmodi sunt delectationes corporales. Quae quidem rationis usum impediunt, sicut supra dictum est, et per contrarietatem appetitus, qui quiescit in eo quod repugnat rationi, et ex hoc habet delectatio quod sit moraliter mala, vel secundum quandam ligationem rationis, sicut in concubitu coniugali delectatio, quamvis sit in eo quod convenit rationi, tamen impedit rationis usum, propter corporalem transmutationem adiunctam. Sed ex hoc non consequitur malitiam moralem, sicut nec somnus quo ligatur usus rationis, moraliter est malus, si sit secundum rationem receptus, nam et ipsa ratio hoc habet, ut quandoque rationis usus intercipiatur. Dicimus tamen quod huiusmodi ligamentum rationis ex delectatione in actu coniugali, etsi non habeat malitiam moralem, quia non est peccatum mortale nec veniale; provenit tamen ex quadam morali malitia, scilicet ex peccato primi parentis, nam hoc in statu innocentiae non erat, ut patet ex his quae in primo dicta sunt.

AD SECUNDUM dicendum quod temperatus non fugit omnes delectationes, sed immoderatas, et rationi non convenientes. Quod autem pueri et bestiae delectationes prosequantur, non ostendit eas universaliter esse malas, quia in eis est naturalis appetitus a Deo, qui movetur in id quod est eis conveniens.

AD TERTIUM dicendum quod non omnis boni est ars, sed exteriorum factibilium, ut infra dicetur. Circa operationes autem et passiones quae sunt in nobis, magis est

appetite rests in that which is discordant from reason and the law of God. The second reason can be found by considering the actions, some of which are good, some evil. Now pleasures which are conjoined to actions are more akin to those actions, than desires, which precede them in point of time. Wherefore, since the desires of good actions are good, and of evil actions, evil; much more are the pleasures of good actions good, and those of evil actions evil.

Reply to Objection 1: As stated above (I-II, q. 33, a. 3), it is not the pleasures which result from an act of reason, that hinder the reason or destroy prudence, but extraneous pleasures, such as the pleasures of the body. These indeed hinder the use of reason, as stated above (I-II, q. 33, a. 3), either by contrariety of the appetite that rests in something repugnant to reason, which makes the pleasure morally bad; or by fettering the reason: thus in conjugal intercourse, though the pleasure be in accord with reason, yet it hinders the use of reason, on account of the accompanying bodily change. But in this case the pleasure is not morally evil; as neither is sleep, whereby the reason is fettered, morally evil, if it be taken according to reason: for reason itself demands that the use of reason be interrupted at times. We must add, however, that although this fettering of the reason through the pleasure of conjugal intercourse has no moral malice, since it is neither a mortal nor a venial sin; yet it proceeds from a kind of moral malice, namely, from the sin of our first parent; because, as stated in the I, q. 98, a. 2, the case was different in the state of innocence.

Reply to Objection 2: The temperate man does not shun all pleasures, but those that are immoderate, and contrary to reason. The fact that children and dumb animals seek pleasures, does not prove that all pleasures are evil: because they have from God their natural appetite, which is moved to that which is naturally suitable to them.

Reply to Objection 3: Art is not concerned with all kinds of good, but with the making of external things, as we shall state further on (I-II, q. 57, a. 3). But actions and passions, which are within us, are more

prudentia et virtus quam ars. Et tamen aliqua ars est factiva delectationis; scilicet *pulmentaria et pigmentaria,* ut dicitur in VII Ethic.

Articulus 2

Ad secundum sic proceditur. Videtur quod omnis delectatio sit bona. Sicut enim in primo dictum est, bonum in tria dividitur, scilicet honestum, utile et delectabile. Sed honestum omne est bonum; et similiter omne utile. Ergo et omnis delectatio est bona.

Praeterea, illud est per se bonum, quod non quaeritur propter aliud, ut dicitur in I Ethic. Sed delectatio non quaeritur propter aliud, ridiculum enim videtur ab aliquo quaerere quare vult delectari. Ergo delectatio est per se bonum. Sed quod per se praedicatur de aliquo, universaliter praedicatur de eo. Ergo omnis delectatio est bona.

Praeterea, id quod ab omnibus desideratur, videtur esse per se bonum, nam bonum est *quod omnia appetunt,* ut dicitur in I Ethic. Sed omnes appetunt aliquam delectationem, etiam pueri et bestiae. Ergo delectatio est secundum se bonum. Omnis ergo delectatio est bona.

Sed contra est quod dicitur Prov. II, *qui laetantur cum malefecerint, et exultant in rebus pessimis.*

Respondeo dicendum quod, sicut aliqui Stoicorum posuerunt omnes delectationes esse malas, ita Epicurei posuerunt delectationem secundum se esse bonum, et per consequens delectationes omnes esse bonas. Qui ex hoc decepti esse videntur, quod non distinguebant inter id quod est bonum simpliciter, et id quod est bonum quoad hunc. Simpliciter quidem bonum est quod secundum se bonum est. Contingit autem quod non est secundum se bonum, esse huic bonum, dupliciter. Uno modo, quia est ei conveniens secundum dispositionem in qua nunc est, quae tamen non est naturalis, sicut leproso bonum est quandoque comedere aliqua venenosa, quae non sunt

the concern of prudence and virtue than of art. Nevertheless there is an art of making pleasure, namely, "the art of cookery and the art of making unguents," as stated in Ethic. vii, 12.

Article 2
Whether every pleasure is good?

Objection 1: It would seem that every pleasure is good. Because as stated in the I, q. 5, a. 6, there are three kinds of good: the virtuous, the useful, and the pleasant. But everything virtuous is good; and in like manner everything useful is good. Therefore also every pleasure is good.

Objection 2: Further, that which is not sought for the sake of something else, is good in itself, as stated in Ethic. i, 6, 7. But pleasure is not sought for the sake of something else; for it seems absurd to ask anyone why he seeks to be pleased. Therefore pleasure is good in itself. Now that which is predicated to a thing considered in itself, is predicated thereof universally. Therefore every pleasure is good.

Objection 3: Further, that which is desired by all, seems to be good of itself: because good is "what all things seek," as stated in Ethic. i, 1. But everyone seeks some kind of pleasure, even children and dumb animals. Therefore pleasure is good in itself: and consequently all pleasure is good.

On the contrary, It is written (Prov. 2:14): "Who are glad when they have done evil, and rejoice in most wicked things."

I answer that, While some of the Stoics maintained that all pleasures are evil, the Epicureans held that pleasure is good in itself, and that consequently all pleasures are good. They seem to have thus erred through not discriminating between that which is good simply, and that which is good in respect of a particular individual. That which is good simply, is good in itself. Now that which is not good in itself, may be good in respect of some individual in two ways. In one way, because it is suitable to him by reason of a disposition in which he is now, which disposition, however, is not natural: thus it is sometimes good for a leper to eat things that are poisonous, which are not

simpliciter convenientia complexioni humanae. Alio modo, quia id quod non est conveniens, aestimatur ut conveniens. Et quia delectatio est quies appetitus in bono, si sit bonum simpliciter illud in quo quiescit appetitus, erit simpliciter delectatio, et simpliciter bona. Si autem non sit bonum simpliciter, sed quoad hunc, tunc nec delectatio est simpliciter, sed huic, nec simpliciter est bona, sed bona secundum quid, vel apparens bona.

AD PRIMUM ergo dicendum quod honestum et utile dicuntur secundum rationem, et ideo nihil est honestum vel utile, quod non sit bonum. Delectabile autem dicitur secundum appetitum, qui quandoque in illud tendit quod non est conveniens rationi. Et ideo non omne delectabile est bonum bonitate morali, quae attenditur secundum rationem.

AD SECUNDUM dicendum quod ideo delectatio non quaeritur propter aliud, quia et quies in fine. Finem autem contingit esse bonum et malum quamvis nunquam sit finis nisi secundum quod est bonum quoad hunc. Ita etiam est de delectatione.

AD TERTIUM dicendum quod hoc modo omnia appetunt delectationem, sicut et bonum, cum delectatio sit quies appetitus in bono. Sed sicut contingit non omne bonum quod appetitur, esse per se et vere bonum; ita non omnis delectatio est per se et vere bona.

suitable simply to the human temperament. In another way, through something unsuitable being esteemed suitable. And since pleasure is the repose of the appetite in some good, if the appetite reposes in that which is good simply, the pleasure will be pleasure simply, and good simply. But if a man's appetite repose in that which is good, not simply, but in respect of that particular man, then his pleasure will not be pleasure simply, but a pleasure to him; neither will it be good simply, but in a certain respect, or an apparent good.

Reply to Objection 1: The virtuous and the useful depend on accordance with reason, and consequently nothing is virtuous or useful, without being good. But the pleasant depends on agreement with the appetite, which tends sometimes to that which is discordant from reason. Consequently not every object of pleasure is good in the moral order which depends on the order of reason.

Reply to Objection 2: The reason why pleasure is not sought for the sake of something else is because it is repose in the end. Now the end may be either good or evil; although nothing can be an end except in so far as it is good in respect of such and such a man: and so too with regard to pleasure.

Reply to Objection 3: All things seek pleasure in the same way as they seek good: since pleasure is the repose of the appetite in good. But, just as it happens that not every good which is desired, is of itself and verily good; so not every pleasure is of itself and verily good.

ARTICULUS 3

AD TERTIUM sic proceditur. Videtur quod nulla delectatio sit optimum. Nulla enim generatio est optimum, nam generatio non potest esse ultimus finis. Sed delectatio consequitur generationem, nam ex eo quod aliquid constituitur in suam naturam, delectatur, ut supra dictum est. Ergo nulla delectatio potest esse optimum.

ARTICLE 3
Whether any pleasure is the greatest good?

Objection 1: It would seem that no pleasure is the greatest good. Because nothing generated is the greatest good: since generation cannot be the last end. But pleasure is a consequence of generation: for the fact that a thing takes pleasure is due to its being established in its own nature, as stated above (I-II, q. 31, a. 1). Therefore no pleasure is the greatest good.

PRAETEREA, illud quod est optimum, nullo addito potest fieri melius. Sed delectatio aliquo addito fit melior, est enim melior delectatio cum virtute quam sine virtute. Ergo delectatio non est optimum.

PRAETEREA, id quod est optimum, est universaliter bonum, sicut per se bonum existens, nam quod est per se, est prius et potius eo quod est per accidens. Sed delectatio non est universaliter bonum, ut dictum est. Ergo delectatio non est optimum.

SED CONTRA beatitudo est optimum, cum sit finis humanae vitae. Sed beatitudo non est sine delectatione, dicitur enim in Psalmo XV, *adimplebis me laetitia cum vultu tuo; delectationes in dextera tua usque in finem.*

RESPONDEO dicendum quod Plato non posuit omnes delectationes esse malas, sicut Stoici; neque omnes esse bonas, sicut Epicurei; sed quasdam esse bonas, et quasdam esse malas; ita tamen quod nulla sit summum bonum, vel optimum. Sed quantum ex eius rationibus datur intelligi, in duobus deficit. In uno quidem quia, cum videret delectationes sensibiles et corporales in quodam motu et generatione consistere, sicut patet in repletione ciborum et huiusmodi; aestimavit omnes delectationes consequi generationem et motum. Unde, cum generatio et motus sint actus imperfecti, sequeretur quod delectatio non haberet rationem ultimae perfectionis. Sed hoc manifeste apparet falsum in delectationibus intellectualibus. Aliquis enim non solum delectatur in generatione scientiae, puta cum addiscit aut miratur, sicut supra dictum est; sed etiam in contemplando secundum scientiam iam acquisitam. Alio vero modo, quia dicebat optimum illud quod est simpliciter summum bonum, quod scilicet est ipsum bonum quasi abstractum et non participatum, sicut ipse Deus est summum bonum. Nos autem loquimur de optimo in rebus humanis. Optimum autem in unaquaque re est ultimus finis. Finis autem, ut supra dictum est, dupliciter dicitur, scilicet ipsa res,

Objection 2: Further, that which is the greatest good cannot be made better by addition. But pleasure is made better by addition; since pleasure together with virtue is better than pleasure without virtue. Therefore pleasure is not the greatest good.

Objection 3: Further, that which is the greatest good is universally good, as being good of itself: since that which is such of itself is prior to and greater than that which is such accidentally. But pleasure is not universally good, as stated above (I-II, q. 34, a. 2). Therefore pleasure is not the greatest good.

On the contrary, Happiness is the greatest good: since it is the end of man's life. But Happiness is not without pleasure: for it is written (Ps. 15:11): "Thou shalt fill me with joy with Thy countenance; at Thy right hand are delights even to the end."

I answer that, Plato held neither with the Stoics, who asserted that all pleasures are evil, nor with the Epicureans, who maintained that all pleasures are good; but he said that some are good, and some evil; yet, so that no pleasure be the sovereign or greatest good. But, judging from his arguments, he fails in two points. First, because, from observing that sensible and bodily pleasure consists in a certain movement and "becoming," as is evident in satiety from eating and the like; he concluded that all pleasure arises from some "becoming" and movement: and from this, since "becoming" and movement are the acts of something imperfect, it would follow that pleasure is not of the nature of ultimate perfection. But this is seen to be evidently false as regards intellectual pleasures: because one takes pleasure, not only in the "becoming" of knowledge, for instance, when one learns or wonders, as stated above (I-II, q. 32, a. 8, ad 2); but also in the act of contemplation, by making use of knowledge already acquired. Secondly, because by greatest good he understood that which is the supreme good simply, i.e., the good as existing apart from, and unparticipated by, all else, in which sense God is the Supreme Good; whereas we are speaking of the greatest good in human things. Now the greatest good of everything is its last end. And the end, as stated above (I-II, q. 1, a. 8; q. 2, a. 7) is twofold; namely,

et usus rei; sicut finis avari est vel pecunia, vel possessio pecuniae. Et secundum hoc, ultimus finis hominis dici potest vel ipse Deus, qui est summum bonum simpliciter; vel fruitio ipsius, quae importat delectationem quandam in ultimo fine. Et per hunc modum aliqua delectatio hominis potest dici optimum inter bona humana.

AD PRIMUM ergo dicendum quod non omnis delectatio consequitur generationem; sed aliquae delectationes consequuntur operationes perfectas, ut dictum est. Et ideo nihil prohibet aliquam delectationem esse optimum, etsi non omnis sit talis.

AD SECUNDUM dicendum quod ratio illa procedit de optimo simpliciter, per cuius participationem omnia sunt bona, unde ex nullius additione fit melius. Sed in aliis bonis universaliter verum est quod quodlibet bonum ex additione alterius fit melius. Quamvis posset dici quod delectatio non est aliquid extraneum ab operatione virtutis, sed concomitans ipsam, ut in I Ethic. dicitur.

AD TERTIUM dicendum quod delectatio non habet quod sit optimum ex hoc quod est delectatio, sed ex hoc quod est perfecta quies in optimo. Unde non oportet quod omnis delectatio sit optima, aut etiam bona. Sicut aliqua scientia est optima, non tamen omnis.

the thing itself, and the use of that thing; thus the miser's end is either money or the possession of money. Accordingly, man's last end may be said to be either God Who is the Supreme Good simply; or the enjoyment of God, which implies a certain pleasure in the last end. And in this sense a certain pleasure of man may be said to be the greatest among human goods.

Reply to Objection 1: Not every pleasure arises from a "becoming"; for some pleasures result from perfect operations, as stated above. Accordingly nothing prevents some pleasure being the greatest good, although every pleasure is not such.

Reply to Objection 2: This argument is true of the greatest good simply, by participation of which all things are good; wherefore no addition can make it better: whereas in regard to other goods, it is universally true that any good becomes better by the addition of another good. Moreover it might be said that pleasure is not something extraneous to the operation of virtue, but that it accompanies it, as stated in Ethic. i, 8.

Reply to Objection 3: That pleasure is the greatest good is due not to the mere fact that it is pleasure, but to the fact that it is perfect repose in the perfect good. Hence it does not follow that every pleasure is supremely good, or even good at all. Thus a certain science is supremely good, but not every science is.

ARTICULUS 4

AD QUARTUM sic proceditur. Videtur quod delectatio non sit mensura vel regula boni et mali moralis. *Omnia enim mensurantur primo sui generis,* ut dicitur in X Metaphys. Sed delectatio non est primum in genere moralium, sed praecedunt ipsam amor et desiderium. Non ergo est regula bonitatis et malitiae in moralibus.

PRAETEREA, mensuram et regulam oportet esse uniformem, et ideo motus qui est maxime uniformis, est mensura et regula omnium motuum, ut dicitur in X Metaphys. Sed delectatio est varia et multiformis, cum quaedam earum sint bonae, et quaedam

ARTICLE 4
Whether pleasure is the measure or rule by which to judge of moral good or evil?

Objection 1: It would seem that pleasure is not the measure or rule of moral good and evil. Because "that which is first in a genus is the measure of all the rest" (Metaph. x, 1). But pleasure is not the first thing in the moral genus, for it is preceded by love and desire. Therefore it is not the rule of goodness and malice in moral matters.

Objection 2: Further, a measure or rule should be uniform; hence that movement which is the most uniform, is the measure and rule of all movements (Metaph. x, 1). But pleasures are various and multiform: since some of them are good, and some

malae. Ergo delectatio non est mensura et regula moralium.

PRAETEREA, certius iudicium sumitur de effectu per causam, quam e converso. Sed bonitas vel malitia operationis est causa bonitatis vel malitiae delectationis, quia *bonae delectationes sunt quae consequuntur bonas operationes, malae autem quae malas,* ut dicitur in X Ethic. Ergo delectationes non sunt regula et mensura bonitatis et malitiae in moralibus.

SED CONTRA est quod Augustinus dicit, super illud Psalmi VII, *scrutans corda et renes Deus, finis curae et cogitationis est delectatio ad quam quis nititur pervenire.* Et philosophus dicit, in VII Ethic., quod *delectatio est finis architecton,* idest principalis, *ad quem respicientes, unumquodque hoc quidem malum, hoc autem bonum simpliciter dicimus.*

RESPONDEO dicendum quod bonitas vel malitia moralis principaliter in voluntate consistit, ut supra dictum est. Utrum autem voluntas sit bona vel mala, praecipue ex fine cognoscitur. Id autem habetur pro fine, in quo voluntas quiescit. Quies autem voluntatis, et cuiuslibet appetitus, in bono, est delectatio. Et ideo secundum delectationem voluntatis humanae, praecipue iudicatur homo bonus vel malus; est enim bonus et virtuosus qui gaudet in operibus virtutum; malus autem qui in operibus malis. Delectationes autem appetitus sensitivi non sunt regula bonitatis vel malitiae moralis, nam cibus communiter delectabilis est secundum appetitum sensitivum, bonis et malis. Sed voluntas bonorum delectatur in eis secundum convenientiam rationis, quam non curat voluntas malorum.

AD PRIMUM ergo dicendum quod amor et desiderium sunt priora delectatione in via generationis. Sed delectatio est prior secundum rationem finis, qui in operabilibus habet rationem principii, a quo maxime sumitur iudicium, sicut a regula vel mensura.

evil. Therefore pleasure is not the measure and rule of morals.

Objection 3: Further, judgment of the effect from its cause is more certain than judgment of cause from effect. Now goodness or malice of operation is the cause of goodness or malice of pleasure: because "those pleasures are good which result from good operations, and those are evil which arise from evil operations," as stated in Ethic. x, 5. Therefore pleasures are not the rule and measure of moral goodness and malice.

On the contrary, Augustine, commenting on Ps. 7:10 "The searcher of hearts and reins is God," says: "The end of care and thought is the pleasure which each one aims at achieving." And the Philosopher says (Ethic. vii, 11) that "pleasure is the architect," i.e., the principal, "end,[*] in regard to which, we say absolutely that this is evil, and that, good."

I answer that, Moral goodness or malice depends chiefly on the will, as stated above (I-II, q. 20, a. 1); and it is chiefly from the end that we discern whether the will is good or evil. Now the end is taken to be that in which the will reposes: and the repose of the will and of every appetite in the good is pleasure. And therefore man is reckoned to be good or bad chiefly according to the pleasure of the human will; since that man is good and virtuous, who takes pleasure in the works of virtue; and that man evil, who takes pleasure in evil works. On the other hand, pleasures of the sensitive appetite are not the rule of moral goodness and malice; since food is universally pleasurable to the sensitive appetite both of good and of evil men. But the will of the good man takes pleasure in them in accordance with reason, to which the will of the evil man gives no heed.

Reply to Objection 1: Love and desire precede pleasure in the order of generation. But pleasure precedes them in the order of the end, which serves a principle in actions; and it is by the principle, which is the rule and measure of such matters, that we form our judgment.

---

[*] St. Thomas took *finis* as being the nominative, whereas it is the genitive—τοῦ τέλους (*tou telous*); and the Greek reads "He" (i.e., the political philosopher), "is the architect of the end."

AD SECUNDUM dicendum quod omnis delectatio in hoc est uniformis, quod est quies in aliquo bono, et secundum hoc potest esse regula vel mensura. Nam ille bonus est cuius voluntas quiescit in vero bono; malus autem, cuius voluntas quiescit in malo.

AD TERTIUM dicendum quod, cum delectatio perficiat operationem per modum finis, ut supra dictum est; non potest esse operatio perfecte bona, nisi etiam adsit delectatio in bono, nam bonitas rei dependet ex fine. Et sic quodammodo bonitas delectationis est causa bonitas in operatione.

Reply to Objection 2: All pleasures are uniform in the point of their being the repose of the appetite in something good: and in this respect pleasure can be a rule or measure. Because that man is good, whose will rests in the true good: and that man evil, whose will rests in evil.

Reply to Objection 3: Since pleasure perfects operation as its end, as stated above (I-II, q. 33, a. 4); an operation cannot be perfectly good, unless there be also pleasure in good: because the goodness of a thing depends on its end. And thus, in a way, the goodness of the pleasure is the cause of goodness in the operation.

QUAESTIO XXXV

Deinde considerandum est de dolore et tristitia. Et circa hoc, *primo* considerandum est de tristitia, seu dolore, secundum se; *secundo,* de causis eius; *tertio,* de effectibus ipsius; *quarto,* de remediis eius; *quinto,* de bonitate vel malitia eius. Circa primum quaeruntur octo. *Primo,* utrum dolor sit passio animae. *Secundo,* utrum tristitia sit idem quod dolor. *Tertio,* utrum tristitia, seu dolor, sit contraria delectationi. *Quarto,* utrum omnis tristitia omni delectationi contrarietur. *Quinto,* utrum delectationi contemplationis sit aliqua tristitia contraria. *Sexto,* utrum magis fugienda sit tristitia, quam delectatio appetenda. *Septimo,* utrum dolor exterior sit maior quam dolor interior. *Octavo,* de speciebus tristitiae.

QUESTION 35
Of Pain or Sorrow, in Itself

We have now to consider pain and sorrow: concerning which we must consider: 1. Sorrow or pain in itself; 2. Its cause; 3. Its effects; 4. Its remedies; 5. Its goodness or malice. Under the first head there are eight points of inquiry: 1. Whether pain is a passion of the soul? 2. Whether sorrow is the same as pain? 3. Whether sorrow or pain is contrary in pleasure? 4. Whether all sorrow is contrary to all pleasure? 5. Whether there is a sorrow contrary to the pleasure of contemplation? 6. Whether sorrow is to be shunned more than pleasure is to be sought? 7. Whether exterior pain is greater than interior? 8. Of the species of sorrow.

ARTICULUS 1

AD PRIMUM sic proceditur. Videtur quod dolor non sit passio animae. Nulla enim passio animae est in corpore. Sed dolor potest esse in corpore, dicit enim Augustinus, in libro de vera Relig., quod *dolor qui dicitur corporis, est corruptio repentina salutis eius rei, quam, male utendo, anima corruptioni obnoxiavit.* Ergo dolor non est passio animae.

PRAETEREA, omnis passio animae pertinet ad vim appetitivam. Sed dolor non pertinet ad vim appetitivam, sed magis ad apprehensivam, dicit enim Augustinus, in libro

ARTICLE 1
Whether pain is a passion of the soul?

Objection 1: It would seem that pain is not a passion of the soul. Because no passion of the soul is in the body. But pain can be in the body, since Augustine says (De Vera Relig. xii), that "bodily pain is a sudden corruption of the well-being of that thing which the soul, by making evil use of it, made subject to corruption." Therefore pain is not a passion of the soul.

Objection 2: Further, every passion of the soul belongs to the appetitive faculty. But pain does not belong to the appetitive, but rather to the apprehensive part: for Augustine

says (De Nat. Boni xx) that "bodily pain is caused by the sense resisting a more powerful body." Therefore pain is not a passion of the soul.

Objection 3: Further, every passion of the soul belongs to the animal appetite. But pain does not belong to the animal appetite, but rather to the natural appetite; for Augustine says (Gen. ad lit. viii, 14): "Had not some good remained in nature, we should feel no pain in being punished by the loss of good." Therefore pain is not a passion of the soul.

On the contrary, Augustine (De Civ. Dei xiv, 8) reckons pain among the passions of the soul; quoting Virgil (Aeneid, vi, 733): "hence wild desires and grovelling fears / And human laughter, human tears."*

I answer that, Just as two things are requisite for pleasure; namely, conjunction with good and perception of this conjunction; so also two things are requisite for pain: namely, conjunction with some evil (which is in so far evil as it deprives one of some good), and perception of this conjunction. Now whatever is conjoined, if it have not the aspect of good or evil in regard to the being to which it is conjoined, cannot cause pleasure or pain. Whence it is evident that something under the aspect of good or evil is the object of the pleasure or pain. But good and evil, as such, are objects of the appetite. Consequently it is clear that pleasure and pain belong to the appetite. Now every appetitive movement or inclination consequent to apprehension, belongs to the intellective or sensitive appetite: since the inclination of the natural appetite is not consequent to an apprehension of the subject of that appetite, but to the apprehension of another, as stated in the I, q. 103, a. 1; a. 3. Since then pleasure and pain presuppose some sense or apprehension in the same subject, it is evident that pain, like pleasure, is in the intellective or sensitive appetite. Again every movement of the sensitive appetite is called a passion, as stated above (I-II, q. 22, a. 1; a. 3): and especially those which tend to some defect. Consequently pain, according as it is in the sensitive appetite, is most

de natura boni, quod *dolorem in corpore facit sensus resistens corpori potentiori.* Ergo dolor non est passio animae.

Praeterea, omnis passio animae pertinet ad appetitum animalem. Sed dolor non pertinet ad appetitum animalem, sed magis ad appetitum naturalem, dicit enim Augustinus, VIII super Gen. ad Litt., *nisi aliquod bonum remansisset in natura, nullius boni amissi esset dolor in poena.* Ergo dolor non est passio animae.

Sed contra est quod Augustinus, XIV de Civ. Dei, ponit dolorem inter passiones animae, inducens illud Virgilii, *hinc metuunt, cupiunt, gaudentque dolentque.*

Respondeo dicendum quod, sicut ad delectationem duo requiruntur, scilicet coniunctio boni, et perceptio huiusmodi coniunctionis; ita etiam ad dolorem duo requiruntur, scilicet coniunctio alicuius mali (quod ea ratione est malum, quia privat aliquod bonum); et perceptio huiusmodi coniunctionis. Quidquid autem coniungitur, si non habeat, respectu eius cui coniungitur, rationem boni vel mali, non potest causare delectationem vel dolorem. Ex quo patet quod aliquid sub ratione boni vel mali, est obiectum delectationis et doloris. Bonum autem et malum, inquantum huiusmodi, sunt obiecta appetitus. Unde patet quod delectatio et dolor ad appetitum pertinent. Omnis autem motus appetitivus, seu inclinatio consequens apprehensionem, pertinet ad appetitum intellectivum vel sensitivum, nam inclinatio appetitus naturalis non consequitur apprehensionem ipsius appetentis, sed alterius, ut in primo dictum est. Cum igitur delectatio et dolor praesupponant in eodem subiecto sensum vel apprehensionem aliquam, manifestum est quod dolor, sicut et delectatio, est in appetitu intellectivo vel sensitivo. Omnis autem motus appetitus sensitivi dicitur passio, ut supra dictum est. Et praecipue illi qui in defectum sonant. Unde dolor, secundum quod est in appetitu sensitivo, propriissime dicitur passio animae, sicut

---

* Translation: Conington.

molestiae corporales proprie passiones corporis dicuntur. Unde et Augustinus, XIV de Civ. Dei, dolorem specialiter aegritudinem nominat.

AD PRIMUM ergo dicendum quod dolor dicitur esse corporis, quia causa doloris est in corpore, puta cum patimur aliquod nocivum corpori. Sed motus doloris semper est in anima, nam *corpus non potest dolere nisi dolente anima,* ut Augustinus dicit.

AD SECUNDUM dicendum quod dolor dicitur esse sensus, non quia sit actus sensitivae virtutis, sed quia requiritur ad dolorem corporalem, sicut ad delectationem.

AD TERTIUM dicendum quod dolor de amissione boni demonstrat bonitatem naturae, non quia dolor sit actus naturalis appetitus, sed quia natura aliquid appetit ut bonum, quod cum removeri sentitur, sequitur doloris passio in appetitu sensitivo.

properly called a passion of the soul: just as

bodily ailments are properly called passions of the body. Hence Augustine* (De Civ. Dei xiv, 7, 8) reckons pain especially as being a kind of ailment.

Reply to Objection 1: We speak of the body, because the cause of pain is in the body: as when we suffer something hurtful to the body. But the movement of pain is always in the soul; since "the body cannot feel pain unless the soul feel it," as Augustine says (Super Psalm 87:4).

Reply to Objection 2: We speak of pain of the senses, not as though it were an act of the sensitive power; but because the senses are required for bodily pain, in the same way as for bodily pleasure.

Reply to Objection 3: Pain at the loss of good proves the goodness of the nature, not because pain is an act of the natural appetite, but because nature desires something as good, the removal of which being perceived, there results the passion of pain in the sensitive appetite.

ARTICULUS 2

AD SECUNDUM sic proceditur. Videtur quod tristitia non sit dolor. Dicit enim Augustinus, XIV de Civ. Dei, quod *dolor in corporibus dicitur.* Tristitia autem dicitur magis in anima. Ergo tristitia non est dolor.

PRAETEREA, dolor non est nisi de praesenti malo. Sed tristitia potest esse de praeterito et de futuro, sicut poenitentia est tristitia de praeterito, et anxietas de futuro. Ergo tristitia omnino a dolore differt.

PRAETEREA, dolor non videtur consequi nisi sensum tactus. Sed tristitia potest consequi ex omnibus sensibus. Ergo tristitia non est dolor, sed se habet in pluribus.

SED CONTRA est quod apostolus dicit, ad Rom. IX, tristitia est mihi magna, et continuus dolor cordi meo, pro eodem utens tristitia et dolore.

ARTICLE 2
Whether sorrow is the same as pain?

Objection 1: It would seem that sorrow is not pain. For Augustine says (De Civ. Dei xiv, 7) that "pain is used to express bodily suffering." But sorrow is used more in reference to the soul. Therefore sorrow is not pain.

Objection 2: Further, pain is only in respect of present evil. But sorrow can refer to both past and future evil: thus repentance is sorrow for the past, and anxiety for the future. Therefore sorrow is quite different from pain.

Objection 3: Further, pain seems not to follow save from the sense of touch. But sorrow can arise from all the senses. Therefore sorrow is not pain, and extends to more objects.

On the contrary, The Apostle says (Rom. 9:2): "I have great sorrow† and continual pain‡ in my heart," thus denoting the same thing by sorrow and pain.

---

* Quoting Cicero.
† Douay: 'sadness.'
‡ Douay: 'sorrow.'

RESPONDEO dicendum quod delectatio et dolor ex duplici apprehensione causari possunt, scilicet ex apprehensione exterioris sensus, et ex apprehensione interiori sive intellectus sive imaginationis. Interior autem apprehensio ad plura se extendit quam exterior, eo quod quaecumque cadunt sub exteriori apprehensione, cadunt sub interiori, sed non e converso. Sola igitur illa delectatio quae ex interiori apprehensione causatur, **gaudium nominatur, ut supra dictum est.** Et similiter ille solus dolor qui ex apprehensione interiori causatur, nominatur tristitia. Et sicut illa delectatio quae ex exteriori apprehensione causatur, delectatio quidem nominatur, non autem gaudium; ita ille dolor qui ex exteriori apprehensione causatur, nominatur quidem dolor, non autem tristitia. Sic igitur tristitia est quaedam species doloris, sicut gaudium delectationis.

AD PRIMUM ergo dicendum quod Augustinus loquitur ibi quantum ad usum vocabuli, quia *dolor* magis usitatur in corporalibus doloribus, qui sunt magis noti, quam in doloribus spiritualibus.

AD SECUNDUM dicendum quod sensus exterior non percipit nisi praesens, vis autem cognitiva interior potest percipere praesens, praeteritum et futurum. Et ideo tristitia potest esse de praesenti, praeterito et futuro, dolor autem corporalis, qui sequitur apprehensionem sensus exterioris, non potest esse nisi de praesenti.

AD TERTIUM dicendum quod sensibilia tactus sunt dolorosa, non solum inquantum sunt improportionata virtuti apprehensivae, sed etiam inquantum contrariantur naturae. Aliorum vero sensuum sensibilia possunt quidem esse improportionata virtuti apprehensivae, non tamen contrariantur naturae, nisi in ordine ad sensibilia tactus. Unde solus homo, qui est animal perfectum in cognitione, delectatur in sensibilibus aliorum sensuum secundum se ipsa, alia vero animalia non delectantur in eis nisi secundum quod referuntur ad sensibilia tactus, ut dicitur in III Ethic. Et ideo de sensibilibus aliorum sensuum non dicitur esse dolor, secundum quod contrariatur delectationi naturali, sed magis tristitia, quae contrariatur

I answer that, Pleasure and pain can arise from a twofold apprehension, namely, from the apprehension of an exterior sense; and from the interior apprehension of the intellect or of the imagination. Now the interior apprehension extends to more objects than the exterior apprehension: because whatever things come under the exterior apprehension, come under the interior, but not conversely. Consequently that pleasure alone which is **caused by an interior apprehension is called** joy, as stated above (I-II, q. 31, a. 3): and in like manner that pain alone which is caused by an interior apprehension, is called sorrow. And just as that pleasure which is caused by an exterior apprehension, is called pleasure but not joy; so too that pain which is caused by an exterior apprehension, is called pain indeed but not sorrow. Accordingly sorrow is a species of pain, as joy is a species of pleasure.

Reply to Objection 1: Augustine is speaking there of the use of the word: because "pain" is more generally used in reference to bodily pains, which are better known, than in reference to spiritual pains.

Reply to Objection 2: External sense perceives only what is present; but the interior cognitive power can perceive the present, past and future. Consequently sorrow can regard present, past and future: whereas bodily pain, which follows apprehension of the external sense, can only regard something present.

Reply to Objection 3: The sensibles of touch are painful, not only in so far as they are disproportionate to the apprehensive power, but also in so far as they are contrary to nature: whereas the objects of the other senses can indeed be disproportionate to the apprehensive power, but they are not contrary to nature, save as they are subordinate to the sensibles of touch. Consequently man alone, who is a perfectly cognizant animal, takes pleasure in the objects of the other senses for their own sake; whereas other animals take no pleasure in them save as referable to the sensibles of touch, as stated in Ethic. iii, 10. Accordingly, in referring to the objects of the other senses, we do not speak of pain in so far as it is contrary to natural pleasure: but rather of sorrow, which is contrary to

gaudio animali. Sic igitur si dolor accipiatur pro corporali dolore, quod usitatius est, dolor ex opposito dividitur contra tristitiam, secundum distinctionem apprehensionis interioris et exterioris; licet, quantum ad obiecta, delectatio ad plura se extendat quam dolor corporalis. Si vero dolor accipiatur communiter, sic dolor est genus tristitiae, ut dictum est.

joy. So then if pain be taken as denoting bodily pain, which is its more usual meaning, then it is contrasted with sorrow, according to the distinction of interior and exterior apprehension; although, on the part of the objects, pleasure extends further than does bodily pain. But if pain be taken in a wide sense, then it is the genus of sorrow, as stated above.

Articulus 3

AD TERTIUM sic proceditur. Videtur quod dolor delectationi non contrarietur. Unum enim contrariorum non est causa alterius. Sed tristitia potest esse causa delectationis, dicitur enim Matth. V, *beati qui lugent, quoniam ipsi consolabuntur.* Ergo non sunt contraria.

PRAETEREA, unum contrariorum non denominat aliud. Sed in quibusdam ipse dolor vel tristitia est delectabilis, sicut Augustinus dicit, in III Confess., quod dolor in spectaculis delectat. Et IV Confess., dicit quod fletus amara res est, et tamen quandoque delectat. Ergo dolor non contrariatur delectationi.

PRAETEREA, unum contrariorum non est materia alterius, quia contraria simul esse non possunt. Sed dolor potest esse materia delectationis, dicit enim Augustinus, in libro de poenitentia, *semper poenitens doleat, et de dolore gaudeat.* Et philosophus dicit, in IX Ethic., quod e converso *malus dolet de eo quod delectatus est.* Ergo delectatio et dolor non sunt contraria.

SED CONTRA est quod Augustinus dicit, XIV de Civ. Dei, quod *laetitia est voluntas in eorum consensione quae volumus, tristitia autem est voluntas in dissensione ab his quae nolumus.* Sed consentire et dissentire sunt contraria. Ergo laetitia et tristitia sunt contraria.

RESPONDEO dicendum quod, sicut philosophus dicit X Metaphys., contrarietas est differentia secundum formam. Forma autem, seu species, passionis et motus sumitur ex obiecto vel termino. Unde, cum obiecta delectationis et tristitiae, seu doloris,

Article 3
Whether sorrow or pain is contrary to pleasure?

Objection 1: It would seem that sorrow is not contrary to pleasure. For one of two contraries is not the cause of the other. But sorrow can be the cause of pleasure; for it is written (Mat. 5:5): "Blessed are they that mourn, for they shall be comforted." Therefore they are not contrary to one another.

Objection 2: Further, one contrary does not denominate the other. But to some, pain or sorrow gives pleasure: thus Augustine says (Confess. iii, 2) that in stage-plays sorrow itself gives pleasure: and (Confess. iv, 5) that "weeping is a bitter thing, and yet it sometimes pleases us." Therefore pain is not contrary to pleasure.

Objection 3: Further, one contrary is not the matter of the other; because contraries cannot co-exist together. But sorrow can be the matter of pleasure; for Augustine says (De Poenit. xiii): "The penitent should ever sorrow, and rejoice in his sorrow." The Philosopher too says (Ethic. ix, 4) that, on the other hand, "the evil man feels pain at having been pleased." Therefore pleasure and pain are not contrary to one another.

On the contrary, Augustine says (De Civ. Dei xiv, 6) that "joy is the volition of consent to the things we wish: and that sorrow is the volition of dissent from the things we do not wish." But consent and dissent are contraries. Therefore pleasure and sorrow are contrary to one another.

I answer that, As the Philosopher says (Metaph. x, 4), contrariety is a difference in respect of a form. Now the form or species of a passion or movement is taken from the object or term. Consequently, since the objects of pleasure and sorrow or pain,

sint contraria, scilicet bonum praesens et malum praesens, sequitur quod dolor et delectatio sint contraria.

AD PRIMUM ergo dicendum quod nihil prohibet unum contrariorum esse causam alterius per accidens. Sic autem tristitia potest esse causa delectationis. Uno quidem modo, inquantum tristitia de absentia alicuius rei, vel de praesentia contrarii, vehementius quaerit id in quo delectetur, sicut sitiens vehementius quaerit delectationem potus, ut remedium contra tristitiam quam patitur. Alio modo, inquantum ex magno desiderio delectationis alicuius, non recusat aliquis tristitias perferre, ut ad illam delectationem perveniat. Et utroque modo luctus praesens ad consolationem futurae vitae perducit. Quia ex hoc ipso quod homo luget pro peccatis, vel pro dilatione gloriae, meretur consolationem aeternam. Similiter etiam meretur eam aliquis ex hoc quod, ad ipsam consequendam, non refugit labores et angustias propter ipsam sustinere.

AD SECUNDUM dicendum quod dolor ipse potest esse delectabilis per accidens, inquantum scilicet habet adiunctam admirationem, ut in spectaculis; vel inquantum facit recordationem rei amatae, et facit percipere amorem eius, de cuius absentia doletur. Unde, cum amor sit delectabilis, et dolor et omnia quae ex amore consequuntur, inquantum in eis sentitur amor, sunt delectabilia. Et propter hoc etiam dolores in spectaculis possunt esse delectabiles, inquantum in eis sentitur aliquis amor conceptus ad illos qui in spectaculis commemorantur.

AD TERTIUM dicendum quod voluntas et ratio supra suos actus reflectuntur, inquantum ipsi actus voluntatis et rationis accipiuntur sub ratione boni vel mali. Et hoc modo tristitia potest esse materia delectationis, vel e converso, non per se, sed per accidens, inquantum scilicet utrumque accipitur in ratione boni vel mali.

viz. present good and present evil, are contrary to one another, it follows that pain and pleasure are contrary to one another.

Reply to Objection 1: Nothing hinders one contrary causing the other accidentally: and thus sorrow can be the cause of pleasure. In one way, in so far as from sorrow at the absence of something, or at the presence of its contrary, one seeks the more eagerly for something pleasant: thus a thirsty man seeks more eagerly the pleasure of a drink, as a remedy for the pain he suffers. In another way, in so far as, from a strong desire for a certain pleasure, one does not shrink from undergoing pain, so as to obtain that pleasure. In each of these ways, the sorrows of the present life lead us to the comfort of the future life. Because by the mere fact that man mourns for his sins, or for the delay of glory, he merits the consolation of eternity. In like manner a man merits it when he shrinks not from hardships and straits in order to obtain it.

Reply to Objection 2: Pain itself can be pleasurable accidentally in so far as it is accompanied by wonder, as in stage-plays; or in so far as it recalls a beloved object to one's memory, and makes one feel one's love for the thing, whose absence gives us pain. Consequently, since love is pleasant, both pain and whatever else results from love, forasmuch as they remind us of our love, are pleasant. And, for this reason, we derive pleasure even from pains depicted on the stage: in so far as, in witnessing them, we perceive ourselves to conceive a certain love for those who are there represented.

Reply to Objection 3: The will and the reason reflect on their own acts, inasmuch as the acts themselves of the will and reason are considered under the aspect of good or evil. In this way sorrow can be the matter of pleasure, or vice versa, not essentially but accidentally: that is, in so far as either of them is considered under the aspect of good or evil.

Articulus 4

Ad quartum sic proceditur. Videtur quod omnis tristitia omni delectationi contrarietur. Sicut enim albedo et nigredo sunt contrariae species coloris, ita delectatio et tristitia sunt contrariae species animae passionum. Sed albedo et nigredo universaliter sibi opponuntur. Ergo etiam delectatio et tristitia.

Praeterea, medicinae per contraria fiunt. Sed quaelibet delectatio est medicina contra quamlibet tristitiam, ut patet per philosophum, in VII Ethic. Ergo quaelibet delectatio cuilibet tristitiae contrariatur.

Praeterea, contraria sunt quae se invicem impediunt. Sed quaelibet tristitia impedit quamlibet delectationem, ut patet per illud quod dicitur X Ethic. Ergo quaelibet tristitia cuilibet delectationi contrariatur.

Sed contra, contrariorum non est eadem causa. Sed ab eodem habitu procedit quod aliquis gaudeat de uno, et tristetur de opposito, ex caritate enim contingit *gaudere cum gaudentibus,* et *flere cum flentibus,* ut dicitur Rom. XII. Ergo non omnis tristitia omni delectationi contrariatur.

Respondeo dicendum quod, sicut dicitur in X Metaphys., contrarietas est differentia secundum formam. Forma autem est et generalis, et specialis. Unde contingit esse aliqua contraria secundum formam generis, sicut virtus et vitium; et secundum formam speciei, sicut iustitia et iniustitia. Est autem considerandum quod quaedam specificantur secundum formas absolutas, sicut substantiae et qualitates, quaedam vero specificantur per comparationem ad aliquid extra, sicut passiones et motus recipiunt speciem ex terminis sive ex obiectis. In his ergo quorum species considerantur secundum formas absolutas, contingit quidem species quae continentur sub contrariis generibus, non esse contrarias secundum rationem speciei, non tamen contingit quod habeant aliquam affinitatem vel convenientiam ad invicem. Intemperantia enim et iustitia, quae sunt in contrariis generibus, virtute scilicet et vitio, non

Article 4
Whether all sorrow is contrary to all pleasure?

Objection 1: It would seem that all sorrow is contrary to all pleasure. Because, just as whiteness and blackness are contrary species of color, so pleasure and sorrow are contrary species of the soul's passions. But whiteness and blackness are universally contrary to one another. Therefore pleasure and sorrow are so too.

Objection 2: Further, remedies are made of things contrary (to the evil). But every pleasure is a remedy for all manner of sorrow, as the Philosopher declares (Ethic. vii, 14). Therefore every pleasure is contrary to every sorrow.

Objection 3: Further, contraries are hindrances to one another. But every sorrow hinders any kind of pleasure: as is evident from Ethic. x, 5. Therefore every sorrow is contrary to every pleasure.

On the contrary, The same thing is not the cause of contraries. But joy for one thing, and sorrow for the opposite thing, proceed from the same habit: thus from charity it happens that we "rejoice with them that rejoice," and "weep with them that weep" (Rom. 12:15). Therefore not every sorrow is contrary to every pleasure.

I answer that, As stated in Metaph. x, 4 contrariety is a difference in respect of a form. Now a form may be generic or specific. Consequently things may be contraries in respect of a generic form, as virtue and vice; or in respect of a specific form, as justice and injustice. Now we must observe that some things are specified by absolute forms, e.g., substances and qualities; whereas other things are specified in relation to something extrinsic, e.g., passions and movements, which derive their species from their terms or objects. Accordingly in those things that are specified by absolute forms, it happens that species contained under contrary genera are not contrary as to their specific nature: but it does not happen for them to have any affinity or fittingness to one another. For intemperance and justice, which are in the contrary genera of virtue and vice, are not

contrariantur ad invicem secundum rationem propriae speciei, nec tamen habent aliquam affinitatem vel convenientiam ad invicem. Sed in illis quorum species sumuntur secundum habitudinem ad aliquid extrinsecum, contingit quod species contrariorum generum non solum non sunt contrariae ad invicem, sed etiam habent quandam convenientiam et affinitatem ad invicem, eo quod eodem modo se habere ad contraria, contrarietatem inducit, sicut accedere ad album et accedere ad nigrum habent rationem contrarietatis; sed contrario modo se habere ad contraria, habet rationem similitudinis, sicut recedere ab albo et accedere ad nigrum. Et hoc maxime apparet in contradictione, quae est principium oppositionis, nam in affirmatione et negatione eiusdem consistit oppositio, sicut *album* et *non album*; in affirmatione autem unius oppositorum et negatione alterius, attenditur convenientia et similitudo, ut si dicam *nigrum* et *non album*. Tristitia autem et delectatio, cum sint passiones, specificantur ex obiectis. Et quidem secundum genus suum, contrarietatem habent, nam unum pertinet ad *prosecutionem,* aliud vero ad *fugam,* quae se *habent in appetitu sicut affirmatio et negatio in ratione,* ut dicitur in VI Ethic. Et ideo tristia et delectatio quae sunt de eodem, habent oppositionem ad invicem secundum speciem. Tristitia vero et delectatio de diversis, si quidem illa diversa non sint opposita, sed disparata, non habent oppositionem ad invicem secundum rationem speciei, sed sunt etiam disparatae, sicut tristari de morte amici, et delectari in contemplatione. Si vero illa diversa sint contraria, tunc delectatio et tristitia non solum non habent contrarietatem secundum rationem speciei, sed etiam habent convenientiam et affinitatem, sicut gaudere de bono, et tristari de malo.

AD PRIMUM ergo dicendum quod albedo et nigredo non habent speciem ex habitudine ad aliquid exterius, sicut delectatio et tristitia. Unde non est eadem ratio.

contrary to one another in respect of their specific nature; and yet they have no affinity or fittingness to one another. On the other hand, in those things that are specified in relation to something extrinsic, it happens that species belonging to contrary genera, are not only not contrary to one another, but also that they have a certain mutual affinity or fittingness. The reason of this is that where there is one same relation to two contraries, there is contrariety; e.g., to approach to a white thing, and to approach to a black thing, are contraries; whereas contrary relations to contrary things, implies a certain likeness, e.g., to recede from something white, and to approach to something black. This is most evident in the case of contradiction, which is the principle of opposition: because opposition consists in affirming and denying the same thing, e.g., "white" and "non-white"; while there is fittingness and likeness in the affirmation of one contrary and the denial of the other, as, if I were to say "black" and "not white." Now sorrow and pleasure, being passions, are specified by their objects. According to their respective genera, they are contrary to one another: since one is a kind of "pursuit," the other a kind of "avoidance," which "are to the appetite, what affirmation and denial are to the intellect" (Ethic. vi, 2). Consequently sorrow and pleasure in respect of the same object, are specifically contrary to one another: whereas sorrow and pleasure in respect of objects that are not contrary but disparate, are not specifically contrary to one another, but are also disparate; for instance, sorrow at the death of a friend, and pleasure in contemplation. If, however, those diverse objects be contrary to one another, then pleasure and sorrow are not only specifically contrary, but they also have a certain mutual fittingness and affinity: for instance to rejoice in good and to sorrow for evil.

Reply to Objection 1: Whiteness and blackness do not take their species from their relationship to something extrinsic, as pleasure and sorrow do: wherefore the comparison does not hold.

AD SECUNDUM dicendum quod genus sumitur ex materia, ut patet in VIII Metaphys. In accidentibus autem loco materiae est subiectum. Dictum est autem quod delectatio et tristitia contrariantur secundum genus. Et ideo in qualibet tristitia est contraria dispositio subiecti dispositioni quae est in qualibet delectatione, nam in qualibet delectatione appetitus se habet ut acceptans id quod habet; in qualibet autem tristitia se habet ut fugiens. Et ideo ex parte subiecti quaelibet delectatio est medicina contra quamlibet tristitiam, et quaelibet tristitia est impeditiva cuiuslibet delectationis, praecipue tamen quando delectatio tristitiae contrariatur etiam secundum speciem.

Unde patet solutio ad tertium. Vel aliter dicendum quod, etsi non omnis tristitia contrarietur omni delectationi secundum speciem, tamen quantum ad effectum contrariantur, nam ex uno confortatur natura animalis, ex alio vero quodammodo molestatur.

Reply to Objection 2: Genus is taken from matter, as is stated in Metaph. viii, 2; and in accidents the subject takes the place of matter. Now it has been said above that pleasure and sorrow are generically contrary to one another. Consequently in every sorrow the subject has a disposition contrary to the disposition of the subject of pleasure: because in every pleasure the appetite is viewed as accepting what it possesses, and in every sorrow, as avoiding it. And therefore on the part of the subject every pleasure is a remedy for any kind of sorrow, and every sorrow is a hindrance of all manner of pleasure: but chiefly when pleasure is opposed to sorrow specifically.

Wherefore the Reply to the Third Objection is evident. Or we may say that, although not every sorrow is specifically contrary to every pleasure, yet they are contrary to one another in regard to their effects: since one has the effect of strengthening the animal nature, while the other results in a kind of discomfort.

ARTICULUS 5

AD QUINTUM sic proceditur. Videtur quod delectationi contemplationis sit aliqua tristitia contraria. Dicit enim apostolus, II ad Cor. VII, *quae secundum Deum est tristitia, poenitentiam in salutem stabilem operatur.* Sed respicere ad Deum pertinet ad superiorem rationem, cuius est contemplationi vacare, secundum Augustinum, in XII de Trin. Ergo delectationi contemplationis opponitur tristitia.

PRAETEREA, contrariorum contrarii sunt effectus. Si ergo unum contrariorum contemplatum est causa delectationis, aliud erit causa tristitiae. Et sic delectationi contemplationis erit tristitia contraria.

PRAETEREA, sicut obiectum delectationis est bonum, ita obiectum tristitiae est malum. Sed contemplatio potest habere mali rationem, dicit enim philosophus, in XII Metaphys., quod *quaedam inconveniens est meditari.* Ergo contemplationis delectationi potest esse contraria tristitia.

ARTICLE 5
Whether there is any sorrow contrary to the pleasure of contemplation?

Objection 1: It would seem that there is a sorrow that is contrary to the pleasure of contemplation. For the Apostle says (2 Cor. 7:10): "The sorrow that is according to God, worketh penance steadfast unto salvation." Now to look at God belongs to the higher reason, whose act is to give itself to contemplation, according to Augustine (De Trin. xii, 3,4). Therefore there is a sorrow contrary to the pleasure of contemplation.

Objection 2: Further, contrary things have contrary effects. If therefore the contemplation of one contrary gives pleasure, the other contrary will give sorrow: and so there will be a sorrow contrary to the pleasure of contemplation.

Objection 3: Further, as the object of pleasure is good, so the object of sorrow is evil. But contemplation can be an evil: since the Philosopher says (Metaph. xii, 9) that "it is unfitting to think of certain things." Therefore sorrow can be contrary to the pleasure of contemplation.

PRAETEREA, operatio quaelibet, secundum quod non est impedita, est causa delectationis, ut dicitur in VII et X Ethic. Sed operatio contemplationis potest multipliciter impediri, vel ut totaliter non sit, vel ut cum difficultate sit. Ergo in contemplatione potest esse tristitia delectationi contraria.

PRAETEREA, carnis afflictio est causa tristitiae. Sed sicut dicitur Eccle. ult., *frequens meditatio carnis est afflictio*. Ergo contemplatio habet tristitiam delectationi contrariam.

SED CONTRA est quod dicitur Sap. VIII, *non habet amaritudinem conversatio illius,* scilicet sapientiae, *nec taedium convictus eius; sed laetitiam et gaudium.* Conversatio autem et convictus sapientiae est per contemplationem. Ergo nulla tristitia est quae sit contraria delectationi contemplationis.

RESPONDEO dicendum quod delectatio contemplationis potest intelligi dupliciter. Uno modo, ita quod contemplatio sit delectationis causa, et non obiectum. Et tunc delectatio non est de ipsa contemplatione, sed de re contemplata. Contingit autem contemplari aliquid nocivum et contristans, sicut et aliquid conveniens et delectans. Unde si sic delectatio contemplationis accipiatur, nihil prohibet delectationi contemplationis esse tristitiam contrariam. Alio modo potest dici delectatio contemplationis, quia contemplatio est eius obiectum et causa, puta cum aliquis delectatur de hoc ipso quod contemplatur. Et sic, ut dicit Gregorius Nyssenus, *ei delectationi quae est secundum contemplationem, non opponitur aliqua tristitia*. Et hoc idem philosophus dicit, in I Topic. et in X Ethic. Sed hoc est intelligendum, per se loquendo. Cuius ratio est, quia tristitia per se contrariatur delectationi quae est de contrario obiecto, sicut delectationi quae est de calore, contrariatur tristitia quae est de frigore. Obiecto autem contemplationis nihil est contrarium, contrariorum enim rationes, secundum quod sunt apprehensae, non sunt contrariae, sed unum contrarium est ratio cognoscendi

Objection 4: Further, any work, so far as it is unhindered, can be a cause of pleasure, as stated in Ethic. vii, 12,13; x, 4. But the work of contemplation can be hindered in many ways, either so as to destroy it altogether, or as to make it difficult. Therefore in contemplation there can be a sorrow contrary to the pleasure.

Objection 5: Further, affliction of the flesh is a cause of sorrow. But, as it is written (Eccles. 12:12) "much study is an affliction of the flesh." Therefore contemplation admits of sorrow contrary to its pleasure.

On the contrary, It is written (Wis. 8:16): "Her," i.e., wisdom's, "conversation hath no bitterness nor her company any tediousness; but joy and gladness." Now the conversation and company of wisdom are found in contemplation. Therefore there is no sorrow contrary to the pleasure of contemplation.

I answer that, The pleasure of contemplation can be understood in two ways. In one way, so that contemplation is the cause, but not the object of pleasure: and then pleasure is taken not in contemplating but in the thing contemplated. Now it is possible to contemplate something harmful and sorrowful, just as to contemplate something suitable and pleasant. Consequently if the pleasure of contemplation be taken in this way, nothing hinders some sorrow being contrary to the pleasure of contemplation. In another way, the pleasure of contemplation is understood, so that contemplation is its object and cause; as when one takes pleasure in the very act of contemplating. And thus, according to Gregory of Nyssa,* "no sorrow is contrary to that pleasure which is about contemplation": and the Philosopher says the same (Topic. i, 13; Ethic. x, 3). This, however, is to be understood as being the case properly speaking. The reason is because sorrow is of itself contrary to pleasure in a contrary object: thus pleasure in heat is contrary to sorrow caused by cold. But there is no contrary to the object of contemplation: because contraries, as apprehended by the mind, are not contrary, but one is the means of knowing

---

* Nemesius, De Nat. Hom. xviii.

aliud. Unde delectationi quae est in contemplando, non potest, per se loquendo, esse aliqua tristitia contraria. Sed nec etiam habet tristitiam annexam, sicut corporales delectationes, quae sunt ut medicinae quaedam contra aliquas molestias, sicut aliquis delectatur in potu ex hoc quod anxiatur siti, quando autem iam tota sitis est repulsa, etiam cessat delectatio potus. Delectatio enim contemplationis non causatur ex hoc quod excluditur aliqua molestia, sed ex hoc quod est secundum seipsam delectabilis, non est enim generatio, sed operatio quaedam perfecta, ut dictum est. Per accidens autem admiscetur tristitia delectationi apprehensionis. Et hoc dupliciter, uno modo, ex parte organi; alio modo, ex impedimento apprehensionis. Ex parte quidem organi, admiscetur tristitia vel dolor apprehensioni, directe quidem in viribus apprehensivis sensitivae partis, quae habent organum corporale, vel ex sensibili, quod est contrarium debitae complexioni organi, sicut gustus rei amarae et olfactus rei foetidae; vel ex continuitate sensibilis convenientis, quod per assiduitatem facit superexcrescentiam naturalis habitus, ut supra dictum est, et sic redditur apprehensio sensibilis quae prius erat delectabilis, taediosa. Sed haec duo directe in contemplatione mentis locum non habent, quia mens non habet organum corporale. Unde dictum est in auctoritate inducta, quod non habet contemplatio mentis nec *amaritudinem* nec *taedium*. Sed quia mens humana utitur in contemplando viribus apprehensivis sensitivis, in quarum actibus accidit lassitudo; ideo indirecte admiscetur aliqua afflictio vel dolor contemplationi. Sed neutro modo tristitia contemplationi per accidens adiuncta, contrariatur delectationi eius. Nam tristitia quae est de impedimento contemplationis, non contrariatur delectationi contemplationis, sed magis habet affinitatem et convenientiam cum ipsa, ut ex supradictis patet. Tristitia vero vel afflictio quae est de lassitudine corporali,

the other. Wherefore, properly speaking, there cannot be a sorrow contrary to the pleasure of contemplation. Nor has it any sorrow annexed to it, as bodily pleasures have, which are like remedies against certain annoyances; thus a man takes pleasure in drinking through being troubled with thirst, but when the thirst is quite driven out, the pleasure of drinking ceases also. Because the pleasure of contemplation is not caused by one's being quit of an annoyance, but by the fact that contemplation is pleasant in itself: for pleasure is not a "becoming" but a perfect operation, as stated above (I-II, q. 31, a. 1). Accidentally, however, sorrow is mingled with the pleasure of contemplation; and this in two ways: first, on the part of an organ, secondly, through some impediment in the apprehension. On the part of an organ, sorrow or pain is mingled with apprehension, directly, as regards the apprehensive powers of the sensitive part, which have a bodily organ; either from the sensible object disagreeing with the normal condition of the organ, as the taste of something bitter, and the smell of something foul; or from the sensible object, though agreeable, being so continuous in its action on the sense, that it exceeds the normal condition of the organ, as stated above (I-II, q. 33, a. 2), the result being that an apprehension which at first was pleasant becomes tedious. But these two things cannot occur directly in the contemplation of the mind; because the mind has no corporeal organ: wherefore it was said in the authority quoted above that intellectual contemplation has neither "bitterness," nor "tediousness." Since, however, the human mind, in contemplation, makes use of the sensitive powers of apprehension, to whose acts weariness is incidental; therefore some affliction or pain is indirectly mingled with contemplation. Nevertheless, in neither of these ways, is the pain thus accidentally mingled with contemplation, contrary to the pleasure thereof. Because pain caused by a hindrance to contemplation, is not contrary to the pleasure of contemplation, but rather is in affinity and in harmony with it, as is evident from what has been said above (I-II, q. 35, a. 4): while pain or sorrow caused by bodily weariness, does

non ad idem genus refertur, unde est penitus disparata. Et sic manifestum est quod delectationi quae est de ipsa contemplatione, nulla tristitia contrariatur; nec adiungitur ei aliqua tristitia nisi per accidens.

AD PRIMUM ergo dicendum quod *illa tristitia quae est secundum Deum,* non est de ipsa contemplatione mentis, sed est de aliquo quod mens contemplatur, scilicet de peccato, quod mens considerat ut contrarium dilectioni divinae.

AD SECUNDUM dicendum quod ea quae sunt contraria in rerum natura, secundum quod sunt in mente, non habent contrarietatem. Non enim rationes contrariorum sunt contrariae, sed magis unum contrarium est ratio cognoscendi aliud. Propter quod est una scientia contrariorum.

AD TERTIUM dicendum quod contemplatio, secundum se, nunquam habet rationem mali, cum contemplatio nihil aliud sit quam consideratio veri, quod est bonum intellectus, sed per accidens tantum, inquantum scilicet contemplatio vilioris impedit contemplationem melioris; vel ex parte rei contemplatae, ad quam inordinatae appetitus afficitur.

AD QUARTUM dicendum quod tristitia quae est de impedimento contemplationis, non contrariatur delectationi contemplationis, sed est ei affinis, ut dictum est.

AD QUINTUM dicendum quod afflictio carnis per accidens et indirecte se habet ad contemplationem mentis, ut dictum est.

not belong to the same genus, wherefore it is altogether disparate. Accordingly it is evident that no sorrow is contrary to pleasure taken in the very act of contemplation; nor is any sorrow connected with it save accidentally.

Reply to Objection 1: The "sorrow which is according to God," is not caused by the very act of intellectual contemplation, but by something which the mind contemplates: *viz.* by sin, which the mind considers as contrary to the love of God.

Reply to Objection 2: Things which are contrary according to nature are not contrary according as they exist in the mind: for things that are contrary in reality are not contrary in the order of thought; indeed rather is one contrary the reason for knowing the other. Hence one and the same science considers contraries.

Reply to Objection 3: Contemplation, in itself, is never evil, since it is nothing else than the consideration of truth, which is the good of the intellect: it can, however, be evil accidentally, i.e., in so far as the contemplation of a less noble object hinders the contemplation of a more noble object; or on the part of the object contemplated, to which the appetite is inordinately attached.

Reply to Objection 4: Sorrow caused by a hindrance to contemplation, is not contrary to the pleasure of contemplation, but is in harmony with it, as stated above.

Reply to Objection 5: Affliction of the flesh affects contemplation accidentally and indirectly, as stated above.

ARTICULUS 6

AD SEXTUM sic proceditur. Videtur quod magis sit fugienda tristitia, quam delectatio appetenda. Dicit enim Augustinus, in libro octoginta trium quaest., *nemo est qui non magis dolorem fugiat, quam appetat voluptatem.* Illud autem in quo communiter omnia consentiunt, videtur esse naturale. Ergo naturale est et conveniens quod plus tristitia fugiatur, quam delectatio appetatur.

ARTICLE 6
Whether sorrow is to be shunned more than pleasure is to be sought?

Objection 1: It would seem that sorrow is to be shunned more than pleasure is to be sought. For Augustine says (QQ. 83, qu. 63): "There is nobody that does not shun sorrow more than he seeks pleasure." Now that which all agree in doing, seems to be natural. Therefore it is natural and right for sorrow to be shunned more than pleasure is sought.

Praeterea, actio contrarii facit ad velocitatem et intensionem motus, *aqua enim calida citius et fortius congelatur,* ut dicit philosophus, in libro Meteor. Sed fuga tristitiae est ex contrarietate contristantis, appetitus autem delectationis non est ex aliqua contrarietate, sed magis procedit ex convenientia delectantis. Ergo maior est fuga tristitiae quam appetitus delectationis.

Praeterea, quanto aliquis secundum rationem fortiori passioni repugnat, tanto laudabilior est et virtuosior, quia *virtus est circa difficile et bonum,* ut dicitur in II Ethic. Sed fortis, qui resistit motui quo fugitur dolor, est virtuosior quam temperatus, qui resistit motui quo appetitur delectatio, dicit enim philosophus, in II Rhetoric., quod *fortes et iusti maxime honorantur.* Ergo vehementior est motus quo fugitur tristitia, quam motus quo appetitur delectatio.

Sed contra, bonum est fortius quam malum, ut patet per Dionysium, IV cap. de Div. Nom. Sed delectatio est appetibilis propter bonum, quod est eius obiectum, fuga autem tristitiae est propter malum. Ergo fortior est appetitus delectationis quam fuga tristitiae.

Respondeo dicendum quod, per se loquendo, appetitus delectationis est fortior quam fuga tristitiae. Cuius ratio est, quia causa delectationis est bonum conveniens, causa autem doloris sive tristitiae est aliquod malum repugnans. Contingit autem aliquod bonum esse conveniens absque omni dissonantia, non autem potest esse aliquod malum totaliter, absque omni convenientia, repugnans. Unde delectatio potest esse integra et perfecta, tristitia autem est semper secundum partem. Unde naturaliter maior est appetitus delectationis quam fuga tristitiae. Alia vero ratio est, quia bonum, quod est obiectum delectationis, propter seipsum appetitur, malum autem, quod est obiectum tristitiae, est fugiendum inquantum est privatio boni. Quod autem est per se, potius est illo quod est per aliud. Cuius etiam signum apparet in motibus naturalibus.

Objection 2: Further, the action of a contrary conduces to rapidity and intensity of movement: for "hot water freezes quicker and harder," as the Philosopher says (Meteor. i, 12). But the shunning of sorrow is due to the contrariety of the cause of sorrow; whereas the desire for pleasure does not arise from any contrariety, but rather from the suitableness of the pleasant object. Therefore sorrow is shunned more eagerly than pleasure is sought.

Objection 3: Further, the stronger the passion which a man resists according to reason, the more worthy is he of praise, and the more virtuous: since "virtue is concerned with the difficult and the good" (Ethic. ii, 3). But the brave man who resists the movement of shunning sorrow, is more virtuous than the temperate man, who resists the movement of desire for pleasure: since the Philosopher says (Rhet. ii, 4) that "the brave and the just are chiefly praised." Therefore the movement of shunning sorrow is more eager than the movement of seeking pleasure.

On the contrary, Good is stronger than evil, as Dionysius declares (Div. Nom. iv). But pleasure is desirable for the sake of the good which is its object; whereas the shunning of sorrow is on account of evil. Therefore the desire for pleasure is more eager than the shunning of sorrow.

I answer that, The desire for pleasure is of itself more eager than the shunning of sorrow. The reason of this is that the cause of pleasure is a suitable good; while the cause of pain or sorrow is an unsuitable evil. Now it happens that a certain good is suitable without any repugnance at all: but it is not possible for any evil to be so unsuitable as not to be suitable in some way. Wherefore pleasure can be entire and perfect: whereas sorrow is always partial. Therefore desire for pleasure is naturally greater than the shunning of sorrow. Another reason is because the good, which is the object of pleasure, is sought for its own sake: whereas the evil, which is the object of sorrow, is to be shunned as being a privation of good: and that which is by reason of itself is stronger than that which is by reason of something else. Moreover we find a confirmation of this in natural movements.

Nam omnis motus naturalis intensior est in fine, cum appropinquat ad terminum suae naturae convenientem, quam in principio, cum recedit a termino suae naturae non convenienti, quasi natura magis tendat in id quod est sibi conveniens, quam fugiat id quod est sibi repugnans. Unde et inclinatio appetitivae virtutis, per se loquendo, vehementius tendit in delectationem quam fugiat tristitiam. Sed per accidens contingit quod **tristitiam aliquis magis fugit, quam delectationem appetat.** Et hoc tripliciter. Primo quidem, ex parte apprehensionis. Quia, ut Augustinus dicit, X de Trin., *amor magis sentitur, cum eum prodit indigentia.* Ex indigentia autem amati procedit tristitia, quae est ex amissione alicuius boni amati, vel ex incursu alicuius mali contrarii. Delectatio autem non habet indigentiam boni amati, sed quiescit in eo iam adepto. Cum igitur amor sit causa delectationis et tristitiae, tanto magis fugitur tristitia, quanto magis sentitur amor ex eo quod contrariatur amori. Secundo, ex parte causae contristantis, vel dolorem inferentis, quae repugnat bono magis amato quam sit bonum illud in quo delectamur. Magis enim amamus consistentiam corporis naturalem, quam delectationem cibi. Et ideo timore doloris qui provenit ex flagellis vel aliis huiusmodi, quae contrariantur bonae consistentiae corporis, dimittimus delectationem ciborum vel aliorum huiusmodi. Tertio, ex parte effectus, inquantum scilicet tristitia impedit non unam tantum delectationem, sed omnes.

AD PRIMUM ergo dicendum quod illud quod Augustinus dicit, quod *dolor magis fugitur quam voluptas appetatur,* est verum per accidens, et non per se. Et hoc patet ex eo quod subdit, *quandoquidem videmus etiam immanissimas bestias a maximis voluptatibus absterreri dolorum metu,* qui contrariatur vitae, quae maxime amatur.

AD SECUNDUM dicendum quod aliter est in motu qui est ab interiori, et aliter in motu qui est ab exteriori. Motus enim qui est ab interiori, magis tendit in id quod est conveniens, quam recedat a contrario, sicut supra dictum est de motu naturali. Sed motus qui est ab extrinseco,

For every natural movement is more intense in the end, when a thing approaches the term that is suitable to its nature, than at the beginning, when it leaves the term that is unsuitable to its nature: as though nature were more eager in tending to what is suitable to it, than in shunning what is unsuitable. Therefore the inclination of the appetitive power is, of itself, more eager in tending to pleasure than in shunning sorrow. But it happens **accidentally that a man shuns sorrow more eagerly than he seeks pleasure:** and this for three reasons. First, on the part of the apprehension. Because, as Augustine says (De Trin. x, 12), "love is felt more keenly, when we lack that which we love." Now from the lack of what we love, sorrow results, which is caused either by the loss of some loved good, or by the presence of some contrary evil. But pleasure suffers no lack of the good loved, for it rests in possession of it. Since then love is the cause of pleasure and sorrow, the latter is more the shunned, according as love is the more keenly felt on account of that which is contrary to it. Secondly, on the part of the cause of sorrow or pain, which cause is repugnant to a good that is more loved than the good in which we take pleasure. For we love the natural well-being of the body more than the pleasure of eating: and consequently we would leave the pleasure of eating and the like, from fear of the pain occasioned by blows or other such causes, which are contrary to the well-being of the body. Thirdly, on the part of the effect: namely, in so far as sorrow hinders not only one pleasure, but all.

Reply to Objection 1: The saying of Augustine that "sorrow is shunned more than pleasure is sought" is true accidentally but not simply. And this is clear from what he says after: "Since we see that the most savage animals are deterred from the greatest pleasures by fear of pain," which pain is contrary to life which is loved above all.

Reply to Objection 2: It is not the same with movement from within and movement from without. For movement from within tends to what is suitable more than it recedes from that which is unsuitable; as we remarked above in regard to natural movement. But movement from without

intenditur ex ipsa contrarietate, quia unumquodque suo modo nititur ad resistendum contrario, sicut ad conservationem sui ipsius. Unde motus violentus intenditur in principio, et remittitur in fine. Motus autem appetitivae partis est ab intrinseco, cum sit ab anima ad res. Et ideo, per se loquendo, magis appetitur delectatio quam fugiatur tristitia. Sed motus sensitivae partis est ab exteriori, quasi a rebus ad animam. Unde magis sentitur quod est magis contrarium. Et sic etiam per accidens, inquantum sensus requiritur ad delectationem et tristitiam, magis fugitur tristitia quam delectatio appetatur.

AD TERTIUM dicendum quod fortis non laudatur ex eo quod secundum rationem non vincitur a dolore vel tristitia quacumque, sed ea quae consistit in periculis mortis. Quae quidem tristitia magis fugitur quam appetatur delectatio ciborum vel venereorum, circa quam est temperantia, sicut vita magis amatur quam cibus vel coitus. Sed temperatus magis laudatur ex hoc quod non prosequitur delectationes tactus, quam ex hoc quod non fugit tristitias contrarias, ut patet in III Ethic.

is intensified by the very opposition: because each thing strives in its own way to resist anything contrary to it, as aiming at its own preservation. Hence violent movement is intense at first, and slackens towards the end. Now the movement of the appetitive faculty is from within: since it tends from the soul to the object. Consequently pleasure is, of itself, more to be sought than sorrow is to be shunned. But the movement of the sensitive faculty is from without, as it were from the object of the soul. Consequently the more contrary a thing is the more it is felt. And then too, accidentally, in so far as the senses are requisite for pleasure and pain, pain is shunned more than pleasure is sought.

Reply to Objection 3: A brave man is not praised because, in accordance with reason, he is not overcome by any kind of sorrow or pain whatever, but because he is not overcome by that which is concerned with the dangers of death. And this kind of sorrow is more shunned, than pleasures of the table or of sexual intercourse are sought, which latter pleasures are the object of temperance: thus life is loved more than food and sexual pleasure. But the temperate man is praised for refraining from pleasures of touch, more than for not shunning the pains which are contrary to them, as is stated in Ethic. iii, 11.

Articulus 7

AD SEPTIMUM sic proceditur. Videtur quod dolor exterior sit maior quam dolor cordis interior. Dolor enim exterior causatur ex causa repugnante bonae consistentiae corporis, in quo est vita, dolor autem interior causatur ex aliqua imaginatione mali. Cum ergo vita magis ametur quam imaginatum bonum, videtur, secundum praedicta, quod dolor exterior sit maior quam dolor interior.

PRAETEREA, res magis movet quam rei similitudo. Sed dolor exterior provenit ex reali coniunctione alicuius contrarii, dolor autem interior ex similitudine contrarii apprehensa. Ergo maior est dolor exterior quam dolor interior.

Article 7
Whether outward pain is greater than interior sorrow?

Objection 1: It would seem that outward pain is greater than interior sorrow of the heart. Because outward pain arises from a cause repugnant to the well-being of the body in which is life: whereas interior sorrow is caused by some evil in the imagination. Since, therefore, life is loved more than an imagined good, it seems that, according to what has been said above (I-II, q. 35, a. 6), outward pain is greater than interior sorrow.

Objection 2: Further, the reality moves more than its likeness does. But outward pain arises from the real conjunction of some contrary; whereas inward sorrow arises from the apprehended likeness of a contrary. Therefore outward pain is greater than inward sorrow.

Praeterea, causa ex effectu cognoscitur. Sed dolor exterior habet fortiores effectus, facilius enim homo moritur propter dolores exteriores quam propter dolorem interiorem. Ergo exterior dolor est maior, et magis fugitur, quam dolor interior.

Sed contra est quod dicitur Eccli. XXV, *omnis plaga tristitia cordis est, et omnis malitia nequitia mulieris.* Ergo, sicut nequitia mulieris alias nequitias superat, ut ibi intenditur; ita tristitia cordis omnem plagam exteriorem excedit.

Respondeo dicendum quod dolor interior et exterior in uno conveniunt, et in duobus differunt. Conveniunt quidem in hoc, quod uterque est motus appetitivae virtutis, ut supra dictum est. Differunt autem secundum illa duo quae ad tristitiam et delectationem requiruntur, scilicet secundum causam, quae est bonum vel malum coniunctum; et secundum apprehensionem. Causa enim doloris exterioris est malum coniunctum quod repugnat corpori, causa autem interioris doloris est malum coniunctum quod repugnat appetitui. Dolor etiam exterior sequitur apprehensionem sensus, et specialiter tactus, dolor autem interior sequitur apprehensionem interiorem, imaginationis scilicet vel etiam rationis. Si ergo comparatur causa interioris doloris ad causam exterioris, una per se pertinet ad appetitum, cuius est uterque dolor, alia vero per aliud. Nam dolor interior est ex hoc quod aliquid repugnat ipsi appetitui, exterior autem dolor, ex hoc quod repugnat appetitui quia repugnat corpori. Semper autem quod est per se, prius est eo quod est per aliud. Unde ex parte ista, dolor interior praeeminet dolori exteriori. Similiter etiam ex parte apprehensionis. Nam apprehensio rationis et imaginationis altior est quam apprehensio sensu tactus. Unde simpliciter et per se loquendo, dolor interior potior est quam dolor exterior. Cuius signum est, quod etiam dolores exteriores aliquis voluntarie suscipit, ut evitet

Objection 3: Further, a cause is known by its effect. But outward pain has more striking effects: since man dies sooner of outward pain than of interior sorrow. Therefore outward pain is greater and is shunned more than interior sorrow.

On the contrary, it is written (Ecclus. 25:17): "The sadness of the heart is every wound,* and the wickedness of a woman is all evil." Therefore, just as the wickedness of a woman surpasses all other wickedness, as the text implies; so sadness of the heart surpasses every outward wound.

I answer that, Interior and exterior pain agree in one point and differ in two. They agree in this, that each is a movement of the appetitive power, as stated above (I-II, q. 35, a. 1). But they differ in respect of those two things which are requisite for pain and pleasure; namely, in respect of the cause, which is a conjoined good or evil; and in respect of the apprehension. For the cause of outward pain is a conjoined evil repugnant to the body; while the cause of inward pain is a conjoined evil repugnant to the appetite. Again, outward pain arises from an apprehension of sense, chiefly of touch; while inward pain arises from an interior apprehension, of the imagination or of the reason. If then we compare the cause of inward pain to the cause of outward pain, the former belongs, of itself, to the appetite to which both these pains belong: while the latter belongs to the appetite directly. Because inward pain arises from something being repugnant to the appetite itself, while outward pain arises from something being repugnant to the appetite, through being repugnant to the body. Now, that which is of itself is always prior to that which is by reason of another. Wherefore, from this point of view, inward pain surpasses outward pain. In like manner also on the part of apprehension: because the apprehension of reason and imagination is of a higher order than the apprehension of the sense of touch. Consequently inward pain is, simply and of itself, more keen than outward pain: a sign whereof is that one willingly undergoes outward pain in order to avoid

---

* Douay: 'plague'

interiorem dolorem. Et inquantum non repugnat dolor exterior interiori appetitui, fit quodammodo delectabilis et iucundus interiori gaudio. Quandoque tamen dolor exterior est cum interiori dolore, et tunc dolor augetur. Non solum enim interior dolor est maior quam exterior, sed etiam universalior. Quidquid enim est repugnans corpori, potest esse repugnans interiori appetitui; et quidquid apprehenditur sensu, potest apprehendi imaginatione et ratione; sed non convertitur. Et ideo signanter in auctoritate adducta dicitur, *omnis plaga tristitia cordis est,* quia etiam dolores exteriorum plagarum sub interiori cordis tristitia comprehenduntur.

AD PRIMUM ergo dicendum quod dolor interior potest etiam esse de his quae contrariantur vitae. Et sic comparatio doloris interioris ad exteriorem non est accipienda secundum diversa mala quae sunt causa doloris, sed secundum diversam comparationem huius causae doloris ad appetitum.

AD SECUNDUM dicendum quod tristitia interior non procedit ex similitudine rei apprehensa, sicut ex causa, non enim homo tristatur interius de ipsa similitudine apprehensa, sed de re cuius est similitudo. Quae quidem res tanto perfectius apprehenditur per aliquam similitudinem, quanto similitudo est magis immaterialis et abstracta. Et ideo dolor interior, per se loquendo, est maior, tanquam de maiori malo existens; propter hoc quod interiori apprehensione magis cognoscitur malum.

AD TERTIUM dicendum quod immutationes corporales magis causantur ex dolore exteriori, tum quia causa doloris exterioris est corrumpens coniunctum corporaliter, quod exigit apprehensio tactus. Tum etiam quia sensus exterior est magis corporalis quam sensus interior, sicut et appetitus sensitivus quam intellectivus. Et propter hoc, ut supra dictum est, ex motu appetitus sensitivi magis corpus immutatur. Et similiter ex dolore exteriori, magis quam ex dolore interiori.

inward pain: and in so far as outward pain is not repugnant to the interior appetite, it becomes in a manner pleasant and agreeable by way of inward joy. Sometimes, however, outward pain is accompanied by inward pain, and then the pain is increased. Because inward pain is not only greater than outward pain, it is also more universal: since whatever is repugnant to the body, can be repugnant to the interior appetite; and whatever is apprehended by sense may be apprehended by imagination and reason, but not conversely. Hence in the passage quoted above it is said expressively: "Sadness of the heart is every wound," because even the pains of outward wounds are comprised in the interior sorrows of the heart.

Reply to Objection 1: Inward pain can also arise from things that are destructive of life. And then the comparison of inward to outward pain must not be taken in reference to the various evils that cause pain; but in regard to the various ways in which this cause of pain is compared to the appetite.

Reply to Objection 2: Inward pain is not caused by the apprehended likeness of a thing: for a man is not inwardly pained by the apprehended likeness itself, but by the thing which the likeness represents. And this thing is all the more perfectly apprehended by means of its likeness, as this likeness is more immaterial and abstract. Consequently inward pain is, of itself, greater, as being caused by a greater evil, forasmuch as evil is better known by an inward apprehension.

Reply to Objection 3: Bodily changes are more liable to be caused by outward pain, both from the fact that outward pain is caused by a corruptive conjoined corporally, which is a necessary condition of the sense of touch; and from the fact that the outward sense is more material than the inward sense, just as the sensitive appetite is more material than the intellective. For this reason, as stated above (I-II, q. 22, a. 3; q. 31, a. 5), the body undergoes a greater change from the movement of the sensitive appetite: and, in like manner, from outward than from inward pain.

Articulus 8

Ad octavum sic proceditur. Videtur quod Damascenus inconvenienter quatuor tristitiae species assignet, quae sunt *acedia, achthos* (vel *anxietas* secundum Gregorium Nyssenum), *misericordia* et *invidia*. Tristitia enim delectationi opponitur. Sed delectationis non assignantur aliquae species. Ergo nec tristitiae species debent assignari.

Praeterea, *poenitentia* est quaedam species tristitiae. Similiter etiam *nemesis* et *zelus,* ut dicit philosophus, II Rhetoric. Quae quidem sub his speciebus non comprehenduntur. Ergo insufficiens est eius praedicta divisio.

Praeterea, omnis divisio debet esse per opposita. Sed praedicta non habent oppositionem ad invicem. Nam secundum Gregorium *acedia est tristitia vocem amputans; anxietas vero est tristitia aggravans; invidia vero est tristitia in alienis bonis; misericordia autem est tristitia in alienis malis.* Contingit autem aliquem tristari et de alienis malis, et de alienis bonis et simul cum hoc interius aggravari, et exterius vocem amittere. Ergo praedicta divisio non est conveniens.

Sed contra est auctoritas utriusque, scilicet Gregorii Nysseni et Damasceni.

Respondeo dicendum quod ad rationem speciei pertinet quod se habeat ex additione ad genus. Sed generi potest aliquid addi dupliciter. Uno modo, quod per se ad ipsum pertinet, et virtute continetur in ipso, sicut *rationale* additur *animali.* Et talis additio facit veras species alicuius generis, ut per philosophum patet, in VII et VIII Metaphys. Aliquid vero additur generi quasi aliquid extraneum a ratione ipsius, sicut si *album animali* addatur, vel aliquid huiusmodi. Et talis additio non facit veras species generis, secundum quod communiter loquimur de genere et

Article 8
Whether there are only four species of sorrow?

Objection 1: It would seem that Damascene's (De Fide Orth. ii, 14) division of sorrow into four species is incorrect; *viz.* into "torpor," distress," which Gregory of Nyssa* calls "anxiety,"—"pity," and "envy." For sorrow is contrary to pleasure. But there are not several species of pleasure. Therefore it is incorrect to assign different species of sorrow.

Objection 2: Further, "Repentance" is a species of sorrow; and so are "indignation" and "jealousy," as the Philosopher states (Rhet. ii, 9,11). But these are not included in the above species. Therefore this division is insufficient.

Objection 3: Further, the members of a division should be things that are opposed to one another. But these species are not opposed to one another. For according to Gregory,† "torpor is sorrow depriving of speech; anxiety is the sorrow that weighs down; envy is sorrow for another's good; pity is sorrow for another's wrongs." But it is possible for one to sorrow for another's wrongs, and for another's good, and at the same time to be weighed down inwardly, and outwardly to be speechless. Therefore this division is correct.

On the contrary, stands the twofold authority of Gregory of Nyssa‡ and of Damascene.

I answer that, It belongs to the notion of a species that it is something added to the genus. But a thing can be added to a genus in two ways. First, as something belonging of itself to the genus, and virtually contained therein: thus "rational" is added to "animal." Such an addition makes true species of a genus: as the Philosopher says (Metaph. vii, 12; viii, 2,3). But, secondly, a thing may be added to a genus, that is, as it were, foreign to the notion conveyed by that genus: thus "white" or something of the kind may be added to "animal." Such an addition does not make true species of the genus, according to the usual sense in which we speak of genera and

---

* Nemesius, De Nat. Hom. xix.
† Ibid.
‡ Nemesius

speciebus. Interdum tamen dicitur aliquid esse species alicuius generis propter hoc quod habet aliquid extraneum ad quod applicatur generis ratio, sicut carbo et flamma dicuntur esse species ignis, propter applicationem naturae ignis ad materiam alienam. Et simili modo loquendi dicuntur astrologia et perspectiva species mathematicae, inquantum principia mathematica applicantur ad materiam naturalem. Et hoc modo loquendi assignantur hic species tristitiae, per applicationem rationis tristitiae ad aliquid extraneum. Quod quidem extraneum accipi potest vel ex parte causae, obiecti; vel ex parte effectus. Proprium enim obiectum tristitiae est *proprium malum*. Unde extraneum obiectum tristitiae accipi potest vel secundum alterum tantum, quia scilicet est malum, sed non proprium, et sic est *misericordia*, quae est tristitia de alieno malo, inquantum tamen aestimatur ut proprium. Vel quantum ad utrumque, quia neque est de proprio, neque de malo, sed de bono alieno, inquantum tamen bonum alienum aestimatur ut proprium malum, et sic est *invidia*. Proprius autem effectus tristitiae consistit in quadam *fuga appetitus*. Unde extraneum circa effectum tristitiae, potest accipi quantum ad alterum tantum, quia scilicet tollitur fuga, et sic est *anxietas* quae sic aggravat animum, ut non appareat aliquod refugium, unde alio nomine dicitur *angustia*. Si vero intantum procedat talis aggravatio, ut etiam exteriora membra immobilitet ab opere, quod pertinet ad *acediam;* sic erit extraneum quantum ad utrumque, quia nec est fuga, nec est in appetitu. Ideo autem specialiter acedia dicitur vocem amputare, quia vox inter omnes exteriores motus magis exprimit interiorem conceptum et affectum, non solum in hominibus, sed etiam in aliis animalibus, ut dicitur in I Polit.

Ad primum ergo dicendum quod delectatio causatur ex bono, quod uno modo dicitur. Et ideo delectationis non assignantur tot species sicut tristitiae, quae causatur ex malo, quod *multifariam contingit*, ut dicit Dionysius, IV cap. de Div. Nom.

species. But sometimes a thing is said to be a species of a certain genus, through having something foreign to that genus indeed, but to which the notion of that genus is applicable: thus a live coal or a flame is said to be a species of fire, because in each of them the nature of fire is applied to a foreign matter. In like manner we speak of astronomy and perspective as being species of mathematics, inasmuch as the principles of mathematics are applied to natural matter. In accordance with this manner of speaking, the species of sorrow are reckoned by an application of the notion of sorrow to something foreign to it. This foreign matter may be taken on the part of the cause or the object, or of the effect. For the proper object of sorrow is "one's own evil." Hence sorrow may be concerned for an object foreign to it either through one's being sorry for an evil that is not one's own; and thus we have "pity" which is sorrow for another's evil, considered, however, as one's own: or through one's being sorry for something that is neither evil nor one's own, but another's good, considered, however, as one's own evil: and thus we have "envy." The proper effect of sorrow consists in a certain "flight of the appetite." Wherefore the foreign element in the effect of sorrow, may be taken so as to affect the first part only, by excluding flight: and thus we have "anxiety" which weighs on the mind, so as to make escape seem impossible: hence it is also called "perplexity." If, however, the mind be weighed down so much, that even the limbs become motionless, which belongs to "torpor," then we have the foreign element affecting both, since there is neither flight, nor is the effect in the appetite. And the reason why torpor especially is said to deprive one of speech is because of all the external movements the voice is the best expression of the inward thought and desire, not only in men, but also in other animals, as is stated in Polit. i, 1.

Reply to Objection 1: Pleasure is caused by good, which has only one meaning: and so pleasure is not divided into several species as sorrow is; for the latter is caused by evil, which "happens in many ways," as Dionysius says (Div. Nom. iv).

AD SECUNDUM dicendum quod poenitentia est de malo proprio, quod per se est obiectum tristitiae. Unde non pertinet ad has species. Zelus vero et Nemesis sub invidia continentur, ut infra patebit.

AD TERTIUM dicendum quod divisio ista non sumitur secundum oppositiones specierum, sed secundum diversitatem extraneorum ad quae trahitur ratio tristitiae, ut dictum est.

Reply to Objection 2: Repentance is for one's own evil, which is the proper object of sorrow: wherefore it does not belong to these species. Jealousy and indignation are included in envy, as we shall explain later (II-II, q. 36, a. 2).

Reply to Objection 3: This division is not according to opposite species; but according to the diversity of foreign matter to which the notion of sorrow is applied, as stated above.

QUAESTIO XXXVI

Deinde considerandum est de causis tristitiae. Et circa hoc quaeruntur quatuor. *Primo,* utrum causa doloris sit bonum amissum, vel magis malum coniunctum. *Secundo,* utrum concupiscentia sit causa doloris. *Tertio,* utrum appetitus unitatis sit causa doloris. *Quarto,* utrum potestas cui resisti non potest, sit causa doloris.

QUESTION 36
Of the Causes of Sorrow or Pain

We must now consider the causes of sorrow: under which head there are four points of inquiry: 1. Whether sorrow is caused by the loss of a good or rather by the presence of an evil? 2. Whether desire is a cause of sorrow? 3. Whether the craving for unity is a cause of sorrow? 4. Whether an irresistible power is a cause of sorrow?

ARTICULUS 1

AD PRIMUM sic proceditur. Videtur quod bonum amissum sit magis causa doloris quam malum coniunctum. Dicit enim Augustinus, in libro de octo quaestionibus Dulcitii, dolorem esse de amissione bonorum temporalium. Eadem ergo ratione, quilibet dolor ex amissione alicuius boni contingit.

PRAETEREA, supra dictum est quod dolor qui delectationi contrariatur, est de eodem de quo est delectatio. Sed delectatio est de bono, sicut supra dictum est. Ergo dolor est principaliter de amissione boni.

PRAETEREA, secundum Augustinum, XIV de Civ. Dei, amor est causa tristitiae, sicut et aliarum affectionum animae. Sed obiectum amoris est bonum. Ergo dolor vel tristitia magis respicit bonum amissum quam malum coniunctum.

SED CONTRA est quod Damascenus dicit, in II libro, quod *expectatum malum timorem constituit, praesens vero tristitiam.*

ARTICLE 1
Whether sorrow is caused by the loss of good or by the presence of evil?

Objection 1: It would seem that sorrow is caused by the loss of a good rather than by the presence of an evil. For Augustine says (De viii QQ. Dulcit. qu. 1) that sorrow is caused by the loss of temporal goods. Therefore, in like manner, every sorrow is caused by the loss of some good.

Objection 2: Further, it was said above (I-II, q. 35, a. 4) that the sorrow which is contrary to a pleasure, has the same object as that pleasure. But the object of pleasure is good, as stated above (I-II, q. 23, a. 4; q. 31, a. 1; q. 35, a. 3). Therefore sorrow is caused chiefly by the loss of good.

Objection 3: Further, according to Augustine (De Civ. Dei xiv, 7,9), love is the cause of sorrow, as of the other emotions of the soul. But the object of love is good. Therefore pain or sorrow is felt for the loss of good rather than for an evil that is present.

On the contrary, Damascene says (De Fide Orth. ii, 12) that "the dreaded evil gives rise to fear, the present evil is the cause of sorrow."

RESPONDEO dicendum quod, si hoc modo se haberent privationes in apprehensione animae, sicut se habent in ipsis rebus, ista quaestio nullius momenti esse videretur. Malum enim, ut in primo libro habitum est, est privatio boni, privatio autem, in rerum natura, nihil est aliud quam carentia oppositi habitus, secundum hoc ergo, idem esset tristari de bono amisso, et de malo habito. Sed tristitia est motus appetitus apprehensionem sequentis. In apprehensione autem ipsa privatio habet rationem cuiusdam entis, unde dicitur *ens rationis*. Et sic malum, cum sit privatio, se habet per modum *contrarii*. Et ideo, quantum ad motum appetitivum, differt utrum respiciat principalius malum coniunctum, vel bonum amissum. Et quia motus appetitus animalis hoc modo se habet in operibus animae, sicut motus naturalis in rebus naturalibus; ex consideratione naturalium motuum veritas accipi potest. Si enim accipiamus in motibus naturalibus accessum et recessum, accessus per se respicit id quod est conveniens naturae; recessus autem per se respicit id quod est contrarium; sicut grave per se recedit a loco superiori, accedit autem naturaliter ad locum inferiorem. Sed si accipiamus causam utriusque motus, scilicet gravitatem, ipsa gravitas per prius inclinat ad locum deorsum, quam retrahat a loco sursum, a quo recedit ut deorsum tendat. Sic igitur, cum tristitia in motibus appetitivis se habeat per modum fugae vel recessus, delectatio autem per modum prosecutionis vel accessus; sicut delectatio per prius respicit bonum adeptum, quasi proprium obiectum, ita tristitia respicit malum coniunctum. Sed causa delectationis et tristitiae, scilicet amor, per prius respicit bonum quam malum. Sic ergo eo modo quo obiectum est causa passionis, magis proprie est causa tristitiae vel doloris malum coniunctum, quam bonum amissum.

AD PRIMUM ergo dicendum quod ipsa amissio boni apprehenditur sub ratione mali, sicut et amissio mali apprehenditur sub ratione boni. Et ideo

I answer that, If privations, as considered by the mind, were what they are in reality, this question would seem to be of no importance. For, as stated in the I, q. 14, a. 10 and I, q. 48, a. 3, evil is the privation of good: and privation is in reality nothing else than the lack of the contrary habit; so that, in this respect, to sorrow for the loss of good, would be the same as to sorrow for the presence of evil. But sorrow is a movement of the appetite in consequence of an apprehension: and even a privation, as apprehended, has the aspect of a being, wherefore it is called "a being of reason." And in this way evil, being a privation, is regarded as a "contrary." Accordingly, so far as the movement of the appetite is concerned, it makes a difference which of the two it regards chiefly, the present evil or the good which is lost. Again, since the movement of the animal appetite holds the same place in the actions of the soul, as natural movement in natural things; the truth of the matter is to be found by considering natural movements. For if, in natural movements, we observe those of approach and withdrawal, approach is of itself directed to something suitable to nature; while withdrawal is of itself directed to something contrary to nature; thus a heavy body, of itself, withdraws from a higher place, and approaches naturally to a lower place. But if we consider the cause of both these movements, *viz.* gravity, then gravity itself inclines towards the lower place more than it withdraws from the higher place, since withdrawal from the latter is the reason for its downward tendency. Accordingly, since, in the movements of the appetite, sorrow is a kind of flight or withdrawal, while pleasure is a kind of pursuit or approach; just as pleasure regards first the good possessed, as its proper object, so sorrow regards the evil that is present. On the other hand love, which is the cause of pleasure and sorrow, regards good rather than evil: and therefore, forasmuch as the object is the cause of a passion, the present evil is more properly the cause of sorrow or pain, than the good which is lost.

Reply to Objection 1: The loss itself of good is apprehended as an evil, just as the loss of evil is apprehended as a good: and in this

Augustinus dicit dolorem provenire ex amissione temporalium bonorum.

AD SECUNDUM dicendum quod delectatio et dolor ei contrarius respiciunt idem, sed sub contraria ratione, nam si delectatio est de praesentia alicuius, tristitia est de absentia eiusdem. In uno autem contrariorum includitur privatio alterius, ut patet in X Metaphys. Et inde est quod tristitia quae est de contrario, est quodammodo de eodem sub contraria ratione.

AD TERTIUM dicendum quod, quando ex una causa proveniunt multi motus, non oportet quod omnes principalius respiciant illud quod principalius respicit causa, sed primus tantum. Unusquisque autem aliorum principalius respicit illud quod est ei conveniens secundum propriam rationem.

ARTICULUS 2

AD SECUNDUM sic proceditur. Videtur quod concupiscentia non sit causa doloris seu tristitiae. Tristitia enim per se respicit malum, ut dictum est. Concupiscentia autem est motus quidam appetitus in bonum. Motus autem qui est in unum contrarium, non est causa motus qui respicit aliud contrarium. Ergo concupiscentia non est causa doloris.

PRAETEREA, dolor, secundum Damascenum, est de praesenti, concupiscentia autem est de futuro. Ergo concupiscentia non est causa doloris.

PRAETEREA, id quod est per se delectabile, non est causa doloris. Sed concupiscentia est secundum seipsam delectabilis, ut philosophus dicit, in I Rhetoric. Ergo concupiscentia non est causa doloris seu tristitiae.

SED CONTRA est quod Augustinus dicit, in Enchirid., *subintrantibus ignorantia agendarum rerum, et concupiscentia noxiarum, comites subinferuntur error et dolor.* Sed ignorantia est causa erroris. Ergo concupiscentia est causa doloris.

RESPONDEO dicendum quod tristitia est motus quidam appetitus animalis. Motus autem appetitivus habet, sicut dictum est, similitudinem appetitus naturalis.

sense Augustine says that pain results from the loss of temporal goods.

Reply to Objection 2: Pleasure and its contrary pain have the same object, but under contrary aspects: because if the presence of a particular thin be the object of pleasure, the absence of that same thing is the object of sorrow. Now one contrary includes the privation of the other, as stated in Metaph. x, 4: and consequently sorrow in respect of one contrary is, in a way, directed to the same thing under a contrary aspect.

Reply to Objection 3: When many movements arise from one cause, it does not follow that they all regard chiefly that which the cause regards chiefly, but only the first of them. And each of the others regards chiefly that which is suitable to it according to its own nature.

ARTICLE 2
Whether desire is a cause of sorrow?

Objection 1: It would seem that desire is not a cause of pain or sorrow. Because sorrow of itself regards evil, as stated above (I-II, q. 36, a. 1): whereas desire is a movement of the appetite towards good. Now movement towards one contrary is not a cause of movement towards the other contrary. Therefore desire is not a cause of pain.

Objection 2: Further, pain, according to Damascene (De Fide Orth. ii, 12), is caused by something present; whereas the object of desire is something future. Therefore desire is not a cause of pain.

Objection 3: Further, that which is pleasant in itself is not a cause of pain. But desire is pleasant in itself, as the Philosopher says (Rhet. i, 11). Therefore desire is not a cause of pain or sorrow.

On the contrary, Augustine says (Enchiridion xxiv): "When ignorance of things necessary to be done, and desire of things hurtful, found their way in: error and pain stole an entrance in their company." But ignorance is the cause of error. Therefore desire is a cause of sorrow.

I answer that, Sorrow is a movement of the animal appetite. Now, as stated above (I-II, q. 36, a. 1), the appetitive movement is likened to the natural appetite; a likeness,

Cuius duplex causa assignari potest, una per modum finis; alia sicut unde est principium motus. Sicut descensionis corporis gravis causa sicut finis, est locus deorsum, principium autem motus est inclinatio naturalis, quae est ex gravitate. Causa autem motus appetitivi per modum finis, est eius obiectum. Et sic supra dictum est quod causa doloris seu tristitiae est malum coniunctum. Causa autem sicut unde est principium talis motus, est interior inclinatio appetitus. Qui quidem per prius inclinatur ad bonum; et ex consequenti ad repudiandum malum contrarium. Et ideo huiusmodi motus appetitivi primum principium est amor, qui est prima inclinatio appetitus ad bonum consequendum, secundum autem principium est odium, quod est inclinatio prima appetitus ad malum fugiendum. Sed quia concupiscentia vel cupiditas est primus effectus amoris, quo maxime delectamur, ut supra dictum est; ideo frequenter Augustinus cupiditatem vel concupiscentiam pro amore ponit, ut etiam supra dictum est. Et hoc modo concupiscentiam dicit esse universalem causam doloris. Sed ipsa concupiscentia, secundum propriam rationem considerata, est interdum causa doloris. Omne enim quod impedit motum ne perveniat ad terminum, est contrarium motui. Illud autem quod est contrarium motui appetitus, est contristans. Et sic per consequens concupiscentia fit causa tristitiae, inquantum de retardatione boni concupiti, vel totali ablatione, tristamur. Universalis autem causa doloris esse non potest, quia magis dolemus de subtractione bonorum praesentium, in quibus iam delectamur, quam futurorum, quae concupiscimus.

AD PRIMUM ergo dicendum quod inclinatio appetitus ad bonum consequendum, est causa inclinationis appetitus ad malum fugiendum, sicut dictum est. Et ex hoc contingit quod motus appetitivi qui respiciunt bonum, ponuntur causa motuum appetitus qui respiciunt malum.

that may be assigned to a twofold cause; one, on the part of the end, the other, on the part of the principle of movement. Thus, on the part of the end, the cause of a heavy body's downward movement is the lower place; while the principle of that movement is a natural inclination resulting from gravity. Now the cause of the appetitive movement, on the part of the end, is the object of that movement. And thus, it has been said above (I-II, q. 36, a. 1) that the cause of pain or sorrow is a present evil. On the other hand, the cause, by way or principle, of that movement, is the inward inclination of the appetite; which inclination regards, first of all, the good, and in consequence, the rejection of a contrary evil. Hence the first principle of this appetitive movement is love, which is the first inclination of the appetite towards the possession of good: while the second principle is hatred, which is the first inclination of the appetite towards the avoidance of evil. But since concupiscence or desire is the first effect of love, which gives rise to the greatest pleasure, as stated above (I-II, q. 32, a. 6); hence it is that Augustine often speaks of desire or concupiscence in the sense of love, as was also stated (I-II, q. 30, a. 2, ad 2): and in this sense he says that desire is the universal cause of sorrow. Sometimes, however, desire taken in its proper sense, is the cause of sorrow. Because whatever hinders a movement from reaching its end is contrary to that movement. Now that which is contrary to the movement of the appetite, is a cause of sorrow. Consequently, desire becomes a cause of sorrow, in so far as we sorrow for the delay of a desired good, or for its entire removal. But it cannot be a universal cause of sorrow: since we sorrow more for the loss of present good, in which we have already taken pleasure, than for the withdrawal of future good which we desire to have.

Reply to Objection 1: The inclination of the appetite to the possession of good causes the inclination of the appetite to fly from evil, as stated above. And hence it is that the appetitive movements that regard good, are reckoned as causing the appetitive movements that regard evil.

Ad secundum dicendum quod illud quod concupiscitur, etsi realiter sit futurum, est tamen quodammodo praesens, inquantum speratur. Vel potest dici quod, licet ipsum bonum concupitum sit futurum, tamen impedimentum praesentialiter apponitur, quod dolorem causat.

Ad tertium dicendum quod concupiscentia est delectabilis, quandiu manet spes adipiscendi quod concupiscitur. Sed, subtracta spe per impedimentum appositum, concupiscentia dolorem causat.

Reply to Objection 2: That which is desired, though really future, is, nevertheless, in a way, present, inasmuch as it is hoped for. Or we may say that although the desired good itself is future, yet the hindrance is reckoned as present, and so gives rise to sorrow.

Reply to Objection 3: Desire gives pleasure, so long as there is hope of obtaining that which is desired. But, when hope is removed through the presence of an obstacle, desire causes sorrow.

Articulus 3

Ad tertium sic proceditur. Videtur quod appetitus unitatis non sit causa doloris. Dicit enim philosophus, in X Ethic., quod *haec opinio,* quae posuit repletionem esse causam delectationis, et incisionem causam tristitiae, *videtur esse facta ex delectationibus et tristitiis quae sunt circa cibum.* Sed non omnis delectatio vel tristitia est huiusmodi. Ergo appetitus unitatis non est causa universalis doloris, cum repletio ad unitatem pertineat, incisio vero multitudinem inducat.

Praeterea, quaelibet separatio unitati opponitur. Si ergo dolor causaretur ex appetitu unitatis, nulla separatio esset delectabilis. Quod patet esse falsum in separatione omnium superfluorum.

Praeterea, eadem ratione appetimus coniunctionem boni, et remotionem mali. Sed sicut coniunctio pertinet ad unitatem, cum sit unio quaedam; ita separatio est contrarium unitati. Ergo appetitus unitatis non magis debet poni causa doloris quam appetitus separationis.

Sed contra est quod Augustinus dicit, in III de libero arbitrio, quod *ex dolore quem bestiae sentiunt, satis apparet in regendis animandisque suis corporibus, quam sint animae appetentes unitatis. Quid enim est aliud dolor, nisi quidam sensus divisionis vel corruptionis impatiens?*

Article 3
Whether the craving for unity is a cause of sorrow?

Objection 1: It would seem that the craving for unity is not a cause of sorrow. For the Philosopher says (Ethic. x, 3) that "this opinion," which held repletion to be the cause of pleasure, and division,* the cause of sorrow, "seems to have originated in pains and pleasures connected with food." But not every pleasure or sorrow is of this kind. Therefore the craving for unity is not the universal cause of sorrow; since repletion pertains to unity, and division is the cause of multitude.

Objection 2: Further, every separation is opposed to unity. If therefore sorrow were caused by a craving for unity, no separation would be pleasant: and this is clearly untrue as regards the separation of whatever is superfluous.

Objection 3: Further, for the same reason we desire the conjunction of good and the removal of evil. But as conjunction regards unity, since it is a kind of union; so separation is contrary to unity. Therefore the craving for unity should not be reckoned, rather than the craving for separation, as causing sorrow.

On the contrary, Augustine says (De Lib. Arb. iii, 23), that "from the pain that dumb animals feel, it is quite evident how their souls desire unity, in ruling and quickening their bodies. For what else is pain but a feeling of impatience of division or corruption?"

---

* Aristotle wrote ἔνδειαν (*endeian*), 'want'; St. Thomas, in the Latin version, read *incisionem;* should he have read *indigentiam?*

Respondeo dicendum quod eo modo quo concupiscentia vel cupiditas boni est causa doloris, etiam appetitus unitatis, vel amor, causa doloris ponendus est. Bonum enim uniuscuiusque rei in quadam unitate consistit, prout scilicet unaquaeque res habet in se unita illa ex quibus consistit eius perfectio, unde et Platonici posuerunt *unum* esse principium, sicut et *bonum*. Unde naturaliter unumquodque appetit unitatem, sicut et bonitatem. Et propter hoc, sicut amor vel appetitus boni est causa doloris, ita etiam amor vel appetitus unitatis.

Ad primum ergo dicendum quod non omnis unio perficit rationem boni, sed solum illa a qua dependet esse perfectum rei. Et propter hoc etiam, non cuiuslibet appetitus unitatis est causa doloris vel tristitiae, ut quidam opinabantur. Quorum opinionem ibi philosophus excludit per hoc, quod quaedam repletiones non sunt delectabiles, sicut repleti cibis non delectantur in ciborum sumptione. Talis enim repletio, sive unio, magis repugnaret ad perfectum esse, quam ipsum constitueret. Unde dolor non causatur ex appetitu cuiuslibet unitatis, sed eius in qua consistit perfectio naturae.

Ad secundum dicendum quod separatio potest esse delectabilis, vel inquantum removetur illud quod est contrarium perfectioni rei, vel inquantum separatio habet aliquam unionem adiunctam, puta sensibilis ad sensum.

Ad tertium dicendum quod separatio nocivorum et corrumpentium appetitur, inquantum tollunt debitam unitatem. Unde appetitus huiusmodi separationis non est prima causa doloris, sed magis appetitus unitatis.

I answer that, Forasmuch as the desire or craving for good is reckoned as a cause of sorrow, so must a craving for unity, and love, be accounted as causing sorrow. Because the good of each thing consists in a certain unity, inasmuch as each thing has, united in itself, the elements of which its perfection consists: wherefore the Platonists held that "one" is a principle, just as "good" is. Hence everything naturally desires unity, just as it desires goodness: and therefore, just as love or desire for good is a cause of sorrow, so also is the love or craving for unity.

Reply to Objection 1: Not every kind of union causes perfect goodness, but only that on which the perfect being of a thing depends. Hence neither does the desire of any kind of unity cause pain or sorrow, as some have maintained: whose opinion is refuted by the Philosopher from the fact that repletion is not always pleasant; for instance, when a man has eaten to repletion, he takes no further pleasure in eating; because repletion or union of this kind, is repugnant rather than conducive to perfect being. Consequently sorrow is caused by the craving, not for any kind of unity, but for that unity in which the perfection of nature consists.

Reply to Objection 2: Separation can be pleasant, either because it removes something contrary to a thing's perfection, or because it has some union connected with it, such as union of the sense to its object.

Reply to Objection 3: Separation from things hurtful and corruptive is desired, in so far as they destroy the unity which is due. Wherefore the desire for such like separation is not the first cause of sorrow, whereas the craving for unity is.

Articulus 4

Ad quartum sic proceditur. Videtur quod potestas maior non debeat poni causa doloris. Quod enim est in potestate agentis, nondum est praesens, sed futurum. Dolor autem est de malo praesenti. Ergo potestas maior non est causa doloris.

Article 4
Whether an irresistible power is a cause of sorrow?

Objection 1: It would seem that a greater power should not be reckoned a cause of sorrow. For that which is in the power of the agent is not present but future. But sorrow is for present evil. Therefore a greater power is not a cause of sorrow.

PRAETEREA, nocumentum illatum est causa doloris. Sed nocumentum potest inferri etiam a potestate minore. Ergo potestas maior non debet poni causa doloris.

PRAETEREA, causae appetitivorum motuum sunt interiores inclinationes animae. Potestas autem maior est aliquid exterius. Ergo non debet poni causa doloris.

SED CONTRA est quod Augustinus dicit, in libro de natura boni, *in animo dolorem facit voluntas resistens potestati maiori; in corpore dolorem facit sensus resistens corpori potentiori.*

RESPONDEO dicendum quod, sicut supra dictum est, malum coniunctum est causa doloris vel tristitiae per modum obiecti. Id ergo quod est causa coniunctionis mali, debet poni causa doloris vel tristitiae. Manifestum est autem hoc esse contra inclinationem appetitus, ut malo praesentialiter inhaereat. Quod autem est contra inclinationem alicuius, nunquam advenit ei nisi per actionem alicuius fortioris. Et ideo potestas maior ponitur esse causa doloris ab Augustino. Sed sciendum est quod, si potestas fortior intantum invalescat quod mutet contrariam inclinationem in inclinationem propriam, iam non erit aliqua repugnantia vel violentia, sicut quando agens fortius, corrumpendo corpus grave, aufert ei inclinationem qua tendit deorsum; et tunc ferri sursum non est ei violentum, sed naturale. Sic igitur si aliqua potestas maior intantum invalescat quod auferat inclinationem voluntatis vel appetitus sensitivi, ex ea non sequitur dolor vel tristitia, sed tunc solum sequitur, quando remanet inclinatio appetitus in contrarium. Et inde est quod Augustinus dicit quod voluntas *resistens potestati fortiori,* causat dolorem, si enim non resisteret, sed cederet consentiendo, non sequeretur dolor, sed delectatio.

AD PRIMUM ergo dicendum quod maior potestas dolorem causat, non secundum quod est agens in potentia, sed secundum quod est agens actu, dum scilicet facit coniunctionem mali corruptivi.

Objection 2: Further, hurt inflicted is the cause of sorrow. But hurt can be inflicted even by a lesser power. Therefore a greater power should not be reckoned as a cause of sorrow.

Objection 3: Further, the interior inclinations of the soul are the causes of the movements of appetite. But a greater power is something external. Therefore it should not be reckoned as a cause of sorrow.

On the contrary, Augustine says (De Nat. Boni xx): "Sorrow in the soul is caused by the will resisting a stronger power: while pain in the body is caused by sense resisting a stronger body."

I answer that, As stated above (I-II, q. 36, a. 1), a present evil, is cause of sorrow or pain, by way of object. Therefore that which is the cause of the evil being present, should be reckoned as causing pain or sorrow. Now it is evident that it is contrary to the inclination of the appetite to be united with a present evil: and whatever is contrary to a thing's inclination does not happen to it save by the action of something stronger. Wherefore Augustine reckons a greater power as being the cause of sorrow. But it must be noted that if the stronger power goes so far as to transform the contrary inclination into its own inclination there will be no longer repugnance or violence: thus if a stronger agent, by its action on a heavy body, deprives it of its downward tendency, its consequent upward tendency is not violent but natural to it. Accordingly if some greater power prevail so far as to take away from the will or the sensitive appetite, their respective inclinations, pain or sorrow will not result therefrom; such is the result only when the contrary inclination of the appetite remains. And hence Augustine says (De Nat. Boni xx) that sorrow is caused by the will "resisting a stronger power": for were it not to resist, but to yield by consenting, the result would be not sorrow but pleasure.

Reply to Objection 1: A greater power causes sorrow, as acting not potentially but actually, i.e., by causing the actual presence of the corruptive evil.

AD SECUNDUM dicendum quod nihil prohibet aliquam potestatem quae non est maior simpliciter, esse maiorem quantum ad aliquid. Et secundum hoc, aliquod nocumentum inferre potest. Si autem nullo modo maior esset, nullo modo posset nocere. Unde non posset causam doloris inferre.

AD TERTIUM dicendum quod exteriora agentia possunt esse causa motuum appetitivorum, inquantum causant praesentiam obiecti. Et hoc modo potestas maior ponitur causa doloris.

Reply to Objection 2: Nothing hinders a power which is not simply greater, from being greater in some respect: and accordingly it is able to inflict some harm. But if it be nowise stronger, it can do no harm at all: wherefore it cannot bring about that which causes sorrow.

Reply to Objection 3: External agents can be the causes of appetitive movements, in so far as they cause the presence of the object: and it is thus that a greater power is reckoned to be the cause of sorrow.

QUAESTIO XXXVII

Deinde considerandum est de effectibus doloris vel tristitiae. Et circa hoc quaeruntur quatuor. *Primo,* utrum dolor auferat facultatem addiscendi. *Secundo,* utrum aggravatio animi sit effectus tristitiae vel doloris. *Tertio,* utrum tristitia vel dolor debilitet omnem operationem. *Quarto,* utrum tristitia noceat corpori magis quam aliae passiones animae.

QUESTION 37
Of the Effects of Pain or Sorrow

We must now consider the effects of pain or of sorrow: under which head there are four points of inquiry: 1. Whether pain deprives one of the power to learn? 2. Whether the effect of sorrow or pain is to burden the soul? 3. Whether sorrow or pain weakens all activity? 4. Whether sorrow is more harmful to the body than all the other passions of the soul?

ARTICULUS 1

AD PRIMUM sic proceditur. Videtur quod dolor non auferat facultatem addiscendi. Dicitur enim Isaiae XXVI, *cum feceris iudicia tua in terra, iustitiam discent omnes habitatores orbis.* Et infra, *in tribulatione murmuris doctrina tua eis,* sed ex iudiciis Dei, et tribulatione, sequitur dolor seu tristitia in cordibus hominum. Ergo dolor vel tristitia non tollit, sed magis auget facultatem addiscendi.

PRAETEREA, Isaiae XXVIII, dicitur, *quem docebit scientiam? Et quem intelligere faciet auditum? Ablactatos a lacte, avulsos ab uberibus* idest a delectationibus. Sed dolor et tristitia maxime tollunt delectationes, impedit enim tristitia omnem delectationem, ut dicitur in VII Ethic.; et Eccli. XI dicitur quod *malitia unius horae oblivionem facit luxuriae maximae.*

ARTICLE 1
Whether pain deprives one of the power to learn?

Objection 1: It would seem that pain does not deprive one of the power to learn. For it is written (Is. 26:9): "When Thou shalt do Thy judgments on the earth, the inhabitants of the world shall learn justice": and further on (verse 16): "In the tribulation of murmuring Thy instruction was with them." But the judgments of God and tribulation cause sorrow in men's hearts. Therefore pain or sorrow, far from destroying, increases the power of learning.

Objection 2: Further, it is written (Is. 28:9): "Whom shall He teach knowledge? And whom shall He make to understand the hearing? Them that are weaned from the milk, that are drawn away from the breasts," i.e., from pleasures. But pain and sorrow are most destructive of pleasure; since sorrow hinders all pleasure, as stated in Ethic. vii, 14: and (Ecclus. 11:29) it is stated that "the affliction of an hour maketh one forget great delights."

Ergo dolor non tollit, sed magis praebet facultatem addiscendi.

PRAETEREA, tristitia interior praeeminet dolori exteriori, ut supra dictum est. Sed simul cum tristitia potest homo addiscere. Ergo multo magis simul cum dolore corporali.

SED CONTRA est quod Augustinus dicit, in I Soliloq., *quanquam acerrimo dolore dentium his diebus torquerer, non quidem sinebar animo volvere nisi ea quae iam forte didiceram. A discendo autem penitus impediebar, ad quod mihi tota intentione animi opus erat.*

RESPONDEO dicendum quod, quia omnes potentiae animae in una essentia animae radicantur, necesse est quod, quando intentio animae vehementer trahitur ad operationem unius potentiae, retrahatur ab operatione alterius, unius enim animae non potest esse nisi una intentio. Et propter hoc, si aliquid ad se trahat totam intentionem animae, vel magnam partem ipsius, non compatitur secum aliquid aliud quod magnam attentionem requirat. Manifestum est autem quod dolor sensibilis maxime trahit ad se intentionem animae, quia naturaliter unumquodque tota intentione tendit ad repellendum contrarium, sicut etiam in rebus naturalibus apparet. Similiter etiam manifestum est quod ad addiscendum aliquid de novo, requiritur studium et conatus cum magna intentione, ut patet per illud quod dicitur Prov. II, *si quaesieris sapientiam quasi pecuniam, et sicut thesauros effoderis eam, tunc intelliges disciplinam*. Et ideo si sit dolor intensus, impeditur homo ne tunc aliquid addiscere possit. Et tantum potest intendi, quod nec etiam, instante dolore, potest homo aliquid considerare etiam quod prius scivit. In hoc tamen attenditur diversitas secundum diversitatem amoris quem homo habet ad addiscendum vel considerandum, qui quanto maior fuerit, magis retinet intentionem animi, ne omnino feratur ad dolorem.

AD PRIMUM ergo dicendum quod tristitia moderata, quae excludit evagationem animi,

Therefore pain, instead of taking away, increases the faculty of learning.

Objection 3: Further, inward sorrow surpasses outward pain, as stated above (I-II, q. 35, a. 7). But man can learn while sorrowful. Much more, therefore, can he learn while in bodily pain.

On the contrary, Augustine says (Soliloq. i, 12): "Although during those days I was tormented with a violent tooth-ache, I was not able to turn over in my mind other things than those I had already learnt; and as to learning anything, I was quite unequal to it, because it required undivided attention."

I answer that, Since all the powers of the soul are rooted in the one essence of the soul, it must needs happen, when the intention of the soul is strongly drawn towards the action of one power, that it is withdrawn from the action of another power: because the soul, being one, can only have one intention. The result is that if one thing draws upon itself the entire intention of the soul, or a great portion thereof, anything else requiring considerable attention is incompatible therewith. Now it is evident that sensible pain above all draws the soul's attention to itself; because it is natural for each thing to tend wholly to repel whatever is contrary to it, as may be observed even in natural things. It is likewise evident that in order to learn anything new, we require study and effort with a strong intention, as is clearly stated in Prov. 2:4, 5: "If thou shalt seek wisdom as money, and shall dig for her as for a treasure, then shalt thou understand learning.*" Consequently if the pain be acute, man is prevented at the time from learning anything: indeed it can be so acute, that, as long as it lasts, a man is unable to give his attention even to that which he knew already. However a difference is to be observed according to the difference of love that a man has for learning or for considering: because the greater his love, the more will he retain the intention of his mind so as to prevent it from turning entirely to the pain.

Reply to Objection 1: Moderate sorrow, that does not cause the mind to wander,

---

* Vulg: 'the fear of the Lord'

potest conferre ad disciplinam suscipiendam, et praecipue eorum per quae homo sperat se posse a tristitia liberari. Et hoc modo *in tribulatione murmuris* homines doctrinam Dei magis recipiunt.

AD SECUNDUM dicendum quod tam delectatio quam dolor, inquantum ad se trahunt animae intentionem, impediunt considerationem rationis, unde in VII Ethic. dicitur quod *impossibile est in ipsa delectatione venereorum, aliquid intelligere.* Sed tamen dolor magis trahit ad se intentionem animae quam delectatio, sicut etiam videmus in rebus naturalibus, quod actio corporis naturalis magis intenditur in contrarium; sicut aqua calefacta magis patitur a frigido, ut fortius congeletur. Si ergo dolor seu tristitia fuerit moderata, per accidens potest conferre ad addiscendum, inquantum aufert superabundantiam delectationum. Sed per se impedit, et si intendatur, totaliter aufert.

AD TERTIUM dicendum quod dolor exterior accidit ex laesione corporali, et ita magis habet transmutationem corporalem adiunctam quam dolor interior, qui tamen est maior secundum illud quod est formale in dolore, quod est ex parte animae. Et ideo dolor corporalis magis impedit contemplationem, quae requirit omnimodam quietem, quam dolor interior. Et tamen etiam dolor interior, si multum intendatur, ita trahit intentionem, ut non possit homo de novo aliquid addiscere. Unde et Gregorius propter tristitiam intermisit Ezechielis expositionem.

can conduce to the acquisition of learning especially in regard to those things by which a man hopes to be freed from sorrow. And thus, "in the tribulation of murmuring," men are more apt to be taught by God.

Reply to Objection 2: Both pleasure and pain, in so far as they draw upon themselves the soul's intention, hinder the reason from the act of consideration, wherefore it is stated in Ethic. vii, 11 that "in the moment of sexual pleasure, a man cannot understand anything." Nevertheless pain attracts the soul's intention more than pleasure does: thus we observe in natural things that the action of a natural body is more intense in regard to its contrary; for instance, hot water is more accessible to the action of cold, and in consequence freezes harder. If therefore pain or sorrow be moderate, it can conduce accidentally to the facility of learning, in so far as it takes away an excess of pleasure. But, of itself, it is a hindrance; and if it be intense, it prevents it altogether.

Reply to Objection 3: External pain arises from hurt done to the body, so that it involves bodily transmutation more than inward sorrow does: and yet the latter is greater in regard to the formal element of pain, which belongs to the soul. Consequently bodily pain is a greater hindrance to contemplation which requires complete repose, than inward sorrow is. Nevertheless if inward sorrow be very intense, it attracts the intention, so that man is unable to learn anything for the first time: wherefore on account of sorrow Gregory interrupted his commentary on Ezechiel (Hom. xxii in Ezechiel).

ARTICULUS 2

AD SECUNDUM sic proceditur. Videtur quod aggravatio animi non sit effectus tristitiae. Dicit enim apostolus, II ad Cor. VII, *ecce hoc ipsum, contristari vos secundum Deum, quantam in vobis operatur sollicitudinem, sed defensionem, sed indignationem,* et cetera. Sed sollicitudo et indignatio ad quandam erectionem animi pertinent, quae aggravationi opponitur. Non ergo aggravatio est effectus tristitiae.

ARTICLE 2
Whether the effect of sorrow or pain is to burden the soul?

Objection 1: It would seem that it is not an effect of sorrow to burden the soul. For the Apostle says (2 Cor. 7:11): "Behold this self-same thing, that you were made sorrowful according to God, how great carefulness it worketh in you: yea, defence, yea indignation," etc. Now carefulness and indignation imply that the soul is uplifted, which is contrary to being depressed. Therefore depression is not an effect of sorrow.

Praeterea, tristitia delectationi opponitur. Sed effectus delectationis est dilatatio, cui non opponitur aggravatio, sed constrictio. Ergo effectus tristitiae non debet poni aggravatio.

Praeterea, ad tristitiam pertinet absorbere, ut patet per illud quod apostolus dicit, II ad Cor. II, *ne forte abundantiori tristitia absorbeatur qui est eiusmodi.* Sed quod aggravatur, non absorbetur, quinimmo sub aliquo ponderoso deprimitur; quod autem absorbetur, intra absorbens includitur. Ergo aggravatio non debet poni effectus tristitiae.

Sed contra est quod Gregorius Nyssenus et Damascenus ponunt *tristitiam aggravantem.*

Respondeo dicendum quod effectus passionum animae quandoque metaphorice nominantur, secundum similitudinem sensibilium corporum, eo quod motus appetitus animalis sunt similes inclinationibus appetitus naturalis. Et per hunc modum fervor attribuitur amori, dilatatio delectationi, et aggravatio tristitiae. Dicitur enim homo aggravari, ex eo quod aliquo pondere impeditur a proprio motu. Manifestum est autem ex praedictis quod tristitia contingit ex aliquo malo praesenti. Quod quidem, ex hoc ipso quod repugnat motui voluntatis, aggravat animum, inquantum impedit ipsum ne fruatur eo quod vult. Et si quidem non sit tanta vis mali contristantis ut auferat spem evadendi, licet animus aggravetur quantum ad hoc, quod in praesenti non potitur eo quod vult; remanet tamen motus ad repellendum nocivum contristans. Si vero superexcrescat vis mali intantum ut spem evasionis excludat, tunc simpliciter impeditur etiam interior motus animi angustiati, ut neque hac neque illac divertere valeat. Et quandoque etiam impeditur exterior motus corporis, ita quod remaneat homo stupidus in seipso.

Objection 2: Further, sorrow is contrary to pleasure. But the effect of pleasure is expansion: the opposite of which is not depression but contraction. Therefore depression should not be reckoned as an effect of sorrow.

Objection 3: Further, sorrow consumes those who are inflicted therewith, as may be gathered from the words of the Apostle (2 Cor. 2:7): "Lest perhaps such an one be swallowed up with overmuch sorrow." But that which is depressed is not consumed; nay, it is weighed down by something heavy, whereas that which is consumed enters within the consumer. Therefore depression should not be reckoned an effect of sorrow.

On the contrary, Gregory of Nyssa* and Damascene (De Fide Orth. ii, 14) speak of "depressing sorrow."

I answer that, The effects of the soul's passions are sometimes named metaphorically, from a likeness to sensible bodies: for the reason that the movements of the animal appetite are like the inclinations of the natural appetite. And in this way fervor is ascribed to love, expansion to pleasure, and depression to sorrow. For a man is said to be depressed, through being hindered in his own movement by some weight. Now it is evident from what has been said above (I-II, q. 23, a. 4; q. 25, a. 4; q. 36, a. 1) that sorrow is caused by a present evil: and this evil, from the very fact that it is repugnant to the movement of the will, depresses the soul, inasmuch as it hinders it from enjoying that which it wishes to enjoy. And if the evil which is the cause of sorrow be not so strong as to deprive one of the hope of avoiding it, although the soul be depressed in so far as, for the present, it fails to grasp that which it craves for; yet it retains the movement whereby to repulse that evil. If, on the other hand, the strength of the evil be such as to exclude the hope of evasion, then even the interior movement of the afflicted soul is absolutely hindered, so that it cannot turn aside either this way or that. Sometimes even the external movement of the body is paralyzed, so that a man becomes completely stupefied.

---

* Nemesius, De Nat. Hom. xix.

AD PRIMUM ergo dicendum quod illa erectio animi provenit ex tristitia quae est secundum Deum, propter spem adiunctam de remissione peccati.

AD SECUNDUM dicendum quod, quantum ad motum appetitivum pertinet, ad idem refertur constrictio et aggravatio. Ex hoc enim quod aggravatur animus, ut ad exteriora libere progredi non possit, ad seipsum retrahitur, quasi in seipso constrictus.

AD TERTIUM dicendum quod tristitia absorbere hominem dicitur, quando sic totaliter vis contristantis mali afficit animam, ut omnem spem evasionis excludat. Et sic etiam eodem modo aggravat et absorbet. Quaedam enim se consequuntur in his quae metaphorice dicuntur, quae sibi repugnare videntur, si secundum proprietatem accipiantur.

Reply to Objection 1: That uplifting of the soul ensues from the sorrow which is according to God, because it brings with it the hope of the forgiveness of sin.

Reply to Objection 2: As far as the movement of the appetite is concerned, contraction and depression amount to the same: because the soul, through being depressed so as to be unable to attend freely to outward things, withdraws to itself, closing itself up as it were.

Reply to Objection 3: Sorrow is said to consume man, when the force of the afflicting evil is such as to shut out all hope of evasion: and thus also it both depresses and consumes at the same time. For certain things, taken metaphorically, imply one another, which taken literally, appear to exclude one another.

ARTICULUS 3

AD TERTIUM sic proceditur. Videtur quod tristitia non impediat omnem operationem. Sollicitudo enim ex tristitia causatur, ut patet per auctoritatem apostoli inductam. Sed sollicitudo adiuvat ad bene operandum, unde apostolus dicit, II ad Tim. II, *sollicite cura teipsum exhibere operarium inconfusibilem.* Ergo tristitia non impedit operationem, sed magis adiuvat ad bene operandum.

PRAETEREA, tristitia causat in multis concupiscentiam, ut dicitur in VII Ethic. Sed concupiscentia facit ad intensionem operationis. Ergo et tristitia.

PRAETEREA, sicut quaedam operationes propriae sunt gaudentium, ita etiam quaedam operationes his qui tristantur, sicut lugere. Sed unumquodque augetur ex sibi convenienti. Ergo aliquae operationes non impediuntur, sed meliorantur propter tristitiam.

SED CONTRA est quod philosophus dicit, in X Ethic., quod *delectatio perficit operationem,* sed e contrario *tristitia impedit.*

RESPONDEO dicendum quod, sicut iam dictum est, tristitia quandoque non ita aggravat vel absorbet animum, ut omnem motum interiorem et exteriorem excludat; sed aliqui

ARTICLE 3
Whether sorrow or pain weakens all activity?

Objection 1: It would seem that sorrow does not weaken all activity. Because carefulness is caused by sorrow, as is clear from the passage of the Apostle quoted above (I-II, q. 37, a. 2, ad 1). But carefulness conduces to good work: wherefore the Apostle says (2 Tim. 2:15): "Carefully study to present thyself . . . a workman that needeth not to be ashamed." Therefore sorrow is not a hindrance to work, but helps one to work well.

Objection 2: Further, sorrow causes desire in many cases, as stated in Ethic. vii, 14. But desire causes intensity of action. Therefore sorrow does too.

Objection 3: Further, as some actions are proper to the joyful, so are others proper to the sorrowful; for instance, to mourn. Now a thing is improved by that which is suitable to it. Therefore certain actions are not hindered but improved by reason of sorrow.

On the contrary, The Philosopher says (Ethic. x, 4) that "pleasure perfects action," whereas on the other hand, "sorrow hinders it" (Ethic. x, 5).

I answer that, As stated above (I-II, q. 37, a. 2), sorrow at times does not depress or consume the soul, so as to shut out all movement, internal or external; but certain

motus quandoque ex ipsa tristitia causantur. Sic ergo operatio ad tristitiam dupliciter potest comparari. Uno modo, sicut ad id de quo est tristitia. Et sic tristitia quamlibet operationem impedit, nunquam enim illud quod cum tristitia facimus, ita bene facimus sicut illud quod facimus cum delectatione, vel sine tristitia. Cuius ratio est, quia voluntas est causa operationis humanae, unde quando operatio est de qua aliquis contristatur, necesse est quod actio debilitetur. Alio modo comparatur operatio ad tristitiam sicut ad principium et causam. Et sic necesse est quod operatio talis ex tristitia augeatur, sicut quanto aliquis magis tristatur de re aliqua, tanto magis conatur ad expellendam tristitiam, dummodo remaneat spes expellendi, alioquin nullus motus vel operatio ex tristitia causaretur.

Et per hoc patet responsio ad obiecta.

Articulus 4

Ad quartum sic proceditur. Videtur quod tristitia non inferat maxime corpori nocumentum. Tristitia enim habet esse spirituale in anima. Sed ea quae habent tantum esse spirituale, non causant transmutationem corporalem, sicut patet de intentionibus colorum quae sunt in aere, a quibus nullum corpus coloratur. Ergo tristitia non facit aliquod corporale nocumentum.

Praeterea, si facit aliquod corporale nocumentum, hoc non est nisi inquantum habet corporalem transmutationem adiunctam. Sed corporalis transmutatio invenitur in omnibus animae passionibus, ut supra dictum est. Ergo non magis tristitia quam aliae animae passiones, corpori nocet.

Praeterea, philosophus dicit, in VII Ethic., quod *irae et concupiscentiae quibusdam insanias faciunt,* quod videtur esse maximum nocumentum, cum ratio sit excellentissimum eorum quae sunt in homine. Desperatio etiam videtur esse magis nociva quam tristitia, cum sit causa tristitiae. Ergo tristitia non magis nocet corpori quam aliae animae passiones.

movements are sometimes caused by sorrow itself. Accordingly action stands in a twofold relation to sorrow. First, as being the object of sorrow: and thus sorrow hinders any action: for we never do that which we do with sorrow, so well as that which we do with pleasure, or without sorrow. The reason for this is that the will is the cause of human actions: and consequently when we do something that gives pain, the action must of necessity be weakened in consequence. Secondly, action stands in relation to sorrow, as to its principle and cause: and such action must needs be improved by sorrow: thus the more one sorrows on account of a certain thing, the more one strives to shake off sorrow, provided there is a hope of shaking it off: otherwise no movement or action would result from that sorrow.

From what has been said the replies to the objections are evident.

Article 4
Whether sorrow is more harmful to the body than the other passions of the soul?

Objection 1: It would seem that sorrow is not most harmful to the body. For sorrow has a spiritual existence in the soul. But those things which have only a spiritual existence do not cause a transmutation in the body: as is evident with regard to the images of colors, which images are in the air and do not give color to bodies. Therefore sorrow is not harmful to the body.

Objection 2: Further if it be harmful to the body, this can only be due to its having a bodily transmutation in conjunction with it. But bodily transmutation takes place in all the passions of the soul, as stated above (I-II, q. 22, a. 1; a. 3). Therefore sorrow is not more harmful to the body than the other passions of the soul.

Objection 3: Further, the Philosopher says (Ethic. vii, 3) that "anger and desire drive some to madness": which seems to be a very great harm, since reason is the most excellent thing in man. Moreover, despair seems to be more harmful than sorrow; for it is the cause of sorrow. Therefore sorrow is not more harmful to the body than the other passions of the soul.

Sed contra est quod dicitur Prov. XVII, *animus gaudens aetatem floridam facit, spiritus tristis exsiccat ossa*. Et Prov. XXV, *sicut tinea vestimento, et vermis ligno, ita tristitia viri nocet cordi*. Et Eccli. XXXVIII, *a tristitia festinat mors*.

Respondeo dicendum quod tristitia, inter omnes animae passiones, magis corpori nocet. Cuius ratio est, quia tristitia repugnat humanae vitae quantum ad speciem sui motus; et non solum quantum ad mensuram seu quantitatem, sicut aliae animae passiones. Consistit enim humana vita in quadam motione, quae a corde in cetera membra diffunditur, quae quidem motio convenit naturae humanae secundum aliquam determinatam mensuram. Si ergo ista motio procedat ultra mensuram debitam, repugnabit humanae vitae secundum quantitatis mensuram; non autem secundum similitudinem speciei. Si autem impediatur processus huius motionis, repugnabit vitae secundum suam speciem. Est autem attendendum in omnibus animae passionibus, quod transmutatio corporalis, quae est in eis materialis, est conformis et proportionata motui appetitus, qui est formalis, sicut in omnibus materia proportionatur formae. Illae ergo animae passiones quae important motum appetitus ad prosequendum aliquid, non repugnant vitali motioni secundum speciem, sed possunt repugnare secundum quantitatem, ut amor, gaudium, desiderium, et huiusmodi. Et ideo ista secundum speciem suam iuvant naturam corporis, sed propter excessum possunt nocere. Passiones autem quae important motum appetitus cum fuga vel retractione quadam, repugnant vitali motioni non solum secundum quantitatem, sed etiam secundum speciem motus, et ideo simpliciter nocent, sicut timor et desperatio, et prae omnibus tristitia, quae aggravat animum ex malo praesenti, cuius est fortior impressio quam futuri.

Ad primum ergo dicendum quod, quia anima naturaliter movet corpus, spiritualis motus animae naturaliter est causa

On the contrary, It is written (Prov. 17:22): "A joyful mind maketh age flourishing: a sorrowful spirit drieth up the bones": and (Prov. 25:20): "As a moth doth by a garment, and a worm by the wood: so the sadness of a man consumeth the heart": and (Ecclus. 38:19): "Of sadness cometh death."

I answer that, Of all the soul's passions, sorrow is most harmful to the body. The reason of this is because sorrow is repugnant to man's life in respect of the species of its movement, and not merely in respect of its measure or quantity, as is the case with the other passions of the soul. For man's life consists in a certain movement, which flows from the heart to the other parts of the body: and this movement is befitting to human nature according to a certain fixed measure. Consequently if this movement goes beyond the right measure, it will be repugnant to man's life in respect of the measure of quantity; but not in respect of its specific character: whereas if this movement be hindered in its progress, it will be repugnant to life in respect of its species. Now it must be noted that, in all the passions of the soul, the bodily transmutation which is their material element, is in conformity with and in proportion to the appetitive movement, which is the formal element: just as in everything matter is proportionate to form. Consequently those passions that imply a movement of the appetite in pursuit of something, are not repugnant to the vital movement as regards its species, but they may be repugnant thereto as regards its measure: such are love, joy, desire and the like; wherefore these passions conduce to the well-being of the body; though, if they be excessive, they may be harmful to it. On the other hand, those passions which denote in the appetite a movement of flight or contraction, are repugnant to the vital movement, not only as regards its measure, but also as regards its species; wherefore they are simply harmful: such are fear and despair, and above all sorrow which depresses the soul by reason of a present evil, which makes a stronger impression than future evil.

Reply to Objection 1: Since the soul naturally moves the body, the spiritual movement of the soul is naturally the cause of

transmutationis corporalis. Nec est simile de spiritualibus intentionibus, quae non habent naturaliter ordinem movendi alia corpora, quae non sunt nata moveri ab anima.

AD SECUNDUM dicendum quod aliae passiones habent transmutationem corporalem conformem, secundum suam speciem, motioni vitali, sed tristitia contrariam, ut supra dictum est.

AD TERTIUM dicendum quod ex leviori causa impeditur usus rationis quam corrumpatur vita, cum videamus multas aegritudines usum rationis tollere, quae nondum adimunt vitam. Et tamen timor et ira maxime nocumentum corporale afferunt ex permixtione tristitiae, propter absentiam eius quod cupitur. Ipsa etiam tristitia quandoque rationem aufert, sicut patet in his qui propter dolorem in melancholiam vel in maniam incidunt.

bodily transmutation. Nor is there any parallel with spiritual images, because they are not naturally ordained to move such other bodies as are not naturally moved by the soul.

Reply to Objection 2: Other passions imply a bodily transmutation which is specifically in conformity with the vital movement: whereas sorrow implies a transmutation that is repugnant thereto, as stated above.

Reply to Objection 3: A lesser cause suffices to hinder the use of reason, than to destroy life: since we observe that many ailments deprive one of the use of reason, before depriving one of life. Nevertheless fear and anger cause very great harm to the body, by reason of the sorrow which they imply, and which arises from the absence of the thing desired. Moreover sorrow too sometimes deprives man of the use of reason: as may be seen in those who through sorrow become a prey to melancholy or madness.

QUAESTIO XXXVIII

Deinde considerandum est de remediis doloris seu tristitiae. Et circa hoc quaeruntur quinque. Primo, utrum dolor vel tristitia mitigetur per quamlibet delectationem. Secundo, utrum mitigetur per fletum. Tertio, utrum per compassionem amicorum. Quarto, utrum per contemplationem veritatis. Quinto, utrum per somnum et balnea.

QUESTION 38
Of the Remedies of Sorrow or Pain

We must now consider the remedies of pain or sorrow: under which head there are five points of inquiry: 1. Whether pain or sorrow is assuaged by every pleasure? 2. Whether it is assuaged by weeping? 3. Whether it is assuaged by the sympathy of friends? 4. Whether it is assuaged by contemplating the truth? 5. Whether it is assuaged by sleep and baths?

ARTICULUS 1

AD PRIMUM sic proceditur. Videtur quod non quaelibet delectatio mitiget quemlibet dolorem seu tristitiam. Non enim delectatio tristitiam mitigat, nisi inquantum ei contrariatur, *medicinae enim fiunt per contraria,* ut dicitur in II Ethic. Sed non quaelibet delectatio contrariatur cuilibet tristitiae, ut supra dictum est. Ergo non quaelibet delectatio mitigat quamlibet tristitiam.

PRAETEREA, illud quod causat tristitiam, non mitigat tristitiam. Sed aliquae delectationes causant tristitiam, quia, ut dicitur in

ARTICLE 1
Whether pain or sorrow is assuaged by every pleasure?

Objection 1: It would seem that not every pleasure assuages every pain or sorrow. For pleasure does not assuage sorrow, save in so far as it is contrary to it: for "remedies work by contraries" (Ethic. ii, 3). But not every pleasure is contrary to every sorrow; as stated above (I-II, q. 35, a. 4). Therefore not every pleasure assuages every sorrow.

Objection 2: Further, that which causes sorrow does not assuage it. But some pleasures cause sorrow; since, as stated in

IX Ethic., *malus tristatur quoniam delectatus est.* Non ergo omnis delectatio mitigat tristitiam.

PRAETEREA, Augustinus dicit, in IV Confess., quod ipse fugit de patria, in qua conversari solitus erat cum amico suo iam mortuo, *minus enim quaerebant eum oculi eius, ubi videre non solebant.* Ex quo accipi potest quod illa in quibus nobis amici mortui vel absentes communicaverunt, efficiuntur nobis, de eorum morte vel absentia dolentibus, onerosa. Sed maxime communicaverunt nobis in delectationibus. Ergo ipsae delectationes efficiuntur nobis dolentibus onerosae. Non ergo quaelibet delectatio mitigat quamlibet tristitiam.

SED CONTRA est quod philosophus dicit, in VII Ethic., quod *expellit delectatio tristitiam, et quae contraria, et quae contingens, si sit fortis.*

RESPONDEO dicendum quod, sicut ex praedictis patet, delectatio est quaedam quies appetitus in bono convenienti; tristitia autem est ex eo quod repugnat appetitui. Unde sic se habet delectatio ad tristitiam in motibus appetitivis, sicut se habet in corporibus quies ad fatigationem, quae accidit ex aliqua transmutatione innaturali, nam et ipsa tristitia fatigationem quandam, seu aegritudinem appetitivae virtutis importat. Sicut igitur quaelibet quies corporis remedium affert contra quamlibet fatigationem, ex quacumque causa innaturali provenientem; ita quaelibet delectatio remedium affert ad mitigandam quamlibet tristitiam, ex quocumque procedat.

AD PRIMUM ergo dicendum quod, licet non omnis delectatio contrarietur omni tristitiae secundum speciem, contrariatur tamen secundum genus, ut supra dictum est. Et ideo ex parte dispositionis subiecti, quaelibet tristitia per quamlibet delectationem mitigari potest.

AD SECUNDUM dicendum quod delectationes malorum non causant tristitiam in praesenti, sed in futuro, inquantum scilicet mali poenitent de malis de quibus laetitiam habuerunt. Et huic tristitiae subvenitur per contrarias delectationes.

Ethic. ix, 4, "the wicked man feels pain at having been pleased." Therefore not every pleasure assuages sorrow.

Objection 3: Further, Augustine says (Confess. iv, 7) that he fled from his country, where he had been wont to associate with his friend, now dead: "for so should his eyes look for him less, where they were not wont to see him." Hence we may gather that those things which united us to our dead or absent friends, become burdensome to us when we mourn their death or absence. But nothing united us more than the pleasures we enjoyed in common. Therefore these very pleasures become burdensome to us when we mourn. Therefore not every pleasure assuages every sorrow.

On the contrary, The Philosopher says (Ethic. vii, 14) that "sorrow is driven forth by pleasure, both by a contrary pleasure and by any other, provided it be intense."

I answer that, As is evident from what has been said above (I-II, q. 23, a. 4), pleasure is a kind of repose of the appetite in a suitable good; while sorrow arises from something unsuited to the appetite. Consequently in movements of the appetite pleasure is to sorrow, what, in bodies, repose is to weariness, which is due to a non-natural transmutation; for sorrow itself implies a certain weariness or ailing of the appetitive faculty. Therefore just as all repose of the body brings relief to any kind of weariness, ensuing from any non-natural cause; so every pleasure brings relief by assuaging any kind of sorrow, due to any cause whatever.

Reply to Objection 1: Although not every pleasure is specifically contrary to every sorrow, yet it is generically, as stated above (I-II, q. 35, a. 4). And consequently, on the part of the disposition of the subject, any sorrow can be assuaged by any pleasure.

Reply to Objection 2: The pleasures of wicked men are not a cause of sorrow while they are enjoyed, but afterwards: that is to say, in so far as wicked men repent of those things in which they took pleasure. This sorrow is healed by contrary pleasures.

AD TERTIUM dicendum quod, quando sunt duae causae ad contrarios motus inclinantes, utraque alteram impedit, et tamen illa finaliter vincit, quae fortior est et diuturnior. In eo autem qui tristatur de his in quibus simul cum amico mortuo vel absente delectari consuevit, duae causae in contrarium moventes inveniuntur. Nam mors vel absentia amici recogitata, inclinat ad dolorem, bonum autem praesens inclinat ad delectationem. Unde utrumque per alterum minuitur. Sed tamen, quia fortius movet sensus praesentis quam memoria praeteriti, et amor sui ipsius quam amor alterius diuturnius manet; inde est quod finaliter delectatio tristitiam expellit. Unde post pauca subdit ibidem Augustinus quod *pristinis generibus delectationum cedebat dolor eius.*

Reply to Objection 3: When there are two causes inclining to contrary movements, each hinders the other; yet the one which is stronger and more persistent, prevails in the end. Now when a man is made sorrowful by those things in which he took pleasure in common with a deceased or absent friend, there are two causes producing contrary movements. For the thought of the friend's death or absence, inclines him to sorrow: whereas the present good inclines him to pleasure. Consequently each is modified by the other. And yet, since the perception of the present moves more strongly than the memory of the past, and since love of self is more persistent than love of another; hence it is that, in the end, the pleasure drives out the sorrow. Wherefore a little further on (Confess. iv, 8) Augustine says that his "sorrow gave way to his former pleasures."

ARTICULUS 2

AD SECUNDUM sic proceditur. Videtur quod fletus non mitiget tristitiam. Nullus enim effectus diminuit suam causam. Sed fletus, vel gemitus, est effectus tristitiae. Ergo non minuit tristitiam.

PRAETEREA, sicut fletus vel gemitus est effectus tristitiae, ita risus est effectus laetitiae. Sed risus non minuit laetitiam. Ergo fletus non mitigat tristitiam.

PRAETEREA, in fletu repraesentatur nobis malum contristans. Sed imaginatio rei contristantis auget tristitiam, sicut imaginatio rei delectantis auget laetitiam. Ergo videtur quod fletus non mitiget tristitiam.

SED CONTRA est quod Augustinus dicit, in IV Confess., quod quando dolebat de morte amici, *in solis gemitibus et lacrimis erat ei aliquantula requies.*

RESPONDEO dicendum quod lacrimae et gemitus naturaliter mitigant tristitiam. Et hoc duplici ratione. Primo quidem, quia omne nocivum interius clausum magis affligit, quia magis multiplicatur intentio animae circa ipsum, sed quando ad exteriora diffunditur, tunc animae intentio ad exteriora quodammodo disgregatur, et sic interior dolor minuitur. Et propter hoc, quando homines

ARTICLE 2
Whether pain or sorrow is assuaged by tears?

Objection 1: It would seem that tears do not assuage sorrow. Because no effect diminishes its cause. But tears or groans are an effect of sorrow. Therefore they do not diminish sorrow.

Objection 2: Further, just as tears or groans are an effect of sorrow, so laughter is an effect of joy. But laughter does not lessen joy. Therefore tears do not lessen sorrow.

Objection 3: Further, when we weep, the evil that saddens us is present to the imagination. But the image of that which saddens us increases sorrow, just as the image of a pleasant thing adds to joy. Therefore it seems that tears do not assuage sorrow.

On the contrary, Augustine says (Confess. iv, 7) that when he mourned the death of his friend, "in groans and in tears alone did he find some little refreshment."

I answer that, Tears and groans naturally assuage sorrow: and this for two reasons. First, because a hurtful thing hurts yet more if we keep it shut up, because the soul is more intent on it: whereas if it be allowed to escape, the soul's intention is dispersed as it were on outward things, so that the inward sorrow is lessened. This is why men,

qui sunt in tristitiis, exterius suam tristitiam manifestant vel fletu aut gemitu, vel etiam verbo, mitigatur tristitia. Secundo, quia semper operatio conveniens homini secundum dispositionem in qua est, sibi est delectabilis. Fletus autem et gemitus sunt quaedam operationes convenientes tristato vel dolenti. Et ideo efficiuntur ei delectabiles. Cum igitur omnis delectatio aliqualiter mitiget tristitiam vel dolorem, ut dictum est, sequitur quod per planctum et gemitum tristitia mitigetur.

AD PRIMUM ergo dicendum quod ipsa habitudo causae ad effectum contrariatur habitudini contristantis ad contristatum, nam omnis effectus est conveniens suae causae, et per consequens est ei delectabilis; contristans autem contrariatur contristato. Et ideo effectus tristitiae habet contrariam habitudinem ad contristatum, quam contristans ad ipsum. Et propter hoc, mitigatur tristitia per effectum tristitiae, ratione contrarietatis praedictae.

AD SECUNDUM dicendum quod habitudo effectus ad causam est similis habitudini delectantis ad delectatum, quia utrobique convenientia invenitur. Omne autem simile auget suum simile. Et ideo per risum et alios effectus laetitiae augetur laetitia, nisi forte per accidens, propter excessum.

AD TERTIUM dicendum quod imaginatio rei contristantis, quantum est de se, nata est augere tristitiam, sed ex hoc ipso quod homo imaginatur quod facit illud quod convenit sibi secundum talem statum, consurgit inde quaedam delectatio. Et eadem ratione, si alicui subrepat risus in statu in quo videtur sibi esse lugendum, ex hoc ipso dolet, tanquam faciat id quod non convenit, ut Tullius dicit, in III de Tuscul. quaestionibus.

ARTICULUS 3

AD TERTIUM sic proceditur. Videtur quod dolor amici compatientis non mitiget tristitiam. Contrariorum enim contrarii sunt effectus. Sed sicut Augustinus dicit, VIII Confess., *quando cum multis gaudetur,*

burdened with sorrow, make outward show of their sorrow, by tears or groans or even by words, their sorrow is assuaged. Secondly, because an action, that befits a man according to his actual disposition, is always pleasant to him. Now tears and groans are actions befitting a man who is in sorrow or pain; and consequently they become pleasant to him. Since then, as stated above (I-II, q. 38, a. 1), every pleasure assuages sorrow or pain somewhat, it follows that sorrow is assuaged by weeping and groans.

Reply to Objection 1: This relation of the cause to effect is opposed to the relation existing between the cause of sorrow and the sorrowing man. For every effect is suited to its cause, and consequently is pleasant to it; but the cause of sorrow is disagreeable to him that sorrows. Hence the effect of sorrow is not related to him that sorrows in the same way as the cause of sorrow is. For this reason sorrow is assuaged by its effect, on account of the aforesaid contrariety.

Reply to Objection 2: The relation of effect to cause is like the relation of the object of pleasure to him that takes pleasure in it: because in each case the one agrees with the other. Now every like thing increases its like. Therefore joy is increased by laughter and the other effects of joy: except they be excessive, in which case, accidentally, they lessen it.

Reply to Objection 3: The image of that which saddens us, considered in itself, has a natural tendency to increase sorrow: yet from the very fact that a man imagines himself to be doing that which is fitting according to his actual state, he feels a certain amount of pleasure. For the same reason if laughter escapes a man when he is so disposed that he thinks he ought to weep, he is sorry for it, as having done something unbecoming to him, as Cicero says (De Tusc. Quaest. iii, 27).

ARTICLE 3
Whether pain or sorrow are assuaged by the sympathy of friends?

Objection 1: It would seem that the sorrow of sympathizing friends does not assuage our own sorrow. For contraries have contrary effects. Now as Augustine says (Confess. viii, 4), "when many rejoice together,

in singulis uberius est gaudium, quia fervere faciunt se, et inflammantur ex alterutro. Ergo, pari ratione, quando multi simul tristantur, videtur quod sit maior tristitia.

Praeterea, hoc requirit amicitia, ut amoris vicem quis rependat, ut Augustinus dicit, IV Confess. Sed amicus condolens dolet de dolore amici dolentis. Ergo ipse dolor amici condolentis est causa amico prius dolenti de proprio malo, alterius doloris. Et sic, duplicato dolore, videtur tristitia crescere.

Praeterea, omne malum amici est contristans, sicut et malum proprium, nam *amicus est alter ipse.* Sed dolor est quoddam malum. Ergo dolor amici condolentis auget tristitiam amico cui condoletur.

Sed contra est quod philosophus dicit, in IX Ethic., quod in tristitiis amicus condolens consolatur.

Respondeo dicendum quod naturaliter amicus condolens in tristitiis, est consolativus. Cuius duplicem rationem tangit philosophus in IX Ethic. Quarum prima est quia, cum ad tristitiam pertineat aggravare, habet rationem cuiusdam oneris, a quo aliquis aggravatus alleviari conatur. Cum ergo aliquis videt de sua tristitia alios contristatos, fit ei quasi quaedam imaginatio quod illud onus alii cum ipso ferant, quasi conantes ad ipsum ab onere alleviandum et ideo levius fert tristitiae onus, sicut etiam in portandis oneribus corporalibus contingit. Secunda ratio, et melior, est quia per hoc quod amici contristantur ei, percipit se ab eis amari; quod est delectabile, ut supra dictum est. Unde, cum omnis delectatio mitiget tristitiam, sicut supra dictum est, sequitur quod amicus condolens tristitiam mitiget.

Ad primum ergo dicendum quod in utroque amicitia manifestatur, scilicet et quod congaudet gaudenti, et quod condolet

each one has more exuberant joy, for they are kindled and inflamed one by the other." Therefore, in like manner, when many are sorrowful, it seems that their sorrow is greater.

Objection 2: Further, friendship demands mutual love, as Augustine declares (Confess. iv, 9). But a sympathizing friend is pained at the sorrow of his friend with whom he sympathizes. Consequently the pain of a sympathizing friend becomes, to the friend in sorrow, a further cause of sorrow: so that, his pain being doubled his sorrow seems to increase.

Objection 3: Further, sorrow arises from every evil affecting a friend, as though it affected oneself: since "a friend is one's other self" (Ethic. ix, 4, 9). But sorrow is an evil. Therefore the sorrow of the sympathizing friend increases the sorrow of the friend with whom he sympathizes.

On the contrary, The Philosopher says (Ethic. ix, 11) that those who are in pain are consoled when their friends sympathize with them.

I answer that, When one is in pain, it is natural that the sympathy of a friend should afford consolation: whereof the Philosopher indicates a twofold reason (Ethic. ix, 11). The first is because, since sorrow has a depressing effect, it is like a weight whereof we strive to unburden ourselves: so that when a man sees others saddened by his own sorrow, it seems as though others were bearing the burden with him, striving, as it were, to lessen its weight; wherefore the load of sorrow becomes lighter for him: something like what occurs in the carrying of bodily burdens. The second and better reason is because when a man's friends condole with him, he sees that he is loved by them, and this affords him pleasure, as stated above (I-II, q. 32, a. 5). Consequently, since every pleasure assuages sorrow, as stated above (I-II, q. 38. a. 1), it follows that sorrow is mitigated by a sympathizing friend.

Reply to Objection 1: In either case there is a proof of friendship, *viz.* when a man rejoices with the joyful, and when he sorrows

dolenti. Et ideo utrumque ratione causae redditur delectabile.

AD SECUNDUM dicendum quod ipse dolor amici secundum se contristaret. Sed consideratio causae eius, quae est amor, magis delectat.

Et per hoc patet responsio ad tertium.

ARTICULUS 4

AD QUARTUM sic proceditur. Videtur quod contemplatio veritatis non mitiget dolorem. Dicitur enim Eccle. I, *qui addit scientiam, addit et dolorem.* Sed scientia ad contemplationem veritatis pertinet. Non ergo contemplatio veritatis mitigat dolorem.

PRAETEREA, contemplatio veritatis ad intellectum speculativum pertinet. Sed *intellectus speculativus non movet,* ut dicitur in III de anima. Cum igitur gaudium et dolor sint quidam motus animi, videtur quod contemplatio veritatis nihil faciat ad mitigationem doloris.

PRAETEREA, remedium aegritudinis apponendum est ubi est aegritudo. Sed contemplatio veritatis est in intellectu. Non ergo mitigat dolorem corporalem, qui est in sensu.

SED CONTRA est quod Augustinus dicit, in I Soliloq., *videbatur mihi, si se ille mentibus nostris veritatis fulgor aperiret, aut non me sensurum fuisse illum dolorem, aut certe pro nihilo toleraturum.*

RESPONDEO dicendum quod, sicut supra dictum est, in contemplatione veritatis maxima delectatio consistit. Omnis autem delectatio dolorem mitigat, ut supra dictum est. Et ideo contemplatio veritatis mitigat tristitiam vel dolorem, et tanto magis, quanto perfectius aliquis est amator sapientiae. Et ideo homines ex contemplatione divina et futurae beatitudinis, in tribulationibus gaudent; secundum illud Iacobi I, *omne gaudium existimate, fratres mei, cum*

with the sorrowful. Consequently each becomes an object of pleasure by reason of its cause.

Reply to Objection 2: The friend's sorrow itself would be a cause of sorrow: but consideration of its cause, *viz.* his love, gives rise rather to pleasure.

And this suffices for the reply to the Third Objection.

ARTICLE 4
Whether pain and sorrow are assuaged by the contemplation of truth?

Objection 1: It would seem that the contemplation of truth does not assuage sorrow. For it is written (Eccles. 1:18): "He that addeth knowledge addeth also sorrow.*" But knowledge pertains to the contemplation of truth. Therefore the contemplation of truth does not assuage sorrow.

Objection 2: Further, the contemplation of truth belongs to the speculative intellect. But "the speculative intellect is not a principle of movement"; as stated in De Anima iii, 11. Therefore, since joy and sorrow are movements of the soul, it seems that the contemplation of truth does not help to assuage sorrow.

Objection 3: Further, the remedy for an ailment should be applied to the part which ails. But contemplation of truth is in the intellect. Therefore it does not assuage bodily pain, which is in the senses.

On the contrary, Augustine says (Soliloq. i, 12): "It seemed to me that if the light of that truth were to dawn on our minds, either I should not feel that pain, or at least that pain would seem nothing to me."

I answer that, As stated above (I-II, q. 3, a. 5), the greatest of all pleasures consists in the contemplation of truth. Now every pleasure assuages pain as stated above (I-II, q. 38, a. 1): hence the contemplation of truth assuages pain or sorrow, and the more so, the more perfectly one is a lover of wisdom. And therefore in the midst of tribulations men rejoice in the contemplation of Divine things and of future Happiness, according to James 1:2: "My brethren, count it all joy, when you shall

---

* Vulg.: 'labor'

in tentationes varias incideritis. Et quod est amplius, etiam inter corporis cruciatus huiusmodi gaudium invenitur, sicut *Tiburtius martyr, cum nudatis plantis super ardentes prunas incederet, dixit, videtur mihi quod super roseos flores incedam, in nomine Iesu Christi.*

AD PRIMUM ergo dicendum quod *qui addit scientiam, addit dolorem,* vel propter difficultatem et defectum inveniendae veritatis, vel propter hoc, quod per scientiam homo cognoscit multa quae voluntati contrariantur. Et sic ex parte rerum cognitarum, scientia dolorem causat, ex parte autem contemplationis veritatis, delectationem.

AD SECUNDUM dicendum quod intellectus speculativus non movet animum ex parte rei speculatae, movet tamen animum ex parte ipsius speculationis, quae est quoddam bonum hominis, et naturaliter delectabilis.

AD TERTIUM dicendum quod in viribus animae fit redundantia a superiori ad inferius. Et secundum hoc, delectatio contemplationis, quae est in superiori parte, redundat ad mitigandum etiam dolorem qui est in sensu.

Articulus 5

AD QUINTUM sic proceditur. Videtur quod somnus et balneum non mitigent tristitiam. Tristitia enim in anima consistit. Sed somnus et balneum ad corpus pertinent. Non ergo aliquid faciunt ad mitigationem tristitiae.

PRAETEREA, idem effectus non videtur causari ex contrariis causis. Sed huiusmodi, cum sint corporalia, repugnant contemplationi veritatis, quae est causa mitigationis tristitiae, ut dictum est. Non ergo per huiusmodi tristitia mitigatur.

PRAETEREA, tristitia et dolor, secundum quod pertinent ad corpus, in quadam transmutatione cordis consistunt. Sed huiusmodi remedia magis videntur pertinere ad exteriores sensus et membra, quam ad interiorem

fall into divers temptations": and, what is more, even in the midst of bodily tortures this joy is found; as the "martyr Tiburtius, when he was walking barefoot on the burning coals, said: Methinks, I walk on roses, in the name of Jesus Christ."*

Reply to Objection 1: "He that addeth knowledge, addeth sorrow," either on account of the difficulty and disappointment in the search for truth; or because knowledge makes man acquainted with many things that are contrary to his will. Accordingly, on the part of the things known, knowledge causes sorrow: but on the part of the contemplation of truth, it causes pleasure.

Reply to Objection 2: The speculative intellect does not move the mind on the part of the thing contemplated: but on the part of contemplation itself, which is man's good and naturally pleasant to him.

Reply to Objection 3: In the powers of the soul there is an overflow from the higher to the lower powers: and accordingly, the pleasure of contemplation, which is in the higher part, overflows so as to mitigate even that pain which is in the senses.

Article 5
Whether pain and sorrow are assuaged by sleep and baths?

Objection 1: It would seem that sleep and baths do not assuage sorrow. For sorrow is in the soul: whereas sleep and baths regard the body. Therefore they do not conduce to the assuaging of sorrow.

Objection 2: Further, the same effect does not seem to ensue from contrary causes. But these, being bodily things, are incompatible with the contemplation of truth which is a cause of the assuaging of sorrow, as stated above (I-II, q. 38, a. 4). Therefore sorrow is not mitigated by the like.

Objection 3: Further, sorrow and pain, in so far as they affect the body, denote a certain transmutation of the heart. But such remedies as these seem to pertain to the outward senses and limbs, rather than to the interior

---

* Cf. Dominican Breviary, August 11th, commemoration of St. Tiburtius.

cordis dispositionem. Non ergo per huiusmodi tristitia mitigatur.

SED CONTRA est quod Augustinus dicit, IX Confess., *audieram balnei nomen inde dictum, quod anxietatem pellat ex animo* et infra, *dormivi, et evigilavi, et non parva ex parte mitigatum inveni dolorem meum.* Et inducit quod in hymno Ambrosii dicitur, quod *quies artus solutos reddit laboris usui, mentesque fessas allevat, luctusque solvit anxios.*

RESPONDEO dicendum quod, sicut supra dictum est, tristitia secundum suam speciem repugnat vitali motioni corporis. Et ideo illa quae reformant naturam corporalem in debitum statum vitalis motionis, repugnant tristitiae, et ipsam mitigant. Per hoc etiam quod huiusmodi remediis reducitur natura ad debitum statum, causatur ex his delectatio, hoc enim est quod delectationem facit, ut supra dictum est. Unde, cum omnis delectatio tristitiam mitiget, per huiusmodi remedia corporalia tristitia mitigatur.

AD PRIMUM ergo dicendum quod ipsa debita corporis dispositio, inquantum sentitur, delectationem causat, et per consequens tristitiam mitigat.

AD SECUNDUM dicendum quod delectationum una aliam impedit, ut supra dictum est, et tamen omnis delectatio tristitiam mitigat. Unde non est inconveniens quod ex causis se invicem impedientibus tristitia mitigetur.

AD TERTIUM dicendum quod omnis bona dispositio corporis redundat quodammodo ad cor, sicut ad principium et finem corporalium motionum, ut dicitur in libro de causa motus animalium.

disposition of the heart. Therefore they do not assuage sorrow.

On the contrary, Augustine says (Confess. ix, 12): "I had heard that the bath had its name* ... from the fact of its driving sadness from the mind." And further on, he says: "I slept, and woke up again, and found my grief not a little assuaged": and quotes the words from the hymn of Ambrose,† in which it is said that "Sleep restores the tired limbs to labor, refreshes the weary mind, and banishes sorrow."

I answer that, As stated above (I-II, q. 37, a. 4), sorrow, by reason of its specific nature, is repugnant to the vital movement of the body; and consequently whatever restores the bodily nature to its due state of vital movement, is opposed to sorrow and assuages it. Moreover such remedies, from the very fact that they bring nature back to its normal state, are causes of pleasure; for this is precisely in what pleasure consists, as stated above (I-II, q. 31, a. 1). Therefore, since every pleasure assuages sorrow, sorrow is assuaged by such like bodily remedies.

Reply to Objection 1: The normal disposition of the body, so far as it is felt, is itself a cause of pleasure, and consequently assuages sorrow.

Reply to Objection 2: As stated above (I-II, q. 31, a. 8), one pleasure hinders another; and yet every pleasure assuages sorrow. Consequently it is not unreasonable that sorrow should be assuaged by causes which hinder one another.

Reply to Objection 3: Every good disposition of the body reacts somewhat on the heart, which is the beginning and end of bodily movements, as stated in De Causa Mot. Animal. xi.

---

* *Balneum,* from the Greek βαλανεῖον (*balaneion*)
† Cf. Sarum Breviary: First Sunday after the octave of the Epiphany, Hymn for first Vespers.

Quaestio XXXIX

Deinde considerandum est de bonitate et malitia doloris vel tristitiae. Et circa hoc quaeruntur quatuor. *Primo,* utrum omnis tristitia sit malum. *Secundo,* utrum possit esse bonum honestum. *Tertio,* utrum possit esse bonum utile. *Quarto,* utrum dolor corporis sit summum malum.

Articulus 1

Ad primum sic proceditur. Videtur quod omnis tristitia sit mala. Dicit enim Gregorius Nyssenus, *omnis tristitia malum est, sui ipsius natura.* Sed quod naturaliter est malum, semper et ubique est malum. Ergo omnis tristitia est mala.

Praeterea, illud quod omnes fugiunt, etiam virtuosi, est malum. Sed tristitiam omnes fugiunt, etiam virtuosi, quia, ut dicitur in VII Ethic., *etsi prudens non intendat delectari, tamen intendit non tristari.* Ergo tristitia est malum.

Praeterea, sicut malum corporale est obiectum et causa doloris corporalis, ita malum spirituale est obiectum et causa tristitiae spiritualis. Sed omnis dolor corporalis est malum corporis. Ergo omnis tristitia spiritualis est malum animae.

Sed contra, tristitia de malo contrariatur delectationi de malo. Sed delectatio de malo est mala, unde in detestationem quorundam dicitur Prov. II, quod *laetantur cum malefecerint.* Ergo tristitia de malo est bona.

Respondeo dicendum quod aliquid esse bonum vel malum, potest dici dupliciter. Uno modo, simpliciter et secundum se. Et sic omnis tristitia est quoddam malum, hoc enim ipsum quod est appetitum hominis anxiari de malo praesenti, rationem mali habet; impeditur enim per hoc quies appetitus in bono. Alio modo dicitur aliquid bonum vel malum, ex suppositione alterius, sicut verecundia dicitur esse bonum, ex suppositione alicuius turpis commissi, ut dicitur in IV Ethic. Sic igitur, supposito aliquo contristabili vel

Question 39
Of the Goodness and Malice of Sorrow or Pain

We must now consider the goodness and malice of pain or sorrow: under which head there are four points of inquiry: 1. Whether all sorrow is evil? 2. Whether sorrow can be a virtuous good? 3. Whether it can be a useful good? 4. Whether bodily pain is the greatest evil?

Article 1
Whether all sorrow is evil?

Objection 1: It would seem that all sorrow is evil. For Gregory of Nyssa[*] says: "All sorrow is evil, from its very nature." Now what is naturally evil, is evil always and everywhere. Therefore, all sorrow is evil.

Objection 2: Further, that which all, even the virtuous, avoid, is evil. But all avoid sorrow, even the virtuous, since as stated in Ethic. vii, 11, "though the prudent man does not aim at pleasure, yet he aims at avoiding sorrow." Therefore sorrow is evil.

Objection 3: Further, just as bodily evil is the object and cause of bodily pain, so spiritual evil is the object and cause of sorrow in the soul. But every bodily pain is a bodily evil. Therefore every spiritual sorrow is an evil of the soul.

On the contrary, Sorrow for evil is contrary to pleasure in evil. But pleasure in evil is evil: wherefore in condemnation of certain men, it is written (Prov. 2:14), that "they were glad when they had done evil." Therefore sorrow for evil is good.

I answer that, A thing may be good or evil in two ways: first considered simply and in itself; and thus all sorrow is an evil, because the mere fact of a man's appetite being uneasy about a present evil, is itself an evil, because it hinders the response of the appetite in good. Secondly, a thing is said to be good or evil, on the supposition of something else: thus shame is said to be good, on the supposition of a shameful deed done, as stated in Ethic. iv, 9. Accordingly, supposing the presence of something saddening or

---

[*] Nemesius, De Nat. Hom. xix.

doloroso, ad bonitatem pertinet quod aliquis de malo praesenti tristetur vel doleat. Quod enim non tristaretur vel non doleret, non posset esse nisi quia vel non sentiret, vel quia non reputaret sibi repugnans, et utrumque istorum est malum manifeste. Et ideo ad bonitatem pertinet ut, supposita praesentia mali, sequatur tristitia vel dolor. Et hoc est quod Augustinus dicit, VIII super Gen. ad Litt., *adhuc est bonum quod dolet amissum bonum, nam nisi aliquod bonum remansisset in natura, nullius boni amissi dolor esset in poena.* Sed quia sermones morales sunt in singularibus, quorum sunt operationes, illud quod est ex suppositione bonum, debet bonum iudicari, sicut quod est ex suppositione voluntarium, iudicatur voluntarium, ut dicitur in III Ethic., et supra habitum est.

AD PRIMUM ergo dicendum quod Gregorius Nyssenus loquitur de tristitia ex parte mali tristantis, non autem ex parte sentientis et repudiantis malum. Et ex hac etiam parte omnes fugiunt tristitiam, inquantum fugiunt malum, sed sensum et refutationem mali non fugiunt. Et sic etiam dicendum est de dolore corporali, nam sensus et recusatio mali corporalis attestatur naturae bonae.

Unde patet responsio ad secundum et tertium.

ARTICULUS 2

AD SECUNDUM sic proceditur. Videtur quod tristitia non habeat rationem boni honesti. Quod enim ad Inferos deducit, contrariatur honesto. Sed sicut dicit Augustinus, XII super Gen. ad Litt., *Iacob hoc timuisse videtur, ne nimia tristitia sic perturbaretur, ut non ad requiem beatorum iret, sed ad Inferos peccatorum.* Ergo tristitia non habet rationem boni honesti.

PRAETEREA, bonum honestum habet rationem laudabilis et meritorii. Sed tristitia diminuit rationem laudis et meriti, dicit enim

painful, it is a sign of goodness if a man is in sorrow or pain on account of this present evil. For if he were not to be in sorrow or pain, this could only be either because he feels it not, or because he does not reckon it as something unbecoming, both of which are manifest evils. Consequently it is a condition of goodness, that, supposing an evil to be present, sorrow or pain should ensue. Wherefore Augustine says (Gen. ad lit. viii, 14): "It is also a good thing that he sorrows for the good he has lost: for had not some good remained in his nature, he could not be punished by the loss of good." Because, however, in the science of Morals, we consider things individually—for actions are concerned about individuals—that which is good on some supposition, should be considered as good: just as that which is voluntary on some supposition, is judged to be voluntary, as stated in Ethic. iii, 1, and likewise above (I-II, q. 6, a. 6).

Reply to Objection 1: Gregory of Nyssa* is speaking of sorrow on the part of the evil that causes it, but not on the part of the subject that feels and rejects the evil. And from this point of view, all shun sorrow, inasmuch as they shun evil: but they do not shun the perception and rejection of evil. The same also applies to bodily pain: because the perception and rejection of bodily evil is the proof of the goodness of nature.

This suffices for the Replies to the Second and Third Objections.

ARTICLE 2
Whether sorrow can be a virtuous good?
Objection 1: It would seem that sorrow is not a virtuous good. For that which leads to hell is not a virtuous good. But, as Augustine says (Gen. ad lit. xii, 33), "Jacob seems to have feared lest he should be troubled overmuch by sorrow, and so, instead of entering into the rest of the blessed, be consigned to the hell of sinners." Therefore sorrow is not a virtuous good.

Objection 2: Further, the virtuous good is praiseworthy and meritorious. But sorrow lessens praise or merit: for the

---
* Nemesius

apostolus, II ad Cor. IX, *unusquisque prout destinavit in corde suo, non ex tristitia aut ex necessitate.* Ergo tristitia non est bonum honestum.

PRAETEREA, sicut Augustinus dicit, XIV de Civ. Dei, *tristitia est de his quae, nobis nolentibus, accidunt.* Sed non velle ea quae praesentialiter fiunt, est habere voluntatem repugnantem ordinationi divinae, cuius providentiae subiacent omnia quae aguntur. Ergo, cum conformitas humanae voluntatis ad divinam pertineat ad rectitudinem voluntatis, ut supra dictum est; videtur quod tristitia contrarietur rectitudini voluntatis. Et sic non habet rationem honesti.

SED CONTRA, omne quod meretur praemium vitae aeternae, habet rationem honesti. Sed tristitia est huiusmodi, ut patet per id quod dicitur Matth. V, *beati qui lugent, quoniam ipsi consolabuntur.* Ergo tristitia est bonum honestum.

RESPONDEO dicendum quod, secundum illam rationem qua tristitia est bonum, potest esse bonum honestum. Dictum est enim quod tristitia est bonum secundum cognitionem et recusationem mali. Quae quidem duo in dolore corporali, attestantur bonitati naturae, ex qua provenit quod sensus sentit, et natura refugit laesivum, quod causat dolorem. In interiori vero tristitia, cognitio mali quandoque quidem est per rectum iudicium rationis; et recusatio mali est per voluntatem bene dispositam detestantem malum. Omne autem bonum honestum ex his duobus procedit, scilicet ex rectitudine rationis et voluntatis. Unde manifestum est quod tristitia potest habere rationem boni honesti.

AD PRIMUM ergo dicendum quod omnes passiones animae regulari debent secundum regulam rationis, quae est radix boni honesti. Quam transcendit immoderata tristitia, de qua loquitur Augustinus. Et ideo recedit a ratione boni honesti.

AD SECUNDUM dicendum quod, sicut tristitia de malo procedit ex voluntate et ratione recta, quae detestatur malum; ita tristitia de bono procedit ex ratione et voluntate perversa, quae detestatur bonum. Et ideo talis tristitia impedit laudem vel meritum

Apostle says (2 Cor. 9:7): "Everyone, as he hath determined in his heart, not with sadness, or of necessity." Therefore sorrow is not a virtuous good.

Objection 3: Further, as Augustine says (De Civ. Dei xiv, 15), "sorrow is concerned about those things which happen against our will." But not to will those things which are actually taking place, is to have a will opposed to the decree of God, to Whose providence whatever is done is subject. Since, then, conformity of the human to the Divine will is a condition of the rectitude of the will, as stated above (I-II, q. 19, a. 9), it seems that sorrow is incompatible with rectitude of the will, and that consequently it is not virtuous.

On the contrary, Whatever merits the reward of eternal life is virtuous. But such is sorrow; as is evident from Mat. 5:5: "Blessed are they that mourn, for they shall be comforted." Therefore sorrow is a virtuous good.

I answer that, In so far as sorrow is good, it can be a virtuous good. For it has been said above (I-II, q. 39, a. 1) that sorrow is a good inasmuch as it denotes perception and rejection of evil. These two things, as regards bodily pain, are a proof of the goodness of nature, to which it is due that the senses perceive, and that nature shuns, the harmful thing that causes pain. As regards interior sorrow, perception of the evil is sometimes due to a right judgment of reason; while the rejection of the evil is the act of the will, well disposed and detesting that evil. Now every virtuous good results from these two things, the rectitude of the reason and the will. Wherefore it is evident that sorrow may be a virtuous good.

Reply to Objection 1: All the passions of the soul should be regulated according to the rule of reason, which is the root of the virtuous good; but excessive sorrow, of which Augustine is speaking, oversteps this rule, and therefore it fails to be a virtuous good.

Reply to Objection 2: Just as sorrow for an evil arises from a right will and reason, which detest the evil, so sorrow for a good is due to a perverse reason and will, which detest the good. Consequently such sorrow is an obstacle to the praise and merit of the

boni honesti, sicut cum quis facit cum tristitia eleemosynam.

AD TERTIUM dicendum quod aliqua praesentialiter eveniunt, quae non fiunt Deo volente, sed Deo permittente, sicut peccata. Unde voluntas repugnans peccato existenti vel in se vel in alio, non discordat a voluntate Dei. Mala vero poenalia praesentialiter contingunt, etiam Deo volente. Non tamen exigitur ad rectitudinem voluntatis, quod ea secundum se homo velit, sed solum quod non contranitatur ordini divinae iustitiae, ut supra dictum est.

ARTICULUS 3

AD TERTIUM sic proceditur. Videtur quod tristitia non possit esse bonum utile. Dicitur enim Eccli. XXX, *multos occidit tristitia, et non est utilitas in illa.*

PRAETEREA, electio est de eo quod est utile ad finem aliquem. Sed tristitia non est eligibilis, quinimmo *idem sine tristitia, quam cum tristitia, est magis eligendum,* ut dicitur in III Topic. Ergo tristitia non est bonum utile.

PRAETEREA, *omnis res est propter suam operationem,* ut dicitur in II de coelo. Sed *tristitia impedit operationem,* ut dicitur in X Ethic. Ergo tristitia non habet rationem boni utilis.

SED CONTRA, sapiens non quaerit nisi utilia. Sed sicut dicitur Eccle. VII, *cor sapientum ubi tristitia, et cor stultorum ubi laetitia.* Ergo tristitia est utilis.

RESPONDEO dicendum quod ex malo praesenti insurgit duplex appetitivus motus. Unus quidem est quo appetitus contrariatur malo praesenti. Et ex ista parte tristitia non habet utilitatem, quia id quod est praesens, non potest non esse praesens. Secundus motus consurgit in appetitu ad fugiendum vel repellendum malum contristans. Et quantum ad hoc, tristitia habet utilitatem, si sit de aliquo quod est fugiendum. Est enim aliquid fugiendum dupliciter. Uno modo, propter seipsum, ex contrarietate quam habet ad bonum; sicut peccatum. Et ideo tristitia

virtuous good; for instance, when a man gives an alms sorrowfully.

Reply to Objection 3: Some things do actually happen, not because God wills, but because He permits them to happen—such as sins. Consequently a will that is opposed to sin, whether in oneself or in another, is not discordant from the Divine will. Penal evils happen actually, even by God's will. But it is not necessary for the rectitude of his will, that man should will them in themselves: but only that he should not revolt against the order of Divine justice, as stated above (I-II, q. 19, a. 10).

ARTICLE 3
Whether sorrow can be a useful good?

Objection 1: It would seem that sorrow cannot be a useful good. For it is written (Ecclus. 30:25): "Sadness hath killed many, and there is no profit in it."

Objection 2: Further, choice is of that which is useful to an end. But sorrow is not an object of choice; in fact, "a thing without sorrow is to be chosen rather than the same thing with sorrow" (Topic. iii, 2). Therefore sorrow is not a useful good.

Objection 3: Further, "Everything is for the sake of its own operation," as stated in De Coel. ii, 3. But "sorrow hinders operation," as stated in Ethic. x, 5. Therefore sorrow is not a useful good.

On the contrary, The wise man seeks only that which is useful. But according to Eccles. 7:5, "the heart of the wise is where there is mourning, and the heart of fools where there is mirth." Therefore sorrow is useful.

I answer that, A twofold movement of the appetite ensues from a present evil. One is that whereby the appetite is opposed to the present evil; and, in this respect, sorrow is of no use; because that which is present, cannot be not present. The other movement arises in the appetite to the effect of avoiding or expelling the saddening evil: and, in this respect, sorrow is of use, if it be for something which ought to be avoided. Because there are two reasons for which it may be right to avoid a thing. First, because it should be avoided in itself, on account of its being contrary to good; for instance, sin. Wherefore sorrow

de peccato utilis est ad hoc quod homo fugiat peccatum, sicut apostolus dicit, II ad Cor. VII, *gaudeo, non quia contristati estis, sed quia contristati estis ad poenitentiam.* Alio modo est aliquid fugiendum, non quia sit secundum se malum, sed quia est occasio mali; dum vel homo nimis inhaeret ei per amorem, vel etiam ex hoc praecipitatur in aliquod malum, sicut patet in bonis temporalibus. Et secundum hoc, tristitia de bonis temporalibus potest esse utilis, sicut dicitur Eccle. VII, *melius est ire ad domum luctus quam ad domum convivii, in illa enim finis cunctorum admonetur hominum.* Ideo autem tristitia in omni fugiendo est utilis, quia geminatur fugiendi causa. Nam ipsum malum secundum se fugiendum est, ipsam autem tristitiam secundum se omnes fugiunt, sicut etiam bonum omnes appetunt, et delectationem de bono. Sicut ergo delectatio de bono facit ut bonum avidius quaeratur, ita tristitia de malo facit ut malum vehementius fugiatur.

AD PRIMUM ergo dicendum quod auctoritas illa intelligitur de immoderata tristitia, quae animum absorbet. Huiusmodi enim tristitia immobilitat animum, et impedit fugam mali, ut supra dictum est.

AD SECUNDUM dicendum quod, sicut quodlibet eligibile fit minus eligibile propter tristitiam, ita quodlibet fugiendum redditur magis fugiendum propter tristitiam. Et quantum ad hoc, tristitia est utilis.

AD TERTIUM dicendum quod tristitia de operatione aliqua, impedit operationem, sed tristitia de cessatione operationis, facit avidius operari.

ARTICULUS 4

AD QUARTUM sic proceditur. Videtur quod tristitia sit summum malum. *Optimo enim opponitur pessimum,* ut dicitur in VIII Ethic. Sed quaedam delectatio est optimum, quae scilicet pertinet ad felicitatem. Ergo aliqua tristitia est summum malum.

PRAETEREA, beatitudo est summum bonum hominis, quia est ultimus hominis finis. Sed beatitudo consistit in hoc quod homo

for sin is useful as inducing a man to avoid sin: hence the Apostle says (2 Cor. 7:9): "I am glad: not because you were made sorrowful, but because you were made sorrowful unto penance." Secondly, a thing is to be avoided, not as though it were evil in itself, but because it is an occasion of evil; either through one's being attached to it, and loving it too much, or through one's being thrown headlong thereby into an evil, as is evident in the case of temporal goods. And, in this respect, sorrow for temporal goods may be useful; according to Eccles. 7:3: "It is better to go to the house of mourning, than to the house of feasting: for in that we are put in mind of the end of all." Moreover, sorrow for that which ought to be avoided is always useful, since it adds another motive for avoiding it. Because the very evil is in itself a thing to be avoided: while everyone avoids sorrow for its own sake, just as everyone seeks the good, and pleasure in the good. Therefore just as pleasure in the good makes one seek the good more earnestly, so sorrow for evil makes one avoid evil more eagerly.

Reply to Objection 1: This passage is to be taken as referring to excessive sorrow, which consumes the soul: for such sorrow paralyzes the soul, and hinders it from shunning evil, as stated above (I-II, q. 37, a. 2).

Reply to Objection 2: Just as any object of choice becomes less eligible by reason of sorrow, so that which ought to be shunned is still more to be shunned by reason of sorrow: and, in this respect, sorrow is useful.

Reply to Objection 3: Sorrow caused by an action hinders that action: but sorrow for the cessation of an action, makes one do it more earnestly.

ARTICLE 4
Whether bodily pain is the greatest evil?

Objection 1: It would seem that pain is the greatest evil. Because "the worst is contrary to the best" (Ethic. viii, 10). But a certain pleasure is the greatest good, *viz.* the pleasure of bliss. Therefore a certain pain is the greatest evil.

Objection 2: Further, happiness is man's greatest good, because it is his last end. But man's Happiness consists in his

habeat quidquid velit, et nihil mali velit, ut supra dictum est. Ergo summum bonum hominis est impletio voluntatis ipsius. Sed tristitia consistit in hoc quod accidit aliquid contra voluntatem, ut patet per Augustinum, XIV de Civ. Dei. Ergo tristitia est summum malum hominis.

PRAETEREA, Augustinus sic argumentatur in Soliloq., *ex duabus partibus compositi sumus, ex anima scilicet et corpore, quarum pars deterior corpus est. Summum autem bonum est melioris partis optimum, summum autem malum, pessimum deterioris. Est autem optimum in animo sapientia, in corpore pessimum dolor. Summum igitur bonum hominis est sapere, summum malum dolere.*

SED CONTRA, culpa est magis malum quam poena, ut in primo habitum est. Sed tristitia seu dolor pertinet ad poenam peccati; sicut frui rebus mutabilibus est malum culpae. Dicit enim Augustinus, in libro de vera religione, *quis est dolor qui dicitur animi, nisi carere mutabilibus rebus quibus fruebatur, aut frui se posse speraverat? Et hoc est totum quod dicitur malum, idest peccatum, et poena peccati.* Ergo tristitia seu dolor non est summum malum hominis.

RESPONDEO dicendum quod impossibile est aliquam tristitiam seu dolorem esse summum hominis malum. Omnis enim tristitia seu dolor aut est de hoc quod est vere malum, aut est de aliquo apparenti malo, quod est vere bonum. Dolor autem seu tristitia quae est de vere malo, non potest esse summum malum, est enim aliquid eo peius, scilicet vel non iudicare esse malum illud quod vere est malum, vel etiam non refutare illud. Tristitia autem vel dolor qui est de apparenti malo, quod est vere bonum, non potest esse summum malum, quia peius esset omnino alienari a vero bono. Unde impossibile est quod aliqua tristitia vel dolor sit summum hominis malum.

AD PRIMUM ergo dicendum quod duo bona sunt communia et delectationi et tristitiae, scilicet iudicium verum de bono et malo; et ordo debitus voluntatis approbantis bonum et recusantis malum. Et sic patet quod in dolore vel tristitia est aliquod bonum per

"having whatever he will, and in willing naught amiss," as stated above (I-II, q. 3, a. 4, ad 5; q. 5, a. 8, ad 3). Therefore man's greatest good consists in the fulfilment of his will. Now pain consists in something happening contrary to the will, as Augustine declares (De Civ. Dei xiv, 6, 15). Therefore pain is man's greatest evil.

Objection 3: Further, Augustine argues thus (Soliloq. i, 12): "We are composed of two parts, i.e., of a soul and a body, whereof the body is the inferior. Now the sovereign good is the greatest good of the better part: while the supreme evil is the greatest evil of the inferior part. But wisdom is the greatest good of the soul; while the worst thing in the body is pain. Therefore man's greatest good is to be wise: while his greatest evil is to suffer pain."

On the contrary, Guilt is a greater evil than punishment, as was stated in the I, q. 48, a. 6. But sorrow or pain belongs to the punishment of sin, just as the enjoyment of changeable things is an evil of guilt. For Augustine says (De Vera Relig. xii): "What is pain of the soul, except for the soul to be deprived of that which it was wont to enjoy, or had hoped to enjoy? And this is all that is called evil, i.e., sin, and the punishment of sin." Therefore sorrow or pain is not man's greatest evil.

I answer that, It is impossible for any sorrow or pain to be man's greatest evil. For all sorrow or pain is either for something that is truly evil, or for something that is apparently evil, but good in reality. Now pain or sorrow for that which is truly evil cannot be the greatest evil: for there is something worse, namely, either not to reckon as evil that which is really evil, or not to reject it. Again, sorrow or pain, for that which is apparently evil, but really good, cannot be the greatest evil, for it would be worse to be altogether separated from that which is truly good. Hence it is impossible for any sorrow or pain to be man's greatest evil.

Reply to Objection 1: Pleasure and sorrow have two good points in common: namely, a true judgment concerning good and evil; and the right order of the will in approving of good and rejecting evil. Thus it is clear that in pain or sorrow there is a good, by the

cuius privationem potest fieri deterius. Sed non in omni delectatione est aliquod malum, per cuius remotionem possit fieri melius. Unde delectatio aliqua potest esse summum hominis bonum, eo modo quo supra dictum est, tristitia autem non potest esse summum hominis malum.

AD SECUNDUM dicendum quod hoc ipsum quod est voluntatem repugnare malo, est quoddam bonum. Et propter hoc, tristitia vel dolor non potest esse summum malum, quia habet aliquam permixtionem boni.

AD TERTIUM dicendum quod peius est quod nocet meliori, quam quod nocet peiori. Malum autem dicitur *quia nocet,* ut dicit Augustinus in Enchirid. Unde maius malum est quod est malum animae, quam quod est malum corporis. Unde non est efficax, ratio, quam Augustinus inducit non ex sensu suo sed ex sensu alterius.

removal of which they become worse: and yet there is not an evil in every pleasure, by the removal of which the pleasure is better. Consequently, a pleasure can be man's highest good, in the way above stated (I-II, q. 34, a. 3): whereas sorrow cannot be man's greatest evil.

Reply to Objection 2: The very fact of the will being opposed to evil is a good. And for this reason, sorrow or pain cannot be the greatest evil; because it has an admixture of good.

Reply to Objection 3: That which harms the better thing is worse than that which harms the worse. Now a thing is called evil "because it harms," as Augustine says (Enchiridion xii). Therefore that which is an evil to the soul is a greater evil than that which is an evil to the body. Therefore this argument does not prove: nor does Augustine give it as his own, but as taken from another.*

QUAESTIO XL

Consequenter considerandum est de passionibus irascibilis, et *primo,* de spe et desperatione; *secundo,* de timore et audacia; *tertio,* de ira. Circa primum quaeruntur octo. *Primo,* utrum spes sit idem quod desiderium vel cupiditas. *Secundo,* utrum spes sit in vi apprehensiva, vel in vi appetitiva. *Tertio,* utrum spes sit in brutis animalibus. *Quarto,* utrum spei contrarietur desperatio. *Quinto,* utrum causa spei sit experientia. *Sexto,* utrum in iuvenibus et ebriosis spes abundet. *Septimo,* de ordine spei ad amorem. *Octavo,* utrum spes conferat ad operationem.

QUESTION 40
Of the Irascible Passions, and First, of Hope and Despair

We must now consider the irascible passions: 1. Hope and despair; 2. Fear and daring; 3. Anger. Under first head there are eight points of inquiry: 1. Whether hope is the same as desire or cupidity? 2. Whether hope is in the apprehensive, or in the appetitive faculty? 3. Whether hope is in dumb animals? 4. Whether despair is contrary to hope? 5. Whether experience is a cause of hope? 6. Whether hope abounds in young men and drunkards? 7. Concerning the order of hope to love; 8. Whether love conduces to action?

ARTICULUS 1

AD PRIMUM sic proceditur. Videtur quod spes sit idem quod desiderium sive cupiditas. Spes enim ponitur una quatuor principalium passionum. Sed Augustinus, enumerans quatuor principales passiones, ponit cupiditatem

ARTICLE 1
Whether hope is the same as desire of cupidity?

Objection 1: It would seem that hope is the same as desire or cupidity. Because hope is reckoned as one of the four principal passions. But Augustine in setting down the four principal passions puts cupidity in the

---

* Cornelius Celsus

loco spei, ut patet in XIV de Civ. Dei. Ergo spes est idem quod cupiditas sive desiderium.

PRAETEREA, passiones differunt secundum obiecta. Sed idem est obiectum spei, et cupiditatis sive desiderii, scilicet bonum futurum. Ergo spes est idem quod cupiditas sive desiderium.

SI DICATUR quod spes addit supra desiderium possibilitatem adipiscendi bonum futurum, contra, id quod per accidens se habet ad obiectum, non variat speciem passionis. Sed possibile se habet per accidens ad bonum futurum, quod est obiectum cupiditatis vel desiderii, et spei. Ergo spes non est passio specie differens a desiderio vel cupiditate.

SED CONTRA, diversarum potentiarum sunt diversae passiones specie differentes. Sed spes est in irascibili; desiderium autem et cupiditas in concupiscibili. Ergo spes differt specie a desiderio seu cupiditate.

RESPONDEO dicendum quod species passionis ex obiecto consideratur circa obiectum autem spei quatuor conditiones attenduntur. Primo quidem, quod sit bonum, non enim, proprie loquendo, est spes nisi de bono. Et per hoc differt spes a timore, qui est de malo. Secundo, ut sit futurum, non enim spes est de praesenti iam habito. Et per hoc differt spes a gaudio, quod est de bono praesenti. Tertio, requiritur quod sit aliquid arduum cum difficultate adipiscibile, non enim aliquis dicitur aliquid sperare minimum, quod statim est in sua potestate ut habeat. Et per hoc differt spes a desiderio vel cupiditate, quae est de bono futuro absolute, unde pertinet ad concupiscibilem, spes autem ad irascibilem. Quarto, quod illud arduum sit possibile adipisci, non enim aliquis sperat id quod omnino adipisci non potest. Et secundum hoc differt spes a desperatione. Sic ergo patet quod spes differt a desiderio, sicut differunt passiones irascibilis a passionibus concupiscibilis. Et propter hoc, spes praesupponit desiderium, sicut et omnes passiones irascibilis praesupponunt passiones concupiscibilis, ut supra dictum est.

place of hope (De Civ. Dei xiv, 3,7). Therefore hope is the same as cupidity or desire.

Objection 2: Further, passions differ according to their objects. But the object of hope is the same as the object of cupidity or desire, *viz.* the future good. Therefore hope is the same as cupidity or desire.

Objection 3: If it be said that hope, in addition to desire, denotes the possibility of obtaining the future good; on the contrary, whatever is accidental to the object does not make a different species of passion. But possibility of acquisition is accidental to a future good, which is the object of cupidity or desire, and of hope. Therefore hope does not differ specifically from desire or cupidity.

On the contrary, To different powers belong different species of passions. But hope is in the irascible power; whereas desire or cupidity is in the concupiscible. Therefore hope differs specifically from desire or cupidity.

I answer that, The species of a passion is taken from the object. Now, in the object of hope, we may note four conditions. First, that it is something good; since, properly speaking, hope regards only the good; in this respect, hope differs from fear, which regards evil. Secondly, that it is future; for hope does not regard that which is present and already possessed: in this respect, hope differs from joy which regards a present good. Thirdly, that it must be something arduous and difficult to obtain, for we do not speak of any one hoping for trifles, which are in one's power to have at any time: in this respect, hope differs from desire or cupidity, which regards the future good absolutely: wherefore it belongs to the concupiscible, while hope belongs to the irascible faculty. Fourthly, that this difficult thing is something possible to obtain: for one does not hope for that which one cannot get at all: and, in this respect, hope differs from despair. It is therefore evident that hope differs from desire, as the irascible passions differ from the concupiscible. For this reason, moreover, hope presupposes desire: just as all irascible passions presuppose the passions of the concupiscible faculty, as stated above (I-II, q. 25, a. 1).

Ad primum ergo dicendum quod Augustinus ponit cupiditatem loco spei, propter hoc quod utrumque respicit bonum futurum, et quia bonum quod non est arduum, quasi nihil reputatur; ut sic cupiditas maxime videatur tendere in bonum arduum, in quod etiam tendit spes.

Ad secundum dicendum quod obiectum spei non est bonum futurum absolute, sed cum arduitate et difficultate adipiscendi, ut dictum est.

Ad tertium dicendum quod obiectum spei non tantum addit possibilitatem super obiectum desiderii, sed etiam arduitatem, quae ad aliam potentiam facit spem pertinere, scilicet ad irascibilem, quae respicit arduum, ut in primo dictum est. Possibile autem et impossibile non omnino per accidens se habent ad obiectum appetitivae virtutis. Nam appetitus est principium motionis, nihil autem movetur ad aliquid nisi sub ratione possibilis; nullus enim movetur ad id quod existimat impossibile adipisci. Et propter hoc, spes differt a desperatione secundum differentiam possibilis et impossibilis.

Reply to Objection 1: Augustine mentions desire instead of hope, because each regards future good; and because the good which is not arduous is reckoned as nothing: thus implying that desire seems to tend chiefly to the arduous good, to which hope tends likewise.

Reply to Objection 1: The object of hope is the future good considered, not absolutely, but as arduous and difficult of attainment, as stated above.

Reply to Objection 3: The object of hope adds not only possibility to the object of desire, but also difficulty: and this makes hope belong to another power, *viz.* the irascible, which regards something difficult, as stated in the I, q. 81, a. 2. Moreover, possibility and impossibility are not altogether accidental to the object of the appetitive power: because the appetite is a principle of movement; and nothing is moved to anything except under the aspect of being possible; for no one is moved to that which he reckons impossible to get. Consequently hope differs from despair according to the difference of possible and impossible.

Articulus 2

Ad secundum sic proceditur. Videtur quod spes pertineat ad vim cognitivam. Spes enim videtur esse expectatio quaedam, dicit enim apostolus, Rom. VIII, *si autem quod non videmus speramus, per patientiam expectamus.* Sed expectatio videtur ad vim cognitivam pertinere, cuius est exspectare. Ergo spes ad cognitivam pertinet.

Praeterea, idem est, ut videtur, spes quod fiducia, unde et sperantes confidentes vocamus, quasi pro eodem utentes eo quod est confidere et sperare. Sed fiducia, sicut et fides, videtur ad vim cognitivam pertinere. Ergo et spes.

Praeterea, certitudo est proprietas cognitivae virtutis. Sed certitudo attribuitur spei. Ergo spes ad vim cognitivam pertinet.

Article 2
Whether hope is in the apprehensive or in the appetitive power?

Objection 1: It would seem that hope belongs to the cognitive power. Because hope, seemingly, is a kind of awaiting; for the Apostle says (Rom. 8:25): "If we hope for that which we see not; we wait for it with patience." But awaiting seems to belong to the cognitive power, which we exercise by "looking out." Therefore hope belongs to the cognitive power.

Objection 2: Further, apparently hope is the same as confidence; hence when a man hopes he is said to be confident, as though to hope and to be confident were the same thing. But confidence, like faith, seems to belong to the cognitive power. Therefore hope does too.

Objection 3: Further, certainty is a property of the cognitive power. But certainty is ascribed to hope. Therefore hope belongs to the cognitive power.

Sed contra, spes est de bono, sicut dictum est. Bonum autem, inquantum huiusmodi, non est obiectum cognitivae, sed appetitivae virtutis. Ergo spes non pertinet ad cognitivam, sed ad appetitivam virtutem.

Respondeo dicendum quod, cum spes importet extensionem quandam appetitus in bonum, manifeste pertinet ad appetitivam virtutem, motus enim ad res pertinet proprie ad appetitum. Actio vero virtutis cognitivae perficitur non secundum motum cognoscentis ad res, sed potius secundum quod res cognitae sunt in cognoscente. Sed quia vis cognitiva movet appetitivam, repraesentando ei suum obiectum; secundum diversas rationes obiecti apprehensi, subsequuntur diversi motus in vi appetitiva. Alius enim motus sequitur in appetitu ex apprehensione boni, et alius ex apprehensione mali, et similiter alius motus ex apprehensione praesentis et futuri, absoluti et ardui, possibilis et impossibilis. Et secundum hoc, spes est motus appetitivae virtutis consequens apprehensionem boni futuri ardui possibilis adipisci, scilicet extensio appetitus in huiusmodi obiectum.

Ad primum ergo dicendum quod, quia spes respicit ad bonum possibile, insurgit dupliciter homini motus spei, sicut dupliciter est ei aliquid possibile, scilicet secundum propriam virtutem, et secundum virtutem alterius. Quod ergo aliquis sperat per propriam virtutem adipisci, non dicitur expectare, sed sperare tantum. Sed proprie dicitur expectare quod sperat ex auxilio virtutis alienae, ut dicatur exspectare quasi ex alio spectare, inquantum scilicet vis apprehensiva praecedens non solum respicit ad bonum quod intendit adipisci, sed etiam ad illud cuius virtute adipisci sperat; secundum illud Eccli. li, *respiciens eram ad adiutorium hominum.* Motus ergo spei quandoque dicitur

On the contrary, Hope regards good, as stated above (I-II, q. 40, a. 1). Now good, as such, is not the object of the cognitive, but of the appetitive power. Therefore hope belongs, not to the cognitive, but to the appetitive power.

I answer that, Since hope denotes a certain stretching out of the appetite towards good, it evidently belongs to the appetitive power; since movement towards things belongs properly to the appetite: whereas the action of the cognitive power is accomplished not by the movement of the knower towards things, but rather according as the things known are in the knower. But since the cognitive power moves the appetite, by presenting its object to it; there arise in the appetite various movements according to various aspects of the apprehended object. For the apprehension of good gives rise to one kind of movement in the appetite, while the apprehension of evil gives rise to another: in like manner various movements arise from the apprehension of something present and of something future; of something considered absolutely, and of something considered as arduous; of something possible, and of something impossible. And accordingly hope is a movement of the appetitive power ensuing from the apprehension of a future good, difficult but possible to obtain; namely, a stretching forth of the appetite to such a good.

Reply to Objection 1: Since hope regards a possible good, there arises in man a twofold movement of hope; for a thing may be possible to him in two ways, *viz.* by his own power, or by another's. Accordingly when a man hopes to obtain something by his own power, he is not said to wait for it, but simply to hope for it. But, properly speaking, he is said to await that which he hopes to get by another's help as though to await [*exspectare*] implied keeping one's eyes on another [*ex alio spectare*], in so far as the apprehensive power, by going ahead, not only keeps its eye on the good which man intends to get, but also on the thing by whose power he hopes to get it; according to Ecclus. 51:10, "I looked for the succor of men." Wherefore the movement of hope is sometimes called

expectatio, propter inspectionem virtutis cognitivae praecedentem.

AD SECUNDUM dicendum quod illud quod homo desiderat, et aestimat se posse adipisci, credit se adepturum, et ex tali fide in cognitiva praecedente, motus sequens in appetitu fiducia nominatur. Denominatur enim motus appetitivus a cognitione praecedente, sicut effectus ex causa magis nota, magis enim cognoscit vis apprehensiva suum actum quam actum appetitivae.

AD TERTIUM dicendum quod certitudo attribuitur motui non solum appetitus sensitivi, sed etiam appetitus naturalis, sicut dicitur quod lapis certitudinaliter tendit deorsum. Et hoc propter infallibilitatem quam habet ex certitudine cognitionis quae praecedit motum appetitus sensitivi, vel etiam naturalis.

expectation, on account of the preceding inspection of the cognitive power.

Reply to Objection 2: When a man desires a thing and reckons that he can get it, he believes that he can get it, he believes that he will get it; and from this belief which precedes in the cognitive power, the ensuing movement in the appetite is called confidence. Because the movement of the appetite takes its name from the knowledge that precedes it, as an effect from a cause which is better known; for the apprehensive power knows its own act better than that of the appetite.

Reply to Objection 3: Certainty is ascribed to the movement, not only of the sensitive, but also of the natural appetite; thus we say that a stone is certain to tend downwards. This is owing to the inerrancy which the movement of the sensitive or even natural appetite derives from the certainty of the knowledge that precedes it.

ARTICULUS 3

AD TERTIUM sic proceditur. Videtur quod in brutis animalibus non sit spes. Spes enim est de futuro bono, ut Damascenus dicit. Sed cognoscere futurum non pertinet ad animalia bruta, quae habent solum cognitionem sensitivam, quae non est futurorum. Ergo spes non est in brutis animalibus.

PRAETEREA, obiectum spei est bonum possibile adipisci. Sed possibile et impossibile sunt quaedam differentiae veri et falsi, quae solum sunt in mente, ut philosophus dicit in VI Metaphys. Ergo spes non est in brutis animalibus, in quibus non est mens.

PRAETEREA, Augustinus dicit, super Gen. ad Litt., quod *animalia moventur visis*. Sed spes non est de eo quod videtur, *nam quod videt quis, quid sperat?* Ut dicitur Rom. VIII. Ergo spes non est in brutis animalibus.

SED CONTRA, spes est passio irascibilis. Sed in brutis animalibus est irascibilis. Ergo et spes.

ARTICLE 3
Whether hope is in dumb animals?

Objection 1: It would seem that there is no hope in dumb animals. Because hope is for some future good, as Damascene says (De Fide Orth. ii, 12). But knowledge of the future is not in the competency of dumb animals, whose knowledge is confined to the senses and does not extend to the future. Therefore there is no hope in dumb animals.

Objection 2: Further, the object of hope is a future good, possible of attainment. But possible and impossible are differences of the true and the false, which are only in the mind, as the Philosopher states (Metaph. vi, 4). Therefore there is no hope in dumb animals, since they have no mind.

Objection 3: Further, Augustine says (Gen. ad lit. ix, 14) that "animals are moved by the things that they see." But hope is of things unseen: "for what a man seeth, why doth he hope for?" (Rom. 8:24). Therefore there is no hope in dumb animals.

On the contrary, Hope is an irascible passion. But the irascible faculty is in dumb animals. Therefore hope is also.

Respondeo dicendum quod interiores passiones animalium ex exterioribus motibus deprehendi possunt. Ex quibus apparet quod in animalibus brutis est spes. Si enim canis videat leporem, aut accipiter avem, nimis distantem, non movetur ad ipsam, quasi non sperans se eam posse adipisci, si autem sit in propinquo, movetur, quasi sub spe adipiscendi. Ut enim supra dictum est, appetitus sensitivus brutorum animalium, et etiam appetitus naturalis rerum insensibilium, sequuntur apprehensionem alicuius intellectus, sicut et appetitus naturae intellectivae, qui dicitur voluntas. Sed in hoc est differentia, quod voluntas movetur ex apprehensione intellectus coniuncti, sed motus appetitus naturalis sequitur apprehensionem intellectus separati, qui naturam instituit; et similiter appetitus sensitivus brutorum animalium, quae etiam quodam instinctu naturali agunt. Unde in operibus brutorum animalium, et aliarum rerum naturalium, apparet similis processus sicut et in operibus artis. Et per hunc modum in animalibus brutis est spes et desperatio.

Ad primum ergo dicendum quod, quamvis bruta animalia non cognoscant futurum, tamen ex instinctu naturali movetur animal ad aliquid in futurum, ac si futurum praevideret. Huiusmodi enim instinctus est eis inditus ab intellectu divino praevidente futura.

Ad secundum dicendum quod obiectum spei non est possibile, prout est quaedam differentia veri, sic enim consequitur habitudinem praedicati ad subiectum. Sed obiectum spei est possibile quod dicitur secundum aliquam potentiam. Sic enim distinguitur possibile in V Metaphys., scilicet in duo possibilia praedicta.

Ad tertium dicendum quod, licet id quod est futurum, non cadat sub visu; tamen ex his quae videt animal in praesenti, movetur eius appetitus in aliquod futurum vel prosequendum vel vitandum.

I answer that, The internal passions of animals can be gathered from their outward movements: from which it is clear that hope is in dumb animals. For if a dog see a hare, or a hawk see a bird, too far off, it makes no movement towards it, as having no hope to catch it: whereas, if it be near, it makes a movement towards it, as being in hopes of catching it. Because as stated above (I-II, q. 1, a. 2; q. 26, a. 1; q. 35, a. 1), the sensitive appetite of dumb animals, and likewise the natural appetite of insensible things, result from the apprehension of an intellect, just as the appetite of the intellectual nature, which is called the will. But there is a difference, in that the will is moved by an apprehension of the intellect in the same subject; whereas the movement of the natural appetite results from the apprehension of the separate Intellect, Who is the Author of nature; as does also the sensitive appetite of dumb animals, who act from a certain natural instinct. Consequently, in the actions of irrational animals and of other natural things, we observe a procedure which is similar to that which we observe in the actions of art: and in this way hope and despair are in dumb animals.

Reply to Objection 1: Although dumb animals do not know the future, yet an animal is moved by its natural instinct to something future, as though it foresaw the future. Because this instinct is planted in them by the Divine Intellect that foresees the future.

Reply to Objection 2: The object of hope is not the possible as differentiating the true, for thus the possible ensues from the relation of a predicate to a subject. The object of hope is the possible as compared to a power. For such is the division of the possible given in Metaph. v, 12, i.e., into the two kinds we have just mentioned.

Reply to Objection 3: Although the thing which is future does not come under the object of sight; nevertheless through seeing something present, an animal's appetite is moved to seek or avoid something future.

Articulus 4

Ad quartum sic proceditur. Videtur quod desperatio non sit contraria spei. *Uni enim unum est contrarium,* ut dicitur in X Metaphys. Sed spei contrariatur timor. Non ergo contrariatur ei desperatio.

Praeterea, contraria videntur esse circa idem. Sed spes et desperatio non sunt circa idem, nam spes respicit bonum, desperatio autem est propter aliquod malum impeditivum adeptionis boni. Ergo spes non contrariatur desperationi.

Praeterea, motui contrariatur motus, quies vero opponitur motui ut privatio. Sed desperatio magis videtur importare immobilitatem quam motum. Ergo non contrariatur spei, quae importat motum extensionis in bonum speratum.

Sed contra est quod *desperatio* nominatur per contrarium spei.

Respondeo dicendum quod, sicut supra dictum est, in mutationibus invenitur duplex contrarietas. Una secundum accessum ad contrarios terminos, et talis contrarietas sola invenitur in passionibus concupiscibilis, sicut amor et odium contrariantur. Alio modo, per accessum et per recessum respectu eiusdem termini, et talis contrarietas invenitur in passionibus irascibilis, sicut supra dictum est. Obiectum autem spei, quod est bonum arduum, habet quidem rationem attractivi, prout consideratur cum possibilitate adipiscendi, et sic tendit in ipsum spes, quae importat quendam accessum. Sed secundum quod consideratur cum impossibilitate obtinendi, habet rationem repulsivi, quia, ut dicitur in III Ethic., *cum ventum fuerit ad aliquid impossibile, tunc homines discedunt.* Et sic respicit hoc obiectum desperatio. Unde importat motum cuiusdam recessus. Et propter hoc, contrariatur spei sicut recessus accessui.

Ad primum ergo dicendum quod timor contrariatur spei secundum contrarietatem obiectorum, scilicet boni et mali, haec enim contrarietas invenitur in passionibus irascibilis, secundum quod derivantur a passionibus

Article 4
Whether despair is contrary to hope?

Objection 1: It would seem that despair is not contrary to hope. Because "to one thing there is one contrary" (Metaph. x, 5). But fear is contrary to hope. Therefore despair is not contrary to hope.

Objection 2: Further, contraries seem to bear on the same thing. But hope and despair do not bear on the same thing: since hope regards the good, whereas despair arises from some evil that is in the way of obtaining good. Therefore hope is not contrary to despair.

Objection 3: Further, movement is contrary to movement: while repose is in opposition to movement as a privation thereof. But despair seems to imply immobility rather than movement. Therefore it is not contrary to hope, which implies movement of stretching out towards the hoped-for good.

On the contrary, The very name of despair [*desperatio*] implies that it is contrary to hope [*spes*].

I answer that, As stated above (I-II, q. 23, a. 2), there is a twofold contrariety of movements. One is in respect of approach to contrary terms: and this contrariety alone is to be found in the concupiscible passions, for instance between love and hatred. The other is according to approach and withdrawal with regard to the same term; and is to be found in the irascible passions, as stated above (I-II, q. 23, a. 2). Now the object of hope, which is the arduous good, has the character of a principle of attraction, if it be considered in the light of something attainable; and thus hope tends thereto, for it denotes a kind of approach. But in so far as it is considered as unobtainable, it has the character of a principle of repulsion, because, as stated in Ethic. iii, 3, "when men come to an impossibility they disperse." And this is how despair stands in regard to this object, wherefore it implies a movement of withdrawal: and consequently it is contrary to hope, as withdrawal is to approach.

Reply to Objection 1: Fear is contrary to hope, because their objects, i.e., good and evil, are contrary: for this contrariety is found in the irascible passions, according as they ensue from the passions of the

concupiscibilis. Sed desperatio contrariatur ei solum secundum contrarietatem accessus et recessus.

AD SECUNDUM dicendum quod desperatio non respicit malum sub ratione mali, sed per accidens quandoque respicit malum, inquantum facit impossibilitatem adipiscendi. Potest autem esse desperatio ex solo superexcessu boni.

AD TERTIUM dicendum quod desperatio non importat solam privationem spei; sed importat quendam recessum a re desiderata, propter aestimatam impossibilitatem adipiscendi. Unde desperatio praesupponit desiderium, sicut et spes, de eo enim quod sub desiderio nostro non cadit, neque spem neque desperationem habemus. Et propter hoc etiam, utrumque eorum est de bono, quod sub desiderio cadit.

concupiscible. But despair is contrary to hope, only by contrariety of approach and withdrawal.

Reply to Objection 2: Despair does not regard evil as such; sometimes however it regards evil accidentally, as making the difficult good impossible to obtain. But it can arise from the mere excess of good.

Reply to Objection 3: Despair implies not only privation of hope, but also a recoil from the thing desired, by reason of its being esteemed impossible to get. Hence despair, like hope, presupposes desire; because we neither hope for nor despair of that which we do not desire to have. For this reason, too, each of them regards the good, which is the object of desire.

ARTICULUS 5

AD QUINTUM sic proceditur. Videtur quod experientia non sit causa spei. Experientia enim ad vim cognitivam pertinet, unde philosophus dicit, in II Ethic., quod *virtus intellectualis indiget experimento et tempore.* Spes autem non est in vi cognitiva, sed in appetitiva, ut dictum est. Ergo experientia non est causa spei.

PRAETEREA, philosophus dicit, in II Rhetoric., quod *senes sunt difficilis spei, propter experientiam,* ex quo videtur quod experientia sit causa defectus spei. Sed non est idem causa oppositorum. Ergo experientia non est causa spei.

PRAETEREA, philosophus dicit, in II de caelo, quod *de omnibus enuntiare aliquid, et nihil praetermittere, quandoque est signum stultitiae.* Sed quod homo tentet omnia, ad magnitudinem spei pertinere videtur, stultitia autem provenit ex inexperientia. Ergo inexperientia videtur esse magis causa spei quam experientia.

SED CONTRA est quod philosophus dicit, in III Ethic., quod *aliqui sunt bonae spei, propter multoties et multos vicisse,* quod ad experientiam pertinet. Ergo experientia est causa spei.

ARTICLE 5
Whether experience is a cause of hope?

Objection 1: It would seem that experience is not a cause of hope. Because experience belongs to the cognitive power; wherefore the Philosopher says (Ethic. ii, 1) that "intellectual virtue needs experience and time." But hope is not in the cognitive power, but in the appetite, as stated above (I-II, q. 40, a. 2). Therefore experience is not a cause of hope.

Objection 2: Further, the Philosopher says (Rhet. ii, 13) that "the old are slow to hope, on account of their experience"; whence it seems to follow that experience causes want of hope. But the same cause is not productive of opposites. Therefore experience is not a cause of hope.

Objection 3: Further, the Philosopher says (De Coel. ii, 5) that "to have something to say about everything, without leaving anything out, is sometimes a proof of folly." But to attempt everything seems to point to great hopes; while folly arises from inexperience. Therefore inexperience, rather than experience, seems to be a cause of hope.

On the contrary, The Philosopher says (Ethic. iii, 8) "some are hopeful, through having been victorious often and over many opponents": which seems to pertain to experience. Therefore experience is a cause of hope.

Respondeo dicendum quod, sicut supra dictum est, spei obiectum est bonum futurum arduum possibile adipisci. Potest ergo aliquid esse causa spei, vel quia facit homini aliquid esse possibile, vel quia facit eum existimare aliquid esse possibile. Primo modo est causa spei omne illud quod auget potestatem hominis, sicut divitiae, fortitudo, et, inter cetera, etiam experientia, nam per experientiam homo acquirit facultatem aliquid de facili faciendi, et ex hoc sequitur spes. Unde Vegetius dicit, in libro de re militari, *nemo facere metuit quod se bene didicisse confidit*. Alio modo est causa spei omne illud quod facit alicui existimationem quod aliquid sit sibi possibile. Et hoc modo et doctrina, et persuasio quaelibet potest esse causa spei. Et sic etiam experientia est causa spei, inquantum scilicet per experientiam fit homini existimatio quod aliquid sit sibi possibile, quod impossibile ante experientiam reputabat. Sed per hunc modum experientia potest etiam esse causa defectus spei. Quia sicut per experientiam fit homini existimatio quod aliquid sibi sit possibile, quod reputabat impossibile; ita e converso per experientiam fit homini existimatio quod aliquid non sit sibi possibile, quod possibile existimabat. Sic ergo experientia est causa spei duobus modis, causa autem defectus spei, uno modo. Et propter hoc, magis dicere possumus eam esse causam spei.

Ad primum ergo dicendum quod experientia in operabilibus non solum causat scientiam; sed etiam causat quendam habitum, propter consuetudinem, qui facit operationem faciliorem. Sed et ipsa virtus intellectualis facit ad potestatem facile operandi, demonstrat enim aliquid esse possibile. Et sic causat spem.

Ad secundum dicendum quod in senibus est defectus spei propter experientiam, inquantum experientia facit existimationem impossibilis. Unde ibidem subditur quod *eis multa evenerunt in deterius*.

Ad tertium dicendum quod stultitia et inexperientia possunt esse causa spei quasi per accidens, removendo scilicet scientiam per quam vere existimatur aliquid esse non possibile. Unde ea ratione inexperientia est

I answer that, As stated above (I-II, q. 40, a. 1), the object of hope is a future good, difficult but possible to obtain. Consequently a thing may be a cause of hope, either because it makes something possible to a man: or because it makes him think something possible. In the first way hope is caused by everything that increases a man's power; e.g., riches, strength, and, among others, experience: since by experience man acquires the faculty of doing something easily, and the result of this is hope. Wherefore Vegetius says (De Re Milit. i): "No one fears to do that which he is sure of having learned well." In the second way, hope is caused by everything that makes man think that he can obtain something: and thus both teaching and persuasion may be a cause of hope. And then again experience is a cause of hope, in so far as it makes him reckon something possible, which before his experience he looked upon as impossible. However, in this way, experience can cause a lack of hope: because just as it makes a man think possible what he had previously thought impossible; so, conversely, experience makes a man consider as impossible that which hitherto he had thought possible. Accordingly experience causes hope in two ways, despair in one way: and for this reason we may say rather that it causes hope.

Reply to Objection 1: Experience in matters pertaining to action not only produces knowledge; it also causes a certain habit, by reason of custom, which renders the action easier. Moreover, the intellectual virtue itself adds to the power of acting with ease: because it shows something to be possible; and thus is a cause of hope.

Reply to Objection 2: The old are wanting in hope because of their experience, in so far as experience makes them think something impossible. Hence he adds (Rhet. ii, 13) that "many evils have befallen them."

Reply to Objection 3: Folly and inexperience can be a cause of hope accidentally as it were, by removing the knowledge which would help one to judge truly a thing to be impossible. Wherefore inexperience is a

causa spei, qua experientia est causa defectus spei.

Articulus 6

Ad sextum sic proceditur. Videtur quod iuventus et ebrietas non sint causa spei. Spes enim importat quandam certitudinem et firmitatem, unde ad Heb. VI, spes comparatur ancorae. Sed iuvenes et ebrii deficiunt a firmitate, habent enim animum de facili mutabilem. Ergo iuventus et ebrietas non est causa spei.

Praeterea, ea quae augent potestatem, maxime sunt causa spei, ut supra dictum est. Sed iuventus et ebrietas quandam infirmitatem habent adiunctam. Ergo non sunt causa spei.

Praeterea, experientia est causa spei, ut dictum est. Sed iuvenibus experientia deficit. Ergo iuventus non est causa spei.

Sed contra est quod philosophus dicit, in III Ethic., quod *inebriati sunt bene sperantes*. Et in II Rhetoric. dicitur quod *iuvenes sunt bonae spei.*

Respondeo dicendum quod iuventus est causa spei propter tria, ut philosophus dicit in II Rhetoric. Et haec tria possunt accipi secundum tres conditiones boni quod est obiectum spei, quod est futurum, et arduum, et possibile, ut dictum est. Iuvenes enim multum habent de futuro, et parum de praeterito. Et ideo, quia memoria est praeteriti, spes autem futuri; parum habent de memoria, sed multum vivunt in spe. Iuvenes etiam, propter caliditatem naturae, habent multos spiritus, et ita in eis cor ampliatur. Ex amplitudine autem cordis est quod aliquis ad ardua tendat. Et ideo iuvenes sunt animosi et bonae spei. Similiter etiam illi qui non sunt passi repulsam, nec experti impedimenta in suis conatibus, de facili reputant aliquid sibi possibile. Unde et iuvenes, propter inexperientiam impedimentorum et defectuum, de facili reputant aliquid sibi possibile. Et ideo sunt bonae spei. Duo etiam istorum sunt

cause of hope, for the same reason as experience causes lack of hope.

Article 6
Whether hope abounds in young men and drunkards?

Objection 1: It would seem that youth and drunkenness are not causes of hope. Because hope implies certainty and steadiness; so much so that it is compared to an anchor (Heb. 6:19). But young men and drunkards are wanting in steadiness; since their minds are easily changed. Therefore youth and drunkenness are not causes of hope.

Objection 2: Further, as stated above (I-II, q. 40, a. 5), the cause of hope is chiefly whatever increases one's power. But youth and drunkenness are united to weakness. Therefore they are not causes of hope.

Objection 3: Further, experience is a cause of hope, as stated above (I-II, q. 40, a. 5). But youth lacks experience. Therefore it is not a cause of hope.

On the contrary, The Philosopher says (Ethic. iii, 8) that "drunken men are hopeful": and (Rhet. ii, 12) that "the young are full of hope."

I answer that, Youth is a cause of hope for three reasons, as the Philosopher states in Rhet. ii, 12: and these three reasons may be gathered from the three conditions of the good which is the object of hope—namely, that it is future, arduous and possible, as stated above (I-II, q. 40, a. 1). For youth has much of the future before it, and little of the past: and therefore since memory is of the past, and hope of the future, it has little to remember and lives very much in hope. Again, youths, on account of the heat of their nature, are full of spirit; so that their heart expands: and it is owing to the heart being expanded that one tends to that which is arduous; wherefore youths are spirited and hopeful. Likewise they who have not suffered defeat, nor had experience of obstacles to their efforts, are prone to count a thing possible to them. Wherefore youths, through inexperience of obstacles and of their own shortcomings, easily count a thing possible; and consequently are of good hope. Two of these causes are also in those who are

in ebriis, scilicet caliditas et multiplicatio spirituum, propter vinum; et iterum inconsideratio periculorum vel defectuum. Et propter eandem rationem etiam omnes stulti, et deliberatione non utentes, omnia tentant, et sunt bonae spei.

Ad primum ergo dicendum quod in iuvenibus et in ebriis licet non sit firmitas secundum rei veritatem, est tamen in eis secundum eorum aestimationem, reputant enim se firmiter assecuturos illud quod sperant.

Et similiter dicendum ad secundum, quod iuvenes et ebrii habent quidem infirmitatem secundum rei veritatem, sed secundum eorum existimationem, habent potestatem; quia suos defectus non cognoscunt.

Ad tertium dicendum quod non solum experientia, sed etiam inexperientia est quodammodo causa spei, ut dictum est.

Articulus 7

Ad septimum sic proceditur. Videtur quod spes non sit causa amoris. Quia secundum Augustinum, XIV de Civ. Dei, prima affectionum animae est amor. Sed spes est quaedam affectio animae. Amor ergo praecedit spem. Non ergo spes causat amorem.

Praeterea, desiderium praecedit spem. Sed desiderium causatur ex amore, ut dictum est. Ergo etiam spes sequitur amorem. Non ergo causat ipsum.

Praeterea, spes causat delectationem, ut supra dictum est. Sed delectatio non est nisi de bono amato. Ergo amor praecedit spem.

Sed contra est quod Matth. I, super illud, *Abraham genuit Isaac, Isaac autem genuit Iacob*, dicit Glossa, idest, *fides spem, spes caritatem*. Caritas autem est amor. Ergo amor causatur a spe.

Respondeo dicendum quod spes duo respicere potest. Respicit enim sicut obiectum, bonum speratum. Sed quia bonum speratum est arduum possibile; aliquando autem fit aliquod arduum possibile nobis, non per nos, sed per alios; ideo spes etiam respicit illud per quod

in drink—*viz.* heat and high spirits, on account of wine, and heedlessness of dangers and shortcomings. For the same reason all foolish and thoughtless persons attempt everything and are full of hope.

Reply to Objection 1: Although youths and men in drink lack steadiness in reality, yet they are steady in their own estimation, for they think that they will steadily obtain that which they hope for.

In like manner, in reply to the Second Objection, we must observe that young people and men in drink are indeed unsteady in reality: but, in their own estimation, they are capable, for they know not their shortcomings.

Reply to Objection 3: Not only experience, but also lack of experience, is, in some way, a cause of hope, as explained above (I-II, q. 40, a. 5, ad 3).

Article 7
Whether hope is a cause of love?

Objection 1: It would seem that hope is not a cause of love. Because, according to Augustine (De Civ. Dei xiv, 7, 9), love is the first of the soul's emotions. But hope is an emotion of the soul. Therefore love precedes hope, and consequently hope does not cause love.

Objection 2: Further, desire precedes hope. But desire is caused by love, as stated above (I-II, q. 25, a. 2). Therefore hope, too, follows love, and consequently is not its cause.

Objection 3: Further, hope causes pleasure, as stated above (I-II, q. 32, a. 3). But pleasure is only of the good that is loved. Therefore love precedes hope.

On the contrary, The gloss commenting on Mat. 1:2, "Abraham begot Isaac, and Isaac begot Jacob," says, i.e., "faith begets hope, and hope begets charity." But charity is love. Therefore love is caused by hope.

I answer that, Hope can regard two things. For it regards as its object, the good which one hopes for. But since the good we hope for is something difficult but possible to obtain; and since it happens sometimes that what is difficult becomes possible to us, not through ourselves but through others; hence it is that hope regards also that by which

fit nobis aliquid possibile. Inquantum igitur spes respicit bonum speratum, spes ex amore causatur, non enim est spes nisi de bono desiderato et amato. Inquantum vero spes respicit illum per quem fit aliquid nobis possibile, sic amor causatur ex spe, et non e converso. Ex hoc enim quod per aliquem speramus nobis posse provenire bona, movemur in ipsum sicut in bonum nostrum, et sic incipimus ipsum amare. Ex hoc autem quod amamus aliquem, non speramus de eo, nisi per accidens, inquantum scilicet credimus nos redamari ab ipso. Unde amari ab aliquo facit nos sperare de eo, sed amor eius causatur ex spe quam de eo habemus.

something becomes possible to us. In so far, then, as hope regards the good we hope to get, it is caused by love: since we do not hope save for that which we desire and love. But in so far as hope regards one through whom something becomes possible to us, love is caused by hope, and not vice versa. Because by the very fact that we hope that good will accrue to us through someone, we are moved towards him as to our own good; and thus we begin to love him. Whereas from the fact that we love someone we do not hope in him, except accidentally, that is, in so far as we think that he returns our love. Wherefore the fact of being loved by another makes us hope in him; but our love for him is caused by the hope we have in him.

Et per haec patet responsio ad obiecta.

Wherefore the Replies to the Objections are evident.

Articulus 8

Article 8
Whether hope is a help or a hindrance to action?

Ad octavum sic proceditur. Videtur quod spes non adiuvet operationem, sed magis impediat. Ad spem enim securitas pertinet. Sed securitas parit negligentiam, quae impedit operationem. Ergo spes impedit operationem.

Objection 1: It would seem that hope is not a help but a hindrance to action. Because hope implies security. But security begets negligence which hinders action. Therefore hope is a hindrance to action.

Praeterea, tristitia impedit operationem, ut supra dictum est. Sed spes quandoque causat tristitiam, dicitur enim Prov. XIII, *spes quae differtur, affligit animam.* Ergo spes impedit operationem.

Objection 2: Further, sorrow hinders action, as stated above (I-II, q. 37, a. 3). But hope sometimes causes sorrow: for it is written (Prov. 13:12): "Hope that is deferred afflicteth the soul." Therefore hope hinders action.

Praeterea, desperatio contrariatur spei, ut dictum est. Sed desperatio, maxime in rebus bellicis, adiuvat operationem, dicitur enim II Reg. II, quod *periculosa res est desperatio.* Ergo spes facit contrarium effectum, impediendo scilicet operationem.

Objection 3: Further, despair is contrary to hope, as stated above (I-II, q. 40, a. 4). But despair, especially in matters of war, conduces to action; for it is written (2 Kings 2:26), that "it is dangerous to drive people to despair." Therefore hope has a contrary effect, namely, by hindering action.

Sed contra est quod dicitur I ad Cor. IX, quod *qui arat, debet arare in spe fructus percipiendi.* Et eadem ratio est in omnibus aliis.

On the contrary, It is written (1 Cor. 9:10) that "he that plougheth should plough in hope . . . to receive fruit": and the same applies to all other actions.

Respondeo dicendum quod spes per se habet quod adiuvet operationem, intendendo ipsam. Et hoc ex duobus. Primo quidem, ex ratione sui obiecti, quod est bonum arduum possibile. Existimatio enim ardui excitat

I answer that, Hope of its very nature is a help to action by making it more intense: and this for two reasons. First, by reason of its object, which is a good, difficult but possible. For the thought of its being difficult arouses

attentionem, existimatio vero possibilis non retardat conatum. Unde sequitur quod homo intente operetur propter spem. Secundo vero, ex ratione sui effectus. Spes enim, ut supra dictum est, causat delectationem, quae adiuvat operationem, ut supra dictum est. Unde spes operationem adiuvat.

AD PRIMUM ergo dicendum quod spes respicit bonum consequendum, securitas autem respicit malum vitandum. Unde securitas magis videtur opponi timori, quam ad spem pertinere. Et tamen securitas non causat negligentiam, nisi inquantum diminuit existimationem ardui, in quo etiam diminuitur ratio spei. Illa enim in quibus homo nullum impedimentum timet, quasi iam non reputantur ardua.

AD SECUNDUM dicendum quod spes per se causat delectationem, sed per accidens est ut causet tristitiam, ut supra dictum est.

AD TERTIUM dicendum quod desperatio in bello fit periculosa, propter aliquam spem adiunctam. Illi enim qui desperant de fuga, debilitantur in fugiendo, sed sperant mortem suam vindicare. Et ideo ex hac spe acrius pugnant, unde periculosi hostibus fiunt.

our attention; while the thought that it is possible is no drag on our effort. Hence it follows that by reason of hope man is intent on his action. Secondly, on account of its effect. Because hope, as stated above (I-II, q. 32, a. 3), causes pleasure; which is a help to action, as stated above (I-II, q. 33, a. 4). Therefore hope is conducive to action.

Reply to Objection 1: Hope regards a good to be obtained; security regards an evil to be avoided. Wherefore security seems to be contrary to fear rather than to belong to hope. Yet security does not beget negligence, save in so far as it lessens the idea of difficulty: whereby it also lessens the character of hope: for the things in which a man fears no hindrance, are no longer looked upon as difficult.

Reply to Objection 2: Hope of itself causes pleasure; it is by accident that it causes sorrow, as stated above (I-II, q. 32, a. 3, ad 2).

Reply to Objection 3: Despair threatens danger in war, on account of a certain hope that attaches to it. For they who despair of flight, strive less to fly, but hope to avenge their death: and therefore in this hope they fight the more bravely, and consequently prove dangerous to the foe.

Quaestio XLI

Consequenter considerandum est, primo, de timore; et secundo, de audacia. Circa timorem consideranda sunt quatuor, *primo*, de ipso timore; *secundo*, de obiecto eius; *tertio*, de causa ipsius; *quarto*, de effectu. Circa primum quaeruntur quatuor. *Primo*, utrum timor sit passio animae. *Secundo*, utrum sit specialis passio. *Tertio*, utrum sit aliquis timor naturalis. *Quarto*, de speciebus timoris.

Articulus 1

Ad primum sic proceditur. Videtur quod timor non sit passio animae. Dicit enim Damascenus, in libro III, quod *timor est virtus secundum systolen* idest contractionem, *essentiae desiderativa*. Sed nulla virtus est passio, ut probatur in II Ethic. Ergo timor non est passio.

Praeterea, omnis passio est effectus ex praesentia agentis proveniens. Sed timor non est de aliquo praesenti, sed de futuro, ut Damascenus dicit in II libro. Ergo timor non est passio.

Praeterea, omnis passio animae est motus appetitus sensitivi, qui sequitur apprehensionem sensus. Sensus autem non est apprehensivus futuri, sed praesentis. Cum ergo timor sit de malo futuro, videtur quod non sit passio animae.

Sed contra est quod Augustinus, in XIV de Civ. Dei, enumerat timorem inter alias animae passiones.

Respondeo dicendum quod, inter ceteros animae motus, post tristitiam, timor magis rationem obtinet passionis. Ut enim supra dictum est, ad rationem passionis primo quidem pertinet quod sit motus passivae virtutis, ad quam scilicet comparetur suum obiectum per modum activi moventis, eo quod passio est effectus agentis. Et per hunc modum, etiam *sentire* et *intelligere* dicuntur pati. Secundo, magis proprie dicitur passio motus appetitivae virtutis. Et adhuc magis proprie, motus appetitivae virtutis habentis organum corporale, qui fit cum aliqua transmutatione corporali. Et adhuc

Question 41
Of Fear, in Itself

We must now consider, in the first place, fear; and, secondly, daring. With regard to fear, four things must be considered: 1. Fear, in itself; 2. Its object; 3. Its cause; 4. Its effect. Under the first head there are four points of inquiry: 1. Whether fear is a passion of the soul? 2. Whether fear is a special passion? 3. Whether there is a natural fear? 4. Of the species of fear.

Article 1
Whether fear is a passion of the soul?

Objection 1: It would seem that fear is not a passion of the soul. For Damascene says (De Fide Orth. iii, 23) that "fear is a power, by way of συστολή (*systole*)"—i.e., of contraction—"desirous of vindicating nature." But no virtue is a passion, as is proved in Ethic. ii, 5. Therefore fear is not a passion.

Objection 2: Further, every passion is an effect due to the presence of an agent. But fear is not of something present, but of something future, as Damascene declares (De Fide Orth. ii, 12). Therefore fear is not a passion.

Objection 3: Further, every passion of the soul is a movement of the sensitive appetite, in consequence of an apprehension of the senses. But sense apprehends, not the future but the present. Since, then, fear is of future evil, it seems that it is not a passion of the soul.

On the contrary, Augustine (De Civ. Dei xiv, 5, seqq.) reckons fear among the other passions of the soul.

I answer that, Among the other passions of the soul, after sorrow, fear chiefly has the character of passion. For as we have stated above (I-II, q. 22), the notion of passion implies first of all a movement of a passive power—i.e., of a power whose object is compared to it as its active principle: since passion is the effect of an agent. In this way, both "to feel" and "to understand" are passions. Secondly, more properly speaking, passion is a movement of the appetitive power; and more properly still, it is a movement of an appetitive power that has a bodily organ, such movement being accompanied by a bodily transmutation. And, again,

propriissime illi motus passiones dicuntur, qui important aliquod nocumentum. Manifestum est autem quod timor, cum sit de malo, ad appetitivam potentiam pertinet, quae per se respicit bonum et malum. Pertinet autem ad appetitum sensitivum, fit enim cum quadam transmutatione, scilicet cum contractione, ut Damascenus dicit. Et importat etiam habitudinem ad malum, secundum quod malum habet quodammodo victoriam super aliquod bonum. Unde verissime sibi competit ratio passionis. Tamen post tristitiam, quae est de malo praesenti, nam timor est de malo futuro, quod non ita movet sicut praesens.

AD PRIMUM ergo dicendum quod virtus nominat quoddam principium actionis, et ideo, inquantum interiores motus appetitivae virtutis sunt principia exteriorum actuum, dicuntur virtutes. Philosophus autem negat passionem esse virtutem quae est habitus.

AD SECUNDUM dicendum quod, sicut passio corporis naturalis provenit ex corporali praesentia agentis, ita passio animae provenit ex animali praesentia agentis, absque praesentia corporali vel reali, inquantum scilicet malum quod est futurum realiter, est praesens secundum apprehensionem animae.

AD TERTIUM dicendum quod sensus non apprehendit futurum, sed ex eo quod apprehendit praesens, animal naturali instinctu movetur ad sperandum futurum bonum, vel timendum futurum malum.

ARTICULUS 2

AD SECUNDUM sic proceditur. Videtur quod timor non sit specialis passio. Dicit enim Augustinus, in libro octoginta trium quaest., quod *quem non exanimat metus, nec cupiditas eum vastat, nec aegritudo,* idest tristitia, *macerat, nec ventilat gestiens et vana laetitia.* Ex quo videtur quod, remoto timore, omnes aliae passiones removentur. Non ergo passio est specialis, sed generalis.

PRAETEREA, philosophus dicit, in VI Ethic., quod *ita se habet in appetitu prosecutio et fuga, sicut in intellectu affirmatio et negatio.* Sed negatio non est aliquid speciale in intellectu, sicut nec affirmatio,

most properly those movements are called passions, which imply some deterioration. Now it is evident that fear, since it regards evil, belongs to the appetitive power, which of itself regards good and evil. Moreover, it belongs to the sensitive appetite: for it is accompanied by a certain transmutation—i.e., contraction—as Damascene says (cf. arg. 1). Again, it implies relation to evil as overcoming, so to speak, some particular good. Wherefore it has most properly the character of passion; less, however, than sorrow, which regards the present evil: because fear regards future evil, which is not so strong a motive as present evil.

Reply to Objection 1: Virtue denotes a principle of action: wherefore, in so far as the interior movements of the appetitive faculty are principles of external action, they are called virtues. But the Philosopher denies that passion is a virtue by way of habit.

Reply to Objection 2: Just as the passion of a natural body is due to the bodily presence of an agent, so is the passion of the soul due to the agent being present to the soul, although neither corporally nor really present: that is to say, in so far as the evil which is really future, is present in the apprehension of the soul.

Reply to Objection 3: The senses do not apprehend the future: but from apprehending the present, an animal is moved by natural instinct to hope for a future good, or to fear a future evil.

ARTICLE 2
Whether fear is a special passion?

Objection 1: It would seem that fear is not a special passion. For Augustine says (QQ. 83, qu. 33) that "the man who is not distraught by fear, is neither harassed by desire, nor wounded by sickness"—i.e., sorrow—"nor tossed about in transports of empty joys." Wherefore it seems that, if fear be set aside, all the other passions are removed. Therefore fear is not a special but a general passion.

Objection 2: Further, the Philosopher says (Ethic. vi, 2) that "pursuit and avoidance in the appetite are what affirmation and denial are in the intellect." But denial is nothing special in the intellect, as neither is affirmation,

sed aliquid commune ad multa. Ergo nec fuga in appetitu. Sed nihil est aliud timor quam fuga quaedam mali. Ergo timor non est passio specialis.

PRAETEREA, si timor esset passio specialis, praecipue in irascibili esset. Est autem timor etiam in concupiscibili. Dicit enim philosophus, in II Rhetoric., quod *timor est tristitia quaedam,* et Damascenus dicit quod *timor est virtus desiderativa,* tristitia autem et desiderium sunt in concupiscibili, ut supra dictum est. Non est ergo passio specialis, cum pertineat ad diversas potentias.

SED CONTRA est quod condividitur aliis passionibus animae; ut patet per Damascenum, in II libro.

RESPONDEO dicendum quod passiones animae recipiunt speciem ex obiectis. Unde specialis passio est quae habet speciale obiectum. Timor autem habet speciale obiectum, sicut et spes. Sicut enim obiectum spei est bonum futurum arduum possibile adipisci; ita obiectum timoris est malum futurum difficile cui resisti non potest. Unde timor est specialis passio animae.

AD PRIMUM ergo dicendum quod omnes passiones animae derivantur ex uno principio, scilicet ex amore, in quo habent ad invicem connexionem. Et ratione huius connexionis, remoto timore, removentur aliae passiones animae, non ideo quia sit passio generalis.

AD SECUNDUM dicendum quod non omnis fuga appetitus est timor, sed fuga ab aliquo speciali obiecto, ut dictum est. Et ideo, licet fuga sit quoddam generale, tamen timor est passio specialis.

AD TERTIUM dicendum quod timor nullo modo est in concupiscibili, non enim respicit malum absolute, sed cum quadam difficultate vel arduitate, ut ei resisti vix possit. Sed quia passiones irascibilis derivantur a passionibus concupiscibilis et ad eas terminantur, ut supra dictum est; ideo timori attribuuntur ea quae sunt concupiscibilis. Dicitur enim timor esse tristitia, inquantum obiectum, timoris est contristans, si praesens fuerit, unde et philosophus dicit ibidem

but something common to many. Therefore neither is avoidance anything special in the appetite. But fear is nothing but a kind of avoidance of evil. Therefore it is not a special passion.

Objection 3: Further, if fear were a special passion, it would be chiefly in the irascible part. But fear is also in the concupiscible: since the Philosopher says (Rhet. ii, 5) that "fear is a kind of sorrow"; and Damascene says (De Fide Orth. iii, 23) that fear is "a power of desire": and both sorrow and desire are in the concupiscible faculty, as stated above (I-II, q. 23, a. 4). Therefore fear is not a special passion, since it belongs to different powers.

On the contrary, Fear is condivided with the other passions of the soul, as is clear from Damascene (De Fide Orth. ii, 12,15).

I answer that, The passions of the soul derive their species from their objects: hence that is a special passion, which has a special object. Now fear has a special object, as hope has. For just as the object of hope is a future good, difficult but possible to obtain; so the object of fear is a future evil, difficult and irresistible. Consequently fear is a special passion of the soul.

Reply to Objection 1: All the passions of the soul arise from one source, *viz.* love, wherein they are connected with one another. By reason of this connection, when fear is put aside, the other passions of the soul are dispersed; not, however, as though it were a general passion.

Reply to Objection 2: Not every avoidance in the appetite is fear, but avoidance of a special object, as stated. Wherefore, though avoidance be something common, yet fear is a special passion.

Reply to Objection 3: Fear is nowise in the concupiscible: for it regards evil, not absolutely, but as difficult or arduous, so as to be almost unavoidable. But since the irascible passions arise from the passions of the concupiscible faculty, and terminate therein, as stated above (I-II, q. 25, a. 1); hence it is that what belongs to the concupiscible is ascribed to fear. For fear is called sorrow, in so far as the object of fear causes sorrow when present: wherefore the Philosopher says (Rhet.

quod timor procedit *ex phantasia futuri mali corruptivi vel contristativi*. Similiter et desiderium attribuitur a Damasceno timori, quia, sicut spes oritur a desiderio boni ita timor ex fuga mali; fuga autem mali oritur ex desiderio boni, ut ex supra dictis patet.

Articulus 3

Ad tertium sic proceditur. Videtur quod timor aliquis sit naturalis. Dicit enim Damascenus, in III libro, quod *est quidam timor naturalis, nolente anima dividi a corpore.*

Praeterea, timor ex amore oritur, ut dictum est. Sed est aliquis amor naturalis, ut Dionysius dicit, IV cap. de Div. Nom. Ergo etiam est aliquis timor naturalis.

Praeterea, timor opponitur spei, ut supra dictum est. Sed est aliqua spes naturae, ut patet per id quod dicitur Rom. IV, de Abraham, quod *contra spem* naturae, *in spem* gratiae *credidit*. Ergo etiam est aliquis timor naturae.

Sed contra, ea quae sunt naturalia, communiter inveniuntur in rebus animatis et inanimatis. Sed timor non invenitur in rebus inanimatis. Ergo timor non est naturalis.

Respondeo dicendum quod aliquis motus dicitur naturalis, quia ad ipsum inclinat natura. Sed hoc contingit dupliciter. Uno modo, quod totum perficitur a natura, absque aliqua operatione apprehensivae virtutis, sicut moveri sursum est motus naturalis ignis, et augeri est motus naturalis animalium et plantarum. Alio modo dicitur motus naturalis, ad quem natura inclinat, licet non perficiatur nisi per apprehensionem, quia, sicut supra dictum est, motus cognitivae et appetitivae virtutis reducuntur in naturam, sicut in principium primum. Et per hunc modum, etiam ipsi actus apprehensivae virtutis, ut intelligere, sentire et memorari, et etiam motus appetitus animalis, quandoque dicuntur naturales. Et per hunc modum potest dici timor naturalis.

ii, 5) that fear arises "from the representation of a future evil which is either corruptive or painful." In like manner desire is ascribed by Damascene to fear, because just as hope arises from the desire of good, so fear arises from avoidance of evil; while avoidance of evil arises from the desire of good, as is evident from what has been said above (I-II, q. 25, a. 2; q. 29, a. 2; q. 36, a. 2).

Article 3
Whether there is a natural fear?

Objection 1: It would seem that there is a natural fear. For Damascene says (De Fide Orth. iii, 23) that "there is a natural fear, through the soul refusing to be severed from the body."

Objection 2: Further, fear arises from love, as stated above (I-II, q. 41, a. 2, ad 1). But there is a natural love, as Dionysius says (Div. Nom. iv). Therefore there is also a natural fear.

Objection 3: Further, fear is opposed to hope, as stated above (I-II, q. 40, a. 4, ad 1). But there is a hope of nature, as is evident from Rom. 4:18, where it is said of Abraham that "against hope" of nature, "he believed in hope" of grace. Therefore there is also a fear of nature.

On the contrary, That which is natural is common to things animate and inanimate. But fear is not in things inanimate. Therefore there is no natural fear.

I answer that, A movement is said to be natural, because nature inclines thereto. Now this happens in two ways. First, so that it is entirely accomplished by nature, without any operation of the apprehensive faculty: thus to have an upward movement is natural to fire, and to grow is the natural movement of animals and plants. Secondly, a movement is said to be natural, if nature inclines thereto, though it be accomplished by the apprehensive faculty alone: since, as stated above (I-II, q. 10, a. 1), the movements of the cognitive and appetitive faculties are reducible to nature as to their first principle. In this way, even the acts of the apprehensive power, such as understanding, feeling, and remembering, as well as the movements of the animal appetite, are sometimes said to be natural.

Et distinguitur a timore non naturali, secundum diversitatem obiecti. Est enim, ut philosophus dicit in II Rhetoric., timor de *malo corruptivo,* quod natura refugit propter naturale desiderium essendi, et talis timor dicitur naturalis. Est iterum de *malo contristativo,* quod non repugnat naturae, sed desiderio appetitus, et talis timor non est naturalis. Sicut etiam supra amor, concupiscentia et delectatio distincta sunt per naturale et non naturale. Sed secundum primam acceptionem *naturalis,* sciendum est quod quaedam de passionibus animae quandoque dicuntur naturales, ut amor, desiderium et spes, aliae vero naturales dici non possunt. Et hoc ideo, quia amor et odium, desiderium et fuga, important inclinationem quandam ad prosequendum bonum et fugiendum malum; quae quidem inclinatio pertinet etiam ad appetitum naturalem. Et ideo est amor quidam naturalis, et desiderium vel spes potest quodammodo dici etiam in rebus naturalibus cognitione carentibus. Sed aliae passiones animae important quosdam motus ad quos nullo modo sufficit inclinatio naturalis. Vel quia de ratione harum passionum est sensus seu cognitio, sicut dictum est quod apprehensio requiritur ad rationem delectationis et doloris, unde quae carent cognitione, non possunt dici delectari vel dolere. Aut quia huiusmodi motus sunt contra rationem inclinationis naturalis, puta quod desperatio refugit bonum propter aliquam difficultatem; et timor refugit impugnationem mali contrarii, ad quod est inclinatio naturalis. Et ideo huiusmodi passiones nullo modo attribuuntur rebus inanimatis.

Et per hoc patet responsio ad obiecta.

And in this sense we may say that there is a natural fear; and it is distinguished from non-natural fear, by reason of the diversity of its object. For, as the Philosopher says (Rhet. ii, 5), there is a fear of "corruptive evil," which nature shrinks from on account of its natural desire to exist; and such fear is said to be natural. Again, there is a fear of "painful evil," which is repugnant not to nature, but to the desire of the appetite; and such fear is not natural. In this sense we have stated above (I-II, q. 26, a. 1; q. 30, a. 3; q. 31, a. 7) that love, desire, and pleasure are divisible into natural and non-natural. But in the first sense of the word "natural," we must observe that certain passions of the soul are sometimes said to be natural, as love, desire, and hope; whereas the others cannot be called natural. The reason of this is because love and hatred, desire and avoidance, imply a certain inclination to pursue what is good or to avoid what is evil; which inclination is to be found in the natural appetite also. Consequently there is a natural love; while we may also speak of desire and hope as being even in natural things devoid of knowledge. On the other hand the other passions of the soul denote certain movements, whereto the natural inclination is nowise sufficient. This is due either to the fact that perception or knowledge is essential to these passions (thus we have said q. 31, a. 1; a. 3; q. 35, a. 1, that apprehension is a necessary condition of pleasure and sorrow), wherefore things devoid of knowledge cannot be said to take pleasure or to be sorrowful: or else it is because such like movements are contrary to the very nature of natural inclination: for instance, despair flies from good on account of some difficulty; and fear shrinks from repelling a contrary evil; both of which are contrary to the inclination of nature. Wherefore such like passions are in no way ascribed to inanimate beings.

Thus the Replies to the Objections are evident.

Articulus 4

Ad quartum sic proceditur. Videtur quod inconvenienter Damascenus assignet sex species timoris, scilicet *segnitiem, erubescentiam, verecundiam, admirationem, stuporem, agoniam.* Ut enim philosophus dicit, in II Rhetoric., *timor est de malo contristativo.* Ergo species timoris debent respondere speciebus tristitiae. Sunt autem quatuor species tristitiae, ut supra dictum est. Ergo solum debent esse quatuor species timoris, eis correspondentes.

Praeterea, illud quod in actu nostro consistit, nostrae potestati subiicitur. Sed timor est de malo quod excedit potestatem nostram, ut dictum est. Non ergo segnities et erubescentia et verecundia, quae respiciunt operationem nostram, debent poni species timoris.

Praeterea, timor est de futuro, ut dictum est. Sed *verecundia est de turpi actu iam commisso,* ut Gregorius Nyssenus dicit. Ergo verecundia non est species timoris.

Praeterea, timor non est nisi de malo. Sed admiratio et stupor sunt de magno et insolito, sive bono sive malo. Ergo admiratio et stupor non sunt species timoris.

Praeterea, philosophi ex admiratione sunt moti ad inquirendum veritatem, ut dicitur in principio Metaphys. Timor autem non movet ad inquirendum, sed magis ad fugiendum. Ergo admiratio non est species timoris.

Sed in contrarium sufficiat auctoritas Damasceni et Gregorii Nysseni.

Respondeo dicendum quod, sicut dictum est, timor est de futuro malo quod excedit potestatem timentis, ut scilicet ei resisti non possit. Sicut autem bonum hominis, ita et malum, potest considerari vel in operatione ipsius, vel in exterioribus rebus. In operatione autem ipsius hominis, potest duplex malum timeri. Primo quidem, labor gravans naturam. Et sic causatur *segnities,* cum

Article 4
Whether the species of fear is suitably assigned?

Objection 1: It would seem that six species of fear are unsuitably assigned by Damascene (De Fide Orth. ii, 15); namely, "laziness, shamefacedness, shame, amazement, stupor, and anxiety." Because, as the Philosopher says (Rhet. ii, 5), "fear regards a saddening evil." Therefore the species of fear should correspond to the species of sorrow. Now there are four species of sorrow, as stated above (I-II, q. 35, a. 8). Therefore there should only be four species of fear corresponding to them.

Objection 2: Further, that which consists in an action of our own is in our power. But fear regards an evil that surpasses our power, as stated above (I-II, q. 41, a. 2). Therefore laziness, shamefacedness, and shame, which regard our own actions, should not be reckoned as species of fear.

Objection 3: Further, fear is of the future, as stated above (I-II, q. 41, a. 1; a. 2). But "shame regards a disgraceful deed already done," as Gregory of Nyssa* says. Therefore shame is not a species of fear.

Objection 4: Further, fear is only of evil. But amazement and stupor regard great and unwonted things, whether good or evil. Therefore amazement and stupor are not species of fear.

Objection 5: Further, Philosophers have been led by amazement to seek the truth, as stated in the beginning of Metaphysics. But fear leads to flight rather than to search. Therefore amazement is not a species of fear.

On the contrary suffices the authority of Damascene and Gregory of Nyssa† (cf. arg. 1; arg. 3).

I answer that, As stated above (I-II, q. 41, a. 2), fear regards a future evil which surpasses the power of him that fears, so that it is irresistible. Now man's evil, like his good, may be considered either in his action or in external things. In his action he has a twofold evil to fear. First, there is the toil that burdens his nature: and hence arises "laziness," as

---

* Nemesius, De Nat. Hom. xx.

† Nemesius.

scilicet aliquis refugit operari, propter timorem excedentis laboris. Secundo, turpitudo laedens opinionem. Et sic, si turpitudo timeatur in actu committendo, est *erubescentia,* si autem sit de turpi iam facto, est *verecundia.* Malum autem quod in exterioribus rebus consistit, triplici ratione potest excedere hominis facultatem ad resistendum. Primo quidem, ratione suae magnitudinis, cum scilicet aliquis considerat aliquod magnum malum, cuius exitum considerare non sufficit. Et sic est *admiratio.* Secundo, ratione dissuetudinis, quia scilicet aliquod malum inconsuetum nostrae considerationi offertur, et sic est magnum nostra reputatione. Et hoc modo est *stupor,* qui causatur ex insolita imaginatione. Tertio modo, ratione improvisionis, quia scilicet provideri non potest, sicut futura infortunia timentur. Et talis timor dicitur *agonia.*

AD PRIMUM ergo dicendum quod illae species tristitiae quae supra positae sunt, non accipiuntur secundum diversitatem obiecti, sed secundum effectus, et secundum quasdam speciales rationes. Et ideo non oportet quod illae species tristitiae respondeant istis speciebus timoris, quae accipiuntur secundum divisionem propriam obiecti ipsius timoris.

AD SECUNDUM dicendum quod operatio secundum quod iam fit, subditur potestati operantis. Sed aliquid circa operationem considerari potest facultatem operantis excedens, propter quod aliquis refugit actionem. Et secundum hoc, segnities, erubescentia et verecundia ponuntur species timoris.

AD TERTIUM dicendum quod de actu praeterito potest timeri convitium vel opprobrium futurum. Et secundum hoc, verecundia est species timoris.

AD QUARTUM dicendum quod non quaelibet admiratio et stupor sunt species timoris, sed admiratio quae est de magno malo, et stupor qui est de malo insolito. Vel potest dici quod, sicut segnities refugit laborem exterioris operationis, ita admiratio et stupor refugiunt difficultatem considerationis rei magnae et insolitae, sive sit bona sive mala,

when a man shrinks from work for fear of too much toil. Secondly, there is the disgrace which damages him in the opinion of others. And thus, if disgrace is feared in a deed that is yet to be done, there is "shamefacedness"; if, however, it be a deed already done, there is "shame." On the other hand, the evil that consists in external things may surpass man's faculty of resistance in three ways. First by reason of its magnitude; when, that is to say, a man considers some great evil the outcome of which he is unable to gauge: and then there is "amazement." Secondly, by reason of its being unwonted; because, to wit, some unwonted evil arises before us, and on that account is great in our estimation: and then there is "stupor," which is caused by the representation of something unwonted. Thirdly, by reason of its being unforeseen: thus future misfortunes are feared, and fear of this kind is called "anxiety."

Reply to Objection 1: Those species of sorrow given above are not derived from the diversity of objects, but from the diversity of effects, and for certain special reasons. Consequently there is no need for those species of sorrow to correspond with these species of fear, which are derived from the proper division of the object of fear itself.

Reply to Objection 2: A deed considered as being actually done, is in the power of the doer. But it is possible to take into consideration something connected with the deed, and surpassing the faculty of the doer, for which reason he shrinks from the deed. It is in this sense that laziness, shamefacedness, and shame are reckoned as species of fear.

Reply to Objection 3: The past deed may be the occasion of fear of future reproach or disgrace: and in this sense shame is a species of fear.

Reply to Objection 4: Not every amazement and stupor are species of fear, but that amazement which is caused by a great evil, and that stupor which arises from an unwonted evil. Or else we may say that, just as laziness shrinks from the toil of external work, so amazement and stupor shrink from the difficulty of considering a great and unwonted thing, whether good or evil:

ut hoc modo se habeat admiratio et stupor ad actum intellectus, sicut segnities ad exteriorem actum.

AD QUINTUM dicendum quod admirans refugit in praesenti dare iudicium de eo quod miratur, timens defectum, sed in futurum inquirit. Stupens autem timet et in praesenti iudicare, et in futuro inquirere. Unde admiratio est principium philosophandi, sed stupor est philosophicae considerationis impedimentum.

so that amazement and stupor stand in relation to the act of the intellect, as laziness does to external work.

Reply to Objection 5: He who is amazed shrinks at present from forming a judgment of that which amazes him, fearing to fall short of the truth, but inquires afterwards: whereas he who is overcome by stupor fears both to judge at present, and to inquire afterwards. Wherefore amazement is a beginning of philosophical research: whereas stupor is a hindrance thereto.

QUAESTIO XLII

Deinde considerandum est de obiecto timoris. Et circa hoc quaeruntur sex. *Primo,* utrum bonum sit obiectum timoris, vel malum. *Secundo,* utrum malum naturae sit obiectum timoris. *Tertio,* utrum timor sit de malo culpae. *Quarto,* utrum ipse timor timeri possit. *Quinto,* utrum repentina magis timeantur. *Sexto,* utrum ea contra quae non est remedium, magis timeantur.

QUESTION 42
Of the Object of Fear

We must now consider the object of fear: under which head there are six points of inquiry: 1. Whether good or evil is the object of fear? 2. Whether evil of nature is the object of fear? 3. Whether the evil of sin is an object of fear? 4. Whether fear itself can be feared? 5. Whether sudden things are especially feared? 6. Whether those things are more feared against which there is no remedy?

ARTICULUS 1

AD PRIMUM sic proceditur. Videtur quod bonum sit obiectum timoris. Dicit enim Augustinus, in libro octoginta trium quaest., quod *nihil timemus, nisi ne id quod amamus, aut adeptum amittamus, aut non adipiscamur speratum.* Sed id quod amamus est bonum. Ergo timor respicit bonum sicut proprium obiectum.

PRAETEREA, philosophus dicit, in II Rhetoric., quod *potestas, et super alium ipsum esse, est terribile.* Sed huiusmodi est quoddam bonum. Ergo bonum est obiectum timoris.

PRAETEREA, in Deo nihil malum esse potest. Sed mandatur nobis ut Deum timeamus; secundum illud Psalmi XXXIII, *timete dominum, omnes sancti eius.* Ergo etiam timor est de bono.

SED CONTRA est quod Damascenus dicit, in II libro, quod timor est de malo futuro.

ARTICLE 1
Whether the object of fear is good or evil?

Objection 1: It would seem that good is the object of fear. For Augustine says (QQ. 83, qu. 83) that "we fear nothing save to lose what we love and possess, or not to obtain that which we hope for." But that which we love is good. Therefore fear regards good as its proper object.

Objection 2: Further, the Philosopher says (Rhet. ii, 5) that "power and to be above another is a thing to be feared." But this is a good thing. Therefore good is the object of fear.

Objection 3: Further, there can be no evil in God. But we are commanded to fear God, according to Ps. 33:10: "Fear the Lord, all ye saints." Therefore even the good is an object of fear.

On the contrary, Damascene says (De Fide Orth. ii, 12) that fear is of future evil.

Respondeo dicendum quod timor est quidam motus appetitivae virtutis. Ad virtutem autem appetitivam pertinet prosecutio et fuga, ut dicitur in VI Ethic. Est autem prosecutio boni. Fuga autem mali. Unde quicumque motus appetitivae virtutis importat prosecutionem, habet aliquod bonum pro obiecto, quicumque autem importat fugam, habet malum pro obiecto. Unde, cum timor fugam quandam importet, primo et per se respicit malum sicut proprium obiectum. Potest autem respicere etiam bonum, secundum quod habet habitudinem ad malum. Quod quidem potest esse dupliciter. Uno quidem modo, inquantum per malum privatur bonum. Ex hoc autem ipso est aliquid malum, quod est privativum boni. Unde, cum fugiatur malum quia malum est, sequitur ut fugiatur quia privat bonum quod quis amando prosequitur. Et secundum hoc dicit Augustinus quod nulla est causa timendi, nisi ne amittatur bonum amatum. Alio modo comparatur bonum ad malum, ut causa ipsius, inquantum scilicet aliquod bonum sua virtute potest inducere aliquod nocumentum in bono amato. Et ideo, sicut spes, ut supra dictum est, ad duo respicit, scilicet ad bonum in quod tendit, et ad id per quod sperat se bonum concupitum adipisci; ita etiam timor ad duo respicit, scilicet ad malum quod refugit, et ad illud bonum quod sua virtute potest infligere malum. Et per hunc modum Deus timetur ab homine, inquantum potest infligere poenam, vel spiritualem vel corporalem. Per hunc etiam modum timetur potestas alicuius hominis, maxime quando est laesa, vel quando est iniusta, quia sic in promptu habet nocumentum inferre. Ita etiam timetur *super alium esse,* idest inniti alii, ut scilicet in eius potestate sic constitutum nobis nocumentum inferre, sicut ille qui est conscius criminis, timetur, ne crimen revelet.

Et per hoc patet responsio ad obiecta.

I answer that, Fear is a movement of the appetitive power. Now it belongs to the appetitive power to pursue and to avoid, as stated in Ethic. vi, 2: and pursuit is of good, while avoidance is of evil. Consequently whatever movement of the appetitive power implies pursuit, has some good for its object: and whatever movement implies avoidance, has an evil for its object. Wherefore, since fear implies an avoidance, in the first place and of its very nature it regards evil as its proper object. It can, however, regard good also, in so far as referable to evil. This can be in two ways. In one way, inasmuch as an evil causes privation of good. Now a thing is evil from the very fact that it is a privation of some good. Wherefore, since evil is shunned because it is evil, it follows that it is shunned because it deprives one of the good that one pursues through love thereof. And in this sense Augustine says that there is no cause for fear, save loss of the good we love. In another way, good stands related to evil as its cause: in so far as some good can by its power bring harm to the good we love: and so, just as hope, as stated above (I-II, q. 40, a. 7), regards two things, namely, the good to which it tends, and the thing through which there is a hope of obtaining the desired good; so also does fear regard two things, namely, the evil from which it shrinks, and that good which, by its power, can inflict that evil. In this way God is feared by man, inasmuch as He can inflict punishment, spiritual or corporal. In this way, too, we fear the power of man; especially when it has been thwarted, or when it is unjust, because then it is more likely to do us a harm. In like manner one fears "to be over another," i.e., to lean on another, so that it is in his power to do us a harm: thus a man fears another, who knows him to be guilty of a crime lest he reveal it to others.

This suffices for the Replies to the Objections.

Articulus 2

Ad secundum sic proceditur. Videtur quod timor non sit de malo naturae. Dicit enim philosophus, in II Rhetoric., quod *timor consiliativos facit*. Non autem consiliamur de his quae a natura eveniunt, ut dicitur in III Ethic. Ergo timor non est de malo naturae.

Praeterea, defectus naturales semper homini imminent, ut mors et alia huiusmodi. Si igitur de huiusmodi malis esset timor, oporteret quod homo semper esset in timore.

Praeterea, natura non movet ad contraria. Sed malum naturae provenit ex natura. Ergo quod timendo aliquis refugiat huiusmodi malum, non est a natura. Timor ergo naturalis non est de malo naturae; ad quem tamen hoc malum pertinere videtur.

Sed contra est quod philosophus dicit, in III Ethic., quod *inter omnia terribilissimum est mors,* quae est malum naturae.

Respondeo dicendum quod, sicut philosophus dicit in II Rhetoric., timor provenit ex *phantasia futuri mali corruptivi vel contristativi*. Sicut autem contristativum malum est quod contrariatur voluntati; ita corruptivum malum est quod contrariatur naturae. Et hoc est malum naturae. Unde de malo naturae potest esse timor. Sed considerandum est quod malum naturae quandoque est a causa naturali, et tunc dicitur malum naturae, non solum quia privat naturae bonum, sed etiam quia est effectus naturae; sicut mors naturalis, et alii huiusmodi defectus. Aliquando vero malum naturae provenit ex causa non naturali, sicut mors quae violenter infertur a persecutore. Et utroque modo malum naturae quodammodo timetur, et quodammodo non timetur. Cum enim timor proveniat *ex phantasia futuri mali,* ut dicit philosophus; illud quod removet futuri mali phantasiam, excludit etiam timorem. Quod autem non appareat aliquod malum ut futurum, potest ex duobus contingere. Uno quidem modo, ex hoc quod est remotum et distans, hoc enim, propter distantiam, imaginamur ut non futurum. Et ideo vel non timemus,

Article 2
Whether evil of nature is an object of fear?

Objection 1: It would seem that evil of nature is not an object of fear. For the Philosopher says (Rhet. ii, 5) that "fear makes us take counsel." But we do not take counsel about things which happen naturally, as stated in Ethic. iii, 3. Therefore evil of nature is not an object of fear.

Objection 2: Further, natural defects such as death and the like are always threatening man. If therefore such like evils were an object of fear, man would needs be always in fear.

Objection 3: Further, nature does not move to contraries. But evil of nature is an effect of nature. Therefore if a man shrinks from such like evils through fear thereof, this is not an effect of nature. Therefore natural fear is not of the evil of nature; and yet it seems that it should be.

On the contrary, The Philosopher says (Ethic. iii, 6) that "the most terrible of all things is death," which is an evil of nature.

I answer that, As the Philosopher says (Rhet. ii, 5), fear is caused by the "imagination of a future evil which is either corruptive or painful." Now just as a painful evil is that which is contrary to the will, so a corruptive evil is that which is contrary to nature: and this is the evil of nature. Consequently evil of nature can be the object of fear. But it must be observed that evil of nature sometimes arises from a natural cause; and then it is called evil of nature, not merely from being a privation of the good of nature, but also from being an effect of nature; such are natural death and other like defects. But sometimes evil of nature arises from a non-natural cause; such as violent death inflicted by an assailant. In either case evil of nature is feared to a certain extent, and to a certain extent not. For since fear arises "from the imagination of future evil," as the Philosopher says (Rhet. ii, 5), whatever removes the imagination of the future evil, removes fear also. Now it may happen in two ways that an evil may not appear as about to be. First, through being remote and far off: for, on account of the distance, such a thing is considered as though it were not to be. Hence we either do not fear

vel parum timemus. Ut enim philosophus dicit, in II Rhetoric., *quae valde longe sunt non timentur, sciunt enim omnes, quod morientur; sed quia non prope est, nihil curant.* Alio modo aestimatur aliquod malum quod est futurum, ut non futurum, propter necessitatem, quae facit ipsum aestimare ut praesens. Unde philosophus dicit, in II Rhetoric., quod *illi qui iam decapitantur non timent,* videntes sibi necessitatem mortis imminere; *sed ad hoc quod aliquis timeat, oportet adesse aliquam spem salutis.* Sic igitur malum naturae non timetur, quia non apprehenditur ut futurum. Si vero malum naturae, quod est corruptivum, apprehendatur ut propinquum, et tamen cum aliqua spe evasionis, tunc timebitur.

Ad primum ergo dicendum quod malum naturae quandoque non provenit a natura, ut dictum est. Secundum tamen quod a natura provenit, etsi non ex toto vitari possit, potest tamen differri. Et sub hac spe, potest esse consilium de vitatione ipsius.

Ad secundum dicendum quod malum naturae, etsi semper immineat, non tamen semper imminet de propinquo. Et ideo non semper timetur.

Ad tertium dicendum quod mors et alii defectus naturae proveniunt a natura universali, quibus tamen repugnat natura particularis quantum potest. Et sic ex inclinatione particularis naturae, est dolor et tristitia de huiusmodi malis, cum sunt praesentia; et timor, si immineant in futurum.

it, or fear it but little; for, as the Philosopher says (Rhet. ii, 5), "we do not fear things that are very far off; since all know that they shall die, but as death is not near, they heed it not." Secondly, a future evil is considered as though it were not to be, on account of its being inevitable, wherefore we look upon it as already present. Hence the Philosopher says (Rhet. ii, 5) that "those who are already on the scaffold, are not afraid," seeing that they are on the very point of a death from which there is no escape; "but in order that a man be afraid, there must be some hope of escape for him." Consequently evil of nature is not feared if it be not apprehended as future: but if evil of nature, that is corruptive, be apprehended as near at hand, and yet with some hope of escape, then it will be feared.

Reply to Objection 1: The evil of nature sometimes is not an effect of nature, as stated above. But in so far as it is an effect of nature, although it may be impossible to avoid it entirely, yet it may be possible to delay it. And with this hope one may take counsel about avoiding it.

Reply to Objection 2: Although evil of nature ever threatens, yet it does not always threaten from near at hand: and consequently it is not always feared.

Reply to Objection 3: Death and other defects of nature are the effects of the common nature; and yet the individual nature rebels against them as far as it can. Accordingly, from the inclination of the individual nature arise pain and sorrow for such like evils, when present; fear when threatening in the future.

Articulus 3

Ad tertium sic proceditur. Videtur quod timor possit esse de malo culpae. Dicit enim Augustinus, super canonicam Ioan., quod *timore casto timet homo separationem a Deo.* Sed nihil separat nos a Deo nisi culpa; secundum illud Isaiae LIX. *Peccata vestra diviserunt inter vos et Deum vestrum.* Ergo timor potest esse de malo culpae.

Article 3
Whether the evil of sin is an object of fear?

Objection 1: It would seem that the evil of sin can be an object of fear. For Augustine says on the canonical Epistle of John (Tract. ix), that "by chaste fear man fears to be severed from God." Now nothing but sin severs us from God; according to Is. 59:2: "Your iniquities have divided between you and your God." Therefore the evil of sin can be an object of fear.

PRAETEREA, Tullius dicit, in IV de Tusculanis quaest., quod *de illis timemus, cum futura sunt, de quorum praesentia tristamur.* Sed de malo culpae potest aliquis dolere vel tristari. Ergo etiam malum culpae aliquis potest timere.

PRAETEREA, spes timori opponitur. Sed spes potest esse de bono virtutis, ut patet per philosophum in IX Ethic. Et apostolus dicit, ad Gal. V, *confido de vobis in domino, quod nihil aliud sapietis.* Ergo etiam timor potest esse de malo culpae.

PRAETEREA, verecundia est quaedam species timoris, ut supra dictum est. Sed verecundia est de turpi facto. Quod est malum culpae. Ergo et timor.

SED CONTRA est quod philosophus dicit, in II Rhetoric., quod *non omnia mala timentur, puta si aliquis erit iniustus, aut tardus.*

RESPONDEO dicendum quod, sicut supra dictum est, sicut obiectum spei est bonum futurum arduum quod quis potest adipisci; ita timor est de malo futuro arduo quod non potest de facili vitari. Ex quo potest accipi quod id quod omnino subiacet potestati et voluntati nostrae, non habet rationem terribilis, sed illud solum est terribile, quod habet causam extrinsecam. Malum autem culpae propriam causam habet voluntatem humanam. Et ideo proprie non habet rationem terribilis. Sed quia voluntas humana ab aliquo exteriori potest inclinari ad peccandum; si illud inclinans habeat magnam vim ad inclinandum, secundum hoc poterit esse timor de malo culpae, inquantum est ab exteriori causa, puta cum aliquis timet commorari in societate malorum, ne ab eis ad peccandum inducatur. Sed proprie loquendo, in tali dispositione magis timet homo seductionem quam culpam secundum propriam rationem, idest inquantum est voluntaria, sic enim non habet ut timeatur.

AD PRIMUM ergo dicendum quod separatio a Deo est quaedam poena consequens peccatum, et omnis poena aliquo modo est ab exteriori causa.

AD SECUNDUM dicendum quod tristitia et timor in uno conveniunt, quia utrumque est de malo, differunt autem in duobus. In uno

Objection 2: Further, Cicero says (Quaest. Tusc. iv, 4, 6) that "we fear when they are yet to come, those things which give us pain when they are present." But it is possible for one to be pained or sorrowful on account of the evil of sin. Therefore one can also fear the evil of sin.

Objection 3: Further, hope is contrary to fear. But the good of virtue can be the object of hope, as the Philosopher declares (Ethic. ix, 4): and the Apostle says (Gal. 5:10): "I have confidence in you in the Lord, that you will not be of another mind." Therefore fear can regard evil of sin.

Objection 4: Further, shame is a kind of fear, as stated above (I-II, q. 41, a. 4). But shame regards a disgraceful deed, which is an evil of sin. Therefore fear does so likewise.

On the contrary, The Philosopher says (Rhet. ii, 5) that "not all evils are feared, for instance that someone be unjust or slow."

I answer that, As stated above (I-II, q. 40, a. 1; q. 41, a. 2), as the object of hope is a future good difficult but possible to obtain, so the object of fear is a future evil, arduous and not to be easily avoided. From this we may gather that whatever is entirely subject to our power and will, is not an object of fear; and that nothing gives rise to fear save what is due to an external cause. Now human will is the proper cause of the evil of sin: and consequently evil of sin, properly speaking, is not an object of fear. But since the human will may be inclined to sin by an extrinsic cause; if this cause have a strong power of inclination, in that respect a man may fear the evil of sin, in so far as it arises from that extrinsic cause: as when he fears to dwell in the company of wicked men, lest he be led by them to sin. But, properly speaking, a man thus disposed, fears the being led astray rather than the sin considered in its proper nature, i.e., as a voluntary act; for considered in this light it is not an object of fear to him.

Reply to Objection 1: Separation from God is a punishment resulting from sin: and every punishment is, in some way, due to an extrinsic cause.

Reply to Objection 2: Sorrow and fear agree in one point, since each regards evil: they differ, however, in two points. First,

quidem, quia tristitia est de malo praesenti, timor de malo futuro. In alio vero, quia tristitia, cum sit in concupiscibili, respicit malum absolute, unde potest esse de quocumque malo, sive parvo sive magno. Timor vero, cum sit in irascibili, respicit malum cum quadam arduitate seu difficultate, quae tollitur, inquantum aliquid subiacet voluntati. Et ideo non omnia timemus quae sunt futura, de quibus tristamur cum sunt praesentia, sed aliqua, quae scilicet sunt ardua.

AD TERTIUM dicendum quod spes est de bono quod quis potest adipisci. Potest autem aliquis adipisci bonum vel per se, vel per alium, et ideo spes potest esse de actu virtutis, qui est in potestate nostra constitutus. Sed timor est de malo quod non subiacet nostrae potestati, et ideo semper malum quod timetur, est a causa extrinseca. Bonum autem quod speratur, potest esse et a causa intrinseca, et a causa extrinseca.

AD QUARTUM dicendum quod, sicut supra dictum est, verecundia non est timor de actu ipso peccati, sed de turpitudine vel ignominia quae consequitur ipsum, quae est a causa extrinseca.

because sorrow is about present evil, whereas fear is future evil. Secondly, because sorrow, being in the concupiscible faculty, regards evil absolutely; wherefore it can be about any evil, great or small; whereas fear, being in the irascible part, regards evil with the addition of a certain arduousness or difficulty; which difficulty ceases in so far as a thing is subject to the will. Consequently not all things that give us pain when they are present, make us fear when they are yet to come, but only some things, namely, those that are difficult.

Reply to Objection 3: Hope is of good that is obtainable. Now one may obtain a good either of oneself, or through another: and so, hope may be of an act of virtue, which lies within our own power. On the other hand, fear is of an evil that does not lie in our own power: and consequently the evil which is feared is always from an extrinsic cause; while the good that is hoped for may be both from an intrinsic and from an extrinsic cause.

Reply to Objection 4: As stated above (I-II, q. 41, a. 4, ad 2; ad 3), shame is not fear of the very act of sin, but of the disgrace or ignominy which arises therefrom, and which is due to an extrinsic cause.

ARTICULUS 4

AD QUARTUM sic proceditur. Videtur quod timor timeri non possit. Omne enim quod timetur, timendo custoditur, ne amittatur, sicut ille qui timet amittere sanitatem timendo custodit eam. Si igitur timor timeatur, timendo se custodiet homo ne timeat. Quod videtur esse inconveniens.

PRAETEREA, timor est quaedam fuga. Sed nihil fugit seipsum. Ergo timor non timet timorem.

PRAETEREA, timor est de futuro. Sed ille qui timet, iam habet timorem. Non ergo potest timere timorem.

SED CONTRA est quod homo potest amare amorem, et dolere de dolore. Ergo etiam, pari ratione, potest timere timorem.

RESPONDEO dicendum quod, sicut dictum est, illud solum habet rationem terribilis, quod ex causa extrinseca provenit, non autem quod provenit ex voluntate nostra. Timor autem partim provenit ex

ARTICLE 4
Whether fear itself can be feared?

Objection 1: It would seem that fear cannot be feared. For whatever is feared, is prevented from being lost, through fear thereof: thus a man who fears to lose his health, keeps it, through fearing its loss. If therefore a man be afraid of fear, he will keep himself from fear by being afraid: which seems absurd.

Objection 2: Further, fear is a kind of flight. But nothing flies from itself. Therefore fear cannot be the object of fear.

Objection 3: Further, fear is about the future. But fear is present to him that fears. Therefore it cannot be the object of his fear.

On the contrary, A man can love his own love, and can grieve at his own sorrow. Therefore, in like manner, he can fear his own fear.

I answer that, As stated above (I-II, q. 42, a. 3), nothing can be an object of fear, save what is due to an extrinsic cause; but not that which ensues from our own will. Now fear partly arises from an

causa extrinseca, et partim subiacet voluntati. Provenit quidem ex causa extrinseca, inquantum est passio quaedam consequens phantasiam imminentis mali. Et secundum hoc, potest aliquis timere timorem, ne scilicet immineat ei necessitas timendi, propter ingruentiam alicuius excellentis mali. Subiacet autem voluntati, inquantum appetitus inferior obedit rationi, unde homo potest timorem repellere. Et secundum hoc, timor non potest timeri, ut dicit Augustinus, in libro octoginta trium quaest. Sed quia rationibus quas inducit, aliquis posset uti ad ostendendum quod timor nullo modo timeatur, ideo ad eas respondendum est.

AD PRIMUM ergo dicendum quod, non omnis timor est unus timor, sed secundum diversa quae timentur, sunt diversi timores. Nihil ergo prohibet quin uno timore aliquis praeservet se ab alio timore, et sic custodiat se non timentem illo timore.

AD SECUNDUM dicendum quod, cum sit alius timor quo timetur malum imminens, et alius timor quo timetur ipse timor mali imminentis; non sequitur quod idem fugiat seipsum, vel quod sit idem fuga sui ipsius.

AD TERTIUM dicendum quod propter diversitatem timorum iam dictam, timore praesenti potest homo timere futurum timorem.

ARTICULUS 5

AD QUINTUM sic proceditur. Videtur quod insolita et repentina non sint magis terribilia. Sicut enim spes est de bono, ita timor est de malo. Sed experientia facit ad augmentum spei in bonis. Ergo etiam facit ad augmentum timoris in malis.

PRAETEREA, philosophus dicit, in II Rhetoric., quod *magis timentur non qui acutae sunt irae, sed mites et astuti.* Constat autem quod illi qui acutae irae sunt, magis habent subitos motus. Ergo ea quae sunt subita, sunt minus terribilia.

PRAETEREA, quae sunt subita, minus considerari possunt. Sed tanto aliqua magis timentur, quanto magis considerantur,

extrinsic cause, and is partly subject to the will. It is due to an extrinsic cause, in so far as it is a passion resulting from the imagination of an imminent evil. In this sense it is possible for fear to be the object of fear, i.e., a man may fear lest he should be threatened by the necessity of fearing, through being assailed by some great evil. It is subject to the will, in so far as the lower appetite obeys reason; wherefore man is able to drive fear away. In this sense fear cannot be the object of fear, as Augustine says (QQ. 83, qu. 33). Lest, however, anyone make use of his arguments, in order to prove that fear cannot be at all be the object of fear, we must add a solution to the same.

Reply to Objection 1: Not every fear is identically the same; there are various fears according to the various objects of fear. Nothing, then, prevents a man from keeping himself from fearing one thing, by fearing another, so that the fear which he has preserves him from the fear which he has not.

Reply to Objection 2: Since fear of an imminent evil is not identical with the fear of the fear of imminent evil; it does not follow that a thing flies from itself, or that it is the same flight in both cases.

Reply to Objection 3: On account of the various kinds of fear already alluded to (ad 2) a man's present fear may have a future fear for its object.

ARTICLE 5
Whether sudden things are especially feared?

Objection 1: It would seem that unwonted and sudden things are not especially feared. Because, as hope is about good things, so fear is about evil things. But experience conduces to the increase of hope in good things. Therefore it also adds to fear in evil things.

Objection 2: Further, the Philosopher says (Rhet. ii, 5) that "those are feared most, not who are quick-tempered, but who are gentle and cunning." Now it is clear that those who are quick-tempered are more subject to sudden emotions. Therefore sudden things are less to be feared.

Objection 3: Further, we think less about things that happen suddenly. But the more we think about a thing, the more we fear it;

unde philosophus dicit, in III Ethic., quod *aliqui videntur fortes propter ignorantiam, qui, si cognoverint quod aliud sit quam suspicantur, fugiunt.* Ergo repentina minus timentur.

Sed contra est quod Augustinus dicit, in II Confess., *timor insolita et repentina exhorrescit, rebus quae amantur adversantia, dum praecavet securitati.*

Respondeo dicendum quod, sicut supra dictum est, obiectum timoris est malum imminens quod non de facili repelli potest. Hoc autem ex duobus contingit, scilicet ex magnitudine mali, et ex debilitate timentis. Ad utrumque autem horum operatur quod aliquid sit insolitum et repentinum. Primo quidem, facit ad hoc quod malum imminens maius appareat. Omnia enim corporalia, et bona et mala, quanto magis considerantur, minora apparent. Et ideo, sicut propter diuturnitatem dolor praesentis mali mitigatur, ut patet per Tullium in III de Tusculanis quaest.; ita etiam ex praemeditatione minuitur timor futuri mali. Secundo, aliquid esse insolitum et repentinum facit ad debilitatem timentis, inquantum subtrahit remedia quae homo potest praeparare ad repellendum futurum malum, quae esse non possunt quando ex improviso malum occurrit.

Ad primum ergo dicendum quod obiectum spei est bonum quod quis potest adipisci. Et ideo ea quae augmentant potestatem hominis, nata sunt augere spem, et eadem ratione, diminuere timorem, quia timor est de malo cui non de facili potest resisti. Quia igitur experientia facit hominem magis potentem ad operandum, ideo, sicut auget spem, ita diminuit timorem.

Ad secundum dicendum quod illi qui habent iram acutam, non occultant eam, et ideo nocumenta ab eis illata non ita sunt repentina, quin praevideantur. Sed homines mites et astuti occultant iram, et ideo nocumentum quod ab eis imminet, non potest praevideri, sed ex improviso advenit. Et propter hoc philosophus dicit quod tales magis timentur.

hence the Philosopher says (Ethic. iii, 8) that "some appear to be courageous through ignorance, but as soon as they discover that the case is different from what they expected, they run away." Therefore sudden things are feared less.

On the contrary, Augustine says (Confess. ii, 6): "Fear is startled at things unwonted and sudden, which endanger things beloved, and takes forethought for their safety."

I answer that, As stated above (I-II, q. 42, a. 3; q. 41, a. 2), the object of fear is an imminent evil, which can be repelled, but with difficulty. Now this is due to one of two causes: to the greatness of the evil, or to the weakness of him that fears; while unwontedness and suddenness conduce to both of these causes. First, it helps an imminent evil to seem greater. Because all material things, whether good or evil, the more we consider them, the smaller they seem. Consequently, just as sorrow for a present evil is mitigated in course of time, as Cicero states (De Quaest. Tusc. iii, 30); so, too, fear of a future evil is diminished by thinking about it beforehand. Secondly, unwontedness and suddenness increase the weakness of him that fears, in so far as they deprive him of the remedies with which he might otherwise provide himself to forestall the coming evil, were it not for the evil taking him by surprise.

Reply to Objection 1: The object of hope is a good that is possible to obtain. Consequently whatever increases a man's power, is of a nature to increase hope, and, for the same reason, to diminish fear, since fear is about an evil which cannot be easily repelled. Since, therefore, experience increases a man's power of action, therefore, as it increases hope, so does it diminish fear.

Reply to Objection 2: Those who are quick-tempered do not hide their anger; wherefore the harm they do others is not so sudden, as not to be foreseen. On the other hand, those who are gentle or cunning hide their anger; wherefore the harm which may be impending from them, cannot be foreseen, but takes one by surprise. For this reason the Philosopher says that such men are feared more than others.

AD TERTIUM dicendum quod, per se loquendo, bona vel mala corporalia in principio maiora apparent. Cuius ratio est, quia unumquodque magis apparet, contrario iuxta se posito. Unde cum aliquis statim a paupertate ad divitias transit, propter paupertatem praeexistentem divitias magis aestimat, et e contrario divites statim ad paupertatem devenientes, eam magis horrent. Et propter hoc, malum repentinum magis timetur, quia **magis videtur esse malum.** Sed potest propter aliquod accidens contingere quod magnitudo alicuius mali lateat, puta cum hostes se insidiose occultant. Et tunc verum est quod malum ex diligenti consideratione fit terribilius.

Reply to Objection 3: Bodily good or evil, considered in itself, seems greater at first. The reason for this is that a thing is more obvious when seen in juxtaposition with its contrary. Hence, when a man passes unexpectedly from penury to wealth, he thinks more of his wealth on account of his previous poverty: while, on the other hand, the rich man who suddenly becomes poor, finds poverty all the more disagreeable. For this reason sudden evil is feared more, **because it seems more to be evil.** However, it may happen through some accident that the greatness of some evil is hidden; for instance if the foe hides himself in ambush: and then it is true that evil inspires greater fear through being much thought about.

Articulus 6

AD SEXTUM sic proceditur. Videtur quod ea quae non habent remedium, non sint magis timenda. Ad timorem enim requiritur quod remaneat aliqua spes salutis, ut supra dictum est. Sed in malis quae non habent remedium, nulla remanet spes salutis. Ergo talia mala nullo modo timentur.

PRAETEREA, malo mortis nullum remedium adhiberi potest, non enim, secundum naturam, potest esse reditus a morte ad vitam. Non tamen mors maxime timetur, ut dicit philosophus, in II Rhetoric. Non ergo ea magis timentur quae remedium non habent.

PRAETEREA, philosophus dicit, in I Ethic., quod *non est magis bonum quod est diuturnius, eo quod est unius diei, neque quod est perpetuum, eo quod non est perpetuum.* Ergo, eadem ratione, neque maius malum. Sed ea quae non habent remedium, non videntur differre ab aliis nisi propter diuturnitatem vel perpetuitatem. Ergo propter hoc non sunt peiora, vel magis timenda.

SED CONTRA est quod philosophus dicit, in II Rhetoric., quod *omnia timenda sunt terribiliora quaecumque, si peccaverint, corrigi non contingit; aut quorum auxilia non sunt; aut non facilia.*

Article 6
Whether those things are more feared, for which there is no remedy?

Objection 1: It would seem that those things are not more to be feared, for which there is no remedy. Because it is a condition of fear, that there be some hope of safety, as stated above (I-II, q. 42, a. 2). But an evil that cannot be remedied leaves no hope of escape. Therefore such things are not feared at all.

Objection 2: Further, there is no remedy for the evil of death: since, in the natural course of things, there is no return from death to life. And yet death is not the most feared of all things, as the Philosopher says (Rhet. ii, 5). Therefore those things are not feared most, for which there is no remedy.

Objection 3: Further, the Philosopher says (Ethic. i, 6) that "a thing which lasts long is no better than that which lasts but one day: nor is that which lasts for ever any better than that which is not everlasting": and the same applies to evil. But things that cannot be remedied seem to differ from other things, merely in the point of their lasting long or for ever. Consequently they are not therefore any worse or more to be feared.

On the contrary, the Philosopher says (Rhet. ii, 5) that "those things are most to be feared which when done wrong cannot be put right ... or for which there is no help, or which are not easy."

Respondeo dicendum quod obiectum timoris est malum, unde illud quod facit ad augmentum mali, facit ad augmentum timoris. Malum autem augetur non solum secundum speciem ipsius mali, sed etiam secundum circumstantias, ut ex supra dictis apparet. Inter ceteras autem circumstantias, diuturnitas, vel etiam perpetuitas, magis videtur facere ad augmentum mali. Ea enim quae sunt in tempore, secundum durationem temporis quodammodo mensurantur, unde si pati aliquid in tanto tempore est malum, pati idem in duplo tempore apprehenditur ut duplatum. Et secundum hanc rationem, pati idem in infinito tempore, quod est perpetuo pati, habet quodammodo infinitum augmentum. Mala autem quae, postquam advenerint, non possunt habere remedium, vel non de facili, accipiuntur ut perpetua vel diuturna. Et ideo maxime redduntur timenda.

Ad primum ergo dicendum quod remedium mali est duplex. Unum, per quod impeditur futurum malum, ne adveniat. Et tali remedio sublato, aufertur spes, et per consequens timor. Unde de tali remedio nunc non loquimur. Aliud remedium mali est, quo malum iam praesens removetur. Et de tali remedio nunc loquimur.

Ad secundum dicendum quod, licet mors sit irremediabile malum, tamen, quia non imminet de prope, non timetur, ut supra dictum est.

Ad tertium dicendum quod philosophus ibi loquitur de per se bono, quod est bonum secundum speciem suam. Sic autem non fit aliquid magis bonum propter diuturnitatem vel perpetuitatem, sed propter naturam ipsius boni.

I answer that, The object of fear is evil: consequently whatever tends to increase evil, conduces to the increase of fear. Now evil is increased not only in its species of evil, but also in respect of circumstances, as stated above (I-II, q. 18, a. 3). And of all the circumstances, longlastingness, or even everlastingness, seems to have the greatest bearing on the increase of evil. Because things that exist in time are measured, in a way, according to the duration of time: wherefore if it be an evil to suffer something for a certain length of time, we should reckon the evil doubled, if it be suffered for twice that length of time. And accordingly, to suffer the same thing for an infinite length of time, i.e., for ever, implies, so to speak, an infinite increase. Now those evils which, after they have come, cannot be remedied at all, or at least not easily, are considered as lasting for ever or for a long time: for which reason they inspire the greatest fear.

Reply to Objection 1: Remedy for an evil is twofold. One, by which a future evil is warded off from coming. If such a remedy be removed, there is an end to hope and consequently to fear; wherefore we do not speak now of remedies of that kind. The other remedy is one by which an already present evil is removed: and of such a remedy we speak now.

Reply to Objection 2: Although death be an evil without remedy, yet, since it threatens not from near, it is not feared, as stated above (I-II, q. 42, a. 2).

Reply to Objection 3: The Philosopher is speaking there of things that are good in themselves, i.e., good specifically. And such like good is no better for lasting long or for ever: its goodness depends on its very nature.

Quaestio XLIII

Deinde considerandum est de causa timoris. Et circa hoc quaeruntur duo. *Primo,* utrum causa timoris sit amor. *Secundo,* utrum causa timoris sit defectus.

Articulus 1

AD PRIMUM sic proceditur. Videtur quod amor non sit causa timoris. Illud enim quod introducit aliquid, est causa eius. Sed *timor introducit amorem caritatis,* ut Augustinus dicit, super canonicam Ioan. Ergo timor est causa amoris, et non e converso.

PRAETEREA, philosophus dicit, in II Rhetoric., quod *illi maxime timentur, a quibus expectamus imminere nobis aliqua mala.* Sed per hoc quod ab aliquo expectamus malum, magis provocamur ad odium eius quam ad amorem. Ergo timor magis causatur ab odio quam ab amore.

PRAETEREA, supra dictum est quod ea quae sunt a nobis ipsis, non habent rationem terribilium. Sed ea quae sunt ex amore, maxime proveniunt ex intimo cordis. Ergo timor ex amore non causatur.

SED CONTRA est quod Augustinus dicit, in libro octoginta trium quaest., *nulli dubium est non aliam esse metuendi causam, nisi ne id quod amamus, aut adeptum amittamus, aut non adipiscamur speratum.* Omnis ergo timor causatur ex hoc quod aliquid amamus. Amor igitur est causa timoris.

RESPONDEO dicendum quod obiecta passionum animae se habent ad eas tanquam formae ad res naturales vel artificiales, quia passiones animae speciem recipiunt ab obiectis, sicut res praedictae a suis formis. Sicut igitur quidquid est causa formae, est causa rei constitutae per ipsam; ita etiam quidquid, et quocumque modo, est causa obiecti, est causa passionis. Contingit autem aliquid esse causam obiecti vel per modum causae efficientis, vel per modum dispositionis materialis. Sicut obiectum delectationis est bonum apparens conveniens coniunctum, cuius causa efficiens est illud quod facit coniunctionem, vel quod facit convenientiam vel bonitatem, vel apparentiam

Question 43
Of the Cause of Fear

We must now consider the cause of fear: under which head there are two points of inquiry: 1. Whether love is the cause of fear? 2. Whether defect is the cause of fear?

Article 1
Whether love is the cause of fear?

Objection 1: It would seem that love is not the cause of fear. For that which leads to a thing is its cause. But "fear leads to the love of charity" as Augustine says on the canonical epistle of John (Tract. ix). Therefore fear is the cause of love, and not conversely.

Objection 2: Further, the Philosopher says (Rhet. ii, 5) that "those are feared most from whom we dread the advent of some evil." But the dread of evil being caused by someone, makes us hate rather than love him. Therefore fear is caused by hate rather than by love.

Objection 3: Further, it has been stated above (I-II, q. 42, a. 3) that those things which occur by our own doing are not fearful. But that which we do from love, is done from our inmost heart. Therefore fear is not caused by love.

On the contrary, Augustine says (QQ. 83, qu. 33): "There can be no doubt that there is no cause for fear save the loss of what we love, when we possess it, or the failure to obtain what we hope for." Therefore all fear is caused by our loving something: and consequently love is the cause of fear.

I answer that, The objects of the soul's passions stand in relation thereto as the forms to things natural or artificial: because the passions of the soul take their species from their objects, as the aforesaid things do from their forms. Therefore, just as whatever is a cause of the form, is a cause of the thing constituted by that form, so whatever is a cause, in any way whatever, of the object, is a cause of the passion. Now a thing may be a cause of the object, either by way of efficient cause, or by way of material disposition. Thus the object of pleasure is good apprehended as suitable and conjoined: and its efficient cause is that which causes the conjunction, or the suitableness, or goodness, or apprehension

huiusmodi boni; causa autem per modum dispositionis materialis, est habitus, vel quaecumque dispositio secundum quam fit alicui conveniens aut apparens illud bonum quod est ei coniunctum. Sic igitur, in proposito, obiectum timoris est aestimatum malum futurum propinquum cui resisti de facili non potest. Et ideo illud quod potest inferre tale malum, est causa effectiva obiecti timoris, et per consequens ipsius timoris. Illud autem per quod aliquis ita disponitur ut aliquid sit ei tale, est causa timoris, et obiecti eius, per modum dispositionis materialis. Et hoc modo amor est causa timoris, ex hoc enim quod aliquis amat aliquod bonum, sequitur quod privativum talis boni sit ei malum, et per consequens quod timeat ipsum tanquam malum.

AD PRIMUM ergo dicendum quod, sicut supra dictum est, timor per se et primo respicit ad malum, quod refugit, quod opponitur alicui bono amato. Et sic per se timor nascitur ex amore. Secundario vero respicit ad id per quod provenit tale malum. Et sic per accidens quandoque timor inducit amorem, inquantum scilicet homo qui timet puniri a Deo, servat mandata eius, et sic incipit sperare, et spes introducit amorem, ut supra dictum est.

AD SECUNDUM dicendum quod ille a quo expectantur mala, primo quidem odio habetur, sed postquam ab ipso iam incipiunt sperari bona, tunc incipit amari. Bonum autem cui contrariatur malum quod timetur, a principio amabatur.

AD TERTIUM dicendum quod ratio illa procedit de eo quod est causa mali terribilis per modum efficientis. Amor autem est causa eius per modum materialis dispositionis, ut dictum est.

of that good thing; while its cause by way of material disposition, is a habit or any sort of disposition by reason of which this conjoined good becomes suitable or is apprehended as such. Accordingly, as to the matter in question, the object of fear is something reckoned as an evil to come, near at hand and difficult to avoid. Therefore that which can inflict such an evil, is the efficient cause of the object of fear, and, consequently, of fear itself. While that which renders a man so disposed that thing is such an evil to him, is a cause of fear and of its object, by way of material disposition. And thus it is that love causes fear: since it is through his loving a certain good, that whatever deprives a man of that good is an evil to him, and that consequently he fears it as an evil.

Reply to Objection 1: As stated above (I-II, q. 42, a. 1), fear, of itself and in the first place, regards the evil from which it recoils as being contrary to some loved good: and thus fear, of itself, is born of love. But, in the second place, it regards the cause from which that evil ensues: so that sometimes, accidentally, fear gives rise to love; in so far as, for instance, through fear of God's punishments, man keeps His commandments, and thus begins to hope, while hope leads to love, as stated above (I-II, q. 40, a. 7).

Reply to Objection 2: He, from whom evil is expected, is indeed hated at first; but afterwards, when once we begin to hope for good from him, we begin to love him. But the good, the contrary evil of which is feared, was loved from the beginning.

Reply to Objection 3: This argument is true of that which is the efficient cause of the evil to be feared: whereas love causes fear by way of material disposition, as stated above.

ARTICULUS 2

AD SECUNDUM sic proceditur. Videtur quod defectus non sit causa timoris. Illi enim qui potentiam habent, maxime timentur. Sed defectus contrariatur potentiae. Ergo defectus non est causa timoris.

ARTICLE 2
Whether defect is the cause of fear?

Objection 1: It would seem that defect is not a cause of fear. Because those who are in power are very much feared. But defect is contrary to power. Therefore defect is not a cause of fear.

PRAETEREA, illi qui iam decapitantur, maxime sunt in defectu. Sed tales non timent. Ut dicitur in II Rhetoric. Ergo defectus non est causa timoris.

PRAETEREA, decertare ex fortitudine provenit, non ex defectu. Sed *decertantes timent eos qui pro eisdem decertant,* ut dicitur in II Rhetoric. Ergo defectus non est causa timoris.

SED CONTRA, contrariorum contrariae sunt causae. Sed *divitiae, et robur, et multitudo amicorum, et potestas, excludunt timorem,* ut dicitur in II Rhetoric. Ergo ex defectu horum timor causatur.

RESPONDEO dicendum quod, sicut supra dictum est, duplex causa timoris accipi potest, una quidem per modum materialis dispositionis, ex parte eius qui timet; alia per modum causae efficientis, ex parte eius qui timetur. Quantum igitur ad primum, defectus, per se loquendo, est causa timoris, ex aliquo enim defectu virtutis contingit quod non possit aliquis de facili repellere imminens malum. Sed tamen ad causandum timorem requiritur defectus cum aliqua mensura. Minor enim est defectus qui causat timorem futuri mali, quam defectus consequens malum praesens, de quo est tristitia. Et adhuc esset maior defectus, si totaliter sensus mali auferretur, vel amor boni cuius contrarium timetur. Quantum vero ad secundum, virtus et robur, per se loquendo, est causa timoris, ex hoc enim quod aliquid quod apprehenditur ut nocivum, est virtuosum, contingit quod eius effectus repelli non potest. Contingit tamen per accidens quod aliquis defectus ex ista parte causat timorem, inquantum ex aliquo defectu contingit quod aliquis velit nocumentum inferre, puta propter iniustitiam, vel quia ante laesus fuit, vel quia timet laedi.

AD PRIMUM ergo dicendum quod ratio illa procedit de causa timoris ex parte causae efficientis.

AD SECUNDUM dicendum quod illi qui iam decapitantur, sunt in passione praesentis mali. Et ideo iste defectus excedit mensuram timoris.

Objection 2: Further, the defect of those who are already being executed is extreme. But such like do not fear as stated in Rhet. ii, 5. Therefore defect is not a cause of fear.

Objection 3: Further, contests arise from strength not from defect. But "those who contend fear those who contend with them" (Rhet. ii, 5). Therefore defect is not a cause of fear.

On the contrary, Contraries ensue from contrary causes. But "wealth, strength, a multitude of friends, and power drive fear away" (Rhet. ii, 5). Therefore fear is caused by lack of these.

I answer that, As stated above (I-II, q. 42, a. 1), fear may be set down to a twofold cause: one is by way of a material disposition, on the part of him that fears; the other is by way of efficient cause, on the part of the person feared. As to the first then, some defect is, of itself, the cause of fear: for it is owing to some lack of power that one is unable easily to repulse a threatening evil. And yet, in order to cause fear, this defect must be according to a measure. For the defect which causes fear of a future evil, is less than the defect caused by evil present, which is the object of sorrow. And still greater would be the defect, if perception of the evil, or love of the good whose contrary is feared, were entirely absent. But as to the second, power and strength are, of themselves, the cause of fear: because it is owing to the fact that the cause apprehended as harmful is powerful, that its effect cannot be repulsed. It may happen, however, in this respect, that some defect causes fear accidentally, in so far as owing to some defect someone wishes to hurt another; for instance, by reason of injustice, either because that other has already done him a harm, or because he fears to be harmed by him.

Reply to Objection 1: This argument is true of the cause of fear, on the part of the efficient cause.

Reply to Objection 2: Those who are already being executed, are actually suffering from a present evil; wherefore their defect exceeds the measure of fear.

AD TERTIUM dicendum quod decertantes timent non propter potentiam, qua decertare possunt, sed propter defectum potentiae, ex quo contingit quod se superaturos non confidunt.

Reply to Objection 3: Those who contend with one another are afraid, not on account of the power which enables them to contend: but on account of the lack of power, owing to which they are not confident of victory.

Quaestio XLIV

Deinde considerandum est de effectibus timoris. Et circa hoc quaeruntur quatuor. *Primo,* utrum timor faciat contractionem. *Secundo,* utrum faciat consiliativos. *Tertio,* utrum faciat tremorem. *Quarto,* utrum impediat operationem.

Question 44
Of the Effects of Fear

We must now consider the effects of fear: under which head there are four points of inquiry: 1. Whether fear causes contraction? 2. Whether it makes men suitable for counsel? 3. Whether it makes one tremble? 4. Whether it hinders action?

Articulus 1

AD PRIMUM sic proceditur. Videtur quod timor non faciat contractionem. Contractione enim facta, calor et spiritus ad interiora revocantur. Sed ex multitudine caloris et spirituum in interioribus, magnificatur cor ad audacter aliquid aggrediendum, ut patet in iratis, cuius contrarium in timore accidit. Non ergo timor facit contractionem.

PRAETEREA, multiplicatis spiritibus et calore in interioribus per contractionem, sequitur quod homo in vocem prorumpat, ut patet in dolentibus. Sed timentes non emittunt vocem, sed magis redduntur taciturni. Ergo timor non facit contractionem.

PRAETEREA, verecundia est quaedam species timoris, ut supra dictum est. Sed *verecundati rubescunt,* ut dicit Tullius, IV de Tusculanis quaest., et philosophus in IV Ethic. Rubor autem faciei non attestatur contractioni, sed contrario. Non ergo contractio est effectus timoris.

SED CONTRA est quod Damascenus dicit, in III libro, quod *timor est virtus secundum systolen,* idest secundum contractionem.

RESPONDEO dicendum quod, sicut supra dictum est, in passionibus animae est sicut formale ipse motus appetitivae potentiae, sicut autem materiale transmutatio corporalis, quorum unum alteri

Article 1
Whether fear causes contraction?

Objection 1: It would seem that fear does not cause contraction. For when contraction takes place, the heat and vital spirits are withdrawn inwardly. But accumulation of heat and vital spirits in the interior parts of the body, dilates the heart unto endeavors of daring, as may be seen in those who are angered: while the contrary happens in those who are afraid. Therefore fear does not cause contraction.

Objection 2: Further, when, as a result of contraction, the vital spirits and heat are accumulated in the interior parts, man cries out, as may be seen in those who are in pain. But those who fear utter nothing: on the contrary they lose their speech. Therefore fear does not cause contraction.

Objection 3: Further, shame is a kind of fear, as stated above (I-II, q. 41, a. 4). But "those who are ashamed blush," as Cicero (De Quaest. Tusc. iv, 8), and the Philosopher (Ethic. iv, 9) observe. But blushing is an indication, not of contraction, but of the reverse. Therefore contraction is not an effect of fear.

On the contrary, Damascene says (De Fide Orth. ii, 23) that "fear is a power according to συστολή (*systole*)," i.e., contraction.

I answer that, As stated above (I-II, q. 28, a. 5), in the passions of the soul, the formal element is the movement of the appetitive power, while the bodily transmutation is the material element. Both of these are mutually

proportionatur. Unde secundum similitudinem et rationem appetitivi motus, sequitur corporalis transmutatio. Quantum autem ad animalem motum appetitus, timor contractionem quandam importat. Cuius ratio est, quia timor provenit ex phantasia alicuius mali imminentis quod difficile repelli potest, ut supra dictum est. Quod autem aliquid difficile possit repelli, provenit ex debilitate virtutis, ut supra dictum est. Virtus autem, **quanto est debilior, tanto ad pauciora se potest extendere**. Et ideo ex ipsa imaginatione quae causat timorem, sequitur quaedam contractio in appetitu. Sicut etiam videmus in morientibus quod natura retrahitur ad interiora, propter debilitatem virtutis, et videmus etiam in civitatibus quod, quando cives timent, retrahunt se ab exterioribus, et recurrunt, quantum possunt, ad interiora. Et secundum similitudinem huius contractionis, quae pertinet ad appetitum animalem, sequitur etiam in timore ex parte corporis, contractio caloris et spirituum ad interiora.

AD PRIMUM ergo dicendum quod, sicut philosophus dicit in libro de problematibus, licet in timentibus retrahantur spiritus ab exterioribus ad interiora, non tamen est idem motus spirituum in iratis et timentibus. Nam in iratis, propter calorem et subtilitatem spirituum, quae proveniunt ex appetitu vindictae, interius fit spirituum motus ab inferioribus ad superiora, et ideo congregantur spiritus et calor circa cor. Ex quo sequitur quod irati redduntur prompti et audaces ad invadendum. Sed in timentibus, propter frigiditatem ingrossantem, spiritus moventur a superioribus ad inferiora, quae quidem frigiditas contingit ex imaginatione defectus virtutis. Et ideo non multiplicantur calor et spiritus circa cor, sed magis a corde refugiunt. Et propter hoc, timentes non prompte invadunt, sed magis refugiunt.

AD SECUNDUM dicendum quod naturale est cuilibet dolenti, sive homini sive animali, quod utatur quocumque auxilio potest, ad repellendum nocivum praesens quod infert dolorem, unde videmus quod animalia

proportionate; and consequently the bodily transmutation assumes a resemblance to and the very nature of the appetitive movement. Now, as to the appetitive movement of the soul, fear implies a certain contraction: the reason of which is that fear arises from the imagination of some threatening evil which is difficult to repel, as stated above (I-II, q. 41, a. 2). But that a thing be difficult to repel is due to lack of power, as stated above (I-II, q. 43, a. 2): and **the weaker a power is, the fewer the things to which it extends**. Wherefore from the very imagination that causes fear there ensues a certain contraction in the appetite. Thus we observe in one who is dying that nature withdraws inwardly, on account of the lack of power: and again we see the inhabitants of a city, when seized with fear, leave the outskirts, and, as far as possible, make for the inner quarters. It is in resemblance to this contraction, which pertains to the appetite of the soul, that in fear a similar contraction of heat and vital spirits towards the inner parts takes place in regard to the body.

Reply to Objection 1: As the Philosopher says (De Problem. xxvii, 3), although in those who fear, the vital spirits recede from outer to the inner parts of the body, yet the movement of vital spirits is not the same in those who are angry and those who are afraid. For in those who are angry, by reason of the heat and subtlety of the vital spirits, which result from the craving for vengeance, the inward movement has an upward direction: wherefore the vital spirits and heat concentrate around the heart: the result being that an angry man is quick and brave in attacking. But in those who are afraid, on account of the condensation caused by cold, the vital spirits have a downward movement; the said cold being due to the imagined lack of power. Consequently the heat and vital spirits abandon the heart instead of concentrating around it: the result being that a man who is afraid is not quick to attack, but is more inclined to run away.

Reply to Objection 2: To everyone that is in pain, whether man or animal, it is natural to use all possible means of repelling the harmful thing that causes pain but its presence: thus we observe that animals,

dolentia percutiunt vel faucibus vel cornibus. Maximum autem auxilium ad omnia in animalibus est calor et spiritus. Et ideo in dolore natura conservat calorem et spiritum interius, ut hoc utatur ad repellendum nocivum. Et ideo philosophus dicit, in libro de problematibus, quod multiplicatis introrsum spiritibus et calore, necesse est quod emittantur per vocem. Et propter hoc, dolentes vix se possunt continere quin clament. Sed in timentibus fit motus interioris caloris et spirituum a corde ad inferiora, ut dictum est. Et ideo timor contrariatur formationi vocis, quae fit per emissionem spirituum ad superiora per os. Et propter hoc, timor tacentes facit. Et inde est etiam quod timor *trementes facit,* ut dicit philosophus, in libro de problematibus.

when in pain, attack with their jaws or with their horns. Now the greatest help for all purposes, in animals, is heat and vital spirits: wherefore when they are in pain, their nature stores up the heat and vital spirits within them, in order to make use thereof in repelling the harmful object. Hence the Philosopher says (De Problem. xxvii, 9) when the vital spirits and heat are concentrated together within, they require to find a vent in the voice: for which reason those who are in pain can scarcely refrain from crying aloud. On the other hand, in those who are afraid, the internal heat and vital spirits move from the heart downwards, as stated above (ad 1): wherefore fear hinders speech which ensues from the emission of the vital spirits in an upward direction through the mouth: the result being that fear makes its subject speechless. For this reason, too, fear "makes its subject tremble," as the Philosopher says (De Problem. xxvii, 1, 6, 7).

AD TERTIUM dicendum quod pericula mortis non solum contrariantur appetitui animali, sed etiam contrariantur naturae. Et propter hoc, in huiusmodi timore non solum fit contractio ex parte appetitus, sed etiam ex parte naturae corporalis, sic enim disponitur animal ex imaginatione mortis contrahens calorem ad interiora, sicut quando naturaliter mors imminet. Et inde est quod *timentes mortem pallescunt,* ut dicitur in IV Ethic. Sed malum quod timet verecundia, non opponitur naturae, sed solum appetitui animali. Et ideo fit quidem contractio secundum appetitum animalem, non autem secundum naturam corporalem, sed magis anima, quasi in se contracta, vacat ad motionem spirituum et caloris, unde fit eorum diffusio ad exteriora. Et propter hoc, verecundati rubescunt.

Reply to Objection 3: Mortal perils are contrary not only to the appetite of the soul, but also to nature. Consequently in such like fear, there is contraction not only in the appetite, but also in the corporeal nature: for when an animal is moved by the imagination of death, it experiences a contraction of heat towards the inner parts of the body, as though it were threatened by a natural death. Hence it is that "those who are in fear of death turn pale" (Ethic. iv, 9). But the evil that shame fears, is contrary, not to nature, but only to the appetite of the soul. Consequently there results a contraction in this appetite, but not in the corporeal nature; in fact, the soul, as though contracted in itself, is free to set the vital spirits and heat in movement, so that they spread to the outward parts of the body: the result being that those who are ashamed blush.

ARTICULUS 2

AD SECUNDUM sic proceditur. Videtur quod timor non faciat consiliativos. Non enim est eiusdem consiliativos facere, et consilium impedire. Sed timor consilium impedit, omnis enim passio perturbat quietem, quae requiritur ad bonum usum

ARTICLE 2
Whether fear makes one suitable for counsel?
Objection 1: It would seem that fear does not make one suitable for counsel. For the same thing cannot be conducive to counsel, and a hindrance thereto. But fear hinders counsel: because every passion disturbs repose, which is requisite for the good use of

rationis. Ergo timor non facit consiliativos.

Praeterea, consilium est actus rationis de futuris cogitantis et deliberantis. Sed aliquis timor *est excutiens cogitata, et mentem a suo loco removet,* ut Tullius dicit, in IV de Tusculanis quaest. Ergo timor non facit consiliativos, sed magis impedit consilium.

Praeterea, sicut consilium adhibetur ad **vitanda mala, ita etiam adhibetur ad consequenda bona.** Sed sicut timor est de malis vitandis, ita spes est de bonis consequendis. Ergo timor non facit magis consiliativos quam spes.

Sed contra est quod philosophus dicit, in II Rhetoric., quod *timor consiliativos facit.*

Respondeo dicendum quod aliquis potest dici consiliativus dupliciter. Uno modo, a voluntate seu sollicitudine consiliandi. Et sic timor consiliativos facit. Quia, ut philosophus in III Ethic. dicit, *consiliamur de magnis, in quibus quasi nobis ipsis discredimus.* Ea autem quae timorem incutiunt, non sunt simpliciter mala, sed habent quandam magnitudinem, tum ex eo quod apprehenduntur ut quae difficiliter repelli possunt; tum etiam quia apprehenduntur ut de prope existentia, sicut iam dictum est. Unde homines maxime in timoribus quaerunt consiliari. Alio modo dicitur aliquis consiliativus, a facultate bene consiliandi. Et sic nec timor, nec aliqua passio consiliativos facit. Quia homini affecto secundum aliquam passionem, videtur aliquid vel maius vel minus quam sit secundum rei veritatem, sicut amanti videntur ea quae amat, meliora; et timenti, ea quae timet, terribiliora. Et sic ex defectu rectitudinis iudicii, quaelibet passio, quantum est de se, impedit facultatem bene consiliandi.

Et per hoc patet responsio ad primum.

Ad secundum dicendum quod quanto aliqua passio est fortior, tanto magis homo secundum ipsam affectus, impeditur. Et ideo quando timor fuerit fortis, vult quidem homo consiliari, sed adeo perturbatur in suis cogitationibus, quod consilium adinvenire non potest. Si autem sit parvus timor,

reason. Therefore fear does not make a man suitable for counsel.

Objection 2: Further, counsel is an act of reason, in thinking and deliberating about the future. But a certain fear "drives away all thought, and dislocates the mind," as Cicero observes (De Quaest. Tusc. iv, 8). Therefore fear does not conduce to counsel, but hinders it.

Objection 3: Further, just as we have recourse to counsel in order to avoid evil, so do we, in order to attain good things. But whereas fear is of evil to be avoided, so is hope of good things to be obtained. Therefore fear is not more conducive to counsel, than hope is.

On the contrary, The Philosopher says (Rhet. ii, 5) that "fear makes men of counsel."

I answer that, A man of counsel may be taken in two ways. First, from his being willing or anxious to take counsel. And thus fear makes men of counsel. Because, as the Philosopher says (Ethic. iii, 3), "we take counsel on great matters, because therein we distrust ourselves." Now things which make us afraid, are not simply evil, but have a certain magnitude, both because they seem difficult to repel, and because they are apprehended as near to us, as stated above (I-II, q. 42, a. 2). Wherefore men seek for counsel especially when they are afraid. Secondly, a man of counsel means one who is apt for giving good counsel: and in this sense, neither fear nor any passion makes men of counsel. Because when a man is affected by a passion, things seem to him greater or smaller than they really are: thus to a lover, what he loves seems better; to him that fears, what he fears seems more dreadful. Consequently owing to the want of right judgment, every passion, considered in itself, hinders the faculty of giving good counsel.

This suffices for the Reply to the First Objection.

Reply to Objection 2: The stronger a passion is, the greater the hindrance is it to the man who is swayed by it. Consequently, when fear is intense, man does indeed wish to take counsel, but his thoughts are so disturbed, that he can find no counsel. If, however, the fear be slight,

qui sollicitudinem consiliandi inducat, nec multum rationem conturbet; potest etiam conferre ad facultatem bene consiliandi, ratione sollicitudinis consequentis.

AD TERTIUM dicendum quod etiam spes facit consiliativos, quia, ut in II Rhetoric. philosophus dicit, *nullus consiliatur de his de quibus desperat;* sicut nec de impossibilibus, ut dicitur in III Ethic. Timor tamen facit magis consiliativos quam spes. Quia spes est de bono, prout possumus ipsum consequi, timor autem de malo, prout vix repelli potest, et ita magis respicit rationem difficilis timor quam spes. In difficilibus autem, maxime in quibus nobis non confidimus, consiliamur, sicut dictum est.

so as to make a man wish to take counsel, without gravely disturbing the reason; it may even make it easier for him to take good counsel, by reason of his ensuing carefulness.

Reply to Objection 3: Hope also makes man a good counsellor: because, as the Philosopher says (Rhet. ii, 5), "no man takes counsel in matters he despairs of," nor about impossible things, as he says in Ethic. iii, 3. But fear incites to counsel more than hope does. Because hope is of good things, as being possible of attainment; whereas fear is of evil things, as being difficult to repel, so that fear regards the aspect of difficulty more than hope does. And it is in matters of difficulty, especially when we distrust ourselves, that we take counsel, as stated above.

ARTICULUS 3

AD TERTIUM sic proceditur. Videtur quod tremor non sit effectus timoris. Tremor enim ex frigore accidit, videmus enim infrigidatos tremere. Timor autem non videtur causare frigus, sed magis calorem desiccantem, cuius signum est quod timentes sitiunt, et praecipue in maximis timoribus, sicut patet in illis qui ad mortem ducuntur. Ergo timor non causat tremorem.

PRAETEREA, emissio superfluitatum ex calore accidit, unde, ut plurimum, medicinae laxativae sunt calidae. Sed huiusmodi emissiones superfluitatum ex timore frequenter contingunt. Ergo timor videtur causare calorem. Et sic non causat tremorem.

PRAETEREA, in timore calor ab exterioribus ad interiora revocatur. Si igitur propter huiusmodi revocationem caloris, in exterioribus homo tremit; videtur quod similiter in omnibus exterioribus membris deberet causari tremor ex timore. Hoc autem non videtur. Non ergo tremor corporis est effectus timoris.

SED CONTRA est quod Tullius dicit, in IV de Tusculanis quaest., quod *terrorem sequitur tremor, et pallor, et dentium crepitus.*

RESPONDEO dicendum quod, sicut supra dictum est, in timore fit quaedam contractio ab exterioribus ad interiora, et ideo

ARTICLE 3
Whether fear makes one tremble?

Objection 1: It would seem that trembling is not an effect of fear. Because trembling is occasioned by cold; thus we observe that a cold person trembles. Now fear does not seem to make one cold, but rather to cause a parching heat: a sign whereof is that those who fear are thirsty, especially if their fear be very great, as in the case of those who are being led to execution. Therefore fear does not cause trembling.

Objection 2: Further, faecal evacuation is occasioned by heat; hence laxative medicines are generally warm. But these evacuations are often caused by fear. Therefore fear apparently causes heat; and consequently does not cause trembling.

Objection 3: Further, in fear, the heat is withdrawn from the outer to the inner parts of the body. If, therefore, man trembles in his outward parts, through the heat being withdrawn thus; it seems that fear should cause this trembling in all the external members. But such is not the case. Therefore trembling of the body is not caused by fear.

On the contrary, Cicero says (De Quaest. Tusc. iv, 8) that "fear is followed by trembling, pallor and chattering of the teeth."

I answer that, As stated above (I-II, q. 44, a. 1), in fear there takes place a certain contraction from the outward to the inner parts of the body, the result being that the

exteriora frigida remanent. Et propter hoc in eis accidit tremor, qui causatur ex debilitate virtutis continentis membra, ad huiusmodi autem debilitatem maxime facit defectus caloris, qui est instrumentum quo anima movet, ut dicitur in II de anima.

AD PRIMUM ergo dicendum quod, calore ab exterioribus ad interiora revocato, multiplicatur calor interius, et maxime versus inferiora, idest circa nutritivam. Et ideo, consumpto humido, consequitur sitis, et etiam interdum solutio ventris, et urinae emissio, et quandoque etiam seminis. Vel huiusmodi emissio superfluitatum accidit propter contractionem ventris et testiculorum, ut philosophus dicit, in libro de problematibus.

Unde patet solutio ad secundum.

AD TERTIUM dicendum quod, quia in timore calor deserit cor, a superioribus ad inferiora tendens, ideo timentibus maxime tremit cor, et membra quae habent aliquam connexionem ad pectus, ubi est cor. Unde timentes maxime tremunt in voce, propter vicinitatem vocalis arteriae ad cor. Tremit etiam labium inferius, et tota inferior mandibula, propter continuationem ad cor, unde et crepitus dentium sequitur. Et eadem ratione brachia et manus tremunt. Vel etiam quia huiusmodi membra sunt magis mobilia. Propter quod et genua tremunt timentibus; secundum illud Isaiae XXXV, *confortate manus dissolutas, et genua trementia roborate*.

outer parts become cold; and for this reason trembling is occasioned in these parts, being caused by a lack of power in controlling the members: which lack of power is due to the want of heat, which is the instrument whereby the soul moves those members, as stated in De Anima ii, 4.

Reply to Objection 1: When the heat withdraws from the outer to the inner parts, the inward heat increases, especially in the inferior or nutritive parts. Consequently the humid element being spent, thirst ensues; sometimes indeed the result is a loosening of the bowels, and urinary or even seminal evacuation. Or else such like evacuations are due to contraction of the abdomen and testicles, as the Philosopher says (De Problem. xxii, 11).

This suffices for the Reply to the Second Objection.

Reply to Objection 3: In fear, heat abandons the heart, with a downward movement: hence in those who are afraid the heart especially trembles, as also those members which are connected with the breast where the heart resides. Hence those who fear tremble especially in their speech, on account of the tracheal artery being near the heart. The lower lip, too, and the lower jaw tremble, through their connection with the heart; which explains the chattering of the teeth. For the same reason the arms and hands tremble. Or else because the aforesaid members are more mobile. For which reason the knees tremble in those who are afraid, according to Is. 35:3: "Strengthen ye the feeble hands, and confirm the trembling* knees."

ARTICULUS 4

AD QUARTUM sic proceditur. Videtur quod timor impediat operationem. Operatio enim maxime impeditur ex perturbatione rationis, quae dirigit in opere. Sed timor perturbat rationem, ut dictum est. Ergo timor impedit operationem.

PRAETEREA, illi qui faciunt aliquid cum timore, facilius in operando deficiunt, sicut si aliquis incedat super trabem in alto positam,

ARTICLE 4
Whether fear hinders action?

Objection 1: It would seem that fear hinders action. For action is hindered chiefly by a disturbance in the reason, which directs action. But fear disturbs reason, as stated above (I-II, q. 44, a. 2). Therefore fear hinders action.

Objection 2: Further, those who fear while doing anything, are more apt to fail: thus a man who walks on a plank placed aloft,

---

* Vulg.: 'weak'

propter timorem de facili cadit; non autem caderet, si incederet super eandem trabem in imo positam, propter defectum timoris. Ergo timor impedit operationem.

PRAETEREA, pigritia, sive segnities, est quaedam species timoris. Sed pigritia impedit operationem. Ergo et timor.

SED CONTRA est quod apostolus dicit, ad Philipp. II, *cum metu et tremore vestram salutem operamini,* quod non diceret, si timor bonam operationem impediret. Timor ergo non impedit bonam operationem.

RESPONDEO dicendum quod operatio hominis exterior causatur quidem ab anima sicut a primo movente, sed a membris corporeis sicut ab instrumentis. Contingit autem operationem impediri et propter defectum instrumenti, et propter defectum principalis moventis. Ex parte igitur instrumentorum corporalium, timor, quantum est de se, semper natus est impedire exteriorem operationem, propter defectum caloris qui ex timore accidit in exterioribus membris. Sed ex parte animae, si sit timor moderatus, non multum rationem perturbans; confert ad bene operandum, inquantum causat quandam sollicitudinem, et facit hominem attentius consiliari et operari. Si vero timor tantum increscat quod rationem perturbet, impedit operationem etiam ex parte animae. Sed de tali timore apostolus non loquitur.

Et per haec patet responsio ad primum.

AD SECUNDUM dicendum quod illi qui cadunt de trabe in alto posita, patiuntur perturbationem imaginationis, propter timorem casus imaginati.

AD TERTIUM dicendum quod omnis timens refugit id quod timet, et ideo, cum pigritia sit timor de ipsa operatione, inquantum est laboriosa, impedit operationem, quia retrahit voluntatem ab ipsa. Sed timor qui est de aliis rebus, intantum adiuvat operationem, inquantum inclinat voluntatem ad operandum ea per quae homo effugit id quod timet.

easily falls through fear; whereas, if he were to walk on the same plank down below, he would not fall, through not being afraid. Therefore fear hinders action.

Objection 3: Further, laziness or sloth is a kind of fear. But laziness hinders action. Therefore fear does too.

On the contrary, The Apostle says (Phil. 2:12): "With fear and trembling work out your salvation": and he would not say this if fear were a hindrance to a good work. Therefore fear does not hinder a good action.

I answer that, Man's exterior actions are caused by the soul as first mover, but by the bodily members as instruments. Now action may be hindered both by defect of the instrument, and by defect of the principal mover. On the part of the bodily instruments, fear, considered in itself, is always apt to hinder exterior action, on account of the outward members being deprived, through fear, of their heat. But on the part of the soul, if the fear be moderate, without much disturbance of the reason, it conduces to working well, in so far as it causes a certain solicitude, and makes a man take counsel and work with greater attention. If, however, fear increases so much as to disturb the reason, it hinders action even on the part of the soul. But of such a fear the Apostle does not speak.

This suffices for the Reply to the First Objection.

Reply to Objection 2: He that falls from a plank placed aloft, suffers a disturbance of his imagination, through fear of the fall that is pictured to his imagination.

Reply to Objection 3: Everyone in fear shuns that which he fears: and therefore, since laziness is a fear of work itself as being toilsome, it hinders work by withdrawing the will from it. But fear of other things conduces to action, in so far as it inclines the will to do that whereby a man escapes from what he fears.

Quaestio XLV

Deinde considerandum est de audacia. Et circa hoc quaeruntur quatuor. *Primo,* utrum audacia sit contraria timori. *Secundo,* quomodo audacia se habeat ad spem. *Tertio,* de causa audaciae. *Quarto,* de effectus ipsius.

Articulus 1

Ad primum sic proceditur. Videtur quod audacia non contrarietur timori. Dicit enim Augustinus, in libro octoginta trium quaest., quod *audacia vitium est.* Vitium autem virtuti contrariatur. Cum ergo timor non sit virtus, sed passio, videtur quod timori non contrarietur audacia.

Praeterea, uni unum est contrarium. Sed timori contrariatur spes. Non ergo contrariatur ei audacia.

Praeterea, unaquaeque passio excludit passionem oppositam. Sed id quod excluditur per timorem, est securitas, dicit enim Augustinus, II Confess., quod *timor securitati praecavet.* Ergo securitas contrariatur timori. Non ergo audacia.

Sed contra est quod philosophus dicit, in II Rhetoric., quod *audacia est timori contraria.*

Respondeo dicendum quod de ratione contrariorum est quod *maxime a se distent,* ut dicitur in X Metaphys. Illud autem quod maxime distat a timore, est audacia, timor enim refugit nocumentum futurum, propter eius victoriam super ipsum timentem; sed audacia aggreditur periculum imminens, propter victoriam sui supra ipsum periculum. Unde manifeste timori contrariatur audacia.

Ad primum ergo dicendum quod ira et audacia, et omnium passionum nomina, dupliciter accipi possunt. Uno modo, secundum quod important absolute motus appetitus sensitivi in aliquod obiectum bonum vel malum, et sic sunt nomina passionum. Alio modo, secundum quod simul cum huiusmodi motu important recessum ab ordine rationis, et sic sunt nomina vitiorum. Et hoc modo loquitur Augustinus de audacia, sed nos loquimur nunc de audacia secundum primum modum.

Question 45
Of Daring

We must now consider daring: under which head there are four points of inquiry: 1. Whether daring is contrary to fear? 2. How is daring related to hope? 3. Of the cause of daring; 4. Of its effect.

Article 1
Whether daring is contrary to fear?

Objection 1: It would seem that daring is not contrary to fear. For Augustine says (QQ. 83, qu. 31) that "daring is a vice." Now vice is contrary to virtue. Since, therefore, fear is not a virtue but a passion, it seems that daring is not contrary to fear.

Objection 2: Further, to one thing there is one contrary. But hope is contrary to fear. Therefore daring is not contrary to fear.

Objection 3: Further, every passion excludes its opposite. But fear excludes safety; for Augustine says (Confess. ii, 6) that "fear takes forethought for safety." Therefore safety is contrary to fear. Therefore daring is not contrary to fear.

On the contrary, The Philosopher says (Rhet. ii, 5) that "daring is contrary to fear."

I answer that, It is of the essence of contraries to be "farthest removed from one another," as stated in Metaph. x, 4. Now that which is farthest removed from fear, is daring: since fear turns away from the future hurt, on account of its victory over him that fears it; whereas daring turns on threatened danger because of its own victory over that same danger. Consequently it is evident that daring is contrary to fear.

Reply to Objection 1: Anger, daring and all the names of the passions can be taken in two ways. First, as denoting absolutely movements of the sensitive appetite in respect of some object, good or bad: and thus they are names of passions. Secondly, as denoting besides this movement, a straying from the order of reason: and thus they are names of vices. It is in this sense that Augustine speaks of daring: but we are speaking of it in the first sense.

AD SECUNDUM dicendum quod uni secundum idem, non sunt plura contraria, sed secundum diversa, nihil prohibet uni plura contrariari. Et sic dictum est supra quod passiones irascibilis habent duplicem contrarietatem, unam secundum oppositionem boni et mali, et sic timor contrariatur spei; aliam secundum oppositionem accessus et recessus, et sic timori contrariatur audacia, spei vero desperatio.

AD TERTIUM dicendum quod securitas non significat aliquid contrarium timori, sed solam timoris exclusionem, ille enim dicitur esse securus, qui non timet. Unde securitas opponitur timori sicut privatio, audacia autem sicut contrarium. Et sicut contrarium includit in se privationem, ita audacia securitatem.

Reply to Objection 2: To one thing, in the same respect, there are not several contraries; but in different respects nothing prevents one thing having several contraries. Accordingly it has been said above (I-II, q. 23, a. 2; q. 40, a. 4) that the irascible passions admit of a twofold contrariety: one, according to the opposition of good and evil, and thus fear is contrary to hope: the other, according to the opposition of approach and withdrawal, and thus daring is contrary to fear, and despair contrary to hope.

Reply to Objection 3: Safety does not denote something contrary to fear, but merely the exclusion of fear: for he is said to be safe, who fears not. Wherefore safety is opposed to fear, as a privation: while daring is opposed thereto as a contrary. And as contrariety implies privation, so daring implies safety.

ARTICULUS 2

AD SECUNDUM sic proceditur. Videtur quod audacia non consequatur spem. Audacia enim est respectu malorum et terribilium, ut dicitur in III Ethic. Spes autem respicit bonum. Ut supra dictum est. Ergo habent diversa obiecta, et non sunt unius ordinis. Non ergo audacia consequitur spem.

PRAETEREA, sicut audacia contrariatur timori, ita desperatio spei. Sed timor non sequitur desperationem, quinimmo desperatio excludit timorem. Ut philosophus dicit, in II Rhetoric. Ergo audacia non consequitur spem.

PRAETEREA, audacia intendit quoddam bonum, scilicet victoriam. Sed tendere in bonum arduum pertinet ad spem. Ergo audacia est idem spei. Non ergo consequitur ad spem.

SED CONTRA est quod philosophus dicit, in III Ethic., quod *illi qui sunt bonae spei, sunt audaces.* Videtur ergo audacia consequi spem.

RESPONDEO dicendum quod, sicut iam pluries dictum est, omnes huiusmodi passiones animae ad appetitivam potentiam pertinent. Omnis autem motus appetitivae potentiae reducitur ad prosecutionem vel

ARTICLE 2
Whether daring ensues from hope?

Objection 1: It would seem that daring does not ensue from hope. Because daring regards evil and fearful things, as stated in Ethic. iii, 7. But hope regards good things, as stated above (I-II, q. 40, a. 1). Therefore they have different objects and are not in the same order. Therefore daring does not ensue from hope.

Objection 2: Further, just as daring is contrary to fear, so is despair contrary to hope. But fear does not ensue from despair: in fact, despair excludes fear, as the Philosopher says (Rhet. ii, 5). Therefore daring does not result from hope.

Objection 3: Further, daring is intent on something good, *viz.* victory. But it belongs to hope to tend to that which is good and difficult. Therefore daring is the same as hope; and consequently does not result from it.

On the contrary, The Philosopher says (Ethic. iii, 8) that "those are hopeful are full of daring." Therefore it seems that daring ensues from hope.

I answer that, As we have often stated (I-II, q. 22, a. 2; q. 35, a. 1; q. 41, a. 1), all these passions belong to the appetitive power. Now every movement of the appetitive power is reducible to one either of pursuit or of

fugam. Prosecutio autem vel fuga est alicuius et per se, et per accidens, per se quidem est prosecutio boni, fuga vero mali; per accidens autem potest prosecutio esse mali, propter aliquod bonum adiunctum, et fuga boni, propter aliquod malum adiunctum. Quod autem est per accidens, sequitur ad id quod est per se. Et ideo prosecutio mali, sequitur prosecutionem boni, sicut et fuga boni sequitur fugam mali. Haec autem quatuor **pertinent ad quatuor passiones, nam** prosecutio boni pertinet ad spem, fuga mali ad timorem, insecutio mali terribilis pertinet ad audaciam, fuga vero boni pertinet ad desperationem. Unde sequitur quod audacia consequitur ad spem, ex hoc enim quod aliquis sperat superare terribile imminens, ex hoc audacter insequitur ipsum. Ad timorem vero sequitur desperatio, ideo enim aliquis desperat, quia timet difficultatem quae est circa bonum sperandum.

AD PRIMUM ergo dicendum quod ratio sequeretur, si bonum et malum essent obiecta non habentia ordinem ad invicem. Sed quia malum habet aliquem ordinem ad bonum, est enim posterius bono, sicut privatio habitu; ideo audacia, quae insequitur malum, est post spem, quae insequitur bonum.

AD SECUNDUM dicendum quod, etsi bonum simpliciter sit prius quam malum, tamen fuga per prius debetur malo quam bono, sicut insecutio per prius debetur bono quam malo. Et ideo sicut spes est prior quam audacia, ita timor est prior quam desperatio. Et sicut ex timore non semper sequitur desperatio, sed quando fuerit intensus; ita ex spe non semper sequitur audacia, sed quando fuerit vehemens.

AD TERTIUM dicendum quod audacia, licet sit circa malum cui coniunctum est bonum victoriae secundum aestimationem audacis, tamen respicit malum, bonum vero adiunctum respicit spes. Et similiter desperatio respicit bonum directe, quod refugit, malum vero adiunctum respicit timor. Unde, proprie loquendo, audacia non est pars spei, sed eius effectus, sicut nec desperatio est pars timoris, sed eius effectus. Et

avoidance. Again, pursuit or avoidance is of something either by reason of itself or by reason of something else. By reason of itself, good is the object of pursuit, and evil, the object of avoidance: but by reason of something else, evil can be the object of pursuit, through some good attaching to it; and good can be the object of avoidance, through some evil attaching to it. Now that which is by reason of something else, follows that which is by **reason of itself. Consequently pursuit of evil** follows pursuit of good; and avoidance of good follows avoidance of evil. Now these four things belong to four passions, since pursuit of good belongs to hope, avoidance of evil to fear, the pursuit of the fearful evil belongs to daring, and the avoidance of good to despair. It follows, therefore, that daring results from hope; since it is in the hope of overcoming the threatening object of fear, that one attacks it boldly. But despair results from fear: since the reason why a man despairs is because he fears the difficulty attaching to the good he should hope for.

Reply to Objection 1: This argument would hold, if good and evil were not co-ordinate objects. But because evil has a certain relation to good, since it comes after good, as privation comes after habit; consequently daring which pursues evil, comes after hope which pursues good.

Reply to Objection 2: Although good, absolutely speaking, is prior to evil, yet avoidance of evil precedes avoidance of good; just as the pursuit of good precedes the pursuit of evil. Consequently just as hope precedes daring, so fear precedes despair. And just as fear does not always lead to despair, but only when it is intense; so hope does not always lead to daring, save only when it is strong.

Reply to Objection 3: Although the object of daring is an evil to which, in the estimation of the daring man, the good of victory is conjoined; yet daring regards the evil, and hope regards the conjoined good. In like manner despair regards directly the good which it turns away from, while fear regards the conjoined evil. Hence, properly speaking, daring is not a part of hope, but its effect: just as despair is an effect, not a part, of fear.

propter hoc etiam audacia principalis passio esse non potest.

For this reason, too, daring cannot be a principal passion.

Articulus 3

Ad tertium sic proceditur. Videtur quod defectus aliquis sit causa audaciae. Dicit enim philosophus, in libro de problematibus, quod *amatores vini sunt fortes et audaces.* Sed ex vino sequitur defectus ebrietatis. Ergo audacia causatur ex aliquo defectu.

Praeterea, philosophus dicit, in II Rhetoric., quod *inexperti periculorum sunt audaces.* Sed inexperientia defectus quidam est. Ergo audacia ex defectu causatur.

Praeterea, iniusta passi audaciores esse solent; *sicut etiam bestiae cum percutiuntur,* ut dicitur in III Ethic. Sed iniustum pati ad defectum pertinet. Ergo audacia ex aliquo defectu causatur.

Sed contra est quod philosophus dicit, in II Rhetoric., quod causa audaciae est, *cum in phantasia spes fuerit salutarium ut prope existentium, timendorum autem aut non entium, aut longe entium.* Sed id quod pertinet ad defectum, vel pertinet ad salutarium remotionem, vel ad terribilium propinquitatem. Ergo nihil quod ad defectum pertinet, est causa audaciae.

Respondeo dicendum quod, sicut supra dictum est, audacia consequitur spem, et contrariatur timori, unde quaecumque nata sunt causare spem, vel excludere timorem, sunt causa audaciae. Quia vero timor et spes, et etiam audacia, cum sint passiones quaedam, consistunt in motu appetitus et in quadam transmutatione corporali; dupliciter potest accipi causa audaciae,
 sive quantum ad provocationem spei, sive quantum ad exclusionem timoris, uno modo quidem, ex parte appetitivi motus; alio vero modo, ex parte transmutationis corporalis. Ex parte quidem appetitivi motus, qui sequitur apprehensionem, provocatur spes causans audaciam, per ea quae faciunt nos aestimare quod possibile sit adipisci victoriam; vel secundum propriam potentiam, sicut fortitudo corporis, experientia

Article 3
Whether some defect is a cause of daring?

Objection 1: It would seem that some defect is a cause of daring. For the Philosopher says (De Problem. xxvii, 4) that "lovers of wine are strong and daring." But from wine ensues the effect of drunkenness. Therefore daring is caused by a defect.

Objection 2: Further, the Philosopher says (Rhet. ii, 5) that "those who have no experience of danger are bold." But want of experience is a defect. Therefore daring is caused by a defect.

Objection 3: Further, those who have suffered wrongs are wont to be daring; "like the beasts when beaten," as stated in Ethic. iii, 5. But the suffering of wrongs pertains to defect. Therefore daring is caused by a defect.

On the contrary, The Philosopher says (Rhet. ii, 5) that the cause of daring "is the presence in the imagination of the hope that the means of safety are nigh, and that the things to be feared are either non-existent or far off." But anything pertaining to defect implies either the removal of the means of safety, or the proximity of something to be feared. Therefore nothing pertaining to defect is a cause of daring.

I answer that, As stated above (I-II, q. 45, a. 1; a. 2) daring results from hope and is contrary to fear: wherefore whatever is naturally apt to cause hope or banish fear, is a cause of daring. Since, however, fear and hope, and also daring, being passions, consist in a movement of the appetite, and in a certain bodily transmutation; a thing may be considered as the cause of daring in two ways, whether by raising hope, or by banishing fear; in one way, in the part of the appetitive movement; in another way, on the part of the bodily transmutation. On the part of the appetitive movement which follows apprehension, hope that leads to daring is roused by those things that make us reckon victory as possible. Such things regard either our own power, as bodily strength, experience

in periculis, multitudo pecuniarum, et alia huiusmodi; sive per potentiam aliorum, sicut multitudo amicorum vel quorumcumque auxiliantium, et praecipue si homo confidat de auxilio divino; unde *illi qui se bene habent ad divina, audaciores sunt*, ut etiam philosophus dicit, in II Rhetoric. Timor autem excluditur, secundum istum modum, per remotionem terribilium appropinquantium, puta quia homo non habet inimicos, quia nulli nocuit, quia non videt aliquod periculum imminere; illis enim videntur maxime pericula imminere, qui aliis nocuerunt. Ex parte vero transmutationis corporalis, causatur audacia per provocationem spei et exclusionem timoris, ex his quae faciunt caliditatem circa cor. Unde philosophus dicit, in libro de partibus animalium, quod *illi qui habent parvum cor secundum quantitatem, sunt magis audaces; et animalia habentia magnum cor secundum quantitatem, sunt timida, quia calor naturalis non tantum potest calefacere magnum cor; sicut parvum, sicut ignis non tantum potest calefacere magnam domum, sicut parvam*. Et in libro de problematibus dicit quod *habentes pulmonem sanguineum, sunt audaciores, propter caliditatem cordis exinde consequentem*. Et ibidem dicit quod *vini amatores sunt magis audaces, propter caliditatem vini*, unde et supra dictum est quod ebrietas facit ad bonitatem spei, caliditas enim cordis repellit timorem, et causat spem, propter cordis extensionem et amplificationem.

AD PRIMUM ergo dicendum quod ebrietas causat audaciam, non inquantum est defectus, sed inquantum facit cordis dilatationem, et inquantum etiam facit aestimationem cuiusdam magnitudinis.

AD SECUNDUM dicendum quod illi qui sunt inexperti periculorum, sunt audaciores, non propter defectum, sed per accidens, inquantum scilicet, propter inexperientiam, neque debilitatem suam cognoscunt, neque praesentiam periculorum. Et ita, per subtractionem causae timoris, sequitur audacia.

of dangers, abundance of wealth, and the like; or they regard the powers of others, such as having a great number of friends or any other means of help, especially if a man trust in the Divine assistance: wherefore "those are more daring, with whom it is well in regard to godlike things," as the Philosopher says (Rhet. ii, 5). Fear is banished, in this way, by the removal of threatening causes of fear; for instance, by the fact that a man has not enemies, through having harmed nobody, so that he is not aware of any imminent danger; since those especially appear to be threatened by danger, who have harmed others. On the part of the bodily transmutation, daring is caused through the incitement of hope and the banishment of fear, by those things which raise the temperature about the heart. Wherefore the Philosopher says (De Part. Animal. iii, 4) that "those whose heart is small in size, are more daring; while animals whose heart is large are timid; because the natural heat is unable to give the same degree of temperature to a large as to a small heart; just as a fire does not heat a large house as well as it does a small house." He says also (De Problem. xxvii, 4), that "those whose lungs contain much blood, are more daring, through the heat in the heart that results therefrom." He says also in the same passage that "lovers of wine are more daring, on account of the heat of the wine": hence it has been said above (I-II, q. 40, a. 6) that drunkenness conduces to hope, since the heat in the heart banishes fear and raises hope, by reason of the dilatation and enlargement of the heart.

Reply to Objection 1: Drunkenness causes daring, not through being a defect, but through dilating the heart: and again through making a man think greatly of himself.

Reply to Objection 2: Those who have no experience of dangers are more daring, not on account of a defect, but accidentally, i.e., in so far as through being inexperienced they do not know their own failings, nor the dangers that threaten. Hence it is that the removal of the cause of fear gives rise to daring.

Ad tertium dicendum quod, sicut philosophus dicit in II Rhetoric., *iniustum passi redduntur audaciores, quia aestimant quod Deus iniustum passis auxilium ferat.* Et sic patet quod nullus defectus causat audaciam nisi per accidens, inquantum scilicet habet adiunctam aliquam excellentiam, vel veram vel aestimatam, vel ex parte sui vel ex parte alterius.

Articulus 4

Ad quartum sic proceditur. Videtur quod audaces non sint promptiores in principio quam in ipsis periculis. Tremor enim ex timore causatur, qui contrariatur audaciae, ut ex dictis patet. Sed audaces quandoque in principio tremunt, ut philosophus dicit, in libro de problematibus. Ergo non sunt promptiores in principio quam in ipsis periculis existentes.

Praeterea, per augmentum obiecti augetur passio, sicut si bonum est amabile, et magis bonum est magis amabile. Sed arduum est obiectum audaciae. Augmentato ergo arduo, augmentatur audacia. Sed magis fit arduum et difficile periculum, quando est praesens. Ergo debet tunc magis crescere audacia.

Praeterea, ex vulneribus inflictis provocatur ira. Sed ira causat audaciam, dicit enim philosophus, in II Rhetoric., quod *ira est ausivum.* Ergo quando iam sunt in ipsis periculis, et percutiuntur, videtur quod magis audaces reddantur.

Sed contra est quod dicitur in III Ethic., quod *audaces praevolantes sunt et volentes ante pericula, in ipsis autem discedunt.*

Respondeo dicendum quod audacia, cum sit quidam motus appetitus sensitivi, sequitur apprehensionem sensitivae virtutis. Virtus autem sensitiva non est collativa nec inquisitiva singulorum quae circumstant rem, sed subitum habet iudicium. Contingit autem quandoque quod secundum subitam apprehensionem non possunt cognosci omnia quae difficultatem in aliquo negotio afferunt, unde surgit audaciae motus ad aggrediendum

Reply to Objection 3: As the Philosopher says (Rhet. ii, 5) "those who have been wronged are courageous, because they think that God comes to the assistance of those who suffer unjustly." Hence it is evident that no defect causes daring except accidentally, i.e., in so far as some excellence attaches thereto, real or imaginary, either in oneself or in another.

Article 4
Whether the brave are more eager at first than in the midst of danger?

Objection 1: It would seem that the daring are not more eager at first than in the midst of danger. Because trembling is caused by fear, which is contrary to daring, as stated above (I-II, q. 45, a. 1; q. 44, a. 3). But the daring sometimes tremble at first, as the Philosopher says (De Problem. xxvii, 3). Therefore they are not more eager at first than in the midst of danger.

Objection 2: Further, passion is intensified by an increase in its object: thus since a good is lovable, what is better is yet more lovable. But the object of daring is something difficult. Therefore the greater the difficulty, the greater the daring. But danger is more arduous and difficult when present. It is then therefore that daring is greatest.

Objection 3: Further, anger is provoked by the infliction of wounds. But anger causes daring; for the Philosopher says (Rhet. ii, 5) that "anger makes man bold." Therefore when man is in the midst of danger and when he is being beaten, then is he most daring.

On the contrary, It is said in Ethic. iii, 7 that "the daring are precipitate and full of eagerness before the danger, yet in the midst of dangers they stand aloof."

I answer that, Daring, being a movement of the sensitive appetite, follows an apprehension of the sensitive faculty. But the sensitive faculty cannot make comparisons, nor can it inquire into circumstances; its judgment is instantaneous. Now it happens sometimes that it is impossible for a man to take note in an instant of all the difficulties of a certain situation: hence there arises the movement of daring to face the

periculum. Unde quando iam experiuntur ipsum periculum, sentiunt maiorem difficultatem quam aestimaverunt. Et ideo deficiunt. Sed ratio est discussiva omnium quae afferunt difficultatem negotio. Et ideo fortes, qui ex iudicio rationis aggrediuntur pericula, in principio videntur remissi, quia non passi, sed cum deliberatione debita aggrediuntur. Quando autem sunt in ipsis periculis, non experiuntur aliquid improvisum; sed quandoque minora illis quae praecogitaverunt. Et ideo magis persistunt. Vel etiam quia propter bonum virtutis pericula aggrediuntur, cuius boni voluntas in eis perseverat, quantacumque sint pericula. Audaces autem, propter solam aestimationem facientem spem et excludentem timorem, sicut dictum est.

AD PRIMUM ergo dicendum quod etiam in audacibus accidit tremor, propter revocationem caloris ab exterioribus ad interiora, sicut etiam in timentibus. Sed in audacibus revocatur calor ad cor, in timentibus autem, ad inferiora.

AD SECUNDUM dicendum quod obiectum amoris est simpliciter bonum, unde augmentatum simpliciter augmentat amorem. Sed obiectum audaciae est compositum ex bono et malo; et motus audaciae in malum, praesupponit motum spei in bonum. Et ideo si tantum addatur de arduitate ad periculum quod excedat spem, non sequetur motus audaciae, sed diminuetur. Si tamen sit motus audaciae, quanto maius est periculum, tanto maior audacia reputatur.

AD TERTIUM dicendum quod ex laesione non causatur ira, nisi supposita aliqua spe, ut infra dicetur. Et ideo si fuerit tantum periculum quod excedat spem victoriae, non sequetur ira. Sed verum est quod, si ira sequatur, audacia augebitur.

danger; so that when he comes to experience the danger, he feels the difficulty to be greater than he expected, and so gives way. On the other hand, reason discusses all the difficulties of a situation. Consequently men of fortitude who face danger according to the judgment of reason, at first seem slack, because they face the danger not from passion but with due deliberation. Yet when they are in the midst of danger, they experience nothing unforeseen, but sometimes the difficulty turns out to be less than they anticipated; wherefore they are more persevering. Moreover, it may be because they face the danger on account of the good of virtue which is the abiding object of their will, however great the danger may prove: whereas men of daring face the danger on account of a mere thought giving rise to hope and banishing fear, as stated above (I-II, q. 45, a. 3).

Reply to Objection 1: Trembling does occur in men of daring, on account of the heat being withdrawn from the outer to the inner parts of the body, as occurs also in those who are afraid. But in men of daring the heat withdraws to the heart; whereas in those who are afraid, it withdraws to the inferior parts.

Reply to Objection 2: The object of love is good simply, wherefore if it be increased, love is increased simply. But the object of daring is a compound of good and evil; and the movement of daring towards evil presupposes the movement of hope towards good. If, therefore, so much difficulty be added to the danger that it overcomes hope, the movement of daring does not ensue, but fails. But if the movement of daring does ensue, the greater the danger, the greater is the daring considered to be.

Reply to Objection 3: Hurt does not give rise to anger unless there be some kind of hope, as we shall see later on (I-II, q. 46, a. 1). Consequently if the danger be so great as to banish all hope of victory, anger does not ensue. It is true, however, that if anger does ensue, there will be greater daring.

Quaestio XLVI

Deinde considerandum est de ira. Et *primo,* de ira secundum se; *secundo,* de causa factiva irae, et remedio eius; *tertio,* de effectu eius. Circa primum quaeruntur octo. *Primo,* utrum ira sit passio specialis. *Secundo,* utrum obiectum irae sit bonum, an malum. *Tertio,* utrum ira sit in concupiscibili. *Quarto,* utrum ira sit cum ratione. *Quinto,* utrum ira sit naturalior quam concupiscentia. *Sexto,* utrum ira sit gravior quam odium. *Septimo,* utrum ira solum sit ad illos ad quos est iustitia. *Octavo,* de speciebus irae.

Articulus 1

Ad primum sic proceditur. Videtur quod ira non sit passio specialis. Ab ira enim denominatur potentia irascibilis. Sed huius potentiae non est una tantum passio, sed multae. Ergo ira non est una passio specialis.

Praeterea, cuilibet passioni speciali est aliquid contrarium; ut patet inducenti per singula. Sed irae non est aliqua passio contraria, ut supra dictum est. Ergo ira non est passio specialis.

Praeterea, una specialis passio non includit aliam. Sed ira includit multas passiones, est enim cum tristitia, et cum delectatione, et cum spe, ut patet per philosophum, in II Rhetoric. Ergo ira non est passio specialis.

Sed contra est quod Damascenus ponit iram specialem passionem. Et similiter Tullius, IV de Tusculanis quaest.

Respondeo dicendum quod aliquid dicitur generale dupliciter. Uno modo, per praedicationem, sicut *animal* est generale ad omnia animalia. Alio modo, per causam, sicut sol est causa generalis omnium quae generantur in his inferioribus, secundum Dionysium, in IV cap. de Div. Nom. Sicut enim genus continet multas differentias potestate, secundum similitudinem materiae; ita causa agens continet multos effectus secundum virtutem activam. Contingit autem aliquem effectum ex concursu diversarum causarum produci, et quia omnis causa

Question 46
Of Anger, in Itself

We must now consider anger: and 1. anger in itself; 2. the cause of anger and its remedy; 3. the effect of anger. Under the first head there are eight points of inquiry: 1. Whether anger is a special passion? 2. Whether the object of anger is good or evil? 3. Whether anger is in the concupiscible faculty? 4. Whether anger is accompanied by an act of reason? 5. Whether anger is more natural than desire? 6. Whether anger is more grievous than hatred? 7. Whether anger is only towards those with whom we have a relation of justice? 8. Of the species of anger.

Article 1
Whether anger is a special passion?

Objection 1: It would seem that anger is not a special passion. For the irascible power takes its name from anger [*ira*]. But there are several passions in this power, not only one. Therefore anger is not one special passion.

Objection 2: Further, to every special passion there is a contrary passion; as is evident by going through them one by one. But no passion is contrary to anger, as stated above (I-II, q. 23, a. 3). Therefore anger is not a special passion.

Objection 3: Further, one special passion does not include another. But anger includes several passions: since it accompanies sorrow, pleasure, and hope, as the Philosopher states (Rhet. ii, 2). Therefore anger is not a special passion.

On the contrary, Damascene (De Fide Orth. ii, 16) calls anger a special passion: and so does Cicero (De Quaest. Tusc. iv, 7).

I answer that, A thing is said to be general in two ways. First, by predication; thus "animal" is general in respect of all animals. Secondly, by causality; thus the sun is the general cause of all things generated here below, according to Dionysius (Div. Nom. iv). Because just as a genus contains potentially many differences, according to a likeness of matter; so an efficient cause contains many effects according to its active power. Now it happens that an effect is produced by the concurrence of various causes; and since every cause

aliquo modo in effectu manet, potest etiam dici, tertio modo, quod effectus ex congregatione multarum causarum productus, habet quandam generalitatem, inquantum continet multas causas quodammodo in actu. Primo ergo modo, ira non est passio generalis, sed condivisa aliis passionibus, ut supra dictum est. Similiter autem nec secundo modo. Non est enim causa aliarum passionum, sed per hunc modum potest dici generalis passio amor, ut patet per Augustinum, in XIV libro de Civ. Dei; amor enim est prima radix omnium passionum, ut supra dictum est. Sed tertio modo potest ira dici passio generalis, inquantum ex concursu multarum passionum causatur. Non enim insurgit motus irae nisi propter aliquam tristitiam illatam et nisi adsit desiderium et spes ulciscendi, quia, ut philosophus dicit in II Rhetoric., *iratus habet spem puniendi; appetit enim vindictam ut sibi possibilem*. Unde si fuerit multum excellens persona quae nocumentum intulit, non sequitur ira, sed solum tristitia, ut Avicenna dicit, in libro de anima.

AD PRIMUM ergo dicendum quod, vis irascibilis denominatur ab ira, non quia omnis motus huius potentiae sit ira, sed quia ad iram terminantur omnes motus huius potentiae; et inter alios eius motus, iste est manifestior.

AD SECUNDUM dicendum quod ex hoc ipso quod ira causatur ex contrariis passionibus, scilicet a spe, quae est boni, et a tristitia, quae est mali, includit in seipsa contrarietatem, et ideo non habet contrarium extra se. Sicut etiam in mediis coloribus non invenitur contrarietas, nisi quae est simplicium colorum, ex quibus causantur.

AD TERTIUM dicendum quod ira includit multas passiones, non quidem sicut genus species, sed magis secundum continentiam causae et effectus.

remains somewhat in its effect, we may say that, in yet a third way, an effect which is due to the concurrence of several causes, has a certain generality, inasmuch as several causes are, in a fashion, actually existing therein. Accordingly in the first way, anger is not a general passion but is condivided with the other passions, as stated above (I-II, q. 23, a. 4). In like manner, neither is it in the second way: since it is not a cause of the other passions. But in this way, love may be called a general passion, as Augustine declares (De Civ. Dei xiv, 7, 9), because love is the primary root of all the other passions, as stated above (I-II, q. 27, a. 4). But, in a third way, anger may be called a general passion, inasmuch as it is caused by a concurrence of several passions. Because the movement of anger does not arise save on account of some pain inflicted, and unless there be desire and hope of revenge: for, as the Philosopher says (Rhet. ii, 2), "the angry man hopes to punish; since he craves for revenge as being possible." Consequently if the person, who inflicted the injury, excel very much, anger does not ensue, but only sorrow, as Avicenna states (De Anima iv, 6).

Reply to Objection 1: The irascible power takes its name from *ira* [anger], not because every movement of that power is one of anger; but because all its movements terminate in anger; and because, of all these movements, anger is the most patent.

Reply to Objection 2: From the very fact that anger is caused by contrary passions, i.e., by hope, which is of good, and by sorrow, which is of evil, it includes in itself contrariety: and consequently it has no contrary outside itself. Thus also in mixed colors there is no contrariety, except that of the simple colors from which they are made.

Reply to Objection 3: Anger includes several passions, not indeed as a genus includes several species; but rather according to the inclusion of cause and effect.

Articulus 2

AD SECUNDUM sic proceditur. Videtur quod obiectum irae sit malum. Dicit enim Gregorius Nyssenus quod ira est quasi *armigera concupiscentiae,* inquantum scilicet impugnat id quod concupiscentiam impedit. Sed omne impedimentum habet rationem mali. Ergo ira respicit malum tanquam obiectum.

PRAETEREA, ira et odium conveniunt in effectu, utriusque enim est inferre nocumentum alteri. Sed odium respicit malum tanquam obiectum, ut supra dictum est. Ergo etiam et ira.

PRAETEREA, ira causatur ex tristitia, unde philosophus dicit, in VII Ethic., quod *ira operatur cum tristitia.* Sed tristitiae obiectum est malum. Ergo et irae.

SED CONTRA est quod Augustinus dicit, in II Confess., quod *ira appetit vindictam.* Sed appetitus vindictae est appetitus boni, cum vindicta ad iustitiam pertineat. Ergo obiectum irae est bonum.

PRAETEREA, ira semper est cum spe, unde et delectationem causat, ut dicit philosophus, in II Rhetoric. Sed spei et delectationis obiectum est bonum. Ergo et irae.

RESPONDEO dicendum quod motus appetitivae virtutis sequitur actum virtutis apprehensivae. Vis autem apprehensiva dupliciter aliquid apprehendit, uno modo, per modum incomplexi, sicut cum intelligimus quid est homo; alio modo, per modum complexi, sicut cum intelligimus album inesse homini. Unde utroque modo vis appetitiva potest tendere in bonum et malum. Per modum quidem simplicis et incomplexi, cum appetitus simpliciter sequitur vel inhaeret bono, vel refugit malum. Et tales motus sunt desiderium et spes, delectatio et tristitia, et alia huiusmodi. Per modum autem complexi, sicut cum appetitus fertur in hoc quod aliquod bonum vel malum insit vel fiat circa alterum, vel tendendo in hoc, vel refugiendo ab hoc. Sicut manifeste apparet in amore et odio, amamus enim aliquem, inquantum

Article 2
Whether the object of anger is good or evil?

Objection 1: It would seem that the object of anger is evil. For Gregory of Nyssa says* that anger is "the sword-bearer of desire," inasmuch, to wit, as it assails whatever obstacle stands in the way of desire. But an obstacle has the character of evil. Therefore anger regards evil as its object.

Objection 2: Further, anger and hatred agree in their effect, since each seeks to inflict harm on another. But hatred regards evil as its object, as stated above (I-II, q. 29, a. 1). Therefore anger does also.

Objection 3: Further, anger arises from sorrow; wherefore the Philosopher says (Ethic. viii, 6) that "anger acts with sorrow." But evil is the object of sorrow. Therefore it is also the object of anger.

On the contrary, Augustine says (Confess. ii, 6) that "anger craves for revenge." But the desire for revenge is a desire for something good: since revenge belongs to justice. Therefore the object of anger is good.

Moreover, anger is always accompanied by hope, wherefore it causes pleasure, as the Philosopher says (Rhet. ii, 2). But the object of hope and of pleasure is good. Therefore good is also the object of anger.

I answer that, The movement of the appetitive power follows an act of the apprehensive power. Now the apprehensive power apprehends a thing in two ways. First, by way of an incomplex object, as when we understand what a man is; secondly, by way of a complex object, as when we understand that whiteness is in a man. Consequently in each of these ways the appetitive power can tend to both good and evil: by way of a simple and incomplex object, when the appetite simply follows and adheres to good, or recoils from evil: and such movements are desire, hope, pleasure, sorrow, and so forth: by way of a complex object, as when the appetite is concerned with some good or evil being in, or being done to, another, either seeking this or recoiling from it. This is evident in the case of love and hatred: for we love someone, in so

---
* Nemesius, De Nat. Hom. xxi.

volumus ei inesse aliquod bonum; odimus autem aliquem, inquantum volumus ei inesse aliquod malum. Et similiter est in ira, quicumque enim irascitur, quaerit vindicari de aliquo. Et sic motus irae tendit in duo, scilicet in ipsam vindictam, quam appetit et sperat sicut quoddam bonum, unde et de ipsa delectatur, tendit etiam in illum de quo quaerit vindictam, sicut in contrarium et nocivum, quod pertinet ad rationem mali. Est tamen **duplex differentia attendenda circa hoc, irae ad odium et ad amorem.** Quarum prima est, quod ira semper respicit duo obiecta, amor vero et odium quandoque respiciunt unum obiectum tantum, sicut cum dicitur aliquis amare vinum vel aliquid huiusmodi, aut etiam odire. Secunda est, quia utrumque obiectorum quod respicit amor, est bonum, vult enim amans bonum alicui, tanquam sibi convenienti. Utrumque vero eorum quae respicit odium, habet rationem mali, vult enim odiens malum alicui, tamquam cuidam inconvenienti. Sed ira respicit unum obiectum secundum rationem boni, scilicet vindictam, quam appetit, et aliud secundum rationem mali, scilicet hominem nocivum, de quo vult vindicari. Et ideo est passio quodammodo composita ex contrariis passionibus.

Et per hoc patet responsio ad obiecta.

far as we wish some good to be in him; and we hate someone, in so far as we wish some evil to be in him. It is the same with anger; for when a man is angry, he wishes to be avenged on someone. Hence the movement of anger has a twofold tendency: viz. to vengeance itself, which it desires and hopes for as being a good, wherefore it takes pleasure in it; and to the person on whom it seeks vengeance, as to something contrary and hurtful, **which bears the character of evil. We must, however, observe a twofold difference in this respect, between anger on the one side, and hatred and love on the other.** The first difference is that anger always regards two objects: whereas love and hatred sometimes regard but one object, as when a man is said to love wine or something of the kind, or to hate it. The second difference is, that both the objects of love are good: since the lover wishes good to someone, as to something agreeable to himself: while both the objects of hatred bear the character of evil: for the man who hates, wishes evil to someone, as to something disagreeable to him. Whereas anger regards one object under the aspect of evil, *viz.* the noxious person, on whom it seeks to be avenged. Consequently it is a passion somewhat made up of contrary passions.

This suffices for the Replies to the Objections.

Articulus 3

AD TERTIUM sic proceditur. Videtur quod ira sit in concupiscibili. Dicit enim Tullius, in IV de Tusculanis quaest., quod ira est *libido* quaedam. Sed libido est in concupiscibili. Ergo et ira.

PRAETEREA, Augustinus dicit, in regula, quod *ira crescit in odium.* Et Tullius dicit, in eodem libro, quod *odium est ira inveterata.* Sed odium est in concupiscibili, sicut amor. Ergo ira est in concupiscibili.

PRAETEREA, Damascenus et Gregorius Nyssenus dicunt quod *ira componitur ex*

Article 3
Whether anger is in the concupiscible faculty?

Objection 1: It would seem that anger is in the concupiscible faculty. For Cicero says (De Quaest. Tusc. iv, 9) that anger is a kind of "desire." But desire is in the concupiscible faculty. Therefore anger is too.

Objection 2: Further, Augustine says in his Rule, that "anger grows into hatred": and Cicero says (De Quaest. Tusc. iv, 9) that "hatred is inveterate anger." But hatred, like love, is a concupiscible passion. Therefore anger is in the concupiscible faculty.

Objection 3: Further, Damascene (De Fide Orth. ii, 16) and Gregory of Nyssa* say that "anger is made up of

---

* Nemesius, De Nat. Hom. xxi.

tristitia et desiderio. Sed utrumque horum est in concupiscibili. Ergo ira est in concupiscibili.

SED CONTRA, vis concupiscibilis est alia ab irascibili. Si igitur ira esset in concupiscibili, non denominaretur ab ea vis irascibilis.

RESPONDEO dicendum quod, sicut supra dictum est, passiones irascibilis in hoc differunt a passionibus concupiscibilis, quod obiecta passionum concupiscibilis sunt bonum et malum absolute; obiecta autem passionum irascibilis sunt bonum et malum cum quadam elevatione vel arduitate. Dictum est autem quod ira respicit duo obiecta, scilicet vindictam, quam appetit; et eum de quo vindictam quaerit. Et circa utrumque quandam arduitatem ira requirit, non enim insurgit motus irae, nisi aliqua magnitudine circa utrumque existente; *quaecumque enim nihil sunt, aut modica valde nullo digna aestimamus,* ut dicit philosophus, in II Rhetoric. Unde manifestum est quod ira non est in concupiscibili, sed in irascibili.

AD PRIMUM ergo dicendum quod Tullius libidinem nominat appetitum cuiuscumque boni futuri non habita discretione ardui vel non ardui. Et secundum hoc, ponit iram sub libidine, inquantum est appetitus vindictae. Sic autem libido communis est ad irascibilem et concupiscibilem.

AD SECUNDUM dicendum quod ira dicitur crescere in odium, non quod eadem numero passio quae prius fuit ira, postmodum fiat odium per quandam inveterationem, sed per quandam causalitatem. Ira enim, per diuturnitatem, causat odium.

AD TERTIUM dicendum quod ira dicitur componi ex tristitia et desiderio, non sicut ex partibus, sed sicut ex causis. Dictum est autem supra quod passiones concupiscibilis sunt causae passionum irascibilis.

sorrow and desire." Both of these are in the concupiscible faculty. Therefore anger is a concupiscible passion.

On the contrary, The concupiscible is distinct from the irascible faculty. If, therefore, anger were in the concupiscible power, the irascible would not take its name from it.

I answer that, As stated above (I-II, q. 23, a. 1), the passions of the irascible part differ from the passions of the concupiscible faculty, in that the objects of the concupiscible passions are good and evil absolutely considered, whereas the objects of the irascible passions are good and evil in a certain elevation or arduousness. Now it has been stated (I-II, q. 23, a. 2) that anger regards two objects: *viz.* the vengeance that it seeks; and the person on whom it seeks vengeance; and in respect of both, anger requires a certain arduousness: for the movement of anger does not arise, unless there be some magnitude about both these objects; since "we make no ado about things that are naught or very minute," as the Philosopher observes (Rhet. ii, 2). It is therefore evident that anger is not in the concupiscible, but in the irascible faculty.

Reply to Objection 1: Cicero gives the name of desire to any kind of craving for a future good, without discriminating between that which is arduous and that which is not. Accordingly he reckons anger as a kind of desire, inasmuch as it is a desire of vengeance. In this sense, however, desire is common to the irascible and concupiscible faculties.

Reply to Objection 2: Anger is said to grow into hatred, not as though the same passion which at first was anger, afterwards becomes hatred by becoming inveterate; but by a process of causality. For anger when it lasts a long time engenders hatred.

Reply to Objection 3: Anger is said to be composed of sorrow and desire, not as though they were its parts, but because they are its causes: and it has been said above (I-II, q. 25, a. 2) that the concupiscible passions are the causes of the irascible passions.

Articulus 4

AD QUARTUM sic proceditur. Videtur quod ira non sit cum ratione. Ira enim, cum sit passio quaedam, est in appetitu sensitivo. Sed appetitus sensitivus non sequitur rationis apprehensionem, sed sensitivae partis. Ergo ira non est cum ratione.

PRAETEREA, animalia bruta carent ratione. Et tamen in eis invenitur ira. Ergo ira non est cum ratione.

PRAETEREA, ebrietas ligat rationem. Adiuvat autem ad iram. Ergo ira non est cum ratione.

SED CONTRA est quod philosophus dicit, in VII Ethic., quod *ira consequitur rationem aliqualiter*.

RESPONDEO dicendum quod, sicut supra dictum est, ira est appetitus vindictae. Haec autem collationem importat poenae infligendae ad nocumentum sibi illatum, unde, in VII Ethic., dicit philosophus quod *syllogizans quoniam oportet talem oppugnare, irascitur confestim*. Conferre autem et syllogizare est rationis. Et ideo ira est quodammodo cum ratione.

AD PRIMUM ergo dicendum quod motus appetitivae virtutis potest esse cum ratione dupliciter. Uno modo, cum ratione praecipiente, et sic voluntas est cum ratione; unde et dicitur appetitus rationalis. Alio modo, cum ratione denuntiante, et sic ira est cum ratione. Dicit enim philosophus, in libro de Problemat., quod *ira est cum ratione, non sicut praecipiente ratione, sed ut manifestante iniuriam*. Appetitus enim sensitivus immediate rationi non obedit, sed mediante voluntate.

AD SECUNDUM dicendum quod bruta animalia habent instinctum naturalem ex divina ratione eis inditum, per quem habent motus interiores et exteriores similes motibus rationis, sicut supra dictum est.

Article 4
Whether anger requires an act of reason?

Objection 1: It would seem that anger does not require an act of reason. For, since anger is a passion, it is in the sensitive appetite. But the sensitive appetite follows an apprehension, not of reason, but of the sensitive faculty. Therefore anger does not require an act of reason.

Objection 2: Further, dumb animals are devoid of reason: and yet they are seen to be angry. Therefore anger does not require an act of reason.

Objection 3: Further, drunkenness fetters the reason; whereas it is conducive to anger. Therefore anger does not require an act of reason.

On the contrary, The Philosopher says (Ethic. vii, 6) that "anger listens to reason somewhat."

I answer that, As stated above (I-II, q. 46, a. 2), anger is a desire for vengeance. Now vengeance implies a comparison between the punishment to be inflicted and the hurt done; wherefore the Philosopher says (Ethic. vii, 6) that "anger, as if it had drawn the inference that it ought to quarrel with such a person, is therefore immediately exasperated." Now to compare and to draw an inference is an act of reason. Therefore anger, in a fashion, requires an act of reason.

Reply to Objection 1: The movement of the appetitive power may follow an act of reason in two ways. In the first way, it follows the reason in so far as the reason commands: and thus the will follows reason, wherefore it is called the rational appetite. In another way, it follows reason in so far as the reason denounces, and thus anger follows reason. For the Philosopher says (De Problem. xxviii, 3) that "anger follows reason, not in obedience to reason's command, but as a result of reason's denouncing the injury." Because the sensitive appetite is subject to the reason, not immediately but through the will.

Reply to Objection 2: Dumb animals have a natural instinct imparted to them by the Divine Reason, in virtue of which they are gifted with movements, both internal and external, like unto rational movements, as stated above (I-II, q. 40, a. 3).

AD TERTIUM dicendum quod, sicut dicitur in VII Ethic., *ira audit aliqualiter rationem,* sicut nuntiantem quod iniuriatum est ei, *sed non perfecte audit,* quia non observat regulam rationis in rependendo vindictam. Ad iram ergo requiritur aliquis actus rationis; et additur impedimentum rationis. Unde philosophus dicit, in libro de Problemat., quod illi qui sunt multum ebrii, tanquam nihil habentes de iudicio rationis, non irascuntur, sed quando sunt parum ebrii, irascuntur, tanquam habentes iudicium rationis, sed impeditum.

Reply to Objection 3: As stated in Ethic. vii, 6, "anger listens somewhat to reason" in so far as reason denounces the injury inflicted, "but listens not perfectly," because it does not observe the rule of reason as to the measure of vengeance. Anger, therefore, requires an act of reason; and yet proves a hindrance to reason. Wherefore the Philosopher says (De Problem. iii, 2, 27) that whose who are very drunk, so as to be incapable of the use of reason, do not get angry: but those who are slightly drunk, do get angry, through being still able, though hampered, to form a judgment of reason.

ARTICULUS 5

AD QUINTUM sic proceditur. Videtur quod ira non sit naturalior quam concupiscentia. Proprium enim hominis dicitur quod sit animal mansuetum natura. Sed *mansuetudo opponitur irae,* ut dicit philosophus, in II Rhetoric. Ergo ira non est naturalior quam concupiscentia, sed omnino videtur esse contra hominis naturam.

PRAETEREA, ratio contra naturam dividitur, ea enim quae secundum rationem agunt, non dicimus secundum naturam agere. Sed *ira est cum ratione, concupiscentia autem sine ratione,* ut dicitur in VII Ethic. Ergo concupiscentia est naturalior quam ira.

PRAETEREA, ira est appetitus vindictae, concupiscentia autem maxime est appetitus delectabilium secundum tactum, scilicet ciborum et venereorum. Haec autem sunt magis naturalia homini quam vindicta. Ergo concupiscentia est naturalior quam ira.

SED CONTRA est quod philosophus dicit, in VII Ethic., quod *ira est naturalior quam concupiscentia.*

RESPONDEO dicendum quod *naturale* dicitur illud quod causatur a natura, ut patet in II Physic. Unde utrum aliqua passio sit magis vel minus naturalis, considerari non potest nisi ex causa sua. Causa autem passionis, ut supra dictum est, dupliciter accipi potest, uno modo, ex parte obiecti; alio modo, ex parte

ARTICLE 5
Whether anger is more natural than desire?

Objection 1: It would seem that anger is not more natural than desire. Because it is proper to man to be by nature a gentle animal. But "gentleness is contrary to anger," as the Philosopher states (Rhet. ii, 3). Therefore anger is no more natural than desire, in fact it seems to be altogether unnatural to man.

Objection 2: Further, reason is contrasted with nature: since those things that act according to reason, are not said to act according to nature. Now "anger requires an act of reason, but desire does not," as stated in Ethic. vii, 6. Therefore desire is more natural than anger.

Objection 3: Further, anger is a craving for vengeance: while desire is a craving for those things especially which are pleasant to the touch, *viz.* for pleasures of the table and for sexual pleasures. But these things are more natural to man than vengeance. Therefore desire is more natural than anger.

On the contrary, The Philosopher says (Ethic. vii, 6) that "anger is more natural than desire."

I answer that, By "natural" we mean that which is caused by nature, as stated in Phys. ii, 1. Consequently the question as to whether a particular passion is more or less natural cannot be decided without reference to the cause of that passion. Now the cause of a passion, as stated above (I-II, q. 36, a. 2), may be considered in two ways: first, on the part of the object; secondly, on the part of the

subiecti. Si ergo consideretur causa irae et concupiscentiae ex parte obiecti, sic concupiscentia, et maxime ciborum et venereorum, naturalior est quam ira, inquantum ista sunt magis naturalia quam vindicta. Si autem consideretur causa irae ex parte subiecti, sic quodammodo ira est naturalior, et quodammodo concupiscentia. Potest enim natura alicuius hominis considerari vel secundum naturam generis, vel secundum naturam speciei, vel secundum complexionem propriam individui. Si igitur consideretur natura generis, quae est natura huius hominis inquantum est animal; sic naturalior est concupiscentia quam ira, quia ex ipsa natura communi habet homo quandam inclinationem ad appetendum ea quae sunt conservativa vitae, vel secundum speciem vel secundum individuum. Si autem consideremus naturam hominis ex parte speciei, scilicet inquantum est rationalis; sic ira est magis naturalis homini quam concupiscentia, inquantum ira est cum ratione magis quam concupiscentia. Unde philosophus dicit, in IV Ethic., quod *humanius est punire,* quod pertinet ad iram, *quam mansuetum esse,* unumquodque enim naturaliter insurgit contra contraria et nociva. Si vero consideretur natura huius individui secundum propriam complexionem, sic ira naturalior est quam concupiscentia, quia scilicet habitudinem naturalem ad irascendum, quae est ex complexione, magis de facili sequitur ira, quam concupiscentia vel aliqua alia passio. Est enim homo dispositus ad irascendum, secundum quod habet cholericam complexionem, cholera autem, inter alios humores, citius movetur; assimilatur enim igni. Et ideo magis est in promptu ut ille qui est dispositus secundum naturalem complexionem ad iram, irascatur; quam de eo qui est dispositus ad concupiscendum, quod concupiscat. Et propter hoc philosophus dicit, in VII Ethic., quod ira magis traducitur a parentibus in filios, quam concupiscentia.

subject. If then we consider the cause of anger and of desire, on the part of the object, thus desire, especially of pleasures of the table, and of sexual pleasures, is more natural than anger; in so far as these pleasures are more natural to man than vengeance. If, however, we consider the cause of anger on the part of the subject, thus anger, in a manner, is more natural; and, in a manner, desire is more natural. Because the nature of an individual man may be considered either as to the generic, or as to the specific nature, or again as to the particular temperament of the individual. If then we consider the generic nature, i.e., the nature of this man considered as an animal; thus desire is more natural than anger; because it is from this very generic nature that man is inclined to desire those things which tend to preserve in him the life both of the species and of the individual. If, however, we consider the specific nature, i.e., the nature of this man as a rational being; then anger is more natural to man than desire, in so far as anger follows reason more than desire does. Wherefore the Philosopher says (Ethic. iv, 5) that "revenge" which pertains to anger "is more natural to man than meekness": for it is natural to everything to rise up against things contrary and hurtful. And if we consider the nature of the individual, in respect of his particular temperament, thus anger is more natural than desire; for the reason that anger is prone to ensue from the natural tendency to anger, more than desire, or any other passion, is to ensue from a natural tendency to desire, which tendencies result from a man's individual temperament. Because disposition to anger is due to a bilious temperament; and of all the humors, the bile moves quickest; for it is like fire. Consequently he that is temperamentally disposed to anger is sooner incensed with anger, than he that is temperamentally disposed to desire, is inflamed with desire: and for this reason the Philosopher says (Ethic. vii, 6) that a disposition to anger is more liable to be transmitted from parent to child, than a disposition to desire.

Ad primum ergo dicendum quod in homine considerari potest et naturalis complexio ex parte corporis, quae est temperata; et ipsa ratio. Ex parte igitur complexionis corporalis, naturaliter homo, secundum suam speciem, est non habens superexcellentiam neque irae neque alicuius alterius passionis, propter temperamentum suae complexionis. Alia vero animalia, secundum quod recedunt ab hac qualitate complexionis ad dispositionem alicuius complexionis extremae, secundum hoc etiam naturaliter disponuntur ad excessum alicuius passionis, ut leo ad audaciam, canis ad iram, lepus ad timorem, et sic de aliis. Ex parte vero rationis, est naturale homini et irasci et mansuetum esse, secundum quod ratio quodammodo causat iram, inquantum nuntiat causam irae; et quodammodo sedat iram, inquantum iratus *non totaliter audit imperium rationis,* ut supra dictum est.

Ad secundum dicendum quod ipsa ratio pertinet ad naturam hominis. Unde ex hoc ipso quod ira est cum ratione, sequitur quod secundum aliquem modum sit homini naturalis.

Ad tertium dicendum quod ratio illa procedit de ira et concupiscentia, ex parte obiecti.

Reply to Objection 1: We may consider in man both the natural temperament on the part of the body, and the reason. On the part of the bodily temperament, a man, considered specifically, does not naturally excel others either in anger or in any other passion, on account of the moderation of his temperament. But other animals, for as much as their temperament recedes from this moderation and approaches to an extreme disposition, are naturally disposed to some excess of passion, such as the lion in daring, the hound in anger, the hare in fear, and so forth. On the part of reason, however, it is natural to man, both to be angry and to be gentle: in so far as reason somewhat causes anger, by denouncing the injury which causes anger; and somewhat appeases anger, in so far as the angry man "does not listen perfectly to the command of reason," as stated above (I-II, q. 46, a. 4, ad 3).

Reply to Objection 2: Reason itself belongs to the nature of man: wherefore from the very fact that anger requires an act of reason, it follows that it is, in a manner, natural to man.

Reply to Objection 3: This argument regards anger and desire on the part of the object.

Articulus 6

Ad sextum sic proceditur. Videtur quod ira sit gravior quam odium. Dicitur enim Prov. XXVII, quod *ira non habet misericordiam, nec erumpens furor.* Odium autem quandoque habet misericordiam. Ergo ira est gravior quam odium.

Praeterea, maius est pati malum et de malo dolere, quam simpliciter pati. Sed illi qui habet aliquem odio, sufficit quod ille quem odit, patiatur malum, irato autem non sufficit, sed quaerit quod cognoscat illud et de illo doleat, ut dicit philosophus, in II Rhetoric. Ergo ira est gravior quam odium.

Article 6
Whether anger is more grievous than hatred?

Objection 1: It would seem that anger is more grievous than hatred. For it is written (Prov. 27:4) that "anger hath no mercy, nor fury when it breaketh forth." But hatred sometimes has mercy. Therefore anger is more grievous than hatred.

Objection 2: Further, it is worse to suffer evil and to grieve for it, than merely to suffer it. But when a man hates, he is contented if the object of his hatred suffer evil: whereas the angry man is not satisfied unless the object of his anger know it and be aggrieved thereby, as the Philosopher says (Rhet. ii, 4). Therefore, anger is more grievous than hatred.

PRAETEREA, quanto ad constitutionem alicuius plura concurrunt, tanto videtur esse stabilius, sicut habitus permanentior est qui ex pluribus actibus causatur. Sed ira causatur ex concursu plurium passionum, ut supra dictum est, non autem odium. Ergo ira est stabilior et gravior quam odium.

SED CONTRA est quod Augustinus, in regula, odium comparat *trabi,* iram vero *festucae.*

RESPONDEO dicendum quod species passionis, et ratio ipsius, ex obiecto pensatur. Est autem obiectum irae et odii idem subiecto, nam sicut odiens appetit malum ei quem odit, ita iratus ei contra quem irascitur. Sed non eadem ratione, sed odiens appetit malum inimici, inquantum est malum; iratus autem appetit malum eius contra quem irascitur, non inquantum est malum, sed inquantum habet quandam rationem boni, scilicet prout aestimat illud esse iustum, inquantum est vindicativum. Unde etiam supra dictum est quod odium est per applicationem mali ad malum; ira autem per applicationem boni ad malum. Manifestum est autem quod appetere malum sub ratione iusti, minus habet de ratione mali quam velle malum alicuius simpliciter. Velle enim malum alicuius sub ratione iusti, potest esse etiam secundum virtutem iustitiae, si praecepto rationis obtemperetur, sed ira in hoc solum deficit, quod non obedit rationis praecepto in ulciscendo. Unde manifestum est quod odium est multo deterius et gravius quam ira.

AD PRIMUM ergo dicendum quod in ira et odio duo possunt considerari, scilicet ipsum quod desideratur, et intensio desiderii. Quantum igitur ad id quod desideratur, ira habet magis misericordiam quam odium. Quia enim odium appetit malum alterius secundum se, nulla mensura mali satiatur, ea enim quae secundum se appetuntur, sine mensura appetuntur, ut philosophus dicit I Politic., sicut avarus divitias. Unde dicitur Eccli. XII, *inimicus si invenerit tempus, non satiabitur*

Objection 3: Further, a thing seems to be so much the more firm according as more things concur to set it up: thus a habit is all the more settled through being caused by several acts. But anger is caused by the concurrence of several passions, as stated above (I-II, q. 46, a. 1): whereas hatred is not. Therefore anger is more settled and more grievous than hatred.

On the contrary, Augustine, in his Rule, compares hatred to "a beam," but anger to "a mote."

I answer that, The species and nature of a passion are taken from its object. Now the object of anger is the same in substance as the object of hatred; since, just as the hater wishes evil to him whom he hates, so does the angry man wish evil to him with whom he is angry. But there is a difference of aspect: for the hater wishes evil to his enemy, as evil, whereas the angry man wishes evil to him with whom he is angry, not as evil but in so far as it has an aspect of good, that is, in so far as he reckons it as just, since it is a means of vengeance. Wherefore also it has been said above (I-II, q. 46, a. 2) that hatred implies application of evil to evil, whereas anger denotes application of good to evil. Now it is evident that to seek evil under the aspect of justice, is a lesser evil, than simply to seek evil to someone. Because to wish evil to someone under the aspect of justice, may be according to the virtue of justice, if it be in conformity with the order of reason; and anger fails only in this, that it does not obey the precept of reason in taking vengeance. Consequently it is evident that hatred is far worse and graver than anger.

Reply to Objection 1: In anger and hatred two points may be considered: namely, the thing desired, and the intensity of the desire. As to the thing desired, anger has more mercy than hatred has. For since hatred desires another's evil for evil's sake, it is satisfied with no particular measure of evil: because those things that are desired for their own sake, are desired without measure, as the Philosopher states (Polit. i, 3), instancing a miser with regard to riches. Hence it is written (Ecclus. 12:16): "An enemy . . . if he find an opportunity, will not be satisfied with

sanguine. Sed ira non appetit malum nisi sub ratione iusti vindicativi. Unde quando malum illatum excedit mensuram iustitiae, secundum aestimationem irascentis, tunc miseretur. Unde philosophus dicit, in II Rhetoric., quod *iratus, si fiant multa, miserebitur, odiens autem pro nullo.* Quantum vero ad intensionem desiderii, ira magis excludit misericordiam quam odium, quia motus irae est impetuosior, propter cholerae inflammationem. Unde statim subditur, *impetum concitati spiritus ferre quis poterit?*

AD SECUNDUM dicendum quod, sicut dictum est, iratus appetit malum alicuius, inquantum habet rationem iusti vindicativi. Vindicta autem fit per illationem poenae. Est autem de ratione poenae quod sit contraria voluntati, et quod sit afflictiva, et quod pro aliqua culpa inferatur. Et ideo iratus hoc appetit, ut ille cui nocumentum infert, percipiat, et doleat, et quod cognoscat propter iniuriam illatam sibi hoc provenire. Sed odiens de hoc nihil curat, quia appetit malum alterius inquantum huiusmodi. Non est autem verum quod id de quo quis tristatur, sit peius, *iniustitia enim et imprudentia, cum sint mala,* quia tamen sunt voluntaria, *non contristant eos quibus insunt,* ut dicit philosophus, in II Rhetoric.

AD TERTIUM dicendum quod id quod ex pluribus causis causatur, tunc est stabilius, quando causae accipiuntur unius rationis, sed una causa potest praevalere multis aliis. Odium autem provenit ex permanentiori causa quam ira. Nam ira provenit ex aliqua commotione animi propter laesionem illatam, sed odium procedit ex aliqua dispositione hominis, secundum quam reputat sibi contrarium et nocivum id quod odit. Et ideo sicut passio citius transit quam dispositio vel habitus, ita ira citius transit quam odium; quamvis etiam odium sit passio ex tali dispositione proveniens. Et propter hoc philosophus dicit, in II Rhetoric., quod *odium est magis insanabile quam ira.*

blood." Anger, on the other hand, seeks evil only under the aspect of a just means of vengeance. Consequently when the evil inflicted goes beyond the measure of justice according to the estimate of the angry man, then he has mercy. Wherefore the Philosopher says (Rhet. ii, 4) that "the angry man is appeased if many evils befall, whereas the hater is never appeased." As to the intensity of the desire, anger excludes mercy more than hatred does; because the movement of anger is more impetuous, through the heating of the bile. Hence the passage quoted continues: "Who can bear the violence of one provoked?"

Reply to Objection 2: As stated above, an angry man wishes evil to someone, in so far as this evil is a means of just vengeance. Now vengeance is wrought by the infliction of a punishment: and the nature of punishment consists in being contrary to the will, painful, and inflicted for some fault. Consequently an angry man desires this, that the person whom he is hurting, may feel it and be in pain, and know that this has befallen him on account of the harm he has done the other. The hater, on the other hand, cares not for all this, since he desires another's evil as such. It is not true, however, that an evil is worse through giving pain: because "injustice and imprudence, although evil," yet, being voluntary, "do not grieve those in whom they are," as the Philosopher observes (Rhet. ii, 4).

Reply to Objection 3: That which proceeds from several causes, is more settled when these causes are of one kind: but it may be that one cause prevails over many others. Now hatred ensues from a more lasting cause than anger does. Because anger arises from an emotion of the soul due to the wrong inflicted; whereas hatred ensues from a disposition in a man, by reason of which he considers that which he hates to be contrary and hurtful to him. Consequently, as passion is more transitory than disposition or habit, so anger is less lasting than hatred; although hatred itself is a passion ensuing from this disposition. Hence the Philosopher says (Rhet. ii, 4) that "hatred is more incurable than anger."

ARTICULUS 7

AD SEPTIMUM sic proceditur. Videtur quod ira non solum sit ad illos ad quos est iustitia. Non enim est iustitia hominis ad res irrationales. Sed tamen homo quandoque irascitur rebus irrationalibus, puta cum scriptor ex ira proiicit pennam, vel eques percutit equum. Ergo ira non solum est ad illos ad quos est iustitia.

PRAETEREA, *non est iustitia hominis ad seipsum, nec ad ea quae sui ipsius sunt,* ut dicitur in V Ethic. Sed homo quandoque sibi ipsi irascitur, sicut poenitens propter peccatum, unde dicitur in Psalmo IV, *irascimini, et nolite peccare.* Ergo ira non solum est ad quos est iustitia.

PRAETEREA, iustitia et iniustitia potest esse alicuius ad totum aliquod genus, vel ad totam aliquam communitatem, puta cum civitas aliquem laesit. Sed ira non est ad aliquod genus, sed solum ad aliquod singularium, ut dicit philosophus, in II Rhetoric. Ergo ira non proprie est ad quos est iustitia et iniustitia.

SED CONTRARIUM accipi potest a philosopho in II Rhetoric.

RESPONDEO dicendum quod, sicut supra dictum est, ira appetit malum, inquantum habet rationem iusti vindicativi. Et ideo ad eosdem est ira, ad quos est iustitia et iniustitia. Nam inferre vindictam ad iustitiam pertinet, laedere autem aliquem pertinet ad iniustitiam. Unde tam ex parte causae, quae est laesio illata ab altero; quam etiam ex parte vindictae, quam appetit iratus; manifestum est quod ad eosdem pertinet ira, ad quos iustitia et iniustitia.

AD PRIMUM ergo dicendum quod, sicut supra dictum est, ira, quamvis sit cum ratione, potest tamen etiam esse in brutis animalibus, quae ratione carent, inquantum naturali instinctu per imaginationem moventur ad aliquid simile operibus rationis. Sic igitur, cum in homine sit et ratio et imaginatio, dupliciter in homine potest motus irae insurgere.

ARTICLE 7
Whether anger is only towards those to whom one has an obligation of justice?

Objection 1: It would seem that anger is not only towards those to whom one has an obligation of justice. For there is no justice between man and irrational beings. And yet sometimes one is angry with irrational beings; thus, out of anger, a writer throws away his pen, or a rider strikes his horse. Therefore anger is not only towards those to whom one has an obligation of justice.

Objection 2: Further, "there is no justice towards oneself . . . nor is there justice towards one's own" (Ethic. v, 6). But sometimes a man is angry with himself; for instance, a penitent, on account of his sin; hence it is written (Ps. 4:5): "Be ye angry and sin not." Therefore anger is not only towards those with whom one has a relation of justice.

Objection 3: Further, justice and injustice can be of one man towards an entire class, or a whole community: for instance, when the state injures an individual. But anger is not towards a class but only towards an individual, as the Philosopher states (Rhet. ii, 4). Therefore properly speaking, anger is not towards those with whom one is in relation of justice or injustice.

The contrary, however, may be gathered from the Philosopher (Rhet. ii, 2,3).

I answer that, As stated above (I-II, q. 46, a. 6), anger desires evil as being a means of just vengeance. Consequently, anger is towards those to whom we are just or unjust: since vengeance is an act of justice, and wrong-doing is an act of injustice. Therefore both on the part of the cause, *viz.* the harm done by another, and on the part of the vengeance sought by the angry man, it is evident that anger concerns those to whom one is just or unjust.

Reply to Objection 1: As stated above (I-II, q. 46, a. 4, ad 2), anger, though it follows an act of reason, can nevertheless be in dumb animals that are devoid of reason, in so far as through their natural instinct they are moved by their imagination to something like rational action. Since then in man there is both reason and imagination, the movement of anger can be aroused in man in two ways.

Uno modo, ex sola imaginatione nuntiante laesionem. Et sic insurgit aliquis motus irae etiam ad res irrationales et inanimatas, secundum similitudinem illius motus qui est in animalibus contra quodlibet nocivum. Alio modo, ex ratione nuntiante laesionem. Et sic, ut philosophus dicit II Rhetoric., *nullo modo potest esse ira ad res insensibiles, neque ad mortuos.* Tum quia non dolent, quod maxime quaerunt irati in eis quibus irascuntur. Tum etiam quia non est ad eos vindicta, cum eorum non sit iniuriam facere.

AD SECUNDUM dicendum quod, sicut philosophus dicit in V Ethic., *quaedam metaphorica iustitia et iniustitia est hominis ad seipsum,* inquantum scilicet ratio regit irascibilem et concupiscibilem. Et secundum hoc etiam homo dicitur de seipso vindictam facere, et per consequens sibi ipsi irasci. Proprie autem et per se, non contingit aliquem sibi ipsi irasci.

AD TERTIUM dicendum quod philosophus, in II Rhetoric., assignat unam differentiam inter odium et iram, quod *odium potest esse ad aliquod genus, sicut habemus odio omne latronum genus, sed ira non est nisi ad aliquod singulare.* Cuius ratio est, quia odium causatur ex hoc quod qualitas alicuius rei apprehenditur ut dissonans nostrae dispositioni, et hoc potest esse vel in universali, vel in particulari. Sed ira causatur ex hoc quod aliquis nos laesit per suum actum. Actus autem omnes sunt singularium. Et ideo ira semper est circa aliquod singulare. Cum autem tota civitas nos laeserit, tota civitas computatur sicut unum singulare.

First, when only his imagination denounces the injury: and, in this way, man is aroused to a movement of anger even against irrational and inanimate beings, which movement is like that which occurs in animals against anything that injures them. Secondly, by the reason denouncing the injury: and thus, according to the Philosopher (Rhet. ii, 3), "it is impossible to be angry with insensible things, or with the dead": both because they feel no pain, which is, above all, what the angry man seeks in those with whom he is angry: and because there is no question of vengeance on them, since they can do us no harm.

Reply to Objection 2: As the Philosopher says (Ethic. v, 11), "metaphorically speaking there is a certain justice and injustice between a man and himself," in so far as the reason rules the irascible and concupiscible parts of the soul. And in this sense a man is said to be avenged on himself, and consequently, to be angry with himself. But properly, and in accordance with the nature of things, a man is never angry with himself.

Reply to Objection 3: The Philosopher (Rhet. ii, 4) assigns as one difference between hatred and anger, that "hatred may be felt towards a class, as we hate the entire class of thieves; whereas anger is directed only towards an individual." The reason is that hatred arises from our considering a quality as disagreeing with our disposition; and this may refer to a thing in general or in particular. Anger, on the other hand, ensues from someone having injured us by his action. Now all actions are the deeds of individuals: and consequently anger is always pointed at an individual. When the whole state hurts us, the whole state is reckoned as one individual.*

ARTICULUS 8

AD OCTAVUM sic proceditur. Videtur quod Damascenus inconvenienter assignet tres species irae, scilicet *fel, maniam* et *furorem.* Nullius enim generis species diversificantur secundum aliquod accidens. Sed ista tria

ARTICLE 8
Whether the species of anger are suitably assigned?

Objection 1: It would seem that Damascene (De Fide Orth. ii, 16) unsuitably assigns three species of anger—"wrath," "ill-will" and "rancor." For no genus derives its specific differences from accidents. But these three

---

* Cf. I-II, q. 29, a. 6.

diversificantur secundum aliquod accidens, *principium enim motus irae fel vocatur; ira autem permanens dicitur mania; furor autem est ira observans tempus in vindictam.* Ergo non sunt diversae species irae.

PRAETEREA, Tullius, in IV de Tusculanis quaest., dicit quod *excandescentia Graece dicitur thymosis; et est ira modo nascens et modo desistens.* Thymosis autem secundum Damascenum, est idem quod furor. Non ergo furor tempus quaerit ad vindictam, sed tempore deficit.

PRAETEREA, Gregorius, XXI Moral., ponit tres gradus irae, scilicet *iram sine voce, et iram cum voce, et iram cum verbo expresso,* secundum illa tria quae dominus ponit Matth. V, *qui irascitur fratri suo,* ubi tangitur *ira sine voce*; et postea subdit, *qui dixerit fratri suo, raca,* ubi tangitur *ira cum voce, sed necdum pleno verbo formata*; et postea dicit, *qui autem dixerit fratri suo, fatue,* ubi expletur *vox perfectione sermonis.* Ergo insufficienter divisit Damascenus iram, nihil ponens ex parte vocis.

SED CONTRA est auctoritas Damasceni et Gregorii Nysseni.

RESPONDEO dicendum quod tres species irae quas Damascenus ponit, et etiam Gregorius Nyssenus, sumuntur secundum ea quae dant irae aliquod augmentum. Quod quidem contingit tripliciter. Uno modo, ex facilitate ipsius motus, et talem iram vocat *fel,* quia cito accenditur. Alio modo, ex parte tristitiae causantis iram, quae diu in memoria manet, et haec pertinet ad *maniam,* quae a *manendo* dicitur. Tertio, ex parte eius quod iratus appetit, scilicet vindictae, et haec pertinet ad *furorem,* qui nunquam quiescit donec puniat. Unde philosophus,

are diversified in respect of an accident: because "the beginning of the movement of anger is called wrath (χόλος / *cholos*), if anger continue it is called ill-will (μῆνις / *menis*); while rancor (κότος / *kotos*) is anger waiting for an opportunity of vengeance." Therefore these are not different species of anger.

Objection 2: Further, Cicero says (De Quaest. Tusc. iv, 9) that "*excandescentia* [irascibility] is what the Greeks call θυμῶσις (*thymosis*), and is a kind of anger that arises and subsides intermittently"; while according to Damascene θυμῶσις is the same as the Greek κότος / *kotos* [rancor]. Therefore κότος does not bide its time for taking vengeance, but in course of time spends itself.

Objection 3: Further, Gregory (Moral. xxi, 4) gives three degrees of anger, namely, "anger without utterance, anger with utterance, and anger with perfection of speech," corresponding to the three degrees mentioned by Our Lord (Mat. 5:22): "Whosoever is angry with his brother" (thus implying "anger without utterance"), and then, "whosoever shall say to his brother, 'Raca'" (implying "anger with utterance yet without full expression"), and lastly, "whosoever shall say 'Thou fool'" (where we have "perfection of speech"). Therefore Damascene's division is imperfect, since it takes no account of utterance.

On the contrary, stands the authority of Damascene (De Fide Orth. ii, 16) and Gregory of Nyssa.*

I answer that, The species of anger given by Damascene and Gregory of Nyssa are taken from those things which give increase to anger. This happens in three ways. First from facility of the movement itself, and he calls this kind of anger χόλος /*cholos* [bile] because it is quickly aroused. Secondly, on the part of the grief that causes anger, and which dwells some time in the memory; this belongs to μῆνις / *menis* [ill-will] which is derived from μένειν / *menein* [to dwell]. Thirdly, on the part of that which the angry man seeks, *viz.* vengeance; and this pertains to κότος / *kotos* [rancor] which never rests until it is avenged.† Hence the Philosopher

---

* Nemesius, De Nat. Hom. xxi.
† Eph. 4:31: "Let all bitterness and anger and indignation . . . be put away from you."

in IV Ethic., quosdam irascentium vocat *acutos,* quia cito irascuntur; quosdam *amaros,* quia diu retinent iram; quosdam *difficiles,* quia nunquam quiescunt nisi puniant.

AD PRIMUM ergo dicendum quod omnia illa per quae ira recipit aliquam perfectionem, non omnino per accidens se habent ad iram. Et ideo nihil prohibet secundum ea species irae assignari.

AD SECUNDUM dicendum quod excandescentia, quam Tullius ponit, magis videtur pertinere ad primam speciem irae, quae perficitur secundum velocitatem irae, quam ad furorem. Nihil autem prohibet ut *thymosis* Graece, quod Latine *furor* dicitur, utrumque importet, et velocitatem ad irascendum et firmitatem propositi ad puniendum.

AD TERTIUM dicendum quod gradus illi irae distinguuntur secundum effectum irae, non autem secundum diversam perfectionem ipsius motus irae.

(Ethic. iv, 5) calls some angry persons ἀκρόχολοι / *akrocholoi* [choleric], because they are easily angered; some he calls πικροί / *pikroi* [bitter], because they retain their anger for a long time; and some he calls χαλεποί / *chalepoi* [ill-tempered], because they never rest until they have retaliated.*

Reply to Objection 1: All those things which give anger some kind of perfection are not altogether accidental to anger; and consequently nothing prevents them from causing a certain specific difference thereof.

Reply to Objection 2: Irascibility, which Cicero mentions, seems to pertain to the first species of anger, which consists in a certain quickness of temper, rather than to rancor [*furor*]. And there is no reason why the Greek θυμῶσις (*thymosis*), which is denoted by the Latin *furor,* should not signify both quickness to anger, and firmness of purpose in being avenged.

Reply to Objection 3: These degrees are distinguished according to various effects of anger; and not according to degrees of perfection in the very movement of anger.

---

* Cf. II-II, q. 158, a. 5

Quaestio XLVII

Deinde considerandum est de causa effectiva irae, et de remediis eius. Et circa hoc quaeruntur quatuor. *Primo*, utrum semper motivum irae sit aliquid factum contra eum qui irascitur. *Secundo*, utrum sola parvipensio vel despectio sit motivum irae. *Tertio*, de causa irae ex parte irascentis. *Quarto*, de causa irae ex parte eius contra quem aliquis irascitur.

Articulus 1

Ad primum sic proceditur. Videtur quod non semper aliquis irascatur propter aliquid contra se factum. Homo enim, peccando, nihil contra Deum facere potest, dicitur enim Iob XXXV, *si multiplicatae fuerint iniquitates tuae, quid facies contra illum?* Dicitur tamen Deus irasci contra homines propter peccata; secundum illud Psalmi CV, *iratus est furore dominus in populum suum.* Ergo non semper aliquis irascitur propter aliquid contra se factum.

Praeterea, ira est appetitus vindictae. Sed aliquis appetit vindictam facere etiam de his quae contra alios fiunt. Ergo non semper motivum irae est aliquid contra nos factum.

Praeterea, sicut philosophus dicit, in II Rhetoric., homines irascuntur praecipue contra eos *qui despiciunt ea circa quae ipsi maxime student, sicut qui student in philosophia, irascuntur contra eos qui philosophiam despiciunt,* et simile est in aliis. Sed despicere philosophiam non est nocere ipsi studenti. Non ergo semper irascimur propter id quod contra nos fit.

Praeterea, ille qui tacet contra contumeliantem, magis ipsum ad iram provocat, ut dicit Chrysostomus. Sed

Question 47
Of the Cause That Provokes Anger, and of the Remedies of Anger[*]

We must now consider the cause that provokes anger, and its remedies. Under this head there are four points of inquiry: 1. Whether the motive of anger is always something done against the one who is angry? 2. Whether slight or contempt is the sole motive of anger? 3. Of the cause of anger on the part of the angry person; 4. Of the cause of anger on the part of the person with whom one is angry.

Article 1
Whether the motive of anger is always something done against the one who is angry?

Objection 1: It would seem that the motive of anger is not always something done against the one who is angry. Because man, by sinning, can do nothing against God; since it is written (Job 35:6): "If thy iniquities be multiplied, what shalt thou do against Him?" And yet God is spoken of as being angry with man on account of sin, according to Ps. 105:40: "The Lord was exceedingly angry with His people." Therefore it is not always on account of something done against him, that a man is angry.

Objection 2: Further, anger is a desire for vengeance. But one may desire vengeance for things done against others. Therefore we are not always angry on account of something done against us.

Objection 3: Further, as the Philosopher says (Rhet. ii, 2) man is angry especially with those "who despise what he takes a great interest in; thus men who study philosophy are angry with those who despise philosophy," and so forth. But contempt of philosophy does not harm the philosopher. Therefore it is not always a harm done to us that makes us angry.

Objection 4: Further, he that holds his tongue when another insults him, provokes him to greater anger, as Chrysostom observes (Hom. xxii, in Ep. ad Rom.). But

---
[*] There is no further mention of these remedies in the text, except in a. 4.

in hoc contra ipsum nihil agit, quod tacet. Ergo non semper ira alicuius provocatur propter aliquid quod contra ipsum fit.

SED CONTRA est quod philosophus dicit, in II Rhetoric., quod *ira fit semper ex his quae ad seipsum. Inimicitia autem et sine his quae ad ipsum, si enim putemus talem esse odimus.*

RESPONDEO dicendum quod, sicut supra dictum est, ira est appetitus nocendi alteri sub ratione iusti vindicativi. Vindicta autem locum non habet nisi ubi praecessit iniuria. Nec iniuria omnis ad vindictam provocat, sed illa sola quae ad eum pertinet qui appetit vindictam, sicut enim unumquodque naturaliter appetit proprium bonum, ita etiam naturaliter repellit proprium malum. Iniuria autem ab aliquo facta non pertinet ad aliquem, nisi aliquid fecerit quod aliquo modo sit contra ipsum. Unde sequitur quod motivum irae alicuius semper sit aliquid contra ipsum factum.

AD PRIMUM ergo dicendum quod ira non dicitur in Deo secundum passionem animi, sed secundum iudicium iustitiae, prout vult vindictam facere de peccato. Peccator enim, peccando, Deo nihil nocere effective potest, tamen ex parte sua dupliciter contra Deum agit. Primo quidem, inquantum eum in suis mandatis contemnit. Secundo, inquantum nocumentum aliquod infert alicui, vel sibi vel alteri, quod ad Deum pertinet, prout ille cui nocumentum infertur, sub Dei providentia et tutela continetur.

AD SECUNDUM dicendum quod irascimur contra illos qui aliis nocent et vindictam appetimus, inquantum illi quibus nocetur, aliquo modo ad nos pertinent, vel per aliquam affinitatem, vel per amicitiam, vel saltem per communionem naturae.

AD TERTIUM dicendum quod id in quo maxime studemus, reputamus esse bonum nostrum. Et ideo, cum illud despicitur, reputamus nos quoque despici, et arbitramur nos laesos.

AD QUARTUM dicendum quod tunc aliquis tacens ad iram provocat iniuriantem, quando videtur ex contemptu tacere, quasi

by holding his tongue he does the other no harm. Therefore a man is not always provoked to anger by something done against him.

On the contrary, The Philosopher says (Rhet. ii, 4) that "anger is always due to something done to oneself: whereas hatred may arise without anything being done to us, for we hate a man simply because we think him such."

I answer that, As stated above (I-II, q. 46, a. 6), anger is the desire to hurt another for the purpose of just vengeance. Now unless some injury has been done, there is no question of vengeance: nor does any injury provoke one to vengeance, but only that which is done to the person who seeks vengeance: for just as everything naturally seeks its own good, so does it naturally repel its own evil. But injury done by anyone does not affect a man unless in some way it be something done against him. Consequently the motive of a man's anger is always something done against him.

Reply to Objection 1: We speak of anger in God, not as of a passion of the soul but as of judgment of justice, inasmuch as He wills to take vengeance on sin. Because the sinner, by sinning, cannot do God any actual harm: but so far as he himself is concerned, he acts against God in two ways. First, in so far as he despises God in His commandments. Secondly, in so far as he harms himself or another; which injury redounds to God, inasmuch as the person injured is an object of God's providence and protection.

Reply to Objection 2: If we are angry with those who harm others, and seek to be avenged on them, it is because those who are injured belong in some way to us: either by some kinship or friendship, or at least because of the nature we have in common.

Reply to Objection 3: When we take a very great interest in a thing, we look upon it as our own good; so that if anyone despise it, it seems as though we ourselves were despised and injured.

Reply to Objection 4: Silence provokes the insulter to anger when he thinks it is due to contempt, as though

parvipendat alterius iram. Ipsa autem parvipensio quidam actus est.

Articulus 2

Ad secundum sic proceditur. Videtur quod non sola parvipensio vel despectio sit motivum irae. Dicit enim Damascenus quod *iniuriam passi, vel aestimantes pati, irascimur.* Sed homo potest iniuriam pati etiam absque despectu vel parvipensione. Ergo non sola parvipensio est irae motivum.

Praeterea, eiusdem est appetere honorem, et contristari de parvipensione. Sed bruta animalia non appetunt honorem. Ergo non contristantur de parvipensione. Et tamen *in eis provocatur ira propter hoc quod vulnerantur,* ut dicit philosophus, in III Ethic. Ergo non sola parvipensio videtur esse motivum irae.

Praeterea, philosophus, in II Rhetoric., ponit multas alias causas irae, puta *oblivionem, et exultationem in infortuniis, denuntiationem malorum, impedimentum consequendae propriae voluntatis.* Non ergo sola parvipensio est provocativum irae.

Sed contra est quod philosophus dicit, in II Rhetoric., quod ira est *appetitus cum tristitia punitionis, propter apparentem parvipensionem non convenienter factam.*

Respondeo dicendum quod omnes causae irae reducuntur ad parvipensionem. Sunt enim tres species parvipensionis, ut dicitur in II Rhetoric., scilicet *despectus, epereasmus,* idest impedimentum voluntatis implendae, et *contumeliatio,* et ad haec tria omnia motiva irae reducuntur. Cuius ratio potest accipi duplex. Prima est, quia ira appetit nocumentum alterius, inquantum habet rationem iusti vindicativi, et ideo intantum quaerit vindictam, inquantum videtur esse iusta. Iusta autem vindicta non fit nisi de eo quod est iniuste factum, et ideo provocativum ad iram semper est aliquid sub ratione iniusti. Unde dicit philosophus, in II Rhetoric., quod *si homines putaverint eos qui laeserunt, esse iuste passos, non irascuntur,*

his anger were slighted: and a slight is an action.

Article 2
Whether the sole motive of anger is slight or contempt?

Objection 1: It would seem that slight or contempt is not the sole motive of anger. For Damascene says (De Fide Orth. ii, 16) that we are angry "when we suffer, or think that we are suffering, an injury." But one may suffer an injury without being despised or slighted. Therefore a slight is not the only motive of anger.

Objection 2: Further, desire for honor and grief for a slight belong to the same subject. But dumb animals do not desire honor. Therefore they are not grieved by being slighted. And yet "they are roused to anger, when wounded," as the Philosopher says (Ethic. iii, 8). Therefore a slight is not the sole motive of anger.

Objection 3: Further, the Philosopher (Rhet. ii, 2) gives many other causes of anger, for instance, "being forgotten by others; that others should rejoice in our misfortunes; that they should make known our evils; being hindered from doing as we like." Therefore being slighted is not the only motive for being angry.

On the contrary, The Philosopher says (Rhet. ii, 2) that anger is "a desire, with sorrow, for vengeance, on account of a seeming slight done unbecomingly."

I answer that, All the causes of anger are reduced to slight. For slight is of three kinds, as stated in Rhet. ii, 2, *viz.* "contempt," "despiteful treatment," i.e., hindering one from doing one's will, and "insolence": and all motives of anger are reduced to these three. Two reasons may be assigned for this. First, because anger seeks another's hurt as being a means of just vengeance: wherefore it seeks vengeance in so far as it seems just. Now just vengeance is taken only for that which is done unjustly; hence that which provokes anger is always something considered in the light of an injustice. Wherefore the Philosopher says (Rhet. ii, 3) that "men are not angry—if they think they have wronged some one and are suffering justly on that account;

non enim fit ira ad iustum. Contingit autem tripliciter nocumentum alicui inferri, scilicet ex ignorantia, ex passione, et ex electione. Tunc autem aliquis maxime iniustum facit, quando ex electione vel industria, vel ex certa malitia nocumentum infert, ut dicitur in V Ethic. Et ideo maxime irascimur contra illos quos putamus ex industria nobis nocuisse. Si enim putemus aliquos vel per ignorantiam, vel ex passione nobis intulisse iniuriam, vel non irascimur contra eos, vel multo minus, agere enim aliquid ex ignorantia vel ex passione, diminuit rationem iniuriae, et est quodammodo provocativum misericordiae et veniae. Illi autem qui ex industria nocumentum inferunt, ex contemptu peccare videntur, et ideo contra eos maxime irascimur. Unde philosophus dicit, in II Rhetoric., quod *his qui propter iram aliquid fecerunt, aut non irascimur, aut minus irascimur, non enim propter parvipensionem videntur egisse.* Secunda ratio est, quia parvipensio excellentiae hominis opponitur, quae enim homines putant nullo digna esse, parvipendunt, ut dicitur in II Rhetoric. Ex omnibus autem bonis nostris aliquam excellentiam quaerimus. Et ideo quodcumque nocumentum nobis inferatur, inquantum excellentiae derogat, videtur ad parvipensionem pertinere.

AD PRIMUM ergo dicendum quod ex quacumque alia causa aliquis iniuriam patiatur quam ex contemptu, illa causa minuit rationem iniuriae. Sed solus contemptus, vel parvipensio, rationem irae auget. Et ideo est per se causa irascendi.

AD SECUNDUM dicendum quod, licet animal brutum non appetat honorem sub ratione honoris, appetit tamen naturaliter quandam excellentiam, et irascitur contra ea quae illi excellentiae derogant.

AD TERTIUM dicendum quod omnes illae causae ad quandam parvipensionem reducuntur. Oblivio enim parvipensionis est evidens signum, ea enim quae magna aestimamus, magis memoriae infigimus. Similiter ex quadam parvipensione est quod aliquis non vereatur contristare aliquem, denuntiando sibi aliqua tristia. Qui etiam in infortuniis alicuius hilaritatis signa ostendit, videtur

because there is no anger at what is just." Now injury is done to another in three ways: namely, through ignorance, through passion, and through choice. Then, most of all, a man does an injustice, when he does an injury from choice, on purpose, or from deliberate malice, as stated in Ethic. v, 8. Wherefore we are most of all angry with those who, in our opinion, have hurt us on purpose. For if we think that some one has done us an injury through ignorance or through passion, either we are not angry with them at all, or very much less: since to do anything through ignorance or through passion takes away from the notion of injury, and to a certain extent calls for mercy and forgiveness. Those, on the other hand, who do an injury on purpose, seem to sin from contempt; wherefore we are angry with them most of all. Hence the Philosopher says (Rhet. ii, 3) that "we are either not angry at all, or not very angry with those who have acted through anger, because they do not seem to have acted slightingly." The second reason is because a slight is opposed to a man's excellence: because "men think little of things that are not worth much ado" (Rhet. ii, 2). Now we seek for some kind of excellence from all our goods. Consequently whatever injury is inflicted on us, in so far as it is derogatory to our excellence, seems to savor of a slight.

Reply to Objection 1: Any other cause, besides contempt, through which a man suffers an injury, takes away from the notion of injury: contempt or slight alone adds to the motive of anger, and consequently is of itself the cause of anger.

Reply to Objection 2: Although a dumb animal does not seek honor as such, yet it naturally seeks a certain superiority, and is angry with anything derogatory thereto.

Reply to Objection 3: Each of those causes amounts to some kind of slight. Thus forgetfulness is a clear sign of slight esteem, for the more we think of a thing the more is it fixed in our memory. Again if a man does not hesitate by his remarks to give pain to another, this seems to show that he thinks little of him: and those too who show signs of hilarity when another is in misfortune, seem

parum curare de bono vel malo eius. Similiter etiam qui impedit aliquem a sui propositi assecutione, non propter aliquam utilitatem sibi inde provenientem, non videtur multum curare de amicitia eius. Et ideo omnia talia, inquantum sunt signa contemptus, sunt provocativa irae.

to care little about his good or evil. Again he that hinders another from carrying out his will, without deriving thereby any profit to himself, seems not to care much for his friendship. Consequently all those things, in so far as they are signs of contempt, provoke anger.

Articulus 3

AD TERTIUM sic proceditur. Videtur quod excellentia alicuius non sit causa quod facilius irascatur. Dicit enim philosophus, in II Rhetoric., quod *maxime aliqui irascuntur cum tristantur, ut infirmi, et egentes, et qui non habent id quod concupiscunt.* Sed omnia ista ad defectum pertinere videntur. Ergo magis facit pronum ad iram defectus quam excellentia.

PRAETEREA, philosophus dicit ibidem quod *tunc aliqui maxime irascuntur, quando in eis despicitur id de quo potest esse suspicio quod vel non insit eis, vel quod insit eis debiliter, sed cum putant se multum excellere in illis in quibus despiciuntur, non curant.* Sed praedicta suspicio ex defectu provenit. Ergo defectus est magis causa quod aliquis irascatur, quam excellentia.

PRAETEREA, ea quae ad excellentiam pertinent, maxime faciunt homines iucundos et bonae spei esse. Sed philosophus dicit, in II Rhetoric., quod *in ludo, in risu, in festo, in prosperitate, in consummatione operum, in delectatione non turpi, et in spe optima, homines non irascuntur.* Ergo excellentia non est causa irae.

SED CONTRA est quod philosophus, in eodem libro, dicit quod homines propter excellentiam indignantur.

RESPONDEO dicendum quod causa irae in eo qui irascitur, dupliciter accipi potest. Uno modo, secundum habitudinem ad motivum irae. Et sic excellentia est causa ut aliquis de facili irascatur. Est enim motivum irae iniusta parvipensio, ut dictum est. Constat autem quod quanto aliquis est excellentior, iniustius parvipenditur in hoc in quo excellit. Et ideo illi qui sunt in aliqua excellentia,

Article 3
Whether a man's excellence is the cause of his being angry?

Objection 1: It would seem that a man's excellence is not the cause of his being more easily angry. For the Philosopher says (Rhet. ii, 2) that "some are angry especially when they are grieved, for instance, the sick, the poor, and those who are disappointed." But these things seem to pertain to defect. Therefore defect rather than excellence makes one prone to anger.

Objection 2: Further, the Philosopher says (Rhet. ii, 2) that "some are very much inclined to be angry when they are despised for some failing or weakness of the existence of which there are grounds for suspicion; but if they think they excel in those points, they do not trouble." But a suspicion of this kind is due to some defect. Therefore defect rather than excellence is a cause of a man being angry.

Objection 3: Further, whatever savors of excellence makes a man agreeable and hopeful. But the Philosopher says (Rhet. ii, 3) that "men are not angry when they play, make jokes, or take part in a feast, nor when they are prosperous or successful, nor in moderate pleasures and well-founded hope." Therefore excellence is not a cause of anger.

On the contrary, The Philosopher says (Rhet. ii, 9) that excellence makes men prone to anger.

I answer that, The cause of anger, in the man who is angry, may be taken in two ways. First in respect of the motive of anger: and thus excellence is the cause of a man being easily angered. Because the motive of anger is an unjust slight, as stated above (I-II, q. 47, a. 2). Now it is evident that the more excellent a man is, the more unjust is a slight offered him in the matter in which he excels. Consequently those who excel in any matter,

maxime irascuntur, si parvipendantur, puta si dives parvipenditur in pecunia, et rhetor in loquendo, et sic de aliis. Alio modo potest considerari causa irae in eo qui irascitur, ex parte dispositionis quae in eo relinquitur ex tali motivo. Manifestum est autem quod nihil movet ad iram, nisi nocumentum quod contristat. Ea autem quae ad defectum pertinent, maxime sunt contristantia, quia homines defectibus subiacentes facilius laeduntur. Et ista est causa quare homines qui sunt infirmi, vel in aliis defectibus, facilius irascuntur, quia facilius contristantur.

Et per hoc patet responsio ad primum.

AD SECUNDUM dicendum quod ille qui despicitur in eo in quo manifeste multum excellit, non reputat se aliquam iacturam pati, et ideo non contristatur, et ex hac parte minus irascitur. Sed ex alia parte, inquantum indignius despicitur, habet maiorem rationem irascendi. Nisi forte reputet se non invideri vel subsannari propter despectum; sed propter ignorantiam, vel propter aliud huiusmodi.

AD TERTIUM dicendum quod omnia illa impediunt iram, inquantum impediunt tristitiam. Sed ex alia parte, nata sunt provocare iram, secundum quod faciunt hominem inconvenientius despici.

are most of all angry, if they be slighted in that matter; for instance, a wealthy man in his riches, or an orator in his eloquence, and so forth. Secondly, the cause of anger, in the man who is angry, may be considered on the part of the disposition produced in him by the motive aforesaid. Now it is evident that nothing moves a man to anger except a hurt that grieves him: while whatever savors of defect is above all a cause of grief; since men who suffer from some defect are more easily hurt. And this is why men who are weak, or subject to some other defect, are more easily angered, since they are more easily grieved.

This suffices for the Reply to the First Objection.

Reply to Objection 2: If a man be despised in a matter in which he evidently excels greatly, he does not consider himself the loser thereby, and therefore is not grieved: and in this respect he is less angered. But in another respect, in so far as he is more undeservedly despised, he has more reason for being angry: unless perhaps he thinks that he is envied or insulted not through contempt but through ignorance, or some other like cause.

Reply to Objection 3: All these things hinder anger in so far as they hinder sorrow. But in another respect they are naturally apt to provoke anger, because they make it more unseemly to insult anyone.

ARTICULUS 4

AD QUARTUM sic proceditur. Videtur quod defectus alicuius non sit causa ut contra ipsum facilius irascamur. Dicit enim philosophus, in II Rhetoric., quod *his qui confitentur et poenitent et humiliantur, non irascimur, sed magis ad eos mitescimus. Unde et canes non mordent eos qui resident.* Sed haec pertinent ad parvitatem et defectum. Ergo parvitas alicuius est causa ut ei minus irascamur.

PRAETEREA, nullus est maior defectus quam mortis. Sed ad mortuos desinit ira. Ergo defectus alicuius non est causa provocativa irae contra ipsum.

ARTICLE 4
Whether a person's defect is a reason for being more easily angry with him?

Objection 1: It would seem that a person's defect is not a reason for being more easily angry with him. For the Philosopher says (Rhet. ii, 3) that "we are not angry with those who confess and repent and humble themselves; on the contrary, we are gentle with them. Wherefore dogs bite not those who sit down." But these things savor of littleness and defect. Therefore littleness of a person is a reason for being less angry with him.

Objection 2: Further, there is no greater defect than death. But anger ceases at the sight of death. Therefore defect of a person does not provoke anger against him.

Praeterea, nullus aestimat aliquem parvum ex hoc quod est sibi amicus. Sed ad amicos, si nos offenderint, vel si non iuverint, magis offendimur, unde dicitur in Psalmo LIV, *si inimicus meus maledixisset mihi, sustinuissem utique.* Ergo defectus alicuius non est causa ut contra ipsum facilius irascamur.

Sed contra est quod philosophus dicit, in II Rhetoric., quod *dives irascitur contra pauperem, si eum despiciat; et principans contra subiectum.*

Respondeo dicendum quod, sicut supra dictum est, indigna despectio est maxime provocativa irae. Defectus igitur vel parvitas eius contra quem irascimur, facit ad augmentum irae, inquantum auget indignam despectionem. Sicut enim quanto aliquis est maior, tanto indignius despicitur; ita quanto aliquis est minor, tanto indignius despicit. Et ideo nobiles irascuntur si despiciantur a rusticis, vel sapientes ab insipientibus, vel domini a servis. Si vero parvitas vel defectus diminuat despectionem indignam, talis parvitas non auget, sed diminuit iram. Et hoc modo illi qui poenitent de iniuriis factis, et confitentur se male fecisse, et humiliantur et veniam petunt, mitigant iram, secundum illud Prov. XV, *responsio mollis frangit iram,* inquantum scilicet tales videntur non despicere, sed magis magnipendere eos quibus se humiliant.

Et per hoc patet responsio ad primum.

Ad secundum dicendum quod duplex est causa quare ad mortuos cessat ira. Una, quia non possunt dolere et sentire, quod maxime quaerunt irati in his quibus irascuntur. Alio modo, quia iam videntur ad ultimum malorum pervenisse. Unde etiam ad quoscumque graviter laesos cessat ira, inquantum eorum malum excedit mensuram iustae retributionis.

Objection 3: Further, no one thinks little of a man through his being friendly towards him. But we are more angry with friends, if they offend us or refuse to help us; hence it is written (Ps. 54:13): "If my enemy had reviled me I would verily have borne with it." Therefore a person's defect is not a reason for being more easily angry with him.

On the contrary, The Philosopher says (Rhet. ii, 2) that "the rich man is angry with the poor man, if the latter despise him; and in like manner the prince is angry with his subject."

I answer that, As stated above (I-II, q. 47, a. 2; a. 3) unmerited contempt more than anything else is a provocative of anger. Consequently deficiency or littleness in the person with whom we are angry, tends to increase our anger, in so far as it adds to the unmeritedness of being despised. For just as the higher a man's position is, the more undeservedly he is despised; so the lower it is, the less reason he has for despising. Thus a nobleman is angry if he be insulted by a peasant; a wise man, if by a fool; a master, if by a servant. If, however, the littleness or deficiency lessens the unmerited contempt, then it does not increase but lessens anger. In this way those who repent of their ill-deeds, and confess that they have done wrong, who humble themselves and ask pardon, mitigate anger, according to Prov. 15:1: "A mild answer breaketh wrath": because, to wit, they seem not to despise, but rather to think much of those before whom they humble themselves.

This suffices for the Reply to the First Objection.

Reply to Objection 2: There are two reasons why anger ceases at the sight of death. One is because the dead are incapable of sorrow and sensation; and this is chiefly what the angry seek in those with whom they are angered. Another reason is because the dead seem to have attained to the limit of evils. Hence anger ceases in regard to all who are grievously hurt, in so far as this hurt surpasses the measure of just retaliation.

AD TERTIUM dicendum quod etiam despectio quae est ab amicis, videtur esse magis indigna. Et ideo ex simili causa magis irascimur contra eos, si despiciant, vel nocendo vel non iuvando, sicut et contra minores.

Reply to Objection 3: To be despised by one's friends seems also a greater indignity. Consequently if they despise us by hurting or by failing to help, we are angry with them for the same reason for which we are angry with those who are beneath us.

Quaestio XLVIII

Deinde considerandum est de effectibus irae. Et circa hoc quaeruntur quatuor. *Primo,* utrum ira causet delectationem. *Secundo,* utrum maxime causet fervorem in corde. *Tertio,* utrum maxime impediat rationis usum. *Quarto,* utrum causet taciturnitatem.

Question 48
Of the Effects of Anger

We must now consider the effects of anger: under which head there are four points of inquiry: 1. Whether anger causes pleasure? 2. Whether above all it causes heat in the heart? 3. Whether above all it hinders the use of reason? 4. Whether it causes taciturnity?

Articulus 1

AD PRIMUM sic proceditur. Videtur quod ira non causet delectationem. Tristitia enim delectationem excludit. Sed ira est semper cum tristitia, quia, ut dicitur in VII Ethic., *omnis qui facit aliquid per iram, facit tristatus.* Ergo ira non causat delectationem.

PRAETEREA, philosophus dicit, in IV Ethic., quod *punitio quietat impetum irae, delectationem pro tristitia faciens,* ex quo potest accipi quod delectatio irato provenit ex punitione, punitio autem excludit iram. Ergo, adveniente delectatione, ira tollitur. Non est ergo effectus delectationi coniunctus.

PRAETEREA, nullus effectus impedit causam suam, cum sit suae causae conformis. Sed delectationes impediunt iram, ut dicitur in II Rhetoric. Ergo delectatio non est effectus irae.

SED CONTRA est quod philosophus, in eodem libro, inducit proverbium, quod ira *multo dulcior melle distillante in pectoribus virorum crescit.*

RESPONDEO dicendum quod, sicut philosophus dicit in VII Ethic., delectationes, maxime sensibiles et corporales, sunt medicinae quaedam contra tristitiam, et ideo quanto per delectationem contra maiorem tristitiam vel anxietatem remedium praestatur, tanto delectatio magis percipitur; sicut patet quod

Article 1
Whether anger causes pleasure?

Objection 1: It would seem that anger does not cause pleasure. Because sorrow excludes pleasure. But anger is never without sorrow, since, as stated in Ethic. vii, 6, "everyone that acts from anger, acts with pain." Therefore anger does not cause pleasure.

Objection 2: Further, the Philosopher says (Ethic. iv, 5) that "vengeance makes anger to cease, because it substitutes pleasure for pain": whence we may gather that the angry man derives pleasure from vengeance, and that vengeance quells his anger. Therefore on the advent of pleasure, anger departs: and consequently anger is not an effect united with pleasure.

Objection 3: Further, no effect hinders its cause, since it is conformed to its cause. But pleasure hinders anger as stated in Rhet. ii, 3. Therefore pleasure is not an effect of anger.

On the contrary, The Philosopher (Ethic. iv, 5) quotes the saying that anger is "Sweet to the soul as honey to the taste" (Iliad, xviii, 109).*

I answer that, As the Philosopher says (Ethic. vii, 14), pleasures, chiefly sensible and bodily pleasures, are remedies against sorrow: and therefore the greater the sorrow or anxiety, the more sensible are we to the pleasure which heals it, as is evident in the

---

* Trl. Pope

quando aliquis sitit, delectabilior fit ei potus. Manifestum est autem ex praedictis quod motus irae insurgit ex aliqua illata iniuria contristante; cui quidem tristitiae remedium adhibetur per vindictam. Et ideo ad praesentiam vindictae delectatio sequitur, et tanto maior, quanto maior fuit tristitia. Si igitur vindicta fuerit praesens realiter, fit perfecta delectatio, quae totaliter excludit tristitiam, et per hoc quietat motum irae. Sed antequam vindicta sit praesens realiter, fit irascenti praesens dupliciter. Uno modo, per spem, quia nullus irascitur nisi sperans vindictam, ut supra dictum est. Alio modo, secundum continuam cogitationem. Unicuique enim concupiscenti est delectabile immorari in cogitatione eorum quae concupiscit, propter quod etiam imaginationes somniorum sunt delectabiles. Et ideo, cum iratus multum in animo suo cogitet de vindicta, ex hoc delectatur. Tamen delectatio non est perfecta, quae tollat tristitiam, et per consequens iram.

AD PRIMUM ergo dicendum quod non de eodem iratus tristatur et gaudet, sed tristatur de illata iniuria, delectatur autem de vindicta cogitata et sperata. Unde tristitia se habet ad iram sicut principium, sed delectatio sicut effectus vel terminus.

AD SECUNDUM dicendum quod obiectio illa procedit de delectatione quae causatur ex reali praesentia vindictae, quae totaliter tollit iram.

AD TERTIUM dicendum quod delectationes praecedentes impediunt ne sequatur tristitia; et per consequens impediunt iram. Sed delectatio de vindicta consequitur ipsam.

case of thirst which increases the pleasure of drink. Now it is clear from what has been said (I-II, q. 47, a. 1; a. 3), that the movement of anger arises from a wrong done that causes sorrow, for which sorrow vengeance is sought as a remedy. Consequently as soon as vengeance is present, pleasure ensues, and so much the greater according as the sorrow was greater. Therefore if vengeance be really present, perfect pleasure ensues, entirely excluding sorrow, so that the movement of anger ceases. But before vengeance is really present, it becomes present to the angry man in two ways: in one way, by hope; because none is angry except he hopes for vengeance, as stated above (I-II, q. 46, a. 1); in another way, by thinking of it continually, for to everyone that desires a thing it is pleasant to dwell on the thought of what he desires; wherefore the imaginings of dreams are pleasant. Accordingly an angry man takes pleasure in thinking much about vengeance. This pleasure, however, is not perfect, so as to banish sorrow and consequently anger.

Reply to Objection 1: The angry man does not grieve and rejoice at the same thing; he grieves for the wrong done, while he takes pleasure in the thought and hope of vengeance. Consequently sorrow is to anger as its beginning; while pleasure is the effect or terminus of anger.

Reply to Objection 2: This argument holds in regard to pleasure caused by the real presence of vengeance, which banishes anger altogether.

Reply to Objection 3: Pleasure that precedes hinders sorrow from ensuing, and consequently is a hindrance to anger. But pleasure felt in taking vengeance follows from anger.

ARTICULUS 2

AD SECUNDUM sic proceditur. Videtur quod fervor non sit maxime effectus irae. Fervor enim, sicut supra dictum est, pertinet ad amorem. Sed amor, sicut supra dictum est, principium est et causa omnium passionum. Cum ergo causa sit potior

ARTICLE 2
Whether anger above all causes fervor in the heart?

Objection 1: It would seem that heat is not above all the effect of anger. For fervor, as stated above (I-II, q. 28, a. 5; q. 37, a. 2), belongs to love. But love, as above stated, is the beginning and cause of all the passions. Since then the cause is more powerful than

its effect, it seems that anger is not the chief cause of fervor.

Objection 2: Further, those things which, of themselves, arouse fervor, increase as time goes on; thus love grows stronger the longer it lasts. But in course of time anger grows weaker; for the Philosopher says (Rhet. ii, 3) that "time puts an end to anger." Therefore fervor is not the proper effect of anger.

Objection 3: Further, fervor added to fervor produces greater fervor. But "the addition of a greater anger banishes already existing anger," as the Philosopher says (Rhet. ii, 3). Therefore anger does not cause fervor.

On the contrary, Damascene says (De Fide Orth. ii, 16) that "anger is fervor of the blood around the heart, resulting from an exhalation of the bile."

I answer that, As stated above (I-II, q. 44, a. 1), the bodily transmutation that occurs in the passions of the soul is proportionate to the movement of the appetite. Now it is evident that every appetite, even the natural appetite, tends with greater force to repel that which is contrary to it, if it be present: hence we see that hot water freezes harder, as though the cold acted with greater force on the hot object. Since then the appetitive movement of anger is caused by some injury inflicted, as by a contrary that is present; it follows that the appetite tends with great force to repel the injury by the desire of vengeance; and hence ensues great vehemence and impetuosity in the movement of anger. And because the movement of anger is not one of recoil, which corresponds to the action of cold, but one of prosecution, which corresponds to the action of heat, the result is that the movement of anger produces fervor of the blood and vital spirits around the heart, which is the instrument of the soul's passions. And hence it is that, on account of the heart being so disturbed by anger, those chiefly who are angry betray signs thereof in their outer members. For, as Gregory says (Moral. v, 30) "the heart that is inflamed with the stings of its own anger beats quick, the body trembles, the tongue stammers, the countenance takes fire, the eyes grow fierce, they that are well known are not recognized. With the mouth indeed he shapes a sound,

effectu, videtur quod ira non faciat maxime fervorem.

PRAETEREA, illa quae de se excitant fervorem, per temporis assiduitatem magis augentur, sicut amor diuturnitate convalescit. Sed ira per tractum temporis debilitatur, dicit enim philosophus, in II Rhetoric., quod *tempus quietat iram.* Ergo ira non proprie causat fervorem.

PRAETEREA, fervor additus fervori, augmentat fervorem. Sed *maior ira superveniens facit iram mitescere,* ut philosophus dicit, in II Rhetoric. Ergo ira non causat fervorem.

SED CONTRA est quod Damascenus dicit, quod *ira est fervor eius qui circa cor est sanguinis, ex evaporatione fellis fiens.*

RESPONDEO dicendum quod, sicut dictum est, corporalis transmutatio quae est in passionibus animae, proportionatur motui appetitus. Manifestum est autem quod quilibet appetitus, etiam naturalis, fortius tendit in id quod est sibi contrarium, si fuerit praesens, unde videmus quod aqua calefacta magis congelatur, quasi frigido vehementius in calidum agente. Motus autem appetitivus irae causatur ex aliqua iniuria illata, sicut ex quodam contrario iniacente. Et ideo appetitus potissime tendit ad repellendum iniuriam per appetitum vindictae, et ex hoc sequitur magna vehementia et impetuositas in motu irae. Et quia motus irae non est per modum retractionis, cui proportionatur frigus; sed magis per modum insecutionis, cui proportionatur calor; consequenter fit motus irae causativus cuiusdam fervoris sanguinis et spirituum circa cor, quod est instrumentum passionum animae. Et exinde est quod, propter magnam perturbationem cordis quae est in ira, maxime apparent in iratis indicia quaedam in exterioribus membris. Ut enim Gregorius dicit, in V Moral., *irae suae stimulis accensum cor palpitat, corpus tremit, lingua se praepedit, facies ignescit, exasperantur oculi, et nequaquam recognoscuntur noti, ore quidem clamorem format,*

sed sensus quid loquatur, ignorat.

AD PRIMUM ergo dicendum quod *amor ipse non ita sentitur, nisi cum eum prodit indigentia,* ut Augustinus dicit, in X de Trin. Et ideo quando homo patitur detrimentum amatae excellentiae propter iniuriam illatam, magis sentitur amor; et ideo ferventius cor mutatur ad removendum impedimentum rei amatae; ut sic fervor ipse amoris per iram crescat, et magis sentiatur. Et tamen fervor qui consequitur calorem, alia ratione pertinet ad amorem, et ad iram. Nam fervor amoris est cum quadam dulcedine et lenitate, est enim in bonum amatum. Et ideo assimilatur calori aeris et sanguinis, propter quod, sanguinei sunt magis amativi; et dicitur quod *cogit amare iecur,* in quo fit quaedam generatio sanguinis. Fervor autem irae est cum amaritudine, ad consumendum, quia tendit ad punitionem contrarii. Unde assimilatur calori ignis et cholerae, et propter hoc Damascenus dicit quod *procedit ex evaporatione fellis, et fellea nominatur.*

AD SECUNDUM dicendum quod omne illud cuius causa per tempus diminuitur, necesse est quod tempore debilitetur. Manifestum est autem quod memoria tempore diminuitur, quae enim antiqua sunt, a memoria de facili excidunt. Ira autem causatur ex memoria iniuriae illatae. Et ideo causa irae per tempus paulatim diminuitur, quousque totaliter tollatur. Maior etiam videtur iniuria quando primo sentitur; et paulatim diminuitur eius aestimatio, secundum quod magis receditur a praesenti sensu iniuriae. Et similiter etiam est de amore, si amoris causa remaneat in sola memoria, unde philosophus dicit, in VIII Ethic., quod *si diuturna fiat amici absentia, videtur amicitiae oblivionem facere.* Sed in praesentia amici, semper per tempus multiplicatur causa amicitiae, et ideo amicitia crescit. Et similiter esset de ira, si continue multiplicaretur causa ipsius.

but the understanding knows not what it says."

Reply to Objection 1: "Love itself is not felt so keenly as in the absence of the beloved," as Augustine observes (De Trin. x, 12). Consequently when a man suffers from a hurt done to the excellence that he loves, he feels his love thereof the more: the result being that his heart is moved with greater heat to remove the hindrance to the object of his love; so that anger increases the fervor of love and makes it to be felt more. Nevertheless, the fervor arising from heat differs according as it is to be referred to love or to anger. Because the fervor of love has a certain sweetness and gentleness; for it tends to the good that one loves: whence it is likened to the warmth of the air and of the blood. For this reason sanguine temperaments are more inclined to love; and hence the saying that "love springs from the liver," because of the blood being formed there. On the other hand, the fervor of anger has a certain bitterness with a tendency to destroy, for it seeks to be avenged on the contrary evil: whence it is likened to the heat of fire and of the bile, and for this reason Damascene says (De Fide Orth. ii, 16) that it "results from an exhalation of the bile whence it takes its name χολή (*chole*)."

Reply to Objection 2: Time, of necessity, weakens all those things, the causes of which are impaired by time. Now it is evident that memory is weakened by time; for things which happened long ago easily slip from our memory. But anger is caused by the memory of a wrong done. Consequently the cause of anger is impaired little by little as time goes on, until at length it vanishes altogether. Moreover a wrong seems greater when it is first felt; and our estimate thereof is gradually lessened the further the sense of present wrong recedes into the past. The same applies to love, so long as the cause of love is in the memory alone; wherefore the Philosopher says (Ethic. viii, 5) that "if a friend's absence lasts long, it seems to make men forget their friendship." But in the presence of a friend, the cause of friendship is continually being multiplied by time: wherefore the friendship increases: and the same would apply to anger, were its cause continually multiplied.

Tamen hoc ipsum quod ira cito consumitur, attestatur vehementi fervori ipsius. Sicut enim ignis magnus cito extinguitur, consumpta materia; ita etiam ira, propter suam vehementiam, cito deficit.

AD TERTIUM dicendum quod omnis virtus divisa in plures partes, diminuitur. Et ideo quando aliquis iratus alicui, irascitur postmodum alteri, ex hoc ipso diminuitur ira ad primum. Et praecipue si ad secundum fuerit maior ira, nam iniuria quae excitavit iram ad primum, videbitur, comparatione secundae iniuriae, quae aestimatur maior, esse parva vel nulla.

Nevertheless the very fact that anger soon spends itself proves the strength of its fervor: for as a great fire is soon spent having burnt up all the fuel; so too anger, by reason of its vehemence, soon dies away.

Reply to Objection 3: Every power that is divided in itself is weakened. Consequently if a man being already angry with one, becomes angry with another, by this very fact his anger with the former is weakened. Especially is this so if his anger in the second case be greater: because the wrong done which aroused his former anger, will, in comparison with the second wrong, which is reckoned greater, seem to be of little or no account.

ARTICULUS 3

AD TERTIUM sic proceditur. Videtur quod ira non impediat rationem. Illud enim quod est cum ratione, non videtur esse rationis impedimentum. Sed *ira est cum ratione,* ut dicitur in VII Ethic. Ergo ira non impedit rationem.

PRAETEREA, quanto magis impeditur ratio, tanto diminuitur manifestatio. Sed philosophus dicit in VII Ethic., quod *iracundus non est insidiator, sed manifestus.* Ergo ira non videtur impedire usum rationis, sicut concupiscentia; quae est insidiosa, ut ibidem dicitur.

PRAETEREA, iudicium rationis evidentius fit ex adiunctione contrarii, quia contraria iuxta se posita magis elucescunt. Sed ex hoc etiam crescit ira, dicit enim philosophus, in II Rhetoric., quod *magis homines irascuntur, si contraria praeexistunt, sicut honorati si dehonorentur;* et sic de aliis. Ergo ex eodem et ira crescit, et iudicium rationis adiuvatur. Non ergo ira impedit iudicium rationis.

SED CONTRA est quod Gregorius dicit, in V Moral., quod ira *intelligentiae lucem subtrahit, cum mentem permovendo confundit.*

RESPONDEO dicendum quod mens vel ratio quamvis non utatur organo corporali in

ARTICLE 3
Whether anger above all hinders the use of reason?

Objection 1: It would seem that anger does not hinder the use of reason. Because that which presupposes an act of reason, does not seem to hinder the use of reason. But "anger listens to reason," as stated in Ethic. vii, 6. Therefore anger does not hinder reason.

Objection 2: Further, the more the reason is hindered, the less does a man show his thoughts. But the Philosopher says (Ethic. vii, 6) that "an angry man is not cunning but is open." Therefore anger does not seem to hinder the use of reason, as desire does; for desire is cunning, as he also states (Ethic. vii, 6.).

Objection 3: Further, the judgment of reason becomes more evident by juxtaposition of the contrary: because contraries stand out more clearly when placed beside one another. But this also increases anger: for the Philosopher says (Rhet. ii, 2) that "men are more angry if they receive unwonted treatment; for instance, honorable men, if they be dishonored": and so forth. Therefore the same cause increases anger, and facilitates the judgment of reason. Therefore anger does not hinder the judgment of reason.

On the contrary, Gregory says (Moral. v, 30) that anger "withdraws the light of understanding, while by agitating it troubles the mind."

I answer that, Although the mind or reason makes no use of a bodily organ in

suo proprio actu; tamen, quia indiget ad sui actum quibusdam viribus sensitivis, quorum actus impediuntur corpore perturbato; necesse est quod perturbationes corporales etiam iudicium rationis impediant, sicut patet in ebrietate et somno. Dictum est autem quod ira maxime facit perturbationem corporalem circa cor, ita ut etiam usque ad exteriora membra derivetur. Unde ira, inter ceteras passiones, manifestius impedit iudicium rationis; secundum illud Psalmi XXX, *conturbatus est in ira oculus meus.*

AD PRIMUM ergo dicendum quod a ratione est principium irae, quantum ad motum appetitivum, qui est formalis in ira. Sed perfectum iudicium rationis passio irae praeoccupat quasi non perfecte rationem audiens, propter commotionem caloris velociter impellentis, quae est materialis in ira. Et quantum ad hoc, impedit iudicium rationis.

AD SECUNDUM dicendum quod iracundus dicitur esse manifestus, non quia manifestum sit sibi quid facere debeat, sed quia manifeste operatur, non quaerens aliquam occultationem. Quod partim contingit propter impedimentum rationis, quae non potest discernere quid sit occultandum et quid manifestandum, nec etiam excogitare occultandi vias. Partim vero est ex ampliatione cordis, quae pertinet ad magnanimitatem, quam facit ira, unde et de magnanimo philosophus dicit, in IV Ethic., quod *est manifestus oditor et amator et manifeste dicit et operatur.* Concupiscentia autem dicitur esse latens et insidiosa, quia, ut plurimum, delectabilia quae concupiscuntur, habent turpitudinem quandam et mollitiem, in quibus homo vult latere. In his autem quae sunt virilitatis et excellentiae, cuiusmodi sunt vindictae, quaerit homo manifestus esse.

AD TERTIUM dicendum quod, sicut dictum est, motus irae a ratione incipit, et ideo secundum idem appositio contrarii ad contrarium adiuvat iudicium rationis, et auget iram. Cum enim aliquis habet

its proper act, yet, since it needs certain sensitive powers for the execution of its act, the acts of which powers are hindered when the body is disturbed, it follows of necessity that any disturbance in the body hinders even the judgment of reason; as is clear in the case of drunkenness or sleep. Now it has been stated (I-II, q. 48, a. 2) that anger, above all, causes a bodily disturbance in the region of the heart, so much as to effect even the outward members. Consequently, of all the passions, anger is the most manifest obstacle to the judgment of reason, according to Ps. 30:10: "My eye is troubled with wrath."

Reply to Objection 1: The beginning of anger is in the reason, as regards the appetitive movement, which is the formal element of anger. But the passion of anger forestalls the perfect judgment of reason, as though it listened but imperfectly to reason, on account of the commotion of the heat urging to instant action, which commotion is the material element of anger. In this respect it hinders the judgment of reason.

Reply to Objection 2: An angry man is said to be open, not because it is clear to him what he ought to do, but because he acts openly, without thought of hiding himself. This is due partly to the reason being hindered, so as not to discern what should be hidden and what done openly, nor to devise the means of hiding; and partly to the dilatation of the heart which pertains to magnanimity which is an effect of anger: wherefore the Philosopher says of the magnanimous man (Ethic. iv, 3) that "he is open in his hatreds and his friendships . . . and speaks and acts openly." Desire, on the other hand, is said to lie low and to be cunning, because, in many cases, the pleasurable things that are desired, savor of shame and voluptuousness, wherein man wishes not to be seen. But in those things that savor of manliness and excellence, such as matters of vengeance, man seeks to be in the open.

Reply to Objection 3: As stated above (ad 1), the movement of anger begins in the reason, wherefore the juxtaposition of one contrary with another facilitates the judgment of reason, on the same grounds as it increases anger. For when a man who is possessed of

honorem vel divitias, et postea incurrit alicuius detrimentum, illud detrimentum apparet maius, tum propter vicinitatem contrarii; tum quia erat inopinatum. Et ideo causat maiorem tristitiam, sicut etiam magna bona ex inopinato venientia, causant maiorem delectationem. Et secundum augmentum tristitiae praecedentis, consequenter augetur et ira.

honor or wealth, suffers a loss therein, the loss seems all the greater, both on account of the contrast, and because it was unforeseen. Consequently it causes greater grief: just as a great good, through being received unexpectedly, causes greater delight. And in proportion to the increase of the grief that precedes, anger is increased also.

Articulus 4

Ad quartum sic proceditur. Videtur quod ira non causet taciturnitatem. Taciturnitas enim locutioni opponitur. Sed per crementum irae usque ad locutionem pervenitur, ut patet per gradus irae quos dominus assignat, Matth. V, dicens, *qui irascitur fratri suo;* et, *qui dixerit fratri suo, raca;* et, *qui dixerit fratri suo, fatue.* Ergo ira non causat taciturnitatem.

Praeterea, ex hoc quod custodia rationis deficit, contingit quod homo prorumpat ad verba inordinata, unde dicitur Prov. XXV, *sicut urbs patens et absque murorum ambitu, ita vir qui non potest cohibere in loquendo spiritum suum.* Sed ira maxime impedit iudicium rationis, ut dictum est. Ergo facit maxime profluere in verba inordinata. Non ergo causat taciturnitatem.

Praeterea, Matth. XII dicitur, *ex abundantia cordis os loquitur.* Sed per iram cor maxime perturbatur, ut dictum est. Ergo maxime causat locutionem. Non ergo causat taciturnitatem.

Sed contra est quod Gregorius dicit, in V Moral., quod *ira per silentium clausa, intra mentem vehementius aestuat.*

Respondeo dicendum quod ira, sicut iam dictum est, et cum ratione est, et impedit rationem. Et ex utraque parte, potest taciturnitatem causare. Ex parte quidem rationis, quando iudicium rationis intantum viget quod, etsi non cohibeat affectum ab inordinato appetitu

Article 4
Whether anger above all causes taciturnity?

Objection 1: It would seem that anger does not cause taciturnity. Because taciturnity is opposed to speech. But increase in anger conduces to speech; as is evident from the degrees of anger laid down by Our Lord (Mat. 5:22): where He says: "Whosoever is angry with his brother"; and " . . . whosoever shall say to his brother, 'Raca'"; and " . . . whosoever shall say to his brother, 'Thou fool.'" Therefore anger does not cause taciturnity.

Objection 2: Further, through failing to obey reason, man sometimes breaks out into unbecoming words: hence it is written (Prov. 25:28): "As a city that lieth open and is not compassed with walls, so is a man that cannot refrain his own spirit in speaking." But anger, above all, hinders the judgment of reason, as stated above (I-II, q. 48, a. 3). Consequently above all it makes one break out into unbecoming words. Therefore it does not cause taciturnity.

Objection 3: Further, it is written (Mat. 12:34): "Out of the abundance of the heart the mouth speaketh." But anger, above all, causes a disturbance in the heart, as stated above (I-II, q. 48, a. 2). Therefore above all it conduces to speech. Therefore it does not cause taciturnity.

On the contrary, Gregory says (Moral. v, 30) that "when anger does not vent itself outwardly by the lips, inwardly it burns the more fiercely."

I answer that, As stated above (I-II, q. 48, a. 3; q. 46, a. 4), anger both follows an act of reason, and hinders the reason: and in both respects it may cause taciturnity. On the part of the reason, when the judgment of reason prevails so far, that although it does not curb the appetite in its inordinate desire

vindictae, cohibet tamen linguam ab inordinata locutione. Unde Gregorius, in V Moral., dicit, *aliquando ira perturbato animo, quasi ex iudicio, silentium indicit*. Ex parte vero impedimenti rationis, quia, sicut dictum est, perturbatio irae usque ad exteriora membra perducitur; et maxime ad illa membra in quibus expressius relucet vestigium cordis, sicut in oculis et in facie et in lingua; unde, sicut dictum est, *lingua se praepedit, facies ignescit, exasperantur oculi*. Potest ergo esse tanta perturbatio irae, quod omnino impediatur lingua ab usu loquendi. Et tunc sequitur taciturnitas.

AD PRIMUM ergo dicendum quod augmentum irae quandoque est usque ad impediendum rationem a cohibitione linguae. Quandoque autem ultra procedit, usque ad impediendum motum linguae, et aliorum membrorum exteriorum.

Et per hoc etiam patet solutio ad secundum.

AD TERTIUM dicendum quod perturbatio cordis quandoque potest superabundare usque ad hoc, quod per inordinatum motum cordis impediatur motus exteriorum membrorum. Et tunc causatur taciturnitas, et immobilitas exteriorum membrorum, et quandoque etiam mors. Si autem non fuerit tanta perturbatio, tunc *ex abundantia perturbationis cordis*, sequitur oris locutio.

for vengeance, yet it curbs the tongue from unbridled speech. Wherefore Gregory says (Moral. v, 30): "Sometimes when the mind is disturbed, anger, as if in judgment, commands silence." On the part of the impediment to reason because, as stated above (I-II, q. 48, a. 2), the disturbance of anger reaches to the outward members, and chiefly to those members which reflect more distinctly the emotions of the heart, such as the eyes, face and tongue; wherefore, as observed above (I-II, q. 48, a. 2), "the tongue stammers, the countenance takes fire, the eyes grow fierce." Consequently anger may cause such a disturbance, that the tongue is altogether deprived of speech; and taciturnity is the result.

Reply to Objection 1: Anger sometimes goes so far as to hinder the reason from curbing the tongue: but sometimes it goes yet farther, so as to paralyze the tongue and other outward members.

And this suffices for the Reply to the Second Objection.

Reply to Objection 3: The disturbance of the heart may sometimes superabound to the extend that the movements of the outward members are hindered by the inordinate movement of the heart. Thence ensue taciturnity and immobility of the outward members; and sometimes even death. If, however, the disturbance be not so great, then "out of the abundance of the heart" thus disturbed, the mouth proceeds to speak.

TREATISE ON HABITS

Quaestio XLIX

Post actus et passiones, considerandum est de principiis humanorum actuum. Et primo, de principiis intrinsecis; secundo, de principiis extrinsecis. Principium autem intrinsecum est potentia et habitus; sed quia de potentiis in prima parte dictum est, nunc restat de habitibus considerandum. Et primo quidem, in generali; secundo vero, de virtutibus et vitiis, et aliis huiusmodi habitibus, qui sunt humanorum actuum principia. Circa ipsos autem habitus in generali, quatuor consideranda sunt, primo quidem, de ipsa substantia habituum, secundo, de subiecto eorum; tertio, de causa generationis, augmenti et corruptionis ipsorum; quarto, de distinctione ipsorum. Circa primum quaeruntur quatuor. *Primo,* utrum habitus sit qualitas. *Secundo,* utrum sit determinata species qualitatis. *Tertio,* utrum habitus importet ordinem ad actum. *Quarto,* de necessitate habitus.

Question 49
Of Habits in General, as to Their Substance

After treating of human acts and passions, we now pass on to the consideration of the principles of human acts, and firstly of intrinsic principles, secondly of extrinsic principles. The intrinsic principle is power and habit; but as we have treated of powers in the I, q. 77, seqq., it remains for us to consider them in general: in the second place we shall consider virtues and vices and other like habits, which are the principles of human acts. Concerning habits in general there are four points to consider: First, the substance of habits; second, their subject; third, the cause of their generation, increase, and corruption; fourth, how they are distinguished from one another. Under the first head, there are four points of inquiry: 1. Whether habit is a quality? 2. Whether it is a distinct species of quality? 3. Whether habit implies an order to an act? 4. Of the necessity of habit.

Articulus 1

Ad primum sic proceditur. Videtur quod habitus non sit qualitas. Dicit enim Augustinus, in libro octoginta trium quaest., quod *hoc nomen habitus dictum est ab hoc verbo quod est habere.* Sed *habere* non solum pertinet ad qualitatem, sed ad alia genera, dicimur enim *habere* etiam quantitatem, et pecuniam, et alia huiusmodi. Ergo habitus non est qualitas.

Praeterea, habitus ponitur unum praedicamentum; ut patet in libro praedicamentorum. Sed unum praedicamentum non continetur sub alio. Ergo habitus non est qualitas.

Praeterea, *omnis habitus est dispositio,* ut dicitur in praedicamentis. Sed dispositio est *ordo habentis partes,* ut dicitur in V Metaphys. Hoc autem pertinet ad praedicamentum situs. Ergo habitus non est qualitas.

Article 1
Whether habit is a quality?

Objection 1: It would seem that habit is not a quality. For Augustine says (QQ. lxxxiii, qu. 73): "this word 'habit' is derived from the verb 'to have.'" But "to have" belongs not only to quality, but also to the other categories: for we speak of ourselves as "having" quantity and money and other like things. Therefore habit is not a quality.

Objection 2: Further, habit is reckoned as one of the predicaments; as may be clearly seen in the Book of the Predicaments (Categor. vi). But one predicament is not contained under another. Therefore habit is not a quality.

Objection 3: Further, "every habit is a disposition," as is stated in the Book of the Predicaments (Categor. vi). Now disposition is "the order of that which has parts," as stated in Metaph. v, text. 24. But this belongs to the predicament Position. Therefore habit is not a quality.

SED CONTRA est quod philosophus dicit, in praedicamentis, quod *habitus est qualitas de difficili mobilis.*

RESPONDEO dicendum quod hoc nomen *habitus* ab *habendo* est sumptum. A quo quidem nomen *habitus* dupliciter derivatur, uno quidem modo, secundum quod homo, vel quaecumque alia res, dicitur aliquid *habere;* alio modo, secundum quod aliqua **res aliquo modo se habet in seipsa vel ad aliquid aliud.** Circa primum autem, considerandum est quod *habere,* secundum quod dicitur respectu cuiuscumque quod *habetur,* commune est ad diversa genera. Unde philosophus inter post praedicamenta *habere* ponit, quae scilicet diversa rerum genera consequuntur; sicut sunt opposita, et prius et posterius, et alia huiusmodi. Sed inter ea quae habentur, talis videtur esse distinctio, quod quaedam sunt in quibus nihil est medium inter habens et id quod habetur, sicut inter subiectum et qualitatem vel quantitatem nihil est medium. Quaedam vero sunt in quibus est aliquid medium inter utrumque, sed sola relatio, sicut dicitur aliquis habere socium vel amicum. Quaedam vero sunt inter quae est aliquid medium, non quidem actio vel passio, sed aliquid per modum actionis vel passionis, prout scilicet unum est ornans vel tegens, et aliud ornatum aut tectum, unde philosophus dicit, in V Metaphys., quod *habitus dicitur tanquam actio quaedam habentis et habiti, sicut est in illis quae circa nos habemus.* Et ideo in his constituitur unum speciale genus rerum, quod dicitur praedicamentum *habitus,* de quo dicit philosophus, in V Metaphys., quod *inter habentem indumentum, et indumentum quod habetur, est habitus medius.* Si autem sumatur *habere* prout res aliqua dicitur quodam modo se habere in seipsa vel ad aliud; cum iste modus se habendi sit secundum aliquam qualitatem, hoc modo habitus quaedam qualitas est, de quo philosophus, in V Metaphys., dicit quod *habitus dicitur dispositio secundum quam bene vel male disponitur dispositum, et aut secundum*

On the contrary, The Philosopher says in the Book of Predicaments (Categor. vi) that "habit is a quality which is difficult to change."

I answer that, This word *habitus* [habit] is derived from *habere* [to have]. Now habit is taken from this word in two ways; in one way, inasmuch as man, or any other thing, is said to "have" something; in another way, inasmuch as a particular thing has a relation [*se habet*] **either in regard to itself, or in regard to something else.** Concerning the first, we must observe that "to have," as said in regard to anything that is "had," is common to the various predicaments. And so the Philosopher puts "to have" among the "post-predicaments," so called because they result from the various predicaments; as, for instance, opposition, priority, posterity, and such like. Now among things which are had, there seems to be this distinction, that there are some in which there is no medium between the "haver" and that which is had: as, for instance, there is no medium between the subject and quality or quantity. Then there are some in which there is a medium, but only a relation: as, for instance, a man is said to have a companion or a friend. And, further, there are some in which there is a medium, not indeed an action or passion, but something after the manner of action or passion: thus, for instance, something adorns or covers, and something else is adorned or covered: wherefore the Philosopher says (Metaph. v, text. 25) that "a habit is said to be, as it were, an action or a passion of the haver and that which is had"; as is the case in those things which we have about ourselves. And therefore these constitute a special genus of things, which are comprised under the predicament of "habit": of which the Philosopher says (Metaph. v, text. 25) that "there is a habit between clothing and the man who is clothed." But if "to have" be taken according as a thing has a relation in regard to itself or to something else; in that case habit is a quality; since this mode of having is in respect of some quality: and of this the Philosopher says (Metaph. v, text. 25) that "habit is a disposition whereby that which is disposed is disposed well or ill, and this, either in regard

se aut ad aliud, ut sanitas habitus quidam est. Et sic loquimur nunc de habitu. Unde dicendum est quod habitus est qualitas.

AD PRIMUM ergo dicendum quod obiectio illa procedit de *habere* communiter sumpto, sic enim est commune ad multa genera, ut dictum est.

AD SECUNDUM dicendum quod ratio illa procedit de habitu secundum quod intelligitur aliquid medium inter habens et id quod habetur, sic enim est quoddam praedicamentum, ut dictum est.

AD TERTIUM dicendum quod dispositio quidem semper importat ordinem alicuius habentis partes, sed hoc contingit tripliciter, ut statim ibidem philosophus subdit, scilicet *aut secundum locum, aut secundum potentiam, aut secundum speciem. In quo,* ut Simplicius dicit in commento praedicamentorum, *comprehendit omnes dispositiones. Corporales quidem, in eo quod dicit secundum locum,* et hoc pertinet ad praedicamentum *situs,* qui est ordo partium in loco. *Quod autem dicit secundum potentiam, includit illas dispositiones quae sunt in praeparatione et idoneitate nondum perfecte,* sicut scientia et virtus inchoata. *Quod autem dicit secundum speciem, includit perfectas dispositiones, quae dicuntur habitus,* sicut scientia et virtus complete.

to itself or in regard to another: thus health is a habit." And in this sense we speak of habit now. Wherefore we must say that habit is a quality.

Reply to Objection 1: This argument takes "to have" in the general sense: for thus it is common to many predicaments, as we have said.

Reply to Objection 2: This argument takes habit in the sense in which we understand it to be a medium between the haver, and that which is had: and in this sense it is a predicament, as we have said.

Reply to Objection 3: Disposition does always, indeed, imply an order of that which has parts: but this happens in three ways, as the Philosopher goes on at once to says (Metaph. v, text. 25): namely, "either as to place, or as to power, or as to species." "In saying this," as Simplicius observes in his Commentary on the Predicaments, "he includes all dispositions: bodily dispositions, when he says 'as to place,'" and this belongs to the predicament "Position," which is the order of parts in a place: "when he says 'as to power,' he includes all those dispositions which are in course of formation and not yet arrived at perfect usefulness," such as inchoate science and virtue: "and when he says, 'as to species,' he includes perfect dispositions, which are called habits," such as perfected science and virtue.

ARTICULUS 2

AD SECUNDUM sic proceditur. Videtur quod habitus non sit determinata species qualitatis. Quia, ut dictum est, habitus, secundum quod est qualitas, dicitur *dispositio secundum quam bene aut male disponitur dispositum.* Sed hoc contingit secundum quamlibet qualitatem, nam et secundum figuram contingit aliquid bene vel male esse dispositum, et similiter secundum calorem et frigus, et secundum omnia huiusmodi. Ergo habitus non est determinata species qualitatis.

PRAETEREA, philosophus, in praedicamentis, caliditatem et frigiditatem dicit esse dispositiones vel habitus, sicut aegritudinem et sanitatem. Sed calor

ARTICLE 2
Whether habit is a distinct species of quality?

Objection 1: It would seem that habit is not a distinct species of quality. Because, as we have said (I-II, q. 49, a. 1), habit, in so far as it is a quality, is "a disposition whereby that which is disposed is disposed well or ill." But this happens in regard to any quality: for a thing happens to be well or ill disposed in regard also to shape, and in like manner, in regard to heat and cold, and in regard to all such things. Therefore habit is not a distinct species of quality.

Objection 2: Further, the Philosopher says in the Book of the Predicaments (Categor. vi), that heat and cold are dispositions or habits, just as sickness and health. But heat

et frigus sunt in tertia specie qualitatis. Ergo habitus vel dispositio non distinguuntur ab aliis speciebus qualitatis.

Praeterea, *difficile mobile* non est differentia pertinens ad genus qualitatis, sed magis pertinet ad motum vel passionem. Nullum autem genus determinatur ad speciem per differentiam alterius generis; sed *oportet differentias per se advenire generi,* ut philosophus dicit, in VII Metaphys. Ergo, cum habitus dicatur esse *qualitas difficile mobilis,* videtur quod non sit determinata species qualitatis.

Sed contra est quod philosophus dicit, in praedicamentis, quod *una species qualitatis est habitus et dispositio.*

Respondeo dicendum quod philosophus, in praedicamentis, ponit inter quatuor species qualitatis primam, dispositionem et habitum. Quarum quidem specierum differentias sic assignat Simplicius, in commento praedicamentorum, dicens quod *qualitatum quaedam sunt naturales, quae secundum naturam insunt, et semper, quaedam autem sunt adventitiae, quae ab extrinseco efficiuntur, et possunt amitti. Et haec quidem,* quae sunt adventitiae, *sunt habitus et dispositiones, secundum facile et difficile amissibile differentes. Naturalium autem qualitatum quaedam sunt secundum id quod aliquid est in potentia, et sic est secunda species qualitatis. Quaedam vero secundum quod aliquid est in actu, et hoc vel in profundum, vel secundum superficiem. Si in profundum quidem, sic est tertia species qualitatis, secundum vero superficiem, est quarta species qualitatis, sicut figura et forma, quae est figura animati.* Sed ista distinctio specierum qualitatis inconveniens videtur. Sunt enim multae figurae et qualitates passibiles non naturales, sed adventitiae, et multae dispositiones non adventitiae, sed naturales, sicut sanitas et pulchritudo et huiusmodi. Et praeterea hoc non convenit ordini specierum, semper enim quod naturalius est, prius est. Et ideo aliter accipienda est distinctio dispositionum et habituum ab aliis qualitatibus. Proprie enim qualitas importat quendam

and cold are in the third species of quality. Therefore habit or disposition is not distinct from the other species of quality.

Objection 3: Further, "difficult to change" is not a difference belonging to the predicament of quality, but rather to movement or passion. Now, no genus should be contracted to a species by a difference of another genus; but "differences should be proper to a genus," as the Philosopher says in Metaph. vii, text. 42. Therefore, since habit is "a quality difficult to change," it seems not to be a distinct species of quality.

On the contrary, The Philosopher says in the Book of the Predicaments (Categor. vi) that "one species of quality is habit and disposition."

I answer that, The Philosopher in the Book of Predicaments (Categor. vi) reckons disposition and habit as the first species of quality. Now Simplicius, in his Commentary on the Predicaments, explains the difference of these species as follows. He says "that some qualities are natural, and are in their subject in virtue of its nature, and are always there: but some are adventitious, being caused from without, and these can be lost. Now the latter," i.e., those which are adventitious, "are habits and dispositions, differing in the point of being easily or difficultly lost. As to natural qualities, some regard a thing in the point of its being in a state of potentiality; and thus we have the second species of quality: while others regard a thing which is in act; and this either deeply rooted therein or only on its surface. If deeply rooted, we have the third species of quality: if on the surface, we have the fourth species of quality, as shape, and form which is the shape of an animated being." But this distinction of the species of quality seems unsuitable. For there are many shapes, and passion-like qualities, which are not natural but adventitious: and there are also many dispositions which are not adventitious but natural, as health, beauty, and the like. Moreover, it does not suit the order of the species, since that which is the more natural is always first. Therefore we must explain otherwise the distinction of dispositions and habits from other qualities. For quality, properly speaking, implies a certain

modum substantiae. Modus autem est, ut dicit Augustinus, super Gen. ad litteram, *quem mensura praefigit,* unde importat quandam determinationem secundum aliquam mensuram. Et ideo sicut id secundum quod determinatur potentia materiae secundum esse substantiale dicitur qualitas quae est differentia substantiae; ita id secundum quod determinatur potentia subiecti secundum esse accidentale, dicitur qualitas accidentalis, quae est etiam quaedam differentia, ut patet per philosophum in V Metaphys. Modus autem sive determinatio subiecti secundum esse accidentale, potest accipi vel in ordine ad ipsam naturam subiecti; vel secundum actionem et passionem quae consequuntur principia naturae, quae sunt materia et forma; vel secundum quantitatem. Si autem accipiatur modus vel determinatio subiecti secundum quantitatem, sic est quarta species qualitatis. Et quia quantitas, secundum sui rationem, est sine motu, et sine ratione boni et mali; ideo ad quartam speciem qualitatis non pertinet quod aliquid sit bene vel male, cito vel tarde transiens. Modus autem sive determinatio subiecti secundum actionem et passionem, attenditur in secunda et tertia specie qualitatis. Et ideo in utraque consideratur quod aliquid facile vel difficile fiat, vel quod sit cito transiens aut diuturnum. Non autem consideratur in his aliquid pertinens ad rationem boni vel mali, quia motus et passiones non habent rationem finis, bonum autem et malum dicitur per respectum ad finem. Sed modus et determinatio subiecti in ordine ad naturam rei, pertinet ad primam speciem qualitatis, quae est habitus et dispositio, dicit enim philosophus, in VII Physic., loquens de habitibus animae et corporis, quod sunt *dispositiones quaedam perfecti ad optimum; dico autem perfecti, quod est dispositum secundum naturam.* Et quia ipsa forma et natura rei est finis et cuius causa fit aliquid, ut dicitur in II Physic., ideo in prima specie consideratur

mode of substance. Now mode, as Augustine says (Gen. ad lit. iv, 3), "is that which a measure determines": wherefore it implies a certain determination according to a certain measure. Therefore, just as that in accordance with which the material potentiality [*potentia materiae*] is determined to its substantial being, is called quality, which is a difference affecting the substance, so that, in accordance with the potentiality of the subject is determined to its accidental being, is called an accidental quality, which is also a kind of difference, as is clear from the Philosopher (Metaph. v, text. 19). Now the mode of determination of the subject to accidental being may be taken in regard to the very nature of the subject, or in regard to action, and passion resulting from its natural principles, which are matter and form; or again in regard to quantity. If we take the mode or determination of the subject in regard to quantity, we shall then have the fourth species of quality. And because quantity, considered in itself, is devoid of movement, and does not imply the notion of good or evil, so it does not concern the fourth species of quality whether a thing be well or ill disposed, nor quickly or slowly transitory. But the mode of determination of the subject, in regard to action or passion, is considered in the second and third species of quality. And therefore in both, we take into account whether a thing be done with ease or difficulty; whether it be transitory or lasting. But in them, we do not consider anything pertaining to the notion of good or evil: because movements and passions have not the aspect of an end, whereas good and evil are said in respect of an end. On the other hand, the mode or determination of the subject, in regard to the nature of the thing, belongs to the first species of quality, which is habit and disposition: for the Philosopher says (Phys. vii, text. 17), when speaking of habits of the soul and of the body, that they are "dispositions of the perfect to the best; and by perfect I mean that which is disposed in accordance with its nature." And since the form itself and the nature of a thing is the end and the cause why a thing is made (Phys. ii, text. 25), therefore in the first species we consider

et bonum et malum; et etiam facile et difficile mobile, secundum quod aliqua natura est finis generationis et motus. Unde in V Metaphys. philosophus definit habitum, quod est *dispositio secundum quam aliquis disponitur bene vel male.* Et in II Ethic. dicit quod *habitus sunt secundum quos ad passiones nos habemus bene vel male.* Quando enim est modus conveniens naturae rei, tunc habet rationem boni, quando autem non convenit, tunc habet rationem mali. Et quia natura est id quod primum consideratur in re, ideo habitus ponitur prima species qualitatis.

AD PRIMUM ergo dicendum quod dispositio ordinem quendam importat, ut dictum est. Unde non dicitur aliquis disponi per qualitatem, nisi in ordine ad aliquid. Et si addatur bene vel male, quod pertinet ad rationem habitus, oportet quod attendatur ordo ad naturam, quae est finis. Unde secundum figuram, vel secundum calorem vel frigus, non dicitur aliquis disponi bene vel male, nisi secundum ordinem ad naturam rei, secundum quod est conveniens vel non conveniens. Unde et ipsae figurae et passibiles qualitates, secundum quod considerantur ut convenientes vel non convenientes naturae rei, pertinent ad habitus vel dispositiones, nam figura, prout convenit naturae rei, et color, pertinent ad pulchritudinem; calor autem et frigus, secundum quod conveniunt naturae rei, pertinent ad sanitatem. Et hoc modo caliditas et frigiditas ponuntur a philosopho in prima specie qualitatis.

Unde patet solutio ad secundum. Licet a quibusdam aliter solvatur, ut Simplicius dicit, in commento praedicamentorum.

AD TERTIUM dicendum quod ista differentia, *difficile mobile,* non diversificat habitum ab aliis speciebus qualitatis, sed a dispositione. Dispositio autem dupliciter accipitur, uno modo, secundum quod est genus habitus, nam in V Metaphys. dispositio ponitur in definitione habitus; alio modo, secundum quod est aliquid contra habitum divisum. Et potest intelligi dispositio proprie dicta condividi contra habitum, dupliciter. Uno modo, sicut perfectum et

both evil and good, and also changeableness, whether easy or difficult; inasmuch as a certain nature is the end of generation and movement. And so the Philosopher (Metaph. v, text. 25) defines habit, a "disposition whereby someone is disposed, well or ill"; and in Ethic. ii, 4, he says that by "habits we are directed well or ill in reference to the passions." For when the mode is suitable to the thing's nature, it has the aspect of good: and when it is unsuitable, it has the aspect of evil. And since nature is the first object of consideration in anything, for this reason habit is reckoned as the first species of quality.

Reply to Objection 1: Disposition implies a certain order, as stated above (I-II, q. 49, a. 1, ad 3). Wherefore a man is not said to be disposed by some quality except in relation to something else. And if we add "well or ill," which belongs to the essential notion of habit, we must consider the quality's relation to the nature, which is the end. So in regard to shape, or heat, or cold, a man is not said to be well or ill disposed, except by reason of a relation to the nature of a thing, with regard to its suitability or unsuitability. Consequently even shapes and passion-like qualities, in so far as they are considered to be suitable or unsuitable to the nature of a thing, belong to habits or dispositions: for shape and color, according to their suitability to the nature of thing, concern beauty; while heat and cold, according to their suitability to the nature of a thing, concern health. And in this way heat and cold are put, by the Philosopher, in the first species of quality.

Wherefore it is clear how to answer the second objection: though some give another solution, as Simplicius says in his Commentary on the Predicaments.

Reply to Objection 3: This difference, "difficult to change," does not distinguish habit from the other species of quality, but from disposition. Now disposition may be taken in two ways; in one way, as the genus of habit, for disposition is included in the definition of habit (Metaph. v, text. 25): in another way, according as it is divided against habit. Again, disposition, properly so called, can be divided against habit in two ways: first, as perfect and

imperfectum in eadem specie, ut scilicet dispositio dicatur, retinens nomen commune, quando imperfecte inest, ita quod de facili amittitur; habitus autem, quando perfecte inest, ut non de facili amittatur. Et sic dispositio fit habitus, sicut puer fit vir. Alio modo possunt distingui sicut diversae species unius generis subalterni, ut dicantur dispositiones illae qualitates primae speciei, quibus convenit secundum propriam rationem ut de facili amittantur, quia habent causas transmutabiles, ut aegritudo et sanitas; habitus vero dicuntur illae qualitates quae secundum suam rationem habent quod non de facili transmutentur, quia habent causas immobiles, sicut scientiae et virtutes. Et secundum hoc dispositio non fit habitus. Et hoc videtur magis consonum intentioni Aristotelis. Unde ad huius distinctionis probationem inducit communem loquendi consuetudinem, secundum quam qualitates quae secundum rationem suam sunt facile mobiles, si ex aliquo accidenti difficile mobiles reddantur, habitus dicuntur, et e converso est de qualitatibus quae secundum suam rationem sunt difficile mobiles; nam si aliquis imperfecte habeat scientiam, ut de facili possit ipsam amittere, magis dicitur disponi ad scientiam quam scientiam habere. Ex quo patet quod nomen *habitus* diuturnitatem quandam importat; non autem nomen *dispositionis*. Nec impeditur quin secundum hoc facile et difficile mobile sint specificae differentiae, propter hoc quod ista pertinent ad passionem et motum, et non ad genus qualitatis. Nam istae differentiae, quamvis per accidens videantur se habere ad qualitatem, designant tamen proprias et per se differentias qualitatum. Sicut etiam in genere substantiae frequenter accipiuntur differentiae accidentales loco substantialium, inquantum per eas designantur principia essentialia.

imperfect within the same species; and thus we call it a disposition, retaining the name of the genus, when it is had imperfectly, so as to be easily lost: whereas we call it a habit, when it is had perfectly, so as not to be lost easily. And thus a disposition becomes a habit, just as a boy becomes a man. Secondly, they may be distinguished as diverse species of the one subaltern genus: so that we call dispositions, those qualities of the first species, which by reason of their very nature are easily lost, because they have changeable causes; e.g., sickness and health: whereas we call habits those qualities which, by reason of their very nature, are not easily changed, in that they have unchangeable causes, e.g., sciences and virtues. And in this sense, disposition does not become habit. The latter explanation seems more in keeping with the intention of Aristotle: for in order to confirm this distinction he adduces the common mode of speaking, according to which, when a quality is, by reason of its nature, easily changeable, and, through some accident, becomes difficultly changeable, then it is called a habit: while the contrary happens in regard to qualities, by reason of their nature, difficultly changeable: for supposing a man to have a science imperfectly, so as to be liable to lose it easily, we say that he is disposed to that science, rather than that he has the science. From this it is clear that the word "habit" implies a certain lastingness: while the word "disposition" does not. Nor does it matter that thus to be easy and difficult to change are specific differences [of a quality], although they belong to passion and movement, and not the genus of quality. For these differences, though apparently accidental to quality, nevertheless designate differences which are proper and essential to quality. In the same way, in the genus of substance we often take accidental instead of substantial differences, in so far as by the former, essential principles are designated.

Articulus 3

AD TERTIUM sic proceditur. Videtur quod habitus non importet ordinem ad actum. Unumquodque enim agit secundum quod est actu. Sed philosophus dicit, in III de anima, quod *cum aliquis fit sciens secundum habitum, est etiam tunc in potentia, aliter tamen quam ante addiscere.* Ergo habitus non importat habitudinem principii ad actum.

PRAETEREA, illud quod ponitur in definitione alicuius, per se convenit illi. Sed esse principium actionis ponitur in definitione potentiae; ut patet in V Metaphys. Ergo esse principium actus per se convenit potentiae. Quod autem est per se, est primum in unoquoque genere. Si ergo etiam habitus sit principium actus, sequitur quod sit posterior quam potentia. Et sic non erit prima species qualitatis habitus vel dispositio.

PRAETEREA, sanitas quandoque est habitus, et similiter macies et pulchritudo. Sed ista non dicuntur per ordinem ad actum. Non ergo est de ratione habitus quod sit principium actus.

SED CONTRA est quod Augustinus dicit, in libro de bono coniugali, quod *habitus est quo aliquid agitur cum opus est.* Et Commentator dicit, in III de anima, quod *habitus est quo quis agit cum voluerit.*

RESPONDEO dicendum quod habere ordinem ad actum potest competere habitui et secundum rationem habitus; et secundum rationem subiecti in quo est habitus. Secundum quidem rationem habitus, convenit omni habitui aliquo modo habere ordinem ad actum. Est enim de ratione habitus ut importet habitudinem quandam in ordine ad naturam rei, secundum quod convenit vel non convenit. Sed natura rei, quae est finis generationis, ulterius etiam ordinatur ad alium finem, qui vel est operatio, vel aliquod operatum, ad quod quis pervenit per operationem. Unde habitus non solum importat ordinem ad ipsam naturam rei, sed etiam consequenter ad operationem, inquantum est finis naturae, vel perducens ad finem. Unde et in V Metaphys. dicitur in definitione habitus, quod est dispositio secundum quam bene vel male disponitur

Article 3
Whether habit implies order to an act?

Objection 1: It would seem that habit does not imply order to an act. For everything acts according as it is in act. But the Philosopher says (De Anima iii, text 8), that "when one is become knowing by habit, one is still in a state of potentiality, but otherwise than before learning." Therefore habit does not imply the relation of a principle to an act.

Objection 2: Further, that which is put in the definition of a thing, belongs to it essentially. But to be a principle of action, is put in the definition of power, as we read in Metaph. v, text. 17. Therefore to be the principle of an act belongs to power essentially. Now that which is essential is first in every genus. If therefore, habit also is a principle of act, it follows that it is posterior to power. And so habit and disposition will not be the first species of quality.

Objection 3: Further, health is sometimes a habit, and so are leanness and beauty. But these do not indicate relation to an act. Therefore it is not essential to habit to be a principle of act.

On the contrary, Augustine says (De Bono Conjug. xxi) that "habit is that whereby something is done when necessary." And the Commentator says (De Anima iii) that "habit is that whereby we act when we will."

I answer that, To have relation to an act may belong to habit, both in regard to the nature of habit, and in regard to the subject in which the habit is. In regard to the nature of habit, it belongs to every habit to have relation to an act. For it is essential to habit to imply some relation to a thing's nature, in so far as it is suitable or unsuitable thereto. But a thing's nature, which is the end of generation, is further ordained to another end, which is either an operation, or the product of an operation, to which one attains by means of operation. Wherefore habit implies relation not only to the very nature of a thing, but also, consequently, to operation, inasmuch as this is the end of nature, or conducive to the end. Whence also it is stated (Metaph. v, text. 25) in the definition of habit, that it is a disposition whereby that which is disposed, is well or ill disposed

dispositum aut secundum se, idest secundum suam naturam, aut ad aliud, idest in ordine ad finem. Sed sunt quidam habitus qui etiam ex parte subiecti in quo sunt, primo et principaliter important ordinem ad actum. Quia ut dictum est, habitus primo et per se importat habitudinem ad naturam rei. Si igitur natura rei in qua est habitus, consistat in ipso ordine ad actum, sequitur quod habitus principaliter importet ordinem ad actum. Manifestum est autem quod natura et ratio potentiae est ut sit principium actus. Unde omnis habitus qui est alicuius potentiae ut subiecti, principaliter importat ordinem ad actum.

AD PRIMUM ergo dicendum quod habitus est actus quidam, inquantum est qualitas, et secundum hoc potest esse principium operationis. Sed est in potentia per respectum ad operationem. Unde habitus dicitur actus primus, et operatio actus secundus; ut patet in II de anima.

AD SECUNDUM dicendum quod non est de ratione habitus quod respiciat potentiam, sed quod respiciat naturam. Et quia natura praecedit actionem, quam respicit potentia; ideo prior species qualitatis ponitur habitus quam potentia.

AD TERTIUM dicendum quod sanitas dicitur habitus, vel habitualis dispositio, in ordine ad naturam, sicut dictum est. Inquantum tamen natura est principium actus, ex consequenti importat ordinem ad actum. Unde philosophus dicit, in X de historia Animal., quod homo dicitur sanus, vel membrum aliquod, *quando potest facere operationem sani.* Et est simile in aliis.

ARTICULUS 4

AD QUARTUM sic proceditur. Videtur quod non sit necessarium esse habitus. Habitus enim sunt quibus aliquid disponitur bene vel male ad aliquid, sicut dictum est. Sed per suam formam aliquid bene vel male disponitur, nam secundum formam aliquid est bonum, sicut et ens. Ergo nulla necessitas est habituum.

PRAETEREA, habitus importat ordinem ad actum. Sed potentia importat principium actus sufficienter, nam et potentiae naturales

either in regard to itself, that is to its nature, or in regard to something else, that is to the end. But there are some habits, which even on the part of the subject in which they are, imply primarily and principally relation to an act. For, as we have said, habit primarily and of itself implies a relation to the thing's nature. If therefore the nature of a thing, in which the habit is, consists in this very relation to an act, it follows that the habit principally implies relation to an act. Now it is clear that the nature and the notion of power is that it should be a principle of act. Wherefore every habit is subjected in a power, implies principally relation to an act.

Reply to Objection 1: Habit is an act, in so far as it is a quality: and in this respect it can be a principle of operation. It is, however, in a state of potentiality in respect to operation. Wherefore habit is called first act, and operation, second act; as it is explained in De Anima ii, text. 5.

Reply to Objection 2: It is not the essence of habit to be related to power, but to be related to nature. And as nature precedes action, to which power is related, therefore habit is put before power as a species of quality.

Reply to Objection 3: Health is said to be a habit, or a habitual disposition, in relation to nature, as stated above. But in so far as nature is a principle of act, it consequently implies a relation to act. Wherefore the Philosopher says (De Hist. Animal. x, 1), that man, or one of his members, is called healthy, "when he can perform the operation of a healthy man." And the same applies to other habits.

ARTICLE 4
Whether habits are necessary?

Objection 1: It would seem that habits are not necessary. For by habits we are well or ill disposed in respect of something, as stated above. But a thing is well or ill disposed by its form: for in respect of its form a thing is good, even as it is a being. Therefore there is no necessity for habits.

Objection 2: Further, habit implies relation to an act. But power implies sufficiently a principle of act: for even the natural powers,

I, q. 49, a. 4, arg. 2

absque habitibus sunt principia actuum. Ergo non fuit necessarium habitus esse.

PRAETEREA, sicut potentia se habet ad bonum et malum, ita et habitus, et sicut potentia non semper agit, ita nec habitus. Existentibus igitur potentiis, superfluum fuit habitum esse.

SED CONTRA est quod habitus sunt perfectiones quaedam, ut dicitur in VII Physic. Sed perfectio est maxime necessaria rei, cum **habeat rationem finis. Ergo necessarium fuit habitus esse.**

RESPONDEO dicendum quod, sicut supra dictum est, habitus importat dispositionem quandam in ordine ad naturam rei, et ad operationem vel finem eius, secundum quam bene vel male aliquid ad hoc disponitur. Ad hoc autem quod aliquid indigeat disponi ad alterum, tria requiruntur. Primo quidem, ut id quod disponitur, sit alterum ab eo ad quod disponitur; et sic se habeat ad ipsum ut potentia ad actum. Unde si aliquid sit cuius natura non sit composita ex potentia et actu, et cuius substantia sit sua operatio, et ipsum sit propter seipsum; ibi habitus vel dispositio locum non habet, sicut patet in Deo. Secundo requiritur quod id quod est in potentia ad alterum, possit pluribus modis determinari, et ad diversa. Unde si aliquid sit in potentia ad alterum, ita tamen quod non sit in potentia nisi ad ipsum, ibi dispositio et habitus locum non habet, quia tale subiectum ex sua natura habet debitam habitudinem ad talem actum. Unde si corpus caeleste sit compositum ex materia et forma, cum illa materia non sit in potentia ad aliam formam, ut in primo dictum est, non habet ibi locum dispositio vel habitus ad formam; aut etiam ad operationem, quia natura caelestis corporis non est in potentia nisi ad unum motum determinatum. Tertio requiritur quod plura concurrant ad disponendum subiectum ad unum eorum ad quae est in potentia, quae diversis modis commensurari possunt, ut sic disponatur bene vel male ad formam vel ad operationem. Unde qualitates simplices

HABITS IN GENERAL, AS TO THEIR SUBSTANCE

without any habits, are principles of acts. Therefore there was no necessity for habits.

Objection 3: Further, as power is related to good and evil, so also is habit: and as power does not always act, so neither does habit. Given, therefore, the powers, habits become superfluous.

On the contrary, Habits are perfections (Phys. vii, text. 17). But perfection is of the greatest necessity to a thing: since it is in the **nature of an end. Therefore it is necessary that there should be habits.**

I answer that, As we have said above (I-II, q. 49, a. 2; a. 3), habit implies a disposition in relation to a thing's nature, and to its operation or end, by reason of which disposition a thing is well or ill disposed thereto. Now for a thing to need to be disposed to something else, three conditions are necessary. The first condition is that which is disposed should be distinct from that to which it is disposed; and so, that it should be related to it as potentiality is to act. Whence, if there is a being whose nature is not composed of potentiality and act, and whose substance is its own operation, which itself is for itself, there we can find no room for habit and disposition, as is clearly the case in God. The second condition is, that that which is in a state of potentiality in regard to something else, be capable of determination in several ways and to various things. Whence if something be in a state of potentiality in regard to something else, but in regard to that only, there we find no room for disposition and habit: for such a subject from its own nature has the due relation to such an act. Wherefore if a heavenly body be composed of matter and form, since that matter is not in a state of potentiality to another form, as we said in the I, q. 56, a. 2, there is no need for disposition or habit in respect of the form, or even in respect of operation, since the nature of the heavenly body is not in a state of potentiality to more than one fixed movement. The third condition is that in disposing the subject to one of those things to which it is in potentiality, several things should occur, capable of being adjusted in various ways: so as to dispose the subject well or ill to its form or to its operation. Wherefore the simple qualities

elementorum, quae secundum unum modum determinatum naturis elementorum conveniunt, non dicimus dispositiones vel habitus, sed *simplices qualitates,* dicimus autem dispositiones vel habitus sanitatem, pulchritudinem et alia huiusmodi, quae important quandam commensurationem plurium quae diversis modis commensurari possunt. Propter quod philosophus dicit, in V Metaphys., quod *habitus est dispositio,* et dispositio est *ordo habentis partes vel secundum locum, vel secundum potentiam, vel secundum speciem;* ut supra dictum est. Quia igitur multa sunt entium ad quorum naturas et operationes necesse est plura concurrere quae diversis modis commensurari possunt, ideo necesse est habitus esse.

AD PRIMUM ergo dicendum quod per formam perficitur natura rei, sed oportet quod in ordine ad ipsam formam disponatur subiectum aliqua dispositione. Ipsa tamen forma ordinatur ulterius ad operationem, quae vel est finis, vel via in finem. Et si quidem habeat forma determinate unam tantum operationem determinatam, nulla alia dispositio requiritur ad operationem praeter ipsam formam. Si autem sit talis forma quae possit diversimode operari, sicut est anima; oportet quod disponatur ad suas operationes per aliquos habitus.

AD SECUNDUM dicendum quod potentia quandoque se habet ad multa, et ideo oportet quod aliquo alio determinetur. Si vero sit aliqua potentia quae non se habeat ad multa, non indiget habitu determinante, ut dictum est. Et propter hoc vires naturales non agunt operationes suas mediantibus aliquibus habitibus, quia secundum seipsas sunt determinatae ad unum.

AD TERTIUM dicendum quod non idem habitus se habet ad bonum et malum, sicut infra patebit. Eadem autem potentia se habet ad bonum et malum. Et ideo necessarii sunt habitus ut potentiae determinentur ad bonum.

of the elements which suit the natures of the elements in one single fixed way, are not called dispositions or habits, but "simple qualities": but we call dispositions or habits, such things as health, beauty, and so forth, which imply the adjustment of several things which may vary in their relative adjustability. For this reason the Philosopher says (Metaph. v, text. 24, 25) that "habit is a disposition": and disposition is "the order of that which has parts either as to place, or as to potentiality, or as to species," as we have said above (I-II, q. 49, a. 1, ad 3). Wherefore, since there are many things for whose natures and operations several things must concur which may vary in their relative adjustability, it follows that habit is necessary.

Reply to Objection 1: By the form the nature of a thing is perfected: yet the subject needs to be disposed in regard to the form by some disposition. But the form itself is further ordained to operation, which is either the end, or the means to the end. And if the form is limited to one fixed operation, no further disposition, besides the form itself, is needed for the operation. But if the form be such that it can operate in diverse ways, as the soul; it needs to be disposed to its operations by means of habits.

Reply to Objection 2: Power sometimes has a relation to many things: and then it needs to be determined by something else. But if a power has not a relation to many things, it does not need a habit to determine it, as we have said. For this reason the natural forces do not perform their operations by means of habits: because they are of themselves determined to one mode of operation.

Reply to Objection 3: The same habit has not a relation to good and evil, as will be made clear further on (I-II, q. 54, a. 3): whereas the same power has a relation to good and evil. And, therefore, habits are necessary that the powers be determined to good.

Quaestio L

Deinde considerandum est de subiecto habituum. Et circa hoc quaeruntur sex. *Primo,* utrum in corpore sit aliquis habitus. *Secundo,* utrum anima sit subiectum habitus secundum suam essentiam, vel secundum suam potentiam. *Tertio,* utrum in potentiis sensitivae partis possit esse aliquis habitus. *Quarto,* utrum in ipso intellectu sit aliquis habitus. *Quinto,* utrum in voluntate sit aliquis habitus. *Sexto,* utrum in substantiis separatis.

Articulus 1

Ad primum sic proceditur. Videtur quod in corpore non sit aliquis habitus. Ut enim Commentator dicit, in III de anima, *habitus est quo quis agit cum voluerit.* Sed actiones corporales non subiacent voluntati, cum sint naturales. Ergo in corpore non potest esse aliquis habitus.

Praeterea, omnes dispositiones corporales sunt facile mobiles. Sed habitus est qualitas difficile mobilis. Ergo nulla dispositio corporalis potest esse habitus.

Praeterea, omnes dispositiones corporales subiacent alterationi. Sed alteratio non est nisi in tertia specie qualitatis, quae dividitur contra habitum. Ergo nullus habitus est in corpore.

Sed contra est quod philosophus, in praedicamentis, sanitatem corporis, vel infirmitatem insanabilem, habitum nominari dicit.

Respondeo dicendum quod, sicut supra dictum est, habitus est quaedam dispositio alicuius subiecti existentis in potentia vel ad formam, vel ad operationem. Secundum ergo quod habitus importat dispositionem ad operationem, nullus habitus est principaliter in corpore sicut in subiecto. Omnis enim operatio corporis est aut a naturali qualitate corporis; aut est ab anima movente corpus. Quantum igitur ad illas operationes quae sunt a natura, non disponitur corpus per aliquem habitum, quia virtutes naturales sunt determinatae ad unum; dictum est autem

Question 50
Of the Subjects of Habits

We consider next the subject of habits: and under this head there are six points of inquiry: 1. Whether there is a habit in the body? 2. Whether the soul is a subject of habit, in respect of its essence or in respect of its power? 3. Whether in the powers of the sensitive part there can be a habit? 4. Whether there is a habit in the intellect? 5. Whether there is a habit in the will? 6. Whether there is a habit in separate substances?

Article 1
Whether there is a habit in the body?

Objection 1: It would seem that there is not a habit in the body. For, as the Commentator says (De Anima iii), "a habit is that whereby we act when we will." But bodily actions are not subject to the will, since they are natural. Therefore there can be no habit in the body.

Objection 2: Further, all bodily dispositions are easy to change. But habit is a quality, difficult to change. Therefore no bodily disposition can be a habit.

Objection 3: Further, all bodily dispositions are subject to change. But change can only be in the third species of quality, which is divided against habit. Therefore there is no habit in the body.

On the contrary, The Philosopher says in the Book of Predicaments (De Categor. vi) that health of the body and incurable disease are called habits.

I answer that, As we have said above (I-II, q. 49, a. 2, seqq.), habit is a disposition of a subject which is in a state of potentiality either to form or to operation. Therefore in so far as habit implies disposition to operation, no habit is principally in the body as its subject. For every operation of the body proceeds either from a natural quality of the body or from the soul moving the body. Consequently, as to those operations which proceed from its nature, the body is not disposed by a habit: because the natural forces are determined to one mode of operation; and we have already said (I-II, q. 49, a. 4)

quod habitualis dispositio requiritur ubi subiectum est in potentia ad multa. Operationes vero quae sunt ab anima per corpus, principaliter quidem sunt ipsius animae, secundario vero ipsius corporis. Habitus autem proportionantur operationibus, unde *ex similibus actibus similes habitus causantur,* ut dicitur in II Ethic. Et ideo dispositiones ad tales operationes principaliter sunt in anima. In corpore vero possunt esse secundario, inquantum scilicet corpus disponitur et habilitatur ad prompte deserviendum operationibus animae. Si vero loquamur de dispositione subiecti ad formam, sic habitualis dispositio potest esse in corpore, quod comparatur ad animam sicut subiectum ad formam. Et hoc modo sanitas et pulchritudo, et huiusmodi, habituales dispositiones dicuntur. Non tamen perfecte habent rationem habituum, quia causae eorum ex sua natura de facili transmutabiles sunt. Alexander vero posuit nullo modo habitum vel dispositionem primae speciei esse in corpore, ut Simplicius refert in commento Praedicament., sed dicebat primam speciem qualitatis pertinere tantum ad animam. Et quod Aristoteles inducit in praedicamentis de sanitate et aegritudine, non inducit quasi haec pertineant ad primam speciem qualitatis, sed per modum exempli, ut sit sensus quod sicut aegritudo et sanitas possunt esse facile vel difficile mobiles, ita etiam qualitates primae speciei, quae dicuntur habitus et dispositio. Sed patet hoc esse contra intentionem Aristotelis. Tum quia eodem modo loquendi utitur exemplificando de sanitate et aegritudine, et de virtute et de scientia. Tum quia in VII Physic. expresse ponit inter habitus pulchritudinem et sanitatem.

AD PRIMUM ergo dicendum quod obiectio illa procedit de habitu secundum quod est dispositio ad operationem, et de actibus corporis qui sunt a natura, non autem de his qui sunt ab anima, quorum principium est voluntas.

AD SECUNDUM dicendum quod dispositiones corporales non sunt simpliciter difficile mobiles, propter mutabilitatem corporalium causarum. Possunt tamen esse difficile mobiles per comparationem ad tale subiectum,

that it is when the subject is in potentiality to many things that a habitual disposition is required. As to the operations which proceed from the soul through the body, they belong principally to the soul, and secondarily to the body. Now habits are in proportion to their operations: whence "by like acts like habits are formed" (Ethic. ii, 1, 2). And therefore the dispositions to such operations are principally in the soul. But they can be secondarily in the body: to wit, in so far as the body is disposed and enabled with promptitude to help in the operations of the soul. If, however, we speak of the disposition of the subject to form, thus a habitual disposition can be in the body, which is related to the soul as a subject is to its form. And in this way health and beauty and such like are called habitual dispositions. Yet they have not the nature of habit perfectly: because their causes, of their very nature, are easily changeable. On the other hand, as Simplicius reports in his Commentary on the Predicaments, Alexander denied absolutely that habits or dispositions of the first species are in the body: and held that the first species of quality belonged to the soul alone. And he held that Aristotle mentions health and sickness in the Book on the Predicaments not as though they belonged to the first species of quality, but by way of example: so that he would mean that just as health and sickness may be easy or difficult to change, so also are all the qualities of the first species, which are called habits and dispositions. But this is clearly contrary to the intention of Aristotle: both because he speaks in the same way of health and sickness as examples, as of virtue and science; and because in Phys. vii, text. 17, he expressly mentions beauty and health among habits.

Reply to Objection 1: This objection runs in the sense of habit as a disposition to operation, and of those actions of the body which are from nature: but not in the sense of those actions which proceed from the soul, and the principle of which is the will.

Reply to Objection 2: Bodily dispositions are not simply difficult to change on account of the changeableness of their bodily causes. But they may be difficult to change by comparison to such a subject,

I-II, q. 50, a. 1, ad 2

quia scilicet, tali subiecto durante, amoveri non possunt, vel quia sunt difficile mobiles per comparationem ad alias dispositiones. Sed qualitates animae sunt simpliciter difficile mobiles, propter immobilitatem subiecti. Et ideo non dicit quod sanitas difficile mobilis simpliciter sit habitus, sed quod est *ut habitus,* sicut in Graeco habetur. Qualitates autem animae dicuntur simpliciter habitus.

AD TERTIUM dicendum quod dispositiones corporales quae sunt in prima specie qualitatis, ut quidam posuerunt, differunt a qualitatibus tertiae speciei in hoc, quod qualitates tertiae speciei sunt ut in fieri et ut in motu, unde dicuntur passiones vel passibiles qualitates. Quando autem iam pervenerint ad perfectum, quasi ad speciem, tunc iam sunt in prima specie qualitatis. Sed hoc improbat Simplicius, in commento praedicamentorum, quia secundum hoc calefactio esset in tertia specie qualitatis, calor autem in prima, Aristoteles autem ponit calorem in tertia. Unde Porphyrius dicit, sicut idem Simplicius refert, quod passio vel passibilis qualitas, et dispositio et habitus, differunt in corporibus secundum intensionem et remissionem. Quando enim aliquid recipit caliditatem secundum calefieri tantum, non autem ut calefacere possit; tunc est passio, si sit cito transiens, vel passibilis qualitas, si sit manens. Quando autem iam ad hoc perducitur quod potest etiam alterum calefacere, tunc est dispositio, si autem ulterius intantum confirmetur quod sit difficile mobilis, tunc erit habitus, ut sic dispositio sit quaedam intensio seu perfectio passionis vel passibilis qualitatis, habitus autem dispositionis. Sed hoc improbat Simplicius, quia talis intensio et remissio non important diversitatem ex parte ipsius formae, sed ex diversa participatione subiecti. Et ita non diversificarentur per hoc species qualitatis. Et ideo aliter dicendum est quod, sicut supra dictum est,

THE SUBJECTS OF HABITS

because, to wit, as long as such a subject endures, they cannot be removed; or because they are difficult to change, by comparison to other dispositions. But qualities of the soul are simply difficult to change, on account of the unchangeableness of the subject. And therefore he does not say that health which is difficult to change is a habit simply: but that it is "as a habit," as we read in the Greek.* On the other hand, the qualities of the soul are called habits simply.

Reply to Objection 3: Bodily dispositions which are in the first species of quality, as some maintained, differ from qualities of the third species, in this, that the qualities of the third species consist in some "becoming" and movement, as it were, wherefore they are called passions or passible qualities. But when they have attained to perfection (specific perfection, so to speak), they have then passed into the first species of quality. But Simplicius in his Commentary disapproves of this; for in this way heating would be in the third species, and heat in the first species of quality; whereas Aristotle puts heat in the third. Wherefore Porphyrius, as Simplicius reports (Commentary), says that passion or passion-like quality, disposition and habit, differ in bodies by way of intensity and remissness. For when a thing receives heat in this only that it is being heated, and not so as to be able to give heat, then we have passion, if it is transitory; or passion-like quality if it is permanent. But when it has been brought to the point that it is able to heat something else, then it is a disposition; and if it goes so far as to be firmly fixed and to become difficult to change, then it will be a habit: so that disposition would be a certain intensity of passion or passion-like quality, and habit an intensity or disposition. But Simplicius disapproves of this, for such intensity and remissness do not imply diversity on the part of the form itself, but on the part of the diverse participation thereof by the subject; so that there would be no diversity among the species of quality. And therefore we must say otherwise that, as was explained above (I-II, q. 49, a. 2, ad 1),

---

* ἴσως ἕξιν / *isos hexin* (Categor. viii)

commensuratio ipsarum qualitatum passibilium secundum convenientiam ad naturam, habet rationem dispositionis, et ideo, facta alteratione circa ipsas qualitates passibiles, quae sunt calidum et frigidum, humidum et siccum, fit ex consequenti alteratio secundum aegritudinem et sanitatem. Primo autem et per se non est alteratio secundum huiusmodi habitus et dispositiones.

Articulus 2

Ad secundum sic proceditur. Videtur quod habitus sint in anima magis secundum essentiam quam secundum potentiam. Dispositiones enim et habitus dicuntur in ordine ad naturam, ut dictum est. Sed natura magis attenditur secundum essentiam animae quam secundum potentias, quia anima secundum suam essentiam est natura corporis talis, et forma eius. Ergo habitus sunt in anima secundum eius essentiam et non secundum potentiam.

Praeterea, accidentis non est accidens. Habitus autem est quoddam accidens. Sed potentiae animae sunt de genere accidentium, ut in primo dictum est. Ergo habitus non est in anima ratione suae potentiae.

Praeterea, subiectum est prius eo quod est in subiecto. Sed habitus, cum pertineat ad primam speciem qualitatis, est prior quam potentia, quae pertinet ad secundam speciem. Ergo habitus non est in potentia animae sicut in subiecto.

Sed contra est quod philosophus, in I Ethic., ponit diversos habitus in diversis partibus animae.

Respondeo dicendum quod, sicut supra dictum est, habitus importat dispositionem quandam in ordine ad naturam, vel ad operationem. Si ergo accipiatur habitus secundum quod habet ordinem ad naturam, sic non potest esse in anima, si tamen de natura humana loquamur, quia ipsa anima est forma completiva humanae naturae; unde secundum hoc, magis potest esse aliquis habitus vel dispositio in corpore per ordinem ad animam, quam in anima per ordinem ad corpus.

the adjustment of the passion-like qualities themselves, according to their suitability to nature, implies the notion of disposition: and so, when a change takes place in these same passion-like qualities, which are heat and cold, moisture and dryness, there results a change as to sickness and health. But change does not occur in regard to like habits and dispositions, primarily and of themselves.

Article 2
Whether the soul is the subject of habit in respect of its essence or in respect of its power?

Objection 1: It would seem that habit is in the soul in respect of its essence rather than in respect of its powers. For we speak of dispositions and habits in relation to nature, as stated above (I-II, q. 49, a. 2). But nature regards the essence of the soul rather than the powers; because it is in respect of its essence that the soul is the nature of such a body and the form thereof. Therefore habits are in the soul in respect of its essence and not in respect of its powers.

Objection 2: Further, accident is not the subject of accident. Now habit is an accident. But the powers of the soul are in the genus of accident, as we have said in the I, q. 77, a. 1, ad 5. Therefore habit is not in the soul in respect of its powers.

Objection 3: Further, the subject is prior to that which is in the subject. But since habit belongs to the first species of quality, it is prior to power, which belongs to the second species. Therefore habit is not in a power of the soul as its subject.

On the contrary, The Philosopher (Ethic. i, 13) puts various habits in the various powers of the soul.

I answer that, As we have said above (I-II, q. 49, a. 2; a. 3), habit implies a certain disposition in relation to nature or to operation. If therefore we take habit as having a relation to nature, it cannot be in the soul—that is, if we speak of human nature: for the soul itself is the form completing the human nature; so that, regarded in this way, habit or disposition is rather to be found in the body by reason of its relation to the soul, than in the soul by reason of its relation to the body.

Sed si loquamur de aliqua superiori natura, cuius homo potest esse particeps, secundum illud II Petr. I, *ut simus consortes naturae divinae,* sic nihil prohibet in anima secundum suam essentiam esse aliquem habitum, scilicet gratiam, ut infra dicetur. Si vero accipiatur habitus in ordine ad operationem, sic maxime habitus inveniuntur in anima, inquantum anima non determinatur ad unam operationem, sed se habet ad multas, quod requiritur ad habitum, ut supra dictum est. Et quia anima est principium operationum per suas potentias, ideo secundum hoc, habitus sunt in anima secundum suas potentias.

AD PRIMUM ergo dicendum quod essentia animae pertinet ad naturam humanam, non sicut subiectum disponendum ad aliquid aliud, sed sicut forma et natura ad quam aliquis disponitur.

AD SECUNDUM dicendum quod accidens per se non potest esse subiectum accidentis. Sed quia etiam in ipsis accidentibus est ordo quidam, subiectum secundum quod est sub uno accidente, intelligitur esse subiectum alterius. Et sic dicitur unum accidens esse subiectum alterius, ut superficies coloris. Et hoc modo potest potentia esse subiectum habitus.

AD TERTIUM dicendum quod habitus praemittitur potentiae, secundum quod importat dispositionem ad naturam, potentia autem semper importat ordinem ad operationem, quae est posterior, cum natura sit operationis principium. Sed habitus cuius potentia est subiectum, non importat ordinem ad naturam, sed ad operationem. Unde est posterior potentia. Vel potest dici quod habitus praeponitur potentiae sicut completum incompleto, et actus potentiae. Actus enim naturaliter est prior; quamvis potentia sit prior ordine generationis et temporis, ut dicitur in VII et IX Metaphys.

But if we speak of a higher nature, of which man may become a partaker, according to 2 Pet. 1, "that we may be partakers of the Divine Nature": thus nothing hinders some habit, namely, grace, from being in the soul in respect of its essence, as we shall state later on (I-II, q. 110, a. 4). On the other hand, if we take habit in its relation to operation, it is chiefly thus that habits are found in the soul: in so far as the soul is not determined to one operation, but is indifferent to many, which is a condition for a habit, as we have said above (I-II, q. 49, a. 4). And since the soul is the principle of operation through its powers, therefore, regarded in this sense, habits are in the soul in respect of its powers.

Reply to Objection 1: The essence of the soul belongs to human nature, not as a subject requiring to be disposed to something further, but as a form and nature to which someone is disposed.

Reply to Objection 2: Accident is not of itself the subject of accident. But since among accidents themselves there is a certain order, the subject, according as it is under one accident, is conceived as the subject of a further accident. In this way we say that one accident is the subject of another; as superficies is the subject of color, in which sense power is the subject of habit.

Reply to Objection 3: Habit takes precedence of power, according as it implies a disposition to nature: whereas power always implies a relation to operation, which is posterior, since nature is the principle of operation. But the habit whose subject is a power, does not imply relation to nature, but to operation. Wherefore it is posterior to power. Or, we may say that habit takes precedence of power, as the complete takes precedence of the incomplete, and as act takes precedence of potentiality. For act is naturally prior to potentiality, though potentiality is prior in order of generation and time, as stated in Metaph. vii, text. 17; ix, text. 13.

Articulus 3

Ad tertium sic proceditur. Videtur quod in potentiis sensitivae partis non possit esse aliquis habitus. Sicut enim potentia nutritiva pars est irrationalis, ita et sensitiva. Sed in potentiis nutritivae partis non ponitur aliquis habitus. Ergo nec in potentiis sensitivae partis aliquis habitus debet poni.

Praeterea, sensitivae partes sunt communes nobis et brutis. Sed in brutis non sunt aliqui habitus, quia non est in eis voluntas, quae in definitione habitus ponitur, ut supra dictum est. Ergo in potentiis sensitivis non sunt aliqui habitus.

Praeterea, habitus animae sunt scientiae et virtutes, et sicut scientia refertur ad vim apprehensivam, ita virtus ad vim appetitivam. Sed in potentiis sensitivis non sunt aliquae scientiae, cum scientia sit universalium, quae vires sensitivae apprehendere non possunt. Ergo etiam nec habitus virtutum in partibus sensitivis esse possunt.

Sed contra est quod philosophus dicit, in III Ethic., quod *aliquae virtutes,* scilicet temperantia et fortitudo, sunt irrationabilium partium.

Respondeo dicendum quod vires sensitivae dupliciter possunt considerari, uno modo, secundum quod operantur ex instinctu naturae; alio modo, secundum quod operantur ex imperio rationis. Secundum igitur quod operantur ex instinctu naturae, sic ordinantur ad unum, sicut et natura. Et ideo sicut in potentiis naturalibus non sunt aliqui habitus, ita etiam nec in potentiis sensitivis, secundum quod ex instinctu naturae operantur. Secundum vero quod operantur ex imperio rationis, sic ad diversa ordinari possunt. Et sic possunt in eis esse aliqui habitus, quibus bene aut male ad aliquid disponuntur.

Ad primum ergo dicendum quod vires nutritivae partis non sunt natae obedire imperio rationis, et ideo

Article 3
Whether there can be any habits in the powers of the sensitive parts?

Objection 1: It would seem that there cannot be any habits in the powers of the sensitive part. For as the nutritive power is an irrational part, so is the sensitive power. But there can be no habits in the powers of the nutritive part. Therefore we ought not to put any habit in the powers of the sensitive part.

Objection 2: Further, the sensitive parts are common to us and the brutes. But there are not any habits in brutes: for in them there is no will, which is put in the definition of habit, as we have said above (I-II, q. 49, a. 3). Therefore there are no habits in the sensitive powers.

Objection 3: Further, the habits of the soul are sciences and virtues: and just as science is related to the apprehensive power, so it virtue related to the appetitive power. But in the sensitive powers there are no sciences: since science is of universals, which the sensitive powers cannot apprehend. Therefore, neither can there be habits of virtue in the sensitive part.

On the contrary, The Philosopher says (Ethic. iii, 10) that "some virtues," namely, temperance and fortitude, "belong to the irrational part."

I answer that, The sensitive powers can be considered in two ways: first, according as they act from natural instinct: secondly, according as they act at the command of reason. According as they act from natural instinct, they are ordained to one thing, even as nature is. And therefore just as there are no habits in natural powers, neither are there any in sensitive powers according as they operate from the instinct of nature.* But according as they act at the command of reason, they can be ordained to various things. And thus there can be habits in them, by which they are well or ill disposed in regard to something.

Reply to Objection 1: The powers of the nutritive part have not an inborn aptitude to obey the command of reason, and therefore

---

* *Sentence missing in English source text; supplied by editors.*

non sunt in eis aliqui habitus. Sed vires sensitivae natae sunt obedire imperio rationis, et ideo in eis esse possunt aliqui habitus; nam secundum quod obediunt rationi, quodammodo rationales dicuntur, ut in I Ethic. dicitur.

AD SECUNDUM dicendum quod vires sensitivae in brutis animalibus non operantur ex imperio rationis; sed si sibi relinquantur bruta animalia, operantur ex instinctu naturae. Et sic in brutis animalibus non sunt aliqui habitus ordinati ad operationes. Sunt tamen in eis aliquae dispositiones in ordine ad naturam, ut sanitas et pulchritudo. Sed quia bruta animalia a ratione hominis per quandam consuetudinem disponuntur ad aliquid operandum sic vel aliter, hoc modo in brutis animalibus habitus quodammodo poni possunt, unde Augustinus dicit, in libro octoginta trium quaest., quod *videmus immanissimas bestias a maximis voluptatibus absterreri dolorum metu, quod cum in earum consuetudinem verterit, domitae et mansuetae vocantur.* Deficit tamen ratio habitus quantum ad usum voluntatis, quia non habent dominium utendi vel non utendi, quod videtur ad rationem habitus pertinere. Et ideo, proprie loquendo, in eis habitus esse non possunt.

AD TERTIUM dicendum quod appetitus sensitivus natus est moveri ab appetitu rationali, ut dicitur in III de anima, sed vires rationales apprehensivae natae sunt accipere a viribus sensitivis. Et ideo magis convenit quod habitus sint in viribus sensitivis appetitivis quam in viribus sensitivis apprehensivis, cum in viribus sensitivis appetitivis non sint habitus nisi secundum quod operantur ex imperio rationis. Quamvis etiam in ipsis interioribus viribus sensitivis apprehensivis possint poni aliqui habitus, secundum quos homo fit bene memorativus vel cogitativus vel imaginativus, unde etiam philosophus dicit, in cap. de memoria, quod *consuetudo multum operatur ad bene memorandum,* quia etiam istae vires moventur ad operandum ex imperio rationis. Vires autem apprehensivae exteriores, ut visus et auditus et huiusmodi, non sunt susceptivae

there are no habits in them. But the sensitive powers have an inborn aptitude to obey the command of reason; and therefore habits can be in them: for in so far as they obey reason, in a certain sense they are said to be rational, as stated in Ethic. i, 13.

Reply to Objection 2: The sensitive powers of dumb animals do not act at the command of reason; but if they are left to themselves, such animals act from natural instinct: and so in them there are no habits ordained to operations. There are in them, however, certain dispositions in relation to nature, as health and beauty. But whereas by man's reason brutes are disposed by a sort of custom to do things in this or that way, so in this sense, to a certain extent, we can admit the existence of habits in dumb animals: wherefore Augustine says (QQ. lxxxiii, qu. 36): "We find the most untamed beasts, deterred by fear of pain, from that wherein they took the keenest pleasure; and when this has become a custom in them, we say that they are tame and gentle." But the habit is incomplete, as to the use of the will, for they have not that power of using or of refraining, which seems to belong to the notion of habit: and therefore, properly speaking, there can be no habits in them.

Reply to Objection 3: The sensitive appetite has an inborn aptitude to be moved by the rational appetite, as stated in De Anima iii, text. 57: but the rational powers of apprehension have an inborn aptitude to receive from the sensitive powers. And therefore it is more suitable that habits should be in the powers of sensitive appetite than in the powers of sensitive apprehension, since in the powers of sensitive appetite habits do not exist except according as they act at the command of the reason. And yet even in the interior powers of sensitive apprehension, we may admit of certain habits whereby man has a facility of memory, thought or imagination: wherefore also the Philosopher says (De Memor. et Remin. ii) that "custom conduces much to a good memory": the reason of which is that these powers also are moved to act at the command of the reason. On the other hand the exterior apprehensive powers, as sight, hearing and the like, are not susceptible

Articulus 4

AD QUARTUM sic proceditur. Videtur quod in intellectu non sint aliqui habitus. Habitus enim operationibus conformantur, ut dictum est. Sed operationes hominis sunt communes animae et corpori, ut dicitur in I de anima. Ergo et habitus. Sed intellectus non est actus corporis, ut dicitur in III de anima. Ergo intellectus non est subiectum alicuius habitus.

PRAETEREA, omne quod est in aliquo, est in eo per modum eius in quo est. Sed id quod est forma sine materia, est actus tantum, quod autem est compositum ex forma et materia, habet potentiam et actum simul. Ergo in eo quod est forma tantum, non potest esse aliquid quod sit simul in potentia et actu, sed solum in eo quod est compositum ex materia et forma. Sed intellectus est forma sine materia. Ergo habitus, qui habet potentiam simul cum actu, quasi medium inter utrumque existens, non potest esse in intellectu; sed solum in *coniuncto,* quod est compositum ex anima et corpore.

PRAETEREA, habitus est dispositio secundum quam aliquis bene vel male disponitur ad aliquid, ut dicitur in V Metaph. Sed quod aliquis bene vel male sit dispositus ad actum intellectus, provenit ex aliqua corporis dispositione, unde etiam in II de anima dicitur quod *molles carne bene aptos mente videmus.* Ergo habitus cognoscitivi non sunt in intellectu, qui est separatus; sed in aliqua potentia quae est actus alicuius partis corporis.

SED CONTRA est quod philosophus, in VI Ethic., ponit scientiam et sapientiam et intellectum, qui est habitus principiorum, in ipsa intellectiva parte animae.

Article 4
Whether there is any habit in the intellect?

Objection 1: It would seem that there are no habits in the intellect. For habits are in conformity with operations, as stated above (I-II, q. 50, a. 1). But the operations of man are common to soul and body, as stated in De Anima i, text. 64. Therefore also are habits. But the intellect is not an act of the body (De Anima iii, text. 6). Therefore the intellect is not the subject of a habit.

Objection 2: Further, whatever is in a thing, is there according to the mode of that in which it is. But that which is form without matter, is act only: whereas what is composed of form and matter, has potentiality and act at the same time. Therefore nothing at the same time potential and actual can be in that which is form only, but only in that which is composed of matter and form. Now the intellect is form without matter. Therefore habit, which has potentiality at the same time as act, being a sort of medium between the two, cannot be in the intellect; but only in the person [*coniunctum*], which is composed of soul and body.

Objection 3: Further, habit is a disposition whereby we are well or ill disposed in regard to something, as is said (Metaph. v, text. 25). But that anyone should be well or ill disposed to an act of the intellect is due to some disposition of the body: wherefore also it is stated (De Anima ii, text. 94) that "we observe men with soft flesh to be quick witted." Therefore the habits of knowledge are not in the intellect, which is separate, but in some power which is the act of some part of the body.

On the contrary, The Philosopher (Ethic. vi, 2, 3, 10) puts science, wisdom and understanding, which is the habit of first principles, in the intellective part of the soul.

Respondeo dicendum quod circa habitus cognoscitivos diversimode sunt aliqui opinati. Quidam enim, ponentes intellectum possibilem esse unum in omnibus hominibus, coacti sunt ponere quod habitus cognoscitivi non sunt in ipso intellectu, sed in viribus interioribus sensitivis. Manifestum est enim quod homines in habitibus diversificantur, unde non possunt habitus cognoscitivi directe poni in eo quod, unum numero existens, est omnibus hominibus commune. Unde si intellectus possibilis sit unus numero omnium hominum, habitus scientiarum, secundum quos homines diversificantur, non poterunt esse in intellectu possibili sicut in subiecto, sed erunt in viribus interioribus sensitivis, quae sunt diversae in diversis. Sed ista positio, primo quidem, est contra intentionem Aristotelis. Manifestum est enim quod vires sensitivae non sunt rationales per essentiam, sed solum per participationem, ut dicitur in I Ethic. Philosophus autem ponit intellectuales virtutes, quae sunt sapientia, scientia et intellectus, in eo quod est rationale per essentiam. Unde non sunt in viribus sensitivis, sed in ipso intellectu. Expresse etiam dicit, in III de anima, quod intellectus possibilis, *cum sic fiat singula*, idest cum reducatur in actum singulorum per species intelligibiles, *tunc fit secundum actum eo modo quo sciens dicitur esse in actu, quod quidem accidit cum aliquis possit operari per seipsum*, scilicet considerando. *Est quidem igitur et tunc potentia quodammodo; non tamen similiter ut ante addiscere aut invenire.* Ipse ergo intellectus possibilis est in quo est habitus scientiae quo potest considerare etiam cum non considerat. Secundo etiam, haec positio est contra rei veritatem. Sicut enim eius est potentia cuius est operatio, ita etiam eius est habitus cuius est operatio. Intelligere autem et considerare est proprius actus intellectus. Ergo et habitus quo consideratur, est proprie in ipso intellectu.

Ad primum ergo dicendum quod quidam dixerunt, ut Simplicius refert in commento praedicamentorum, quod quia omnis

I answer that, concerning intellective habits there have been various opinions. Some, supposing that there was only one possible* intellect for all men, were bound to hold that habits of knowledge are not in the intellect itself, but in the interior sensitive powers. For it is manifest that men differ in habits; and so it was impossible to put the habits of knowledge directly in that, which, being only one, would be common to all men. Wherefore if there were but one single possible intellect of all men, the habits of science, in which men differ from one another, could not be in the possible intellect as their subject, but would be in the interior sensitive powers, which differ in various men. Now, in the first place, this supposition is contrary to the mind of Aristotle. For it is manifest that the sensitive powers are rational, not by their essence, but only by participation (Ethic. i, 13). Now the Philosopher puts the intellectual virtues, which are wisdom, science and understanding, in that which is rational by its essence. Wherefore they are not in the sensitive powers, but in the intellect itself. Moreover he says expressly (De Anima iii, text. 8, 18) that when the possible intellect "is thus identified with each thing," that is, when it is reduced to act in respect of singulars by the intelligible species, "then it is said to be in act, as the knower is said to be in act; and this happens when the intellect can act of itself," i.e., by considering: "and even then it is in potentiality in a sense; but not in the same way as before learning and discovering." Therefore the possible intellect itself is the subject of the habit of science, by which the intellect, even though it be not actually considering, is able to consider. In the second place, this supposition is contrary to the truth. For as to whom belongs the operation, belongs also the power to operate, belongs also the habit. But to understand and to consider is the proper act of the intellect. Therefore also the habit whereby one considers is properly in the intellect itself.

Reply to Objection 1: Some said, as Simplicius reports in his Commentary on the Predicaments, that, since every

---

* I, q. 79, a. 2, ad 2

operatio hominis est quodammodo coniuncti, ut philosophus dicit in I de anima; ideo nullus habitus est animae tantum, sed coniuncti. Et per hoc sequitur quod nullus habitus sit in intellectu, cum intellectus sit separatus, ut ratio proposita procedebat. Sed ista ratio non cogit. Habitus enim non est dispositio obiecti ad potentiam, sed magis dispositio potentiae ad obiectum, unde habitus oportet quod sit in ipsa potentia quae est principium actus, non autem in eo quod comparatur ad potentiam sicut obiectum. Ipsum autem intelligere non dicitur commune esse animae et corpori, nisi ratione phantasmatis, ut dicitur in I de anima. Patet autem quod phantasma comparatur ad intellectum possibilem ut obiectum, ut dicitur in III de anima. Unde relinquitur quod habitus intellectivus sit principaliter ex parte ipsius intellectus, non autem ex parte phantasmatis, quod est commune animae et corpori. Et ideo dicendum est quod intellectus possibilis est subiectum habitus, illi enim competit esse subiectum habitus, quod est in potentia ad multa; et hoc maxime competit intellectui possibili. Unde intellectus possibilis est subiectum habituum intellectualium.

AD SECUNDUM dicendum quod, sicut potentia ad esse sensibile convenit materiae corporali, ita potentia ad esse intelligibile convenit intellectui possibili. Unde nihil prohibet in intellectu possibili esse habitum, qui est medius inter puram potentiam et actum perfectum.

AD TERTIUM dicendum quod, quia vires apprehensivae interius praeparant intellectui possibili proprium obiectum; ideo ex bona dispositione harum virium, ad quam cooperatur bona dispositio corporis, redditur homo habilis ad intelligendum. Et sic habitus intellectivus secundario potest esse in istis viribus. Principaliter autem est in intellectu possibili.

operation of man is to a certain extent an operation of the *conjunctum*, as the Philosopher says (De Anima i, text. 64); therefore no habit is in the soul only, but in the *conjunctum*. And from this it follows that no habit is in the intellect, for the intellect is separate, as ran the argument, given above. But the argument is no cogent. For habit is not a disposition of the object to the power, but rather a disposition of the power to the object: wherefore the habit needs to be in that power which is principle of the act, and not in that which is compared to the power as its object. Now the act of understanding is not said to be common to soul and body, except in respect of the phantasm, as is stated in De Anima, text. 66. But it is clear that the phantasm is compared as object to the passive intellect (De Anima iii, text. 3, 39). Whence it follows that the intellective habit is chiefly on the part of the intellect itself; and not on the part of the phantasm, which is common to soul and body. And therefore we must say that the possible intellect is the subject of habit, which is in potentiality to many: and this belongs, above all, to the possible intellect. Wherefore the possible intellect is the subject of intellectual habits.

Reply to Objection 2: As potentiality to sensible being belongs to corporeal matter, so potentiality to intellectual being belongs to the possible intellect. Wherefore nothing forbids habit to be in the possible intellect, for it is midway between pure potentiality and perfect act.

Reply to Objection 3: Because the apprehensive powers inwardly prepare their proper objects for the possible intellect, therefore it is by the good disposition of these powers, to which the good disposition of the body cooperates, that man is rendered apt to understand. And so in a secondary way the intellective habit can be in these powers. But principally it is in the possible intellect.

Articulus 5

Ad quintum sic proceditur. Videtur quod in voluntate non sit aliquis habitus. Habitus enim qui in intellectu est, sunt species intelligibiles, quibus intelligit actu. Sed voluntas non operatur per aliquas species. Ergo voluntas non est subiectum alicuius habitus.

Praeterea, in intellectu agente non ponitur aliquis habitus, sicut in intellectu possibili, quia est potentia activa. Sed voluntas est maxime potentia activa, quia movet omnes potentias ad suos actus, ut supra dictum est. Ergo in ipsa non est aliquis habitus.

Praeterea, in potentiis naturalibus non est aliquis habitus, quia ex sua natura sunt ad aliquid determinatae. Sed voluntas ex sua natura ordinatur ad hoc quod tendat in bonum ordinatum ratione. Ergo in voluntate non est aliquis habitus.

Sed contra est quod iustitia est habitus quidam. Sed iustitia est in voluntate, *est enim iustitia habitus secundum quem aliqui volunt et operantur iusta,* ut dicitur in V Ethic. Ergo voluntas est subiectum alicuius habitus.

Respondeo dicendum quod omnis potentia quae diversimode potest ordinari ad agendum, indiget habitu quo bene disponatur ad suum actum. Voluntas autem, cum sit potentia rationalis, diversimode potest ad agendum ordinari. Et ideo oportet in voluntate aliquem habitum ponere, quo bene disponatur ad suum actum. Ex ipsa etiam ratione habitus apparet quod habet quendam principalem ordinem ad voluntatem, prout *habitus est quo quis utitur cum voluerit,* ut supra dictum est.

Ad primum ergo dicendum quod, sicut in intellectu est aliqua species quae est similitudo obiecti, ita oportet in voluntate, et in qualibet vi appetitiva, esse aliquid quo inclinetur in suum obiectum, cum nihil aliud sit actus appetitivae virtutis quam inclinatio quaedam, ut supra dictum est. Ad ea ergo ad quae sufficienter inclinatur per naturam ipsius potentiae, non indiget aliqua qualitate inclinante. Sed quia necessarium est ad finem

Article 5
Whether any habit is in the will?

Objection 1: It would seem that there is not a habit in the will. For the habit which is in the intellect is the intelligible species, by means of which the intellect actually understands. But the will does not act by means of species. Therefore the will is not the subject of habit.

Objection 2: Further, no habit is allotted to the active intellect, as there is to the possible intellect, because the former is an active power. But the will is above all an active power, because it moves all the powers to their acts, as stated above (I-II, q. 9, a. 1). Therefore there is no habit in the will.

Objection 3: Further, in the natural powers there is no habit, because, by reason of their nature, they are determinate to one thing. But the will, by reason of its nature, is ordained to tend to the good which reason directs. Therefore there is no habit in the will.

On the contrary, Justice is a habit. But justice is in the will; for it is "a habit whereby men will and do that which is just" (Ethic. v, 1). Therefore the will is the subject of a habit.

I answer that, Every power which may be variously directed to act, needs a habit whereby it is well disposed to its act. Now since the will is a rational power, it may be variously directed to act. And therefore in the will we must admit the presence of a habit whereby it is well disposed to its act. Moreover, from the very nature of habit, it is clear that it is principally related to the will; inasmuch as habit "is that which one uses when one wills," as stated above (I-II, q. 50, a. 1).

Reply to Objection 1: Even as in the intellect there is a species which is the likeness of the object; so in the will, and in every appetitive power there must be something by which the power is inclined to its object; for the act of the appetitive power is nothing but a certain inclination, as we have said above (I-II, q. 6, a. 4; q. 22, a. 2). And therefore in respect of those things to which it is inclined sufficiently by the nature of the power itself, the power needs no quality to incline it. But since it is necessary, for the end of

humanae vitae, quod vis appetitiva inclinetur in aliquid determinatum, ad quod non inclinatur ex natura potentiae, quae se habet ad multa et diversa; ideo necesse est quod in voluntate, et in aliis viribus appetitivis, sint quaedam qualitates inclinantes, quae dicuntur habitus.

AD SECUNDUM dicendum quod intellectus agens est agens tantum, et nullo modo patiens. Sed voluntas, et quaelibet vis appetitiva, est movens motum, ut dicitur in III de anima. Et ideo non est similis ratio de utroque, nam esse susceptivum habitus convenit ei quod est quodammodo in potentia.

AD TERTIUM dicendum quod voluntas ex ipsa natura potentiae inclinatur in bonum rationis. Sed quia hoc bonum multipliciter diversificatur, necessarium est ut ad aliquod determinatum bonum rationis voluntas per aliquem habitum inclinetur, ad hoc quod sequatur promptior operatio.

ARTICULUS 6

AD SEXTUM sic proceditur. Videtur quod in angelis non sint habitus. Dicit enim maximus, Commentator Dionysii, in VII cap. de Cael. Hier., *non convenit arbitrari virtutes intellectuales, idest spirituales, more accidentium, quemadmodum et in nobis sunt, in divinis intellectibus, scilicet angelis, esse, ut aliud in alio sit sicut in subiecto, accidens enim omne illinc repulsum est.* Sed omnis habitus est accidens. Ergo in angelis non sunt habitus.

PRAETEREA, sicut Dionysius dicit, in IV cap. de Cael. Hier., *sanctae caelestium essentiarum dispositiones super omnia alia Dei bonitatem participant.* Sed semper quod est per se, est prius et potius eo quod est per aliud. Ergo angelorum essentiae per seipsas perficiuntur ad conformitatem Dei. Non ergo per aliquos habitus. Et haec videtur esse ratio Maximi, qui ibidem subdit, si enim hoc esset, non utique maneret in semetipsa harum essentia, nec deificari per se, quantum foret possibile, valuisset.

human life, that the appetitive power be inclined to something fixed, to which it is not inclined by the nature of the power, which has a relation to many and various things, therefore it is necessary that, in the will and in the other appetitive powers, there be certain qualities to incline them, and these are called habits.

Reply to Objection 2: The active intellect is active only, and in no way passive. But the will, and every appetitive power, is both mover and moved (De Anima iii, text. 54). And therefore the comparison between them does not hold; for to be susceptible of habit belongs to that which is somehow in potentiality.

Reply to Objection 3: The will from the very nature of the power inclined to the good of the reason. But because this good is varied in many ways, the will needs to be inclined, by means of a habit, to some fixed good of the reason, in order that action may follow more promptly.

ARTICLE 6
Whether there are habits in the angels?

Objection 1: It would seem that there are no habits in the angels. For Maximus, commentator of Dionysius (Coel. Hier. vii), says: "It is not proper to suppose that there are intellectual (i.e., spiritual) powers in the divine intelligences (i.e., in the angels) after the manner of accidents, as in us: as though one were in the other as in a subject: for accident of any kind is foreign to them." But every habit is an accident. Therefore there are no habits in the angels.

Objection 2: Further, as Dionysius says (Coel. Hier. iv): "The holy dispositions of the heavenly essences participate, above all other things, in God's goodness." But that which is of itself [*per se*] is prior to and more power than that which is by another [*per aliud*]. Therefore the angelic essences are perfected of themselves unto conformity with God, and therefore not by means of habits. And this seems to have been the reasoning of Maximus, who in the same passage adds: "For if this were the case, surely their essence would not remain in itself, nor could it have been as far as possible deified of itself."

PRAETEREA, habitus est dispositio quaedam, ut dicitur in V Metaphys. Sed dispositio, ut ibidem dicitur, *est ordo habentis partes.* Cum ergo angeli sint simplices substantiae, videtur quod in eis non sint dispositiones et habitus.

SED CONTRA est quod Dionysius dicit, VII cap. Cael. Hier., quod angeli primae hierarchiae nominantur *calefacientes et throni et effusio sapientiae, manifestatio deiformis ipsorum habituum.*

RESPONDEO dicendum quod quidam posuerunt in angelis non esse habitus; sed quaecumque dicuntur de eis, essentialiter dicuntur. Unde Maximus, post praedicta verba quae induximus, dicit, *habitudines earum, atque virtutes quae in eis sunt, essentiales sunt, propter immaterialitatem.* Et hoc etiam Simplicius dicit, in commento praedicamentorum, *sapientia quae est in anima, habitus est, quae autem in intellectu, substantia. Omnia enim quae sunt divina, et per se sufficientia sunt, et in seipsis existentia.* Quae quidem positio partim habet veritatem, et partim continet falsitatem. Manifestum est enim ex praemissis quod subiectum habitus non est nisi ens in potentia. Considerantes igitur praedicti commentatores quod angeli sunt substantiae immateriales, et quod non est in illis potentia materiae; secundum hoc, ab eis habitum excluserunt, et omne accidens. Sed quia, licet in angelis non sit potentia materiae, est tamen in eis aliqua potentia (esse enim actum purum est proprium Dei); ideo inquantum invenitur in eis de potentia, intantum in eis possunt habitus inveniri. Sed quia potentia materiae et potentia intellectualis substantiae non est unius rationis, ideo per consequens nec habitus unius rationis est utrobique. Unde Simplicius dicit, in commento praedicamentorum, quod *habitus intellectualis substantiae non sunt similes his qui sunt hic habitibus; sed magis sunt similes simplicibus et immaterialibus speciebus quas continet in seipsa.* Circa huiusmodi tamen habitum aliter se habet intellectus angelicus, et aliter intellectus humanus. Intellectus enim humanus, cum sit infimus in ordine intellectuum, est in potentia respectu omnium intelligibilium, sicut materia prima respectu omnium formarum sensibilium, et ideo ad

Objection 3: Further, habit is a disposition (Metaph. v, text. 25). But disposition, as is said in the same book, is "the order of that which has parts." Since, therefore, angels are simple substances, it seems that there are no dispositions and habits in them.

On the contrary, Dionysius says (Coel. Hier. vii) that the angels are of the first hierarchy are called: "Fire-bearers and Thrones and Outpouring of Wisdom, by which is indicated the godlike nature of their habits."

I answer that, Some have thought that there are no habits in the angels, and that whatever is said of them, is said essentially. Whence Maximus, after the words which we have quoted, says: "Their dispositions, and the powers which are in them, are essential, through the absence of matter in them." And Simplicius says the same in his Commentary on the Predicaments: "Wisdom which is in the soul is its habit: but that which is in the intellect, is its substance. For everything divine is sufficient of itself, and exists in itself." Now this opinion contains some truth, and some error. For it is manifest from what we have said (I-II, q. 49, a. 4) that only a being in potentiality is the subject of habit. So the above-mentioned commentators considered that angels are immaterial substances, and that there is no material potentiality in them, and on that account, excluded from them habit and any kind of accident. Yet since though there is no material potentiality in angels, there is still some potentiality in them (for to be pure act belongs to God alone), therefore, as far as potentiality is found to be in them, so far may habits be found in them. But because the potentiality of matter and the potentiality of intellectual substance are not of the same kind. Whence, Simplicius says in his Commentary on the Predicaments that: "The habits of the intellectual substance are not like the habits here below, but rather are they like simple and immaterial images which it contains in itself." However, the angelic intellect and the human intellect differ with regard to this habit. For the human intellect, being the lowest in the intellectual order, is in potentiality as regards all intelligible things, just as primal matter is in respect of all sensible forms; and therefore for

omnia intelligenda indiget aliquo habitu. Sed intellectus angelicus non se habet sicut pura potentia in genere intelligibilium, sed sicut actus quidam, non autem sicut actus purus (hoc enim solius Dei est), sed cum permixtione alicuius potentiae, et tanto minus habet de potentialitate, quanto est superior. Et ideo, ut in primo dictum est, inquantum est in potentia, indiget perfici habitualiter per aliquas species intelligibiles ad operationem propriam, sed inquantum est actu, per essentiam suam potest aliqua intelligere, ad minus seipsum, et alia secundum modum suae substantiae, ut dicitur in Lib. de causis, et tanto perfectius, quanto est perfectior. Sed quia nullus angelus pertingit ad perfectionem Dei, sed in infinitum distat; propter hoc, ad attingendum ad ipsum Deum per intellectum et voluntatem, indigent aliquibus habitibus, tanquam in potentia existentes respectu illius puri actus. Unde Dionysius dicit habitus eorum esse *deiformes,* quibus scilicet Deo conformantur. Habitus autem qui sunt dispositiones ad esse naturale, non sunt in angelis, cum sint immateriales.

the understanding of all things, it needs some habit. But the angelic intellect is not as a pure potentiality in the order of intelligible things, but as an act; not indeed as pure act (for this belongs to God alone), but with an admixture of some potentiality: and the higher it is, the less potentiality it has. And therefore, as we said in the I, q. 55, a. 1, so far as it is in potentiality, so far is it in need of habitual perfection by means of intelligible species in regard to its proper operation: but so far as it is in act, through its own essence it can understand some things, at least itself, and other things according to the mode of its substance, as stated in De Causis: and the more perfect it is, the more perfectly will it understand. But since no angel attains to the perfection of God, but all are infinitely distant therefrom; for this reason, in order to attain to God Himself, through intellect and will, the angels need some habits, being as it were in potentiality in regard to that Pure Act. Wherefore Dionysius says (Coel. Hier. vii) that their habits are "godlike," that is to say, that by them they are made like to God. But those habits that are dispositions to the natural being are not in angels, since they are immaterial.

AD PRIMUM ergo dicendum quod verbum maximi intelligendum est de habitibus et accidentibus materialibus.

AD SECUNDUM dicendum quod quantum ad hoc quod convenit angelis per suam essentiam, non indigent habitu. Sed quia non ita sunt per seipsos entes, quin participent sapientiam et bonitatem divinam; ideo inquantum indigent participare aliquid ab exteriori, intantum necesse est in eis ponere habitus.

AD TERTIUM dicendum quod in angelis non sunt partes essentiae, sed sunt partes secundum potentiam, inquantum intellectus eorum per plures species perficitur, et voluntas eorum se habet ad plura.

Reply to Objection 1: This saying of Maximus must be understood of material habits and accidents.

Reply to Objection 2: As to that which belongs to angels by their essence, they do not need a habit. But as they are not so far beings of themselves, as not to partake of Divine wisdom and goodness, therefore, so far as they need to partake of something from without, so far do they need to have habits.

Reply to Objection 3: In angels there are no essential parts: but there are potential parts, in so far as their intellect is perfected by several species, and in so far as their will has a relation to several things.

Quaestio LI

Deinde considerandum est de causa habituum. Et primo, quantum ad generationem ipsorum; secundo, quantum ad augmentum; tertio, quantum ad diminutionem et corruptionem. Circa primum quaeruntur quatuor. *Primo,* utrum aliquis habitus sit a natura. *Secundo,* utrum aliquis habitus ex actibus causetur. *Tertio,* utrum per unum actum possit generari habitus. *Quarto,* utrum aliqui habitus sint in hominibus infusi a Deo.

Articulus 1

Ad primum sic proceditur. Videtur quod nullus habitus sit a natura. Eorum enim quae sunt a natura, usus non subiacet voluntati. Sed habitus *est quo quis utitur cum voluerit,* ut dicit Commentator, in III de anima. Ergo habitus non est a natura.

Praeterea, natura non facit per duo quod per unum potest facere. Sed potentiae animae sunt a natura. Si igitur habitus potentiarum a natura essent, habitus et potentia essent unum.

Praeterea, natura non deficit in necessariis. Sed habitus sunt necessarii ad bene operandum, ut supra dictum est. Si igitur habitus aliqui essent a natura, videtur quod natura non deficeret quin omnes habitus necessarios causaret. Patet autem hoc esse falsum. Ergo habitus non sunt a natura.

Sed contra est quod in VI Ethic., inter alios habitus ponitur intellectus principiorum, qui est a natura, unde et principia prima dicuntur naturaliter cognita.

Respondeo dicendum quod aliquid potest esse naturale alicui dupliciter. Uno modo, secundum naturam speciei, sicut naturale est homini esse risibile, et igni ferri sursum. Alio modo, secundum naturam individui, sicut naturale est Socrati vel Platoni esse aegrotativum vel sanativum, secundum propriam complexionem. Rursus, secundum utramque naturam potest dici aliquid naturale dupliciter, uno modo, quia totum est a natura; alio modo, quia secundum aliquid est a natura, et secundum aliquid est ab

Question 51
Of the Cause of Habits, as to Their Formation

We must next consider the cause of habits: and firstly, as to their formation; secondly, as to their increase; thirdly, as to their diminution and corruption. Under the first head there are four points of inquiry: 1. Whether any habit is from nature? 2. Whether any habit is caused by acts? 3. Whether any habit can be caused by one act? 4. Whether any habits are infused in man by God?

Article 1
Whether any habit is from nature?

Objection 1: It would seem that no habit is from nature. For the use of those things which are from nature does not depend on the will. But habit "is that which we use when we will," as the Commentator says on De Anima iii. Therefore habit is not from nature.

Objection 2: Further, nature does not employ two where one is sufficient. But the powers of the soul are from nature. If therefore the habits of the powers were from nature, habit and power would be one.

Objection 3: Further, nature does not fail in necessaries. But habits are necessary in order to act well, as we have stated above (I-II, q. 49, a. 4). If therefore any habits were from nature, it seems that nature would not fail to cause all necessary habits: but this is clearly false. Therefore habits are not from nature.

On the contrary, In Ethic. vi, 6, among other habits, place is given to understanding of first principles, which habit is from nature: wherefore also first principles are said to be known naturally.

I answer that, One thing can be natural to another in two ways. First in respect of the specific nature, as the faculty of laughing is natural to man, and it is natural to fire to have an upward tendency. Secondly, in respect of the individual nature, as it is natural to Socrates or Plato to be prone to sickness or inclined to health, in accordance with their respective temperaments. Again, in respect of both natures, something may be called natural in two ways: first, because it entirely is from the nature; secondly, because it is partly from nature, and partly from an

exteriori principio. Sicut cum aliquis sanatur per seipsum, tota sanitas est a natura, cum autem aliquis sanatur auxilio medicinae, sanitas partim est a natura, partim ab exteriori principio. Sic igitur si loquamur de habitu secundum quod est dispositio subiecti in ordine ad formam vel naturam, quolibet praedictorum modorum contingit habitum esse naturalem. Est enim aliqua dispositio naturalis quae debetur humanae speciei, extra quam nullus homo invenitur. Et haec est naturalis secundum naturam speciei. Sed quia talis dispositio quandam latitudinem habet, contingit diversos gradus huiusmodi dispositionis convenire diversis hominibus secundum naturam individui. Et huiusmodi dispositio potest esse vel totaliter a natura, vel partim a natura et partim ab exteriori principio, sicut dictum est de his qui sanantur per artem. Sed habitus qui est dispositio ad operationem, cuius subiectum est potentia animae, ut dictum est, potest quidem esse naturalis et secundum naturam speciei, et secundum naturam individui. Secundum quidem naturam speciei, secundum quod se tenet ex parte ipsius animae, quae, cum sit forma corporis, est principium specificum. Secundum autem naturam individui, ex parte corporis, quod est materiale principium. Sed tamen neutro modo contingit in hominibus esse habitus naturales ita quod sint totaliter a natura. In angelis siquidem contingit, eo quod habent species intelligibiles naturaliter inditas, quod non competit animae humanae, ut in primo dictum est. Sunt ergo in hominibus aliqui habitus naturales, tanquam partim a natura existentes et partim ab exteriori principio; aliter quidem in apprehensivis potentiis, et aliter in appetitivis. In apprehensivis enim potentiis potest esse habitus naturalis secundum inchoationem, et secundum naturam speciei, et secundum naturam individui. Secundum quidem naturam speciei, ex parte ipsius animae, sicut intellectus principiorum dicitur esse habitus naturalis. Ex ipsa enim natura animae intellectualis, convenit homini quod statim, cognito quid est

extrinsic principle. For instance, when a man is healed by himself, his health is entirely from nature; but when a man is healed by means of medicine, health is partly from nature, partly from an extrinsic principle. Thus, then, if we speak of habit as a disposition of the subject in relation to form or nature, it may be natural in either of the foregoing ways. For there is a certain natural disposition demanded by the human species, so that no man can be without it. And this disposition is natural in respect of the specific nature. But since such a disposition has a certain latitude, it happens that different grades of this disposition are becoming to different men in respect of the individual nature. And this disposition may be either entirely from nature, or partly from nature, and partly from an extrinsic principle, as we have said of those who are healed by means of art. But the habit which is a disposition to operation, and whose subject is a power of the soul, as stated above (I-II, q. 50, a. 2), may be natural whether in respect of the specific nature or in respect of the individual nature: in respect of the specific nature, on the part of the soul itself, which, since it is the form of the body, is the specific principle; but in respect of the individual nature, on the part of the body, which is the material principle. Yet in neither way does it happen that there are natural habits in man, so that they be entirely from nature. In the angels, indeed, this does happen, since they have intelligible species naturally impressed on them, which cannot be said of the human soul, as we have said in the I, q. 55, a. 2; q. 84, a. 3. There are, therefore, in man certain natural habits, owing their existence, partly to nature, and partly to some extrinsic principle: in one way, indeed, in the apprehensive powers; in another way, in the appetitive powers. For in the apprehensive powers there may be a natural habit by way of a beginning, both in respect of the specific nature, and in respect of the individual nature. This happens with regard to the specific nature, on the part of the soul itself: thus the understanding of first principles is called a natural habit. For it is owing to the very nature of the intellectual soul that man, having once grasped what is a whole and what is a

totum et quid est pars, cognoscat quod omne totum est maius sua parte, et simile est in ceteris. Sed quid sit totum, et quid sit pars, cognoscere non potest nisi per species intelligibiles a phantasmatibus acceptas. Et propter hoc philosophus, in fine posteriorum, ostendit quod cognitio principiorum provenit nobis ex sensu. Secundum vero naturam individui, est aliquis habitus cognoscitivus secundum inchoationem naturalis, inquantum unus homo, ex dispositione organorum, est magis aptus ad bene intelligendum quam alius, inquantum ad operationem intellectus indigemus virtutibus sensitivis. In appetitivis autem potentiis non est aliquis habitus naturalis secundum inchoationem, ex parte ipsius animae, quantum ad ipsam substantiam habitus, sed solum quantum ad principia quaedam ipsius, sicut principia iuris communis dicuntur esse *seminalia virtutum*. Et hoc ideo, quia inclinatio ad obiecta propria, quae videtur esse inchoatio habitus, non pertinet ad habitum, sed magis pertinet ad ipsam rationem potentiarum. Sed ex parte corporis, secundum naturam individui, sunt aliqui habitus appetitivi secundum inchoationes naturales. Sunt enim quidam dispositi ex propria corporis complexione ad castitatem vel mansuetudinem, vel ad aliquid huiusmodi.

AD PRIMUM ergo dicendum quod obiectio illa procedit de natura secundum quod dividitur contra rationem et voluntatem, cum tamen ipsa ratio et voluntas ad naturam hominis pertineant.

AD SECUNDUM dicendum quod aliquid etiam naturaliter potest superaddi potentiae, quod tamen ad ipsam potentiam pertinere non potest. Sicut in angelis non potest pertinere ad ipsam potentiam intellectivam quod sit per se cognoscitiva omnium, quia oporteret quod esset actus omnium, quod solius Dei est. Id enim quo aliquid cognoscitur, oportet esse actualem similitudinem eius quod cognoscitur, unde sequeretur, si potentia angeli per seipsam cognosceret omnia, quod esset similitudo et actus omnium. Unde oportet quod superaddantur potentiae intellectivae ipsius aliquae species intelligibiles, quae sunt similitudines rerum intellectarum, quia per participationem

part, should at once perceive that every whole is larger than its part: and in like manner with regard to other such principles. Yet what is a whole, and what is a part—this he cannot know except through the intelligible species which he has received from phantasms: and for this reason, the Philosopher at the end of the Posterior Analytics shows that knowledge of principles comes to us from the senses. But in respect of the individual nature, a habit of knowledge is natural as to its beginning, in so far as one man, from the disposition of his organs of sense, is more apt than another to understand well, since we need the sensitive powers for the operation of the intellect. In the appetitive powers, however, no habit is natural in its beginning, on the part of the soul itself, as to the substance of the habit; but only as to certain principles thereof, as, for instance, the principles of common law are called the "seeds of virtue." The reason of this is because the inclination to its proper objects, which seems to be the beginning of a habit, does not belong to the habit, but rather to the very nature of the powers. But on the part of the body, in respect of the individual nature, there are some appetitive habits by way of natural beginnings. For some are disposed from their own bodily temperament to chastity or meekness or such like.

Reply to Objection 1: This objection takes nature as divided against reason and will; whereas reason itself and will belong to the nature of man.

Reply to Objection 2: Something may be added even naturally to the nature of a power, while it cannot belong to the power itself. For instance, with regard to the angels, it cannot belong to the intellective power itself capable of knowing all things: for thus it would have to be the act of all things, which belongs to God alone. Because that by which something is known, must needs be the actual likeness of the thing known: whence it would follow, if the power of the angel knew all things by itself, that it was the likeness and act of all things. Wherefore there must needs be added to the angels' intellective power, some intelligible species, which are likenesses of things understood: for it is by participation

divinae sapientiae, et non per essentiam propriam, possunt intellectus eorum esse actu ea quae intelligunt. Et sic patet quod non omne id quod pertinet ad habitum naturalem, potest ad potentiam pertinere.

AD TERTIUM dicendum quod natura non aequaliter se habet ad causandas omnes diversitates habituum, quia quidam possunt causari a natura, quidam non, ut supra dictum est. Et ideo non sequitur, si aliqui habitus sint naturales, quod omnes sint naturales.

Articulus 2

AD SECUNDUM sic proceditur. Videtur quod nullus habitus possit ex actu causari. Habitus enim est qualitas quaedam, ut supra dictum est. Omnis autem qualitas causatur in aliquo subiecto, inquantum est alicuius receptivum. Cum igitur agens ex hoc quod agit, non recipiat aliquid, sed magis ex se emittat; videtur quod non possit aliquis habitus in agente ex propriis actibus generari.

PRAETEREA, illud in quo causatur aliqua qualitas, movetur ad qualitatem illam, sicut patet in re calefacta vel infrigidata, quod autem producit actum causantem qualitatem, movet, ut patet de calefaciente vel infrigidante. Si igitur in aliquo causaretur habitus per actum sui ipsius, sequeretur quod idem esset movens et motum, agens et patiens. Quod est impossibile, ut dicitur in VII Physic.

PRAETEREA, effectus non potest esse nobilior sua causa. Sed habitus est nobilior quam actus praecedens habitum, quod patet ex hoc, quod nobiliores actus reddit. Ergo habitus non potest causari ab actu praecedente habitum.

SED CONTRA est quod philosophus, in II Ethic., docet habitus virtutum et vitiorum ex actibus causari.

RESPONDEO dicendum quod in agente quandoque est solum activum principium sui actus, sicut in igne est solum principium activum calefaciendi. Et in tali agente non potest aliquis habitus causari ex proprio actu, et inde est quod res naturales non possunt aliquid consuescere vel dissuescere, ut dicitur in II Ethic. Invenitur autem aliquod agens in quo est principium activum et

of the Divine wisdom and not by their own essence, that their intellect can be actually those things which they understand. And so it is clear that not everything belonging to a natural habit can belong to the power.

Reply to Objection 3: Nature is not equally inclined to cause all the various kinds of habits: since some can be caused by nature, and some not, as we have said above. And so it does not follow that because some habits are natural, therefore all are natural.

Article 2
Whether any habit is caused by acts?

Objection 1: It would seem that no habit is caused by acts. For habit is a quality, as we have said above (I-II, q. 49, a. 1). Now every quality is caused in a subject, according to the latter's receptivity. Since then the agent, inasmuch as it acts, does not receive but rather gives: it seems impossible for a habit to be caused in an agent by its own acts.

Objection 2: Further, the thing wherein a quality is caused is moved to that quality, as may be clearly seen in that which is heated or cooled: whereas that which produces the act that causes the quality, moves, as may be seen in that which heats or cools. If therefore habits were caused in anything by its own act, it would follow that the same would be mover and moved, active and passive: which is impossible, as stated in Physics iii, 8.

Objection 3: Further, the effect cannot be more noble than its cause. But habit is more noble than the act which precedes the habit; as is clear from the fact that the latter produces more noble acts. Therefore habit cannot be caused by an act which precedes the habit.

On the contrary, The Philosopher (Ethic. ii, 1, 2) teaches that habits of virtue and vice are caused by acts.

I answer that, In the agent there is sometimes only the active principle of its act: for instance in fire there is only the active principle of heating. And in such an agent a habit cannot be caused by its own act: for which reason natural things cannot become accustomed or unaccustomed, as is stated in Ethic. ii, 1. But a certain agent is to be found, in which there is both the active and

passivum sui actus, sicut patet in actibus humanis. Nam actus appetitivae virtutis procedunt a vi appetitiva secundum quod movetur a vi apprehensiva repraesentante obiectum, et ulterius vis intellectiva, secundum quod ratiocinatur de conclusionibus, habet sicut principium activum propositionem per se notam. Unde ex talibus actibus possunt in agentibus aliqui habitus causari, non quidem quantum ad primum activum principium, sed quantum ad principium actus quod movet motum. Nam omne quod patitur et movetur ab alio, disponitur per actum agentis, unde ex multiplicatis actibus generatur quaedam qualitas in potentia passiva et mota, quae nominatur habitus. Sicut habitus virtutum moralium causantur in appetitivis potentiis, secundum quod moventur a ratione, et habitus scientiarum causantur in intellectu, secundum quod movetur a primis propositionibus.

AD PRIMUM ergo dicendum quod agens, inquantum est agens, non recipit aliquid. Sed inquantum agit motum ab alio, sic recipit aliquid a movente, et sic causatur habitus.

AD SECUNDUM dicendum quod idem, secundum idem, non potest esse movens et motum. Nihil autem prohibet idem a seipso moveri secundum diversa, ut in VIII Physic. probatur.

AD TERTIUM dicendum quod actus praecedens habitum inquantum procedit a principio activo, procedit a nobiliori principio quam sit habitus generatus, sicut ipsa ratio est nobilius principium quam sit habitus virtutis moralis in vi appetitiva per actuum consuetudines generatus; et intellectus principiorum est nobilius principium quam scientia conclusionum.

the passive principle of its act, as we see in human acts. For the acts of the appetitive power proceed from that same power according as it is moved by the apprehensive power presenting the object: and further, the intellective power, according as it reasons about conclusions, has, as it were, an active principle in a self-evident proposition. Wherefore by such acts habits can be caused in their agents; not indeed with regard to the first active principle, but with regard to that principle of the act, which principle is a mover moved. For everything that is passive and moved by another, is disposed by the action of the agent; wherefore if the acts be multiplied a certain quality is formed in the power which is passive and moved, which quality is called a habit: just as the habits of moral virtue are caused in the appetitive powers, according as they are moved by the reason, and as the habits of science are caused in the intellect, according as it is moved by first propositions.

Reply to Objection 1: The agent, as agent, does not receive anything. But in so far as it moves through being moved by another, it receives something from that which moves it: and thus is a habit caused.

Reply to Objection 2: The same thing, and in the same respect, cannot be mover and moved; but nothing prevents a thing from being moved by itself as to different respects, as is proved in Physics viii, text. 28, 29.

Reply to Objection 3: The act which precedes the habit, in so far as it comes from an active principle, proceeds from a more excellent principle than is the habit caused thereby: just as the reason is a more excellent principle than the habit of moral virtue produced in the appetitive power by repeated acts, and as the understanding of first principles is a more excellent principle than the science of conclusions.

Articulus 3

AD TERTIUM sic proceditur. Videtur quod per unum actum possit habitus generari. Demonstratio enim actus rationis est. Sed per unam demonstrationem causatur scientia quae est habitus conclusionis unius. Ergo habitus potest causari ex uno actu.

PRAETEREA, sicut contingit actus crescere per multiplicationem, ita contingit actum crescere per intensionem. Sed multiplicatis actibus, generatur habitus. Ergo etiam si multum intendatur unus actus, poterit esse causa generativa habitus.

PRAETEREA, sanitas et aegritudo sunt habitus quidam. Sed ex uno actu contingit hominem vel sanari vel infirmari. Ergo unus actus potest habitum causare.

SED CONTRA est quod philosophus dicit, in I Ethic., quod *una hirundo ver non facit, nec una dies, ita utique nec beatum nec felicem una dies, nec paucum tempus.* Sed *beatitudo est operatio secundum habitum perfectae virtutis,* ut dicitur in I Ethic. Ergo habitus virtutis, et eadem ratione alius habitus, non causatur per unum actum.

RESPONDEO dicendum quod, sicut iam dictum est, habitus per actum generatur inquantum potentia passiva movetur ab aliquo principio activo. Ad hoc autem quod aliqua qualitas causetur in passivo, oportet quod activum totaliter vincat passivum. Unde videmus quod, quia ignis non potest statim vincere suum combustibile, non statim inflammat ipsum, sed paulatim abiicit contrarias dispositiones, ut sic totaliter vincens ipsum, similitudinem suam ipsi imprimat. Manifestum est autem quod principium activum quod est ratio, non totaliter potest supervincere appetitivam potentiam in uno actu, eo quod appetitiva potentia se habet diversimode et ad multa; iudicatur autem per rationem, in uno actu, aliquid appetendum secundum determinatas rationes et circumstantias. Unde ex hoc non totaliter vincitur appetitiva potentia, ut feratur in idem ut in pluribus, per modum naturae, quod pertinet ad habitum virtutis. Et ideo habitus virtutis non potest causari per unum actum, sed per multos. In apprehensivis

Article 3
Whether a habit can be caused by one act?

Objection 1: It would seem that a habit can be caused by one act. For demonstration is an act of reason. But science, which is the habit of one conclusion, is caused by one demonstration. Therefore habit can be caused by one act.

Objection 2: Further, as acts happen to increase by multiplication so do they happen to increase by intensity. But a habit is caused by multiplication of acts. Therefore also if an act be very intense, it can be the generating cause of a habit.

Objection 3: Further, health and sickness are habits. But it happens that a man is healed or becomes ill, by one act. Therefore one act can cause a habit.

On the contrary, The Philosopher says (Ethic. i, 7): "As neither does one swallow nor one day make spring: so neither does one day nor a short time make a man blessed and happy." But "happiness is an operation in respect of a habit of perfect virtue" (Ethic. i, 7, 10, 13). Therefore a habit of virtue, and for the same reason, other habits, is not caused by one act.

I answer that, As we have said already (I-II, q. 51, a. 2), habit is caused by act, because a passive power is moved by an active principle. But in order that some quality be caused in that which is passive the active principle must entirely overcome the passive. Whence we see that because fire cannot at once overcome the combustible, it does not enkindle at once; but it gradually expels contrary dispositions, so that by overcoming it entirely, it may impress its likeness on it. Now it is clear that the active principle which is reason, cannot entirely overcome the appetitive power in one act: because the appetitive power is inclined variously, and to many things; while the reason judges in a single act, what should be willed in regard to various aspects and circumstances. Wherefore the appetitive power is not thereby entirely overcome, so as to be inclined like nature to the same thing, in the majority of cases; which inclination belongs to the habit of virtue. Therefore a habit of virtue cannot be caused by one act, but only by many. But in the apprehensive

autem potentiis considerandum est quod duplex est passivum, unum quidem ipse intellectus possibilis; aliud autem intellectus quem vocat Aristoteles *passivum,* qui est *ratio particularis,* idest vis cogitativa cum memorativa et imaginativa. Respectu igitur primi passivi, potest esse aliquod activum quod uno actu totaliter vincit potentiam sui passivi, sicut una propositio per se nota convincit intellectum ad assentiendum firmiter conclusioni; quod quidem non facit propositio probabilis. Unde ex multis actibus rationis oportet causari habitum opinativum, etiam ex parte intellectus possibilis, habitum autem scientiae possibile est causari ex uno rationis actu, quantum ad intellectum possibilem. Sed quantum ad inferiores vires apprehensivas, necessarium est eosdem actus pluries reiterari, ut aliquid firmiter memoriae imprimatur. Unde philosophus, in libro de memoria et reminiscentia, dicit quod *meditatio confirmat memoriam.* Habitus autem corporales possibile est causari ex uno actu, si activum fuerit magnae virtutis, sicut quandoque medicina fortis statim inducit sanitatem.

powers, we must observe that there are two passive principles: one is the possible* intellect itself; the other is the intellect which Aristotle (De Anima iii, text. 20) calls "passive," and is the "particular reason," that is the cogitative power, with memory and imagination. With regard then to the former passive principle, it is possible for a certain active principle to entirely overcome, by one act, the power of its passive principle: thus one self-evident proposition convinces the intellect, so that it gives a firm assent to the conclusion, but a probable proposition cannot do this. Wherefore a habit of opinion needs to be caused by many acts of the reason, even on the part of the possible intellect: whereas a habit of science can be caused by a single act of the reason, so far as the possible intellect is concerned. But with regard to the lower apprehensive powers, the same acts need to be repeated many times for anything to be firmly impressed on the memory. And so the Philosopher says (De Memor. et Remin. 1) that "meditation strengthens memory." Bodily habits, however, can be caused by one act, if the active principle is of great power: sometimes, for instance, a strong dose of medicine restores health at once.

Et per hoc patet responsio ad obiecta.

Hence the solutions to the objections are clear.

Articulus 4

Ad quartum sic proceditur. Videtur quod nullus habitus hominibus infundatur a Deo. Deus enim aequaliter se habet ad omnes. Si igitur quibusdam infundit habitus aliquos, omnibus eos infunderet. Quod patet esse falsum.

Praeterea, Deus operatur in omnibus secundum modum qui convenit naturae ipsorum, quia *divinae providentiae est naturam salvare,* ut dicit Dionysius, IV cap. de Div. Nom. Sed habitus in homine naturaliter causantur ex actibus, ut dictum est. Non ergo causat Deus in hominibus aliquos habitus absque actibus.

Article 4
Whether any habits are infused in man by God?

Objection 1: It would seem that no habit is infused in man by God. For God treats all equally. If therefore He infuses habits into some, He would infuse them into all: which is clearly untrue.

Objection 2: Further, God works in all things according to the mode which is suitable to their nature: for "it belongs to Divine providence to preserve nature," as Dionysius says (Div. Nom. iv). But habits are naturally caused in man by acts, as we have said above (I-II, q. 51, a. 4). Therefore God does not cause habits to be in man except by acts.

---

* See I, q. 79, a. 2, ad 2

Praeterea, si aliquis habitus a Deo infunditur, per illum habitum homo potest multos actus producere. Sed *ex illis actibus causatur similis habitus,* ut in II Ethic. dicitur. Sequitur ergo duos habitus eiusdem speciei esse in eodem, unum acquisitum, et alterum infusum. Quod videtur esse impossibile, non enim duae formae unius speciei possunt esse in eodem subiecto. Non ergo habitus aliquis infunditur homini a Deo.

Sed contra est quod dicitur Eccli. XV, *implevit eum dominus spiritu sapientiae et intellectus.* Sed sapientia et intellectus quidam habitus sunt. Ergo aliqui habitus homini a Deo infunduntur.

Respondeo dicendum quod duplici ratione aliqui habitus homini a Deo infunduntur. Prima ratio est, quia aliqui habitus sunt quibus homo bene disponitur ad finem excedentem facultatem humanae naturae, qui est ultima et perfecta hominis beatitudo, ut supra dictum est. Et quia habitus oportet esse proportionatos ei ad quod homo disponitur secundum ipsos, ideo necesse est quod etiam habitus ad huiusmodi finem disponentes, excedant facultatem humanae naturae. Unde tales habitus nunquam possunt homini inesse nisi ex infusione divina, sicut est de omnibus gratuitis virtutibus. Alia ratio est, quia Deus potest producere effectus causarum secundarum absque ipsis causis secundis, ut in primo dictum est. Sicut igitur quandoque, ad ostensionem suae virtutis, producit sanitatem absque naturali causa, quae tamen per naturam posset causari; ita etiam quandoque, ad ostendendam suam virtutem, infundit homini illos etiam habitus qui naturali virtute possunt causari. Sicut apostolis dedit scientiam Scripturarum et omnium linguarum, quam homines per studium vel consuetudinem acquirere possunt, licet non ita perfecte.

Ad primum ergo dicendum quod Deus, quantum ad suam naturam, aequaliter se habet ad omnes, sed secundum ordinem suae sapientiae certa ratione quaedam tribuit aliquibus, quae non tribuit aliis.

Ad secundum dicendum quod hoc quod Deus in omnibus operatur secundum modum eorum, non excludit quin Deus quaedam operetur quae natura operari non potest, sed

Objection 3: Further, if any habit be infused into man by God, man can by that habit perform many acts. But "from those acts a like habit is caused" (Ethic. ii, 1, 2). Consequently there will be two habits of the same species in the same man, one acquired, the other infused. Now this seems impossible: for the two forms of the same species cannot be in the same subject. Therefore a habit is not infused into man by God.

On the contrary, it is written (Ecclus. 15:5): "God filled him with the spirit of wisdom and understanding." Now wisdom and understanding are habits. Therefore some habits are infused into man by God.

I answer that, Some habits are infused by God into man, for two reasons. The first reason is because there are some habits by which man is disposed to an end which exceeds the proportion of human nature, namely, the ultimate and perfect happiness of man, as stated above (I-II, q. 5, a. 5). And since habits need to be in proportion with that to which man is disposed by them, therefore is it necessary that those habits, which dispose to this end, exceed the proportion of human nature. Wherefore such habits can never be in man except by Divine infusion, as is the case with all gratuitous virtues. The other reason is, because God can produce the effects of second causes, without these second causes, as we have said in the I, q. 105, a. 6. Just as, therefore, sometimes, in order to show His power, He causes health, without its natural cause, but which nature could have caused, so also, at times, for the manifestation of His power, He infuses into man even those habits which can be caused by a natural power. Thus He gave to the apostles the science of the Scriptures and of all tongues, which men can acquire by study or by custom, but not so perfectly.

Reply to Objection 1: God, in respect of His Nature, is the same to all, but in respect of the order of His Wisdom, for some fixed motive, gives certain things to some, which He does not give to others.

Reply to Objection 2: That God works in all according to their mode, does not hinder God from doing what nature cannot do: but

ex hoc sequitur quod nihil operatur contra id quod naturae convenit.

Ad tertium dicendum quod actus qui producuntur ex habitu infuso, non causant aliquem habitum, sed confirmant habitum praeexistentem, sicut medicinalia remedia adhibita homini sano per naturam, non causant aliquam sanitatem, sed sanitatem prius habitam corroborant.

it follows from this that He does nothing contrary to that which is suitable to nature.

Reply to Objection 3: Acts produced by an infused habit, do not cause a habit, but strengthen the already existing habit; just as the remedies of medicine given to a man who is naturally health, do not cause a kind of health, but give new strength to the health he had before.

Quaestio LII

Deinde considerandum est de augmento habituum. Et circa hoc quaeruntur tria. *Primo,* utrum habitus augeantur. *Secundo,* utrum augeantur per additionem. *Tertio,* utrum quilibet actus augeat habitum.

Question 52
Of the Increase of Habits

We have now to consider the increase of habits; under which head there are three points of inquiry: 1. Whether habits increase? 2. Whether they increase by addition? 3. Whether each act increases the habit?

Articulus 1

Ad primum sic proceditur. Videtur quod habitus augeri non possint. Augmentum enim est circa quantitatem, ut dicitur in V Physic. Sed habitus non sunt in genere quantitatis, sed in genere qualitatis. Ergo circa eos augmentum esse non potest.

Praeterea, habitus est perfectio quaedam, ut dicitur in VII Physic. Sed perfectio, cum importet finem et terminum, non videtur posse recipere magis et minus. Ergo habitus augeri non potest.

Praeterea, in his quae recipiunt magis et minus, contingit esse alterationem, alterari enim dicitur quod de minus calido fit magis calidum. Sed in habitibus non est alteratio, ut probatur in VII Physic. Ergo habitus augeri non possunt.

Sed contra est quod fides est quidam habitus, et tamen augetur, unde discipuli domino dicunt, *domine, adauge nobis fidem,* ut habetur Luc. XVII. Ergo habitus augentur.

Respondeo dicendum quod augmentum, sicut et alia ad quantitatem pertinentia, a quantitatibus corporalibus ad res spirituales intelligibiles transfertur; propter connaturalitatem intellectus nostri ad res corporeas, quae sub imaginatione cadunt. Dicitur autem in quantitatibus corporeis aliquid

Article 1
Whether habits increase?

Objection 1: It would seem that habits cannot increase. For increase concerns quantity (Phys. v, text. 18). But habits are not in the genus quantity, but in that of quality. Therefore there can be no increase of habits.

Objection 2: Further, habit is a perfection (Phys. vii, text. 17,18). But since perfection conveys a notion of end and term, it seems that it cannot be more or less. Therefore a habit cannot increase.

Objection 3: Further, those things which can be more or less are subject to alteration: for that which from being less hot becomes more hot, is said to be altered. But in habits there is no alteration, as is proved in Phys. vii, text. 15, 17. Therefore habits cannot increase.

On the contrary, Faith is a habit, and yet it increases: wherefore the disciples said to our Lord (Lk. 17:5): "Lord, increase our faith." Therefore habits increase.

I answer that, Increase, like other things pertaining to quantity, is transferred from bodily quantities to intelligible spiritual things, on account of the natural connection of the intellect with corporeal things, which come under the imagination. Now in corporeal quantities, a thing is said to be

magnum, secundum quod ad debitam perfectionem quantitatis perducitur, unde aliqua quantitas reputatur magna in homine, quae non reputatur magna in elephante. Unde et in formis dicimus aliquid magnum, ex hoc quod est perfectum. Et quia bonum habet rationem perfecti, propter hoc *in his quae non mole magna sunt, idem est esse maius quod melius,* ut Augustinus dicit, in VI de Trin. Perfectio autem formae dupliciter potest considerari, uno modo, secundum ipsam formam; alio modo, secundum quod subiectum participat formam. Inquantum igitur attenditur perfectio formae secundum ipsam formam, sic dicitur ipsa esse *parva* vel *magna;* puta magna vel parva sanitas vel scientia. Inquantum vero attenditur perfectio formae secundum participationem subiecti, dicitur *magis* et *minus;* puta magis vel minus album vel sanum. Non autem ista distinctio procedit secundum hoc, quod forma habeat esse praeter materiam aut subiectum, sed quia alia est consideratio eius secundum rationem speciei suae, et alia secundum quod participatur in subiecto. Secundum hoc igitur, circa intensionem et remissionem habituum et formarum, fuerunt quatuor opiniones apud philosophos, ut Simplicius narrat in commento praedicamentorum. Plotinus enim et alii Platonici ponebant ipsas qualitates et habitus suscipere magis et minus, propter hoc quod materiales erant, et ex hoc habebant indeterminationem quandam, propter materiae infinitatem. Alii vero in contrarium ponebant quod ipsae qualitates et habitus secundum se non recipiebant magis et minus; sed qualia dicuntur magis et minus, secundum diversam participationem; puta quod iustitia non dicatur magis et minus, sed iustum. Et hanc opinionem tangit Aristoteles in praedicamentis. Tertia fuit opinio Stoicorum, media inter has. Posuerunt enim quod aliqui habitus secundum se recipiunt magis et minus, sicuti artes; quidam autem non, sicut virtutes. Quarta opinio fuit quorundam dicentium quod qualitates et formae immateriales non recipiunt magis

great, according as it reaches the perfection of quantity due to it; wherefore a certain quantity is reputed great in man, which is not reputed great in an elephant. And so also in forms, we say a thing is great because it is perfect. And since good has the nature of perfection, therefore "in things which are great, but not in quantity, to be greater is the same as to be better," as Augustine says (De Trin. vi, 8). Now the perfection of a form may be considered in two ways: first, in respect of the form itself: secondly, in respect of the participation of the form by its subject. In so far as we consider the perfections of a form in respect of the form itself, thus the form is said to be "little" or "great": for instance great or little health or science. But in so far as we consider the perfection of a form in respect of the participation thereof by the subject, it is said to be "more" or "less": for instance more or less white or healthy. Now this distinction is not to be understood as implying that the form has a being outside its matter or subject, but that it is one thing to consider the form according to its specific nature, and another to consider it in respect of its participation by a subject. In this way, then, there were four opinions among philosophers concerning intensity and remission of habits and forms, as Simplicius relates in his Commentary on the Predicaments. For Plotinus and the other Platonists held that qualities and habits themselves were susceptible of more or less, for the reason that they were material and so had a certain want of definiteness, on account of the infinity of matter. Others, on the contrary, held that qualities and habits of themselves were not susceptible of more or less; but that the things affected by them [*qualia*] are said to be more or less, in respect of the participation of the subject: that, for instance, justice is not more or less, but the just thing. Aristotle alludes to this opinion in the Predicaments (Categor. vi). The third opinion was that of the Stoics, and lies between the two preceding opinions. For they held that some habits are of themselves susceptible of more and less, for instance, the arts; and that some are not, as the virtues. The fourth opinion was held by some who said that qualities and immaterial forms

et minus, materiales autem recipiunt. Ut igitur huius rei veritas manifestetur, considerandum est quod illud secundum quod sortitur aliquid speciem, oportet esse fixum et stans, et quasi indivisibile, quaecumque enim ad illud attingunt, sub specie continentur; quaecumque autem recedunt ab illo, vel in plus vel in minus, pertinent ad aliam speciem, vel perfectiorem vel imperfectiorem. Unde philosophus dicit, in VIII Metaphys., *quod species rerum sunt sicut numeri, in quibus additio vel diminutio variat speciem.* Si igitur aliqua forma, vel quaecumque res, secundum seipsam vel secundum aliquid sui, sortiatur rationem speciei; necesse est quod, secundum se considerata, habeat determinatam rationem, quae neque in plus excedere, neque in minus deficere possit. Et huiusmodi sunt calor et albedo, et aliae huiusmodi qualitates quae non dicuntur in ordine ad aliud, et multo magis substantia, quae est per se ens. Illa vero quae recipiunt speciem ex aliquo ad quod ordinantur, possunt secundum seipsa diversificari in plus vel in minus, et nihilominus sunt eadem specie, propter unitatem eius ad quod ordinantur, ex quo recipiunt speciem. Sicut motus secundum se est intensior et remissior, et tamen remanet eadem species, propter unitatem termini, ex quo specificatur. Et idem potest considerari in sanitate, nam corpus pertingit ad rationem sanitatis, secundum quod habet dispositionem convenientem naturae animalis, cui possunt dispositiones diversae convenientes esse; unde potest variari dispositio in plus vel in minus, et tamen semper remanet ratio sanitatis. Unde philosophus dicit, in X Ethic., quod *sanitas ipsa recipit magis et minus, non enim eadem est commensuratio in omnibus, neque in uno et eodem semper; sed remissa permanet sanitas usque ad aliquid.* Huiusmodi autem diversae dispositiones vel commensurationes sanitatis se habent secundum excedens et excessum, unde si nomen sanitatis esset impositum soli perfectissimae commensurationi, tunc ipsa sanitas non diceretur maior vel minor. Sic igitur

are not susceptible of more or less, but that material forms are. In order that the truth in this matter be made clear, we must observe that, in respect of which a thing receives its species, must be something fixed and stationary, and as it were indivisible: for whatever attains to that thing, is contained under the species, and whatever recedes from it more or less, belongs to another species, more or less perfect. Wherefore, the Philosopher says (Metaph. viii, text. 10) that species of things are like numbers, in which addition or subtraction changes the species. If, therefore, a form, or anything at all, receives its specific nature in respect of itself, or in respect of something belonging to it, it is necessary that, considered in itself, it be something of a definite nature, which can be neither more nor less. Such are heat, whiteness or other like qualities which are not denominated from a relation to something else: and much more so, substance, which is *per se* being. But those things which receive their species from something to which they are related, can be diversified, in respect of themselves, according to more or less: and nonetheless they remain in the same species, on account of the oneness of that to which they are related, and from which they receive their species. For example, movement is in itself more intense or more remiss: and yet it remains in the same species, on account of the oneness of the term by which it is specified. We may observe the same thing in health; for a body attains to the nature of health, according as it has a disposition suitable to an animal's nature, to which various dispositions may be suitable; which disposition is therefore variable as regards more or less, and withal the nature of health remains. Whence the Philosopher says (Ethic. x, 2, 3): "Health itself may be more or less: for the measure is not the same in all, nor is it always the same in one individual; but down to a certain point it may decrease and still remain health." Now these various dispositions and measures of health are by way of excess and defect: wherefore if the name of health were given to the most perfect measure, then we should not speak of health as greater or less. Thus therefore

patet qualiter aliqua qualitas vel forma possit secundum seipsam augeri vel minui, et qualiter non. Si vero consideremus qualitatem vel formam secundum participationem subiecti, sic etiam inveniuntur quaedam qualitates et formae recipere magis et minus, et quaedam non. Huiusmodi autem diversitatis causam Simplicius assignat ex hoc, quod substantia secundum seipsam non potest recipere magis et minus, quia est ens per se. Et ideo omnis forma quae substantialiter participatur in subiecto, caret intensione et remissione, unde in genere substantiae nihil dicitur secundum magis et minus. Et quia quantitas propinqua est substantiae, et figura etiam consequitur quantitatem; inde est quod neque etiam in istis dicitur aliquid secundum magis aut minus. Unde philosophus dicit, in VII Physic., quod cum aliquid accipit formam et figuram, non dicitur alterari, sed magis fieri. Aliae vero qualitates, quae sunt magis distantes a substantia, et coniunguntur passionibus et actionibus, recipiunt magis et minus secundum participationem subiecti. Potest autem et magis explicari huiusmodi diversitatis ratio. Ut enim dictum est, id a quo aliquid habet speciem, oportet manere fixum et stans in indivisibili. Duobus igitur modis potest contingere quod forma non participatur secundum magis et minus. Uno modo, quia participans habet speciem secundum ipsam. Et inde est quod nulla forma substantialis participatur secundum magis et minus. Et propter hoc philosophus dicit, in VIII Metaphys., quod, *sicut numerus non habet magis neque minus, sic neque substantia quae est secundum speciem,* idest quantum ad participationem formae specificae; sed *si quidem quae cum materia,* idest, secundum materiales dispositiones, *invenitur magis et minus in substantia.* Alio modo potest contingere ex hoc quod ipsa indivisibilitas est de ratione formae, unde oportet quod, si aliquid participet formam illam, quod participet illam secundum rationem indivisibilitatis. Et inde est quod species numeri non dicuntur secundum magis et minus, quia unaquaeque species in eis constituitur per indivisibilem unitatem. Et eadem ratio est de speciebus

it is clear how a quality or form may increase or decrease of itself, and how it cannot. But if we consider a quality or form in respect of its participation by the subject, thus again we find that some qualities and forms are susceptible of more or less, and some not. Now Simplicius assigns the cause of this diversity to the fact that substance in itself cannot be susceptible of more or less, because it is *per se* being. And therefore every form which is participated substantially by its subject, cannot vary in intensity and remission: wherefore in the genus of substance nothing is said to be more or less. And because quantity is nigh to substance, and because shape follows on quantity, therefore is it that neither in these can there be such a thing as more or less. Whence the Philosopher says (Phys. vii, text. 15) that when a thing receives form and shape, it is not said to be altered, but to be made. But other qualities which are further removed from quantity, and are connected with passions and actions, are susceptible of more or less, in respect of their participation by the subject. Now it is possible to explain yet further the reason of this diversity. For, as we have said, that from which a thing receives its species must remain indivisibly fixed and constant in something indivisible. Wherefore in two ways it may happen that a form cannot be participated more or less. First because the participator has its species in respect of that form. And for this reason no substantial form is participated more or less. Wherefore the Philosopher says (Metaph. viii, text. 10) that, "as a number cannot be more or less, so neither can that which is in the species of substance," that is, in respect of its participation of the specific form: "but in so far as substance may be with matter," i.e., in respect of material dis-positions, "more or less are found in substance." Secondly this may happen from the fact that the form is essentially indivisible: wherefore if anything participate that form, it must needs participate it in respect of its indivisibility. For this reason we do not speak of the species of number as varying in respect of more or less; because each species thereof is constituted by an indivisible unity. The same is to be said of the species of

quantitatis continuae quae secundum numeros accipiuntur ut bicubitum et tricubitum; et de relationibus, ut duplum et triplum; et de figuris, ut trigonum et tetragonum. Et hanc rationem ponit Aristoteles in praedicamentis, ubi, assignans rationem quare figurae non recipiunt magis et minus, dicit, *quae quidem enim recipiunt trigoni rationem et circuli, similiter trigona vel circuli sunt,* quia scilicet indivisibilitas est de ipsa eorum ratione, unde **quaecumque participant rationem eorum,** oportet quod indivisibiliter participent. Sic igitur patet quod, cum habitus et dispositiones dicantur secundum ordinem ad aliquid, ut dicitur in VII Physic., dupliciter potest intensio et remissio in habitibus et dispositionibus considerari. Uno modo, secundum se, prout dicitur maior vel minor sanitas; vel maior vel minor scientia, quae ad plura vel pauciora se extendit. Alio modo, secundum participationem subiecti, prout scilicet aequalis scientia vel sanitas magis recipitur in uno quam in alio, secundum diversam aptitudinem vel ex natura vel ex consuetudine. Non enim habitus et dispositio dat speciem subiecto, neque iterum in sui ratione includit indivisibilitatem. Quomodo autem circa virtutes se habeat, infra dicetur.

AD PRIMUM ergo dicendum quod, sicut nomen *magnitudinis* derivatur a quantitatibus corporalibus ad intelligibiles perfectiones formarum; ita etiam et nomen *augmenti,* cuius terminus est magnum.

AD SECUNDUM dicendum quod habitus quidem perfectio est, non tamen talis perfectio quae sit terminus sui subiecti, puta dans ei esse specificum. Neque etiam in sui ratione terminum includit, sicut species numerorum. Unde nihil prohibet quin recipiat magis et minus.

AD TERTIUM dicendum quod alteratio primo quidem est in qualitatibus tertiae speciei. In qualitatibus vero primae speciei potest esse alteratio per posterius, facta enim alteratione secundum calidum et frigidum, sequitur animal alterari secundum sanum et aegrum. Et similiter, facta alteratione secundum

continuous quantity, which are denominated from numbers, as two-cubits-long, three-cubits-long, and of relations of quantity, as double and treble, and of figures of quantity, as triangle and tetragon. This same explanation is given by Aristotle in the Predicaments (Categor. vi), where in explaining why figures are not susceptible of more or less, he says: "Things which are given the nature of a triangle or a circle, are accordingly triangles and circles": to wit, because indivisibility is essential to the notion of such, wherefore whatever participates their nature must participate it in its indivisibility. It is clear, therefore, since we speak of habits and dispositions in respect of a relation to something (Phys. vii, text. 17), that in two ways intensity and remission may be observed in habits and dispositions. First, in respect of the habit itself: thus, for instance, we speak of greater or less health; greater or less science, which extends to more or fewer things. Secondly, in respect of participation by the subject: in so far as equal science or health is participated more in one than in another, according to a diverse aptitude arising either from nature, or from custom. For habit and disposition do not give species to the subject: nor again do they essentially imply indivisibility. We shall say further on (I-II, q. 66, a. 1) how it is with the virtues.

Reply to Objection 1: As the word "great" is taken from corporeal quantities and applied to the intelligible perfections of forms; so also is the word "growth," the term of which is something great.

Reply to Objection 2: Habit is indeed a perfection, but not a perfection which is the term of its subject; for instance, a term giving the subject its specific being. Nor again does the nature of a habit include the notion of term, as do the species of numbers. Wherefore there is nothing to hinder it from being susceptible of more or less.

Reply to Objection 3: Alteration is primarily indeed in the qualities of the third species; but secondarily it may be in the qualities of the first species: for, supposing an alteration as to hot and cold, there follows in an animal an alteration as to health and sickness. In like manner, if an alteration take place in

passiones appetitus sensitivi, vel secundum vires sensitivas apprehensivas, sequitur alteratio secundum scientias et virtutes, ut dicitur in VII Physic.

Articulus 2

Ad secundum sic proceditur. Videtur quod augmentum habituum fiat per additionem. Nomen enim *augmenti*, ut dictum est, a quantitatibus corporalibus transfertur ad formas. Sed in quantitatibus corporalibus non fit augmentum sine additione, unde in I de Generat. dicitur quod *augmentum est praeexistenti magnitudini additamentum*. Ergo et in habitibus non fit augmentum nisi per additionem.

Praeterea, habitus non augetur nisi aliquo agente. Sed omne agens aliquid facit in subiecto patiente, sicut calefaciens facit calorem in ipso calefacto. Ergo non potest esse augmentum nisi aliqua fiat additio.

Praeterea, sicut id quod non est album, est in potentia ad album; ita id quod est minus album, est in potentia ad magis album. Sed id quod non est album, non fit album nisi per adventum albedinis. Ergo id quod est minus album, non fit magis album nisi per aliquam aliam albedinem supervenientem.

Sed contra est quod philosophus dicit, in IV Physic., *ex calido fit magis calidum, nullo facto in materia calido, quod non esset calidum quando erat minus calidum*. Ergo, pari ratione, nec in aliis formis quae augentur, est aliqua additio.

Respondeo dicendum quod huius quaestionis solutio dependet ex praemissa. Dictum est enim supra quod augmentum et diminutio in formis quae intenduntur et remittuntur, accidit uno modo non ex parte ipsius formae secundum se consideratae, sed ex diversa participatione subiecti. Et ideo huiusmodi augmentum habituum et aliarum formarum, non fit per additionem formae ad formam; sed fit per hoc quod subiectum magis vel minus perfecte participat unam et eandem formam. Et sicut per agens quod est actu, fit aliquid actu calidum,

the passions of the sensitive appetite, or the sensitive powers of apprehension, an alteration follows as to science and virtue (Phys. viii, text. 20).

Article 2
Whether habits increases by addition?

Objection 1: It would seem that the increase of habits is by way of addition. For the word "increase," as we have said, is transferred to forms, from corporeal quantities. But in corporeal quantities there is no increase without addition: wherefore (De Gener. i, text. 31) it is said that "increase is an addition to a magnitude already existing." Therefore in habits also there is no increase without addition.

Objection 2: Further, habit is not increased except by means of some agent. But every agent does something in the passive subject: for instance, that which heats, causes heat in that which is heated. Therefore there is no increase without addition.

Objection 3: Further, as that which is not white, is in potentiality to be white: so that which is less white, is in potentiality to be more white. But that which is not white, is not made white except by the addition of whiteness. Therefore that which is less white, is not made more white, except by an added whiteness.

On the contrary, The Philosopher says (Phys. iv, text. 84): "That which is hot is made hotter, without making, in the matter, something hot, that was not hot, when the thing was less hot." Therefore, in like manner, neither is any addition made in other forms when they increase.

I answer that, The solution of this question depends on what we have said above (I-II, q. 52, a. 1). For we said that increase and decrease in forms which are capable of intensity and remissness, happen in one way not on the part of the very form considered in itself, through the diverse participation thereof by the subject. Wherefore such increase of habits and other forms, is not caused by an addition of form to form; but by the subject participating more or less perfectly, one and the same form. And just as, by an agent which is in act, something is made actually hot,

quasi de novo incipiens participare formam, non quod fiat ipsa forma, ut probatur VII Metaphys.; ita per actionem intensam ipsius agentis efficitur magis calidum, tanquam perfectius participans formam, non tanquam formae aliquid addatur. Si enim per additionem intelligeretur huiusmodi augmentum in formis, hoc non posset esse nisi vel ex parte ipsius formae, vel ex parte subiecti. Si autem ex parte ipsius formae, iam dictum est quod talis additio vel subtractio speciem variaret; sicut variatur species coloris, quando de pallido fit album. Si vero huiusmodi additio intelligatur ex parte subiecti, hoc non posset esse nisi vel quia aliqua pars subiecti recipit formam quam prius non habebat, ut si dicatur frigus crescere in homine qui prius frigebat in una parte, quando iam in pluribus partibus friget, vel quia aliquod aliud subiectum additur participans eandem formam, sicut si calidum adiungatur calido, vel album albo. Sed secundum utrumque istorum duorum modorum, non dicitur aliquid magis album vel calidum, sed maius. Sed quia quaedam accidentia augentur secundum seipsa, ut supra dictum est, in quibusdam eorum fieri potest augmentum per additionem. Augetur enim motus per hoc quod ei aliquid additur vel secundum tempus in quo est, vel secundum viam per quam est, et tamen manet eadem species, propter unitatem termini. Augetur etiam nihilominus motus per intensionem, secundum participationem subiecti, inquantum scilicet idem motus potest vel magis vel minus expedite aut prompte fieri. Similiter etiam et scientia potest augeri secundum seipsam per additionem, sicut cum aliquis plures conclusiones geometriae addiscit, augetur in eo habitus eiusdem scientiae secundum speciem. Augetur nihilominus scientia in aliquo, secundum participationem subiecti, per intensionem, prout scilicet expeditius et clarius unus homo se habet alio in eisdem conclusionibus considerandis. In habitibus autem corporalibus non multum videtur fieri augmentum per additionem.

beginning, as it were, to participate a form, not as though the form itself were made, as is proved in Metaph. vii, text. 32, so, by an intense action of the agent, something is made more hot, as it were participating the form more perfectly, not as though something were added to the form. For if this increase in forms were understood to be by way of addition, this could only be either in the form itself or in the subject. If it be understood of the form itself, it has already been stated (I-II, a. 52, a. 1) that such an addition or subtraction would change the species; even as the species of color is changed when a thing from being pale becomes white. If, on the other hand, this addition be understood as applying to the subject, this could only be either because one part of the subject receives a form which it had not previously (thus we may say cold increases in a man who, after being cold in one part of his body, is cold in several parts), or because some other subject is added sharing in the same form (as when a hot thing is added to another, or one white thing to another). But in either of these two ways we have not a more white or a more hot thing, but a greater white or hot thing. Since, however, as stated above (I-II, q. 52, a. 1), certain accidents are of themselves susceptible of more or less, in some of these we may find increase by addition. For movement increases by an addition either to the time it lasts, or to the course it follows: and yet the species remains the same on account of the oneness of the term. Yet movement increases the intensity as to participation in its subject: i.e., in so far as the same movement can be executed more or less speedily or readily. In like manner, science can increase in itself by addition; thus when anyone learns several conclusions of geometry, the same specific habit of science increases in that man. Yet a man's science increases, as to the subject's participation thereof, in intensity, in so far as one man is quicker and readier than another in considering the same conclusions. As to bodily habits, it does not seem very probable that they receive increase by way of addition.

Quia non dicitur animal sanum simpliciter, aut pulchrum, nisi secundum omnes partes suas sit tale. Quod autem ad perfectiorem commensurationem perducatur, hoc contingit secundum transmutationem simplicium qualitatum; quae non augentur nisi secundum intensionem, ex parte subiecti participantis. Quomodo autem se habeat circa virtutes, infra dicetur.

AD PRIMUM ergo dicendum quod etiam in magnitudine corporali contingit dupliciter esse augmentum. Uno modo, per additionem subiecti ad subiectum; sicut est in augmento viventium. Alio modo, per solam intensionem, absque omni additione; sicut est in his quae rarefiunt, ut dicitur in IV Physic.

AD SECUNDUM dicendum quod causa augens habitum, facit quidem semper aliquid in subiecto, non autem novam formam. Sed facit quod subiectum perfectius participet formam praeexistentem, aut quod amplius se extendat.

AD TERTIUM dicendum quod id quod nondum est album, est in potentia ad formam ipsam, tanquam nondum habens formam, et ideo agens causat novam formam in subiecto. Sed id quod est minus calidum aut album, non est in potentia ad formam, cum iam actu formam habeat, sed est in potentia ad perfectum participationis modum. Et hoc consequitur per actionem agentis.

For an animal is not said to be simply healthy or beautiful, unless it be such in all its parts. And if it be brought to a more perfect measure, this is the result of a change in the simple qualities, which are not susceptible of increase save in intensity on the part of the subject partaking of them. How this question affects virtues we shall state further on (I-II, q. 66, a. 1).

Reply to Objection 1: Even in bodily bulk increase is twofold. First, by addition of one subject to another; such is the increase of living things. Secondly, by mere intensity, without any addition at all; such is the case with things subject to rarefaction, as is stated in Phys. iv, text. 63.

Reply to Objection 2: The cause that increases a habit, always effects something in the subject, but not a new form. But it causes the subject to partake more perfectly of a pre-existing form, or it makes the form to extend further.

Reply to Objection 3: What is not already white, is potentially white, as not yet possessing the form of whiteness: hence the agent causes a new form in the subject. But that which is less hot or white, is not in potentiality to those forms, since it has them already actually: but it is in potentiality to a perfect mode of participation; and this it receives through the agent's action.

ARTICULUS 3

AD TERTIUM sic proceditur. Videtur quod quilibet actus augeat habitum. Multiplicata enim causa, multiplicatur effectus. Sed actus sunt causa habituum aliquorum, ut supra dictum est. Ergo habitus augetur, multiplicatis actibus.

PRAETEREA, de similibus idem est iudicium. Sed omnes actus ab eodem habitu procedentes sunt similes, ut dicitur in II Ethic. Ergo, si aliqui actus augeant habitum, quilibet actus augebit ipsum.

PRAETEREA, simile augetur suo simili. Sed quilibet actus est similis habitui a quo procedit. Ergo quilibet actus auget habitum.

ARTICLE 3
Whether every act increases its habit?

Objection 1: It would seem that every act increases its habit. For when the cause is increased the effect is increased. Now acts are causes of habits, as stated above (I-II, q. 51, a. 2). Therefore a habit increases when its acts are multiplied.

Objection 2: Further, of like things a like judgment should be formed. But all the acts proceeding from one and the same habit are alike (Ethic. ii, 1, 2). Therefore if some acts increase a habit, every act should increase it.

Objection 3: Further, like is increased by like. But any act is like the habit whence it proceeds. Therefore every act increases the habit.

I-II, q. 52, a. 2, s. c.

SED CONTRA, idem non est contrariorum causa. Sed, sicut dicitur in II Ethic., aliqui actus ab habitu procedentes diminuunt ipsum; utpote cum negligenter fiunt. Ergo non omnis actus habitum auget.

RESPONDEO dicendum quod *similes actus similes habitus causant,* ut dicitur in II Ethic. Similitudo autem et dissimilitudo non solum attenditur secundum qualitatem eandem vel diversam; sed etiam secundum eundem vel diversum participationis modum. Est enim dissimile non solum nigrum albo, sed etiam minus album magis albo, nam etiam motus fit a minus albo in magis album, tanquam ex opposito in oppositum, ut dicitur in V Physic. Quia vero usus habituum in voluntate hominis consistit, ut ex supradictis patet; sicut contingit quod aliquis habens habitum non utitur illo, vel etiam agit actum contrarium; ita etiam potest contingere quod utitur habitu secundum actum non respondentem proportionaliter intensioni habitus. Si igitur intensio actus proportionaliter aequetur intensioni habitus, vel etiam superexcedat; quilibet actus vel auget habitum, vel disponit ad augmentum ipsius; ut loquamur de augmento habituum ad similitudinem augmenti animalis. Non enim quodlibet alimentum assumptum actu auget animal, sicut nec quaelibet gutta cavat lapidem, sed, multiplicato alimento, tandem fit augmentum. Ita etiam, multiplicatis actibus, crescit habitus. Si vero intensio actus proportionaliter deficiat ab intensione habitus, talis actus non disponit ad augmentum habitus, sed magis ad diminutionem ipsius.

Et per hoc patet responsio ad obiecta.

THE INCREASE OF HABITS

On the contrary, Opposite effects do not result from the same cause. But according to Ethic. ii, 2, some acts lessen the habit whence they proceed, for instance if they be done carelessly. Therefore it is not every act that increases a habit.

I answer that, "Like acts cause like habits" (Ethic. ii, 1, 2). Now things are like or unlike not only in respect of their qualities being the same or various, but also in respect of the same or a different mode of participation. For it is not only black that is unlike white, but also less white is unlike more white, since there is movement from less white to more white, even as from one opposite to another, as stated in Phys. v, text. 52. But since use of habits depends on the will, as was shown above (I-II, q. 50, a. 5); just as one who has a habit may fail to use it or may act contrary to it; so may he happen to use the habit by performing an act that is not in proportion to the intensity of the habit. Accordingly, if the intensity of the act correspond in proportion to the intensity of the habit, or even surpass it, every such act either increases the habit or disposes to an increase thereof, if we may speak of the increase of habits as we do of the increase of an animal. For not every morsel of food actually increases the animal's size as neither does every drop of water hollow out the stone: but the multiplication of food results at last in an increase of the body. So, too, repeated acts cause a habit to grow. If, however, the act falls short of the intensity of the habit, such an act does not dispose to an increase of that habit, but rather to a lessening thereof.

From this it is clear how to solve the objections.

Quaestio LIII

Deinde considerandum est de corruptione et diminutione habituum. Et circa hoc quaeruntur tria. *Primo,* utrum habitus corrumpi possit. *Secundo,* utrum possit diminui. *Tertio,* de modo corruptionis et diminutionis.

Articulus 1

AD PRIMUM sic proceditur. Videtur quod habitus corrumpi non possit. Habitus enim inest sicut natura quaedam, unde operationes secundum habitum sunt delectabiles. Sed natura non corrumpitur, manente eo cuius est natura. Ergo neque habitus corrumpi potest, manente subiecto.

PRAETEREA, omnis corruptio formae vel est per corruptionem subiecti, vel est a contrario, sicut aegritudo corrumpitur corrupto animali, vel etiam superveniente sanitate. Sed scientia, quae est quidam habitus, non potest corrumpi per corruptionem subiecti, quia *intellectus,* qui est subiectum eius, *est substantia quaedam, et non corrumpitur,* ut dicitur in I de anima. Similiter etiam non potest corrumpi a contrario, nam species intelligibiles non sunt ad invicem contrariae, ut dicitur in VII Metaphys. Ergo habitus scientiae nullo modo corrumpi potest.

PRAETEREA, omnis corruptio est per aliquem motum. Sed habitus scientiae, qui est in anima, non potest corrumpi per motum per se ipsius animae, quia anima per se non movetur. Movetur autem per accidens per motum corporis. Nulla autem transmutatio corporalis videtur posse corrumpere species intelligibiles existentes in intellectu, cum intellectus sit per se locus specierum, sine corpore, unde ponitur quod nec per senium nec per mortem corrumpuntur habitus. Ergo scientia corrumpi non potest. Et per consequens, nec habitus virtutis, qui etiam est in anima rationali, et, sicut philosophus dicit in I Ethic., *virtutes sunt permanentiores disciplinis.*

Question 53
How Habits Are Corrupted or Diminished

We must now consider how habits are lost or weakened; and under this head there are three points of inquiry: 1. Whether a habit can be corrupted? 2. Whether it can be diminished? 3. How are habits corrupted or diminished?

Article 1
Whether a habit can be corrupted?

Objection 1: It would seem that a habit cannot be corrupted. For habit is within its subject like a second nature; wherefore it is pleasant to act from habit. Now so long as a thing is, its nature is not corrupted. Therefore neither can a habit be corrupted so long as its subject remains.

Objection 2: Further, whenever a form is corrupted, this is due either to corruption of its subject, or to its contrary: thus sickness ceases through corruption of the animal, or through the advent of health. Now science, which is a habit, cannot be lost through corruption of its subject: since "the intellect," which is its subject, "is a substance that is incorruptible" (De Anima i, text. 65). In like manner, neither can it be lost through the action of its contrary: since intelligible species are not contrary to one another (Metaph. vii, text. 52). Therefore the habit of science can nowise be lost.

Objection 3: Further, all corruption results from some movement. But the habit of science, which is in the soul, cannot be corrupted by a direct movement of the soul itself, since the soul is not moved directly. It is, however, moved indirectly through the movement of the body: and yet no bodily change seems capable of corrupting the intelligible species residing in the intellect: since the intellect independently of the body is the proper abode of the species; for which reason it is held that habits are not lost either through old age or through death. Therefore science cannot be corrupted. For the same reason neither can habits of virtue be corrupted, since they also are in the rational soul, and, as the Philosopher declares (Ethic. i, 10), "virtue is more lasting than learning."

I-II, q. 53, a. 1, s. c.

SED CONTRA est quod philosophus dicit, in libro de longitudine et brevitate vitae, quod *scientiae corruptio est oblivio et deceptio*. Peccando etiam aliquis habitum virtutis amittit. Et ex contrariis actibus virtutes generantur et corrumpuntur, ut dicitur II Ethic.

RESPONDEO dicendum quod secundum se dicitur aliqua forma corrumpi per contrarium suum, per accidens autem, per corruptionem sui subiecti. Si igitur fuerit aliquis **habitus cuius subiectum est corruptibile, et cuius causa habet contrarium, utroque modo corrumpi poterit**, sicut patet de habitibus corporalibus, scilicet sanitate et aegritudine. Illi vero habitus quorum subiectum est incorruptibile, non possunt corrumpi per accidens. Sunt tamen habitus quidam qui, etsi principaliter sint in subiecto incorruptibili, secundario tamen sunt in subiecto corruptibili, sicut habitus scientiae, qui principaliter est quidem in intellectu possibili, secundario autem in viribus apprehensivis sensitivis, ut supra dictum est. Et ideo ex parte intellectus possibilis, habitus scientiae non potest corrumpi per accidens; sed solum ex parte inferiorum virium sensitivarum. Est igitur considerandum si possunt huiusmodi habitus per se corrumpi. Si igitur fuerit aliquis habitus qui habeat aliquod contrarium, vel ex parte sua vel ex parte suae causae, poterit per se corrumpi, si vero non habet contrarium, non poterit per se corrumpi. Manifestum est autem quod species intelligibilis in intellectu possibili existens, non habet aliquid contrarium. Neque iterum intellectui agenti, qui est causa eius, potest aliquid esse contrarium. Unde si aliquis habitus sit in intellectu possibili immediate ab intellectu agente causatus, talis habitus est incorruptibilis et per se et per accidens. Huiusmodi autem sunt habitus primorum principiorum, tam speculabilium quam practicorum, qui nulla oblivione vel deceptione corrumpi possunt, sicut philosophus dicit, in VI Ethic., de prudentia, quod *non perditur per oblivionem*. Aliquis vero habitus est in intellectu possibili ex ratione causatus, scilicet habitus conclusionum, qui dicitur scientia, cuius causae dupliciter potest aliquid contrarium esse. Uno modo, ex parte ipsarum propositionum ex quibus ratio procedit, etenim

On the contrary, The Philosopher says (De Long. et Brev. Vitae ii) that "forgetfulness and deception are the corruption of science." Moreover, by sinning a man loses a habit of virtue: and again, virtues are engendered and corrupted by contrary acts (Ethic. ii, 2).

I answer that, A form is said to be corrupted directly by its contrary; indirectly, through its subject being corrupted. When therefore a habit has a corruptible subject, **and a cause that has a contrary, it can be corrupted both ways.** This is clearly the case with bodily habits—for instance, health and sickness. But those habits that have an incorruptible subject, cannot be corrupted indirectly. There are, however, some habits which, while residing chiefly in an incorruptible subject, reside nevertheless secondarily in a corruptible subject; such is the habit of science which is chiefly indeed in the possible intellect, but secondarily in the sensitive powers of apprehension, as stated above (I-II, q. 50, a. 3, ad 3). Consequently the habit of science cannot be corrupted indirectly, on the part of the possible intellect, but only on the part of the lower sensitive powers. We must therefore inquire whether habits of this kind can be corrupted directly. If then there be a habit having a contrary, either on the part of itself or on the part of its cause, it can be corrupted directly: but if it has no contrary, it cannot be corrupted directly. Now it is evident that an intelligible species residing in the possible intellect, has no contrary; nor can the active intellect, which is the cause of that species, have a contrary. Wherefore if in the possible intellect there be a habit caused immediately by the active intellect, such a habit is incorruptible both directly and indirectly. Such are the habits of the first principles, both speculative and practical, which cannot be corrupted by any forgetfulness or deception whatever: even as the Philosopher says about prudence (Ethic. vi, 5) that "it cannot be lost by being forgotten." There is, however, in the possible intellect a habit caused by the reason, to wit, the habit of conclusions, which is called science, to the cause of which something may be contrary in two ways. First, on the part of those very propositions which are the starting point of the reason: for the

enuntiationi quae est, *bonum est bonum,* contraria est ea quae est, *bonum non est bonum,* secundum philosophum, in II Periherm. Alio modo, quantum ad ipsum processum rationis; prout syllogismus sophisticus opponitur syllogismo dialectico vel demonstrativo. Sic igitur patet quod per falsam rationem potest corrumpi habitus verae opinionis, aut etiam scientiae. Unde philosophus dicit quod *deceptio est corruptio scientiae,* sicut supra dictum est. Virtutum vero quaedam sunt intellectuales, quae sunt in ipsa ratione, ut dicitur in VI Ethic., de quibus est eadem ratio quae est de scientia vel opinione. Quaedam vero sunt in parte animae appetitiva, quae sunt virtutes morales, et eadem ratio est de vitiis oppositis. Habitus autem appetitivae partis causantur per hoc quod ratio nata est appetitivam partem movere. Unde per iudicium rationis in contrarium moventis quocumque modo, scilicet sive ex ignorantia, sive ex passione, vel etiam ex electione, corrumpitur habitus virtutis vel vitii.

Ad primum ergo dicendum quod, sicut dicitur in VII Ethic., habitus similitudinem habet naturae, deficit tamen ab ipsa. Et ideo, cum natura rei nullo modo removeatur ab ipsa, habitus difficile removetur.

Ad secundum dicendum quod, etsi speciebus intelligibilibus non sit aliquid contrarium, enuntiationibus tamen et processui rationis potest aliquid esse contrarium, ut dictum est.

Ad tertium dicendum quod scientia non removetur per motum corporalem quantum ad ipsam radicem habitus, sed solum quantum ad impedimentum actus; inquantum intellectus indiget in suo actu viribus sensitivis, quibus impedimentum affertur per corporalem transmutationem. Sed per intelligibilem motum rationis potest corrumpi habitus scientiae, etiam quantum ad ipsam radicem habitus. Et similiter etiam potest corrumpi habitus virtutis. Tamen quod dicitur, *virtutes esse permanentiores disciplinis,* intelligendum est non ex parte subiecti vel causae, sed ex parte actus, nam virtutum usus est continuus per totam vitam, non autem usus disciplinarum.

assertion "Good is not good" is contrary to the assertion "Good is good" (Peri Herm. ii). Secondly, on the part of the process of reasoning; forasmuch as a sophistical syllogism is contrary to a dialectic or demonstrative syllogism. Wherefore it is clear that a false reason can corrupt the habit of a true opinion or even of science. Hence the Philosopher, as stated above, says that "deception is the corruption of science." As to virtues, some of them are intellectual, residing in reason itself, as stated in Ethic. vi, 1: and to these applies what we have said of science and opinion. Some, however, *viz.* the moral virtues, are in the appetitive part of the soul; and the same may be said of the contrary vices. Now the habits of the appetitive part are caused therein because it is natural to it to be moved by the reason. Therefore a habit either of virtue or of vice, may be corrupted by a judgment of reason, whenever its motion is contrary to such vice or virtue, whether through ignorance, passion or deliberate choice.

Reply to Objection 1: As stated in Ethic. vii, 10, a habit is like a second nature, and yet it falls short of it. And so it is that while the nature of a thing cannot in any way be taken away from a thing, a habit is removed, though with difficulty.

Reply to Objection 2: Although there is no contrary to intelligible species, yet there can be a contrary to assertions and to the process of reason, as stated above.

Reply to Objection 3: Science is not taken away by movement of the body, if we consider the root itself of the habit, but only as it may prove an obstacle to the act of science; in so far as the intellect, in its act, has need of the sensitive powers, which are impeded by corporal transmutation. But the intellectual movement of the reason can corrupt the habit of science, even as regards the very root of the habit. In like manner a habit of virtue can be corrupted. Nevertheless when it is said that "virtue is more lasting than learning," this must be understood in respect, not of the subject or cause, but of the act: because the use of virtue continues through the whole of life, whereas the use of learning does not.

ARTICULUS 2

AD SECUNDUM sic proceditur. Videtur quod habitus diminui non possit. Habitus enim est quaedam qualitas et forma simplex. Simplex autem aut totum habetur, aut totum amittitur. Ergo habitus, etsi corrumpi possit, diminui non potest.

PRAETEREA, omne quod convenit accidenti, convenit eidem secundum se, vel ratione sui subiecti. Habitus autem secundum seipsum non intenditur et remittitur, alioquin sequeretur quod aliqua species de suis individuis praedicaretur secundum magis et minus. Si igitur secundum participationem subiecti diminui possit, sequeretur quod aliquid accidat habitui proprium, quod non sit commune ei et subiecto. Cuicumque autem formae convenit aliquid proprium praeter suum subiectum, illa forma est separabilis, ut dicitur in I de anima. Sequitur ergo quod habitus sit forma separabilis, quod est impossibile.

PRAETEREA, ratio et natura habitus, sicut et cuiuslibet accidentis, consistit in concretione ad subiectum, unde et quodlibet accidens definitur per suum subiectum. Si igitur habitus secundum seipsum non intenditur neque remittitur, neque etiam secundum concretionem sui ad subiectum diminui poterit. Et ita nullo modo diminuetur.

SED CONTRA est quod contraria nata sunt fieri circa idem. Augmentum autem et diminutio sunt contraria. Cum igitur habitus possit augeri, videtur quod etiam possit diminui.

RESPONDEO dicendum quod habitus dupliciter diminuuntur, sicut et augentur, ut ex supradictis patet. Et sicut ex eadem causa augentur ex qua generantur, ita ex eadem causa diminuuntur ex qua corrumpuntur, nam diminutio habitus est quaedam via ad corruptionem, sicut e converso generatio habitus est quoddam fundamentum augmenti ipsius.

AD PRIMUM ergo dicendum quod habitus secundum se consideratus, est forma simplex, et secundum hoc non accidit ei diminutio, sed secundum diversum modum participandi, qui provenit ex

ARTICLE 2
Whether a habit can diminish?

Objection 1: It would seem that a habit cannot diminish. Because a habit is a simple quality and form. Now a simple thing is possessed either wholly or not at all. Therefore although a habit can be lost it cannot diminish.

Objection 2: Further, if a thing is befitting an accident, this is by reason either of the accident or of its subject. Now a habit does not become more or less intense by reason of itself; else it would follow that a species might be predicated of its individuals more or less. And if it can become less intense as to its participation by its subject, it would follow that something is accidental to a habit, proper thereto and not common to the habit and its subject. Now whenever a form has something proper to it besides its subject, that form can be separate, as stated in De Anima i, text. 13. Hence it follows that a habit is a separable form; which is impossible.

Objection 3: Further, the very notion and nature of a habit as of any accident, is inherence in a subject: wherefore any accident is defined with reference to its subject. Therefore if a habit does not become more or less intense in itself, neither can it in its inherence in its subject: and consequently it will be nowise less intense.

On the contrary, It is natural for contraries to be applicable to the same thing. Now increase and decrease are contraries. Since therefore a habit can increase, it seems that it can also diminish.

I answer that, Habits diminish, just as they increase, in two ways, as we have already explained (I-II, q. 52, a. 1). And since they increase through the same cause as that which engenders them, so too they diminish by the same cause as that which corrupts them: since the diminishing of a habit is the road which leads to its corruption, even as, on the other hand, the engendering of a habit is a foundation of its increase.

Reply to Objection 1: A habit, considered in itself, is a simple form. It is not thus that it is subject to decrease; but according to the different ways in which its subject participates in it. This is due to the fact that

indeterminatione potentiae ipsius participantis, quae scilicet diversimode potest unam formam participare, vel quae potest ad plura vel ad pauciora extendi.

AD SECUNDUM dicendum quod ratio illa procederet, si ipsa essentia habitus nullo modo diminueretur. Hoc autem non ponimus, sed quod quaedam diminutio essentiae habitus non habet principium ab habitu, sed a participante.

AD TERTIUM dicendum quod, quocumque modo significetur accidens, habet dependentiam ad subiectum secundum suam rationem, aliter tamen et aliter. Nam accidens significatum in abstracto, importat habitudinem ad subiectum quae incipit ab accidente, et terminatur ad subiectum, nam *albedo dicitur qua aliquid est album*. Et ideo in definitione accidentis abstracti non ponitur subiectum quasi prima pars definitionis, quae est genus; sed quasi secunda, quae est differentia; dicimus enim quod *simitas* est *curvitas nasi*. Sed in concretis incipit habitudo a subiecto, et terminatur ad accidens, dicitur enim *album quod habet albedinem*. Propter quod in definitione huiusmodi accidentis ponitur subiectum tanquam genus, quod est prima pars definitionis, dicimus enim quod *simum* est *nasus curvus*. Sic igitur id quod convenit accidentibus ex parte subiecti, non autem ex ipsa ratione accidentis, non attribuitur accidenti in abstracto, sed in concreto. Et huiusmodi est intensio et remissio in quibusdam accidentibus, unde albedo non dicitur magis et minus, sed album. Et eadem ratio est in habitibus et aliis qualitatibus, nisi quod quidam habitus augentur vel diminuuntur per quandam additionem, ut ex supradictis patet.

the subject's potentiality is indeterminate, through its being able to participate a form in various ways, or to extend to a greater or a smaller number of things.

Reply to Objection 2: This argument would hold, if the essence itself of a habit were nowise subject to decrease. This we do not say; but that a certain decrease in the essence of a habit has its origin, not in the habit, but in its subject.

Reply to Objection 3: No matter how we take an accident, its very notion implies dependence on a subject, but in different ways. For if we take an accident in the abstract, it implies relation to a subject, which relation begins in the accident and terminates in the subject: for "whiteness is that whereby a thing is white." Accordingly in defining an accident in the abstract, we do not put the subject as though it were the first part of the definition, *viz.* the genus; but we give it the second place, which is that of the difference; thus we say that *simitas* is "a curvature of the nose." But if we take accidents in the concrete, the relation begins in the subject and terminates in the concrete, the relation begins in the subject and terminates at the accident: for "a white thing" is "something that has whiteness." Accordingly in defining this kind of accident, we place the subject as the genus, which is the first part of a definition; for we say that a *simum* is a "snub-nose." Accordingly whatever is befitting an accident on the part of the subject, but is not of the very essence of the accident, is ascribed to that accident, not in the abstract, but in the concrete. Such are increase and decrease in certain accidents: wherefore to be more or less white is not ascribed to whiteness but to a white thing. The same applies to habits and other qualities; save that certain habits increase or diminish by a kind of addition, as we have already clearly explained (I-II, q. 52, a. 2).

Articulus 3

Ad tertium sic proceditur. Videtur quod habitus non corrumpatur aut diminuatur per solam cessationem ab opere. Habitus enim permanentiores sunt quam passibiles qualitates, ut ex supradictis apparet. Sed passibiles qualitates non corrumpuntur neque diminuuntur per cessationem ab actu, non enim albedo diminuitur si visum non immutet, neque calor si non calefaciat. Ergo neque habitus diminuuntur vel corrumpuntur per cessationem ab actu.

Praeterea, corruptio et diminutio sunt quaedam mutationes. Sed nihil mutatur absque aliqua causa movente. Cum igitur cessatio ab actu non importet aliquam causam moventem, non videtur quod per cessationem ab actu possit esse diminutio vel corruptio habitus.

Praeterea, habitus scientiae et virtutis sunt in anima intellectiva, quae est supra tempus. Ea vero quae sunt supra tempus, non corrumpuntur neque diminuuntur per temporis diuturnitatem. Ergo neque huiusmodi habitus corrumpuntur vel diminuuntur per temporis diuturnitatem, si diu aliquis absque exercitio permaneat.

Sed contra est quod philosophus, in libro de Longit. et Brevit. vitae, dicit quod *corruptio scientiae* non solum est *deceptio,* sed etiam *oblivio.* Et in VIII Ethic. dicitur quod *multas amicitias inappellatio dissolvit.* Et eadem ratione, alii habitus virtutum per cessationem ab actu diminuuntur vel tolluntur.

Respondeo dicendum quod, sicut dicitur in VIII Physic., aliquid potest esse movens dupliciter, uno modo, per se, quod scilicet movet secundum rationem propriae formae, sicut ignis calefacit; alio modo, per accidens, sicut id quod removet prohibens. Et hoc modo cessatio ab actu causat corruptionem vel diminutionem habituum, inquantum scilicet removetur actus qui prohibebat causas corrumpentes vel diminuentes habitum. Dictum est enim quod habitus per se corrumpuntur vel diminuuntur

Article 3
Whether a habit is corrupted or diminished through mere cessation from act?

Objection 1: It would seem that a habit is not corrupted or diminished through mere cessation from act. For habits are more lasting than passion-like qualities, as we have explained above (I-II, q. 49, a. 2, ad 3; q. 50, a. 1). But passion-like qualities are neither corrupted nor diminished by cessation from act: for whiteness is not lessened through not affecting the sight, nor heat through ceasing to make something hot. Therefore neither are habits diminished or corrupted through cessation from act.

Objection 2: Further, corruption and diminution are changes. Now nothing is changed without a moving cause. Since therefore cessation from act does not imply a moving cause, it does not appear how a habit can be diminished or corrupted through cessation from act.

Objection 3: Further, the habits of science and virtue are in the intellectual soul which is above time. Now those things that are above time are neither destroyed nor diminished by length of time. Neither, therefore, are such habits destroyed or diminished through length of time, if one fails for long to exercise them.

On the contrary, The Philosopher says (De Long. et Brev. Vitae ii) that not only "deception," but also "forgetfulness, is the corruption of science." Moreover he says (Ethic. viii, 5) that "want of intercourse has dissolved many a friendship." In like manner other habits of virtue are diminished or destroyed through cessation from act.

I answer that, As stated in Phys. vii, text. 27, a thing is a cause of movement in two ways. First, directly; and such a thing causes movement by reason of its proper form; thus fire causes heat. Secondly, indirectly; for instance, that which removes an obstacle. It is in this latter way that the destruction or diminution of a habit results through cessation from act, in so far, to wit, as we cease from exercising an act which overcame the causes that destroyed or weakened that habit. For it has been stated (I-II, q. 53, a. 1) that habits are destroyed or diminished directly

ex contrario agente. Unde quorumcumque habituum contraria subcrescunt per temporis tractum, quae oportet subtrahi per actum ab habitu procedentem; huiusmodi habitus diminuuntur, vel etiam tolluntur totaliter, per diuturnam cessationem ab actu; ut patet et in scientia et in virtute. Manifestum est enim quod habitus virtutis moralis facit hominem promptum ad eligendum medium in operationibus et passionibus. Cum autem aliquis non utitur habitu virtutis ad moderandas passiones vel operationes proprias, necesse est quod proveniant multae passiones et operationes praeter modum virtutis, ex inclinatione appetitus sensitivi, et aliorum quae exterius movent. Unde corrumpitur virtus, vel diminuitur, per cessationem ab actu. Similiter etiam est ex parte habituum intellectualium, secundum quos est homo promptus ad recte iudicandum de imaginatis. Cum igitur homo cessat ab usu intellectualis habitus, insurgunt imaginationes extraneae, et quandoque ad contrarium ducentes; ita quod, nisi per frequentem usum intellectualis habitus, quodammodo succidantur vel comprimantur, redditur homo minus aptus ad recte iudicandum, et quandoque totaliter disponitur ad contrarium. Et sic per cessationem ab actu diminuitur, vel etiam corrumpitur intellectualis habitus.

AD PRIMUM ergo dicendum quod ita etiam calor per cessationem a calefaciendo corrumperetur, si per hoc incresceret frigidum, quod est calidi corruptivum.

AD SECUNDUM dicendum quod cessatio ab actu est movens ad corruptionem vel diminutionem, sicut removens prohibens, ut dictum est.

AD TERTIUM dicendum quod pars intellectiva animae secundum se est supra tempus, sed pars sensitiva subiacet tempori. Et ideo per temporis cursum, transmutatur quantum ad passiones appetitivae partis et etiam quantum ad vires apprehensivas. Unde philosophus dicit, in IV Physic., quod tempus est causa oblivionis.

through some contrary agency. Consequently all habits that are gradually undermined by contrary agencies which need to be counteracted by acts proceeding from those habits, are diminished or even destroyed altogether by long cessation from act, as is clearly seen in the case both of science and of virtue. For it is evident that a habit of moral virtue makes a man ready to choose the mean in deeds and passions. And when a man fails to make use of his virtuous habit in order to moderate his own passions or deeds, the necessary result is that many passions and deeds fail to observe the mode of virtue, by reason of the inclination of the sensitive appetite and of other external agencies. Wherefore virtue is destroyed or lessened through cessation from act. The same applies to the intellectual habits, which render man ready to judge aright of those things that are pictured by his imagination. Hence when man ceases to make use of his intellectual habits, strange fancies, sometimes in opposition to them, arise in his imagination; so that unless those fancies be, as it were, cut off or kept back by frequent use of his intellectual habits, man becomes less fit to judge aright, and sometimes is even wholly disposed to the contrary, and thus the intellectual habit is diminished or even wholly destroyed by cessation from act.

Reply to Objection 1: Even heat would be destroyed through ceasing to give heat, if, for this same reason, cold which is destructive of heat were to increase.

Reply to Objection 2: Cessation from act is a moving cause, conducive of corruption or diminution, by removing the obstacles, thereto, as explained above.

Reply to Objection 3: The intellectual part of the soul, considered in itself, is above time, but the sensitive part is subject to time, and therefore in course of time it undergoes change as to the passions of the sensitive part, and also as to the powers of apprehension. Hence the Philosopher says (Phys. iv. text. 117) that time makes us forget.

Quaestio LIV

Deinde considerandum est de distinctione habituum. Et circa hoc quaeruntur quatuor. *Primo,* utrum multi habitus possint esse in una potentia. *Secundo,* utrum habitus distinguantur secundum obiecta. *Tertio,* utrum habitus distinguantur secundum bonum et malum. *Quarto,* utrum unus habitus ex multis habitibus constituatur.

Articulus 1

Ad primum sic proceditur. Videtur quod non possint esse multi habitus in una potentia. Eorum enim quae secundum idem distinguuntur multiplicato uno, multiplicatur et aliud. Sed secundum idem potentiae et habitus distinguuntur, scilicet secundum actus et obiecta. Similiter ergo multiplicantur. Non ergo possunt esse multi habitus in una potentia.

Praeterea, potentia est virtus quaedam simplex. Sed in uno subiecto simplici non potest esse diversitas accidentium, quia subiectum est causa accidentis; ab uno autem simplici non videtur procedere nisi unum. Ergo in una potentia non possunt esse multi habitus.

Praeterea, sicut corpus formatur per figuram, ita potentia formatur per habitum. Sed unum corpus non potest simul formari diversis figuris. Ergo neque una potentia potest simul formari diversis habitibus. Non ergo plures habitus possunt simul esse in una potentia.

Sed contra est quod intellectus est una potentia, in qua tamen sunt diversarum scientiarum habitus.

Respondeo dicendum quod, sicut supra dictum est, habitus sunt dispositiones quaedam alicuius in potentia existentis ad aliquid, sive ad naturam, sive ad operationem vel finem naturae. Et de illis quidem habitibus qui sunt dispositiones ad naturam, manifestum est quod possunt plures esse in uno subiecto, eo quod unius subiecti possunt diversimode partes accipi, secundum quarum dispositionem habitus dicuntur. Sicut, si accipiantur humani corporis partes humores, prout disponuntur secundum

Question 54
Of the Distinction of Habits

We have now to consider the distinction of habits; and under this head there are four points of inquiry: 1. Whether many habits can be in one power? 2. Whether habits are distinguished by their objects? 3. Whether habits are divided into good and bad? 4. Whether one habit may be made up of many habits?

Article 1
Whether many habits can be in one power?

Objection 1: It would seem that there cannot be many habits in one power. For when several things are distinguished in respect of the same thing, if one of them be multiplied, the others are too. Now habits and powers are distinguished in respect of the same thing, *viz.* their acts and objects. Therefore they are multiplied in like manner. Therefore there cannot be many habits in one power.

Objection 2: Further, a power is a simple force. Now in one simple subject there cannot be diversity of accidents; for the subject is the cause of its accidents; and it does not appear how diverse effects can proceed from one simple cause. Therefore there cannot be many habits in one power.

Objection 3: Further, just as the body is informed by its shape, so is a power informed by a habit. But one body cannot be informed at the same time by various shapes. Therefore neither can a power be informed at the same time by many habits. Therefore several habits cannot be at the same time in one power.

On the contrary, The intellect is one power; wherein, nevertheless, are the habits of various sciences.

I answer that, As stated above (I-II, q. 49, a. 4), habits are dispositions of a thing that is in potentiality to something, either to nature, or to operation, which is the end of nature. As to those habits which are dispositions to nature, it is clear that several can be in one same subject: since in one subject we may take parts in various ways, according to the various dispositions of which parts there are various habits. Thus, if we take the humors as being parts of the human body, according to their disposition in respect of

naturam humanam, est habitus vel dispositio sanitatis, si vero accipiantur partes similes ut nervi et ossa et carnes, earum dispositio in ordine ad naturam, est fortitudo aut macies, si vero accipiantur membra, ut manus et pes et huiusmodi, earum dispositio naturae conveniens, est pulchritudo. Et sic sunt plures habitus vel dispositiones in eodem. Si vero loquamur de habitibus qui sunt dispositiones ad opera, qui proprie pertinent ad potentias; sic etiam contingit unius potentiae esse habitus plures. Cuius ratio est, quia subiectum habitus est potentia passiva, ut supra dictum est, potentia enim activa tantum non est alicuius habitus subiectum, ut ex supradictis patet. Potentia autem passiva comparatur ad actum determinatum unius speciei, sicut materia ad formam, eo quod, sicut materia determinatur ad unam formam per unum agens, ita etiam potentia passiva a ratione unius obiecti activi determinatur ad unum actum secundum speciem. Unde sicut plura obiecta possunt movere unam potentiam passivam, ita una potentia passiva potest esse subiectum diversorum actuum vel perfectionum secundum speciem. Habitus autem sunt quaedam qualitates aut formae inhaerentes potentiae, quibus inclinatur potentia ad determinatos actus secundum speciem. Unde ad unam potentiam possunt plures habitus pertinere, sicut et plures actus specie differentes.

AD PRIMUM ergo dicendum quod, sicut in rebus naturalibus diversitas specierum est secundum formam, diversitas autem generum est secundum materiam, ut dicitur in V Metaphys. (ea enim sunt diversa genere, quorum est materia diversa), ita etiam diversitas obiectorum secundum genus, facit distinctionem potentiarum (unde philosophus dicit, in VI Ethic., quod *ad ea quae sunt genere altera, sunt etiam animae particulae aliae*); diversitas vero obiectorum secundum speciem, facit diversitatem actuum secundum speciem, et per consequens habituum. Quaecumque autem sunt diversa genere, sunt etiam specie diversa, sed non convertitur. Et ideo diversarum potentiarum sunt diversi actus specie, et diversi habitus, non autem oportet quod diversi habitus sint diversarum potentiarum, sed possunt esse plures unius.

human nature, we have the habit or disposition of health: while, if we take like parts, such as nerves, bones, and flesh, the disposition of these in respect of nature is strength or weakness; whereas, if we take the limbs, i.e., the hands, feet, and so on, the disposition of these in proportion to nature, is beauty: and thus there are several habits or dispositions in the same subject. If, however, we speak of those habits that are dispositions to operation, and belong properly to the powers; thus, again, there may be several habits in one power. The reason for this is that the subject of a habit is a passive power, as stated above (I-II, q. 51, a. 2): for it is only an active power that cannot be the subject of a habit, as was clearly shown above (I-II, q. 51, a. 2). Now a passive power is compared to the determinate act of any species, as matter to form: because, just as matter is determinate to one form by one agent, so, too, is a passive power determined by the nature of one active object to an act specifically one. Wherefore, just as several objects can move one passive power, so can one passive power be the subject of several acts or perfections specifically diverse. Now habits are qualities or forms adhering to a power, and inclining that power to acts of a determinate species. Consequently several habits, even as several specifically different acts, can belong to one power.

Reply to Objection 1: Even as in natural things, diversity of species is according to the form, and diversity of genus, according to matter, as stated in Metaph. v, text. 33 (since things that differ in matter belong to different genera): so, too, generic diversity of objects entails a difference of powers (wherefore the Philosopher says in Ethic. vi, 1, that "those objects that differ generically belong to different departments of the soul"); while specific difference of objects entails a specific difference of acts, and consequently of habits also. Now things that differ in genus differ in species, but not vice versa. Wherefore the acts and habits of different powers differ in species: but it does not follow that different habits are in different powers, for several can be in one power.

Et sicut sunt genera generum, et species specierum; ita etiam contingit esse diversas species habituum et potentiarum.

Ad secundum dicendum quod potentia, etsi sit quidem simplex secundum essentiam, est tamen multiplex virtute, secundum quod ad multos actus specie differentes se extendit. Et ideo nihil prohibet in una potentia esse multos habitus specie differentes.

Ad tertium dicendum quod corpus formatur per figuram sicut per propriam terminationem, habitus autem non est terminatio potentiae, sed est dispositio ad actum sicut ad ultimum terminum. Et ideo non possunt esse unius potentiae simul plures actus, nisi forte secundum quod unus comprehenditur sub alio, sicut nec unius corporis plures figurae, nisi secundum quod una est in alia, sicut trigonum in tetragono. Non enim potest intellectus simul multa *actu* intelligere. Potest tamen simul *habitu* multa scire.

And even as several genera may be included in one genus, and several species be contained in one species; so does it happen that there are several species of habits and powers.

Reply to Objection 2: Although a power is simple as to its essence, it is multiple virtually, inasmuch as it extends to many specifically different acts. Consequently there is nothing to prevent many superficially different habits from being in one power.

Reply to Objection 3: A body is informed by its shape as by its own terminal boundaries: whereas a habit is not the terminal boundary of a power, but the disposition of a power to an act as to its ultimate term. Consequently one same power cannot have several acts at the same time, except in so far as perchance one act is comprised in another; just as neither can a body have several shapes, save in so far as one shape enters into another, as a three-sided in a four-sided figure. For the intellect cannot understand several things at the same time "actually"; and yet it can know several things at the same time "habitually."

Articulus 2

Ad secundum sic proceditur. Videtur quod habitus non distinguantur secundum obiecta. Contraria enim sunt specie differentia. Sed idem habitus scientiae est contrariorum, sicut medicina sani et aegri. Non ergo secundum obiecta specie differentia, habitus distinguuntur.

Praeterea, diversae scientiae sunt diversi habitus. Sed idem scibile pertinet ad diversas scientias, sicut terram esse rotundam demonstrat et naturalis et astrologus, ut dicitur in II Physic. Ergo habitus non distinguuntur secundum obiecta.

Praeterea, eiusdem actus est idem obiectum. Sed idem actus potest pertinere ad diversos habitus virtutum, si ad diversos fines referatur, sicut dare pecuniam alicui, si sit propter Deum, pertinet ad caritatem; si vero sit propter debitum solvendum, pertinet ad iustitiam. Ergo etiam idem obiectum potest

Article 2
Whether habits are distinguished by their objects?

Objection 1: It would seem that habits are not distinguished by their objects. For contraries differ in species. Now the same habit of science regards contraries: thus medicine regards the healthy and the unhealthy. Therefore habits are not distinguished by objects specifically distinct.

Objection 2: Further, different sciences are different habits. But the same scientific truth belongs to different sciences: thus both the physicist and the astronomer prove the earth to be round, as stated in Phys. ii, text. 17. Therefore habits are not distinguished by their objects.

Objection 3: Further, wherever the act is the same, the object is the same. But the same act can belong to different habits of virtue, if it be directed to different ends; thus to give money to anyone, if it be done for God's sake, is an act of charity; while, if it be done in order to pay a debt, it is an act of justice. Therefore the same object can also

ad diversos habitus pertinere. Non ergo est diversitas habituum secundum diversitatem obiectorum.

SED CONTRA, actus differunt specie secundum diversitatem obiectorum, ut supra dictum est. Sed habitus sunt dispositiones quaedam ad actus. Ergo etiam habitus distinguuntur secundum diversa obiecta.

RESPONDEO dicendum quod habitus et est forma quaedam, et est habitus. Potest ergo distinctio habituum secundum speciem attendi aut secundum communem modum quo formae specie distinguuntur; aut secundum proprium modum distinctionis habituum. Distinguuntur siquidem formae ad invicem secundum diversa principia activa, eo quod omne agens facit simile secundum speciem. Habitus autem importat ordinem ad aliquid. Omnia autem quae dicuntur secundum ordinem ad aliquid, distinguuntur secundum distinctionem eorum ad quae dicuntur. Est autem habitus dispositio quaedam ad duo ordinata, scilicet ad naturam, et ad operationem consequentem naturam. Sic igitur secundum tria, habitus specie distinguuntur. Uno quidem modo, secundum principia activa talium dispositionum; alio vero modo, secundum naturam; tertio vero modo, secundum obiecta specie differentia; ut per sequentia explicabitur.

AD PRIMUM ergo dicendum quod in distinctione potentiarum, vel etiam habituum, non est considerandum ipsum obiectum materialiter; sed ratio obiecti differens specie, vel etiam genere. Quamvis autem contraria specie differant diversitate rerum, tamen eadem ratio est cognoscendi utrumque, quia unum per aliud cognoscitur. Et ideo inquantum conveniunt in una ratione cognoscibilis, pertinent ad unum habitum cognoscitivum.

AD SECUNDUM dicendum quod terram esse rotundam per aliud medium demonstrat naturalis, et per aliud astrologus, astrologus enim hoc demonstrat per media mathematica, sicut per figuras eclipsium, vel per aliud huiusmodi; naturalis vero hoc demonstrat per medium naturale, sicut per motum gravium ad medium, vel per aliud huiusmodi. Tota autem virtus demonstrationis, quae est

belong to different habits. Therefore diversity of habits does not follow diversity of objects.

On the contrary, Acts differ in species according to the diversity of their objects, as stated above (I-II, q. 18, a. 5). But habits are dispositions to acts. Therefore habits also are distinguished according to the diversity of objects.

I answer that, A habit is both a form and a habit. Hence the specific distinction of habits may be taken in the ordinary way in which forms differ specifically; or according to that mode of distinction which is proper to habits. Accordingly forms are distinguished from one another in reference to the diversity of their active principles, since every agent produces its like in species. Habits, however, imply order to something: and all things that imply order to something, are distinguished according to the distinction of the things to which they are ordained. Now a habit is a disposition implying a twofold order: *viz.* to nature and to an operation consequent to nature. Accordingly habits are specifically distinct in respect of three things. First, in respect of the active principles of such dispositions; secondly, in respect of nature; thirdly, in respect of specifically different objects, as will appear from what follows.

Reply to Objection 1: In distinguishing powers, or also habits, we must consider the object not in its material but in its formal aspect, which may differ in species or even in genus. And though the distinction between specific contraries is a real distinction yet they are both known under one aspect, since one is known through the other. And consequently in so far as they concur in the one aspect of cognoscibility, they belong to one cognitive habit.

Reply to Objection 2: The physicist proves the earth to be round by one means, the astronomer by another: for the latter proves this by means of mathematics, e.g., by the shapes of eclipses, or something of the sort; while the former proves it by means of physics, e.g., by the movement of heavy bodies towards the center, and so forth. Now the whole force of a demonstration, which is

I-II, q. 53, a. 2, ad 2

syllogismus faciens scire, ut dicitur in I Poster., dependet ex medio. Et ideo diversa media sunt sicut diversa principia activa, secundum quae habitus scientiarum diversificantur.

AD TERTIUM dicendum quod, sicut philosophus dicit, in II Physic. et in VII Ethic., ita se habet finis in operabilibus, sicut principium in demonstrativis. Et ideo diversitas finium diversificat virtutes sicut et diversitas **activorum principiorum.** Sunt etiam ipsi fines obiecta actuum interiorum, qui maxime pertinent ad virtutes, ut ex supradictis patet.

ARTICULUS 3

AD TERTIUM sic proceditur. Videtur quod habitus non distinguantur secundum bonum et malum. Bonum enim et malum sunt contraria. Sed idem habitus est contrariorum, ut supra habitum est. Ergo habitus non distinguuntur secundum bonum et malum.

PRAETEREA, bonum convertitur cum ente, et sic, cum sit commune omnibus, non potest sumi ut differentia alicuius speciei; ut patet per philosophum in IV Topic. Similiter etiam malum, cum sit privatio et non ens, non potest esse alicuius entis differentia. Non ergo secundum bonum et malum possunt habitus specie distingui.

PRAETEREA, circa idem obiectum contingit esse diversos habitus malos, sicut circa concupiscentias intemperantiam et insensibilitatem, et similiter etiam plures habitus bonos, scilicet virtutem humanam et virtutem heroicam sive divinam, ut patet per philosophum in VII Ethic. Non ergo distinguuntur habitus secundum bonum et malum.

SED CONTRA est quod habitus bonus contrariatur habitui malo, sicut virtus vitio. Sed contraria sunt diversa secundum speciem. Ergo habitus differunt specie secundum differentiam boni et mali.

RESPONDEO dicendum quod, sicut dictum est, habitus specie distinguuntur non solum secundum obiecta et principia activa, sed etiam in ordine ad naturam. Quod

THE DISTINCTION OF HABITS

"a syllogism producing science," as stated in Poster. i, text. 5, depends on the mean. And consequently various means are as so many active principles, in respect of which the habits of science are distinguished.

Reply to Objection 3: As the Philosopher says (Phys. ii, text. 89; Ethic. vii, 8), the end is, in practical matters, what the principle is in speculative matters. Consequently diversity of ends demands a diversity of virtues, even **as diversity of active principles does.** Moreover the ends are objects of the internal acts, with which, above all, the virtues are concerned, as is evident from what has been said (I-II, q. 18, a. 6; q. 19, a. 2, ad 1; q. 34, a. 4).

ARTICLE 3
Whether habits are divided into good and bad?

Objection 1: It would seem that habits are not divided into good and bad. For good and bad are contraries. Now the same habit regards contraries, as was stated above (I-II, q. 54, a. 2, arg. 1). Therefore habits are not divided into good and bad.

Objection 2: Further, good is convertible with being; so that, since it is common to all, it cannot be accounted a specific difference, as the Philosopher declares (Topic. iv). Again, evil, since it is a privation and a non-being, cannot differentiate any being. Therefore habits cannot be specifically divided into good and evil.

Objection 3: Further, there can be different evil habits about one same object; for instance, intemperance and insensibility about matters of concupiscence: and in like manner there can be several good habits; for instance, human virtue and heroic or godlike virtue, as the Philosopher clearly states (Ethic. vii, 1). Therefore, habits are not divided into good and bad.

On the contrary, A good habit is contrary to a bad habit, as virtue to vice. Now contraries are divided specifically into good and bad habits.

I answer that, As stated above (I-II, q. 54, a. 2), habits are specifically distinct not only in respect of their objects and active principles, but also in their relation to nature. Now,

quidem contingit dupliciter. Uno modo, secundum convenientiam ad naturam, vel etiam secundum disconvenientiam ab ipsa. Et hoc modo distinguuntur specie habitus bonus et malus, nam habitus bonus dicitur qui disponit ad actum convenientem naturae agentis; habitus autem malus dicitur qui disponit ad actum non convenientem naturae. Sicut actus virtutum naturae humanae conveniunt, eo quod sunt secundum rationem, actus vero vitiorum, cum sint contra rationem, a natura humana discordant. Et sic manifestum est quod secundum differentiam boni et mali, habitus specie distinguuntur. Alio modo secundum naturam habitus distinguuntur, ex eo quod habitus unus disponit ad actum convenientem naturae inferiori; alius autem habitus disponit ad actum convenientem naturae superiori. Et sic virtus humana, quae disponit ad actum convenientem naturae humanae, distinguitur a divina virtute vel heroica, quae disponit ad actum convenientem cuidam superiori naturae.

AD PRIMUM ergo dicendum quod contrariorum potest esse unus habitus, secundum quod contraria conveniunt in una ratione. Nunquam tamen contingit quod habitus contrarii sint unius speciei, contrarietas enim habituum est secundum contrarias rationes. Et ita secundum bonum et malum habitus distinguuntur, scilicet inquantum unus habitus est bonus et alius malus, non autem ex hoc quod unus est boni et alius mali.

AD SECUNDUM dicendum quod bonum commune omni enti non est differentia constituens speciem alicuius habitus, sed quoddam bonum determinatum, quod est secundum convenientiam ad determinatam naturam, scilicet humanam. Similiter etiam malum quod est differentia constitutiva habitus, non est privatio pura, sed est aliquid determinatum repugnans determinatae naturae.

AD TERTIUM dicendum quod plures habitus boni circa idem specie, distinguuntur secundum convenientiam ad diversas naturas, ut dictum est. Plures vero habitus mali distinguuntur circa idem agendum secundum diversas repugnantias ad id quod est secundum naturam, sicut

this happens in two ways. First, by reason of their suitableness or unsuitableness to nature. In this way a good habit is specifically distinct from a bad habit: since a good habit is one which disposes to an act suitable to the agent's nature, while an evil habit is one which disposes to an act unsuitable to nature. Thus, acts of virtue are suitable to human nature, since they are according to reason, whereas acts of vice are discordant from human nature, since they are against reason. Hence it is clear that habits are distinguished specifically by the difference of good and bad. Secondly, habits are distinguished in relation to nature, from the fact that one habit disposes to an act that is suitable to a lower nature, while another habit disposes to an act befitting a higher nature. And thus human virtue, which disposes to an act befitting human nature, is distinct from godlike or heroic virtue, which disposes to an act befitting some higher nature.

Reply to Objection 1: The same habit may be about contraries in so far as contraries agree in one common aspect. Never, however, does it happen that contrary habits are in one species: since contrariety of habits follows contrariety of aspect. Accordingly habits are divided into good and bad, namely, inasmuch as one habit is good, and another bad; but not by reason of one habit being something good, and another about something bad.

Reply to Objection 2: It is not the good which is common to every being, that is a difference constituting the species of a habit; but some determinate good by reason of suitability to some determinate, *viz.* the human, nature. In like manner the evil that constitutes a difference of habits is not a pure privation, but something determinate repugnant to a determinate nature.

Reply to Objection 3: Several good habits about one same specific thing are distinct in reference to their suitability to various natures, as stated above. But several bad habits in respect of one action are distinct in reference to their diverse repugnance to that which is in keeping with nature: thus,

I-II, q. 53, a. 3, ad 3

uni virtuti contrariantur diversa vitia circa eandem materiam.

various vices about one same matter are contrary to one virtue.

Articulus 4

Ad quartum sic proceditur. Videtur quod unus habitus ex pluribus habitibus constituatur. Illud enim cuius generatio non simul perficitur, sed successive, videtur constitui ex pluribus partibus. Sed generatio habitus non est simul, sed successive ex pluribus actibus, ut supra habitum est. Ergo unus habitus constituitur ex pluribus habitibus.

Praeterea, ex partibus constituitur totum. Sed uni habitui assignantur multae partes, sicut Tullius ponit multas partes fortitudinis, temperantiae et aliarum virtutum. Ergo unus habitus constituitur ex pluribus.

Praeterea, de una sola conclusione potest scientia haberi et actu et habitu. Sed multae conclusiones pertinent ad unam scientiam totam, sicut ad geometriam vel arithmeticam. Ergo unus habitus constituitur ex multis.

Sed contra, habitus, cum sit qualitas quaedam, est forma simplex. Sed nullum simplex constituitur ex pluribus. Ergo unus habitus non constituitur ex pluribus habitibus.

Respondeo dicendum quod habitus ad operationem ordinatus, de quo nunc principaliter intendimus, est perfectio quaedam potentiae. Omnis autem perfectio proportionatur suo perfectibili. Unde sicut potentia, cum sit una, ad multa se extendit secundum quod conveniunt in aliquo uno, idest in generali quadam ratione obiecti; ita etiam habitus ad multa se extendit secundum quod habent ordinem ad aliquod unum, puta ad unam specialem rationem obiecti, vel unam naturam, vel unum principium, ut ex supradictis patet. Si igitur consideremus habitum secundum ea ad quae se extendit, sic inveniemus in eo quandam multiplicitatem. Sed quia illa multiplicitas est ordinata ad aliquid unum, ad quod principaliter respicit habitus, inde est quod habitus est qualitas simplex, non constituta ex pluribus habitibus, etiam si ad multa se extendat. Non enim unus habitus

Article 4
Whether one habit is made up of many habits?

Objection 1: It would seem that one habit is made up of many habits. For whatever is engendered, not at once, but little by little, seems to be made up of several parts. But a habit is engendered, not at once, but little by little out of several acts, as stated above (I-II, q. 51, a. 3). Therefore one habit is made up of several.

Objection 2: Further, a whole is made up of its parts. Now many parts are assigned to one habit: thus Tully assigns many parts of fortitude, temperance, and other virtues. Therefore one habit is made up of many.

Objection 3: Further, one conclusion suffices both for an act and for a habit of scientific knowledge. But many conclusions belong to but one science, to geometry, for instance, or to arithmetic. Therefore one habit is made up of many.

On the contrary, A habit, since it is a quality, is a simple form. But nothing simple is made up of many. Therefore one habit is not made up of many.

I answer that, A habit directed to operation, such as we are chiefly concerned with at present, is a perfection of a power. Now every perfection should be in proportion with that which it perfects. Hence, just as a power, while it is one, extends to many things, in so far as they have something in common, i.e., some general objective aspect, so also a habit extends to many things, in so far as they are related to one, for instance, to some specific objective aspect, or to one nature, or to one principle, as was clearly stated above (I-II, q. 54, a. 2; a. 3). If then we consider a habit as to the extent of its object, we shall find a certain multiplicity therein. But since this multiplicity is directed to one thing, on which the habit is chiefly intent, hence it is that a habit is a simple quality, not composed to several habits, even though it extend to many things. For a habit does not

se extendit ad multa, nisi in ordine ad unum, ex quo habet unitatem.

Ad primum ergo dicendum quod successio in generatione habitus non contingit ex hoc quod pars eius generetur post partem, sed ex eo quod subiectum non statim consequitur dispositionem firmam et difficile mobilem; et ex eo quod primo imperfecte incipit esse in subiecto, et paulatim perficitur. Sicut etiam est de aliis qualitatibus.

Ad secundum dicendum quod partes quae singulis virtutibus cardinalibus assignantur, non sunt partes integrales, ex quibus constituatur totum sed partes subiectivae sive potentiales, ut infra patebit.

Ad tertium dicendum quod ille qui in aliqua scientia acquirit per demonstrationem scientiam conclusionis unius, habet quidem habitum, sed imperfecte. Cum vero acquirit per aliquam demonstrationem scientiam conclusionis alterius, non aggeneratur in eo alius habitus; sed habitus qui prius inerat fit perfectior, utpote ad plura se extendens; eo quod conclusiones et demonstrationes unius scientiae ordinatae sunt, et una derivatur ex alia.

extend to many things save in relation to one, whence it derives its unity.

Reply to Objection 1: That a habit is engendered little by little, is due, not to one part being engendered after another, but to the fact that the subject does not acquire all at once a firm and difficultly changeable disposition; and also to the fact that it begins by being imperfectly in the subject, and is gradually perfected. The same applies to other qualities.

Reply to Objection 2: The parts which are assigned to each cardinal virtue, are not integral parts that combine to form a whole; but subjective or potential parts, as we shall explain further on (I-II, q. 57, a. 6, ad 4; II-II, q. 48).

Reply to Objection 3: In any science, he who acquires, by demonstration, scientific knowledge of one conclusion, has the habit indeed, yet imperfectly. And when he obtains, by demonstration, the scientific knowledge of another conclusion, no additional habit is engendered in him: but the habit which was in him previously is perfected, forasmuch as it has increased in extent; because the conclusions and demonstrations of one science are coordinate, and one flows from another.

TREATISE ON HABITS IN PARTICULAR
Good Habits, i.e., Virtues

Quaestio LV

Consequenter considerandum est de habitibus in speciali. Et quia habitus, ut dictum est, distinguuntur per bonum et malum, primo dicendum est de habitibus bonis, qui sunt virtutes et alia eis adiuncta, scilicet dona, beatitudines et fructus; secundo, de habitibus malis, scilicet de vitiis et peccatis. Circa virtutes autem quinque consideranda sunt, *primo*, de essentia virtutis; *secundo*, de subiecto eius; *tertio*, de divisione virtutum; *quarto*, de causa virtutis; *quinto*, de quibusdam proprietatibus virtutis. Circa primum quaeruntur quatuor. *Primo*, utrum virtus humana sit habitus. *Secundo*, utrum sit habitus operativus. *Tertio*, utrum sit habitus bonus. *Quarto*, de definitione virtutis.

Articulus 1

Ad primum sic proceditur. Videtur quod virtus humana non sit habitus. Virtus enim est *ultimum potentiae,* ut dicitur in I de caelo. Sed ultimum uniuscuiusque reducitur ad genus illud cuius est ultimum, sicut punctum ad genus lineae. Ergo virtus reducitur ad genus potentiae, et non ad genus habitus.

Praeterea, Augustinus dicit, in II de libero Arbit., quod *virtus est bonus usus liberi arbitrii.* Sed usus liberi arbitrii est actus. Ergo virtus non est habitus, sed actus.

Praeterea, habitibus non meremur, sed actibus, alioquin homo mereretur continue, etiam dormiendo. Sed virtutibus meremur. Ergo virtutes non sunt habitus, sed actus.

Praeterea, Augustinus dicit, in libro de moribus Eccles., quod *virtus est ordo amoris.* Et in libro octoginta trium quaest., dicit quod *ordinatio quae virtus vocatur, est fruendis frui, et utendis uti.* Ordo autem, seu ordinatio, nominat vel actum, vel

Question 55
Of the Virtues, as to Their Essence

We come now to the consideration of habits specifically. And since habits, as we have said (I-II, q. 54, a. 3), are divided into good and bad, we must speak in the first place of good habits, which are virtues, and of other matters connected with them, namely the Gifts, Beatitudes and Fruits; in the second place, of bad habits, namely of vices and sins. Now five things must be considered about virtues: 1. the essence of virtue; 2. its subject; 3. the division of virtue; 4. the cause of virtue; 5. certain properties of virtue. Under the first head, there are four points of inquiry: 1. Whether human virtue is a habit? 2. Whether it is an operative habit? 3. Whether it is a good habit? 4. Of the definition of virtue.

Article 1
Whether human virtue is a habit?

Objection 1: It would seem that human virtue is not a habit: For virtue is "the limit of power" (De Coelo i, text. 116). But the limit of anything is reducible to the genus of that of which it is the limit; as a point is reducible to the genus of line. Therefore virtue is reducible to the genus of power, and not to the genus of habit.

Objection 2: Further, Augustine says (De Lib. Arb. ii*) that "virtue is good use of free-will." But use of free-will is an act. Therefore virtue is not a habit, but an act.

Objection 3: Further, we do not merit by our habits, but by our actions: otherwise a man would merit continually, even while asleep. But we do merit by our virtues. Therefore virtues are not habits, but acts.

Objection 4: Further, Augustine says (De Moribus Eccl. xv) that "virtue is the order of love," and (QQ. lxxxiii, qu. 30) that "the ordering which is called virtue consists in enjoying what we ought to enjoy, and using what we ought to use." Now order, or ordering, denominates either an action or

---

* Retract. ix; cf. De Lib. Arb. ii, 19.

relationem. Ergo virtus non est habitus, sed actus vel relatio.

PRAETEREA, sicut inveniuntur virtutes humanae, ita et virtutes naturales. Sed virtutes naturales non sunt habitus, sed potentiae quaedam. Ergo etiam neque virtutes humanae.

SED CONTRA est quod philosophus, in libro Praedicament., scientiam et virtutem ponit esse habitus.

RESPONDEO dicendum quod virtus nominat quandam potentiae perfectionem. Uniuscuiusque autem perfectio praecipue consideratur in ordine ad suum finem. Finis autem potentiae actus est. Unde potentia dicitur esse perfecta, secundum quod determinatur ad suum actum. Sunt autem quaedam potentiae quae secundum seipsas sunt determinatae ad suos actus; sicut potentiae naturales activae. Et ideo huiusmodi potentiae naturales secundum seipsas dicuntur virtutes. Potentiae autem rationales, quae sunt propriae hominis, non sunt determinatae ad unum, sed se habent indeterminate ad multa, determinantur autem ad actus per habitus, sicut ex supradictis patet. Et ideo virtutes humanae habitus sunt.

AD PRIMUM ergo dicendum quod quandoque virtus dicitur id ad quod est virtus, scilicet vel obiectum virtutis, vel actus eius, sicut fides dicitur quandoque id quod creditur, quandoque vero ipsum credere, quandoque autem ipse habitus quo creditur. Unde quando dicitur quod *virtus est ultimum potentiae,* sumitur virtus pro obiecto virtutis. Id enim in quod ultimo potentia potest, est id ad quod dicitur virtus rei, sicut si aliquis potest ferre centum libras et non plus, virtus eius consideratur secundum centum libras, non autem secundum sexaginta. Obiectio autem procedebat ac si essentialiter virtus esset ultimum potentiae.

AD SECUNDUM dicendum quod bonus usus liberi arbitrii dicitur esse virtus, secundum eandem rationem, quia scilicet est id ad quod ordinatur virtus sicut ad proprium

a relation. Therefore virtue is not a habit, but an action or a relation.

Objection 5: Further, just as there are human virtues, so are there natural virtues. But natural virtues are not habits, but powers. Neither therefore are human virtues habits.

On the contrary, The Philosopher says (Categor. vi) that science and virtue are habits.

I answer that, Virtue denotes a certain perfection of a power. Now a thing's perfection is considered chiefly in regard to its end. But the end of power is act. Wherefore power is said to be perfect, according as it is determinate to its act. Now there are some powers which of themselves are determinate to their acts; for instance, the active natural powers. And therefore these natural powers are in themselves called virtues. But the rational powers, which are proper to man, are not determinate to one particular action, but are inclined indifferently to many: and they are determinate to acts by means of habits, as is clear from what we have said above (I-II, q. 49, a. 4). Therefore human virtues are habits.

Reply to Objection 1: Sometimes we give the name of a virtue to that to which the virtue is directed, namely, either to its object, or to its act: for instance, we give the name Faith, to that which we believe, or to the act of believing, as also to the habit by which we believe. When therefore we say that "virtue is the limit of power," virtue is taken for the object of virtue. For the furthest point to which a power can reach, is said to be its virtue; for instance, if a man can carry a hundredweight and not more, his virtue* is put at a hundredweight, and not at sixty. But the objection takes virtue as being essentially the limit of power.

Reply to Objection 2: Good use of freewill is said to be a virtue, in the same sense as above (ad 1); that is to say, because it is that to which virtue is directed as to its

---

* In English we should say 'strength,' which is the original signification of the Latin *virtus:* thus we speak of an engine being so many horse-power, to indicate its 'strength.'

actum. Nihil est enim aliud actus virtutis quam bonus usus liberi arbitrii.

Ad tertium dicendum quod aliquo dicimur mereri dupliciter. Uno modo, sicut ipso merito, eo modo quo dicimur currere cursu, et hoc modo meremur actibus. Alio modo dicimur mereri aliquo sicut principio merendi, sicut dicimur currere potentia motiva, et sic dicimur mereri virtutibus et habitibus.

Ad quartum dicendum quod virtus dicitur ordo vel ordinatio amoris, sicut id ad quod est virtus, per virtutem enim ordinatur amor in nobis.

Ad quintum dicendum quod potentiae naturales sunt de se determinatae ad unum, non autem potentiae rationales. Et ideo non est simile, ut dictum est.

proper act. For the act of virtue is nothing else than the good use of free-will.

Reply to Objection 3: We are said to merit by something in two ways. First, as by merit itself, just as we are said to run by running; and thus we merit by acts. Secondly, we are said to merit by something as by the principle whereby we merit, as we are said to run by the motive power; and thus are we said to merit by virtues and habits.

Reply to Objection 4: When we say that virtue is the order or ordering of love, we refer to the end to which virtue is ordered: because in us love is set in order by virtue.

Reply to Objection 5: Natural powers are of themselves determinate to one act: not so the rational powers. And so there is no comparison, as we have said.

Articulus 2

Ad secundum sic proceditur. Videtur quod non sit de ratione virtutis humanae quod sit habitus operativus. Dicit enim Tullius, in IV de Tuscul. quaest., quod sicut est sanitas et pulchritudo corporis, ita est virtus animae. Sed sanitas et pulchritudo non sunt habitus operativi. Ergo neque etiam virtus.

Praeterea, in rebus naturalibus invenitur virtus non solum ad agere, sed etiam ad esse, ut patet per philosophum, in I de caelo, quod quaedam habent virtutem ut sint semper, quaedam vero non ad hoc quod sint semper, sed aliquo tempore determinato. Sed sicut se habet virtus naturalis in rebus naturalibus, ita se habet virtus humana in rationalibus. Ergo etiam virtus humana non solum est ad agere, sed etiam ad esse.

Praeterea, philosophus dicit, in VII Physic., quod virtus *est dispositio perfecti ad optimum.* Optimum autem ad quod hominem oportet disponi per virtutem, est ipse Deus, ut probat Augustinus in libro II de moribus Eccles.; ad quem disponitur anima per assimilationem ad ipsum. Ergo videtur quod virtus dicatur qualitas quaedam animae in ordine ad Deum, tanquam assimilativa ad ipsum, non autem in ordine ad operationem. Non igitur est habitus operativus.

Article 2
Whether human virtue is an operative habit?

Objection 1: It would seem that it is not essential to human virtue to be an operative habit. For Tully says (Tuscul. iv) that as health and beauty belong to the body, so virtue belongs to the soul. But health and beauty are not operative habits. Therefore neither is virtue.

Objection 2: Further, in natural things we find virtue not only in reference to act, but also in reference to being: as is clear from the Philosopher (De Coelo i), since some have a virtue to be always, while some have a virtue to be not always, but at some definite time. Now as natural virtue is in natural things, so is human virtue in rational beings. Therefore also human virtue is referred not only to act, but also to being.

Objection 3: Further, the Philosopher says (Phys. vii, text. 17) that virtue "is the disposition of a perfect thing to that which is best." Now the best thing to which man needs to be disposed by virtue is God Himself, as Augustine proves (De Moribus Eccl. 3, 6, 14) to Whom the soul is disposed by being made like to Him. Therefore it seems that virtue is a quality of the soul in reference to God, likening it, as it were, to Him; and not in reference to operation. It is not, therefore, an operative habit.

SED CONTRA est quod philosophus dicit, in II Ethic., quod *virtus uniuscuiusque rei est quae opus eius bonum reddit.*

RESPONDEO dicendum quod virtus, ex ipsa ratione nominis, importat quandam perfectionem potentiae, ut supra dictum est. Unde, cum duplex sit potentia, scilicet potentia ad esse et potentia ad agere, utriusque potentiae perfectio virtus vocatur. Sed potentia ad esse se tenet ex parte materiae, quae est ens in potentia, potentia autem ad agere se tenet ex parte formae, quae est principium agendi, eo quod unumquodque agit inquantum est actu. In constitutione autem hominis, corpus se habet sicut materia, anima vero sicut forma. Et quantum quidem ad corpus, homo communicat cum aliis animalibus; et similiter quantum ad vires quae sunt animae et corpori communes; solae autem illae vires quae sunt propriae animae, scilicet rationales, sunt hominis tantum. Et ideo virtus humana, de qua loquimur, non potest pertinere ad corpus; sed pertinet tantum ad id quod est proprium animae. Unde virtus humana non importat ordinem ad esse, sed magis ad agere. Et ideo de ratione virtutis humanae est quod sit habitus operativus.

AD PRIMUM ergo dicendum quod modus actionis sequitur dispositionem agentis, unumquodque enim quale est, talia operatur. Et ideo, cum virtus sit principium aliqualis operationis, oportet quod in operante praeexistat secundum virtutem aliqua conformis dispositio. Facit autem virtus operationem ordinatam. Et ideo ipsa virtus est quaedam dispositio ordinata in anima, secundum scilicet quod potentiae animae ordinantur aliqualiter ad invicem, et ad id quod est extra. Et ideo virtus, inquantum est conveniens dispositio animae, assimilatur sanitati et pulchritudini, quae sunt debitae dispositiones corporis. Sed per hoc non excluditur quin virtus etiam sit operationis principium.

AD SECUNDUM dicendum quod virtus quae est ad esse, non est propria hominis, sed

On the contrary, The Philosopher (Ethic. ii, 6) says that "virtue of a thing is that which makes its work good."

I answer that, Virtue, from the very nature of the word, implies some perfection of power, as we have said above (I-II, q. 55, a. 1). Wherefore, since power* is of two kinds, namely, power in reference to being, and power in reference to act; the perfection of each of these is called virtue. But power in reference to being is on the part of matter, which is potential being, whereas power in reference to act, is on the part of the form, which is the principle of action, since everything acts in so far as it is in act. Now man is so constituted that the body holds the place of matter, the soul that of form. The body, indeed, man has in common with other animals; and the same is to be said of the forces which are common to the soul and body: and only those forces which are proper to the soul, namely, the rational forces, belong to man alone. And therefore, human virtue, of which we are speaking now, cannot belong to the body, but belongs only to that which is proper to the soul. Wherefore human virtue does not imply reference to being, but rather to act. Consequently it is essential to human virtue to be an operative habit.

Reply to Objection 1: Mode of action follows on the disposition of the agent: for such as a thing is, such is its act. And therefore, since virtue is the principle of some kind of operation, there must needs pre-exist in the operator in respect of virtue some corresponding disposition. Now virtue causes an ordered operation. Therefore virtue itself is an ordered disposition of the soul, in so far as, to wit, the powers of the soul are in some way ordered to one another, and to that which is outside. Hence virtue, inasmuch as it is a suitable disposition of the soul, is like health and beauty, which are suitable dispositions of the body. But this does not hinder virtue from being a principle of operation.

Reply to Objection 2: Virtue which is referred to being is not proper to man; but

---

* The one Latin word *potentia* is rendered 'potentiality' in the first case, and 'power' in the second.

solum virtus quae est ad opera rationis, quae sunt propria hominis.

Ad tertium dicendum quod, cum Dei substantia sit eius actio, summa assimilatio hominis ad Deum est secundum aliquam operationem. Unde, sicut supra dictum est, felicitas sive beatitudo, per quam homo maxime Deo conformatur, quae est finis humanae vitae, in operatione consistit.

only that virtue which is referred to works of reason, which are proper to man.

Reply to Objection 3: As God's substance is His act, the highest likeness of man to God is in respect of some operation. Wherefore, as we have said above (I-II, q. 3, a. 2), happiness or bliss by which man is made most perfectly conformed to God, and which is the end of human life, consists in an operation.

Articulus 3

Ad tertium sic proceditur. Videtur quod non sit de ratione virtutis quod sit habitus bonus. Peccatum enim in malo semper sumitur. Sed etiam peccati est aliqua virtus; secundum illud I ad Cor. XV, *virtus peccati lex*. Ergo virtus non semper est habitus bonus.

Praeterea, virtus potentiae respondet. Sed potentia non solum se habet ad bonum, sed etiam ad malum; secundum illud Isaiae V, *vae, qui potentes estis ad bibendum vinum, et viri fortes ad miscendam ebrietatem*. Ergo etiam virtus se habet et ad bonum et ad malum.

Praeterea, secundum apostolum, II ad Cor. XII, *virtus in infirmitate perficitur*. Sed infirmitas est quoddam malum. Ergo virtus non solum se habet ad bonum, sed etiam ad malum.

Sed contra est quod Augustinus dicit, in libro de moribus Eccles., *nemo autem dubitaverit quod virtus animam facit optimam*. Et philosophus dicit, in II Ethic., quod *virtus est quae bonum facit habentem, et opus eius bonum reddit*.

Respondeo dicendum quod, sicut supra dictum est, virtus importat perfectionem potentiae, unde virtus cuiuslibet rei determinatur ad ultimum in quod res potest, ut dicitur in I de caelo. Ultimum autem in quod unaquaeque potentia potest, oportet quod sit bonum, nam omne malum defectum quendam importat; unde Dionysius dicit, in IV cap. de Div. Nom., quod omne malum est infirmum. Et propter hoc oportet quod virtus cuiuslibet rei dicatur in ordine ad bonum. Unde virtus humana, quae est habitus operativus, est bonus habitus, et boni operativus.

Article 3
Whether human virtue is a good habit?

Objection 1: It would seem that it is not essential to virtue that it should be a good habit. For sin is always taken in a bad sense. But there is a virtue even of sin; according to 1 Cor. 15:56: "The virtue* of sin is the Law." Therefore virtue is not always a good habit.

Objection 2: Further, Virtue corresponds to power. But power is not only referred to good, but also to evil: according to Is. 5: "Woe to you that are mighty to drink wine, and stout men at drunkenness." Therefore virtue also is referred to good and evil.

Objection 3: Further, according to the Apostle (2 Cor. 12:9): "Virtue† is made perfect in infirmity." But infirmity is an evil. Therefore virtue is referred not only to good, but also to evil.

On the contrary, Augustine says (De Moribus Eccl. vi): "No one can doubt that virtue makes the soul exceeding good": and the Philosopher says (Ethic. ii, 6): "Virtue is that which makes its possessor good, and his work good likewise."

I answer that, As we have said above (I-II, q. 55, a. 1), virtue implies a perfection of power: wherefore the virtue of a thing is fixed by the limit of its power (De Coelo i). Now the limit of any power must needs be good: for all evil implies defect; wherefore Dionysius says (Div. Hom. ii) that every evil is a weakness. And for this reason the virtue of a thing must be regarded in reference to good. Therefore human virtue which is an operative habit, is a good habit, productive of good works.

---

* Douay: 'strength'
† Douay: 'power'

AD PRIMUM ergo dicendum quod sicut perfectum, ita et bonum dicitur metaphorice in malis, dicitur enim et perfectus fur sive latro, et bonus fur sive latro; ut patet per philosophum, in V Metaphys. Secundum hoc ergo, etiam virtus metaphorice in malis dicitur. Et sic virtus peccati dicitur lex, inquantum scilicet per legem occasionaliter est peccatum augmentatum, et quasi ad maximum suum posse pervenit.

AD SECUNDUM dicendum quod malum ebrietatis et nimiae potationis, consistit in defectu ordinis rationis. Contingit autem, cum defectu rationis, esse aliquam potentiam inferiorem perfectam ad id quod est sui generis, etiam cum repugnantia vel cum defectu rationis. Perfectio autem talis potentiae, cum sit cum defectu rationis, non posset dici virtus humana.

AD TERTIUM dicendum quod tanto ratio perfectior esse ostenditur, quanto infirmitates corporis et inferiorum partium magis potest vincere seu tolerare. Et ideo virtus humana, quae rationi attribuitur, *in infirmitate perfici* dicitur, non quidem rationis, sed in infirmitate corporis et inferiorum partium.

Reply to Objection 1: Just as bad things are said metaphorically to be perfect, so are they said to be good: for we speak of a perfect thief or robber; and of a good thief or robber, as the Philosopher explains (Metaph. v, text. 21). In this way therefore virtue is applied to evil things: so that the "virtue" of sin is said to be law, in so far as occasionally sin is aggravated through the law, so as to attain to the limit of its possibility.

Reply to Objection 2: The evil of drunkenness and excessive drink, consists in a falling away from the order of reason. Now it happens that, together with this falling away from reason, some lower power is perfect in reference to that which belongs to its own kind, even in direct opposition to reason, or with some falling away therefrom. But the perfection of that power, since it is compatible with a falling away from reason, cannot be called a human virtue.

Reply to Objection 3: Reason is shown to be so much the more perfect, according as it is able to overcome or endure more easily the weakness of the body and of the lower powers. And therefore human virtue, which is attributed to reason, is said to be "made perfect in infirmity," not of the reason indeed, but of the body and of the lower powers.

ARTICULUS 4

AD QUARTUM sic proceditur. Videtur quod non sit conveniens definitio virtutis quae solet assignari, scilicet, *virtus est bona qualitas mentis, qua recte vivitur, qua nullus male utitur, quam Deus in nobis sine nobis operatur.* Virtus enim est bonitas hominis, ipsa enim est quae bonum facit habentem. Sed bonitas non videtur esse bona, sicut nec albedo est alba. Igitur inconvenienter dicitur quod virtus est *bona qualitas.*

PRAETEREA, nulla differentia est communior suo genere, cum sit generis divisiva. Sed bonum est communius quam qualitas, convertitur enim cum ente. Ergo *bonum* non debet poni in definitione virtutis, ut differentia qualitatis.

ARTICLE 4
Whether virtue is suitably defined?

Objection 1: It would seem that the definition, usually given, of virtue, is not suitable, to wit: "Virtue is a good quality of the mind, by which we live righteously, of which no one can make bad use, which God works in us, without us." For virtue is man's goodness, since virtue it is that makes its subject good. But goodness does not seem to be good, as neither is whiteness white. It is therefore unsuitable to describe virtue as a "good quality."

Objection 2: Further, no difference is more common than its genus; since it is that which divides the genus. But good is more common than quality, since it is convertible with being. Therefore "good" should not be put in the definition of virtue, as a difference of quality.

I-II, q. 55, a. 4, arg. 3 THE VIRTUES, AS TO THEIR ESSENCE

PRAETEREA, sicut Augustinus dicit, in XII de Trin., *ubi primo occurrit aliquid quod non sit nobis pecoribusque commune, illud ad mentem pertinet.* Sed quaedam virtutes sunt etiam irrationabilium partium; ut philosophus dicit, in III Ethic. Non ergo omnis virtus est bona qualitas *mentis.*

PRAETEREA, rectitudo videtur ad iustitiam pertinere, unde idem dicuntur recti, et iusti. Sed iustitia est species virtutis. Inconvenienter ergo ponitur *rectum* in definitione virtutis, cum dicitur, *qua recte vivitur.*

PRAETEREA, quicumque superbit de aliquo, male utitur eo. Sed multi superbiunt de virtute, dicit enim Augustinus, in regula, quod *superbia etiam bonis operibus insidiatur, ut pereant.* Falsum est ergo quod *nemo virtute male utatur.*

PRAETEREA, homo per virtutem iustificatur. Sed Augustinus dicit, super illud Ioan., *maiora horum faciet, qui creavit te sine te, non iustificabit te sine te.* Inconvenienter ergo dicitur quod *virtutem Deus in nobis sine nobis operatur.*

SED CONTRA est auctoritas Augustini, ex cuius verbis praedicta definitio colligitur, et praecipue in II de libero arbitrio.

RESPONDEO dicendum quod ista definitio perfecte complectitur totam rationem virtutis. Perfecta enim ratio uniuscuiusque rei colligitur ex omnibus causis eius. Comprehendit autem praedicta definitio omnes causas virtutis. Causa namque formalis virtutis, sicut et cuiuslibet rei, accipitur ex eius genere et differentia, cum dicitur *qualitas bona,* genus enim virtutis *qualitas* est, differentia autem *bonum.* Esset tamen convenientior definitio, si loco *qualitatis habitus* poneretur, qui est genus propinquum. Virtus autem non habet materiam *ex qua,* sicut nec alia accidentia, sed habet materiam *circa quam;* et materiam *in qua,* scilicet subiectum. Materia autem circa quam est obiectum virtutis; quod non

Objection 3: Further, as Augustine says (De Trin. xii, 3): "When we come across anything that is not common to us and the beasts of the field, it is something appertaining to the mind." But there are virtues even of the irrational parts; as the Philosopher says (Ethic. iii, 10). Every virtue, therefore, is not a good quality "of the mind."

Objection 4: Further, righteousness seems to belong to justice; whence the righteous are called just. But justice is a species of virtue. It is therefore unsuitable to put "righteous" in the definition of virtue, when we say that virtue is that "by which we live righteously."

Objection 5: Further, whoever is proud of a thing, makes bad use of it. But many are proud of virtue, for Augustine says in his Rule, that "pride lies in wait for good works in order to slay them." It is untrue, therefore, "that no one can make bad use of virtue."

Objection 6: Further, man is justified by virtue. But Augustine commenting on Jn. 15:11: "He shall do greater things than these," says*: "He who created thee without thee, will not justify thee without thee." It is therefore unsuitable to say that "God works virtue in us, without us."

On the contrary, We have the authority of Augustine from whose words this definition is gathered, and principally in De Libero Arbitrio ii, 19.

I answer that, This definition comprises perfectly the whole essential notion of virtue. For the perfect essential notion of anything is gathered from all its causes. Now the above definition comprises all the causes of virtue. For the formal cause of virtue, as of everything, is gathered from its genus and difference, when it is defined as "a good quality": for "quality" is the genus of virtue, and the difference, "good." But the definition would be more suitable if for "quality" we substitute "habit," which is the proximate genus. Now virtue has no matter "out of which" it is formed, as neither has any other accident; but it has matter "about which" it is concerned, and matter "in which" it exits, namely, the subject. The matter about which virtue is concerned is its object, and this could not be

---

* Tract. xxvii in Joan.: Serm. xv de Verb. Ap. 11

potuit in praedicta definitione poni, eo quod per obiectum determinatur virtus ad speciem; hic autem assignatur definitio virtutis in communi. Unde ponitur subiectum loco causae materialis, cum dicitur quod est bona qualitas *mentis*. Finis autem virtutis, cum sit habitus operativus, est ipsa operatio. Sed notandum quod habituum operativorum aliqui sunt semper ad malum, sicut habitus vitiosi; aliqui vero quandoque ad bonum, et quandoque ad malum, sicut opinio se habet ad verum et ad falsum; virtus autem est habitus semper se habens ad bonum. Et ideo, ut discernatur virtus ab his quae semper se habent ad malum, dicitur, *qua recte vivitur*, ut autem discernatur ab his quae se habent quandoque ad bonum, quandoque ad malum, dicitur, *qua nullus male utitur*. Causa autem efficiens virtutis infusae, de qua definitio datur, Deus est. Propter quod dicitur, *quam Deus in nobis sine nobis operatur*. Quae quidem particula si auferatur, reliquum definitionis erit commune omnibus virtutibus, et acquisitis et infusis.

AD PRIMUM ergo dicendum quod id quod primo cadit in intellectu, est ens, unde unicuique apprehenso a nobis attribuimus quod sit ens; et per consequens quod sit unum et bonum, quae convertuntur cum ente. Unde dicimus quod essentia est ens et una et bona; et quod unitas est ens et una et bona; et similiter de bonitate. Non autem hoc habet locum in specialibus formis, sicut est albedo et sanitas, non enim omne quod apprehendimus, sub ratione albi et sani apprehendimus. Sed tamen considerandum quod sicut accidentia et formae non subsistentes dicuntur entia, non quia ipsa habeant esse, sed quia eis aliquid est; ita etiam dicuntur bona vel una, non quidem aliqua alia bonitate vel unitate, sed quia eis est aliquid bonum vel unum. Sic igitur et virtus dicitur bona, quia ea aliquid est bonum.

AD SECUNDUM dicendum quod bonum quod ponitur in definitione virtutis, non est bonum commune, quod convertitur cum ente, et est in plus quam qualitas, sed

included in the above definition, because the object fixes the virtue to a certain species, and here we are giving the definition of virtue in general. And so for material cause we have the subject, which is mentioned when we say that virtue is a good quality "of the mind." The end of virtue, since it is an operative habit, is operation. But it must be observed that some operative habits are always referred to evil, as vicious habits: others are sometimes referred to good, sometimes to evil; for instance, opinion is referred both to the true and to the untrue: whereas virtue is a habit which is always referred to good: and so the distinction of virtue from those habits which are always referred to evil, is expressed in the words "by which we live righteously": and its distinction from those habits which are sometimes directed unto good, sometimes unto evil, in the words, "of which no one makes bad use." Lastly, God is the efficient cause of infused virtue, to which this definition applies; and this is expressed in the words "which God works in us without us." If we omit this phrase, the remainder of the definition will apply to all virtues in general, whether acquired or infused.

Reply to Objection 1: That which is first seized by the intellect is being: wherefore everything that we apprehend we consider as being, and consequently as one, and as good, which are convertible with being. Wherefore we say that essence is being and is one and is good; and that oneness is being and one and good: and in like manner goodness. But this is not the case with specific forms, as whiteness and health; for everything that we apprehend, is not apprehended with the notion of white and healthy. We must, however, observe that, as accidents and non-subsistent forms are called beings, not as if they themselves had being, but because things are by them; so also are they called good or one, not by some distinct goodness or oneness, but because by them something is good or one. So also is virtue called good, because by it something is good.

Reply to Objection 2: Good, which is put in the definition of virtue, is not good in general which is convertible with being, and which extends further than quality, but the

est bonum rationis, secundum quod Dionysius dicit, in IV cap. de Div. Nom., quod *bonum animae est secundum rationem esse.*

AD TERTIUM dicendum quod virtus non potest esse in irrationali parte animae, nisi inquantum participat rationem, ut dicitur in I Ethic. Et ideo ratio, sive mens, est proprium subiectum virtutis humanae.

AD QUARTUM dicendum quod iustitiae est propria rectitudo quae constituitur circa res exteriores quae in usum hominis veniunt, quae sunt propria materia iustitiae, ut infra patebit. Sed rectitudo quae importat ordinem ad finem debitum et ad legem divinam, quae est regula voluntatis humanae, ut supra dictum est, communis est omni virtuti.

AD QUINTUM dicendum quod virtute potest aliquis male uti tanquam obiecto, puta cum male sentit de virtute, cum odit eam, vel superbit de ea, non autem tanquam principio usus, ita scilicet quod malus sit actus virtutis.

AD SEXTUM dicendum quod virtus infusa causatur in nobis a Deo sine nobis agentibus, non tamen sine nobis consentientibus. Et sic est intelligendum quod dicitur, *quam Deus in nobis sine nobis operatur.* Quae vero per nos aguntur, Deus in nobis causat non sine nobis agentibus, ipse enim operatur in omni voluntate et natura.

good as fixed by reason, with regard to which Dionysius says (Div. Nom. iv) "that the good of the soul is to be in accord with reason."

Reply to Objection 3: Virtue cannot be in the irrational part of the soul, except in so far as this participates in the reason (Ethic. i, 13). And therefore reason, or the mind, is the proper subject of virtue.

Reply to Objection 4: Justice has a righteousness of its own by which it puts those outward things right which come into human use, and are the proper matter of justice, as we shall show further on (I-II, q. 60, a. 2; II-II, q. 58, a. 8). But the righteousness which denotes order to a due end and to the Divine law, which is the rule of the human will, as stated above (I-II, q. 19, a. 4), is common to all virtues.

Reply to Objection 5: One can make bad use of a virtue objectively, for instance by having evil thoughts about a virtue, e.g., by hating it, or by being proud of it: but one cannot make bad use of virtue as principle of action, so that an act of virtue be evil.

Reply to Objection 6: Infused virtue is caused in us by God without any action on our part, but not without our consent. This is the sense of the words, "which God works in us without us." As to those things which are done by us, God causes them in us, yet not without action on our part, for He works in every will and in every nature.

Quaestio LVI

Deinde considerandum est de subiecto virtutis. Et circa hoc quaeruntur sex. *Primo,* utrum virtus sit in potentia animae sicut in subiecto. *Secundo,* utrum una virtus possit esse in pluribus potentiis. *Tertio,* utrum intellectus possit esse subiectum virtutis. *Quarto,* utrum irascibilis et concupiscibilis. *Quinto,* utrum vires apprehensivae sensitivae. *Sexto,* utrum voluntas.

Articulus 1

Ad primum sic proceditur. Videtur quod virtus non sit in potentia animae sicut in subiecto. Dicit enim Augustinus, in II de Lib. Arbit., quod *virtus est qua recte vivitur.* Vivere autem non est per potentiam animae, sed per eius essentiam. Ergo virtus non est in potentia animae, sed in eius essentia.

Praeterea, philosophus dicit, in II Ethic., *virtus est quae bonum facit habentem, et opus eius bonum reddit.* Sed sicut opus constituitur per potentiam, ita habens virtutem constituitur per essentiam animae. Ergo virtus non magis pertinet ad potentiam animae, quam ad eius essentiam.

Praeterea, potentia est in secunda specie qualitatis. Virtus autem est quaedam qualitas, ut supra dictum est. Qualitatis autem non est qualitas. Ergo virtus non est in potentia animae sicut in subiecto.

Sed contra, *virtus est ultimum potentiae,* ut dicitur in I de caelo. Sed ultimum est in eo cuius est ultimum. Ergo virtus est in potentia animae.

Respondeo dicendum quod virtutem pertinere ad potentiam animae, ex tribus potest esse manifestum. Primo quidem, ex ipsa ratione virtutis, quae importat perfectionem potentiae, perfectio autem est in eo cuius est perfectio. Secundo, ex hoc quod est habitus operativus, ut supra dictum est, omnis autem operatio est ab anima per aliquam potentiam. Tertio, ex hoc

Question 56
Of the Subject of Virtue

We now have to consider the subject of virtue, about which there are six points of inquiry: 1. Whether the subject of virtue is a power of the soul? 2. Whether one virtue can be in several powers? 3. Whether the intellect can be the subject of virtue? 4. Whether the irascible and concupiscible faculties can be the subject of virtue? 5. Whether the sensitive powers of apprehension can be the subject of virtue? 6. Whether the will can be the subject of virtue?

Article 1
Whether the subject of virtue is a power of the soul?

Objection 1: It would seem that the subject of virtue is not a power of the soul. For Augustine says (De Lib. Arb. ii, 19) that "virtue is that by which we live righteously." But we live by the essence of the soul, and not by a power of the soul. Therefore virtue is not a power, but in the essence of the soul.

Objection 2: Further, the Philosopher says (Ethic. ii, 6) that "virtue is that which makes its possessor good, and his work good likewise." But as work is set up by power, so he that has a virtue is set up by the essence of the soul. Therefore virtue does not belong to the power, any more than to the essence of the soul.

Objection 3: Further, power is in the second species of quality. But virtue is a quality, as we have said above (I-II, q. 55, a. 4): and quality is not the subject of quality. Therefore a power of the soul is not the subject of virtue.

On the contrary, "Virtue is the limit of power" (De Coelo ii). But the limit is in that of which it is the limit. Therefore virtue is in a power of the soul.

I answer that, It can be proved in three ways that virtue belongs to a power of the soul. First, from the notion of the very essence of virtue, which implies perfection of a power; for perfection is in that which it perfects. Secondly, from the fact that virtue is an operative habit, as we have said above (I-II, q. 55, a. 2): for all operation proceeds from the soul through a power. Thirdly, from the fact

quod disponit ad optimum, optimum autem est finis, qui vel est operatio rei, vel aliquid consecutum per operationem a potentia egredientem. Unde virtus humana est in potentia animae sicut in subiecto.

AD PRIMUM ergo dicendum quod *vivere* dupliciter sumitur. Quandoque enim dicitur vivere ipsum esse viventis, et sic pertinet ad essentiam animae, quae est viventi essendi principium. Alio modo *vivere* dicitur operatio viventis, et sic virtute recte vivitur, inquantum per eam aliquis recte operatur.

AD SECUNDUM dicendum quod bonum vel est finis, vel in ordine ad finem dicitur. Et ideo, cum bonum operantis consistat in operatione, hoc etiam ipsum quod virtus facit operantem bonum, refertur ad operationem, et per consequens ad potentiam.

AD TERTIUM dicendum quod unum accidens dicitur esse in alio sicut in subiecto, non quia accidens per seipsum possit sustentare aliud accidens, sed quia unum accidens inhaeret substantiae mediante alio accidente, ut color corpori mediante superficie; unde superficies dicitur esse subiectum coloris. Et eo modo potentia animae dicitur esse subiectum virtutis.

that virtue disposes to that which is best: for the best is the end, which is either a thing's operation, or something acquired by an operation proceeding from the thing's power. Therefore a power of the soul is the subject of virtue.

Reply to Objection 1: "To live" may be taken in two ways. Sometimes it is taken for the very existence of the living thing: in this way it belongs to the essence of the soul, which is the principle of existence in the living thing. But sometimes "to live" is taken for the operation of the living thing: in this sense, by virtue we live righteously, inasmuch as by virtue we perform righteous actions.

Reply to Objection 2: Good is either the end, or something referred to the end. And therefore, since the good of the worker consists in the work, this fact also, that virtue makes the worker good, is referred to the work, and consequently, to the power.

Reply to Objection 3: One accident is said to be the subject of another, not as though one accident could uphold another; but because one accident inheres to substance by means of another, as color to the body by means of the surface; so that surface is said to be the subject of color. In this way a power of the soul is said to be the subject of virtue.

ARTICULUS 2

AD SECUNDUM sic proceditur. Videtur quod una virtus possit esse in duabus potentiis. Habitus enim cognoscuntur per actus. Sed unus actus progreditur diversimode a diversis potentiis, sicut ambulatio procedit a ratione ut a dirigente, a voluntate sicut a movente, et a potentia motiva sicut ab exequente. Ergo etiam unus habitus virtutis potest esse in pluribus potentiis.

PRAETEREA, philosophus dicit, in II Ethic., quod ad virtutem tria requiruntur, scilicet *scire, velle et immobiliter operari.* Sed *scire* pertinet ad intellectum, *velle* ad voluntatem. Ergo virtus potest esse in pluribus potentiis.

ARTICLE 2
Whether one virtue can be in several powers?

Objection 1: It would seem that one virtue can be in several powers. For habits are known by their acts. But one act proceeds in various way from several powers: thus walking proceeds from the reason as directing, from the will as moving, and from the motive power as executing. Therefore also one habit can be in several powers.

Objection 2: Further, the Philosopher says (Ethic. ii, 4) that three things are required for virtue, namely: "to know, to will, and to work steadfastly." But "to know" belongs to the intellect, and "to will" belongs to the will. Therefore virtue can be in several powers.

Praeterea, prudentia est in ratione, cum sit *recta ratio agibilium,* ut dicitur in VI Ethic. Est etiam in voluntate, quia non potest esse cum voluntate perversa, ut in eodem libro dicitur. Ergo una virtus potest esse in duabus potentiis.

Sed contra, virtus est in potentia animae sicut in subiecto. Sed idem accidens non potest esse in pluribus subiectis. Ergo una virtus non potest esse in pluribus potentiis animae.

Respondeo dicendum quod aliquid esse in duobus, contingit dupliciter. Uno modo, sic quod ex aequo sit in utroque. Et sic impossibile est unam virtutem esse in duabus potentiis, quia diversitas potentiarum attenditur secundum generales conditiones obiectorum, diversitas autem habituum secundum speciales; unde ubicumque est diversitas potentiarum, est diversitas habituum, sed non convertitur. Alio modo potest esse aliquid in duobus vel pluribus, non ex aequo, sed ordine quodam. Et sic una virtus pertinere potest ad plures potentias; ita quod in una sit principaliter, et se extendat ad alias per modum diffusionis, vel per modum dispositionis; secundum quod una potentia movetur ab alia, et secundum quod una potentia accipit ab alia.

Ad primum ergo dicendum quod idem actus non potest aequaliter, et eodem ordine, pertinere ad diversas potentias, sed secundum diversas rationes, et diverso ordine.

Ad secundum dicendum quod *scire* praeexigitur ad virtutem moralem, inquantum virtus moralis operatur secundum rationem rectam. Sed essentialiter in appetendo virtus moralis consistit.

Ad tertium dicendum quod prudentia realiter est in ratione sicut in subiecto, sed praesupponit rectitudinem voluntatis sicut principium, ut infra dicetur.

Articulus 3

Ad tertium sic proceditur. Videtur quod intellectus non sit subiectum virtutis. Dicit enim Augustinus, in libro de moribus Eccles., quod omnis virtus est amor. Subiectum autem amoris non est

Objection 3: Further, prudence is in the reason since it is "the right reason of things to be done" (Ethic. vi, 5). And it is also in the will: for it cannot exist together with a perverse will (Ethic. vi, 12). Therefore one virtue can be in two powers.

On the contrary, The subject of virtue is a power of the soul. But the same accident cannot be in several subjects. Therefore one virtue cannot be in several powers of the soul.

I answer that, It happens in two ways that one thing is subjected in two. First, so that it is in both on an equal footing. In this way it is impossible for one virtue to be in two powers: since diversity of powers follows the generic conditions of the objects, while diversity of habits follows the specific conditions thereof: and so wherever there is diversity of powers, there is diversity of habits; but not vice versa. In another way one thing can be subjected in two or more, not on an equal footing, but in a certain order. And thus one virtue can belong to several powers, so that it is in one chiefly, while it extends to others by a kind of diffusion, or by way of a disposition, in so far as one power is moved by another, and one power receives from another.

Reply to Objection 1: One act cannot belong to several powers equally, and in the same degree; but only from different points of view, and in various degrees.

Reply to Objection 2: "To know" is a condition required for moral virtue, inasmuch as moral virtue works according to right reason. But moral virtue is essentially in the appetite.

Reply to Objection 3: Prudence is really subjected in reason: but it presupposes as its principle the rectitude of the will, as we shall see further on (I-II, q. 56, a. 3; q. 57, a. 4).

Article 3
Whether the intellect can be the subject of virtue?

Objection 1: It would seem that the intellect is not the subject of virtue. For Augustine says (De Moribus Eccl. xv) that all virtue is love. But the subject of love is not

I-II, q. 56, a. 3, arg. 1

intellectus, sed solum vis appetitiva. Ergo nulla virtus est in intellectu.

PRAETEREA, virtus ordinatur ad bonum, sicut ex supradictis patet. Bonum autem non est obiectum intellectus, sed appetitivae virtutis. Ergo subiectum virtutis non est intellectus, sed appetitiva virtus.

PRAETEREA, virtus est *quae bonum facit habentem,* ut philosophus dicit. Sed habitus perficiens intellectum non facit bonum habentem, non enim propter scientiam vel artem dicitur homo bonus. Ergo intellectus non est subiectum virtutis.

SED CONTRA est quod mens maxime dicitur intellectus. Subiectum autem virtutis est mens; ut patet ex definitione virtutis supra inducta. Ergo intellectus est subiectum virtutis.

RESPONDEO dicendum quod, sicut supra dictum est, virtus est habitus quo quis bene operatur. Dupliciter autem habitus aliquis ordinatur ad bonum actum. Uno modo, inquantum per huiusmodi habitum acquiritur homini facultas ad bonum actum, sicut per habitum grammaticae habet homo facultatem recte loquendi. Non tamen grammatica facit ut homo semper recte loquatur, potest enim grammaticus barbarizare aut soloecismum facere. Et eadem ratio est in aliis scientiis et artibus. Alio modo, aliquis habitus non solum facit facultatem agendi, sed etiam facit quod aliquis recte facultate utatur, sicut iustitia non solum facit quod homo sit promptae voluntatis ad iusta operandum, sed etiam facit ut iuste operetur. Et quia bonum, sicut et ens, non dicitur simpliciter aliquid secundum id quod est in potentia, sed secundum id quod est in actu; ideo ab huiusmodi habitibus simpliciter dicitur homo bonum operari, et esse bonus, puta quia est iustus vel temperatus; et eadem ratio est de similibus. Et quia virtus est *quae bonum facit habentem, et opus eius bonum reddit,* huiusmodi habitus simpliciter dicuntur virtutes, quia reddunt bonum opus in actu, et simpliciter faciunt bonum habentem. Primi vero habitus non simpliciter dicuntur virtutes, quia non reddunt bonum opus nisi in

THE SUBJECT OF VIRTUE

the intellect, but the appetitive power alone. Therefore no virtue is in the intellect.

Objection 2: Further, virtue is referred to good, as is clear from what has been said above (I-II, q. 55, a. 3). Now good is not the object of the intellect, but of the appetitive power. Therefore the subject of virtue is not the intellect, but the appetitive power.

Objection 3: Further, virtue is that "which makes its possessor good," as the Philosopher says (Ethic. ii, 6). But the habit which perfects the intellect does not make its possessor good: since a man is not said to be a good man on account of his science or his art. Therefore the intellect is not the subject of virtue.

On the contrary, The mind is chiefly called the intellect. But the subject of virtue is the mind, as is clear from the definition, above given, of virtue (I-II, q. 55, a. 4). Therefore the intellect is the subject of virtue.

I answer that, As we have said above (I-II, q. 55, a. 3), a virtue is a habit by which we work well. Now a habit may be directed to a good act in two ways. First, in so far as by the habit a man acquires an aptness to a good act; for instance, by the habit of grammar man has the aptness to speak correctly. But grammar does not make a man always speak correctly: for a grammarian may be guilty of a barbarism or make a solecism: and the case is the same with other sciences and arts. Secondly, a habit may confer not only aptness to act, but also the right use of that aptness: for instance, justice not only gives man the prompt will to do just actions, but also makes him act justly. And since good, and, in like manner, being, is said of a thing simply, in respect, not of what it is potentially, but of what it is actually: therefore from having habits of the latter sort, man is said simply to do good, and to be good; for instance, because he is just, or temperate; and in like manner as regards other such virtues. And since virtue is that "which makes its possessor good, and his work good likewise," these latter habits are called virtuous simply: because they make the work to be actually good, and the subject good simply. But the first kind of habits are not called virtues simply: because they do not make the work good except in regard

quadam facultate, nec simpliciter faciunt bonum habentem. Non enim dicitur simpliciter aliquis homo bonus, ex hoc quod est sciens vel artifex, sed dicitur bonus solum secundum quid, puta bonus grammaticus, aut bonus faber. Et propter hoc, plerumque scientia et ars contra virtutem dividitur, quandoque autem virtutes dicuntur, ut patet in VI Ethic. Subiectum igitur habitus qui secundum quid dicitur virtus, potest esse intellectus, non solum practicus, sed etiam intellectus speculativus, absque omni ordine ad voluntatem, sic enim philosophus, in VI Ethic., scientiam, sapientiam et intellectum, et etiam artem, ponit esse intellectuales virtutes. Subiectum vero habitus qui simpliciter dicitur virtus, non potest esse nisi voluntas; vel aliqua potentia secundum quod est mota a voluntate. Cuius ratio est, quia voluntas movet omnes alias potentias quae aliqualiter sunt rationales, ad suos actus, ut supra habitum est, et ideo quod homo actu bene agat, contingit ex hoc quod homo habet bonam voluntatem. Unde virtus quae facit bene agere in actu, non solum in facultate, oportet quod vel sit in ipsa voluntate; vel in aliqua potentia secundum quod est a voluntate mota. Contingit autem intellectum a voluntate moveri, sicut et alias potentias, considerat enim aliquis aliquid actu, eo quod vult. Et ideo intellectus, secundum quod habet ordinem ad voluntatem, potest esse subiectum virtutis simpliciter dictae. Et hoc modo intellectus speculativus, vel ratio, est subiectum fidei, movetur enim intellectus ad assentiendum his quae sunt fidei, ex imperio voluntatis; *nullus enim credit nisi volens*. Intellectus vero practicus est subiectum prudentiae. Cum enim prudentia sit recta ratio agibilium, requiritur ad prudentiam quod homo se bene habeat ad principia huius rationis agendorum, quae sunt fines; ad quos bene se habet homo per rectitudinem voluntatis, sicut ad principia speculabilium per naturale lumen intellectus agentis. Et ideo sicut subiectum scientiae, quae est ratio recta

to a certain aptness, nor do they make their possessor good simply. For through being gifted in science or art, a man is said to be good, not simply, but relatively; for instance, a good grammarian or a good smith. And for this reason science and art are often divided against virtue; while at other times they are called virtues (Ethic. vi, 2). Hence the subject of a habit which is called a virtue in a relative sense, can be the intellect, and not only the practical intellect, but also the speculative, without any reference to the will: for thus the Philosopher (Ethic. vi, 3) holds that science, wisdom and understanding, and also art, are intellectual virtues. But the subject of a habit which is called a virtue simply, can only be the will, or some power in so far as it is moved by the will. And the reason of this is, that the will moves to their acts all those other powers that are in some way rational, as we have said above (I-II, q. 9, a. 1; q. 17, a. 1; a. 5; I, q. 82, a. 4): and therefore if man do well actually, this is because he has a good will. Therefore the virtue which makes a man to do well actually, and not merely to have the aptness to do well, must be either in the will itself; or in some power as moved by the will. Now it happens that the intellect is moved by the will, just as are the other powers: for a man considers something actually, because he wills to do so. And therefore the intellect, in so far as it is subordinate to the will, can be the subject of virtue absolutely so called. And in this way the speculative intellect, or the reason, is the subject of Faith: for the intellect is moved by the command of the will to assent to what is of faith: for "no man believeth, unless he will."* But the practical intellect is the subject of prudence. For since prudence is the right reason of things to be done, it is a condition thereof that man be rightly disposed in regard to the principles of this reason of things to be done, that is in regard to their ends, to which man is rightly disposed by the rectitude of the will, just as to the principles of speculative truth he is rightly disposed by the natural light of the active intellect. And therefore as the subject of science, which is the right reason of

---

* Augustine: Tract. xxvi in Joan.

speculabilium, est intellectus speculativus in ordine ad intellectum agentem; ita subiectum prudentiae est intellectus practicus in ordine ad voluntatem rectam.

AD PRIMUM ergo dicendum quod verbum Augustini intelligendum est de virtute simpliciter dicta non quod omnis talis virtus sit simpliciter amor; sed quia dependet aliqualiter ab amore, inquantum dependet a voluntate, cuius prima affectio est amor, ut supra dictum est.

AD SECUNDUM dicendum quod bonum uniuscuiusque est finis eius, et ideo, cum verum sit finis intellectus, cognoscere verum est bonus actus intellectus. Unde habitus perficiens intellectum ad verum cognoscendum, vel in speculativis vel in practicis, dicitur virtus.

AD TERTIUM dicendum quod ratio illa procedit de virtute simpliciter dicta.

Articulus 4

AD QUARTUM sic proceditur. Videtur quod irascibilis et concupiscibilis non possint esse subiectum virtutis. Huiusmodi enim vires sunt communes nobis et brutis. Sed nunc loquimur de virtute secundum quod est propria homini, sic enim dicitur virtus humana. Non igitur humanae virtutis potest esse subiectum irascibilis et concupiscibilis, quae sunt partes appetitus sensitivi, ut in primo dictum est.

PRAETEREA, appetitus sensitivus est vis utens organo corporali. Sed bonum virtutis non potest esse in corpore hominis, dicit enim apostolus, Rom. VII, *scio quod non habitat in carne mea bonum*. Ergo appetitus sensitivus non potest esse subiectum virtutis.

PRAETEREA, Augustinus probat, in libro de moribus Eccles., quod virtus non est in corpore, sed in anima, eo quod per animam corpus regitur, unde quod aliquis corpore bene utatur, totum refertur ad animam; *sicut si mihi auriga obtemperans, equos quibus praeest, recte regit, hoc totum mihi debetur*. Sed sicut anima regit corpus, ita

speculative truths, is the speculative intellect in its relation to the active intellect, so the subject of prudence is the practical intellect in its relation to the right will.

Reply to Objection 1: The saying of Augustine is to be understood of virtue simply so called: not that every virtue is love simply: but that it depends in some way on love, in so far as it depends on the will, whose first movement consists in love, as we have said above (I-II, q. 25, a. 1; a. 2; a. 3; q. 27, a. 4; I, q. 20, a. 1).

Reply to Objection 2: The good of each thing is its end: and therefore, as truth is the end of the intellect, so to know truth is the good act of the intellect. Whence the habit, which perfects the intellect in regard to the knowledge of truth, whether speculative or practical, is a virtue.

Reply to Objection 3: This objection considers virtue simply so called.

Article 4
Whether the irascible and concupiscible powers are the subject of virtue?

Objection 1: It would seem that the irascible and concupiscible powers cannot be the subject of virtue. For these powers are common to us and dumb animals. But we are now speaking of virtue as proper to man, since for this reason it is called human virtue. It is therefore impossible for human virtue to be in the irascible and concupiscible powers which are parts of the sensitive appetite, as we have said in the I, q. 81, a. 2.

Objection 2: Further, the sensitive appetite is a power which makes use of a corporeal organ. But the good of virtue cannot be in man's body: for the Apostle says (Rom. 7): "I know that good does not dwell in my flesh." Therefore the sensitive appetite cannot be the subject of virtue.

Objection 3: Further, Augustine proves (De Moribus Eccl. v) that virtue is not in the body but in the soul, for the reason that the body is ruled by the soul: wherefore it is entirely due to his soul that a man make good use of his body: "For instance, if my coachman, through obedience to my orders, guides well the horses which he is driving; this is all due to me." But just as the soul rules the body, so

etiam ratio regit appetitum sensitivum. Ergo totum rationali parti debetur, quod irascibilis et concupiscibilis recte regantur. Sed *virtus est qua recte vivitur,* ut supra dictum est. Virtus igitur non est in irascibili et concupiscibili, sed solum in parte rationali.

Praeterea, *principalis actus virtutis moralis est electio,* ut dicitur in VIII Ethic. Sed electio non est actus irascibilis et concupiscibilis, sed rationis, ut supra dictum est. Ergo virtus moralis non est in irascibili et concupiscibili, sed in ratione.

Sed contra est quod fortitudo ponitur esse in irascibili, temperantia autem in concupiscibili. Unde philosophus dicit, in III Ethic., quod *hae virtutes sunt irrationabilium partium.*

Respondeo dicendum quod irascibilis et concupiscibilis dupliciter considerari possunt. Uno modo secundum se, inquantum sunt partes appetitus sensitivi. Et hoc modo, non competit eis quod sint subiectum virtutis. Alio modo possunt considerari inquantum participant rationem, per hoc quod natae sunt rationi obedire. Et sic irascibilis vel concupiscibilis potest esse subiectum virtutis humanae, sic enim est principium humani actus, inquantum participat rationem. Et in his potentiis necesse est ponere virtutes. Quod enim in irascibili et concupiscibili sint aliquae virtutes, patet. Actus enim qui progreditur ab una potentia secundum quod est ab alia mota, non potest esse perfectus, nisi utraque potentia sit bene disposita ad actum, sicut actus artificis non potest esse congruus, nisi et artifex sit bene dispositus ad agendum, et etiam ipsum instrumentum. In his igitur circa quae operatur irascibilis et concupiscibilis secundum quod sunt a ratione motae, necesse est ut aliquis habitus perficiens ad bene agendum sit non solum in ratione, sed etiam in irascibili et concupiscibili. Et quia bona dispositio potentiae moventis motae, attenditur secundum conformitatem ad potentiam moventem; ideo virtus quae est in

also does the reason rule the sensitive appetite. Therefore that the irascible and concupiscible powers are rightly ruled, is entirely due to the rational powers. Now "virtue is that by which we live rightly," as we have said above (I-II, q. 55, a. 4). Therefore virtue is not in the irascible and concupiscible powers, but only in the rational powers.

Objection 4: Further, "the principal act of moral virtue is choice" (Ethic. viii, 13). Now choice is not an act of the irascible and concupiscible powers, but of the rational power, as we have said above (I-II, q. 13, a. 2). Therefore moral virtue is not in the irascible and concupiscible powers, but in the reason.

On the contrary, Fortitude is assigned to the irascible power, and temperance to the concupiscible power. Whence the Philosopher (Ethic. iii, 10) says that "these virtues belong to the irrational part of the soul."

I answer that, The irascible and concupiscible powers can be considered in two ways. First, in themselves, in so far as they are parts of the sensitive appetite: and in this way they are not competent to be the subject of virtue. Secondly, they can be considered as participating in the reason, from the fact that they have a natural aptitude to obey reason. And thus the irascible or concupiscible power can be the subject of human virtue: for, in so far as it participates in the reason, it is the principle of a human act. And to these powers we must needs assign virtues. For it is clear that there are some virtues in the irascible and concupiscible powers. Because an act, which proceeds from one power according as it is moved by another power, cannot be perfect, unless both powers be well disposed to the act: for instance, the act of a craftsman cannot be successful unless both the craftsman and his instrument be well disposed to act. Therefore in the matter of the operations of the irascible and concupiscible powers, according as they are moved by reason, there must needs be some habit perfecting in respect of acting well, not only the reason, but also the irascible and concupiscible powers. And since the good disposition of the power which moves through being moved, depends on its conformity with the power that moves it: therefore the virtue which is in the

irascibili et concupiscibili, nihil aliud est quam quaedam habitualis conformitas istarum potentiarum ad rationem.

AD PRIMUM ergo dicendum quod irascibilis et concupiscibilis secundum se consideratae, prout sunt partes appetitus sensitivi, communes sunt nobis et brutis. Sed secundum quod sunt rationales per participationem, ut obedientes rationi, sic sunt propriae hominis. Et hoc modo possunt esse subiectum virtutis humanae.

AD SECUNDUM dicendum quod, sicut caro hominis ex se quidem non habet bonum virtutis, fit tamen instrumentum virtuosi actus, inquantum, movente ratione, *membra nostra exhibemus ad serviendum iustitiae,* ita etiam irascibilis et concupiscibilis ex se quidem non habent bonum virtutis sed magis infectionem *fomitis;* inquantum vero conformantur rationi, sic in eis adgeneratur bonum virtutis moralis.

AD TERTIUM dicendum quod alia ratione regitur corpus ab anima, et irascibilis et concupiscibilis a ratione. Corpus enim ad nutum obedit animae absque contradictione, in his in quibus natum est ab anima moveri, unde philosophus dicit, in I Polit., quod *anima regit corpus despotico principatu,* idest sicut dominus servum. Et ideo totus motus corporis refertur ad animam. Et propter hoc in corpore non est virtus, sed solum in anima. Sed irascibilis et concupiscibilis non ad nutum obediunt rationi, sed habent proprios motus suos, quibus interdum rationi repugnant, unde in eodem libro philosophus dicit quod *ratio regit irascibilem et concupiscibilem principatu politico,* quo scilicet reguntur liberi, qui habent in aliquibus propriam voluntatem. Et propter hoc etiam oportet in irascibili et concupiscibili esse aliquas virtutes, quibus bene disponantur ad actum.

AD QUARTUM dicendum quod in electione duo sunt, scilicet intentio finis, quae pertinet ad virtutem moralem; et praeacceptio eius quod est ad finem, quod pertinet ad prudentiam; ut dicitur in VI Ethic.

irascible and concupiscible powers is nothing else but a certain habitual conformity of these powers to reason.

Reply to Objection 1: The irascible and concupiscible powers considered in themselves, as parts of the sensitive appetite, are common to us and dumb animals. But in so far as they are rational by participation, and are obedient to the reason, they are proper to man. And in this way they can be the subject of human virtue.

Reply to Objection 2: Just as human flesh has not of itself the good of virtue, but is made the instrument of a virtuous act, inasmuch as being moved by reason, we "yield our members to serve justice"; so also, the irascible and concupiscible powers, of themselves indeed, have not the good of virtue, but rather the infection of the *fomes:* whereas, inasmuch as they are in conformity with reason, the good of reason is begotten in them.

Reply to Objection 3: The body is ruled by the soul, and the irascible and concupiscible powers by the reason, but in different ways. For the body obeys the soul blindly without any contradiction, in those things in which it has a natural aptitude to be moved by the soul: whence the Philosopher says (Polit. i, 3) that the "soul rules the body with a despotic command" as the master rules his slave: wherefore the entire movement of the body is referred to the soul. For this reason virtue is not in the body, but in the soul. But the irascible and concupiscible powers do not obey the reason blindly; on the contrary, they have their own proper movements, by which, at times, they go against reason, whence the Philosopher says (Polit. i, 3) that the "reason rules the irascible and concupiscible powers by a political command" such as that by which free men are ruled, who have in some respects a will of their own. And for this reason also must there be some virtues in the irascible and concupiscible powers, by which these powers are well disposed to act.

Reply to Objection 4: In choice there are two things, namely, the intention of the end, and this belongs to the moral virtue; and the preferential choice of that which is unto the end, and this belongs to prudence (Ethic. vi,

Quod autem habeat rectam intentionem finis circa passiones animae, hoc contingit ex bona dispositione irascibilis et concupiscibilis. Et ideo virtutes morales circa passiones, sunt in irascibili et concupiscibili, sed prudentia est in ratione.

2, 5). But that the irascible and concupiscible powers have a right intention of the end in regard to the passions of the soul, is due to the good disposition of these powers. And therefore those moral virtues which are concerned with the passions are in the irascible and concupiscible powers, but prudence is in the reason.

Articulus 5

Ad quintum sic proceditur. Videtur quod in viribus sensitivis apprehensivis interius, possit esse aliqua virtus. Appetitus enim sensitivus potest esse subiectum virtutis, inquantum obedit rationi. Sed vires sensitivae apprehensivae interius, rationi obediunt, ad imperium enim rationis operatur et imaginativa et cogitativa et memorativa. Ergo in his viribus potest esse virtus.

Praeterea, sicut appetitus rationalis, qui est voluntas, in suo actu potest impediri, vel etiam adiuvari, per appetitum sensitivum; ita etiam intellectus vel ratio potest impediri, vel etiam iuvari, per vires praedictas. Sicut ergo in viribus sensitivis appetitivis potest esse virtus, ita etiam in apprehensivis.

Praeterea, prudentia est quaedam virtus, cuius partem ponit Tullius memoriam, in sua rhetorica. Ergo etiam in vi memorativa potest esse aliqua virtus. Et eadem ratione, in aliis interioribus apprehensivis viribus.

Sed contra est quod omnes virtutes vel sunt intellectuales, vel morales, ut dicitur in II Ethic. Morales autem virtutes omnes sunt in parte appetitiva, intellectuales autem in intellectu vel ratione, sicut patet in VI Ethic. Nulla ergo virtus est in viribus sensitivis apprehensivis interius.

Respondeo dicendum quod in viribus sensitivis apprehensivis interius, ponuntur aliqui habitus. Quod patet ex hoc praecipue quod philosophus dicit, in libro de memoria, quod *in memorando unum post aliud, operatur consuetudo, quae est quasi quaedam*

Article 5
Whether the sensitive powers of apprehension are the subject of virtue?

Objection 1: It would seem that it is possible for virtue to be in the interior sensitive powers of apprehension. For the sensitive appetite can be the subject of virtue, in so far as it obeys reason. But the interior sensitive powers of apprehension obey reason: for the powers of imagination, of cogitation, and of memory* act at the command of reason. Therefore in these powers there can be virtue.

Objection 2: Further, as the rational appetite, which is the will, can be hindered or helped in its act, by the sensitive appetite, so also can the intellect or reason be hindered or helped by the powers mentioned above. As, therefore, there can be virtue in the interior powers of appetite, so also can there be virtue in the interior powers of apprehension.

Objection 3: Further, prudence is a virtue, of which Cicero (De Invent. Rhetor. ii) says that memory is a part. Therefore also in the power of memory there can be a virtue: and in like manner, in the other interior sensitive powers of apprehension.

On the contrary, All virtues are either intellectual or moral (Ethic. ii, 1). Now all the moral virtues are in the appetite; while the intellectual virtues are in the intellect or reason, as is clear from Ethic. vi, 1. Therefore there is no virtue in the interior sensitive powers of apprehension.

I answer that, In the interior sensitive powers of apprehension there are some habits. And this is made clear principally from what the Philosopher says (De Memoria ii), that "in remembering one thing after another, we become used to it; and use is a second

---

* Cf. I, q. 78, a. 4.

natura, nihil autem est aliud habitus consuetudinalis quam habitudo acquisita per consuetudinem, quae est in modum naturae. Unde de virtute dicit Tullius, in sua rhetorica, quod *est habitus in modum naturae, rationi consentaneus.* In homine tamen id quod ex consuetudine acquiritur in memoria, et in aliis viribus sensitivis apprehensivis, non est habitus per se; sed aliquid annexum habitibus intellectivae partis, ut supra dictum est. Sed tamen si qui sunt habitus in talibus viribus, virtutes dici non possunt. Virtus enim est habitus perfectus, quo non contingit nisi bonum operari, unde oportet quod virtus sit in illa potentia quae est consummativa boni operis. Cognitio autem veri non consummatur in viribus sensitivis apprehensivis; sed huiusmodi vires sunt quasi praeparatoriae ad cognitionem intellectivam. Et ideo in huiusmodi viribus non sunt virtutes, quibus cognoscitur verum; sed magis in intellectu vel ratione.

AD PRIMUM ergo dicendum quod appetitus sensitivus se habet ad voluntatem, quae est appetitus rationis, sicut motus ab eo. Et ideo opus appetitivae virtutis consummatur in appetitu sensitivo. Et propter hoc, appetitus sensitivus est subiectum virtutis. Virtutes autem sensitivae apprehensivae magis se habent ut moventes respectu intellectus, eo quod phantasmata se habent ad animam intellectivam, sicut colores ad visum, ut dicitur in III de anima. Et ideo opus cognitionis in intellectu terminatur. Et propter hoc, virtutes cognoscitivae sunt in ipso intellectu vel ratione.

Et per hoc patet solutio ad secundum.

AD TERTIUM dicendum quod memoria non ponitur pars prudentiae, sicut species est pars generis, quasi ipsa memoria sit quaedam virtus per se, sed quia unum eorum quae requiruntur ad prudentiam, est bonitas memoriae; ut sic quodammodo se habeat per modum partis integralis.

nature." Now a habit of use is nothing else than a habit acquired by use, which is like unto nature. Wherefore Tully says of virtue in his Rhetoric that "it is a habit like a second nature in accord with reason." Yet, in man, that which he acquires by use, in his memory and other sensitive powers of apprehension, is not a habit properly so called, but something annexed to the habits of the intellective faculty, as we have said above (I-II, q. 50, a. 4, ad 3). Nevertheless even if there be habits in such powers, they cannot be virtues. For virtue is a perfect habit, by which it never happens that anything but good is done: and so virtue must needs be in that power which consummates the good act. But the knowledge of truth is not consummated in the sensitive powers of apprehension: for such powers prepare the way to the intellective knowledge. And therefore in these powers there are none of the virtues, by which we know truth: these are rather in the intellect or reason.

Reply to Objection 1: The sensitive appetite is related to the will, which is the rational appetite, through being moved by it. And therefore the act of the appetitive power is consummated in the sensitive appetite: and for this reason the sensitive appetite is the subject of virtue. Whereas the sensitive powers of apprehension are related to the intellect rather through moving it; for the reason that the phantasms are related to the intellective soul, as colors to sight (De Anima iii, text. 18). And therefore the act of knowledge is terminated in the intellect; and for this reason the cognoscitive virtues are in the intellect itself, or the reason.

And thus is made clear the *Reply to* the Second Objection.

Reply to Objection 3: Memory is not a part of prudence, as species is of a genus, as though memory were a virtue properly so called: but one of the conditions required for prudence is a good memory; so that, in a fashion, it is after the manner of an integral part.

Articulus 6

AD SEXTUM sic proceditur. Videtur quod voluntas non sit subiectum alicuius virtutis. Ad id enim quod convenit potentiae ex ipsa ratione potentiae, non requiritur aliquis habitus. Sed de ipsa ratione voluntatis, cum sit in ratione, secundum philosophum in III de anima, est quod tendat in id quod est bonum secundum rationem, ad quod ordinatur omnis virtus, quia unumquodque naturaliter appetit proprium bonum, *virtus enim est habitus per modum naturae, consentaneus rationi,* ut Tullius dicit in sua rhetorica. Ergo voluntas non est subiectum virtutis.

PRAETEREA, omnis virtus aut est intellectualis, aut moralis, ut dicitur in I et II Ethic. Sed virtus intellectualis est, sicut in subiecto, in intellectu et ratione, non autem in voluntate, virtus autem moralis est, sicut in subiecto, in irascibili et concupiscibili, quae sunt rationales per participationem. Ergo nulla virtus est in voluntate sicut in subiecto.

PRAETEREA, omnes actus humani, ad quos virtutes ordinantur, sunt voluntarii. Si igitur respectu aliquorum humanorum actuum sit aliqua virtus in voluntate, pari ratione respectu omnium actuum humanorum erit virtus in voluntate. Aut ergo in nulla alia potentia erit aliqua virtus, aut ad eundem actum ordinabuntur duae virtutes, quod videtur inconveniens. Voluntas ergo non potest esse subiectum virtutis.

SED CONTRA est quod maior perfectio requiritur in movente quam in moto. Sed voluntas movet irascibilem et concupiscibilem. Multo ergo magis debet esse virtus in voluntate, quam in irascibili et concupiscibili.

RESPONDEO dicendum quod, cum per habitum perficiatur potentia ad agendum, ibi indiget potentia habitu perficiente ad bene agendum, qui quidem habitus est virtus, ubi ad hoc non sufficit propria ratio potentiae. Omnis autem potentiae propria ratio attenditur in ordine ad obiectum. Unde cum, sicut dictum est, obiectum voluntati sit bonum rationis voluntati proportionatum, quantum ad hoc non indiget voluntas virtute perficiente.

Article 6
Whether the will can be the subject of virtue?

Objection 1: It would seem that the will is not the subject of virtue. Because no habit is required for that which belongs to a power by reason of its very nature. But since the will is in the reason, it is of the very essence of the will, according to the Philosopher (De Anima iii, text. 42), to tend to that which is good, according to reason. And to this good every virtue is ordered, since everything naturally desires its own proper good; for virtue, as Tully says in his Rhetoric, is a "habit like a second nature in accord with reason." Therefore the will is not the subject of virtue.

Objection 2: Further, every virtue is either intellectual or moral (Ethic. i, 13; ii, 1). But intellectual virtue is subjected in the intellect and reason, and not in the will: while moral virtue is subjected in the irascible and concupiscible powers which are rational by participation. Therefore no virtue is subjected in the will.

Objection 3: Further, all human acts, to which virtues are ordained, are voluntary. If therefore there be a virtue in the will in respect of some human acts, in like manner there will be a virtue in the will in respect of all human acts. Either, therefore, there will be no virtue in any other power, or there will be two virtues ordained to the same act, which seems unreasonable. Therefore the will cannot be the subject of virtue.

On the contrary, Greater perfection is required in the mover than in the moved. But the will moves the irascible and concupiscible powers. Much more therefore should there be virtue in the will than in the irascible and concupiscible powers.

I answer that, Since the habit perfects the power in reference to act, then does the power need a habit perfecting it unto doing well, which habit is a virtue, when the power's own proper nature does not suffice for the purpose. Now the proper nature of a power is seen in its relation to its object. Since, therefore, as we have said above (I-II, q. 19, a. 3), the object of the will is the good of reason proportionate to the will, in respect of this the will does not need a virtue perfecting it.

Sed si quod bonum immineat homini volendum, quod excedat proportionem volentis; sive quantum ad totam speciem humanam, sicut bonum divinum, quod transcendit limites humanae naturae, sive quantum ad individuum, sicut bonum proximi; ibi voluntas indiget virtute. Et ideo huiusmodi virtutes quae ordinant affectum hominis in Deum vel in proximum, sunt in voluntate sicut in subiecto; ut caritas, iustitia et huiusmodi.

AD PRIMUM ergo dicendum quod ratio illa habet locum de virtute quae ordinat ad bonum proprium ipsius volentis, sicut temperantia et fortitudo, quae sunt circa passiones humanas et alia huiusmodi, ut ex dictis patet.

AD SECUNDUM dicendum quod rationale per participationem non solum est irascibilis et concupiscibilis; sed *omnino*, idest universaliter, *appetitivum*, ut dicitur in I Ethic. Sub appetitivo autem comprehenditur voluntas. Et ideo, si qua virtus est in voluntate, erit moralis, nisi sit theologica, ut infra patebit.

AD TERTIUM dicendum quod quaedam virtutes ordinantur ad bonum passionis moderatae, quod est proprium huius vel illius hominis, et in talibus non est necessarium quod sit aliqua virtus in voluntate, cum ad hoc sufficiat natura potentiae, ut dictum est. Sed hoc solum necessarium est in illis virtutibus quae ordinantur ad aliquod bonum extrinsecum.

But if man's will is confronted with a good that exceeds its capacity, whether as regards the whole human species, such as Divine good, which transcends the limits of human nature, or as regards the individual, such as the good of one's neighbor, then does the will need virtue. And therefore such virtues as those which direct man's affections to God or to his neighbor are subjected in the will, as charity, justice, and such like.

Reply to Objection 1: This objection is true of those virtues which are ordained to the willer's own good; such as temperance and fortitude, which are concerned with the human passions, and the like, as is clear from what we have said (I-II, q. 35, a. 6).

Reply to Objection 2: Not only the irascible and concupiscible powers are rational by participation but "the appetitive power altogether," i.e., in its entirety (Ethic. i, 13). Now the will is included in the appetitive power. And therefore whatever virtue is in the will must be a moral virtue, unless it be theological, as we shall see later on (I-II, q. 62, a. 3).

Reply to Objection 3: Some virtues are directed to the good of moderated passion, which is the proper good of this or that man: and in these cases there is no need for virtue in the will, for the nature of the power suffices for the purpose, as we have said. This need exists only in the case of virtues which are directed to some extrinsic good.

Quaestio LVII

Deinde considerandum est de distinctione virtutum. Et *primo,* quantum ad virtutes intellectuales; *secundo,* quantum ad morales; *tertio,* quantum ad theologicas. Circa primum quaeruntur sex. *Primo,* utrum habitus intellectuales speculativi sint virtutes. *Secundo,* utrum sint tres, scilicet sapientia, scientia et intellectus. *Tertio,* utrum habitus intellectualis qui est ars, sit virtus. *Quarto,* utrum prudentia sit virtus distincta ab arte. *Quinto,* utrum prudentia sit virtus necessaria homini. *Sexto,* utrum eubulia, synesis et gnome sint virtutes adiunctae prudentiae.

Articulus 1

Ad primum sic proceditur. Videtur quod habitus intellectuales speculativi non sint virtutes. Virtus enim est habitus operativus, ut supra dictum est. Sed habitus speculativi non sunt operativi, distinguitur enim speculativum a practico, idest operativo. Ergo habitus intellectuales speculativi non sunt virtutes.

Praeterea, virtus est eorum per quae fit homo felix sive beatus, eo quod *felicitas est virtutis praemium,* ut dicitur in I Ethic. Sed habitus intellectuales non considerant actus humanos, aut alia bona humana, per quae homo beatitudinem adipiscitur, sed magis res naturales et divinas. Ergo huiusmodi habitus virtutes dici non possunt.

Praeterea, scientia est habitus speculativus. Sed scientia et virtus distinguuntur sicut diversa genera non subalternatim posita; ut patet per philosophum, in IV Topic. Ergo habitus speculativi non sunt virtutes.

Sed contra, soli habitus speculativi considerant necessaria quae impossibile est aliter se habere. Sed philosophus ponit, in VI Ethic., quasdam virtutes intellectuales in parte animae quae considerat necessaria quae non possunt aliter se habere. Ergo habitus intellectuales speculativi sunt virtutes.

Question 57
Of the Intellectual Virtues

We now have to consider the various kinds of virtue: and 1. the intellectual virtues; 2. the moral virtues; 3. the theological virtues. Concerning the first there are six points of inquiry: 1. Whether habits of the speculative intellect are virtues? 2. Whether they are three, namely, wisdom, science and understanding? 3. Whether the intellectual habit, which is art, is a virtue? 4. Whether prudence is a virtue distinct from art? 5. Whether prudence is a virtue necessary to man? 6. Whether *eubulia, synesis* and *gnome* are virtues annexed to prudence?

Article 1
Whether the habits of the speculative intellect are virtues?

Objection 1: It would seem that the habits of the speculative intellect are not virtues. For virtue is an operative habit, as we have said above (I-II, q. 55, a. 2). But speculative habits are not operative: for speculative matter is distinct from practical, i.e., operative matter. Therefore the habits of the speculative intellect are not virtues.

Objection 2: Further, virtue is about those things by which man is made happy or blessed: for "happiness is the reward of virtue" (Ethic. i, 9). Now intellectual habits do not consider human acts or other human goods, by which man acquires happiness, but rather things pertaining to nature or to God. Therefore such like habits cannot be called virtues.

Objection 3: Further, science is a speculative habit. But science and virtue are distinct from one another as genera which are not subalternate, as the Philosopher proves in Topic. iv. Therefore speculative habits are not virtues.

On the contrary, The speculative habits alone consider necessary things which cannot be otherwise than they are. Now the Philosopher (Ethic. vi, 1) places certain intellectual virtues in that part of the soul which considers necessary things that cannot be otherwise than they are. Therefore the habits of the speculative intellect are virtues.

RESPONDEO dicendum quod, cum omnis virtus dicatur in ordine ad bonum, sicut supra dictum est, duplici ratione aliquis habitus dicitur virtus, ut supra dictum est, uno modo, quia facit facultatem bene operandi; alio modo, quia cum facultate, facit etiam usum bonum. Et hoc, sicut supra dictum est, pertinet solum ad illos habitus qui respiciunt partem appetitivam, eo quod vis appetitiva animae est quae facit uti omnibus potentiis et habitibus. Cum igitur habitus intellectuales speculativi non perficiant partem appetitivam, nec aliquo modo ipsam respiciant, sed solam intellectivam; possunt quidem dici virtutes inquantum faciunt facultatem bonae operationis, quae est consideratio veri (hoc enim est bonum opus intellectus), non tamen dicuntur virtutes secundo modo, quasi facientes bene uti potentia seu habitu. Ex hoc enim quod aliquis habet habitum scientiae speculativae, non inclinatur ad utendum, sed fit potens speculari verum in his quorum habet scientiam, sed quod utatur scientia habita, hoc est movente voluntate. Et ideo virtus quae perficit voluntatem, ut caritas vel iustitia, facit etiam bene uti huiusmodi speculativis habitibus. Et secundum hoc etiam, in actibus horum habituum potest esse meritum, si ex caritate fiant, sicut Gregorius dicit, in VI Moral., quod *contemplativa est maioris meriti quam activa.*

AD PRIMUM ergo dicendum quod duplex est opus, scilicet exterius, et interius. Practicum ergo, vel operativum, quod dividitur contra speculativum, sumitur ab opere exteriori, ad quod non habet ordinem habitus speculativus. Sed tamen habet ordinem ad interius opus intellectus, quod est speculari verum. Et secundum hoc est habitus operativus.

AD SECUNDUM dicendum quod virtus est aliquorum dupliciter. Uno modo, sicut obiectorum. Et sic huiusmodi virtutes speculativae non sunt eorum per quae homo fit beatus; nisi forte secundum quod ly *per* dicit causam efficientem vel obiectum completae beatitudinis, quod est Deus, quod est

I answer that, Since every virtue is ordained to some good, as stated above (I-II, q. 55, a. 3), a habit, as we have already observed (I-II, q. 56, a. 3), may be called a virtue for two reasons: first, because it confers aptness in doing good; secondly, because besides aptness, it confers the right use of it. The latter condition, as above stated (I-II, q. 55, a. 3), belongs to those habits alone which affect the appetitive part of the soul: since it is the soul's appetitive power that puts all the powers and habits to their respective uses. Since, then, the habits of the speculative intellect do not perfect the appetitive part, nor affect it in any way, but only the intellective part; they may indeed be called virtues in so far as they confer aptness for a good work, *viz.* the consideration of truth (since this is the good work of the intellect): yet they are not called virtues in the second way, as though they conferred the right use of a power or habit. For if a man possess a habit of speculative science, it does not follow that he is inclined to make use of it, but he is made able to consider the truth in those matters of which he has scientific knowledge: that he make use of the knowledge which he has, is due to the motion of his will. Consequently a virtue which perfects the will, as charity or justice, confers the right use of these speculative habits. And in this way too there can be merit in the acts of these habits, if they be done out of charity: thus Gregory says (Moral. vi) that the "contemplative life has greater merit than the active life."

Reply to Objection 1: Work is of two kinds, exterior and interior. Accordingly the practical or active faculty which is contrasted with the speculative faculty, is concerned with exterior work, to which the speculative habit is not ordained. Yet it is ordained to the interior act of the intellect which is to consider the truth. And in this way it is an operative habit.

Reply to Objection 2: Virtue is about certain things in two ways. In the first place a virtue is about its object. And thus these speculative virtues are not about those things whereby man is made happy; except perhaps, in so far as the word "whereby" indicates the efficient cause or object of complete happiness, i.e., God, Who is the

summum speculabile. Alio modo dicitur virtus esse aliquorum sicut actuum. Et hoc modo virtutes intellectuales sunt eorum per quae homo fit beatus. Tum quia actus harum virtutum possunt esse meritorii, sicut dictum est. Tum etiam quia sunt quaedam inchoatio perfectae beatitudinis, quae in contemplatione veri consistit, sicut supra dictum est.

AD TERTIUM dicendum quod scientia dividitur contra virtutem secundo modo dictam, quae pertinet ad vim appetitivam.

supreme object of contemplation. Secondly, a virtue is said to be about its acts: and in this sense the intellectual virtues are about those things whereby a man is made happy; both because the acts of these virtues can be meritorious, as stated above, and because they are a kind of beginning of perfect bliss, which consists in the contemplation of truth, as we have already stated (I-II, q. 30, a. 7).

Reply to Objection 3: Science is contrasted with virtue taken in the second sense, wherein it belongs to the appetitive faculty.

ARTICULUS 2

AD SECUNDUM sic proceditur. Videtur quod inconvenienter distinguantur tres virtutes intellectuales speculativae, scilicet sapientia, scientia et intellectus. Species enim non debet condividi generi. Sed sapientia est quaedam scientia, ut dicitur in VI Ethic. Ergo sapientia non debet condividi scientiae, in numero virtutum intellectualium.

PRAETEREA, in distinctione potentiarum, habituum et actuum, quae attenditur secundum obiecta, attenditur principaliter distinctio quae est secundum rationem formalem obiectorum, ut ex supradictis patet. Non ergo diversi habitus debent distingui secundum materiale obiectum; sed secundum rationem formalem illius obiecti. Sed principium demonstrationis est ratio sciendi conclusiones. Non ergo intellectus principiorum debet poni habitus alius, aut alia virtus, a scientia conclusionum.

PRAETEREA, virtus intellectualis dicitur quae est in ipso rationali per essentiam. Sed ratio, etiam speculativa, sicut ratiocinatur syllogizando demonstrative; ita etiam ratiocinatur syllogizando dialectice. Ergo sicut scientia, quae causatur ex syllogismo demonstrativo, ponitur virtus intellectualis speculativa; ita etiam et opinio.

SED CONTRA est quod philosophus, VI Ethic., ponit has solum tres virtutes intellectuales speculativas, scilicet sapientiam, scientiam et intellectum.

ARTICLE 2
Whether there are only three habits of the speculative intellect, viz. wisdom, science and understanding?

Objection 1: It would seem unfitting to distinguish three virtues of the speculative intellect, *viz.* wisdom, science and understanding. Because a species is a kind of science, as stated in Ethic. vi, 7. Therefore wisdom should not be condivided with science among the intellectual virtues.

Objection 2: Further, in differentiating powers, habits and acts in respect of their objects, we consider chiefly the formal aspect of these objects, as we have already explained (I, q. 77, a. 3). Therefore diversity of habits is taken, not from their material objects, but from the formal aspect of those objects. Now the principle of a demonstration is the formal aspect under which the conclusion is known. Therefore the understanding of principles should not be set down as a habit or virtue distinct from the knowledge of conclusions.

Objection 3: Further, an intellectual virtue is one which resides in the essentially rational faculty. Now even the speculative reason employs the dialectic syllogism for the sake of argument, just as it employs the demonstrative syllogism. Therefore as science, which is the result of a demonstrative syllogism, is set down as an intellectual virtue, so also should opinion be.

On the contrary, The Philosopher (Ethic. vi, 1) reckons these three alone as being intellectual virtues, *viz.* wisdom, science and understanding.

I-II, q. 57, a. 2, co.

Respondeo dicendum quod, sicut iam dictum est, virtus intellectualis speculativa est per quam intellectus speculativus perficitur ad considerandum verum, hoc enim est bonum opus eius. Verum autem est dupliciter considerabile, uno modo, sicut per se notum; alio modo, sicut per aliud notum. Quod autem est per se notum, se habet ut *principium*; et percipitur statim ab intellectu. Et ideo habitus perficiens intellectum ad huiusmodi veri considerationem, vocatur *intellectus*, qui est habitus principiorum. Verum autem quod est per aliud notum, non statim percipitur ab intellectu, sed per inquisitionem rationis, et se habet in ratione *termini*. Quod quidem potest esse dupliciter, uno modo, ut sit ultimum in aliquo genere; alio modo, ut sit ultimum respectu totius cognitionis humanae. Et quia *ea quae sunt posterius nota quoad nos, sunt priora et magis nota secundum naturam,* ut dicitur in I Physic.; ideo id quod est ultimum respectu totius cognitionis humanae, est id quod est primum et maxime cognoscibile secundum naturam. Et circa huiusmodi est *sapientia,* quae considerat altissimas causas, ut dicitur in I Metaphys. Unde convenienter iudicat et ordinat de omnibus, quia iudicium perfectum et universale haberi non potest nisi per resolutionem ad primas causas. Ad id vero quod est ultimum in hoc vel in illo genere cognoscibilium, perficit intellectum *scientia*. Et ideo secundum diversa genera scibilium, sunt diversi habitus scientiarum, cum tamen sapientia non sit nisi una.

Ad primum ergo dicendum quod sapientia est quaedam scientia, inquantum habet id quod est commune omnibus scientiis, ut scilicet ex principiis conclusiones demonstret. Sed quia habet aliquid proprium supra alias scientias, inquantum scilicet de omnibus iudicat; et non solum quantum ad conclusiones, sed etiam quantum ad prima principia, ideo habet rationem perfectioris virtutis quam scientia.

Ad secundum dicendum quod quando ratio obiecti sub uno actu refertur ad potentiam vel habitum, tunc non distinguuntur habitus vel potentiae penes

THE INTELLECTUAL VIRTUES

I answer that, As already stated (I-II, q. 57, a. 1), the virtues of the speculative intellect are those which perfect the speculative intellect for the consideration of truth: for this is its good work. Now a truth is subject to a twofold consideration—as known in itself, and as known through another. What is known in itself, is as a "principle," and is at once understood by the intellect: wherefore the habit that perfects the intellect for the consideration of such truth is called "understanding," which is the habit of principles. On the other hand, a truth which is known through another, is understood by the intellect, not at once, but by means of the reason's inquiry, and is as a "term." This may happen in two ways: first, so that it is the last in some particular genus; secondly, so that it is the ultimate term of all human knowledge. And, since "things that are knowable last from our standpoint, are knowable first and chiefly in their nature" (Phys. i, text. 2, 3); hence that which is last with respect to all human knowledge, is that which is knowable first and chiefly in its nature. And about these is "wisdom," which considers the highest causes, as stated in Metaph. i, 1, 2. Wherefore it rightly judges all things and sets them in order, because there can be no perfect and universal judgment that is not based on the first causes. But in regard to that which is last in this or that genus of knowable matter, it is "science" which perfects the intellect. Wherefore according to the different kinds of knowable matter, there are different habits of scientific knowledge; whereas there is but one wisdom.

Reply to Objection 1: Wisdom is a kind of science, in so far as it has that which is common to all the sciences; *viz.* to demonstrate conclusions from principles. But since it has something proper to itself above the other sciences, inasmuch as it judges of them all, not only as to their conclusions, but also as to their first principles, therefore it is a more perfect virtue than science.

Reply to Objection 2: When the formal aspect of the object is referred to a power or habit by one same act, there is no distinction of habit or power in respect of the

rationem obiecti et obiectum materiale, sicut ad eandem potentiam visivam pertinet videre colorem, et lumen, quod est ratio videndi colorem et simul cum ipso videtur. Principia vero demonstrationis possunt seorsum considerari, absque hoc quod considerentur conclusiones. Possunt etiam considerari simul cum conclusionibus, prout principia in conclusiones deducuntur. Considerare ergo hoc secundo modo principia, pertinet ad scientiam, quae considerat etiam conclusiones, sed considerare principia secundum seipsa, pertinet ad intellectum. Unde, si quis recte consideret, istae tres virtutes non ex aequo distinguuntur ab invicem, sed ordine quodam; sicut accidit in totis potentialibus, quorum una pars est perfectior altera, sicut anima rationalis est perfectior quam sensibilis, et sensibilis quam vegetabilis. Hoc enim modo, scientia dependet ab intellectu sicut a principaliori. Et utrumque dependet a sapientia sicut a principalissimo, quae sub se continet et intellectum et scientiam, ut de conclusionibus scientiarum diiudicans, et de principiis earundem.

formal aspect and of the material object: thus it belongs to the same power of sight to see both color, and light, which is the formal aspect under which color is seen, and is seen at the same time as the color. On the other hand, the principles of a demonstration can be considered apart, without the conclusion being considered at all. Again they can be considered together with the conclusions, since the conclusions can be deduced from them. Accordingly, to consider the principles in this second way, belongs to science, which considers the conclusions also: while to consider the principles in themselves belongs to understanding. Consequently, if we consider the point aright, these three virtues are distinct, not as being on a par with one another, but in a certain order. The same is to be observed in potential wholes, wherein one part is more perfect than another; for instance, the rational soul is more perfect than the sensitive soul; and the sensitive, than the vegetal. For it is thus that science depends on understanding as on a virtue of higher degree: and both of these depend on wisdom, as obtaining the highest place, and containing beneath itself both understanding and science, by judging both of the conclusions of science, and of the principles on which they are based.

AD TERTIUM dicendum quod, sicut supra dictum est, habitus virtutis determinate se habet ad bonum, nullo autem modo ad malum. Bonum autem intellectus est verum, malum autem eius est falsum. Unde soli illi habitus virtutes intellectuales dicuntur, quibus semper dicitur verum, et nunquam falsum. Opinio vero et suspicio possunt esse veri et falsi. Et ideo non sunt intellectuales virtutes, ut dicitur in VI Ethic.

Reply to Objection 3: As stated above (I-II, q. 55, a. 3; a. 4), a virtuous habit has a fixed relation to good, and is nowise referable to evil. Now the good of the intellect is truth, and falsehood is its evil. Wherefore those habits alone are called intellectual virtues, whereby we tell the truth and never tell a falsehood. But opinion and suspicion can be about both truth and falsehood: and so, as stated in Ethic. vi, 3, they are not intellectual virtues.

Articulus 3

AD TERTIUM sic proceditur. Videtur quod ars non sit virtus intellectualis. Dicit enim Augustinus, in libro de libero arbitrio, quod *virtute nullus male utitur.* Sed arte aliquis male utitur, potest enim aliquis artifex, secundum scientiam artis suae, male operari. Ergo ars non est virtus.

Article 3
Whether the intellectual habit, art, is a virtue?

Objection 1: It would seem that art is not an intellectual virtue. For Augustine says (De Lib. Arb. ii, 18,19) that "no one makes bad use of virtue." But one may make bad use of art: for a craftsman can work badly according to the knowledge of his art. Therefore art is not a virtue.

I-II, q. 57, a. 3, arg. 2

Praeterea, virtutis non est virtus. *Artis autem est aliqua virtus,* ut dicitur in VI Ethic. Ergo ars non est virtus.

Praeterea, artes liberales sunt excellentiores quam artes mechanicae. Sed sicut artes mechanicae sunt practicae, ita artes liberales sunt speculativae. Ergo si ars esset virtus intellectualis, deberet virtutibus speculativis annumerari.

Sed contra est quod philosophus, in VI Ethic., ponit artem esse virtutem; nec tamen connumerat eam virtutibus speculativis, quarum subiectum ponit scientificam partem animae.

Respondeo dicendum quod ars nihil aliud est quam *ratio recta aliquorum operum faciendorum.* Quorum tamen bonum non consistit in eo quod appetitus humanus aliquo modo se habet, sed in eo quod ipsum opus quod fit, in se bonum est. Non enim pertinet ad laudem artificis, inquantum artifex est, qua voluntate opus faciat; sed quale sit opus quod facit. Sic igitur ars, proprie loquendo, habitus operativus est. Et tamen in aliquo convenit cum habitibus speculativis, quia etiam ad ipsos habitus speculativos pertinet qualiter se habeat res quam considerant, non autem qualiter se habeat appetitus humanus ad illas. Dummodo enim verum geometra demonstret, non refert qualiter se habeat secundum appetitivam partem, utrum sit laetus vel iratus, sicut nec in artifice refert, ut dictum est. Et ideo eo modo ars habet rationem virtutis, sicut et habitus speculativi, inquantum scilicet nec ars, nec habitus speculativus, faciunt bonum opus quantum ad usum, quod est proprium virtutis perficientis appetitum; sed solum quantum ad facultatem bene agendi.

Ad primum ergo dicendum quod, cum aliquis habens artem operatur malum artificium, hoc non est opus artis, immo est contra artem, sicut etiam cum aliquis sciens verum mentitur, hoc quod dicit non est secundum scientiam, sed contra scientiam. Unde sicut scientia se habet semper ad bonum, ut dictum est, ita et ars, et secundum hoc dicitur

Objection 2: Further, there is no virtue of a virtue. But "there is a virtue of art," according to the Philosopher (Ethic. vi, 5). Therefore art is not a virtue.

Objection 3: Further, the liberal arts excel the mechanical arts. But just as the mechanical arts are practical, so the liberal arts are speculative. Therefore, if art were an intellectual virtue, it would have to be reckoned among the speculative virtues.

On the contrary, The Philosopher (Ethic. vi, 3, 4) says that art is a virtue; and yet he does not reckon it among the speculative virtues, which, according to him, reside in the scientific part of the soul.

I answer that, Art is nothing else but "the right reason about certain works to be made." And yet the good of these things depends, not on man's appetitive faculty being affected in this or that way, but on the goodness of the work done. For a craftsman, as such, is commendable, not for the will with which he does a work, but for the quality of the work. Art, therefore, properly speaking, is an operative habit. And yet it has something in common with the speculative habits: since the quality of the object considered by the latter is a matter of concern to them also, but not how the human appetite may be affected towards that object. For as long as the geometrician demonstrates the truth, it matters not how his appetitive faculty may be affected, whether he be joyful or angry: even as neither does this matter in a craftsman, as we have observed. And so art has the nature of a virtue in the same way as the speculative habits, in so far, to wit, as neither art nor speculative habit makes a good work as regards the use of the habit, which is the property of a virtue that perfects the appetite, but only as regards the aptness to work well.

Reply to Objection 1: When anyone endowed with an art produces bad workmanship, this is not the work of that art, in fact it is contrary to the art: even as when a man lies, while knowing the truth, his words are not in accord with his knowledge, but contrary thereto. Wherefore, just as science has always a relation to good, as stated above (I-II, q. 57, a. 2, ad 3), so it is with art: and it is for this reason that it is called a

virtus. In hoc tamen deficit a perfecta ratione virtutis, quia non facit ipsum bonum usum, sed ad hoc aliquid aliud requiritur, quamvis bonus usus sine arte esse non possit.

AD SECUNDUM dicendum quod, quia ad hoc ut homo bene utatur arte quam habet, requiritur bona voluntas, quae perficitur per virtutem moralem; ideo philosophus dicit quod artis est virtus, scilicet moralis, inquantum ad bonum usum eius aliqua virtus moralis requiritur. Manifestum est enim quod artifex per iustitiam, quae facit voluntatem rectam, inclinatur ut opus fidele faciat.

AD TERTIUM dicendum quod etiam in ipsis speculabilibus est aliquid per modum cuiusdam operis, puta constructio syllogismi aut orationis congruae aut opus numerandi vel mensurandi. Et ideo quicumque ad huiusmodi opera rationis habitus speculativi ordinantur, dicuntur per quandam similitudinem artes, sed *liberales;* ad differentiam illarum artium quae ordinantur ad opera per corpus exercita, quae sunt quodammodo serviles, inquantum corpus serviliter subditur animae, et homo secundum animam est liber. Illae vero scientiae quae ad nullum huiusmodi opus ordinantur, simpliciter scientiae dicuntur, non autem artes. Nec oportet, si liberales artes sunt nobiliores, quod magis eis conveniat ratio artis.

virtue. And yet it falls short of being a perfect virtue, because it does not make its possessor to use it well; for which purpose something further is requisite: although there cannot be a good use without the art.

Reply to Objection 2: In order that man may make good use of the art he has, he needs a good will, which is perfected by moral virtue; and for this reason the Philosopher says that there is a virtue of art; namely, a moral virtue, in so far as the good use of art requires a moral virtue. For it is evident that a craftsman is inclined by justice, which rectifies his will, to do his work faithfully.

Reply to Objection 3: Even in speculative matters there is something by way of work: e.g., the making of a syllogism or of a fitting speech, or the work of counting or measuring. Hence whatever habits are ordained to such like works of the speculative reason, are, by a kind of comparison, called arts indeed, but "liberal" arts, in order to distinguish them from those arts that are ordained to works done by the body, which arts are, in a fashion, servile, inasmuch as the body is in servile subjection to the soul, and man, as regards his soul, is free [*liber*]. On the other hand, those sciences which are not ordained to any such like work, are called sciences simply, and not arts. Nor, if the liberal arts be more excellent, does it follow that the notion of art is more applicable to them.

ARTICULUS 4

AD QUARTUM sic proceditur. Videtur quod prudentia non sit alia virtus ab arte. Ars enim est ratio recta aliquorum operum. Sed diversa genera operum non faciunt ut aliquid amittat rationem artis, sunt enim diversae artes circa opera valde diversa. Cum igitur etiam prudentia sit quaedam ratio recta operum, videtur quod etiam ipsa debeat dici ars.

PRAETEREA, prudentia magis convenit cum arte quam habitus speculativi, utrumque enim eorum est *circa contingens aliter se habere,* ut dicitur in VI Ethic. Sed quidam

ARTICLE 4
Whether prudence is a distinct virtue from art?

Objection 1: It would seem that prudence is not a distinct virtue from art. For art is the right reason about certain works. But diversity of works does not make a habit cease to be an art; since there are various arts about works widely different. Since therefore prudence is also right reason about works, it seems that it too should be reckoned a virtue.

Objection 2: Further, prudence has more in common with art than the speculative habits have; for they are both "about contingent matters that may be otherwise than they are" (Ethic. vi, 4, 5). Now some

habitus speculativi dicuntur artes. Ergo multo magis prudentia debet dici ars.

PRAETEREA, ad prudentiam *pertinet bene consiliari,* ut dicitur in VI Ethic. Sed etiam in quibusdam artibus consiliari contingit, ut dicitur in III Ethic., sicut in arte militari, et gubernativa, et medicinali. Ergo prudentia ab arte non distinguitur.

SED CONTRA est quod philosophus distinguit prudentiam ab arte, in VI Ethic.

RESPONDEO dicendum quod ubi invenitur diversa ratio virtutis, ibi oportet virtutes distingui. Dictum est autem supra quod aliquis habitus habet rationem virtutis ex hoc solum quod facit facultatem boni operis, aliquis autem ex hoc quod facit non solum facultatem boni operis, sed etiam usum. Ars autem facit solum facultatem boni operis, quia non respicit appetitum. Prudentia autem non solum facit boni operis facultatem, sed etiam usum, respicit enim appetitum, tanquam praesupponens rectitudinem appetitus. Cuius differentiae ratio est, quia ars est *recta ratio factibilium;* prudentia vero est *recta ratio agibilium.* Differt autem *facere* et *agere* quia, ut dicitur in IX Metaphys., *factio* est actus transiens in exteriorem materiam, sicut *aedificare, secare,* et huiusmodi; *agere* autem est actus permanens in ipso agente, sicut *videre, velle,* et huiusmodi. Sic igitur hoc modo se habet prudentia ad huiusmodi actus humanos, qui sunt usus potentiarum et habituum, sicut se habet ars ad exteriores factiones, quia utraque est perfecta ratio respectu illorum ad quae comparatur. Perfectio autem et rectitudo rationis in speculativis, dependet ex principiis, ex quibus ratio syllogizat, sicut dictum est quod scientia dependet ab intellectu, qui est habitus principiorum, et praesupponit ipsum. In humanis autem actibus se habent fines sicut principia in speculativis, ut dicitur in VII Ethic. Et ideo ad prudentiam, quae est recta ratio agibilium, requiritur quod homo sit bene dispositus circa fines, quod quidem est per appetitum rectum. Et ideo ad prudentiam requiritur

speculative habits are called arts. Much more, therefore, should prudence be called an art.

Objection 3: Further, it belongs to prudence, "to be of good counsel" (Ethic. vi, 5). But counselling takes place in certain arts also, as stated in Ethic. iii, 3, e.g., in the arts of warfare, of seamanship, and of medicine. Therefore prudence is not distinct from art.

On the contrary, The Philosopher distinguishes prudence from art (Ethic. vi, 5).

I answer that, Where the nature of virtue differs, there is a different kind of virtue. Now it has been stated above (I-II, q. 57, a. 1; q. 56, a. 3) that some habits have the nature of virtue, through merely conferring aptness for a good work: while some habits are virtues, not only through conferring aptness for a good work, but also through conferring the use. But art confers the mere aptness for good work; since it does not regard the appetite; whereas prudence confers not only aptness for a good work, but also the use: for it regards the appetite, since it presupposes the rectitude thereof. The reason for this difference is that art is the "right reason of things to be made"; whereas prudence is the "right reason of things to be done." Now "making" and "doing" differ, as stated in Metaph. ix, text. 16, in that "making" is an action passing into outward matter, e.g., "to build," "to saw," and so forth; whereas "doing" is an action abiding in the agent, e.g., "to see," "to will," and the like. Accordingly prudence stands in the same relation to such like human actions, consisting in the use of powers and habits, as art does to outward making: since each is the perfect reason about the things with which it is concerned. But perfection and rectitude of reason in speculative matters, depend on the principles from which reason argues; just as we have said above (I-II, q. 57, a. 2, ad 2) that science depends on and presupposes understanding, which is the habit of principles. Now in human acts the end is what the principles are in speculative matters, as stated in Ethic. vii, 8. Consequently, it is requisite for prudence, which is right reason about things to be done, that man be well disposed with regard to the ends: and this depends on the rectitude of his appetite. Wherefore, for prudence there is need of a

moralis virtus, per quam fit appetitus rectus. Bonum autem artificialium non est bonum appetitus humani, sed bonum ipsorum operum artificialium, et ideo ars non praesupponit appetitum rectum. Et inde est quod magis laudatur artifex qui volens peccat, quam qui peccat nolens; magis autem contra prudentiam est quod aliquis peccet volens, quam nolens, quia rectitudo voluntatis est de ratione prudentiae, non autem de ratione artis. Sic igitur patet quod prudentia est virtus distincta ab arte.

AD PRIMUM ergo dicendum quod diversa genera artificialium omnia sunt extra hominem, et ideo non diversificatur ratio virtutis. Sed prudentia est recta ratio ipsorum actuum humanorum, unde diversificatur ratio virtutis, ut dictum est.

AD SECUNDUM dicendum quod prudentia magis convenit cum arte quam habitus speculativi, quantum ad subiectum et materiam, utrumque enim est in opinativa parte animae, et circa contingens aliter se habere. Sed ars magis convenit cum habitibus speculativis in ratione virtutis, quam cum prudentia, ut ex dictis patet.

AD TERTIUM dicendum quod prudentia est bene consiliativa de his quae pertinent ad totam vitam hominis, et ad ultimum finem vitae humanae. Sed in artibus aliquibus est consilium de his quae pertinent ad fines proprios illarum artium. Unde aliqui, inquantum sunt bene consiliativi in rebus bellicis vel nauticis, dicuntur prudentes duces vel gubernatores, non autem prudentes simpliciter, sed illi solum qui bene consiliantur de his quae conferunt ad totam vitam.

ARTICULUS 5

AD QUINTUM sic proceditur. Videtur quod prudentia non sit virtus necessaria ad bene vivendum. Sicut enim se habet ars ad factibilia, quorum est ratio recta; ita se habet prudentia ad agibilia, secundum quae vita hominis consideratur, est enim eorum recta ratio prudentia, ut dicitur in VI Ethic. Sed ars non est necessaria in rebus

moral virtue, which rectifies the appetite. On the other hand the good things made by art is not the good of man's appetite, but the good of those things themselves: wherefore art does not presuppose rectitude of the appetite. The consequence is that more praise is given to a craftsman who is at fault willingly, than to one who is unwillingly; whereas it is more contrary to prudence to sin willingly than unwillingly, since rectitude of the will is essential to prudence, but not to art. Accordingly it is evident that prudence is a virtue distinct from art.

Reply to Objection 1: The various kinds of things made by art are all external to man: hence they do not cause a different kind of virtue. But prudence is right reason about human acts themselves: hence it is a distinct kind of virtue, as stated above.

Reply to Objection 2: Prudence has more in common with art than a speculative habit has, if we consider their subject and matter: for they are both in the thinking part of the soul, and about things that may be otherwise than they are. But if we consider them as virtues, then art has more in common with the speculative habits, as is clear from what has been said.

Reply to Objection 3: Prudence is of good counsel about matters regarding man's entire life, and the end of human life. But in some arts there is counsel about matters concerning the ends proper to those arts. Hence some men, in so far as they are good counselors in matters of warfare, or seamanship, are said to be prudent officers or pilots, but not simply prudent: only those are simply prudent who give good counsel about all the concerns of life.

ARTICLE 5
Whether prudence is a virtue necessary to man?

Objection 1: It would seem that prudence is not a virtue necessary to lead a good life. For as art is to things that are made, of which it is the right reason, so is prudence to things that are done, in respect of which we judge of a man's life: for prudence is the right reason about these things, as stated in Ethic. vi, 5. Now art is not necessary in things

factibilibus nisi ad hoc quod fiant, non autem postquam sunt factae. Ergo nec prudentia est necessaria homini ad bene vivendum, postquam est virtuosus, sed forte solum quantum ad hoc quod virtuosus fiat.

Praeterea, *prudentia est per quam recte consiliamur,* ut dicitur in VI Ethic. Sed homo potest ex bono consilio agere non solum proprio, sed etiam alieno. Ergo non est necessarium ad bene vivendum quod ipse homo habeat prudentiam; sed sufficit quod prudentum consilia sequatur.

Praeterea, virtus intellectualis est secundum quam contingit semper dicere verum, et nunquam falsum. Sed hoc non videtur contingere secundum prudentiam, non enim est humanum quod in consiliando de agendis nunquam erretur; cum humana agibilia sint contingentia aliter se habere. Unde dicitur Sap. IX, *cogitationes mortalium timidae, et incertae providentiae nostrae.* Ergo videtur quod prudentia non debeat poni intellectualis virtus.

Sed contra est quod Sap. VIII, connumeratur aliis virtutibus necessariis ad vitam humanam, cum dicitur de divina sapientia, *sobrietatem et prudentiam docet, iustitiam et virtutem, quibus utilius nihil est in vita hominibus.*

Respondeo dicendum quod prudentia est virtus maxime necessaria ad vitam humanam. Bene enim vivere consistit in bene operari. Ad hoc autem quod aliquis bene operetur, non solum requiritur quid faciat, sed etiam quomodo faciat; ut scilicet secundum electionem rectam operetur, non solum ex impetu aut passione. Cum autem electio sit eorum quae sunt ad finem, rectitudo electionis duo requirit, scilicet debitum finem; et id quod convenienter ordinatur ad debitum finem. Ad debitum autem finem homo convenienter disponitur per virtutem quae perficit partem animae appetitivam, cuius obiectum est bonum et finis. Ad id autem quod convenienter in finem debitum ordinatur, oportet quod homo directe disponatur per habitum rationis, quia consiliari et eligere, quae sunt eorum quae sunt ad finem, sunt actus rationis. Et ideo

that are made, save in order that they be made, but not after they have been made. Neither, therefore is prudence necessary to man in order to lead a good life, after he has become virtuous; but perhaps only in order that he may become virtuous.

Objection 2: Further, "It is by prudence that we are of good counsel," as stated in Ethic. vi, 5. But man can act not only from his own, but also from another's good counsel. Therefore man does not need prudence in order to lead a good life, but it is enough that he follow the counsels of prudent men.

Objection 3: Further, an intellectual virtue is one by which one always tells the truth, and never a falsehood. But this does not seem to be the case with prudence: for it is not human never to err in taking counsel about what is to be done; since human actions are about things that may be otherwise than they are. Hence it is written (Wis. 9:14): "The thoughts of mortal men are fearful, and our counsels uncertain." Therefore it seems that prudence should not be reckoned an intellectual virtue.

On the contrary, It is reckoned with other virtues necessary for human life, when it is written (Wis. 8:7) of Divine Wisdom: "She teacheth temperance and prudence and justice and fortitude, which are such things as men can have nothing more profitable in life."

I answer that, Prudence is a virtue most necessary for human life. For a good life consists in good deeds. Now in order to do good deeds, it matters not only what a man does, but also how he does it; to wit, that he do it from right choice and not merely from impulse or passion. And, since choice is about things in reference to the end, rectitude of choice requires two things: namely, the due end, and something suitably ordained to that due end. Now man is suitably directed to his due end by a virtue which perfects the soul in the appetitive part, the object of which is the good and the end. And to that which is suitably ordained to the due end man needs to be rightly disposed by a habit in his reason, because counsel and choice, which are about things ordained to the end, are acts of the reason. Consequently

necesse est in ratione esse aliquam virtutem intellectualem, per quam perficiatur ratio ad hoc quod convenienter se habeat ad ea quae sunt ad finem. Et haec virtus est prudentia. Unde prudentia est virtus necessaria ad bene vivendum.

AD PRIMUM ergo dicendum quod bonum artis consideratur non in ipso artifice, sed magis in ipso artificiato, cum ars sit ratio recta factibilium, factio enim, in exteriorem materiam transiens, non est perfectio facientis, sed facti, sicut motus est actus mobilis; ars autem circa factibilia est. Sed prudentiae bonum attenditur in ipso agente, cuius perfectio est ipsum agere, est enim prudentia recta ratio agibilium, ut dictum est. Et ideo ad artem non requiritur quod artifex bene operetur, sed quod bonum opus faciat. Requireretur autem magis quod ipsum artificiatum bene operaretur, sicut quod cultellus bene incideret, vel serra bene secaret; si proprie horum esset agere, et non magis agi, quia non habent dominium sui actus. Et ideo ars non est necessaria ad bene vivendum ipsi artificis; sed solum ad faciendum artificiatum bonum, et ad conservandum ipsum. Prudentia autem est necessaria homini ad bene vivendum, non solum ad hoc quod fiat bonus.

AD SECUNDUM dicendum quod, cum homo bonum operatur non secundum propriam rationem, sed motus ex consilio alterius; nondum est omnino perfecta operatio ipsius, quantum ad rationem dirigentem, et quantum ad appetitum moventem. Unde si bonum operetur, non tamen simpliciter bene; quod est bene vivere.

AD TERTIUM dicendum quod verum intellectus practici aliter accipitur quam verum intellectus speculativi, ut dicitur in VI Ethic. Nam verum intellectus speculativi accipitur per conformitatem intellectus ad rem. Et quia intellectus non potest infallibiliter conformari rebus in contingentibus, sed solum in necessariis; ideo nullus habitus speculativus contingentium est intellectualis virtus, sed

an intellectual virtue is needed in the reason, to perfect the reason, and make it suitably affected towards things ordained to the end; and this virtue is prudence. Consequently prudence is a virtue necessary to lead a good life.

Reply to Objection 1: The good of an art is to be found, not in the craftsman, but in the product of the art, since art is right reason about things to be made: for since the making of a thing passes into external matter, it is a perfection not of the maker, but of the thing made, even as movement is the act of the thing moved: and art is concerned with the making of things. On the other hand, the good of prudence is in the active principle, whose activity is its perfection: for prudence is right reason about things to be done, as stated above (I-II, q. 57, a. 4). Consequently art does not require of the craftsman that his act be a good act, but that his work be good. Rather would it be necessary for the thing made to act well (e.g., that a knife should carve well, or that a saw should cut well), if it were proper to such things to act, rather than to be acted on, because they have not dominion over their actions. Wherefore the craftsman needs art, not that he may live well, but that he may produce a good work of art, and have it in good keeping: whereas prudence is necessary to man, that he may lead a good life, and not merely that he may be a good man.

Reply to Objection 2: When a man does a good deed, not of his own counsel, but moved by that of another, his deed is not yet quite perfect, as regards his reason in directing him and his appetite in moving him. Wherefore, if he do a good deed, he does not do well simply; and yet this is required in order that he may lead a good life.

Reply to Objection 3: As stated in Ethic. vi, 2, truth is not the same for the practical as for the speculative intellect. Because the truth of the speculative intellect depends on conformity between the intellect and the thing. And since the intellect cannot be infallibly in conformity with things in contingent matters, but only in necessary matters, therefore no speculative habit about contingent things is an intellectual virtue, but

I-II, q. 57, a. 5, ad 3

solum est circa necessaria. Verum autem intellectus practici accipitur per conformitatem ad appetitum rectum. Quae quidem conformitas in necessariis locum non habet, quae voluntate humana non fiunt, sed solum in contingentibus quae possunt a nobis fieri, sive sint agibilia interiora, sive factibilia exteriora. Et ideo circa sola contingentia ponitur virtus intellectus practici, circa factibilia quidem, ars; circa agibilia vero prudentia.

only such as is about necessary things. On the other hand, the truth of the practical intellect depends on conformity with right appetite. This conformity has no place in necessary matters, which are not affected by the human will; but only in contingent matters which can be effected by us, whether they be matters of interior action, or the products of external work. Hence it is only about contingent matters that an intellectual virtue is assigned to the practical intellect, *viz.* art, as regards things to be made, and prudence, as regards things to be done.

Articulus 6

Ad sextum sic proceditur. Videtur quod inconvenienter adiungantur prudentiae *eubulia, synesis* et *gnome*. *Eubulia* enim est *habitus quo bene consiliamur,* ut dicitur in VI Ethic. Sed *bene consiliari pertinet ad prudentiam,* ut in eodem libro dicitur. Ergo *eubulia* non est virtus adiuncta prudentiae, sed magis est ipsa prudentia.

Praeterea, ad superiorem pertinet de inferioribus iudicare. Illa ergo virtus videtur suprema, cuius est actus iudicium. Sed *synesis* est bene iudicativa. Ergo *synesis* non est virtus adiuncta prudentiae, sed magis ipsa est principalis.

Praeterea, sicut diversa sunt ea de quibus est iudicandum, ita etiam diversa sunt ea de quibus est consiliandum. Sed circa omnia consiliabilia ponitur una virtus, scilicet *eubulia*. Ergo ad bene iudicandum de agendis, non oportet ponere, praeter *synesim*, aliam virtutem, scilicet *gnomen*.

Praeterea, Tullius ponit, in sua rhetorica, tres alias partes prudentiae, scilicet *memoriam praeteritorum, intelligentiam praesentium, et providentiam futurorum*. Macrobius etiam ponit, super somnium Scipionis, quasdam alias partes prudentiae, scilicet *cautionem, docilitatem,* et alia

Article 6
Whether eubulia, synesis, and gnome are virtues annexed to prudence?*

Objection 1: It would seem that εὐβουλία (*euboulia*), σύνεσις (*synesis*), and γνώμη (*gnome*) are unfittingly assigned as virtues annexed to prudence. For εὐβουλία is "a habit whereby we take good counsel" (Ethic. vi, 9). Now it "belongs to prudence to take good counsel," as stated (Ethic. vi, 9). Therefore εὐβουλία is not a virtue annexed to prudence, but rather is prudence itself.

Objection 2: Further, it belongs to the higher to judge the lower. The highest virtue would therefore seem to be the one whose act is judgment. Now σύνεσις (*synesis*) enables us to judge well. Therefore σύνεσις is not a virtue annexed to prudence, but rather is a principal virtue.

Objection 3: Further, just as there are various matters to pass judgment on, so are there different points on which one has to take counsel. But there is one virtue referring to all matters of counsel, namely εὐβουλία (*euboulia*). Therefore, in order to judge well of what has to be done, there is no need, besides σύνεσις (*synesis*) of the virtue of γνώμη (*gnome*).

Objection 4: Further, Cicero (De Invent. Rhet. iii) mentions three other parts of prudence; *viz.* "memory of the past, understanding of the present, and foresight of the future." Moreover, Macrobius (Super Somn. Scip. 1) mentions yet others: *viz.* "caution, docility," and the like.

---

* εὐβουλία, σύνεσις, γνώμη

huiusmodi. Non videntur igitur solae huiusmodi virtutes prudentiae adiungi.

SED CONTRA est auctoritas philosophi, in VI Ethic., qui has tres virtutes ponit prudentiae adiunctas.

RESPONDEO dicendum quod in omnibus potentiis ordinatis illa est principalior, quae ad principaliorem actum ordinatur. Circa agibilia autem humana tres actus rationis inveniuntur, quorum primus est consiliari, secundus iudicare, tertius est praecipere. Primi autem duo respondent actibus intellectus speculativi qui sunt inquirere et iudicare, nam consilium inquisitio quaedam est. Sed tertius actus proprius est practici intellectus, inquantum est operativus, non enim ratio habet praecipere ea quae per hominem fieri non possunt. Manifestum est autem quod in his quae per hominem fiunt, principalis actus est praecipere, ad quem alii ordinantur. Et ideo virtuti quae est bene praeceptiva, scilicet prudentiae, tanquam principaliori, adiunguntur tanquam secundariae, *eubulia,* quae est bene consiliativa, et *synesis* et *gnome,* quae sunt partes iudicativae; de quarum distinctione dicetur.

AD PRIMUM ergo dicendum quod prudentia est bene consiliativa, non quasi bene consiliari sit immediate actus eius, sed quia hunc actum perficit mediante virtute sibi subiecta, quae est *eubulia.*

AD SECUNDUM dicendum quod iudicium in agendis ad aliquid ulterius ordinatur, contingit enim aliquem bene iudicare de aliquo agendo, et tamen non recte exequi. Sed ultimum complementum est, quando ratio iam bene praecipit de agendis.

AD TERTIUM dicendum quod iudicium de unaquaque re fit per propria principia eius. Inquisitio autem nondum est per propria principia, quia his habitis, non esset opus inquisitione, sed iam res esset inventa. Et ideo una sola virtus ordinatur ad

Therefore it seems that the above are not the only virtues annexed to prudence.

On the contrary, stands the authority of the Philosopher (Ethic. vi, 9, 10, 11), who assigns these three virtues as being annexed to prudence.

I answer that, Wherever several powers are subordinate to one another, that power is the highest which is ordained to the highest act. Now there are three acts of reason in respect of anything done by man: the first of these is counsel; the second, judgment; the third, command. The first two correspond to those acts of the speculative intellect, which are inquiry and judgment, for counsel is a kind of inquiry: but the third is proper to the practical intellect, in so far as this is ordained to operation; for reason does not have to command in things that man cannot do. Now it is evident that in things done by man, the chief act is that of command, to which all the rest are subordinate. Consequently, that virtue which perfects the command, *viz.* prudence, as obtaining the highest place, has other secondary virtues annexed to it, *viz.* εὐβουλία (*euboulia*), which perfects counsel; and σύνεσις (*synesis*) and γνώμη (*gnome*), which are parts of prudence in relation to judgment, and of whose distinction we shall speak further on (ad 3).

Reply to Objection 1: Prudence makes us be of good counsel, not as though its immediate act consisted in being of good counsel, but because it perfects the latter act by means of a subordinate virtue, *viz.* εὐβουλία (*euboulia*).

Reply to Objection 2: Judgment about what is to be done is directed to something further: for it may happen in some matter of action that a man's judgment is sound, while his execution is wrong. The matter does not attain to its final complement until the reason has commanded aright in the point of what has to be done.

Reply to Objection 3: Judgment of anything should be based on that thing's proper principles. But inquiry does not reach to the proper principles: because, if we were in possession of these, we should need no more to inquire, the truth would be already discovered. Hence only one virtue is directed to being of good

I-II, q. 57, a. 6, ad 3

bene consiliandum, duae autem virtutes ad bene iudicandum, quia distinctio non est in communibus principiis, sed in propriis. Unde et in speculativis una est dialectica inquisitiva de omnibus, scientiae autem demonstrativae, quae sunt iudicativae, sunt diversae de diversis. Distinguuntur autem *synesis* et *gnome* secundum diversas regulas quibus iudicatur, nam *synesis* est iudicativa de agendis secundum communem legem; *gnome* autem secundum ipsam rationem naturalem, in his in quibus deficit lex communis; sicut plenius infra patebit.

AD QUARTUM dicendum quod memoria, intelligentia et providentia, similiter etiam cautio et docilitas, et alia huiusmodi, non sunt virtutes diversae a prudentia, sed quodammodo comparantur ad ipsam sicut partes integrales, inquantum omnia ista requiruntur ad perfectionem prudentiae. Sunt etiam et quaedam partes subiectivae, seu species prudentiae, sicut oeconomica, regnativa, et huiusmodi. Sed praedicta tria sunt quasi partes potentiales prudentiae, quia ordinantur sicut secundarium ad principale. Et de his infra dicetur.

counsel, wheres there are two virtues for good judgment: because difference is based not on common but on proper principles. Consequently, even in speculative matters, there is one science of dialectics, which inquires about all matters; whereas demonstrative sciences, which pronounce judgment, differ according to their different objects. Σύνεσις (*synesis*) and γνώμη (*gnome*) differ in respect of the different rules on which judgment is based: for σύνεσις judges of actions according to the common law; while γνώμη bases its judgment on the natural law, in those cases where the common law fails to apply, as we shall explain further on (II-II, q. 51, a. 4).

Reply to Objection 4: Memory, understanding and foresight, as also caution and docility and the like, are not virtues distinct from prudence: but are, as it were, integral parts thereof, in so far as they are all requisite for perfect prudence. There are, moreover, subjective parts or species of prudence, e.g., domestic and political economy, and the like. But the three first names are, in a fashion, potential parts of prudence; because they are subordinate thereto, as secondary virtues to a principal virtue: and we shall speak of them later (II-II, q. 48, seqq.).

Quaestio LVIII

Deinde considerandum est de virtutibus moralibus. Et *primo,* de distinctione earum a virtutibus intellectualibus; *secundo,* de distinctione earum ab invicem, secundum propriam materiam; *tertio,* de distinctione principalium, vel cardinalium, ab aliis. Circa primum quaeruntur quinque. *Primo,* utrum omnis virtus sit virtus moralis. *Secundo,* utrum virtus moralis distinguatur ab intellectuali. *Tertio,* utrum sufficienter dividatur virtus per intellectualem et moralem. *Quarto,* utrum moralis virtus possit esse sine intellectuali. *Quinto,* utrum e converso, intellectualis virtus possit esse sine morali.

Articulus 1

Ad primum sic proceditur. Videtur quod omnis virtus sit moralis. Virtus enim moralis dicitur a more, idest consuetudine. Sed omnium virtutum actus consuescere possumus. Ergo omnis virtus est moralis.

Praeterea, philosophus dicit, in II Ethic., quod virtus moralis est *habitus electivus in medietate rationis consistens.* Sed omnis virtus videtur esse habitus electivus, quia actus cuiuslibet virtutis possumus ex electione facere. Omnis etiam virtus aliqualiter in medio rationis consistit, ut infra patebit. Ergo omnis virtus est moralis.

Praeterea, Tullius dicit, in sua rhetorica, quod *virtus est habitus in modum naturae, rationi consentaneus.* Sed cum omnis virtus humana ordinetur ad bonum hominis, oportet quod sit consentanea rationi, cum bonum hominis *sit secundum rationem esse,* ut Dionysius dicit. Ergo omnis virtus est moralis.

Sed contra est quod philosophus dicit, in I Ethic., *dicentes de moribus, non dicimus quoniam sapiens vel intelligens; sed quoniam mitis vel sobrius.* Sic igitur sapientia et intellectus non sunt morales. Quae tamen sunt

Question 58
Of the Difference Between Moral and Intellectual Virtues

We must now consider moral virtues. We shall speak 1. of the difference between them and intellectual virtues; 2. of their distinction, one from another, in respect of their proper matter; 3. of the difference between the chief or cardinal virtues and the others. Under the first head there are five points of inquiry:
1. Whether every virtue is a moral virtue?
2. Whether moral virtue differs from intellectual virtue? 3. Whether virtue is adequately divided into moral and intellectual virtue? 4 Whether there can be moral without intellectual virtue? 5. Whether, on the other hand, there can be intellectual without moral virtue?

Article 1
Whether every virtue is a moral virtue?

Objection 1: It would seem that every virtue is a moral virtue. Because moral virtue is so called from the Latin *mos,* i.e. custom. Now, we can accustom ourselves to the acts of all the virtues. Therefore every virtue is a moral virtue.

Objection 2: Further, the Philosopher says (Ethic. ii, 6) that moral virtue is "a habit of choosing the rational mean." But every virtue is a habit of choosing: since the acts of any virtue can be done from choice. And, moreover, every virtue consists in following the rational mean in some way, as we shall explain further on (I-II, q. 64, a. 1; a. 2; a. 3). Therefore every virtue is a moral virtue.

Objection 3: Further, Cicero says (De Invent. Rhet. ii) that "virtue is a habit like a second nature, in accord with reason." But since every human virtue is directed to man's good, it must be in accord with reason: since man's good "consists in that which agrees with his reason," as Dionysius states (Div. Nom. iv). Therefore every virtue is a moral virtue.

On the contrary, The Philosopher (Ethic. i, 13): "When we speak of a man's morals, we do not say that he is wise or intelligent, but that he is gentle or sober." Accordingly, then, wisdom and understanding are not moral virtues: and yet they are vir-

virtutes, sicut supra dictum est. Non ergo omnis virtus est moralis.

Respondeo dicendum quod ad huius evidentiam, considerare oportet quid sit *mos*, sic enim scire poterimus quid sit *moralis* virtus. *Mos* autem duo significat. Quandoque enim significat consuetudinem, sicut dicitur Act. XV, *nisi circumcidamini secundum morem Moysi, non poteritis salvi fieri*. Quandoque vero significat inclinationem quandam naturalem, vel quasi naturalem, ad aliquid agendum, unde etiam et brutorum animalium dicuntur aliqui mores; unde dicitur II Machab. XI, quod *leonum more irruentes in hostes, prostraverunt eos*. Et sic accipitur mos in Psalmo LXVII, ubi dicitur, *qui habitare facit unius moris in domo*. Et hae quidem duae significationes in nullo distinguuntur, apud Latinos, quantum ad vocem. In Graeco autem distinguuntur, nam *ethos*, quod apud nos *morem* significat, quandoque habet primam longam, et scribitur per eta, Graecam litteram; quandoque habet primam correptam, et scribitur per epsilon. Dicitur autem virtus *moralis* a *more*, secundum quod mos significat quandam inclinationem naturalem, vel quasi naturalem, ad aliquid agendum. Et huic significationi *moris* propinqua est alia significatio, qua significat *consuetudinem*, nam consuetudo quodammodo vertitur in naturam, et facit inclinationem similem naturali. Manifestum est autem quod inclinatio ad actum proprie convenit appetitivae virtuti, cuius est movere omnes potentias ad agendum, ut ex supradictis patet. Et ideo non omnis virtus dicitur moralis, sed solum illa quae est in vi appetitiva.

Ad primum ergo dicendum quod obiectio illa procedit de *more*, secundum quod significat *consuetudinem*.

Ad secundum dicendum quod omnis actus virtutis potest ex electione agi, sed electionem rectam agit sola virtus quae est in appetitiva parte animae, dictum est enim supra quod eligere est actus appetitivae partis. Unde habitus electivus, qui scilicet est electionis principium, est solum ille qui perficit vim appetitivam, quamvis

tues, as stated above (I-II, q. 57, a. 2). Therefore not every virtue is a moral virtue.

I answer that, In order to answer this question clearly, we must consider the meaning of the Latin word *mos*; for thus we shall be able to discover what a "moral" virtue is. Now *mos* has a twofold meaning. For sometimes it means custom, in which sense we read (Acts 15:1): "Except you be circumcised after the manner [*morem*] of Moses, you cannot be saved." Sometimes it means a natural or quasi-natural inclination to do some particular action, in which sense the word is applied to dumb animals. Thus we read (2 Macc. 1:2) that "rushing violently upon the enemy, like lions,* they slew them": and the word is used in the same sense in Ps. 67:7, where we read: "Who maketh men of one manner [*moris*] to dwell in a house." For both these significations there is but one word in Latin; but in the Greek there is a distinct word for each, for the word *ethos* is written sometimes with a long, and sometimes a short "e." Now "moral" virtue is so called from *mos* in the sense of a natural or quasi-natural inclination to do some particular action. And the other meaning of *mos*, i.e. "custom," is akin to this: because custom becomes a second nature, and produces an inclination similar to a natural one. But it is evident that inclination to an action belongs properly to the appetitive power, whose function it is to move all the powers to their acts, as explained above (I-II, q. 9, a. 1). Therefore not every virtue is a moral virtue, but only those that are in the appetitive faculty.

Reply to Objection 1: This argument takes *mos* in the sense of "custom."

Reply to Objection 2: Every act of virtue can be done from choice: but no virtue makes us choose aright, save that which is in the appetitive part of the soul: for it has been stated above that choice is an act of the appetitive faculty (I-II, q. 13, a. 1). Wherefore a habit of choosing, i.e., a habit which is the principle whereby we choose, is that habit alone which perfects the appetitive faculty: although the

---

* *Leonum more*, i.e., as lions are in the habit of doing.

etiam aliorum habituum actus sub electione cadere possint.

AD TERTIUM dicendum quod *natura est principium motus,* sicut dicitur in II Physic. Movere autem ad agendum proprium est appetitivae partis. Et ideo assimilari naturae in consentiendo rationi, est proprium virtutum quae sunt in vi appetitiva.

acts of other habits also may be a matter of choice.

Reply to Objection 3: "Nature is the principle of movement" (Phys. ii, text. 3). Now to move the faculties to act is the proper function of the appetitive power. Consequently to become as a second nature by consenting to the reason, is proper to those virtues which are in the appetitive faculty.

ARTICULUS 2

AD SECUNDUM sic proceditur. Videtur quod virtus moralis ab intellectuali non distinguatur. Dicit enim Augustinus, in libro de Civ. Dei, quod *virtus est ars recte vivendi.* Sed ars est virtus intellectualis. Ergo virtus moralis ab intellectuali non differt.

PRAETEREA, plerique in definitione virtutum moralium ponunt scientiam, sicut quidam definiunt quod perseverantia est *scientia vel habitus eorum quibus est immanendum vel non immanendum;* et sanctitas est *scientia faciens fideles et servantes quae ad Deum iusta.* Scientia autem est virtus intellectualis. Ergo virtus moralis non debet distingui ab intellectuali.

PRAETEREA, Augustinus dicit, in I Soliloq., quod *virtus est recta et perfecta ratio.* Sed hoc pertinet ad virtutem intellectualem, ut patet in VI Ethic. ergo virtus moralis non est distincta ab intellectuali.

PRAETEREA, nihil distinguitur ab eo quod in eius definitione ponitur. Sed virtus intellectualis ponitur in definitione virtutis moralis, dicit enim philosophus, in II Ethic., quod *virtus moralis est habitus electivus existens in medietate determinata ratione, prout sapiens determinabit.* Huiusmodi autem recta ratio determinans medium virtutis moralis, pertinet ad virtutem intellectualem, ut dicitur in VI Ethic. Ergo virtus moralis non distinguitur ab intellectuali.

SED CONTRA est quod dicitur in I Ethic., *determinatur virtus secundum differentiam hanc, dicimus enim harum has quidem intellectuales, has vero morales.*

ARTICLE 2
Whether moral virtue differs from intellectual virtue?

Objection 1: It would seem that moral virtue does not differ from intellectual virtue. For Augustine says (De Civ. Dei iv, 21) "that virtue is the art of right conduct." But art is an intellectual virtue. Therefore moral and intellectual virtue do not differ.

Objection 2: Further, some authors put science in the definition of virtues: thus some define perseverance as a "science or habit regarding those things to which we should hold or not hold"; and holiness as "a science which makes man to be faithful and to do his duty to God." Now science is an intellectual virtue. Therefore moral virtue should not be distinguished from intellectual virtue.

Objection 3: Further, Augustine says (Soliloq. i, 6) that "virtue is the rectitude and perfection of reason." But this belongs to the intellectual virtues, as stated in Ethic. vi, 13. Therefore moral virtue does not differ from intellectual.

Objection 4: Further, a thing does not differ from that which is included in its definition. But intellectual virtue is included in the definition of moral virtue: for the Philosopher says (Ethic. ii, 6) that "moral virtue is a habit of choosing the mean appointed by reason as a prudent man would appoint it." Now this right reason that fixes the mean of moral virtue, belongs to an intellectual virtue, as stated in Ethic. vi, 13. Therefore moral virtue does not differ from intellectual.

On the contrary, It is stated in Ethic. i, 13 that "there are two kinds of virtue: some we call intellectual; some moral."

RESPONDEO dicendum quod omnium humanorum operum principium primum ratio est, et quaecumque alia principia humanorum operum inveniantur, quodammodo rationi obediunt; diversimode tamen. Nam quaedam rationi obediunt omnino ad nutum, absque omni contradictione, sicut corporis membra, si fuerint in sua natura consistentia; statim enim ad imperium rationis, manus aut pes movetur ad opus. Unde philosophus dicit, in I Polit., quod *anima regit corpus despotico principatu,* idest sicut dominus servum, qui ius contradicendi non habet. Posuerunt igitur quidam quod omnia principia activa quae sunt in homine, hoc modo se habent ad rationem. Quod quidem si verum esset, sufficeret quod ratio esset perfecta, ad bene agendum. Unde, cum virtus sit habitus quo perficimur ad bene agendum, sequeretur quod in sola ratione esset, et sic nulla virtus esset nisi intellectualis. Et haec fuit opinio Socratis, qui dixit *omnes virtutes esse prudentias,* ut dicitur in VI Ethic. Unde ponebat quod homo, scientia in eo existente, peccare non poterat; sed quicumque peccabat, peccabat propter ignorantiam. Hoc autem procedit ex suppositione falsi. Pars enim appetitiva obedit rationi non omnino ad nutum, sed cum aliqua contradictione, unde philosophus dicit, in I Polit., quod *ratio imperat appetitivae principatu politico,* quo scilicet aliquis praeest liberis, qui habent ius in aliquo contradicendi. Unde Augustinus dicit, super Psalm., quod *interdum praecedit intellectus, et sequitur tardus aut nullus affectus,* intantum quod quandoque passionibus vel habitibus appetitivae partis hoc agitur, ut usus rationis in particulari impediatur. Et secundum hoc, aliqualiter verum est quod Socrates dixit, quod scientia praesente, non peccatur, si tamen hoc extendatur usque ad usum rationis in particulari eligibili. Sic igitur ad hoc quod homo bene agat, requiritur quod non solum ratio sit bene disposita per habitum virtutis intellectualis; sed etiam quod vis appetitiva sit bene disposita per habitum virtutis moralis. Sicut igitur

I answer that, Reason is the first principle of all human acts; and whatever other principles of human acts may be found, they obey reason somewhat, but in various ways. For some obey reason blindly and without any contradiction whatever: such are the limbs of the body, provided they be in a healthy condition, for as soon as reason commands, the hand or the foot proceeds to action. Hence the Philosopher says (Polit. i, 3) that "the soul **rules the body like a despot,**" i.e., as a **master rules his slave,** who has no right to rebel. Accordingly some held that all the active principles in man are subordinate to reason in this way. If this were true, for man to act well it would suffice that his reason be perfect. Consequently, since virtue is a habit perfecting man in view of his doing good actions, it would follow that it is only in the reason, so that there would be none but intellectual virtues. This was the opinion of Socrates, who said "every virtue is a kind of prudence," as stated in Ethic. vi, 13. Hence he maintained that as long as man is in possession of knowledge, he cannot sin; and that every one who sins, does so through ignorance. Now this is based on a false supposition. Because the appetitive faculty obeys the reason, not blindly, but with a certain power of opposition; wherefore the Philosopher says (Polit. i, 3) that "reason commands the appetitive faculty by a politic power," whereby a man rules over subjects that are free, having a certain right of opposition. Hence Augustine says on Ps. 118 (Serm. 8) that "sometimes we understand [what is right] while desire is slow, or follows not at all," in so far as the habits or passions of the appetitive faculty cause the use of reason to be impeded in some particular action. And in this way, there is some truth in the saying of Socrates that so long as a man is in possession of knowledge he does not sin: provided, however, that this knowledge is made to include the use of reason in this individual act of choice. Accordingly for a man to do a good deed, it is requisite not only that his reason be well disposed by means of a habit of intellectual virtue; but also that his appetite be well disposed by means of a habit of moral virtue. And so

appetitus distinguitur a ratione, ita virtus moralis distinguitur ab intellectuali. Unde sicut appetitus est principium humani actus secundum quod participat aliqualiter rationem, ita habitus moralis habet rationem virtutis humanae, inquantum rationi conformatur.

AD PRIMUM ergo dicendum quod Augustinus communiter accipit *artem,* pro qualibet recta ratione. Et sic sub arte includitur etiam prudentia, quae ita est recta ratio agibilium, sicut ars est recta ratio factibilium. Et secundum hoc, quod dicit quod *virtus est ars recte vivendi,* essentialiter convenit prudentiae, participative autem aliis virtutibus, prout secundum prudentiam diriguntur.

AD SECUNDUM dicendum quod tales definitiones, a quibuscumque inveniantur datae, processerunt ex opinione Socratica, et sunt exponendae eo modo quo de arte praedictum est.

Et similiter dicendum est ad tertium.

AD QUARTUM dicendum quod recta ratio, quae est secundum prudentiam, ponitur in definitione virtutis moralis, non tanquam pars essentiae eius, sed sicut quiddam participatum in omnibus virtutibus moralibus, inquantum prudentia dirigit omnes virtutes morales.

moral differs from intellectual virtue, even as the appetite differs from the reason. Hence just as the appetite is the principle of human acts, in so far as it partakes of reason, so are moral habits to be considered virtues in so far as they are in conformity with reason.

Reply to Objection 1: Augustine usually applies the term "art" to any form of right reason; in which sense art includes prudence which is the right reason about things to be done, even as art is the right reason about things to be made. Accordingly, when he says that "virtue is the art of right conduct," this applies to prudence essentially; but to other virtues, by participation, for as much as they are directed by prudence.

Reply to Objection 2: All such definitions, by whomsoever given, were based on the Socratic theory, and should be explained according to what we have said about art (ad 1).

The same applies to the Third Objection.

Reply to Objection 4: Right reason which is in accord with prudence is included in the definition of moral virtue, not as part of its essence, but as something belonging by way of participation to all the moral virtues, in so far as they are all under the direction of prudence.

ARTICULUS 3

AD TERTIUM sic proceditur. Videtur quod virtus humana non sufficienter dividatur per virtutem moralem et intellectualem. Prudentia enim videtur esse aliquid medium inter virtutem moralem et intellectualem, connumeratur enim virtutibus intellectualibus in VI Ethic.; et etiam ab omnibus communiter connumeratur inter quatuor virtutes cardinales, quae sunt morales, ut infra patebit. Non ergo sufficienter dividitur virtus per intellectualem et moralem, sicut per immediata.

PRAETEREA, continentia et perseverantia, et etiam patientia, non computantur inter virtutes intellectuales. Nec etiam sunt virtutes morales, quia non tenent medium in passionibus, sed abundant in eis passiones. Non ergo sufficienter dividitur virtus per intellectuales et morales.

ARTICLE 3
Whether virtue is adequately divided into moral and intellectual?

Objection 1: It would seem that virtue is not adequately divided into moral and intellectual. For prudence seems to be a mean between moral and intellectual virtue, since it is reckoned among the intellectual virtues (Ethic. vi, 3, 5); and again is placed by all among the four cardinal virtues, which are moral virtues, as we shall show further on (I-II, q. 61, a. 1). Therefore virtue is not adequately divided into intellectual and moral, as though there were no mean between them.

Objection 2: Further, contingency, perseverance, and patience are not reckoned to be intellectual virtues. Yet neither are they moral virtues; since they do not reduce the passions to a mean, and are consistent with an abundance of passion. Therefore virtue is not adequately divided into intellectual and moral.

PRAETEREA, fides, spes et caritas quaedam virtutes sunt. Non tamen sunt virtutes intellectuales, hae enim solum sunt quinque, scilicet scientia, sapientia, intellectus, prudentia et ars, ut dictum est. Nec etiam sunt virtutes morales, quia non sunt circa passiones, circa quas maxime est moralis virtus. Ergo virtus non sufficienter dividitur per intellectuales et morales.

SED CONTRA est quod philosophus dicit, in II Ethic., *duplicem esse virtutem, hanc quidem intellectualem, illam autem moralem.*

RESPONDEO dicendum quod virtus humana est quidam habitus perficiens hominem ad bene operandum. Principium autem humanorum actuum in homine non est nisi duplex, scilicet intellectus sive ratio, et appetitus, haec enim sunt duo moventia in homine, ut dicitur in III de anima. Unde omnis virtus humana oportet quod sit perfectiva alicuius istorum principiorum. Si quidem igitur sit perfectiva intellectus speculativi vel practici ad bonum hominis actum, erit virtus intellectualis, si autem sit perfectiva appetitivae partis, erit virtus moralis. Unde relinquitur quod omnis virtus humana vel est intellectualis vel moralis.

AD PRIMUM ergo dicendum quod prudentia, secundum essentiam suam, est intellectualis virtus. Sed secundum materiam, convenit cum virtutibus moralibus, est enim recta ratio agibilium, ut supra dictum est. Et secundum hoc, virtutibus moralibus connumeratur.

AD SECUNDUM dicendum quod continentia et perseverantia non sunt perfectiones appetitivae virtutis sensitivae. Quod ex hoc patet, quod in continente et perseverante superabundant inordinatae passiones, quod non esset, si appetitus sensitivus esset perfectus aliquo habitu conformante ipsum rationi. Est autem continentia, seu perseverantia, perfectio rationalis partis, quae se tenet contra passiones ne deducatur. Deficit tamen a ratione virtutis, quia virtus intellectiva quae facit rationem se bene habere circa moralia, praesupponit appetitum rectum finis, ut recte se habeat circa principia, idest fines, ex

Objection 3: Further, faith, hope, and charity are virtues. Yet they are not intellectual virtues: for there are only five of these, viz. science, wisdom, understanding, prudence, and art, as stated above (I-II, q. 57, a. 2; a. 3; a. 5). Neither are they moral virtues; since they are not about the passions, which are the chief concern of moral virtue. Therefore virtue is not adequately divided into intellectual and moral.

On the contrary, The Philosopher says (Ethic. ii, 1) that "virtue is twofold, intellectual and moral."

I answer that, Human virtue is a habit perfecting man in view of his doing good deeds. Now, in man there are but two principles of human actions, *viz.* the intellect or reason and the appetite: for these are the two principles of movement in man as stated in De Anima iii, text. 48. Consequently every human virtue must needs be a perfection of one of these principles. Accordingly if it perfects man's speculative or practical intellect in order that his deed may be good, it will be an intellectual virtue: whereas if it perfects his appetite, it will be a moral virtue. It follows therefore that every human virtue is either intellectual or moral.

Reply to Objection 1: Prudence is essentially an intellectual virtue. But considered on the part of its matter, it has something in common with the moral virtues: for it is right reason about things to be done, as stated above (I-II, q. 57, a. 4). It is in this sense that it is reckoned with the moral virtues.

Reply to Objection 2: Contingency and perseverance are not perfections of the sensitive appetite. This is clear from the fact that passions abound in the continent and persevering man, which would not be the case if his sensitive appetite were perfected by a habit making it conformable to reason. Contingency and perseverance are, however, perfections of the rational faculty, and withstand the passions lest reason be led astray. But they fall short of being virtues: since intellectual virtue, which makes reason to hold itself well in respect of moral matters, presupposes a right appetite of the end, so that it may hold itself aright in respect of principles, i.e., the ends, on

quibus ratiocinatur; quod continenti et perseveranti deest. Neque etiam potest esse perfecta operatio quae a duabus potentiis procedit, nisi utraque potentia perficiatur per debitum habitum, sicut non sequitur perfecta actio alicuius agentis per instrumentum, si instrumentum non sit bene dispositum, quantumcumque principale agens sit perfectum. Unde si appetitus sensitivus, quem movet rationalis pars, non sit perfectus; quantumcumque rationalis pars sit perfecta, actio consequens non erit perfecta. Unde nec principium actionis erit virtus. Et propter hoc, continentia a delectationibus, et perseverantia a tristitiis, non sunt virtutes, sed aliquid minus virtute, ut philosophus dicit, in VII Ethic.

AD TERTIUM dicendum quod fides, spes et caritas sunt supra virtutes humanas, sunt enim virtutes hominis prout est factus particeps divinae gratiae.

which it builds its argument: and this is wanting in the continent and persevering man. Nor again can an action proceeding from two principles be perfect, unless each principle be perfected by the habit corresponding to that operation: thus, however perfect be the principal agent employing an instrument, it will produce an imperfect effect, if the instrument be not well disposed also. Hence if the sensitive faculty, which is moved by the rational faculty, is not perfect; however perfect the rational faculty may be, the resulting action will be imperfect: and consequently the principle of that action will not be a virtue. And for this reason, contingency, desisting from pleasures, and perseverance in the midst of pains, are not virtues, but something less than a virtue, as the Philosopher maintains (Ethic. vii, 1,9).

Reply to Objection 3: Faith, hope, and charity are superhuman virtues: for they are virtues of man as sharing in the grace of God.

Articulus 4

AD QUARTUM sic proceditur. Videtur quod virtus moralis possit esse sine intellectuali. Virtus enim moralis, ut dicit Tullius, est *habitus in modum naturae, rationi consentaneus.* Sed natura etsi consentiat alicui superiori rationi moventi, non tamen oportet quod illa ratio naturae coniungatur in eodem, sicut patet in rebus naturalibus cognitione carentibus. Ergo potest esse in homine virtus moralis in modum naturae, inclinans ad consentiendum rationi, quamvis illius hominis ratio non sit perfecta per virtutem intellectualem.

PRAETEREA, per virtutem intellectualem homo consequitur rationis usum perfectum. Sed quandoque contingit quod aliqui in quibus non multum viget usus rationis, sunt virtuosi et Deo accepti. Ergo videtur quod virtus moralis possit esse sine virtute intellectuali.

PRAETEREA, virtus moralis facit inclinationem ad bene operandum. Sed quidam

Article 4
Whether there can be moral without intellectual virtue?

Objection 1: It would seem that moral can be without intellectual virtue. Because moral virtue, as Cicero says (De Invent. Rhet. ii) is "a habit like a second nature in accord with reason." Now though nature may be in accord with some sovereign reason that moves it, there is no need for that reason to be united to nature in the same subject, as is evident of natural things devoid of knowledge. Therefore in a man there may be a moral virtue like a second nature, inclining him to consent to his reason, without his reason being perfected by an intellectual virtue.

Objection 2: Further, by means of intellectual virtue man obtains perfect use of reason. But it happens at times that men are virtuous and acceptable to God, without being vigorous in the use of reason. Therefore it seems that moral virtue can be without intellectual.

Objection 3: Further, moral virtue makes us inclined to do good works. But some,

habent naturalem inclinationem ad bene operandum, etiam absque rationis iudicio. Ergo virtutes morales possunt esse sine intellectuali.

Sed contra est quod Gregorius dicit, in XXII Moral., quod *ceterae virtutes, nisi ea quae appetunt, prudenter agant, virtutes esse nequaquam possunt.* Sed prudentia est virtus intellectualis, ut supra dictum est. Ergo virtutes morales non possunt esse sine intellectualibus.

Respondeo dicendum quod virtus moralis potest quidem esse sine quibusdam intellectualibus virtutibus, sicut sine sapientia, scientia et arte, non autem potest esse sine intellectu et prudentia. Sine prudentia quidem esse non potest moralis virtus, quia moralis virtus est habitus electivus, idest faciens bonam electionem. Ad hoc autem quod electio sit bona, duo requiruntur. Primo, ut sit debita intentio finis, et hoc fit per virtutem moralem, quae vim appetitivam inclinat ad bonum conveniens rationi, quod est finis debitus. Secundo, ut homo recte accipiat ea quae sunt ad finem, et hoc non potest esse nisi per rationem recte consiliantem, iudicantem et praecipientem; quod pertinet ad prudentiam et ad virtutes sibi annexas, ut supra dictum est. Unde virtus moralis sine prudentia esse non potest. Et per consequens nec sine intellectu. Per intellectum enim cognoscuntur principia naturaliter nota, tam in speculativis quam in operativis. Unde sicut recta ratio in speculativis, inquantum procedit ex principiis naturaliter cognitis, praesupponit intellectum principiorum; ita etiam prudentia, quae est recta ratio agibilium.

Ad primum ergo dicendum quod inclinatio naturae in rebus carentibus ratione, est absque electione, et ideo talis inclinatio non requirit ex necessitate rationem. Sed inclinatio virtutis moralis est cum electione, et ideo ad suam perfectionem indiget quod sit ratio perfecta per virtutem intellectualem.

Ad secundum dicendum quod in virtuoso non oportet quod vigeat usus rationis quantum ad omnia, sed solum quantum ad ea quae sunt agenda

without depending on the judgment of reason, have a natural inclination to do good works. Therefore moral virtues can be without intellectual virtues.

On the contrary, Gregory says (Moral. xxii) that "the other virtues, unless we do prudently what we desire to do, cannot be real virtues." But prudence is an intellectual virtue, as stated above (I-II, q. 57, a. 5). Therefore moral virtues cannot be without intellectual virtues.

I answer that, Moral virtue can be without some of the intellectual virtues, *viz.* wisdom, science, and art; but not without understanding and prudence. Moral virtue cannot be without prudence, because it is a habit of choosing, i.e., making us choose well. Now in order that a choice be good, two things are required. First, that the intention be directed to a due end; and this is done by moral virtue, which inclines the appetitive faculty to the good that is in accord with reason, which is a due end. Secondly, that man take rightly those things which have reference to the end: and this he cannot do unless his reason counsel, judge and command aright, which is the function of prudence and the virtues annexed to it, as stated above (I-II, q. 57, a. 5; a. 6). Wherefore there can be no moral virtue without prudence: and consequently neither can there be without understanding. For it is by the virtue of understanding that we know self-evident principles both in speculative and in practical matters. Consequently just as right reason in speculative matters, in so far as it proceeds from naturally known principles, presupposes the understanding of those principles, so also does prudence, which is the right reason about things to be done.

Reply to Objection 1: The inclination of nature in things devoid of reason is without choice: wherefore such an inclination does not of necessity require reason. But the inclination of moral virtue is with choice: and consequently in order that it may be perfect it requires that reason be perfected by intellectual virtue.

Reply to Objection 2: A man may be virtuous without having full use of reason as to everything, provided he have it with regard to those things which have to be done

secundum virtutem. Et sic usus rationis viget in omnibus virtuosis. Unde etiam qui videntur simplices, eo quod carent mundana astutia, possunt esse prudentes; secundum illud Matth. X, *estote prudentes sicut serpentes, et simplices sicut columbae.*

AD TERTIUM dicendum quod naturalis inclinatio ad bonum virtutis, est quaedam inchoatio virtutis, non autem est virtus perfecta. Huiusmodi enim inclinatio, quanto est fortior, tanto potest esse periculosior, nisi recta ratio adiungatur, per quam fiat recta electio eorum quae conveniunt ad debitum finem, sicut equus currens, si sit caecus, tanto fortius impingit et laeditur, quanto fortius currit. Et ideo, etsi virtus moralis non sit ratio recta, ut Socrates dicebat; non tamen solum est *secundum rationem rectam,* inquantum inclinat ad id quod est secundum rationem rectam, ut Platonici posuerunt; sed etiam oportet quod sit *cum ratione recta,* ut Aristoteles dicit, in VI Ethic.

virtuously. In this way all virtuous men have full use of reason. Hence those who seem to be simple, through lack of worldly cunning, may possibly be prudent, according to Mat. 10:16: "Be ye therefore prudent* as serpents, and simple as doves."

Reply to Objection 3: The natural inclination to a good of virtue is a kind of beginning of virtue, but is not perfect virtue. For the stronger this inclination is, the more perilous may it prove to be, unless it be accompanied by right reason, which rectifies the choice of fitting means towards the due end. Thus if a running horse be blind, the faster it runs the more heavily will it fall, and the more grievously will it be hurt. And consequently, although moral virtue be not right reason, as Socrates held, yet not only is it "according to right reason," in so far as it inclines man to that which is, according to right reason, as the Platonists maintained;† but also it needs to be "joined with right reason," as Aristotle declares (Ethic. vi, 13).

ARTICULUS 5

AD QUINTUM sic proceditur. Videtur quod virtus intellectualis possit esse sine virtute morali. Perfectio enim prioris non dependet a perfectione posterioris. Sed ratio est prior appetitu sensitivo, et movens ipsum. Ergo virtus intellectualis quae est perfectio rationis, non dependet a virtute morali, quae est perfectio appetitivae partis. Potest ergo esse sine ea.

PRAETEREA, moralia sunt materia prudentiae, sicut factibilia sunt materia artis. Sed ars potest esse sine propria materia, sicut faber sine ferro. Ergo et prudentia potest esse sine virtutibus moralibus, quae tamen inter omnes intellectuales virtutes, maxime moralibus coniuncta videtur.

PRAETEREA, prudentia est *virtus bene consiliativa,* ut dicitur in VI Ethic. Sed multi bene consiliantur, quibus tamen virtutes morales desunt. Ergo prudentia potest esse sine virtute morali.

ARTICLE 5
Whether there can be intellectual without moral virtue?

Objection 1: It would seem that there can be intellectual without moral virtue. Because perfection of what precedes does not depend on the perfection of what follows. Now reason precedes and moves the sensitive appetite. Therefore intellectual virtue, which is a perfection of the reason, does not depend on moral virtue, which is a perfection of the appetitive faculty; and can be without it.

Objection 2: Further, morals are the matter of prudence, even as things makeable are the matter of art. Now art can be without its proper matter, as a smith without iron. Therefore prudence can be without the moral virtue, although of all the intellectual virtues, it seems most akin to the moral virtues.

Objection 3: Further, prudence is "a virtue whereby we are of good counsel" (Ethic. vi, 9). Now many are of good counsel without having the moral virtues. Therefore prudence can be without a moral virtue.

---

* Douay: 'wise'
† Cf. Plato, Meno xli.

Sed contra, velle malum facere opponitur directe virtuti morali; non autem opponitur alicui quod sine virtute morali esse potest. Opponitur autem prudentiae quod *volens peccet,* ut dicitur in VI Ethic. Non ergo prudentia potest esse sine virtute morali.

Respondeo dicendum quod aliae virtutes intellectuales sine virtute morali esse possunt, sed prudentia sine virtute morali esse non potest. Cuius ratio est, quia prudentia est **recta ratio agibilium**; non autem solum in universali, sed etiam in particulari, in quibus sunt actiones. Recta autem ratio praeexigit principia ex quibus ratio procedit. Oportet autem rationem circa particularia procedere non solum ex principiis universalibus, sed etiam ex principiis particularibus. Circa principia quidem universalia agibilium, homo recte se habet per naturalem intellectum principiorum, per quem homo cognoscit quod nullum malum est agendum; vel etiam per aliquam scientiam practicam. Sed hoc non sufficit ad recte ratiocinandum circa particularia. Contingit enim quandoque quod huiusmodi universale principium cognitum per intellectum vel scientiam, corrumpitur in particulari per aliquam passionem, sicut concupiscenti, quando concupiscentia vincit, videtur hoc esse bonum quod concupiscit, licet sit contra universale iudicium rationis. Et ideo, sicut homo disponitur ad recte se habendum circa principia universalia, per intellectum naturalem vel per habitum scientiae; ita ad hoc quod recte se habeat circa principia particularia agibilium, quae sunt fines, oportet quod perficiatur per aliquos habitus secundum quos fiat quodammodo homini connaturale recte iudicare de fine. Et hoc fit per virtutem moralem, virtuosus enim recte iudicat de fine virtutis, quia *qualis unusquisque est, talis finis videtur ei,* ut dicitur in III Ethic. Et ideo ad rectam rationem agibilium, quae est prudentia, requiritur quod homo habeat virtutem moralem.

Ad primum ergo dicendum quod ratio, secundum quod est apprehensiva finis, praecedit appetitum finis, sed appetitus finis praecedit rationem ratiocinantem ad eligendum ea quae sunt ad finem, quod pertinet ad prudentiam. Sicut etiam in speculativis,

On the contrary, To wish to do evil is directly opposed to moral virtue; and yet it is not opposed to anything that can be without moral virtue. Now it is contrary to prudence "to sin willingly" (Ethic. vi, 5). Therefore prudence cannot be without moral virtue.

I answer that, Other intellectual virtues can, but prudence cannot, be without moral virtue. The reason for this is that prudence is the right reason about things to be done (and this, not merely in general, but also in particular); about which things actions are. Now right reason demands principles from which reason proceeds to argue. And when reason argues about particular cases, it needs not only universal but also particular principles. As to universal principles of action, man is rightly disposed by the natural understanding of principles, whereby he understands that he should do no evil; or again by some practical science. But this is not enough in order that man may reason aright about particular cases. For it happens sometimes that the aforesaid universal principle, known by means of understanding or science, is destroyed in a particular case by a passion: thus to one who is swayed by concupiscence, when he is overcome thereby, the object of his desire seems good, although it is opposed to the universal judgment of his reason. Consequently, as by the habit of natural understanding or of science, man is made to be rightly disposed in regard to the universal principles of action; so, in order that he be rightly disposed with regard to the particular principles of action, *viz.* the ends, he needs to be perfected by certain habits, whereby it becomes connatural, as it were, to man to judge aright to the end. This is done by moral virtue: for the virtuous man judges aright of the end of virtue, because "such a man is, such does the end seem to him" (Ethic. iii, 5). Consequently the right reason about things to be done, *viz.* prudence, requires man to have moral virtue.

Reply to Objection 1: Reason, as apprehending the end, precedes the appetite for the end: but appetite for the end precedes the reason, as arguing about the choice of the means, which is the concern of prudence. Even so, in speculative matters the

intellectus principiorum est principium rationis syllogizantis.

Ad secundum dicendum quod principia artificialium non diiudicantur a nobis bene vel male secundum dispositionem appetitus nostri, sicut fines, qui sunt moralium principia, sed solum per considerationem rationis. Et ideo ars non requirit virtutem perficientem appetitum, sicut requirit prudentia.

Ad tertium dicendum quod prudentia non solum est bene consiliativa, sed etiam bene iudicativa et bene praeceptiva. Quod esse non potest, nisi removeatur impedimentum passionum corrumpentium iudicium et praeceptum prudentiae; et hoc per virtutem moralem.

understanding of principles is the foundation on which the syllogism of the reason is based.

Reply to Objection 2: It does not depend on the disposition of our appetite whether we judge well or ill of the principles of art, as it does, when we judge of the end which is the principle in moral matters: in the former case our judgment depends on reason alone. Hence art does not require a virtue perfecting the appetite, as prudence does.

Reply to Objection 3: Prudence not only helps us to be of good counsel, but also to judge and command well. This is not possible unless the impediment of the passions, destroying the judgment and command of prudence, be removed; and this is done by moral virtue.

Quaestio LIX

Deinde considerandum est de distinctione moralium virtutum ad invicem. Et quia virtutes morales quae sunt circa passiones, distinguuntur secundum diversitatem passionum, oportet *primo* considerare comparationem virtutis ad passionem; *secundo,* distinctionem moralium virtutum secundum passiones. Circa primum quaeruntur quinque. *Primo,* utrum virtus moralis sit passio. *Secundo,* utrum virtus moralis possit esse cum passione. *Tertio,* utrum possit esse cum tristitia. *Quarto,* utrum omnis virtus moralis sit circa passionem. *Quinto,* utrum aliqua virtus moralis possit esse sine passione.

Question 59
Of Moral Virtue in Relation to the Passions

We must now consider the difference of one moral virtue from another. And since those moral virtues which are about the passions, differ accordingly to the difference of passions, we must consider 1. the relation of virtue to passion; 2. the different kinds of moral virtue in relation to the passions. Under the first head there are five points of inquiry: 1. Whether moral virtue is a passion? 2. Whether there can be moral virtue with passion? 3. Whether sorrow is compatible with moral virtue? 4. Whether every moral virtue is about a passion? 5. Whether there can be moral virtue without passion?

Articulus 1

Ad primum sic proceditur. Videtur quod virtus moralis sit passio. Medium enim est eiusdem generis cum extremis. Sed virtus moralis est medium inter passiones. Ergo virtus moralis est passio.

Praeterea, virtus et vitium, cum sint contraria, sunt in eodem genere. Sed quaedam passiones vitia esse dicuntur, ut invidia et ira. Ergo etiam quaedam passiones sunt virtutes.

Praeterea, misericordia quaedam passio est, est enim tristitia de alienis malis, ut supra dictum est. Hanc autem *Cicero,*

Article 1
Whether moral virtue is a passion?

Objection 1: It would seem that moral virtue is a passion. Because the mean is of the same genus as the extremes. But moral virtue is a mean between two passions. Therefore moral virtue is a passion.

Objection 2: Further, virtue and vice, being contrary to one another, are in the same genus. But some passions are reckoned to be vices, such as envy and anger. Therefore some passions are virtues.

Objection 3: Further, pity is a passion, since it is sorrow for another's ills, as stated above (I-II, q. 35, a. 8). Now "Cicero the

locutor egregius, non dubitavit appellare virtutem; ut Augustinus dicit, in IX de Civ. Dei. Ergo passio potest esse virtus moralis.

SED CONTRA est quod dicitur in II Ethic., quod *passiones neque virtutes sunt neque malitiae.*

RESPONDEO dicendum quod virtus moralis non potest esse passio. Et hoc patet triplici ratione. Primo quidem, quia passio est motus quidam appetitus sensitivi, ut supra dictum est. Virtus autem moralis non est motus aliquis, sed magis principium appetitivi motus, habitus quidam existens. Secundo quia passiones ex seipsis non habent rationem boni vel mali. Bonum enim vel malum hominis est secundum rationem, unde passiones, secundum se consideratae, se habent et ad bonum et ad malum, secundum quod possunt convenire rationi vel non convenire. Nihil autem tale potest esse virtus, cum virtus solum ad bonum se habeat, ut supra dictum est. Tertio quia, dato quod aliqua passio se habeat solum ad bonum, vel solum ad malum, secundum aliquem modum; tamen motus passionis, inquantum passio est, principium habet in ipso appetitu, et terminum in ratione, in cuius conformitatem appetitus tendit. Motus autem virtutis est e converso, principium habens in ratione et terminum in appetitu, secundum quod a ratione movetur. Unde in definitione virtutis moralis dicitur, in II Ethic., quod est *habitus electivus in medietate consistens determinata ratione, prout sapiens determinabit.*

AD PRIMUM ergo dicendum quod virtus, secundum suam essentiam, non est medium inter passiones, sed secundum suum effectum, quia scilicet inter passiones medium constituit.

AD SECUNDUM dicendum quod, si vitium dicatur habitus secundum quem quis male operatur, manifestum est quod nulla passio est vitium. Si vero dicatur vitium peccatum, quod est actus vitiosus, sic nihil prohibet passionem esse vitium, et e contrario concurrere ad actum virtutis; secundum quod passio vel contrariatur rationi, vel sequitur actum rationis.

AD TERTIUM dicendum quod misericordia dicitur esse virtus, idest virtutis actus, secundum *quod motus ille animi rationi servit,*

renowned orator did not hesitate to call pity a virtue," as Augustine states in De Civ. Dei ix, 5. Therefore a passion may be a moral virtue.

On the contrary, It is stated in Ethic. ii, 5 that "passions are neither virtues nor vices."

I answer that, Moral virtue cannot be a passion. This is clear for three reasons. First, because a passion is a movement of the sensitive appetite, as stated above (I-II, q. 22, a. 3): whereas moral virtue is not a movement, but rather a principle of the movement of the appetite, being a kind of habit. Secondly, because passions are not in themselves good or evil. For man's good or evil is something in reference to reason: wherefore the passions, considered in themselves, are referable both to good and evil, for as much as they may accord or disaccord with reason. Now nothing of this sort can be a virtue: since virtue is referable to good alone, as stated above (I-II, q. 55, a. 3). Thirdly, because, granted that some passions are, in some way, referable to good only, or to evil only; even then the movement of passion, as passion, begins in the appetite, and ends in the reason, since the appetite tends to conformity with reason. On the other hand, the movement of virtue is the reverse, for it begins in the reason and ends in the appetite, inasmuch as the latter is moved by reason. Hence the definition of moral virtue (Ethic. ii, 6) states that it is "a habit of choosing the mean appointed by reason as a prudent man would appoint it."

Reply to Objection 1: Virtue is a mean between passions, not by reason of its essence, but on account of its effect; because, to wit, it establishes the mean between passions.

Reply to Objection 2: If by vice we understand a habit of doing evil deeds, it is evident that no passion is a vice. But if vice is taken to mean sin which is a vicious act, nothing hinders a passion from being a vice, or, on the other hand, from concurring in an act of virtue; in so far as a passion is either opposed to reason or in accordance with reason.

Reply to Objection 3: Pity is said to be a virtue, i.e., an act of virtue, in so far as "that movement of the soul is obedient to reason";

quando scilicet *ita praebetur misericordia, ut iustitia conservetur, sive cum indigenti tribuitur, sive cum ignoscitur poenitenti,* ut Augustinus dicit ibidem. Si tamen misericordia dicatur aliquis habitus quo homo perficitur ad rationabiliter miserendum, nihil prohibet misericordiam sic dictam esse virtutem. Et eadem est ratio de similibus passionibus.

viz. "when pity is bestowed without violating right, as when the poor are relieved, or the penitent forgiven," as Augustine says (De Civ. Dei ix, 5). But if by pity we understand a habit perfecting man so that he bestows pity reasonably, nothing hinders pity, in this sense, from being a virtue. The same applies to similar passions.

Articulus 2

Ad secundum sic proceditur. Videtur quod virtus moralis cum passione esse non possit. Dicit enim philosophus, in IV Topic., quod *mitis est qui non patitur, patiens autem qui patitur et non deducitur.* Et eadem ratio est de omnibus virtutibus moralibus. Ergo omnis virtus moralis est sine passione.

Praeterea, virtus est quaedam recta habitudo animae, sicut sanitas corporis, ut dicitur in VII Physic., unde *virtus quaedam sanitas animae esse videtur,* ut Tullius dicit, in IV de Tuscul. quaest. Passiones autem animae dicuntur *morbi quidam animae,* ut in eodem libro Tullius dicit. Sanitas autem non compatitur secum morbum. Ergo neque virtus compatitur animae passionem.

Praeterea, virtus moralis requirit perfectum usum rationis etiam in particularibus. Sed hoc impeditur per passiones, dicit enim philosophus, in VI Ethic., quod *delectationes corrumpunt existimationem prudentiae*; et Sallustius dicit, in Catilinario, quod *non facile verum perspicit animus, ubi illa officiunt, scilicet animi passiones.* Virtus ergo moralis non potest esse cum passione.

Sed contra est quod Augustinus dicit, in XIV de Civ. Dei, *si perversa est voluntas, perversos habebit hos motus,* scilicet passionum, *si autem recta est, non solum inculpabiles, verum etiam laudabiles erunt.* Sed nullum laudabile excluditur per virtutem moralem. Virtus ergo moralis non excludit passiones, sed potest esse cum ipsis.

Respondeo dicendum quod circa hoc fuit discordia inter Stoicos et Peripateticos, sicut Augustinus dicit, IX de Civ. Dei. Stoici

Article 2
Whether there can be moral virtue with passion?

Objection 1: It would seem that moral virtue cannot be with passion. For the Philosopher says (Topic. iv) that "a gentle man is one who is not passionate; but a patient man is one who is passionate but does not give way." The same applies to all the moral virtues. Therefore all moral virtues are without passion.

Objection 2: Further, virtue is a right affection of the soul, as health is to the body, as stated Phys. vii, text. 17: wherefore "virtue is a kind of health of the soul," as Cicero says (Quaest. Tusc. iv). But the soul's passions are "the soul's diseases," as he says in the same book. Now health is incompatible with disease. Therefore neither is passion compatible with virtue.

Objection 3: Further, moral virtue requires perfect use of reason even in particular matters. But the passions are an obstacle to this: for the Philosopher says (Ethic. vi, 5) that "pleasures destroy the judgment of prudence": and Sallust says (Catilin.) that "when they," i.e., the soul's passions, "interfere, it is not easy for the mind to grasp the truth." Therefore passion is incompatible with moral virtue.

On the contrary, Augustine says (De Civ. Dei xiv, 6): "If the will is perverse, these movements," *viz.* the passions, "are perverse also: but if it is upright, they are not only blameless, but even praiseworthy." But nothing praiseworthy is incompatible with moral virtue. Therefore moral virtue does not exclude the passions, but is consistent with them.

I answer that, The Stoics and Peripatetics disagreed on this point, as Augustine relates (De Civ. Dei ix, 4). For the Stoics

enim posuerunt quod passiones animae non possunt esse in sapiente, sive virtuoso, Peripatetici vero, quorum sectam Aristoteles instituit, ut Augustinus dicit in IX de Civ. Dei, posuerunt quod passiones simul cum virtute morali esse possunt, sed ad medium reductae. Haec autem diversitas, sicut Augustinus ibidem dicit, magis erat secundum verba, quam secundum eorum sententias. Quia enim Stoici non distinguebant inter **appetitum intellectivum, qui est voluntas**, et inter **appetitum sensitivum, qui per irascibilem et concupiscibilem dividitur**; non distinguebant in hoc passiones animae ab aliis affectionibus humanis, quod passiones animae sint motus appetitus sensitivi, aliae vero affectiones, quae non sunt passiones animae, sunt motus appetitus intellectivi, qui dicitur voluntas, sicut Peripatetici distinxerunt, sed solum quantum ad hoc quod passiones esse dicebant quascumque affectiones rationi repugnantes. Quae si ex deliberatione oriantur, in sapiente, seu in virtuoso, esse non possunt. Si autem subito oriantur, hoc in virtuoso potest accidere, eo quod *animi visa quae appellant phantasias, non est in potestate nostra utrum aliquando incidant animo; et cum veniunt ex terribilibus rebus, necesse est ut sapientis animum moveant, ita ut paulisper vel pavescat metu, vel tristitia contrahatur, tanquam his passionibus praevenientibus rationis officium; nec tamen approbant ista, eisque consentiunt*; ut Augustinus narrat in IX de Civ. Dei, ab Agellio dictum. Sic igitur, si passiones dicantur inordinatae affectiones, non possunt esse in virtuoso, ita quod post deliberationem eis consentiatur; ut Stoici posuerunt. Si vero passiones dicantur quicumque motus appetitus sensitivi, sic possunt esse in virtuoso, secundum quod sunt a ratione ordinati. Unde Aristoteles dicit, in II Ethic., quod *non bene quidam determinant virtutes impassibilitates quasdam et quietes, quoniam simpliciter dicunt*, sed deberent dicere quod sunt quietes a passionibus *quae sunt ut non oportet, et quando non oportet*.

held that the soul's passions cannot be in a wise or virtuous man: whereas the Peripatetics, who were founded by Aristotle, as Augustine says (De Civ. Dei ix, 4), maintained that the passions are compatible with moral virtue, if they be reduced to the mean. This difference, as Augustine observes (De Civ. Dei ix, 4), was one of words rather than of opinions. Because the Stoics, through not discriminating between the intellective appetite, i.e., **the will**, and **the sensitive appetite**, which is divided into irascible and concupiscible, did not, as the Peripatetics did, distinguish the passions from the other affections of the human soul, in the point of their being movements of the sensitive appetite, whereas the other emotions of the soul, which are not passions, are movements of the intellective appetite or will; but only in the point of the passions being, as they maintained, any emotions in disaccord with reason. These emotions could not be in a wise or virtuous man if they arose deliberately: while it would be possible for them to be in a wise man, if they arose suddenly: because, in the words of Aulus Gellius,[*] quoted by Augustine (De Civ. Dei ix, 4), "it is not in our power to call up the visions of the soul, known as its fancies; and when they arise from awesome things, they must needs disturb the mind of a wise man, so that he is slightly startled by fear, or depressed with sorrow," in so far as "these passions forestall the use of reason without his approving of such things or consenting thereto." Accordingly, if the passions be taken for inordinate emotions, they cannot be in a virtuous man, so that he consent to them deliberately; as the Stoics maintained. But if the passions be taken for any movements of the sensitive appetite, they can be in a virtuous man, in so far as they are subordinate to reason. Hence Aristotle says (Ethic. ii, 3) that "some describe virtue as being a kind of freedom from passion and disturbance; this is incorrect, because the assertion should be qualified": they should have said virtue is freedom from those passions "that are not as they should be as to manner and time."

---

[*] Noct. Attic. xix, 1

AD PRIMUM ergo dicendum quod philosophus exemplum illud inducit, sicut et multa alia in libris logicalibus, non secundum opinionem propriam, sed secundum opinionem aliorum. Haec autem fuit opinio Stoicorum, quod virtutes essent sine passionibus animae. Quam opinionem philosophus excludit in II Ethic., dicens virtutes non esse impassibilitates. Potest tamen dici quod, cum dicitur quod *mitis non patitur,* intelligendum est secundum passionem inordinatam.

AD SECUNDUM dicendum quod ratio illa, et omnes similes quas Tullius ad hoc inducit in IV libro de Tuscul. quaest., procedit de passionibus secundum quod significant inordinatas affectiones.

AD TERTIUM dicendum quod passio praeveniens iudicium rationis, si in animo praevaleat ut ei consentiatur, impedit consilium et iudicium rationis. Si vero sequatur, quasi ex ratione imperata, adiuvat ad exequendum imperium rationis.

Reply to Objection 1: The Philosopher quotes this, as well as many other examples in his books on Logic, in order to illustrate, not his own mind, but that of others. It was the opinion of the Stoics that the passions of the soul were incompatible with virtue: and the Philosopher rejects this opinion (Ethic. ii, 3), when he says that virtue is not freedom from passion. It may be said, however, that when he says "a gentle man is not passionate," we are to understand this of inordinate passion.

Reply to Objection 2: This and all similar arguments which Tully brings forward in De Tusc. Quaest. iv take the passions in the execution of reason's command.

Reply to Objection 3: When a passion forestalls the judgment of reason, so as to prevail on the mind to give its consent, it hinders counsel and the judgment of reason. But when it follows that judgment, as through being commanded by reason, it helps towards the execution of reason's command.

ARTICULUS 3

AD TERTIUM sic proceditur. Videtur quod virtus cum tristitia esse non possit. Virtutes enim sunt sapientiae effectus, secundum illud Sap. VIII, *sobrietatem et iustitiam docet, scilicet divina sapientia, prudentiam et virtutem.* Sed *sapientiae convictus non habet amaritudinem,* ut postea subditur. Ergo nec virtutes cum tristitia esse possunt.

PRAETEREA, tristitia est impedimentum operationis; ut patet per philosophum, in VII et X Ethic. Sed impedimentum bonae operationis repugnat virtuti. Ergo tristitia repugnat virtuti.

PRAETEREA, tristitia est quaedam animi aegritudo; ut Tullius eam vocat, in III de Tuscul. quaest. Sed aegritudo animae contrariatur virtuti, quae est bona animae habitudo. Ergo tristitia contrariatur virtuti, nec potest simul esse cum ea.

SED CONTRA est quod Christus fuit perfectus virtute. Sed in eo fuit tristitia, dicit enim, ut habetur Matth. XXVI, *tristis est anima mea*

ARTICLE 3
Whether sorrow is compatible with moral virtue?

Objection 1: It would seem that sorrow is incompatible with virtue. Because the virtues are effects of wisdom, according to Wis. 8:7: "She," i.e., Divine wisdom, "teacheth temperance, and prudence, and justice, and fortitude." Now the "conversation" of wisdom "hath no bitterness," as we read further on (verse 16). Therefore sorrow is incompatible with virtue also.

Objection 2: Further, sorrow is a hindrance to work, as the Philosopher states (Ethic. vii, 13; x, 5). But a hindrance to good works is incompatible with virtue. Therefore sorrow is incompatible with virtue.

Objection 3: Further, Tully calls sorrow a disease of the mind (De Tusc. Quaest. iv). But disease of the mind is incompatible with virtue, which is a good condition of the mind. Therefore sorrow is opposed to virtue and is incompatible with it.

On the contrary, Christ was perfect in virtue. But there was sorrow in Him, for He said (Mat. 26:38): "My soul is sorrowful

usque ad mortem. Ergo tristitia potest esse cum virtute.

Respondeo dicendum quod sicut dicit Augustinus, XIV de Civ. Dei, Stoici voluerunt, pro tribus perturbationibus, in animo sapientis esse tres *eupathias,* idest tres bonas passiones, pro cupiditate scilicet *voluntatem;* pro laetitia, *gaudium;* pro metu, *cautionem.* Pro tristitia vero, negaverunt posse aliquid esse in animo sapientis, duplici ratione. Primo quidem, quia tristitia est de malo quod iam accidit. Nullum autem malum aestimant posse accidere sapienti, crediderunt enim quod, sicut solum hominis bonum est virtus, bona autem corporalia nulla bona hominis sunt; ita solum inhonestum est hominis malum, quod in virtuoso esse non potest. Sed hoc irrationabiliter dicitur. Cum enim homo sit ex anima et corpore compositus, id quod confert ad vitam corporis conservandam, aliquod bonum hominis est, non tamen maximum, quia eo potest homo male uti. Unde et malum huic bono contrarium in sapiente esse potest, et tristitiam moderatam inducere. Praeterea, etsi virtuosus sine gravi peccato esse possit, nullus tamen invenitur qui absque levibus peccatis vitam ducat, secundum illud I Ioan. I, *si dixerimus quia peccatum non habemus, nos ipsos seducimus.* Tertio, quia virtuosus, etsi peccatum non habeat, forte quandoque habuit. Et de hoc laudabiliter dolet; secundum illud II ad Cor. VII, *quae secundum Deum est tristitia, poenitentiam in salutem stabilem operatur.* Quarto, quia potest etiam dolere laudabiliter de peccato alterius. Unde eo modo quo virtus moralis compatitur alias passiones ratione moderatas, compatitur etiam tristitiam. Secundo, movebantur ex hoc, quod tristitia est de praesenti malo, timor autem de malo futuro, sicut delectatio de bono praesenti, desiderium vero de bono futuro. Potest autem hoc ad virtutem pertinere, quod aliquis bono habito fruatur, vel non habitum habere desideret, vel quod etiam malum futurum caveat. Sed quod malo praesenti animus hominis substernatur, quod fit per tristitiam, omnino videtur contrarium rationi, unde cum virtute esse non potest. Sed hoc irrationabiliter dicitur. Est enim aliquod malum quod potest

even unto death." Therefore sorrow is compatible with virtue.

I answer that, As Augustine says (De Civ. Dei xiv, 8), the Stoics held that in the mind of the wise man there are three εὐπάθιαι (*eupatheiai*), i.e., three good passions, in place of the three disturbances: *viz.* instead of covetousness, "desire"; instead of mirth, "joy"; instead of fear, "caution." But they denied that anything corresponding to sorrow could be in the mind of a wise man, for two reasons. First, because sorrow is for an evil that is already present. Now they held that no evil can happen to a wise man: for they thought that, just as man's only good is virtue, and bodily goods are no good to man; so man's only evil is vice, which cannot be in a virtuous man. But this is unreasonable. For, since man is composed of soul and body, whatever conduces to preserve the life of the body, is some good to man; yet not his supreme good, because he can abuse it. Consequently the evil which is contrary to this good can be in a wise man, and can cause him moderate sorrow. Again, although a virtuous man can be without grave sin, yet no man is to be found to live without committing slight sins, according to 1 Jn. 1:8: "If we say that we have no sin, we deceive ourselves." A third reason is because a virtuous man, though not actually in a state of sin, may have been so in the past. And he is to be commended if he sorrow for that sin, according to 2 Cor. 7:10: "The sorrow that is according to God worketh penance steadfast unto salvation." Fourthly, because he may praiseworthily sorrow for another's sin. Therefore sorrow is compatible with moral virtue in the same way as the other passions are when moderated by reason. Their second reason for holding this opinion was that sorrow is about evil present, whereas fear is for evil to come: even as pleasure is about a present good, while desire is for a future good. Now the enjoyment of a good possessed, or the desire to have good that one possesses not, may be consistent with virtue: but depression of the mind resulting from sorrow for a present evil, is altogether contrary to reason: wherefore it is incompatible with virtue. But this is unreasonable. For there is an evil which

esse virtuoso praesens, ut dictum est. Quod quidem malum ratio detestatur. Unde appetitus sensitivus in hoc sequitur detestationem rationis, quod de huiusmodi malo tristatur, moderate tamen, secundum rationis iudicium. Hoc autem pertinet ad virtutem, ut appetitus sensitivus rationi conformetur, ut dictum est. Unde ad virtutem pertinet quod tristetur moderate in quibus tristandum est, sicut etiam philosophus dicit in II Ethic. Et hoc etiam utile est ad fugiendum mala. Sicut enim bona propter delectationem promptius quaeruntur, ita mala propter tristitiam fortius fugiuntur. Sic igitur dicendum est quod tristitia de his quae conveniunt virtuti, non potest simul esse cum virtute, quia virtus in propriis delectatur. Sed de his quae quocumque modo repugnant virtuti, virtus moderate tristatur.

AD PRIMUM ergo dicendum quod ex illa auctoritate habetur quod de sapientia sapiens non tristetur. Tristatur tamen de his quae sunt impeditiva sapientiae. Et ideo in beatis, in quibus nullum impedimentum sapientiae esse potest, tristitia locum non habet.

AD SECUNDUM dicendum quod tristitia impedit operationem de qua tristamur, sed adiuvat ad ea promptius exequenda per quae tristitia fugitur.

AD TERTIUM dicendum quod tristitia immoderata est animae aegritudo, tristitia autem moderata ad bonam habitudinem animae pertinet, secundum statum praesentis vitae.

can be present to the virtuous man, as we have just stated; which evil is rejected by reason. Wherefore the sensitive appetite follows reason's rejection by sorrowing for that evil; yet moderately, according as reason dictates. Now it pertains to virtue that the sensitive appetite be conformed to reason, as stated above (I-II, q. 59, a. 1, ad 2). Wherefore moderated sorrow for an object which ought to make us sorrowful, is a mark of virtue; as also the Philosopher says (Ethic. ii, 6, 7). Moreover, this proves useful for avoiding evil: since, just as good is more readily sought for the sake of pleasure, so is evil more undauntedly shunned on account of sorrow. Accordingly we must allow that sorrow for things pertaining to virtue is incompatible with virtue: since virtue rejoices in its own. On the other hand, virtue sorrows moderately for all that thwarts virtue, no matter how.

Reply to Objection 1: The passage quoted proves that the wise man is not made sorrowful by wisdom. Yet he sorrows for anything that hinders wisdom. Consequently there is no room for sorrow in the blessed, in whom there can be no hindrance to wisdom.

Reply to Objection 2: Sorrow hinders the work that makes us sorrowful: but it helps us to do more readily whatever banishes sorrow.

Reply to Objection 3: Immoderate sorrow is a disease of the mind: but moderate sorrow is the mark of a well-conditioned mind, according to the present state of life.

ARTICULUS 4

AD QUARTUM sic proceditur. Videtur quod omnis virtus moralis sit circa passiones. Dicit enim philosophus, in II Ethic., quod *circa voluptates et tristitias est moralis virtus.* Sed delectatio et tristitia sunt passiones, ut supra dictum est. Ergo omnis virtus moralis est circa passiones.

PRAETEREA, rationale per participationem est subiectum moralium virtutum, ut dicitur

ARTICLE 4
Whether all the moral virtues are about the passions?

Objection 1: It would seem that all the moral virtues are about the passions. For the Philosopher says (Ethic. ii, 3) that "moral virtue is about objects of pleasure and sorrow." But pleasure and sorrow are passions, as stated above (I-II, q. 23, a. 4; q. 31, a. 1; q. 35, a. 1; a. 2). Therefore all the moral virtues are about the passions.

Objection 2: Further, the subject of the moral virtues is a faculty which is rational by participation, as the Philosopher states

in I Ethic. Sed huiusmodi pars animae est in qua sunt passiones, ut supra dictum est. Ergo omnis virtus moralis est circa passiones.

Praeterea, in omni virtute morali est invenire aliquam passionem. Aut ergo omnes sunt circa passiones, aut nulla. Sed aliquae sunt circa passiones, ut fortitudo et temperantia, ut dicitur in III Ethic. Ergo omnes virtutes morales sunt circa passiones.

Sed contra est quod iustitia, quae est virtus moralis, non est circa passiones, ut dicitur in V Ethic.

Respondeo dicendum quod virtus moralis perficit appetitivam partem animae ordinando ipsam in bonum rationis. Est autem rationis bonum id quod est secundum rationem moderatum seu ordinatum. Unde circa omne id quod contingit ratione ordinari et moderari, contingit esse virtutem moralem. Ratio autem ordinat non solum passiones appetitus sensitivi; sed etiam ordinat operationes appetitus intellectivi, qui est voluntas, quae non est subiectum passionis, ut supra dictum est. Et ideo non omnis virtus moralis est circa passiones; sed quaedam circa passiones, quaedam circa operationes.

Ad primum ergo dicendum quod non omnis virtus moralis est circa delectationes et tristitias sicut circa propriam materiam, sed sicut circa aliquid consequens proprium actum. Omnis enim virtuosus delectatur in actu virtutis, et tristatur in contrario. Unde philosophus post praemissa verba subdit quod, *si virtutes sunt circa actus et passiones; omni autem passioni et omni actui sequitur delectatio et tristitia; propter hoc virtus erit circa delectationes et tristitias,* scilicet sicut circa aliquid consequens.

Ad secundum dicendum quod rationale per participationem non solum est appetitus sensitivus, qui est subiectum passionum; sed etiam voluntas, in qua non sunt passiones, ut dictum est.

Ad tertium dicendum quod in quibusdam virtutibus sunt passiones sicut propria materia, in quibusdam autem non. Unde non est eadem ratio de omnibus, ut infra ostendetur.

(Ethic. i, 13). But the passions are in this part of the soul, as stated above (I-II, q. 22, a. 3). Therefore every moral virtue is about the passions.

Objection 3: Further, some passion is to be found in every moral virtue: and so either all are about the passions, or none are. But some are about the passions, as fortitude and temperance, as stated in Ethic. iii, 6, 10. Therefore all the moral virtues are about the passions.

On the contrary, Justice, which is a moral virtue, is not about the passions; as stated in Ethic. v, 1, seqq.

I answer that, Moral virtue perfects the appetitive part of the soul by directing it to good as defined by reason. Now good as defined by reason is that which is moderated or directed by reason. Consequently there are moral virtues about all matters that are subject to reason's direction and moderation. Now reason directs, not only the passions of the sensitive appetite, but also the operations of the intellective appetite, i.e., the will, which is not the subject of a passion, as stated above (I-II, q. 22, a. 3). Therefore not all the moral virtues are about passions, but some are about passions, some about operations.

Reply to Objection 1: The moral virtues are not all about pleasures and sorrows, as being their proper matter; but as being something resulting from their proper acts. For every virtuous man rejoices in acts of virtue, and sorrows for the contrary. Hence the Philosopher, after the words quoted, adds, "if virtues are about actions and passions; now every action and passion is followed by pleasure or sorrow, so that in this way virtue is about pleasures and sorrows," *viz.* as about something that results from virtue.

Reply to Objection 2: Not only the sensitive appetite which is the subject of the passions, is rational by participation, but also the will, where there are no passions, as stated above.

Reply to Objection 3: Some virtues have passions as their proper matter, but some virtues not. Hence the comparison does not hold for all cases.

Articulus 5

AD QUINTUM sic proceditur. Videtur quod virtus moralis possit esse absque passione. Quanto enim virtus moralis est perfectior, tanto magis superat passiones. Ergo in suo perfectissimo esse, est omnino absque passionibus.

PRAETEREA, tunc unumquodque est perfectum, quando est remotum a suo contrario, et ab his quae ad contrarium inclinant. Sed passiones inclinant ad peccatum, quod virtuti contrariatur, unde Rom. VII, nominantur *passiones peccatorum*. Ergo perfecta virtus est omnino absque passione.

PRAETEREA, secundum virtutem Deo conformamur; ut patet per Augustinum, in libro de moribus Eccles. Sed Deus omnia operatur sine passione. Ergo virtus perfectissima est absque omni passione.

SED CONTRA est quod *nullus iustus est qui non gaudet iusta operatione,* ut dicitur in I Ethic. Sed gaudium est passio. Ergo iustitia non potest esse sine passione. Et multo minus aliae virtutes.

RESPONDEO dicendum quod, si passiones dicamus inordinatas affectiones, sicut Stoici posuerunt; sic manifestum est quod virtus perfecta est sine passionibus. Si vero passiones dicamus omnes motus appetitus sensitivi, sic planum est quod virtutes morales quae sunt circa passiones sicut circa propriam materiam, sine passionibus esse non possunt. Cuius ratio est, quia secundum hoc, sequeretur quod virtus moralis faceret appetitum sensitivum omnino otiosum. Non autem ad virtutem pertinet quod ea quae sunt subiecta rationi, a propriis actibus vacent, sed quod exequantur imperium rationis, proprios actus agendo. Unde sicut virtus membra corporis ordinat ad actus exteriores debitos, ita appetitum sensitivum ad motus proprios ordinatos. Virtutes vero morales quae non sunt circa passiones, sed circa operationes, possunt esse sine passionibus (et huiusmodi virtus est iustitia), quia per eas applicatur voluntas ad proprium actum, qui non est passio. Sed tamen ad actum iustitiae sequitur gaudium, ad minus in voluntate, quod non est passio.

Article 5
Whether there can be moral virtue without passion?

Objection 1: It would seem that moral virtue can be without passion. For the more perfect moral virtue is, the more does it overcome the passions. Therefore at its highest point of perfection it is altogether without passion.

Objection 2: Further, then is a thing perfect, when it is removed from its contrary and from whatever inclines to its contrary. Now the passions incline us to sin which is contrary to virtue: hence (Rom. 7:5) they are called "passions of sins." Therefore perfect virtue is altogether without passion.

Objection 3: Further, it is by virtue that we are conformed to God, as Augustine declares (De Moribus Eccl. vi, xi, xiii). But God does all things without passion at all. Therefore the most perfect virtue is without any passion.

On the contrary, "No man is just who rejoices not in his deeds," as stated in Ethic. i, 8. But joy is a passion. Therefore justice cannot be without passion; and still less can the other virtues be.

I answer that, If we take the passions as being inordinate emotions, as the Stoics did, it is evident that in this sense perfect virtue is without the passions. But if by passions we understand any movement of the sensitive appetite, it is plain that moral virtues, which are about the passions as about their proper matter, cannot be without passions. The reason for this is that otherwise it would follow that moral virtue makes the sensitive appetite altogether idle: whereas it is not the function of virtue to deprive the powers subordinate to reason of their proper activities, but to make them execute the commands of reason, by exercising their proper acts. Wherefore just as virtue directs the bodily limbs to their due external acts, so does it direct the sensitive appetite to its proper regulated movements. Those moral virtues, however, which are not about the passions, but about operations, can be without passions. Such a virtue is justice: because it applies the will to its proper act, which is not a passion. Nevertheless, joy results from the act of justice; at least in the will, in which case it is not a passion.

Et si hoc gaudium multiplicetur per iustitiae perfectionem, fiet gaudii redundantia usque ad appetitum sensitivum; secundum quod vires inferiores sequuntur motum superiorum, ut supra dictum est. Et sic per redundantiam huiusmodi, quanto virtus fuerit perfectior, tanto magis passionem causat.

AD PRIMUM ergo dicendum quod virtus passiones inordinatas superat, moderatas autem producit.

AD SECUNDUM dicendum quod passiones inordinatae inducunt ad peccandum, non autem si sunt moderatae.

AD TERTIUM dicendum quod bonum in unoquoque consideratur secundum conditionem suae naturae. In Deo autem et angelis non est appetitus sensitivus, sicut est in homine. Et ideo bona operatio Dei et angeli est omnino sine passione, sicut et sine corpore, bona autem operatio hominis est cum passione, sicut et cum corporis ministerio.

And if this joy be increased through the perfection of justice, it will overflow into the sensitive appetite; in so far as the lower powers follow the movement of the higher, as stated above (I-II, q. 17, a. 7; q. 24, a. 3). Wherefore by reason of this kind of overflow, the more perfect a virtue is, the more does it cause passion.

Reply to Objection 1: Virtue overcomes inordinate passion; it produces ordinate passion.

Reply to Objection 2: It is inordinate, not ordinate, passion that leads to sin.

Reply to Objection 3: The good of anything depends on the condition of its nature. Now there is no sensitive appetite in God and the angels, as there is in man. Consequently good operation in God and the angels is altogether without passion, as it is without a body: whereas the good operation of man is with passion, even as it is produced with the body's help.

QUAESTIO LX

Deinde considerandum est de distinctione virtutum moralium ad invicem. Et circa hoc quaeruntur quinque. *Primo,* utrum sit tantum una virtus moralis. *Secundo,* utrum distinguantur virtutes morales quae sunt circa operationes, ab his quae sunt circa passiones. *Tertio,* utrum circa operationes sit una tantum moralis virtus. *Quarto,* utrum circa diversas passiones sint diversae morales virtutes. *Quinto,* utrum virtutes morales distinguantur secundum diversa obiecta passionum.

QUESTION 60
How the Moral Virtues Differ from One Another

We must now consider how the moral virtues differ from one another: under which head there are five points of inquiry: 1. Whether there is only one moral virtue? 2. Whether those moral virtues which are about operations, are distinct from those which are about passions? 3. Whether there is but one moral virtue about operations? 4. Whether there are different moral virtues about different passions? 5. Whether the moral virtues differ in point of the various objects of the passions?

ARTICULUS 1

AD PRIMUM sic proceditur. Videtur quod sit una tantum moralis virtus. Sicut enim in actibus moralibus directio pertinet ad rationem, quae est subiectum intellectualium virtutum; ita inclinatio pertinet ad vim appetitivam, quae est subiectum moralium virtutum. Sed una est intellectualis virtus dirigens in omnibus moralibus actibus,

ARTICLE 1
Whether there is only one moral virtue?

Objection 1: It would seem that there is only one moral virtue. Because just as the direction of moral actions belongs to reason which is the subject of the intellectual virtues; so does their inclination belong to the appetite which is the subject of moral virtues. But there is only one intellectual virtue to direct all moral acts,

scilicet prudentia. Ergo etiam una tantum est moralis virtus inclinans in omnibus moralibus actibus.

PRAETEREA, habitus non distinguuntur secundum materialia obiecta, sed secundum formales rationes obiectorum. Formalis autem ratio boni ad quod ordinatur virtus moralis, est unum, scilicet modus rationis. Ergo videtur quod sit una tantum moralis virtus.

PRAETEREA, moralia recipiunt speciem a fine, ut supra dictum est. Sed finis omnium virtutum moralium communis est unus, scilicet felicitas; proprii autem et propinqui sunt infiniti. Non sunt autem infinitae virtutes morales. Ergo videtur quod sit una tantum.

SED CONTRA est quod unus habitus non potest esse in diversis potentiis, ut supra dictum est. Sed subiectum virtutum moralium est pars appetitiva animae, quae per diversas potentias distinguitur, ut in primo dictum est. Ergo non potest esse una tantum virtus moralis.

RESPONDEO dicendum quod, sicut supra dictum est, virtutes morales sunt habitus quidam appetitivae partis. Habitus autem specie differunt secundum speciales differentias obiectorum, ut supra dictum est. Species autem obiecti appetibilis, sicut et cuiuslibet rei, attenditur secundum formam specificam, quae est ab agente. Est autem considerandum quod materia patientis se habet ad agens dupliciter. Quandoque enim recipit formam agentis secundum eandem rationem, prout est in agente, sicut est in omnibus agentibus univocis. Et sic necesse est quod, si agens est unum specie, quod materia recipiat formam unius speciei, sicut ab igne non generatur univoce nisi aliquid existens in specie ignis. Aliquando vero materia recipit formam ab agente non secundum eandem rationem, prout est in agente, sicut patet in generantibus non univocis, ut animal generatur a sole. Et tunc formae receptae in materia ab eodem agente, non sunt unius speciei sed diversificantur secundum diversam proportionem materiae ad recipiendum influxum agentis, sicut videmus quod ab

viz. prudence. Therefore there is also but one moral virtue to give all moral acts their respective inclinations.

Objection 2: Further, habits differ, not in respect of their material objects, but according to the formal aspect of their objects. Now the formal aspect of the good to which moral virtue is directed, is one thing, *viz.* the mean defined by reason. Therefore, seemingly, there is but one moral virtue.

Objection 3: Further, things pertaining to morals are specified by their end, as stated above (I-II, q. 1, a. 3). Now there is but one common end of all moral virtues, *viz.* happiness, while the proper and proximate ends are infinite in number. But the moral virtues themselves are not infinite in number. Therefore it seems that there is but one.

On the contrary, One habit cannot be in several powers, as stated above (I-II, q. 56, a. 2). But the subject of the moral virtues is the appetitive part of the soul, which is divided into several powers, as stated in the I, q. 80, a. 2; q. 81, a. 2. Therefore there cannot be only one moral virtue.

I answer that, As stated above (I-II, q. 58, a. 1; a. 2; a. 3), the moral virtues are habits of the appetitive faculty. Now habits differ specifically according to the specific differences of their objects, as stated above (I-II, q. 54, a. 2). Again, the species of the object of appetite, as of any thing, depends on its specific form which it receives from the agent. But we must observe that the matter of the passive subject bears a twofold relation to the agent. For sometimes it receives the form of the agent, in the same kind specifically as the agent has that form, as happens with all univocal agents, so that if the agent be one specifically, the matter must of necessity receive a form specifically one: thus the univocal effect of fire is of necessity something in the species of fire. Sometimes, however, the matter receives the form from the agent, but not in the same kind specifically as the agent, as is the case with non-univocal causes of generation: thus an animal is generated by the sun. In this case the forms received into matter are not of one species, but vary according to the adaptability of the matter to receive the influx of the agent: for instance, we see that owing to the

una actione solis generantur per putrefactionem animalia diversarum specierum secundum diversam proportionem materiae. Manifestum est autem quod in moralibus ratio est sicut imperans et movens; vis autem appetitiva est sicut imperata et mota. Non autem appetitus recipit impressionem rationis quasi univoce, quia non fit rationale per essentiam, sed per participationem, ut dicitur in I Ethic. Unde appetibilia secundum **motionem rationis constituuntur in diversis speciebus**, secundum quod diversimode se habent ad rationem. Et ita sequitur quod virtutes morales sint diversae secundum speciem, et non una tantum.

Ad primum ergo dicendum quod obiectum rationis est verum. Est autem eadem ratio veri in omnibus moralibus, quae sunt contingentia agibilia. Unde est una sola virtus in eis dirigens, scilicet prudentia. Obiectum autem appetitivae virtutis est bonum appetibile. Cuius est diversa ratio, secundum diversam habitudinem ad rationem dirigentem.

Ad secundum dicendum quod illud formale est unum genere, propter unitatem agentis. Sed diversificatur specie, propter diversas habitudines recipientium, ut supra dictum est.

Ad tertium dicendum quod moralia non habent speciem a fine ultimo sed a finibus proximis, qui quidem, etsi infiniti sint numero, non tamen infiniti sunt specie.

Articulus 2

Ad secundum sic proceditur. Videtur quod virtutes morales non distinguantur ab invicem per hoc quod quaedam sunt circa operationes, quaedam circa passiones. Dicit enim philosophus, in II Ethic., quod *virtus moralis est circa delectationes et tristitias optimorum operativa*. Sed voluptates et tristitiae sunt passiones quaedam, ut supra dictum est. Ergo eadem virtus quae est circa passiones, est etiam circa operationes, utpote operativa existens.

Praeterea, passiones sunt principia exteriorum operationum. Si ergo

one action of the sun, animals of various species are produced by putrefaction according to the various adaptability of matter. Now it is evident that in moral matters the reason holds the place of commander and mover, while the appetitive power is commanded and moved. But the appetite does not receive the direction of reason univocally so to say; because it is rational, not essentially, but by participation (Ethic. i, 13). Consequently **objects made appetible by the direction of reason belong to various species**, according to their various relations to reason: so that it follows that moral virtues are of various species and are not one only.

Reply to Objection 1: The object of the reason is truth. Now in all moral matters, which are contingent matters of action, there is but one kind of truth. Consequently, there is but one virtue to direct all such matters, *viz.* prudence. On the other hand, the object of the appetitive power is the appetible good, which varies in kind according to its various relations to reason, the directing power.

Reply to Objection 2: This formal element is one generically, on account of the unity of the agent: but it varies in species, on account of the various relations of the receiving matter, as explained above.

Reply to Objection 3: Moral matters do not receive their species from the last end, but from their proximate ends: and these, although they be infinite in number, are not infinite in species.

Article 2
Whether moral virtues about operations are different from those that are about passions?

Objection 1: It would seem that moral virtues are not divided into those which are about operations and those which are about passions. For the Philosopher says (Ethic. ii, 3) that moral virtue is "an operative habit whereby we do what is best in matters of pleasure or sorrow." Now pleasure and sorrow are passions, as stated above (I-II, q. 31, a. 1; q. 35, a. 1). Therefore the same virtue which is about passions is also about operations, since it is an operative habit.

Objection 2: Further, the passions are principles of external action. If therefore

aliquae virtutes rectificant passiones, oportet quod etiam per consequens rectificent operationes. Eaedem ergo virtutes morales sunt circa passiones et operationes.

Praeterea, ad omnem operationem exteriorem movetur appetitus sensitivus bene vel male. Sed motus appetitus sensitivi sunt passiones. Ergo eaedem virtutes quae sunt circa operationes, sunt circa passiones.

Sed contra est quod philosophus ponit iustitiam circa operationes; temperantiam autem et fortitudinem et mansuetudinem, circa passiones quasdam.

Respondeo dicendum quod operatio et passio dupliciter potest comparari ad virtutem. Uno modo, sicut effectus. Et hoc modo, omnis moralis virtus habet aliquas operationes bonas, quarum est productiva; et delectationem aliquam vel tristitiam, quae sunt passiones, ut supra dictum est. Alio modo potest comparari operatio ad virtutem moralem, sicut materia circa quam est. Et secundum hoc, oportet alias esse virtutes morales circa operationes, et alias circa passiones. Cuius ratio est, quia bonum et malum in quibusdam operationibus attenditur secundum seipsas, qualitercumque homo afficiatur ad eas, inquantum scilicet bonum in eis et malum accipitur secundum rationem commensurationis ad alterum. Et in talibus oportet quod sit aliqua virtus directiva operationum secundum seipsas, sicut sunt emptio et venditio, et omnes huiusmodi operationes in quibus attenditur ratio debiti vel indebiti ad alterum. Et propter hoc, iustitia et partes eius proprie sunt circa operationes sicut circa propriam materiam. In quibusdam vero operationibus bonum et malum attenditur solum secundum commensurationem ad operantem. Et ideo oportet in his bonum et malum considerari, secundum quod homo bene vel male afficitur circa huiusmodi. Et propter hoc, oportet quod virtutes in talibus sint principaliter circa interiores affectiones, quae dicuntur animae passiones, sicut patet de temperantia, fortitudine et aliis huiusmodi. Contingit autem quod in operationibus quae sunt ad alterum, praetermittatur bonum virtutis propter inordinatam

some virtues regulate the passions, they must, as a consequence, regulate operations also. Therefore the same moral virtues are about both passions and operations.

Objection 3: Further, the sensitive appetite is moved well or ill towards every external operation. Now movements of the sensitive appetite are passions. Therefore the same virtues that are about operations are also about passions.

On the contrary, The Philosopher reckons justice to be about operations; and temperance, fortitude and gentleness, about passions (Ethic. ii, 3, 7; v, 1, seqq.).

I answer that, Operation and passion stand in a twofold relation to virtue. First, as its effects; and in this way every moral virtue has some good operations as its product; and a certain pleasure or sorrow which are passions, as stated above (I-II, q. 59, a. 4, ad 1). Secondly, operation may be compared to moral virtue as the matter about which virtue is concerned: and in this sense those moral virtues which are about operations must needs differ from those which are about passions. The reason for this is that good and evil, in certain operations, are taken from the very nature of those operations, no matter how man may be affected towards them: *viz.* in so far as good and evil in them depend on their being commensurate with someone else. In operations of this kind there needs to be some power to regulate the operations in themselves: such are buying and selling, and all such operations in which there is an element of something due or undue to another. For this reason justice and its parts are properly about operations as their proper matter. On the other hand, in some operations, good and evil depend only on commensuration with the agent. Consequently good and evil in these operations depend on the way in which man is affected to them. And for this reason in such like operations virtue must needs be chiefly about internal emotions which are called the passions of the soul, as is evidently the case with temperance, fortitude and the like. It happens, however, in operations which are directed to another, that the good of virtue is overlooked by reason of some inordinate

animi passionem. Et tunc, inquantum corrumpitur commensuratio exterioris operationis, est corruptio iustitiae, inquantum autem corrumpitur commensuratio interiorum passionum, est corruptio alicuius alterius virtutis. Sicut cum propter iram aliquis alium percutit, in ipsa percussione indebita corrumpitur iustitia, in immoderantia vero irae corrumpitur mansuetudo. Et idem patet in aliis.

Et per hoc patet responsio ad obiecta. Nam prima ratio procedit de operatione, secundum quod est effectus virtutis. Aliae vero duae rationes procedunt ex hoc, quod ad idem concurrunt operatio et passio. Sed in quibusdam virtus est principaliter circa operationem, in quibusdam circa passionem, ratione praedicta.

passion of the soul. In such cases justice is destroyed in so far as the due measure of the external act is destroyed: while some other virtue is destroyed in so far as the internal passions exceed their due measure. Thus when through anger, one man strikes another, justice is destroyed in the undue blow; while gentleness is destroyed by the immoderate anger. The same may be clearly applied to other virtues.

This suffices for the Replies to the Objections. For the first considers operations as the effect of virtue, while the other two consider operation and passion as concurring in the same effect. But in some cases virtue is chiefly about operations, in others, about passions, for the reason given above.

Articulus 3

Ad tertium sic proceditur. Videtur quod sit una tantum virtus moralis circa operationes. Rectitudo enim omnium operationum exteriorum videtur ad iustitiam pertinere. Sed iustitia est una virtus. Ergo una sola virtus est circa operationes.

Praeterea, operationes maxime differentes esse videntur quae ordinantur ad bonum unius, et quae ordinantur ad bonum multitudinis. Sed ista diversitas non diversificat virtutes morales, dicit enim philosophus, in V Ethic., quod iustitia legalis, quae ordinat actus hominum ad commune bonum, non est aliud a virtute quae ordinat actus hominis ad unum tantum, nisi secundum rationem. Ergo diversitas operationum non causat diversitatem virtutum moralium.

Praeterea, si sunt diversae virtutes morales circa diversas operationes, oporteret quod secundum diversitatem operationum, esset diversitas virtutum moralium. Sed hoc patet esse falsum, nam ad iustitiam pertinet in diversis generibus commutationum rectitudinem statuere, et etiam in distributionibus, ut patet in V Ethic. Non ergo diversae virtutes sunt diversarum operationum.

Article 3
Whether there is only one moral virtue about operations?

Objection 1: It would seem that there is but one moral virtue about operations. Because the rectitude of all external operations seems to belong to justice. Now justice is but one virtue. Therefore there is but one virtue about operations.

Objection 2: Further, those operations seem to differ most, which are directed on the one side to the good of the individual, and on the other to the good of the many. But this diversity does not cause diversity among the moral virtues: for the Philosopher says (Ethic. v, 1) that legal justice, which directs human acts to the common good, does not differ, save logically, from the virtue which directs a man's actions to one man only. Therefore diversity of operations does not cause a diversity of moral virtues.

Objection 3: Further, if there are various moral virtues about various operations, diversity of moral virtues would needs follow diversity of operations. But this is clearly untrue: for it is the function of justice to establish rectitude in various kinds of commutations, and again in distributions, as is set down in Ethic. v, 2. Therefore there are not different virtues about different operations.

Sed contra est quod religio est alia virtus a pietate, quarum tamen utraque est circa operationes quasdam.

Respondeo dicendum quod omnes virtutes morales quae sunt circa operationes, conveniunt in quadam generali ratione iustitiae, quae attenditur secundum debitum ad alterum, distinguuntur autem secundum diversas speciales rationes. Cuius ratio est quia in operationibus exterioribus ordo rationis instituitur sicut dictum est, non secundum proportionem ad affectionem hominis, sed secundum ipsam convenientiam rei in seipsa; secundum quam convenientiam accipitur ratio debiti, ex quo constituitur ratio iustitiae, ad iustitiam enim pertinere videtur ut quis debitum reddat. Unde omnes huiusmodi virtutes quae sunt circa operationes, habent aliquo modo rationem iustitiae. Sed debitum non est unius rationis in omnibus, aliter enim debetur aliquid aequali, aliter superiori, aliter minori; et aliter ex pacto, vel ex promisso, vel ex beneficio suscepto. Et secundum has diversas rationes debiti, sumuntur diversae virtutes, puta *religio* est per quam redditur debitum Deo; *pietas* est per quam redditur debitum parentibus vel patriae; *gratia* est per quam redditur debitum benefactoribus; et sic de aliis.

Ad primum ergo dicendum quod iustitia proprie dicta est una specialis virtus, quae attendit perfectam rationem debiti, quod secundum aequivalentiam potest restitui. Dicitur tamen et ampliato nomine iustitia, secundum quamcumque debiti redditionem. Et sic non est una specialis virtus.

Ad secundum dicendum quod iustitia quae intendit bonum commune, est alia virtus a iustitia quae ordinatur ad bonum privatum alicuius, unde et ius commune distinguitur a iure privato; et Tullius ponit unam specialem virtutem, pietatem, quae ordinat ad bonum patriae. Sed iustitia ordinans hominem ad bonum commune, est generalis per imperium, quia omnes actus virtutum ordinat ad finem suum, scilicet ad bonum commune. Virtus autem secundum quod

On the contrary, Religion is a moral virtue distinct from piety, both of which are about operations.

I answer that, All the moral virtues that are about operations agree in one general notion of justice, which is in respect of something due to another: but they differ in respect of various special notions. The reason for this is that in external operations, the order of reason is established, as we have stated (I-II, q. 60, a. 2), not according as how man is affected towards such operations, but according to the becomingness of the thing itself; from which becomingness we derive the notion of something due which is the formal aspect of justice: for, seemingly, it pertains to justice that a man give another his due. Wherefore all such virtues as are about operations, bear, in some way, the character of justice. But the thing due is not of the same kind in all these virtues: for something is due to an equal in one way, to a superior, in another way, to an inferior, in yet another; and the nature of a debt differs according as it arises from a contract, a promise, or a favor already conferred. And corresponding to these various kinds of debt there are various virtues: e.g., "Religion" whereby we pay our debt to God; "Piety," whereby we pay our debt to our parents or to our country; "Gratitude," whereby we pay our debt to our benefactors, and so forth.

Reply to Objection 1: Justice properly so called is one special virtue, whose object is the perfect due, which can be paid in the equivalent. But the name of justice is extended also to all cases in which something due is rendered: in this sense it is not as a special virtue.

Reply to Objection 2: That justice which seeks the common good is another virtue from that which is directed to the private good of an individual: wherefore common right differs from private right; and Tully (De Inv. ii) reckons as a special virtue, piety which directs man to the good of his country. But that justice which directs man to the common good is a general virtue through its act of command: since it directs all the acts of the virtues to its own end, *viz.* the common good. And the virtues, in so far as

a tali iustitia imperatur, etiam iustitiae nomen accipit. Et sic virtus a iustitia legali non differt nisi ratione, sicut sola ratione differt virtus operans secundum seipsam, et virtus operans ad imperium alterius.

AD TERTIUM dicendum quod in omnibus operationibus ad iustitiam specialem pertinentibus, est eadem ratio debiti. Et ideo est eadem virtus iustitiae, praecipue quantum ad commutationes. Forte enim distributiva est alterius speciei a commutativa, sed de hoc infra quaeretur.

they are commanded by that justice, receive the name of justice: so that virtue does not differ, save logically, from legal justice; just as there is only a logical difference between a virtue that is active of itself, and a virtue that is active through the command of another virtue.

Reply to Objection 3: There is the same kind of due in all the operations belonging to special justice. Consequently, there is the same virtue of justice, especially in regard to commutations. For it may be that distributive justice is of another species from commutative justice; but about this we shall inquire later on (II-II, q. 61, a. 1).

ARTICULUS 4

AD QUARTUM sic proceditur. Videtur quod circa diversas passiones non sint diversae virtutes morales. Eorum enim quae conveniunt in principio et fine, unus est habitus, sicut patet maxime in scientiis. Sed omnium passionum unum est principium, scilicet amor; et omnes ad eundem finem terminantur, scilicet ad delectationem vel tristitiam; ut supra habitum est. Ergo circa omnes passiones est una tantum moralis virtus.

PRAETEREA, si circa diversas passiones essent diversae virtutes morales, sequeretur quod tot essent virtutes morales quot passiones. Sed hoc patet esse falsum, quia circa oppositas passiones est una et eadem virtus moralis, sicut fortitudo circa timores et audacias, temperantia circa delectationes et tristitias. Non ergo oportet quod circa diversas passiones sint diversae virtutes morales.

PRAETEREA, amor, concupiscentia et delectatio sunt passiones specie differentes, ut supra habitum est. Sed circa omnes has est una virtus, scilicet temperantia. Ergo virtutes morales non sunt diversae circa diversas passiones.

SED CONTRA est quod fortitudo est circa timores et audacias; temperantia circa concupiscentias; mansuetudo circa iras; ut dicitur in III et IV Ethic.

ARTICLE 4
Whether there are different moral virtues about different passions?

Objection 1: It would seem that there are not different moral virtues about different passions. For there is but one habit about things that concur in their source and end: as is evident especially in the case of sciences. But the passions all concur in one source, *viz.* love; and they all terminate in the same end, *viz.* joy or sorrow, as we stated above (I-II, q. 25, a. 1; a. 2; a. 4; q. 27, a. 4). Therefore there is but one moral virtue about all the passions.

Objection 2: Further, if there were different moral virtues about different passions, it would follow that there are as many moral virtues as passions. But this clearly is not the case: since there is one moral virtue about contrary passions; namely, fortitude, about fear and daring; temperance, about pleasure and sorrow. Therefore there is no need for different moral virtues about different passions.

Objection 3: Further, love, desire, and pleasure are passions of different species, as stated above (I-II, q. 23, a. 4). Now there is but one virtue about all these three, *viz.* temperance. Therefore there are not different moral virtues about different passions.

On the contrary, Fortitude is about fear and daring; temperance about desire; meekness about anger; as stated in Ethic. iii, 6,10; iv, 5.

RESPONDEO dicendum quod non potest dici quod circa omnes passiones sit una sola virtus moralis, sunt enim quaedam passiones ad diversas potentias pertinentes; aliae namque pertinent ad irascibilem, aliae ad concupiscibilem, ut supra dictum est. Nec tamen oportet quod omnis diversitas passionum sufficiat ad virtutes morales diversificandas. Primo quidem, quia quaedam passiones sunt quae sibi opponuntur secundum contrarietatem, sicut gaudium et tristitia, timor et audacia, et alia huiusmodi. Et circa huiusmodi passiones sic oppositas, oportet esse unam et eandem virtutem. Cum enim virtus moralis in quadam medietate consistat, medium in contrariis passionibus secundum eandem rationem instituitur, sicut et in naturalibus idem est medium inter contraria, ut inter album et nigrum. Secundo, quia diversae passiones inveniuntur secundum eundem modum rationi repugnantes, puta secundum impulsum ad id quod est contra rationem; vel secundum retractionem ab eo quod est secundum rationem. Et ideo diversae passiones concupiscibilis non pertinent ad diversas virtutes morales, quia earum motus secundum quendam ordinem se invicem consequuntur, utpote ad idem ordinati, scilicet ad consequendum bonum, vel ad fugiendum malum; sicut ex amore procedit concupiscentia, et ex concupiscentia pervenitur ad delectationem. Et eadem ratio est de oppositis, quia ex odio sequitur fuga vel abominatio, quae perducit ad tristitiam. Sed passiones irascibilis non sunt unius ordinis, sed ad diversa ordinantur, nam audacia et timor ordinantur ad aliquod magnum periculum; spes et desperatio ad aliquod bonum arduum; ira autem ad superandum aliquod contrarium quod nocumentum intulit. Et ideo circa has passiones diversae virtutes ordinantur, utpote temperantia circa passiones concupiscibilis; fortitudo circa timores et audacias; magnanimitas circa spem et desperationem; mansuetudo circa iras.

AD PRIMUM ergo dicendum quod omnes passiones conveniunt in uno principio et fine communi, non autem in uno proprio principio seu fine. Unde hoc non sufficit ad unitatem virtutis moralis.

I answer that, It cannot be said that there is only one moral virtue about all the passions: since some passions are not in the same power as other passions; for some belong to the irascible, others to the concupiscible faculty, as stated above (I-II, q. 23, a. 1). On the other hand, neither does every diversity of passions necessarily suffice for a diversity of moral virtues. First, because some passions are in contrary opposition to one another, such as joy and sorrow, fear and daring, and so on. About such passions as are thus in opposition to one another there must needs be one same virtue. Because, since moral virtue consists in a kind of mean, the mean in contrary passions stands in the same ratio to both, even as in the natural order there is but one mean between contraries, e.g., between black and white. Secondly, because there are different passions contradicting reason in the same manner, e.g., by impelling to that which is contrary to reason, or by withdrawing from that which is in accord with reason. Wherefore the different passions of the concupiscible faculty do not require different moral virtues, because their movements follow one another in a certain order, as being directed to the one same thing, *viz.* the attainment of some good or the avoidance of some evil: thus from love proceeds desire, and from desire we arrive at pleasure; and it is the same with the opposite passions, for hatred leads to avoidance or dislike, and this leads to sorrow. On the other hand, the irascible passions are not all of one order, but are directed to different things: for daring and fear are about some great danger; hope and despair are about some difficult good; while anger seeks to overcome something contrary which has wrought harm. Consequently there are different virtues about such like passions: e.g., temperance, about the concupiscible passions; fortitude, about fear and daring; magnanimity, about hope and despair; meekness, about anger.

Reply to Objection 1: All the passions concur in one common principle and end; but not in one proper principle or end: and so this does not suffice for the unity of moral virtue.

AD SECUNDUM dicendum quod, sicut in naturalibus idem est principium quo receditur ab uno principio, et acceditur ad aliud; et in rationalibus est eadem ratio contrariorum, ita etiam virtus moralis, quae in modum naturae rationi consentit, est eadem contrariarum passionum.

AD TERTIUM dicendum quod illae tres passiones ad idem obiectum ordinantur secundum quendam ordinem, ut dictum est. Et ideo ad eandem virtutem moralem pertinent.

ARTICULUS 5

AD QUINTUM sic proceditur. Videtur quod virtutes morales non distinguantur secundum obiecta passionum. Sicut enim sunt obiecta passionum, ita sunt obiecta operationum. Sed virtutes morales quae sunt circa operationes, non distinguuntur secundum obiecta operationum, ad eandem enim virtutem iustitiae pertinet emere vel vendere domum, et equum. Ergo etiam nec virtutes morales quae sunt circa passiones, diversificantur per obiecta passionum.

PRAETEREA, passiones sunt quidam actus vel motus appetitus sensitivi. Sed maior diversitas requiritur ad diversitatem habituum, quam ad diversitatem actuum. Diversa igitur obiecta quae non diversificant speciem passionis, non diversificabunt speciem virtutis moralis. Ita scilicet quod de omnibus delectabilibus erit una virtus moralis, et similiter est de aliis.

PRAETEREA, magis et minus non diversificant speciem. Sed diversa delectabilia non differunt nisi secundum magis et minus. Ergo omnia delectabilia pertinent ad unam speciem virtutis. Et eadem ratione, omnia terribilia, et similiter de aliis. Non ergo virtus moralis distinguitur secundum obiecta passionum.

PRAETEREA, sicut virtus est operativa boni, ita est impeditiva mali. Sed circa concupiscentias bonorum sunt diversae virtutes, sicut temperantia circa concupiscentias

Reply to Objection 2: Just as in the natural order the same principle causes movement from one extreme and movement towards the other; and as in the intellectual order contraries have one common ratio; so too between contrary passions there is but one moral virtue, which, like a second nature, consents to reason's dictates.

Reply to Objection 3: Those three passions are directed to the same object in a certain order, as stated above: and so they belong to the same virtue.

ARTICLE 5
Whether the moral virtues differ in point of the various objects of the passions?

Objection 1: It would seem that the moral virtues do not differ according to the objects of the passions. For just as there are objects of passions, so are there objects of operations. Now those moral virtues that are about operations, do not differ according to the objects of those operations: for the buying and selling either of a house or of a horse belong to the one same virtue of justice. Therefore neither do those moral virtues that are about passions differ according to the objects of those passions.

Objection 2: Further, the passions are acts or movements of the sensitive appetite. Now it needs a greater difference to differentiate habits than acts. Hence diverse objects which do not diversify the species of passions, do not diversify the species of moral virtue: so that there is but one moral virtue about all objects of pleasure, and the same applies to the other passions.

Objection 3: Further, more or less do not change a species. Now various objects of pleasure differ only by reason of being more or less pleasurable. Therefore all objects of pleasure belong to one species of virtue: and for the same reason so do all fearful objects, and the same applies to others. Therefore moral virtue is not diversified according to the objects of the passions.

Objection 4: Further, virtue hinders evil, even as it produces good. But there are various virtues about the desires for good things: thus temperance is about desires for the

delectationum tactus, et *eutrapelia* circa delectationes ludi. Ergo etiam circa timores malorum debent esse diversae virtutes.

SED CONTRA est quod castitas est circa delectabilia venereorum; abstinentia vero est circa delectabilia ciborum; et *eutrapelia* circa delectabilia ludorum.

RESPONDEO dicendum quod perfectio virtutis ex ratione dependet, perfectio autem passionis, ex ipso appetitu sensitivo. Unde oportet quod virtutes diversificentur secundum ordinem ad rationem, passiones autem, secundum ordinem ad appetitum. Obiecta igitur passionum, secundum quod diversimode comparantur ad appetitum sensitivum, causant diversas passionum species, secundum vero quod comparantur ad rationem, causant diversas species virtutum. Non est autem idem motus rationis, et appetitus sensitivi. Unde nihil prohibet aliquam differentiam obiectorum causare diversitatem passionum, quae non causat diversitatem virtutum, sicut quando una virtus est circa multas passiones, ut dictum est, et aliquam etiam differentiam obiectorum causare diversitatem virtutum, quae non causat diversitatem passionum, cum circa unam passionem, puta delectationem, diversae virtutes ordinentur. Et quia diversae passiones ad diversas potentias pertinentes, semper pertinent ad diversas virtutes, ut dictum est; ideo diversitas obiectorum quae respicit diversitatem potentiarum, semper diversificat species virtutum; puta quod aliquid sit bonum absolute, et aliquid bonum cum aliqua arduitate. Et quia ordine quodam ratio inferiores hominis partes regit, et etiam se ad exteriora extendit; ideo etiam secundum quod unum obiectum passionis apprehenditur sensu vel imaginatione, aut etiam ratione; et secundum etiam quod pertinet ad animam, corpus, vel exteriores res; diversam habitudinem habet ad rationem; et per consequens natum est diversificare virtutes. Bonum igitur hominis, quod est obiectum amoris, concupiscentiae et delectationis, potest accipi vel ad sensum corporis pertinens; vel ad interiorem

pleasure of touch, and *eutrapelia** about pleasures in games. Therefore there should be different virtues about fears of evils.

On the contrary, Chastity is about sexual pleasures, abstinence about pleasures of the table, and *eutrapelia* about pleasures in games.

I answer that, The perfection of a virtue depends on the reason; whereas the perfection of a passion depends on the sensitive appetite. Consequently virtues must needs be differentiated according to their relation to reason, but the passions according to their relation to the appetite. Hence the objects of the passions, according as they are variously related to the sensitive appetite, cause the different species of passions: while, according as they are related to reason, they cause the different species of virtues. Now the movement of reason is not the same as that of the sensitive appetite. Wherefore nothing hinders a difference of objects from causing diversity of passions, without causing diversity of virtues, as when one virtue is about several passions, as stated above (I-II, q. 60, a. 4); and again, a difference of objects from causing different virtues, without causing a difference of passions, since several virtues are directed about one passion, e.g., pleasure. And because diverse passions belonging to diverse powers, always belong to diverse virtues, as stated above (I-II, q. 60, a. 4); therefore a difference of objects that corresponds to a difference of powers always causes a specific difference of virtues—for instance the difference between that which is good absolutely speaking, and that which is good and difficult to obtain. Moreover since the reason rules man's lower powers in a certain order, and even extends to outward things; hence, one single object of the passions, according as it is apprehended by sense, imagination, or reason, and again, according as it belongs to the soul, body, or external things, has various relations to reason, and consequently is of a nature to cause a difference of virtues. Consequently man's good which is the object of love, desire and pleasure, may be taken as referred either to a bodily sense, or to the inner

---

* εὐτραπελία (*eutrapelia*)

animae apprehensionem. Et hoc, sive ordinetur ad bonum hominis in seipso, vel quantum ad corpus vel quantum ad animam; sive ordinetur ad bonum hominis in ordine ad alios. Et omnis talis diversitas, propter diversum ordinem ad rationem, diversificat virtutem. Sic igitur si consideretur aliquod bonum, si quidem sit per sensum tactus apprehensum, et ad consistentiam humanae vitae pertinens in individuo vel in specie, sicut sunt **delectabilia ciborum et venereorum; erit pertinens ad virtutem** *temperantiae.* Delectationes autem aliorum sensuum, cum non sint vehementes, non praestant aliquam difficultatem rationi, et ideo circa eas non ponitur aliqua virtus, *quae est circa difficile, sicut et ars,* ut dicitur in II Ethic. Bonum autem non sensu, sed interiori virtute apprehensum, ad ipsum hominem pertinens secundum seipsum, est sicut pecunia et honor; quorum pecunia ordinabilis est de se ad bonum corporis; honor autem consistit in apprehensione animae. Et haec quidem bona considerari possunt vel absolute, secundum quod pertinent ad concupiscibilem; vel cum arduitate quadam, secundum quod pertinent ad irascibilem. Quae quidem distinctio non habet locum in bonis quae delectant tactum, quia huiusmodi sunt quaedam infima, et competunt homini secundum quod convenit cum brutis. Circa bonum igitur pecuniae absolute sumptum, secundum quod est obiectum concupiscentiae vel delectationis aut amoris, est *liberalitas.* Circa bonum autem huiusmodi cum arduitate sumptum, secundum quod est obiectum spei, est *magnificentia.* Circa bonum vero quod est honor, si quidem sit absolute sumptum, secundum quod est obiectum amoris, sic est quaedam virtus quae vocatur *philotimia,* idest *amor honoris.* Si vero cum arduitate consideretur, secundum quod est obiectum spei, sic est *magnanimitas.* Unde liberalitas et *philotimia* videntur esse in concupiscibili, magnificentia vero et magnanimitas in irascibili. Bonum vero hominis in ordine ad alium,

apprehension of the mind: and this same good may be directed to man's good in himself, either in his body or in his soul, or to man's good in relation to other men. And every such difference, being differently related to reason, differentiates virtues. Accordingly, if we take a good, and it be something discerned by the sense of touch, and something pertaining to the upkeep of human life either in the individual or in the species, such as the **pleasures of the table or of sexual intercourse**, it will belong to the virtue of "temperance." As regards the pleasures of the other senses, they are not intense, and so do not present much difficulty to the reason: hence there is no virtue corresponding to them; for virtue, "like art, is about difficult things" (Ethic. ii, 3). On the other hand, good discerned not by the senses, but by an inner power, and belonging to man in himself, is like money and honor; the former, by its very nature, being employable for the good of the body, while the latter is based on the apprehension of the mind. These goods again may be considered either absolutely, in which way they concern the concupiscible faculty, or as being difficult to obtain, in which way they belong to the irascible part: which distinction, however, has no place in pleasurable objects of touch; since such are of base condition, and are becoming to man in so far as he has something in common with irrational animals. Accordingly in reference to money considered as a good absolutely, as an object of desire, pleasure, or love, there is "liberality": but if we consider this good as difficult to get, and as being the object of our hope, there is "magnificence."* With regard to that good which we call honor, taken absolutely, as the object of love, we have a virtue called *philotimia,*† i.e., "love of honor": while if we consider it as hard to attain, and as an object of hope, then we have "magnanimity." Wherefore liberality and *philotimia* seem to be in the concupiscible part, while magnificence and magnanimity are in the irascible. As regards man's good in relation to other men,

---

* μεγαλοπρέπεια (*megaloprepeia*), liberality of expenditure, with good taste, observing the mean between vulgar ostentation and narrow pettiness.

† φιλοτιμία (*philotimia*)

non videtur arduitatem habere, sed accipitur ut absolute sumptum, prout est obiectum passionum concupiscibilis. Quod quidem bonum potest esse alicui delectabile secundum quod praebet se alteri vel in his quae serio fiunt, idest in actionibus per rationem ordinatis ad debitum finem; vel in his quae fiunt ludo, idest in actionibus ordinatis ad delectationem tantum, quae non eodem modo se habent ad rationem sicut prima. In seriis autem se exhibet aliquis alteri dupliciter. Uno modo, ut delectabilem decentibus verbis et factis, et hoc pertinet ad quandam virtutem quam Aristoteles nominat *amicitiam;* et potest dici affabilitas. Alio modo praebet se aliquis alteri ut manifestum, per dicta et facta, et hoc pertinet ad aliam virtutem, quam nominat *veritatem*. Manifestatio enim propinquius accedit ad rationem quam delectatio; et seria quam iocosa. Unde et circa delectationes ludorum est alia virtus, quam philosophus *eutrapeliam* nominat. Sic igitur patet quod, secundum Aristotelem, sunt decem virtutes morales circa passiones, scilicet fortitudo, temperantia, liberalitas, magnificentia, magnanimitas, *philotimia,* mansuetudo, amicitia, veritas et *eutrapelia*. Et distinguuntur secundum diversas materias vel secundum diversas passiones; vel secundum diversa obiecta. Si igitur addatur *iustitia,* quae est circa operationes, erunt omnes undecim.

AD PRIMUM ergo dicendum quod omnia obiecta eiusdem operationis secundum speciem, eandem habitudinem habent ad rationem; non autem omnia obiecta eiusdem passionis secundum speciem, quia operationes non repugnant rationi, sicut passiones.

AD SECUNDUM dicendum quod alia ratione diversificantur passiones, et alia virtutes, sicut dictum est.

AD TERTIUM dicendum quod magis et minus non diversificant speciem, nisi propter diversam habitudinem ad rationem.

AD QUARTUM dicendum quod bonum fortius est ad movendum quam malum quia malum non agit nisi virtute boni, ut Dionysius dicit, IV cap. de Div. Nom. Unde

it does not seem hard to obtain, but is considered absolutely, as the object of the concupiscible passions. This good may be pleasurable to a man in his behavior towards another either in some serious matter, in actions, to wit, that are directed by reason to a due end, or in playful actions, *viz.* that are done for mere pleasure, and which do not stand in the same relation to reason as the former. Now one man behaves towards another in serious matters, in two ways. First, as being pleasant in his regard, by becoming speech and deeds: and this belongs to a virtue which Aristotle (Ethic. ii, 7) calls "friendship,"* and may be rendered "affability." Secondly, one man behaves towards another by being frank with him, in words and deeds: this belongs to another virtue which (Ethic. iv, 7) he calls "truthfulness."† For frankness is more akin to the reason than pleasure, and serious matters than play. Hence there is another virtue about the pleasures of games, which the Philosopher calls *eutrapelia*.‡ (Ethic. iv, 8). It is therefore evident that, according to Aristotle, there are ten moral virtues about the passions, *viz.* fortitude, temperance, liberality, magnificence, magnanimity, *philotimia,* gentleness, friendship, truthfulness, and *eutrapelia,* all of which differ in respect of their diverse matter, passions, or objects: so that if we add "justice," which is about operations, there will be eleven in all.

Reply to Objection 1: All objects of the same specific operation have the same relation to reason: not so all the objects of the same specific passion; because operations do not thwart reason as the passions do.

Reply to Objection 2: Passions are not differentiated by the same rule as virtues are, as stated above.

Reply to Objection 3: More and less do not cause a difference of species, unless they bear different relations to reason.

Reply to Objection 4: Good is a more potent mover than evil: because evil does not cause movement save in virtue of good, as Dionysius states (Div. Nom. iv). Hence an

---

* φιλία (*philia*)
† ἀλήθεια (*aletheia*)
‡ εὐτραπελία (*eutrapelia*)

malum non facit difficultatem rationi quae requirat virtutem, nisi sit excellens, quod videtur esse unum in uno genere passionis. Unde circa iras non ponitur nisi una virtus, scilicet mansuetudo, et similiter circa audacias una sola, scilicet fortitudo. Sed bonum ingerit difficultatem, quae requirit virtutem, etiam si non sit excellens in genere talis passionis. Et ideo circa concupiscentias ponuntur diversae virtutes morales, ut dictum est.

evil does not prove an obstacle to reason, so as to require virtues unless that evil be great; there being, seemingly, one such evil corresponding to each kind of passion. Hence there is but one virtue, meekness, for every form of anger; and, again, but one virtue, fortitude, for all forms of daring. On the other hand, good involves difficulty, which requires virtue, even if it be not a great good in that particular kind of passion. Consequently there are various moral virtues about desires, as stated above.

Quaestio LXI

Deinde considerandum est de virtutibus cardinalibus. Et circa hoc quaeruntur quinque. *Primo,* utrum virtutes morales debeant dici cardinales, vel principales. *Secundo,* de numero earum. *Tertio,* quae sint. *Quarto,* utrum differant ab invicem. *Quinto,* utrum dividantur convenienter in virtutes politicas, et purgatorias, et purgati animi, et exemplares.

Question 61
Of the Cardinal Virtues

We must now consider the cardinal virtues: under which head there are five points of inquiry: 1. Whether the moral virtues should be called cardinal or principal virtues? 2. Of their number; 3. Which are they? 4. Whether they differ from one another? 5. Whether they are fittingly divided into social, perfecting, perfect, and exemplar virtues?

Articulus 1

Ad primum sic proceditur. Videtur quod virtutes morales non debeant dici cardinales, seu principales. *Quae enim ex opposito dividuntur, sunt simul natura,* ut dicitur in praedicamentis, et sic unum non est altero principalius. Sed omnes virtutes ex opposito dividunt genus *virtutis.* Ergo nullae earum debent dici principales.

Praeterea, finis principalior est his quae sunt ad finem. Sed virtutes theologicae sunt circa finem, virtutes autem morales circa ea quae sunt ad finem. Ergo virtutes morales non debent dici principales, seu cardinales; sed magis theologicae.

Praeterea, principalius est quod est per essentiam, quam quod est per participationem. Sed virtutes intellectuales pertinent ad rationale per essentiam, virtutes autem morales ad rationale per participationem, ut supra dictum est. Ergo

Article 1
Whether the moral virtues should be called cardinal or principal virtues?

Objection 1: It would seem that moral virtues should not be called cardinal or principal virtues. For "the opposite members of a division are by nature simultaneous" (Categor. x), so that one is not principal rather than another. Now all the virtues are opposite members of the division of the genus "virtue." Therefore none of them should be called principal.

Objection 2: Further, the end is principal as compared to the means. But the theological virtues are about the end; while the moral virtues are about the means. Therefore the theological virtues, rather than the moral virtues, should be called principal or cardinal.

Objection 3: Further, that which is essentially so is principal in comparison with that which is so by participation. But the intellectual virtues belong to that which is essentially rational: whereas the moral virtues belong to that which is rational by participation, as stated above (I-II, q. 58, a. 3). Therefore the

virtutes morales non sunt principales, sed magis virtutes intellectuales.

SED CONTRA est quod Ambrosius dicit, super Lucam, exponens illud, *beati pauperes spiritu, scimus virtutes esse quatuor cardinales, scilicet temperantiam, iustitiam, prudentiam, fortitudinem.* Hae autem sunt virtutes morales. Ergo virtutes morales sunt cardinales.

RESPONDEO dicendum quod, cum simpliciter de virtute loquimur, intelligimur loqui de virtute humana. Virtus autem humana, ut supra dictum est, secundum perfectam rationem virtutis dicitur, quae requirit rectitudinem appetitus, huiusmodi enim virtus non solum facit facultatem bene agendi, sed ipsum etiam usum boni operis causat. Sed secundum imperfectam rationem virtutis dicitur virtus quae non requirit rectitudinem appetitus, quia solum facit facultatem bene agendi, non autem causat boni operis usum. Constat autem quod perfectum est principalius imperfecto. Et ideo virtutes quae continent rectitudinem appetitus, dicuntur principales. Huiusmodi autem sunt virtutes morales; et inter intellectuales, sola prudentia, quae etiam quodammodo moralis est, secundum materiam, ut ex supradictis patet, unde convenienter inter virtutes morales ponuntur illae quae dicuntur principales, seu cardinales.

AD PRIMUM ergo dicendum quod, quando genus univocum dividitur in suas species, tunc partes divisionis ex aequo se habent secundum rationem generis; licet secundum naturam rei, una species sit principalior et perfectior alia, sicut homo aliis animalibus. Sed quando est divisio alicuius analogi, quod dicitur de pluribus secundum prius et posterius; tunc nihil prohibet unum esse principalius altero, etiam secundum communem rationem; sicut substantia principalius dicitur ens quam accidens. Et talis est divisio virtutum in diversa genera virtutum, eo quod bonum rationis non secundum eundem ordinem invenitur in omnibus.

AD SECUNDUM dicendum quod virtutes theologicae sunt supra hominem, ut supra

intellectual virtues are principal, rather than the moral virtues.

On the contrary, Ambrose in explaining the words, "Blessed are the poor in spirit" (Lk. 6:20) says: "We know that there are four cardinal virtues, *viz.* temperance, justice, prudence, and fortitude." But these are moral virtues. Therefore the moral virtues are cardinal virtues.

I answer that, When we speak of virtue simply, we are understood to speak of human virtue. Now human virtue, as stated above (I-II, q. 56, a. 3), is one that answers to the perfect idea of virtue, which requires rectitude of the appetite: for such like virtue not only confers the faculty of doing well, but also causes the good deed done. On the other hand, the name virtue is applied to one that answers imperfectly to the idea of virtue, and does not require rectitude of the appetite: because it merely confers the faculty of doing well without causing the good deed to be done. Now it is evident that the perfect is principal as compared to the imperfect: and so those virtues which imply rectitude of the appetite are called principal virtues. Such are the moral virtues, and prudence alone, of the intellectual virtues, for it is also something of a moral virtue, as was clearly shown above (I-II, q. 57, a. 4). Consequently, those virtues which are called principal or cardinal are fittingly placed among the moral virtues.

Reply to Objection 1: When a univocal genus is divided into its species, the members of the division are on a par in the point of the generic idea; although considered in their nature as things, one species may surpass another in rank and perfection, as man in respect of other animals. But when we divide an analogous term, which is applied to several things, but to one before it is applied to another, nothing hinders one from ranking before another, even in the point of the generic idea; as the notion of being is applied to substance principally in relation to accident. Such is the division of virtue into various kinds of virtue: since the good defined by reason is not found in the same way in all things.

Reply to Objection 2: The theological virtues are above man, as stated above

dictum est. Unde non proprie dicuntur virtutes humanae, sed *superhumanae,* vel divinae.

AD TERTIUM dicendum, quod aliae virtutes intellectuales a prudentia, etsi sint principaliores quam morales quantum ad subiectum; non tamen sunt principaliores quantum ad rationem virtutis, quae respicit bonum, quod est obiectum appetitus.

ARTICULUS 2

AD SECUNDUM sic proceditur. Videtur quod non sint quatuor virtutes cardinales. Prudentia enim est directiva aliarum virtutum moralium, ut ex supradictis patet. Sed id quod est directivum aliorum, principalius est. Ergo prudentia sola est virtus principalis.

PRAETEREA, virtutes principales sunt aliquo modo morales. Sed ad operationes morales ordinamur per rationem practicam, et appetitum rectum, ut dicitur in VI Ethic. Ergo solae duae virtutes cardinales sunt.

PRAETEREA, inter alias etiam virtutes una est principalior altera. Sed ad hoc quod virtus dicatur principalis, non requiritur quod sit principalis respectu omnium, sed respectu quarundam. Ergo videtur quod sint multo plures principales virtutes.

SED CONTRA est quod Gregorius dicit, in II Moral., *in quatuor virtutibus tota boni operis structura consurgit.*

RESPONDEO dicendum quod numerus aliquorum accipi potest aut secundum principia formalia aut secundum subiecta, et utroque modo inveniuntur quatuor cardinales virtutes. Principium enim formale virtutis de qua nunc loquimur, est rationis bonum. Quod quidem dupliciter potest considerari. Uno modo, secundum quod in ipsa consideratione rationis consistit. Et sic erit una virtus principalis, quae dicitur *prudentia.* Alio modo, secundum quod circa aliquid ponitur rationis ordo. Et hoc vel circa operationes, et sic est *iustitia,* vel circa passiones, et sic necesse est esse duas virtutes. Ordinem enim rationis necesse est ponere circa passiones, considerata repugnantia ipsarum ad rationem. Quae quidem potest esse dupliciter.

(I-II, q. 58, a. 3, ad 3). Hence they should properly be called not human, but "super-human" or godlike virtues.

Reply to Objection 3: Although the intellectual virtues, except in prudence, rank before the moral virtues, in the point of their subject, they do not rank before them as virtues; for a virtue, as such, regards good, which is the object of the appetite.

ARTICLE 2
Whether there are four cardinal virtues?

Objection 1: It would seem that there are not four cardinal virtues. For prudence is the directing principle of the other moral virtues, as is clear from what has been said above (I-II, q. 58, a. 4). But that which directs other things ranks before them. Therefore prudence alone is a principal virtue.

Objection 2: Further, the principal virtues are, in a way, moral virtues. Now we are directed to moral works both by the practical reason, and by a right appetite, as stated in Ethic. vi, 2. Therefore there are only two cardinal virtues.

Objection 3: Further, even among the other virtues one ranks higher than another. But in order that a virtue be principal, it needs not to rank above all the others, but above some. Therefore it seems that there are many more principal virtues.

On the contrary, Gregory says (Moral. ii): "The entire structure of good works is built on four virtues."

I answer that, Things may be numbered either in respect of their formal principles, or according to the subjects in which they are: and either way we find that there are four cardinal virtues. For the formal principle of the virtue of which we speak now is good as defined by reason; which good is considered in two ways. First, as existing in the very act of reason: and thus we have one principal virtue, called "Prudence." Secondly, according as the reason puts its order into something else; either into operations, and then we have "Justice"; or into passions, and then we need two virtues. For the need of putting the order of reason into the passions is due to their thwarting reason: and this occurs in two ways.

Uno modo secundum quod passio impellit ad aliquid contrarium rationi, et sic necesse est quod passio reprimatur, et ab hoc denominatur *temperantia*. Alio modo, secundum quod passio retrahit ab eo quod ratio dictat, sicut timor periculorum vel laborum, et sic necesse est quod homo firmetur in eo quod est rationis, ne recedat; et ab hoc denominatur *fortitudo*. Similiter secundum subiecta, idem numerus invenitur. Quadruplex enim invenitur subiectum huius virtutis de qua nunc loquimur, scilicet rationale per essentiam, quod *prudentia* perficit; et rationale per participationem, quod dividitur in tria; idest in voluntatem, quae est subiectum *iustitiae*; et in concupiscibilem, quae est subiectum *temperantiae*; et in irascibilem, quae est subiectum *fortitudinis*.

Ad primum ergo dicendum quod prudentia est simpliciter principalior omnibus. Sed aliae ponuntur principales unaquaeque in suo genere.

Ad secundum dicendum quod rationale per participationem dividitur in tria, ut dictum est.

Ad tertium dicendum quod omnes aliae virtutes, quarum una est principalior alia, reducuntur ad praedictas quatuor, et quantum ad subiectum, et quantum ad rationes formales.

First, by the passions inciting to something against reason, and then the passions need a curb, which we call "Temperance." Secondly, by the passions withdrawing us from following the dictate of reason, e.g., through fear of danger or toil: and then man needs to be strengthened for that which reason dictates, lest he turn back; and to this end there is "Fortitude." In like manner, we find the same number if we consider the subjects of virtue. For there are four subjects of the virtue we speak of now: *viz.* the power which is rational in its essence, and this is perfected by "Prudence"; and that which is rational by participation, and is threefold, the will, subject of "Justice," the concupiscible faculty, subject of "Temperance," and the irascible faculty, subject of "Fortitude."

Reply to Objection 1: Prudence is the principal of all the virtues simply. The others are principal, each in its own genus.

Reply to Objection 2: That part of the soul which is rational by participation is threefold, as stated above.

Reply to Objection 3: All the other virtues among which one ranks before another, are reducible to the above four, both as to the subject and as to the formal principle.

Articulus 3

Ad tertium sic proceditur. Videtur quod aliae virtutes debeant dici magis principales quam istae. Id enim quod est maximum in unoquoque genere, videtur esse principalius. Sed *magnanimitas operatur magnum in omnibus virtutibus,* ut dicitur in IV Ethic. Ergo magnanimitas maxime debet dici principalis virtus.

Praeterea, illud per quod aliae virtutes firmantur, videtur esse maxime principalis virtus. Sed humilitas est huiusmodi, dicit enim Gregorius quod *qui ceteras virtutes sine humilitate congregat, quasi paleas in ventum portat*. Ergo humilitas videtur esse maxime principalis.

Article 3
Whether any other virtues should be called principal rather than these?

Objection 1: It would seem that other virtues should be called principal rather than these. For, seemingly, the greatest is the principal in any genus. Now "magnanimity has a great influence on all the virtues" (Ethic. iv, 3). Therefore magnanimity should more than any be called a principal virtue.

Objection 2: Further, that which strengthens the other virtues should above all be called a principal virtue. But such is humility: for Gregory says (Hom. iv in Ev.) that "he who gathers the other virtues without humility is as one who carries straw against the wind." Therefore humility seems above all to be a principal virtue.

PRAETEREA, illud videtur esse principale, quod est perfectissimum. Sed hoc pertinet ad patientiam; secundum illud Iacobi I, *patientia opus perfectum habet*. Ergo patientia debet poni principalis.

SED CONTRA est quod Tullius, in sua rhetorica, ad has quatuor omnes alias reducit.

RESPONDEO dicendum quod sicut supra dictum est, huiusmodi quatuor virtutes cardinales accipiuntur secundum quatuor formales rationes virtutis de qua loquimur. Quae quidem in aliquibus actibus vel passionibus principaliter inveniuntur. Sicut bonum consistens in consideratione rationis, principaliter invenitur in ipso rationis imperio; non autem in consilio, neque in iudicio, ut supra dictum est. Similiter autem bonum rationis prout ponitur in operationibus secundum rationem recti et debiti, principaliter invenitur in commutationibus vel distributionibus quae sunt ad alterum cum aequalitate. Bonum autem refraenandi passiones principaliter invenitur in passionibus quas maxime difficile est reprimere, scilicet in delectationibus tactus. Bonum autem firmitatis ad standum in bono rationis contra impetum passionum, praecipue invenitur in periculis mortis, contra quae difficillimum est stare. Sic igitur praedictas quatuor virtutes dupliciter considerare possumus. Uno modo, secundum communes rationes formales. Et secundum hoc, dicuntur principales, quasi generales ad omnes virtutes, utputa quod omnis virtus quae facit bonum in consideratione rationis, dicatur prudentia; et quod omnis virtus quae facit bonum debiti et recti in operationibus, dicatur iustitia; et omnis virtus quae cohibet passiones et deprimit, dicatur temperantia; et omnis virtus quae facit firmitatem animi contra quascumque passiones, dicatur fortitudo. Et sic multi loquuntur de istis virtutibus, tam sacri doctores quam etiam philosophi. Et sic aliae virtutes sub ipsis continentur unde cessant omnes obiectiones. Alio vero modo possunt accipi, secundum quod istae virtutes denominantur ab eo quod est praecipuum in unaquaque materia. Et sic sunt speciales virtutes, contra alias divisae. Dicuntur tamen principales respectu aliarum, propter principalitatem

Objection 3: Further, that which is most perfect seems to be principal. But this applies to patience, according to James 1:4: "Patience hath a perfect work." Therefore patience should be reckoned a principal virtue.

On the contrary, Cicero reduces all other virtues to these four (De Invent. Rhet. ii).

I answer that, As stated above (I-II, q. 61, a. 2), these four are reckoned as cardinal virtues, in respect of the four formal principles of virtue as we understand it now. These principles are found chiefly in certain acts and passions. Thus the good which exists in the act of reason, is found chiefly in reason's command, but not in its counsel or its judgment, as stated above (I-II, q. 57, a. 6). Again, good as defined by reason and put into our operations as something right and due, is found chiefly in commutations and distributions in respect of another person, and on a basis of equality. The good of curbing the passions is found chiefly in those passions which are most difficult to curb, *viz.* in the pleasures of touch. The good of being firm in holding to the good defined by reason, against the impulse of passion, is found chiefly in perils of death, which are most difficult to withstand. Accordingly the above four virtues may be considered in two ways. First, in respect of their common formal principles. In this way they are called principal, being general, as it were, in comparison with all the virtues: so that, for instance, any virtue that causes good in reason's act of consideration, may be called prudence; every virtue that causes the good of right and due in operation, be called justice; every virtue that curbs and represses the passions, be called temperance; and every virtue that strengthens the mind against any passions whatever, be called fortitude. Many, both holy doctors, as also philosophers, speak about these virtues in this sense: and in this way the other virtues are contained under them. Wherefore all the objections fail. Secondly, they may be considered in point of their being denominated, each one from that which is foremost in its respective matter, and thus they are specific virtues, condivided with the others. Yet they are called principal in comparison with the other virtues, on account of the importance

materiae, puta quod prudentia dicatur quae praeceptiva est; iustitia, quae est circa actiones debitas inter aequales; temperantia, quae reprimit concupiscentias delectationum tactus; fortitudo, quae firmat contra pericula mortis.

Et sic etiam cessant obiectiones, quia aliae virtutes possunt habere aliquas alias principalitates, sed istae dicuntur principales ratione materiae, ut supra dictum est.

of their matter: so that prudence is the virtue which commands; justice, the virtue which is about due actions between equals; temperance, the virtue which suppresses desires for the pleasures of touch; and fortitude, the virtue which strengthens against dangers of death.

Thus again do the objections fail: because the other virtues may be principal in some other way, but these are called principal by reason of their matter, as stated above.

Articulus 4

Ad quartum sic proceditur. Videtur quod quatuor praedictae virtutes non sint diversae virtutes, et ab invicem distinctae. Dicit enim Gregorius, in XXII Moral., *prudentia vera non est, quae iusta, temperans et fortis non est; nec perfecta temperantia, quae fortis, iusta et prudens non est; nec fortitudo integra, quae prudens, temperans et iusta non est; nec vera iustitia, quae prudens, fortis et temperans non est*. Hoc autem non contingeret, si praedictae quatuor virtutes essent ab invicem distinctae, diversae enim species eiusdem generis non denominant se invicem. Ergo praedictae virtutes non sunt ab invicem distinctae.

Praeterea, eorum quae ab invicem sunt distincta, quod est unius, non attribuitur alteri. Sed illud quod est temperantiae, attribuitur fortitudini, dicit enim Ambrosius, in I libro de Offic., *iure ea fortitudo vocatur, quando unusquisque seipsum vincit, nullis illecebris emollitur atque inflectitur*. De temperantia etiam dicit quod *modum vel ordinem servat omnium quae vel agenda vel dicenda arbitramur*. Ergo videtur quod huiusmodi virtutes non sunt ab invicem distinctae.

Praeterea, philosophus dicit, in II Ethic., quod ad virtutem haec requiruntur, primum quidem, *si sciens; deinde, si eligens, et eligens propter hoc; tertium autem, si firme et immobiliter habeat et operetur*. Sed horum primum videtur ad prudentiam pertinere, quae est recta ratio agibilium; secundum, scilicet eligere, ad temperantiam,

Article 4
Whether the four cardinal virtues differ from one another?

Objection 1: It would seem that the above four virtues are not diverse and distinct from one another. For Gregory says (Moral. xxii, 1): "There is no true prudence, unless it be just, temperate and brave; no perfect temperance, that is not brave, just and prudent; no sound fortitude, that is not prudent, temperate and just; no real justice, without prudence, fortitude and temperance." But this would not be so, if the above virtues were distinct from one another: since the different species of one genus do not qualify one another. Therefore the aforesaid virtues are not distinct from one another.

Objection 2: Further, among things distinct from one another the function of one is not attributed to another. But the function of temperance is attributed to fortitude: for Ambrose says (De Offic. xxxvi): "Rightly do we call it fortitude, when a man conquers himself, and is not weakened and bent by any enticement." And of temperance he says (De Offic. xliii, xlv) that it "safeguards the manner and order in all things that we decide to do and say." Therefore it seems that these virtues are not distinct from one another.

Objection 3: Further, the Philosopher says (Ethic. ii, 4) that the necessary conditions of virtue are first of all "that a man should have knowledge; secondly, that he should exercise choice for a particular end; thirdly, that he should possess the habit and act with firmness and steadfastness." But the first of these seems to belong to prudence which is rectitude of reason in things to be done; the second, i.e., choice, belongs to temperance,

I-II, q. 61, a. 4, arg. 3

ut aliquis non ex passione, sed ex electione agat, passionibus refraenatis; tertium, ut aliquis propter debitum finem operetur, rectitudinem quandam continet, quae videtur ad iustitiam pertinere aliud, scilicet firmitas et immobilitas, pertinet ad fortitudinem. Ergo quaelibet harum virtutum est generalis ad omnes virtutes. Ergo non distinguuntur ad invicem.

Sed contra est quod Augustinus dicit, in libro de moribus Eccles., quod *quadripartita dicitur virtus, ex ipsius amoris vario affectu,* et subiungit de praedictis quatuor virtutibus. Praedictae ergo quatuor virtutes sunt ab invicem distinctae.

Respondeo dicendum quod, sicut supra dictum est, praedictae quatuor virtutes dupliciter a diversis accipiuntur. Quidam enim accipiunt eas, prout significant quasdam generales conditiones humani animi, quae inveniuntur in omnibus virtutibus, ita scilicet quod prudentia nihil sit aliud quam quaedam rectitudo discretionis in quibuscumque actibus vel materiis; iustitia vero sit quaedam rectitudo animi, per quam homo operatur quod debet in quacumque materia; temperantia vero sit quaedam dispositio animi quae modum quibuscumque passionibus vel operationibus imponit, ne ultra debitum efferantur; fortitudo vero sit quaedam dispositio animae per quam firmetur in eo quod est secundum rationem, contra quoscumque impetus passionum vel operationum labores. Haec autem quatuor sic distincta, non important diversitatem habituum virtuosorum quantum ad iustitiam, temperantiam et fortitudinem. Cuilibet enim virtuti morali, ex hoc quod est *habitus,* convenit quaedam firmitas, ut a contrario non moveatur, quod dictum est ad fortitudinem pertinere. Ex hoc vero quod est *virtus,* habet quod ordinetur ad bonum, in quo importatur ratio recti vel debiti, quod dicebatur ad iustitiam pertinere. In hoc vero quod est *virtus moralis* rationem participans, habet quod modum rationis in omnibus servet, et ultra se non extendat, quod dicebatur pertinere ad temperantiam. Solum autem hoc quod est discretionem habere, quod attribuebatur prudentiae, videtur distingui ab aliis tribus, inquantum hoc est

THE CARDINAL VIRTUES

whereby a man, holding his passions on the curb, acts, not from passion but from choice; the third, that a man should act for the sake of a due end, implies a certain rectitude, which seemingly belongs to justice; while the last, *viz.* firmness and steadfastness, belongs to fortitude. Therefore each of these virtues is general in comparison to other virtues. Therefore they are not distinct from one another.

On the contrary, Augustine says (De Moribus Eccl. xi) that "there are four virtues, corresponding to the various emotions of love," and he applies this to the four virtues mentioned above. Therefore the same four virtues are distinct from one another.

I answer that, As stated above (I-II, q. 61, a. 3), these four virtues are understood differently by various writers. For some take them as signifying certain general conditions of the human mind, to be found in all the virtues: so that, to wit, prudence is merely a certain rectitude of discretion in any actions or matters whatever; justice, a certain rectitude of the mind, whereby a man does what he ought in any matters; temperance, a disposition of the mind, moderating any passions or operations, so as to keep them within bounds; and fortitude, a disposition whereby the soul is strengthened for that which is in accord with reason, against any assaults of the passions, or the toil involved by any operations. To distinguish these four virtues in this way does not imply that justice, temperance and fortitude are distinct virtuous habits: because it is fitting that every moral virtue, from the fact that it is a "habit," should be accompanied by a certain firmness so as not to be moved by its contrary: and this, we have said, belongs to fortitude. Moreover, inasmuch as it is a "virtue," it is directed to good which involves the notion of right and due; and this, we have said, belongs to justice. Again, owing to the fact that it is a "moral virtue" partaking of reason, it observes the mode of reason in all things, and does not exceed its bounds, which has been stated to belong to temperance. It is only in the point of having discretion, which we ascribed to prudence, that there seems to be a distinction from the other three, inasmuch

ipsius rationis per essentiam; alia vero tria important quandam participationem rationis, per modum applicationis cuiusdam ad passiones vel operationes. Sic igitur, secundum praedicta, prudentia quidem esset virtus distincta ab aliis tribus, sed aliae tres non essent virtutes distinctae ab invicem; manifestum est enim quod una et eadem virtus et est habitus, et est virtus, et est moralis. Alii vero, et melius, accipiunt has quatuor virtutes secundum quod determinantur ad materias speciales; unaquaeque quidem illarum ad unam materiam, in qua principaliter laudatur illa generalis conditio a qua nomen virtutis accipitur, ut supra dictum est. Et secundum hoc, manifestum est quod praedictae virtutes sunt diversi habitus, secundum diversitatem obiectorum distincti.

AD PRIMUM ergo dicendum quod Gregorius loquitur de praedictis quatuor virtutibus secundum primam acceptionem. Vel potest dici quod istae quatuor virtutes denominantur ab invicem per redundantiam quandam. Id enim quod est prudentiae, redundat in alias virtutes, inquantum a prudentia diriguntur. Unaquaeque vero aliarum redundat in alias ea ratione, quod qui potest quod est difficilius, potest et id quod minus est difficile. Unde qui potest refraenare concupiscentias delectabilium secundum tactum, ne modum excedant, quod est difficillimum; ex hoc ipso redditur habilior ut refraenet audaciam in periculis mortis, ne ultra modum procedat, quod est longe facilius; et secundum hoc, fortitudo dicitur temperata. Temperantia etiam dicitur fortis, ex redundantia fortitudinis in temperantiam, inquantum scilicet ille qui per fortitudinem habet animum firmum contra pericula mortis, quod est difficillimum, est habilior ut retineat animi firmitatem contra impetus delectationum; quia, ut dicit Tullius in I de Offic., *non est consentaneum ut qui metu non frangitur, cupiditate frangatur; nec qui invictum se a labore praestiterit, vinci a voluptate.*

Et per hoc etiam patet responsio ad secundum. Sic enim temperantia in omnibus modum servat, et fortitudo contra illecebras voluptatum animum servat inflexum,

as discretion belongs essentially to reason; whereas the other three imply a certain share of reason by way of a kind of application (of reason) to passions or operations. According to the above explanation, then, prudence would be distinct from the other three virtues: but these would not be distinct from one another; for it is evident that one and the same virtue is both habit, and virtue, and moral virtue. Others, however, with better reason, take these four virtues, according as they have their special determinate matter; each of its own matter, in which special commendation is given to that general condition from which the virtue's name is taken as stated above (I-II, q. 61, a. 3). In this way it is clear that the aforesaid virtues are distinct habits, differentiated in respect of their diverse objects.

Reply to Objection 1: Gregory is speaking of these four virtues in the first sense given above. It may also be said that these four virtues qualify one another by a kind of overflow. For the qualities of prudence overflow on to the other virtues in so far as they are directed by prudence. And each of the others overflows on to the rest, for the reason that whoever can do what is harder, can do what is less difficult. Wherefore whoever can curb his desires for the pleasures of touch, so that they keep within bounds, which is a very hard thing to do, for this very reason is more able to check his daring in dangers of death, so as not to go too far, which is much easier; and in this sense fortitude is said to be temperate. Again, temperance is said to be brave, by reason of fortitude overflowing into temperance: in so far, to wit, as he whose mind is strengthened by fortitude against dangers of death, which is a matter of very great difficulty, is more able to remain firm against the onslaught of pleasures; for as Cicero says (De Offic. i), "it would be inconsistent for a man to be unbroken by fear, and yet vanquished by cupidity; or that he should be conquered by lust, after showing himself to be unconquered by toil."

From this the Reply to the Second Objection is clear. For temperance observes the mean in all things, and fortitude keeps the mind unbent by the enticements of pleasures,

I-II, q. 61, a. 4, ad 2

vel inquantum istae virtutes denominant quasdam generales conditiones virtutum; vel per redundantiam praedictam.

AD TERTIUM dicendum quod illae quatuor generales virtutum conditiones quas ponit philosophus, non sunt propriae praedictis virtutibus. Sed possunt eis appropriari, secundum modum iam dictum.

either in so far as these virtues are taken to denote certain general conditions of virtue, or in the sense that they overflow on to one another, as explained above.

Reply to Objection 3: These four general conditions of virtue set down by the Philosopher, are not proper to the aforesaid virtues. They may, however, be appropriated to them, in the way above stated.

ARTICULUS 5

AD QUINTUM sic proceditur. Videtur quod inconvenienter huiusmodi quatuor virtutes dividantur in virtutes exemplares, purgati animi, purgatorias, et politicas. Ut enim Macrobius dicit, in I super somnium Scipionis, *virtutes exemplares sunt quae in ipsa divina mente consistunt.* Sed philosophus, in X Ethic., dicit quod *ridiculum est Deo iustitiam, fortitudinem, temperantiam et prudentiam attribuere.* Ergo virtutes huiusmodi non possunt esse exemplares.

PRAETEREA, virtutes *purgati animi* dicuntur quae sunt absque passionibus, dicit enim ibidem Macrobius quod *temperantiae purgati animi est terrenas cupiditates non reprimere, sed penitus oblivisci; fortitudinis autem passiones ignorare, non vincere.* Dictum est autem supra quod huiusmodi virtutes sine passionibus esse non possunt. Ergo huiusmodi virtutes *purgati animi* esse non possunt.

PRAETEREA, virtutes *purgatorias* dicit esse eorum qui quadam humanorum *fuga solis se inserunt divinis.* Sed hoc videtur esse vitiosum, dicit enim Tullius, in I de Offic., quod *qui despicere se dicunt ea quae plerique mirantur imperia et magistratus, his non modo non laudi, verum etiam vitio dandum puto.* Ergo non sunt aliquae virtutes *purgatoriae.*

ARTICLE 5
Whether the cardinal virtues are fittingly divided into social virtues, perfecting, perfect, and exemplar virtues?

Objection 1: It would seem that these four virtues are unfittingly divided into exemplar virtues, perfecting virtues, perfect virtues, and social virtues. For as Macrobius says (Super Somn. Scip. 1), the "exemplar virtues are such as exist in the mind of God." Now the Philosopher says (Ethic. x, 8) that "it is absurd to ascribe justice, fortitude, temperance, and prudence to God." Therefore these virtues cannot be exemplar.

Objection 2: Further, the "perfect" virtues are those which are without any passion: for Macrobius says (Super Somn. Scip. 1) that "in a soul that is cleansed, temperance has not to check worldly desires, for it has forgotten all about them: fortitude knows nothing about the passions; it does not have to conquer them." Now it was stated above (I-II, q. 59, a. 5) that the aforesaid virtues cannot be without passions. Therefore there is no such thing as "perfect" virtue.

Objection 3: Further, he says (Macrobius: Super Somn. Scip. 1) that the "perfecting" virtues are those of the man "who flies from human affairs and devotes himself exclusively to the things of God." But it seems wrong to do this, for Cicero says (De Offic. i): "I reckon that it is not only unworthy of praise, but wicked for a man to say that he despises what most men admire, *viz.* power and office." Therefore there are no "perfecting" virtues.

PRAETEREA, virtutes *politicas* esse dicit *quibus boni viri reipublicae consulunt, urbesque tuentur*. Sed ad bonum commune sola iustitia legalis ordinatur; ut philosophus dicit, in V Ethic. Ergo aliae virtutes non debent dici *politicae*.

SED CONTRA est quod Macrobius ibidem dicit, *Plotinus, inter philosophiae professores cum Platone princeps, quatuor sunt, inquit, quaternarum genera virtutum. Ex his primae politicae vocantur; secundae, purgatoriae; tertiae autem, iam purgati animi; quartae, exemplares.*

RESPONDEO dicendum quod, sicut Augustinus dicit in libro de moribus Eccles., *oportet quod anima aliquid sequatur, ad hoc quod ei possit virtus innasci, et hoc Deus est, quem si sequimur, bene vivimus*. Oportet igitur quod exemplar humanae virtutis in Deo praeexistat, sicut et in eo praeexistunt omnium rerum rationes. Sic igitur virtus potest considerari vel prout est exemplariter in Deo, et sic dicuntur virtutes *exemplares*. Ita scilicet quod ipsa divina mens in Deo dicatur prudentia; temperantia vero, conversio divinae intentionis ad seipsum, sicut in nobis temperantia dicitur per hoc quod concupiscibilis conformatur rationi; fortitudo autem Dei est eius immutabilitas; iustitia vero Dei est observatio legis aeternae in suis operibus, sicut Plotinus dixit. Et quia homo secundum suam naturam est animal politicum, virtutes huiusmodi, prout in homine existunt secundum conditionem suae naturae, *politicae* vocantur, prout scilicet homo secundum has virtutes recte se habet in rebus humanis gerendis. Secundum quem modum hactenus de his virtutibus locuti sumus.

Objection 4: Further, he says (Macrobius: Super Somn. Scip. 1) that the "social" virtues are those "whereby good men work for the good of their country and for the safety of the city." But it is only legal justice that is directed to the common weal, as the Philosopher states (Ethic. v, 1). Therefore other virtues should not be called "social."

On the contrary, Macrobius says (Super Somn. Scip. 1): "Plotinus, together with Plato foremost among teachers of philosophy, says: 'The four kinds of virtue are fourfold: In the first place there are social* virtues; secondly, there are perfecting virtues;[†] thirdly, there are perfect[‡] virtues; and fourthly, there are exemplar virtues.'"

I answer that, As Augustine says (De Moribus Eccl. vi), "the soul needs to follow something in order to give birth to virtue: this something is God: if we follow Him we shall live aright." Consequently the exemplar of human virtue must needs pre-exist in God, just as in Him pre-exist the types of all things. Accordingly virtue may be considered as existing originally in God, and thus we speak of "exemplar" virtues: so that in God the Divine Mind itself may be called prudence; while temperance is the turning of God's gaze on Himself, even as in us it is that which conforms the appetite to reason. God's fortitude is His unchangeableness; His justice is the observance of the Eternal Law in His works, as Plotinus states (Cf. Macrobius, Super Somn. Scip. 1). Again, since man by his nature is a social[§] animal, these virtues, in so far as they are in him according to the condition of his nature, are called "social" virtues; since it is by reason of them that man behaves himself well in the conduct of human affairs. It is in this sense that we have been speaking of these virtues until now.

---

* Cf. Chrysostom's fifteenth homily on St. Matthew, where he says: "The gentle, the modest, the merciful, the just man does not shut up his good deeds within himself. ...He that is clean of heart and peaceful, and suffers persecution for the sake of the truth, lives for the common weal."

† *Virtutes purgatoriae:* literally meaning, cleansing virtues.

‡ *Virtutes purgati animi:* literally, virtues of the clean soul.

§ See above note on Chrysostom.

I-II, q. 61, a. 5, co.

Sed quia ad hominem pertinet ut etiam ad divina se trahat quantum potest, ut etiam philosophus dicit, in X Ethic.; et hoc nobis in sacra Scriptura multipliciter commendatur, ut est illud Matth. V, *estote perfecti, sicut et pater vester caelestis perfectus est*, necesse est ponere quasdam virtutes medias inter politicas, quae sunt virtutes humanae, et exemplares, quae sunt virtutes divinae. Quae quidem virtutes distinguuntur secundum **diversitatem motus et termini. Ita scilicet quod quaedam sunt virtutes transeuntium** et in divinam similitudinem tendentium, et hae vocantur virtutes *purgatoriae*. Ita scilicet quod prudentia omnia mundana divinorum contemplatione despiciat, omnemque animae cogitationem in divina sola dirigat; temperantia vero relinquat, inquantum natura patitur, quae corporis usus requirit; fortitudinis autem est ut anima non terreatur propter excessum a corpore, et accessum ad superna; iustitia vero est ut tota anima consentiat ad huius propositi viam. Quaedam vero sunt virtutes iam assequentium divinam similitudinem, quae vocantur virtutes iam *purgati animi*. Ita scilicet quod prudentia sola divina intueatur; temperantia terrenas cupiditates nesciat; fortitudo passiones ignoret; iustitia cum divina mente perpetuo foedere societur, eam scilicet imitando. Quas quidem virtutes dicimus esse beatorum, vel aliquorum in hac vita perfectissimorum.

AD PRIMUM ergo dicendum quod philosophus loquitur de his virtutibus secundum quod sunt circa res humanas, puta iustitia circa emptiones et venditiones, fortitudo circa timores, temperantia circa concupiscentias. Sic enim ridiculum est eas Deo attribuere.

AD SECUNDUM dicendum quod virtutes humanae sunt circa passiones, scilicet virtutes hominum in hoc mundo conversantium. Sed virtutes eorum qui plenam beatitudinem assequuntur, sunt absque passionibus. Unde Plotinus dicit quod *passiones politicae virtutes molliunt,* idest ad medium reducunt; *secundae,* scilicet purgatoriae, *auferunt; tertiae,* quae sunt purgati animi, *obliviscuntur;*

But since it behooves a man to do his utmost to strive onward even to Divine things, as even the Philosopher declares in Ethic. x, 7, and as Scripture often admonishes us—for instance: "Be ye . . . perfect, as your heavenly Father is perfect" (Mat. 5:48), we must needs place some virtues between the social or human virtues, and the exemplar virtues which are Divine. Now these virtues differ by reason of a difference of movement and term: **so that some are virtues of men who are on their way and tending towards the Divine similitude; and these are called "perfecting"** virtues. Thus prudence, by contemplating the things of God, counts as nothing all things of the world, and directs all the thoughts of the soul to God alone: temperance, so far as nature allows, neglects the needs of the body; fortitude prevents the soul from being afraid of neglecting the body and rising to heavenly things; and justice consists in the soul giving a whole-hearted consent to follow the way thus proposed. Besides these there are the virtues of those who have already attained to the Divine similitude: these are called the "perfect virtues." Thus prudence sees nought else but the things of God; temperance knows no earthly desires; fortitude has no knowledge of passion; and justice, by imitating the Divine Mind, is united thereto by an everlasting covenant. Such as the virtues attributed to the Blessed, or, in this life, to some who are at the summit of perfection.

Reply to Objection 1: The Philosopher is speaking of these virtues according as they relate to human affairs; for instance, justice, about buying and selling; fortitude, about fear; temperance, about desires; for in this sense it is absurd to attribute them to God.

Reply to Objection 2: Human virtues, that is to say, virtues of men living together in this world, are about the passions. But the virtues of those who have attained to perfect bliss are without passions. Hence Plotinus says (Cf. Macrobius, Super Somn. Scip. 1) that "the social virtues check the passions," i.e., they bring them to the relative mean; "the second kind," *viz.* the perfecting virtues, "uproot them"; "the third kind," *viz.* the perfect virtues, "forget them;

in quartis, scilicet exemplaribus, *nefas est nominari.* Quamvis dici possit quod loquitur hic de passionibus secundum quod significant aliquos inordinatos motus.

AD TERTIUM dicendum quod deserere res humanas ubi necessitas imponitur, vitiosum est, alias est virtuosum. Unde parum supra Tullius praemittit, *his forsitan concedendum est rempublicam non capessentibus, qui excellenti ingenio doctrinae se dederunt; et his qui aut valetudinis imbecillitate, aut aliqua graviori causa impediti, a republica recesserunt; cum eius administrandae potestatem aliis laudemque concederent.* Quod consonat ei quod Augustinus dicit, XIX de Civ. Dei, *otium sanctum quaerit caritas veritatis; negotium iustum suscipit necessitas caritatis. Quam sarcinam si nullus imponit, percipiendae atque intuendae vacandum est veritati, si autem imponitur, suscipienda est, propter caritatis necessitatem.*

AD QUARTUM dicendum quod sola iustitia legalis directe respicit bonum commune, sed per imperium omnes alias virtutes ad bonum commune trahit, ut in V Ethic. dicit philosophus. Est enim considerandum quod ad politicas virtutes, secundum quod hic dicuntur, pertinet non solum bene operari ad commune, sed etiam bene operari ad partes communis, scilicet ad domum, vel aliquam singularem personam.

while it is impious to mention them in connection with virtues of the fourth kind," *viz.* the exemplar virtues. It may also be said that here he is speaking of passions as denoting inordinate emotions.

Reply to Objection 3: To neglect human affairs when necessity forbids is wicked; otherwise it is virtuous. Hence Cicero says a little earlier: "Perhaps one should make allowances for those who by reason of their exceptional talents have devoted themselves to learning; as also to those who have retired from public life on account of failing health, or for some other yet weightier motive; when such men yielded to others the power and renown of authority." This agrees with what Augustine says (De Civ. Dei xix, 19): "The love of truth demands a hollowed leisure; charity necessitates good works. If no one lays this burden on us we may devote ourselves to the study and contemplation of truth; but if the burden is laid on us it is to be taken up under the pressure of charity."

Reply to Objection 4: Legal justice alone regards the common weal directly: but by commanding the other virtues it draws them all into the service of the common weal, as the Philosopher declares (Ethic. v, 1). For we must take note that it concerns the human virtues, as we understand them here, to do well not only towards the community, but also towards the parts of the community, *viz.* towards the household, or even towards one individual.

Quaestio LXII

Deinde considerandum est de virtutibus theologicis. Et circa hoc quaeruntur quatuor. *Primo,* utrum sint aliquae virtutes theologicae. *Secundo,* utrum virtutes theologicae distinguantur ab intellectualibus et moralibus. *Tertio,* quot, et quae sint. *Quarto,* de ordine earum.

Articulus 1

AD PRIMUM sic proceditur. Videtur quod non sint aliquae virtutes theologicae. Ut enim dicitur in VII Physic., *virtus est dispositio perfecti ad optimum, dico autem perfectum, quod est dispositum secundum naturam.* Sed id quod est divinum, est supra naturam hominis. Ergo virtutes theologicae non sunt virtutes hominis.

PRAETEREA, virtutes theologicae dicuntur quasi virtutes divinae. Sed virtutes divinae sunt exemplares, ut dictum est, quae quidem non sunt in nobis, sed in Deo. Ergo virtutes theologicae non sunt virtutes hominis.

PRAETEREA, virtutes theologicae dicuntur quibus ordinamur in Deum, qui est primum principium et ultimus finis rerum. Sed homo ex ipsa natura rationis et voluntatis, habet ordinem ad primum principium et ultimum finem. Non ergo requiruntur aliqui habitus virtutum theologicarum, quibus ratio et voluntas ordinetur in Deum.

SED CONTRA est quod praecepta legis sunt de actibus virtutum. Sed de actibus fidei, spei et caritatis dantur praecepta in lege divina, dicitur enim Eccli. II, *qui timetis Deum, credite illi;* item, *sperate in illum;* item, *diligite illum.* Ergo fides, spes et caritas sunt virtutes in Deum ordinantes. Sunt ergo theologicae.

RESPONDEO dicendum quod per virtutem perficitur homo ad actus quibus in beatitudinem ordinatur, ut ex supradictis patet. Est autem duplex hominis beatitudo sive felicitas, ut supra dictum est. Una quidem proportionata humanae naturae, ad quam scilicet homo pervenire potest per principia suae naturae. Alia autem est beatitudo

Question 62
Of the Theological Virtues

We must now consider the Theological Virtues: under which head there are four points of inquiry: 1. Whether there are any theological virtues? 2. Whether the theological virtues are distinct from the intellectual and moral virtues? 3. How many, and which are they? 4. Of their order.

Article 1
Whether there are any theological virtues?

Objection 1: It would seem that there are not any theological virtues. For according to Phys. vii, text. 17, "virtue is the disposition of a perfect thing to that which is best: and by perfect, I mean that which is disposed according to nature." But that which is Divine is above man's nature. Therefore the theological virtues are not virtues of a man.

Objection 2: Further, theological virtues are quasi-Divine virtues. But the Divine virtues are exemplars, as stated above (I-II, q. 61, a. 5), which are not in us but in God. Therefore the theological virtues are not virtues of man.

Objection 3: Further, the theological virtues are so called because they direct us to God, Who is the first beginning and last end of all things. But by the very nature of his reason and will, man is directed to his first beginning and last end. Therefore there is no need for any habits of theological virtue, to direct the reason and will to God.

On the contrary, The precepts of the Law are about acts of virtue. Now the Divine Law contains precepts about the acts of faith, hope, and charity: for it is written (Ecclus. 2:8, seqq.): "Ye that fear the Lord believe Him," and again, "hope in Him," and again, "love Him." Therefore faith, hope, and charity are virtues directing us to God. Therefore they are theological virtues.

I answer that, Man is perfected by virtue, for those actions whereby he is directed to happiness, as was explained above (I-II, q. 5, a. 7). Now man's happiness is twofold, as was also stated above (I-II, q. 5, a. 5). One is proportionate to human nature, a happiness, to wit, which man can obtain by means of his natural principles. The other is a happiness

naturam hominis excedens, ad quam homo sola divina virtute pervenire potest, secundum quandam divinitatis participationem; secundum quod dicitur II Petr. I, quod per Christum facti sumus *consortes divinae naturae.* Et quia huiusmodi beatitudo proportionem humanae naturae excedit, principia naturalia hominis, ex quibus procedit ad bene agendum secundum suam proportionem, non sufficiunt ad ordinandum hominem in beatitudinem praedictam. Unde oportet quod superaddantur homini divinitus aliqua principia, per quae ita ordinetur ad beatitudinem supernaturalem, sicut per principia naturalia ordinatur ad finem connaturalem, non tamen absque adiutorio divino. Et huiusmodi principia virtutes dicuntur *theologicae,* tum quia habent Deum pro obiecto, inquantum per eas recte ordinamur in Deum; tum quia a solo Deo nobis infunduntur; tum quia sola divina revelatione, in sacra Scriptura, huiusmodi virtutes traduntur.

AD PRIMUM ergo dicendum quod aliqua natura potest attribui alicui rei dupliciter. Uno modo, essentialiter, et sic huiusmodi virtutes theologicae excedunt hominis naturam. Alio modo, participative, sicut lignum ignitum participat naturam ignis, et sic quodammodo fit homo particeps divinae naturae, ut dictum est. Et sic istae virtutes conveniunt homini secundum naturam participatam.

AD SECUNDUM dicendum quod istae virtutes non dicuntur divinae, sicut quibus Deus sit virtuosus, sed sicut quibus nos efficimur virtuosi a Deo, et in ordine ad Deum. Unde non sunt exemplares, sed exemplatae.

AD TERTIUM dicendum quod ad Deum naturaliter ratio et voluntas ordinatur prout est naturae principium et finis, secundum tamen proportionem naturae. Sed ad ipsum secundum quod est obiectum beatitudinis supernaturalis, ratio et voluntas secundum suam naturam non ordinantur sufficienter.

surpassing man's nature, and which man can obtain by the power of God alone, by a kind of participation of the Godhead, about which it is written (2 Pet. 1:4) that by Christ we are made "partakers of the Divine nature." And because such happiness surpasses the capacity of human nature, man's natural principles which enable him to act well according to his capacity, do not suffice to direct man to this same happiness. Hence it is necessary for man to receive from God some additional principles, whereby he may be directed to supernatural happiness, even as he is directed to his connatural end, by means of his natural principles, albeit not without Divine assistance. Such like principles are called "theological virtues": first, because their object is God, inasmuch as they direct us aright to God: secondly, because they are infused in us by God alone: thirdly, because these virtues are not made known to us, save by Divine revelation, contained in Holy Writ.

Reply to Objection 1: A certain nature may be ascribed to a certain thing in two ways. First, essentially: and thus these theological virtues surpass the nature of man. Secondly, by participation, as kindled wood partakes of the nature of fire: and thus, after a fashion, man becomes a partaker of the Divine Nature, as stated above: so that these virtues are proportionate to man in respect of the Nature of which he is made a partaker.

Reply to Objection 2: These virtues are called Divine, not as though God were virtuous by reason of them, but because of them God makes us virtuous, and directs us to Himself. Hence they are not exemplar but exemplate virtues.

Reply to Objection 3: The reason and will are naturally directed to God, inasmuch as He is the beginning and end of nature, but in proportion to nature. But the reason and will, according to their nature, are not sufficiently directed to Him in so far as He is the object of supernatural happiness.

Articulus 2

Ad secundum sic proceditur. Videtur quod virtutes theologicae non distinguantur a moralibus et intellectualibus. Virtutes enim theologicae, si sunt in anima humana, oportet quod perficiant ipsam vel secundum partem intellectivam vel secundum partem appetitivam. Sed virtutes quae perficiunt partem intellectivam, dicuntur intellectuales, virtutes autem quae perficiunt partem appetitivam, sunt morales. Ergo virtutes theologicae non distinguuntur a virtutibus moralibus et intellectualibus.

Praeterea, virtutes theologicae dicuntur quae ordinant nos ad Deum. Sed inter intellectuales virtutes est aliqua quae ordinat nos ad Deum, scilicet sapientia, quae est de divinis, utpote causam altissimam considerans. Ergo virtutes theologicae ab intellectualibus virtutibus non distinguuntur.

Praeterea, Augustinus, in libro de moribus Eccles., manifestat in quatuor virtutibus cardinalibus quod sunt *ordo amoris*. Sed amor est caritas, quae ponitur virtus theologica. Ergo virtutes morales non distinguuntur a theologicis.

Sed contra, id quod est supra naturam hominis, distinguitur ab eo quod est secundum naturam hominis. Sed virtutes theologicae sunt super naturam hominis, cui secundum naturam conveniunt virtutes intellectuales et morales, ut ex supradictis patet. Ergo distinguuntur ab invicem.

Respondeo dicendum quod, sicut supra dictum est, habitus specie distinguuntur secundum formalem differentiam obiectorum. Obiectum autem theologicarum virtutum est ipse Deus, qui est ultimus rerum finis, prout nostrae rationis cognitionem excedit. Obiectum autem virtutum intellectualium et moralium est aliquid quod humana ratione comprehendi potest. Unde virtutes theologicae specie distinguuntur a moralibus et intellectualibus.

Article 2
Whether the theological virtues are distinct from the intellectual and moral virtues?

Objection 1: It would seem that the theological virtues are not distinct from the moral and intellectual virtues. For the theological virtues, if they be in a human soul, must needs perfect it, either as to the intellective, or as to the appetitive part. Now the virtues which perfect the intellective part are called intellectual; and the virtues which perfect the appetitive part, are called moral. Therefore, the theological virtues are not distinct from the moral and intellectual virtues.

Objection 2: Further, the theological virtues are those which direct us to God. Now, among the intellectual virtues there is one which directs us to God: this is wisdom, which is about Divine things, since it considers the highest cause. Therefore the theological virtues are not distinct from the intellectual virtues.

Objection 3: Further, Augustine (De Moribus Eccl. xv) shows how the four cardinal virtues are the "order of love." Now love is charity, which is a theological virtue. Therefore the moral virtues are not distinct from the theological.

On the contrary, That which is above man's nature is distinct from that which is according to his nature. But the theological virtues are above man's nature; while the intellectual and moral virtues are in proportion to his nature, as clearly shown above (I-II, q. 58, a. 3). Therefore they are distinct from one another.

I answer that, As stated above (I-II, q. 54, a. 2, ad 1), habits are specifically distinct from one another in respect of the formal difference of their objects. Now the object of the theological virtues is God Himself, Who is the last end of all, as surpassing the knowledge of our reason. On the other hand, the object of the intellectual and moral virtues is something comprehensible to human reason. Wherefore the theological virtues are specifically distinct from the moral and intellectual virtues.

Ad primum ergo dicendum quod virtutes intellectuales et morales perficiunt intellectum et appetitum hominis secundum proportionem naturae humanae, sed theologicae supernaturaliter.

Ad secundum dicendum quod sapientia quae a philosopho ponitur intellectualis virtus, considerat divina secundum quod sunt investigabilia ratione humana. Sed theologica virtus est circa ea secundum quod rationem humanam excedunt.

Ad tertium dicendum quod, licet caritas sit amor, non tamen omnis amor est caritas. Cum ergo dicitur quod omnis virtus est ordo amoris, potest intelligi vel de amore communiter dicto; vel de amore caritatis. Si de amore communiter dicto, sic dicitur quaelibet virtus esse ordo amoris, inquantum ad quamlibet cardinalium virtutum requiritur ordinata affectio, omnis autem affectionis radix et principium est amor, ut supra dictum est. Si autem intelligatur de amore caritatis, non datur per hoc intelligi quod quaelibet alia virtus essentialiter sit caritas, sed quod omnes aliae virtutes aliqualiter a caritate dependeant, ut infra patebit.

Reply to Objection 1: The intellectual and moral virtues perfect man's intellect and appetite according to the capacity of human nature; the theological virtues, supernatually.

Reply to Objection 2: The wisdom which the Philosopher (Ethic. vi, 3, 7) reckons as an intellectual virtue, considers Divine things so far as they are open to the research of human reason. Theological virtue, on the other hand, is about those same things so far as they surpass human reason.

Reply to Objection 3: Though charity is love, yet love is not always charity. When, then, it is stated that every virtue is the order of love, this can be understood either of love in the general sense, or of the love of charity. If it be understood of love, commonly so called, then each virtue is stated to be the order of love, in so far as each cardinal virtue requires ordinate emotions; and love is the root and cause of every emotion, as stated above (I-II, q. 27, a. 4; q. 28, a. 6, ad 2; q. 41, a. 2, ad 1). If, however, it be understood of the love of charity, it does not mean that every other virtue is charity essentially: but that all other virtues depend on charity in some way, as we shall show further on (I-II, q. 65, a. 2; a. 5; II-II, q. 23, a. 7).

Articulus 3

Ad tertium sic proceditur. Videtur quod inconvenienter ponantur tres virtutes theologicae, fides, spes et caritas. Virtutes enim theologicae se habent in ordine ad beatitudinem divinam, sicut inclinatio naturae ad finem connaturalem. Sed inter virtutes ordinatas ad finem connaturalem, ponitur una sola virtus naturalis, scilicet intellectus principiorum. Ergo debet poni una sola virtus theologica.

Praeterea, theologicae virtutes sunt perfectiores virtutibus intellectualibus et moralibus. Sed inter intellectuales virtutes fides non ponitur, sed est aliquid minus virtute, cum sit cognitio imperfecta. Similiter etiam inter virtutes morales non ponitur spes, sed est aliquid

Article 3
Whether faith, hope, and charity are fittingly reckoned as theological virtues?

Objection 1: It would seem that faith, hope, and charity are not fittingly reckoned as three theological virtues. For the theological virtues are in relation to Divine happiness, what the natural inclination is in relation to the connatural end. Now among the virtues directed to the connatural end there is but one natural virtue, *viz.* the understanding of principles. Therefore there should be but one theological virtue.

Objection 2: Further, the theological virtues are more perfect than the intellectual and moral virtues. Now faith is not reckoned among the intellectual virtues, but is something less than a virtue, since it is imperfect knowledge. Likewise hope is not reckoned among the moral virtues, but is something

minus virtute, cum sit passio. Ergo multo minus debent poni virtutes theologicae.

PRAETEREA, virtutes theologicae ordinant animam hominis ad Deum. Sed ad Deum non potest anima hominis ordinari nisi per intellectivam partem, in qua est intellectus et voluntas. Ergo non debent esse nisi duae virtutes theologicae, una quae perficiat intellectum, alia quae perficiat voluntatem.

SED CONTRA est quod apostolus dicit, I ad Cor. XIII, *nunc autem manent fides, spes, caritas, tria haec.*

RESPONDEO dicendum quod, sicut supra dictum est, virtutes theologicae hoc modo ordinant hominem ad beatitudinem supernaturalem, sicut per naturalem inclinationem ordinatur homo in finem sibi connaturalem. Hoc autem contingit secundum duo. Primo quidem, secundum rationem vel intellectum, inquantum continet prima principia universalia cognita nobis per naturale lumen intellectus, ex quibus procedit ratio tam in speculandis quam in agendis. Secundo, per rectitudinem voluntatis naturaliter tendentis in bonum rationis. Sed haec duo deficiunt ab ordine beatitudinis supernaturalis; secundum illud I ad Cor. II, *oculus non vidit, et auris non audivit, et in cor hominis non ascendit, quae praeparavit Deus diligentibus se.* Unde oportuit quod quantum ad utrumque, aliquid homini supernaturaliter adderetur, ad ordinandum ipsum in finem supernaturalem. Et primo quidem, quantum ad intellectum, adduntur homini quaedam principia supernaturalia, quae divino lumine capiuntur, et haec sunt credibilia, de quibus est fides. Secundo vero, voluntas ordinatur in illum finem et quantum ad motum intentionis, in ipsum tendentem sicut in id quod est possibile consequi, quod pertinet ad spem, et quantum ad unionem quandam spiritualem, per quam quodammodo transformatur in illum finem, quod fit per caritatem. Appetitus enim uniuscuiusque rei naturaliter movetur et tendit in finem sibi connaturalem, et iste motus provenit ex quadam conformitate rei ad suum finem.

AD PRIMUM ergo dicendum quod intellectus indiget speciebus intelligibilibus, per quas intelligat, et ideo oportet quod in eo

less than a virtue, since it is a passion. Much less therefore should they be reckoned as theological virtues.

Objection 3: Further, the theological virtues direct man's soul to God. Now man's soul cannot be directed to God, save through the intellective part, wherein are the intellect and will. Therefore there should be only two theological virtues, one perfecting the intellect, the other, the will.

On the contrary, The Apostle says (1 Cor. 13:13): "Now there remain faith, hope, charity, these three."

I answer that, As stated above (I-II, q. 62, a. 1), the theological virtues direct man to supernatural happiness in the same way as by the natural inclination man is directed to his connatural end. Now the latter happens in respect of two things. First, in respect of the reason or intellect, in so far as it contains the first universal principles which are known to us by the natural light of the intellect, and which are reason's starting-point, both in speculative and in practical matters. Secondly, through the rectitude of the will which tends naturally to good as defined by reason. But these two fall short of the order of supernatural happiness, according to 1 Cor. 2:9: "The eye hath not seen, nor ear heard, neither hath it entered into the heart of man, what things God hath prepared for them that love Him." Consequently in respect of both the above things man needed to receive in addition something supernatural to direct him to a supernatural end. First, as regards the intellect, man receives certain supernatural principles, which are held by means of a Divine light: these are the articles of faith, about which is faith. Secondly, the will is directed to this end, both as to that end as something attainable—and this pertains to hope—and as to a certain spiritual union, whereby the will is, so to speak, transformed into that end— and this belongs to charity. For the appetite of a thing is moved and tends towards its connatural end naturally; and this movement is due to a certain conformity of the thing with its end.

Reply to Objection 1: The intellect requires intelligible species whereby to understand: consequently there is

ponatur aliquis habitus naturalis superadditus potentiae. Sed ipsa natura voluntatis sufficit ad naturalem ordinem in finem, sive quantum ad intentionem finis, sive quantum ad conformitatem ad ipsum. Sed in ordine ad ea quae supra naturam sunt, ad nihil horum sufficit natura potentiae. Et ideo oportet fieri superadditionem habitus supernaturalis quantum ad utrumque.

AD SECUNDUM dicendum quod fides et spes imperfectionem quandam important, quia fides est de his quae non videntur, et spes de his quae non habentur. Unde habere fidem et spem de his quae subduntur humanae potestati, deficit a ratione virtutis. Sed habere fidem et spem de his quae sunt supra facultatem naturae humanae, excedit omnem virtutem homini proportionatam; secundum illud I ad Cor. I, *quod infirmum est Dei, fortius est hominibus.*

AD TERTIUM dicendum quod ad appetitum duo pertinent, scilicet motus in finem; et conformatio ad finem per amorem. Et sic oportet quod in appetitu humano duae virtutes theologicae ponantur, scilicet spes et caritas.

ARTICULUS 4

AD QUARTUM sic proceditur. Videtur quod non sit hic ordo theologicarum virtutum, quod fides sit prior spe, et spes prior caritate. Radix enim est prior eo quod est ex radice. Sed caritas est radix omnium virtutum; secundum illud ad Ephes. III, *in caritate radicati et fundati.* Ergo caritas est prior aliis.

PRAETEREA, Augustinus dicit, in I de Doct. Christ., *non potest aliquis diligere quod esse non crediderit. Porro si credit et diligit, bene agendo efficit ut etiam speret.* Ergo videtur quod fides praecedat caritatem, et caritas spem.

PRAETEREA, amor est principium omnis affectionis, ut supra dictum est. Sed spes nominat quandam affectionem; est enim quaedam passio, ut supra dictum est. Ergo caritas, quae est amor, est prior spe.

need of a natural habit in addition to the power. But the very nature of the will suffices for it to be directed naturally to the end, both as to the intention of the end and as to its conformity with the end. But the nature of the power is insufficient in either of these respects, for the will to be directed to things that are above its nature. Consequently there was need for an additional supernatural habit in both respects.

Reply to Objection 2: Faith and hope imply a certain imperfection: since faith is of things unseen, and hope, of things not possessed. Hence faith and hope, in things that are subject to human power, fall short of the notion of virtue. But faith and hope in things which are above the capacity of human nature surpass all virtue that is in proportion to man, according to 1 Cor. 1:25: "The weakness of God is stronger than men."

Reply to Objection 3: Two things pertain to the appetite, *viz.* movement to the end, and conformity with the end by means of love. Hence there must needs be two theological virtues in the human appetite, namely, hope and charity.

ARTICLE 4
Whether faith precedes hope, and hope charity?

Objection 1: It would seem that the order of the theological virtues is not that faith precedes hope, and hope charity. For the root precedes that which grows from it. Now charity is the root of all the virtues, according to Eph. 3:17: "Being rooted and founded in charity." Therefore charity precedes the others.

Objection 2: Further, Augustine says (De Doctr. Christ. i): "A man cannot love what he does not believe to exist. But if he believes and loves, by doing good works he ends in hoping." Therefore it seems that faith precedes charity, and charity hope.

Objection 3: Further, love is the principle of all our emotions, as stated above (I-II, q. 62, a. 2, ad 3). Now hope is a kind of emotion, since it is a passion, as stated above (I-II, q. 25, a. 2). Therefore charity, which is love, precedes hope.

I-II, q. 62, a. 4, s. c.

Sed contra est ordo quo apostolus ista enumerat, dicens, *nunc autem manent fides, spes, caritas.*

Respondeo dicendum quod duplex est ordo, scilicet generationis, et perfectionis. Ordine quidem generationis, quo materia est prior forma, et imperfectum perfecto, in uno et eodem; fides praecedit spem, et spes caritatem, secundum actus (nam habitus simul infunduntur). Non enim potest in aliquid **motus appetitivus tendere vel sperando vel amando, nisi quod est apprehensum sensu aut intellectu.** Per fidem autem apprehendit intellectus ea quae sperat et amat. Unde oportet quod, ordine generationis, fides praecedat spem et caritatem. Similiter autem ex hoc homo aliquid amat, quod apprehendit illud ut bonum suum. Per hoc autem quod homo ab aliquo sperat se bonum consequi posse, reputat ipsum in quo spem habet, quoddam bonum suum. Unde ex hoc ipso quod homo sperat de aliquo, procedit ad amandum ipsum. Et sic, ordine generationis, secundum actus, spes praecedit caritatem. Ordine vero perfectionis, caritas praecedit fidem et spem, eo quod tam fides quam spes per caritatem formatur, et perfectionem virtutis acquirit. Sic enim caritas est mater omnium virtutum et radix, inquantum est omnium virtutum forma, ut infra dicetur.

Et per hoc patet responsio ad primum.

Ad secundum dicendum quod Augustinus loquitur de spe qua quis sperat ex meritis iam habitis se ad beatitudinem perventurum, quod est spei formatae, quae sequitur caritatem. Potest autem aliquis sperare antequam habeat caritatem, non ex meritis quae iam habet, sed quae sperat se habiturum.

Ad tertium dicendum quod, sicut supra dictum est, cum de passionibus ageretur, spes respicit duo. Unum quidem sicut principale obiectum, scilicet bonum quod speratur. Et respectu huius, semper amor praecedit spem, nunquam enim speratur aliquod bonum nisi desideratum et amatum. Respicit etiam spes illum a quo se sperat posse consequi

THE THEOLOGICAL VIRTUES

On the contrary, The Apostle enumerates them thus (1 Cor. 13:13): "Now there remain faith, hope, charity."

I answer that, Order is twofold: order of generation, and order of perfection. By order of generation, in respect of which matter precedes form, and the imperfect precedes the perfect, in one same subject faith precedes hope, and hope charity, as to their acts: because habits are all infused together. For **the movement of the appetite cannot tend to anything, either by hoping or loving, unless that thing be apprehended by the sense or by the intellect.** Now it is by faith that the intellect apprehends the object of hope and love. Hence in the order of generation, faith precedes hope and charity. In like manner a man loves a thing because he apprehends it as his good. Now from the very fact that a man hopes to be able to obtain some good through someone, he looks on the man in whom he hopes as a good of his own. Hence for the very reason that a man hopes in someone, he proceeds to love him: so that in the order of generation, hope precedes charity as regards their respective acts. But in the order of perfection, charity precedes faith and hope: because both faith and hope are quickened by charity, and receive from charity their full complement as virtues. For thus charity is the mother and the root of all the virtues, inasmuch as it is the form of them all, as we shall state further on (II-II, q. 23, a. 8).

This suffices for the Reply to the First Objection.

Reply to Objection 2: Augustine is speaking of that hope whereby a man hopes to obtain bliss through the merits which he has already: this belongs to hope quickened by and following charity. But it is possible for a man before having charity, to hope through merits not already possessed, but which he hopes to possess.

Reply to Objection 3: As stated above (I-II, q. 40, a. 7), in treating of the passions, hope regards two things. One as its principal object, *viz.* the good hoped for. With regard to this, love always precedes hope: for good is never hoped for unless it be desired and loved. Hope also regards the person from whom a man hopes to be able to obtain some

bonum. Et respectu huius, primo quidem spes praecedit amorem; quamvis postea ex ipso amore spes augeatur. Per hoc enim quod aliquis reputat per aliquem se posse consequi aliquod bonum, incipit amare ipsum, et ex hoc ipso quod ipsum amat, postea fortius de eo sperat.

good. With regard to this, hope precedes love at first; though afterwards hope is increased by love. Because from the fact that a man thinks that he can obtain a good through someone, he begins to love him: and from the fact that he loves him, he then hopes all the more in him.

Quaestio LXIII

Deinde considerandum est de causa virtutum. Et circa hoc quaeruntur quatuor. *Primo,* utrum virtus sit in nobis a natura. *Secundo,* utrum aliqua virtus causetur in nobis ex assuetudine operum. *Tertio,* utrum aliquae virtutes morales sint in nobis per infusionem. *Quarto,* utrum virtus quam acquirimus ex assuetudine operum, sit eiusdem speciei cum virtute infusa.

Question 63
Of the Cause of Virtues

We must now consider the cause of virtues; and under this head there are four points of inquiry: 1. Whether virtue is in us by nature? 2. Whether any virtue is caused in us by habituation? 3. Whether any moral virtues are in us by infusion? 4. Whether virtue acquired by habituation, is of the same species as infused virtue?

Articulus 1

Ad primum sic proceditur. Videtur quod virtus sit in nobis a natura. Dicit enim Damascenus, in III libro, *naturales sunt virtutes, et aequaliter insunt omnibus.* Et Antonius dicit, in sermone ad monachos, *si naturam voluntas mutaverit, perversitas est; conditio servetur, et virtus est.* Et Matth. IV, super illud, *circuibat Iesus* etc., dicit Glossa, *docet naturales iustitias, scilicet castitatem, iustitiam, humilitatem, quas naturaliter habet homo.*

Praeterea, bonum virtutis est secundum rationem esse, ut ex dictis patet. Sed id quod est secundum rationem, est homini naturale, cum ratio sit hominis natura. Ergo virtus inest homini a natura.

Praeterea, illud dicitur esse nobis naturale, quod nobis a nativitate inest. Sed virtutes quibusdam a nativitate insunt, dicitur enim Iob XXXI, *ab infantia crevit mecum miseratio, et de utero egressa est mecum.* Ergo virtus inest homini a natura.

Article 1
Whether virtue is in us by nature?

Objection 1: It would seem that virtue is in us by nature. For Damascene says (De Fide Orth. iii, 14): "Virtues are natural to us and are equally in all of us." And Antony says in his sermon to the monks: "If the will contradicts nature it is perverse, if it follow nature it is virtuous." Moreover, a gloss on Mat. 4:23, "Jesus went about," etc., says: "He taught them natural virtues, i.e., chastity, justice, humility, which man possesses naturally."

Objection 2: Further, the virtuous good consists in accord with reason, as was clearly shown above (I-II, q. 55, a. 4, ad 2). But that which accords with reason is natural to man; since reason is part of man's nature. Therefore virtue is in man by nature.

Objection 3: Further, that which is in us from birth is said to be natural to us. Now virtues are in some from birth: for it is written (Job 31:18): "From my infancy mercy grew up with me; and it came out with me from my mother's womb." Therefore virtue is in man by nature.

I-II, q. 63, a. 1, s. c.

Sed contra, id quod inest homini a natura, est omnibus hominibus commune, et non tollitur per peccatum, quia etiam in Daemonibus bona naturalia manent, ut Dionysius dicit, in IV cap. de Div. Nom. Sed virtus non inest omnibus hominibus; et abiicitur per peccatum. Ergo non inest homini a natura.

Respondeo dicendum quod circa formas corporales, aliqui dixerunt quod sunt totaliter ab intrinseco, sicut ponentes *latitationem formarum*. Aliqui vero, quod totaliter sint ab extrinseco, sicut ponentes formas corporales esse ab aliqua causa separata. Aliqui vero, quod partim sint ab intrinseco, inquantum scilicet praeexistunt in materia in potentia; et partim ab extrinseco, inquantum scilicet reducuntur ad actum per agens. Ita etiam circa scientias et virtutes, aliqui quidem posuerunt eas totaliter esse ab intrinseco, ita scilicet quod omnes virtutes et scientiae naturaliter praeexistunt in anima; sed per disciplinam et exercitium impedimenta scientiae et virtutis tolluntur, quae adveniunt animae ex corporis gravitate; sicut cum ferrum clarificatur per limationem. Et haec fuit opinio Platonicorum. Alii vero dixerunt quod sunt totaliter ab extrinseco, idest ex influentia intelligentiae agentis, ut ponit Avicenna. Alii vero dixerunt quod secundum aptitudinem scientiae et virtutes sunt in nobis a natura, non autem secundum perfectionem, ut philosophus dicit, in II Ethic. Et hoc verius est. Ad cuius manifestationem, oportet considerare quod aliquid dicitur alicui homini naturale dupliciter, uno modo, ex natura speciei; alio modo, ex natura individui. Et quia unumquodque habet speciem secundum suam formam, individuatur vero secundum materiam; forma vero hominis est anima rationalis, materia vero corpus, id quod convenit homini secundum animam rationalem, est ei naturale secundum rationem speciei; id vero quod est ei naturale secundum determinatam corporis complexionem, est ei naturale secundum

THE CAUSE OF VIRTUES

On the contrary, Whatever is in man by nature is common to all men, and is not taken away by sin, since even in the demons natural gifts remain, as Dionysius states (Div. Nom. iv). But virtue is not in all men; and is cast out by sin. Therefore it is not in man by nature.

I answer that, With regard to corporeal forms, it has been maintained by some that they are wholly from within, by those, for instance, who upheld the theory of "latent forms."* Others held that forms are entirely from without, those, for instance, who thought that corporeal forms originated from some separate cause. Others, however, esteemed that they are partly from within, in so far as they pre-exist potentially in matter; and partly from without, in so far as they are brought into act by the agent. In like manner with regard to sciences and virtues, some held that they are wholly from within, so that all virtues and sciences would pre-exist in the soul naturally, but that the hindrances to science and virtue, which are due to the soul being weighed down by the body, are removed by study and practice, even as iron is made bright by being polished. This was the opinion of the Platonists. Others said that they are wholly from without, being due to the inflow of the active intellect, as Avicenna maintained. Others said that sciences and virtues are within us by nature, so far as we are adapted to them, but not in their perfection: this is the teaching of the Philosopher (Ethic. ii, 1), and is nearer the truth. To make this clear, it must be observed that there are two ways in which something is said to be natural to a man; one is according to his specific nature, the other according to his individual nature. And, since each thing derives its species from its form, and its individuation from matter, and, again, since man's form is his rational soul, while his matter is his body, whatever belongs to him in respect of his rational soul, is natural to him in respect of his specific nature; while whatever belongs to him in respect of the particular temperament of his body, is natural to him in respect of

---

* Anaxagoras; Cf. I, q. 45, a. 8; q. 65, a. 4.

naturam individui. Quod enim est naturale homini ex parte corporis secundum speciem, quodammodo refertur ad animam, inquantum scilicet tale corpus est tali animae proportionatum. Utroque autem modo virtus est homini naturalis secundum quandam inchoationem. Secundum quidem naturam speciei, inquantum in ratione homini insunt naturaliter quaedam principia naturaliter cognita tam scibilium quam agendorum, quae sunt quaedam seminalia intellectualium virtutum et moralium; et inquantum in voluntate inest quidam naturalis appetitus boni quod est secundum rationem. Secundum vero naturam individui, inquantum ex corporis dispositione aliqui sunt dispositi vel melius vel peius ad quasdam virtutes, prout scilicet vires quaedam sensitivae actus sunt quarundam partium corporis, ex quarum dispositione adiuvantur vel impediuntur huiusmodi vires in suis actibus, et per consequens vires rationales, quibus huiusmodi sensitivae vires deserviunt. Et secundum hoc, unus homo habet naturalem aptitudinem ad scientiam, alius ad fortitudinem, alius ad temperantiam. Et his modis tam virtutes intellectuales quam morales, secundum quandam aptitudinis inchoationem, sunt in nobis a natura. Non autem consummatio earum. Quia natura determinatur ad unum, consummatio autem huiusmodi virtutum non est secundum unum modum actionis, sed diversimode, secundum diversas materias in quibus virtutes operantur, et secundum diversas circumstantias. Sic ergo patet quod virtutes in nobis sunt a natura secundum aptitudinem et inchoationem, non autem secundum perfectionem, praeter virtutes theologicas, quae sunt totaliter ab extrinseco.

Et per hoc patet responsio ad obiecta. Nam primae duae rationes procedunt secundum quod seminalia virtutum insunt nobis a natura, inquantum rationales sumus. Tertia vero ratio procedit secundum quod ex naturali dispositione corporis, quam habet ex nativitate, unus habet aptitudinem ad miserendum, alius ad temperate vivendum, alius ad aliam virtutem.

his individual nature. For whatever is natural to man in respect of his body, considered as part of his species, is to be referred, in a way, to the soul, in so far as this particular body is adapted to this particular soul. In both these ways virtue is natural to man inchoatively. This is so in respect of the specific nature, in so far as in man's reason are to be found instilled by nature certain naturally known principles of both knowledge and action, which are the nurseries of intellectual and moral virtues, and in so far as there is in the will a natural appetite for good in accordance with reason. Again, this is so in respect of the individual nature, in so far as by reason of a disposition in the body, some are disposed either well or ill to certain virtues: because, to wit, certain sensitive powers are acts of certain parts of the body, according to the disposition of which these powers are helped or hindered in the exercise of their acts, and, in consequence, the rational powers also, which the aforesaid sensitive powers assist. In this way one man has a natural aptitude for science, another for fortitude, another for temperance: and in these ways, both intellectual and moral virtues are in us by way of a natural aptitude, inchoatively, but not perfectly, since nature is determined to one, while the perfection of these virtues does not depend on one particular mode of action, but on various modes, in respect of the various matters, which constitute the sphere of virtue's action, and according to various circumstances. It is therefore evident that all virtues are in us by nature, according to aptitude and inchoation, but not according to perfection, except the theological virtues, which are entirely from without.

This suffices for the Replies to the Objections. For the first two argue about the nurseries of virtue which are in us by nature, inasmuch as we are rational beings. The third objection must be taken in the sense that, owing to the natural disposition which the body has from birth, one has an aptitude for pity, another for living temperately, another for some other virtue.

Articulus 2

Ad secundum sic proceditur. Videtur quod virtutes in nobis causari non possint ex assuetudine operum. Quia super illud Rom. XIV, *omne quod non est ex fide, peccatum est,* dicit Glossa Augustini, *omnis infidelium vita peccatum est; et nihil est bonum sine summo bono. Ubi deest cognitio veritatis, falsa est virtus etiam in optimis moribus.* Sed fides non potest acquiri ex operibus, sed causatur in nobis a Deo; secundum illud Ephes. II, *gratia estis salvati per fidem.* Ergo nulla virtus potest in nobis acquiri ex assuetudine operum.

Praeterea, peccatum, cum contrarietur virtuti, non compatitur secum virtutem. Sed homo non potest vitare peccatum nisi per gratiam Dei; secundum illud Sap. VIII, *didici quod non possum esse aliter continens, nisi Deus det.* Ergo nec virtutes aliquae possunt in nobis causari ex assuetudine operum; sed solum dono Dei.

Praeterea, actus qui sunt in virtutem, deficiunt a perfectione virtutis. Sed effectus non potest esse perfectior causa. Ergo virtus non potest causari ex actibus praecedentibus virtutem.

Sed contra est quod Dionysius dicit, IV cap. de Div. Nom., quod bonum est virtuosius quam malum. Sed ex malis actibus causantur habitus vitiorum. Ergo multo magis ex bonis actibus possunt causari habitus virtutum.

Respondeo dicendum quod de generatione habituum ex actibus, supra in generali dictum est. Nunc autem specialiter quantum ad virtutem, considerandum est quod sicut supra dictum est, virtus hominis perficit ipsum ad bonum. Cum autem ratio boni consistat in *modo, specie et ordine,* ut Augustinus dicit in libro de natura boni; sive in *numero, pondere et mensura,* ut dicitur Sap. XI, oportet quod bonum hominis secundum aliquam regulam consideretur. Quae quidem est duplex, ut supra dictum est, scilicet ratio humana, et

Article 2
Whether any virtue is caused in us by habituation?

Objection 1: It would seem that virtues can not be caused in us by habituation. Because a gloss of Augustine* commenting on Rom. 14:23, "All that is not of faith is sin," says: "The whole life of an unbeliever is a sin: and there is no good without the Sovereign Good. Where knowledge of the truth is lacking, virtue is a mockery even in the best behaved people." Now faith cannot be acquired by means of works, but is caused in us by God, according to Eph. 2:8: "By grace you are saved through faith." Therefore no acquired virtue can be in us by habituation.

Objection 2: Further, sin and virtue are contraries, so that they are incompatible. Now man cannot avoid sin except by the grace of God, according to Wis. 8:21: "I knew that I could not otherwise be continent, except God gave it." Therefore neither can any virtues be caused in us by habituation, but only by the gift of God.

Objection 3: Further, actions which lead toward virtue, lack the perfection of virtue. But an effect cannot be more perfect than its cause. Therefore a virtue cannot be caused by actions that precede it.

On the contrary, Dionysius says (Div. Nom. iv) that good is more efficacious than evil. But vicious habits are caused by evil acts. Much more, therefore, can virtuous habits be caused by good acts.

I answer that, We have spoken above (I-II, q. 51, a. 2; a. 3) in a general way about the production of habits from acts; and speaking now in a special way of this matter in relation to virtue, we must take note that, as stated above (I-II, q. 55, a. 3; a. 4), man's virtue perfects him in relation to good. Now since the notion of good consists in "mode, species, and order," as Augustine states (De Nat. Boni. iii) or in "number, weight, and measure," as expressed in Wis. 11:21, man's good must needs be appraised with respect to some rule. Now this rule is twofold, as stated above (I-II, q. 19, a. 3; a. 4), *viz.* human reason and

---

* Cf. Lib. Sentent. Prosperi cvi.

lex divina. Et quia lex divina est superior regula, ideo ad plura se extendit, ita quod quidquid regulatur ratione humana, regulatur etiam lege divina, sed non convertitur. Virtus igitur hominis ordinata ad bonum quod modificatur secundum regulam rationis humanae, potest ex actibus humanis causari, inquantum huiusmodi actus procedunt a ratione, sub cuius potestate et regula tale bonum consistit. Virtus vero ordinans hominem ad bonum secundum quod modificatur per legem divinam, et non per rationem humanam, non potest causari per actus humanos, quorum principium est ratio, sed causatur solum in nobis per operationem divinam. Et ideo, huiusmodi virtutem definiens, Augustinus posuit in definitione virtutis, *quam Deus in nobis sine nobis operatur.*

Et de huiusmodi etiam virtutibus prima ratio procedit.

AD SECUNDUM dicendum quod virtus divinitus infusa, maxime si in sua perfectione consideretur, non compatitur secum aliquod peccatum mortale. Sed virtus humanitus acquisita potest secum compati aliquem actum peccati, etiam mortalis, quia usus habitus in nobis est nostrae voluntati subiectus, ut supra dictum est; non autem per unum actum peccati corrumpitur habitus virtutis acquisitae; habitui enim non contrariatur directe actus, sed habitus. Et ideo, licet sine gratia homo non possit peccatum mortale vitare, ita quod nunquam peccet mortaliter; non tamen impeditur quin possit habitum virtutis acquirere, per quam a malis operibus abstineat ut in pluribus, et praecipue ab his quae sunt valde rationi contraria. Sunt etiam quaedam peccata mortalia quae homo sine gratia nullo modo potest vitare, quae scilicet directe opponuntur virtutibus theologicis, quae ex dono gratiae sunt in nobis. Hoc tamen infra manifestius fiet.

AD TERTIUM dicendum quod, sicut dictum est, virtutum acquisitarum praeexistunt in nobis quaedam semina sive principia, secundum naturam. Quae quidem prin-cipia sunt nobiliora virtutibus eorum virtute acquisitis, sicut intellectus principiorum speculabilium est nobilior scientia conclusionum; et naturalis rectitudo rationis

Divine Law. And since Divine Law is the higher rule, it extends to more things, so that whatever is ruled by human reason, is ruled by the Divine Law too; but the converse does not hold. It follows that human virtue directed to the good which is defined according to the rule of human reason can be caused by human acts: inasmuch as such acts proceed from reason, by whose power and rule the aforesaid good is established. On the other hand, virtue which directs man to good as defined by the Divine Law, and not by human reason, cannot be caused by human acts, the principle of which is reason, but is produced in us by the Divine operation alone. Hence Augustine in giving the definition of the latter virtue inserts the words, "which God works in us without us" (Super Ps. 118, Serm. xxvi).

It is also of these virtues that the First Objection holds good.

Reply to Objection 2: Mortal sin is incompatible with divinely infused virtue, especially if this be considered in its perfect state. But actual sin, even mortal, is compatible with humanly acquired virtue; because the use of a habit in us is subject to our will, as stated above (I-II, q. 49, a. 3): and one sinful act does not destroy a habit of acquired virtue, since it is not an act but a habit, that is directly contrary to a habit. Wherefore, though man cannot avoid mortal sin without grace, so as never to sin mortally, yet he is not hindered from acquiring a habit of virtue, whereby he may abstain from evil in the majority of cases, and chiefly in matters most opposed to reason. There are also certain mortal sins which man can nowise avoid without grace, those, namely, which are directly opposed to the theological virtues, which are in us through the gift of grace. This, however, will be more fully explained later (I-II, q. 109, a. 4).

Reply to Objection 3: As stated above (I-II, q. 63, a. 1; q. 51, a. 1), certain seeds or principles of acquired virtue pre-exist in us by nature. These principles are more excellent than the virtues acquired through them: thus the understanding of speculative principles is more excellent than the science of conclusions, and the natural rectitude of the reason

est nobilior rectificatione appetitus quae fit per participationem rationis, quae quidem rectificatio pertinet ad virtutem moralem. Sic igitur actus humani, inquantum procedunt ex altioribus principiis, possunt causare virtutes acquisitas humanas.

Articulus 3

Ad tertium sic proceditur. Videtur quod praeter virtutes theologicas, non sint aliae virtutes nobis infusae a Deo. Ea enim quae possunt fieri a causis secundis, non fiunt immediate a Deo, nisi forte aliquando miraculose, quia, ut Dionysius dicit, *lex divinitatis est ultima per media adducere*. Sed virtutes intellectuales et morales possunt in nobis causari per nostros actus, ut dictum est. Non ergo convenienter causantur in nobis per infusionem.

Praeterea, in operibus Dei multo minus est aliquid superfluum quam in operibus naturae. Sed ad ordinandum nos in bonum supernaturale, sufficiunt virtutes theologicae. Ergo non sunt aliae virtutes supernaturales, quas oporteat in nobis causari a Deo.

Praeterea, natura non facit per duo, quod potest facere per unum, et multo minus Deus. Sed Deus inseruit animae nostrae semina virtutum, ut dicit Glossa Heb. I. Ergo non oportet quod aliae virtutes in nobis per infusionem causet.

Sed contra est quod dicitur Sap. VIII, *sobrietatem et iustitiam docet, prudentiam et virtutem*.

Respondeo dicendum quod oportet effectus esse suis causis et principiis proportionatos. Omnes autem virtutes tam intellectuales quam morales, quae ex nostris actibus acquiruntur, procedunt ex quibusdam naturalibus principiis in nobis praeexistentibus, ut supra dictum est. Loco quorum naturalium principiorum, conferuntur nobis a Deo virtutes theologicae, quibus ordinamur ad finem supernaturalem, sicut supra dictum est. Unde oportet quod

is more excellent than the rectification of the appetite which results through the appetite partaking of reason, which rectification belongs to moral virtue. Accordingly human acts, in so far as they proceed from higher principles, can cause acquired human virtues.

Article 3
Whether any moral virtues are in us by infusion?

Objection 1: It would seem that no virtues besides the theological virtues are infused in us by God. Because God does not do by Himself, save perhaps sometimes miraculously, those things that can be done by second causes; for, as Dionysius says (Coel. Hier. iv), "it is God's rule to bring about extremes through the mean." Now intellectual and moral virtues can be caused in us by our acts, as stated above (I-II, q. 63, a. 2). Therefore it is not reasonable that they should be caused in us by infusion.

Objection 2: Further, much less superfluity is found in God's works than in the works of nature. Now the theological virtues suffice to direct us to supernatural good. Therefore there are no other supernatural virtues needing to be caused in us by God.

Objection 3: Further, nature does not employ two means where one suffices: much less does God. But God sowed the seeds of virtue in our souls, according to a gloss on Heb. 1.[*] Therefore it is unfitting for Him to cause in us other virtues by means of infusion.

On the contrary, It is written (Wis. 8:7): "She teacheth temperance and prudence and justice and fortitude."

I answer that, Effects must needs be proportionate to their causes and principles. Now all virtues, intellectual and moral, that are acquired by our actions, arise from certain natural principles pre-existing in us, as above stated (I-II, q. 63, a. 1; q. 51, a. 1): instead of which natural principles, God bestows on us the theological virtues, whereby we are directed to a supernatural end, as stated (I-II, q. 62, a. 1). Wherefore

---

[*] Cf. Jerome on Gal. 1: 15, 16.

his etiam virtutibus theologicis proportionaliter respondeant alii habitus divinitus causati in nobis, qui sic se habeant ad virtutes theologicas sicut se habent virtutes morales et intellectuales ad principia naturalia virtutum.

Ad primum ergo dicendum quod aliquae quidem virtutes morales et intellectuales possunt causari in nobis ex nostris actibus, tamen illae non sunt proportionatae virtutibus theologicis. Et ideo oportet alias, eis proportionatas, immediate a Deo causari.

Ad secundum dicendum quod virtutes theologicae sufficienter nos ordinant in finem supernaturalem, secundum quandam inchoationem, quantum scilicet ad ipsum Deum immediate. Sed oportet quod per alias virtutes infusas perficiatur anima circa alias res, in ordine tamen ad Deum.

Ad tertium dicendum quod virtus illorum principiorum naturaliter inditorum, non se extendit ultra proportionem naturae. Et ideo in ordine ad finem supernaturalem, indiget homo perfici per alia principia superaddita.

we need to receive from God other habits corresponding, in due proportion, to the theological virtues, which habits are to the theological virtues, what the moral and intellectual virtues are to the natural principles of virtue.

Reply to Objection 1: Some moral and intellectual virtues can indeed be caused in us by our actions: but such are not proportionate to the theological virtues. Therefore it was necessary for us to receive, from God immediately, others that are proportionate to these virtues.

Reply to Objection 2: The theological virtues direct us sufficiently to our supernatural end, inchoatively: i.e., to God Himself immediately. But the soul needs further to be perfected by infused virtues in regard to other things, yet in relation to God.

Reply to Objection 3: The power of those naturally instilled principles does not extend beyond the capacity of nature. Consequently man needs in addition to be perfected by other principles in relation to his supernatural end.

Articulus 4

Ad quartum sic proceditur. Videtur quod virtutes infusae non sint alterius speciei a virtutibus acquisitis. Virtus enim acquisita et virtus infusa, secundum praedicta, non videntur differre nisi secundum ordinem ad ultimum finem. Sed habitus et actus humani non recipiunt speciem ab ultimo fine, sed a proximo. Non ergo virtutes morales vel intellectuales infusae differunt specie ab acquisitis.

Praeterea, habitus per actus cognoscuntur. Sed idem est actus temperantiae infusae, et acquisitae, scilicet moderari concupiscentias tactus. Ergo non differunt specie.

Praeterea, virtus acquisita et infusa differunt secundum illud quod est immediate a Deo factum, et a creatura. Sed idem est specie homo quem Deus formavit, et quem generat

Article 4

Whether virtue by habituation belongs to the same species as infused virtue?

Objection 1: It would seem that infused virtue does not differ in species from acquired virtue. Because acquired and infused virtues, according to what has been said (I-II, q. 63, a. 3), do not differ seemingly, save in relation to the last end. Now human habits and acts are specified, not by their last, but by their proximate end. Therefore the infused moral or intellectual virtue does not differ from the acquired virtue.

Objection 2: Further, habits are known by their acts. But the act of infused and acquired temperance is the same, *viz.* to moderate desires of touch. Therefore they do not differ in species.

Objection 3: Further, acquired and infused virtue differ as that which is wrought by God immediately, from that which is wrought by a creature. But the man whom God made, is of the same species as a man begotten

I-II, q. 63, a. 4, arg. 3

natura; et oculus quem caeco nato dedit, et quem virtus formativa causat. Ergo videtur quod est eadem specie virtus acquisita, et infusa.

Sed contra, quaelibet differentia in definitione posita, mutata diversificat speciem. Sed in definitione virtutis infusae ponitur, *quam Deus in nobis sine nobis operatur,* ut supra dictum est. Ergo virtus acquisita, cui hoc non convenit, non est eiusdem speciei cum infusa.

Respondeo dicendum quod dupliciter habitus distinguuntur specie. Uno modo, sicut praedictum est, secundum speciales et formales rationes obiectorum. Obiectum autem virtutis cuiuslibet est bonum consideratum in materia propria, sicut temperantiae obiectum est bonum delectabilium in concupiscentiis tactus. Cuius quidem obiecti formalis ratio est a ratione, quae instituit modum in his concupiscentiis, materiale autem est id quod est ex parte concupiscentiarum. Manifestum est autem quod alterius rationis est modus qui imponitur in huiusmodi concupiscentiis secundum regulam rationis humanae, et secundum regulam divinam. Puta in sumptione ciborum, ratione humana modus statuitur ut non noceat valetudini corporis, nec impediat rationis actum, secundum autem regulam legis divinae, requiritur quod homo *castiget corpus suum, et in servitutem redigat,* per abstinentiam cibi et potus, et aliorum huiusmodi. Unde manifestum est quod temperantia infusa et acquisita differunt specie, et eadem ratio est de aliis virtutibus. Alio modo habitus distinguuntur specie secundum ea ad quae ordinantur, non enim est eadem specie sanitas hominis et equi, propter diversas naturas ad quas ordinantur. Et eodem modo dicit philosophus, in III Polit., quod diversae sunt virtutes civium, secundum quod bene se habent ad diversas politias. Et per hunc etiam modum differunt specie virtutes morales infusae, per quas homines

naturally; and the eye which He gave to the man born blind, as one produced by the power of generation. Therefore it seems that acquired and infused virtue belong to the same species.

On the contrary, Any change introduced into the difference expressed in a definition involves a difference of species. But the definition of infused virtue contains the words, "which God works in us without us," as stated above (I-II, q. 55, a. 4). Therefore acquired virtue, to which these words cannot apply, is not of the same species as infused virtue.

I answer that, There is a twofold specific difference among habits. The first, as stated above (I-II, q. 54, a. 2; q. 56, a. 2; q. 60, a. 1), is taken from the specific and formal aspects of their objects. Now the object of every virtue is a good considered as in that virtue's proper matter: thus the object of temperance is a good in respect of the pleasures connected with the concupiscence of touch. The formal aspect of this object is from reason which fixes the mean in these concupiscences: while the material element is something on the part of the concupiscences. Now it is evident that the mean that is appointed in such like concupiscences according to the rule of human reason, is seen under a different aspect from the mean which is fixed according to Divine rule. For instance, in the consumption of food, the mean fixed by human reason, is that food should not harm the health of the body, nor hinder the use of reason: whereas, according to the Divine rule, it behooves man to "chastise his body, and bring it into subjection" (1 Cor. 9:27), by abstinence in food, drink and the like. It is therefore evident that infused and acquired temperance differ in species; and the same applies to the other virtues. The other specific differences among habits is taken from the things to which they are directed: for a man's health and a horse's are not of the same species, on account of the difference between the natures to which their respective healths are directed. In the same sense, the Philosopher says (Polit. iii, 3) that citizens have diverse virtues according as they are well directed to diverse forms of government. In the same way, too, those infused moral virtues, whereby men

bene se habent in ordine ad hoc quod sint *cives sanctorum et domestici Dei*; et aliae virtutes acquisitae, secundum quas homo se bene habet in ordine ad res humanas.

AD PRIMUM ergo dicendum quod virtus infusa et acquisita non solum differunt secundum ordinem ad ultimum finem; sed etiam secundum ordinem ad propria obiecta, ut dictum est.

AD SECUNDUM dicendum quod alia ratione modificat concupiscentias delectabilium tactus temperantia acquisita, et temperantia infusa, ut dictum est. Unde non habent eundem actum.

AD TERTIUM dicendum quod oculum caeci nati Deus fecit ad eundem actum ad quem formantur alii oculi secundum naturam, et ideo fuit eiusdem speciei. Et eadem ratio esset, si Deus vellet miraculose causare in homine virtutes quales acquiruntur ex actibus. Sed ita non est in proposito, ut dictum est.

behave well in respect of their being "fellow-citizens with the saints, and of the household* of God" (Eph. 2:19), differ from the acquired virtues, whereby man behaves well in respect of human affairs.

Reply to Objection 1: Infused and acquired virtue differ not only in relation to the ultimate end, but also in relation to their proper objects, as stated.

Reply to Objection 2: Both acquired and infused temperance moderate desires for pleasures of touch, but for different reasons, as stated: wherefore their respective acts are not identical.

Reply to Objection 3: God gave the man born blind an eye for the same act as the act for which other eyes are formed naturally: consequently it was of the same species. It would be the same if God wished to give a man miraculously virtues, such as those that are acquired by acts. But the case is not so in the question before us, as stated.

---

* Douay: 'domestics'

Question 64
Of the Mean of Virtue

We must now consider the properties of virtues: and 1. the mean of virtue, 2. the connection between virtues, 3. equality of virtues, 4. the duration of virtues. Under the first head there are four points of inquiry: 1. Whether moral virtue observes the mean? 2. Whether the mean of moral virtue is the real mean or the rational mean? 3. Whether the intellectual virtues observe the mean? 4. Whether the theological virtues do?

Article 1
Whether moral virtues observe the mean?

Objection 1: It would seem that moral virtue does not observe the mean. For the nature of a mean is incompatible with that which is extreme. Now the nature of virtue is to be something extreme; for it is stated in De Coelo i that "virtue is the limit of power." Therefore moral virtue does not observe the mean.

Objection 2: Further, the maximum is not a mean. Now some moral virtues tend to a maximum: for instance, magnanimity to very great honors, and magnificence to very large expenditure, as stated in Ethic. iv, 2,3. Therefore not every moral virtue observes the mean.

Objection 3: Further, if it is essential to a moral virtue to observe the mean, it follows that a moral virtue is not perfected, but the contrary corrupted, through tending to something extreme. Now some moral virtues are perfected by tending to something extreme; thus virginity, which abstains from all sexual pleasure, observes the extreme, and is the most perfect chastity: and to give all to the poor is the most perfect mercy or liberality. Therefore it seems that it is not essential to moral virtue that it should observe the mean.

On the contrary, The Philosopher says (Ethic. ii, 6) that "moral virtue is a habit of choosing the mean."

I answer that, As already explained (I-II, q. 55, a. 3), the nature of virtue is that it should direct man to good. Now moral virtue is properly a perfection of the appetitive part of the soul in regard to some determinate

materiam. Mensura autem et regula appetitivi motus circa appetibilia, est ipsa ratio. Bonum autem cuiuslibet mensurati et regulati consistit in hoc quod conformetur suae regulae, sicut bonum in artificiatis est ut consequantur regulam artis. Malum autem per consequens in huiusmodi est per hoc quod aliquid discordat a sua regula vel mensura. Quod quidem contingit vel per hoc quod superexcedit mensuram, vel per hoc quod deficit ab ea, sicut manifeste apparet in omnibus regulatis et mensuratis. Et ideo patet quod bonum virtutis moralis consistit in adaequatione ad mensuram rationis. Manifestum est autem quod inter excessum et defectum medium est aequalitas sive conformitas. Unde manifeste apparet quod virtus moralis in medio consistit.

AD PRIMUM ergo dicendum quod virtus moralis bonitatem habet ex regula rationis, pro materia autem habet passiones vel operationes. Si ergo comparetur virtus moralis ad rationem, sic, secundum id quod rationis est, habet rationem extremi unius, quod est conformitas, excessus vero et defectus habet rationem alterius extremi, quod est difformitas. Si vero consideretur virtus moralis secundum suam materiam, sic habet rationem medii, inquantum passionem reducit ad regulam rationis. Unde philosophus dicit, in II Ethic., quod *virtus secundum substantiam medietas est,* inquantum regula virtutis ponitur circa propriam materiam, *secundum optimum autem et bene, est extremitas,* scilicet secundum conformitatem rationis.

AD SECUNDUM dicendum quod medium et extrema considerantur in actionibus et passionibus secundum diversas circumstantias, unde nihil prohibet in aliqua virtute esse extremum secundum unam circumstantiam, quod tamen est medium secundum alias circumstantias, per conformitatem ad rationem. Et sic est in magnificentia et magnanimitate. Nam si consideretur quantitas absoluta eius in quod tendit magnificus et magnanimus, dicetur extremum et maximum, sed si consideretur hoc ipsum per comparationem ad alias circumstantias, sic habet rationem medii; quia in hoc tendunt huiusmodi virtutes secundum regulam rationis, idest *ubi* oportet, et *quando*

matter: and the measure or rule of the appetitive movement in respect of appetible objects is the reason. But the good of that which is measured or ruled consists in its conformity with its rule: thus the good things made by art is that they follow the rule of art. Consequently, in things of this sort, evil consists in discordance from their rule or measure. Now this may happen either by their exceeding the measure or by their falling short of it; as is clearly the case in all things ruled or measured. Hence it is evident that the good of moral virtue consists in conformity with the rule of reason. Now it is clear that between excess and deficiency the mean is equality or conformity. Therefore it is evident that moral virtue observes the mean.

Reply to Objection 1: Moral virtue derives goodness from the rule of reason, while its matter consists in passions or operations. If therefore we compare moral virtue to reason, then, if we look at that which is has of reason, it holds the position of one extreme, *viz.* conformity; while excess and defect take the position of the other extreme, *viz.* deformity. But if we consider moral virtue in respect of its matter, then it holds the position of mean, in so far as it makes the passion conform to the rule of reason. Hence the Philosopher says (Ethic. ii, 6) that "virtue, as to its essence, is a mean state," in so far as the rule of virtue is imposed on its proper matter: "but it is an extreme in reference to the 'best' and the 'excellent,'" *viz.* as to its conformity with reason.

Reply to Objection 2: In actions and passions the mean and the extremes depend on various circumstances: hence nothing hinders something from being extreme in a particular virtue as to one circumstance, while the same thing is a mean in respect of other circumstances, through being in conformity with reason. This is the case with magnanimity and magnificence. For if we look at the absolute quantity of the respective objects of these virtues, we shall call it an extreme and a maximum: but if we consider the quantity in relation to other circumstances, then it has the character of a mean: since these virtues tend to this maximum in accordance with the rule of reason, i.e., "where" it is right, "when"

oportet, et *propter quod* oportet. Excessus autem, si in hoc maximum tendatur *quando* non oportet, vel *ubi* non oportet, vel *propter quod* non oportet; defectus autem est, si non tendatur in hoc maximum *ubi* oportet, et *quando* oportet. Et hoc est quod philosophus dicit, in IV Ethic., quod *magnanimus est quidem magnitudine extremus; eo autem quod ut oportet, medius.*

Ad tertium dicendum quod eadem ratio est de virginitate et paupertate, quae est de magnanimitate. Abstinet enim virginitas ab omnibus venereis, et paupertas ab omnibus divitiis, propter quod oportet, et secundum quod oportet; idest secundum mandatum Dei, et propter vitam aeternam. Si autem hoc fiat secundum quod non oportet, idest secundum aliquam superstitionem illicitam, vel etiam propter inanem gloriam; erit superfluum. Si autem non fiat quando oportet, vel secundum quod oportet, est vitium per defectum, ut patet in transgredientibus votum virginitatis vel paupertatis.

it is right, and for an "end" that is right. There will be excess, if one tends to this maximum "when" it is not right, or "where" it is not right, or for an undue "end"; and there will be deficiency if one fails to tend thereto "where" one ought, and "when" one aught. This agrees with the saying of the Philosopher (Ethic. iv, 3) that the "magnanimous man observes the extreme in quantity, but the mean in the right mode of his action."

Reply to Objection 3: The same is to be said of virginity and poverty as of magnanimity. For virginity abstains from all sexual matters, and poverty from all wealth, for a right end, and in a right manner, i.e., according to God's word, and for the sake of eternal life. But if this be done in an undue manner, i.e., out of unlawful superstition, or again for vainglory, it will be in excess. And if it be not done when it ought to be done, or as it ought to be done, it is a vice by deficiency: for instance, in those who break their vows of virginity or poverty.

Articulus 2

Ad secundum sic proceditur. Videtur quod medium virtutis moralis non sit medium rationis, sed medium rei. Bonum enim virtutis moralis consistit in hoc quod est in medio. Bonum autem, ut dicitur in VI Metaphys., est in rebus ipsis. Ergo medium virtutis moralis est medium rei.

Praeterea, ratio est vis apprehensiva. Sed virtus moralis non consistit in medio apprehensionum; sed magis in medio operationum et passionum. Ergo medium virtutis moralis non est medium rationis, sed medium rei.

Praeterea, medium quod accipitur secundum proportionem arithmeticam vel geometricam, est medium rei. Sed tale est medium iustitiae, ut dicitur in V Ethic. Ergo medium virtutis moralis non est medium rationis, sed rei.

Sed contra est quod philosophus dicit, in II Ethic., quod *virtus moralis in medio consistit quoad nos, determinata ratione.*

Article 2
Whether the mean of moral virtue is the real mean, or the rational mean?

Objection 1: It would seem that the mean of moral virtue is not the rational mean, but the real mean. For the good of moral virtue consists in its observing the mean. Now, good, as stated in Metaph. ii, text. 8, is in things themselves. Therefore the mean of moral virtue is a real mean.

Objection 2: Further, the reason is a power of apprehension. But moral virtue does not observe a mean between apprehensions, but rather a mean between operations or passions. Therefore the mean of moral virtue is not the rational, but the real mean.

Objection 3: Further, a mean that is observed according to arithmetical or geometrical proportion is a real mean. Now such is the mean of justice, as stated in Ethic. v, 3. Therefore the mean of moral virtue is not the rational, but the real mean.

On the contrary, The Philosopher says (Ethic. ii, 6) that "moral virtue observes the mean fixed, in our regard, by reason."

Respondeo dicendum quod medium rationis dupliciter potest intelligi. Uno modo, secundum quod medium in ipso actu rationis existit, quasi ipse actus rationis ad medium reducatur. Et sic, quia virtus moralis non perficit actum rationis, sed actum virtutis appetitivae; medium virtutis moralis non est medium rationis. Alio modo potest dici medium rationis id quod a ratione ponitur in aliqua materia. Et sic omne medium virtutis moralis est medium rationis, quia, sicut dictum est, virtus moralis dicitur consistere in medio, per conformitatem ad rationem rectam. Sed quandoque contingit quod medium rationis est etiam medium rei, et tunc oportet quod virtutis moralis medium sit medium rei; sicut est in iustitia. Quandoque autem medium rationis non est medium rei, sed accipitur per comparationem ad nos, et sic est medium in omnibus aliis virtutibus moralibus. Cuius ratio est quia iustitia est circa operationes, quae consistunt in rebus exterioribus, in quibus rectum institui debet simpliciter et secundum se, ut supra dictum est, et ideo medium rationis in iustitia est idem cum medio rei, inquantum scilicet iustitia dat unicuique quod debet, et non plus nec minus. Aliae vero virtutes morales consistunt circa passiones interiores, in quibus non potest rectum constitui eodem modo, propter hoc quod homines diversimode se habent ad passiones, et ideo oportet quod rectitudo rationis in passionibus instituatur per respectum ad nos, qui afficimur secundum passiones.

Et per hoc patet responsio ad obiecta. Nam, primae duae rationes procedunt de medio rationis quod scilicet invenitur in ipso actu rationis. Tertia vero ratio procedit de medio iustitiae.

I answer that, The rational mean can be understood in two ways. First, according as the mean is observed in the act itself of reason, as though the very act of reason were made to observe the mean: in this sense, since moral virtue perfects not the act of reason, but the act of the appetitive power, the mean of moral virtue is not the rational mean. Secondly, the mean of reason may be considered as that which the reason puts into some particular matter. In this sense every mean of moral virtue is a rational mean, since, as above stated (I-II, q. 64, a. 1), moral virtue is said to observe the mean, through conformity with right reason. But it happens sometimes that the rational mean is also the real mean: in which case the mean of moral virtue is the real mean, for instance, in justice. On the other hand, sometimes the rational mean is not the real mean, but is considered in relation to us: and such is the mean in all the other moral virtues. The reason for this is that justice is about operations, which deal with external things, wherein the right has to be established simply and absolutely, as stated above (I-II, q. 60, a. 2): wherefore the rational mean in justice is the same as the real mean, in so far, to wit as justice gives to each one his due, neither more nor less. But the other moral virtues deal with interior passions wherein the right cannot be established in the same way, since men are variously situated in relation to their passions; hence the rectitude of reason has to be established in the passions, with due regard to us, who are moved in respect of the passions.

This suffices for the Replies to the Objections. For the first two arguments take the rational mean as being in the very act of reason, while the third argues from the mean of justice.

Articulus 3

Ad tertium sic proceditur. Videtur quod virtutes intellectuales non consistant in medio. Virtutes enim morales consistunt in medio, inquantum conformantur regulae rationis. Sed virtutes intellectuales sunt in

Article 3
Whether the intellectual virtues observe the mean?

Objection 1: It would seem that the intellectual virtues do not observe the mean. Because moral virtue observes the mean by conforming to the rule of reason. But the intellectual virtues are in

I-II, q. 64, a. 3, arg. 1

ipsa ratione; et sic non videntur habere superiorem regulam. Ergo virtutes intellectuales non consistunt in medio.

Praeterea, medium virtutis moralis determinatur a virtute intellectuali, dicitur enim in II Ethic., quod *virtus consistit in medietate determinata ratione, prout sapiens determinabit.* Si igitur virtus intellectualis iterum consistat in medio, oportet quod determinetur sibi medium per aliquam aliam virtutem. Et sic procedetur in infinitum in virtutibus.

Praeterea, medium proprie est inter contraria; ut patet per philosophum, in X Metaphys. Sed in intellectu non videtur esse aliqua contrarietas, cum etiam ipsa contraria, secundum quod sunt in intellectu, non sint contraria, sed simul intelligantur, ut album et nigrum, sanum et aegrum. Ergo in intellectualibus virtutibus non est medium.

Sed contra est quod ars est virtus intellectualis, ut dicitur in VI Ethic.; et tamen artis est aliquod medium, ut dicitur in II Ethic. Ergo etiam virtus intellectualis consistit in medio.

Respondeo dicendum quod bonum alicuius rei consistit in medio, secundum quod conformatur regulae vel mensurae quam contingit transcendere et ab ea deficere, sicut dictum est. Virtus autem intellectualis ordinatur ad bonum, sicut et moralis, ut supra dictum est. Unde secundum quod bonum virtutis intellectualis se habet ad mensuram, sic se habet ad rationem medii. Bonum autem virtutis intellectualis est verum, speculativae quidem virtutis, verum absolute, ut in VI Ethic. dicitur; practicae autem virtutis, verum secundum conformitatem ad appetitum rectum. Verum autem intellectus nostri absolute consideratum, est sicut mensuratum a re, res enim est mensura intellectus nostri, ut dicitur in X Metaphys.; ex eo enim quod res est vel non est, veritas est in opinione et in oratione. Sic igitur bonum virtutis intellectualis speculativae consistit in quodam medio, per conformitatem ad ipsam rem, secundum quod dicit esse quod est, vel non esse quod non est;

THE MEAN OF VIRTUE

reason itself, so that they seem to have no higher rule. Therefore the intellectual virtues do not observe the mean.

Objection 2: Further, the mean of moral virtue is fixed by an intellectual virtue: for it is stated in Ethic. ii, 6, that "virtue observes the mean appointed by reason, as a prudent man would appoint it." If therefore intellectual virtue also observe the mean, this mean will have to be appointed for them by another virtue, so that there would be an indefinite series of virtues.

Objection 3: Further, a mean is, properly speaking, between contraries, as the Philosopher explains (Metaph. x, text. 22, 23). But there seems to be no contrariety in the intellect; since contraries themselves, as they are in the intellect, are not in opposition to one another, but are understood together, as white and black, healthy and sick. Therefore there is no mean in the intellectual virtues.

On the contrary, Art is an intellectual virtue; and yet there is a mean in art (Ethic. ii, 6). Therefore also intellectual virtue observes the mean.

I answer that, The good of anything consists in its observing the mean, by conforming with a rule or measure in respect of which it may happen to be excessive or deficient, as stated above (I-II, q. 64, a. 1). Now intellectual virtue, like moral virtue, is directed to the good, as stated above (I-II, q. 56, a. 3). Hence the good of an intellectual virtue consists in observing the mean, in so far as it is subject to a measure. Now the good of intellectual virtue is the true; in the case of contemplative virtue, it is the true taken absolutely (Ethic. vi, 2); in the case of practical virtue, it is the true in conformity with a right appetite. Now truth apprehended by our intellect, if we consider it absolutely, is measured by things; since things are the measure of our intellect, as stated in Metaph. x, text. 5; because there is truth in what we think or say, according as the thing is so or not. Accordingly the good of speculative intellectual virtue consists in a certain mean, by way of conformity with things themselves, in so far as the intellect expresses them as being what they are, or as not being what they are not:

in quo ratio veri consistit. Excessus autem est secundum affirmationem falsam, per quam dicitur esse quod non est, defectus autem accipitur secundum negationem falsam, per quam dicitur non esse quod est. Verum autem virtutis intellectualis practicae, comparatum quidem ad rem, habet rationem mensurati. Et sic eodem modo accipitur medium per conformitatem ad rem, in virtutibus intellectualibus practicis, sicut in speculativis. Sed respectu appetitus, habet rationem regulae et mensurae. Unde idem medium, quod est virtutis moralis, etiam est ipsius prudentiae, scilicet rectitudo rationis, sed prudentiae quidem est istud medium ut regulantis et mensurantis; virtutis autem moralis, ut mensuratae et regulatae. Similiter excessus et defectus accipitur diversimode utrobique.

AD PRIMUM ergo dicendum quod etiam virtus intellectualis habet suam mensuram, ut dictum est, et per conformitatem ad ipsam, accipitur in ipsa medium.

AD SECUNDUM dicendum quod non est necesse in infinitum procedere in virtutibus, quia mensura et regula intellectualis virtutis non est aliquod aliud genus virtutis, sed ipsa res.

AD TERTIUM dicendum quod ipsae res contrariae non habent contrarietatem in anima, quia unum est ratio cognoscendi alterum, et tamen in intellectu est contrarietas affirmationis et negationis, quae sunt contraria, ut dicitur in fine peri hermeneias. Quamvis enim *esse* et *non esse* non sint contraria, sed contradictorie opposita, si considerentur ipsa significata prout sunt in rebus, quia alterum est *ens,* et alterum est pure *non ens,* tamen si referantur ad actum animae, utrumque ponit aliquid. Unde *esse* et *non esse* sunt contradictoria, sed opinio qua opinamur quod *bonum est bonum,* est contraria opinioni qua opinamur quod *bonum non est bonum.* Et inter huiusmodi contraria medium est virtus intellectualis.

and it is in this that the nature of truth consists. There will be excess if something false is affirmed, as though something were, which in reality it is not: and there will be deficiency if something is falsely denied, and declared not to be, whereas in reality it is. The truth of practical intellectual virtue, if we consider it in relation to things, is by way of that which is measured; so that both in practical and in speculative intellectual virtues, the mean consists in conformity with things. But if we consider it in relation to the appetite, it has the character of a rule and measure. Consequently the rectitude of reason is the mean of moral virtue, and also the mean of prudence—of prudence as ruling and measuring, of moral virtue, as ruled and measured by that mean. In like manner the difference between excess and deficiency is to be applied in both cases.

Reply to Objection 1: Intellectual virtues also have their measure, as stated, and they observe the mean according as they conform to that measure.

Reply to Objection 2: There is no need for an indefinite series of virtues: because the measure and rule of intellectual virtue is not another kind of virtue, but things themselves.

Reply to Objection 3: The things themselves that are contrary have no contrariety in the mind, because one is the reason for knowing the other: nevertheless there is in the intellect contrariety of affirmation and negation, which are contraries, as stated at the end of Peri Hermenias. For though "to be" and "not to be" are not in contrary, but in contradictory opposition to one another, so long as we consider their signification in things themselves, for on the one hand we have "being" and on the other we have simply "non-being"; yet if we refer them to the act of the mind, there is something positive in both cases. Hence "to be" and "not to be" are contradictory: but the opinion stating that "good is good" is contrary to the opinion stating that "good is not good": and between two such contraries intellectual virtue observes the mean.

Articulus 4

Ad quartum sic proceditur. Videtur quod virtus theologica consistat in medio. Bonum enim aliarum virtutum consistit in medio. Sed virtus theologica excedit in bonitate alias virtutes. Ergo virtus theologica multo magis est in medio.

Praeterea, medium virtutis accipitur, moralis quidem secundum quod appetitus regulatur per rationem; intellectualis vero secundum quod intellectus noster mensuratur a re. Sed virtus theologica et perficit intellectum, et appetitum, ut supra dictum est. Ergo etiam virtus theologica consistit in medio.

Praeterea, spes quae est virtus theologica, medium est inter desperationem et praesumptionem. Similiter etiam fides incedit media inter contrarias haereses, ut Boetius dicit, in libro de duabus naturis, quod enim confitemur in Christo unam personam et duas naturas, medium est inter haeresim Nestorii, qui dicit duas personas et duas naturas; et haeresim Eutychis, qui dicit unam personam et unam naturam. Ergo virtus theologica consistit in medio.

Sed contra, in omnibus in quibus consistit virtus in medio, contingit peccare per excessum, sicut et per defectum. Sed circa Deum, qui est obiectum virtutis theologicae, non contingit peccare per excessum, dicitur enim Eccli. XLIII, *benedicentes Deum, exaltate illum quantum potestis, maior enim est omni laude*. Ergo virtus theologica non consistit in medio.

Respondeo dicendum quod, sicut dictum est, medium virtutis accipitur per conformitatem ad suam regulam vel mensuram, secundum quod contingit ipsam transcendere vel ab ea deficere. Virtutis autem theologicae duplex potest accipi mensura. Una quidem secundum ipsam rationem virtutis. Et sic mensura et regula virtutis theologicae est ipse Deus, fides enim nostra regulatur secundum veritatem divinam, caritas autem secundum bonitatem eius, spes autem secundum magnitudinem omnipotentiae et pietatis eius. Et ista est mensura excellens omnem humanam

Article 4
Whether the theological virtues observe the mean?

Objection 1: It would seem that theological virtue observes the mean. For the good of other virtues consists in their observing the mean. Now the theological virtues surpass the others in goodness. Therefore much more does theological virtue observe the mean.

Objection 2: Further, the mean of moral virtue depends on the appetite being ruled by reason; while the mean of intellectual virtue consists in the intellect being measured by things. Now theological virtue perfects both intellect and appetite, as stated above (I-II, q. 62, a. 3). Therefore theological virtue also observes the mean.

Objection 3: Further, hope, which is a theological virtue, is a mean between despair and presumption. Likewise faith holds a middle course between contrary heresies, as Boethius states (De Duab. Natur. vii): thus, by confessing one Person and two natures in Christ, we observe the mean between the heresy of Nestorius, who maintained the existence of two persons and two natures, and the heresy of Eutyches, who held to one person and one nature. Therefore theological virtue observes the mean.

On the contrary, Wherever virtue observes the mean it is possible to sin by excess as well as by deficiency. But there is no sinning by excess against God, Who is the object of theological virtue: for it is written (Ecclus. 43:33): "Blessing the Lord, exalt Him as much as you can: for He is above all praise." Therefore theological virtue does not observe the mean.

I answer that, As stated above (I-II, q. 64, a. 1), the mean of virtue depends on conformity with virtue's rule or measure, in so far as one may exceed or fall short of that rule. Now the measure of theological virtue may be twofold. One is taken from the very nature of virtue, and thus the measure and rule of theological virtue is God Himself: because our faith is ruled according to Divine truth; charity, according to His goodness; hope, according to the immensity of His omnipotence and loving kindness. This measure surpasses all human

facultatem, unde nunquam potest homo tantum diligere Deum quantum diligi debet, nec tantum credere aut sperare in ipsum, quantum debet. Unde multo minus potest ibi esse excessus. Et sic bonum talis virtutis non consistit in medio, sed tanto est melius, quanto magis acceditur ad summum. Alia vero regula vel mensura virtutis theologicae est ex parte nostra, quia etsi non possumus ferri in Deum quantum debemus, debemus tamen ferri in ipsum credendo, sperando et amando, secundum mensuram nostrae conditionis. Unde per accidens potest in virtute theologica considerari medium et extrema, ex parte nostra.

AD PRIMUM ergo dicendum quod bonum virtutum intellectualium et moralium consistit in medio per conformitatem ad regulam vel mensuram quam transcendere contingit. Quod non est in virtutibus theologicis, per se loquendo, ut dictum est.

AD SECUNDUM dicendum quod virtutes morales et intellectuales perficiunt intellectum et appetitum nostrum in ordine ad mensuram et regulam creatam, virtutes autem theologicae in ordine ad mensuram et regulam increatam. Unde non est similis ratio.

AD TERTIUM dicendum quod spes est media inter praesumptionem et desperationem, ex parte nostra, inquantum scilicet aliquis praesumere dicitur ex eo quod sperat a Deo bonum quod excedit suam conditionem; vel non sperat quod secundum suam conditionem sperare posset. Non autem potest esse superabundantia spei ex parte Dei, cuius bonitas est infinita. Similiter etiam fides est media inter contrarias haereses, non per comparationem ad obiectum, quod est Deus, cui non potest aliquis nimis credere, sed inquantum ipsa opinio humana est media inter contrarias opiniones, ut ex supradictis patet.

power: so that never can we love God as much as He ought to be loved, nor believe and hope in Him as much as we should. Much less therefore can there be excess in such things. Accordingly the good of such virtues does not consist in a mean, but increases the more we approach to the summit.

The other rule or measure of theological virtue is by comparison with us: for although we cannot be borne towards God as much as we ought, yet we should approach to Him by believing, hoping and loving, according to the measure of our condition. Consequently it is possible to find a mean and extremes in theological virtue, accidentally and in reference to us.

Reply to Objection 1: The good of intellectual and moral virtues consists in a mean of reason by conformity with a measure that may be exceeded: whereas this is not so in the case of theological virtue, considered in itself, as stated above.

Reply to Objection 2: Moral and intellectual virtues perfect our intellect and appetite in relation to a created measure and rule; whereas the theological virtues perfect them in relation to an uncreated rule and measure. Wherefore the comparison fails.

Reply to Objection 3: Hope observes the mean between presumption and despair, in relation to us, in so far, to wit, as a man is said to be presumptuous, through hoping to receive from God a good in excess of his condition; or to despair through failing to hope for that which according to his condition he might hope for. But there can be no excess of hope in comparison with God, Whose goodness is infinite. In like manner faith holds a middle course between contrary heresies, not by comparison with its object, which is God, in Whom we cannot believe too much; but in so far as human opinion itself takes a middle position between contrary opinions, as was explained above.

Question 65
Of the Connection of Virtues

We must now consider the connection of virtues: under which head there are five points of inquiry: 1. Whether the moral virtues are connected with one another? 2. Whether the moral virtues can be without charity? 3. Whether charity can be without them? 4. Whether faith and hope can be without charity? 5. Whether charity can be without them?

Article 1
Whether the moral virtues are connected with one another?

Objection 1: It would seem that the moral virtues are not connected with one another. Because moral virtues are sometimes caused by the exercise of acts, as is proved in Ethic. ii, 1, 2. But man can exercise himself in the acts of one virtue, without exercising himself in the acts of some other virtue. Therefore it is possible to have one moral virtue without another.

Objection 2: Further, magnificence and magnanimity are moral virtues. Now a man may have other moral virtues without having magnificence or magnanimity: for the Philosopher says (Ethic. iv, 2, 3) that "a poor man cannot be magnificent," and yet he may have other virtues; and (Ethic. iv) that "he who is worthy of small things, and so accounts his worth, is modest, but not magnanimous." Therefore the moral virtues are not connected with one another.

Objection 3: Further, as the moral virtues perfect the appetitive part of the soul, so do the intellectual virtues perfect the intellective part. But the intellectual virtues are not mutually connected: since we may have one science, without having another. Neither, therefore, are the moral virtues connected with one another.

Objection 4: Further, if the moral virtues are mutually connected, this can only be because they are united together in prudence. But this does not suffice to connect the moral virtues together. For, seemingly, one may be prudent about things to be done in relation to one virtue, without being prudent in those that concern another virtue: even as one

THE CONNECTION OF VIRTUES

aliquis potest habere artem circa quaedam factibilia, sine hoc quod habeat artem circa alia. Prudentia autem est recta ratio agibilium. Ergo non est necessarium virtutes morales esse connexas.

SED CONTRA est quod Ambrosius dicit, super Lucam, *connexae sibi sunt, concatenataeque virtutes, ut qui unam habet, plures habere videatur.* Augustinus etiam dicit, in VI de Trin., quod *virtutes quae sunt in animo humano, nullo modo separantur ab invicem.* Et Gregorius dicit, XXII Moral., quod *una virtus sine aliis aut omnino nulla est, aut imperfecta.* Et Tullius dicit, in II de Tuscul. quaest., *si unam virtutem confessus es te non habere, nullam necesse est te habiturum.*

RESPONDEO dicendum quod virtus moralis potest accipi vel perfecta vel imperfecta. Imperfecta quidem moralis virtus, ut temperantia vel fortitudo, nihil aliud est quam aliqua inclinatio in nobis existens ad opus aliquod de genere bonorum faciendum, sive talis inclinatio sit in nobis a natura, sive ex assuetudine. Et hoc modo accipiendo virtutes morales, non sunt connexae, videmus enim aliquem ex naturali complexione, vel ex aliqua consuetudine, esse promptum ad opera liberalitatis, qui tamen non est promptus ad opera castitatis. Perfecta autem virtus moralis est habitus inclinans in bonum opus bene agendum. Et sic accipiendo virtutes morales, dicendum est eas connexas esse; ut fere ab omnibus ponitur. Cuius ratio duplex assignatur, secundum quod diversimode aliqui virtutes cardinales distinguunt. Ut enim dictum est, quidam distinguunt eas secundum quasdam generales conditiones virtutum, utpote quod discretio pertineat ad prudentiam, rectitudo ad iustitiam, moderantia ad temperantiam, firmitas animi ad fortitudinem, in quacumque materia ista considerentur. Et secundum hoc, manifeste apparet ratio connexionis, non enim firmitas habet laudem virtutis, si sit sine moderatione, vel rectitudine, aut discretione; et eadem ratio est de aliis. Et hanc rationem connexionis assignat Gregorius, XXII Moral., dicens quod *virtutes, si sint disiunctae, non possunt esse perfectae*, secundum rationem virtutis,

I-II, q. 65, a. 1, co.

may have the art of making certain things, without the art of making certain others. Now prudence is right reason about things to be done. Therefore the moral virtues are not necessarily connected with one another.

On the contrary, Ambrose says on Lk. 6:20: "The virtues are connected and linked together, so that whoever has one, is seen to have several": and Augustine says (De Trin. vi, 4) that "the virtues that reside in the human mind are quite inseparable from one another": and Gregory says (Moral. xxii, 1) that "one virtue without the other is either of no account whatever, or very imperfect": and Cicero says (Quaest. Tusc. ii): "If you confess to not having one particular virtue, it must needs be that you have none at all."

I answer that, Moral virtue may be considered either as perfect or as imperfect. An imperfect moral virtue, temperance for instance, or fortitude, is nothing but an inclination in us to do some kind of good deed, whether such inclination be in us by nature or by habituation. If we take the moral virtues in this way, they are not connected: since we find men who, by natural temperament or by being accustomed, are prompt in doing deeds of liberality, but are not prompt in doing deeds of chastity. But the perfect moral virtue is a habit that inclines us to do a good deed well; and if we take moral virtues in this way, we must say that they are connected, as nearly as all are agreed in saying. For this two reasons are given, corresponding to the different ways of assigning the distinction of the cardinal virtues. For, as we stated above (I-II, q. 61, a. 3; a. 4), some distinguish them according to certain general properties of the virtues: for instance, by saying that discretion belongs to prudence, rectitude to justice, moderation to temperance, and strength of mind to fortitude, in whatever matter we consider these properties to be. In this way the reason for the connection is evident: for strength of mind is not commended as virtuous, if it be without moderation or rectitude or discretion: and so forth. This, too, is the reason assigned for the connection by Gregory, who says (Moral. xxii, 1) that "a virtue cannot be perfect" as a virtue, "if isolated from the others:

I-II, q. 65, a. 1, co.

quia nec prudentia vera est quae iusta, temperans et fortis non est; et idem subdit de aliis virtutibus. Et similem rationem assignat Augustinus, in VI de Trin. Alii vero distinguunt praedictas virtutes secundum materias. Et secundum hoc assignatur ratio connexionis ab Aristotele, in VI Ethic. Quia sicut supra dictum est, nulla virtus moralis potest sine prudentia haberi, eo quod proprium virtutis moralis est facere electionem rectam, cum sit habitus electivus; ad rectam autem electionem non solum sufficit inclinatio in debitum finem, quod est directe per habitum virtutis moralis; sed etiam quod aliquis directe eligat ea quae sunt ad finem, quod fit per prudentiam, quae est consiliativa et iudicativa et praeceptiva eorum quae sunt ad finem. Similiter etiam prudentia non potest haberi nisi habeantur virtutes morales, cum prudentia sit *recta ratio agibilium,* quae, sicut ex principiis, procedit ex finibus agibilium, ad quos aliquis recte se habet per virtutes morales. Unde sicut scientia speculativa non potest haberi sine intellectu principiorum, ita nec prudentia sine virtutibus moralibus. Ex quo manifeste sequitur virtutes morales esse connexas.

AD PRIMUM ergo dicendum quod virtutum moralium quaedam perficiunt hominem secundum communem statum, scilicet quantum ad ea quae communiter in omni vita hominum occurrunt agenda. Unde oportet quod homo simul exercitetur circa materias omnium virtutum moralium. Et si quidem circa omnes exercitetur bene operando, acquiret habitus omnium virtutum moralium. Si autem exercitetur bene operando circa unam materiam, non autem circa aliam, puta bene se habendo circa iras, non autem circa concupiscentias; acquiret quidem habitum aliquem ad refrenandum iras, qui tamen non habebit rationem virtutis, propter defectum prudentiae, quae circa concupiscentias corrumpitur. Sicut etiam naturales inclinationes non habent perfectam rationem virtutis, si prudentia desit.

THE CONNECTION OF VIRTUES

for there can be no true prudence without temperance, justice and fortitude": and he continues to speak in like manner of the other virtues (cf. q. 61, a. 4, arg. 1). Augustine also gives the same reason (De Trin. vi, 4). Others, however, differentiate these virtues in respect of their matters, and it is in this way that Aristotle assigns the reason for their connection (Ethic. vi, 13). Because, as stated above (I-II, q. 58, a. 4), no moral virtue can be without prudence; since it is proper to moral virtue to make a right choice, for it is an elective habit. Now right choice requires not only the inclination to a due end, which inclination is the direct outcome of moral virtue, but also correct choice of things conducive to the end, which choice is made by prudence, that counsels, judges, and commands in those things that are directed to the end. In like manner one cannot have prudence unless one has the moral virtues: since prudence is "right reason about things to be done," and the starting point of reason is the end of the thing to be done, to which end man is rightly disposed by moral virtue. Hence, just as we cannot have speculative science unless we have the understanding of the principles, so neither can we have prudence without the moral virtues: and from this it follows clearly that the moral virtues are connected with one another.

Reply to Objection 1: Some moral virtues perfect man as regards his general state, in other words, with regard to those things which have to be done in every kind of human life. Hence man needs to exercise himself at the same time in the matters of all moral virtues. And if he exercise himself, by good deeds, in all such matters, he will acquire the habits of all the moral virtues. But if he exercise himself by good deeds in regard to one matter, but not in regard to another, for instance, by behaving well in matters of anger, but not in matters of concupiscence; he will indeed acquire a certain habit of restraining his anger; but this habit will lack the nature of virtue, through the absence of prudence, which is wanting in matters of concupiscence. In the same way, natural inclinations fail to have the complete character of virtue, if prudence be lacking.

Quaedam vero virtutes morales sunt quae perficiunt hominem secundum aliquem eminentem statum, sicut magnificentia, et magnanimitas. Et quia exercitium circa materias harum virtutum non occurrit unicuique communiter, potest aliquis habere alias virtutes morales, sine hoc quod habitus harum virtutum habeat actu, loquendo de virtutibus acquisitis. Sed tamen, acquisitis aliis virtutibus, habet istas virtutes in potentia propinqua. Cum enim aliquis per exercitium adeptus est liberalitatem circa mediocres donationes et sumptus, si superveniat ei abundantia pecuniarum, modico exercitio acquiret magnificentiae habitum, sicut geometer modico studio acquirit scientiam alicuius conclusionis quam nunquam consideravit. Illud autem habere dicimur, quod in promptu est ut habeamus; secundum illud philosophi, in II Physic., *quod parum deest, quasi nihil deesse videtur.*

Et per hoc patet responsio ad secundum.

AD TERTIUM dicendum quod virtutes intellectuales sunt circa diversas materias ad invicem non ordinatas, sicut patet in diversis scientiis et artibus. Et ideo non invenitur in eis connexio quae invenitur in virtutibus moralibus existentibus circa passiones et operationes, quae manifeste habent ordinem ad invicem. Nam omnes passiones, a quibusdam primis procedentes, scilicet amore et odio, ad quasdam alias terminantur, scilicet delectationem et tristitiam. Et similiter omnes operationes quae sunt virtutis moralis materia, habent ordinem ad invicem, et etiam ad passiones. Et ideo tota materia moralium virtutum sub una ratione prudentiae cadit. Habent tamen omnia intelligibilia ordinem ad prima principia. Et secundum hoc, omnes virtutes intellectuales dependent ab intellectu principiorum; sicut prudentia a virtutibus moralibus, ut dictum est. Principia autem universalia, quorum est intellectus principiorum, non dependent a conclusionibus, de quibus sunt reliquae intellectuales virtutes; sicut morales dependent a prudentia, eo quod

But there are some moral virtues which perfect man with regard to some eminent state, such as magnificence and magnanimity; and since it does not happen to all in common to be exercised in the matter of such virtues, it is possible for a man to have the other moral virtues, without actually having the habits of these virtues—provided we speak of acquired virtue. Nevertheless, when once a man has acquired those other virtues he possesses these in proximate potentiality. Because when, by practice, a man has acquired liberality in small gifts and expenditure, if he were to come in for a large sum of money, he would acquire the habit of magnificence with but little practice: even as a geometrician, by dint of little study, acquires scientific knowledge about some conclusion which had never been presented to his mind before. Now we speak of having a thing when we are on the point of having it, according to the saying of the Philosopher (Phys. ii, text. 56): "That which is scarcely lacking is not lacking at all."

This suffices for the Reply to the Second Objection.

Reply to Objection 3: The intellectual virtues are about divers matters having no relation to one another, as is clearly the case with the various sciences and arts. Hence we do not observe in them the connection that is to be found among the moral virtues, which are about passions and operations, that are clearly related to one another. For all the passions have their rise in certain initial passions, *viz.* love and hatred, and terminate in certain others, *viz.* pleasure and sorrow. In like manner all the operations that are the matter of moral virtue are related to one another, and to the passions. Hence the whole matter of moral virtues falls under the one rule of prudence. Nevertheless, all intelligible things are related to first principles. And in this way, all the intellectual virtues depend on the understanding of principles; even as prudence depends on the moral virtues, as stated. On the other hand, the universal principles which are the object of the virtue of understanding of principles, do not depend on the conclusions, which are the objects of the other intellectual virtues, as do the moral virtues depend on prudence, because the ap-

appetitus movet quodammodo rationem, et ratio appetitum, ut supra dictum est.

AD QUARTUM dicendum quod ea ad quae inclinant virtutes morales, se habent ad prudentiam sicut principia, non autem factibilia se habent ad artem sicut principia, sed solum sicut materia. Manifestum est autem quod, etsi ratio possit esse recta in una parte materiae, et non in alia; nullo tamen modo potest dici ratio recta, si sit defectus cuiuscumque principii. Sicut si quis erraret circa hoc principium, *omne totum est maius sua parte,* non posset habere scientiam geometricam, quia oporteret multum recedere a veritate in sequentibus. Et praeterea, *agibilia* sunt ordinata ad invicem; non autem *factibilia,* ut dictum est. Et ideo defectus prudentiae circa unam partem agibilium, induceret defectum etiam circa alia agibilia. Quod in factibilibus non contingit.

petite, in a fashion, moves the reason, and the reason the appetite, as stated above (I-II, q. 9, a. 1; q. 58, a. 5, ad 1).

Reply to Objection 4: Those things to which the moral virtues incline, are as the principles of prudence: whereas the products of art are not the principles, but the matter of art. Now it is evident that, though reason may be right in one part of the matter, and not in another, yet in no way can it be called **right reason,** if it be deficient in any principle whatever. Thus, if a man be wrong about the principle, "A whole is greater than its part," he cannot acquire the science of geometry, because he must necessarily wander from the truth in his conclusion. Moreover, things "done" are related to one another, but not things "made," as stated above (ad 3). Consequently the lack of prudence in one department of things to be done, would result in a deficiency affecting other things to be done: whereas this does not occur in things to be made.

ARTICULUS 2

AD SECUNDUM sic proceditur. Videtur quod virtutes morales possint esse sine caritate. Dicitur enim in libro sententiarum prosperi, quod *omnis virtus praeter caritatem, potest esse communis bonis et malis.* Sed *caritas non potest esse nisi in bonis,* ut dicitur ibidem. Ergo aliae virtutes possunt haberi sine caritate.

PRAETEREA, virtutes morales possunt acquiri ex actibus humanis, ut dicitur in II Ethic. Sed caritas non habetur nisi ex infusione; secundum illud Rom. V, *caritas Dei diffusa est in cordibus nostris per spiritum sanctum, qui datus est nobis.* Ergo aliae virtutes possunt haberi sine caritate.

PRAETEREA, virtutes morales connectuntur ad invicem, inquantum dependent a prudentia. Sed caritas non dependet a prudentia; immo prudentiam excedit, secundum illud Ephes. III, *supereminentem scientiae caritatem Christi.* Ergo virtutes morales non connectuntur caritati, sed sine ea esse possunt.

ARTICLE 2
Whether moral virtues can be without charity?

Objection 1: It would seem that moral virtues can be without charity. For it is stated in the Liber Sentent. Prosperi vii, that "every virtue save charity may be common to the good and bad." But "charity can be in none except the good," as stated in the same book. Therefore the other virtues can be had without charity.

Objection 2: Further, moral virtues can be acquired by means of human acts, as stated in Ethic. ii, 1, 2, whereas charity cannot be had otherwise than by infusion, according to Rom. 5:5: "The charity of God is poured forth in our hearts by the Holy Ghost Who is given to us." Therefore it is possible to have the other virtues without charity.

Objection 3: Further, the moral virtues are connected together, through depending on prudence. But charity does not depend on prudence; indeed, it surpasses prudence, according to Eph. 3:19: "The charity of Christ, which surpasseth all knowledge." Therefore the moral virtues are not connected with charity, and can be without it.

SED CONTRA est quod dicitur I Ioan. III, *qui non diligit, manet in morte.* Sed per virtutes perficitur vita spiritualis, ipsae enim sunt *quibus recte vivitur,* ut Augustinus dicit, in II de Lib. Arbit. Ergo non possunt esse sine dilectione caritatis.

RESPONDEO dicendum quod, sicut supra dictum est, virtutes morales prout sunt operativae boni in ordine ad finem qui non excedit facultatem naturalem hominis, possunt per opera humana acquiri. Et sic acquisitae sine caritate esse possunt, sicut fuerunt in multis gentilibus. Secundum autem quod sunt operativae boni in ordine ad ultimum finem supernaturalem, sic perfecte et vere habent rationem virtutis; et non possunt humanis actibus acquiri, sed infunduntur a Deo. Et huiusmodi virtutes morales sine caritate esse non possunt. Dictum est enim supra quod aliae virtutes morales non possunt esse sine prudentia; prudentia autem non potest esse sine virtutibus moralibus, inquantum virtutes morales faciunt bene se habere ad quosdam fines, ex quibus procedit ratio prudentiae. Ad rectam autem rationem prudentiae multo magis requiritur quod homo bene se habeat circa ultimum finem, quod fit per caritatem, quam circa alios fines, quod fit per virtutes morales, sicut ratio recta in speculativis maxime indiget primo principio indemonstrabili, quod est *contradictoria non simul esse vera.* Unde manifestum fit quod nec prudentia infusa potest esse sine caritate; nec aliae virtutes morales consequenter, quae sine prudentia esse non possunt. Patet igitur ex dictis quod solae virtutes infusae sunt perfectae, et simpliciter dicendae virtutes, quia bene ordinant hominem ad finem ultimum simpliciter. Aliae vero virtutes, scilicet acquisitae, sunt secundum quid virtutes, non autem simpliciter, ordinant enim hominem bene respectu finis ultimi in aliquo genere, non autem respectu finis ultimi simpliciter.

On the contrary, It is written (1 Jn. 3:14): "He that loveth not, abideth in death." Now the spiritual life is perfected by the virtues, since it is "by them" that "we lead a good life," as Augustine states (De Lib. Arb. ii, 17, 19). Therefore they cannot be without the love of charity.

I answer that, As stated above (I-II, q. 63, a. 2), it is possible by means of human works to acquire moral virtues, in so far as they produce good works that are directed to an end not surpassing the natural power of man: and when they are acquired thus, they can be without charity, even as they were in many of the Gentiles. But in so far as they produce good works in proportion to a supernatural last end, thus they have the character of virtue, truly and perfectly; and cannot be acquired by human acts, but are infused by God. Such like moral virtues cannot be without charity. For it has been stated above (I-II, q. 65, a. 1; q. 58, a. 4; a. 5) that the other moral virtues cannot be without prudence; and that prudence cannot be without the moral virtues, because these latter make man well disposed to certain ends, which are the starting-point of the procedure of prudence. Now for prudence to proceed aright, it is much more necessary that man be well disposed towards his ultimate end, which is the effect of charity, than that he be well disposed in respect of other ends, which is the effect of moral virtue: just as in speculative matters right reason has greatest need of the first indemonstrable principle, that "contradictories cannot both be true at the same time." It is therefore evident that neither can infused prudence be without charity; nor, consequently, the other moral virtues, since they cannot be without prudence. It is therefore clear from what has been said that only the infused virtues are perfect, and deserve to be called virtues simply: since they direct man well to the ultimate end. But the other virtues, those, namely, that are acquired, are virtues in a restricted sense, but not simply: for they direct man well in respect of the last end in some particular genus of action, but not in respect of the last end simply.

Unde Rom. XIV super illud, *omne quod non est ex fide, peccatum est,* dicit Glossa Augustini, *ubi deest agnitio veritatis, falsa est virtus etiam in bonis moribus.*

AD PRIMUM ergo dicendum quod virtutes ibi accipiuntur secundum imperfectam rationem virtutis. Alioquin, si virtus moralis secundum perfectam rationem virtutis accipiatur, *bonum facit habentem*; et per consequens in malis esse non potest.

AD SECUNDUM dicendum quod ratio illa procedit de virtutibus moralibus acquisitis.

AD TERTIUM dicendum quod, etsi caritas excedat scientiam et prudentiam, tamen prudentia dependet a caritate, ut dictum est. Et per consequens, omnes virtutes morales infusae.

Hence a gloss of Augustine* on the words, "All that is not of faith is sin" (Rom. 14:23), says: "He that fails to acknowledge the truth, has no true virtue, even if his conduct be good."

Reply to Objection 1: Virtue, in the words quoted, denotes imperfect virtue. Else if we take moral virtue in its perfect state, "it makes its possessor good," and consequently cannot be in the wicked.

Reply to Objection 2: This argument holds good of virtue in the sense of acquired virtue.

Reply to Objection 3: Though charity surpasses science and prudence, yet prudence depends on charity, as stated: and consequently so do all the infused moral virtues.

ARTICULUS 3

AD TERTIUM sic proceditur. Videtur quod caritas sine aliis virtutibus moralibus haberi possit. Ad id enim ad quod sufficit unum, indebitum est quod plura ordinentur. Sed sola caritas sufficit ad omnia opera virtutis implenda, ut patet per id quod dicitur I ad Cor. XIII, *caritas patiens est, benigna est,* et cetera. Ergo videtur quod, habita caritate, aliae virtutes superfluerent.

PRAETEREA, qui habet habitum virtutis, de facili operatur ea quae sunt virtutis, et ei secundum se placent, unde et *signum habitus est delectatio quae fit in opere,* ut dicitur in II Ethic. Sed multi habent caritatem, absque peccato mortali existentes, qui tamen difficultatem in operibus virtutum patiuntur, neque eis secundum se placent, sed solum secundum quod referuntur ad caritatem. Ergo multi habent caritatem, qui non habent alias virtutes.

PRAETEREA, caritas in omnibus sanctis invenitur. Sed quidam sunt sancti qui tamen aliquibus virtutibus carent, dicit enim Beda quod sancti magis humiliantur de virtutibus quas non habent, quam de virtutibus quas habent, glorientur. Ergo

ARTICLE 3
Whether charity can be without moral virtue?

Objection 1: It would seem possible to have charity without the moral virtues. For when one thing suffices for a certain purpose, it is superfluous to employ others. Now charity alone suffices for the fulfilment of all the works of virtue, as is clear from 1 Cor. 13:4, seqq.: "Charity is patient, is kind," etc. Therefore it seems that if one has charity, other virtues are superfluous.

Objection 2: Further, he that has a habit of virtue easily performs the works of that virtue, and those works are pleasing to him for their own sake: hence "pleasure taken in a work is a sign of habit" (Ethic. ii, 3). Now many have charity, being free from mortal sin, and yet they find it difficult to do works of virtue; nor are these works pleasing to them for their own sake, but only for the sake of charity. Therefore many have charity without the other virtues.

Objection 3: Further, charity is to be found in every saint: and yet there are some saints who are without certain virtues. For Bede says (on Lk. 17:10) that the saints are more humbled on account of their not having certain virtues, than rejoiced at the virtues they have. Therefore,

---

* Cf. Lib. Sentent. Prosperi cvi.

non est necessarium quod qui habet caritatem, omnes virtutes morales habeat.

SED CONTRA est quod per caritatem tota lex impletur, dicitur enim Rom. XIII, qui *diligit proximum, legem implevit.* Sed tota lex impleri non potest nisi per omnes virtutes morales, quia lex praecipit de omnibus actibus virtutum, ut dicitur in V Ethic. Ergo qui habet caritatem, habet omnes virtutes morales. Augustinus etiam dicit, in quadam epistola, quod caritas includit in se omnes virtutes cardinales.

RESPONDEO dicendum quod cum caritate simul infunduntur omnes virtutes morales. Cuius ratio est quia Deus non minus perfecte operatur in operibus gratiae, quam in operibus naturae. Sic autem videmus in operibus naturae, quod non invenitur principium aliquorum operum in aliqua re, quin inveniantur in ea quae sunt necessaria ad huiusmodi opera perficienda, sicut in animalibus inveniuntur organa quibus perfici possunt opera ad quae peragenda anima habet potestatem. Manifestum est autem quod caritas, inquantum ordinat hominem ad finem ultimum, est principium omnium bonorum operum quae in finem ultimum ordinari possunt. Unde oportet quod cum caritate simul infundantur omnes virtutes morales, quibus homo perficit singula genera bonorum operum. Et sic patet quod virtutes morales infusae non solum habent connexionem propter prudentiam; sed etiam propter caritatem. Et quod qui amittit caritatem per peccatum mortale, amittit omnes virtutes morales infusas.

AD PRIMUM ergo dicendum quod ad hoc quod actus inferioris potentiae sit perfectus, requiritur quod non solum adsit perfectio in superiori potentia, sed etiam in inferiori, si enim principale agens debito modo se haberet, non sequeretur actio perfecta, si instrumentum non esset bene dispositum. Unde oportet ad hoc quod homo bene operetur in his quae sunt ad finem, quod non solum habeat virtutem qua bene se habeat circa finem, sed etiam virtutes quibus bene se habeat circa ea quae sunt ad finem, nam virtus quae est circa finem, se habet ut principalis et motiva respectu

if a man has charity, it does not follow of necessity that he has all the moral virtues.

On the contrary, The whole Law is fulfilled through charity, for it is written (Rom. 13:8): "He that loveth his neighbor, hath fulfilled the Law." Now it is not possible to fulfil the whole Law, without having all the moral virtues: since the law contains precepts about all acts of virtue, as stated in Ethic. v, 1, 2. Therefore he that has charity, has all the moral virtues. Moreover, Augustine says in a letter (Epis. clxvii)* that charity contains all the cardinal virtues.

I answer that, All the moral virtues are infused together with charity. The reason for this is that God operates no less perfectly in works of grace than in works of nature. Now, in the works of nature, we find that whenever a thing contains a principle of certain works, it has also whatever is necessary for their execution: thus animals are provided with organs whereby to perform the actions that their souls empower them to do. Now it is evident that charity, inasmuch as it directs man to his last end, is the principle of all the good works that are referable to his last end. Wherefore all the moral virtues must needs be infused together with charity, since it is through them that man performs each different kind of good work. It is therefore clear that the infused moral virtues are connected, not only through prudence, but also on account of charity: and, again, that whoever loses charity through mortal sin, forfeits all the infused moral virtues.

Reply to Objection 1: In order that the act of a lower power be perfect, not only must there be perfection in the higher, but also in the lower power: for if the principal agent were well disposed, perfect action would not follow, if the instrument also were not well disposed. Consequently, in order that man work well in things referred to the end, he needs not only a virtue disposing him well to the end, but also those virtues which dispose him well to whatever is referred to the end: for the virtue which regards the end is the chief and moving principle in respect

---

* Cf. Serm. xxxix and xlvi de Temp.

earum quae sunt ad finem. Et ideo cum caritate necesse est etiam habere alias virtutes morales.

AD SECUNDUM dicendum quod quandoque contingit quod aliquis habens habitum, patitur difficultatem in operando, et per consequens non sentit delectationem et complacentiam in actu, propter aliquod impedimentum extrinsecus superveniens, sicut ille qui habet habitum scientiae, patitur difficultatem in intelligendo, propter somnolentiam vel aliquam infirmitatem. Et similiter habitus moralium virtutum infusarum patiuntur interdum difficultatem in operando, propter aliquas dispositiones contrarias ex praecedentibus actibus relictas. Quae quidem difficultas non ita accidit in virtutibus moralibus acquisitis, quia per exercitium actuum, quo acquiruntur, tolluntur etiam contrariae dispositiones.

AD TERTIUM dicendum quod aliqui sancti dicuntur aliquas virtutes non habere, inquantum patiuntur difficultatem in actibus earum, ratione iam dicta; quamvis habitus omnium virtutum habeant.

of those things that are referred to the end. Therefore it is necessary to have the moral virtues together with charity.

Reply to Objection 2: It happens sometimes that a man who has a habit, finds it difficult to act in accordance with the habit, and consequently feels no pleasure and complacency in the act, on account of some impediment supervening from without: thus a man who has a habit of science, finds it difficult to understand, through being sleepy or unwell. In like manner sometimes the habits of moral virtue experience difficulty in their works, by reason of certain ordinary dispositions remaining from previous acts. This difficulty does not occur in respect of acquired moral virtue: because the repeated acts by which they are acquired, remove also the contrary dispositions.

Reply to Objection 3: Certain saints are said not to have certain virtues, in so far as they experience difficulty in the acts of those virtues, for the reason stated; although they have the habits of all the virtues.

ARTICULUS 4

AD QUARTUM sic proceditur. Videtur quod fides et spes nunquam sint sine caritate. Cum enim sint virtutes theologicae, digniores esse videntur virtutibus moralibus, etiam infusis. Sed virtutes morales infusae non possunt esse sine caritate. Ergo neque fides et spes.

PRAETEREA, *nullus credit nisi volens,* sed caritas est in voluntate ut Augustinus dicit, super Ioan. Sicut perfectio eius, ut supra dictum est. Ergo fides non potest esse sine caritate.

PRAETEREA, Augustinus dicit, in Enchirid., quod *spes sine amore esse non potest.* Amor autem est caritas, de hoc enim amore ibi loquitur. Ergo spes non potest esse sine caritate.

SED CONTRA est quod Matth. I, dicitur in Glossa quod *fides generat spem, spes vero caritatem.* Sed generans est prius generato, et potest esse sine eo. Ergo fides potest esse sine spe; et spes sine caritate.

ARTICLE 4
Whether faith and hope can be without charity?

Objection 1: It would seem that faith and hope are never without charity. Because, since they are theological virtues, they seem to be more excellent than even the infused moral virtues. But the infused moral virtues cannot be without charity. Neither therefore can faith and hope be without charity.

Objection 2: Further, "no man believes unwillingly" as Augustine says (Tract. xxvi in Joan.). But charity is in the will as a perfection thereof, as stated above (I-II, q. 62, a. 3). Therefore faith cannot be without charity.

Objection 3: Further, Augustine says (Enchiridion viii) that "there can be no hope without love." But love is charity: for it is of this love that he speaks. Therefore hope cannot be without charity.

On the contrary, A gloss on Mat. 1:2 says that "faith begets hope, and hope, charity." Now the begetter precedes the begotten, and can be without it. Therefore faith can be without hope; and hope, without charity.

RESPONDEO dicendum quod fides et spes, sicut et virtutes morales, dupliciter considerari possunt. Uno modo, secundum inchoationem quandam; alio modo, secundum perfectum esse virtutis. Cum enim virtus ordinetur ad bonum opus agendum, virtus quidem perfecta dicitur ex hoc quod potest in opus perfecte bonum, quod quidem est dum non solum bonum est quod fit, sed etiam bene fit. Alioquin, si bonum sit quod fit, non autem bene fiat, non erit perfecte bonum, unde nec habitus qui est talis operis principium, habebit perfecte rationem virtutis. Sicut si aliquis operetur iusta, bonum quidem facit, sed non erit opus perfectae virtutis, nisi hoc bene faciat, idest secundum electionem rectam, quod est per prudentiam, et ideo iustitia sine prudentia non potest esse virtus perfecta. Sic igitur fides et spes sine caritate possunt quidem aliqualiter esse, perfectae autem virtutis rationem sine caritate non habent. Cum enim fidei opus sit credere Deo; credere autem sit alicui propria voluntate assentire, si non debito modo velit, non erit fidei opus perfectum. Quod autem debito modo velit, hoc est per caritatem, quae perficit voluntatem, omnis enim rectus motus voluntatis ex recto amore procedit, ut Augustinus dicit, in XIV de Civ. Dei. Sic igitur fides est quidem sine caritate, sed non perfecta virtus, sicut temperantia vel fortitudo sine prudentia. Et similiter dicendum est de spe. Nam actus spei est expectare futuram beatitudinem a Deo. Qui quidem actus perfectus est, si fiat ex meritis quae quis habet, quod non potest esse sine caritate. Si autem hoc expectet ex meritis quae nondum habet, sed proponit in futurum acquirere, erit actus imperfectus, et hoc potest esse sine caritate. Et ideo fides et spes possunt esse sine caritate, sed sine caritate, proprie loquendo, virtutes non sunt; nam ad rationem virtutis pertinet ut non solum secundum ipsam aliquod bonum operemur, sed etiam bene, ut dicitur in II Ethic.

AD PRIMUM ergo dicendum quod virtutes morales dependent a prudentia, prudentia autem infusa nec rationem prudentiae habere potest absque caritate, utpote deficiente debita habitudine ad primum principium,

I answer that, Faith and hope, like the moral virtues, can be considered in two ways; first in an inchoate state; secondly, as complete virtues. For since virtue is directed to the doing of good works, perfect virtue is that which gives the faculty of doing a perfectly good work, and this consists in not only doing what is good, but also in doing it well. Else, if what is done is good, but not well done, it will not be perfectly good; wherefore neither will the habit that is the principle of such an act, have the perfect character of virtue. For instance, if a man do what is just, what he does is good: but it will not be the work of a perfect virtue unless he do it well, i.e., by choosing rightly, which is the result of prudence; for which reason justice cannot be a perfect virtue without prudence. Accordingly faith and hope can exist indeed in a fashion without charity: but they have not the perfect character of virtue without charity. For, since the act of faith is to believe in God; and since to believe is to assent to someone of one's own free will: to will not as one ought, will not be a perfect act of faith. To will as one ought is the outcome of charity which perfects the will: since every right movement of the will proceeds from a right love, as Augustine says (De Civ. Dei xiv, 9). Hence faith may be without charity, but not as a perfect virtue: just as temperance and fortitude can be without prudence. The same applies to hope. Because the act of hope consists in looking to God for future bliss. This act is perfect, if it is based on the merits which we have; and this cannot be without charity. But to expect future bliss through merits which one has not yet, but which one proposes to acquire at some future time, will be an imperfect act; and this is possible without charity. Consequently, faith and hope can be without charity; yet, without charity, they are not virtues properly so-called; because the nature of virtue requires that by it, we should not only do what is good, but also that we should do it well (Ethic. ii, 6).

Reply to Objection 1: Moral virtue depends on prudence: and not even infused prudence has the character of prudence without charity; for this involves the absence of due order to the first principle,

quod est ultimus finis. Fides autem et spes, secundum proprias rationes, nec a prudentia nec a caritate dependent. Et ideo sine caritate esse possunt; licet non sint virtutes sine caritate, ut dictum est.

AD SECUNDUM dicendum quod ratio illa procedit de fide quae habet perfectam rationem virtutis.

AD TERTIUM dicendum quod Augustinus loquitur ibi de spe, secundum quod aliquis expectat futuram beatitudinem per merita quae iam habet, quod non est sine caritate.

viz. the ultimate end. On the other hand faith and hope, as such, do not depend either on prudence or charity; so that they can be without charity, although they are not virtues without charity, as stated.

Reply to Objection 2: This argument is true of faith considered as a perfect virtue.

Reply to Objection 3: Augustine is speaking here of that hope whereby we look to gain future bliss through merits which we have already; and this is not without charity.

ARTICULUS 5

AD QUINTUM sic proceditur. Videtur quod caritas possit esse sine fide et spe. Caritas enim est amor Dei. Sed Deus potest a nobis amari naturaliter, etiam non praesupposita fide, vel spe futurae beatitudinis. Ergo caritas potest esse sine fide et spe.

PRAETEREA, caritas est radix omnium virtutum; secundum illud Ephes. III, *in caritate radicati et fundati.* Sed radix aliquando est sine ramis. Ergo caritas potest esse aliquando sine fide et spe et aliis virtutibus.

PRAETEREA, in Christo fuit perfecta caritas. Ipse tamen non habuit fidem et spem, quia fuit perfectus comprehensor, ut infra dicetur. Ergo caritas potest esse sine fide et spe.

SED CONTRA est quod apostolus dicit, Heb. XI, *sine fide impossibile est placere Deo;* quod maxime pertinet ad caritatem, ut patet; secundum illud Proverb. VIII, *ego diligentes me diligo.* Spes etiam est quae introducit ad caritatem, ut supra dictum est. Ergo caritas non potest haberi sine fide et spe.

RESPONDEO dicendum quod caritas non solum significat amorem Dei, sed etiam amicitiam quandam ad ipsum; quae quidem super amorem addit mutuam redamationem cum quadam mutua communicatione, ut dicitur in VIII Ethic. Et quod hoc ad caritatem pertineat, patet per id quod dicitur I Ioan. IV, *qui manet in caritate, in Deo manet, et Deus in eo.* Et I ad Cor. I dicitur, *fidelis Deus,*

ARTICLE 5
Whether charity can be without faith and hope?

Objection 1: It would seem that charity can be without faith and hope. For charity is the love of God. But it is possible for us to love God naturally, without already having faith, or hope in future bliss. Therefore charity can be without faith and hope.

Objection 2: Further, charity is the root of all the virtues, according to Eph. 3:17: "Rooted and founded in charity." Now the root is sometimes without branches. Therefore charity can sometimes be without faith and hope, and the other virtues.

Objection 3: Further, there was perfect charity in Christ. And yet He had neither faith nor hope: because He was a perfect comprehensor, as we shall explain further on (III, q. 7, a. 3; a. 4). Therefore charity can be without faith and hope.

On the contrary, The Apostle says (Heb. 11:6): "Without faith it is impossible to please God"; and this evidently belongs most to charity, according to Prov. 8:17: "I love them that love me." Again, it is by hope that we are brought to charity, as stated above (I-II, q. 62, a. 4). Therefore it is not possible to have charity without faith and hope.

I answer that, Charity signifies not only the love of God, but also a certain friendship with Him; which implies, besides love, a certain mutual return of love, together with mutual communion, as stated in Ethic. viii, 2. That this belongs to charity is evident from 1 Jn. 4:16: "He that abideth in charity, abideth in God, and God in him," and from 1 Cor. 1:9, where it is written: "God is faithful,

per quem vocati estis in societatem filii eius. Haec autem societas hominis ad Deum, quae est quaedam familiaris conversatio cum ipso, inchoatur quidem hic in praesenti per gratiam, perficietur autem in futuro per gloriam, quorum utrumque fide et spe tenetur. Unde sicut aliquis non posset cum aliquo amicitiam habere, si discrederet vel desperaret se posse habere aliquam societatem vel familiarem conversationem cum ipso; ita aliquis non potest habere amicitiam ad Deum, quae est caritas, nisi fidem habeat, per quam credat huiusmodi societatem et conversationem hominis cum Deo, et speret se ad hanc societatem pertinere. Et sic caritas sine fide et spe nullo modo esse potest.

Ad primum ergo dicendum quod caritas non est qualiscumque amor Dei, sed amor Dei quo diligitur ut beatitudinis obiectum, ad quod ordinamur per fidem et spem.

Ad secundum dicendum quod caritas est radix fidei et spei, inquantum dat eis perfectionem virtutis. Sed fides et spes, secundum rationem propriam, praesupponuntur ad caritatem, ut supra dictum est. Et sic caritas sine eis esse non potest.

Ad tertium dicendum quod Christo defuit fides et spes, propter id quod est imperfectionis in eis. Sed loco fidei, habuit apertam visionem; et loco spei, plenam comprehensionem. Et sic fuit perfecta caritas in eo.

by Whom you are called unto the fellowship of His Son." Now this fellowship of man with God, which consists in a certain familiar colloquy with Him, is begun here, in this life, by grace, but will be perfected in the future life, by glory; each of which things we hold by faith and hope. Wherefore just as friendship with a person would be impossible, if one disbelieved in, or despaired of, the possibility of their fellowship or familiar colloquy; so too, friendship with God, which is charity, is impossible without faith, so as to believe in this fellowship and colloquy with God, and to hope to attain to this fellowship. Therefore charity is quite impossible without faith and hope.

Reply to Objection 1: Charity is not any kind of love of God, but that love of God, by which He is loved as the object of bliss, to which object we are directed by faith and hope.

Reply to Objection 2: Charity is the root of faith and hope, in so far as it gives them the perfection of virtue. But faith and hope as such are the precursors of charity, as stated above (I-II, q. 62, a. 4), and so charity is impossible without them.

Reply to Objection 3: In Christ there was neither faith nor hope, on account of their implying an imperfection. But instead of faith, He had manifest vision, and instead of hope, full comprehension:* so that in Him was perfect charity.

---

* See above, I-II, q. 4, a. 3.

Quaestio LXVI

Deinde considerandum est de aequalitate virtutum. Et circa hoc quaeruntur sex. *Primo,* utrum virtus possit esse maior vel minor. *Secundo,* utrum omnes virtutes simul in eodem existentes, sint aequales. *Tertio,* de comparatione virtutum moralium ad intellectuales. *Quarto,* de comparatione virtutum moralium ad invicem. *Quinto,* de comparatione virtutum intellectualium ad invicem. *Sexto,* de comparatione virtutum theologicarum ad invicem.

Articulus 1

Ad primum sic proceditur. Videtur quod virtus non possit esse maior vel minor. Dicitur enim in Apoc. XXI, quod latera civitatis Ierusalem sunt aequalia. Per haec autem significantur virtutes, ut Glossa dicit ibidem. Ergo omnes virtutes sunt aequales. Non ergo potest esse virtus maior virtute.

Praeterea, omne illud cuius ratio consistit in maximo, non potest esse maius vel minus. Sed ratio virtutis consistit in maximo, est enim virtus *ultimum potentiae,* ut philosophus dicit in I de caelo; et Augustinus etiam dicit, in II de Lib. Arb., quod *virtutes sunt maxima bona, quibus nullus potest male uti.* Ergo videtur quod virtus non possit esse maior neque minor.

Praeterea, quantitas effectus pensatur secundum virtutem agentis. Sed virtutes perfectae, quae sunt virtutes infusae, sunt a Deo, cuius virtus est uniformis et infinita. Ergo videtur quod virtus non possit esse maior virtute.

Sed contra, ubicumque potest esse augmentum et superabundantia, potest esse inaequalitas. Sed in virtutibus invenitur superabundantia et augmentum, dicitur enim Matth. V, *nisi abundaverit iustitia vestra plus quam Scribarum et Pharisaeorum, non intrabitis in regnum caelorum;* et Proverb. XV dicitur, *in abundanti iustitia virtus maxima est.* Ergo videtur quod virtus possit esse maior vel minor.

Question 66
Of Equality Among the Virtues

We must now consider equality among the virtues: under which head there are six points of inquiry: 1. Whether one virtue can be greater or less than another? 2. Whether all the virtues existing together in one subject are equal? 3. Of moral virtue in comparison with intellectual virtue; 4. Of the moral virtues as compared with one another; 5. Of the intellectual virtues in comparison with one another; 6. Of the theological virtues in comparison with one another.

Article 1
Whether one virtue can be greater or less than another?

Objection 1: It would seem that one virtue cannot be greater or less than another. For it is written (Apoc. 21:16) that the sides of the city of Jerusalem are equal; and a gloss says that the sides denote the virtues. Therefore all virtues are equal; and consequently one cannot be greater than another.

Objection 2: Further, a thing that, by its nature, consists in a maximum, cannot be more or less. Now the nature of virtue consists in a maximum, for virtue is "the limit of power," as the Philosopher states (De Coelo i, text. 116); and Augustine says (De Lib. Arb. ii, 19) that "virtues are very great boons, and no one can use them to evil purpose." Therefore it seems that one virtue cannot be greater or less than another.

Objection 3: Further, the quantity of an effect is measured by the power of the agent. But perfect, *viz.* infused virtues, are from God Whose power is uniform and infinite. Therefore it seems that one virtue cannot be greater than another.

On the contrary, Wherever there can be increase and greater abundance, there can be inequality. Now virtues admit of greater abundance and increase: for it is written (Mat. 5:20): "Unless your justice abound more than that of the Scribes and Pharisees, you shall not enter into the kingdom of heaven": and (Prov. 15:5): "In abundant justice there is the greatest strength [*virtus*]." Therefore it seems that a virtue can be greater or less than another.

RESPONDEO dicendum quod cum quaeritur utrum virtus una possit esse maior alia, dupliciter intelligi potest quaestio. Uno modo, in virtutibus specie differentibus. Et sic manifestum est quod una virtus est alia maior. Semper enim est potior causa suo effectu, et in effectibus, tanto aliquid est potius, quanto est causae propinquius. Manifestum est autem ex dictis quod causa et radix humani boni est ratio. Et ideo prudentia, quae perficit rationem, praefertur in bonitate aliis virtutibus moralibus, perficientibus vim appetitivam inquantum participat rationem. Et in his etiam tanto est una altera melior, quanto magis ad rationem accedit. Unde et iustitia, quae est in voluntate, praefertur aliis virtutibus moralibus, et fortitudo, quae est in irascibili, praefertur temperantiae, quae est in concupiscibili, quae minus participat rationem, ut patet in VII Ethic. Alio modo potest intelligi quaestio in virtute eiusdem speciei. Et sic, secundum ea quae dicta sunt supra, cum de intensionibus habituum ageretur, virtus potest dupliciter dici maior et minor, uno modo, secundum seipsam; alio modo, ex parte participantis subiecti. Si igitur secundum seipsam consideretur, magnitudo vel parvitas eius attenditur secundum ea ad quae se extendit. Quicumque autem habet aliquam virtutem, puta temperantiam, habet ipsam quantum ad omnia ad quae se temperantia extendit. Quod de scientia et arte non contingit, non enim quicumque est grammaticus, scit omnia quae ad grammaticam pertinent. Et secundum hoc bene dixerunt Stoici, ut Simplicius dicit in commento praedicamentorum, quod virtus non recipit magis et minus, sicut scientia vel ars; eo quod ratio virtutis consistit in maximo. Si vero consideretur virtus ex parte subiecti participantis, sic contingit virtutem esse maiorem vel minorem, sive secundum diversa tempora, in eodem; sive in diversis hominibus. Quia ad attingendum medium virtutis, quod est secundum rationem rectam, unus est melius dispositus quam alius, vel propter maiorem assuetudinem, vel propter meliorem dispositionem naturae, vel propter perspicacius iudicium rationis, aut etiam propter maius gratiae donum, quod unicuique donatur

I answer that, When it is asked whether one virtue can be greater than another, the question can be taken in two senses. First, as applying to virtues of different species. In this sense it is clear that one virtue is greater than another; since a cause is always more excellent than its effect; and among effects, those nearest to the cause are the most excellent. Now it is clear from what has been said (I-II, q. 18, a. 5; q. 61, a. 2) that the cause and root of human good is the reason. Hence prudence which perfects the reason, surpasses in goodness the other moral virtues which perfect the appetitive power, in so far as it partakes of reason. And among these, one is better than another, according as it approaches nearer to the reason. Consequently justice, which is in the will, excels the remaining moral virtues; and fortitude, which is in the irascible part, stands before temperance, which is in the concupiscible, which has a smaller share of reason, as stated in Ethic. vii, 6. The question can be taken in another way, as referring to virtues of the same species. In this way, according to what was said above (I-II, q. 52, a. 1), when we were treating of the intensity of habits, virtue may be said to be greater or less in two ways: first, in itself; secondly with regard to the subject that partakes of it. If we consider it in itself, we shall call it greater or little, according to the things to which it extends. Now whosoever has a virtue, e.g., temperance, has it in respect of whatever temperance extends to. But this does not apply to science and art: for every grammarian does not know everything relating to grammar. And in this sense the Stoics said rightly, as Simplicius states in his Commentary on the Predicaments, that virtue cannot be more or less, as science and art can; because the nature of virtue consists in a maximum. If, however, we consider virtue on the part of the subject, it may then be greater or less, either in relation to different times, or in different men. Because one man is better disposed than another to attain to the mean of virtue which is defined by right reason; and this, on account of either greater habituation, or a better natural disposition, or a more discerning judgment of reason, or again a greater gift of grace, which is given to each

secundum mensuram donationis Christi, ut dicitur ad Ephes. IV. Et in hoc deficiebant Stoici, aestimantes nullum esse virtuosum dicendum, nisi qui summe fuerit dispositus ad virtutem. Non enim exigitur ad rationem virtutis, quod attingat rectae rationis medium in indivisibili, sicut Stoici putabant, sed sufficit prope medium esse, ut in II Ethic. dicitur. Idem etiam indivisibile signum unus propinquius et promptius attingit quam alius, sicut etiam patet in sagittatoribus trahentibus ad certum signum.

AD PRIMUM ergo dicendum quod aequalitas illa non est secundum quantitatem absolutam, sed est secundum proportionem intelligenda, quia omnes virtutes proportionaliter crescunt in homine, ut infra dicetur.

AD SECUNDUM dicendum quod illud *ultimum* quod pertinet ad virtutem, potest habere rationem *magis* vel *minus* boni secundum praedictos modos, cum non sit ultimum indivisibile, ut dictum est.

AD TERTIUM dicendum quod Deus non operatur secundum necessitatem naturae, sed secundum ordinem suae sapientiae, secundum quam diversam mensuram virtutis hominibus largitur, secundum illud ad Ephes. IV, *unicuique vestrum data est gratia secundum mensuram donationis Christi*.

one "according to the measure of the giving of Christ," as stated in Eph. 4:9. And here the Stoics erred, for they held that no man should be deemed virtuous, unless he were, in the highest degree, disposed to virtue. Because the nature of virtue does not require that man should reach the mean of right reason as though it were an indivisible point, as the Stoics thought; but it is enough that he should approach the mean, as stated in Ethic. ii, 6. Moreover, one same indivisible mark is reached more nearly and more readily by one than by another: as may be seen when several arches aim at a fixed target.

Reply to Objection 1: This equality is not one of absolute quantity, but of proportion: because all virtues grow in a man proportionately, as we shall see further on (I-II, q. 66, a. 2).

Reply to Objection 2: This "limit" which belongs to virtue, can have the character of something "more" or "less" good, in the ways explained above: since, as stated, it is not an indivisible limit.

Reply to Objection 3: God does not work by necessity of nature, but according to the order of His wisdom, whereby He bestows on men various measures of virtue, according to Eph. 4:7: "To every one of you* is given grace according to the measure of the giving of Christ."

ARTICULUS 2

AD SECUNDUM sic proceditur. Videtur quod non omnes virtutes in uno et eodem sint aequaliter intensae. Dicit enim apostolus, I ad Cor. VII, *unusquisque habet proprium donum a Deo, alius quidem sic, alius autem sic*. Non esset autem unum donum magis proprium alicui quam aliud, si omnes virtutes dono Dei infusas quilibet aequaliter haberet. Ergo videtur quod non omnes virtutes sint aequales in uno et eodem.

PRAETEREA, si omnes virtutes essent aeque intensae in uno et eodem, sequeretur quod quicumque excederet aliquem in una virtute, excederet ipsum in omnibus aliis

ARTICLE 2
Whether all the virtues that are together in one man, are equal?

Objection 1: It would seem that the virtues in one same man are not all equally intense. For the Apostle says (1 Cor. 7:7): "Everyone hath his proper gift from God; one after this manner, and another after that." Now one gift would not be more proper than another to a man, if God infused all the virtues equally into each man. Therefore it seems that the virtues are not all equal in one and the same man.

Objection 2: Further, if all the virtues were equally intense in one and the same man, it would follow that whoever surpasses another in one virtue, would surpass him in all the

---

* Vulg.: 'us'

virtutibus. Sed hoc patet esse falsum, quia diversi sancti de diversis virtutibus praecipue laudantur; sicut Abraham de fide, Moyses de mansuetudine, Iob de patientia. Unde et de quolibet confessore cantatur in Ecclesia, *non est inventus similis illi, qui conservaret legem excelsi;* eo quod quilibet habuit praerogativam alicuius virtutis. Non ergo omnes virtutes sunt aequales in uno et eodem.

PRAETEREA, quanto habitus est intensior, tanto homo secundum ipsum delectabilius et promptius operatur. Sed experimento patet quod unus homo delectabilius et promptius operatur actum unius virtutis quam actum alterius. Non ergo omnes virtutes sunt aequales in uno et eodem.

SED CONTRA est quod Augustinus dicit, in VI de Trin., quod *quicumque sunt aequales in fortitudine, aequales sunt in prudentia et temperantia;* et sic de aliis. Hoc autem non esset, nisi omnes virtutes unius hominis essent aequales. Ergo omnes virtutes unius hominis sunt aequales.

RESPONDEO dicendum quod quantitas virtutum, sicut ex dictis patet, potest attendi dupliciter. Uno modo, secundum rationem speciei. Et sic non est dubium quod una virtus unius hominis sit maior quam alia, sicut caritas fide et spe. Alio modo potest attendi secundum participationem subiecti, prout scilicet intenditur vel remittitur in subiecto. Et secundum hoc, omnes virtutes unius hominis sunt aequales quadam aequalitate proportionis, inquantum aequaliter crescunt in homine, sicut digiti manus sunt inaequales secundum quantitatem, sed sunt aequales secundum proportionem, cum proportionaliter augeantur. Huiusmodi autem aequalitatis oportet eodem modo rationem accipere, sicut et connexionis, aequalitas enim est quaedam connexio virtutum secundum quantitatem. Dictum est autem supra quod ratio connexionis virtutum dupliciter assignari potest. Uno modo, secundum intellectum eorum qui intelligunt per has quatuor virtutes, quatuor conditiones generales virtutum, quarum una simul invenitur cum aliis in qualibet materia.

others. But this is clearly not the case: since various saints are specially praised for different virtues; e.g., Abraham for faith (Rom. 4), Moses for his meekness (Num. 7:3), Job for his patience (Tob. 2:12). This is why of each Confessor the Church sings: "There was not found his like in keeping the law of the most High,"* since each one was remarkable for some virtue or other. Therefore the virtues are not all equal in one and the same man.

Objection 3: Further, the more intense a habit is, the greater one's pleasure and readiness in making use of it. Now experience shows that a man is more pleased and ready to make use of one virtue than of another. Therefore the virtues are not all equal in one and the same man.

On the contrary, Augustine says (De Trin. vi, 4) that "those who are equal in fortitude are equal in prudence and temperance," and so on. Now it would not be so, unless all the virtues in one man were equal. Therefore all virtues are equal in one man.

I answer that, As explained above (I-II, q. 66, a. 1), the comparative greatness of virtues can be understood in two ways. First, as referring to their specific nature: and in this way there is no doubt that in a man one virtue is greater than another, for example, charity, than faith and hope. Secondly, it may be taken as referring to the degree of participation by the subject, according as a virtue becomes intense or remiss in its subject. In this sense all the virtues in one man are equal with an equality of proportion, in so far as their growth in man is equal: thus the fingers are unequal in size, but equal in proportion, since they grow in proportion to one another. Now the nature of this equality is to be explained in the same way as the connection of virtues; for equality among virtues is their connection as to greatness. Now it has been stated above (I-II, q. 65, a. 1) that a twofold connection of virtues may be assigned. The first is according to the opinion of those who understood these four virtues to be four general properties of virtues, each of which is found together with the other in any matter.

---

* See Lesson in the Mass *Statuit* (Dominican Missal).

Et sic virtus in qualibet materia non potest aequalis dici, nisi habeat omnes istas conditiones aequales. Et hanc rationem aequalitatis virtutum assignat Augustinus, in VI de Trin., dicens, *si dixeris aequales esse istos fortitudine, sed illum praestare prudentia; sequitur quod huius fortitudo minus prudens sit. Ac per hoc, nec fortitudine aequales sunt, quando est illius fortitudo prudentior. Atque ita de ceteris virtutibus invenies, si omnes eadem consideratione percurras.* Alio modo assignata est ratio connexionis virtutum secundum eos qui intelligunt huiusmodi virtutes habere materias determinatas. Et secundum hoc, ratio connexionis virtutum moralium accipitur ex parte prudentiae, et ex parte caritatis quantum ad virtutes infusas, non autem ex parte inclinationis, quae est ex parte subiecti, ut supra dictum est. Sic igitur et ratio aequalitatis virtutum potest accipi ex parte prudentiae, quantum ad id quod est formale in omnibus virtutibus moralibus, existente enim ratione aequaliter perfecta in uno et eodem, oportet quod proportionaliter secundum rationem rectam medium constituatur in qualibet materia virtutum. Quantum vero ad id quod est materiale in virtutibus moralibus, scilicet inclinationem ipsam ad actum virtutis; potest esse unus homo magis promptus ad actum unius virtutis quam ad actum alterius, vel ex natura, vel ex consuetudine, vel etiam ex gratiae dono.

AD PRIMUM ergo dicendum quod verbum apostoli potest intelligi de donis gratiae gratis datae, quae non sunt communia omnibus, nec omnia aequalia in uno et eodem. Vel potest dici quod refertur ad mensuram gratiae gratum facientis; secundum quam unus abundat in omnibus virtutibus plus quam alius, propter maiorem abundantiam prudentiae, vel etiam caritatis, in qua connectuntur omnes virtutes infusae.

AD SECUNDUM dicendum quod unus sanctus laudatur praecipue de una virtute, et alius de alia, propter excellentiorem promptitudinem ad actum unius virtutis, quam ad actum alterius.

In this way virtues cannot be said to be equal in any matter unless they have all these properties equal. Augustine alludes to this kind of equality (De Trin. vi, 4) when he says: "If you say these men are equal in fortitude, but that one is more prudent than the other; it follows that the fortitude of the latter is less prudent. Consequently they are not really equal in fortitude, since the former's fortitude is more prudent. You will find that this applies to the other virtues if you run over them all in the same way." The other kind of connection among virtues followed the opinion of those who hold these virtues to have their own proper respective matters (I-II, q. 65, a. 1; a. 2). In this way the connection among moral virtues results from prudence, and, as to the infused virtues, from charity, and not from the inclination, which is on the part of the subject, as stated above (I-II, q. 65, a. 1). Accordingly the nature of the equality among virtues can also be considered on the part of prudence, in regard to that which is formal in all the moral virtues: for in one and the same man, so long as his reason has the same degree of perfection, the mean will be proportionately defined according to right reason in each matter of virtue. But in regard to that which is material in the moral virtues, *viz.* the inclination to the virtuous act, one may be readier to perform the act of one virtue, than the act of another virtue, and this either from nature, or from habituation, or again by the grace of God.

Reply to Objection 1: This saying of the Apostle may be taken to refer to the gifts of gratuitous grace, which are not common to all, nor are all of them equal in the one same subject. We might also say that it refers to the measure of sanctifying grace, by reason of which one man has all the virtues in greater abundance than another man, on account of his greater abundance of prudence, or also of charity, in which all the infused virtues are connected.

Reply to Objection 2: One saint is praised chiefly for one virtue, another saint for another virtue, on account of his more admirable readiness for the act of one virtue than for the act of another virtue.

Et per hoc etiam patet responsio ad tertium.

Articulus 3

Ad tertium sic proceditur. Videtur quod virtutes morales praeemineant intellectualibus. Quod enim magis est necessarium, et permanentius, est melius. Sed virtutes morales sunt *permanentiores etiam disciplinis,* quae sunt virtutes intellectuales, et sunt etiam magis necessariae ad vitam humanam. Ergo sunt praeferendae virtutibus intellectualibus.

Praeterea, de ratione virtutis est quod *bonum faciat habentem.* Sed secundum virtutes morales dicitur homo bonus, non autem secundum virtutes intellectuales, nisi forte secundum solam prudentiam. Ergo virtus moralis est melior quam intellectualis.

Praeterea, finis est nobilior his quae sunt ad finem. Sed sicut dicitur in VI Ethic., *virtus moralis facit rectam intentionem finis; prudentia autem facit rectam electionem eorum quae sunt ad finem.* Ergo virtus moralis est nobilior prudentia, quae est virtus intellectualis circa moralia.

Sed contra, virtus moralis est in rationali per participationem; virtus autem intellectualis in rationali per essentiam, sicut dicitur in I Ethic. Sed rationale per essentiam est nobilius quam rationale per participationem. Ergo virtus intellectualis est nobilior virtute morali.

Respondeo dicendum quod aliquid potest dici maius vel minus, dupliciter, uno modo, simpliciter; alio modo, secundum quid. Nihil enim prohibet aliquid esse melius simpliciter, ut *philosophari quam ditari,* quod tamen non est melius secundum quid, idest *necessitatem patienti.* Simpliciter autem consideratur unumquodque, quando consideratur secundum propriam rationem suae speciei. Habet autem virtus speciem ex obiecto, ut ex dictis patet. Unde, simpliciter loquendo, illa virtus nobilior est quae habet nobilius obiectum. Manifestum est autem

This suffices for the Reply to the Third Objection.

Article 3
Whether the moral virtues are better than the intellectual virtues?

Objection 1: It would seem that the moral virtues are better than the intellectual. Because that which is more necessary, and more lasting, is better. Now the moral virtues are "more lasting even than the sciences" (Ethic. i) which are intellectual virtues: and, moreover, they are more necessary for human life. Therefore they are preferable to the intellectual virtues.

Objection 2: Further, virtue is defined as "that which makes its possessor good." Now man is said to be good in respect of moral virtue, and art in respect of intellectual virtue, except perhaps in respect of prudence alone. Therefore moral is better than intellectual virtue.

Objection 3: Further, the end is more excellent than the means. But according to Ethic. vi, 12, "moral virtue gives right intention of the end; whereas prudence gives right choice of the means." Therefore moral virtue is more excellent than prudence, which is the intellectual virtue that regards moral matters.

On the contrary, Moral virtue is in that part of the soul which is rational by participation; while intellectual virtue is in the essentially rational part, as stated in Ethic. i, 13. Now rational by essence is more excellent than rational by participation. Therefore intellectual virtue is better than moral virtue.

I answer that, A thing may be said to be greater or less in two ways: first, simply; secondly, relatively. For nothing hinders something from being better simply, e.g., "learning than riches," and yet not better relatively, i.e., "for one who is in want."* Now to consider a thing simply is to consider it in its proper specific nature. Accordingly, a virtue takes its species from its object, as explained above (I-II, q. 54, a. 2; q. 60, a. 1). Hence, speaking simply, that virtue is more excellent, which has the more excellent object. Now it is evident

---

* Aristotle, Topic. iii.

quod obiectum rationis est nobilius quam obiectum appetitus, ratio enim apprehendit aliquid in universali; sed appetitus tendit in res, quae habent esse particulare. Unde, simpliciter loquendo, virtutes intellectuales, quae perficiunt rationem, sunt nobiliores quam morales, quae perficiunt appetitum. Sed si consideretur virtus in ordine ad actum, sic virtus moralis, quae perficit appetitum, cuius est movere alias potentias ad actum, ut supra dictum est, nobilior est. Et quia virtus dicitur ex eo quod est principium alicuius actus, cum sit perfectio potentiae, sequitur etiam quod ratio virtutis magis competat virtutibus moralibus quam virtutibus intellectualibus, quamvis virtutes intellectuales sint nobiliores habitus simpliciter.

AD PRIMUM ergo dicendum quod virtutes morales sunt magis permanentes quam intellectuales, propter exercitium earum in his quae pertinent ad vitam communem. Sed manifestum est quod obiecta disciplinarum, quae sunt necessaria et semper eodem modo se habentia, sunt permanentiora quam obiecta virtutum moralium, quae sunt quaedam particularia agibilia. Quod autem virtutes morales sunt magis necessariae ad vitam humanam, non ostendit eas esse nobiliores simpliciter, sed quoad hoc. Quinimmo virtutes intellectuales speculativae, ex hoc ipso quod non ordinantur ad aliud sicut utile ordinatur ad finem, sunt digniores. Hoc enim contingit quia secundum eas quodammodo inchoatur in nobis beatitudo, quae consistit in cognitione veritatis, sicut supra dictum est.

AD SECUNDUM dicendum quod secundum virtutes morales dicitur homo bonus simpliciter, et non secundum intellectuales, ea ratione, quia appetitus movet alias potentias ad suum actum, ut supra dictum est. Unde per hoc etiam non probatur nisi quod virtus moralis sit melior secundum quid.

AD TERTIUM dicendum quod prudentia non solum dirigit virtutes morales in eligendo ea quae sunt ad finem, sed etiam in praestituendo finem. Est autem finis uniuscuiusque virtutis moralis attingere medium in propria materia, quod quidem medium

that the object of the reason is more excellent than the object of the appetite: since the reason apprehends things in the universal, while the appetite tends to things themselves, whose being is restricted to the particular. Consequently, speaking simply, the intellectual virtues, which perfect the reason, are more excellent than the moral virtues, which perfect the appetite. But if we consider virtue in its relation to act, then moral virtue, which perfects the appetite, whose function it is to move the other powers to act, as stated above (I-II, q. 9, a. 1), is more excellent. And since virtue is so called from its being a principle of action, for it is the perfection of a power, it follows again that the nature of virtue agrees more with moral than with intellectual virtue, though the intellectual virtues are more excellent habits, simply speaking.

Reply to Objection 1: The moral virtues are more lasting than the intellectual virtues, because they are practised in matters pertaining to the life of the community. Yet it is evident that the objects of the sciences, which are necessary and invariable, are more lasting than the objects of moral virtue, which are certain particular matters of action. That the moral virtues are more necessary for human life, proves that they are more excellent, not simply, but relatively. Indeed, the speculative intellectual virtues, from the very fact that they are not referred to something else, as a useful thing is referred to an end, are more excellent. The reason for this is that in them we have a kind of beginning of that happiness which consists in the knowledge of truth, as stated above (I-II, q. 3, a. 6).

Reply to Objection 2: The reason why man is said to be good simply, in respect of moral virtue, but not in respect of intellectual virtue, is because the appetite moves the other powers to their acts, as stated above (I-II, q. 56, a. 3). Wherefore this argument, too, proves merely that moral virtue is better relatively.

Reply to Objection 3: Prudence directs the moral virtues not only in the choice of the means, but also in appointing the end. Now the end of each moral virtue is to attain the mean in the matter proper to that virtue; which mean is

determinatur secundum rectam rationem prudentiae, ut dicitur in II et VI Ethic.

Articulus 4

AD QUARTUM sic proceditur. Videtur quod iustitia non sit praecipua inter virtutes morales. Maius enim est dare alicui de proprio, quam reddere alicui quod ei debetur. Sed primum pertinet ad liberalitatem; secundum autem ad iustitiam. Ergo videtur quod liberalitas sit maior virtus quam iustitia.

PRAETEREA, illud videtur esse maximum in unoquoque, quod est perfectissimum in ipso. Sed sicut dicitur Iac. I, *patientia opus perfectum habet.* Ergo videtur quod patientia sit maior quam iustitia.

PRAETEREA, magnanimitas operatur magnum, in omnibus virtutibus, ut dicitur in IV Ethic. Ergo magnificat etiam ipsam iustitiam. Est igitur maior quam iustitia.

SED CONTRA est quod philosophus dicit, in V Ethic., quod *iustitia est praeclarissima virtutum.*

RESPONDEO dicendum quod virtus aliqua secundum suam speciem potest dici maior vel minor, vel simpliciter, vel secundum quid. Simpliciter quidem virtus dicitur maior, secundum quod in ea maius bonum rationis relucet, ut supra dictum est. Et secundum hoc, iustitia inter omnes virtutes morales praecellit, tanquam propinquior rationi. Quod patet et ex subiecto, et ex obiecto. Ex subiecto quidem, quia est in voluntate sicut in subiecto, voluntas autem est appetitus rationalis, ut ex dictis patet. Secundum autem obiectum sive materiam, quia est circa operationes, quibus homo ordinatur non solum in seipso, sed etiam ad alterum. Unde *iustitia est praeclarissima virtutum,* ut dicitur in V Ethic. Inter alias autem virtutes morales, quae sunt circa passiones, tanto in unaquaque magis relucet rationis bonum, quanto circa maiora motus appetitivus subditur rationi. Maximum autem in his quae ad hominem pertinent, est vita, a qua omnia alia dependent. Et ideo fortitudo, quae appetitivum motum subdit rationi in his quae ad mortem et vitam pertinent, primum locum tenet inter virtutes morales quae sunt circa

appointed according to the right ruling of prudence, as stated in Ethic. ii, 6; vi, 13.

Article 4
Whether justice is the chief of the moral virtues?

Objection 1: It would seem that justice is not the chief of the moral virtues. For it is better to give of one's own than to pay what is due. Now the former belongs to liberality, the latter to justice. Therefore liberality is apparently a greater virtue than justice.

Objection 2: Further, the chief quality of a thing is, seemingly, that in which it is most perfect. Now, according to Jam. 1:4, "Patience hath a perfect work." Therefore it would seem that patience is greater than justice.

Objection 3: Further, "Magnanimity has a great influence on every virtue," as stated in Ethic. iv, 3. Therefore it magnifies even justice. Therefore it is greater than justice.

On the contrary, The Philosopher says (Ethic. v, 1) that "justice is the most excellent of the virtues."

I answer that, A virtue considered in its species may be greater or less, either simply or relatively. A virtue is said to be greater simply, whereby a greater rational good shines forth, as stated above (I-II, q. 66, a. 1). In this way justice is the most excellent of all the moral virtues, as being most akin to reason. This is made evident by considering its subject and its object: its subject, because this is the will, and the will is the rational appetite, as stated above (I-II, q. 8, a. 1; q. 26, a. 1): its object or matter, because it is about operations, whereby man is set in order not only in himself, but also in regard to another. Hence "justice is the most excellent of virtues" (Ethic. v, 1). Among the other moral virtues, which are about the passions, the more excellent the matter in which the appetitive movement is subjected to reason, so much the more does the rational good shine forth in each. Now in things touching man, the chief of all is life, on which all other things depend. Consequently fortitude which subjects the appetitive movement to reason in matters of life and death, holds the first place among those moral virtues that are about the

passiones, tamen ordinatur infra iustitiam. Unde philosophus dicit, in I Rhetoric., quod *necesse est maximas esse virtutes, quae sunt aliis honoratissimae, siquidem est virtus potentia benefactiva. Propter hoc, fortes et iustos maxime honorant, haec quidem enim in bello,* scilicet fortitudo; *haec autem,* scilicet iustitia, *et in bello et in pace utilis est.* Post fortitudinem autem ordinatur temperantia, quae subiicit rationi appetitum circa ea quae immediate ordinantur ad vitam, vel in eodem secundum numerum, vel in eodem secundum speciem, scilicet in cibis et venereis. Et sic istae tres virtutes, simul cum prudentia, dicuntur esse principales etiam dignitate. Secundum quid autem dicitur aliqua virtus esse maior, secundum quod adminiculum vel ornamentum praebet principali virtuti. Sicut substantia est simpliciter dignior accidente; aliquod tamen accidens est secundum quid dignius substantia, inquantum perficit substantiam in aliquo esse accidentali.

AD PRIMUM ergo dicendum quod actus liberalitatis oportet quod fundetur super actum iustitiae, *non enim esset liberalis datio, si non de proprio daret,* ut in II Polit. dicitur. Unde liberalitas sine iustitia esse non posset, quae secernit *suum* a *non suo.* Iustitia autem potest esse sine liberalitate. Unde iustitia simpliciter est maior liberalitate, tanquam communior, et fundamentum ipsius, liberalitas autem est secundum quid maior, cum sit quidam ornatus iustitiae, et complementum eius.

AD SECUNDUM dicendum quod patientia dicitur habere *opus perfectum* in tolerantia malorum, in quibus non solum excludit iniustam vindictam, quam etiam excludit iustitia; neque solum odium quod facit caritas; neque solum iram, quod facit mansuetudo; sed etiam excludit tristitiam inordinatam, quae est radix omnium praedictorum. Et ideo in hoc est perfectior et maior, quod in hac materia extirpat radicem. Non autem est simpliciter perfectior omnibus aliis virtutibus. Quia fortitudo non solum sustinet molestias absque perturbatione, quod est patientiae, sed etiam ingerit se eis, cum opus fuerit. Unde quicumque est fortis, est patiens, sed non convertitur, est enim patientia quaedam fortitudinis pars.

passions, but is subordinate to justice. Hence the Philosopher says (Rhet. 1) that "those virtues must needs be greatest which receive the most praise: since virtue is a power of doing good. Hence the brave man and the just man are honored more than others; because the former," i.e., fortitude, "is useful in war, and the latter," i.e., justice, "both in war and in peace." After fortitude comes temperance, which subjects the appetite to reason in matters directly relating to life, in the one individual, or in the one species, *viz.* in matters of food and of sex. And so these three virtues, together with prudence, are called principal virtues, in excellence also. A virtue is said to be greater relatively, by reason of its helping or adorning a principal virtue: even as substance is more excellent simply than accident: and yet relatively some particular accident is more excellent than substance in so far as it perfects substance in some accidental mode of being.

Reply to Objection 1: The act of liberality needs to be founded on an act of justice, for "a man is not liberal in giving, unless he gives of his own" (Polit. ii, 3). Hence there could be no liberality apart from justice, which discerns between *meum* and *tuum:* whereas justice can be without liberality. Hence justice is simply greater than liberality, as being more universal, and as being its foundation: while liberality is greater relatively since it is an ornament and an addition to justice.

Reply to Objection 2: Patience is said to have "a perfect work," by enduring evils, wherein it excludes not only unjust revenge, which is also excluded by justice; not only hatred, which is also suppressed by charity; nor only anger, which is calmed by gentleness; but also inordinate sorrow, which is the root of all the above. Wherefore it is more perfect and excellent through plucking up the root in this matter. It is not, however, more perfect than all the other virtues simply. Because fortitude not only endures trouble without being disturbed, but also fights against it if necessary. Hence whoever is brave is patient; but the converse does not hold, for patience is a part of fortitude.

Ad tertium dicendum quod magnanimitas non potest esse nisi aliis virtutibus praeexistentibus, ut dicitur in IV Ethic. Unde comparatur ad alias sicut ornatus earum. Et sic secundum quid est maior omnibus aliis, non tamen simpliciter.

Reply to Objection 3: There can be no magnanimity without the other virtues, as stated in Ethic. iv, 3. Hence it is compared to them as their ornament, so that relatively it is greater than all the others, but not simply.

Articulus 5

Ad quintum sic proceditur. Videtur quod sapientia non sit maxima inter virtutes intellectuales. Imperans enim maius est eo cui imperatur. Sed prudentia videtur imperare sapientiae, dicitur enim I Ethic., quod *quales disciplinarum debitum est esse in civitatibus, et quales unumquemque addiscere, et usquequo, haec praeordinat, scilicet politica, quae ad prudentiam pertinet,* ut dicitur in VI Ethic. Cum igitur inter disciplinas etiam sapientia contineatur, videtur quod prudentia sit maior quam sapientia.

Praeterea, de ratione virtutis est quod ordinet hominem ad felicitatem, est enim virtus *dispositio perfecti ad optimum,* ut dicitur in VII Physic. Sed prudentia est *recta ratio agibilium,* per quae homo ad felicitatem perducitur, sapientia autem non considerat humanos actus, quibus ad beatitudinem pervenitur. Ergo prudentia est maior virtus quam sapientia.

Praeterea, quanto cognitio est perfectior, tanto videtur esse maior. Sed perfectiorem cognitionem habere possumus de rebus humanis, de quibus est scientia, quam de rebus divinis, de quibus est sapientia, ut distinguit Augustinus in XII de Trin., quia divina incomprehensibilia sunt, secundum illud Iob XXXVI, *ecce Deus magnus, vincens scientiam nostram.* Ergo scientia est maior virtus quam sapientia.

Praeterea, cognitio principiorum est dignior quam cognitio conclusionum. Sed sapientia concludit ex principiis indemonstrabilibus, quorum est intellectus; sicut et aliae scientiae. Ergo intellectus est maior virtus quam sapientia.

Article 5
Whether wisdom is the greatest of the intellectual virtues?

Objection 1: It would seem that wisdom is not the greatest of the intellectual virtues. Because the commander is greater than the one commanded. Now prudence seems to command wisdom, for it is stated in Ethic. i, 2 that political science, which belongs to prudence (Ethic. vi, 8), "orders that sciences should be cultivated in states, and to which of these each individual should devote himself, and to what extent." Since, then, wisdom is one of the sciences, it seems that prudence is greater than wisdom.

Objection 2: Further, it belongs to the nature of virtue to direct man to happiness: because virtue is "the disposition of a perfect thing to that which is best," as stated in Phys. vii, text. 17. Now prudence is "right reason about things to be done," whereby man is brought to happiness: whereas wisdom takes no notice of human acts, whereby man attains happiness. Therefore prudence is a greater virtue than wisdom.

Objection 3: Further, the more perfect knowledge is, the greater it seems to be. Now we can have more perfect knowledge of human affairs, which are the subject of science, than of Divine things, which are the object of wisdom, which is the distinction given by Augustine (De Trin. xii, 14): because Divine things are incomprehensible, according to Job 26:26: "Behold God is great, exceeding our knowledge." Therefore science is a greater virtue than wisdom.

Objection 4: Further, knowledge of principles is more excellent than knowledge of conclusions. But wisdom draws conclusions from indemonstrable principles which are the object of the virtue of understanding, even as other sciences do. Therefore understanding is a greater virtue than wisdom.

I-II, q. 66, a. 5, s. c.

SED CONTRA est quod philosophus dicit, in VI Ethic., quod sapientia est sicut *caput* inter *virtutes intellectuales.*

RESPONDEO dicendum quod, sicut dictum est, magnitudo virtutis secundum suam speciem, consideratur ex obiecto. Obiectum autem sapientiae praecellit inter obiecta omnium virtutum intellectualium, considerat enim causam altissimam, quae Deus est, ut dicitur in principio Metaphys. Et quia per causam iudicatur de effectu, et per causam superiorem de causis inferioribus; inde est quod sapientia habet iudicium de omnibus aliis virtutibus intellectualibus; et eius est ordinare omnes; et ipsa est quasi architectonica respectu omnium.

AD PRIMUM ergo dicendum quod, cum prudentia sit circa res humanas, sapientia vero circa causam altissimam; impossibile est quod prudentia sit maior virtus quam sapientia, *nisi,* ut dicitur in VI Ethic., *maximum eorum quae sunt in mundo, esset homo.* Unde dicendum est, sicut in eodem libro dicitur, quod prudentia non imperat ipsi sapientiae, sed potius e converso, quia *spiritualis iudicat omnia, et ipse a nemine iudicatur,* ut dicitur I ad Cor. II. Non enim prudentia habet se intromittere de altissimis, quae considerat sapientia, sed imperat de his quae ordinantur ad sapientiam, scilicet quomodo homines debeant ad sapientiam pervenire. Unde in hoc est prudentia, seu politica, ministra sapientiae, introducit enim ad eam, praeparans ei viam, sicut ostiarius ad regem.

AD SECUNDUM dicendum quod prudentia considerat ea quibus pervenitur ad felicitatem, sed sapientia considerat ipsum obiectum felicitatis, quod est altissimum intelligibile. Et si quidem esset perfecta consideratio sapientiae respectu sui obiecti, esset perfecta felicitas in actu sapientiae. Sed quia actus sapientiae in hac vita est imperfectus respectu principalis obiecti, quod est Deus; ideo actus sapientiae est quaedam inchoatio seu participatio futurae felicitatis. Et sic propinquius se habet ad felicitatem quam prudentia.

AD TERTIUM dicendum quod, sicut philosophus dicit, in I de anima, *una notitia praefertur alteri aut ex eo quod est nobiliorum, aut propter certitudinem.* Si igitur subiecta sint aequalia in

EQUALITY AMONG THE VIRTUES

On the contrary, The Philosopher says (Ethic. vi, 7) that wisdom is "the head" among "the intellectual virtues."

I answer that, As stated above (I-II, q. 66, a. 3), the greatness of a virtue, as to its species, is taken from its object. Now the object of wisdom surpasses the objects of all the intellectual virtues: because wisdom considers the Supreme Cause, which is God, as stated at the beginning of the Metaphysics. And since it is by the cause that we judge of an effect, and by the higher cause that we judge of the lower effects; hence it is that wisdom exercises judgment over all the other intellectual virtues, directs them all, and is the architect of them all.

Reply to Objection 1: Since prudence is about human affairs, and wisdom about the Supreme Cause, it is impossible for prudence to be a greater virtue than wisdom, "unless," as stated in Ethic. vi, 7, "man were the greatest thing in the world." Wherefore we must say, as stated in the same book (Ethic. vi), that prudence does not command wisdom, but vice versa: because "the spiritual man judgeth all things; and he himself is judged by no man" (1 Cor. 2:15). For prudence has no business with supreme matters which are the object of wisdom: but its command covers things directed to wisdom, *viz.* how men are to obtain wisdom. Wherefore prudence, or political science, is, in this way, the servant of wisdom; for it leads to wisdom, preparing the way for her, as the doorkeeper for the king.

Reply to Objection 2: Prudence considers the means of acquiring happiness, but wisdom considers the very object of happiness, *viz.* the Supreme Intelligible. And if indeed the consideration of wisdom were perfect in respect of its object, there would be perfect happiness in the act of wisdom: but as, in this life, the act of wisdom is imperfect in respect of its principal object, which is God, it follows that the act of wisdom is a beginning or participation of future happiness, so that wisdom is nearer than prudence to happiness.

Reply to Objection 3: As the Philosopher says (De Anima i, text. 1), "one knowledge is preferable to another, either because it is about a higher object, or because it is more certain." Hence if the objects be equally

bonitate et nobilitate, illa quae est certior, erit maior virtus. Sed illa quae est minus certa de altioribus et maioribus, praefertur ei quae est magis certa de inferioribus rebus. Unde philosophus dicit, in II de caelo, quod *magnum est de rebus caelestibus aliquid posse cognoscere etiam debili et topica ratione.* Et in I de partibus Animal., dicit quod *amabile est magis parvum aliquid cognoscere de rebus nobilioribus quam multa cognoscere de rebus ignobilioribus.* Sapientia igitur ad quam pertinet Dei cognitio, homini, maxime in statu huius vitae, non potest perfecte advenire, ut sit quasi eius possessio; sed hoc *solius Dei est,* ut dicitur in I Metaphys. Sed tamen illa modica cognitio quae per sapientiam de Deo haberi potest, omni alii cognitioni praefertur.

good and sublime, that virtue will be greater which possesses more certain knowledge. But a virtue which is less certain about a higher and better object, is preferable to that which is more certain about an object of inferior degree. Wherefore the Philosopher says (De Coelo ii, text. 60) that "it is a great thing to be able to know something about celestial beings, though it be based on weak and probable reasoning"; and again (De Part. Animal. i, 5) that "it is better to know a little about sublime things, than much about mean things." Accordingly wisdom, to which knowledge about God pertains, is beyond the reach of man, especially in this life, so as to be his possession: for this "belongs to God alone" (Metaph. i, 2): and yet this little knowledge about God which we can have through wisdom is preferable to all other knowledge.

AD QUARTUM dicendum quod veritas et cognitio principiorum indemonstrabilium dependet ex ratione terminorum, cognito enim quid est totum et quid pars, statim cognoscitur quod omne totum est maius sua parte. Cognoscere autem rationem entis et non entis, et totius et partis, et aliorum quae consequuntur ad ens, ex quibus sicut ex terminis constituuntur principia indemonstrabilia, pertinet ad sapientiam, quia ens commune est proprius effectus causae altissimae, scilicet Dei. Et ideo sapientia non solum utitur principiis indemonstrabilibus, quorum est intellectus, concludendo ex eis, sicut aliae scientiae; sed etiam iudicando de eis, et disputando contra negantes. Unde sequitur quod sapientia sit maior virtus quam intellectus.

Reply to Objection 4: The truth and knowledge of indemonstrable principles depends on the meaning of the terms: for as soon as we know what is a whole, and what is a part, we know at once that every whole is greater than its part. Now to know the meaning of being and non-being, of whole and part, and of other things consequent to being, which are the terms whereof indemonstrable principles are constituted, is the function of wisdom: since universal being is the proper effect of the Supreme Cause, which is God. And so wisdom makes use of indemonstrable principles which are the object of understanding, not only by drawing conclusions from them, as other sciences do, but also by passing its judgment on them, and by vindicating them against those who deny them. Hence it follows that wisdom is a greater virtue than understanding.

ARTICULUS 6

ARTICLE 6
Whether charity is the greatest of the theological virtues?

AD SEXTUM sic proceditur. Videtur quod caritas non sit maxima inter virtutes theologicas. Cum enim fides sit in intellectu, spes autem et caritas in vi appetitiva, ut supra dictum est; videtur quod fides comparetur ad spem et caritatem, sicut virtus intellectualis ad moralem. Sed virtus intellectualis est

Objection 1: It would seem that charity is not the greatest of the theological virtues. Because, since faith is in the intellect, while hope and charity are in the appetitive power, it seems that faith is compared to hope and charity, as intellectual to moral virtue. Now intellectual virtue is

maior morali, ut ex dictis patet. Ergo fides est maior spe et caritate.

Praeterea, quod se habet ex additione ad aliud, videtur esse maius eo. Sed spes, ut videtur, se habet ex additione ad caritatem, praesupponit enim spes amorem, ut Augustinus dicit in Enchirid.; addit autem quendam motum protensionis in rem amatam. Ergo spes est maior caritate.

Praeterea, causa est potior effectu. Sed fides et spes sunt causa caritatis, dicitur enim Matth. I, in Glossa, quod *fides generat spem, et spes caritatem*. Ergo fides et spes sunt maiores caritate.

Sed contra est quod apostolus dicit, I ad Cor. XIII, *nunc autem manent fides, spes, caritas, tria haec; maior autem horum est caritas.*

Respondeo dicendum quod, sicut supra dictum est, magnitudo virtutis secundum suam speciem, consideratur ex obiecto. Cum autem tres virtutes theologicae respiciant Deum sicut proprium obiectum, non potest una earum dici maior altera ex hoc quod sit circa maius obiectum; sed ex eo quod una se habet propinquius ad obiectum quam alia. Et hoc modo caritas est maior aliis. Nam aliae important in sui ratione quandam distantiam ab obiecto, est enim fides de non visis, spes autem de non habitis. Sed amor caritatis est de eo quod iam habetur, est enim amatum quodammodo in amante, et etiam amans per affectum trahitur ad unionem amati; propter quod dicitur I Ioan. IV, *qui manet in caritate, in Deo manet, et Deus in eo.*

Ad primum ergo dicendum quod non hoc modo se habent fides et spes ad caritatem, sicut prudentia ad virtutem moralem. Et hoc propter duo. Primo quidem, quia virtutes theologicae habent obiectum quod est supra animam humanam, sed prudentia et virtutes morales sunt circa ea quae sunt infra hominem. In his autem quae sunt supra hominem, nobilior est dilectio quam cognitio. Perficitur enim cognitio, secundum quod cognita sunt in cognoscente, dilectio vero, secundum

greater than moral virtue, as was made evident above (I-II, q. 62, a. 3). Therefore faith is greater than hope and charity.

Objection 2: Further, when two things are added together, the result is greater than either one. Now hope results from something added to charity; for it presupposes love, as Augustine says (Enchiridion viii), and it adds a certain movement of stretching forward to the beloved. Therefore hope is greater than charity.

Objection 3: Further, a cause is more noble than its effect. Now faith and hope are the cause of charity: for a gloss on Mat. 1:3 says that "faith begets hope, and hope charity." Therefore faith and hope are greater than charity.

On the contrary, The Apostle says (1 Cor. 13:13): "Now there remain faith, hope, charity, these three; but the greatest of these is charity."

I answer that, As stated above (I-II, q. 66, a. 3), the greatness of a virtue, as to its species, is taken from its object. Now, since the three theological virtues look at God as their proper object, it cannot be said that any one of them is greater than another by reason of its having a greater object, but only from the fact that it approaches nearer than another to that object; and in this way charity is greater than the others. Because the others, in their very nature, imply a certain distance from the object: since faith is of what is not seen, and hope is of what is not possessed. But the love of charity is of that which is already possessed: since the beloved is, in a manner, in the lover, and, again, the lover is drawn by desire to union with the beloved; hence it is written (1 Jn. 4:16): "He that abideth in charity, abideth in God, and God in him."

Reply to Objection 1: Faith and hope are not related to charity in the same way as prudence to moral virtue; and for two reasons. First, because the theological virtues have an object surpassing the human soul: whereas prudence and the moral virtues are about things beneath man. Now in things that are above man, to love them is more excellent than to know them. Because knowledge is perfected by the known being in the knower: whereas love is perfected by

quod diligens trahitur ad rem dilectam. Id autem quod est supra hominem, nobilius est in seipso quam sit in homine, quia unumquodque est in altero per modum eius in quo est. E converso autem est in his quae sunt infra hominem. Secundo, quia prudentia moderatur motus appetitivos ad morales virtutes pertinentes, sed fides non moderatur motum appetitivum tendentem in Deum, qui pertinet ad virtutes theologicas; sed solum ostendit obiectum. Motus autem appetitivus in obiectum, excedit cognitionem humanam; secundum illud ad Ephes. III, *supereminentem scientiae caritatem Christi*.

AD SECUNDUM dicendum quod spes praesupponit amorem eius quod quis adipisci se sperat, qui est amor concupiscentiae, quo quidem amore magis se amat qui concupiscit bonum, quam aliquid aliud. Caritas autem importat amorem amicitiae, ad quam pervenitur spe, ut supra dictum est.

AD TERTIUM dicendum quod causa perficiens est potior effectu, non autem causa disponens. Sic enim calor ignis esset potior quam anima, ad quam disponit materiam, quod patet esse falsum. Sic autem fides generat spem, et spes caritatem, secundum scilicet quod una disponit ad alteram.

the lover being drawn to the beloved. Now that which is above man is more excellent in itself than in man: since a thing is contained according to the mode of the container. But it is the other way about in things beneath man. Secondly, because prudence moderates the appetitive movements pertaining to the moral virtues, whereas faith does not moderate the appetitive movement tending to God, which movement belongs to the theological virtues: it only shows the object. And this appetitive movement towards its object surpasses human knowledge, according to Eph. 3:19: "The charity of Christ which surpasseth all knowledge."

Reply to Objection 2: Hope presupposes love of that which a man hopes to obtain; and such love is love of concupiscence, whereby he who desires good, loves himself rather than something else. On the other hand, charity implies love of friendship, to which we are led by hope, as stated above (I-II, q. 62, a. 4).

Reply to Objection 3: An efficient cause is more noble than its effect: but not a disposing cause. For otherwise the heat of fire would be more noble than the soul, to which the heat disposes the matter. It is in this way that faith begets hope, and hope charity: in the sense, to wit, that one is a disposition to the other.

Question 67
Of the Duration of Virtues After This Life

We must now consider the duration of virtues after this life, under which head there are six points of inquiry: 1. Whether the moral virtues remain after this life? 2. Whether the intellectual virtues remain? 3. Whether faith remains? 4. Whether hope remains? 5. Whether anything remains of faith or hope? 6. Whether charity remains?

Article 1
Whether the moral virtues remain after this life?

Objection 1: It would seem that the moral virtues doe not remain after this life. For in the future state of glory men will be like angels, according to Mat. 22:30. But it is absurd to put moral virtues in the angels,* as stated in Ethic. x, 8. Therefore neither in man will there be moral virtues after this life.

Objection 2: Further, moral virtues perfect man in the active life. But the active life does not remain after this life: for Gregory says (Moral. iv, 18): "The works of the active life pass away from the body." Therefore moral virtues do not remain after this life.

Objection 3: Further, temperance and fortitude, which are moral virtues, are in the irrational parts of the soul, as the Philosopher states (Ethic. iii, 10). Now the irrational parts of the soul are corrupted, when the body is corrupted: since they are acts of bodily organs. Therefore it seems that the moral virtues do not remain after this life.

On the contrary, It is written (Wis. 1:15) that "justice is perpetual and immortal."

I answer that, As Augustine says (De Trin. xiv, 9), Cicero held that the cardinal virtues do not remain after this life; and that, as Augustine says (De Trin. xiv, 9), "in the other life men are made happy by the mere knowledge of that nature, than which nothing is better or more lovable, that Nature, to wit, which created all others." Afterwards he concludes that these four virtues remain in the future life, but after a different

---

* "Whatever relates to moral action is petty, and unworthy of the gods" (Ethic. x, 8).

modo. Ad cuius evidentiam, sciendum est quod in huiusmodi virtutibus aliquid est formale; et aliquid quasi materiale. Materiale quidem est in his virtutibus inclinatio quaedam partis appetitivae ad passiones vel operationes secundum modum aliquem. Sed quia iste modus determinatur a ratione, ideo formale in omnibus virtutibus est ipse ordo rationis. Sic igitur dicendum est quod huiusmodi virtutes morales in futura vita non manent, quantum ad id quod est materiale in eis. Non enim habebunt in futura vita locum concupiscentiae et delectationes ciborum et venereorum; neque etiam timores et audaciae circa pericula mortis; neque etiam distributiones et communicationes rerum quae veniunt in usum praesentis vitae. Sed quantum ad id quod est formale, remanebunt in beatis perfectissimae post hanc vitam, inquantum ratio uniuscuiusque rectissima erit circa ea quae ad ipsum pertinent secundum statum illum; et vis appetitiva omnino movebitur secundum ordinem rationis, in his quae ad statum illum pertinent. Unde Augustinus ibidem dicit quod *prudentia ibi erit sine ullo periculo erroris; fortitudo, sine molestia tolerandorum malorum; temperantia, sine repugnatione libidinum. Ut prudentiae sit nullum bonum Deo praeponere vel aequare; fortitudinis, ei firmissime cohaerere; temperantiae, nullo defectu noxio delectari.* De iustitia vero manifestius est quem actum ibi habebit, scilicet *esse subditum Deo,* quia etiam in hac vita ad iustitiam pertinet esse subditum superiori.

AD PRIMUM ergo dicendum quod philosophus loquitur ibi de huiusmodi virtutibus moralibus, quantum ad id quod materiale est in eis, sicut de iustitia, quantum ad *commutationes et depositiones;* de fortitudine, quantum ad *terribilia et pericula;* de temperantia, quantum ad *concupiscentias pravas.*

Et similiter dicendum est ad secundum. Ea enim quae sunt activae vitae, materialiter se habent ad virtutes.

AD TERTIUM dicendum quod status post hanc vitam est duplex, unus quidem ante resurrectionem, quando animae erunt a corporibus separatae; alius autem post resurrectionem, quando animae iterato

manner. In order to make this evident, we must note that in these virtues there is a formal element, and a quasi-material element. The material element in these virtues is a certain inclination of the appetitive part to the passions and operations according to a certain mode: and since this mode is fixed by reason, the formal element is precisely this order of reason. Accordingly we must say that these moral virtues do not remain in the future life, as regards their material element. For in the future life there will be no concupiscences and pleasures in matters of food and sex; nor fear and daring about dangers of death; nor distributions and commutations of things employed in this present life. But, as regards the formal element, they will remain most perfect, after this life, in the Blessed, in as much as each one's reason will have most perfect rectitude in regard to things concerning him in respect of that state of life: and his appetitive power will be moved entirely according to the order of reason, in things pertaining to that same state. Hence Augustine says (De Trin. xiv, 9) that "prudence will be there without any danger of error; fortitude, without the anxiety of bearing with evil; temperance, without the rebellion of the desires: so that prudence will neither prefer nor equal any good to God; fortitude will adhere to Him most steadfastly; and temperance will delight in Him Who knows no imperfection." As to justice, it is yet more evident what will be its act in that life, *viz.* "to be subject to God": because even in this life subjection to a superior is part of justice.

Reply to Objection 1: The Philosopher is speaking there of these moral virtues, as to their material element; thus he speaks of justice, as regards "commutations and distributions"; of fortitude, as to "matters of terror and danger"; of temperance, in respect of "lewd desires."

The same applies to the Second Objection. For those things that concern the active life, belong to the material element of the virtues.

Reply to Objection 3: There is a twofold state after this life; one before the resurrection, during which the soul will be separate from the body; the other, after the resurrection, when the souls will be

reunited to their bodies. In this state of resurrection, the irrational powers will be in the bodily organs, just as they now are. Hence it will be possible for fortitude to be in the irascible, and temperance in the concupiscible part, in so far as each power will be perfectly disposed to obey the reason. But in the state preceding the resurrection, the irrational parts will not be in the soul actually, but only radically in its essence, as stated in the I, q. 77, a. 8. Wherefore neither will these virtues be actually, but only in their root, i.e., in the reason and will, wherein are certain nurseries of these virtues, as stated above (I-II, q. 63, a. 1). Justice, however, will remain because it is in the will. Hence of justice it is specially said that it is "perpetual and immortal"; both by reason of its subject, since the will is incorruptible; and because its act will not change, as stated.

ARTICLE 2
Whether the intellectual virtues remain after this life?

Objection 1: It would seem that the intellectual virtues do not remain after this life. For the Apostle says (1 Cor. 13:8, 9) that "knowledge shall be destroyed," and he states the reason to be because "we know in part." Now just as the knowledge of science is in part, i.e., imperfect; so also is the knowledge of the other intellectual virtues, as long as this life lasts. Therefore all the intellectual virtues will cease after this life.

Objection 2: Further, the Philosopher says (Categor. vi) that since science is a habit, it is a quality difficult to remove: for it is not easily lost, except by reason of some great change or sickness. But no bodily change is so great as that of death. Therefore science and the other intellectual virtues do not remain after death.

Objection 3: Further, the intellectual virtues perfect the intellect so that it may perform its proper act well. Now there seems to be no act of the intellect after this life, since "the soul understands nothing without a phantasm" (De Anima iii, text. 30); and, after this life, the phantasms do not remain, since their only subject is an

organis corporeis. Ergo virtutes intellectuales non manent post hanc vitam.

SED CONTRA est quod firmior est cognitio universalium et necessariorum, quam particularium et contingentium. Sed in homine remanet post hanc vitam cognitio particularium contingentium, puta eorum quae quis fecit vel passus est; secundum illud Luc. XVI, *recordare quia recepisti bona in vita tua, et Lazarus similiter mala.* Ergo multo magis remanet cognitio universalium et necessariorum, quae pertinent ad scientiam et ad alias virtutes intellectuales.

RESPONDEO dicendum quod, sicut in primo dictum est, quidam posuerunt quod species intelligibiles non permanent in intellectu possibili nisi quandiu actu intelligit, nec est aliqua conservatio specierum, cessante consideratione actuali, nisi in viribus sensitivis, quae sunt actus corporalium organorum, scilicet in imaginativa et memorativa. Huiusmodi autem vires corrumpuntur, corrupto corpore. Et ideo secundum hoc, scientia nullo modo post hanc vitam remanebit, corpore corrupto; neque aliqua alia intellectualis virtus. Sed haec opinio est contra sententiam Aristotelis, qui in III de anima dicit quod *intellectus possibilis est in actu, cum fit singula, sicut sciens; cum tamen sit in potentia ad considerandum in actu.* Est etiam contra rationem, quia species intelligibiles recipiuntur in intellectu possibili immobiliter, secundum modum recipientis. Unde et intellectus possibilis dicitur *locus specierum,* quasi species intelligibiles conservans. Sed phantasmata, ad quae respiciendo homo intelligit in hac vita, applicando ad ipsa species intelligibiles, ut in primo dictum est, corrupto corpore corrumpuntur. Unde quantum ad ipsa phantasmata, quae sunt quasi materialia in virtutibus intellectualibus, virtutes intellectuales destruuntur, destructo corpore, sed quantum ad species intelligibiles, quae sunt in intellectu possibili, virtutes intellectuales manent. Species autem

organ of the body. Therefore the intellectual virtues do not remain after this life.

On the contrary, The knowledge of what is universal and necessary is more constant than that of particular and contingent things. Now the knowledge of contingent particulars remains in man after this life; for instance, the knowledge of what one has done or suffered, according to Lk. 16:25: "Son, remember that thou didst receive good things in thy life-time, and likewise Lazarus evil things." Much more, therefore, does the knowledge of universal and necessary things remain, which belong to science and the other intellectual virtues.

I answer that, As stated in the I, q. 79, a. 6, some have held that the intelligible species do not remain in the passive intellect except when it actually understands; and that so long as actual consideration ceases, the species are not preserved save in the sensitive powers which are acts of bodily organs, *viz.* in the powers of imagination and memory. Now these powers cease when the body is corrupted: and consequently, according to this opinion, neither science nor any other intellectual virtue will remain after this life when once the body is corrupted. But this opinion is contrary to the mind of Aristotle, who states (De Anima iii, text. 8) that "the possible intellect is in act when it is identified with each thing as knowing it; and yet, even then, it is in potentiality to consider it actually." It is also contrary to reason, because intelligible species are contained by the possible intellect immovably, according to the mode of their container. Hence the possible intellect is called "the abode of the species" (De Anima iii) because it preserves the intelligible species. And yet the phantasms, by turning to which man understands in this life, by applying the intelligible species to them as stated in the I, q. 84, a. 7; q. 85, a. 1, ad 5, cease as soon as the body is corrupted. Hence, so far as the phantasms are concerned, which are the quasi-material element in the intellectual virtues, these latter cease when the body is destroyed: but as regards the intelligible species, which are in the possible intellect, the intellectual virtues remain. Now the species

se habent in virtutibus intellectualibus sicut formales. Unde intellectuales virtutes manent post hanc vitam, quantum ad id quod est formale in eis, non autem quantum ad id quod est materiale, sicut et de moralibus dictum est.

Ad primum ergo dicendum quod verbum apostoli est intelligendum quantum ad id quod est materiale in scientia, et quantum ad modum intelligendi, quia scilicet neque **phantasmata remanebunt, destructo corpore**; neque erit usus scientiae per conversionem ad phantasmata.

Ad secundum dicendum quod per aegritudinem corrumpitur habitus scientiae quantum ad id quod est materiale in eo, scilicet quantum ad phantasmata, non autem quantum ad species intelligibiles, quae sunt in intellectu possibili.

Ad tertium dicendum quod anima separata post mortem habet alium modum intelligendi quam per conversionem ad phantasmata, ut in primo dictum est. Et sic scientia manet, non tamen secundum eundem modum operandi, sicut et de virtutibus moralibus dictum est.

are the quasi-formal element of the intellectual virtues. Therefore these remain after this life, as regards their formal element, just as we have stated concerning the moral virtues (I-II, q. 67, a. 1).

Reply to Objection 1: The saying of the Apostle is to be understood as referring to the material element in science, and to the mode of understanding; because, to it, **neither do the phantasms remain, when the body is destroyed**; nor will science be applied by turning to the phantasms.

Reply to Objection 2: Sickness destroys the habit of science as to its material element, *viz.* the phantasms, but not as to the intelligible species, which are in the possible intellect.

Reply to Objection 3: As stated in the I, q. 89, a. 1, the separated soul has a mode of understanding, other than by turning to the phantasms. Consequently science remains, yet not as to the same mode of operation; as we have stated concerning the moral virtues (I-II, q. 67, a. 1).

Articulus 3

Ad tertium sic proceditur. Videtur quod fides maneat post hanc vitam. Nobilior enim est fides quam scientia. Sed scientia manet post hanc vitam, ut dictum est. Ergo et fides.

Praeterea, I ad Cor. III, dicitur, *fundamentum aliud nemo potest ponere, praeter id quod positum est, quod est Christus Iesus,* idest fides Christi Iesu. Sed sublato fundamento, non remanet id quod superaedificatur. Ergo, si fides non remanet post hanc vitam, nulla alia virtus remaneret.

Praeterea, cognitio fidei et cognitio gloriae differunt secundum perfectum et imperfectum. Sed cognitio imperfecta potest esse simul cum cognitione perfecta, sicut in angelo simul potest esse cognitio vespertina cum cognitione matutina; et aliquis homo

Article 3
Whether faith remains after this life?

Objection 1: It would seem that faith remains after this life. Because faith is more excellent than science. Now science remains after this life, as stated above (I-II, q. 67, a. 2). Therefore faith remains also.

Objection 2: Further, it is written (1 Cor. 3:11): "Other foundation no man can lay, but that which is laid; which is Christ Jesus," i.e., faith in Jesus Christ. Now if the foundation is removed, that which is built upon it remains no more. Therefore, if faith remains not after this life, no other virtue remains.

Objection 3: Further, the knowledge of faith and the knowledge of glory differ as perfect from imperfect. Now imperfect knowledge is compatible with perfect knowledge: thus in an angel there can be "evening" and "morning" knowledge;[*] and a man

---

[*] Cf. I, q. 58, a. 6.

potest simul habere de eadem conclusione scientiam per syllogismum demonstrativum, et opinionem per syllogismum dialecticum. Ergo etiam fides simul esse potest, post hanc vitam, cum cognitione gloriae.

SED CONTRA est quod apostolus dicit, II ad Cor. V, *quandiu sumus in corpore, peregrinamur a domino, per fidem enim ambulamus, et non per speciem.* Sed illi qui sunt in gloria, non peregrinantur a domino, sed sunt ei praesentes. Ergo fides non manet post hanc vitam in gloria.

RESPONDEO dicendum quod oppositio est per se et propria causa quod unum excludatur ab alio, inquantum scilicet in omnibus oppositis includitur oppositio affirmationis et negationis. Invenitur autem in quibusdam oppositio secundum contrarias formas, sicut in coloribus album et nigrum. In quibusdam autem, secundum perfectum et imperfectum, unde in alterationibus magis et minus accipiuntur ut contraria, ut cum de minus calido fit magis calidum, ut dicitur in V Physic. Et quia perfectum et imperfectum opponuntur, impossibile est quod simul, secundum idem, sit perfectio et imperfectio. Est autem considerandum quod imperfectio quidem quandoque est de ratione rei, et pertinet ad speciem ipsius, sicut defectus rationis pertinet ad rationem speciei equi vel bovis. Et quia unum et idem numero manens non potest transferri de una specie in aliam, inde est quod, tali imperfectione sublata, tollitur species rei, sicut iam non esset bos vel equus, si esset rationalis. Quandoque vero imperfectio non pertinet ad rationem speciei, sed accidit individuo secundum aliquid aliud, sicut alicui homini quandoque accidit defectus rationis, inquantum impeditur in eo rationis usus, propter somnum vel ebrietatem vel aliquid huiusmodi. Patet autem quod, tali imperfectione remota, nihilominus substantia rei manet. Manifestum est autem quod imperfectio cognitionis est de ratione fidei. Ponitur enim in eius definitione, fides enim est *substantia sperandarum rerum,*

can have science through a demonstrative syllogism, together with opinion through a probable syllogism, about one same conclusion. Therefore after this life faith also is compatible with the knowledge of glory.

On the contrary, The Apostle says (2 Cor. 5:6, 7): "While we are in the body, we are absent from the Lord: for we walk by faith and not by sight." But those who are in glory are not absent from the Lord, but present to Him. Therefore after this life faith does not remain in the life of glory.

I answer that, Opposition is of itself the proper cause of one thing being excluded from another, in so far, to wit, as wherever two things are opposite to one another, we find opposition of affirmation and negation. Now in some things we find opposition in respect of contrary forms; thus in colors we find white and black. In others we find opposition in respect of perfection and imperfection: wherefore in alterations, more and less are considered to be contraries, as when a thing from being less hot is made more hot (Phys. v, text. 19). And since perfect and imperfect are opposite to one another, it is impossible for perfection and imperfection to affect the same thing at the same time. Now we must take note that sometimes imperfection belongs to a thing's very nature, and belongs to its species: even as lack of reason belongs to the very specific nature of a horse and an ox. And since a thing, so long as it remains the same identically, cannot pass from one species to another, it follows that if such an imperfection be removed, the species of that thing is changed: even as it would no longer be an ox or a horse, were it to be rational. Sometimes, however, the imperfection does not belong to the specific nature, but is accidental to the individual by reason of something else; even as sometimes lack of reason is accidental to a man, because he is asleep, or because he is drunk, or for some like reason; and it is evident, that if such an imperfection be removed, the thing remains substantially. Now it is clear that imperfect knowledge belongs to the very nature of faith: for it is included in its definition; faith being defined as "the substance of things to be hoped for,

argumentum non apparentium, ut dicitur ad Heb. XI. Et Augustinus dicit, *quid est fides? Credere quod non vides.* Quod autem cognitio sit sine apparitione vel visione, hoc ad im-perfectionem cognitionis pertinet. Et sic imperfectio cognitionis est de ratione fidei. Unde manifestum est quod fides non potest esse perfecta cognitio, eadem numero manens. Sed ulterius considerandum est utrum simul possit esse cum cognitione perfecta, **nihil enim prohibet aliquam cognitionem imperfectam simul esse aliquando cum cognitione perfecta.** Est igitur considerandum quod cognitio potest esse imperfecta tripliciter, uno modo, ex parte obiecti cognoscibilis; alio modo, ex parte medii; tertio modo, ex parte subiecti. Ex parte quidem obiecti cognoscibilis, differunt secundum perfectum et imperfectum cognitio matutina et vespertina in angelis, nam cognitio matutina est de rebus secundum quod habent esse in verbo; cognitio autem vespertina est de eis secundum quod habent esse in propria natura, quod est imperfectum respectu primi esse. Ex parte vero medii, differunt secundum perfectum et imperfectum cognitio quae est de aliqua conclusione per medium demonstrativum, et per medium probabile. Ex parte vero subiecti differunt secundum perfectum et imperfectum opinio, fides et scientia. Nam de ratione opinionis est quod accipiatur unum cum formidine alterius oppositi, unde non habet firmam inhaesionem. De ratione vero scientiae est quod habeat firmam inhaesionem cum visione intellectiva, habet enim certitudinem procedentem ex intellectu principiorum. Fides autem medio modo se habet, excedit enim opinionem, in hoc quod habet firmam inhaesionem; deficit vero a scientia, in hoc quod non habet visionem. Manifestum est autem quod perfectum et imperfectum non possunt simul esse secundum idem, sed ea quae differunt secundum perfectum et imperfectum, secundum aliquid idem possunt simul esse in aliquo alio eodem. Sic igitur cognitio perfecta et imperfecta ex parte obiecti, nullo modo possunt esse de eodem obiecto.

the evidence of things that appear not" (Heb. 11:1). Wherefore Augustine says (Tract. xl in Joan.): "Where is faith? Believing without seeing." But it is an imperfect knowledge that is of things unapparent or unseen. Consequently imperfect knowledge belongs to the very nature of faith: therefore it is clear that the knowledge of faith cannot be perfect and remain identically the same. But we must also consider whether it is compatible with **perfect knowledge: for there is nothing** to prevent some kind of imperfect knowledge from being sometimes with perfect knowledge. Accordingly we must observe that knowledge can be imperfect in three ways: first, on the part of the knowable object; secondly, on the part of the medium; thirdly, on the part of the subject. The difference of perfect and imperfect knowledge on the part of the knowable object is seen in the "morning" and "evening" knowledge of the angels: for the "morning" knowledge is about things according to the being which they have in the Word, while the "evening" knowledge is about things according as they have being in their own natures, which being is imperfect in comparison with the First Being. On the part of the medium, perfect and imperfect knowledge are exemplified in the knowledge of a conclusion through a demonstrative medium, and through a probable medium. On the part of the subject the difference of perfect and imperfect knowledge applies to opinion, faith, and science. For it is essential to opinion that we assent to one of two opposite assertions with fear of the other, so that our adhesion is not firm: to science it is essential to have firm adhesion with intellectual vision, for science possesses certitude which results from the understanding of principles: while faith holds a middle place, for it surpasses opinion in so far as its adhesion is firm, but falls short of science in so far as it lacks vision. Now it is evident that a thing cannot be perfect and imperfect in the same respect; yet the things which differ as perfect and imperfect can be together in the same respect in one and the same other thing. Accordingly, knowledge which is perfect on the part of the object is quite incompatible with imperfect knowledge about the same object;

Possunt tamen convenire in eodem medio, et in eodem subiecto, nihil enim prohibet quod unus homo simul et semel per unum et idem medium habeat cognitionem de duobus, quorum unum est perfectum et aliud imperfectum, sicut de sanitate et aegritudine, et bono et malo. Similiter etiam impossibile est quod cognitio perfecta et imperfecta ex parte medii, conveniant in uno medio. Sed nihil prohibet quin conveniant in uno obiecto, et in uno subiecto, potest enim unus homo cognoscere eandem conclusionem per medium probabile, et demonstrativum. Et est similiter impossibile quod cognitio perfecta et imperfecta ex parte subiecti, sint simul in eodem subiecto. Fides autem in sui ratione habet imperfectionem quae est ex parte subiecti, ut scilicet credens non videat id quod credit, beatitudo autem de sui ratione habet perfectionem ex parte subiecti, ut scilicet beatus videat id quo beatificatur, ut supra dictum est. Unde manifestum est quod impossibile est quod fides maneat simul cum beatitudine in eodem subiecto.

but they are compatible with one another in respect of the same medium or the same subject: for nothing hinders a man from having at one and the same time, through one and the same medium, perfect and imperfect knowledge about two things, one perfect, the other imperfect, e.g., about health and sickness, good and evil. In like manner knowledge that is perfect on the part of the medium is incompatible with imperfect knowledge through one and the same medium: but nothing hinders them being about the same subject or in the same subject: for one man can know the same conclusions through a probable and through a demonstrative medium. Again, knowledge that is perfect on the part of the subject is incompatible with imperfect knowledge in the same subject. Now faith, of its very nature, contains an imperfection on the part of the subject, *viz.* that the believer sees not what he believes: whereas bliss, of its very nature, implies perfection on the part of the subject, *viz.* that the Blessed see that which makes them happy, as stated above (I-II, q. 3, a. 8). Hence it is manifest that faith and bliss are incompatible in one and the same subject.

AD PRIMUM ergo dicendum quod fides est nobilior quam scientia, ex parte obiecti, quia eius obiectum est veritas prima. Sed scientia habet perfectiorem modum cognoscendi, qui non repugnat perfectioni beatitudinis, scilicet visioni, sicut repugnat ei modus fidei.

Reply to Objection 1: Faith is more excellent than science, on the part of the object, because its object is the First Truth. Yet science has a more perfect mode of knowing its object, which is not incompatible with vision which is the perfection of happiness, as the mode of faith is incompatible.

AD SECUNDUM dicendum quod fides est fundamentum quantum ad id quod habet de cognitione. Et ideo quando perficietur cognitio, erit perfectius fundamentum.

AD TERTIUM patet solutio ex his quae dicta sunt.

Reply to Objection 2: Faith is the foundation in as much as it is knowledge: consequently when this knowledge is perfected, the foundation will be perfected also.

The Reply to the Third Objection is clear from what has been said.

Articulus 4

AD QUARTUM sic proceditur. Videtur quod spes maneat post mortem in statu gloriae. Spes enim nobiliori modo perficit appetitum humanum quam virtutes morales. Sed virtutes morales manent post hanc vitam, ut patet per Augustinum, in XIV de Trin. Ergo multo magis spes.

Article 4
Whether hope remains after death, in the state of glory?

Objection 1: It would seem that hope remains after death, in the state of glory. Because hope perfects the human appetite in a more excellent manner than the moral virtues. But the moral virtues remain after this life, as Augustine clearly states (De Trin. xiv, 9). Much more then does hope remain.

PRAETEREA, spei opponitur timor. Sed timor manet post hanc vitam, et in beatis quidem timor filialis, qui manet in saeculum; et in damnatis timor poenarum. Ergo spes, pari ratione, potest permanere.

PRAETEREA, sicut spes est futuri boni, ita et desiderium. Sed in beatis est desiderium futuri boni, et quantum ad gloriam corporis, quam animae beatorum desiderant, ut dicit Augustinus, XII super Gen. ad Litt.; et etiam quantum ad gloriam animae, secundum illud Eccli. XXIV, *qui edunt me, adhuc esurient, et qui bibunt me, adhuc sitient*; et I Petr. I, dicitur, *in quem desiderant angeli prospicere*. Ergo videtur quod possit esse spes post hanc vitam in beatis.

SED CONTRA est quod apostolus dicit, Rom. VIII, *quod videt quis, quid sperat?* Sed beati vident id quod est obiectum spei, scilicet Deum. Ergo non sperant.

RESPONDEO dicendum quod, sicut dictum est, id quod de ratione sui importat imperfectionem subiecti, non potest simul stare cum subiecto opposita perfectione perfecto. Sicut patet quod motus in ratione sui importat imperfectionem subiecti, est enim *actus existentis in potentia, inquantum huiusmodi*, unde quando illa potentia reducitur ad actum, iam cessat motus; non enim adhuc albatur, postquam iam aliquid factum est album. Spes autem importat motum quendam in id quod non habetur; ut patet ex his quae supra de passione spei diximus. Et ideo quando habebitur id quod speratur, scilicet divina fruitio, iam spes esse non poterit.

AD PRIMUM ergo dicendum quod spes est nobilior virtutibus moralibus quantum ad obiectum, quod est Deus. Sed actus virtutum moralium non repugnant perfectioni beatitudinis, sicut actus spei; nisi forte ratione materiae, secundum quam non manent. Non enim virtus moralis perficit appetitum solum in id quod nondum habetur; sed etiam circa id quod praesentialiter habetur.

Objection 2: Further, fear is opposed to hope. But fear remains after this life: in the Blessed, filial fear, which abides for ever—in the lost, the fear of punishment. Therefore, in a like manner, hope can remain.

Objection 3: Further, just as hope is of future good, so is desire. Now in the Blessed there is desire for future good; both for the glory of the body, which the souls of the Blessed desire, as Augustine declares (Gen. ad lit. xii, 35); and for the glory of the soul, according to Ecclus. 24:29: "They that eat me, shall yet hunger, and they that drink me, shall yet thirst," and 1 Pet. 1:12: "On Whom the angels desire to look." Therefore it seems that there can be hope in the Blessed after this life is past.

On the contrary, The Apostle says (Rom. 8:24): "What a man seeth, why doth he hope for?" But the Blessed see that which is the object of hope, *viz.* God. Therefore they do not hope.

I answer that, As stated above (I-II, q. 67, a. 3), that which, in its very nature, implies imperfection of its subject, is incompatible with the opposite perfection in that subject. Thus it is evident that movement of its very nature implies imperfection of its subject, since it is "the act of that which is in potentiality as such" (Phys. iii): so that as soon as this potentiality is brought into act, the movement ceases; for a thing does not continue to become white, when once it is made white. Now hope denotes a movement towards that which is not possessed, as is clear from what we have said above about the passion of hope (I-II, q. 40, a. 1; a. 2). Therefore when we possess that which we hope for, *viz.* the enjoyment of God, it will no longer be possible to have hope.

Reply to Objection 1: Hope surpasses the moral virtues as to its object, which is God. But the acts of the moral virtues are not incompatible with the perfection of happiness, as the act of hope is; except perhaps, as regards their matter, in respect of which they do not remain. For moral virtue perfects the appetite, not only in respect of what is not yet possessed, but also as regards something which is in our actual possession.

AD SECUNDUM dicendum quod timor est duplex, servilis et filialis, ut infra dicetur. Servilis quidem est timor poenae, qui non poterit esse in gloria, nulla possibilitate ad poenam remanente. Timor vero filialis habet duos actus, scilicet revereri Deum, et quantum ad hunc actum manet; et timere separationem ab ipso, et quantum ad hunc actum non manet. Separari enim a Deo habet rationem mali, nullum autem malum ibi timebitur, secundum illud Proverb. I, *abundantia perfruetur, malorum timore sublato.* Timor autem opponitur spei oppositione boni et mali, ut supra dictum est, et ideo timor qui remanet in gloria, non opponitur spei. In damnatis autem magis potest esse timor poenae, quam in beatis spes gloriae. Quia in damnatis erit successio poenarum, et sic remanet ibi ratio futuri, quod est obiectum timoris, sed gloria sanctorum est absque successione, secundum quandam aeternitatis participationem, in qua non est praeteritum et futurum, sed solum praesens. Et tamen nec etiam in damnatis est proprie timor. Nam sicut supra dictum est, timor nunquam est sine aliqua spe evasionis, quae omnino in damnatis non erit. Unde nec timor; nisi communiter loquendo, secundum quod quaelibet expectatio mali futuri dicitur timor.

AD TERTIUM dicendum quod quantum ad gloriam animae, non potest esse in beatis desiderium, secundum quod respicit futurum, ratione iam dicta. Dicitur autem ibi esse esuries et sitis, per remotionem fastidii, et eadem ratione dicitur esse desiderium in angelis. Respectu autem gloriae corporis, in animabus sanctorum potest quidem esse desiderium, non tamen spes, proprie loquendo, neque secundum quod spes est virtus theologica, sic enim eius obiectum est Deus, non autem aliquod bonum creatum; neque secundum quod communiter sumitur. Quia obiectum spei est arduum,ut supra dictum est, bonum autem cuius iam inevitabilem causam habemus, non comparatur ad nos in ratione ardui.

Reply to Objection 2: Fear is twofold, servile and filial, as we shall state further on (II-II, q. 19, a. 2). Servile fear regards punishment, and will be impossible in the life of glory, since there will no longer be possibility of being punished. Filial fear has two acts: one is an act of reverence to God, and with regard to this act, it remains: the other is an act of fear lest we be separated from God, and as regards this act, it does not remain. Because separation from God is in the nature of an evil: and no evil will be feared there, according to Prov. 1:33: "He . . . shall enjoy abundance without fear of evils." Now fear is opposed to hope by opposition of good and evil, as stated above (I-II, q. 23, a. 2; q. 40, a. 1), and therefore the fear which will remain in glory is not opposed to hope. In the lost there can be fear of punishment, rather than hope of glory in the Blessed. Because in the lost there will be a succession of punishments, so that the notion of something future remains there, which is the object of fear: but the glory of the saints has no succession, by reason of its being a kind of participation of eternity, wherein there is neither past nor future, but only the present. And yet, properly speaking, neither in the lost is there fear. For, as stated above (I-II, q. 42, a. 2), fear is never without some hope of escape: and the lost have no such hope. Consequently neither will there be fear in them; except speaking in a general way, in so far as any expectation of future evil is called fear.

Reply to Objection 3: As to the glory of the soul, there can be no desire in the Blessed, in so far as desire looks for something future, for the reason already given (ad 2). Yet hunger and thirst are said to be in them because they never weary, and for the same reason desire is said to be in the angels. With regard to the glory of the body, there can be desire in the souls of the saints, but not hope, properly speaking; neither as a theological virtue, for thus its object is God, and not a created good; nor in its general signification. Because the object of hope is something difficult, as stated above (I-II, q. 40, a. 1): while a good whose unerring cause we already possess, is not compared to us as something difficult.

Unde non proprie dicitur aliquis qui habet argentum, sperare se habiturum aliquid quod statim in potestate eius est ut emat. Et similiter illi qui habent gloriam animae, non proprie dicuntur sperare gloriam corporis; sed solum desiderare.

Hence he that has money is not, properly speaking, said to hope for what he can buy at once. In like manner those who have the glory of the soul are not, properly speaking, said to hope for the glory of the body, but only to desire it.

Articulus 5

Ad quintum sic proceditur. Videtur quod aliquid fidei vel spei remaneat in gloria. Remoto enim eo quod est proprium, remanet id quod est commune, sicut dicitur in libro de causis, quod, *remoto rationali, remanet vivum; et remoto vivo, remanet ens.* Sed in fide est aliquid quod habet commune cum beatitudine, scilicet ipsa cognitio, aliquid autem quod est sibi proprium, scilicet aenigma; est enim fides cognitio aenigmatica. Ergo, remoto aenigmate fidei, adhuc remanet ipsa cognitio fidei.

Praeterea, fides est quoddam spirituale lumen animae, secundum illud Ephes. I, *illuminatos oculos cordis vestri in agnitionem Dei;* sed hoc lumen est imperfectum respectu luminis gloriae, de quo dicitur in Psalmo XXXV, *in lumine tuo videbimus lumen.* Lumen autem imperfectum remanet, superveniente lumine perfecto, non enim candela extinguitur, claritate solis superveniente. Ergo videtur quod ipsum lumen fidei maneat cum lumine gloriae.

Praeterea, substantia habitus non tollitur per hoc quod subtrahitur materia, potest enim homo habitum liberalitatis retinere, etiam amissa pecunia; sed actum habere non potest. Obiectum autem fidei est veritas prima non visa. Ergo, hoc remoto per hoc quod videtur veritas prima, adhuc potest remanere ipse habitus fidei.

Sed contra est quod fides est quidam habitus simplex. Simplex autem vel totum tollitur, vel totum manet. Cum igitur fides non totaliter maneat, sed evacuetur, ut dictum est; videtur quod totaliter tollatur.

Article 5
Whether anything of faith or hope remains in glory?

Objection 1: It would seem that something of faith and hope remains in glory. For when that which is proper to a thing is removed, there remains what is common; thus it is stated in De Causis that "if you take away rational, there remains living, and when you remove living, there remains being." Now in faith there is something that it has in common with beatitude, *viz.* knowledge: and there is something proper to it, *viz.* darkness, for faith is knowledge in a dark manner. Therefore, the darkness of faith removed, the knowledge of faith still remains.

Objection 2: Further, faith is a spiritual light of the soul, according to Eph. 1:17, 18: "The eyes of your heart enlightened . . . in the knowledge of God"; yet this light is imperfect in comparison with the light of glory, of which it is written (Ps. 35:10): "In Thy light we shall see light." Now an imperfect light remains when a perfect light supervenes: for a candle is not extinguished when the sun's rays appear. Therefore it seems that the light of faith itself remains with the light of glory.

Objection 3: Further, the substance of a habit does not cease through the withdrawal of its matter: for a man may retain the habit of liberality, though he have lost his money: yet he cannot exercise the act. Now the object of faith is the First Truth as unseen. Therefore when this ceases through being seen, the habit of faith can still remain.

On the contrary, Faith is a simple habit. Now a simple thing is either withdrawn entirely, or remains entirely. Since therefore faith does not remain entirely, but is taken away as stated above (I-II, q. 67, a. 3), it seems that it is withdrawn entirely.

RESPONDEO dicendum quod quidam dixerunt quod spes totaliter tollitur, fides autem partim tollitur, scilicet quantum ad aenigma, et partim manet, scilicet quantum ad substantiam cognitionis. Quod quidem si sic intelligatur quod maneat non idem numero, sed idem genere, verissime dictum est, fides enim cum visione patriae convenit in genere, quod est cognitio. Spes autem non convenit cum beatitudine in genere, comparatur enim spes ad beatitudinis fruitionem, sicut motus ad quietem in termino. Si autem intelligatur quod eadem numero cognitio quae est fidei, maneat in patria; hoc est omnino impossibile. Non enim, remota differentia alicuius speciei, remanet substantia generis eadem numero, sicut, remota differentia constitutiva albedinis, non remanet eadem substantia coloris numero, ut sic idem numero color sit quandoque albedo, quandoque vero nigredo. Non enim comparatur genus ad differentiam sicut materia ad formam, ut remaneat substantia generis eadem numero, differentia remota; sicut remanet eadem numero substantia materiae, remota forma. Genus enim et differentia non sunt partes speciei, alioquin non praedicarentur de specie. Sed sicut species significat totum, idest compositum ex materia et forma in rebus materialibus, ita differentia significat totum, et similiter genus, sed genus denominat totum ab eo quod est sicut materia; differentia vero ab eo quod est sicut forma; species vero ab utroque. Sicut in homine sensitiva natura materialiter se habet ad intellectivam, animal autem dicitur quod habet naturam sensitivam; rationale quod habet intellectivam; homo vero quod habet utrumque. Et sic idem totum significatur per haec tria, sed non ab eodem. Unde patet quod, cum differentia non sit nisi designativa generis, remota differentia, non potest substantia generis eadem remanere, non enim remanet eadem animalitas, si sit alia anima constituens animal. Unde non potest esse quod eadem numero cognitio, quae

I answer that, Some have held that hope is taken away entirely: but that faith is taken away in part, *viz.* as to its obscurity, and remains in part, *viz.* as to the substance of its knowledge. And if this be understood to mean that it remains the same, not identically but generically, it is absolutely true; since faith is of the same genus, *viz.* knowledge, as the beatific vision. On the other hand, hope is not of the same genus as heavenly bliss: because it is compared to the enjoyment of bliss, as movement is to rest in the term of movement. But if it be understood to mean that in heaven the knowledge of faith remains identically the same, this is absolutely impossible. Because when you remove a specific difference, the substance of the genus does not remain identically the same: thus if you remove the difference constituting whiteness, the substance of color does not remain identically the same, as though the identical color were at one time whiteness, and, at another, blackness. The reason is that genus is not related to difference as matter to form, so that the substance of the genus remains identically the same, when the difference is removed, as the substance of matter remains identically the same, when the form is changed: for genus and difference are not the parts of a species, else they would not be predicated of the species. But even as the species denotes the whole, i.e., the compound of matter and form in material things, so does the difference, and likewise the genus; the genus denotes the whole by signifying that which is material; the difference, by signifying that which is formal; the species, by signifying both. Thus, in man, the sensitive nature is as matter to the intellectual nature, and animal is predicated of that which has a sensitive nature, rational of that which has an intellectual nature, and man of that which has both. So that the one same whole is denoted by these three, but not under the same aspect. It is therefore evident that, since the signification of the difference is confined to the genus if the difference be removed, the substance of the genus cannot remain the same: for the same animal nature does not remain, if another kind of soul constitute the animal. Hence it is impossible for the identical knowledge, which

prius fuit aenigmatica, postea fiat visio aperta. Et sic patet quod nihil idem numero vel specie quod est in fide, remanet in patria; sed solum idem genere.

AD PRIMUM ergo dicendum quod, remoto *rationali*, non remanet *vivum* idem numero, sed idem genere, ut ex dictis patet.

AD SECUNDUM dicendum quod imperfectio luminis candelae non opponitur perfectioni solaris luminis, quia non respiciunt idem subiectum. Sed imperfectio fidei et perfectio gloriae opponuntur ad invicem, et respiciunt idem subiectum. Unde non possunt esse simul, sicut nec claritas aeris cum obscuritate eius.

AD TERTIUM dicendum quod ille qui amittit pecuniam, non amittit possibilitatem habendi pecuniam, et ideo convenienter remanet habitus liberalitatis. Sed in statu gloriae non solum actu tollitur obiectum fidei, quod est non visum; sed etiam secundum possibilitatem, propter beatitudinis stabilitatem. Et ideo frustra talis habitus remaneret.

was previously obscure, to become clear vision. It is therefore evident that, in heaven, nothing remains of faith, either identically or specifically the same, but only generically.

Reply to Objection 1: If "rational" be withdrawn, the remaining "living" thing is the same, not identically, but generically, as stated.

Reply to Objection 2: The imperfection of candlelight is not opposed to the perfection of sunlight, since they do not regard the same subject: whereas the imperfection of faith and the perfection of glory are opposed to one another and regard the same subject. Consequently they are incompatible with one another, just as light and darkness in the air.

Reply to Objection 3: He that loses his money does not therefore lose the possibility of having money, and therefore it is reasonable for the habit of liberality to remain. But in the state of glory not only is the object of faith, which is the unseen, removed actually, but even its possibility, by reason of the unchangeableness of heavenly bliss: and so such a habit would remain to no purpose.

ARTICULUS 6

AD SEXTUM sic proceditur. Videtur quod caritas non maneat post hanc vitam in gloria. Quia, ut dicitur I ad Cor. XIII, *cum venerit quod perfectum est, evacuabitur quod ex parte est,* idest quod est imperfectum. Sed caritas viae est imperfecta. Ergo evacuabitur, adveniente perfectione gloriae.

PRAETEREA, habitus et actus distinguuntur secundum obiecta. Sed obiectum amoris est bonum apprehensum. Cum ergo alia sit apprehensio praesentis vitae, et alia apprehensio futurae vitae; videtur quod non maneat eadem caritas utrobique.

PRAETEREA, eorum quae sunt unius rationis, imperfectum potest venire ad aequalitatem perfectionis, per continuum augmentum. Sed caritas viae nunquam potest pervenire ad aequalitatem caritatis patriae, quantumcumque augeatur. Ergo videtur

ARTICLE 6
Whether charity remains after this life, in glory?

Objection 1: It would seem that charity does not remain after this life, in glory. Because according to 1 Cor. 13:10, "when that which is perfect is come, that which is in part," i.e., that which is imperfect, "shall be done away." Now the charity of the wayfarer is imperfect. Therefore it will be done away when the perfection of glory is attained.

Objection 2: Further, habits and acts are differentiated by their objects. But the object of love is good apprehended. Since therefore the apprehension of the present life differs from the apprehension of the life to come, it seems that charity is not the same in both cases.

Objection 3: Further, things of the same kind can advance from imperfection to perfection by continuous increase. But the charity of the wayfarer can never attain to equality with the charity of heaven, however much it be increased. Therefore it seems

quod caritas viae non remaneat in patria.

Sed contra est quod apostolus dicit, I ad Cor. XIII, *caritas nunquam excidit.*

Respondeo dicendum quod, sicut supra dictum est, quando imperfectio alicuius rei non est de ratione speciei ipsius, nihil prohibet idem numero quod prius fuit imperfectum, postea perfectum esse, sicut homo per augmentum perficitur, et albedo per intensionem. Caritas autem est amor; de cuius ratione non est aliqua imperfectio, potest enim esse et habiti et non habiti, et visi et non visi. Unde caritas non evacuatur per gloriae perfectionem, sed eadem numero manet.

Ad primum ergo dicendum quod imperfectio caritatis per accidens se habet ad ipsam, quia non est de ratione amoris imperfectio. Remoto autem eo quod est per accidens, nihilominus remanet substantia rei. Unde, evacuata imperfectione caritatis, non evacuatur ipsa caritas.

Ad secundum dicendum quod caritas non habet pro obiecto ipsam cognitionem, sic enim non esset eadem in via et in patria. Sed habet pro obiecto ipsam rem cognitam, quae est eadem, scilicet ipsum Deum.

Ad tertium dicendum quod caritas viae per augmentum non potest pervenire ad aequalitatem caritatis patriae, propter differentiam quae est ex parte causae, visio enim est quaedam causa amoris, ut dicitur in IX Ethic. Deus autem quanto perfectius cognoscitur, tanto perfectius amatur.

that the charity of the wayfarer does not remain in heaven.

On the contrary, The Apostle says (1 Cor. 13:8): "Charity never falleth away."

I answer that, As stated above (I-II, q. 67, a. 3), when the imperfection of a thing does not belong to its specific nature, there is nothing to hinder the identical thing passing from imperfection to perfection, even as man is perfected by growth, and whiteness by intensity. Now charity is love, the nature of which does not include imperfection, since it may relate to an object either possessed or not possessed, either seen or not seen. Therefore charity is not done away by the perfection of glory, but remains identically the same.

Reply to Objection 1: The imperfection of charity is accidental to it; because imperfection is not included in the nature of love. Now although that which is accidental to a thing be withdrawn, the substance remains. Hence the imperfection of charity being done away, charity itself is not done away.

Reply to Objection 2: The object of charity is not knowledge itself; if it were, the charity of the wayfarer would not be the same as the charity of heaven: its object is the thing known, which remains the same, *viz.* God Himself.

Reply to Objection 3: The reason why charity of the wayfarer cannot attain to the perfection of the charity of heaven, is a difference on the part of the cause: for vision is a cause of love, as stated in Ethic. ix, 5: and the more perfectly we know God, the more perfectly we love Him.

Quaestio LXVIII

Consequenter considerandum est de donis. Et circa hoc quaeruntur octo. *Primo,* utrum dona differant a virtutibus. *Secundo,* de necessitate donorum. *Tertio,* utrum dona sint habitus. *Quarto,* quae, et quot sint. *Quinto,* utrum dona sint connexa. *Sexto,* utrum maneant in patria. *Septimo,* de comparatione eorum ad invicem. *Octavo,* de comparatione eorum ad virtutes.

Articulus 1

Ad primum sic proceditur. Videtur quod dona non distinguantur a virtutibus. Dicit enim Gregorius, in I Moral., exponens illud Iob, *nati sunt ei septem filii, septem nobis nascuntur filii, cum per conceptionem bonae cogitationis, sancti spiritus septem in nobis virtutes oriuntur.* Et inducit illud quod habetur Isaiae XI, *requiescet super eum spiritus intellectus* etc., ubi enumerantur septem spiritus sancti dona. Ergo septem dona spiritus sancti sunt virtutes.

Praeterea, Augustinus dicit, in libro de Quaestionib. Evang., exponens illud quod habetur Matth. XII, *tunc vadit, et assumit septem alios spiritus* etc., *septem vitia sunt contraria septem virtutibus spiritus sancti,* idest septem donis. Sunt autem septem vitia contraria virtutibus communiter dictis. Ergo dona non distinguuntur a virtutibus communiter dictis.

Praeterea, quorum est definitio eadem, ipsa quoque sunt eadem. Sed definitio virtutis convenit donis, unumquodque enim donum est *bona qualitas mentis qua recte vivitur,* et cetera. Similiter definitio doni convenit virtutibus infusis, est enim *donum datio irreddibilis,* secundum philosophum. Ergo virtutes et dona non distinguuntur.

Praeterea, plura eorum quae enumerantur inter dona, sunt virtutes. Nam sicut supra dictum est, sapientia et intellectus et scientia

Question 68
Of the Gifts

We now come to consider the Gifts; under which head there are eight points of inquiry: 1. Whether the Gifts differ from the virtues? 2. Of the necessity of the Gifts? 3. Whether the Gifts are habits? 4. Which, and how many are they? 5. Whether the Gifts are connected? 6. Whether they remain in heaven? 7. Of their comparison with one another; 8. Of their comparison with the virtues.

Article 1
Whether the Gifts differ from the virtues?

Objection 1: It would seem that the gifts do not differ from the virtues. For Gregory commenting on Job 1:2, "There were born to him seven sons," says (Moral. i, 12): "Seven sons were born to us, when through the conception of heavenly thought, the seven virtues of the Holy Ghost take birth in us": and he quotes the words of Is. 11:2, 3: "And the Spirit . . . of understanding . . . shall rest upon him," etc., where the seven gifts of the Holy Ghost are enumerated. Therefore the seven gifts of the Holy Ghost are virtues.

Objection 2: Further, Augustine commenting on Mat. 12:45, "Then he goeth and taketh with him seven other spirits," etc., says (De Quaest. Evang. i, qu. 8): "The seven vices are opposed to the seven virtues of the Holy Ghost," i.e., to the seven gifts. Now the seven vices are opposed to the seven virtues, commonly so called. Therefore the gifts do not differ from the virtues commonly so called.

Objection 3: Further, things whose definitions are the same, are themselves the same. But the definition of virtue applies to the gifts; for each gift is "a good quality of the mind, whereby we lead a good life," etc.*
Likewise the definition of a gift can apply to the infused virtues: for a gift is "an unreturnable giving," according to the Philosopher (Topic. iv, 4). Therefore the virtues and gifts do not differ from one another.

Objection 4: Several of the things mentioned among the gifts, are virtues: for, as stated above (I-II, q. 57, a. 2), wisdom, understanding, and knowledge

---
* Cf. I-II, q. 55, a. 4.

sunt virtutes intellectuales; consilium autem ad prudentiam pertinet; pietas autem species est iustitiae; fortitudo autem quaedam virtus est moralis. Ergo videtur quod virtutes non distinguantur a donis.

SED CONTRA est quod Gregorius, I Moral., distinguit septem dona, quae dicit significari per septem filios Iob, a tribus virtutibus theologicis, quas dicit significari per tres filias Iob. Et in II Moral., distinguit eadem septem dona a quatuor virtutibus cardinalibus, quae dicit significari per quatuor angulos domus.

RESPONDEO dicendum quod, si loquamur de dono et virtute secundum nominis rationem, sic nullam oppositionem habent ad invicem. Nam ratio *virtutis* sumitur secundum quod perficit hominem ad bene agendum, ut supra dictum est, ratio autem *doni* sumitur secundum comparationem ad causam a qua est. Nihil autem prohibet illud quod est ab alio ut donum, esse perfectivum alicuius ad bene operandum, praesertim cum supra dixerimus quod virtutes quaedam nobis sunt infusae a Deo. Unde secundum hoc, donum a virtute distingui non potest. Et ideo quidam posuerunt quod dona non essent a virtutibus distinguenda. Sed eis remanet non minor difficultas, ut scilicet rationem assignent quare quaedam virtutes dicantur dona, et non omnes; et quare aliqua computantur inter dona, quae non computantur inter virtutes, ut patet de timore. Unde alii dixerunt dona a virtutibus esse distinguenda; sed non assignaverunt convenientem distinctionis causam, quae scilicet ita communis esset virtutibus, quod nullo modo donis, aut e converso. Considerantes enim aliqui quod, inter septem dona, quatuor pertinent ad rationem, scilicet sapientia scientia, intellectus et consilium; et tria ad vim appetitivam, scilicet fortitudo, pietas et timor; posuerunt quod dona perficiebant liberum arbitrium secundum quod est facultas rationis, virtutes vero secundum quod est facultas voluntatis, quia invenerunt duas solas virtutes in ratione vel intellectu, scilicet fidem et prudentiam, alias vero in vi appetitiva vel affectiva.

are intellectual virtues, counsel pertains to prudence, piety to a kind of justice, and fortitude is a moral virtue. Therefore it seems that the gifts do not differ from the virtues.

On the contrary, Gregory (Moral. i, 12) distinguishes seven gifts, which he states to be denoted by the seven sons of Job, from the three theological virtues, which, he says, are signified by Job's three daughters. He also distinguishes (Moral. ii, 26) the same seven gifts from the four cardinal virtues, which he says were signified by the four corners of the house.

I answer that, If we speak of gift and virtue with regard to the notion conveyed by the words themselves, there is no opposition between them. Because the word "virtue" conveys the notion that it perfects man in relation to well-doing, while the word "gift" refers to the cause from which it proceeds. Now there is no reason why that which proceeds from one as a gift should not perfect another in well-doing: especially as we have already stated (I-II, q. 63, a. 3) that some virtues are infused into us by God. Wherefore in this respect we cannot differentiate gifts from virtues. Consequently some have held that the gifts are not to be distinguished from the virtues. But there remains no less a difficulty for them to solve; for they must explain why some virtues are called gifts and some not; and why among the gifts there are some, fear, for instance, that are not reckoned virtues. Hence it is that others have said that the gifts should be held as being distinct from the virtues; yet they have not assigned a suitable reason for this distinction, a reason, to wit, which would apply either to all the virtues, and to none of the gifts, or vice versa. For, seeing that of the seven gifts, four belong to the reason, *viz.* wisdom, knowledge, understanding and counsel, and three to the appetite, *viz.* fortitude, piety and fear; they held that the gifts perfect the free-will according as it is a faculty of the reason, while the virtues perfect it as a faculty of the will: since they observed only two virtues in the reason or intellect, *viz.* faith and prudence, the others being in the appetitive power or the affections.

I-II, q. 68, a. 1, co.

Oporteret autem, si haec distinctio esset conveniens, quod omnes virtutes essent in vi appetitiva, et omnia dona in ratione. Quidam vero, considerantes quod Gregorius dicit, in II Moral., quod *donum spiritus sancti, quod in mente sibi subiecta format temperantiam, prudentiam, iustitiam et fortitudinem; eandem mentem munit contra singula tentamenta per septem dona,* dixerunt quod virtutes ordinantur ad bene operandum, dona vero ad resistendum tentationibus. Sed nec ista distinctio sufficit. Quia etiam virtutes tentationibus resistunt, inducentibus ad peccata, quae contrariantur virtutibus, unumquodque enim resistit naturaliter suo contrario. Quod praecipue patet de caritate, de qua dicitur Cantic. VIII, *aquae multae non potuerunt extinguere caritatem.* Alii vero, considerantes quod ista dona traduntur in Scriptura secundum quod fuerunt in Christo, ut patet Isaiae XI; dixerunt quod virtutes ordinantur simpliciter ad bene operandum; sed dona ordinantur ad hoc ut per ea conformemur Christo, praecipue quantum ad ea quae passus est, quia in passione eius praecipue huiusmodi dona resplenduerunt. Sed hoc etiam non videtur esse sufficiens. Quia ipse dominus praecipue nos inducit ad sui conformitatem secundum humilitatem et mansuetudinem, Matth. XI, *discite a me, quia mitis sum et humilis corde;* et secundum caritatem, ut Ioan. XV, *diligatis invicem, sicut dilexi vos.* Et hae etiam virtutes praecipue in passione Christi refulserunt. Et ideo ad distinguendum dona a virtutibus, debemus sequi modum loquendi Scripturae, in qua nobis traduntur non quidem sub nomine *donorum,* sed magis sub nomine *spirituum,* sic enim dicitur Isaiae XI, *requiescet super eum spiritus sapientiae et intellectus,* et cetera. Ex quibus verbis manifeste datur intelligi quod ista septem enumerantur ibi, secundum quod sunt in nobis ab inspiratione divina. Inspiratio autem significat quandam motionem ab exteriori. Est enim considerandum quod in homine est duplex principium movens, unum quidem interius, quod est ratio; aliud autem exterius, quod est Deus, ut supra dictum est; et etiam philosophus hoc dicit, in cap. de bona fortuna.

THE GIFTS

If this distinction were true, all the virtues would have to be in the appetite, and all the gifts in the reason. Others observing that Gregory says (Moral. ii, 26) that "the gift of the Holy Ghost, by coming into the soul endows it with prudence, temperance, justice, and fortitude, and at the same time strengthens it against every kind of temptation by His sevenfold gift," said that the virtues are given us that we may do good works, and the gifts, that we may resist temptation. But neither is this distinction sufficient. Because the virtues also resist those temptations which lead to the sins that are contrary to the virtues; for everything naturally resists its contrary: which is especially clear with regard to charity, of which it is written (Cant 8:7): "Many waters cannot quench charity." Others again, seeing that these gifts are set down in Holy Writ as having been in Christ, according to Is. 11:2, 3, said that the virtues are given simply that we may do good works, but the gifts, in order to conform us to Christ, chiefly with regard to His Passion, for it was then that these gifts shone with the greatest splendor. Yet neither does this appear to be a satisfactory distinction. Because Our Lord Himself wished us to be conformed to Him, chiefly in humility and meekness, according to Mat. 11:29: "Learn of Me, because I am meek and humble of heart," and in charity, according to Jn. 15:12: "Love one another, as I have loved you." Moreover, these virtues were especially resplendent in Christ's Passion. Accordingly, in order to differentiate the gifts from the virtues, we must be guided by the way in which Scripture expresses itself, for we find there that the term employed is "spirit" rather than "gift." For thus it is written (Is. 11:2, 3): "The spirit…of wisdom and of understanding…shall rest upon him," etc.: from which words we are clearly given to understand that these seven are there set down as being in us by Divine inspiration. Now inspiration denotes motion from without. For it must be noted that in man there is a twofold principle of movement, one within him, *viz.* the reason; the other extrinsic to him, *viz.* God, as stated above (I-II, q. 9, a. 4; a. 6): moreover the Philosopher says this in the chapter On Good Fortune (Ethic. Eudem. vii,

Manifestum est autem quod omne quod movetur, necesse est proportionatum esse motori, et haec est perfectio mobilis inquantum est mobile, dispositio qua disponitur ad hoc quod bene moveatur a suo motore. Quanto igitur movens est altior, tanto necesse est quod mobile perfectiori dispositione ei proportionetur, sicut videmus quod perfectius oportet esse discipulum dispositum, ad hoc quod altiorem doctrinam capiat a docente. Manifestum est autem quod virtutes humanae perficiunt hominem secundum quod homo natus est moveri per rationem in his quae interius vel exterius agit. Oportet igitur inesse homini altiores perfectiones, secundum quas sit dispositus ad hoc quod divinitus moveatur. Et istae perfectiones vocantur dona, non solum quia infunduntur a Deo; sed quia secundum ea homo disponitur ut efficiatur prompte mobilis ab inspiratione divina, sicut dicitur Isaiae l, *dominus aperuit mihi aurem; ego autem non contradico, retrorsum non abii*. Et philosophus etiam dicit, in cap. de bona fortuna, quod his qui moventur per instinctum divinum, non expedit consiliari secundum rationem humanam, sed quod sequantur interiorem instinctum, quia moventur a meliori principio quam sit ratio humana. Et hoc est quod quidam dicunt, quod dona perficiunt hominem ad altiores actus quam sint actus virtutum.

AD PRIMUM ergo dicendum quod huiusmodi dona nominantur quandoque virtutes, secundum communem rationem virtutis. Habent tamen aliquid supereminens rationi communi virtutis, inquantum sunt quaedam divinae virtutes, perficientes hominem inquantum est a Deo motus. Unde et philosophus, in VII Ethic., supra virtutem communem ponit quandam *virtutem heroicam* vel *divinam*, secundum quam dicuntur aliqui *divini* viri.

AD SECUNDUM dicendum quod vitia, inquantum sunt contra bonum rationis, contrariantur virtutibus, inquantum autem sunt contra divinum instinctum, contrariantur donis. Idem enim contrariatur Deo et rationi, cuius lumen a Deo derivatur.

8). Now it is evident that whatever is moved must be proportionate to its mover: and the perfection of the mobile as such, consists in a disposition whereby it is disposed to be well moved by its mover. Hence the more exalted the mover, the more perfect must be the disposition whereby the mobile is made proportionate to its mover: thus we see that a disciple needs a more perfect disposition in order to receive a higher teaching from his master. Now it is manifest that human virtues perfect man according as it is natural for him to be moved by his reason in his interior and exterior actions. Consequently man needs yet higher perfections, whereby to be disposed to be moved by God. These perfections are called gifts, not only because they are infused by God, but also because by them man is disposed to become amenable to the Divine inspiration, according to Is. 50:5: "The Lord ... hath opened my ear, and I do not resist; I have not gone back." Even the Philosopher says in the chapter On Good Fortune (Ethic. Eudem., vii, 8) that for those who are moved by Divine instinct, there is no need to take counsel according to human reason, but only to follow their inner promptings, since they are moved by a principle higher than human reason. This then is what some say, *viz.* that the gifts perfect man for acts which are higher than acts of virtue.

Reply to Objection 1: Sometimes these gifts are called virtues, in the broad sense of the word. Nevertheless, they have something over and above the virtues understood in this broad way, in so far as they are Divine virtues, perfecting man as moved by God. Hence the Philosopher (Ethic. vii, 1) above virtue commonly so called, places a kind of "heroic" or "divine virtue,"* in respect of which some men are called "divine."

Reply to Objection 2: The vices are opposed to the virtues, in so far as they are opposed to the good as appointed by reason; but they are opposed to the gifts, in as much as they are opposed to the Divine instinct. For the same thing is opposed both to God and to reason, whose light flows from God.

---

* ἀρετὴ ἡρωϊκή καὶ θεία (*arete heroike kai theia*)

Ad tertium dicendum quod definitio illa datur de virtute secundum communem modum virtutis. Unde si volumus definitionem restringere ad virtutes prout distinguuntur a donis, dicemus quod hoc quod dicitur, *qua recte vivitur,* intelligendum est de rectitudine vitae quae accipitur secundum regulam rationis. Similiter autem donum, prout distinguitur a virtute infusa, potest dici id quod datur a Deo in ordine ad motionem ipsius; quod scilicet facit hominem bene sequentem suos instinctus.

Ad quartum dicendum quod sapientia dicitur intellectualis virtus, secundum quod procedit ex iudicio rationis, dicitur autem donum, secundum quod operatur ex instinctu divino. Et similiter dicendum est de aliis.

Reply to Objection 3: This definition applies to virtue taken in its general sense. Consequently, if we wish to restrict it to virtue as distinguished from the gifts, we must explain the words, "whereby we lead a good life" as referring to the rectitude of life which is measured by the rule of reason. Likewise the gifts, as distinct from infused virtue, may be defined as something given by God in relation to His motion; something, to wit, that makes man to follow well the promptings of God.

Reply to Objection 4: Wisdom is called an intellectual virtue, so far as it proceeds from the judgment of reason: but it is called a gift, according as its work proceeds from the Divine prompting. The same applies to the other virtues.

Articulus 2

Ad secundum sic proceditur. Videtur quod dona non sint necessaria homini ad salutem. Dona enim ordinantur ad quandam perfectionem ultra communem perfectionem virtutis. Non autem est homini necessarium ad salutem ut huiusmodi perfectionem consequatur, quae est ultra communem statum virtutis, quia huiusmodi perfectio non cadit sub praecepto, sed sub consilio. Ergo dona non sunt necessaria homini ad salutem.

Praeterea, ad salutem hominis sufficit quod homo se bene habeat et circa divina et circa humana. Sed per virtutes theologicas homo se habet bene circa divina; per virtutes autem morales, circa humana. Ergo dona non sunt homini necessaria ad salutem.

Praeterea, Gregorius dicit, in II Moral., quod *spiritus sanctus dat sapientiam contra stultitiam, intellectum contra hebetudinem, consilium contra praecipitationem, fortitudinem contra timorem, scientiam contra ignorantiam, pietatem contra duritiam, timorem contra superbiam.* Sed sufficiens remedium potest adhiberi ad omnia ista tollenda per virtutes. Ergo dona non sunt necessaria homini ad salutem.

Article 2
Whether the gifts are necessary to man for salvation?

Objection 1: It would seem that the gifts are not necessary to man for salvation. Because the gifts are ordained to a perfection surpassing the ordinary perfection of virtue. Now it is not necessary for man's salvation that he should attain to a perfection surpassing the ordinary standard of virtue; because such perfection falls, not under the precept, but under a counsel. Therefore the gifts are not necessary to man for salvation.

Objection 2: Further, it is enough, for man's salvation, that he behave well in matters concerning God and matters concerning man. Now man's behavior to God is sufficiently directed by the theological virtues; and his behavior towards men, by the moral virtues. Therefore gifts are not necessary to man for salvation.

Objection 3: Further, Gregory says (Moral. ii, 26) that "the Holy Ghost gives wisdom against folly, understanding against dullness, counsel against rashness, fortitude against fears, knowledge against ignorance, piety against hardness of our heart, and fear against pride." But a sufficient remedy for all these things is to be found in the virtues. Therefore the gifts are not necessary to man for salvation.

SED CONTRA, inter dona summum videtur esse sapientia, infimum autem timor. Utrumque autem horum necessarium est ad salutem, quia de sapientia dicitur, Sap. VII, *neminem diligit Deus nisi eum qui cum sapientia inhabitat;* et de timore dicitur, Eccli. I, *qui sine timore est, non poterit iustificari.* Ergo etiam alia dona media sunt necessaria ad salutem.

RESPONDEO dicendum quod, sicut dictum est, dona sunt quaedam hominis perfectiones, quibus homo disponitur ad hoc quod bene sequatur instinctum divinum. Unde in his in quibus non sufficit instinctus rationis, sed est necessarius spiritus sancti instinctus, per consequens est necessarium donum. Ratio autem hominis est perfecta dupliciter a Deo, primo quidem, naturali perfectione, scilicet secundum lumen naturale rationis; alio modo, quadam supernaturali perfectione, per virtutes theologicas, ut dictum est supra. Et quamvis haec secunda perfectio sit maior quam prima, tamen prima perfectiori modo habetur ab homine quam secunda, nam prima habetur ab homine quasi plena possessio, secunda autem habetur quasi imperfecta; imperfecte enim diligimus et cognoscimus Deum. Manifestum est autem quod unumquodque quod perfecte habet naturam vel formam aliquam aut virtutem, potest per se secundum illam operari, non tamen exclusa operatione Dei, qui in omni natura et voluntate interius operatur. Sed id quod imperfecte habet naturam aliquam vel formam aut virtutem, non potest per se operari, nisi ab altero moveatur. Sicut sol, quia est perfecte lucidus, per seipsum potest illuminare, luna autem, in qua est imperfecte natura lucis, non illuminat nisi illuminata. Medicus etiam, qui perfecte novit artem medicinae, potest per se operari, sed discipulus eius, qui nondum est plene instructus, non potest per se operari, nisi ab eo instruatur. Sic igitur quantum ad ea quae subsunt humanae rationi, in ordine scilicet ad finem connaturalem homini; homo potest operari, per iudicium rationis. Si tamen etiam in hoc homo adiuvetur a Deo per specialem instinctum, hoc erit superabundantis bonitatis, unde secundum

On the contrary, Of all the gifts, wisdom seems to be the highest, and fear the lowest. Now each of these is necessary for salvation: since of wisdom it is written (Wis. 7:28): "God loveth none but him that dwelleth with wisdom"; and of fear (Ecclus. 1:28): "He that is without fear cannot be justified." Therefore the other gifts that are placed between these are also necessary for salvation.

I answer that, As stated above (I-II, q. 68, a. 1), the gifts are perfections of man, whereby he is disposed so as to be amenable to the promptings of God. Wherefore in those matters where the prompting of reason is not sufficient, and there is need for the prompting of the Holy Ghost, there is, in consequence, need for a gift. Now man's reason is perfected by God in two ways: first, with its natural perfection, to wit, the natural light of reason; secondly, with a supernatural perfection, to wit, the theological virtues, as stated above (I-II, q. 62, a. 1). And, though this latter perfection is greater than the former, yet the former is possessed by man in a more perfect manner than the latter: because man has the former in his full possession, whereas he possesses the latter imperfectly, since we love and know God imperfectly. Now it is evident that anything that has a nature or a form or a virtue perfectly, can of itself work according to them: not, however, excluding the operation of God, Who works inwardly in every nature and in every will. On the other hand, that which has a nature, or form, or virtue imperfectly, cannot of itself work, unless it be moved by another. Thus the sun which possesses light perfectly, can shine by itself; whereas the moon which has the nature of light imperfectly, sheds only a borrowed light. Again, a physician, who knows the medical art perfectly, can work by himself; but his pupil, who is not yet fully instructed, cannot work by himself, but needs to receive instructions from him. Accordingly, in matters subject to human reason, and directed to man's connatural end, man can work through the judgment of his reason. If, however, even in these things man receive help in the shape of special promptings from God, this will be out of God's superabundant goodness: hence, according to

philosophos, non quicumque habebat virtutes morales acquisitas, habebat virtutes heroicas vel divinas. Sed in ordine ad finem ultimum supernaturalem, ad quem ratio movet secundum quod est aliqualiter et imperfecte formata per virtutes theologicas; non sufficit ipsa motio rationis, nisi desuper adsit instinctus et motio spiritus sancti; secundum illud Rom. VIII, *qui spiritu Dei aguntur, hi filii Dei sunt; et si filii, et haeredes,* et in Psalmo CXLII, dicitur, *spiritus tuus bonus deducet me in terram rectam;* quia scilicet in haereditatem illius terrae beatorum nullus potest pervenire, nisi moveatur et deducatur a spiritu sancto. Et ideo ad illum finem consequendum, necessarium est homini habere donum spiritus sancti.

AD PRIMUM ergo dicendum quod dona excedunt communem perfectionem virtutum, non quantum ad genus operum, eo modo quo consilia excedunt praecepta, sed quantum ad modum operandi, secundum quod movetur homo ab altiori principio.

AD SECUNDUM dicendum quod per virtutes theologicas et morales non ita perficitur homo in ordine ad ultimum finem, quin semper indigeat moveri quodam superiori instinctu spiritus sancti, ratione iam dicta.

AD TERTIUM dicendum quod rationi humanae non sunt omnia cognita, neque omnia possibilia, sive accipiatur ut perfecta perfectione naturali, sive accipiatur ut perfecta theologicis virtutibus. Unde non potest quantum ad omnia repellere stultitiam, et alia huiusmodi, de quibus ibi fit mentio. Sed Deus cuius scientiae et potestati omnia subsunt, sua motione ab omni stultitia et ignorantia et hebetudine et duritia et ceteris huiusmodi, nos tutos reddit. Et ideo dona spiritus sancti, quae faciunt nos bene sequentes instinctum ipsius, dicuntur contra huiusmodi defectus dari.

the philosophers, not every one that had the acquired moral virtues, had also the heroic or divine virtues. But in matters directed to the supernatural end, to which man's reason moves him, according as it is, in a manner, and imperfectly, informed by the theological virtues, the motion of reason does not suffice, unless it receive in addition the prompting or motion of the Holy Ghost, according to Rom. 8:14, 17: "Whosoever are led by the Spirit of God, they are sons of God . . . and if sons, heirs also": and Ps. 142:10: "Thy good Spirit shall lead me into the right land," because, to wit, none can receive the inheritance of that land of the Blessed, except he be moved and led thither by the Holy Ghost. Therefore, in order to accomplish this end, it is necessary for man to have the gift of the Holy Ghost.

Reply to Objection 1: The gifts surpass the ordinary perfection of the virtues, not as regards the kind of works (as the counsels surpass the commandments), but as regards the manner of working, in respect of man being moved by a higher principle.

Reply to Objection 2: By the theological and moral virtues, man is not so perfected in respect of his last end, as not to stand in continual need of being moved by the yet higher promptings of the Holy Ghost, for the reason already given.

Reply to Objection 3: Whether we consider human reason as perfected in its natural perfection, or as perfected by the theological virtues, it does not know all things, nor all possible things. Consequently it is unable to avoid folly and other like things mentioned in the objection. God, however, to Whose knowledge and power all things are subject, by His motion safeguards us from all folly, ignorance, dullness of mind and hardness of heart, and the rest. Consequently the gifts of the Holy Ghost, which make us amenable to His promptings, are said to be given as remedies to these defects.

Articulus 3

Ad tertium sic proceditur. Videtur quod dona spiritus sancti non sint habitus. Habitus enim est qualitas in homine manens, est enim *qualitas difficile mobilis,* ut dicitur in praedicamentis. Sed proprium Christi est quod dona spiritus sancti in eo requiescant; ut dicitur Isaiae XI. Et Ioan. I, dicitur, *super quem videris spiritum descendentem, et manentem super eum, hic est qui baptizat,* quod exponens Gregorius, in II Moral., dicit, *in cunctis fidelibus spiritus sanctus venit; sed in solo mediatore semper singulariter permanet.* Ergo dona spiritus sancti non sunt habitus.

Praeterea, dona spiritus sancti perficiunt hominem secundum quod agitur a spiritu Dei, sicut dictum est. Sed inquantum homo agitur a spiritu Dei, se habet quodammodo ut instrumentum respectu eius. Non autem convenit ut instrumentum perficiatur per habitum, sed principale agens. Ergo dona spiritus sancti non sunt habitus.

Praeterea, sicut dona spiritus sancti sunt ex inspiratione divina, ita et donum prophetiae. Sed prophetia non est habitus, *non enim semper spiritus prophetiae adest prophetis,* ut Gregorius dicit, in I homilia Ezechielis. Ergo neque etiam dona spiritus sancti sunt habitus.

Sed contra est quod dominus dicit discipulis, de spiritu sancto loquens, Ioan. XIV, *apud vos manebit, et in vobis erit.* Spiritus autem sanctus non est in hominibus absque donis eius. Ergo dona eius manent in hominibus. Ergo non solum sunt actus vel passiones, sed etiam habitus permanentes.

Respondeo dicendum quod, sicut dictum est, dona sunt quaedam perfectiones hominis, quibus disponitur ad hoc quod homo bene sequatur instinctum spiritus sancti. Manifestum est autem ex supradictis quod virtutes morales perficiunt vim appetitivam secundum quod participat aliqualiter rationem, inquantum scilicet nata est moveri per imperium rationis. Hoc igitur modo dona

Article 3
Whether the gifts of the Holy Ghost are habits?

Objection 1: It would seem that the gifts of the Holy Ghost are not habits. Because a habit is a quality abiding in man, being defined as "a quality difficult to remove," as stated in the Predicaments (Categor. vi). Now it is proper to Christ that the gifts of the Holy Ghost rest in Him, as stated in Is. 11:2, 3: "He upon Whom thou shalt see the Spirit descending and remaining upon Him, He it is that baptizeth"; on which words Gregory comments as follows (Moral. ii, 27): "The Holy Ghost comes upon all the faithful; but, in a singular way, He dwells always in the Mediator." Therefore the gifts of the Holy Ghost are not habits.

Objection 2: Further, the gifts of the Holy Ghost perfect man according as he is moved by the Spirit of God, as stated above (I-II, q. 68, a. 1; a. 2). But in so far as man is moved by the Spirit of God, he is somewhat like an instrument in His regard. Now to be perfected by a habit is befitting, not an instrument, but a principal agent. Therefore the gifts of the Holy Ghost are not habits.

Objection 3: Further, as the gifts of the Holy Ghost are due to Divine inspiration, so is the gift of prophecy. Now prophecy is not a habit: for "the spirit of prophecy does not always reside in the prophets," as Gregory states (Hom. i in Ezechiel). Neither, therefore, are the gifts of the Holy Ghost.

On the contrary, Our Lord in speaking of the Holy Ghost said to His disciples (Jn. 14:17): "He shall abide with you, and shall be in you." Now the Holy Ghost is not in a man without His gifts. Therefore His gifts abide in man. Therefore they are not merely acts or passions but abiding habits.

I answer that, As stated above (I-II, q. 68, a. 1), the gifts are perfections of man, whereby he becomes amenable to the promptings of the Holy Ghost. Now it is evident from what has been already said (I-II, q. 56, a. 4; q. 58, a. 2), that the moral virtues perfect the appetitive power according as it partakes somewhat of the reason, in so far, to wit, as it has a natural aptitude to be moved by the command of reason. Accordingly the gifts

spiritus sancti se habent ad hominem in comparatione ad spiritum sanctum, sicut virtutes morales se habent ad vim appetitivam in comparatione ad rationem. Virtutes autem morales habitus quidam sunt, quibus vires appetitivae disponuntur ad prompte obediendum rationi. Unde et dona spiritus sancti sunt quidam habitus, quibus homo perficitur ad prompte obediendum spiritui sancto.

AD PRIMUM ergo dicendum quod Gregorius ibidem solvit, dicens quod *in illis donis sine quibus ad vitam perveniri non potest, spiritus sanctus in electis omnibus semper manet, sed in aliis non semper manet.* Septem autem dona sunt necessaria ad salutem, ut dictum est. Unde quantum ad ea, spiritus sanctus semper manet in sanctis.

AD SECUNDUM dicendum quod ratio illa procedit de instrumento cuius non est agere, sed solum agi. Tale autem instrumentum non est homo; sed sic agitur a spiritu sancto, quod etiam agit, inquantum est liberi arbitrii. Unde indiget habitu.

AD TERTIUM dicendum quod prophetia est de donis quae sunt ad manifestationem spiritus, non autem ad necessitatem salutis. Unde non est simile.

of the Holy Ghost, as compared with the Holy Ghost Himself, are related to man, even as the moral virtues, in comparison with the reason, are related to the appetitive power. Now the moral virtues are habits, whereby the powers of appetite are disposed to obey reason promptly. Therefore the gifts of the Holy Ghost are habits whereby man is perfected to obey readily the Holy Ghost.

Reply to Objection 1: Gregory solves this objection (Moral. ii, 27) by saying that "by those gifts without which one cannot obtain life, the Holy Ghost ever abides in all the elect, but not by His other gifts." Now the seven gifts are necessary for salvation, as stated above (I-II, q. 68, a. 2). Therefore, with regard to them, the Holy Ghost ever abides in holy men.

Reply to Objection 2: This argument holds, in the case of an instrument which has no faculty of action, but only of being acted upon. But man is not an instrument of that kind; for he is so acted upon, by the Holy Ghost, that he also acts himself, in so far as he has a free-will. Therefore he needs a habit.

Reply to Objection 3: Prophecy is one of those gifts which are for the manifestation of the Spirit, not for the necessity of salvation: hence the comparison fails.

ARTICULUS 4

AD QUARTUM sic proceditur. Videtur quod inconvenienter septem dona spiritus sancti enumerentur. In illa enim enumeratione ponuntur quatuor pertinentia ad virtutes intellectuales, scilicet sapientia, intellectus, scientia et consilium, quod pertinet ad prudentiam, nihil autem ibi ponitur quod pertineat ad artem, quae est quinta virtus intellectualis. Similiter etiam ponitur aliquid pertinens ad iustitiam, scilicet pietas, et aliquid pertinens ad fortitudinem, scilicet donum fortitudinis, nihil autem ponitur ibi pertinens ad temperantiam. Ergo insufficienter enumerantur dona.

ARTICLE 4
Whether the seven gifts of the Holy Ghost are suitably enumerated?

Objection 1: It would seem that seven gifts of the Holy Ghost are unsuitably enumerated. For in that enumeration four are set down corresponding to the intellectual virtues, *viz.* wisdom, understanding, knowledge, and counsel, which corresponds to prudence; whereas nothing is set down corresponding to art, which is the fifth intellectual virtue. Moreover, something is included corresponding to justice, *viz.* piety, and something corresponding to fortitude, *viz.* the gift of fortitude; while there is nothing to correspond to temperance. Therefore the gifts are enumerated insufficiently.

PRAETEREA, pietas est pars iustitiae. Sed circa fortitudinem non ponitur aliqua pars eius, sed ipsa fortitudo. Ergo non debuit poni pietas, sed ipsa iustitia.

PRAETEREA, virtutes theologicae maxime ordinant nos ad Deum. Cum ergo dona perficiant hominem secundum quod movetur a Deo, videtur quod debuissent poni aliqua dona pertinentia ad theologicas virtutes.

PRAETEREA, sicut Deus timetur, ita etiam amatur, et in ipsum aliquis sperat, et de eo delectatur. Amor autem, spes et delectatio sunt passiones condivisae timori. Ergo, sicut timor ponitur donum, ita et alia tria debent poni dona.

PRAETEREA, intellectui adiungitur sapientia quae regit ipsum; fortitudini autem consilium, pietati vero scientia. Ergo et timori debuit addi aliquod donum directivum. Inconvenienter ergo septem dona spiritus sancti enumerantur.

SED IN CONTRARIUM est auctoritas Scripturae, Isaiae XI.

RESPONDEO dicendum quod, sicut dictum est, dona sunt quidam habitus perficientes hominem ad hoc quod prompte sequatur instinctum spiritus sancti, sicut virtutes morales perficiunt vires appetitivas ad obediendum rationi. Sicut autem vires appetitivae natae sunt moveri per imperium rationis, ita omnes vires humanae natae sunt moveri per instinctum Dei, sicut a quadam superiori potentia. Et ideo in omnibus viribus hominis quae possunt esse principia humanorum actuum, sicut sunt virtutes, ita etiam sunt dona, scilicet in ratione, et in vi appetitiva. Ratio autem est speculativa et practica, et in utraque consideratur apprehensio veritatis, quae pertinet ad inventionem; et iudicium de veritate. Ad apprehensionem igitur veritatis, perficitur speculativa ratio per *intellectum;* practica vero per *consilium.* Ad recte autem iudicandum, speculativa quidem per *sapientiam,* practica vero per *scientiam* perficitur. Appetitiva autem virtus, in his quidem quae sunt ad alterum,

Objection 2: Further, piety is a part of justice. But no part of fortitude is assigned to correspond thereto, but fortitude itself. Therefore justice itself, and not piety, ought to have been set down.

Objection 3: Further, the theological virtues, more than any, direct us to God. Since, then, the gifts perfect man according as he is moved by God, it seems that some gifts, corresponding to the theological virtues, should have been included.

Objection 4: Further, even as God is an object of fear, so is He of love, of hope, and of joy. Now love, hope, and joy are passions condivided with fear. Therefore, as fear is set down as a gift, so ought the other three.

Objection 5: Further, wisdom is added in order to direct understanding; counsel, to direct fortitude; knowledge, to direct piety. Therefore, some gift should have been added for the purpose of directing fear. Therefore the seven gifts of the Holy Ghost are unsuitably enumerated.

On the contrary, stands the authority of Holy Writ (Is. 11:2,3).

I answer that, As stated above (I-II, q. 68, a. 3), the gifts are habits perfecting man so that he is ready to follow the promptings of the Holy Ghost, even as the moral virtues perfect the appetitive powers so that they obey the reason. Now just as it is natural for the appetitive powers to be moved by the command of reason, so it is natural for all the forces in man to be moved by the instinct of God, as by a superior power. Therefore whatever powers in man can be the principles of human actions, can also be the subjects of gifts, even as they are virtues; and such powers are the reason and appetite. Now the reason is speculative and practical: and in both we find the apprehension of truth (which pertains to the discovery of truth), and judgment concerning the truth. Accordingly, for the apprehension of truth, the speculative reason is perfected by "understanding"; the practical reason, by "counsel." In order to judge aright, the speculative reason is perfected by "wisdom"; the practical reason by "knowledge." The appetitive power, in matters touching a man's relations to another,

perficitur per *pietatem*. In his autem quae sunt ad seipsum, perficitur per *fortitudinem* contra terrorem periculorum, contra concupiscentiam vero inordinatam delectabilium, per *timorem*, secundum illud Proverb. XV, *per timorem domini declinat omnis a malo*; et in Psalmo CXVIII, *confige timore tuo carnes meas, a iudiciis enim tuis timui*. Et sic patet quod haec dona extendunt se ad omnia ad quae se extendunt virtutes tam intellectuales quam morales.

AD PRIMUM ergo dicendum quod dona spiritus sancti perficiunt hominem in his quae pertinent ad bene vivendum, ad quae non ordinatur ars, sed ad exteriora factibilia; est enim ars ratio recta non agibilium, sed factibilium, ut dicitur in VI Ethic. Potest tamen dici quod, quantum ad infusionem donorum, ars pertinet ad spiritum sanctum, qui est principaliter movens; non autem ad homines, qui sunt quaedam organa eius dum ab eo moventur. Temperantiae autem respondet quodammodo donum timoris. Sicut enim ad virtutem temperantiae pertinet, secundum eius propriam rationem, ut aliquis recedat a delectationibus pravis propter bonum rationis; ita ad donum timoris pertinet quod aliquis recedat a delectationibus pravis propter Dei timorem.

AD SECUNDUM dicendum quod nomen iustitiae imponitur a rectitudine rationis, et ideo nomen virtutis est convenientius quam nomen doni. Sed nomen pietatis importat reverentiam quam habemus ad patrem et ad patriam. Et quia pater omnium Deus est, etiam cultus Dei pietas nominatur; ut Augustinus dicit, X de Civ. Dei. Et ideo convenienter donum quo aliquis propter reverentiam Dei bonum operatur ad omnes, pietas nominatur.

AD TERTIUM dicendum quod animus hominis non movetur a spiritu sancto, nisi ei secundum aliquem modum uniatur, sicut instrumentum non movetur ab artifice nisi per contactum, aut per aliquam aliam unionem. Prima autem unio hominis est per fidem, spem et caritatem. Unde istae virtutes praesupponuntur ad dona, sicut radices quaedam donorum. Unde omnia dona pertinent ad has tres virtutes, sicut quaedam derivationes praedictarum virtutum.

is perfected by "piety"; in matters touching himself, it is perfected by "fortitude" against the fear of dangers; and against inordinate lust for pleasures, by "fear," according to Prov. 15:27: "By the fear of the Lord every one declineth from evil," and Ps. 118:120: "Pierce Thou my flesh with Thy fear: for I am afraid of Thy judgments." Hence it is clear that these gifts extend to all those things to which the virtues, both intellectual and moral, extend.

Reply to Objection 1: The gifts of the Holy Ghost perfect man in matters concerning a good life: whereas art is not directed to such matters, but to external things that can be made, since art is the right reason, not about things to be done, but about things to be made (Ethic. vi, 4). However, we may say that, as regards the infusion of the gifts, the art is on the part of the Holy Ghost, Who is the principal mover, and not on the part of men, who are His organs when He moves them. The gift of fear corresponds, in a manner, to temperance: for just as it belongs to temperance, properly speaking, to restrain man from evil pleasures for the sake of the good appointed by reason, so does it belong to the gift of fear, to withdraw man from evil pleasures through fear of God.

Reply to Objection 2: Justice is so called from the rectitude of the reason, and so it is more suitably called a virtue than a gift. But the name of piety denotes the reverence which we give to our father and to our country. And since God is the Father of all, the worship of God is also called piety, as Augustine states (De Civ. Dei x, 1). Therefore the gift whereby a man, through reverence for God, works good to all, is fittingly called piety.

Reply to Objection 3: The mind of man is not moved by the Holy Ghost, unless in some way it be united to Him: even as the instrument is not moved by the craftsman, unless there by contact or some other kind of union between them. Now the primal union of man with God is by faith, hope and charity: and, consequently, these virtues are presupposed to the gifts, as being their roots. Therefore all the gifts correspond to these three virtues, as being derived therefrom.

AD QUARTUM dicendum quod amor et spes et delectatio habent bonum pro obiecto. Summum autem bonum Deus est, unde nomina harum passionum transferuntur ad virtutes theologicas, quibus anima coniungitur Deo. Timoris autem obiectum est malum, quod Deo nullo modo competit, unde non importat coniunctionem ad Deum, sed magis recessum ab aliquibus rebus propter reverentiam Dei. Et ideo non est nomen virtutis theologicae, sed doni, quod eminentius retrahit a malis quam virtus moralis.

AD QUINTUM dicendum quod per sapientiam dirigitur et hominis intellectus, et hominis affectus. Et ideo ponuntur duo correspondentia sapientiae tanquam directivo, ex parte quidem intellectus, donum intellectus; ex parte autem affectus, donum timoris. Ratio enim timendi Deum praecipue sumitur ex consideratione excellentiae divinae, quam considerat sapientia.

Reply to Objection 4: Love, hope and joy have good for their object. Now God is the Sovereign Good: wherefore the names of these passions are transferred to the theological virtues which unite man to God. On the other hand, the object of fear is evil, which can nowise apply to God: hence fear does not denote union with God, but withdrawal from certain things through reverence for God. Hence it does not give its name to a theological virtue, but to a gift, which withdraws us from evil, for higher motives than moral virtue does.

Reply to Objection 5: Wisdom directs both the intellect and the affections of man. Hence two gifts are set down as corresponding to wisdom as their directing principle; on the part of the intellect, the gift of understanding; on the part of the affections, the gift of fear. Because the principal reason for fearing God is taken from a consideration of the Divine excellence, which wisdom considers.

ARTICULUS 5

AD QUINTUM sic proceditur. Videtur quod dona non sint connexa. Dicit enim apostolus, I ad Cor. XII, *alii datur per spiritum sermo sapientiae, alii sermo scientiae secundum eundem spiritum.* Sed sapientia et scientia inter dona spiritus sancti computantur. Ergo dona spiritus sancti dantur diversis, et non connectuntur sibi invicem in eodem.

PRAETEREA, Augustinus dicit, in XIV de Trin., quod *scientia non pollent fideles plurimi, quamvis polleant ipsa fide.* Sed fidem concomitatur aliquod de donis, ad minus donum timoris. Ergo videtur quod dona non sint ex necessitate connexa in uno et eodem.

PRAETEREA, Gregorius, in I Moral., dicit quod *minor est sapientia, si intellectu careat; et valde inutilis est intellectus, si ex sapientia non subsistat. Vile est consilium, cui opus fortitudinis deest; et valde fortitudo destruitur, nisi per consilium fulciatur. Nulla est scientia,*

ARTICLE 5
Whether the gifts of the Holy Ghost are connected?

Objection 1: It would seem that the gifts are not connected, for the Apostle says (1 Cor. 12:8): "To one . . . by the Spirit, is given the word of wisdom, and to another, the word of knowledge, according to the same Spirit." Now wisdom and knowledge are reckoned among the gifts of the Holy Ghost. Therefore the gifts of the Holy Ghost are given to divers men, and are not connected together in the same man.

Objection 2: Further, Augustine says (De Trin. xiv, 1) that "many of the faithful have not knowledge, though they have faith." But some of the gifts, at least the gift of fear, accompany faith. Therefore it seems that the gifts are not necessarily connected together in one and the same man.

Objection 3: Further, Gregory says (Moral. i) that wisdom "is of small account if it lack understanding, and understanding is wholly useless if it be not based upon wisdom…Counsel is worthless, when the strength of fortitude is lacking thereto… and fortitude is very weak if it be not supported by counsel…Knowledge is nought

I-II, q. 68, a. 5, arg. 3

si utilitatem pietatis non habet; et valde inutilis est pietas, si scientiae discretione caret. Timor quoque ipse, si non has virtutes habuerit, ad nullum opus bonae actionis surgit. Ex quibus videtur quod unum donum possit sine alio haberi. Non ergo dona spiritus sancti sunt connexa.

SED CONTRA est quod ibidem Gregorius praemittit, dicens, *illud in hoc filiorum convivio perscrutandum videtur, quod semetipsos invicem pascunt.* Per filios autem Iob, de quibus loquitur, designantur dona spiritus sancti. Ergo dona spiritus sancti sunt connexa, per hoc quod se invicem reficiunt.

RESPONDEO dicendum quod huius quaestionis veritas de facili ex praemissis potest haberi. Dictum est enim supra quod sicut vires appetitivae disponuntur per virtutes morales in comparatione ad regimen rationis, ita omnes vires animae disponuntur per dona in comparatione ad spiritum sanctum moventem. Spiritus autem sanctus habitat in nobis per caritatem, secundum illud Rom. V, *caritas Dei diffusa est in cordibus nostris per spiritum sanctum, qui datus est nobis,* sicut et ratio nostra perficitur per prudentiam. Unde sicut virtutes morales connectuntur sibi invicem in prudentia, ita dona spiritus sancti connectuntur sibi invicem in caritate, ita scilicet quod qui caritatem habet, omnia dona spiritus sancti habet; quorum nullum sine caritate haberi potest.

AD PRIMUM ergo dicendum quod sapientia et scientia uno modo possunt considerari secundum quod sunt gratiae gratis datae, prout scilicet aliquis abundat intantum in cognitione rerum divinarum et humanarum, ut possit et fideles instruere et adversarios confutare. Et sic loquitur ibi apostolus de sapientia et scientia, unde signanter fit mentio de *sermone* sapientiae et scientiae. Alio modo possunt accipi prout sunt dona spiritus sancti. Et sic sapientia et scientia nihil aliud sunt quam quaedam perfectiones humanae mentis, secundum quas disponitur ad sequendum instinctus spiritus sancti in cognitione divinorum vel

THE GIFTS

if it hath not the use of piety...and piety is very useless if it lack the discernment of knowledge...and assuredly, unless it has these virtues with it, fear itself rises up to the doing of no good action": from which it seems that it is possible to have one gift without another. Therefore the gifts of the Holy Ghost are not connected.

On the contrary, Gregory prefaces the passage above quoted, with the following remark: "It is worthy of note in this feast of Job's sons, that by turns they fed one another." Now the sons of Job, of whom he is speaking, denote the gifts of the Holy Ghost. Therefore the gifts of the Holy Ghost are connected together by strengthening one another.

I answer that, The true answer to this question is easily gathered from what has been already set down. For it has been stated (I-II, q. 68, a. 3) that as the powers of the appetite are disposed by the moral virtues as regards the governance of reason, so all the powers of the soul are disposed by the gifts as regards the motion of the Holy Ghost. Now the Holy Ghost dwells in us by charity, according to Rom. 5:5: "The charity of God is poured forth in our hearts by the Holy Ghost, Who is given to us," even as our reason is perfected by prudence. Wherefore, just as the moral virtues are united together in prudence, so the gifts of the Holy Ghost are connected together in charity: so that whoever has charity has all the gifts of the Holy Ghost, none of which can one possess without charity.

Reply to Objection 1: Wisdom and knowledge can be considered in one way as gratuitous graces, in so far, to wit, as man so far abounds in the knowledge of things Divine and human, that he is able both to instruct the believer and confound the unbeliever. It is in this sense that the Apostle speaks, in this passage, about wisdom and knowledge: hence he mentions pointedly the "word" of wisdom and the "word" of knowledge. They may be taken in another way for the gifts of the Holy Ghost: and thus wisdom and knowledge are nothing else but perfections of the human mind, rendering it amenable to the promptings of the Holy Ghost in the knowledge of things Divine and

humanorum. Et sic patet quod huiusmodi dona sunt in omnibus habentibus caritatem.

AD SECUNDUM dicendum quod Augustinus ibi loquitur de scientia exponens praedictam auctoritatem apostoli, unde loquitur de scientia praedicto modo accepta, secundum quod est gratia gratis data. Quod patet ex hoc quod subdit, aliud enim est scire tantummodo quid homo credere debeat propter adipiscendam vitam beatam, quae non nisi aeterna est; aliud autem scire quemadmodum hoc ipsum et piis opituletur, et contra impios defendatur; quam proprio appellare vocabulo scientiam videtur apostolus.

AD TERTIUM dicendum quod, sicut uno modo connexio virtutum cardinalium probatur per hoc quod una earum perficitur quodammodo per aliam, ut supra dictum est; ita Gregorius eodem modo vult probare connexionem donorum, per hoc quod unum sine alio non potest esse perfectum. Unde praemittit dicens, *valde singula quaelibet destituitur, si non una alii virtus virtuti suffragetur.* Non ergo datur intelligi quod unum donum possit esse sine alio, sed quod intellectus, si esset sine sapientia, non esset donum; sicut temperantia, si esset sine iustitia, non esset virtus.

Reply to Objection 2: Augustine is speaking there of knowledge, while expounding the passage of the Apostle quoted above (arg. 1): hence he is referring to knowledge, in the sense already explained, as a gratuitous grace. This is clear from the context which follows: "For it is one thing to know only what a man must believe in order to gain the blissful life, which is no other than eternal life; and another, to know how to impart this to godly souls, and to defend it against the ungodly, which latter the Apostle seems to have styled by the proper name of knowledge."

Reply to Objection 3: Just as the connection of the cardinal virtues is proved in one way from the fact that one is, in a manner, perfected by another, as stated above (I-II, q. 65, a. 1); so Gregory wishes to prove the connection of the gifts, in the same way, from the fact that one cannot be perfect without the other. Hence he had already observed that "each particular virtue is to the last degree destitute, unless one virtue lend its support to another." We are therefore not to understand that one gift can be without another; but that if understanding were without wisdom, it would not be a gift; even as temperance, without justice, would not be a virtue.

ARTICULUS 6

AD SEXTUM sic proceditur. Videtur quod dona spiritus sancti non maneant in patria. Dicit enim Gregorius, in II Moral., quod *spiritus sanctus contra singula tentamenta septem donis erudit mentem.* Sed in patria non erunt aliqua tentamenta; secundum illud Isaiae XI, *non nocebunt et non occident in universo monte sancto meo.* Ergo dona spiritus sancti non erunt in patria.

PRAETEREA, dona spiritus sancti sunt habitus quidam, ut supra dictum est. Frustra autem essent habitus, ubi actus esse non possunt. Actus autem quorundam donorum in patria esse non possunt, dicit enim Gregorius, in I Moral., quod *intellectus facit audita penetrare, et consilium prohibet esse praecipitem, et fortitudo*

ARTICLE 6
Whether the gifts of the Holy Ghost remain in heaven?

Objection 1: It would seem that the gifts of the Holy Ghost do not remain in heaven. For Gregory says (Moral. ii, 26) that by means of His sevenfold gift the "Holy Ghost instructs the mind against all temptations." Now there will be no temptations in heaven, according to Is. 11:9: "They shall not hurt, nor shall they kill in all My holy mountain." Therefore there will be no gifts of the Holy Ghost in heaven.

Objection 2: Further, the gifts of the Holy Ghost are habits, as stated above (I-II, q. 68, a. 3). But habits are of no use, where their acts are impossible. Now the acts of some gifts are not possible in heaven; for Gregory says (Moral. i, 15) that "understanding… penetrates the truths heard…counsel… stays us from acting rashly…fortitude…

I-II, q. 68, a. 6, arg. 2

facit non metuere adversa, et pietas replet cordis viscera operibus misericordiae; haec autem non competunt statui patriae. Ergo huiusmodi dona non erunt in statu gloriae.

PRAETEREA, donorum quaedam perficiunt hominem in vita contemplativa, ut sapientia et intellectus; quaedam in vita activa, ut pietas et fortitudo. Sed activa vita cum hac vita terminatur; ut Gregorius dicit, in VI Moral. Ergo in statu gloriae non erunt omnia dona spiritus sancti.

SED CONTRA est quod Ambrosius dicit, in libro de spiritu sancto, *civitas Dei illa, Ierusalem caelestis, non meatu alicuius fluvii terrestris abluitur; sed ex vitae fonte procedens spiritus sanctus, cuius nos brevi satiamur haustu, in illis caelestibus spiritibus redundantius videtur affluere, pleno septem virtutum spiritualium fervens meatu.*

RESPONDEO dicendum quod de donis dupliciter possumus loqui. Uno modo, quantum ad essentiam donorum, et sic perfectissime erunt in patria, sicut patet per auctoritatem Ambrosii inductam. Cuius ratio est quia dona spiritus sancti perficiunt mentem humanam ad sequendam motionem spiritus sancti, quod praecipue erit in patria, quando Deus erit *omnia in omnibus,* ut dicitur I ad Cor. XV, et quando homo erit totaliter subditus Deo. Alio modo possunt considerari quantum ad materiam circa quam operantur, et sic in praesenti habent operationem circa aliquam materiam circa quam non habebunt operationem in statu gloriae. Et secundum hoc, non manebunt in patria, sicut supra de virtutibus cardinalibus dictum est.

AD PRIMUM ergo dicendum quod Gregorius loquitur ibi de donis secundum quod competunt statui praesenti, sic enim donis protegimur contra tentamenta malorum. Sed in statu gloriae, cessantibus malis, per dona spiritus sancti perficiemur in bono.

AD SECUNDUM dicendum quod Gregorius quasi in singulis donis ponit aliquid quod transit cum statu praesenti, et aliquid quod permanet etiam in futuro. Dicit enim

THE GIFTS

has no fear of adversity…piety satisfies the inmost heart with deeds of mercy," all of which are incompatible with the heavenly state. Therefore these gifts will not remain in the state of glory.

Objection 3: Further, some of the gifts perfect man in the contemplative life, e.g., wisdom and understanding: and some in the active life, e.g., piety and fortitude. Now the active life ends with this as Gregory states (Moral. vi). Therefore not all the gifts of the Holy Ghost will be in the state of glory.

On the contrary, Ambrose says (De Spiritu Sancto i, 20): "The city of God, the heavenly Jerusalem is not washed with the waters of an earthly river: it is the Holy Ghost, of Whose outpouring we but taste, Who, proceeding from the Fount of life, seems to flow more abundantly in those celestial spirits, a seething torrent of sevenfold heavenly virtue."

I answer that, We may speak of the gifts in two ways: first, as to their essence; and thus they will be most perfectly in heaven, as may be gathered from the passage of Ambrose, just quoted. The reason for this is that the gifts of the Holy Ghost render the human mind amenable to the motion of the Holy Ghost: which will be especially realized in heaven, where God will be "all in all" (1 Cor. 15:28), and man entirely subject unto Him. Secondly, they may be considered as regards the matter about which their operations are: and thus, in the present life they have an operation about a matter, in respect of which they will have no operation in the state of glory. Considered in this way, they will not remain in the state of glory; just as we have stated to be the case with regard to the cardinal virtues (I-II, q. 67, a. 1).

Reply to Objection 1: Gregory is speaking there of the gifts according as they are compatible with the present state: for it is thus that they afford us protection against evil temptations. But in the state of glory, where all evil will have ceased, we shall be perfected in good by the gifts of the Holy Ghost.

Reply to Objection 2: Gregory, in almost every gift, includes something that passes away with the present state, and something that remains in the future state. For he says

quod *sapientia mentem de aeternorum spe et certitudine reficit,* quorum duorum spes transit, sed certitudo remanet. Et de intellectu dicit *quod in eo quod audita penetrat, reficiendo cor, tenebras eius illustrat,* quorum auditus transit, quia *non docebit vir fratrem suum,* ut dicitur Ierem. XXXI; sed illustratio mentis manebit. De consilio autem dicit quod *prohibet esse praecipitem,* quod est necessarium in praesenti, et iterum quod *ratione animum replet,* quod est necessarium etiam in futuro. De fortitudine vero dicit quod *adversa non metuit,* quod est necessarium in praesenti, et iterum quod *confidentiae cibos apponit,* quod permanet etiam in futuro. De scientia vero unum tantum ponit, scilicet quod *ignorantiae ieiunium superat,* quod pertinet ad statum praesentem. Sed quod addit, *in ventre mentis,* potest figuraliter intelligi repletio cognitionis, quae pertinet etiam ad statum futurum. De pietate vero dicit quod *cordis viscera misericordiae operibus replet.* Quod quidem secundum verba, pertinet tantum ad statum praesentem. Sed ipse intimus affectus proximorum, per *viscera* designatus, pertinet etiam ad futurum statum; in quo pietas non exhibebit misericordiae opera, sed congratulationis affectum. De timore vero dicit quod *premit mentem, ne de praesentibus superbiat,* quod pertinet ad statum praesentem; et quod *de futuris cibo spei confortat,* quod etiam pertinet ad statum praesentem, quantum ad spem; sed potest etiam ad statum futurum pertinere, quantum ad *confortationem* de rebus hic speratis, et ibi obtentis.

AD TERTIUM dicendum quod ratio illa procedit de donis quantum ad materiam. Opera enim activae vitae non erunt materia donorum, sed omnia habebunt actus suos circa ea quae pertinent ad vitam contemplativam, quae est vita beata.

that "wisdom strengthens the mind with the hope and certainty of eternal things"; of which two, hope passes, and certainty remains. Of understanding, he says "that it penetrates the truths heard, refreshing the heart and enlightening its darkness," of which, hearing passes away, since "they shall teach no more every man . . . his brother" (Jer. 31:3,4); but the enlightening of the mind remains. Of counsel he says that it "prevents us from being impetuous," which is necessary in the present life; and also that "it makes the mind full of reason," which is necessary even in the future state. Of fortitude he says that it "fears not adversity," which is necessary in the present life; and further, that it "sets before us the viands of confidence," which remains also in the future life. With regard to knowledge he mentions only one thing, *viz.* that "she overcomes the void of ignorance," which refers to the present state. When, however, he adds "in the womb of the mind," this may refer figuratively to the fulness of knowledge, which belongs to the future state. Of piety he says that "it satisfies the inmost heart with deeds of mercy." These words taken literally refer only to the present state: yet the inward regard for our neighbor, signified by "the inmost heart," belongs also to the future state, when piety will achieve, not works of mercy, but fellowship of joy. Of fear he say that "it oppresses the mind, lest it pride itself in present things," which refers to the present state, and that "it strengthens it with the meat of hope for the future," which also belongs to the present state, as regards hope, but may also refer to the future state, as regards being "strengthened" for things we hope are here, and obtain there.

Reply to Objection 3: This argument considers the gifts as to their matter. For the matter of the gifts will not be the works of the active life; but all the gifts will have their respective acts about things pertaining to the contemplative life, which is the life of heavenly bliss.

Articulus 7

Ad septimum sic proceditur. Videtur quod dignitas donorum non attenditur secundum enumerationem qua enumerantur Isaiae XI. Illud enim videtur esse potissimum in donis, quod maxime Deus ab homine requirit. Sed maxime requirit Deus ab homine timorem, dicitur enim Deut. X, *et nunc, Israel, quid dominus Deus tuus petit a te, nisi ut timeas dominum Deum tuum?* Et Malach. I, dicitur, *si ego dominus, ubi timor meus?* Ergo videtur quod timor, qui enumeratur ultimo, non sit infimum donorum, sed maximum.

Praeterea, pietas videtur esse quoddam bonum universale, dicit enim apostolus, I ad Tim. IV, quod *pietas ad omnia utilis est.* Sed bonum universale praefertur particularibus bonis. Ergo pietas, quae penultimo enumeratur, videtur esse potissimum donorum.

Praeterea, scientia perficit iudicium hominis; consilium autem ad inquisitionem pertinet. Sed iudicium praeeminet inquisitioni. Ergo scientia est potius donum quam consilium, cum tamen post enumeretur.

Praeterea, fortitudo pertinet ad vim appetitivam; scientia autem ad rationem. Sed ratio est eminentior quam vis appetitiva. Ergo et scientia est eminentius donum quam fortitudo, quae tamen primo enumeratur. Non ergo dignitas donorum attenditur secundum ordinem enumerationis eorum.

Sed contra est quod Augustinus dicit, in libro de Serm. Dom. in monte, videtur mihi septiformis operatio spiritus sancti, de qua Isaias loquitur, his gradibus sententiisque congruere (de quibus fit mentio Matth. V); sed interest ordinis. Nam ibi (scilicet in Isaia) enumeratio ab excellentioribus coepit, hic vero, ab inferioribus.

Respondeo dicendum quod dignitas donorum dupliciter potest attendi, uno modo, simpliciter, scilicet per comparationem ad proprios actus prout

Article 7
Whether the gifts are set down by Isaias in their order of dignity?

Objection 1: It would seem that the gifts are not set down by Isaias in their order of dignity. For the principal gift is, seemingly, that which, more than the others, God requires of man. Now God requires of man fear, more than the other gifts: for it is written (Dt. 10:12): "And now, Israel, what doth the Lord thy God require of thee, but that thou fear the Lord thy God?" and (Malachi 1:6): "If …I be a master, where is My fear?" Therefore it seems that fear, which is mentioned last, is not the lowest but the greatest of the gifts.

Objection 2: Further, piety seems to be a kind of common good; since the Apostle says (1 Tim. 4:8): "Piety* is profitable to all things." Now a common good is preferable to particular goods. Therefore piety, which is given the last place but one, seems to be the most excellent gift.

Objection 3: Further, knowledge perfects man's judgment, while counsel pertains to inquiry. But judgment is more excellent than inquiry. Therefore knowledge is a more excellent gift than counsel; and yet it is set down as being below it.

Objection 4: Further, fortitude pertains to the appetitive power, while science belongs to reason. But reason is a more excellent power than the appetite. Therefore knowledge is a more excellent gift than fortitude; and yet the latter is given the precedence. Therefore the gifts are not set down in their order of dignity.

On the contrary, Augustine says†: "It seems to me that the sevenfold operation of the Holy Ghost, of which Isaias speaks, agrees in degrees and expression with these (of which we read in Mat. 5:3): but there is a difference of order, for there (*viz.* in Isaias) the enumeration begins with the more excellent gifts, here, with the lower gifts."

I answer that, The excellence of the gifts can be measured in two ways: first, simply, *viz.* by comparison to their proper acts as

---

* Douay: 'Godliness'.
† De Serm. Dom. in Monte i, 4.

procedunt a suis principiis; alio modo, secundum quid, scilicet per comparationem ad materiam. Simpliciter autem loquendo de dignitate donorum, eadem est ratio comparationis in ipsis et in virtutibus, quia dona ad omnes actus potentiarum animae perficiunt hominem, ad quos perficiunt virtutes, ut supra dictum est. Unde sicut virtutes intellectuales praeferuntur virtutibus moralibus; et in ipsis virtutibus intellectualibus contemplativae praeferuntur activis, ut sapientia intellectui, et scientia prudentiae et arti; ita tamen quod sapientia praefertur intellectui, et intellectus scientiae, sicut prudentia et synesis eubuliae, ita etiam in donis sapientia et intellectus, scientia et consilium, praeferuntur pietati et fortitudini et timori; in quibus etiam pietas praefertur fortitudini, et fortitudo timori, sicut iustitia fortitudini, et fortitudo temperantiae. Sed quantum ad materiam, fortitudo et consilium praeferuntur scientiae et pietati, quia scilicet fortitudo et consilium in arduis locum habent; pietas autem, et etiam scientia, in communibus. Sic igitur donorum dignitas ordini enumerationis respondet, partim quidem simpliciter, secundum quod sapientia et intellectus omnibus praeferuntur, partim autem secundum ordinem materiae, secundum quod consilium et fortitudo praeferuntur scientiae et pietati.

AD PRIMUM ergo dicendum quod timor maxime requiritur quasi primordium quoddam perfectionis donorum, quia *initium sapientiae timor domini,* non propter hoc quod sit ceteris dignius. Prius enim est, secundum ordinem generationis, ut aliquis recedat a malo, quod fit per timorem, ut dicitur Proverb. XVI; quam quod operetur bonum, quod fit per alia dona.

AD SECUNDUM dicendum quod pietas non comparatur in verbis apostoli, omnibus donis Dei, sed soli *corporali exercitationi,* de qua praemittit quod *ad modicum utilis est.*

proceeding from their principles; secondly, relatively, *viz.* by comparison to their matter. If we consider the excellence of the gifts simply, they follow the same rule as the virtues, as to their comparison one with another; because the gifts perfect man for all the acts of the soul's powers, even as the virtues do, as stated above (I-II, q. 68, a. 4). Hence, as the intellectual virtues have the precedence of the moral virtues, and among the intellectual virtues, the contemplative are preferable to the active, *viz.* wisdom, understanding and science to prudence and art (yet so that wisdom stands before understanding, and understanding before science, and prudence and synesis before eubulia): so also among the gifts, wisdom, understanding, knowledge, and counsel are more excellent than piety, fortitude, and fear; and among the latter, piety excels fortitude, and fortitude fear, even as justice surpasses fortitude, and fortitude temperance. But in regard to their matter, fortitude and counsel precede knowledge and piety: because fortitude and counsel are concerned with difficult matters, whereas piety and knowledge regard ordinary matters. Consequently the excellence of the gifts corresponds with the order in which they are enumerated; but so far as wisdom and understanding are given the preference to the others, their excellence is considered simply, while, so far, as counsel and fortitude are preferred to knowledge and piety, it is considered with regard to their matter.

Reply to Objection 1: Fear is chiefly required as being the foundation, so to speak, of the perfection of the other gifts, for "the fear of the Lord is the beginning of wisdom" (Ps. 110:10; Ecclus. 1:16), and not as though it were more excellent than the others. Because, in the order of generation, man departs from evil on account of fear (Prov. 16:16), before doing good works, and which result from the other gifts.

Reply to Objection 2: In the words quoted from the Apostle, piety is not compared with all God's gifts, but only with "bodily exercise," of which he had said it "is profitable to little."

AD TERTIUM dicendum quod scientia etsi praeferatur consilio ratione iudicii, tamen consilium praefertur ratione materiae, nam consilium non habet locum nisi in arduis, ut dicitur in III Ethic.; sed iudicium scientiae in omnibus locum habet.

AD QUARTUM dicendum quod dona directiva, quae pertinent ad rationem, donis exequentibus digniora sunt, si considerentur per comparationem ad actus prout egrediuntur a potentiis, ratio enim appetitivae praeeminet, ut regulans regulato. Sed ratione materiae, adiungitur consilium fortitudini, sicut directivum exequenti, et similiter scientia pietati, quia scilicet consilium et fortitudo in arduis locum habent, scientia autem et pietas etiam in communibus. Et ideo consilium simul cum fortitudine, ratione materiae, numeratur ante scientiam et pietatem.

Reply to Objection 3: Although knowledge stands before counsel by reason of its judgment, yet counsel is more excellent by reason of its matter: for counsel is only concerned with matters of difficulty (Ethic. iii, 3), whereas the judgment of knowledge embraces all matters.

Reply to Objection 4: The directive gifts which pertain to the reason are more excellent than the executive gifts, if we consider them in relation to their acts as proceeding from their powers, because reason transcends the appetite as a rule transcends the thing ruled. But on the part of the matter, counsel is united to fortitude as the directive power to the executive, and so is knowledge united to piety: because counsel and fortitude are concerned with matters of difficulty, while knowledge and piety are concerned with ordinary matters. Hence counsel together with fortitude, by reason of their matter, are given the preference to knowledge and piety.

ARTICULUS 8

AD OCTAVUM sic proceditur. Videtur quod virtutes sint praeferendae donis. Dicit enim Augustinus, in XV de Trin., de caritate loquens, *nullum est isto Dei dono excellentius. Solum est quod dividit inter filios regni aeterni, et filios perditionis aeternae, dantur et alia per spiritum sanctum munera, sed sine caritate nihil prosunt.* Sed caritas est virtus. Ergo virtus est potior donis spiritus sancti.

PRAETEREA, ea quae sunt priora naturaliter, videntur esse potiora. Sed virtutes sunt priores donis spiritus sancti, dicit enim Gregorius, in II Moral., quod *donum spiritus sancti in subiecta mente ante alia iustitiam, prudentiam, fortitudinem et temperantiam format, et sic eandem mentem septem mox virtutibus* (idest donis) *temperat, ut contra stultitiam, sapientiam; contra hebetudinem, intellectum; contra praecipitationem, consilium; contra timorem, fortitudinem; contra ignorantiam, scientiam; contra duritiam, pietatem; contra superbiam, det timorem.*

ARTICLE 8
Whether the virtues are more excellent than the gifts?

Objection 1: It would seem that the virtues are more excellent than the gifts. For Augustine says (De Trin. xv, 18) while speaking of charity: "No gift of God is more excellent than this. It is this alone which divides the children of the eternal kingdom from the children of eternal damnation. Other gifts are bestowed by the Holy Ghost, but, without charity, they avail nothing." But charity is a virtue. Therefore a virtue is more excellent than the gifts of the Holy Ghost.

Objection 2: Further, that which is first naturally, seems to be more excellent. Now the virtues precede the gifts of the Holy Ghost; for Gregory says (Moral. ii, 26) that "the gift of the Holy Ghost in the mind it works on, forms first of all justice, prudence, fortitude, temperance . . . and doth afterwards give it a temper in the seven virtues" (*viz.* the gifts), "so as against folly to bestow wisdom; against dullness, understanding; against rashness, counsel; against fear, fortitude; against ignorance, knowledge; against hardness of heart, piety; against piety, fear."

Ergo virtutes sunt potiores donis.

Praeterea, virtutibus nullus male uti potest, ut Augustinus dicit. *Donis autem potest aliquis male uti,* dicit enim Gregorius, in I Moral., quod *hostiam nostrae precis immolamus ne sapientia elevet; ne intellectus, dum subtiliter currit, oberret; ne consilium, dum se multiplicat, confundat; ne fortitudo, dum fiduciam praebet, praecipitet; ne scientia, dum novit et non diligit, inflet; ne pietas, dum se extra rectitudinem inclinat, intorqueat; ne timor, dum plus iusto trepidat, in desperationis foveam mergat.* Ergo virtutes sunt digniores donis spiritus sancti.

Sed contra est quod dona dantur in adiutorium virtutum contra defectus, ut patet in auctoritate inducta; et sic videtur quod perficiant quod virtutes perficere non possunt. Sunt ergo dona potiora virtutibus.

Respondeo dicendum quod, sicut ex supradictis patet, virtutes in tria genera distinguuntur, sunt enim quaedam virtutes theologicae, quaedam intellectuales, quaedam morales. Virtutes quidem theologicae sunt quibus mens humana Deo coniungitur; virtutes autem intellectuales sunt quibus ratio ipsa perficitur; virtutes autem morales sunt quibus vires appetitivae perficiuntur ad obediendum rationi. Dona autem spiritus sancti sunt quibus omnes vires animae disponuntur ad hoc quod subdantur motioni divinae. Sic ergo eadem videtur esse comparatio donorum ad virtutes theologicas, per quas homo unitur spiritui sancto moventi; sicut virtutum moralium ad virtutes intellectuales, per quas perficitur ratio, quae est virtutum moralium motiva. Unde sicut virtutes intellectuales praeferuntur virtutibus moralibus, et regulant eas; ita virtutes theologicae praeferuntur donis spiritus sancti, et regulant ea. Unde Gregorius dicit, in I Moral., quod *neque ad denarii perfectionem septem filii* (idest septem dona) *perveniunt,*

Therefore the virtues are more excellent than the gifts.

Objection 3: Further, Augustine says (De Lib. Arb. ii, 19) that "the virtues cannot be used to evil purpose." But it is possible to make evil use of the gifts, for Gregory says (Moral. i, 18): "We offer up the sacrifice of prayer . . . lest wisdom may uplift; or understanding, while it runs nimbly, deviate from the right path; or counsel, while it multiplies itself, grow into confusion; that fortitude, while it gives confidence, may not make us rash; lest knowledge, while it knows and yet loves not, may swell the mind; lest piety, while it swerves from the right line, may become distorted; and lest fear, while it is unduly alarmed, may plunge us into the pit of despair." Therefore the virtues are more excellent than the gifts of the Holy Ghost.

On the contrary, The gifts are bestowed to assist the virtues and to remedy certain defects, as is shown in the passage quoted (arg. 2), so that, seemingly, they accomplish what the virtues cannot. Therefore the gifts are more excellent than the virtues.

I answer that, As was shown above (I-II, q. 58, a. 3; q. 62, a. 1), there are three kinds of virtues: for some are theological, some intellectual, and some moral. The theological virtues are those whereby man's mind is united to God; the intellectual virtues are those whereby reason itself is perfected; and the moral virtues are those which perfect the powers of appetite in obedience to the reason. On the other hand the gifts of the Holy Ghost dispose all the powers of the soul to be amenable to the Divine motion. Accordingly the gifts seem to be compared to the theological virtues, by which man is united to the Holy Ghost his Mover, in the same way as the moral virtues are compared to the intellectual virtues, which perfect the reason, the moving principle of the moral virtues. Wherefore as the intellectual virtues are more excellent than the moral virtues and control them, so the theological virtues are more excellent than the gifts of the Holy Ghost and regulate them. Hence Gregory says (Moral. i, 12) that "the seven sons," i.e., the seven gifts, "never attain the perfection of the number ten,

nisi in fide, spe et caritate fuerit omne quod agunt. Sed si comparemus dona ad alias virtutes intellectuales vel morales, dona praeferuntur virtutibus. Quia dona perficiunt vires animae in comparatione ad spiritum sanctum moventem, virtutes autem perficiunt vel ipsam rationem, vel alias vires in ordine ad rationem. Manifestum est autem quod ad altiorem motorem oportet maiori perfectione mobile esse dispositum. Unde perfectiora sunt dona virtutibus.

AD PRIMUM ergo dicendum quod caritas est virtus theologica; de qua concedimus quod sit potior donis.

AD SECUNDUM dicendum quod aliquid est prius altero dupliciter. Uno modo, ordine perfectionis et dignitatis, sicut dilectio Dei est prior dilectione proximi. Et hoc modo dona sunt priora virtutibus intellectualibus et moralibus, posteriora vero virtutibus theologicis. Alio modo, ordine generationis seu dispositionis, sicut dilectio proximi praecedit dilectionem Dei, quantum ad actum. Et sic virtutes morales et intellectuales praecedunt dona, quia per hoc quod homo bene se habet circa rationem propriam, disponitur ad hoc quod se bene habeat in ordine ad Deum.

AD TERTIUM dicendum quod sapientia et intellectus et alia huiusmodi sunt dona spiritus sancti, secundum quod caritate informantur; quae *non agit perperam,* ut dicitur I ad Cor. XIII. Et ideo sapientia et intellectu et aliis huiusmodi nullus male utitur, secundum quod sunt dona spiritus sancti. Sed ad hoc quod a caritatis perfectione non recedant, unum ab altero adiuvatur. Et hoc est quod Gregorius dicere intendit.

unless all they do be done in faith, hope, and charity." But if we compare the gifts to the other virtues, intellectual and moral, then the gifts have the precedence of the virtues. Because the gifts perfect the soul's powers in relation to the Holy Ghost their Mover; whereas the virtues perfect, either the reason itself, or the other powers in relation to reason: and it is evident that the more exalted the mover, the more excellent the disposition whereby the thing moved requires to be disposed. Therefore the gifts are more perfect than the virtues.

Reply to Objection 1: Charity is a theological virtue; and such we grant to be more perfect than the gifts.

Reply to Objection 2: There are two ways in which one thing precedes another. One is in order of perfection and dignity, as love of God precedes love of our neighbor: and in this way the gifts precede the intellectual and moral virtues, but follow the theological virtues. The other is the order of generation or disposition: thus love of one's neighbor precedes love of God, as regards the act: and in this way moral and intellectual virtues precede the gifts, since man, through being well subordinate to his own reason, is disposed to be rightly subordinate to God.

Reply to Objection 3: Wisdom and understanding and the like are gifts of the Holy Ghost, according as they are quickened by charity, which "dealeth not perversely" (1 Cor. 13:4). Consequently wisdom and understanding and the like cannot be used to evil purpose, in so far as they are gifts of the Holy Ghost. But, lest they depart from the perfection of charity, they assist one another. This is what Gregory means to say.

Quaestio LXIX

Deinde considerandum est de beatitudinibus. Et circa hoc quaeruntur quatuor. *Primo,* utrum beatitudines a donis et virtutibus distinguantur. *Secundo,* de praemiis beatitudinum, utrum pertineant ad hanc vitam. *Tertio,* de numero beatitudinum. *Quarto,* de convenientia praemiorum quae eis attribuuntur.

Articulus 1

Ad primum sic proceditur. Videtur quod beatitudines a virtutibus et donis non distinguantur. Augustinus enim, in libro de Serm. Dom. in monte, attribuit beatitudines in Matthaeo enumeratas, donis spiritus sancti, Ambrosius autem, super Lucam, attribuit beatitudines ibi enumeratas quatuor virtutibus cardinalibus. Ergo beatitudines non distinguuntur a virtutibus et donis.

Praeterea, humanae voluntatis non est nisi duplex regula, scilicet ratio, et lex aeterna, ut supra habitum est. Sed virtutes perficiunt hominem in ordine ad rationem; dona autem in ordine ad legem aeternam spiritus sancti, ut ex dictis patet. Ergo non potest esse aliquid aliud pertinens ad rectitudinem voluntatis humanae, praeter virtutes et dona. Non ergo beatitudines ab eis distinguuntur.

Praeterea, in enumeratione beatitudinum ponitur mititas, et iustitia, et misericordia; quae dicuntur esse quaedam virtutes. Ergo beatitudines non distinguuntur a virtutibus et donis.

Sed contra est quod quaedam enumerantur inter beatitudines, quae nec sunt virtutes nec dona; sicut paupertas, et luctus, et pax. Differunt ergo beatitudines et a virtutibus et a donis.

Respondeo dicendum quod, sicut supra dictum est, beatitudo est ultimus finis humanae vitae. Dicitur autem aliquis iam finem habere, propter spem finis obtinendi,

Question 69
Of the Beatitudes

We must now consider the beatitudes: under which head there are four points of inquiry: 1. Whether the beatitudes differ from the gifts and virtues? 2. Of the rewards of the beatitudes: whether they refer to this life? 3. Of the number of the beatitudes; 4. Of the fittingness of the rewards ascribed to the beatitudes.

Article 1
Whether the beatitudes differ from the virtues and gifts?

Objection 1: It would seem that the beatitudes do not differ from the virtues and gifts. For Augustine (De Serm. Dom. in Monte i, 4) assigns the beatitudes recited by Matthew (v 3, seqq.) to the gifts of the Holy Ghost; and Ambrose in his commentary on Luke 6:20, seqq., ascribes the beatitudes mentioned there, to the four cardinal virtues. Therefore the beatitudes do not differ from the virtues and gifts.

Objection 2: Further, there are but two rules of the human will: the reason and the eternal law, as stated above (I-II, q. 19, a. 3; ; q. 21, a. 1). Now the virtues perfect man in relation to reason; while the gifts perfect him in relation to the eternal law of the Holy Ghost, as is clear from what has been said (I-II, q. 68, a. 1; a. 3, seqq.). Therefore there cannot be anything else pertaining to the rectitude of the human will, besides the virtues and gifts. Therefore the beatitudes do not differ from them.

Objection 3: Further, among the beatitudes are included meekness, justice, and mercy, which are said to be virtues. Therefore the beatitudes do not differ from the virtues and gifts.

On the contrary, Certain things are included among the beatitudes, that are neither virtues nor gifts, e.g., poverty, mourning, and peace. Therefore the beatitudes differ from the virtues and gifts.

I answer that, As stated above (I-II, q. 2, a. 7; q. 3, a. 1), happiness is the last end of human life. Now one is said to possess the end already, when one hopes to possess it;

unde et philosophus dicit, in I Ethic., quod *pueri dicuntur beati propter spem*; et apostolus dicit, Rom. VIII, *spe salvi facti sumus*. Spes autem de fine consequendo insurgit ex hoc quod aliquis convenienter movetur ad finem, et appropinquat ad ipsum, quod quidem fit per aliquam actionem. Ad finem autem beatitudinis movetur aliquis et appropinquat per operationes virtutum; et praecipue per operationes donorum, si loquamur de beatitudine aeterna, ad quam ratio non sufficit, sed in eam inducit spiritus sanctus, ad cuius obedientiam et sequelam per dona perficimur. Et ideo beatitudines distinguuntur quidem a virtutibus et donis, non sicut habitus ab eis distincti, sed sicut actus distinguuntur ab habitibus.

AD PRIMUM ergo dicendum quod Augustinus et Ambrosius attribuunt beatitudines donis et virtutibus, sicut actus attribuuntur habitibus. Dona autem sunt eminentiora virtutibus cardinalibus, ut supra dictum est. Et ideo Ambrosius, exponens beatitudines turbis propositas, attribuit eas virtutibus cardinalibus; Augustinus autem, exponens beatitudines discipulis propositas in monte, tanquam perfectioribus, attribuit eas donis spiritus sancti.

AD SECUNDUM dicendum quod ratio illa probat quod non sunt alii habitus rectificantes humanam vitam, praeter virtutes et dona.

AD TERTIUM dicendum quod mititas accipitur pro actu mansuetudinis, et similiter dicendum est de iustitia et de misericordia. Et quamvis haec videantur esse virtutes, attribuuntur tamen donis, quia etiam dona perficiunt hominem circa omnia circa quae perficiunt virtutes, ut dictum est.

wherefore the Philosopher says (Ethic. i, 9) that "children are said to be happy because they are full of hope"; and the Apostle says (Rom. 8:24): "We are saved by hope." Again, we hope to obtain an end, because we are suitably moved towards that end, and approach thereto; and this implies some action. And a man is moved towards, and approaches the happy end by works of virtue, and above all by the works of the gifts, if we speak of eternal happiness, for which our reason is not sufficient, since we need to be moved by the Holy Ghost, and to be perfected with His gifts that we may obey and follow him. Consequently the beatitudes differ from the virtues and gifts, not as habit, but as act from habit.

Reply to Objection 1: Augustine and Ambrose assign the beatitudes to the gifts and virtues, as acts are ascribed to habits. But the gifts are more excellent than the cardinal virtues, as stated above (I-II, q. 68, a. 8). Wherefore Ambrose, in explaining the beatitudes propounded to the throng, assigns them to the cardinal virtues, whereas Augustine, who is explaining the beatitudes delivered to the disciples on the mountain, and so to those who were more perfect, ascribes them to the gifts of the Holy Ghost.

Reply to Objection 2: This argument proves that no other habits, besides the virtues and gifts, rectify human conduct.

Reply to Objection 3: Meekness is to be taken as denoting the act of meekness: and the same applies to justice and mercy. And though these might seem to be virtues, they are nevertheless ascribed to gifts, because the gifts perfect man in all matters wherein the virtues perfect him, as stated above (I-II, q. 68, a. 2).

ARTICULUS 2

AD SECUNDUM sic proceditur. Videtur quod praemia quae attribuuntur beatitudinibus, non pertineant ad hanc vitam. Dicuntur enim aliqui beati propter spem praemiorum, ut dictum est. Sed obiectum spei beatitudo est futura. Ergo praemia ista pertinent ad vitam futuram.

ARTICLE 2
Whether the rewards assigned to the beatitudes refer to this life?

Objection 1: It would seem that the rewards assigned to the beatitudes do not refer to this life. Because some are said to be happy because they hope for a reward, as stated above (I-II, q. 69, a. 1). Now the object of hope is future happiness. Therefore these rewards refer to the life to come.

THE BEATITUDES

PRAETEREA, Luc. VI, ponuntur quaedam poenae per oppositum ad beatitudines, cum dicitur, *vae vobis qui saturati estis, quia esurietis. Vae vobis qui ridetis nunc, quia lugebitis et flebitis.* Sed istae poenae non intelliguntur in hac vita, quia frequenter homines in hac vita non puniuntur, secundum illud Iob XXI, *ducunt in bonis dies suos.* Ergo nec praemia beatitudinum pertinent ad hanc vitam.

PRAETEREA, regnum caelorum, quod ponitur praemium paupertatis, est beatitudo caelestis; ut Augustinus dicit, XIX de Civ. Dei. *Plena etiam saturitas non nisi in futura vita habetur;* secundum illud Psalmi XVI, *satiabor cum apparuerit gloria tua.* Visio etiam Dei, et manifestatio filiationis divinae, ad vitam futuram pertinent; secundum illud I Ioan. III, *nunc filii Dei sumus, et nondum apparuit quid erimus. Scimus quoniam cum apparuerit, similes ei erimus, quoniam videbimus eum sicuti est.* Ergo praemia illa pertinent ad vitam futuram.

SED CONTRA est quod Augustinus dicit, in libro de Serm. Dom. in monte, *ista quidem in hac vita compleri possunt, sicut completa esse in apostolis credimus. Nam illa omnimoda, et in angelicam formam mutatio, quae post hanc vitam promittitur, nullis verbis exponi potest.*

RESPONDEO dicendum quod circa ista praemia expositores sacrae Scripturae diversimode sunt locuti. Quidam enim omnia ista praemia ad futuram beatitudinem pertinere dicunt, sicut Ambrosius, super Lucam. Augustinus vero dicit ea ad praesentem vitam pertinere. Chrysostomus autem, in suis homiliis, quaedam eorum dicit pertinere ad futuram vitam, quaedam autem ad praesentem. Ad cuius evidentiam, considerandum est quod spes futurae beatitudinis potest esse in nobis propter duo, primo quidem, propter aliquam praeparationem vel dispositionem ad futuram beatitudinem, quod est per modum meriti; alio modo, per quandam inchoationem imperfectam

Objection 2: Further, certain punishments are set down in opposition to the beatitudes, Lk. 6:25, where we read: "Woe to you that are filled; for you shall hunger. Woe to you that now laugh, for you shall mourn and weep." Now these punishments do not refer to this life, because frequently men are not punished in this life, according to Job 21:13: "They spend their days in wealth." Therefore neither do the rewards of the beatitudes refer to this life.

Objection 3: Further, the kingdom of heaven which is set down as the reward of poverty is the happiness of heaven, as Augustine says (De Civ. Dei xix).* Again, abundant fullness is not to be had save in the life to come, according to Ps. 16:15: "I shall be filled† when Thy glory shall appear." Again, it is only in the future life that we shall see God, and that our Divine sonship will be made manifest, according to 1 Jn. 3:2: "We are now the sons of God; and it hath not yet appeared what we shall be. We know that, when He shall appear, we shall be like to Him, because we shall see Him as He is." Therefore these rewards refer to the future life.

On the contrary, Augustine says (De Serm. Dom. in Monte i, 4): "These promises can be fulfilled in this life, as we believe them to have been fulfilled in the apostles. For no words can express that complete change into the likeness even of an angel, which is promised to us after this life."

I answer that, Expounders of Holy Writ are not agreed in speaking of these rewards. For some, with Ambrose (Super Luc. v), hold that all these rewards refer to the life to come; while Augustine (De Serm. Dom. in Monte i, 4) holds them to refer to the present life; and Chrysostom in his homilies (In Matth. xv) says that some refer to the future, and some to the present life. In order to make the matter clear we must take note that hope of future happiness may be in us for two reasons. First, by reason of our having a preparation for, or a disposition to future happiness; and this is by way of merit; secondly, by a kind of imperfect inchoation of

---

* Cf. De Serm. Dom. in Monte i, 1.
† Douay: 'satisfied'

futurae beatitudinis in viris sanctis, etiam in hac vita. Aliter enim habetur spes fructificationis arboris cum virescit frondibus, et aliter cum iam primordia fructuum incipiunt apparere. Sic igitur ea quae in beatitudinibus tanguntur tanquam merita, sunt quaedam praeparationes vel dispositiones ad beatitudinem, vel perfectam vel inchoatam. Ea vero quae ponuntur tanquam praemia, possunt esse vel ipsa beatitudo perfecta, et sic pertinent ad futuram vitam, vel aliqua inchoatio beatitudinis, sicut est in viris perfectis, et sic praemia pertinent ad praesentem vitam. Cum enim aliquis incipit proficere in actibus virtutum et donorum, potest sperari de eo quod perveniet et ad perfectionem viae, et ad perfectionem patriae.

AD PRIMUM ergo dicendum quod spes est de futura beatitudine sicut de ultimo fine, potest etiam esse et de auxilio gratiae, sicut de eo quod ducit ad finem, secundum illud Psalmi XXVII, *in Deo speravit cor meum, et adiutus sum.*

AD SECUNDUM dicendum quod mali, etsi interdum in hac vita temporales poenas non patiantur, patiuntur tamen spirituales. Unde Augustinus dicit, in I Confess., *iussisti, domine, et sic est, ut poena sibi sit inordinatus animus.* Et philosophus dicit, in IX Ethic., de malis, quod *contendit ipsorum anima, et hoc quidem huc trahit, illud autem illuc*; et postea concludit, *si autem sic miserum est malum esse, fugiendum est malitiam intense.* Et similiter e converso boni, etsi in hac vita quandoque non habeant corporalia praemia, nunquam tamen deficiunt a spiritualibus, etiam in hac vita; secundum illud Matth. XIX, et Marc. X, *centuplum accipietis* etiam *in hoc saeculo.*

AD TERTIUM dicendum quod omnia illa praemia perfecte quidem consummabuntur in vita futura, sed interim etiam in hac vita quodammodo inchoantur. Nam *regnum caelorum,* ut Augustinus dicit, potest intelligi perfectae sapientiae initium,

future happiness in holy men, even in this life. For it is one thing to hope that the tree will bear fruit, when the leaves begin to appear, and another, when we see the first signs of the fruit. Accordingly, those things which are set down as merits in the beatitudes, are a kind of preparation for, or disposition to happiness, either perfect or inchoate: while those that are assigned as rewards, may be either perfect happiness, so as to refer to the future life, or some beginning of happiness, such as is found in those who have attained perfection, in which case they refer to the present life. Because when a man begins to make progress in the acts of the virtues and gifts, it is to be hoped that he will arrive at perfection, both as a wayfarer, and as a citizen of the heavenly kingdom.

Reply to Objection 1: Hope regards future happiness as the last end: yet it may also regard the assistance of grace as that which leads to that end, according to Ps. 27:7: "In Him hath my heart hoped, and I have been helped."

Reply to Objection 2: Although sometimes the wicked do not undergo temporal punishment in this life, yet they suffer spiritual punishment. Hence Augustine says (Confess. i): "Thou hast decreed, and it is so, Lord—that the disordered mind should be its own punishment." The Philosopher, too, says of the wicked (Ethic. ix, 4) that "their soul is divided against itself . . . one part pulls this way, another that"; and afterwards he concludes, saying: "If wickedness makes a man so miserable, he should strain every nerve to avoid vice." In like manner, although, on the other hand, the good sometimes do not receive material rewards in this life, yet they never lack spiritual rewards, even in this life, according to Mat. 19:29, and Mk. 10:30: "Ye shall receive a hundred times as much" even "in this time."

Reply to Objection 3: All these rewards will be fully consummated in the life to come: but meanwhile they are, in a manner, begun, even in this life. Because the "kingdom of heaven," as Augustine says (De Civ. Dei xiv);* can denote the beginning of perfect wisdom,

---

* Cf. De Serm. Dom. in Monte, i, 1.

secundum quod incipit in eis *spiritus* regnare. *Possessio* etiam terrae significat affectum bonum animae requiescentis per desiderium in stabilitate haereditatis perpetuae, per *terram* significatae. *Consolantur* autem in hac vita, spiritum sanctum, qui *Paracletus,* idest consolator, dicitur, participando. *Saturantur* etiam in hac vita illo cibo de quo dominus dicit, *meus cibus est ut faciam voluntatem patris mei.* In hac etiam vita *consequuntur* homines *misericordiam* Dei. In hac etiam vita, purgato oculo per donum intellectus, *Deus* quodammodo *videri* potest. Similiter etiam in hac vita qui motus suos *pacificant,* ad similitudinem Dei accedentes, *filii Dei* nominantur. Tamen haec perfectius erunt in patria.

in so far as "the spirit" begins to reign in men. The "possession" of the land denotes the well ordered affections of the soul that rests, by its desire, on the solid foundation of the eternal inheritance, signified by "the land." They are "comforted" in this life, by receiving the Holy Ghost, Who is called the "Paraclete," i.e., the Comforter. They "have their fill," even in this life, of that food of which Our Lord said (Jn. 4:34): "My meat is to do the will of Him that sent Me." Again, in this life, men "obtain" God's "Mercy." Again, the eye being cleansed by the gift of understanding, we can, so to speak, "see God." Likewise, in this life, those who are the "peacemakers" of their own movements, approach to likeness to God, and are called "the children of God." Nevertheless these things will be more perfectly fulfilled in heaven.

Articulus 3

Ad tertium sic proceditur. Videtur quod inconvenienter enumerentur beatitudines. Attribuuntur enim beatitudines donis, ut dictum est. Donorum autem quaedam pertinent ad vitam contemplativam, scilicet sapientia et intellectus, nulla autem beatitudo ponitur in actu contemplationis, sed omnes in his quae pertinent ad vitam activam. Ergo insufficienter beatitudines enumerantur.

Praeterea, ad vitam activam non solum pertinent dona exequentia; sed etiam quaedam dona dirigentia, ut scientia et consilium. Nihil autem ponitur inter beatitudines quod directe ad actum scientiae vel consilii pertinere videatur. Ergo insufficienter beatitudines tanguntur.

Praeterea, inter dona exequentia in vita activa, timor ponitur ad paupertatem pertinere; pietas autem videtur pertinere ad beatitudinem misericordiae. Nihil autem ponitur directe ad fortitudinem pertinens. Ergo insufficienter enumerantur beatitudines.

Article 3
Whether the beatitudes are suitably enumerated?

Objection 1: It would seem that the beatitudes are unsuitably enumerated. For the beatitudes are assigned to the gifts, as stated above (I-II, q. 69, a. 1, ad 1). Now some of the gifts, *viz.* wisdom and understanding, belong to the contemplative life: yet no beatitude is assigned to the act of contemplation, for all are assigned to matters connected with the active life. Therefore the beatitudes are insufficiently enumerated.

Objection 2: Further, not only do the executive gifts belong to the active life, but also some of the directive gifts, e.g., knowledge and counsel: yet none of the beatitudes seems to be directly connected with the acts of knowledge or counsel. Therefore the beatitudes are insufficiently indicated.

Objection 3: Further, among the executive gifts connected with the active life, fear is said to be connected with poverty, while piety seems to correspond to the beatitude of mercy: yet nothing is included directly connected with justice. Therefore the beatitudes are insufficiently enumerated.

PRAETEREA, in sacra Scriptura tanguntur multae aliae beatitudines, sicut Iob V, dicitur, *beatus homo qui corripitur a domino*; et in Psalmo I, *beatus vir qui non abiit in consilio impiorum*; et Proverb. III, *beatus vir qui invenit sapientiam*. Ergo insufficienter beatitudines enumerantur.

SED CONTRA, videtur quod superflue enumerentur. Sunt enim septem dona spiritus sancti. Beatitudines autem tanguntur octo.

PRAETEREA, Luc. VI, ponuntur quatuor tantum beatitudines. Superflue ergo enumerantur septem, vel octo, in Matthaeo.

RESPONDEO dicendum quod beatitudines istae convenientissime enumerantur. Ad cuius evidentiam, est considerandum quod triplicem beatitudinem aliqui posuerunt, quidam enim posuerunt beatitudinem in vita voluptuosa; quidam in vita activa; quidam vero in vita contemplativa. Hae autem tres beatitudines diversimode se habent ad beatitudinem futuram, cuius spe dicimur hic beati. Nam beatitudo voluptuosa, quia falsa est et rationi contraria, impedimentum est beatitudinis futurae. Beatitudo vero activae vitae dispositiva est ad beatitudinem futuram. Beatitudo autem contemplativa, si sit perfecta, est essentialiter ipsa futura beatitudo, si autem sit imperfecta, est quaedam inchoatio eius. Et ideo dominus primo quidem posuit quasdam beatitudines quasi removentes impedimentum voluptuosae beatitudinis. Consistit enim voluptuosa vita in duobus. Primo quidem, in affluentia exteriorum bonorum, sive sint divitiae, sive sint honores. A quibus quidem retrahitur homo per virtutem sic ut moderate eis utatur, per donum autem excellentiori modo, ut scilicet homo totaliter ea contemnat. Unde prima beatitudo ponitur, *beati pauperes spiritu*, quod potest referri vel ad contemptum divitiarum; vel ad contemptum honorum, quod fit per humilitatem. Secundo vero voluptuosa vita consistit in sequendo proprias passiones, sive irascibilis sive concupiscibilis. A sequela autem passionum irascibilis, retrahit virtus

Objection 4: Further, many other beatitudes are mentioned in Holy Writ. Thus, it is written (Job 5:17): "Blessed is the man whom God correcteth"; and (Ps. i, 1): "Blessed is the man who hath not walked in the counsel of the ungodly"; and (Prov. 3:13): "Blessed is the man that findeth wisdom." Therefore the beatitudes are insufficiently enumerated.

Objection 5: On the other hand, it seems that too many are mentioned. For there are seven gifts of the Holy Ghost: whereas eight beatitudes are indicated.

Objection 6: Further, only four beatitudes are indicated in the sixth chapter of Luke. Therefore the seven or eight mentioned in Matthew 5 are too many.

I answer that, These beatitudes are most suitably enumerated. To make this evident it must be observed that beatitude has been held to consist in one of three things: for some have ascribed it to a sensual life, some, to an active life, and some, to a contemplative life.* Now these three kinds of happiness stand in different relations to future beatitude, by hoping for which we are said to be happy. Because sensual happiness, being false and contrary to reason, is an obstacle to future beatitude; while happiness of the active life is a disposition of future beatitude; and contemplative happiness, if perfect, is the very essence of future beatitude, and, if imperfect, is a beginning thereof. And so Our Lord, in the first place, indicated certain beatitudes as removing the obstacle of sensual happiness. For a life of pleasure consists of two things. First, in the affluence of external goods, whether riches or honors; from which man is withdrawn—by a virtue so that he uses them in moderation—and by a gift, in a more excellent way, so that he despises them altogether. Hence the first beatitude is: "Blessed are the poor in spirit," which may refer either to the contempt of riches, or to the contempt of honors, which results from humility. Secondly, the sensual life consists in following the bent of one's passions, whether irascible or concupiscible. From following the irascible passions man is withdrawn—by a virtue,

---

* I-II, q. 3.

so that they are kept within the bounds appointed by the ruling of reason—and by a gift, in a more excellent manner, so that man, according to God's will, is altogether undisturbed by them: hence the second beatitude is: "Blessed are the meek." From following the concupiscible passions, man is withdrawn—by a virtue, so that man uses these passions in moderation—and by gift, so that, if necessary, he casts them aside altogether; nay more, so that, if need be, he makes a deliberate choice of sorrow;[*] hence the third beatitude is: "Blessed are they that mourn." Active life consists chiefly in man's relations with his neighbor, either by way of duty or by way of spontaneous gratuity. To the former we are disposed—by a virtue, so that we do not refuse to do our duty to our neighbor, which pertains to justice—and by a gift, so that we do the same much more heartily, by accomplishing works of justice with an ardent desire, even as a hungry and thirsty man eats and drinks with eager appetite. Hence the fourth beatitude is: "Blessed are they that hunger and thirst after justice." With regard to spontaneous favors we are perfected—by a virtue, so that we give where reason dictates we should give, e.g., to our friends or others united to us; which pertains to the virtue of liberality—and by a gift, so that, through reverence for God, we consider only the needs of those on whom we bestow our gratuitous bounty: hence it is written (Lk. 14:12, 13): "When thou makest a dinner or supper, call not thy friends, nor thy brethren," etc.…"but…call the poor, the maimed," etc.; which, properly, is to have mercy: hence the fifth beatitude is: "Blessed are the merciful." Those things which concern the contemplative life, are either final beatitude itself, or some beginning thereof: wherefore they are included in the beatitudes, not as merits, but as rewards. Yet the effects of the active life, which dispose man for the contemplative life, are included in the beatitudes. Now the effect of the active life, as regards those virtues and gifts whereby man is perfected in himself, is the cleansing of man's heart, so that it is not defiled by the passions: hence the sixth

---

[*] Cf. I-II, q. 35, a. 3.

I-II, q. 69, a. 3, co.

beatitudo ponitur, *beati mundo corde*. Quantum vero ad virtutes et dona quibus homo perficitur in comparatione ad proximum, effectus activae vitae est pax; secundum illud Isaiae XXXII, *opus iustitiae pax*. Et ideo septima beatitudo ponitur, *beati pacifici*.

AD PRIMUM ergo dicendum quod actus donorum pertinentium ad vitam activam, exprimuntur in ipsis meritis, sed actus donorum pertinentium ad vitam contemplativam, exprimuntur in praemiis, ratione iam dicta. *Videre enim Deum* respondet dono intellectus; et conformari Deo quadam *filiatione* adoptiva, pertinet ad donum sapientiae.

AD SECUNDUM dicendum quod in his quae pertinent ad activam vitam, cognitio non quaeritur propter seipsam, sed propter operationem, ut etiam philosophus dicit, in II Ethic. Et ideo, quia beatitudo aliquid ultimum importat, non computantur inter beatitudines actus donorum dirigentium in vita activa, quos scilicet eliciunt, sicut consiliari est actus consilii, et iudicare est actus scientiae, sed magis attribuuntur eis actus operativi in quibus dirigunt, sicut scientiae lugere, et consilio misereri.

AD TERTIUM dicendum quod in attributione beatitudinum ad dona, possunt duo considerari. Quorum unum est conformitas materiae. Et secundum hoc, omnes primae quinque beatitudines possunt attribui scientiae et consilio, tanquam dirigentibus. Sed inter dona exequentia distribuuntur, ita scilicet quod esuries et sitis iustitiae, et etiam misericordia, pertineant ad pietatem, quae perficit hominem in his quae sunt ad alterum; mititas autem ad fortitudinem, dicit enim Ambrosius, super Lucam, quod *fortitudinis est iram vincere, indignationem cohibere,* est enim fortitudo circa passiones irascibilis; paupertas vero et luctus ad donum timoris, quo homo se retrahit a cupiditatibus et delectationibus mundi. Alio modo possumus in his beatitudinibus considerare motiva ipsarum, et sic, quantum ad aliqua eorum, oportet aliter attribuere. Praecipue enim ad mansuetudinem movet reverentia

THE BEATITUDES

beatitude is: "Blessed are the clean of heart." But as regards the virtues and gifts whereby man is perfected in relation to his neighbor, the effect of the active life is peace, according to Is. 32:17: "The work of justice shall be peace": hence the seventh beatitude is "Blessed are the peacemakers."

Reply to Objection 1: The acts of the gifts which belong to the active life are indicated in the merits: but the acts of the gifts pertaining to the contemplative life are indicated in the rewards, for the reason given above. Because to "see God" corresponds to the gift of understanding; and to be like God by being adoptive "children of God," corresponds to the gift of wisdom.

Reply to Objection 2: In things pertaining to the active life, knowledge is not sought for its own sake, but for the sake of operation, as even the Philosopher states (Ethic. ii, 2). And therefore, since beatitude implies something ultimate, the beatitudes do not include the acts of those gifts which direct man in the active life, such acts, to wit, as are elicited by those gifts, as, e.g., to counsel is the act of counsel, and to judge, the act of knowledge: but, on the other hand, they include those operative acts of which the gifts have the direction, as, e.g., mourning in respect of knowledge, and mercy in respect of counsel.

Reply to Objection 3: In applying the beatitudes to the gifts we may consider two things. One is likeness of matter. In this way all the first five beatitudes may be assigned to knowledge and counsel as to their directing principles: whereas they must be distributed among the executive gifts: so that, to wit, hunger and thirst for justice, and mercy too, correspond to piety, which perfects man in his relations to others; meekness to fortitude, for Ambrose says on Lk. 6:22: "It is the business of fortitude to conquer anger, and to curb indignation," fortitude being about the irascible passions: poverty and mourning to the gift of fear, whereby man withdraws from the lusts and pleasures of the world. Secondly, we may consider the motives of the beatitudes: and, in this way, some of them will have to be assigned differently. Because the principal motive for meekness is reverence

ad Deum; quae pertinet ad pietatem. Ad lugendum autem movet praecipue scientia, per quam homo cognoscit defectus suos et rerum mundanarum; secundum illud Eccle. I, *qui addit scientiam, addit et dolorem.* Ad esuriendum autem iustitiae opera, praecipue movet animi fortitudo. Ad miserendum vero praecipue movet consilium Dei; secundum illud Dan. IV, *consilium meum regi placeat, peccata tua eleemosynis redime, et iniquitates tuas misericordiis pauperum.* Et hunc modum attributionis sequitur Augustinus, in libro de Serm. Dom. in monte.

AD QUARTUM dicendum quod necesse est beatitudines omnes quae in sacra Scriptura ponuntur, ad has reduci vel quantum ad merita, vel quantum ad praemia, quia necesse est quod omnes pertineant aliquo modo vel ad vitam activam, vel ad vitam contemplativam. Unde quod dicitur, *beatus vir qui corripitur a domino,* pertinet ad beatitudinem luctus. Quod vero dicitur, *beatus vir qui non abiit in consilio impiorum,* pertinet ad munditiam cordis. Quod vero dicitur, *beatus vir qui invenit sapientiam,* pertinet ad praemium septimae beatitudinis. Et idem patet de omnibus aliis quae possunt induci.

AD QUINTUM dicendum quod octava beatitudo est quaedam confirmatio et manifestatio omnium praecedentium. Ex hoc enim quod aliquis est confirmatus in paupertate spiritus et mititate et aliis sequentibus, provenit quod ab his bonis propter nullam persecutionem recedit. Unde octava beatitudo quodammodo ad septem praecedentes pertinet.

AD SEXTUM dicendum quod Lucas narrat sermonem domini factum esse ad turbas. Unde beatitudines numerantur ab eo secundum capacitatem turbarum, quae solam voluptuosam et temporalem et terrenam beatitudinem noverunt. Unde dominus per quatuor beatitudines quatuor excludit quae ad praedictam beatitudinem pertinere videntur. Quorum primum est abundantia bonorum exteriorum, quod excludit per hoc

for God, which belongs to piety. The chief motive for mourning is knowledge, whereby man knows his failings and those of worldly things, according to Eccles. 1:18: "He that addeth knowledge, addeth also sorrow.[*]" The principal motive for hungering after the works of justice is fortitude of the soul: and the chief motive for being merciful is God's counsel, according to Dan. 4:24: "Let my counsel be acceptable to the king:[†] and redeem thou thy sins with alms, and thy iniquities with works of mercy to the poor." It is thus that Augustine assigns them (De Serm. Dom. in Monte i, 4).

Reply to Objection 4: All the beatitudes mentioned in Holy Writ must be reduced to these, either as to the merits or as to the rewards: because they must all belong either to the active or to the contemplative life. Accordingly, when we read, "Blessed is the man whom the Lord correcteth," we must refer this to the beatitude of mourning: when we read, "Blessed is the man that hath not walked in the counsel of the ungodly," we must refer it to cleanness of heart: and when we read, "Blessed is the man that findeth wisdom," this must be referred to the reward of the seventh beatitude. The same applies to all others that can be adduced.

Reply to Objection 5: The eighth beatitude is a confirmation and declaration of all those that precede. Because from the very fact that a man is confirmed in poverty of spirit, meekness, and the rest, it follows that no persecution will induce him to renounce them. Hence the eighth beatitude corresponds, in a way, to all the preceding seven.

Reply to Objection 6: Luke relates Our Lord's sermon as addressed to the multitude (Lk. 6:17). Hence he sets down the beatitudes according to the capacity of the multitude, who know no other happiness than pleasure, temporal and earthly: wherefore by these four beatitudes Our Lord excludes four things which seem to belong to such happiness. The first of these is abundance of external goods, which he sets aside by

---

[*] Vulg: labor
[†] Vulg: to thee, O king

quod dicit, *beati pauperes*. Secundum est quod sit bene homini quantum ad corpus, in cibis et potibus et aliis huiusmodi, et hoc excludit per secundum quod ponit, *beati qui esuritis*. Tertium est quod sit homini bene quantum ad cordis iucunditatem, et hoc excludit tertio, dicens, *beati qui nunc fletis*. Quartum est exterior hominum favor, et hoc excludit quarto, dicens, *beati eritis cum vos oderint homines*. Et sicut Ambrosius dicit, *paupertas pertinet ad temperantiam, quae illecebrosa non quaerit; esuries ad iustitiam, quia qui esurit, compatitur, et, compatiendo, largitur; fletus ad prudentiam, cuius est flere occidua; pati odium hominum, ad fortitudinem.*

saying: "Blessed are ye poor." The second is that man be well off as to his body, in food and drink, and so forth; this he excludes by saying in the second place: "Blessed are ye that hunger." The third is that it should be well with man as to joyfulness of heart, and this he puts aside by saying: "Blessed are ye that weep now." The fourth is the outward favor of man; and this he excludes, saying, fourthly: "Blessed shall you be, when men shall hate you." And as Ambrose says on Lk. 6:20, "poverty corresponds to temperance, which is unmoved by delights; hunger, to justice, since who hungers is compassionate and, through compassion gives; mourning, to prudence, which deplores perishable things; endurance of men's hatred belongs to fortitude."

Articulus 4

Ad quartum sic proceditur. Videtur quod praemia beatitudinum inconvenienter enumerentur. In regno enim caelorum, quod est vita aeterna, bona omnia continentur. Posito ergo regno caelorum, non oportuit alia praemia ponere.

Praeterea, regnum caelorum ponitur pro praemio et in prima beatitudine et in octava. Ergo, eadem ratione, debuit poni in omnibus.

Praeterea, in beatitudinibus proceditur ascendendo, sicut Augustinus dicit. In praemiis autem videtur procedi descendendo, nam *possessio terrae* est minus quam *regnum caelorum*. Ergo inconvenienter huiusmodi praemia assignantur.

Sed contra est auctoritas ipsius domini, praemia huiusmodi proponentis.

Respondeo dicendum quod praemia ista convenientissime assignantur, considerata conditione beatitudinum secundum tres beatitudines supra assignatas. Tres enim primae beatitudines accipiuntur per retractionem ab his in quibus voluptuosa beatitudo consistit, quam homo desiderat quaerens id quod

Article 4
Whether the rewards of the beatitudes are suitably enumerated?

Objection 1: It would seem that the rewards of the beatitudes are unsuitably enumerated. Because the kingdom of heaven, which is eternal life, contains all good things. Therefore, once given the kingdom of heaven, no other rewards should be mentioned.

Objection 2: Further, the kingdom of heaven is assigned as the reward, both of the first and of the eighth beatitude. Therefore, on the same ground it should have been assigned to all.

Objection 3: Further, the beatitudes are arranged in the ascending order, as Augustine remarks (De Serm. Dom. in Monte i, 4): whereas the rewards seem to be placed in the descending order, since to "possess the land" is less than to possess "the kingdom of heaven." Therefore these rewards are unsuitably enumerated.

On the contrary, stands the authority of Our Lord Who propounded these rewards.

I answer that, These rewards are most suitably assigned, considering the nature of the beatitudes in relation to the three kinds of happiness indicated above (I-II, q. 69, a. 3). For the first three beatitudes concerned the withdrawal of man from those things in which sensual happiness consists: which happiness man desires by seeking the object of

naturaliter desideratur, non ubi quaerere debet, scilicet in Deo, sed in rebus temporalibus et caducis. Et ideo praemia trium primarum beatitudinum accipiuntur secundum ea quae in beatitudine terrena aliqui quaerunt. Quaerunt enim homines in rebus exterioribus, scilicet divitiis et honoribus, excellentiam quandam et abundantiam, quorum utrumque importat regnum caelorum, per quod homo consequitur excellentiam et abundantiam bonorum in Deo. Et ideo regnum caelorum dominus pauperibus spiritu repromisit. Quaerunt autem homines feroces et immites per litigia et bella securitatem sibi acquirere, inimicos suos destruendo. Unde dominus repromisit mitibus securam et quietam possessionem terrae viventium, per quam significatur soliditas aeternorum bonorum. Quaerunt autem homines in concupiscentiis et delectationibus mundi, habere consolationem contra praesentis vitae labores. Et ideo dominus consolationem lugentibus repromittit. Aliae vero duae beatitudines pertinent ad opera activae beatitudinis, quae sunt opera virtutum ordinantium hominem ad proximum, a quibus operibus aliqui retrahuntur propter inordinatum amorem proprii boni. Et ideo dominus attribuit illa praemia his beatitudinibus, propter quae homines ab eis discedunt. Discedunt enim aliqui ab operibus iustitiae, non reddentes debitum, sed potius aliena rapientes ut bonis temporalibus repleantur. Et ideo dominus esurientibus iustitiam, saturitatem repromisit. Discedunt etiam aliqui ab operibus misericordiae, ne se immisceant miseriis alienis. Et ideo dominus misericordibus repromittit misericordiam, per quam ab omni miseria liberentur. Aliae vero duae ultimae beatitudines pertinent ad contemplativam felicitatem seu beatitudinem, et ideo secundum convenientiam dispositionum quae ponuntur in merito, praemia redduntur. Nam munditia oculi disponit ad clare videndum, unde mundis corde divina visio repromittitur. Constituere vero pacem vel in seipso vel inter alios, manifestat hominem esse Dei imitatorem, qui est Deus unitatis et pacis. Et ideo pro praemio redditur ei gloria divinae filiationis,

his natural desire, not where he should seek it, *viz.* in God, but in temporal and perishable things. Wherefore the rewards of the first three beatitudes correspond to these things which some men seek to find in earthly happiness. For men seek in external things, *viz.* riches and honors, a certain excellence and abundance, both of which are implied in the kingdom of heaven, whereby man attains to excellence and abundance of good things in God. Hence Our Lord promised the kingdom of heaven to the poor in spirit. Again, cruel and pitiless men seek by wrangling and fighting to destroy their enemies so as to gain security for themselves. Hence Our Lord promised the meek a secure and peaceful possession of the land of the living, whereby the solid reality of eternal goods is denoted. Again, men seek consolation for the toils of the present life, in the lusts and pleasures of the world. Hence Our Lord promises comfort to those that mourn. Two other beatitudes belong to the works of active happiness, which are the works of virtues directing man in his relations to his neighbor: from which operations some men withdraw through inordinate love of their own good. Hence Our Lord assigns to these beatitudes rewards in correspondence with the motives for which men recede from them. For there are some who recede from acts of justice, and instead of rendering what is due, lay hands on what is not theirs, that they may abound in temporal goods. Wherefore Our Lord promised those who hunger after justice, that they shall have their fill. Some, again, recede from works of mercy, lest they be busied with other people's misery. Hence Our Lord promised the merciful that they should obtain mercy, and be delivered from all misery. The last two beatitudes belong to contemplative happiness or beatitude: hence the rewards are assigned in correspondence with the dispositions included in the merit. For cleanness of the eye disposes one to see clearly: hence the clean of heart are promised that they shall see God. Again, to make peace either in oneself or among others, shows a man to be a follower of God, Who is the God of unity and peace. Hence, as a reward, he is promised the glory of the Divine sonship,

quae est in perfecta coniunctione ad Deum per sapientiam consummatam.

AD PRIMUM ergo dicendum quod, sicut Chrysostomus dicit, omnia praemia ista unum sunt in re, scilicet beatitudo aeterna; quam intellectus humanus non capit. Et ideo oportuit quod per diversa bona nobis nota, describeretur, observata convenientia ad merita quibus praemia attribuuntur.

AD SECUNDUM dicendum quod, sicut octava beatitudo est firmitas quaedam omnium beatitudinum, ita debentur sibi omnium beatitudinum praemia. Et ideo redit ad caput, ut intelligantur sibi consequenter omnia praemia attribui. Vel, secundum Ambrosium, pauperibus spiritu repromittitur regnum caelorum, quantum ad gloriam animae, sed passis persecutionem in corpore, quantum ad gloriam corporis.

AD TERTIUM dicendum quod etiam praemia secundum additionem se habent ad invicem. Nam plus est possidere terram regni caelorum, quam simpliciter habere, multa enim habemus quae non firmiter et pacifice possidemus. Plus est etiam consolari in regno, quam habere et possidere, multa enim cum dolore possidemus. Plus est etiam saturari quam simpliciter consolari, nam saturitas abundantiam consolationis importat. Misericordia vero excedit saturitatem, ut plus scilicet homo accipiat quam meruerit, vel desiderare potuerit. Adhuc autem maius est Deum videre, sicut maior est qui in curia regis non solum prandet, sed etiam faciem regis videt. Summam autem dignitatem in domo regia filius regis habet.

consisting in perfect union with God through consummate wisdom.

Reply to Objection 1: As Chrysostom says (Hom. xv in Matth.), all these rewards are one in reality, *viz.* eternal happiness, which the human intellect cannot grasp. Hence it was necessary to describe it by means of various boons known to us, while observing due proportion to the merits to which those rewards are assigned.

Reply to Objection 2: Just as the eighth beatitude is a confirmation of all the beatitudes, so it deserves all the rewards of the beatitudes. Hence it returns to the first, that we may understand all the other rewards to be attributed to it in consequence. Or else, according to Ambrose (Super Luc. v), the kingdom of heaven is promised to the poor in spirit, as regards the glory of the soul; but to those who suffer persecution in their bodies, it is promised as regards the glory of the body.

Reply to Objection 3: The rewards are also arranged in ascending order. For it is more to possess the land of the heavenly kingdom than simply to have it: since we have many things without possessing them firmly and peacefully. Again, it is more to be comforted in the kingdom than to have and possess it, for there are many things the possession of which is accompanied by sorrow. Again, it is more to have one's fill than simply to be comforted, because fulness implies abundance of comfort. And mercy surpasses satiety, for thereby man receives more than he merited or was able to desire. And yet more is it to see God, even as he is a greater man who not only dines at court, but also sees the king's countenance. Lastly, the highest place in the royal palace belongs to the king's son.

Quaestio LXX

Deinde considerandum est de fructibus. Et circa hoc quaeruntur quatuor. *Primo,* utrum fructus spiritus sancti sint actus. *Secundo,* utrum differant a beatitudinibus. *Tertio,* de eorum numero. *Quarto,* de oppositione eorum ad opera carnis.

Articulus 1

Ad primum sic proceditur. Videtur quod fructus spiritus sancti quos apostolus nominat ad Galat. V, non sint actus. Id enim cuius est alius fructus, non debet dici fructus, sic enim in infinitum iretur. Sed actuum nostrorum est aliquis fructus, dicitur enim Sap. III, *bonorum laborum gloriosus est fructus;* et Ioan. IV, *qui metit, mercedem accipit, et fructum congregat in vitam aeternam.* Ergo ipsi actus nostri non dicuntur fructus.

Praeterea, sicut Augustinus dicit, in X de Trin., fruimur cognitis in quibus voluntas propter ipsa delectata conquiescit. Sed voluntas nostra non debet conquiescere in actibus nostris propter se. Ergo actus nostri fructus dici non debent.

Praeterea, inter fructus spiritus sancti enumerantur ab apostolo aliquae virtutes scilicet caritas, mansuetudo, fides et castitas. Virtutes autem non sunt actus, sed habitus, ut supra dictum est. Ergo fructus non sunt actus.

Sed contra est quod dicitur Matth. XII, *ex fructu arbor cognoscitur;* idest, ex operibus suis homo, ut ibi exponitur a sanctis. Ergo ipsi actus humani dicuntur fructus.

Respondeo dicendum quod nomen *fructus* a corporalibus ad spiritualia est translatum. Dicitur autem in corporalibus fructus, quod ex planta producitur cum ad perfectionem pervenerit, et quandam in se suavitatem habet. Qui quidem fructus ad duo comparari potest, scilicet ad arborem producentem ipsum; et ad hominem qui fructum ex arbore adipiscitur. Secundum hoc

Question 70
Of the Fruits of the Holy Ghost

We must now consider the Fruits of the Holy Ghost: under which head there are four points of inquiry: 1. Whether the fruits of the Holy Ghost are acts? 2. Whether they differ from the beatitudes? 3. Of their number? 4. Of their opposition to the works of the flesh.

Article 1
Whether the fruits of the Holy Ghost which the Apostle enumerates (Gal. 5) are acts?

Objection 1: It would seem that the fruits of the Holy Ghost, enumerated by the Apostle (Gal. 5:22, 23), are not acts. For that which bears fruit, should not itself be called a fruit, else we should go on indefinitely. But our actions bear fruit: for it is written (Wis. 3:15): "The fruit of good labor is glorious," and (Jn. 4:36): "He that reapeth receiveth wages, and gathereth fruit unto life everlasting." Therefore our actions are not to be called fruits.

Objection 2: Further, as Augustine says (De Trin. x, 10), "we enjoy* the things we know, when the will rests by rejoicing in them." But our will should not rest in our actions for their own sake. Therefore our actions should not be called fruits.

Objection 3: Further, among the fruits of the Holy Ghost, the Apostle numbers certain virtues, *viz.* charity, meekness, faith, and chastity. Now virtues are not actions but habits, as stated above (I-II, q. 55, a. 1). Therefore the fruits are not actions.

On the contrary, It is written (Mat. 12:33): "By the fruit the tree is known"; that is to say, man is known by his works, as holy men explain the passage. Therefore human actions are called fruits.

I answer that, The word "fruit" has been transferred from the material to the spiritual world. Now fruit, among material things, is the product of a plant when it comes to perfection, and has a certain sweetness. This fruit has a twofold relation: to the tree that produces it, and to the man who gathers the fruit from the tree. Accordingly,

---

* *Fruimur,* from which verb we have the Latin *fructus* and the English 'fruit.'

igitur, nomen *fructus* in rebus spiritualibus dupliciter accipere possumus, uno modo, ut dicatur fructus hominis, quasi arboris, id quod ab eo producitur; alio modo, ut dicatur fructus hominis id quod homo adipiscitur. Non autem omne id quod adipiscitur homo, habet rationem fructus, sed id quod est ultimum, delectationem habens. Habet enim homo et agrum et arborem, quae fructus non dicuntur; sed solum id quod est ultimum, quod scilicet ex agro et arbore homo intendit habere. Et secundum hoc, fructus hominis dicitur ultimus hominis finis, quo debet frui. Si autem dicatur fructus hominis id quod ex homine producitur, sic ipsi actus humani fructus dicuntur, operatio enim est actus secundus operantis, et delectationem habet, si sit conveniens operanti. Si igitur operatio hominis procedat ab homine secundum facultatem suae rationis, sic dicitur esse fructus rationis. Si vero procedat ab homine secundum altiorem virtutem, quae est virtus spiritus sancti; sic dicitur esse operatio hominis fructus spiritus sancti, quasi cuiusdam divini seminis, dicitur enim I Ioan. III, *omnis qui natus est ex Deo, peccatum non facit, quoniam semen ipsius in eo manet.*

AD PRIMUM ergo dicendum quod, cum fructus habeat quodammodo rationem ultimi et finis, nihil prohibet alicuius fructus esse alium fructum, sicut finis ad finem ordinatur. Opera igitur nostra inquantum sunt effectus quidam spiritus sancti in nobis operantis, habent rationem fructus, sed inquantum ordinantur ad finem vitae aeternae, sic magis habent rationem florum. Unde dicitur Eccli. XXIV, *flores mei fructus honoris et honestatis.*

AD SECUNDUM dicendum quod, cum dicitur voluntas in aliquo propter se delectari, potest intelligi dupliciter. Uno modo, secundum quod ly *propter* dicit causam finalem, et sic propter se non delectatur aliquis nisi in ultimo fine. Alio modo, secundum quod designat causam formalem, et sic propter se aliquis potest delectari in omni eo quod delectabile est secundum suam formam. Sicut patet quod infirmus delectatur in sanitate propter se, sicut in fine; in medicina autem suavi, non sicut in fine, sed sicut in habente saporem delectabilem; in medicina autem austera, nullo modo propter se, sed

in spiritual matters, we may take the word "fruit" in two ways: first, so that the fruit of man, who is likened to the tree, is that which he produces; secondly, so that man's fruit is what he gathers. Yet not all that man gathers is fruit, but only that which is last and gives pleasure. For a man has both a field and a tree, and yet these are not called fruits; but that only which is last, to wit, that which man intends to derive from the field and from the tree. In this sense man's fruit is his last end which is intended for his enjoyment. If, however, by man's fruit we understand a product of man, then human actions are called fruits: because operation is the second act of the operator, and gives pleasure if it is suitable to him. If then man's operation proceeds from man in virtue of his reason, it is said to be the fruit of his reason: but if it proceeds from him in respect of a higher power, which is the power of the Holy Ghost, then man's operation is said to be the fruit of the Holy Ghost, as of a Divine seed, for it is written (1 Jn. 3:9): "Whosoever is born of God, committeth no sin, for His seed abideth in him."

Reply to Objection 1: Since fruit is something last and final, nothing hinders one fruit bearing another fruit, even as one end is subordinate to another. And so our works, in so far as they are produced by the Holy Ghost working in us, are fruits: but, in so far as they are referred to the end which is eternal life, they should rather be called flowers: hence it is written (Ecclus. 24:23): "My flowers are the fruits of honor and riches."

Reply to Objection 2: When the will is said to delight in a thing for its own sake, this may be understood in two ways. First, so that the expression "for the sake of" be taken to designate the final cause; and in this way, man delights in nothing for its own sake, except the last end. Secondly, so that it expresses the formal cause; and in this way, a man may delight in anything that is delightful by reason of its form. Thus it is clear that a sick man delights in health, for its own sake, as in an end; in a nice medicine, not as in an end, but as in something tasty; and in a nasty medicine, nowise for its own sake, but

solum propter aliud. Sic igitur dicendum est quod in Deo delectari debet homo propter se, sicut propter ultimum finem, in actibus autem virtuosis, non sicut propter finem, sed propter honestatem quam continent, delectabilem virtuosis. Unde Ambrosius dicit quod opera virtutum dicuntur fructus, quia *suos possessores sancta et sincera delectatione reficiunt.*

AD TERTIUM dicendum quod nomina virtutum sumuntur quandoque pro actibus earum, sicut Augustinus dicit quod *fides est credere quod non vides;* et *caritas est motus animi ad diligendum Deum et proximum.* Et hoc modo sumuntur nomina virtutum in enumeratione fructuum.

only for the sake of something else. Accordingly we must say that man must delight in God for His own sake, as being his last end, and in virtuous deeds, not as being his end, but for the sake of their inherent goodness which is delightful to the virtuous. Hence Ambrose says (De Parad. xiii) that virtuous deeds are called fruits because "they refresh those that have them, with a holy and genuine delight."

Reply to Objection 3: Sometimes the names of the virtues are applied to their actions: thus Augustine writes (Tract. xl in Joan.): "Faith is to believe what thou seest not"; and (De Doctr. Christ. iii, 10): "Charity is the movement of the soul in loving God and our neighbor." It is thus that the names of the virtues are used in reckoning the fruits.

ARTICULUS 2

AD SECUNDUM sic proceditur. Videtur quod fructus a beatitudinibus non differant. Beatitudines enim attribuuntur donis, ut supra dictum est. Sed dona perficiunt hominem secundum quod movetur a spiritu sancto. Ergo beatitudines ipsae sunt fructus spiritus sancti.

PRAETEREA, sicut se habet fructus vitae aeternae ad beatitudinem futuram, quae est rei; ita se habent fructus praesentis vitae ad beatitudines praesentis vitae, quae sunt spei. Sed fructus vitae aeternae est ipsa beatitudo futura. Ergo fructus vitae praesentis sunt ipsae beatitudines.

PRAETEREA, de ratione fructus est quod sit quiddam ultimum et delectabile. Sed hoc pertinet ad rationem beatitudinis, ut supra dictum est. Ergo eadem ratio est fructus et beatitudinis. Ergo non debent ab invicem distingui.

SED CONTRA, quorum species sunt diversae, ipsa quoque sunt diversa. Sed in diversas partes dividuntur et fructus et beatitudines; ut patet per numerationem utrorumque. Ergo fructus differunt a beatitudinibus.

ARTICLE 2
Whether the fruits differ from the beatitudes?

Objection 1: It would seem that the fruits do not differ from the beatitudes. For the beatitudes are assigned to the gifts, as stated above (I-II, q. 69, a. 1, ad 1). But the gifts perfect man in so far as he is moved by the Holy Ghost. Therefore the beatitudes themselves are fruits of the Holy Ghost.

Objection 2: Further, as the fruit of eternal life is to future beatitude which is that of actual possession, so are the fruits of the present life to the beatitudes of the present life, which are based on hope. Now the fruit of eternal life is identified with future beatitude. Therefore the fruits of the present life are the beatitudes.

Objection 3: Further, fruit is essentially something ultimate and delightful. Now this is the very nature of beatitude, as stated above (I-II, q. 3, a. 1; q. 4, a. 1). Therefore fruit and beatitude have the same nature, and consequently should not be distinguished from one another.

On the contrary, Things divided into different species, differ from one another. But fruits and beatitudes are divided into different parts, as is clear from the way in which they are enumerated. Therefore the fruits differ from the beatitudes.

RESPONDEO dicendum quod plus requiritur ad rationem beatitudinis, quam ad rationem fructus. Nam ad rationem fructus sufficit quod sit aliquid habens rationem ultimi et delectabilis, sed ad rationem beatitudinis, ulterius requiritur quod sit aliquid perfectum et excellens. Unde omnes beatitudines possunt dici fructus, sed non convertitur. Sunt enim fructus quaecumque virtuosa opera, in quibus homo delectatur. Sed beatitudines dicuntur solum perfecta opera, quae etiam, ratione suae perfectionis, magis attribuuntur donis quam virtutibus, ut supra dictum est.

AD PRIMUM ergo dicendum quod ratio illa probat quod beatitudines sint fructus, non autem quod omnes fructus beatitudines sint.

AD SECUNDUM dicendum quod fructus vitae aeternae est simpliciter ultimus et perfectus, et ideo in nullo distinguitur a beatitudine futura. Fructus autem praesentis vitae non sunt simpliciter ultimi et perfecti, et ideo non omnes fructus sunt beatitudines.

AD TERTIUM dicendum quod aliquid amplius est de ratione beatitudinis quam de ratione fructus, ut dictum est.

I answer that, More is required for a beatitude than for a fruit. Because it is sufficient for a fruit to be something ultimate and delightful; whereas for a beatitude, it must be something perfect and excellent. Hence all the beatitudes may be called fruits, but not vice versa. For the fruits are any virtuous deeds in which one delights: whereas the beatitudes are none but perfect works, and which, by reason of their perfection, are assigned to the gifts rather than to the virtues, as already stated (I-II, q. 69, a. 1, ad 1).

Reply to Objection 1: This argument proves the beatitudes to be fruits, but not that all the fruits are beatitudes.

Reply to Objection 2: The fruit of eternal life is ultimate and perfect simply: hence it nowise differs from future beatitude. On the other hand the fruits of the present life are not simply ultimate and perfect; wherefore not all the fruits are beatitudes.

Reply to Objection 3: More is required for a beatitude than for a fruit, as stated.

ARTICULUS 3

AD TERTIUM sic proceditur. Videtur quod apostolus inconvenienter enumeret, ad Galat. V, duodecim fructus. Alibi enim dicit esse tantum unum fructum praesentis vitae; secundum illud Rom. VI, *habetis fructum vestrum in sanctificatione* et Isaiae XXVII dicitur, *hic est omnis fructus, ut auferatur peccatum.* Non ergo ponendi sunt duodecim fructus.

PRAETEREA, fructus est qui ex spirituali semine exoritur, ut dictum est. Sed dominus, Matth. XIII, ponit triplicem terrae bonae fructum ex spirituali semine provenientem, scilicet *centesimum, et sexagesimum,* et *trigesimum.* Ergo non sunt ponendi duodecim fructus.

PRAETEREA, fructus habet in sui ratione quod sit ultimum et delectabile. Sed ratio ista non invenitur in omnibus fructibus ab apostolo enumeratis, patientia enim et longanimitas videntur in rebus contristantibus esse;

ARTICLE 3
Whether the fruits are suitably enumerated by the Apostle?

Objection 1: It would seem that the fruits are unsuitably enumerated by the Apostle (Gal. 5:22,23). Because, elsewhere, he says that there is only one fruit of the present life; according to Rom. 6:22: "You have your fruit unto sanctification." Moreover it is written (Is. 27:9): "This is all the fruit...that the sin ...be taken away." Therefore we should not reckon twelve fruits.

Objection 2: Further, fruit is the product of spiritual seed, as stated (I-II, q. 70, a. 1). But Our Lord mentions (Mat. 13:23) a threefold fruit as growing from a spiritual seed in a good ground, *viz.* "hundredfold, sixtyfold," and "thirtyfold." Therefore one should not reckon twelve fruits.

Objection 3: Further, the very nature of fruit is to be something ultimate and delightful. But this does not apply to all the fruits mentioned by the Apostle: for patience and long-suffering seem to imply a painful object,

fides autem non habet rationem ultimi, sed magis rationem primi fundamenti. Superflue igitur huiusmodi fructus enumerantur.

SED CONTRA, videtur quod insufficienter et diminute enumerentur. Dictum est enim quod omnes beatitudines fructus dici possunt, sed non omnes hic enumerantur. Nihil etiam hic ponitur ad actum sapientiae pertinens, et multarum aliarum virtutum. Ergo videtur quod insufficienter enumerentur fructus.

RESPONDEO dicendum quod numerus duodecim fructuum ab apostolo enumeratorum, conveniens est, et possunt significari per duodecim fructus de quibus dicitur Apoc. ult., *ex utraque parte fluminis lignum vitae, afferens fructus duodecim.* Quia vero fructus dicitur quod ex aliquo principio procedit sicut ex semine vel radice, attendenda est distinctio horum fructuum secundum diversum processum spiritus sancti in nobis. Qui quidem processus attenditur secundum hoc, ut primo mens hominis in seipsa ordinetur; secundo vero, ordinetur ad ea quae sunt iuxta; tertio vero, ad ea quae sunt infra. Tunc autem bene mens hominis disponitur in seipsa, quando mens hominis bene se habet et in bonis et in malis. Prima autem dispositio mentis humanae ad bonum, est per amorem, qui est prima affectio et omnium affectionum radix, ut supra dictum est. Et ideo inter fructus spiritus primo ponitur *caritas*; in qua specialiter spiritus sanctus datur, sicut in propria similitudine, cum et ipse sit amor. Unde dicitur Rom. V, *caritas Dei diffusa est in cordibus nostris per spiritum sanctum, qui datus est nobis.* Ad amorem autem caritatis ex necessitate sequitur gaudium. Omnis enim amans gaudet ex coniunctione amati. Caritas autem semper habet praesentem Deum, quem amat; secundum illud I Ioan. IV, *qui manet in caritate, in Deo manet, et Deus in eo.* Unde sequela caritatis est *gaudium.* Perfectio autem gaudii est pax, quantum ad duo. Primo quidem, quantum ad quietem ab exterioribus conturbantibus, non enim potest perfecte gaudere de bono amato,

while faith is not something ultimate, but rather something primary and fundamental. Therefore too many fruits are enumerated.

Objection 4: On the other hand, It seems that they are enumerated insufficiently and incompletely. For it has been stated (I-II, q. 70, a. 2) that all the beatitudes may be called fruits; yet not all are mentioned here. Nor is there anything corresponding to the acts of wisdom, and of many other virtues. Therefore it seems that the fruits are insufficiently enumerated.

I answer that, The number of the twelve fruits enumerated by the Apostle is suitable, and that there may be a reference to them in the twelve fruits of which it is written (Apoc. 22:2): "On both sides of the river was the tree bearing twelve fruits." Since, however, a fruit is something that proceeds from a source as from a seed or root, the difference between these fruits must be gathered from the various ways in which the Holy Ghost proceeds in us: which process consists in this, that the mind of man is set in order, first of all, in regard to itself; secondly, in regard to things that are near it; thirdly, in regard to things that are below it. Accordingly man's mind is well disposed in regard to itself when it has a good disposition towards good things and towards evil things. Now the first disposition of the human mind towards the good is effected by love, which is the first of our emotions and the root of them all, as stated above (I-II, q. 27, a. 4). Wherefore among the fruits of the Holy Ghost, we reckon "charity," wherein the Holy Ghost is given in a special manner, as in His own likeness, since He Himself is love. Hence it is written (Rom. 5:5): "The charity of God is poured forth in our hearts by the Holy Ghost, Who is given to us." The necessary result of the love of charity is joy: because every lover rejoices at being united to the beloved. Now charity has always actual presence in God Whom it loves, according to 1 Jn. 4:16: "He that abideth in charity, abideth in God, and God in Him": wherefore the sequel of charity is "joy." Now the perfection of joy is peace in two respects. First, as regards freedom from outward disturbance; for it is impossible to rejoice perfectly in the beloved good,

qui in eius fruitione ab aliis perturbatur; et iterum, qui perfecte cor habet in uno pacatum, a nullo alio molestari potest, cum alia quasi nihil reputet; unde dicitur in Psalmo CXVIII, *pax multa diligentibus legem tuam, et non est illis scandalum,* quia scilicet ab exterioribus non perturbantur, quin Deo fruantur. Secundo, quantum ad sedationem desiderii fluctuantis, non enim perfecte gaudet de aliquo, cui non sufficit id de quo gaudet. Haec autem duo importat pax, scilicet ut neque ab exterioribus perturbemur; et ut desideria nostra conquiescant in uno. Unde post caritatem et gaudium, tertio ponitur *pax.* In malis autem bene se habet mens quantum ad duo. Primo quidem, ut non perturbetur mens per imminentiam malorum, quod pertinet ad *patientiam.* Secundo, ut non perturbetur in dilatione bonorum, quod pertinet ad *longanimitatem,* nam *carere bono habet rationem mali,* ut dicitur in V Ethic. Ad id autem quod est iuxta hominem, scilicet proximum, bene disponitur mens hominis, primo quidem, quantum ad voluntatem bene faciendi. Et ad hoc pertinet *bonitas.* Secundo, quantum ad beneficentiae executionem. Et ad hoc pertinet *benignitas,* dicuntur enim benigni quos bonus ignis amoris fervere facit ad benefaciendum proximis. Tertio, quantum ad hoc quod aequanimiter tolerentur mala ab eis illata. Et ad hoc pertinet *mansuetudo,* quae cohibet iras. Quarto, quantum ad hoc quod non solum per iram proximis non noceamus, sed etiam neque per fraudem vel per dolum. Et ad hoc pertinet *fides,* si pro fidelitate sumatur. Sed si sumatur pro fide qua creditur in Deum, sic per hanc ordinatur homo ad id quod est supra se, ut scilicet homo intellectum suum Deo subiiciat, et per consequens omnia quae ipsius sunt. Sed ad id quod infra est, bene disponitur homo, primo quidem, quantum ad exteriores actiones, per *modestiam,* quae in omnibus dictis et factis modum observat. Quantum ad interiores concupiscentias, per *continentiam* et *castitatem,* sive haec duo distinguantur per hoc, quod castitas refrenat hominem ad

if one is disturbed in the enjoyment thereof; and again, if a man's heart is perfectly set at peace in one object, he cannot be disquieted by any other, since he accounts all others as nothing; hence it is written (Ps. 118:165): "Much peace have they that love Thy Law, and to them there is no stumbling-block," because, to wit, external things do not disturb them in their enjoyment of God. Secondly, as regards the calm of the restless desire: **for he does not perfectly rejoice, who is not satisfied with the object of his joy.** Now peace implies these two things, namely, that we be not disturbed by external things, and that our desires rest altogether in one object. Wherefore after charity and joy, "peace" is given the third place. In evil things the mind has a good disposition, in respect of two things. First, by not being disturbed whenever evil threatens: which pertains to "patience"; secondly, by not being disturbed, whenever good things are delayed; which belongs to "long suffering," since "to lack good is a kind of evil" (Ethic. v, 3). Man's mind is well disposed as regards what is near him, *viz.* his neighbor, first, as to the will to do good; and to this belongs "goodness." Secondly, as to the execution of well-doing; and to this belongs "benignity," for the benign are those in whom the salutary flame* of love has enkindled the desire to be kind to their neighbor. Thirdly, as to his suffering with equanimity the evils his neighbor inflicts on him. To this belongs "meekness," which curbs anger. Fourthly, in the point of our refraining from doing harm to our neighbor not only through anger, but also through fraud or deceit. To this pertains "faith," if we take it as denoting fidelity. But if we take it for the faith whereby we believe in God, then man is directed thereby to that which is above him, so that he subject his intellect and, consequently, all that is his, to God. Man is well disposed in respect of that which is below him, as regards external action, by "modesty," whereby we observe the "mode" in all our words and deeds: as regards internal desires, by "continency" and "chastity": whether these two differ because chastity withdraws man from

---

* *bonus ignis*

illicitis, continentia vero etiam a licitis; sive per hoc quod continens patitur concupiscentias sed non deducitur, castus autem neque patitur neque deducitur.

AD PRIMUM ergo dicendum quod sanctificatio fit per omnes virtutes per quas etiam peccata tolluntur. Unde fructus ibi singulariter nominatur propter unitatem generis, quod in multas species dividitur, secundum quas dicuntur multi fructus.

AD SECUNDUM dicendum quod fructus centesimus, sexagesimus et trigesimus non diversificantur secundum diversas species virtuosorum actuum, sed secundum diversos perfectionis gradus etiam unius virtutis. Sicut continentia coniugalis dicitur significari per fructum trigesimum; continentia vidualis per sexagesimum; virginalis autem per centesimum. Et aliis etiam modis sancti distinguunt tres evangelicos fructus secundum tres gradus virtutis. Et ponuntur tres gradus, quia cuiuslibet rei perfectio attenditur secundum principium, medium et finem.

AD TERTIUM dicendum quod ipsum quod est in tristitiis non perturbari, rationem delectabilis habet. Et fides etiam si accipiatur prout est fundamentum, habet quandam rationem ultimi et delectabilis, secundum quod continet certitudinem, unde Glossa exponit, *fides, idest de invisibilibus certitudo.*

AD QUARTUM dicendum quod, sicut Augustinus dicit, super epistolam ad Galat., *apostolus non hoc ita suscepit, ut doceret quod sunt (vel opera carnis, vel fructus spiritus); sed ut ostenderet in quo genere illa vitanda, illa vero sectanda sint.* Unde potuissent vel plures, vel etiam pauciores fructus enumerari. Et tamen omnes donorum et virtutum actus possunt secundum quandam convenientiam ad haec reduci, secundum quod omnes virtutes et dona necesse est quod ordinent mentem aliquo praedictorum modorum. Unde et actus sapientiae, et quorumcumque donorum ordinantium ad bonum, reducuntur ad caritatem, gaudium et pacem. Ideo tamen potius haec quam alia enumeravit, quia hic enumerata magis important vel fruitionem

unlawful desires, contingency also from lawful desires: or because the continent man is subject to concupiscence, but is not led away; whereas the chaste man is neither subject to, nor led away from them.

Reply to Objection 1: Sanctification is effected by all the virtues, by which also sins are taken away. Consequently fruit is mentioned there in the singular, on account of its being generically one, though divided into many species which are spoken of as so many fruits.

Reply to Objection 2: The hundredfold, sixtyfold, and thirtyfold fruits do not differ as various species of virtuous acts, but as various degrees of perfection, even in the same virtue. Thus contingency of the married state is said to be signified by the thirtyfold fruit; the contingency of widowhood, by the sixtyfold; and virginal contingency, by the hundredfold fruit. There are, moreover, other ways in which holy men distinguish three evangelical fruits according to the three degrees of virtue: and they speak of three degrees, because the perfection of anything is considered with respect to its beginning, its middle, and its end.

Reply to Objection 3: The fact of not being disturbed by painful things is something to delight in. And as to faith, if we consider it as the foundation, it has the aspect of being ultimate and delightful, in as much as it contains certainty: hence a gloss expounds thus: "Faith, which is certainly about the unseen."

Reply to Objection 4: As Augustine says on Gal. 5:22, 23, "the Apostle had no intention of teaching us how many (either works of the flesh, or fruits of the Spirit) there are; but to show how the former should be avoided, and the latter sought after." Hence either more or fewer fruits might have been mentioned. Nevertheless, all the acts of the gifts and virtues can be reduced to these by a certain kind of fittingness, in so far as all the virtues and gifts must needs direct the mind in one of the above-mentioned ways. Wherefore the acts of wisdom and of any gifts directing to good, are reduced to charity, joy and peace. The reason why he mentions these rather than others, is that these imply either enjoyment

I-II, q. 70, a. 3, ad 4

bonorum, vel sedationem malorum; quod videtur ad rationem fructus pertinere.

Articulus 4

Ad quartum sic proceditur. Videtur quod fructus non contrarientur operibus carnis quae apostolus enumerat. Contraria enim sunt in eodem genere. Sed opera carnis non dicuntur fructus. Ergo fructus spiritus eis non contrariantur.

Praeterea, unum uni est contrarium. Sed plura enumerat apostolus opera carnis quam fructus spiritus. Ergo fructus spiritus et opera carnis non contrariantur.

Praeterea, inter fructus spiritus primo ponuntur caritas, gaudium, pax, quibus non correspondent ea quae primo enumerantur inter opera carnis, quae sunt fornicatio, immunditia, impudicitia. Ergo fructus spiritus non contrariantur operibus carnis.

Sed contra est quod apostolus dicit ibidem, quod *caro concupiscit adversus spiritum, et spiritus adversus carnem.*

Respondeo dicendum quod opera carnis et fructus spiritus possunt accipi dupliciter. Uno modo, secundum communem rationem. Et hoc modo in communi fructus spiritus sancti contrariantur operibus carnis. Spiritus enim sanctus movet humanam mentem ad id quod est secundum rationem, vel potius ad id quod est supra rationem, appetitus autem carnis, qui est appetitus sensitivus, trahit ad bona sensibilia, quae sunt infra hominem. Unde sicut motus sursum et motus deorsum contrariantur in naturalibus, ita in operibus humanis contrariantur opera carnis fructibus spiritus. Alio modo possunt considerari secundum proprias rationes singulorum fructuum enumeratorum, et operum carnis. Et sic non oportet quod singula singulis contraponantur, quia, sicut dictum est, apostolus non intendit enumerare omnia opera spiritualia, nec omnia opera carnalia. Sed tamen, secundum quandam adaptationem, Augustinus, super epistolam ad Galat.,

of good things, or relief from evils, which things seem to belong to the notion of fruit.

Article 4
Whether the fruits of the Holy Ghost are contrary to the works of the flesh?

Objection 1: It would seem that the fruits of the Holy Ghost are not contrary to the works of the flesh, which the Apostle enumerates (Gal. 5:19, seqq.). Because contraries are in the same genus. But the works of the flesh are not called fruits. Therefore the fruits of the Spirit are not contrary to them.

Objection 2: Further, one thing has a contrary. Now the Apostle mentions more works of the flesh than fruits of the Spirit. Therefore the fruits of the Spirit and the works of the flesh are not contrary to one another.

Objection 3: Further, among the fruits of the Spirit, the first place is given to charity, joy, and peace: to which, fornication, uncleanness, and immodesty, which are the first of the works of the flesh are not opposed. Therefore the fruits of the Spirit are not contrary to the works of the flesh.

On the contrary, The Apostle says (Gal. 5:17) that "the flesh lusteth against the spirit, and the spirit against the flesh."

I answer that, The works of the flesh and the fruits of the Spirit may be taken in two ways. First, in general: and in this way the fruits of the Holy Ghost considered in general are contrary to the works of the flesh. Because the Holy Ghost moves the human mind to that which is in accord with reason, or rather to that which surpasses reason: whereas the fleshly, *viz.* the sensitive, appetite draws man to sensible goods which are beneath him. Wherefore, since upward and downward are contrary movements in the physical order, so in human actions the works of the flesh are contrary to the fruits of the Spirit. Secondly, both fruits and fleshly works as enumerated may be considered singly, each according to its specific nature. And in this they are not of necessity contrary each to each: because, as stated above (I-II, q. 70, a. 3, ad 4), the Apostle did not intend to enumerate all the works, whether spiritual or carnal. However, by a kind of adaptation, Augustine, commenting on Gal. 5:22, 23,

contraponit singulis operibus carnis singulos fructus. Sicut *fornicationi, quae est amor explendae libidinis a legitimo connubio solutus, opponitur caritas, per quam anima coniungitur Deo in qua etiam est vera castitas. Immunditiae autem sunt omnes perturbationes de illa fornicatione conceptae, quibus gaudium tranquillitatis opponitur. Idolorum autem servitus, propter quam bellum est gestum adversus Evangelium Dei, opponitur paci. Contra veneficia autem, et inimicitias et contentiones et aemulationes, animositates et dissensiones, opponuntur longanimitas, ad sustinendum mala hominum inter quos vivimus; et ad curandum, benignitas; et ad ignoscendum, bonitas. Haeresibus autem opponitur fides, invidiae, mansuetudo; ebrietatibus et comessationibus, continentia.*

AD PRIMUM ergo dicendum quod id quod procedit ab arbore contra naturam arboris, non dicitur esse fructus eius, sed magis corruptio quaedam. Et quia virtutum opera sunt connaturalia rationi, opera vero vitiorum sunt contra rationem; ideo opera virtutum fructus dicuntur, non autem opera vitiorum.

AD SECUNDUM dicendum quod *bonum contingit uno modo, malum vero omnifariam,* ut Dionysius dicit, IV cap. de Div. Nom., unde et uni virtuti plura vitia opponuntur. Et propter hoc, non est mirum si plura ponuntur opera carnis quam fructus spiritus.

AD TERTIUM patet solutio ex dictis.

contrasts the fruits with the carnal works, each to each. Thus "to fornication, which is the love of satisfying lust outside lawful wedlock, we may contrast charity, whereby the soul is wedded to God: wherein also is true chastity. By uncleanness we must understand whatever disturbances arise from fornication: and to these the joy of tranquillity is opposed. Idolatry, by reason of which war was waged against the Gospel of God, is opposed to peace. Against witchcrafts, enmities, contentions, emulations, wraths and quarrels, there is longsuffering, which helps us to bear the evils inflicted on us by those among whom we dwell; while kindness helps us to cure those evils; and goodness, to forgive them. In contrast to heresy there is faith; to envy, mildness; to drunkenness and revellings, contingency."

Reply to Objection 1: That which proceeds from a tree against the tree's nature, is not called its fruit, but rather its corruption. And since works of virtue are connatural to reason, while works of vice are contrary to nature, therefore it is that works of virtue are called fruits, but not so works of vice.

Reply to Objection 2: "Good happens in one way, evil in all manner of ways," as Dionysius says (Div. Nom. iv): so that to one virtue many vices are contrary. Consequently we must not be surprised if the works of the flesh are more numerous than the fruits of the spirit.

The Reply to the Third Objection is clear from what has been said.

Made in the USA
Lexington, KY
03 March 2013